The Plays of George Chapman

�֍

The Tragedies
with *Sir Gyles Goosecappe*

THE PLAYS OF
GEORGE CHAPMAN

✤

THE TRAGEDIES
WITH *SIR GYLES GOOSECAPPE*

A Critical Edition

General Editor: Allan Holaday

✤

Assisted by G. Blakemore Evans and Thomas L. Berger

D. S. BREWER

Editorial matter © Contributors 1987

First published 1987 by D. S. Brewer
240 Hills Road, Cambridge
an imprint of Boydell & Brewer Ltd
PO Box 9, Woodbridge, Suffolk IP12 3DF
and Wolfeboro, New Hampshire 03894-2069, USA

ISBN 0 85991 243 4

British Library Cataloguing in Publication Data
Chapman, George, *1559? – 1634*
  The plays of George Chapman: a critical
  edition.
  The tragedies with Sir Gyles Goosecappe.
  I. Title II. Holaday, Allan III. Evans,
  G. Blakemore IV. Berger, Thomas L.
  822'.3   PR2440
  ISBN 0-85991-243-4

Library of Congress Cataloging-in-Publication Data
Chapman, George, 1559?-1634.
  The plays of George Chapman.
  Includes bibliographical references.
  I. Holaday, Allan. II. Evans, G. Blakemore
(Gwynne Blakemore), 1912-   . III. Berger, Thomas L.
IV. Title.
PR2442.H6 1987   822'.3   86-26890
ISBN 0-85991-243-4

Printed in Great Britain by
St Edmundsbury Press, Bury St Edmunds, Suffolk

To the Memory of
John Hazel Smith and Dennis G. Donovan

Contents

✣

Abbreviations

❉

(c)	corrected (state)
conj.	conjecture
ELN	*English Language Notes*
ELR	*English Language Review*
ES	*Englische Studien*
HLQ	*Huntington Library Quarterly*
(i)	inner (forme)
JEGP	*Journal of English and Germanic Philology*
MLN	*Modern Language Notes*
MLR	*Modern Language Review*
MP	*Modern Philology*
N & Q	*Notes and Queries*
NED	*New English Dictionary* (Oxford)
(o)	outer (forme)
om.	omitted
PBSA	*Publications of the Bibliographical Society of America*
PMLA	*Publications of the Modern Language Association* (of America)
(r)	reset
RES	*Review of English Studies*
SB	*Studies in Bibliography*
SD	stage direction
SP	*Studies in Philology*
subs.	substantially
TLS	*Times Literary Supplement*
(u)	uncorrected (state)

General Introduction[1]

❖

Collected editions of Chapman's plays – of which the present one is number four – began with *The Comedies and Tragedies of George Chapman*, presumably edited by R. H. Shepherd, and published in 1873 by John Pearson. Essentially a diplomatic reprint of the original quartos, it has slight textual value. But with its immediate successor, *The Works of George Chapman: Plays* (1875), Shepherd did seriously undertake the business of textual correction, perhaps in part as a result of his decision to modernize spelling and punctuation. Forced by this exacting process occasionally to confront textual cruxes, he ultimately produced a text which, though flawed by errors, is, nonetheless, superior to its predecessor.

But the limitations of this second edition prove crippling. Its textual errors result especially from Shepherd's tendency to misread his copy-text, to emend without warrant, and to overlook obvious quarto mistakes. Having made no systematic collation, he was often unaware of corrected states of the quarto texts. And he provided no textual apparatus whatever. Indeed, even a hasty examination of his work convincingly establishes its limited usefulness for any student of Chapman.

Immediate predecessors to the present edition are T. M. Parrott's *The Tragedies* (1910) and *The Comedies* (1914), two volumes in a projected three-volume work, *The Plays and Poems of George Chapman*.[2] Parrott produced much the best complete text then available and supplied as well useful information about early editions, a record of his collations, and discussions of troublesome cruxes. Noting the inadequacy of quarto stage directions, uncritically reproduced by Shepherd, he corrected many of those that he derived from his copy-text and originated others; several of his interpolations which clarify ambiguous scenes have special textual relevance.

But, despite its evident merit, current readers recognize in Parrott's edition serious limitations, the most conspicuous of which result from our changed editorial standards. The inadequacy of Parrott's textual apparatus, for example, often exasperates scholars, many of whom, for quite sound reasons, also object to his modernized text. But even more serious than these

---

[1] Reprinted, with permission, from *The Plays of George Chapman: The Comedies* (University of Illinois Press, Urbana), 1970.
[2] Volume III, *Poems*, was never published.

1

shortcomings are his numerous errors, several of which directly resulted from a decision to correct for the printer a copy of Shepherd's second edition. He also chose to collate only two or three quarto copies, thereby missing numerous press-variants. And, inevitably, he overlooked some cruxes, misinterpreted others, and sometimes misread. Thus, though he carried Chapman scholarship a great step forward, Parrott left unfulfilled the critical need for sound texts.

Intent upon satisfying that need, editors of the present edition, in addition to textual introductions, have prepared for each play the following four-part apparatus: a table of press-variants, two 'collations', and textual notes. The press-variants (i.e., variations from copy to copy in the copy-text edition) result from changes made in printer's formes during the press run; that is, they derive from printshop efforts to 'correct' the quarto text. One of the two collations, recorded in notes at the bottom of each page, lists all emendations made by the editor in deriving his critical text from his copy-text. These include revision of accidentals as well as substantives, excepting only those covered by a general statement on silent emendations. The other, a 'historical' collation, lists substantive and semi-substantive (but not accidental) variants which differentiate the critical text from specified earlier versions. The textual notes provide a terse commentary on special cruxes and a defense of editorial decisions. Thus the apparatus records various attempts to correct the text, including original printshop revisions as well as those emendations made or conjectured by succeeding editors and commentators.

Since attention to the distinctions among substantive, semi-substantive, and accidental variants promotes successful use of the apparatus, a brief explanation of these terms seems in order. The basic distinction, of course, is that between substantive variants (i.e., those that affect meaning) and accidental variants (i.e., those that involve spelling or punctuation without altering meaning). The term 'semi-substantive' identifies those variations in punctuation or, very occasionally, in spelling that do affect meaning (and hence are substantive) but, because they do not involve diction, resemble accidentals. As a working principle, editors of the present edition follow the now customary practice of accepting as substantive or semi-substantive any emendation which changes copy-text diction, alters copy-text meaning through punctuation, or removes copy-text ambiguity; all other variants are considered accidental.

Recognizing that one rarely reads directly through a collected edition, editors have prefaced each text with whatever information seemed especially pertinent to that play, accepting the duplication of information that occasionally results on the assumption that consequent gains in clarity and convenience for the reader adequately offset the disadvantages. Fortunately, not much information required full repetition; often the complete explanation necessary in one introduction could, in summarized form, serve another. But anyone who does proceed directly through either volume will, on several occasions, recognize that he is covering some of the ground more than once.

Headnotes for each play identify editions cited by sigla in the historical collations; but since variants recorded in the footnotes derive principally from the copy-text, sigla are usually unnecessary here except to distinguish corrected [Q(c)] from uncorrected [Q(u)] states of the copy-text variant or to identify re-set passages [Q(r)] and later quartos (e.g., Q2, Q3). Occurrence in a footnote of an editor's name or an appropriate siglum such as Q(c) immediately after the square bracket designates the originator of the emendation recorded in the lemma and hence adopted in the critical text. Thus, the following footnote specifies that the lemma 'threed', taken from the critical text, derives from a corrected state of the copy-text; 'throat' represents the uncorrected version.

24 threed] Q(c); throat Q(u)

Lack of an editor's name or siglum immediately after the bracket in the footnotes and historical collations implies that the emendation originates with the present text. In the interest of further simplicity, editors, wherever clarity permits, avoid the abbreviation *om.* (omitted) after the bracket to designate an editorial interpolation. Thus, the following footnote,

61 SD Pointing to d'Olive.]

indicates that the stage direction comprising the lemma is an interpolation originating with the critical text. To avoid repeating in the variant words found in the lemma, editors usually substitute a swung dash for each omitted word; a caret indicates that a mark of punctuation occurring in the lemma does not reappear in the variant. Thus, the following note indicates that instead of the comma, Shepherd has a semicolon and Parrott no punctuation whatever.

61 more,] ∼; S; ∼_∧ P

Parenthetical listings, appended to various footnotes, record changes between upper and lower case that result from variations in lineation. Hence, the following note shows that, in emending the prose lineation of Q to verse (after Parrott), the present editor raised the initial letters of 'tel' and 'for' to upper case.

65-67 Hast … all.] Parrott; as prose (tel … for)

And finally, an editor identifies cruxes which, because he has accepted the copy-text reading, would otherwise escape mention in the footnotes, by the following device:

81 seasonable] stet (See Textual Note)

Unrecorded emendations are few in number and without textual significance. They include the normalization of speech heads, of wrong-font letters, and of wrong-font punctuation; correction of turned letters where no ambiguity exists, of printers' substitutions occasioned by type shortages, and of wrong-font type for complete words in the stage directions; expansion of the tilde and ampersand; substitutions of standard types for display capitals and lower case for the capitals that usually follow display letters.

Abbreviations, including abbreviated names and titles, found in the copy-text reappear in the critical texts except for those that prove ambiguous or otherwise confusing. Likewise, editors normally preserve the u-v, i-j spellings

3

of the copy-text, on rare occasions emending to avoid inconvenience to the reader. An example of one such emendation, taken from *The Blind Beggar*, is that from the copy-text spelling, 'loud', to the less confusing 'lou'd'. And, where an 'aside' ends mid-speech, editors conventionally mark the conclusion by a dash.

In general, editorial interpolations (i.e., any passages of one word or more in the critical text that are supplied to remedy a copy-text omission) are bracketed; an exception is material added to a stage direction that exists in the copy-text. Completely interpolated stage directions, however, are bracketed. As a means of identifying the source of any substantive emendation, editors record even bracketed interpolations in both the footnotes and the historical collations.

The need to refer in textual introductions to such units of the copy-text as pages, printer's formes, and sheets necessitated the definition within the critical text of the boundaries of each original page. For example, since an editor in presenting his evidence for a change in compositors between sheets B and C in the copy-text of *Monsieur D'Olive* necessarily refers to special characteristics of these sheets, he obligates himself to provide his reader the means by which to identify all relevant passages. Thus, a slash in the critical text marks the point at which one quarto page ends and another begins. And at the right margin opposite the first line or part of a line representing a new copy-text page, a bracketed signature corresponding to that in the copy-text identifies the page. The title-page reproductions that precede the plays have been standardized in size for use in the present volume.

An attempt further to improve Chapman's dramatic texts seems particularly consistent with intense critical interest in this dramatist and, as a response to the evident needs of students, scholars, and critics, to deserve, at the moment, priority over other useful work. Editors of the present edition, therefore, omitting historical and critical commentaries, have sought to establish reliable texts for all of Chapman's plays. Aware of their advantage in being latest to undertake this task, they have provided a record of their predecessors' answers to the common textual problems. Thus, though the critical text represents in each instance its editor's best solution to textual cruxes, the reader has immediate access through the apparatus to requisite information by which he can assess all editorial decisions.

The present volume of George Chapman's tragedies and *Sir Gyles Goosecappe* (now regularly accepted as by Chapman) complements the volume of his comedies published by the University of Illinois Press in 1970. Together they contain all Chapman's unaided plays now extant and his one masque. His only important collaboration (with John Marston and Ben Jonson), *Eastward Hoe* (1605), has not been included because a carefully edited old-spelling text is easily available in the Herford and Simpson *Ben Jonson*, Vol. IV (Oxford, 1932). Also omitted are *The Ball* (1639), *Alphonsus Emperor of Germany* (1654), and *Revenge for Honour* (1654), which, though provisionally included by T. M. Parrott in *The Plays and Poems of*

George Chapman: The Tragedies (1910), *The Comedies* (1914), because of title page attributions, are no longer considered to have any significant connection with Chapman.

The editors wish to acknowledge with special and personal gratitude the generous financial support toward the publication of this volume given by their several universities: Brandeis University, Harvard University (from the Hyder E. Rollins Fund), University of North Carolina at Chapel Hill (in memory of Dennis G. Donovan), Notre Dame University, Ohio State University, and St Lawrence University. We would also like to thank Professor Marvin Spevack and Professor William P. Williams for their interest in furthering the publication of our work. As in the earlier Comedies volume (1970), we are greatly indebted to those libraries throughout England and America which so kindly furnished us with microfilms of their copies of the seventeenth-century quarto editions (see the headnote to the list of press-variants for each play) and to the Trustees of the British Library for permission to reproduce the title pages of the quartos from copies in the British Library.

A. H.
G. B. E.
T. L. B.

Bussy D'Ambois

edited by John Hazel Smith

❖

TEXTUAL INTRODUCTION

The '*tragedie of Busye D'amboise*, made by George Chapman,' was entered in the *Stationers' Register* on June 3, 1607, as the copyright of William Aspley. Presumably the copy presented by Aspley, or else Aspley orally, is responsible for the attribution to Chapman. No one, I believe, has ever questioned Chapman's authorship of the play, but no surviving text of *Bussy D'Ambois* identified the author by name until a reissue of the 1641 quarto (Q2) with a new title page dated 1657.[1]

After entry, the play was published by Aspley in a quarto that boasted on the title page that it had been '*often presented at Paules.*'[2] The quarto was printed at the Eliot's Court press (in the Old Bailey) owned at that time by Arnold Hatfield and Melchisidec Bradwood.[3] Title pages of this edition survive in two states, dated '1607' and '1608' respectively; the earlier date was 'apparently rejected and the type altered in the course of printing the first sheet' (Greg, I, 378).

---

[1] W. W. Greg, *Bibliography of the English Printed Drama to the Restoration* (London, 1939), I, 377-79, No. 246. In 1652, however, a nonce-collection of *Comedies, Tragi-Comedies, and Tragedies: Written by George Chapman* was made that contained a copy of Q1, including the original (1607) title page; if the collection was actually issued, as the printed title page for the collection might suggest, it would be the first published identification of Chapman.

[2] It is commonly assumed that the release for publication of this and a number of other plays was due to the cessation of playing by Paul's Boys (T. M. Parrott, 'The Date of Chapman's "Bussy D'Ambois",' *MLR*, III [1908], 126; E. K. Chambers, *The Elizabethan Stage* [Oxford, 1923], II, 22). It has been suggested that *Bussy* was originally written for the Children of the Chapel, and was among the plays taken over to Paul's by Edward Kirkham in 1605-6 (Chambers, III, 254).

[3] The printer is not identified on the title page, but Greg identified the press from the printer's device (No. 306 in R. B. McKerrow, *Printers' and Publishers' Devices in England and Scotland 1485-1640* [London, 1913], pp. 119-20, apparently used by the members of the firm indifferently). The identification is confirmed by some identical types that I have found in *Bussy D'Ambois* Q1 and in George Abbot's *Sermon Preached at Westminster May 26, 1608*, admittedly printed by Bradwood: Cf. a 'd' found in *Bussy* Q1 (A3.30; C2.3; E2ᵛ.15; and H2.22) and in Abbot (B2ᵛ.6); an 'n' in *Bussy* (A2ᵛ.5) and in Abbot (B3ᵛ.6); and a 'w' in *Bussy* (C1ᵛ.21; E1ᵛ.11; G1.12; and I2ᵛ.26) and in Abbot (B3ᵛ.27).

The copy for the 1607-8 quarto (Q1) was almost certainly an authorial manuscript – perhaps foul papers, judging from some problems noted below, but on the whole a fairly clean manuscript. The spelling 'ahlas(se)', which has been identified as a Chapman form,[4] occurs several times in Q1; and a number of stage directions contain Latin forms of a type associated particularly with Chapman (e.g., *Procumbit*, A2ᵛ; *Intrat vmbra*, I1ᵛ). W. T. Jewkes found data that he interpreted as evidence that the copy had been worked on by a prompter:

> Although many traces of Chapman's hand remain in the marginal Latin stage directions, the text does not present the usual consistency of other Chapman plays for the boy companies. The first three acts have almost no directions at all; even at the head of scenes they are very brief, often omitting the word 'Enter.' The last two acts, however, have profuse directions. In several instances, English directions seem to have been added to expand original Latin directions, as with 'Intrat vmbra, Comolet to the countesse wrap't in a canopie' (I1r), and 'Exeunt Mons. Guise. Lead her out' (G4r). ... These are all indicative of at least preparation for the stage.[5]

Nicholas Brooke also found it 'just possible that the bookkeeper had made preliminary notes,' but concluded that the characteristics taken as evidence of the bookkeeper's hand may be authorial.[6] I see little reason to believe that anybody other than Chapman had touched the manuscript. Contrary to Jewkes's account of the profusion of directions in the last two acts, there is, as my Textual Notes demonstrate, such a woeful absence of important directions in Act V that it is not possible to know when several important characters enter and leave the stage. Certainly a number of anomalous speech-prefixes would not long have survived a prompter's attentions. On D1, a speech (II.ii.111/61, sandwiched between speeches by *Mons.* and *Mont.*) is assigned to *Mont.* when it can only have been spoken by Tamyra, and the likeliest explanation is an author's change of mind during the writing of the play (Tamyra's speech being an afterthought by Chapman after he had written the speech-prefix for Montsurry's next speech).[7] On G3, an answer to a question by Bussy is assigned to *Mons.* (who has just entered, but who is not represented as being in the same location as Bussy) rather than to Frier or Behemoth (IV.ii.80/100); probably this was a result of crossed wires by Chapman as he was writing. On I1ᵛ and I2, speech-prefixes inconsistently identify Tamyra by her title ('*Count.*') rather than an abbreviation of her name (V.iii.64, 75/V.iv.10, 21). (Inconsistent identifications of the

---

[4] G. Blakemore Evans, ed., *All Fooles*, in *The Plays of George Chapman: The Comedies*, gen. ed. Allan Holaday (Urbana, 1970), p. 228.
[5] *Act Division in Elizabethan and Jacobean Plays 1583-1616* ([Hampden, Conn.], 1958), p. 256.
[6] The Revels ed., *Bussy D'Ambois* (London, 1964), p. lxi.
[7] As explained more fully in the headnote to the Historical Collation, when the line numbers of Q1 and Q2 diverge, my references are dual: The number to the left of the slash refers to my edition of Q1; the number to the right, to my edition of Q2. If a passage is not represented in one quarto, a dash appears before or after the slash to indicate the absence of any comparable words there.

protagonist as '*Buss.*' and the less common '*D'Amb.*' may also have a bearing here.) On both D4 and I3 there are redundant speech-prefixes.[8] Perhaps the best indication that Q1 was printed from foul papers is an incomplete stage direction printed in its uncorrected state at IV.ii.7/–: '*Enter Comolet in a*'; in the corrected state, '*in a*' was deleted. While it is possible that the compositor omitted a word that was in his copy and then corrected the error in the simplest way possible without checking copy, probably the likeliest explanation is that Chapman left the direction unfinished in draft.

The running-titles of Q1 present an unusual problem. Nineteen individual headlines appear in the quarto, each of them (whether on recto or verso) identically worded, '*Bussy D'Ambois*'. They recur through the quarto, mostly one by one, in an irregular way; no pattern of recurrence is evident except that headlines never move from a recto in one forme to a verso in another, or vice versa. The three used in A-outer reappear in the same relative positions in H-inner, and B-outer and D-outer have in common three running-titles in different relative positions; but in each case one or more of the common components had been used in intervening formes in different combinations.

Headline No.	Used on Signatures
I	A2^v, C1^v, E3^v, F4^v, H1^v, I3^v
II	A3, C2, E1, F1, G2, H4, I1
III	A3^v, B4^v, C3^v, D4^v, F3^v, G4^v, I2^v
IV	A4, C1, E3, G4
V	A4^v, C2^v, E1^v, G1^v, H3^v
VI	B1, D3, F4, H3
VII	B1^v, D2^v, F2^v, H2^v
VIII	B2, E4, G3
IX	B2^v, C4^v, E2^v, G2^v, I1^v
X	B3, C4, D1, F3, H2, I3
XI	B3^v
XII	B4
XIII	C3, E2, G1, H1, I2
XIV	D1^v
XV	D2
XVI	D3^v, E4^v, G3^v, H4^v
XVII	D4
XVIII	F1^v, I4^v
XIX	F2, I4

Two headlines (II and III) are used seven times each, five once, the rest varying between those extremes. At times new headlines are set – four (VII, VIII, XI, XII) in B-inner, three (VI, IX, X) in B-outer, one (XIII) in C-outer, another four (XIV-XVII) in D-inner, a pair (XVIII, XIX) in F-inner. Sometimes one can deduce why, and sometimes not. As Sheet C was being

---

[8] T. M. Parrott, however, interpreted the redundancies on D4 as evidence that Q1 'may have been printed from a ms. cut for stage purposes'; as a corollary he suggested that the passage that Q2 adds at that point (III.i.45 ff.) 'may have been in the original ms.' ('Notes on the Text of *Bussy D'Ambois,*' *Englische Studien*, XXXVIII [1907], 375 n.)

imposed, for example, four headlines from Sheet A (IV, I, II, V) were available for C1, C1ᵛ, C2, and C2ᵛ, but no set headlines were available for C3 (the fifth headline from Sheet A having been used in Sheet B, which was apparently still being printed off); thus, a new headline was set for that page. By that time, the headlines from B-outer became available, and no new headlines were needed for the remaining pages of Sheet C. On the other hand, I cannot explain why new headlines were set for D-inner: The running-titles from C-inner should have been available (since the one from C4 had been used on D1), not to mention those from Sheet B; B-outer at least had been printed off and its type distributed by the time C4ᵛ was composed.⁹ Equally puzzling is the fact that three of the four new D-inner running-titles were never re-used; one reappears three times. Alan Craven has suggested to me privately that the printer may have been working on some other job concurrently and sometimes used types from *Bussy*'s headlines in that unknown work, so that they were not always available when it would appear that they should have been. In any case, the running-titles are so far from providing information useful to the editor of the play that they are in themselves a partially inexplicable puzzle.

Spelling tests indicate that two compositors worked on the quarto. The main distinctions between the spellings of the two men (A and B) are as follows: A generally used the spellings 'blood' and 'cloud/croun,' where B used 'bloud' and 'clowd/crown.' For the final [i] sound in words like 'very' and 'cloudy,' A almost invariably used the spelling '-ie' except for the adverbial ending '-ly,' and even for that we sometimes find '-lie' (on B1ᵛ, B2, B3, F1, and F2ᵛ); B, on the other hand, showed a strong (though not exclusive) preference for the '-y' spelling. B alone occasionally used the speech-prefix *Buc.* for *Buss.* and in certain other words preferred single consonants where A tended to use double consonants. A had a preference for the spelling '-our' (e.g., 'honour'), while B used '-our' and '-or' about evenly and in three instances used '-ure' in 'valure.' B used colons more liberally than A, but A more regularly used apostrophes in past forms of words ending in liquids or nasals. In some of these respects B may have been more faithful to copy than A. In any case, by these tests B seems to have set the following pages: C3ᵛ-D1 (plus about seven lines at the top of D1ᵛ), D3ᵛ (except the first eight lines, which conclude Act II) -D4ᵛ, E3-E4ᵛ, F3 (?plus a few lines at the bottom of F2ᵛ which begin Act IV)-F4, G3-G4ᵛ (plus a half-dozen lines on H1), H3 (except perhaps a few lines at the top)-H4ᵛ, and I3-I4ᵛ. A set the rest (including all of the first two sheets¹⁰), except that the evidence is ambiguous for G1ᵛ-G2ᵛ, with

---

⁹ Types from B-outer are found on C4ᵛ as follows: n (seruaɴts), B3.10, on C4ᵛ.31 (aɴd); e (those), B3.30, on C4ᵛ.37 (endure); y (ʏour), B3.8, on C4ᵛ.28 (ʏou). Types from both formes of Sheet B are found early in Sheet D.

¹⁰ It is just possible that a third hand set some of the pages in Sheets A and B. On A3ᵛ and B2 'I'le' appears (and on A4 'Il'e'); everywhere else in the quarto the word is spelled 'Ile'. Again, on B4ᵛ, the unusual forms 'hurl's' and 'Call's' occur for the third-person singular verbs; cf. 'starr's' for 'starrs' (modern 'stars'') on B3. Intriguingly, however, Q2 has the spelling 'let's' in V.iii.43/

a few B spellings ('honor'd,' 'cald,' 'crown'd') scattered among A forms. In other words, to summarize roughly, A set the first half or so of each sheet (after the first two) and B the latter half or so. The likeliest explanation of this pattern of composition, including the fact that the compositors' stints did not always coincide with the end of a page of type, is that (after the first two sheets) the compositors divided up the copy, with A taking the first one or two manuscript leaves (whatever would fill up about four pages of type) and B the next one or two. The compositors apparently estimated quite closely how many lines more or less than an exact four pages of type their portions of the copy would fill. I assume that the compositors worked simultaneously, since the greater speed that would thus result would seem to be the only advantage to such division of the copy. If, then, Compositor B knew that A would have, say, ten lines to set at the top of B's first page, he might set the page leaving room for those ten lines and go on with the rest of his portion; when A reached the end of his portion of the copy and set those ten lines, if B were working at a similar rate, the sheet would be ready for imposition and printing. (Such a sequence might explain why some of the headlines do not occur where we expect them to.) Alternatively, of course, given the same hypothetical circumstance, A could set his last ten lines first, allowing B to finish the page and place the headline into position earlier, but such a procedure seems *a priori* less efficient. In any case, the pattern of composition implies that the men worked seriatim; that implication seems to be confirmed not only by the pattern of the running-titles, but also by the fact that few identifiable types are found in contiguous sheets.

On the whole, Q1 is carefully printed. I have the impression that Compositor A was a more accurate workman than Compositor B, who, however, may have been somewhat more faithful to the spellings in his copy than A. For what it is worth, moreover, most of the stop-press corrections that I have found in the quarto (other than the change of date on the title page) are on pages composed by B. Definite stop-press corrections were made in A-outer (the title page), E-outer (E3), G-inner (G2, one of the pages that I have not certainly assigned to either compositor, and G4), and I-inner (I4); variants that may not be due to corrections exist in D-inner and I-outer. On the other hand, there is some slight evidence of earlier proof sheets;[11] thus, it is possible that we have A's work in a more corrected state than B's. This evidence is not strong, however, since a number of glaring typographical errors remain

V.ii.38. Cf. also the '-lie' spellings on B1ᵛ, B2, and B3. But these anomalies may reflect copy spellings. The spellings of oblique forms with '-'s' may very well be from Chapman himself. My findings differ from those of Nicholas Brooke, who discovered no 'clear evidence of more than one compositor' (p. lxi, n. 2).

[11] On A3ᵛ (I.i.99), about half the copies show typographical disruption of the words 'you breake your fast?'; line 98 ends with very similar words ('you breake for haste,'), and conceivably the disruption resulted from a resetting to correct an earlier error. (As it stands, however, the page does not have an abnormal number of lines of type.) Cf. a similar displacement in some copies on B4ᵛ (II.i.10); lines 9 and 10 both end 'her'. Again, on C1 (II.i.70), the second 'much' in 'much much' is spaced oddly in all copies, raising the possibility that it was added during an earlier proof stage. D. F. McKenzie has argued, of course, that early proof pulls were probably normal: 'Printers of the Mind: Some Notes on Bibliographical Theories and Printing-House Practices,' *SB*, XXII (1969), 42-48.

(including two on E3, for example); the proofreading was apparently not too thorough, and, judging by the kinds of corrections made, need not have involved checking against manuscript.

The second quarto (Q2) was printed in 1641 by A. N. (probably Alice Norton) for Robert Lunne. How Lunne came into possession of the play is not known, since there exists no record of a transfer from Aspley (who died in August, 1640) or his heirs. Berta Sturman suspected foul play. Noting that Aspley was a power in the Stationers' Company, that Lunne was an 'exceedingly obscure publisher' who seems to have published no other works, and that his printer, Alice Norton ('an equally shadowy figure'), printed mostly ephemera rather than books, Sturman speculated that 'Lunne had acquired a copy of the play from the actors somewhat earlier, but, finding himself unable or unwilling to purchase a transfer of Aspley's right, withheld publication until the latter's death removed some of his difficulties.'[12] While not impossible, the argument is not convincing, and is too conjectural to form a valid basis for further argument.

John Freehafer made a more persuasive argument for irregular publication by attributing the release of the text, not to its actors, but to an acting company whose title to it was questionable. Starting from the ownership dispute discussed in the Prologue to the Q2 version (a prologue that Freehafer, unlike most others, attributed to Chapman), he reconstructed the following sequence of events: When Nathan Field, manager of the Lady Elizabeth's Men, left that collapsing company in 1616 and joined the King's Men, he took several plays with him, among them *Bussy*. (Thus far he was essentially restating what is commonly assumed.) Some six years later, Christopher Beeston reconstituted Lady Elizabeth's Men and tried to reclaim those plays. As a part of his effort, he persuaded Chapman to revise the play in order to increase its 'theatrical effectiveness' and thus 'challenge a staging of the original version by the King's Men, a company for which Chapman never wrote.' Beeston soon gave up his effort to regain title to the play, but after his death in 1638, his son William 'apparently decided to retaliate against the King's Men by publishing plays that had once belonged to Lady Elizabeth's Men but were part of the acting repertory of the King's Men.' Among them were *Monsieur Thomas* and *Rollo Duke of Normandy* (both 1639) and *Bussy*:

> Since the new edition was authorized by neither the Stationers' Company nor the King's Men, it is not surprising that its publisher and printer are obscure, and its title page replaces the customary reference to performance by the King's Men with a vague statement that the play 'hath been often Acted with great Applause.'

The King's Men then obtained (on August 7, 1641) an order forbidding unauthorized publication of their plays, especially warning against attempts to publish some 'under another name' (as had happened with *Rollo*).[13] The

---

[12] 'The 1641 Edition of Chapman's *Bussy D'Ambois*,' *HLQ*, XIV (1951), 172-74.
[13] 'The Contention for *Bussy D'Ambois*, 1622-41,' *Theatre Notebook*, XXIII (1968/69), 61-69. It should be noted that Freehafer differs from most other scholars in associating the Prologue and Epilogue with the revisions in the Q2 text.

coincidence of this order and the publication of *Bussy* without a transfer of copyright is suggestive, but is not inconsistent with release by the King's Men themselves. The fact that *Bussy* was published under its original name may be irrelevant (since a change of name would presumably be useful only in getting past the clerk of the Stationers' Company). A possible problem with the theory is that the Q2 version (which Freehafer thus attributed to persons unconnected with the King's Men) may well have been the version that the King's Men performed: At least it was the one that formed the basis for Thomas D'Urfey's adaptation of 1691 (mentioned below), and D'Urfey did not indicate any discrepancy between Q2 and the version he had seen on the stage (to be sure, some sixteen years earlier).

There may be an additional problem for Freehafer's theory in the nature of the copy for Q2. As we shall see, what was submitted to the printer was a copy of Q1 that had been corrected by collation against a prompt-book. It is possible that a prompt-book would have been made for Christopher Beeston's postulated rival production; but why, after the battle for ownership of the play had been long lost (in Freehafer's reconstruction of the events), would William Beeston have gone to all the trouble of collating Q1 against the prompt-book? Evidently companies protected their prompt-books as much as possible, for obvious reasons; but Beeston would presumably have had no further need for a prompt-book. Somehow the circumstances supposed by Freehafer do not seem quite to be in accord with what we know of the release of the Q2 text.

Several issues of Q2 appeared; the title page in each issue after the first is a cancel reset with different type.[14] One issue of 1641 gives an address for Lunne ('next doore to the signe of the Crane on Lambeth Hill at the end of old *Fish-Street*'). A 1646 issue bears a title page printed by T. W. (Thomas Warren the elder?), but apparently sharing some types with the first issue (suggesting to Greg that the printer was Alice Norton's husband). Finally, an issue dated 1657 (and published, according to its title page, by Joshua Kirton) is the first published text of the play (save, possibly, the title page of the 1652 noncecollection cited above, n. 1) to identify Chapman as the author.

Two skeleton formes were used to print Q2. Skeleton I was used to impose A-inner (two headlines only), B-inner (A3^v to B2, A4 to B1^v, and two new headlines, one of which – B4 – has an incorrect roman 'B'), C-outer (B4 to C3, with the roman 'B' corrected to italic), E-inner, and F-inner. Skeleton II imposed A-outer (A4^v only); B-outer (A4^v to B2^v with some types reset); C-inner; both formes of D; E-outer; F-outer; both formes of G, H, and I; and K-outer (three headlines only). For K-inner, two headlines from Skeleton II were used (I1^v to K1^v, I2 to K2) along with one from Skeleton I (last used for F1^v) on K3^v. There are indications that the quarto may have been composed by formes from cast-off copy, at least in part. Many types recur in contiguous sheets, often in the early pages of subsequent sheets. While this evidence should no doubt be discounted somewhat in view of D. F. McKenzie's arguments (pp. 12-22) that, typically, more than one job was printed concurrently,

---

[14] For complete details, see Greg, *loc. cit.*

there is also some evidence from type substitutions: In Sheet I, eight sub-stitutions of 'vv' for 'w' were made (presumably because of a shortage of 'w's in the case), and all of them are in the outer forme (three on I1, four on I2ᵛ, one on I3). On the other hand, in Sheet B, italic colons are substituted for roman on three consecutive pages (three on B3ᵛ, six on B4, three on B4ᵛ). It may be, then, that the pattern of substitutions in Sheet I is accidental; or perhaps Sheet B was composed seriatim though the rest of the book was composed by formes (the pattern of type recurrence from Sheet B to Sheet C is different from the typical pattern in the quarto: Types from B are found no earlier than C3ᵛ, and B-outer types are not found in C at all).

Like Nicholas Brooke, I have found no clear evidence of more than one compositor in Q2. In general, Q2 shows a marked tendency to follow copy closely in its spellings, especially when its copy was a page of Q1 set by Q1's Compositor A. The copy for Q2 was, beyond question, a copy of Q1 (except for revisions, which will be discussed below). Q2 frequently follows Q1 readings even when they are manifestly wrong or are different from the Q2 compositor's normal practices (as shown, sometimes, by later stop-press corrections of those readings). Such a large number of identical readings would be unlikely to have survived a complete transcription of the play. Consider the following examples:

- I.ii.86/93 SD *'Pyrlot'* (error for *'Pyrhot'*; identical in Q2, though the SD is moved
- II.ii.82/32 'Puttofs'; identical in Q2, uncorrected state, then corrected to 'Put-ofs'
- III.ii.129 'yours' (error for 'your'); identical in Q2, uncorrected state, then corrected to 'your'
- III.ii.174/184 'Lord?'; identical in Q2, uncorrected state, then corrected to 'Lord,'
- III.ii.292/299 'vailes'; identical in Q2, uncorrected state, then corrected to 'veiles'
- IV.ii.80/100 *Mons.* (erroneous); identical in Q2
- IV.ii.129/150 *Com.*; identical in Q2, uncorrected state, then corrected to Q2's normal form *'Frier.'*
- V.i.36/40 *Com.*; identical in Q2

Some few pages seem to show unusual kinds of changes, or an abnormally high (or low) proportion of changes from Q1: For example, on C4ᵛ (set from Compositor B's part of Q1), several words that have lower-case initials in Q1 are capitalized; on I3ᵛ (also set from B's work), there are twice as many alterations of punctuation as of spelling and many more than on most pages (altogether there are almost four times as many changes of spelling as of pointing in Q2); on several pages there are fewer than ten accidental variants from Q1, but on some others three or four times that many.[15] It is possible that these variations point to more than one hand at work on Q2, but I have not found any clear pattern that would confirm such a view.

---

[15] Cf., for example, B3 (eight accidental variants) and C4ᵛ (thirty-five variants). Variables other than the compositors are, of course, possible.

The composition in Q2 was somewhat less reliable than that of either man who set Q1. As Nicholas Brooke has shown, the work of the Q2 compositor was especially suspect when he was setting from manuscript,[16] but there are significant numbers of typographical errors in other sections of the quarto as well. About three-fourths of the twenty formes show stop-press corrections – evidence of systematic proofreading, some of it surely against copy, and of some concern for the quality of the work.

The play presented in Q2 is drastically revised from that in Q1. Scores of changes involve the substitution of single words or short phrases, the addition or deletion of small groups of lines (in one or two instances up to fifty or sixty lines), and the relocation of several passages (including the transposition of two scenes in Act V). Where the revisions were brief, they were surely transcribed directly onto the pages of the copy of Q1 that was sent to the printer of Q2, because the contexts of most of the altered words and phrases are formally very similar in Q1 and Q2. Where there were additions of considerable length, or transfers of passages from one page to another, the revisions were presumably written on interleaved manuscript pages (or slips). In either case, but especially when passages were written in the margins, there was always the possibility that the compositor would not know which (if any) of the printed lines on the page were to be deleted; I believe that some deletions were made by mistake.

These manuscript revisions were almost certainly transcribed from a manuscript prompt-book. On B1 of Q2, adjacent to I.i.153-55, appear the words '*Table Chesbord & Tapers behind the Arras.*'; as has been frequently noticed, this note must be a prompter's warning to prepare for the next scene some seventy lines later and is the clearest evidence of prompt-copy. There are other indications only slightly less clear in the numerous references to properties that are added in Q2: '*Tamyra with a Book.*', II.ii.191 (Q1: '*Tamyra.*'); '*Tamyra, with a Chaine of Pearle.*', III.i.SD (Q1: '*Tamyra.*'); '*Monsieur with a Letter,*', IV.i.SD (Q1: '*Monsieur,*'); '*He puts on his robes.*', –/IV.ii.51 (not in Q1; but see my Textual Note *ad loc.*); '*Pages with Tapers.*', V.iii.SD (Q1 V.ii.SD: '*Pages.*'). Because of these indications, several scholars have assumed that the copy for Q2 was itself the prompt-book.[17] But no prompt-book would have long retained the misattribution on H1ᵛ (IV.ii.80/100, cited above); or the redundant speech-prefix ('*Frier.*') on K2ᵛ (V.iii.190/V.iv.153), the result of a transferred speech; or the speech-prefix with the abandoned name '*Com.*' (V.i.36/40, cited above). What we have then, as the copy for Q2,

---

[16] There was, however, considerable variation in reliability, another possible indication of multiple compositors.

[17] T. M. Parrott, ed., *The Plays of George Chapman: The Tragedies* (London, 1910), p. 562 (though earlier, in 'Notes,' p. 394, he had been less precise, saying that the copy was 'a ms. or printed copy of [Q1] which had been revised and corrected by the poet, and perhaps by others'); Hazelton Spencer, ed., *Elizabethan Plays* (Boston, 1933), p. 523, note to I.ii.SD ('the source of Q 1641 was the prompt-copy [or a transcription of it]'); W. W. Greg, *The Shakespeare First Folio* (Oxford, 1955), p. 160, n. 4; Robert J. Lordi, ed., *Bussy D'Ambois*, Nebraska Regents Renaissance Drama Series (Lincoln, 1964), p. xxxi (though he also believed, apparently, that it might have been set at least in part 'from the author's script' – Chapman having 'made his revisions on the pages of a printed copy of Q1').

is a copy of Q1 that had been corrected by collation against a prompt-book (presumably a manuscript) – the collations most probably done in preparation for the publication of Q2.[18]

The prompt-book against which Q1 was collated (and which may have contained an unknown number of additional revisions that were overlooked by the collator) was presumably that used for performances by the King's Men in the 1630s.[19] Whether it was older than that cannot be determined, because the date of the revisions preserved in it is not known – nor, of course, do we know whether the prompt-book used was the one prepared at the time of the revisions or some later transcript of the original. The possible time span is quite large, for the second quarto was printed almost forty years after the play was written.

The usually accepted date for the original version is around 1604 – a year chosen, as Nicholas Brooke observes, almost entirely because of allusions in I.ii: 'their old Queene' (I.ii.12), which has been described as inappropriate unless written after Elizabeth's death in March, 1603; thrusts at James's increases in the ranks of the nobility (I.ii.111/123, 155/171), which parallel, *inter alia*, similar thrusts in *Eastward Ho!* (1605); and 'Tis leape yeare' (I.ii.78/82), which, though part of a bawdy joke, has been thought to indicate performance in a leap year.[20] Some have argued for an earlier date: 1600 (because of a reference to 'trusty *Damboys*' in Dekker's *Satiromastix*, 1601)[21] or 1596-8 (principally because of entries in Henslowe's *Diary* in 1598 for 'Perowes sewt, which Wm Sley w[o]re,' and to costumes for 'The Gwisse').[22]

---

[18] If the acting company decided to release a text for publication, one supposes that they would want the text to be reasonably accurate, but that they would not demand *definitive* care from their copyist. This mixture of care (evidenced by a collation with Q1 against a substantive manuscript that must have taken at least the better part of a day to perform) and carelessness is precisely the set of qualities that may be inferred about the copy for Q2. It is difficult to conceive of any other purpose that such a text would have been intended to serve.

[19] The play was performed at court on April 7, 1634 (Joseph Q. Adams, ed., *The Dramatic Records of Sir Henry Herbert Master of the Revels, 1623-1673* [New Haven, 1917], p. 55); either *Bussy* (probably) or *The Revenge of Bussy D'Ambois* was performed there again on March 27, 1638 (Adams, p. 76). Freehafer, of course, would argue that the prompt-book was from a production by the Lady Elizabeth's Men in the early 1620s.

[20] E.g., T. M. Parrott, 'The Date of Chapman's "Bussy D'Ambois",' *MLR*, III (1908), 126-40; Parrott ed., p. 549, followed by most editors. The most recent affirmation of this date (or, to be more precise, of 1603/4) is by Albert H. Tricomi, 'The Dates of the Plays of George Chapman,' *ELR*, XII (1982), 252-55; he declared other dates to be 'beyond reasonable possibility.'

[21] E.g., E. E. Stoll, 'On the Dates of Some of Chapman's Plays,' *MLN*, XX (1905), 206; W. J. Lawrence, 'Dekker's Theatrical Allusiveness,' *TLS* (January 30, 1937), p. 72, both of whom noted that 1600 was also a leap year. Robert Ornstein countered that Dekker could have been referring to a lost play or to the real personage, who was apparently well known ('The Dates of Chapman's Tragedies, Once More,' *MP*, LIX [1961], 61-64).

[22] E.g., P. C. Hoyt in an unpublished paper reported favorably by F. S. Boas, ed., Bussy D'Ambois *and* The Revenge of Bussy D'Ambois, The Belles-Lettres Series (Boston, 1905), p. xii n.; Ezra Lehman, ed., *The Tragedie of Chabot Admirall of France*, Publications of the University of Pennsylvania, Series in Philology and Literature 10 (Philadelphia, 1906), pp. 6-11; Elias Schwartz, 'The Dates and Order of Chapman's Tragedies,' *MP*, LVII (1959), 80-82; Elias Schwartz, 'The Date of *Bussy D'Ambois*,' *MP*, LXIX (1961), 126-27. Ornstein countered that Chapman's Pero would have worn, not a suit, but a serving maid's farthingale – a doubtful statement: As a maid-in-waiting to a countess, she would certainly have had social status higher than that of a common serving maid. Ornstein argued more plausibly that Henslowe's reference was to a 'Piero or Pierrot's suit (the long-sleeved, white clown costume originated by the *commedia dell'arte* in the late sixteenth century) which had previously belonged to Sly.'

To accommodate the allusions in I.ii, a number of those who argued for an early date supposed a revision of what is now a lost play into the Q1 version around 1604.[23] One factor that may have weakened some scholars' faith in the evidence for 1604 is that it is all concentrated in one scene, into which it could have been interpolated some time after the original composition of the play. I have elsewhere explored evidence from Act V that may bear upon the date.[24] Without repeating the analysis here in detail, I can summarize the argument briefly: Montsurry's distressed reference to a 'new flame' that 'breakes out of the firmament' (V.i.151/159) may be an allusion to the supernova that became visible in the foot of Ophiuchus in late September, 1604. This 'new star' is known as Kepler's star because Johannes Kepler investigated it thoroughly, publishing at least two works about it: a German book published soon after the event (*Von einem vngewohnliches Newen Stern* [Prague, n.d.]) and an encyclopedic study (*De Stella Nova*) published two years later. Though less spectacular visually than the supernova of 1572 in Cassiopeia (Tycho Brahe's star), and probably less shocking because it was not the first, Kepler's star nonetheless evoked much comment, partly because it was near the conjunction of Jupiter and Saturn that in December, 1603, had marked the beginning of the portentous fiery trigon. Though less was made of it in England than on the continent, Ben Jonson's probable allusion in *Volpone* (1606) is worth noting: Among the other prodigies that Sir Politick Would-be asks Peregrine about is 'the new star' (II.i.38). The 'new flame' would have special point in Act V, with its significant star imagery, if it were a reference to a recent event of such significance. If it was a reference to Kepler's star, the date of the play would be moved by perhaps as much as a year – to 1604-5 rather than 1603-4.[25]

The date of the revision is even less certain. The Q2 title page states that the revision was made '*by the Author before his death*'; if Chapman was the author meant, the terminal date is 1634, when Chapman died (and a year when a performance of the play is recorded). But it is only an inference that that phrase means *shortly* before 1634, and in fact most scholars have dated the revision much earlier. The usually accepted date is around 1610-11 because of certain very close parallels between the revised *Bussy* and *The Revenge of Bussy D'Ambois*, which is usually dated then.[26] Albert H. Tricomi, in fact, has recently argued that the parallels are more than that: that, 'far from being unrelated to one another, the two D'Ambois plays were intended to be presented together' in 'thematic counterpoint' to 'demonstrate by dramatic contrast and comparison the superior virtue of Clermont's rational heroism.' Thus, implicitly, though not necessarily, the revision of *Bussy* was made at the very time of the writing of *The Revenge* in order to integrate the

---

[23] E.g., Boas; Lawrence; and R. G. Howarth, 'The Date of "Bussy D'Ambois",' *N & Q*, CLXXVII (July 8, 1939), 25 (who supposed the earlier version to have been called 'Fatall Love, a French Tragedy,' under which title a play by Chapman was entered in the *Stationers' Register* in 1660).
[24] 'On the Date of George Chapman's *Bussy D'Ambois*,' in *Brandeis Essays in Literature*, ed. John Hazel Smith (Waltham, Mass., 1983), pp. 30-36.
[25] For another possible allusion to events in 1604, see the Textual Note to II.ii.122/72.
[26] Parrott, 'Date,' *MLR* (1908), III, 133-40; Peter Ure, 'The Date of the Revision of Chapman's "The Tragedy of Bussy D'Ambois",' *N & Q*, CXCVII (1952), 1-2.

two plays into the one intention.[27] Tricomi's argument is reasonable enough, but cannot now be proved. Nor do the parallels with *The Revenge* prove that the revision was made when *The Revenge* was being written. In his review of Nicholas Brooke's edition, G. K. Hunter noted a 'small point' that may be relevant here: Associating Q1 with boy players and Q2 with an adult company, he pointed out that the transfer of Marston's *Malcontent* from children to adult players produced 'augmentations "to entertain a little more time, and to abridge the not received custom of music in our [sc. adult] theatre". At one point in *Bussy* [IV.ii.SD] the abridgement of music seems to be involved in the textual augmentation, and it may be suspected elsewhere.'[28] If relevant and correct, this argument might put the revision in about 1616, when Field joined the King's Men, presumably taking *Bussy D'Ambois* with him. Again, as we have seen, John Freehafer argued for a revision in 1622-24, during the dispute over ownership that he postulated at that time. None of the arguments for any particular date seems compelling to me, and the only independent evidence that I have found is ambiguous: Middleton's *Game at Chess* (1624) uses a phrase ('tympanous master, swell'd with state-wind') that seems to echo the Q1 reading of *Bussy* at I.i.10 ('Tympanouse statists') – though the *NED* credits Middleton with the first use of 'tympanous'. Unless Middleton came up with the phrase independently (which seems a little unlikely to me), the echo may mean that the Q1 version of *Bussy* was still on the boards in the early 1620s; but it is also possible that Middleton *read* the words in Q1. (See also my Textual Note to V.i.84/91.)

My analysis of the relationship between Q1 and Q2 shows that Nicholas Brooke was certainly correct in his statement (p. lxv) that, on bibliographical grounds, Q1 is the more substantive text. But that evidence will not help us to determine the authoritativeness of the revisions.

Until relatively recently, no one questioned the accuracy of Q2's title page assertion that the play (presumably the version printed in Q2) had been '*much corrected and amended by the Author.*' All editors followed (or normalized to) Q2. Sometimes they seemed a little uncomfortable in doing so: Boas, for example, thought the play in Q2 'not appreciably superior to the original draft,' but accepted the evidence of the Q2 title page.[29] Parrott, however, had no such doubt. He recognized (what later scholars would make much of) the 'theatrical' nature of many changes – the clarifications of motives and actions

---

[27] 'The Revised *Bussy D'Ambois* and *The Revenge of Bussy D'Ambois*: Joint Performance in Thematic Counterpoint,' *ELN*, IX (1972), 253-62. Cf. also Tricomi's 'The Revised Version of Chapman's *Bussy D'Ambois*: A Shift in Point of View,' *SP*, LXX (1973), 288-305. With some reservations, Tricomi's argument is accepted by Gunilla Florby, *The Painful Passage to Virtue: A Study of George Chapman's* The Tragedy of Bussy D'Ambois *and* The Revenge of Bussy D'Ambois, Lund Studies in English 61 (Lund, 1982), pp. 150-80.

[28] *RES*, n.s. XVI (1965), 197. This explanation is challenged by R. Corballis, 'Bussy D'Ambois: The Textual Problem Once More,' *Journal of the Australasian Universities Language and Literature Association*, XLV (1976), 83: The addition to *Bussy*, he argued, was designed to clarify a changed emphasis wanted in the Q2 version.

[29] Boas, p. xlv. Incidentally, the editor of the Pearson reprint (probably R. H. Shepherd) did use Q1 as his copy-text, correcting it (but very inadequately) to agree with Q2; but that was obviously an expedient rather than a policy decision, for he claimed to have followed Q2 (*The Comedies and Tragedies of George Chapman Now First Collected* [London, 1873], II, 2).

– and even supposed advice to Chapman by an actor-playwright with 'practical experience' of the theatre, someone like Nathan Field. But he found Chapman's hand everywhere and thought the revised version 'in every way superior to the first draft; in diction, in freedom of metrical handling, and in its adaptation to the stage' ('Notes,' p. 360). As recently as 1964, Robert Lordi found in Q2 'signs, except in minor cases, of careful revision and of interpolations that bear the stamp of Chapman's genius' (p. xxx). Even more recently, as we have seen, Freehafer and Tricomi have accepted the revision as Chapman's.

In the meantime, however, Berta Sturman in 1951 had published a serious attack on the authority of Q2. Besides raising questions, summarized earlier, about the integrity of the publisher and printer of Q2 (thus casting doubt on the reliability of the title page evidence), she argued that the language of Q2 usually moves toward a simplification that belies Chapman's characteristic methods and his poetic creed; she also noted changes wrought in characterization, particularly of Tamyra and Bussy, that she thought unworthy of Chapman (pp. 175-201).

Sturman was immediately answered by Peter Ure, who analyzed closely each substantive variation between Q1 and Q2 (except some longer passages) and decided that most of the revisions reflect a kind of busy tinkering that does not add up to much. He found forty-three changes possibly due to errors or corrections by the printer or copyist; thirty revisions that weaken the original; four cuts pursuant to the Blasphemy Act of 1606; forty-nine revisions that improved on the original; and about twenty 'indifferent' changes (including those in which one kind of effect is sacrificed for another).[30] For Ure, these circumstances pointed to work by the original author.

The most important argument for following Q1 was presented in 1964 by Nicholas Brooke, who in his fine Revels edition of the play was the first editor ever to follow the earlier version. He dismissed Sturman's argument from the supposed irregularity of Lunne's copyright by noting the difficulty in believing 'that such an elaborate correction of printed copy would have been undertaken except in good faith,' and he found her argument from the relative absence of coinages in the revised passages to be statistically questionable. But he also disagreed with Ure, questioning Ure's implicit assumption that most of the 'numerous neither-better-nor-worse changes were deliberately made.' Conceding that the assumption would force agreement that 'only Chapman himself could have bothered,' Brooke, however, was

> inclined to believe that a great many are so casual as to be accidental, and if that is so they do not necessarily point to Chapman at all. In fact, a considerable group of these changes involve only the substitution of synonymous words or phrases ...; the kind of thing that copyists and even compositors are commonly blamed for.

He found three classes of revision: (1) 'a number where the poetic quality is

---

[30] 'Chapman's "Tragedy of Bussy D'Ambois": Problems of the Revised Quarto,' *MLR*, XLVIII (1953), 257-69.

unmistakably Chapman'; (2) 'a number where the motive is obviously "theatrical" and without poetic merit'; and (3) 'a number which could easily be due to copyists.' But he also found the verges between these classifications so indistinct that he could not go 'right through the revisions assigning each one to its distinct source.' To help to 'simplify' the problem, Brooke posited a 'deliberate reviser' who 'made his revision by copying the whole play out,' being 'freer than the most careless copyist over the changing of unimportant words – sometimes through sheer inadvertence, sometimes because a slight preference struck him as he wrote.' While the 'best candidate for treating the text in such a proprietary manner is Chapman himself,' Brooke found the changes running counter to Chapman's development, in that they altered the play from a highly philosophic exploration of man and destiny into what he considered a melodrama; and the 'one person who could *not* have done this is Chapman himself.' Yet there are some passages of poetry (three of which Brooke took into his edition) that must be by Chapman. Brooke therefore had to conclude that the play was revised twice, once by Chapman and once by someone else. The 'someone else' was capable of writing very like Chapman, both in his poetry and in rare Latin stage directions. This man was

> no hack. He was apparently a man of the theatre; he also had at least small Latin; and some literary talent, albeit imitative ...; he knew Chapman's work well, and very likely had Chapman's general permission for such extensive tampering.

The candidate he tentatively put forward for that 'someone else' was the man Chapman called his 'Loved son,' the man Parrott called Chapman's theatrical advisor, Nathan Field (pp. lxv-lxxiv).

Since Brooke, no editor has followed Q2. Two years after the Revels edition appeared, Maurice Evans found Brooke's argument for a double revision to be 'irrefutable,' and he too followed Q1 but adopted some passages from Q2 – though not exactly the ones adopted by Brooke.[31] In 1976, Russell A. Fraser also followed Q1 because he found 'no certain reason' to think Chapman the reviser.[32] Brooke's edition has been widely, and deservedly, praised. Not everyone has accepted his conclusions, however,[33] and I believe that we must render a Scotch verdict on his solution to what G. K. Hunter called the 'very vexed problem' of the authorship of the *Bussy* revision (pp. 196-97). While it is true that title pages were in part promotional blurbs whose honesty is not beyond challenge, it is also true, as Samuel Schoenbaum has implied, that we ought not to discount their evidence without clear *proof* of their unreliability.[34] In the present case, one may wonder what the publisher

---

[31] Ed., *Bussy D'Ambois*, The New Mermaids (New York, 1966), p. xxxii. My Historical Collation indicates which Q2 passages Brooke and Evans adopted into their editions.

[32] *Drama of the English Renaissance*, ed. R. A. Fraser and Norman Rabkin (New York, 1976), II, 270.

[33] Cf. recent studies by A. H. Tricomi, 'The Problem of Authorship in the Revised *Bussy D'Ambois*,' *ELN*, XVII (Sept. 1979), 22-29; and Florby, pp. 25-69.

[34] *Internal Evidence and Elizabethan Dramatic Authorship: An Essay in Literary History and Method* (Evanston, 1966), p. 150: 'External evidence may and often does provide incontestable proof; internal evidence can only support hypotheses or corroborate external evidence.' Of course, Schoenbaum catalogued the dangers of relying unquestioningly on title pages (pp. 151-53).

had to gain by a false claim that the play had been revised by 'the Author' since he did not also add the name of the author. To disbelieve it and believe Brooke, we would have to accept what Brooke admitted is a very inefficient proposition, perhaps one of the most intricate ever offered in addressing a problem. In effect, Brooke proposed that Q2 is partly a revision by Chapman; partly a revision, probably with Chapman's approval, by someone who writes enough like Chapman to be easily mistakable for Chapman (even to a rare Latin stage direction, 'Exiturus.' at –/III.ii.317, which occurs also in Monsieur D'Olive, V.ii.59); and partly the equivalent of a bad quarto (because some memorial reconstruction was involved as the reviser copied out the play).

I believe that Brooke was right in part, but I do not accept his entire argument. The solution to this problem probably must be inefficient. For example, Parrott's argument that certain redundant speech-prefixes in Q1 – two or three of which occur in or adjacent to points where Q2 interpolates passages missing from Q1 – indicate that in some places, at least, Q1 presents a text that has been cut, while Q2 contains the earlier, uncut version. G. Blakemore Evans called to my attention the intriguing fact that the spellings in some of the passages that are unique to Q2 seem to be in older spellings than the rest of Q2: e.g., in –/II.i.210-15, 'Duchesse', 'bloud', and 'hee'. (Cf. the spelling 'let's', perhaps a Chapman spelling, cited above in n. 10.) In most cases, no doubt, Q2 is the later, revised text. There are many points between 1607 (or, better, 1604-5) and 1641 where accidental corruption, or deliberate alteration, could occur. The simplest to understand are the expurgations of words thought offensive under the Blasphemy Act of 1606 – alterations made, most likely, by the company's bookkeeper. Because Q1 was printed from foul papers, there was presumably at least one recopying to make a fair copy. If that was by Chapman, he could have made some scribal mistakes – but he could also have made *currente calamo* revisions. I suspect that some of the tinkering with individual words may have occurred at that stage – in short, that some Q1 readings never reached the fair copy to become parts of the official play. The person who prepared the copy for Q2 by collating a copy of Q1 with the prompt-book (prepared after revision and conceivably several times removed from Chapman's hand) could have made several kinds of mistakes, and there is no reason to believe that he faithfully recorded *all* the variants between the two texts: The uneven pattern of verbal tinkering from one passage to another – even allowing for the apparent fact that the reviser made more changes in prose passages than in verse – could as easily derive from inadequate collation as from uneven revision.[35] Finally, there was the printshop process. At this final stage some manifest and serious errors occurred: At –/IV.ii.27, for instance, the compositor misread a manuscript

[35] In II.i, Q2 substitutes Montsurry for Beaumond in the opening stage direction, but fails to change 'Beau.' in a speech-prefix and an exit – evidence of incomplete collation. Cf. other confusions or inconsistencies described by R. Corballis (pp. 80-90) and assumed by him to have resulted from the reviser's neglect. For an indication of the reviser's care, see the Textual Note to –/III.ii.316. The likelihood of imperfect collation makes it entirely possible that Q2 preserves some readings that were wrong in Q1 and are not readily detectable because not obviously wrong.

word as 'showne'; later, the word was corrected to 'knowne'. Some other obvious misreadings were not corrected: several in the lines transferred from the end of the play to –/V.iv.146-52, for example. An unknown number of other misreadings may survive uncorrected and not readily detectable because they are not manifestly wrong. There may well have been places where the compositor, failing to understand the collator's marginal markings, deleted too much or too little from the Q1 text. An editor attempting to establish a single *Bussy* text must consider all of these circumstances, but each alteration must be judged by local conditions; this is far different from Brooke's assumption of a *systematic* corrupting process.

Apart from the inferences to be drawn from these many details, it is probably relevant to consider the general circumstances of the collation. Most importantly, we should remember that the collation was made against a prompt-book. It is hard to imagine this collation's being made without the knowledge and consent of the company, and it is perfectly understandable that the company would want to protect its prompt-book against loss or damage by allowing such collation rather than by releasing the prompt-book itself to the publisher. One presumes that the company knew who revised the play; such knowledge is likely (though not certain) even if the revision was made in 1610, before the King's Men came into possession of it. While the company should not be held accountable for words that the publisher elected to put on his title page, the cooperation implicit in the situation as described gives some reason for believing in the truth as well as the truthfulness of the publisher's words.[36]

I have the impression that most previous editors who have seriously deliberated the question have been as much guided by their aesthetic preferences as by anything else. As we have seen, Parrott thought that Q2 presented a 'superior' play. Brooke preferred the Q1 version. That this preference affected his editorial decisions is evident: For example, at II.ii.172/123, he found that the Q2 revision 'might be Chapman's,', but he rejected it as 'hardly an improvement.' But it is by no means impossible for an author, any author, to weaken a work in revision. A critic has the right to tell him he has done so; a producer may have the power to prevent him from doing so; an editor has the right of the critic, but not the power of the producer. I am inclined to agree with the growing number of people who think *Bussy I* somewhat better than *Bussy II* (to use Robert Adams's designations of the two versions[37]), though I think the difference in quality much less marked than some have asserted.[38] But perhaps it is worth mentioning that *Bussy D'Ambois*,

[36] Of course, if the prompt-book belonged to William Beeston rather than to the King's Men, as Freehafer argued, this argument would have less weight.
[37] 'Critical Myths and Chapman's Original *Bussy D'Ambois*,' *Renaissance Drama*, IX (1966), 142.
[38] Cf. William Dean, 'Chapman's "Bussy D'Ambois": A Case for the Aesthetic and Moral Priority of the 1607 Version,' *Journal of the Australasian Universities Language and Literature Association*, XXXVIII (1972), 174: Q2 'weakens the whole experience of tragic irony in this play. ... any discussion of Chapman's achievement in *Bussy D'Ambois* ought preferably to be based on a reading of Q1.' See also R. Corballis (p. 88), who argued on grounds of dramatic confusions that 'the reviser made rather a botch of his job, so that Q1 must be regarded as the superior text'; Corballis, however, found 'no real reason' to question Chapman's responsibility for the revision and left it to editors to decide 'whether or not to respect the author's latest decisions when some

Chapman's earliest surviving tragedy, is in either of its versions almost universally held to be better than any he wrote later. Perhaps he more than many authors should be thought capable of revising away some of the qualities that made the first play superior.

Still, the editorial problems are so severe that any general conclusion must remain a matter of doubt. The fact is that, for every passage (such as –/V.iv.16 ff.) that will embarrass an editor who follows Q2 and will delight his critic, there is another passage (such as –/V.iv.32-35) of which the opposite is true. With the evidence now available, Robert Adams had very good reason for declaring the question 'perhaps insoluble' (p. 142). Faced with this situation, I have felt compelled to respect Adams's astute comment (later echoed by Tricomi[39]) that 'Bussy I and Bussy II are so different from each other that, if we seriously respect the integrity of texts, it is only good sense to treat these plays as two different works of art.' Given the nature and the likely audience of the present collected edition, I have decided that a parallel-text edition of both versions would be more useful to scholars than would yet another editor's *choice* between the two – a choice that, however well founded, would inevitably be at some level arbitrary and intuitive.

These are not, it must be emphasized, diplomatic editions of the two versions. Each text is edited according to the principles that govern all editors whose work appears in these pages. In the first instance, I have attempted to base my editorial judgments for each text on the kinds of assumptions that would obtain if no other version were known. The edition of each version is therefore basically independent of the other. Most of my editorial methods in each case have been very conservative: That is, in general, if a reading makes acceptable sense, I have not abandoned it even if, on some grounds, I have preferred the reading of the other quarto. For example, I strongly suspect that Q1's 'it' in V.i.17/21 is an incorrect interpretation of a manuscript 'y⸱', and that Q2 correctly read it as an abbreviation for 'that'. If I were preparing a single *Bussy* text, I would certainly follow Q2 in this instance. Because 'it' makes acceptable sense, however, I have preserved it for Q1; a Textual Note discusses this place, and others where judgment is called for. On the other hand, if I am convinced that a reading is corrupt, I have considered emendation; if emendation was called for, of course, the other quarto was a resource that was routinely examined to see if it would offer assistance. In those passages, for example, in which the Q2 compositor was probably attempting to decipher MS copy and garbled the readings, it would be pedantic to reject the Q1 readings. Inevitably, there are borderline areas: In a number of places, for example, Q2 presents readings that seem to have been motivated

---

of them were so manifestly misguided.' Louis C. Stagg apparently agreed on the superiority of Q1, for his citations from *Bussy* were based on Brooke's edition, whereas his other Chapman citations were based on Parrott (*Index to the Figurative Language of the Tragedies of Shakespeare's Chief Seventeenth-Century Contemporaries* [Ann Arbor, 1977], p. ix).

[39] 'The Revised Version of Chapman's *Bussy D'Ambois*,' p. 305: '. . . all these [changes] combine to produce what must be acknowledged as a new *Tragedy of Bussy D'Ambois*.' While admitting that the revised version 'is truer to the intentions and outlook of *The Revenge of Bussy D'Ambois* than it is to the values of the original *Bussy*,' Tricomi (unlike Nicholas Brooke) found the shift consistent with Chapman's own philosophic development.

by censorship: 'heaven' for 'God' in V.i.36/40, for example. One must suspect expurgation pursuant to the Blasphemy Act of 1606, and such expurgation would presumably have been done by someone other than the author. If so, these changes represent a special kind of corruption. If I were presenting a single text of *Bussy*, I would tend to follow Q1 in such instances; but once again I have adopted the more conservative policy of allowing each version to present its own reading.

The Historical Collation records all significant differences between the Q1 and Q2 versions (as well as the decisions of all later editors). To provide a more immediate means of identifying the verbal variants, I have printed in **boldface** all such variants in each text. I have arranged the two texts so that counterpart lines appear on facing pages directly opposite each other. A blank space opposite a line or lines in the other text indicates that the passage is unique to one text. Where the words that form a single verse in one text appear in two verses in the other because of lines interpolated in the middle, I have wherever possible broken the single verse, indenting the continuation as in the typography of verses broken between speeches. Lines that appear in both quartos but in different locations could not, of course, be brought together except by disarranging one of the texts; such lines face a blank space, and the rearrangement is noticed in a bracketed comment. In such transferred passages, only variant words are printed in boldface.

There was one later version of this play, a reworking (based on the Q2 version) for Restoration tastes by Thomas D'Urfey; published in 1691 (in a text that, to judge from several prompter's calls, was printed from a prompt-book), it was entitled *Bussy D'Ambois, or The Husband's Revenge*. Of course it has no textual authority for an editor of Chapman's play, but I have collated it as a matter of historical interest and on the chance that, because D'Urfey said that he had seen a production of Chapman's play, it may contain correct readings, or especially stage directions, that had been preserved on the stage but not accurately printed in Q2.

I have been engaged in the work on this edition for an embarrassing number of years. During that time I have been materially and spiritually assisted by many institutions and individuals. Both Marquette University and Brandeis University supported my work in significant and tangible ways. As always, I am indebted to many libraries and their staffs. The Huntington Library in particular was generous enough to provide a fellowship in support of this work, and the University of Illinois Library and the British Library provided their resources during extended periods of time. The staff of the Feldberg Computer Center at Brandeis University also gave unsparingly of their technical assistance – particularly Scott Magoon, John Lavagnino, and Ira Solomon. This project was one of those on which I worked with the subvention, at different times, of the John Simon Guggenheim Memorial Foundation and the American Council of Learned Societies. Berta Nash (née Sturman) kindly supplied me, during the early stages of my work, with a great deal of material supplementary to what she had published on this play, and I am happy to record here my gratitude to her; although I have finally disagreed with her conclusions, she deserves credit for being the first scholar to look at the relationship between the two versions of *Bussy D'Ambois* in a really searching way. As she was original, so she may yet be proved right, for we are still, I judge, in the shakeout phase of the idea that she first presented. In a similar, though less personal, way I am indebted to most of the previous editors of this play, for nearly all of them have forced me to think. Several former graduate students have assisted me in one way or another; those who contributed most substantively to the final result are Robert Wexelblatt, David Leese, and Gideon Rappaport. Professors Alan Craven and the late Charlton Hinman kindly offered criticism of a portion of the work, and each of them saved me from error. Professor Allan Holaday also offered helpful criticism, and his patience. Professor G. Blakemore Evans provided his faith, his help, and the model of his own impeccable scholarship. Finally, my wife has been – my wife, and she has helped more than anyone else.

Bussy D'Ambois:

A
TRAGEDIE:

As

it hath been often presented

at Paules.

LONDON,

Printed for *William Aspley.*

1607.

Reproduced from a copy in the British Library (Ashley 375)

Bussy D'Ambois:

A TRAGEDIE:

As it hath been often Acted with great Applause.

Being much corrected and amended by the Author before his death.

LONDON:
Printed by *A. N.* for *Robert Lunne.*
1 6 4 1.

[DRAMATIS PERSONAE

Bussy D'Ambois
King Henry [= Henri III of France]
Monsieur, brother of the King [= Duc d'Alençon]
Duke of Guise [= Henri le Balafre]
Montsurry, a Count [= Charles de Chambes, Comte de Monsoreau]
Beaumond, a courtier
Barrisor
L'Anou   } courtiers, challengers
Pyrhot (also spelled Pyrrhot)   of Bussy D'Ambois
Brisac
Melynell   } courtiers, supporters of Bussy D'Ambois
Frier, later Umbra Frier (named Comolet in Q1)
Maffe, steward to Monsieur
Behemoth, emperor of the underworld spirits
Cartophylax, spirit of the underworld

Duchess Elenor, wife of the Duke of Guise
Tamyra, Countess of Montsurry [= Françoise de Maridort]
Beaupre, niece to Duchess Elenor
Pyra, a lady of the court (also spelled Pyrha)
Annable, English maid-in-waiting to Duchess Elenor (also spelled -bel)
Pero, maid-in-waiting to Tamyra
Charlotte, maid-in-waiting to Beaupre

Nuncius, attendants, pages, servants, spirits, murtherers]

Dramatis Personae] *See Historical Collation*

Prologue.

Not out of confidence that none but wee
Are able to present this Tragedie,
Nor out of envie at the grace of late
It did receive, nor yet to derogate
From their deserts, who give out boldly, that   5
They move with equall feet on the same flat;
Neither for all, nor any of such ends,
Wee offer it, gracious and noble friends,
To your review, wee farre from emulation
(And charitably judge from imitation)   10
With this work entertaine you, a peece knowne
And still beleev'd in Court to be our owne,
To quit our claime, doubting our right or merit,
Would argue in us poverty of spirit
Which we must not subscribe to: Field is gone   15
Whose Action first did give it name, and one
Who came the neerest to him, is denide
By his gray beard to shew the height and pride /
Of D'Ambois youth and braverie; yet to hold   [A2ᵛ]
Our title still a foot, and not grow cold   20
By giving it o're, a third man with his best
Of care and paines defends our interest;
As Richard he was lik'd, nor doe wee feare,
In personating D'Ambois, hee'le appeare
To faint, or goe lesse, so your free consent   25
As heretofore give him encouragement. /

Prologue] (See Textual Note) ‖ 13 doubting] Q2(c); oubting Q2(u) ‖

Bussy D'Ambois:
A
TRAGEDIE.

Actus primi   Scena prima.

Bussy solus.

[*Buss.*] Fortune, not Reason, rules the state of things,
Reward goes backwards, Honor on his head;
Who is not poore, is monstrous; only Need
Giues forme and worth to euery humane seed.
As Cedars beaten with **incessant** stormes,   5
So great men flourish; and doe imitate
Vnskilfull statuaries, who suppose
(In **forging** a Colossus) if they make him
Stroddle enough, stroote, and looke big, and gape,
Their worke is goodly: so **our Tympanouse statists**   10
(In their affected grauitie of voice,
Sowernesse of countenance, maners crueltie,
Authoritie, wealth, and all the spawne of Fortune)
Thinke they beare all the kingdomes worth before them;
Yet differ not from those Colossicke Statues,   15
Which with Heroique formes, without o'respread,
Within are nought but morter, flint and lead.
Man is a Torch borne in the winde; a Dreame
But of a shadow, summ'd with all his substance;
And as great Seamen vsing all their **powers**   20
And skils in Neptunes deepe inuisible pathes,
In tall ships richly built and ribd with brasse,
To put a Girdle round about the world, /
When they haue done it (comming neere their Hauen)   [A2ᵛ]
Are **glad** to giue a warning peece, and call   25
A poore staid fisher-man, that neuer past
His Contries sight, to waft and guide them in:

I.i.1 *Buss.*] ‖ **4** and] & ‖ **10** Tympanouse statists] *stet* (*See Textual Note*) ‖ **12** maners] *stet*
(*See Textual Note*) ‖ **26** staid] *stet* (*See Textual Note*) ‖

Bussy D'Ambois:
A
TRAGEDIE.

Actus primi   Scena prima.

Enter Bussy D'Ambois poore.

[*Buss.*] Fortune, not Reason, rules the state of things,
Reward goes backwards, Honor on his head;
Who is not poore, is monstrous; only Need
Gives forme and worth to every humane seed.
As Cedars beaten with **continuall** stormes,   5
So great men flourish; and doe imitate
Unskilfull statuaries, who suppose
(In **forming** a Colossus) if they make him
Stroddle enough, stroot, and look bigg, and gape,
Their work is goodly: so **men meerely great**   10
(In their affected gravity of voice,
Sowernesse of countenance, manners cruelty,
Authority, wealth, and all the spawne of Fortune)
Think they beare all the Kingdomes worth before them;
Yet differ not from those Colossick Statues,   15
Which with Heroique formes without o're-spread,
Within are nought but morter, flint and lead.
Man is a Torch borne in the winde; a Dreame
But of a shadow, summ'd with all his substance;
And as great Seamen using all their **wealth**   20
And skills in *Neptunes* deepe invisible pathes, /
In tall ships richly built and ribd with brasse,   [A3ᵛ]
To put a Girdle round about the world,
When they have done it (comming neere their Haven)
Are **faine** to give a warning peece, and call   25
A poore staid fisher-man, that never past
His Countries sight, to waft and guide them in:

I.i.1 *Buss.*] ‖ **10** men meerely great] *stet* (*See Textual Note*) ‖ **12** manners] *stet* (*See Textual Note*) ‖ **26** staid] *stet* (*See Textual Note*) ‖

So when we wander furthest through the waues
Of Glassie Glorie and the Gulfes of State,
Topt with all Titles, spreading all our reaches,   30
As if each priuate Arme would sphere the **world**,
Wee must to Vertue for her guide resort,
Or wee shall shipwracke in our safest Port.   *Procumbit.*
                Monsieur with two Pages.
   [*Mons. Aside.*] There is no second place in Numerous State
That holds more than a Cypher: In a King   35
All places are contain'd. His words and lookes
Are like the flashes and the bolts of Ioue,
His deedes inimitable, like the Sea
That shuts still as it opes, and leaues no tracts,
Nor prints of President for **poore** mens facts: 40
There's but a Thred betwixt me and a Croune;
I would not wish it cut, vnlesse by Nature;
Yet to prepare mee for that **likely** Fortune,
Tis **fit I** get resolued spirits about mee.
I followd D'Ambois to this greene Retreat;   45
A man of spirit beyond the reach of feare,
Who (discontent with his neglected worth)
Neglects the light, and loues obscure Abodes;
But he is yoong and haughtie, apt to take
Fire at aduancement, to beare state and flourish;   50
In his Rise therefore shall my bounties shine:
None lothes the world so much, nor loues to scoffe it,
But gold and grace will make him surfet of it. –
What, D'Ambois?
   Buss.   He sir.
   Mons.   Turn'd to Earth, aliue?
Vp man, the Sunne shines on thee.
   Buss.   Let it shine.   55
I am no mote to play in't, as great men are. /
   Mons. **Think'st** thou men great in state, motes in the   [A3]
      sunne?
They say so that would haue thee freeze in shades,
That (like the grosse Sicilian Gurmundist)
Emptie their Noses in the Cates they loue,   60
That none may eat but they. Do thou but bring
Light to the Banquet Fortune sets before thee,
And thou wilt loth leane Darkenesse like thy Death.
Who would beleeue thy Mettall could let sloth

---

31 world,] ~; (*See Textual Note*) ‖ **32** Vertue] *Shepherd subs.*; vertue ‖ **34** *Mons.*] | SD *Aside.*]
Spencer ‖ **42** Nature] *N. Brooke*; nature ‖ **53** it. –] ~·ₐ ‖

So when we wander furthest through the waves
Of Glassie Glory and the Gulfes of State,
Topt with all Titles, spreading all our reaches,   30
As if each private Arme would sphere the **earth**,
Wee must to Vertue for her guide resort,
Or wee shall shipwrack in our safest Port.   *Procumbit.*
                 Monsieur with two Pages.
  [*Mons. Aside.*] There is no second place in Numerous State
That holds more than a Cypher: In a King   35
All places are contain'd. His words and looks
Are like the flashes and the bolts of *Iove*,
His deeds inimitable, like the Sea
That shuts still as it opes, and leaves no tracts,
Nor prints of President for **meane** mens facts: 40
There's but a Thred betwixt me and a Crowne;
I would not wish it cut, unlesse by Nature;
Yet to prepare me for that **possible** Fortune,
Tis **good to** get resolved spirits about mee.
I follow'd *D'Ambois* to this greene Retreat;   45
A man of spirit beyond the reach of feare,
Who (discontent with his neglected worth)
Neglects the light, and loves obscure Abodes;
But hee is young and haughty, apt to take
Fire at advancement, to beare state, and flourish;   50
In his Rise therefore shall my bounties shine:
None lothes the world so much, nor loves to scoffe it,
But gold and grace will make him surfet of it. –
What, *D'Ambois*?
  Buss.   He sir.
  Mons.   Turn'd to Earth, alive?   54
Up man, the Sunne shines on thee. /
  Buss.   Let it shine.   [A4]
I am no mote to play in't, as great men are.
  Mons. **Call'st** thou men great in state, motes in the
    sunne?
They say so that would have thee freeze in shades,
That (like the grosse Sicilian Gurmundist)
Empty their Noses in the Cates they love,   60
That none may eat but they. Do thou but bring
Light to the Banquet Fortune sets before thee
And thou wilt loath leane Darknesse like thy Death.
Who would beleeve thy mettall could let sloth

---

31 earth] *stet* (*See Textual Note*) ‖ 32 Vertue] *Shepherd subs.*; vertue ‖ 34 *Mons.*] | SD *Aside.*]
Spencer ‖ 42 Nature] *N. Brooke*; nature ‖ 53 it. –] ~.ˬ ‖ 57 Call'st] *Neilson*; Callest ‖

Rust and consume it? If Themistocles   65
Had liu'd obscur'd thus in th'Athenian state,
Xerxes had made both him and it his slaues.
If braue Camillus had lurckt so in Rome,
He had not fiue times beene dictator there,
Nor foure times triumpht. If Epaminondas   70
(Who liu'd twice twentie yeeres obscur'd in Thebs)
Had liu'd so still, he had beene still vnnam'd,
And paid his Countrie nor himselfe their right:
But putting foorth his strength, he rescude both
From imminent ruine; and like Burnisht Steele,   75
After long vse he shin'd; for as the light
Not only serues to shew, but render vs
Mutually profitable; so our liues
In acts exemplarie, not only winne
Our selues good Names, but **doth** to others giue   80
Matter for vertuous Deedes, by which wee liue.
    Buss. What would you wish me **doe**?
    Mons.   Leaue the troubled
   streames,
And liue **as** Thriuers doe, at the Well head.
    Buss. At the Well head? Alas what should I doe
With that enchanted Glasse? See diuels there?   85
Or (like a strumpet) learne to set my lookes
In an eternall Brake, or practise iuggling,
To keepe my face still fast, my hart still loose;
Or beare (like Dame Schoolemistresses their Riddles)
Two Tongues, and be good only for a shift;   90
Flatter great Lords, to put them still in minde
Why they were made Lords: or please **portly** Ladies
With a good carriage, tell them idle Tales, /
To make their Physicke worke; spend a mans life   [A3ᵛ]
In sights and visitations, that will make   95
His eies as hollow as his Mistresse heart:
To doe none good, but those that haue no neede;
To gaine being forward, though you breake for haste
All the Commandements ere you breake your fast,
But Beleeue backewards, make your Period   100
And Creedes last Article, I beleeue in God:
And (hearing villanies preacht) t'vnfold their Art
Learne to commit them? Tis a great mans Part.
Shall I learne this there?
    Mons.   No, thou needst not learne,

---

66 liu'd] liued ‖ **72** beene] *stet* (been *in one copy*) ‖ **82** me doe] *stet* (*See Textual Note*) ‖ **83** doe,]
~ ‖ **89** Dame] *Parrott subs.*; Dames (*See Textual Note*) ‖ **99** ere you] ereyou | fast,] ~? ‖ **101**
Article,] ~; ‖ **103** them?] ~, ‖

Rust and consume it? If *Themistocles*   65
Had liv'd obscur'd thus in th'Athenian state,
Xerxes had made both him and it his slaves.
If brave *Camillus* had lurckt so in Rome,
He had not five times beene Dictator there,
Nor foure times triumpht. If *Epaminondas*   70
(Who liv'd twice twenty yeeres obscur'd in Thebs)
Had liv'd so still, he had beene still unnam'd,
And paid his Country nor himselfe their right:
But putting forth his strength, he rescu'd both
From imminent ruine; and like burnisht Steele,   75
After long use he shin'd; for as the light
Not only serves to shew, but render us
Mutually profitable; so our lives
In acts exemplarie, not only winne
Our selves good Names, but **doe** to others give   80
Matter for vertuous Deeds, by which wee live.
    Buss. What would you wish me?
    Mons.   Leave the troubled
     streames,
And live **where** Thrivers doe, at the Well head.
    Buss. At the Well head? Alas what should I doe
With that enchanted Glasse? See devils there?   85
Or (like a strumpet) learne to set my looks
In an eternall Brake, or practise jugling,
To keepe my face still fast, my heart still loose;
Or beare (like Dame Schoolmistresses their Riddles)
Two Tongues, and be good only for a shift;   90
Flatter great Lords, to put them still in minde /
Why they were made Lords: or please **humorous** Ladies   [A4ᵛ]
With a good carriage, tell them idle Tales,
To make their Physick work; spend a mans life
In sights and visitations, that will make   95
His eyes as hollow as his Mistresse heart:
To doe none good, but those that have no need;
To gaine being forward, though you break for haste
All the Commandements ere you break your fast,
But Beleeve backwards, make your Period   100
And Creeds last Article, I beleeve in God:
And (hearing villanies preacht) t'unfold their Art
Learne to commit them? 'Tis a great mans Part.
Shall I learne this there?
    Mons.   No, thou needst not learne,

---

82 me] *stet* (*See Textual Note*) ‖ 83 doe,] ~. ‖ 89 Dame] *Parrott subs.*; Dames (*See Textual Note*) ‖
99 fast,] ~; ‖ 103 them?] ~, ‖

Thou hast the Theorie, now goe there and practise.   105
    Buss. I, in a thridbare suit; when men come there,
They must haue high Naps, and goe from thence bare:
A man may drowne the parts of ten rich men
In one poore suit; Braue Barks, and outward Glosse
Attract Court **eies**, be in-parts ne're so grosse.   110
    Mons. Thou shalt haue Glosse enough, and all things fit
T'enchase in all shew, thy long-smother'd spirit:
Be rul'd by me then. The **rude** Scythians
Painted blinde Fortunes powerfull hands with wings,
To shew her gifts come swift and suddenly,   115
Which if her Fauorite be not swift to take,
He loses them foreuer. Then be **rul'd**:
Stay but a while heere, and I'le send to thee.
                              Exit Mons. with Pages. Manet Buss.
    Buss. [*Rising.*] What will he send? some Crounes? It is to
        sow them
Vpon my spirit, and make them spring a Croune   120
Worth Millions of the seede Crounes he will send:

But hee's no husband heere; A smooth plaine ground
Will neuer nourish any politicke seede;
I am for honest Actions, not for great:
If I may bring vp a new fashion,   125
And rise in Court **with** vertue, speede his plow:
The King hath knowne me long as well as hee,
Yet could my Fortune neuer fit the length
Of both their vnderstandings till this houre.
There is a deepe nicke in times restlesse wheele /   130
For each mans good, when which nicke comes it strikes;   [A4]
As Rhetoricke, yet workes not perswasion,
But only is a meane to make it worke:
So no man riseth by his reall merit,
But when it cries Clincke in his Raisers spirit: 135
Many will say, that cannot rise at all,
Mans first houres rise, is first steppe to his fall.
I'le venture that; men that fall low must die,
As well as men cast headlong from the skie.

---

110 in-parts] ~ ~ ‖ 112 long-smother'd] long smothered ‖ 118 SD *Exit Mons.*] *placed as in Dilke;
after l.117* | *with Pages.*] *Boas subs.* | *Manet Buss.*] *after l.119* ‖ 119 SD *Rising.*] (*See Textual
Note*) ‖ 126 with] *stet* (*See Textual Note*) | vertue,] ~; ‖ 138 I'le] Il'e ‖

Thou hast the Theorie, now goe there and practise.   105
   Buss. I, in a thrid-bare suit; when men come there,
They must have high Naps, and goe from thence bare:
A man may drowne the parts of ten rich men
In one poore suit; Brave Barks, and outward Glosse
Attract Court **Loves**, be in-parts ne're so grosse.   110
   Mons. Thou shalt have Glosse enough, and all things fit
T'enchase in all shew thy long-smother'd spirit:
Be rul'd by me then. The **old** Scythians
Painted blinde Fortunes powerfull hands with wings,
To shew her gifts come swift and suddenly,   115
Which if her Favorite be not swift to take,
He loses them for ever. Then be **wise**:
Stay but a while here, and I'le send to thee.
                    Exit Mons. with Pages. Manet Buss.
   Buss. [*Rising.*] What will he send? some Crowns? It is to
     sow them
Upon my spirit, and make them spring a Crowne   120
Worth Millions of the seed Crownes he will send.
Like to disparking noble Husbandmen,
Hee'll put his Plow into me, Plow me up:
But his unsweating thrift is policie,
And learning-hating policie is ignorant   125
To fit his seed-land soyl; a smooth plain ground
Will never nourish any politick seed;
I am for honest Actions, not for great: /
If I may bring up a new fashion,   [B1]
And rise in Court **for** vertue, speed his plow: 130
The King hath knowne me long as well as hee,
Yet could my Fortune never fit the length
Of both their understandings till this houre.
There is a deepe nicke in times restlesse wheele
For each mans good, when which nicke comes it strikes;   135
As Rhetorick, yet workes not perswasion,
But only is a meane to make it worke:
So no man riseth by his reall merit,
But when it cries Clincke in his Raisers spirit.
Many will say, that cannot rise at all,   140
Mans first houres rise is first step to his fall:
I'le venture that; men that fall low must die,
As well as men cast headlong from the skie.

---

110 in-parts] ~,~ ‖ 112 long-smother'd] long smothered ‖ 118 SD *Exit Mons.*] *placed as in Dilke;
after l.117* ⌐ *with Pages.*] *Boas subs.* ⌐ *Manet Buss.*] *after l.119* ‖ 119 SD *Rising.*] (*See Textual
Note*) ‖ 122-26 Like … soyl] *stet* (*See Textual Note*) ‖ 127 nourish any] nourishany ‖ 130 for]
stet (*See Textual Note*) ⌐ vertue,] ~; ‖

Ent. Maffe.

[*Maff. Aside.*] Humor of Princes! Is this **man** indu'd   140
With any merit worth a thousand Crounes?
Will my Lord haue me be so ill a Steward
Of his Reuenue, to dispose a summe
So great with so small cause as shewes in him?
I must examine this:– Is your name D'Ambois?   145
   Buss. Sir?
   Maff.   Is your name D'Ambois?
   Buss.   Who haue wee heere?
Serue you the Monsieur?
   Maff.   How?
   Buss.   Serue you the Monsieur?
   Maff. Sir, y'are very hot. I serue the Monsieur;
But in such place as giues me the Command
Of all his other seruants: And because   150
His Graces pleasure is, to giue your good
A Passe through my Command, Me thinks you might
Vse me with more **good fashion**.
   Buss.   Crie you mercie.
Now you haue open'd my dull eies, I see you;
And would be glad to see the good you speake of: 155
What might I call your name?
   Maff.   Monsieur Maffe.
   Buss. Monsieur Maffe? Then good Monsieur Maffe,
Pray let me know you better.
   Maff.   Pray doe so,
That you may vse me better; For your selfe, /   159
By your no better outside, I would iudge you   [A4ᵛ]
To be **a** Poet; Haue you giuen my Lord
Some Pamphlet?
   Buss.   Pamphlet?
   Maff.   Pamphlet sir, I say.
   Buss. Did **his wise excellencie** leaue the good
That is to passe your charge, to my poore vse,
To your discretion?
   Maff.   Though he did not sir,   165
I hope tis no **bad** office to aske reason,
How that his grace giues mee in charge, goes from me?
   Buss. That's very perfect, sir.
   Maff.   Why very good, sir;
I pray then giue me leaue: If for no Pamphlet,
May I not know what other merit in you,   170

---

140 *Maff.*] | SD *Aside.*] *Parrott* | Princes!] ~. ‖ **145** this:–] ~:ˬ ‖ **146** Sir?] ~. ‖ **152** Command,]
~; ‖ **154** open'd] opened ‖ **159** better;] ~, ‖ **168** perfect, ... good,] ~ˬ ... ~ˬ ‖

Ent. Maffe.

[*Maff. Aside.*] Humor of Princes! Is this **wretch** indu'd
With any merit worth a thousand Crownes?   145
Will my Lord have me be so ill a Steward
Of his Revenue, to dispose a summe
So great with so small cause as shewes in him?
I must examine this:– Is your name *D'Ambois*?
  Buss. Sir?
  Maff.   Is your name *D'Ambois*?
  Buss.   Who have we here?   150
Serve you the Monsieur?
  Maff.   How?
  Buss.   Serve you the Monsieur?
  Maff. Sir, y'are very hot. I **doe** serve the Monsieur;
But in such place as gives me the Command
Of all his other servants: And because
His Graces pleasure is, to give your good   155
His Passe through my Command, Me thinks you might
Vse me with more **respect**.
  Buss.   Crie you mercy.
Now you have open'd my dull eies, I see you;
And would be glad to see the good you speake of: /
What might I call your name?   [B1ᵛ]
  Maff.   Monsieur *Maffe.*   160
  Buss. Monsieur *Maffe*? Then good Monsieur *Maffe*,
Pray let me know you better.
  Maff.   Pray doe so,
That you may use me better. For your selfe,
By your no better outside, I would judge you
To be **some** Poet; Have you given my Lord   165
Some Pamphlet?
  Buss.   Pamphlet?
  Maff.   Pamphlet sir, I say.
  Buss. Did **your great Masters goodnesse** leave the good
That is to passe your charge, to my poore use,
To your discretion?
  Maff.   Though he did not sir,
I hope 'tis no **rude** office to aske reason,   170
How that his Grace gives me in charge goes from me?
  Buss. That's very perfect, sir.
  Maff.   Why very good, sir;
I pray then give me leave: If for no Pamphlet,
May I not know what other merit in you,

---

144 *Maff.*] | SD *Aside.*] *Parrott* ‖ **149** this:–] ~:ˌ ‖ **150** Sir?] ~. ‖ **153-55**] *For Q2 prompter's note*
opposite these lines, see I.ii.SD ‖ **156** His] *stet* (*See Textual Note*) ‖ **158** open'd] opened ‖ **172**
perfect, ... good,] ~ˌ ... ~ˌ ‖

Makes his compunction willing to relieue you?
   Buss. No merit in the world sir.
   Maff.   That is strange.
Y'are a poore souldier, are you?
   Buss.   That I am sir.
   Maff. And haue Commanded?
   Buss.   I, and gone without sir.
   Maff. [*Aside.*] I see the man: A hundred Crounes will
   make him   175
Swagger, and drinke healths to his **highnes** bountie;
And sweare he could not be more bountifull.
So ther's nine hundred Crounes, saft;– heere tall souldier,
His grace hath sent you a whole hundred Crounes.
   Buss. A hundred sir? naie doe his Highnes right;   180
I know his hand is larger, and perhaps
I may deserue more than my outside shewes:
I am a **scholar**, as I am a souldier,
And I can Poetise; and (being well encourag'd)
May sing his Fame for giuing; yours for deliuering   185
(Like a most faithfull Steward) what he giues.
   Maff. What shall your subiect be?
   Buss.   I care not much,
If to his **excellence** I sing the praise
Of faire great Noses, And to **your Deserts** /   189
The reuerend vertues of a faithfull Steward;   [B1]
What Qualities haue you sir (beside your chaine
And veluet Iacket)? Can your worship dance?

                                          [*Touching his sword.*]
   Maff. [*Aside.*] A **merrie** Fellow faith: It seemes my Lord
Will haue him for his Iester; And **beleeue it,**
Such men are now no fooles, Tis a Knights place: 195
If I (to saue **my Lord** some Crounes) should vrge him
T'abate his Bountie, I should not be heard;
I would to heauen I were an errant Asse,
For then I should be sure to haue the Eares
Of these great men, where now their Iesters haue them: 200
Tis good to please him, yet Ile take no notice
Of his preferment, but in policie
Will still be graue and serious, lest he thinke
I feare his wodden dagger:– Heere sir Ambo,

175 SD *Aside.*] *Dilke subs.* ‖ **178** saft;–] ~;͵ ‖ **183** scholar] *stet (See Textual Note)* ‖ **192** Iacket)?]
~)͵ | SD *Touching his sword.*] *after D'Urfey (See Textual Note)* ‖ **193** SD *Aside.*] *Dilke subs.* ‖ **196**
my Lord] *stet (See Textual Note)* ‖ **204** dagger:–] ~:͵ | Ambo] *stet (See Textual Note)* ‖

Makes his compunction willing to relieve you?   175
  Buss. No merit in the world sir.
  Maff.   That is strange.
Y'are a poore souldier, are you?
  Buss.   That I am sir.
  Maff. And have Commanded?
  Buss.   I, and gone without sir.
  Maff. [*Aside.*] I see the man: A hundred Crownes will
    make him
Swagger, and drinke healths to his **Graces** bountie;   180
And sweare he could not be more bountifull.
So there's nine hundred Crounes sav'd;– here tall souldier,
His grace hath sent you a whole hundred Crownes.
  Buss. A hundred sir? Nay doe his Highnesse right;
I know his hand is larger, and perhaps   185
I may deserve more than my outside shewes:
I am a **Poet**, as I am a Souldier,
And I can Poetise; and (being well encourag'd) /
May sing his fame for giving; yours for delivering   [B2]
(Like a most faithfull Steward) what he gives.   190
  Maff. What shall your subject be?
  Buss.   I care not much,
If to his **bounteous Grace** I sing the praise
Of faire great Noses, And to **you of long ones**.

What Qualities have you sir (beside your chaine
And velvet Jacket)? Can your worship dance?   195
                   [*Touching his sword.*]
  Maff. [*Aside.*] A **pleasant** fellow faith: It seemes my Lord
Will have him for his Jester; And **berlady**
Such men are now no fooles, 'Tis a Knights place:
If I (to save **his Grace** some Crounes) should urge him
T'abate his Bountie, I should not be heard;   200
I would to heaven I were an errant Asse,
For then I should be sure to have the Eares
Of these great men, where now their Jesters have them:
Tis good to please him, yet Ile take no notice
Of his preferment, but in policie   205
Will still be grave and serious, lest he thinke
I feare his woodden dagger:– Here sir *Ambo*–
  Buss. How, *Ambo* sir?
  Maff.   I, is not your name *Ambo*?

---

179 SD *Aside.*] *Dilke subs.* || **182** sav'd;–] ~; || **187** Poet] *stet (See Textual Note)* || **192** praise] ~, || **195** Jacket)?] ~). | SD *Touching his sword.*] *after D'Urfey (See Textual Note)* || **196** SD *Aside.*] *Dilke subs.* || **200** T'abate] Tabate || **207** dagger:–] ~: | *Ambo*–] Ambo, *(See Textual Note)* || **208** Buss.] *D'Amb. (so through the rest of this scene)* | *Ambo ... Ambo*] Ambo ... Ambo | I,] ~ || **208-10** How ... *D'Amboys.*] *stet (See Textual Note)* || **208** I,] ~ ||

A thousand Crounes I bring you from my Lord;   205
Serue God, play the good husband, you may make
This a good standing liuing, Tis a Bountie,
His Highnes might perhaps haue bestow'd better.
   Buss. Goe, y'are a Rascall; hence, Away you Rogue.
   Maff. What meane you sir?
   Buss.   Hence; prate no more;   210
Or by thy villans blood thou prat'st thy last:
A Barbarous Groome, grudge at his masters Bountie:
But since I know he would as much abhorre
His hinde should argue what he giues his friend,   214
Take that Sir, [*Strikes him.*] for your aptnesse
   to dispute.   *Exit.*
   Maff. These Crounes are **sown** in blood, blood be their
   fruit.   *Exit.*

[I.ii.]

Henry, Guise, Montsurry, Duchess Elenor, Tamyra,
Beaupre, Pero, Charlotte,
Pyra, Annable.

   Henr. Dutchesse of Guise, your Grace is much enricht,
In the attendance of **this** English virgin,   [*Indicating Annable.*]
That will initiate her Prime of youth
(Dispos'd to Court conditions), vnder hand
Of your preferd instructions and Command, /   5
Rather than anie in the English Court,   [B1ᵛ]
Whose Ladies are not matcht in Christendome,
For gracefull and confirm'd behauiours;
More than the Court, where they are bred is equall'd.
   Gui. I like not their Court **forme**, it is too
   crestfalne,   10
In all obseruance; making **Semi**-gods
Of their great Nobles; and of their old Queene
An euer-yoong, and most immortall Goddesse.

206 Serue God] *stet* (*See Textual Note*) ‖ **209, 210** Buss.] *D'Amb.* ‖ **215** SD *Strikes him.*] *Dilke after D'Urfey* ‖ **216** sown] *stet* (*See Textual Note*) ‖ **I.ii.**] *Boas subs. after Dilke* ‖ SD *Duchess Elenor*] *Elenor* | *Pyra*] *Pyr* | *Annable*] *stet* (*See Textual Note*) ‖ **2** SD *Indicating Annable.*] *after Boas note* ‖ **3-4** youth … conditions),] ~, … ~)ₐ ‖ **11** Semi-gods] *stet* (*See Textual Note*) ‖

Buss. You call'd me lately *D'Amboys,* has your Worship
  So short a head?
Maff.   I cry thee mercy *D'Amboys.*   210
A thousand Crownes I bring you from my Lord;
If you be thriftie and play the good husband, you may make
This a good standing living, 'Tis a Bountie,
His Highnesse might perhaps have bestow'd better.
  Buss. Goe, y'are a Rascall; hence, Away you Rogue.   215
  Maff. What meane you sir?
  Buss.   Hence; prate no more;
Or by thy villans bloud thou prat'st thy last:
A Barbarous Groome, grudge at his masters Bountie:
But since I know he would as much abhorre
His hinde should argue what he gives his friend,   220
Take that Sir, [*Strikes him.*] for your aptnesse
  to dispute.   *Exit.*
  Maff. These Crownes are **set** in bloud, bloud be their
  fruit.   *Exit. /*

[I. ii.]

     Henry, Guise, Montsurry, Duchess Elenor, Tamyra,   [B2ᵛ]
       Beaupre, Pero, Charlotte, Pyra, Annable.
         Table, Chesbord, and Tapers.
  Henr. Duchesse of *Guise,* your Grace is much enricht,
In the attendance of **that** English virgin,   [*Indicating Annable.*]
That will initiate her Prime of youth
(Dispos'd to Court conditions), under **the** hand
Of your prefer'd instructions and Command,   5
Rather than any in the English Court,
Whose Ladies are not matcht in Christendome,
For gracefull and confirm'd behaviours;
More than the Court where they are bred is equall'd.
  Gui. I like not their Court-**fashion**, it is too
  crestfalne,   10
In all observance; making **Demi**-gods
Of their great Nobles; and of their old Queene
An ever-yong, and most immortall Goddesse.
  Mont. No question shee's the rarest Queene in Europe.
  Gui. **But what's that to her Immortality?**   15

---

212 If ... and] *stet (See Textual Note)* ‖ **221** SD *Strikes him.*] *Dilke after D'Urfey* ‖ **222** set] *stet*
(See Textual Note) | their] Q2(c); *the* Q2(u) ‖ **I.ii.**] *Boas subs. after Dilke* ‖ SD *Duchess Elenor*]
Elenor | *Annable*] *stet (See Textual Note)* | *Table ... Tapers.*] *placed as in Shepherd; Table*
Chesbord / & Tapers behind / the Arras. / in margin opposite ll. 153-55 (See Textual Note) ‖ **1**
Guise] *Guïse* ‖ **2** SD *Indicating Annable.*] *after Boas note* ‖ **3** youth] *you h one copy (See Press-*
Variants) ‖ **3-4** youth ... conditions),] ~, ... ~), ‖ **11** Demi-gods] *Demi gods some copies (See*
Press-Variants and Textual Note) ‖

   Henr. Assure you Cosen Guise, so great a Courtier,
So full of maiestie and Roiall parts,   15
No Queene in Christendome may **boast** her selfe,
Her Court approoues it, That's a Court indeede;
Not mixt with **Rudenesse** vs'd in common houses;
But, as Courts should be th'abstracts of their kingdomes,
In all the Beautie, State, and Worth they hold;   20
So is hers, amplie, and by her inform'd.
The world is not contracted in a man,
With more proportion and expression
Than in her Court, her Kingdome: Our French Court
Is a meere mirror of confusion to it: 25
The King and subiect, Lord and euerie slaue
Dance a continuall Haie; Our Roomes of State,
Kept like our stables; No place more obseru'd
Than a rude Market place: And though our Custome
Keepe this assur'd **deformitie** from our **sight**,   30
Tis nere the lesse essentiallie vnsightlie,
Which they would soone see, would they change their forme
To this of ours, and then compare them both;
Which we must not affect, because in Kingdomes,
Where the Kings change doth breede the Subiects terror, 35
Pure Innouation is more grosse than error.
   Mont. No Question we shall see them imitate
(Though a farre off) the fashions of our Courts,
As they haue euer Ap't vs in attire;
Neuer were men so wearie of their Skins,   40
And apt to leape out of themselues as they;
Who when they trauell to bring foorth rare men,
Come home deliuer'd of a fine French suit: /
Their Braines lie with their Tailors, and get babies   [B2]
For their most compleat issue; Hee's **first borne**   45
To all the morall vertues, that first greetes
The light with a new fashion, which becomes them
Like Apes, disfigur'd with the attires of men.
   Henr. No Question they much wrong their reall worth,
In affectation of outlandish Scumme;   50
But they haue faults, and wee; They foolish-proud,
To be the Pictures of our vanitie;
We proud, that they are proud of foolerie.

---

17 That's] Thats ‖ **43** deliuer'd] deliuered ‖ **51** wee] *stet (See Textual Note)* ‖ **53** foolerie.] *stet (On the line added in Q2 see Textual Note)* ‖

Henr. Assure you Cosen *Guise*, so great a Courtier,
So full of majestie and Roiall parts,
No Queene in Christendome may **vaunt** her selfe,
Her Court approves it, That's a Court indeed;
Not mixt with **Clowneries** us'd in common houses;   20
But, as Courts should be th'abstracts of their kingdomes,
In all the Beautie, State, and Worth they hold;
So is hers, amplie, and by her inform'd.
The world is not contracted in a man,
With more proportion and expression,   25
Than in her Court, her Kingdome: Our French Court
Is a meere mirror of confusion to it:
The King and subject, Lord and every slave,
Dance a continuall Haie; Our Roomes of State,
Kept like our stables; no place more observ'd   30
Than a rude Market-place: and though our Custome
Keepe this assur'd **confusion** from our **eyes**,
'Tis nere the lesse essentially unsightly,
Which they would soone see, would they change their forme /   34
To this of ours, and then compare them both;   [B3]
Which we must not affect, because in Kingdomes,
Where the Kings change doth breed the Subjects terror,
Pure Innovation is more grosse than error.
    Mont. No Question we shall see them imitate
(Though a farre off) the fashions of our Courts,   40
As they have ever Ap't us in attire;
Never were men so weary of their skins,
And apt to leape out of themselves as they;
Who when they travell to bring forth rare men,
Come home deliver'd of a fine French suit: 45
Their Braines lie with their Tailors, and get babies
For their most compleat issue; Hee's **sole heire**
To all the morall vertues, that first greetes
The light with a new fashion, which becomes them
Like Apes, disfigur'd with the attires of men.   50
    Henr. No Question they much wrong their reall worth,
In affectation of outlandish Scumme;
But they have faults, and we **more**; They foolish-proud,
To **jet in others plumes so haughtely**;
We proud, that they are proud of foolerie,   55
Holding our worthes more compleat for their vaunts.

16 *Guise*] Guise ‖ 45 deliver'd] delivered ‖ 53 we more] *stet (See Textual Note)* ‖ 56 Holding . . .
vaunts] *stet (See Textual Note)* ‖

Enter Monsieur, D'Ambois.

Mons. [*To Bussy.*] Come mine owne sweet heart I will enter
    thee.
[*To Henry.*] Sir, I haue brought **this** Gentleman **t'attend
    you**;   55
And pray, you would vouchsafe to doe him grace.
   Henr. D'Ambois, I thinke.
   Buss.   That's still my name, my Lord,
Though I be something alter'd in attire.
   Henr. I like your alteration, and must tell you,
I haue expected th'offer of your seruice;   60
For we (in feare to make milde Vertue proud)
Vse not to seeke her out in any man.
   Buss. Nor doth she vse to seeke out any man:
He that will winne, must wooe her; **shee's not shamelesse**.
   Mons. I vrg'd her modestie in him, my Lord,   65
And gaue her those Rites, that he saies shee merits.
   Henr. If you haue woo'd and won, then Brother weare
    him.   [*Henry and Guise begin a game of chess.*]
   Mons. [*Aside to Bussy.*] Th'art mine, **my loue**; See here's
the Guises Duches; The Countesse of Mountsurreaue; Beaupres;
come I'le enseame thee; – Ladies, y'are too many to be in   70
Counsell: I haue heere a friend, that I would gladlie enter in your
Graces.

   Duch. If you enter him in our Graces, me thinks by his blunt
behauiour, he should come out of himselfe.
   Tam. Has he neuer beene Courtier, my Lord?   75
   Mons. Neuer, my Ladie.
   Beaup. And why did the Toy take him inth'head now?
   Buss. Tis leape yeere, Ladie, and therefore verie good to /
enter a Courtier.   [B2ᵛ]

   Tam. The man's a Courtier at first sight.   80
   Buss. I can sing prickesong, Ladie, at first sight; and why not
be a Courtier as suddenly?
   Beaup. Heere's a Courtier rotten before he be ripe.
   Buss. Thinke mee not impudent, Ladie, I am yet no Courtier, I

---

54 SD *To Bussy.*] ‖ **55** SD *To Henry.*] *Parrott subs.* ‖ **57** *Buss.*] *D'Amb.* (*so all speech-prefixes
through l. 129*) | That's] Thats ‖ **57-58** That's ... attire] *Dilke; as prose* (though ... some-/thing) ‖
58 alter'd] altered ‖ **61** Vertue] *N. Brooke subs. after D'Urfey*; vertue ‖ **65-66** I ... merits] *Dilke;
as prose* (and) ‖ **67** SD *Henry ... chess.*] *Harrier after Jacquot (See Textual Note)* ‖ **68** SD *Aside
to Bussy.*] *after D'Urfey* ‖ **69** Duches;] ~. | Beaupres;] ~, ‖ **70** thee;–] ~;‸ ‖ **71** haue heere]
haueheere ‖

Enter Monsieur, D'Ambois.

Mons. [*To Bussy.*] Come mine owne sweet heart I will enter
    thee.
[*To Henry.*] Sir, I have brought **a** Gentleman **to**
    court;
And pray, you would vouchsafe to doe him grace.
    Henr. D'Ambois, I thinke.
    Buss.   That's still my name, my Lord,   60
Though I be something alter'd in attire.
    Henr. **We** like your alteration, and must tell you,
We have expected th'offer of your service;
For we (in feare to make mild Vertue proud)
Vse not to seeke her out in any man.   65
    Buss. Nor doth she use to seeke out any man:
They that will winne, must wooe her.
    Mons. I urg'd her modestie in him, my Lord,
And gave her those Rites, that he sayes shee merits.
    Henr. If you have woo'd and won, then Brother weare   70
    him. /   [*Henry and Guise begin a game of chess.*]
    Mons. [*Aside to Bussy.*] Th'art mine, **sweet heart**; See here's   [B3ᵛ]
the *Guises* Duches; The Countesse of *Mountsurreaue*; *Beaupre*;
come I'le enseame thee. – Ladies, y'are too many to be in
Counsell: I have here a friend, that I would gladly enter in your
Graces.   75
    Buss. **'Save you Ladyes.**
    Duch. If you enter him in our Graces, **my Lord,** me thinkes by
his blunt behaviour, he should come out of himselfe.
    Tam. Has he never beene Courtier, my Lord?
    Mons. Never, my Lady.   80
    Beaup. And why did the Toy take him inth'head now?
    Buss. Tis leape yeare, Lady, and therefore very good to enter
a Courtier.
    Henr. [*Looking up from the board.*] **Marke Duchesse of *Guise*,**
there is one is not bashfull.   85
    Duch. **No my Lord, he is much guilty of the bold extremity.**
    Tam. The man's a Courtier at first sight.
    Buss. I can sing pricksong, Lady, at first sight; and why not
be a Courtier as suddenly?
    Beaup. Here's a Courtier rotten before he be ripe.   90
    Buss. Thinke me not impudent, Lady, I am yet no Courtier, I

---

57 SD *To Bussy.*] ‖ **58** SD *To Henry.*] *Parrott subs.* ‖ **60** *Buss.*] *D'Amb. (so through l.145)* ‖
60-61 That's ... attire] *Dilke; as prose (though ... some-/thing)* ‖ **61** alter'd] altered ‖ **64** Vertue]
N. Brooke subs. after D'Urfey; vertue ‖ **67** her.] *stet (See Textual Note to l.–/56)* ‖ **68-69** I ...
merits] *Dilke; as prose* (and) ‖ **70** SD *Henry ... chess.*] *Harrier after Jacquot (See Textual Note)* ‖
71 SD *Aside to Bussy.*] *after D'Urfey* ‖ **72** *Guises*] Guises | *Mountsurreaue;*] Mountsurreaue, ‖
73 thee.–] ~. ‖ **84-86** *Henr. ... extremity*] *stet (See Textual Note)* ‖ **84** SD *Looking ... board.*] |
Guise] Guise ‖

desire to be one, and [*To the Duchess.*] would gladly take entrance   85
(Madam) vnder your Princely Colours.
          Enter Barrisor, L'Anou, Pyrhot. [They converse apart].

Gui. [*Looking up from the board.*] Sir, know you me?
Buss. My Lord?
Gui. I know not you: Whom doe you serue?
Buss. Serue, my Lord?   90
Gui. Go to Companion; Your Courtship's too saucie.
Buss. Saucie? Companion? Tis the Guise, but yet those
termes might haue beene spar'd of the Guiserd. Companion?
Hee's iealous by this light: are you blinde of that side **Sir**?
Ile to her againe for that. – Forth **Madam**, for the honour   95
of Courtship.
Gui. Cease your Courtshippe, or by heauen Ile cut your
throat.
Buss. Cut my throat? cut a whetstone; **good** Accius Nœuius, doe
as much with your tongue as he did with a Rasor; cut my   100
throat?

[Q2 ll. 120-25 = Q1 ll. 108-13.]

Gui. Ile doe't, by this hand.
Buss. That hand dares not doe't; y'aue cut too many throates
alreadie Guise; and robb'd the Realme of many thousand Soules,
more precious than thine owne. – Come Madam, talke on;   105

85 SD *To the Duchess.*] *Parrott subs.* ‖ **86** SD *Enter ... Pyrhot.*] *placed as in Q2; before l. 108 in
Q1 (See Textual Note)* | *Pyrhot*] *after* Shepherd; *Pyrlot* | *They converse apart.*] ‖ **87** SD *Looking
up from the board.*] *after* Baskervill ‖ **92-95** Saucie? ... that] *stet (See Textual Note)* ‖ **93**
Guiserd. Companion] Guiserd. / Companion (*wide space after* Guiserd. *as if verse*) ‖ **95** that.–]
~., ‖ **102** doe't,] ~., ‖ **103-7** That ... it] *prose as in* Shepherd; That ... many / Throates ... Realme of /
Many ... owne. / Come ... talke? / Talke ... it ‖ **104** robb'd] Robb'd ‖ **105** owne.–] ~., ‖

desire to be one, and [*To the Duchess.*] would gladly take entrance
(Madam) under your Princely Colours.

          Enter Barrisor, L'Anou, Pyrhot. [They converse apart].

Duch. Soft sir, you must rise by degrees, first being the
servant of some common Lady or Knights wife, then a little   95
higher to a Lords wife; next a little higher to a Countesse; yet
a little higher to a Duchesse, and then turne the ladder.

Buss. Doe you alow a man then foure mistresses, when the
greatest Mistresse is alowed but three servants?

Duch. Where find you that statute sir?   100

Buss. Why, be judged by the Groome-porters.

Duch. The Groome-porters?

Buss. I Madam, must not they judge of all gamings i'th' Court?

Duch. You talke like a gamester.

Gui. [*Looking up from the board.*] Sir, know you me?   105

Buss. My Lord?

Gui. I know not you: Whom doe you serve?

Buss. Serve, my Lord? /

Gui. Go to Companion; Your Courtship's too saucie.   [B4]

Buss. Saucie? Companion? Tis the *Guise*, but yet those   110
termes might have beene spar'd of the Guiserd. Companion?
He's jealous by this light: are you blind of that side **Duke?**
Ile to her againe for that. – Forth **princely Mistresse,** for the
honour of Courtship. **Another Riddle.**

Gui. Cease your Courtshippe, or by heaven Ile cut your   115
throat.

Buss. Cut my throat? cut a whetstone; **young** *Accius Nœvius,* doe
as much with your tongue as he did with a Rasor; cut my
throat?

Bar. What new-come Gallant have wee heere, that dares mate 120
the *Guise* thus?

L'An. Sfoot tis *D'Ambois*; The Duke mistakes him (on my life)
for some Knight of the new edition.

Buss. Cut my throat? I would the King fear'd thy cutting of
his throat no more than I feare thy cutting of mine.   125

Gui. Ile doe't, by this hand.

Buss. That hand dares not doe't; y'ave cut too many throats
already *Guise,* and robb'd the Realme of many thousand Soules,
more precious than thine owne. – Come Madam, talk on; Sfoot,

92 SD *To the Duchess.*] *N. Brooke after Parrott* ‖ 93 SD *Enter ... Pyrhot.*] *stet* (See Textual Note)
| SD *Pyrhot*] *after Shepherd; Pyrlot* | SD *They converse apart.*] ‖ 94-104 *Duch. ... gamester.*] *stet*
(See Textual Note) ‖ 96 wife;] ~ˏ *one copy* (See Press-Variants) ‖ 98 *Buss.*] *D'Amb.* (*D'Amb ?some
copies* [See Press-Variants]) ‖ 101 Why,] ~ˏ ‖ 105 SD *Looking ... board.*] *after Baskervill* ‖ 110-12
Saucie ... light] *stet* (See Textual Note) ‖ 110 *Guise*] Guise ‖ 111 Guiserd. Companion] Guiserd. /
Companion (*wide space after* Guiserd. *as if verse*) ‖ 113 that.–] ~ˏ ‖ 121 *Guise*] Guise ‖ 126 doe't,]
~ˏ ‖ 127-30 That ... Riddle] *prose as in Shepherd;* That ... many / Throats ... of / Many ...
owne. / Come ... talk? / Talk ... Riddle ‖ 128 *Guise*] Guise ‖ 129 owne.–] ~ˏ ‖

Sfoote, can you not talke? Talke on I say, **more Courtship, as
you loue it**.

Bar. What new-come Gallant haue wee heere, that dares mate
the Guise thus?

L'An. Sfoote tis D'Ambois; The Duke mistakes him (on my   110
life) for some Knight of the new edition.

Buss. Cut my throat? I would the King fear'd thy cutting of
his throat no more than I feare thy cutting of mine.

Gui. So sir, so. /   114

Pyrh. Heere's some strange distemper.   [B3]

Bar. Heere's a sudden transmigration with D'Ambois, out of
the Knights ward, into the Duches bed.

L'An. See what a Metamorphosis a braue suit can worke.

Pyrh. Slight, step to the Guise and discouer him.

Bar. By no meanes, let the new suit worke, wee'll see the   120
issue.

Gui. Leaue your **Courtship**.

Buss. I will not. – I say, mistresse, and I will stand vnto
it, that if a woman may haue three seruants, a man may haue
threescore mistresses.   125

Gui. Sirha, Ile haue you whipt out of the Court for this
insolence.

Buss. Whipt? Such another syllable out a th'presence, if thou
dar'st for thy Dukedome.   129

Gui. Remember, Poultron.   [*Resumes chess game.*]

Mons. [*To Bussy.*] Pray thee forbeare.

Buss. Passion of death! Were not the King heere, he should
strow the Chamber like a rush.

Mons. But leaue Courting his wife then.

Buss. I will not: Ile Court her in despight of him. Not   135
Court her! – Come Madam, talke on; Feare me nothing: [*To
Guise.*] Well maist thou driue thy master from the Court; but
neuer D'Ambois.   [*Whispers with Duchess.*]

Mons. [*Aside.*] His great heart will not downe, tis like
    the Sea

That partly by his owne internall heat,   140
Partly the starr's dailie and nightly motion,
Ardor and light, and partly of the place
The diuers frames; **And** chiefly by the Moone,
Bristled with surges, neuer will be wonne

---

114 *Gui. So Sir, so.*] stet (See Textual Note) ‖ **115** *Pyrh.*] *Pyr.* Q1 text (so throughout); *Pyr:* Q1
catchword ‖ **119** Slight,] ~ ‖ **123** not.–] ~. ǀ say,] ~ ‖ **130** SD *Resumes chess game.*] Baskervill
subs. ‖ **131** SD *To Bussy.*] Parrott ‖ **136** her!–] ~! ‖ **136-37** SD *To Guise.*] Boas subs. ‖ **138** SD
Whispers with Duchess.] ‖ **139** SD *Aside.*] Parrott ‖ **141** starr's] stet (See Textual Note) ‖ **142** place]
~, ‖ **144** wonne] ~, ‖

can you not talk? Talk on I say. **Another Riddle.**   130

[Q1 ll. 105-10 = Q2 ll. 120-25.]

Pyrh. Here's some strange distemper.

Bar. Here's a sudden transmigration with *D'Ambois*, out of the Knights Ward, into the Duches bed.

L'An. See what a Metamorphosis a brave suit can work.

Pyrh. Slight, step to the *Guise* and discover him.   135

Bar. By no meanes, let the new suit work, wee'll see the issue.

Gui. Leave your **Courting**.

Buss. I will not. – I say, Mistresse, and I will stand unto it, that if a woman may have three servants, a man may have   140
threescore Mistresses.

Gui. Sirrha, Ile have you whipt out of the Court for this insolence.

Buss. Whipt? Such another syllable out a th'presence, if thou dar'st for thy Dukedome. /   145

Gui. Remember, Poultron.   [*Resumes chess game.*][B4ᵛ]

Mons. [*To Bussy.*] Pray thee forbeare.

Buss. Passion of death! Were not the King here, he should strow the Chamber like a rush.

Mons. But leaue Courting his wife then.   150

Buss. I wil not: Ile Court her in despight of him. Not Court her! – Come Madam, talk on; Feare me nothing: [*To Guise.*] Well mai'st thou drive thy Master from the Court; but never *D'Ambois.*   [*Whispers with Duchess.*]

Mons. [*Aside.*] His great heart will not down, tis like the Sea   155
That partly by his owne internall heat,
Partly the starr's daily and nightly motion,
Their heat and light, and partly of the place
The divers frames, **but** chiefly by the Moone,
Bristled with surges, never will be wonne   160

130 Another Riddle] *stet* (*See Textual Note; and see the Textual Note on l. 114/– for the possibility that it should have followed this line in Q2*) ‖ 131 Pyrh.] Pyr. *Q2 text (so throughout)* ‖ 135 Slight,] ~. | *Guise*] Guise ‖ 139 not.–] ~., | say,] ~. ‖ 146 SD *Resumes chess game.*] *Baskervill subs.* ‖ 147 SD *To Bussy.*] *Parrott* ‖ 152 her!–] ~! ‖ 152-53 SD *To Guise.*] *Boas subs.* ‖ 154 SD *Whispers with Duchess.*] ‖ 155 SD *Aside.*] *Parrott* ‖ 157 the] he *some copies* (*See Press-Variants*) | starr's] *stet* (*See Textual Note*) ‖ 160 wonne] ~, ‖

(No, not when th'hearts of all those powers are burst)   145
To make retreat into his setled home,
Till he be croun'd with his owne quiet fome.
 Henr. [*To Guise.*] You haue the mate. Another.
 Gui. [*Rising.*] No more.

         *Exit Guise, after him the King and
         Mons. whispering. After them the
         Ladies.* [*Barrisor, L'Anou, and
         Pyrhot converse in stage whispers.*]

 Bar. Why heer's the Lion, skard with the throat of a dunghill   150
Cocke; a fellow that has newlie shak'd off his shackles; / Now
does he crow for that victorie.   [B3ᵛ]
 L'An. Tis one of the best Iigges that euer was acted.
 Pyrh. Whom does the Guise suppose him to be, troe?
 L'An. Out of doubt, some new denizond Lord; and thinks   155
that suit **come new** out a th'Mercers bookes.
 Bar. I haue heard of a fellow, that by a fixt imagination look-
ing vpon a Bulbaiting, had a visible paire of hornes grew out
of his forhead: and I beleeue this Gallant, ouerioied with the
conceit of Monsieurs cast suit, imagines himselfe to be the   160
Monsieur.
 L'An. And why not? as well as the Asse, stalking in the Lions
case, **beare** himselfe like a Lion, **roaring** all the huger beasts out
of the Forrest?
 Pyrh. Peace, he lookes this way.   165
 Bar. Marrie let him looke sir, what will you say now if the
Guise be gone to fetch a blanquet for him?
 L'An. Faith I beleeue it for his honour.
 Pyrh. But, if D'Ambois carrie it cleane?
 Bar. True, when he curuets in the blanquet.   170
 Pyrh. I marie sir.
 L'An. Sfoote, see how he stares on's.
 Bar. [*In mock fright.*] Lord blesse vs, let's away.
 Buss. [*To Barrisor.*] Now sir, take your full view: how does
the Obiect please ye?   175
 Bar. If you aske my opinion sir, I thinke your suit sits as well
as if't had beene made for you.
 Buss. So sir, and was that the subiect of your ridiculous
ioilitie?
 L'An. What's that to you sir?   180

---

148 SD *To Guise.*] ‖ **149** SD *Rising.*] | SD *King and*] King, | SD *After ... Ladies.*] (*See Textual
Note*) | SD *Barrisor ... whispers.*] ‖ **150** dunghill] dung-/hill ‖ **154** be,] ~ˌ ‖ **156** Mercers] stet (*See
Textual Note*) ‖ **159** Gallant,] ~ˌ ‖ **173** SD *In mock fright.*] ‖ **174** SD *To Barrisor.*] ‖ **176** sits] stet
(*See Textual Note*) ‖

(No, not when th'hearts of all those powers are burst)
To make retreat into his setled home,
Till he be crown'd with his owne quiet fome.

Henr. [*To Guise.*] You have the Mate. Another.

Gui. [*Rising.*] No more. ***Flourish short.***

Exit Guise, after him the King and Mons. whispering. After them the Ladies. [*Barrisor, L'Anou, and Pyrhot converse in stage whispers.*]

Bar. Why here's the Lion skar'd with the throat of a dunghill Cock; a fellow that has newly shak'd off his shackles; Now does he crow for that victory.

L'An. Tis one of the best Jiggs that ever was acted.

Pyrh. Whom does the *Guise* suppose him to be, troe?

L'An. Out of doubt, some new denizond Lord; and thinks that suit **newly drawne** out a th'Mercers books.

Bar. I have heard of a fellow, that by a fixt imagination looking upon a Bulbaiting, had a visible paire of hornes grew out of his forhead: and I beleeve this Gallant, overjoyed with the conceit of Monsieurs cast suit, imagines himselfe to be the Monsieur.

L'An. And why not? as well as the Asse, stalking in the Lions case, **bare** himselfe like a Lion, **braying** all the huger beasts out of the Forrest?

Pyrh. Peace, he looks this way.

Bar. Marrie let him look sir; what will you say now if the *Guise* be gone to fetch a blanquet for him? /

L'An. Faith I beleeve it for his honour **sake**. [C1]

Pyrh. But, if *D'Ambois* carrie it cleane?

Bar. True, when he curvets in the blanquet.

Pyrh. I marrie sir.

L'An. Sfoot, see how he stares on's.

Bar. [*In mock fright.*] Lord blesse us, let's away.

Buss. [*To Barrisor.*] Now sir, take your full view: how does the Object please ye?

Bar. If you aske my opinion sir, I think your suit sits as well as if't had beene made for you.

Buss. So sir, and was that the subject of your ridiculous joylity?

L'An. What's that to you sir?

164 SD *To Guise.*] || **165** SD *Rising.*] | SD *King and*] *King,* | SD *After ... Ladies.*] *Exeunt Ladies./* (*after l. 185*) (*See Textual Note*) | SD *Barrisor ... whispers.*] || **166** dunghill] dung-/hill || **170** *Guise*] Guise | be,] ~‸ || **172** Mercers] *stet* (*See Textual Note*) || **175** Gallant,] ~‸ || **183** *Guise*] Guise || **189** SD *In mock fright.*] || **190** SD *To Barrisor.*] || **192** sits] *stet* (*See Textual Note*) || **196** you sir] yousir ||

Buss. Sir, I haue obseru'd all your fleerings; and resolue your selues yee shall giue a strickt account for't.

          Enter Brisac, Melynell. [They listen apart.]

Pyrh. O **strange credulitie**! Doe you thinke your selfe such a singular subiect for laughter, that none can fall into our meriment but you?   185

Bar. This iealousie of yours sir, confesses some close defect in your selfe, that wee neuer dream'd of. /

L'An. We held discourse of a perfum'd Asse, that being dis-   [B4] guis'd **with** a Lions case, imagin'd himselfe a Lion: I hope that toucht not you.   190

Buss. So sir: Your descants doe maruellous well fit this ground, wee shall meete where your Buffonly laughters will cost ye the best blood in your bodies.

Bar. For lifes sake let's be gone; hee'll kill's outright.

Buss. Goe at your pleasures, Ile be your Ghost to haunt you,   195 and yee sleepe an't, hang mee.

L'An. Goe, goe sir, Court your mistresse.

Pyrh. And be aduis'd: we shall haue odds against you.

Buss. Tush, valour stands not in number: Ile maintaine it, that one man may beat three boies.   200

          [Brisac and Melynell come forward.]

Bris. Nay you shall haue no ods of him in number sir: hee's a gentleman as good as the proudest of you, and yee shall not wrong him.

Bar. Not sir?

Mely. Not sir: Though he be not so rich, hee's a better man   205 than the best of you; And I will not endure it.

L'An. [To Brisac.] Not you sir?

Bris. No sir, nor I.

Buss. [To Brisac and Melynell.] I should thanke you for this kindnesse, if I thought these perfum'd muske-Cats (being out of   210 this priuiledge) durst but once mew at vs.

Bar. Does your confident spirit doubt that sir? **Come** follow vs and trie.

L'An. Come sir, wee'll lead you a dance.   *Exeunt.*

        Finis Actus primi.

---

182 SD *Brisac,*] ∼‸ | SD *They ... apart.*] ‖ **183** *Pyrh.*] stet (*See Textual Note*) ‖ **183-85** O ... you] *Dilke*; O ... selfe / Such ... into / Our ... you ‖ **188** *L'An.*] *LAn.* ‖ **200** SD *Brisac ... forward.*] ‖ **204** sir?] ∼. ‖ **207** SD *To Brisac.*] ‖ **209** SD *To ... Melynell.*] *Parrott* ‖

Buss. Sir, I have observ'd all your fleerings; and resolve your
selves yee shall give a strickt account for't.

        Enter Brisac, Melynell. [They listen apart.]

Bar. O **miraculous jealousie!** Doe you think your selfe such a
singular subject for laughter, that none can fall into **the matter of**   200
our merriment but you?

L'An. This jealousie of yours sir, confesses some close defect
in your selfe, that wee never dream'd of.

Pyrh. Wee held discourse of a perfum'd Asse, that being disguis'd **in** a Lions case, imagin'd himself a Lion: I hope that   205
toucht not you.

Buss. So sir: Your descants doe marvellous well fit this ground,
we shall meet where your Buffonly laughters will cost ye the
best blood in your bodies.

Bar. For lifes sake let's be gone; hee'll kill's outright   210
else.

Buss. Goe at your pleasures, Ile be your Ghost to haunt you,
and yee sleepe an't, hang me.

L'An. Goe, goe sir, Court your Mistresse.

Pyrh. And be advis'd: we shall have odds against you.   215

Buss. Tush, valour stands not in number: Ile maintaine it,
that one man may beat three boyes.

        [Brisac and Melynell come forward.]

Bris. Nay, you shall have no ods of him in number sir: hee's
a Gentleman as good as the proudest of you, and yee shall not
wrong him.   220

Bar. Not sir?

Mely. Not sir: Though he be not so rich, hee's a better man
than the best of you; And I will not endure it.

L'An. [To Brisac.] Not you sir? /   224

Bris. No sir, nor I.   [C1ᵛ]

Buss. [To Brisac and Melynell.] I should thank you for this
kindnesse, if I thought these perfum'd musk-Cats (being out of
this priviledge) durst but once mew at us.

Bar. Does your confident spirit doubt that sir? Follow us
and try.   230

L'An. Come sir, wee'll lead you a dance.   *Exeunt.*

        Finis Actus primi.

---

198 SD *They ... apart.*] ‖ **199** *Bar.*] stet (*See Textual Note*) ‖ **199-201** O ... but you] *prose as in
Dilke*; O ... selfe / Such ... into / The ... but you ‖ **217** boyes.] ~, | SD *Brisac ... forward.*] ‖
221 sir?] ~. ‖ **224** SD *To Brisac.*] ‖ **226** SD *To ... Melynell.*] *Parrott* ‖

Actus secundi   Scena prima.

*Henry, Guise, **Beaumond**, and Attendants.*
     Henr. This desperate quarrell sprung out of their enuies
To D'Ambois sudden brauerie, and great spirit.
     Gui. Neither is worth their enuie.
     Henr.   Lesse then either /
Will make the Gall of Enuie ouerflow;   [B4ᵛ]
She feedes on outcast entrailes like a Kite: 5
In which foule heape, if any ill lies hid,
She sticks her beake into it, shakes it vp,
And hurl's it all abroad, that all may view it.
Corruption is her Nutriment; but touch her
With any precious ointment, and you kill her: 10
When she findes any filth in men, she feasts,
And with her blacke throat bruits it through the world
(Being sound and healthfull); But if she but taste
The slenderest pittance of commended vertue,
She surfets of it, and is like a flie,   15
That passes all the bodies soundest parts,
And dwels vpon the sores; or if her squint eie
Haue power to finde none there, she forges some:
She makes that crooked euer which is strait;
Call's valour giddinesse, Iustice Tyrannie: 20
A wise man may shun her, she not her selfe;
Whither soeuer she flies from her Harmes,
She beares her Foe still claspt in her owne Armes:
And therefore cousen Guise let vs auoid her.
                         Enter Nuncius.
     [*Nun.*] What Atlas, or Olympus lifts his head   25
So farre past Couert, that with aire enough
My words may be inform'd? And from **his** height
I may be seene, and heard through all the world?
A tale so worthie, and so fraught with wonder,
Sticks in my iawes, and labours with euent.   30
     Henr. Com'st thou from D'Ambois?
     Nun.   From him, and the rest
His friends and enemies; whose sterne fight I saw,
And heard their words before, and in the fray.
     Henr. Relate at large what thou hast seene and heard.
     Nun. I saw fierce D'Ambois, and his two braue friends   35

II.i. SD *Beaumond*] *stet* (*See Textual Note*) | SD *and Attendants.*] Q2; *Nuncius.* ‖ **2** spirit.] ~:
(?) ‖ **10** kill her] kill   her (*some copies*) ‖ **12-13** world ... healthfull);] ~; ... ~)‸ ‖ **25** *Nun.*] Q2
subs. ‖ **27** his] *stet* (*See Textual Note*) ‖

Actus secundi   Scena prima.

*Henry, Guise, **Montsurry**, and Attendants.*

Henr. This desperate quarrell sprung out of their envies
To *D'Ambois* sudden bravery, and great spirit.
   Gui. Neither is worth their envie.
   Henr.   Lesse than either
Will make the Gall of Envie overflow;
She feeds on outcast entrailes like a Kite: 5
In which foule heape, if any ill lies hid,
She sticks her beak into it, shakes it up,
And hurl's it all abroad, that all may view it.
Corruption is her Nutriment; but touch her
With any precious oyntment, and you kill her: 10
Where she finds any filth in men, she feasts,
And with her black throat bruits it through the world
(Being sound and healthfull); But if she but taste
The slenderest pittance of commended vertue,
She surfets of it, and is like a flie,   15
That passes all the bodies soundest parts,
And dwels upon the sores; or if her squint eie
Have power to find none there, she forges some:
She makes that crooked ever which is strait;
Call's Valour giddinesse, Iustice Tyrannie: 20
A wise man may shun her, she not her selfe;
Whither soever she flies from her Harmes,
She beares her Foe still claspt in her own Armes:
And therefore cousen *Guise* let us avoid her. /
                            Enter Nuncius.   [C2]
   Nun. What *Atlas* or *Olympus* lifts his head   25
So farre past Covert, that with aire enough
My words may be inform'd? And from **their** height
I may be seene, and heard through all the world?
A tale so worthy, and so fraught with wonder,
Sticks in my jawes, and labours with event.   30
   Henr. Com'st thou from *D'Ambois*?
   Nun.   From him, and the rest
His friends and enemies; whose sterne fight I saw,
And heard their words before, and in the fray.
   Henr. Relate at large what thou hast seene and heard.
   Nun. I saw fierce *D'Ambois*, and his two brave friends   35

II.i. secundi] secund. | SD *Montsurry*] *stet* (*See Textual Note*) ‖ **12-13** world . . . healthfull);] ~; . . .
~). ‖ **23** She] Sh *one copy* (*See Press-Variants*) ‖ **24** *Guise*] Guise ‖ **27** their] *stet* (*See Textual Note*) ‖

Enter the Field, and at their heeles their foes;
Which were the famous souldiers, Barrisor,
L'Anou, and Pyrrhot, great in deedes of Armes: /
All which arriu'd at the euenest peece of earth   [C1]
The field affoorded; The three Challengers   40
Turn'd head, drew all their rapiers, and stoode ranckt:
When face to face the three Defendants met them,
Alike prepar'd, and resolute alike;
Like bonfires of Contributorie wood
Euerie mans looke shew'd; Fed with eithers spirit,   45
As one had beene a mirror to another,
Like formes of life and death each tooke from other;
And so were life and death mixt at their heights,
That you could see no feare of death, for life;
Nor loue of life, for death: But in their browes   50
Pyrrho's Opinion in great letters shone,
That life and death in all respects are one.
    Henr. Past there no sort of words at their encounter?
    Nun. As Hector, twixt the Hosts of Greece and Troy
(When Paris and the Spartane King should end   55
The nine yeeres warre), held vp his brasen launce
For signall, that both Hosts should cease from Armes,
And heare him speake: So Barrisor (aduis'd)
Aduanc'd his Naked Rapier twixt both sides,
Ript vp the Quarrell, and compar'd six liues,   60
Then laid in ballance with six idle words,
Offer'd remission and contrition too;
Or else that he and D'Ambois might conclude
The others dangers. D'Ambois lik'd the last;
But Barrisors friends (being equally engag'd   65
In the maine Quarrell) neuer would expose
His life alone, to that they all deseru'd.
And (for the other offer of remission)
D'Ambois (that like a Lawrell put in fire,
Sparkl'd and spit) did much much more than scorne,   70
That his wrong should incense him so like chaffe,
To goe so soone out; and like lighted paper,
Approoue his spirit at once both fire and ashes:
So drew they lots, and in them Fates appointed,
That Barrisor should fight with firie D'Ambois;   75
Pyrhot with Melynell; with Brisac L'Anou: /

37 souldiers,] ~; || **43-44** alike; ... wood] ~, ... ~: (*See Textual Note*) || **45** shew'd;] ~, || **47** death] ~, || **51** shone,] ~; || **54-56** Troy ... warre),] ~, ... ~)ˏ (*See Press-Variants*) || **60** liues,] ~; ||

Enter the Field, and at their heeles their foes;
Which were the famous souldiers, *Barrisor*,
£L'Anou, and *Pyrrhot*, great in deeds of Armes:
All which arriv'd at the evenest peece of earth
The field afforded; The three Challengers   40
Turn'd head, drew all their rapiers, and stood ranckt:
When face to face the three Defendants met them,
Alike prepar'd, and resolute alike;
Like bonfires of Contributorie wood
Every mans look shew'd; Fed with eithers spirit,   45
As one had beene a mirror to another,
Like formes of life and death each took from other;
And so were life and death mixt at their heights,
That you could see no feare of death, for life;
Nor love of life, for death: But in their browes   50
Pyrrho's Opinion in great letters shone,
That life and death in all respects are one.
   Henr. Past there no sort of words at their encounter?
   Nun. As *Hector*, twixt the Hosts of *Greece* and *Troy*
(When *Paris* and the Spartane King should end   55
The nine yeares warre), held up his brasen launce
For signall, that both Hosts should cease from Armes,
And heare him speak: So *Barrisor* (advis'd)
Advanc'd his naked Rapier twixt both sides,
Ript up the Quarrell, and compar'd six lives, /   60
Then laid in ballance with six idle words,   [C2ᵛ]
Offer'd remission and contrition too;
Or else that he and *D'Ambois* might conclude
The others dangers. *D'Ambois* lik'd the last;
But *Barrisors* friends (being equally engag'd   65
In the maine Quarrell) never would expose
His life alone, to that they all deserv'd.
And (for the other offer of remission)
D'Ambois (that like a Lawrell put in fire,
Sparkl'd and spit) did much much more than scorne,   70
That his wrong should incense him so like chaffe,
To goe so soone out; and like lighted paper,
Approve his spirit at once both fire and ashes:
So drew they lots, and in them Fates appointed,
That *Barrisor* should fight with firie *D'Ambois*;   75
Pyrhot with *Melynell*; with *Brisac L'Anou*:

43-44 alike; ... wood] ~, ... ~, (*See Textuaal Note*) ‖ 45 shew'd;] ~, (*See Textual Note*) ‖ 51
shone,] ~; ‖ 54-55 *Greece* ... *Troy* ... *Paris*] Greece ... Troy ... Paris ‖ 54-56 *Troy* ... warre),]
~, [*some copies* ~.] ...). ‖ 70 Sparkl'd] Spakl'd ‖

And then like flame and Powder they commixt,   [C1ᵛ]
So spritely, that I wisht they had beene spirits,
That the ne're-shutting wounds, they needes must open,
Might as they open'd, shut, and neuer kill: 80
But D'Ambois sword (that lightned as it flew)
Shot like a pointed Comet at the face
Of manly Barrisor; and there it stucke:
Thrice pluckt he at it, and thrice drew on thrusts,
From him, that of himselfe was free as fire;   85
Who thrust still as he pluckt, yet (past beliefe!)
He with his subtle eie, hand, bodie, scap't;
At last the deadly bitten point tugg'd off,
On fell his yet vndaunted Foe so fiercely,
That (only made more horrid with his wound)   90
Great D'Ambois shrunke, and gaue a little ground;
But soone return'd, redoubled in his danger,
And at the heart of Barrisor seal'd his anger:
Then, as in Arden I haue seene an Oke
Long shooke with tempests, and his loftie toppe   95
Bent to his roote, which being at length made loose
(Euen groaning with his weight) he gan to Nodde
This way and that: as loth his curled Browes
(Which he had oft wrapt in the skie with stormes)
Should stoope: and yet, his radicall fiuers burst,   ·100
Storme-like he fell, and hid the feare-cold Earth.
So fell stout Barrisor, that had stoode the shockes
Of ten set Battles in your Highnesse warre,
Gainst the sole souldier of the world, Nauarre.
   Gui. O pitious and horrid murther!
   Beaum.   Such a life   105
Me thinkes had mettall in it to suruiue
An age of men.
   Henr.   Such, often soonest end. –
Thy felt report cals on, wee long to know
On what euents the other haue arriu'd.
   Nun. Sorrow and furie, like two opposite fumes   110
Met in the vpper Region of a Cloud,
At the report made by this worthies fall, /
Brake from the earth, and with them rose Reuenge,   [C2]
Entring with fresh powers his two noble friends;
And vnder that ods fell surcharg'd Brisac,   115

---

79 ne're-shutting] ~ˌ~ ‖ **88** tugg'd] tuggd'd ‖ **105** *Beaum.*] *Beau.* ‖ **107** end.–] ~.ˌ ‖ **110** fumes] ~, ‖

And then like flame and Powder they commixt,
So spritely, that I wisht they had beene spirits,
That the ne're-shutting wounds, they needs must open,
Might as they open'd, shut, and never kill: 80
But *D'Ambois* sword (that lightned as it flew)
Shot like a pointed Comet at the face
Of manly *Barrisor*; and there it stucke:
Thrice pluckt he at it, and thrice drew on thrusts,
From him, that of himselfe was free as fire;   85
Who thrust still as he pluckt, yet (past beliefe!)
He with his subtile eye, hand, body, scap't;
At last the deadly bitten point tugg'd off,
On fell his yet undaunted Foe so fiercely,
That (only made more horrid with his wound)   90
Great *D'Ambois* shrunke, and gave a little ground;
But soone return'd, redoubled in his danger,
And at the heart of *Barrisor* seal'd his anger:
Then, as in *Arden* I have seene an Oke
Long shooke with tempests, and his loftie toppe   95
Bent to his root, which being at length made loose
(Even groaning with his weight) he gan to Nodde
This way and that: as loth his curled Browes /
(Which he had oft wrapt in the skie with stormes)   [C3]
Should stoope: and yet, his radicall fivers burst,   100
Storme-like he fell, and hid the feare-cold Earth.
So fell stout *Barrisor*, that had stood the shocks
Of ten set Battels in your Highnesse warre,
'Gainst the sole souldier of the world, *Navarre*.
  Gui. O pitious and horrid murther!
  Mont.   Such a life   105
Me thinks had mettall in it to survive
An age of men.
  Henr.   Such, often soonest end. –
Thy felt report cals on, we long to know
On what events the other have arriv'd.
  Nun. Sorrow and fury, like two opposite fumes   110
Met in the upper Region of a Cloud,
At the report made by this Worthies fall,
Brake from the earth, and with them rose Revenge,
Entring with fresh powers his two noble friends;
And under that ods fell surcharg'd *Brisac*,   115

79 ne're-shutting] ~.~ ‖ 93 seal'd] seal d *some copies (See Press-Variants)* ‖ 94 *Arden*] Arden ‖
104 *Navarre*] Navarre ‖ 105 *Mont.*] *Boas subs.; Beau. (See II.i.SD Textual Note)* ‖ 107 end.–] ~., ‖
110 fumes] ~, ‖

The friend of D'Ambois, before fierce L'Anou;
Which D'Ambois seeing, as I once did see
In my yoong trauels through Armenia,
An angrie Vnicorne in his full carier
Charge with too **quicke an eie** a Ieweller,   120
That watcht him for the Treasure of his browe;
And ere he could get shelter of a tree,
Naile him with his rich Antler to the Earth:
So D'Ambois ranne vpon reueng'd L'Anou,
Who eying th'eager point borne in his face,   125
And giuing backe, fell backe, and in his fall
His foes vncurbed sword stopt in his heart:
By which time all the life strings of **the** tw'other
Were cut, and both fell as their **spirits** flew
Vpwards: and still hunt Honour at the view.   130
And now (of all the six) sole D'Ambois stood
Vntoucht, saue only with the others blood.
    Henr. All slaine outright?
    Nun.   All slaine outright
      but he,
Who kneeling in the warme life of his friends
(All **feebled** with the blood, his Rapier raind),   135
He kist their pale **cheekes**, and bade both farewell;
And see the brauest man the French earth beares.
           Enter Monsieur, D'Amb. bare.
    Buss. Now is the time, y'are Princely vow'd my friend,
Performe it Princely, and obtaine my pardon.
    Mons. Else Heauen, forgiue not me: Come on braue   140
    friend. –   *[They kneel before Henry.]*
If euer Nature held herselfe her owne,
When the great Triall of a King and subiect
Met in one blood, both from one bellie springing:
Now prooue her vertue and her greatnesse One,
Or make the t'one the greater with the t'other   145
(As true Kings should), and for your brothers loue
(Which is a speciall species of true vertue), /
Doe that you could not doe, not being a King.   [C2ᵛ]
    Henr. Brother I know your suit; these wilfull murthers
Are euer past our pardon.
    Mons.   Manly slaughter   150
Should neuer beare th'account of wilfull murther;

---

132 others] stet (*See Textual Note to l. 133*) ‖ 134-35 friends ... raind),] ~, ... ~)ˌ ‖ 135 feebled]
stet (*See Textual Note*) ‖ 140 friend.–] ~.ˌ | SD *They ... Henry.*] *Parrott after Dilke* ‖ 145-46
t'other ... should),] ~, ... ~)ˌ ‖ 146-47 loue ... vertue),] ~, ... ~)ˌ ‖ 151 th'account] th account
some copies (See Press-Variants) ‖

The friend of *D'Ambois*, before fierce *L'Anou*;
Which *D'Ambois* seeing, as I once did see
In my young travels through *Armenia*,
An angrie Vnicorne in his full cariere
Charge with too **swift a foot** a Jeweller,   120
That watcht him for the Treasure of his brow;
And ere he could get shelter of a tree,
Naile him with his rich Antler to the Earth:
So *D'Ambois* ranne upon reveng'd *L'Anou*,
Who eying th'eager point borne in his face,   125
And giving backe, fell back, and in his fall
His foes uncurbed sword stopt in his heart:
By which time all the life strings of **th'tw'other**
Were cut, and both fell as their **spirit** flew
Vpwards: and still hunt Honour at the view.   130
And now (of all the six) sole *D'Ambois* stood
Vntoucht, save only with the others bloud.
    Henr. All slaine outright **but hee?**
    Nun.   All slaine outright
       but he, /
Who kneeling in the warme life of his friends   [C3ᵛ]
(All **freckled** with the bloud his Rapier raind),   135
He kist their pale **lips**, and bade both farewell;
And see the bravest man the French earth beares.
                Enter Monsieur, D'Amb. bare.
    Buss. Now is the time, y'are Princely vow'd my friend,
Performe it Princely, and obtaine my pardon.
    Mons. Else Heaven forgive not me: Come on brave   140
       friend. –   *[They kneel before Henry.]*
If ever Nature held her selfe her owne,
When the great Triall of a King and subject
Met in one bloud, both from one belly springing:
Now prove her vertue and her greatnesse One,
Or make the t'one the greater with the t'other   145
(As true Kings should), and for your brothers love
(Which is a speciall species of true vertue),
Doe that you could not doe, not being a King.
    Henr. Brother I know your suit; these wilfull murthers
Are ever past our pardon.
    Mons.   Manly slaughter   150
Should never beare th'account of wilfull murther;

---

118 *Armenia*] Armenia ‖ **133** but hee?] *stet (See Textual Note)* ‖ **134-35** friends . . . raind),] ~, . . .
~)ˎ ‖ **135** freckled] *stet (See Textual Note)* ‖ **140** friend.–] ~.ˎ | SD *They . . . Henry.] Parrott
after Dilke* ‖ **145-46** t'other . . . should),] ~, . . . ~)ˎ ‖ **146-47** love . . . vertue),] ~, . . . ~)ˎ ‖

It being a spice of iustice, where with life
Offending past law, equall life is laid
In equall ballance, to scourge that offence
By law of reputation, which to men   155
Exceedes all positiue law, and what that leaues
To true mens valours (not prefixing rights
Of satisfaction, suited to their wrongs)
A free mans eminence may supplie and take.
 Henr. This would make euerie man that thinks him
  wrongd,   160
Or is offended, or in wrong or right,
Lay on this violence, and all vaunt themselues
Law-menders and suppliers though meere Butchers,
Should this fact (though of iustice) be forgiuen!
 Mons. O no, my Lord; it would make Cowards feare   165
To touch the reputations of **full** men;
When only they are left to impe the law,
Iustice will soone distinguish murtherous mindes
From iust reuengers: Had my friend beene slaine
(His enemie suruiuing), he should die,   170
Since he had added to a murther'd fame
(Which was in his intent) a murther'd man;
And this had worthily beene wilfull murther:
But my friend only sau'd his fames deare life,
Which is aboue life, taking th'vnder value,   175
Which in the wrong it did, was forfeit to him;
And in this fact only preserues a man
In his vprightnesse, worthie to suruiue
Millions of such as murther men, aliue.
 Henr. Well brother, rise, and raise your friend withall   180
From death to life: –   *[Monsieur and Bussy rise.]*
   and D'Ambois, let your life
(Refin'd by passing through this merited death)
Be purg'd from more such foule pollution;
Nor on your scape, nor valour more presuming, /
To be againe so **violent**.   [C3]
 Buss.   My Lord,   185
I loth as much a deede of vniust death,
As law it selfe doth; and to Tyrannise,
Because I haue a little spirit to dare,
And power to doe, as to be Tyranniz'd;   189

---

162 themselues] ~, ‖ 163-64 Butchers, … forgiuen!] ~; … ~? *(See Textual Note)* ‖ 166 full] *stet*
(See Textual Note) | men;] ~, *(See Textual Note)* ‖ 169-70 slaine … suruiuing),] ~, … ~)ˌ ‖ 172
murther'd] murthered ‖ 178 vprightnesse,] ~; ‖ 181 life:–] ~:ˌ | SD *Monsieur … rise.*] ‖

It being a spice of justice, where with life
Offending past law, equall life is laid
In equall ballance, to scourge that offence
By law of reputation, which to men   155
Exceeds all positive law, and what that leaves
To true mens valours (not prefixing rights
Of satisfaction, suited to their wrongs)
A free mans eminence may supply and take.
   Henr. This would make every man that thinks him
     wrong'd,   160
Or is offended, or in wrong or right,
Lay on this violence, and all vaunt themselves
Law-menders and supplyers though meere Butchers,
Should this fact (though of justice) be forgiven!
   Mons. O no, my Lord; it would make Cowards feare   165
To touch the reputations of **true** men;
When only they are left to impe the law,
Justice will soone distinguish murtherous minds
From just revengers: Had my friend beene slaine /   169
(His enemy surviving), he should die,   [C4]
Since he had added to a murther'd fame
(Which was in his intent) a murther'd man;
And this had worthily beene wilfull murther:
But my friend only sav'd his fames deare life,
Which is above life, taking th'under value,   175
Which in the wrong it did was forfeit to him;
And in this fact only preserves a man
In his uprightnesse, worthy to survive
Millions of such as murther men, alive.
   Henr. Well brother, rise, and raise your friend withall   180
From death to life: –   *[Monsieur and Bussy rise.]*
        and *D'Ambois*, let your life
(Refin'd by passing through this merited death)
Be purg'd from more such foule pollution;
Nor on your scape, nor valour more presuming,
To be againe so **daring**.
   Buss.   My Lord,   185
I lothe as much a deed of unjust death,
As law it selfe doth; and to Tyrannise,
Because I have a little spirit to dare,
And power to doe, as to be Tyranniz'd;   189

---

162 themselves] ~, ‖ 163-64 Butchers, ... forgiven!] ~; ... ~? *(See Textual Note)* ‖ 166 true] *stet* *(See Textual Note)* | men;] ~, *(See Textual Note)* ‖ 169-70 slaine ... surviving),] ~, ... ~)ˏ ‖ 172 murther'd] murthered ‖ 178 uprightnesse,] ~; ‖ 179 men,] ~ˏ ‖ 181 life:–] ~:ˏ | SD *Monsieur ... rise.]* ‖

This is a grace that (on my knees redoubled)   [*Kneels again.*]
I craue to double this my short lifes gift;
And shall your royall bountie Centuple,
That I may so make good what **God** and nature
Haue giuen mee for my good: since I am free
(Offending no iust law), let no law make   195
By any wrong it does, my life her slaue:
When I am wrong'd and that law failes to right me,
Let me be King my selfe (as man was made)
And doe a iustice that exceedes the law:
If my wrong passe the power of single valour   200
To right and expiate, then be you my King,
And doe a Right, exceeding Law and Nature:
Who to himselfe is law, no law doth neede,
Offends no **King**, and is a King indeede.
    Henr. Enioy what thou intreat'st, we giue but ours.   205
    Buss. [*Rising.*] What you haue giuen, my Lord, is euer
       yours.   *Exit Rex [Henry] cum Beaum., Nuncio, Attendants.*
    Gui. **Mort dieu,** who would haue pardon'd such a murther?   *Exit.*
    Mons. Now vanish horrors into Court attractions,
For which let this balme make thee fresh and faire.
    Buss. How shall I quite your loue?
    Mons.   **Be true to the end:**   210
[*Aside.*] **I haue obtain'd a Kingdome with my friend.**
                              Exit Mons. with Bussy.

[II.ii.]

    *Montsur., Tamyra, **Beaupre**, Pero walking apart with a Book,*
                Charlotte, Pyrha.
    Mont. **He will haue pardon sure.**
    Tam.   **Twere pittie else:**

190 SD *Kneels again.*] *N. Brooke* ǁ **193** God] *stet* (*See Textual Note*) ǁ **194-95** free ... law),] ~,
... ~)ˌ ǁ **201** expiate,] ~; ǁ **204** no King] *stet* (*See Textual Note*) ǁ **206** SD *Rising.*] | SD *Exit ...
Attendants.*] (*See Historical Collation*); *Exit Rex / cum Beau.* (*in margin beginning a half-line
below l. 205*) ǁ **207** Mort dieu] *stet* (*See Textual Note*) ǁ **211** SD *Aside.*] | SD *Exit ... Bussy.*]
Exit. ǁ **II.ii.**] *Boas subs.* ǁ SD *Montsur.,*] *Montsur.ˌ* | *walking ... Book*] with a Booke/ *Q2* (*See
Textual Note*) ǁ **1-50** *Mont. He ... vnanswer'd?*] *stet* (*See Textual Note*) ǁ

This is a grace that (on my knees redoubled)   [*Kneels again.*]
I crave to double this my short lifes gift,
And shall your royall bountie Centuple,
That I may so make good what **law** and nature
Have given me for my good: since I am free
(Offending no Just law), let no law make   195
By any wrong it does, my life her slave:
When I am wrong'd and that law failes to right me,
Let me be King my selfe (as man was made)
And doe a justice that exceeds the law:
If my wrong passe the power of single valour   200
To right and expiate, then be you my King,
And doe a Right, exceeding Law and Nature:
Who to himselfe is law, no law doth need,
Offends no **Law**, and is a King indeed.
   Henr. Enjoy what thou intreat'st, we give but ours.   205
   Buss. [*Rising.*] What you have given, my Lord, is ever
      yours.   *Exit Rex [Henry] cum Mont., Nuncio, Attendants. /*
   Gui. Who would have pardon'd such a murther?   *Exit.* [C4ᵛ]
   Mons. Now vanish horrors into Court attractions,
For which let this balme make thee fresh and faire.

And now forth with thy service to the Duchesse,   210
As my long love will *Montsurries* Countesse.   *Exit.*
   Buss. To whom my love hath long been vow'd in heart,
Although in hand for shew I held the Duchesse.
And now through bloud and vengeance, deeds of height,
And hard to be atchiev'd, tis fit I make   215
Attempt of her perfection; I need feare
No check in his Rivality, since her vertues
Are so renown'd, and hee of all Dames hated.   *Exit.*

[II.ii.]

Enter Monsieur, Tamyra, and Pero walking apart **with a Booke.**

---

190 SD *Kneels again.*] *N. Brooke* || 193 law] *stet* (*See Textual Note*) || **194-95** free ... law),] ~,
... ~)ˏ || **201** expiate,] ~; || **204** Law] *stet* (*See Textual Note*) || **206** SD *Rising.*] | SD *Exit ...
Attendants.*] (*See Historical Collation*); *Exit Rex / cum Beau.* (*in margin beginning opposite
l. 205*) || **207** Who] *stet* (*See Textual Note*) | SD *Exit.*] ~: || **210-18** And ... hated.] *stet* (*See
Textual Note*) || **211** *Montsurries*] Montsurries || **216** perfection;] ~, || **II.ii.**] *Boas subs.* || SD
walking apart] (*See Textual Note*) | *On the omission of fifty lines, see Textual Note* ||

For though his great spirit something ouerflow,
All faults are still borne, that from greatnesse grow:
But such a sudden Courtier saw I neuer.
    Beaup. He was too sudden, which indeede was rudenesse.   5
    Tam. True, for it argued his no due conceit /
Both of the place, and greatnesse of the persons: [C3ᵛ]
Nor of our sex: all which (we all being strangers
To his encounter) should haue made more maners
Deserue more welcome.
    Mont.   All this fault is found   10
Because he lou'd the Dutchesse and left you.
    Tam. Ahlas, loue giue her ioy; I am so farre
From Enuie of her honour, that I sweare,
Had he encounterd me with such proud sleight,
I would haue put that proiect face of his   15
To a more test, than did her Dutchesship.
    Beaup. Why (by your leaue my Lord) Ile speake it heere,
(Although she be my ante) she scarce was modest,
When she perceiu'd the Duke her husband take
Those late exceptions to her seruants Courtship   20
To entertaine him.
    Tam.   I, and stand him still,
Letting her husband giue her seruant place:
Though he did manly, she should be a woman.
                   Enter Guise.
    [*Gui.*] D'Ambois is pardond: wher's a king? where law?
See how it runnes, much like a turbulent sea;   25
Heere high, and glorious, as it did contend
To wash the heauens, and make the stars more pure:
And heere so low, it leaues the mud of hell
To euery common view: – come count Montsurry
We must consult of this.
    Tam.   Stay not, sweet Lord.   30
    Mont. Be pleas'd, Ile strait returne.   *Exit cum Guise.*
    Tam. [*Aside.*]   Would that would please
    me.
    Beaup. Ile leaue you Madam to your passions.
I see, ther's change of weather in your lookes.
                   Exit cum suis [Charlotte and Pyrha].
    Tam. I cannot cloake it: but, as when a fume,
Hot, drie and grosse, within the wombe of earth   35

---

14 sleight,] ~: ‖ **19** perceiu'd] perceiued ‖ **21** still,] ~. ‖ **24** *Gui.*] ‖ **29** view:–] ~:ˌ ‖ **31** pleas'd]
pleased ‖ **31** *Tam.*] *Tamy.* (*so through l.99*) | SD *Aside.*] *Spencer* ‖ **33** SD *Charlotte and Pyra.*]
Brooke subs. ‖ **34** but,] ~; ‖ **35** grosse,] ~: ‖

Or in her superficies begot:
When extreame cold hath stroke it to her heart,
The more it is comprest, the more it rageth; /
Exceeds his prisons strength that should containe it;   [C4]
And then it tosseth Temples in the aire,   40
Alle barres made engines, to his insolent fury:
So, of a sudden, my licentious fancy
Riots within me: not my name and house
Nor my religion to this houre obseru'd
Can stand aboue it: I must vtter that   45
That will in parting breake more strings in me,
Than death when life parts: and that holy man
That, from my cradle, counseld for my soule,
I now must make an agent for my bloud.

                       Enter Monsieur.

   Mons. Yet, is my Mistresse gratious?
   Tam.   Yet vnanswer'd?   50
   Mons. Pray thee regard thine owne good, if not mine,
And cheere my Loue for that; you do not know
What you may be by me, nor what without me;
I may haue power t'aduance and pull downe any.
   Tam. That's not my study: one way I am sure   55
You shall not pull downe me: my husbands height
Is crowne to all my hopes: and his retiring
To any meane state, shalbe my aspiring:
Mine honour's in mine owne hands, spite of kings.
   Mons. Honour, what's that? your second maidenhead: 60
And what is that? a word: the word is gone,
The thing remaines: the rose is pluckt, the stalke
Abides: an easie losse where no lack's found:
Beleeue it ther's as small lacke in the losse,
As there is paine i'th'losing: archers euer   65
Haue two strings to a bow: and shall great Cupid
(Archer of archers both in men and women)
Be worse prouided than a common archer?
A husband and a friend all wise wiues haue.
   Tam. Wise wiues they are that on such strings depend,   70
With a firme husband, **weighing** a **dissolute** friend.
   Mons. Still you stand on your husband, so doe all
The common sex of you, when y'are encounterd /
With one ye cannot fancie: all men know   [C4ᵛ]

---

39 it;] ~, ‖ 40 aire,] ~; ‖ 48 soule,] ~: ‖ 50 vnanswer'd] vnanswered ‖ 55 That's] Thats ‖ 60
what's] whats ‖ 61 gone,] ~ˏ ‖ 65 i'th'] ith ‖ 73 y'are] yare ‖

Mons. Pray thee regard thine owne good, if not mine,
And cheere my Love for that; you doe not know
What you may be by me, nor what without me;
I may have power t'advance and pull downe any.
    Tam. That's not my study. One way I am sure   5
You shall not pull downe me; my husbands height
Is crowne to all my hopes, and his retiring
To any meane state, shall be my aspiring:
Mine honour's in mine owne hands, spite of kings.
    Mons. Honour, what's that? your second maydenhead: 10
And what is that? a word; the word is gone,
The thing remaines; the Rose is pluckt, the stalk
Abides: an easie losse where no lack's found.
Beleeve it, there's as small lack in the losse,
As there is paine i'th'losing: Archers ever   15
Have two strings to a bow, and shall great *Cupid*
(Archer of Archers both in men and women)
Be worse provided than a common Archer?
A Husband and a Friend all wise Wives have.
    Tam. Wise wives they are that on such strings depend,   20
With a firme husband **joyning** a **lose** friend.
    Mons. Still you stand on your husband, so doe all
The common sex of you when y'are encounter'd
With one ye cannot fancie: all men know

15 i'th'] ith' ‖ 23 you] Q2(c); ~, Q2(u) ‖

73

You liue in court heere by your owne election,   75
Frequenting all our **solemne** sports and triumphs,
All the most youthfull companie of men:
And wherefore doe you this? To please your husband?
Tis grosse and fulsome: if your husbands pleasure
Be all your Obiect, and you aime at Honour,   80
In liuing close to him, get you from Court,
You may haue him at home; these common Put-ofs
For common women serue: my honor? husband?
Dames maritorious, ne're were meritorious:
Speake plaine and say I do not like you Sir,   85
Y'are an illfauor'd fellow in my eie,
And I am answer'd.
     Tam.   Then I pray be answer'd:
For in good faith my Lord I do not like you
In that sort you like.
     Mons. [*Offering a necklace.*]   Then haue at you heere:
Take (with a politique hand) this rope of Pearle;   90
And though you be not amorous: yet be wise:
Take me for wisdome; he that you can loue
Is neere the further from you.
     Tam. [*Spurning it.*]   Now it comes
So ill prepar'd, that I may take a poison,
Vnder a medicine as good cheape as it: 95
I will not haue it were it worth the world.
     Mons. Horror of death: could I but please your eie,
You would giue me the like, ere you would loose me:
Honor and husband?
     Tam.   By this light my Lord
Y'are a vile fellow: and Ile tell the King   100
Your occupation of dishonouring Ladies
And of his Court: a Lady cannot liue
As she was borne; and with that sort of pleasure
That fits her state: but she must be defam'd
With an infamous Lords detraction: 105
Who would endure the Court if these attempts
Of open and profest lust must be borne? – /
[*Calls.*] Whose there? [*To Pero.*] come on Dame, you are at
     your booke   [D1]
When men are at your mistresse; haue I taught you
Any such waiting womans qualitie?   110

75 election,] ~. *some copies* (*See Press-Variants*) ‖ 82 Put-ofs] Q2(c); Puttofs ‖ 89 SD *Offering a necklace.*] ‖ 93 SD *Spurning it.*] (*See Textual Note*) ‖ 106 attempts] ~, ‖ 107 borne?–] ~?︵ ‖ 108 SD *Calls.*] | SD *To Pero.*] | you] Q2(c); your ‖

You live in Court here by your owne election, /   25
Frequenting all our **common** sports and triumphs,   [D1]
All the most youthfull company of men:
And wherefore doe you this? To please your husband?
Tis grosse and fulsome: if your husbands pleasure
Be all your Object, and you ayme at Honour,   30
In living close to him, Get you from Court,
You may have him at home; these common Put-ofs
For common women serve: my honour? husband?
Dames maritorious, ne're were meritorious:
Speak plaine, and say I doe not like you Sir,   35
Y'are an ill-favour'd fellow in my eye
And I am answer'd.
   Tam.   Then I pray be answer'd:
For in good faith my Lord I doe not like you
In that sort you like.
   Mons. [*Offering a necklace.*]   Then have at you here:
Take (with a politique hand) this rope of Pearle;   40
And though you be not amorous, yet be wise:
Take me for wisedom; he that you can love
Is nere the further from you.
   Tam. [*Spurning it.*]   Now it comes
So ill prepar'd, that I may take a poyson
Under a medicine as good cheap as it: 45
I will not have it were it worth the world.
   Mons. Horror of death: could I but please your eye,
You would give me the like, ere you would loose me:
Honor and husband?
   Tam.   By this light my Lord
Y'are a vile fellow: and Ile tell the King   50
Your occupation of dishonouring Ladies
And of his Court: a Lady cannot live
As she was borne, and with that sort of pleasure
That fits her state, but she must be defam'd
With an infamous Lords detraction: 55
Who would endure the Court if these attempts
Of open and profest lust must be borne? –
[*Calls.*] Whose there? [*To Pero.*] come on Dame, you are at
    your book
When men are at your Mistresse; have I taught you /   59
Any such waiting womans quality?   [D1ᵛ]

32 Put-ofs] *Q2(c)*; Puttofs *Q2(u)* ‖ 39 SD *Offering a necklace.*] ‖ 43 SD *Spurning it.*] (*See Textual Note*) ‖ 44 poyson] *Q2(c)*; ~, *Q2(u)* ‖ 56 attempts] ~, ‖ 57 borne?–] ~?. ‖ 58 SD *Calls.*] | SD *To Pero.*] | you] *Q2(c)*; your *Q2(u)* ‖

Mons. Farewell good husband.   *Exit Mons.*
Tam.   Farewell wicked Lord.
                         Enter Mont.
Mont. Was not the Monsieur heere?
Tam.   Yes, to good purpose.
And your cause is as good to seeke him too
And haunt his company.
   Mont.   Why what's the matter?
   Tam. Matter of death, were I some husbands wife: 115
I cannot liue at quiet in my chamber
For opportunities almost to rapes
Offerd me by him.
   Mont.   Pray thee beare with him:
Thou know'st he is a Bachelor, and a Courtier,
I, and a Prince: and their prerogatiues   120
Are, to their lawes, as to their pardons are
Their reseruations, after Parliaments
One quits another: forme giues al their essence:
That Prince doth high in Vertues reckoning stand
That will entreat a vice, and not command: 125
So far beare with him: should another man
Trust to his priuiledge, he should trust to death:
Take comfort then (my comfort) nay triumph,
And crown thy selfe, thou part'st with victory:
My presence is so only deare to thee,   130
That other mens appeare worse than they be.
For this night yet, beare with my forced absence:
Thou know'st my businesse; and with how much weight,
My vow hath charg'd it.
   Tam.   True my Lord, and neuer
My fruitlesse loue shall let your serious **profit**,   135
Yet, sweet Lord, do not stay, you know my soule
Is so long time without me, and I dead
As you are absent. /
   Mont.   By this kisse, receiue   [D1ᵛ]
My soule for hostage, till I see my loue.
   Tam. The morne shall let me see you?
   Mont.   With the sunne   140
Ile visit thy more comfortable beauties.
   Tam. This is my comfort, that the sunne hath left
The whole worlds beauty ere my sunne leaues me.

---

111 *Tam.*] Q2 (*Tamira.*); *Mont.* (*See Textual Note*) ‖ 122 Parliaments] *stet* (*See Textual Note*) ‖
123 essence] essen e *one copy* (*See Press-Variants*) ‖ 124 Vertues] vertues ‖ 134 charg'd] charged ‖
136 not] *Dilke*; no ‖ 140 you?] ~: ‖

Mons. Farewell good husband.   *Exit Mons.*
Tam.   Farewell wicked Lord.
            Enter Mont.
Mont. Was not the Monsieur here?
Tam.   Yes, to good purpose.
And your cause is as good to seek him too,
And haunt his company.
    Mont.   Why, what's the matter?
Tam. Matter of death, were I some husbands wife: 65
I cannot live at quiet in my chamber
For opportunities almost to rapes
Offerd me by him.
    Mont.   Pray thee beare with him:
Thou know'st he is a Bachelor, and a Courtier,
I, and a Prince: and their prerogatives   70
Are, to their lawes, as to their pardons are
Their reservations, after Parliaments
One quits another: forme gives all their essence:
That Prince doth high in Vertues reckoning stand
That will entreat a vice, and not command: 75
So farre beare with him: should another man
Trust to his priviledge, he should trust to death:
Take comfort then (my comfort) nay triumph,
And crown thy selfe, thou part'st with victory:
My presence is so onely deare to thee,   80
That other mens appeare worse than they be.
For this night yet, beare with my forced absence:
Thou know'st my businesse; and with how much weight,
My vow hath charg'd it.
    Tam.   True my Lord, and never
My fruitlesse love shall let your serious **honour**,   85
Yet, sweet Lord, do not stay, you know my soule
Is so long time without me, and I dead
As you are absent.
    Mont.   By this kisse, receive
My soule for hostage, till I see my love.   89
    Tam. The morne shall let me see you? /
    Mont.   With the sunne   [D2]
Ile visit thy more comfortable beauties.
    Tam. This is my comfort, that the sunne hath left
The whole worlds beauty ere my sunne leaves me.

---

61 *Tam.*] *stet* (*See Textual Note*) ‖ **72** Parliaments] ~, (*See Textual Note*) ‖ **74** Vertues] vertues
(vertu s *one copy* [*See Press-Variants*]) ‖ **78** triumph,] Q2(c); ~. Q2(u) ‖ **84** charg'd] charged ‖ **85**
fruitlesse] fru tlesse *one copy* (*See Press-Variants*) ‖ **86** not] *Dilke*; no ‖ **90** you?] ~. ‖

   Mont. Tis late night now indeed: farewell my light.   *Exit.*
   Tam. Farewell my light and life: [*Aside.*] But not in
     him.   145

Alas, that in the wane of our affections
We should supplie it with a full dissembling,
In which each yoongest maid is growne a mother;
Frailtie is fruitfull, one sinne gets another:
Our loues like sparkles are that brightest shine,   150
When they goe out; most vice shewes most diuine:
[*To Pero.*] Goe maid, to bed, lend me your booke I pray:
Not like your selfe, for forme; Ile this night trouble
None of your seruices: Make sure the doores,
And call your other fellowes to their rest.   155
   Pero. I will, [*Aside.*] yet I will watch to know why you
     watch.   *Exit.*
   Tam. Now all **the** peacefull regents of the night,
Silently-gliding exhalations,
Languishing windes, and murmuring fals of waters,
Sadnesse of heart, and ominous securenesse,   160
Enchantments, dead sleepes, all the friends of rest,
That euer wrought vpon the life of man,
Extend your vtmost strengths; and this charm'd houre
Fix like the Center; make the violent wheeles
Of Time and Fortune stand; and Great Existens   165
(The Makers treasurie) now not seeme to bee,
To all but my approaching friends and mee:
They come, alas they come, feare, feare and hope
Of one thing, at one instant fight in mee:
I loue what most I loath, and cannot liue   170
Vnlesse I compasse that **that** holds my death:
For **loue is hatefull without loue againe**,
And he I loue, will loth me, when he sees
I flie my sex, my vertue, my Renowne, /   174
To runne so madly on a man vnknowne.   *[The vault opens.]* [D2]
See, see **the gulfe** is opening, that **will swallow**

Me and my fame for euer; I will in,

145 SD *Aside.*] *Baskervill* ‖ 146 wane] waue (*See Textual Note*) ‖ 148 mother;] ~, ‖ 151 out;] ~: ‖
152 SD *To Pero.*] *Parrott* ‖ 153 forme;] ~, ‖ 156 *Pero.*] *Per.* (*See Press-Variants*) | SD *Aside.*]
Parrot subs. after Dilke | 157 the] *stet* (*See Press-Variants*) ‖ 175 SD *The vault opens.*] *Q2 after
l.124; placed as in Shepherd* ‖ 176 gulfe] *stet* (*See Textual Note*) ‖

Mont. Tis late night now indeed: farewell my light.   *Exit.*

Tam. Farewell my light and life: [*Aside.*] But not in

him,   95

In mine owne dark love and light bent to another.

Alas, that in the wane of our affections

We should supply it with a full dissembling,

In which each youngest Maid is grown a Mother;

Frailty is fruitfull, one sinne gets another: 100

Our loves like sparkles are that brightest shine,

When they goe out; most vice shewes most divine:

[*To Pero.*] Goe Maid, to bed, lend me your book I pray:

Not like your selfe, for forme; Ile this night trouble

None of your services: Make sure the dores,   105

And call your other fellowes to their rest.

   Pero. I will, [*Aside.*] yet I will watch to know why you

watch.   *Exit.*

   Tam. Now all **yee** peacefull regents of the night,

Silently-gliding exhalations,

Languishing windes, and murmuring falls of waters,   110

Sadnesse of heart, and ominous securenesse,

Enchantments, dead sleepes, all the friends of rest,

That ever wrought upon the life of man,

Extend your utmost strengths, and this charm'd houre

Fix like the Center: make the violent wheeles   115

Of Time and Fortune stand; and Great Existens

(The Makers treasurie) now not seeme to be,

To all but my approaching friends and me:

They come, alas they come, feare, feare and hope

Of one thing, at one instant fight in me: 120

I love what most I loath, and cannot live

Unlesse I compasse that **which** holds my death:

For **life's meere death loving one that loathes me,**

And he I love, will loath me, when he sees

I flie my sex, my vertue, my Renowne,   125

To runne so madly on a man unknowne.   *The Vault opens.*

See, see **a Vault** is opening that **was never** /

Knowne to my Lord and husband, nor to any   [D2ᵛ]

But him that brings the man I love, and me;

How shall I looke on him? how shall I live   130

And not consume in blushes? I will in,

---

95 SD *Aside.*] *Baskervill* | him,] Q2(c); ~. Q2(u) ‖ **96** In … another] *stet* (*See Textual Note*) ‖ **97** wane] *Dilke*; wave (*See Textual Note*) ‖ **99** Mother;] ~, ‖ **103** SD *To Pero.*] *Parrott* ‖ **104** forme;] ~, ‖ **107** SD *Aside.*] *Parrott subs. after Dilke* ‖ **108** yee] *stet* (*See Textual Note*) ‖ **123** life's] lifes ‖ **126** SD *The Vault opens.*] placed as in *Shepherd*; *after l.124* ‖ **127** a Vault] *stet* (*See Textual Note*) ‖ **127-31** was … blushes] *stet* (*See Textual Note*) ‖ **129** me;] Q2(c); ~. Q2(u) ‖ **131** blushes?] ~, | in,] ~; ‖

And cast my selfe off, as I ne're had beene.   *Exit.*
                    [*Ascendit Comolet and D'Ambois.*]
    Com. Come worthiest sonne, I am past measure glad,
That you (whose worth I haue approou'd so long)   180
Should be the Obiect of her fearefull loue;
Since both your wit and spirit can adapt
Their full force to supplie her vtmost weakenesse:
You know her worths and vertues, for Report
Of all that know, is to a man a knowledge: 185
You know besides, that our affections storme,
Rais'd in our blood, no Reason can reforme.
Though she seeke then their satisfaction
(Which she must needes, or rest vnsatisfied),
Your iudgement will esteeme her peace thus wrought,   190
Nothing lesse deare, than if your selfe had sought:
And (with another colour, which my Art
Shall teach you to lay on) your selfe must seeme
The only agent, and the first Orbe Moue,
In this our set, and cunning world of Loue.   195
    Buss. Giue me the colour (my most honour'd Father)
And trust my cunning then to lay it on.
    Com. Tis this, good sonne; Lord Barrisor (whom you slew)
Did loue her dearely, and with all fit meanes
Hath vrg'd his acceptation, of all which   200
She keepes one letter written in his blood:
You must say thus then, That you heard from mee
How much her selfe was toucht in conscience
With a Report (which is in truth disperst)
That your maine quarrell grew about her loue,   205
Lord Barrisor imagining your Courtship
Of the great Guises Duchesse in the Presence,
Was by you made to his elected mistresse:
And so made me your meane now to resolue her,
Chosing (by my direction) this nights depth,   210
For the more cleere auoiding of all note
Of your presumed presence, and with this /
(To cleere her hands of such a louers blood)   [D2ᵛ]
She will so kindely thanke and entertaine you
(Me thinkes I see how), I, and ten to one,   215
Shew you the confirmation in his blood,
Lest you should thinke report and she did faine,
That you shall so haue circumstantiall meanes,

---

178 SD *Ascendit ... D'Ambois.*] Q2 subs. (*Frier*) ‖ **188-89** satisfaction ... vnsatisfied),] ~, ... ~)ₐ ‖
206 Barrisor] ~, ‖ **211** note] ~, ‖ **214-15** you ... how),] ~, ... ~)ₐ ‖

And cast my selfe off, as I ne're had beene.   *Exit.*

        Ascendit Frier and D'Ambois.

   Frier. Come worthiest sonne, I am past measure glad,

That you (whose worth I have approv'd so long)

Should be the Object of her fearefull love;   135

Since both your wit and spirit can adapt

Their full force to supply her utmost weaknesse:

You know her worths and vertues, for Report

Of all that know, is to a man a knowledge:

You know besides, that our affections storme,   140

Rais'd in our blood, no Reason can reforme.

Though she seeke then their satisfaction

(Which she must needs, or rest unsatisfied),

Your judgement will esteeme her peace thus wrought,

Nothing lesse deare, than if your selfe had sought: 145

And (with another colour, which my Art

Shall teach you to lay on) your selfe must seeme

The onely agent, and the first Orbe Move,

In this our set, and cunning world of Love.

   Buss. Give me the colour (my most honour'd Father)   150

And trust my cunning then to lay it on.

   Frier. Tis this, good sonne; Lord *Barrisor* (whom you slew)

Did love her dearely, and with all fit meanes

Hath urg'd his acceptation, of all which

Shee keepes one letter written in his blood: 155

You must say thus then, That you heard from mee

How much her selfe was toucht in conscience

With a Report (which is in truth disperst)

That your maine quarrell grew about her love,

Lord *Barrisor* imagining your Courtship   160

Of the great *Guises* Duchesse in the Presence,

Was by you made to his elected Mistresse;

And so made me your meane now to resolve her,

Chosing (by my direction) this nights depth, /   164

For the more cleare avoiding of all note   [D3]

Of your presumed presence, and with this

(To cleare her hands of such a Lovers blood)

She will so kindly thank and entertaine you

(Me thinks I see how), I, and ten to one,

Shew you the confirmation in his blood,   170

Lest you should think report, and she did faine,

That you shall so have circumstantiall meanes,

---

133 *Frier.*] *stet* (*See Textual Note*) ‖ **138, 140** know her ... know] *Q2(c, second state)*; know ...
know *Q2(c, first state)*; know ... know her *Q2(u)* ‖ **142-43** satisfaction ... unsatisfied),] ~, ...
~)ₐ ‖ **161** *Guises*] Guises ‖ **168-69** you ... how),] ~, ... ~)ₐ ‖

To come to the direct, which must be vsed:
For the direct is crooked; Loue comes flying;   220
The height of loue is still wonne with denying.
   Buss. Thankes honour'd Father.
   Com.   She must neuer know
That you know any thing of any loue
Sustain'd on her part: For learne this of mee;
In any thing a woman does alone,   225
If she dissemble, she thinkes tis not done;
If not dissemble, nor a little chide,
Giue her her wish, she is not satisfi'd;
To haue a man thinke that she neuer seekes,
Does her more good than to haue all she likes: 230
This frailtie sticks in them beyond their sex;
Which to reforme, reason is too perplex:
Vrge reason to them, it will doe no good;
Humour (that is the charriot of our foode
In euerie bodie) must in them be fed,   235
To carrie their affections by it bred.
Stand close.   *[They stand aside.]*
               Enter Tamyra.
   Tam. Alas, I feare my strangenesse will retire him:
If he goe backe, I die; I must preuent it,
And cheare his onset with my sight at least,   240
And that's the most; though euerie step he takes
Goes to my heart, Ile rather die than seeme
Not to be strange to that I most esteeme.
   Com. [*Advancing with Bussy.*] Madam.
   Tam.   Ah.
   Com.   You will pardon me,
     I hope,
That, so beyond your expectation /   245
(And at a time for visitants so vnfit),   [D3]
I (with my noble friend heere) visit you:
You know that my accesse at any time
Hath euer beene admitted; and that friend
That my care will presume to bring with mee,   250
Shall haue all circumstance of worth in him,
To merit as free welcome as my selfe.
   Tam. O father, but at this suspicious houre
You know how apt best men are to suspect vs,
In any cause, that makes suspicious shadow   255

222 *Buss.*] *D'Amb.* (*so also l. 268*) | honour'd] honoured | *Com.*] *Commolet.* ‖ 237 SD *They stand aside.*] *after Parrott* ‖ 241 that's] thats ‖ 244 SD *Advancing with Bussy.*] *after Parrott* ‖ 245-46 expectation ... vnfit),] ~, ... ~)◌ ‖

To come to the direct, which must be used:
For the direct is crooked; Love comes flying;
The height of love is still wonne with denying.   175
   Buss. Thanks honour'd Father.
   Frier.   Shee must never know
That you know any thing of any love
Sustain'd on her part: For learne this of me;
In any thing a woman does alone,
If she dissemble, she thinks tis not done;   180
If not dissemble, nor a little chide,
Give her her wish, she is not satisfi'd;
To have a man think that she never seekes,
Does her more good than to have all she likes:
This frailty sticks in them beyond their sex;   185
Which to reforme, reason is too perplex:
Urge reason to them, it will doe no good;
Humour (that is the charriot of our food
In every body) must in them be fed,
To carry their affections by it bred.   190
Stand close.   [*They stand aside.*]
        Enter Tamyra **with a Book**.
   Tam. Alas, I feare my strangenesse will retire him·
If he goe back, I die; I must prevent it,
And cheare his onset with my sight at least,
And that's the most; though every step he takes   195
Goes to my heart, Ile rather die than seeme
Not to be strange to that I most esteeme.
   Frier. [*Advancing with Bussy.*] Madam.
   Tam.   Ah!
   Frier.   You will pardon me,
    I hope, /
That, so beyond your expectation   [D3ᵛ]
(And at a time for visitants so unfit),   200
I (with my noble friend here) visit you:
You know that my accesse at any time
Hath ever beene admitted; and that friend
That my care will presume to bring with me,
Shall have all circumstance of worth in him,   205
To merit as free welcome as my selfe.
   Tam. O Father, but at this suspicious houre
You know how apt best men are to suspect us,
In any cause, that makes suspicious shadow

---

176 *Buss.*] *D'Amb.* | honour'd] honoured ‖ **177** any thing] ary thing Q2 (?) ‖ **191** SD *They stand aside.*] *after Parrott* ‖ **198** SD *Advancing with Bussy.*] *after Parrott* ‖ **199-200** expectation . . . unfit),] ~, . . . ~)ˏ ‖

No greater than the shadow of a haire:
And y'are to blame: what though my Lord and husband
Lie foorth to night? and since I cannot sleepe
When he is absent, I sit vp to night,
Though all the doores are sure, and all our seruants   260
As sure bound with their sleepes; yet there is one
That **sits** aboue, whose eie no sleepe can binde:
He sees through doores, and darkenesse, and our thoughts;
And therefore as we should auoid with feare,
To thinke amisse our selues before his search;   265
So should we be as curious to shunne
All cause that other thinke not ill of vs.
   Buss. Madam, tis farre from that: I only heard
By this my honour'd father, that your conscience
Was something troubled with a false report: 270
That Barrisors blood should something touch your **hand**,
Since he imagin'd I was courting you,
When I was bold to change words with the Duchesse,
And therefore made his quarrell;

                     which my presence
(Presum'd on with my father at this season,   275
For the more care of your so curious honour)
Can well resolue your Conscience, is most false.
   Tam. And is it therefore that you come good sir?
Then craue I now your pardon and my fathers,
And sweare your presence does me so much **comfort**,   280
That all I haue, it bindes to your requitall:
Indeede sir, tis most true that a report
Is spread, alleaging that his loue to mee /
Was reason of your quarrell, and because   [D3ᵛ]
You shall not thinke I faine it for my glorie,   285
That he importun'd me for his Court seruice,
Ile shew you his owne hand, set downe in blood
To that vaine purpose: Good Sir, then come in.
Father I thanke you now a thousand fold.
                            [Exeunt Tamyra and D'Amb.]
   Com. May it be worth it to you honour'd daughter.   290
                                 [Descendit Com.]

               Finis Actus secundi.

260 and] & ‖ 270 report:] ~; ‖ 274-75 And ... (Presum'd] (And ... Presum'd ‖ 289 SD *Exeunt ... D'Amb.*] Q2 (*Exit Tamira / and D'Amb,*) *beside ll. 244-45; placed as in Dilke* ‖ 290 SD *Descendit Com.*] Q2 (*Fryar*) ‖

No greater than the shadow of a haire: 210
And y'are to blame: what though my Lord and husband
Lie forth to night? and since I cannot sleepe
When he is absent, I sit up to night,
Though all the dores are sure, and all our servants
As sure bound with their sleepes; yet there is one   215
That **wakes** above, whose eye no sleepe can binde:
He sees through dores, and darknesse, and our thoughts;
And therefore as we should avoid with feare,
To think amisse our selves before his search;
So should we be as curious to shunne   220
All cause that other think not ill of us.
  Buss. Madam, 'tis farre from that: I only heard
By this my honour'd Father, that your conscience
Made some deepe scruple with a false report:
That *Barrisors* blood should something touch your **honour,**   225
Since he imagin'd I was courting you,
When I was bold to change words with the Duchesse,
And therefore made his quarrell, **his long love**
And service, as I heare, being deepely vowed
To your perfections, which my **ready** presence,   230
Presum'd on with my Father at this season,
For the more care of your so curious honour,
Can well resolve your Conscience, is most false.
  Tam. And is it therefore that you come good sir?
Then crave I now your pardon and my Fathers,   235
And sweare your presence does me so much **good,** /
That all I have it bindes to your requitall: [D4]
Indeed sir, 'tis most true that a report
Is spread, alleadging that his love to me
Was reason of your quarrell, and because   240
You shall not think I faine it for my glory,
That he importun'd me for his Court service,
I'le shew you his own hand, set down in blood
To that vaine purpose: Good Sir, then come in.
Father I thank you now a thousand fold.   245
                                      Exeunt Tamira and D'Amb.
  Frier. May it be worth it to you honour'd daughter.
                                       Descendit Fryar.

         Finis Actus secundi.

222 *Buss.*] *D'Amb.* ‖ 224 report:] ~; ‖ 230 presence,] ~. ‖ 242 importun'd] Q2(c); importud'd
Q2(u) ‖ 245 SD *Exeunt ... D'Amb.*] *Exit Tamira / and D'Amb,* (*beginning in margin beside
l. 244*) ‖

Actus Tertij   Scena Prima.

Bucy, Tamyra.

Tam. O my deare seruant, in thy close embraces,
I haue set open all the dores of danger
To my encompast honor, and my life:
Before I was secure against death and hell;
But now am subiect to the hartlesse feare   5
Of euery shadow, and of euery breath,
And would change firmnesse with an aspen leafe:
So confident a spotlesse conscience is;
So weake a guilty: O the dangerous siege
Sin laies about vs! and the tyranny   10
He exercises when he hath expugn'd:
Like to the horror of a winters thunder,
Mixt with a gushing storme, that suffer nothing
To stirre abroad on earth, but their own rages,
Is sin, when it hath gather'd head aboue vs: 15
No roofe, no shelter can secure vs so,
But he will drowne our cheeks in feare or woe.
Buss. Sin is a coward Madam, and insults
But on our weaknesse, in his truest valour:
And so our ignorance tames vs, that we let   20
His shadowes fright vs: and like empty clouds
In which our faulty apprehensions fordge
The formes of Dragons, Lions, Elephants,
When they hold no proportion: the slie charmes
Of the witch Policy makes him, like a monster /   25
Kept onely to shew men for **Goddesse** money: [D4]
That false hagge often paints him in her cloth
Ten times more monstrous than he is in troth:
In three of vs, the secret of our meeting,
Is onely guarded, and three friends as one   30
Haue euer beene esteem'd: as our three powers
That in **our** one soule, are as one vnited:
Why should we feare then? for my **truth** I sweare
Sooner shall Torture, be the Sire to Pleasure,
And health be grieuous to **men** long time sicke,   35
Than the deare iewell of your fame in me,

III.i. SD *Bucy*] stet (*See Textual Note*) ‖ **5** feare] ~: ‖ **9** dangerous] daugerous ‖ **10** vs!] ~? ‖ **14** rages,] ~; ‖ **15** gather'd] gathered ‖ **18** *Buss.*] *Buc.* ‖ **25** Policy] *Parrott*; policy ‖ **27** him] ~: ‖ **32** are] ~, ‖ **34** Torture ... Pleasure] *N. Brooke*; torture ... pleasure ‖

Actus Tertij   Scena Prima.

Enter D'Ambois, Tamyra, with a Chaine of Pearle.
Buss. **Sweet Mistresse cease, your conscience is too nice,**
And bites too hotly of the Puritane spice.
   Tam. O my deare servant, in thy close embraces,
I have set open all the dores of danger
To my encompast honour, and my life: 5
Before I was secure against death and hell;
But now am subject to the heartlesse feare
Of every shadow, and of every breath,
And would change firmnesse with an aspen leafe:
So confident a spotlesse conscience is;   10
So weake a guilty: O the dangerous siege
Sinne layes about us! and the tyrannie
He exercises when he hath expugn'd:
Like to the horror of a Winters thunder,
Mixt with a gushing storme, that suffer nothing   15
To stirre abroad on earth, but their own rages,
Is sinne, when it hath gather'd head above us:
No roofe, no shelter can secure us so,
But he will drowne our cheeks in feare or woe.
   Buss. Sin is a coward Madam, and insults   20
But on our weaknesse, in his truest valour:
And so our ignorance tames us, that we let /
His shadowes fright us: and like empty clouds   [D4ᵛ]
In which our faulty apprehensions forge
The formes of Dragons, Lions, Elephants,   25
When they hold no proportion: the slie charmes
Of the witch Policy makes him, like a Monster
Kept onely to shew men for **Servile** money:
That false hagge often paints him in her cloth
Ten times more monstrous than he is in troth: 30
In three of us, the secret of our meeting,
Is onely guarded, and three friends as one
Have ever beene esteem'd: as our three powers
That in [our] one soule, are as one united:
Why should we feare then? for my **selfe** I sweare   35
Sooner shall Torture be the Sire to Pleasure,
And health be grievous to **one** long time sick,
Than the deare jewell of your fame in me,

III.i.1 *Buss.*] *D'Amb.* | (*See Textual Note on ll.–/1-2*) ‖ **6** death] dea h *one copy* (*See Press-Variants*) ‖ **7** feare] ~, ‖ **12** us!] ~? ‖ **17** gather'd] gathered | us:] *Q2(u)* (us:); ~, *Q2(c)* ‖ **20** *Buss.*] *D'Ambois.* ‖ **27** Policy] *Parrott*; policy ‖ **34** in our] *Q1*; in Q2 (*See Textual Note*) | are] ~, ‖ **36** Torture ... Pleasure] *N. Brooke*; torture ... pleasure ‖

Be made an outcast to your infamy;
Nor shall my valure (sacred to your vertues)
Onely giue free course to it, from my selfe:
But make it flie out of the mouths of kings   40
In golden vapours, and with awfull wings.   *Exit D'Amb. Manet Tamy.*
  Tam. It rests as all kings seales were set in thee. –

It is not I, but vrgent destiny,
That (as great states men for their generall end
In politique iustice, make poore men offend)   45
Enforceth my offence to make it iust:
What shall weake Dames doe, when th'whole worke of Nature
Hath a strong finger in each one of vs?
Needs must that sweep away the silly cobweb
Of our still-vndone labours; that laies still   50
Our powers to it: as to the line, the stone,
Not to the stone, the line should be oppos'd;
We cannot keepe our constant course in vertue:
What is alike at all parts? euery day

---

38 valure] *Shepherd* (valour); value (*See Textual Note*) ‖ **41** SD *Exit ... Tamy.*] *opposite ll. 42-43*
‖ **42** thee.–] ~., ‖ **43** It] *Ta.* It (*See Textual Note*) ‖ **47** th'whole] t'whole ‖

Be made an out-cast to your infamy;
Nor shall my valure (sacred to your vertues)   40
Onely give free course to it, from my selfe:
But make it flie out of the mouths of Kings
In golden vapours, and with awfull wings.
   Tam. It rests as all Kings seales were set in thee.
Now let us call my Father, whom I sweare   45
I could extreamly chide, but that I feare
To make him so suspicious of my love,
Of which (sweet servant) doe not let him know
For all the world.
   Buss.   Alas! he will not think it?
   Tam. Come then---- [*Calls.*] ho? Father, ope, and take your
    friend.   50
                  Ascendit Frier.
   Frier. Now honour'd daughter, is your doubt resolv'd.
   Tam. I Father, but you went away too soone.
   Frier. Too soone?
   Tam.   Indeed you did, you should have stayed;
Had not your worthy friend beene of your bringing,
And that containes all lawes to temper me,   55
Not all the fearefull danger that besieg'd us,
Had aw'd my throat from exclamation. /
   Frier. I know your serious disposition well. –   [E1]
Come sonne the morne comes on.
   Buss.   Now honour'd Mistresse
Till farther service call, all blisse supply you.   60
   Tam. [*Giving a necklace*]. And you this chaine of pearle,
    and my love onely.   *Descendit Frier and D'Amb.*
It is not I, but urgent destiny,
That (as great States-men for their generall end
In politique justice, make poore men offend)
Enforceth my offence to make it just: 65
What shall weak Dames doe, when th'whole work of Nature
Hath a strong finger in each one of us?
Needs must that sweep away the silly cobweb
Of our still-undone labours; that layes still
Our powers to it: as to the line, the stone,   70
Not to the stone, the line should be oppos'd.
We cannot keepe our constant course in vertue:
What is alike at all parts? every day

---

40 valure] *Shepherd* (valour); value (*See Textual Note*) ‖ 45-61 Now ... onely] *stet* (*See Textual Note*) ‖ 47 love,] ~. ‖ 49 *Buss.*] *D'Amb.* | it?] *stet* (*See Textual Note*) ‖ 50 SD *Calls.*] ‖ 51 resolv'd] *stet* (*See Textual Note*) ‖ 56 besieg'd] besieged ‖ 58 *Frier.*] Q2 *catchword*; *Fryer./* Q2 *text* | well.–] ~. ‖ 59 *Buss.*] *D'Amb.* ‖ 61 SD *Giving a necklace.*] | SD *Descendit ... D'Amb.*] *placed as in Dilke; after l. 62* ‖

Differs from other: euery houre and minute: 55
I, euery thought in our false clock of life,
Oft times inuerts the whole circumference:
We must be sometimes one, sometimes another:
Our bodies are but thicke clouds to our soules;
Through which they cannot shine when they desire: 60
When all the starres, and euen the sunne himselfe,
Must stay the vapors times that he exhales
Before he can make good his beames to vs: /
O how can we, that are but motes to him,   [D4ᵛ]
Wandring at randon in his orderd rayes,   65
Disperse our passions fumes, with our weake labors,
That are more thick and black than all earths vapors?
                    Enter Mont.
   Mont. Good day, my loue: what vp and ready too!
   Tam. Both (my deare Lord), not all this night made I
My selfe vnready, or could sleepe a winke.   70
   Mont. Ahlasse, what troubled my true loue, my peace,
From being at peace within her better selfe?
Or how could Sleepe forbeare to sease **thy beauties**
When he might challenge them as his iust prise?
   Tam. I am in no powre earthly, but in yours;   75
To what end should I goe to bed my Lord,
That wholly mist the comfort of my bed?
Or how should Sleepe possesse my faculties,
Wanting the proper closer of mine eies?
   Mont. Then will I neuer more sleepe night from thee: 80
All mine owne Businesse, all the Kings affaires
Shall take the day to serue them: Euerie night
Ile euer dedicate to thy delight.
   Tam. Nay, good my Lord esteeme not my desires
Such doters on their humours, that my iudgement   85
Cannot subdue them to your worthier pleasure:
A wiues pleas'd husband must her obiect be
In all her acts, not her sooth'd fantasie.
   Mont. Then come my loue, Now pay those Rites to Sleepe
Thy faire eies owe him: shall we now to bed?   90
   Tam. O no my Lord, your holy Frier saies,
All couplings in the day that touch the bed,
Adulterous are, euen in the married;
Whose graue and worthie doctrine, well I know,

---

60 cannot] cannnot ‖ 67 and] & ‖ 69 Both . . . Lord),] ~, . . . ~), ‖ 71 loue,] ~? (*See Textual Note*) ‖
73 Sleepe] *N. Brooke*; sleepe ‖ 78 Sleepe] sleepe ‖ 89 Sleepe] *N. Brooke*; sleepe ‖

Differs from other: every houre and minute:
I, every thought in our false clock of life,   75
Oft times inverts the whole circumference:
We must be sometimes one, sometimes another:
Our bodies are but thick clouds to our soules;
Through which they cannot shine when they desire:
When all the starres, and even the sunne himselfe,   80
Must stay the vapours times that he exhales
Before he can make good his beames to us:
O how can we, that are but motes to him,
Wandring at randon in his order'd rayes,
Disperse our passions fumes, with our weak labours,   85
That are more thick and black than all earths vapours?
                                   Enter Mont.
    Mont. Good day, my love: what up and ready too!
    Tam. Both (my deare Lord), not all this night made I
My selfe unready, or could sleep a wink.
    Mont. Alas, what troubled my true Love, my peace,   90
From being at peace within her better selfe?
Or how could Sleepe forbeare to seize **thine eyes**
When he might challenge them as his just prise? /
    Tam. I am in no powre earthly, but in yours;   [E1ᵛ]
To what end should I goe to bed my Lord,   95
That wholly mist the comfort of my bed?
Or how should Sleepe possesse my faculties,
Wanting the proper closer of mine eyes?
    Mont. Then will I never more sleepe night from thee:
All mine owne Businesse, all the Kings affaires,   100
Shall take the day to serve them: Every night
Ile ever dedicate to thy delight.
    Tam. Nay, good my Lord esteeme not my desires
Such doters on their humours, that my judgement
Cannot subdue them to your worthier pleasure: 105
A wives pleas'd husband must her object be
In all her acts, not her sooth'd fantasie.
    Mont. Then come my Love, Now pay those Rites to Sleepe
Thy faire eyes owe him: shall we now to bed?
    Tam. O no my Lord, your holy Frier sayes,   110
All couplings in the day that touch the bed,
Adulterous are, even in the married;
Whose grave and worthy doctrine, well I know,

---

84 order'd] ordered ‖ 88 Both... Lord),] ~, ... ~)ₐ ‖ 90 Love,] ~? (*See Textual Note*) ‖ 92 Sleepe]
N. Brooke; sleepe ‖ 97 Sleepe] sleepe ‖ 108 Sleepe] *N. Brooke*; sleepe ‖

Your faith in him will liberally allow.   95
   Mont. Hee's a most learned and Religious man;
Come to the Presence then, and see great D'Ambois
(Fortunes proud mushrome shot vp in a night)
Stand like an Atlas **vnderneath the King**; /   99
Which greatnesse with him Monsieur now enuies   [E1]
As bitterly and deadly as the Guise.
   Tam. What, he that was but yesterday his maker?
His raiser and preseruer?
   Mont.   Euen the same.
Each naturall agent workes but to this end,
To render that it works on, like it selfe;   105
Which since the Monsieur in his act on D'Ambois,
Cannot to his ambitious end effect,
But that (quite opposite) the King hath power
(In his loue borne to D'Ambois) to conuert
The point of Monsieurs aime on his owne breast,   110
He turnes his outward loue to inward hate:
A Princes loue is like the lightnings fume,
Which no man can embrace, but must consume.   *Exeunt.*

[III.ii.]

Henry, D'Ambois, Monsieur, Guise, Duchess Elenor,
Annable, Charlotte, Attendants.

   Henr. Speake home **my** Bussy, thy impartiall wordes
Are like braue Faulcons that dare trusse a Fowle
Much greater than themselues; Flatterers are Kites
That checke at **nothing**; thou shalt be my Eagle,
And beare my thunder vnderneath thy wings: 5
Truths words like iewels hang in th'eares of Kings.
   Buss. Would I might liue to see no Iewes hang there
In steede of iewels; sycophants I meane,
Who vse truth like the Diuell, his true Foe
Cast by the Angell to the pit of feares,   10
And bound in chaines; truth seldome decks Kings eares:
Slaue Flatterie (like a Rippiers legs rowl'd vp
In bootes of haie-ropes) with Kings soothed guts
Swadled and strappl'd, now liues only free.
O tis a subtle knaue; how like the plague   15
Vnfelt, he strikes into the braine of **truth**,

---

99 vnderneath the King] *stet* (*See Textual Note*) ‖ **III.ii.**] *Boas subs.* ‖ SD *Duchess … Attendants.*]
after Q2; Monts.␣ / Elenor, Tam.␣ Pero./ (*cf. l. 59 n.*) ‖ **1** my] *stet* (*See Textual Note*) ‖ **12** Flatterie]
Parrott subs.; flatterie ‖

92

Your faith in him will liberally allow.

  Mont. Hee's a most learned and Religious man: 115
Come to the Presence then, and see great *D'Ambois*
(Fortunes proud mushrome shot up in a night)
Stand like an *Atlas* **under our Kings arme**;
Which greatnesse with him Monsieur now envies
As bitterly and deadly as the *Guise*.   120

  Tam. What, he that was but yesterday his maker?
His raiser and preserver?

  Mont.   Even the same.
Each naturall agent works but to this end,
To render that it works on, like it selfe;
Which since the Monsieur in his act on *D'Ambois*,   125
Cannot to his ambitious end effect,
But that (quite opposite) the King hath power
(In his love borne to *D'Ambois*) to convert
The point of Monsieurs aime on his owne breast,
He turnes his outward love to inward hate: /   130
A Princes love is like the lightnings fume,   [E2]
Which no man can embrace, but must consume.   *Exeunt.*

[III.ii.]

Henry, D'Ambois, Monsieur, Guise, Dutches Elenor,
Annabell, Charlot, Attendants.

  Henr. Speak home *Bussy*, thy impartiall words
Are like brave Faulcons that dare trusse a Fowle
Much greater than themselves; Flatterers are Kites
That check at **Sparrowes**; thou shalt be my Eagle,
And beare my thunder underneath thy wings: 5
Truths words like jewels hang in th'eares of Kings.

  Buss. Would I might live to see no Jewes hang there
In steed of jewels; sycophants I meane,
Who use truth like the Devill, his true Foe,
Cast by the Angell to the pit of feares,   10
And bound in chaines; truth seldome decks Kings eares:
Slave Flattery (like a Rippiers legs rowl'd up
In boots of hay-ropes) with Kings soothed guts
Swadled and strappl'd, now lives only free.
O tis a subtle knave; how like the plague   15
Unfelt, he strikes into the braine of **man**,

---

116 Presence] Pres nce *one copy (See Press-Variants)* ‖ 118 under ... arme] *stet (See Textual Note)* ‖ 120 Guise] Guise ‖ **III.ii.**] *Boas subs.* | SD D'Ambois,] ∼. ?*one copy (See Press-Variants)* | Dutches Elenor,] Dutches‸ ‖ 1 Bussy] *stet (See Textual Note)* ‖ 12 Flattery] *Parrott;* flattery ‖ 16 man] *stet (See Textual Note)* ‖

And rageth in his entrailes when he can,
Worse than the poison of a red-hair'd man.
   Henr. Flie at him and his broode, I cast thee off,
And once more giue thee surname of mine Eagle. /   20
   Buss. Ile make you sport enough then, let me haue   [E1ᵛ]
My lucerns too (or dogges inur'd to hunt
Beasts of most rapine) but to put them vp,
And if I trusse not, let me not be trusted:
Shew me a great man (by the peoples voice,   25
Which is the voice of God) that by his greatnesse
Bumbasts his priuate roofes, with publique riches;
That affects royaltie, rising from a clapdish;
That rules so much more **than** his suffering King,
That he makes kings of his subordinate slaues: 30
Himselfe and them graduate like woodmongers
(Piling a stacke of billets) from the earth,
Raising each other into steeples heights;
Let him conuey this on the turning proppes
Of Protean Law, and (his owne counsell keeping)   35
Keepe all vpright; let me but Hawlke at him,
Ile play the Vulture, and so thumpe his liuer,
That (like a huge vnlading Argosea)
He shall confesse all, and you then may hang him.
Shew me a Clergie man, that is in voice   40
A Larke of Heauen; in heart a Mowle of earth;
That hath good liuing, and a wicked life;
A temperate looke, and a luxurious gut;
Turning the rents of his superfluous Cures
Into your Phesants and your Partriches;   45
Venting their Quintessence as men read Hebrew:
Let me but hawlke at him, and, like the other,
He shall confesse all, and you then may hang him.
Shew me a Lawyer that turnes sacred law
(The equall rendrer of each man his owne,   50
The scourge of Rapine and Extortion,
The Sanctuarie and impregnable defence
Of retir'd learning, and **oppressed** vertue)
Into a Harpye, that eates all but's owne,
Into the damned sins it punisheth;   55
Into the Synagogue of theeues and Atheists;
Blood into gold, and iustice into lust:
Let me but hawlke at him, as at the **tother**, /

18 red-hair'd] ~ˌ~ ‖

And rageth in his entrailes when he can,
Worse than the poison of a red-hair'd man?
  Henr. Fly at him and his brood, I cast thee off,
And once more give thee surname of mine Eagle.   20
  Buss. Ile make you sport enough then, let me have
My lucerns too (or dogs inur'd to hunt
Beasts of most rapine), but to put them up,
And if I trusse not, let me not be trusted:
Shew me a great man (by the peoples voice,   25
Which is the voice of God) that by his greatnesse
Bumbasts his private roofes, with publique riches;
That affects royaltie, rising from a clapdish;
That rules so much more **by** his suffering King,
That he makes Kings of his subordinate slaves: 30
Himselfe and them graduate like woodmongers
(Piling a stack of billets) from the earth,
Raising each other into steeples heights;
Let him convey this on the turning props /   34
Of Protean Law, and (his owne counsell keeping)   [E2ᵛ]
Keepe all upright; let me but hawlk at him,
Ile play the Vulture, and so thump his liver,
That (like a huge unlading Argosea)
He shall confesse all, and you then may hang him.
Shew me a Clergie man, that is in voice   40
A Lark of Heaven, in heart a Mowle of earth;
That hath good living, and a wicked life;
A temperate look, and a luxurious gut;
Turning the rents of his superfluous Cures
Into your Phesants and your Partriches;   45
Venting their Quintessence as men read Hebrew:
Let me but hawlk at him, and, like the other,
He shall confesse all, and you then may hang him.
Shew me a Lawyer that turnes sacred law
(The equall rendrer of each man his owne,   50
The scourge of Rapine and Extortion,
The Sanctuary and impregnable defence
Of retir'd learning, and **besieged** vertue)
Into a Harpy, that eates all but's owne,
Into the damned sinnes it punisheth;   55
Into the Synagogue of theeves and Atheists;
Blood into gold, and justice into lust:
Let me but hawlk at him, as at the **rest**,

---

18 red-hair'd] ~‸~ ‖ 21 have] haye *? some copies* (*See Press-Variants*) ‖ 22-23 too ... rapine),] ~,
... ~)‸ ‖

He shall confesse all, and you then may hang him.   [E2]
       [*Enter Montsurry, Tamyra, and Pero.*]
   Gui. Where will you finde such game as you would hawlke
    at?   60
   Buss. Ile hawlke about your house for one of them.
   Gui. Come, y'are a glorious Ruffin, and runne proud
Of the Kings headlong graces; hold your breath,
Or by that poison'd vapour not the King
Shall backe your murtherous valour against me.   65
   Buss. I would the King would make his presence free
But for one **charge** betwixt vs: By the reuerence
Due to the sacred space twixt kings and subiects,
Heere would I make thee cast that popular purple,
In which thy proud soule sits and braues thy soueraigne.   70
   Mons. Peace, peace, I pray thee peace.
   Buss.   Let him peace
    first
That made the first warre.
   Mons.   Hee's the better man.
   Buss. And therefore may doe worst?
   Mons.   He has more titles.
   Buss. So Hydra had more heads.
   Mons.   Hee's greater knowne.
   Buss. His greatnesse is the peoples, mine's mine owne.   75
   Mons. Hee's noblie borne.
   Buss.   He is not, I am noble.
And noblesse in his blood hath no gradation,
But in his merit.
   Gui.   Th'art not nobly borne,
But bastard to the Cardinall of Ambois.
   Buss. Thou liest proud Guiserd; [*To Henry.*] let me flie
    (my Lord).   80
   Henr. Not in my face (my Eagle); violence flies
The Sanctuaries of a Princes eies.
   Buss. [*To Guise.*] Still shall we chide? and fome vpon this
    bit?
Is the Guise only great in faction?
Stands he not by himselfe? Prooues he th'Opinion   85
That mens soules are without them? Be a duke,
And lead me to the field.
   Gui.   Come, follow me.

---

59 SD *Enter … Pero.*] Q2 subs. (*Mont-Surrey, Tamira*) ‖ **71-72** Let … warre] *Boas; one line*
(that) ‖ **76** noblie] *stet* (*See Textual Note*) ‖ **80** SD *To Henry.*] *after D'Urfey* | Lord).] ~.) ‖ **81** face
(my Eagle);] ~; (~ ~)ˌ ‖ **83** SD *To Guise.*] ‖ **86** duke] *Dilke*; Duke ‖

He shall confesse all, and you then may hang him.
Enter Mont-Surrey, Tamira, and Pero.
 Gui. Where will you find such game as you would hawlk
  at?   60
 Buss. Ile hawlk about your house for one of them.
 Gui. Come, y'are a glorious Ruffin, and runne proud
Of the Kings headlong graces; hold your breath,
Or by that poyson'd vapour not the King
Shall back your murtherous valour against me.   65
 Buss. I would the King would make his presence free
But for one **bout** betwixt us: By the reverence
Due to the sacred space twixt kings and subjects,
Here would I make thee cast that popular purple,
In which thy proud soule sits and braves thy soveraigne. 70
 Mons. Peace, peace, I pray thee peace. /
 Buss.   Let him peace [E3]
  first
That made the first warre.
 Mons.   He's the better man.
 Buss. And therefore may doe worst?
 Mons.   He has more titles.
 Buss. So *Hydra* had more heads.
 Mons.   He's greater knowne.
 Buss. His greatnesse is the peoples, mine's mine owne. 75
 Mons. He's nobly borne.
 Buss.   He is not, I am noble.
And noblesse in his blood hath no gradation,
But in his merit.
 Gui.   Th'art not nobly borne,
But bastard to the Cardinall of *Ambois.*
 Buss. Thou liest proud Guiserd; [*To Henry.*] let me flie
  (my Lord).   80
 Henr. Not in my face (my Eagle); violence flies
The Sanctuaries of a Princes eyes.
 Buss. [*To Guise.*] Still shall we chide? and fome upon this
  bit?
Is the *Guise* onely great in faction?
Stands he not by himselfe? Proves he th'Opinion   85
That mens soules are without them? Be a duke,
And lead me to the field.
 Gui.   Come, follow me.

---

60 *Gui.*] *Gui* ‖ 71-72 Let ... warre] *Boas; one line* (that) ‖ 76 nobly] *stet* (*See Textual Note*) ‖ 78 merit.] ~, ‖ 80 SD *To Henry.*] *after D'Urfey* | Lord).] ~.) ‖ 81 face (my Eagle);] ~; (~ ~) ‖ 83 SD *To Guise.*] ‖ 84 *Guise*] Guise ‖ 86 duke] *Dilke;* Duke ‖

Henr. Stay them, – stay, D'Ambois; – Cosen Guise, I wonder
Your **equall** disposition brookes so ill
A man so good, that only would vphold /   90
Man in his natiue noblesse, from whose fall   [E2ᵛ]
All our dissentions rise; that in himselfe
(Without the outward patches of our frailtie,
Riches and honour) knowes he comprehends
Worth with the greatest: Kings had neuer borne   95
Such boundlesse **eminence** ouer other men,
Had all maintain'd the spirit and state of D'Ambois;
Nor had the full impartiall hand of Nature
That all things gaue in her originall,
Without these definite terms of Mine and Thine,   100
Beene turn'd vniustly to the hand of Fortune:
Had all preseru'd her in her prime, like D'Ambois;
No enuie, no disiunction had dissolu'd,
Or pluck'd **out one sticke** of the golden fagot,
In which the world of Saturne **was compris'd,**   105
Had all beene held together with the nerues,
The genius and th'**ingenuous** soule of D'Ambois.
Let my hand therefore be the Hermean rodde
To part and reconcile, and so conserue you,
As my combin'd embracers and supporters.   110
     Buss. [*To Guise.*] Tis our Kings motion, and wee shall not
          seeme
(To worst eies) womanish, though wee change thus soone
Neuer so great grudge for his greater pleasure.
     Gui. I seale to that, and so the manly freedome
That you so much professe, heereafter prooue not   115
A bold and glorious licence to depraue:
To mee his hand shall **prooue** the Hermean **rodde**
His grace affects, in which submissiue signe
On this his sacred right hand, I lay mine.
                              [*Places his hand on Henry's.*]
     Buss. Tis well my Lord, and so your worthie greatnesse   120
Engender not the greater insolence,
Nor make you thinke it a Prerogatiue,
To racke mens freedomes with the ruder wrongs;
My hand (stucke full of lawrell, in true signe
Tis wholly dedicate to righteous peace)   125
In all submission kisseth th'other side.
                              [*Places his hand on theirs.*]

---

88 them, – stay, D'Ambois;–] ~,. ~. ~;. (*See Textual Note*) ‖ **89** equall] *stet* (*See Textual Note*) ‖
98 Nature] *Boas after D'Urfey*; nature ‖ **104** out one sticke] *stet* (*See Textual Note*) ‖ **107**
ingenuous] *stet* (*See Textual Note*) ‖ **111** SD *To Guise.*] ‖ **119** SD *Places … Henry's.*] ‖ **126** SD
Places … theirs.] ‖

Henr. Stay them, – stay, *D'Ambois*; – Cosen *Guise*, I wonder
Your **honour'd** disposition brooks so ill
A man so good, that only would uphold   90
Man in his native noblesse, from whose fall
All our dissentions rise; that in himselfe
(Without the outward patches of our frailty,
Riches and honour) knowes he comprehends
Worth with the greatest: Kings had never borne   95
Such boundlesse **Empire** over other men,
Had all maintain'd the spirit and state of *D'Ambois*;
Nor had the full impartiall hand of Nature
That all things gave in her originall,
Without these definite terms of Mine and Thine,   100
Beene turn'd unjustly to the hand of Fortune,
Had all preserv'd her in her prime, like *D'Ambois*;
No envie, no disiunction had dissolv'd, /
Or pluck'd **one stick out** of the golden faggot,   [E3ᵛ]
In which the world of *Saturne* **bound our lifes**,   105
Had all becne held together with the nerves,
The genius and th'**ingenious** soule of *D'Ambois*.
Let my hand therefore be the Hermean rod
To part and reconcile, and so conserve you,
As my combin'd embracers and supporters.   110
    Buss. [*To Guise.*] Tis our Kings motion, and we shall not
      seeme
(To worst eies) womanish, though we change thus soone
Never so great grudge for his greater pleasure.
    Gui. I seale to that, and so the manly freedome
That you so much professe, hereafter prove not   115
A bold and glorious licence to deprave,
To me his hand shall **hold** the Hermean **vertue**
His grace affects, in which submissive signe
On this his sacred right hand, I lay mine.
                               [*Places his hand on Henry's.*]
    Buss. Tis well my Lord, and so your worthy greatnesse   120
Decline not **to** the greater insolence,
Nor make you think it a Prerogative,
To rack mens freedomes with the ruder wrongs;
My hand (stuck full of lawrell, in true signe
Tis wholly dedicate to righteous peace)   125
In all submission kisseth th'other side.
                               [*Places his hand on theirs.*]

---

88 them, – stay, *D'Ambois*;–] ~,‿ ~‿ ~;‿ (*See Textual Note*) | *Guise*] Guise ‖ 89 honour'd] *stet* (*See Textual Note*) | disposition] disposit on *one copy* (*See Press-Variants*) ‖ 98 Nature] *Boas after D'Urfey*; nature ‖ 104 one stick out] *stet* (*See Textual Note*) ‖ 107 ingenious] *stet* (*See Textual Note*) ‖ 111 SD *To Guise.*] ‖ 116 deprave,] Q2(c); ~: Q2(u) ‖ 119 SD *Places ... Henry's.*] ‖ 126 SD *Places ... theirs.*] ‖

Henr. Thankes to ye both: and kindly I inuite ye
Both to a banquet where weele sacrifice /
Full cups to confirmation of your loues; –   [E3]
At which (faire Ladies) I entreat your presence.   130

> Exeunt Henry, D'Amb., Duchess Ely., Ta.,
> Pero, Annable, Charlotte, and Attendants.

Mons. What had my bounty drunke when it rais'd him?
Gui. Y'aue stucke vs vp a very **proper** flag
That takes more winde than we with all our sailes.
Mons. O so he spreds and flourishes.
Gui.   He must downe,
Vpstarts should neuer perch too neere a crowne.   135
Mons. Tis true my Lord; and as this doting hand,
Euen out of earth (like Iuno), strooke this giant,
So Ioues great **ordinance** shalbe heere implide
To strike him vnder th'Ætna of his pride:
To which worke lend your hands and let vs cast   140
Where we may set snares for his **gadding** greatnes:
I thinke it best, amongst our greatest women:
For there is no such trap to catch an vpstart
As a loose downfall; **and indeed** their fals
Are th'ends of all mens rising: if great men   145
And wise make scapes to please aduantage
Tis with a woman: women, that woorst may,
Still hold mens candles: they direct and know
All things amisse in all men; and their women
All things amisse in them: through whose charmd mouthes   150
We may see all the close scapes of the Court:
When the most royall beast of chace (being old,

---

129 your] Q2(c); yours | loues;–] ~;. ‖ **130** SD *Exeunt … Ta.,*] *Exeunt / Henry, / D'Amᵇ. / Ely.*.
Ta. / *Q1(c) in margin beginning after l. 130; Q1(u) identical except /DA'mᵇ.* | *Pero … Attendants.*]
Ladies. Q2 ‖ **132** Y'aue] Y'ane ‖ **137** earth (like Iuno),] ~, (~ ~). ‖ **146** wise] Q2(c); ~; (See
Textual Note) ‖ **147** women, … may,] ~. … ~. ‖

Henr. Thanks to ye both: and kindly I invite ye
Both to a banquet where weele sacrifice
Full cups to confirmation of your loves; –
At which (faire Ladies) I entreat your presence.   130
[*To the Duchess.*] **And hope you Madam will take one carowse**
For reconcilement of your Lord and servant.
    Duch. If I should faile, my Lord, some other Lady
Would be found there to doe that for my servant.
    Mons. Any of these here?
    Duch.   Nay, I know not that.   135
    Buss. [*To Tamyra.*] **Think your thoughts, like my Mistresse,**
        honour'd Lady?
    Tam. I think not on you Sir, y'are one I know not.
    Buss. Cry you mercy Madam.
    Mont.   Oh Sir, has she met you?
                    Exeunt Henry, D'Amb., Ladies,
                    and Attendants.
    Mons. What had my bounty drunk when it rais'd him? /   139
    Gui. Y'ave stuck us up a very **worthy** flag,   [E4]
That takes more winde than we with all our sailes.
    Mons. O so he spreds and flourishes.
    Gui.   He must downe,
Upstarts should never perch too neere a crowne.
    Mons. Tis true my Lord; and as this doting hand,
Even out of earth (like *Juno*), struck this Giant,   145
So *Joves* great **ordnance** shall be here implide
To strike him under th'*Ætna* of his pride:
To which work lend your hands and let us cast
Where we may set snares for his **ranging** greatnes:
I think it best, amongst our greatest women: 150
For there is no such trap to catch an upstart
As a loose downfall; **for you know** their falls
Are th'ends of all mens rising: if great men
And wise make scapes to please advantage,
Tis with a woman: women, that worst may,   155
Still hold mens candels: they direct and know
All things amisse in all men; and their women
All things amisse in them: through whose charm'd mouthes
We may see all the close scapes of the Court:
When the most royall beast of chase, **the Hart**   160

---

129 your] *Q2(c)*; yours *Q2(u)* | loves;–] ~;ˏ ‖ **131** SD *To the Duchess.*] ‖ **131-38** And ... met you]
stet (*See Textual Note*) ‖ **133** faile,] ~ˏ ‖ **136** *Buss.*] *D'Amb.* | SD *To Tamyra.*] *Parrott* | Mistresse,
honour'd Lady?] ~, ~ / (~. *Q2(c)* (*the parenthesis marking an overrun*); ~ (~ / ~.) *Q2(u)* ‖
138 *Buss.*] *D'Amb.* | Madam.] *Q2(c)*; ~, *Q2(u)* | SD *Exeunt ... Attendants.*] *Exeunt Henry, /*
D'Amb.ˏ Ladies / (*beginning after* Madam. *in l. 138* ‖ **145** earth ... *Juno*,] ~, ... ~)ˏ ‖ **146**
ordnance] *Q2(c)*; ordinance *Q2(u)* ‖ **154** wise] *Q2(c)*; ~; *Q2(u)* (*See Textual Note*) | advantage,]
Q2(c); ~ˏ *Q2(u)* ‖ **155** women, ... may,] ~ˏ ... ~ˏ | worst] *Q2(c)*; woorst *Q2(u)* ‖

And cunning in his **choice of** layres and haunts)
Can neuer be discouer'd to the bow,
The peece or hound: yet where **his custome is**   155
To beat his **vault**, and **he ruts** with his hinde,
The place is markt, and by his Venery
He still is taken. Shall we then attempt
The chiefest meane to that discouery heere,
And court our greatest Ladies **greatest** women,   160
With shews of loue, and liberall promises?
Tis but our breath. If something giuen in hand,
Sharpen their hopes of more, twilbe well venterd.
    Gui. No doubt of that: and tis **an excellent** point
Of our deuis'd inuestigation. /   165
    Mons. I haue **already broke**   [E3ᵛ]
                                    the ice, **my Lord**,
With the **most trusted** woman
                                    of your **Countesse**,
And hope
          I shall wade **through** to our **discouery**.

    Mont. Take say of her my Lord, she comes most fitly
And we will to the other.
                    Enter Charlot, Anable, Pero.

    Gui. [*To Charlotte.*]   Y'are engag'd.   170

    An. [*To Montsurry.*] Nay pray my Lord forbeare.
    Mont. [*Drawing Annable aside.*]   What
        skittish, seruant?
    An. No my Lord I am not so fit for your seruice.
    Char. [*To Guise, as he draws her aside.*] Pray pardon me now
my Lord, my Lady expects me.
    Gui. Ile satisfie her expectation, as far as an vnkle   175
may.

154 discouer'd] discouered | bow,] ~. ‖ 160 greatest women] *stet* (*See Textual Note*) ‖ 163 more,]
~; ‖ 168 discouery.] ~, ‖ 170 And ... other] *stet* (*See Textual Note*) | SD *To Charlotte.*] ‖ 171
An.] *stet* (*See Textual Note*) | SD *To Montsurry.*] | SD *Drawing Annable aside.*] ‖ 172 seruice.] ~:
‖ 173 SD *To ... aside.*] ‖ 174 Lord,] ~? ‖

(Being old, and cunning in his layres and haunts)
Can never be discover'd to the bow,
The peece or hound: yet where **(behind some Queich)**
He breaks his **gall**, and **rutteth** with his hinde,
The place is markt, and by his Venery   165
He still is taken. Shall we then attempt
The chiefest meane to that discovery here,
And court our greatest Ladies **chiefest** women,
With shewes of love, and liberall promises?
Tis but our breath. If something given in hand,   170
Sharpen their hopes of more, 'twill be well ventur'd.
   Gui. No doubt of that: and tis **the cunningst** point
Of our devis'd investigation.
   Mons. I have **broken**
The yce **to it already**
                    with the woman   175
Of your **chast Lady**,
              and **conceive good** hope, /
I shall wade **thorow** to **some wished shore**   [E4ᵛ]
At our **next meeting.**
   Mont.   **Nay, there's small hope there.**
   Gui. Take say of her my Lord, she comes most fitly.

       Enter Charlot, Anable, Pero. [Seeing the men,
            they turn to go.]
   Mons. [Stopping Pero.] **Starting back?**
   Gui. [Stopping Charlotte.]   Y'are engag'd
   indeed.   180
   Char. Nay, pray my Lord forbeare.
   Mont. [Drawing Annable aside.]   What skittish,
   servant?
   An. No my Lord, I am not so fit for your service.
   Char. [To Guise, as he draws her aside.] Pray pardon me now
my Lord, my Lady expects me.
   Gui. Ile satisfie her expectation, as far as an Vnkle   185
may.

---

162 discover'd] discovered | bow,] ~, ‖ 163 Queich] *stet (See Textual Note)* ‖ 168 chiefest] *stet*
(See Textual Note) ‖ 176 hope,] Q2(c); ~. Q2(u) ‖ 179 fitly.] *stet (See Textual Note on l. 170/–)* |
SD *Enter ... Pero.*] *after* back? *in l. 180; placed as in Parrott after Q1* | *Seeing ... go.*] ‖ 180 SD
Stopping Pero.] *after D'Urfey (See Historical Collation)* | Starting back?] *stet (See Textual Note)* |
SD *Stopping Charlotte.*] *after D'Urfey* ‖ 181 Char.] *stet (See Textual Note)* | SD *Drawing*
Annable aside.] *after Spencer* ‖ 183 SD *To Guise ... aside.*] *after Spencer* ‖ 184 Lord,] Q2(c); ~?
Q2(u) ‖

Mons. [*To Guise.*] Well said:– a spirit of Courtship of all hands: [*Aside to Pero.*] Now mine owne Pero: hast thou remembred mee for the discouery I entreated thee to make **concerning** thy Mistresse? speak boldly, and be sure of all things I haue   180
promised.

Pero. Building on that **you haue sworne** (my Lord) I may speake: and much the rather, because my Lady hath not trusted me with that I can tell you; for now I cannot be said to betray her.

Mons. That's all one: so **it bee not to one that will betray thee**: foorth I beseech thee.   185

Pero. To tell you truth, my Lord, I haue made a strange discouery.

Mons. Excellent Pero thou reuiu'st me: may I sincke quicke **into earth heere**, if my tongue discouer it.   190

Pero. Tis thus then: This last night my Lord lay foorth: and I **wondring** my Ladies sitting vp, stole at midnight from my pallat: and (hauing before made a hole both through the wall and arras to her inmost chamber) I saw D'Ambois and **she set close at a banquet**.   195

Mons. D'Ambois?

Pero. Euen he my Lord.

Mons. Dost thou not dreame wench?

Pero. **No my Lord**, he is the man.

Mons. The diuell he is, [*Aside.*] and thy Lady his dam: 200

infinite re-/gions betwixt a womans tongue and her heart: [E4] is this our Goddesse of chastity? I thought I could not be so sleighted, if shee had not her **freight** besides: and therefore plotted this with her

woman: – deare Pero I will aduance   205 thee for euer: but tell mee now: [*Aside.*] Gods pretious it transformes me with admiration: – sweet Pero, whom should she trust with **his** conueiance? Or, all the doores being made sure, how **could** his conueiance bee **performed**?

Pero. Nay my Lord, that amazes me: I cannot by any study   210 so much as guesse at it.

Mons. Well, let's fauour our apprehensions with forbearing that a little: for if my heart were not hoopt with adamant, the conceipt of this would haue burst it: but hearke thee –

[*Whispers with Pero.*]

---

177 SD *To Guise.*] ‖ 177-81 Well … promised] *prose as in Dilke*; Well … hands: / Now … mee/ For … concerning / Thy [*remainder prose*] ‖ 177 said:–] ~: (*See Textual Note*) | spirit] s pirt ‖ 178 SD *Aside to Pero.*] *after Spencer* ‖ 192 wondring] *stet* (*See Textual Note*) ‖ 194-95 she … banquet] *stet* (*See Textual Note*) ‖ 200 SD *Aside.*] (*See Textual Note and Historical Collation*) ‖ 203 sleighted,] ~: ‖ 205 woman:–] ~: ‖ 206 SD *Aside.*] (*See Textual Note and Historical Collation*) ‖ 207 admiration:–] ~: ‖ 208-9 his … his] *stet* (*See Textual Note*) ‖ 212 let's] lets ‖ 214 thee–] ~. | SD *Whispers with Pero.*] *after Q2* ‖

Mons. [*To Guise.*] Well said:– a spirit of Courtship of all hands: [*Aside to Pero.*] Now mine owne *Pero*: hast thou remembred me for the discovery I entreated thee to make **of** thy Mistresse? speak boldly, and be sure of all things I have **sworne**   190
to thee.

Pero. Building on that **assurance** (my Lord) I may speak: and much the rather, because my Lady hath not trusted me with that I can tell you; for now I cannot be said to betray her.

Mons. That's all one, so **wee reach our objects**: forth I beseech   195
thee.

Pero. To tell you truth, my Lord, I have made a strange discovery.

Mons. Excellent! *Pero* thou reviv'st me: may I sink quick **to perdition**, if my tongue discover it.   200

Pero. Tis thus then: This last night my Lord lay forth: and I **watching** my Ladies sitting up, stole **up** at midnight from my pallat, and (having before made a hole both through the wall and arras to her inmost chamber) I saw *D'Ambois* and **her selfe**
reading a letter.   205

Mons. *D'Ambois?*

Pero. Even he my Lord.

Mons. Do'st thou not dreame wench?

Pero. **I sweare**, he is the man.

Mons. The devill he is, [*Aside.*] and thy Lady his dam: 210
Why this was the happiest shot that ever flew, the just plague
of hypocrisie level'd it; Oh the infinite regions betwixt a womans tongue and her heart! is this our Goddesse of chastity? I thought /
I could not be so sleighted, if she had not her **fraught** besides: [F1]
and therefore plotted this with her woman: **never dreaming of**   215
D'Amboys. – Deare *Pero* I will advance thee for ever: but tell me now: [*Aside.*] Gods pretious it transformes mee with admiration: – sweet *Pero*, whom should she trust with **this** conveyance? Or, all the dores being made sure, how **should** his conveyance be **made**?   220

Pero. Nay my Lord, that amazes me: I cannot by any study so much as guesse at it.

Mons. Well, let's favour our apprehensions with forbearing that a little: for if my heart were not hoopt with adamant, the conceipt of this would have burst it: but heark thee –   225
Whispers *with Pero.*

---

187 SD *To Guise.*] ‖ **187-91** Well ... to thee] *prose as in Dilke*; Well ... hands: / Now ... me/ For [*remainder prose*] ‖ **187** said:–] ~. (*See Textual Note*) ‖ **188** SD *Aside to Pero.*] *after Spencer* ‖ **202** watching] *stet* (*See Textual Note*) ‖ **204-5** her selfe ... letter] *stet* (*See Textual Note*) ‖ **210** SD *Aside.*] (*See Textual Note*) ‖ **211-12** Why ... Oh the] *stet* (*See Textual Note*) ‖ **211** shot ... flew,] Q2(c); ~? ... flewe‸ Q2(u) ‖ **212** it;] ~, ‖ **213** and] Q2(c); aud Q2(u) ‖ heart!] Q2(c); ~: Q2(u) ‖ **214** I could] Q2 *text*; could Q2 *catchword* ‖ **216** D'Amboys.–] ~.‸ ‖ **217** SD *Aside.*] (*See Textual Note*) ‖ **217-18** admiration:–] ~:‸ ‖ **218** this] *stet* (*See Textual Note*) ‖ **225** thee–] ~. ‖ SD *Whispers with Pero.*] *after Parrott*; Whispers. (*See Textual Note to ll. 215-18/–*) ‖

Char. [*Aside to Guise.*] I sweare to your Grace, all that   215
I can coniecture touching my Lady your Neece, is a strong
affection she beares to the English Mylor.

Gui. All quod you? tis enough I assure you, but tell me –

[*Whispers with Charlotte.*]

Mont. [*Aside to Annable.*] I pray thee resolue me: the Duke
will neuer imagine that I am busie about's wife: hath D'Ambois   220
any priuy accesse to her?

An. No my Lord, D'Ambois neglects her (as she takes it) and
is therefore suspicious that either your **Countesse**, or the Lady
Beaupre hath closely entertaind him.

Mont. Ber lady a likely suspition, and very neere the life,   225
if she marks it; especially of my wife.

Mons. [*Aside to Pero.*] Come we'l **put off** all, with seeming
onely to haue courted; – away drie palme: sh'as a liuer as **hard**
as a bisket: a man may goe a whole voyage with her, and get
nothing but tempests **at** her windpipe.   230

Gui. Heer's one (I thinke) has swallowd a porcupine, she casts
pricks from her tongue so.

Mont. And heer's a peacock seemes to haue deuourd one
of the Alpes, she has so swelling a spirit, and is so cold of her
kindnesse.   235

Char. We **be** no windfals my Lord; ye must gather vs with the
ladder of matrimony, or we'l hang till we be rotten.

Mons. Indeed that's the way to make ye right openarses.
But ahlas ye haue no portions fit for such husbands as we wish
you. /   240

Pero. Portions my Lord, yes and such portions as your   [E4ᵛ]
principality cannot purchase.

Mons. What, woman? what are those portions?

Pero. Riddle my riddle my Lord.

Mons. I, marry, wench, I thinke thy portion is a right riddle,   245
a man shall neuer finde it out: but let's heare it.

Pero. You shall my Lord.

       What's that, that being most rar's most cheape?
       That **if** you sow, you neuer reape?
       That when it growes most, most you in it?   250
       And still you lose it when you win it:
       That when tis commonest, tis dearest,
       And when tis farthest off 'tis neerest?

215 SD *Aside to Guise.*] ‖ **218** me–] ~. | SD *Whispers with Charlotte.*] *after N. Brooke (See Textual Note)* ‖ **219** SD *Aside to Annable.*] *Baskervill subs.* ‖ **223** Countesse, ... Lady] *N. Brooke subs.*; Lady ... Lady Q2; Lady ... Coun-/tesse *(See Textual Note)* ‖ **227** SD *Aside to Pero.*] *Parrot subs.* ‖ **228** courted;–] *after Boas*; ~; | liuer as hard] *stet (See Textual Note)* ‖ **231** one] ~: ‖ **243** What,] ~ˌ ‖ **245** I, marry,] ~ˌ ~ˌ ‖ **246** let's] lets ‖

Mont. [*Aside to Annable.*] I pray thee resolve mee: the Duke
will never imagine that I am busie about's wife: hath *D'Ambois*
any privy accesse to her?

An. No my Lord, *D'Ambois* neglects her (as shee takes it) and
is therefore suspicious that either your Countesse, or the Lady   230
Beaupre hath closely entertain'd him.

Mont. Ber lady a likely suspition, and very neere the life;
especially of my wife.

Mons. [*Aside to Pero.*] Come, we'l **disguise** all, with seeming
onely to have courted; – away dry palm: sh'as a livor as **dry**   235
as a bisket: a man may goe a whole voyage with her, and get
nothing but tempests **from** her windpipe.

Gui. Here's one (I think) has swallowed a Porcupine, shee casts
pricks from her tongue so.

Mont. And here's a Peacock seemes to have devour'd one   240
of the Alpes, she has so swelling a spirit, and is so cold of her
kindnes.

Char. We **are** no windfalls my Lord; ye must gather us with the
ladder of matrimony, or we'l hang till we be rotten.

Mons. Indeed that's the way to make ye right openarses.   245
But alas ye have no portions fit for such husbands as we wish
you.

Pero. Portions my Lord, yes and such portions as your
principality cannot purchase.

Mons. What, woman? what are those portions?

Pero. Riddle my riddle my Lord.   250

Mons. I, marry, wench, I think thy portion is a right riddle,
a man shall never finde it out: but let's heare it. /

Pero. You shall my Lord.   [F1ᵛ]

What's that, that being most rar's most cheap?
That **when** you sow, you never reap?   255
That when it growes most, most you in it?
And still you lose it when you win it?
That when tis commonest, tis dearest,
And when tis farthest off, 'tis neerest?

226 SD *Aside to Annable.*] *Baskervill subs.* ‖ 227 busie] Q2(c); a busie Q2(u) ‖ 230 Countesse]
N. Brooke subs.; Lady (*See Textual Note*) ‖ 234 SD *Aside to Pero.*] *Parrott subs.* ‖ 235 courted;–]
after Boas; ~; ‖ 235 livor as dry] *stet* (*See Textual Note*) ‖ 238 one] ~, ‖ 241 and] & ‖ 243 are] *stet*
(*See Textual Note*) ‖ 249 What,] ~ₐ ‖ 251 I, marry,] ~ₐ ~ₐ ‖ 255 when] *stet* (*See Textual Note*) ‖

Mons. Is this your portion?

Pero. Euen this my Lord.   255

Mons. Beleeue me I cannot riddle it.

Pero. No my Lord, tis my chastity, which you shall neither
riddle nor fiddle.

Mons. Your chastity? let me begin with the end of **you**; how is
a womans chastitie neerest a man, when tis furthest off?   260

Pero. Why my Lord, when you cannot get it, it goes toth' heart
on you; and that I thinke comes most neere you: and I am
sure it shall bee farre enough off; and so **I** leaue you to **my**
mercy.   *Exit with Charlotte and Annable.*

Mons. Farewell, riddle.   265

Gui. Farewell, Medlar.

Mont. Farewell, winter plum.

Mons. Now my Lords, what fruit of our inquisition? feele you
nothing budding yet? Speake good my Lord Mountsurry.

Mont. Nothing but this: D'Ambois is negligent in obseruing   270
the Duchesse, and therefore she is suspicious that your Neece
or my wife closely entertaines him.

Mons. Your wife, my Lord? Thinke you that possible?

Mont. Alas, I know she flies him like her last houre.

Mons. Her last houre? why that comes vpon her the more   275
she flies it: Does D'Ambois so, thinke you?

Mont. That's not worth the answering: Tis **horrible** to
think with what monsters womens imaginations engrosse them /
when they are once enamour'd, and what wonders they will   [F1]
worke for their satisfaction. They will make a sheepe valiant,   280
a Lion fearefull.

Mons. And an Asse confident, my Lord, **tis true, and** more
will come forth shortly, get you to the banquet.

                                              Exit Guise cum Mont.

O the vnsounded Sea of womens bloods,
That when tis calmest, is most dangerous;   285
Not any wrincle creaming in their faces,
When in their hearts are Scylla and Charibdis,
Which still are hid in **monster-formed cloudes**,
Where neuer day shines, nothing euer growes,
But weeds and poisons, that no states-man knowes;   290
Not Cerberus euer saw the damned nookes
Hid with the vailes of womens vertuous lookes:

---

264 SD *Exit ... Annable.*] *Exeunt women./* Q2; *Exit.* ‖ **265-67** Farewell, ... Farewell, ...
Farewell,] ~‚ ... ~‚ ... ~‚ ‖ **276** so,] ~‚ ‖ **277** That's] Thats ‖ **283** banquet.] *stet (On the line added
in Q2, see Textual Note on l.–/290)* | SD *cum Mont.*] *overrun beside l. 284* ‖

Mons. Is this your **great** portion?   260
Pero. Even this my Lord.
Mons. Beleeve me I cannot riddle it.
Pero. No my Lord, tis my chastity, which you shall neither
riddle nor fiddle.
Mons. Your chastity? let me begin with the end of **it**; how is   265
a womans chastity neerest a man, when tis furthest off?
Pero. Why my Lord, when you cannot get it, it goes to th'heart
on you; and that I think comes most neere you: and I am
sure it shall be farre enough off; and so **wee** leave you to **our**
mercies.   *Exeunt women.* 270
Mons. Farewell, riddle.
Gui. Farewell, Medlar.
Mont. Farewell, winter plum.
Mons. Now my Lords, what fruit of our inquisition? feele you
nothing budding yet? Speak good my Lord *Mountsurry.*   275
Mont. Nothing but this: *D'Ambois* is **thought** negligent in
observing the Duchesse, and therefore she is suspicious that your
Neece or my wife closely entertaines him.
Mons. Your wife, my Lord? Think you that possible?
Mont. Alas, I know she flies him like her last houre.   280
Mons. Her last houre? why that comes upon her the more
she flies it: Does *D'Ambois* so, think you?
Mont. That's not worth the answering; Tis **miraculous** to
think with what monsters womens imaginations engrosse them
when they are once enamour'd, and what wonders they will   285
work for their satisfaction. They will make a sheepe valiant,
a Lion fearefull.
Mons. And an Asse confident; **well** my Lord, more will come
forth shortly, get you to the banquet.   289
Gui. Come my Lord, I have the blind side of one of them. /
                                      Exit Guise cum Mont. [F2]
Mons. O the unsounded Sea of womens bloods,
That when tis calmest, is most dangerous;
Not any wrinkle creaming in their faces,
When in their hearts are *Scylla* and *Caribdis*,
Which still are hid in **dark and standing foggs**,   295
Where never day shines, nothing ever growes,
But weeds and poysons, that no States-man knowes;
Not *Cerberus* ever saw the damned nookes
Hid with the veiles of womens vertuous lookes.

271-73 Farewell, ... Farewell, ... Farewell,] ~, ... ~, ... ~, ‖ **282** so,] ~, ‖ **283** answering;]
Q2(c); ~: Q2(u) ‖ **288** confident;] ~, ‖ **290** Come ... them] *stet* (*See Textual Note*) ‖ **291** Mons.]
Mouns./ Q2(c); *Mount./* Q2(u) ‖ **299** veiles] Q2(c); vailes Q2(u) ‖

I will conceale all yet, and giue more time
To D'Ambois triall, now vpon my hooke;
He awes my throat; else like Sybillas Caue   295

293-301 I will conceale ... How now] *stet (See Textual Note)* ‖

But what a cloud of sulphur have I drawne   300
Up to my bosome in this dangerous secret?
Which if my hast (with any spark) should light
Ere *D'Ambois* were engag'd in some sure plot
I were blowne up; He would be sure, my death.
Would I had never knowne it, for before   305
I shall perswade th'importance to *Montsurry*,
And make him with some studied stratagem,
Train *D'Ambois* to his wreak, his maid may tell it,
Or I (out of my fiery thirst to play
With the fell Tyger, up in darknesse tyed,   310
And give it some light) make it quite break loose.
I feare it afore heaven, and will not see
D'Ambois againe, till I have told *Montsurry*,
And set a snare with him to free my feares:
[*Calls.*] Whose there?

                      Enter Maffe.

Maffe.   My Lord?
Mons.   Goe call the Count
    Montsurry,   315
And make the dores fast, I will speak with none
Till he come to me.
Maffe.   Well my Lord.   *Exiturus.*
Mons.   Or else
Send you some other, and see all the dores
Made safe your selfe I pray; hast, flie about it.   319
    Maffe. You'l speak with none but with the Count *Montsurry*.
    Mons. With none but hee except it be the *Guise*.
    Maffe. See even by this, there's one exception more;
Your Grace must be more firme in the command, /
Or else shall I as weakly execute.   [F2ᵛ]
The *Guise* shall speak with you?
Mons.   He shall I say.   325
    Maffe. And Count *Montsurry*?
Mons.   I, and Count *Montsurry*.
    Maffe. Your Grace must pardon me, that I am bold
To urge the cleare and full sence of your pleasure;
Which when so ever I have knowne, I hope

300-70 But ... How now] *stet* (*See Textual Note*) ‖ 314-15 And ... there?] *Shepherd subs.; as one line* (whose) ‖ 315 SD *Calls.*] | Lord] Lord ‖ 316 I ... none] *stet* (*See Textual Note*) | with none] withnone ‖ 317 Lord] Lord | SD *Exiturus.*] *stet* (*See Textual Note*) ‖ 319 pray;] ~, ‖ 321 *Mons.*] *Boas; Mont.* | *Guise*] Guise ‖ 322 more;] ~, ‖ 325 *Guise*] Guise ‖ 327 bold] Q2(c); bol Q2(u) ‖

It should breath oracles; I feare him strangely,
And may resemble his aduanced valour
Vnto a spirit rais'd without a circle,
Endangering him that ignorantly rais'd him,
And for whose furie he hath learn'd no limit.   300

Your Grace will say, I hit it to a haire.   330
  Mons. You have.
  Maffe.   I hope so, or I would be glad –
  Mons. I pray thee get thee gone, thou art so tedious
In the strickt forme of all thy services,
That I had better have one negligent.
You hit my pleasure well, when *D'Ambois* hit you,   335
Did you not, think you?
  Maffe.   *D'Ambois*? why my Lord –
  Mons. I pray thee talk no more, but shut the dores.
Doe what I charge thee.
  Maffe.   I will my Lord, and yet
I would be glad the wrong I had of *D'Ambois* –
  Mons. Precious! then it is a Fate that plagues me   340
In this mans foolery, I may be murthered
While he stands on protection of his folly.
Avant about thy charge.
  Maffe.   I goe my Lord.
[*Aside.*] I had my head broke in his faithfull service,
I had no suit the more, nor any thanks,   345
And yet my teeth must still be hit with *D'Ambois*. –
D'Ambois my Lord shall know –
  Mons.   The devill and *D'Ambois*!
                           Exit Maffe.

How am I tortur'd with this trusty foole?
Never was any curious in his place
To doe things justly, but he was an Asse: 350
We cannot finde one trusty that is witty,
And therefore beare their disproportion.
Grant thou great starre, and angell of my life,
A sure lease of it but for some few dayes, /   354
That I may cleare my bosome of the Snake   [F3]
I cherisht there, and I will then defie
All check to it but Natures, and her Altars
Shall crack with vessels crown'd with ev'ry liquor
Drawn from her highest, and most bloudy humors.
I feare him strangely,
             his advanced valour   360
Is like a spirit rais'd without a circle,
Endangering him that ignorantly rais'd him,
And for whose fury he hath learnt no limit.

---

331 glad–] ~.– ‖ 336 Lord–] ~? ‖ 344 SD *Aside.*] *after Dilke* ‖ 346 *D'Ambois*.–] ~. ‖ 347 know–]
~.– | *D'Ambois*!] ~. ‖ 356 I will then] *Q2(c)*; then I will *Q2(u)* ‖ 359 her] *Q2(c)*; the *Q2(u)* ‖

Enter D'Ambois.

How now, what leap'st thou at?
   Buss.   O royall obiect.
   Mons. Thou dream'st awake: Obiect in th'emptie aire?
   Buss. Worthie the **head** of Titan, worth his chaire.
   Mons. Pray thee what mean'st thou?
   Buss.   See you not a Croune
Empale the forehead of the great King Monsieur?   305
   Mons. O fie vpon thee.
   Buss.   **Sir,** that is the Subiect
Of all these your retir'd and sole discourses.
   Mons. Wilt thou not leaue that wrongfull supposition?

This still hath made me doubt thou dost not loue me.
Wilt thou doe one thing **for me then** syncerelie?   310
   Buss. I, any thing, but killing of the King. /
   Mons. Still in that discord, and ill-taken note?   [F1ᵛ]

Buss. **Come,** doe not doubt **me, and command mee all things**.

301 How] *Mons.* How | *Buss.*] *D'Amb. (so through the rest of this scene)* ‖ 312 ill-taken] ∼ ͵∼ ‖
313 Come ... things] *verse as in Evans (N. Brooke unclear); as prose* ‖

Enter Maffe hastily.
Maffe. I cannot help it, what should I do more?
As I was gathering a fit Guard to make   365
My passage to the dores, and the dores sure,
The man of bloud is enter'd.   *[Exit.]*
   Mons.   Rage of death!
If I had told the secret, and he knew it,
Thus had I bin endanger'd: –
               Enter D'Ambois.
              My sweet heart!
How now? what leap'st thou at?
   Buss.   O royall object.   370
   Mons. Thou dream'st awake: Object in th'empty aire?
   Buss. Worthy the **browes** of *Titan*, worth his chaire.
   Mons. Pray thee what mean'st thou?
   Buss.   See you not a Crowne
Empale the forehead of the great King Monsieur?
   Mons. O fie upon thee.
   Buss.   **Prince**, that is the Subject   375
Of all these your retir'd and sole discourses.
   Mons. Wilt thou not leave that wrongfull supposition?
   Buss. **Why wrongfull?** to suppose the **doubtlesse right**
To the succession worth the thinking on.
   Mons. Well, leave these jests; how I am over-joyed   380
With thy wish'd presence, and how fit thou com'st,
For of mine honour I was sending for thee.
   Buss. To what end?
   Mons.   Onely for thy company,
Which I have still in thought, but that's no payment
On thy part made with personall appearance. /   385
Thy absence so long suffer'd oftentimes   [F3ᵛ]
Put me **in some little** doubt thou do'st not love me.
Wilt thou doe one thing **therefore now** sincerely?
   Buss. I, any thing, but killing of the King.
   Mons. Still in that discord, and ill-taken note?   390
How most unseasonable thou playest the Cucko,
In this thy fall of friendship!
   Buss.   **Then** doe not doubt,
That there is any act within my nerves,
But killing of the King that is not yours.

367 SD *Exit.*] *after D'Urfey* | death!] ~. ‖ **369** SD *Enter D'Ambois.*] *placed as in Boas; after* at?
in l.370 ‖ **370** *Buss.*] *D'Amb.* (*so through the rest of this scene*) ‖ **380** jests;] ~, ‖ **386** suffer'd]
suffered ‖ **390** ill-taken] ~‿~ ‖ **392** friendship!] ~? ‖

    Mons. I will not then, **and now** by **all** my loue
Shewne to thy vertues, and by all fruits else   315
Alreadie sprung from that **affection,**

I charge thee vtter (euen with all the freedome
Both of thy noble nature and thy friendship)
The full and plaine state of me in thy thoughts.
    Buss. What, vtter plainly what I thinke of you?   320

Why this swims quite against the streame of
    greatnesse:
Great men would rather heare their flatteries,
And if they be not made fooles, are not wise.
    Mons. I am no such great foole, and therefore charge thee
Euen from the roote of thy free heart, display mee.   325
    Buss. Since you affect it in such serious termes,
If your selfe first will tell me what you thinke
As freely and as heartily of mee,
Ile be as open in my thoughts of you.
    Mons. A bargaine, of mine honour; and make this,   330
That prooue wee in our full dissection
Neuer so foule, liue still the sounder friends.
    Buss. What else Sir? **come begin, and speake** me **simply**.
    Mons. I will I sweare. I thinke thee then a man,
That dares as much as a wilde horse or Tyger;   335
As headstrong and as bloodie; and **to** feede
The rauenous wolfe of thy most Caniball valour,
(Rather than not employ it) thou would'st turne
Hackster to any whore, slaue to a Iew
Or English vsurer, to force possessions,   340
And cut mens throates of morgaged estates;
Or thou would'st tire thee like a Tinkers **wife,**
And murther market folkes, quarrell with sheepe,
And runne as mad as Aiax; serue a Butcher;
Doe any thing but killing of the King: 345
That in thy valour th'art like other naturals,
That haue strange gifts in nature, but no soule
Diffus'd quite through, to make them of a peece, /
But stoppe at humours, that are more absurd,   [F2]
Childish and villanous than that hackster, whore,   350
Slaue, cut-throat, Tinkers bitch, compar'd before:

---

330 bargaine,] ~ˌ ‖ **339** Iew] ~, (*See Textual Note*) ‖ **340-41** possessions, ... throates] *stet* (*See Textual Note*) ‖ **344** Butcher;] ~, ‖

Mons. I will not then; **to prove which** by my love   395
Shewne to thy vertues, and by all fruits else
Already sprung from that **still flourishing tree,**
With whatsoever may hereafter spring,
I charge thee utter (even with all the freedome
Both of thy noble nature and thy friendship)   400
The full and plaine state of me in thy thoughts.
   Buss. What, utter plainly what I think of you?
   Mons. **Plaine as truth.**
   Buss. Why this swims quite against the stream of
      greatnes.
Great men would rather heare their flatteries,   405
And if they be not made fooles, are not wise.
   Mons. I am no such great foole, and therefore charge thee
Even from the root of thy free heart display mee.
   Buss. Since you affect it in such serious termes,
If your selfe first will tell me what you think   410
As freely and as heartily of me,
I'le be as open in my thoughts of you.
   Mons. A bargain, of mine honour; and make this,
That prove we in our full dissection
Never so foule, live still the sounder friends.   415
   Buss. What else Sir? **pay** me **home, ile bide it bravely.**
   Mons. I will I sweare. I think thee then a man,
That dares as much as a wilde horse or Tyger;
As headstrong and as bloody; and to feed
The ravenous wolfe of thy most Caniball valour,   420
(Rather than not employ it) thou would'st turne
Hackster to any whore, slave to a Jew /
Or English usurer, to force possessions,   [F4]
And cut mens throats of morgaged estates;
Or thou would'st tire thee like a Tinkers **strumpet,**   425
And murther market folks, quarrell with sheepe,
And runne as mad as *Ajax*; serve a Butcher;
Doe any thing but killing of the King:
That in thy valour th'art like other naturalls,
That have strange gifts in nature, but no soule   430
Diffus'd quite through, to make them of a peece,
But stop at humours, that are more absurd,
Childish and villanous than that hackster, whore,
Slave, cut-throat, Tinkers bitch, compar'd before:

408 heart] *Q2(c)*; ~, *Q2(u)* ‖ **413** bargain,] ~. ‖ **416** pay] *Parrot conj.*; come pay (*See Textual Note*) ‖ **419** to] *Q1*; so (*See Textual Note*) ‖ **422** Jew] ~, (*See Textual Note*) ‖ **423-24** possessions, ... throats] *stet* (*See Textual Note*) ‖ **427** Butcher;] ~, ‖

And in those humours would'st enuie, betray,
Slander, blaspheme, change each houre a religion;
Doe any thing, but killing of the King;
That in **that** valour (which is still **my** dunghill,   355
To which **I carrie** all filth in thy house)
Th'art more ridiculous and vaine-glorious
Than any Mountibancke; and impudent
Than any painted bawde; which, not to sooth
And glorifie thee like a Iupiter Hammon,   360
Thou eat'st thy heart in vineger; and thy gall
Turns all thy blood to poison, which is cause
Of that Tode-poole that stands in thy complexion;
And makes thee (with a cold and earthie moisture,
Which is the damme of putrifaction,   365
As plague to thy damn'd pride) rot as thou liu'st,
To study calumnies and treacheries;
To thy friends slaughters, like a Scrich-owle sing,
And to all mischiefs, but to kill the King.
   Buss. So: Haue you said?
   Mons.   How thinkest thou? Doe I
   flatter?   370
Speake I not like a trustie friend to thee?
   Buss. That euer any man was blest withall;
So heere's for mee. I thinke you are (at worst)
No diuell, since y'are like to be no king;
Of which, with any friend of yours Ile lay   375
This poore Stilladoe heere, gainst all the starres,
I, and gainst all your treacheries, which are more,
That you did neuer good, but to doe ill;
But ill of all sorts, free and for it selfe:
That (like a murthering peece, making lanes in armies,   380
The first man of a ranke, the whole ranke falling)
If you haue **once** wrong'd one man, **y'are** so farre
From making him amends, that all his race,
Friends and associates fall into your chace:
That y'are for periuries the verie prince /   385
Of all intelligencers; and your voice   [F2ᵛ]
Is like an Easterne winde, that where it flies,
Knits nets of Catterpillars, with which you catch
The prime of all the fruits the kingdome yeeldes.
That your politicall head is the curst fount   390
Of all the violence, rapine, crueltie,

359-60 which, ... Hammon] *stet (See Textual Note)* ‖ **366** liu'st,] ~; ‖ **377** more,] ~; ‖ **380** armies,] ~ˌ ‖ **382** once ... y'are] *stet (See Textual Note)* ‖

And in those humours would'st envie, betray,   435
Slander, blaspheme, change each houre a religion;
Doe any thing, but killing of the King;
That in **thy** valour (which is still **the** dunghill,
To which **hath reference** all filth in thy house)
Th'art more ridiculous and vaine-glorious   440
Than any Mountibank; and impudent
Than any painted Bawd; which, not to sooth
And glorifie thee like a *Iupiter Hammon*,
Thou eat'st thy heart in vineger; and thy gall
Turns all thy blood to poyson, which is cause   445
Of that Toad-poole that stands in thy complexion;
And makes thee (with a cold and earthy moisture,
Which is the damme of putrifaction,
As plague to thy damn'd pride) rot as thou liv'st,
To study calumnies and treacheries;   450
To thy friends slaughters, like a Scrich-owle sing,
And to all mischiefes, but to kill the King.
   Buss. So: Have you said?
   Mons.   How thinkest thou? Doe I
    flatter?
Speak I not like a trusty friend to thee?
   Buss. That ever any man was blest withall;   455
So here's for me. I think you are (at worst)
No devill, since y'are like to be no King;
Of which, with any friend of yours Ile lay
This poore Stillado here, gainst all the starres, /   459
I, and 'gainst all your treacheries, which are more,   [F4ᵛ]
That you did never good, but to doe ill;
But ill of all sorts, free and for it selfe:
That (like a murthering peece, making lanes in Armies,
The first man of a rank, the whole rank falling)
If you have wrong'd one man, **you** are so farre   465
From making him amends, that all his race,
Friends and associates fall into your chace:
That y'are for perjuries the very prince
Of all intelligencers; and your voice
Is like an Easterne winde, that where it flies,   470
Knits nets of Catterpillars, with which you catch
The prime of all the fruits the Kingdome yeelds.
That your politicall head is the curst fount
Of all the violence, rapine, cruelty,

---

438 dunghill] Q2(c); dnnghill Q2(u) ‖ **442-43** which, ... *Hammon*] stet (*See Textual Note*) ‖ **449** liv'st,] ~; ‖ **460** more,] ~; ‖ **463** Armies,] ~. ‖ **465** you are] Q2(c); y'are Q2(u) (*See Textual Note*) ‖

Tyrannie and Atheisme flowing through the realme.
That y'aue a tongue so scandalous, twill cut
A perfect Crystall; and a breath that will
Kill to that wall a spider; you will iest   395
With God, and your soule to the diuell tender
For lust; kisse horror, and with death engender.
That your foule bodie is a Lernean fenne
Of all the maladies breeding in all men.
That you are vtterlie without a soule: 400
And (for your life) the thred of that was spunne,
When Clotho slept, and let her breathing rocke
Fall in the durt; and Lachesis still drawes it,
Dipping her twisting fingers in a boule
Defil'd, and croun'd with Vertues forced soule.   405
And lastly (which I must for Gratitude
Euer remember) That of all my height
And dearest life, you are the onlie spring,
Only in royall hope to kill the king.
   Mons. Why now I see thou lou'st mee, come to the
     banquet.   *[Exeunt.]* 410

Finis Actus tertij.

Actus Quarti   Scena Prima.

Henry, Monsieur, Guise, Montsurry, Bussy, Duchess Elynor,
Tamyra, Beaupre, Pero, Charlotte, Anable,
Pyrha, with foure Pages.
   Henr. Ladies, ye haue not done our banquet right,
Nor lookt vpon it with those cheerefull raies
That lately turnd your breaths to flouds of gold;
Your looks, me thinks, are not drawne out with thoughts,
So cleere and free as heeretofore, but **fare** /   5
As if the thicke complexions of men   [F3]
Gouernd within them.
   Buss.   Tis not like, my Lord,
That men in women rule, but contrary;
For as the Moone (of all things God created)
Not only is the most appropriate image   10
Or glasse to shew them how they wax and wane,
But in her **light** and motion, likewise beares

392 and] & ‖ 405 Vertues] *N. Brooke subs.*; vertues ‖ 410 SD *Exeunt.*] Q2 ‖ **IV.i.** SD *Duchess Elynor*] *Elynor* ‖ 7 like, my Lord,] ~ ~ ~ ‖ 8 rule, but contrary;] ~; ~ ~, ‖ 12 light] *stet (See Textual Note)* ‖

Tyrannie and Atheisme flowing through the realme.   475
That y'ave a tongue so scandalous, 'twill cut
The purest Christall; and a breath that will
Kill to that wall a spider; you will jest
With God, and your soule to the devill tender
For lust; kisse horror, and with death engender.   480
That your foule body is a Lernean fenne
Of all the maladies breeding in all men.
That you are utterly without a soule:
And (for your life) the thred of that was spunne,
When *Clotho* slept, and let her breathing rock   485
Fall in the durt; and *Lachesis* still drawes it,
Dipping her twisting fingers in a boule
Defil'd, and crown'd with Vertues forced soule.
And lastly (which I must for Gratitude
Ever remember) That of all my height   490
And dearest life, you are the onely spring,
Onely in royall hope to kill the King.
   Mons. Why now I see thou lov'st me, come to the
   banquet.   ***Exeunt.***

Finis Actus tertij. /

Actus Quarti   Scena Prima.   [G1]

*Henry, Monsieur **with a Letter**, Guise, Montsurry, Bussy,*
Duchess Elynor, Tamyra, Beaupre, Pero, Charlotte, Anable,
Pyrha, with foure Pages.
   Henr. Ladies, ye have not done our banquet right,
Nor lookt upon it with those cheerefull rayes
That lately turn'd your breaths to flouds of gold;
Your looks, me thinks, are not drawne out with thoughts,
So cleare and free as heretofore, but **foule**   5
As if the thick complexions of men
Govern'd within them.
   Buss.   'Tis not like, my Lord,
That men in women rule, but contrary;
For as the Moone (of all things God created)
Not only is the most appropriate image   10
Or glasse to shew them how they wax and wane,
But in her **height** and motion likewise beares

475 and] & ‖ 486 and] *Q2(c)*; anp *Q2(u)* ‖ 488 Vertues] *N. Brooke subs.*; vertues ‖ 493 banquet.]
~- ‖ **IV.i.** SD *Duchess Elynor*] *Elynor* | *Anable,*] *Q2(c)*; ~ₐ *Q2(u)* ‖ 7 like, my Lord,] ~ₐ ~ ~ₐ ‖ 12
height] *stet (See Textual Note)* ‖

Imperiall influences that command
In all their powers, and make them wax and wane;
So women, that (of all things made of nothing)   15
Are the most perfect **images** of the Moone
(Or still-vnweand sweet Moon-calues with white faces)
Not only are paternes of change to men:
But as the tender Moon-shine of their beauties
Cleeres, or is cloudy, make men glad or sad.   20

    Mons. But heere the Moones are chang'd (as the King notes)
And either men rule in them, or some power
Beyond their voluntary **motions**:
For nothing can recouer their lost faces.
    Buss. None can be alwaies one: our griefes and ioies   25
Hold seuerall scepters in vs, and haue times
For their **predominance**: which griefe now, in them
Doth **claime**, as proper to his diademe:
And grief's a naturall sicknesse of the bloud,
That time to part, asks as his comming had;   30
Onely sleight fooles grieu'd, suddenly are glad;
A man may say t'a dead man, be reuiu'd,
As well as to one sorrowfull, be not grieu'd.
[*To the Duchess.*] And therefore (Princely mistresse) in all
      warres
Against these base foes that insult on weaknesse,   35
And still fight hous'd, behinde the shield of Nature,
Of **tyrannous** law, treachery, or beastly need,
Your seruant cannot helpe; authority heere
Goes with corruption; something like some States,
That back woorst men: Valure to them must creepe   40
That (to themselues left) would feare him asleepe. ˙
    Duch. Ye all take that for granted, that doth rest /
Yet to be prou'd; we all are as we were,   [F3ᵛ]
As merry, and as free in thought as euer.
    Gui. And why then can ye not disclose your thoughts?   45
    Tam. Me thinks the man hath answerd for vs well.
    Mons. The man? why Madam d'ee not know his name?
    Tam. Man is a name of honour for a King:
Additions take away from each chiefe thing:
The Schoole of Modesty, not to learne, learnes Dames: 50
They sit in high formes there, that know mens names.

---

14 and wane] & wane ‖ **23-27** motions . . . predominance] *stet* (*See Textual Note*) ‖ **25** *Buss.*] *stet* (*See Textual Note*) ‖ **28** claime] *stet* (*See Textual Note*) ‖ **32** reuiu'd] reuiu d (*most copies*) ‖ **34** SD *To the Duchess.*] *Baskervill after Dilke* ‖ **40** Valure] valure ‖ **43** were,] ~͵ ‖ **46** *Tam.*] *Tamy.* (*so through l. 61*) ‖

Imperiall influences that command
In all their powers, and make them wax and wane;
So women, that (of all things made of nothing)　　　　15
Are the most perfect **Idols** of the Moone
(Or still-unwean'd sweet Moon-calves with white faces),
Not only are paterns of change to men:
But as the tender Moon-shine of their beauties
Cleares, or is cloudy, make men glad or sad,　　　　20
So then they rule in men, not men in them.
　　Mons. But here the Moons are chang'd (as the King notes)
And either men rule in them, or some power
Beyond their voluntary **faculty**:
For nothing can recover their lost faces.　　　　25
　　Mont. None can be alwayes one: our griefes and joyes
Hold severall scepters in us, and have times
For their **divided Empires**: which griefe now, in them
Doth **prove** as proper to his diadem.
　　Buss. And griefe's a naturall sicknesse of the bloud, /　　　30
That time to part asks, as his comming had;　　　　[G1ᵛ]
Onely sleight fooles griev'd, suddenly are glad;
A man may say t'a dead man, be reviv'd,
As well as to one sorrowfull, be not griev'd.
[*To the Duchess.*] And therefore (Princely Mistresse) in all
　　　warres　　　　35
Against these base foes that insult on weaknesse,
And still fight hous'd, behind the shield of Nature,
Of **priviledge**, law, treachery, or beastly need,
Your servant cannot help; authority here
Goes with corruption; something like some States,　　　40
That back woorst men; Valour to them must creepe
That (to themselves left) would feare him asleepe.
　　Duch. Ye all take that for granted, that doth rest
Yet to be prov'd; we all are as we were,
As merry, and as free in thought as ever.　　　　45
　　Gui. And why then can ye not disclose your thoughts?
　　Tam. Me thinks the man hath answer'd for us well.
　　Mons. The man? why Madam d'ee not know his name?
　　Tam. Man is a name of honour for a King:
Additions take away from each chiefe thing:　　　　50
The Schoole of Modesty, not to learne, learnes Dames:
They sit in high formes there, that know mens names.

16-17 Moone ... faces),] ~, ... ~)‸ ‖ **22** notes)] Q2(c); note‸ Q2(u) ‖ **24** faculty] *stet* (*See Textual Note*) ‖ **26** *Mont.*] *stet* (*See Textual Note*) | joyes] Q2(c); joy Q2(u) ‖ **29** prove] *stet* (*See Textual Note*) ‖ **30** *Buss.*] *D'Amb.* (*so through the rest of this scene*) ‖ **35** SD *To the Duchess.*] *Baskervill after Dilke* | therefore] Q2(c); thereforn Q2(u) ‖ **38** priviledge,] ~‸ (*See Textual Note*) ‖ **41** Valour] valour ‖ **43** granted] grauted ‖ **47** *Tam.*] *Tamy.* (*so through l. 62*) ‖

Mons. [*To Bussy.*] Harke sweet heart, heer's a **bound** set to
    your valure:
It cannot enter heere; no, not to notice
Of what your name is; your great Eagles beake
(Should you flie at her) had as good encounter   55
An Albion cliffe, as her more craggy liuer.
   Buss. Ile not attempt her Sir; her sight and name
(By which I only know her) doth deter me.
   Henr. So do they all men else.
   Mons.   You would say so
If you knew all.
   Tam.   Knew all my Lord? what meane you?   60
   Mons. All that I know Madam.
   Tam.   That you know? speake it.
   Mons. No tis enough I feele it.
   Henr.   But me thinkes
Her Courtship is more pure than heeretofore:
True Courtiers should be modest, **but** not nice:
Bold, but not impudent: pleasure loue, not vice.   65
   Mons. Sweet heart: come hither,

                     [*Draws Bussy aside as others converse.*]
                what if one should make
Horns at Mountsurry? would it strike him iealous
Through all the proofes of his chaste Ladies vertues?
   Buss. **No I thinke** not.
   Mons.   Not if **I** **nam'd** the **man**
With whom I would **make** him **suspicious**   70
His wife hath **armd his forehead**?
   Buss.   So, **you might**

Haue your **great** nose made lesse indeed: and slit:
Your eies thrust out.
   Mons.   Peace, peace, I pray thee peace. /
Who dares doe that? the brother of his King?   [F4]
   Buss. Were your King brother in you: all your powers   75
(Stretcht in the armes of great men and their bawds)
Set close downe by you; all your stormie lawes

---

52 SD *To Bussy.*] Boas | heer's] hee'rs ‖ 57 *Buss.*] *Buc.* (so also ll. 69, 71, 75) ‖ 64 but] *stet* (*See Textual Note*) ‖ 66 SD *Draws … converse.*] ‖ 74 King?] *stet* (*See Textual Note*) ‖

Mons. [*To Bussy.*] Heark sweet heart, here's a **bar** set to
    your valour:
It cannot enter here; no, not to notice
Of what your name is; your great Eagles beak   55
(Should you flie at her) had as good encounter
An *Albion* cliffe, as her more craggy liver.
   Buss. Ile not attempt her Sir; her sight and name
(By which I onely know her) doth deter me.
   Henr. So doe they all men else.
   Mons.   You would say so   60
If you knew all.
   Tam.   Knew all my Lord? what meane you?
   Mons. All that I know Madam.
   Tam.   That you know? speak it.
   Mons. No tis enough I feele it.
   Henr.   But me thinks
Her Courtship is more pure then heretofore: /   64
True Courtiers should be modest, **and** not nice: [G2]
Bold, but not impudent: pleasure love, not vice.
   Mons. Sweet heart, come hither:
                 [*Draws Bussy aside as others converse.*]
               what if one should make
Horns at *Mountsurry*? would it **not** strike him jealous
Through all the proofes of his chaste Ladies vertues?
   Buss. **If he be wise,** not.   70
   Mons. **What?** not if **I should name** the **Gardener,**
That I would have him **think** hath **grafted him?**

   Buss. So **the large licence that your greatnesse uses**
To jest at all men, may be taught indeed
To make a difference of the grounds you play on,   75
Both in the men you scandall, and the matter.
   Mons. **As how? as how?**
   Buss.   **Perhaps led with a traine,**
Where you **may** have your nose made lesse, and slit,
Your eyes thrust out.
   Mons.   Peace, peace, I pray thee peace.
Who dares doe that? the brother of his King?   80
   Buss. Were your King brother in you, all your powers
(Stretcht in the armes of great men and their Bawds)
Set close downe by you, all your stormy lawes

---

53 SD *To Bussy.*] *Boas* ‖ **57** *Albion*] Albion ‖ **61** Lord] Lord ‖ **65** and] *stet* (*See Textual Note*) ‖
67 SD *Draws ... converse.*] ‖ **77-79** Perhaps ... out] *Boas subs.*; Perhaps ... where ... have /
Your ... slit, your ... out ‖ **80** King?] *stet* (*See Textual Note*) ‖

Spouted with Lawyers mouths, and gushing bloud,
Like to so many Torrents: all your glories
(Making you terrible, like enchaunted flames,   80
Fed with bare cockescombes: and with crooked hammes):
All your prerogatiues, your shames and tortures:
All daring heauen, and opening hell about you:
Were I the man, ye wrong'd so and prouok'd
(Though ne're so much beneath you): like a box tree   85
I would (out of the **toughnesse** of my root)
Ramme hardnesse, in my lownesse, and like death
Mounted on earthquakes, I would trot through all
Honors and horrors: **through** fowle and faire,
And from your whole strength tosse you into aire.   90
   Mons. Goe, th'art a diuell; such another spirit
Could not be stild, from all Th'Armenian dragons.
O my Loues glory: heire to all I haue
(That's all I can say, and that all I sweare):
If thou outliue me, as I know thou must,   95
Or else hath Nature no proportiond end
To her great labors: she hath breath'd a **spirit**
Into thy entrailes, of **effect** to swell
Into another great Augustus Cæsar:
Organes, and faculties fitted to her greatnesse: 100
And should that perish like a common spirit,
Nature's a Courtier and regards no merit.
   Henr. Heer's nought but whispering with vs: like a calme
Before a tempest, when the silent aire
Laies her soft eare close to the earth to hearken   105
For that she feares **is comming** to **afflict** her;
Some fate doth ioine our eares to heare it comming.
Come, my braue eagle, let's to Couert flie:
I see Almighty Æther in the smoake
Of all his clowds descending: and the skie   110
Hid in the dimme ostents of Tragedy.
                   Exit Hen. with D'Amb., Pages, and Ladies. /
   Gui. [*Aside to Monsieur.*] Now stirre the humour, and   [F4ᵛ]
    begin the brawle.
   Mont. The King and D'Ambois now are growen all one.
   Mons. Nay, they are two my Lord.
   Mont.   How's that?
   Mons.   No more.

---

78 mouths,] ~; ‖ **79-81** glories . . . hammes):] ~: . . . ~)ˎ ‖ **80** flames,] ~ˎ (*See Textual Note*) ‖ **84-85**
prouok'd . . . you):] ~: . . . ~)ˎ ‖ **86** toughnesse] *stet* (*See Textual Note*) ‖ **93-94** haue (That's . . .
sweare):] ~: ~ . . . ~. ‖ **96** Nature] *Boas;* nature ‖ **111** SD *Pages,*] | *and Ladies.*] Q2 ‖ **112** SD
Aside to Monsieur.] *Parrott* ‖

Spouted with Lawyers mouthes, and gushing bloud,
Like to so many Torrents, all your glories   85
(Making you terrible, like enchanted flames,
Fed with bare cockscombs, and with crooked hammes),
All your prerogatives, your shames and tortures,
All daring heaven, and opening hell about you,
Were I the man ye wrong'd so, and provok'd   90
(Though ne're so much beneath you), like a box tree
I would (out of the **roughnesse** of my root)
Ramme hardnesse, in my lownesse, and like death
Mounted on earthquakes, I would trot through all
Honors and horrors, **thorow** foule and faire,   95
And from your whole strength tosse you into **the** aire.
  Mons. Goe, th'art a devill; such another spirit
Could not be still'd from all th'Armenian dragons.
O my Loves glory: heire to all I have
(That's all I can say, and that all I sweare):   100
If thou out-live me, as I know thou must, /
Or else hath Nature no proportion'd end   [G2ᵛ]
To her great labours: she hath breath'd a **minde**
Into thy entrails, of **desert** to swell
Into another great *Augustus Cæsar*:   105
Organs, and faculties fitted to her greatnesse:
And should that perish like a common spirit,
Nature's a Courtier and regards no merit.
  Henr. Here's nought but whispering with us: like a calme
Before a tempest, when the silent ayre   110
Layes her soft eare close to the earth to hearken
For that she feares **steales on** to **ravish** her;
Some Fate doth joyne our eares to heare it comming.
Come, my brave eagle, let's to Covert flie:
I see Almighty *Æther* in the smoak   115
Of all his clowds descending, and the skie
Hid in the dim ostents of Tragedy.
                              Exit Henr. with D'Amb. Pages, **and Ladies.**
  Gui. [*Aside to Monsieur.*] Now stirre the humour, and begin
    the brawle.
  Mont. The King and *D'Ambois* now are growne all one.
  Mons. Nay, they are two my Lord.
  Mont.   How's that?
  Mons.   No more.   120

85-87 glories ... hammes),] ~, ... ~)ˌ ‖ 86 flames,] *stet (See Textual Note)* ‖ 90-91 provok'd ...
you),] ~, ... ~)ˌ ‖ 92 roughnesse] *stet (See Textual Note)* ‖ 95 thorow] *Q2(c)*; throrow *Q2(u)* ‖
96 the] *stet (See Textual Note)* ‖ 99-100 have (That's ... sweare):] ~: ~ ... ~. ‖ 102 Nature]
Boas; nature ‖ 115 Æther] Æther ‖ 117 SD *Exit ... Ladies.*] *Exit Henr. with / D'Amb. & Ladies./
starting opposite l.116* ‖ 118 SD *Aside to Monsieur.*] *Parrott* ‖ 120 *Mont.* How's ... No more.]
On one line ‖

Mont. I must haue more my Lord.

Mons. [*Making horns.*]   What, more than two?   115

Mont. How monstrous is this!

Mons.   Why?

Mont.   You make me Horns.

Mons. Not I, it is a worke, without my power,

Married mens ensignes are not made with fingers:

Of diuine Fabrique they are, Not mens hands;

Your wife, you know, is a Meere Cynthia,   120

And she must fashion hornes out of her nature.

Mont. But doth she? dare you charge her? speak, false

        Prince.

Mons. I must not speake, my Lord: but if yow'le vse

The learning of a noble man, and read,

Heer's something to those points: [*Producing a paper.*] soft

        you must pawne   125

Your honour hauing read it to returne it.

Mont. Not I, I pawne mine Honour, for a paper?

Mons. You must not buie it vnder.

                Ent. Tamy., Pero.

Mont.   Keepe it then!

And keepe fire in your bosome.   [*Exeunt Guise and Monsieur.*]

Tam.   What saies he?

Mont. You must make good the rest.

Tam.   How fares my Lord?   130

Takes my Loue any thing to heart he saies?

Mont. Come y'are a –

Tam.   What my Lord?

Mont.   The plague of Herod

Feast in his rotten entrailes.

Tam.   Will you wreake

Your angers iust cause giuen by him, on mee?

Mont. By him?

Tam.   By him my Lord, I haue admir'd   135

You could all this time be at concord with him,

That still hath plaid such discords on your honour. /

Mont. Perhaps tis with some proud string of my wiues.   [G1]

Tam. How's that, my Lord?

Mont.   Your tongue will still admire,

Till my head be the miracle of the world.   140

---

115 SD *Making horns.*] *N. Brooke after D'Urfey (See Textual Note)* | What,] ~ || 116 this!] ~? ||
121 nature] Nature || 122 speak,] ~ || 123 speake,] ~ || 124 read,] ~ || 125 SD *Producing a paper.*] ||
128 SD *Tamy.*] *Tamy.* | then!] ~ *(space quad taking ink resembles exclamation point)* || 129 SD
Exeunt ... Monsieur.] Q2 || 132 a–] Q2 (a.–); ~. || 135 *Tam.*] *Tamy.* ||

Mont. I must have more my Lord.

Mons. [*Making horns.*]　　　　　　What, more than two?

Mont. How monstrous is this!

Mons.　　　　　　Why?

Mont.　　　　　　　　You make me Horns.

Mons. Not I, it is a work without my power,
Married mens ensignes are not made with fingers:
Of divine Fabrique they are, Not mens hands;　　　　　125
Your wife, you know, is a meere *Cynthia*,
And she must fashion hornes out of her nature.

　Mont. But doth she? dare you charge her? speak, false
　　Prince.

　Mons. I must not speak, my Lord: but if you'l use
The learning of a noble man, and read,　　　　　130
Here's something to those points: [*Producing a paper.*] soft
　　you must pawne
Your honour having read it to returne it.

　　　　　　　Enter Tamira and Pero.

　Mont. Not I, I pawne mine Honour for a paper?

　Mons. You must not buy it under.　　**Exeunt Guise and Monsieur.** /

Mont.　　　　　　Keepe it then,　　　　　[G3]
And keepe fire in your bosome.

　Tam.　　　　　　What sayes he?　　　　　135

　Mont. You must make good the rest.

　Tam.　　　　　　How fares my Lord?
Takes my Love any thing to heart he sayes?

　Mont. Come y'are a –

　Tam.　　　　　What my Lord?

　Mont.　　　　　　The plague of *Herod*
Feast in his rotten entrailes.

　Tam.　　　　　Will you wreak
Your angers just cause given by him, on me?　　　　　140

　Mont. By him?

　Tam.　　　　By him my Lord, I have admir'd
You could all this time be at concord with him,
That still hath plaid such discords on your honour.

　Mont. Perhaps tis with some proud string of my wives.

　Tam. How's that, my Lord?

　Mont.　　　　　　Your tongue will still admire,　　145
Till my head be the miracle of the world.

121 SD *Making horns.*] *N. Brooke after D'Urfey (See Textual Note)* | What,] ~͜ ‖ 122 this!] ~? ‖
124 fingers:] ~? ‖ 127 nature] Nature ‖ 128 speak,] ~͜ ‖ 129 speak,] ~͜ ‖ 131 SD *Producing a
paper.*] ‖ 132 SD *and*] *&* ‖ 138 *Mont.* Come . . . Lord?] *On one line* | a–] a.— ‖ 141 *Tam.*] *Tamy.* ‖

Tam. O woe is mee.   [*She seems to swoon.*]
   Pero.   What does your Lordship meane? –
Madam, be comforted; my Lord but tries you.
Madam? – Helpe good my Lord, are you not mou'd?
Doe your set lookes print in your words, your thoughts?
Sweete Lord, cleere vp those eies, **for shame of Noblesse:**   145

Mercilesse creature; but it is enough,
You haue shot home, your words are in her heart;
She has not liu'd to beare a triall now.
   Mont. Looke vp my loue, and by this kisse receiue
My soule amongst thy spirits for supplie   150
To thine, chac'd with my furie.
   Tam. [*Seeming to recover.*]   O my Lord,
I haue too long liu'd to heare this from you.
   Mont. Twas from my troubled blood, and not from mee:
[*Aside as she rises.*] I know not how I fare; a sudden
    night
Flowes through my entrailes, and a headlong Chaos   155
Murmurs within mee, which I must digest;
And not drowne her in my confusions,
That was my liues ioy, being best inform'd: –
Sweet, you must needes forgiue me, that my loue
(Like to a fire disdaining his suppression)   160
Rag'd being discourag'd; my whole heart is wounded
When any least thought in you is but touch't,
And shall be till I know your former merits:
Your name and memorie altogether craue
In **loth'd** obliuion their eternall graue;   165
And then you must heare from me, ther's no meane
In any passion I shall feele for you:
Loue is a rasor cleansing being well vs'd,
But fetcheth blood still, being the least abus'd:
To tell you briefly all; The man that left mee   170
When you appear'd, did turne me worse than woman,
And stab'd me to the heart thus, [*Making horns.*] with his
   hand. /
   Tam. O happie woman! Comes my staine from him?   [G1ᵛ]
It is my beautie, and that innocence prooues,
That slew Chymæra, rescu'd Peleus   175

141 SD *She ... swoon.*] Q2 *subs.* | meane?–] ~?ˬ ‖ 143 Madam?–] ~?ˬ ‖ 151 SD *Seeming to recover.*] ‖ 152 from] ftom ‖ 154 SD *Aside*] *Dilke* | *as she rises.*] ‖ 158 inform'd:–] ~:ˬ ‖ 163 merits:] *stet* (See Textual Note) ‖ 165 loth'd] *stet* (See Textual Note) ‖ 169 still,] ~ˬ ‖ 172 SD *Making horns.*] *Parrott* | hand] *stet* (See *Textual Note*) ‖ 173 *Tam.*] *Tamy.* ‖

Tam. O woe is me.   *She seemes to sound.*
   Pero.   What does your Lordship meane? –
Madam, be comforted; my Lord but tries you.
Madam? – Help good my Lord, are you not mov'd?
Doe your set looks print in your words your thoughts?   150
Sweet Lord, cleare up those eyes,
Unbend that masking forehead, whence is it
You rush upon her with these Irish warres,
More full of sound then hurt? but it is enough,
You have shot home, your words are in her heart;   155
She has not liv'd to beare a triall now.
   Mont. Look up my Love, and by this kisse receive
My soule amongst thy spirits for supply
To thine, chac'd with my fury.
   Tam. [*Seeming to recover.*]   O my Lord,
I have too long liv'd to heare this from you.   160
   Mont. 'Twas from my troubled bloud, and not from me:
[*Aside as she rises.*] I know not how I fare; a sudden
   night
Flowes through my entrailes, and a headlong Chaos
Murmurs within me, which I must digest; /   164
And not drowne her in my confusions,   [G3ᵛ]
That was my lives joy, being best inform'd: –
Sweet, you must needs forgive me, that my love
(Like to a fire disdaining his suppression)
Rag'd being discourag'd; my whole heart is wounded
When any least thought in you is but touch't,   170
And shall be till I know your former merits:
Your name and memory altogether crave
In **just** oblivion their eternall grave;
And then you must heare from me, there's no meane
In any passion I shall feele for you: 175
Love is a rasor cleansing being well us'd,
But fetcheth blood still, being the least abus'd:
To tell you briefly all; The man that left me
When you appear'd, did turne me worse than woman,
And stab'd me to the heart thus, [*Making horns.*] with
   his **fingers**.   180
   Tam. O happy woman! Comes my stain from him?
It is my beauty, and that innocence proves,
That slew *Chymæra*, rescu'd *Peleus*

---

147 meane?–] ~?ˌ ‖ **149** Madam?–] ~?ˌ ‖ **151-53** Sweet . . . warres] Sweet . . . unbend . . . forehead, /
Whence . . . you . . . warres (*See Textual Note*) ‖ **153** her] Q2(c); ~, Q2(u) ‖ **154** hurt?] Q2(c); ~:
Q2(u) ‖ **159** SD *Seeming to recover.*] ‖ **162** SD *Aside*] *Dilke* | *as she rises.*] ‖ **166** inform'd:–] ~:ˌ ‖
171 merits:] *stet* (*See Textual Note*) ‖ **173** just] *stet* (*See Textual Note*) ‖ **177** still,] ~ˌ | **180** SD
Making horns.] *Dilke* | fingers] *stet* (*See Textual Note*) ‖ **181** *Tam.*] *Tamy.* ‖

From all the sauage beasts in Peleon;
And rais'd the chaste Athenian prince from Hell:
All suffering with me; they for womens lusts,
I for a mans; that the Augean stable
Of his foule sinne would emptie in my lappe: 180
How his guilt shunn'd me! sacred Innocence
That where thou fear'st, **art** dreadfull; and his face
Turn'd in flight from thee, that had thee in chace:
Come, bring me to him: I will tell the serpent
Euen to his teeth (**whence, in mine honors soile,**   185
A pitcht field starts vp twixt my Lord and mee)
That his throat lies, and he shall curse his fingers,
For being so gouern'd by his filthie soule.
    Mont. I know not, if himselfe will vaunt t'haue beene
The princely author of the slauish sinne,   190
Or any other; he would haue resolu'd mee,
Had you not come; not by his word, but writing,
Would I haue sworne to giue it him againe,
And pawn'd mine honour to him for a paper.
    Tam. See how he flies me still: Tis a foule heart   195
That feares his owne hand: Good my Lord make haste
To see the dangerous paper: **Be not nice**

For any trifle, ieweld with your honour,
To pawne your honor; and with it conferre
My neerest woman heere, in all she knowes;   200
Who (if the sunne or Cerberus could haue seene
Anie staine in mee) might as **much** as they:—
And Pero, heere I charge thee by my loue,
And all proofes of it (which I might call bounties),
By all that thou hast seene seeme good in mee,   205
And all the ill which thou shouldst spit from thee,
By pity of the wound, **my Lord** hath giuen mee,
Not as thy Mistresse now, but a poore woman
(To death giuen ouer): rid me of my paines,
Powre on thy powder: cleere thy breast of me: /   210
My Lord is only heere: heere speake thy worst,   [G2]
Thy best will doe me mischiefe; If thou spar'st mee,
Neuer shine good thought on thy memorie:
Resolue my Lord, and leaue me desperate.

179 Augean] *Shepherd*; Egean (*See Textual Note*) ‖ 181 me!] ~? | Innocence] *Parrott*; innocence ‖
202 they:—] ~: ‖ 204 it … bounties),] ~, … ~). ‖ 209 ouer):] ~:) ‖

From all the savage beasts in *Peleon*;
And rais'd the chaste Athenian Prince from hell: 185
All suffering with me; they for womens lusts,
I for a mans; that the Augean stable
Of his foule sinne would empty in my lap:
How his guilt shunn'd me! sacred Innocence
That where thou fear'st, **are** dreadfull; and his face   190
Turn'd in flight from thee, that had thee in chace:
Come, bring me to him: I will tell the serpent
Even to his **venom'd** teeth **(from whose curst seed**
A pitcht field starts up 'twixt my Lord and me)
That his throat lies, and he shall curse his fingers,   195
For being so govern'd by his filthy soule.
    Mont. I know not, if himselfe will vaunt t'have beene
The princely Author of the slavish sinne,
Or any other; he would have resolv'd me,
Had you not come; not by his word, but writing,   200
Would I have sworne to give it him againe,
And pawn'd mine honour to him for a paper. /
    Tam. See how he flies me still: Tis a foule heart   [G4]
That feares his owne hand: Good my Lord make haste
To see the dangerous paper: **Papers hold**   205
Oft-times the formes, and copies of our soules,
And (though the world despise them) are the prizes
Of all our honors, make your honour **then**
A hostage for it, and with it conferre
My neerest woman here, in all she knowes;   210
Who (if the sunne or *Cerberus* could have seene
Any staine in me) might as **well** as they: –
And *Pero*, here I charge thee by my love,
And all proofes of it (which I might call bounties),
By all that thou hast seene seeme good in mee,   215
And all the ill which thou shouldst spit from thee,
By pity of the wound **this touch** hath given me,
Not as thy Mistresse now, but a poore woman
(To death given over) rid me of my paines,
Powre on thy powder: cleare thy breast of me: 220
My Lord is only here: here speak thy worst,
Thy best will doe me mischiefe; If thou spar'st me,
Never shine good thought on thy memory:
Resolve my Lord, and leave me desperate.

184 *Peleon*] Peleon ‖ **187** Augean] *Shepherd*; Egean (*See Textual Note*) ‖ **189** me!] ~?] |
Innocence] *Parrott*; innocence ‖ **190** are] *stet* (*See Textual Note*) ‖ **199** resolv'd] Q2(c); resolv d
?Q2(u) ‖ **205-9** Papers … for it] *stet* (*See Textual Note*) ‖ **207** them)] Q2(c); ~, Q2(u) ‖ **208** your]
Q2(c); the Q2(u) (*See Textual Note*) ‖ **212** they:–] ~:͵ ‖ **214** it … bounties),] ~, … ~)͵ ‖

Pero. My Lord? My Lord hath plaid a prodigals part,   215
To breake his Stocke for nothing; and an insolent,
To cut a Gordian when he could not loose it:
What violence is this, to put true fire
To a false traine? To blow vp long-crown'd peace
With sudden outrage? and beleeue a man   220
Sworne to the shame of women, gainst a woman
Borne to their honours? **Ile attend your Lordship**.
   Tam. No, I will write (for I shall neuer more
Speake with the fugitiue) where I will defie him,
Were he ten times the brother of my king.   225
                                                          Exeunt.

[IV.ii.]

Musicke: and Tamyra enters with Pero her maid,
bearing a letter.
Tam. Away, deliuer it: [*Exit Pero.*]
              O may my lines

219 long-crown'd] ~ͺ~ ‖ **221** a woman] ~ ~, ‖ **222** honours?] ~: ‖ **IV.ii.**] *Boas subs.* ‖ SD *Tamyra*
enters with Pero] Q2̃ (*Tamira*); *she enters with* (See Textual Note) ‖ **1** SD *Exit Pero.*] Q2 (*after*
lines); *placed as in Boas* ‖

Pero. My Lord? My Lord hath plaid a prodigals part,   225
To break his Stock for nothing; and an insolent,
To cut a Gordian when he could not loose it:
What violence is this, to put true fire
To a false train? To blow up long-crown'd peace
With sudden outrage? and beleeve a man   230
Sworne to the shame of women, 'gainst a woman
Borne to their honours? **but I will to him.**
   Tam. No, I will write (for I shall never more
Meet with the fugitive) where I will defie him,
Were he ten times the brother of my King. –   235
To him my Lord, and ile to cursing him.   *Exeunt.*

[IV.ii.]

Enter D'Ambois and Frier.

   Buss. I am suspitious my most honour'd Father,
By some of Monsieurs cunning passages,
That his still-ranging and contentious nosethrils, /
To scent the haunts of Mischiefe, have so us'd   [G4ᵛ]
The vicious vertue of his busie sence,   5
That he trails hotly of him, and will rowze him,
Driving him all enrag'd, and foming on us,
And therefore have entreated your deepe skill,
In the command of good aeriall spirits,
To assume these Magick rites, and call up one   10
To know if any have reveal'd unto him
Any thing touching my deare Love and me.
   Frier. Good sonne you have amaz'd me but to make
The least doubt of it, it concernes so neerely
The faith and reverence of my name and order.   15
Yet will I justifie upon my soule
All I have done; if any spirit i'th'earth or aire
Can give you the resolve, doe not despaire.
         Musick: and **Tamira** *enters with* **Pero** *her maid,*
                bearing a Letter.
   Tam. Away, deliver it: *Exit Pero.*
        [Aside.] O may my lines

---

229 long-crown'd] ~.~ ‖ 231 woman] ~, ‖ 232 honours?] ~: ‖ 235 King.–] ~., ‖ **IV.ii.**] *Boas subs.* ‖ SD *Enter ... Frier.*] *stet* (*See Textual Note*) ‖ 1 *Buss.*] *D'Amb.* (*so through l.101*) ‖ **1-18** I am ... despaire] *stet* (*See Textual Note*) ‖ 3 still-ranging] ~.~ ‖ 4 Mischiefe] *Parrott;* mischiefe ‖ 17 done;] ~, ‖ i'th'] i'th ‖ 18 SD *Musick:*] *stet* (*See Textual Note*) ‖ Pero] *Dilke;* Pero and (*See Textual Note*) ‖ 19 SD *Exit Pero.*] *placed as in Boas; after* lines ‖ SD *Aside.*] *after Spencer* (*See Textual Note to l.7/0 SD*) ‖

135

(**Fild** with the poison of a womans hate)
When he shall open them shrinke vp his eies
With torturous darkenesse, such as stands in hell,
Stucke full of inward horrors, neuer lighted;   5
With which are all things to be fear'd, affrighted; –
Father?

> *Ascendit Bussy with Comolet in a conjuring robe.*

   Buss. How is it with my honour'd mistresse?
   Tam. O seruant helpe, and saue me from the gripes
Of shame and infamie.

   Buss.   What **insensate stocke,**
Or rude inanimate vapour without fashion,   10
Durst take into his Epimethean breast
A box of such plagues as the danger yeeldes,
Incurd in this discouerie? He had better
Ventur'd his breast in the consuming reach
Of the hot surfets cast out of the cloudes,   15
Or stoode the bullets that (to wreake the skie) /
The Cyclops ramme in Ioues artillerie.   [G2ᵛ]
   Com. Wee soone will take the darkenesse from his face
That did that deede of darkenesse; wee will know
What now the Monsieur and your husband doe;   20
What is contain'd within the secret paper
Offerd by Monsieur, and your loues euents:
To which ends (honour'd daughter) at your motion,
I haue put on these exorcising Rites,
And, by my power of learned holinesse   25
Vouchsaft me from aboue, I will command
Our resolution of a raised spirit.
   Tam. Good father raise him in some beauteous forme,
That with least terror I may brooke his sight.
   Com. Stand sure together then, what ere **ye** see,   30
And stirre not, as ye tender all our liues.
   Occidentalium legionum **spiritalium** imperator (magnus ille
Behemoth) veni, veni, comitatus cum Astaroth locotenente
inuicto. Adiuro te per stygis inscrutabilia arcana, per
ipsos irremeabiles anfractus auerni: adesto ô Behemoth,   35
tu cui peruia sunt Magnatum scrinia; veni, per Noctis et

---

2 Fild] *stet* (*See Textual Note*) ‖ **2-3** hate) . . . them] *Dilke subs.*; ~͵ . . . ~) ‖ **6** affrighted;–] ~;͵ ‖ **7**
SD *Comolet . . . robe.*] *Comolet in a/ Q1(u)*; *Comolet./ Q1(c)* (*See Textual Note*) | *Buss.*]
D'Amb. (*so also l. 9*) ‖ **28** *Tam.*] *Tamy.* ‖ **33** Astaroth] *Dilke*; Asaroth ‖ **36** et] & ‖

(**Fill'd** with the poyson of a womans hate)   20
When he shall open them shrink up his **curst** eyes
With torturous darknesse, such as stands in hell,
Stuck full of inward horrors, never lighted;
With which are all things to be fear'd, affrighted.

[*Bussy and Frier advance.*]
  Buss. How is it with my honour'd Mistresse?   25
  Tam. O servant help, and save me from the gripes
Of shame and infamy. **Our love is knowne,**
Your Monsieur hath a paper where is writ
Some secret tokens that decipher it.
  Buss. What **cold dull Northern brain, what foole but he,**   30

Durst take into his Epimethean breast
A box of such plagues as the danger yeelds,
Incur'd in this discovery? He had better
Ventur'd his breast in the consuming reach
Of the hot surfets cast out of the clouds,   35
Or stood the bullets that (to wreak the skie)
The *Cyclops* ramme in *Ioves* artillerie.
  Frier. We soone will take the darknesse from his face
That did that deed of darknesse; we will know /   39
What now the Monsieur and your husband doe;   [H1]
What is contain'd within the secret paper
Offer'd by Monsieur, and your loves events:
To which ends (honour'd daughter) at your motion
I have put on these exorcising Rites,
And, by my power of learned holinesse   45
Vouchsaft me from above, I will command
Our resolution of a raised spirit.
  Tam. Good father raise him in some beauteous forme,
That with least terror I may brook his sight.
  Frier. Stand sure together then what ere **you** see,   50
And stir not, as ye tender all our lives.   *He puts on his robes.*
*Occidentalium legionum **spiritualium** imperator (magnus ille*
Behemoth) veni, veni, comitatus cum Astaroth locotenente
invicto. Adjuro te per stygis inscrutabilia arcana, per
ipsos irremeabiles anfractus averni: adesto ô Behemoth,   55
tu cui pervia sunt Magnatum scrinia; veni, per Noctis et

---

20 Fill'd] *stet* (*See Textual Note*) ‖ **20-21** hate) ... them] *Dilke subs.*; ~ˌ ... ~) ‖ **24** SD *Bussy ...*
advance.] *after Parrott* (*See Textual Note to l. 7/0 SD*) ‖ **25** How ... Mistresse?] *stet* (*See Textual*
Note to l. 7/– on the omission of Father) ‖ **26** and] *Q2(c)*; end *Q2(u)* ‖ **27** infamy. Our] *Q2(c)*;
infamyˌ our *Q2(u)* | knowne] *Q2(c)*; showne *Q2(u)* ‖ **27-29** Our ... it] *stet* (*See Textual Note*) ‖
30-33 What ... discovery?] *stet* (*See Textual Note*) ‖ **34** consuming] *Q2(c)*; consnming *Q2(u)* ‖
37 *Cyclops*] Cyclops ‖ **48** *Tam.*] Tamy. ‖ **50** you] *stet* (*See Textual Note*) ‖ **51** SD *He ... robes.*]
stet (*See Textual Note*) ‖ **53** Astaroth] *Dilke subs.*; Asaroth ‖ **56** et] & ‖

tenebrarum abdita profundissima; (*Thunder.*) per labentia
sydera; per ipsos motus horarum furtiuos, Hecatesque altum
silentium: Appare in forma spiritali, lucente splendida et
amabili.   40

> *Ascendit Behemoth, with Cartophylax*
> *and other spirits holding torches.*

Beh. What would the holy Frier?
Com.   I would see
What now the Monsieur and Mountsurrie doe;
And see the secret paper that the Monsieur
Offer'd to Count Montsurry, longing much
To know on what euents the secret loues   45
Of these two honor'd persons shall arriue.
    Beh. Why call'dst thou me to this accursed light?
To these light purposes? I am Emperor
Of that inscrutable darkenesse, where are hid
All deepest truths, and secrets neuer seene,   50
All which I know, and command Legions
Of knowing spirits that can doe more than these.
Any of this my guard that circle mee
In these blew fires, and out of whose dim fumes /   54
Vast murmurs vse to breake, and from their soundes   [G3]
Articulat voices, can doe ten parts more
Than open such sleight truths, as you require.
    Com. From the last nights black depth, I cald
        vp one
Of the inferior ablest ministers,
And he could not resolue mee; send one then   60
Out of thine owne command, to fetch the paper
That Monsieur hath to shew to Count Montsurry.
    Beh. I will: – Cartophylax: thou that properly
Hast in thy power all papers so inscribde:
Glide through all barres to it and fetch that paper.   65
    Cart. I will.   *a torch remoues.*
    Com.   Till he returnes (great prince of darknesse)
Tell me, if Monsieur and the Count Montsurry
Are yet encounterd.
    Beh.   Both them and the Guise
Are now together.
    Com.   Shew vs all their persons,
And represent the place, with all their actions.   70

---

37 SD (*Thunder.*)] *Thunder.*/ *in left margin between* tenebrarum ab- / *and* -dita profundissima ‖
38 Hecatesque] Hecatesq; ‖ 39 et] & ‖ 40 SD *Behemoth ... torches.*] *after Boas and N. Brooke* ‖
47 call'dst] Q2(c); calledst ‖ 56 voices,] ~; ‖ 58 one] *stet* (*See Historical Collation*) ‖ 63 will:-]
~:ˎ ‖ 66 *Cart.*] *Car.* ‖

tenebrarum   abdita   profundissima;   per   labentia   sydera;
per   ipsos   motus   horarum   furtivos,   Hecatesque   altum
silentium: Appare   in   forma   spiritali,   lucente   splendida   et
amabili.   60

Thunder. Ascendit Behemoth, with Cartophylax
and other spirits holding torches.

Beh. What would the holy Frier?
Frier.   I would see
What now the Monsieur and *Mountsurrie* doe;
And see the secret paper that the Monsieur
Offer'd to Count *Montsurry*, longing much
To know on what events the secret loves   65
Of these two honour'd persons shall arrive.
    Beh. Why call'dst thou me to this accursed light,
To these light purposes? I am Emperor
Of that inscrutable darknesse, where are hid
All deepest truths, and secrets never seene,   70
All which I know, and command Legions
Of knowing spirits that can doe more then these.
Any of this my guard that circle me
In these blew fires, and out of whose dim fumes
Vast murmurs use to break, and from their sounds   75
Articulat voyces, can doe ten parts more
Than open such sleight truths, as you require. /
    Frier. From the last nights black depth, I call'd   [H1ᵛ]
        up one
Of the inferiour ablest Ministers,
And he could not resolve me; send one then   80
Out of thine owne command, to fetch the paper
That Monsieur hath to shew to Count *Montsurry*.
    Beh. I will: – *Cartophylax*: thou that properly
Hast in thy power all papers so inscrib'd,
Glide through all barres to it, and fetch that paper.   85
    Cart. I will.   *A Torch removes.*
    Frier.   Till he returnes (great prince of darknesse)
Tell me, if Monsieur and the Count *Montsurry*
Are yet encounter'd.
    Beh.   Both them and the *Guise*
Are now together.
    Frier.   Shew us all their persons,
And represent the place, with all their actions.   90

58 *Hecatesque*] Hecatesq; ‖ **59** *et*] & ‖ **60** SD *Ascendit ... torches.*] *after Boas and N. Brooke*;
Ascendit. ‖ **67** call'dst] Q2(c); calledst Q2(u) | light,] Q2(c); ~? Q2(u) ‖ **76** Articulat] Q2(c);
Articular Q2(u) ‖ **78** one] stet (*See Historical Collation*) ‖ **83** will:–] ~:ˌ ‖ **86** *Cart.*] *Car.* ‖ **88**
Guise] Guise ‖

Beh. The spirit will strait returne: and then Ile shew
    thee:

                   [*The torch returns.*]

See he is come; – why broughtst thou not the paper?
    Cart. He hath preuented me, and got a spirit
Rais'd by another, great in our command,
To take the guard of it before I came.   75
    Beh. [*To Comolet.*] This is your slacknesse, not t'inuoke
    our powers
When first your acts, set foorth to their effects;
Yet shall you see it, and themselues: behold
They come heere and the Earle now holds the paper.
            Ent. apart Mons., Gui., Mont.
    Buss. May we not heare them?
    Beh.   No, be still and see.   80
    Buss. I will go fetch the paper.
    Com.   Do not stir:
Ther's too much distance and too many lockes
Twixt you and them (how neere so e're they seeme)
For any man to interrupt their secrets.
    Tam. O honord spirit: flie into the fancie   85
Of my offended Lord: and do not let him
Beleeue what there the wicked man hath written. /
    Beh. Perswasion hath already enterd him   [G3ᵛ]
Beyond reflection; peace till their departure.
    Mons. [*Pointing to a paper.*] There is a glasse of inke
    wherein you see   90
How to make ready black-fac't Tragedy:
You now discerne, I hope through all her paintings
Her gasping wrinkles, and fames sepulchres.
    Gui. Thinke you he faines my Lord? what hold you now?
Doe we maligne your wife: or honour you?   95
    Mons. What stricken dumbe? nay fie, Lord be not danted:
Your case is common: were it ne're so rare
Beare it as rarely: now to laugh were manly:
A woorthy man should imitate the weather
That sings in tempests: and being cleere is silent.   100
    Gui. Goe home my Lord, and force your wife to write
Such louing **stuffe** to D'Ambois as she vsde
When she desir'd his presence.
    Mons.   Doe my Lord,

---

71 SD *The torch returns.*] *after Spencer* ‖ **72** come;–] ~;ᵔ ‖ **74** command,] ~ᵔ ‖ **76** SD *To Comolet.*] |
t'inuoke] t'nuoke ‖ **79** and] & | SD *apart*] (*See Textual Note*) | Mons.,] Mons.ᵔ | Gui., Mont.] Gui.
Mont./ *after* them] *in l. 80* ‖ **80, 81** Buss.] Bus. ‖ **80** Beh.] Dilke; Mons. (*See Textual Note*) ‖
83 and] & | them] ~: ‖ **88** Beh.] Dilke; Pre./ *Q1 text*; Per./ *Q1 catchword* (*See Textual Note*) ‖
90 SD *Pointing … paper.*] *after Dilke* ‖ **91** black-fac't] ~ᵔ~ ‖

Beh. The spirit will strait return, and then Ile shew
    thee:
[The torch returns.]

See he is come; – why brought'st thou not the paper?
    Cart. He hath prevented me, and got a spirit
Rais'd by another, great in our command,
To take the guard of it before I came.   95
    Beh. [*To Frier.*] This is your slacknesse, not t'invoke our
    powers
When first your acts set forth to their effects;
Yet shall you see it, and themselves: behold
They come here and the Earle now holds the paper.
Ent. apart Mons., Gui., Mont. with a paper.

    Buss. May we not heare them?
    Beh.   No, be still and see.   100
    Buss. I will goe fetch the paper.
    Frier.   Doe not stirre.
There's too much distance, and too many locks
Twixt you and them (how neere so e're they seeme)
For any man to interrupt their secrets.
    Tam. O honour'd spirit, flie into the fancie   105
Of my offended Lord: and doe not let him
Beleeve what there the wicked man hath written.
    Beh. Perswasion hath already enter'd him
Beyond reflection; peace till their departure.
    Mons. [*Pointing to the paper.*] There is a glasse of Ink
    where you **may** see /   110
How to make ready black-fac'd Tragedy: [H2]
You now discerne, I hope through all her paintings,
Her gasping wrinkles, and fames sepulchres.
    Gui. Think you he faines my Lord? what hold you now?
Doe we maligne your wife: or honour you?   115
    Mons. What stricken dumb? nay fie, Lord be not danted:
Your case is common: were it ne're so rare
Beare it as rarely: now to laugh were manly:
A worthy man should imitate the weather
That sings in tempests: and being cleare is silent.   120
    Gui. Goe home my Lord, and force your wife to write
Such loving **lines** to *D'Ambois* as she us'd
When she desir'd his presence.
    Mons.   Doe my Lord,

---

91 SD *The torch returns.*] *after Spencer* ‖ **92** is] i ?*one copy (See Press-Variants)* | come;–] ~;ˏ ‖ **96** SD *To Frier.*] ‖ **97** acts] ~, ?*one copy (See Press-Variants)* ‖ **99** and] & | SD *Ent. ... paper.*] *Ent. Mons.ˏ / Gui.ˏ Mont.ˏ / with a paperˏ/ beginning opposite l. 99 (See Textual Note)* ‖ **100** *Beh.*] *Dilke; Mons. (See Textual Note)* ‖ **103** them] ~: ‖ **106** offended] off nded *one copy (See Press-Variants)* ‖ **108** *Beh.*] *Dilke; Pre. (See Textual Note)* ‖ **110** SD *Pointing ... paper.*] *after Dilke* ‖ **111** black-fac'd] ~ˏ~ ‖ **114** *Gui.*] ~ˏ *one copy (See Press-Variants)* ‖

And make her name her conceald messenger:
That close and most inennerable Pander   105
That passeth all our studies to exquire:
By whom conuay the letter to her loue:
And so you shall be sure to haue him come
Within the thirsty reach of your reuenge;
Before which, lodge an ambush in her chamber   110
Behind the arras of your stoutest men
All close and soundly armd: and let them share
A spirit amongst them, that would serue a thousand.
                    [*Enter Pero with a Letter.*]
    Gui. Yet stay a little: see she sends for you.
    Mons. Poore, louing lady, she'le make all good yet, 115
Thinke you not so my Lord?   *Mont. stabs Pero and exit.*
    Gui.   Ahlas poore soule.
    Mons. This was **ill** done y'faith.
    Pero.   T'was nobly done.
And I forgiue his Lordship from my soule.
    Mons. Then much good doo't thee Pero: hast a letter?
    Pero. I hope it be, **at least, if not** a volume   120
Of worthy curses for your periury.

    Mons. [*Reads.*] Now out vpon her. /

    Gui.   Let me see, my Lord.   [G4]
    Mons. You shall presently: – how fares my Pero?
[*Calls.*] Whose there?
                    [*Enter servant.*]
            take in this maid, sh'as caught a clap:
And fetch my surgeon to her; – come my Lord,   125
We'l now peruse our letter.   *Exeunt Mons., Guise.*
    Pero.   Furies rise
Out of the blacke lines, and torment his soule.

                                    Servant leads her out.

    Tam. Hath my Lord slaine my woman?
    Beh.   No, she liues.
    Com. What shall become of vs?
    Beh.   All I can say
Being cald thus late, is briefe, and darkly this: 130
If D'Ambois mistresse, **stay**ne not her white hand

---

113 SD *Enter ... Letter.*] Q2 ‖ 116 SD *Mont. ... exit.*] Q2 *subs.*; *Exit Mont./ after* y'faith. *in l. 117* ‖
122 SD *Reads.*] *Lordi* | vpon] v pon | see,] ~ͺ ‖ 123 presently:–] ~:ͺ ‖ 124 SD *Calls.*] | SD *Enter
servant.*] Q2 | maid,] Q2 (Maid); ~ͺ ‖ 125 her;–] ~;ͺ ‖ 126 SD *Mons.*,] *Mons.*ͺ ‖ 127 SD *Servant ...
out.*] *Parrott subs.*; *Lead her out./ opposite l. 126 under /Exeunt Mons. Guise./ as if a continuation
of SD* ‖ 131 stayne] *Parrott subs.*; stay (*See Textual Note*) ‖

And make her name her conceal'd messenger:
That close and most inennerable Pander   125
That passeth all our studies to exquire:
By whom convay the letter to her love:
And so you shall be sure to have him come
Within the thirsty reach of your revenge;
Before which, lodge an ambush in her chamber   130
Behind the arras of your stoutest men
All close and soundly arm'd: and let them share
A spirit amongst them, that would serve a thousand.
Enter Pero with a Letter.
Gui. Yet stay a little: see she sends for you.
Mons. Poore, loving Lady, she'le make all good yet,   135
Think you not so my Lord?   *Mont.* **stabs Pero and** *exit.*
Gui.   Alas poore soule.
Mons. This was **cruelly** done y'faith.
Pero.   T'was nobly done.
And I forgive his Lordship from my soule.
Mons. Then much good doo't thee *Pero*: hast a letter?
Pero. I hope it **rather** be a **bitter** volume   140
Of worthy curses for your perjury.
Gui. [*Takes the letter.*] **To you my Lord.**
Mons.   **To me?** [*Reads.*] Now
    out upon her.
Gui. Let me see, my Lord. /
Mons. You shall presently: – how fares my *Pero*?   [H2ᵛ]
[*Calls.*] Whose there?
Enter servant.
            take in this Maid, sh'as caught a clap,   145
And fetch my Surgeon to her; – Come my Lord,
We'l now peruse our letter.   *Exeunt Mons., Guise.*
Pero.   Furies rise
Out of the black lines, and torment his soule.

                         Servant leads her out.

Tam. Hath my Lord slaine my woman?
Beh.   No, she lives.
Frier. What shall become of us?
Beh.   All I can say   150
Being call'd thus late, is briefe, and darkly this:
If *D'Ambois* Mistresse **die** not her white hand

---

136 SD *Mont. ... exit.*] *Dilke subs.; Exit Mont. and stabs Pero.* ‖ 142 SD *Takes the letter.*] |
Reads.] *Lordi* ‖ 143 see,] ∼‸ ‖ 144 presently:–] ∼:‸ ‖ 145 SD *Calls.*] | SD *Enter servant.*] *placed as
in Parrott; after l.144* ‖ 146 her;–] ∼;‸ ‖ 147 SD *Mons.,*] *Mons.*‸ ‖ 148 SD *Servant ... out.*]
*Parrott subs.; Lead her out./ after rise in l.147 and under /Exeunt Mons. Guise./ as though a
continuation of that SD* ‖ 150 SD *Frier.*] *Q2(c); Com. / Q2(u)* ‖ 152 die] *stet (See Textual Note)* ‖

With his forst bloud he shall remaine vntoucht:
So father, shall your selfe, but by your selfe:
To make this Augurie plainer: when the voice
Of D'Ambois shall inuoke me I will rise,   135
Shining in greater light: and shew him all
'That will betide ye all; meane time be wise,
And **let him** curb his **rage**, with **policy**.   *Descendit cum suis.*
    Buss. Will he appeare to me, when I inuoke him?
    Com. He will: be sure.
    Buss.   It must be shortly then: 140
For his darke words haue tied my thoughts on knots
Till he dissolue, and free them.
    Tam.   In meane time
Deare seruant, till your powerfull voice reuoke him,
Be sure to vse the policy he aduis'd:
Lest fury in your too quicke knowledge taken   145
Of our abuse, and your defence of me
Accuse me more than any enemy: –
And Father, you must on my Lord impose
Your holiest charges, and the churches power
To temper his hot spirit: and disperse   150
The cruelty and the bloud, I know his hand
Will showre vpon our heads, if you put not
Your finger to the storme, and hold it vp,
As my deare seruant heere must do with Monsieur. /   154
    Buss. Ile sooth his plots: and strow my hate with   [G4ᵛ]
        smiles
Till all at once the close mines of my heart
Rise at full date, and rush into his bloud:
Ile bind his arme in silke, and rub his flesh,
To make the vaine swell, that his soule may gush
Into some kennell, where it longs to lie,   160
And policy shalbe flanckt with policy.
Yet shall the feeling center where wee meet
Grone with the wait of my approaching feet:
Ile make th'inspired threshals of his Court
Sweat with the weather of my horrid steps   165
Before I enter: yet will I appeare
Like calme security, before a ruine;
A politician must like lightening melt
The very marrow, and not **Print** the skin:

---

132 his] *stet* (*See Textual Note*) ‖ 138 rage ... policy] *stet* (*See Textual Note*) | SD *suis.*] *Q1(c)*; ~:
Q1(u) ‖ 139, 140 *Buss.*] *Buc.* ‖ 147 enemy:–] ~:‿ ‖ 155 *Buss.*] *Bus.* ‖ 168 politician] ~, ‖

In his forc'd bloud, he shall remaine untouch:
So Father, shall your selfe, but by your selfe:
To make this Augurie plainer: when the voyce   155
Of *D'Amboys* shall invoke me, I will rise,
Shining in greater light, and shew him all
That will betide ye all; meane time be wise,
And curb his **valour**, with **your policies**.   *Descendit cum suis.*
    Buss. Will he appeare to me, when I invoke him?   160
    Frier. He will: be sure.
    Buss.   It must be shortly then:
For his dark words have tyed my thoughts on knots
Till he dissolve, and free them.
    Tam.   In meane time
Deare servant, till your powerfull voice revoke him,
Be sure to use the policy he advis'd: 165
Lest fury in your too quick knowledge taken
Of our abuse, and your defence of me,
Accuse me more than any enemy: –
And Father, you must on my Lord impose
Your holiest charges, and the Churches power,   170
To temper his hot spirit: and disperse
The cruelty and the bloud, I know his hand
Will showre upon our heads, if you put not
Your finger to the storme, and hold it up,
As my deare servant here must doe with Monsieur.   175
    Buss. Ile sooth his plots, and strow my hate with
      smiles, /
Till all at once the close mines of my heart   [H3]
Rise at full date, and rush into his bloud:
Ile bind his arme in silk, and rub his flesh,
To make the veine swell, that his soule may gush   180
Into some kennell, where it longs to lie,
And policy shall be flanckt with policy.
Yet shall the feeling center where we meet
Groane with the wait of my approaching feet:
Ile make th'inspired threshals of his Court   185
Sweat with the weather of my horrid steps
Before I enter: yet will I appeare
Like calme security, before a ruine:
A Politician must like lightning melt
The very marrow, and not **taint** the skin: 190

---

153 his] *stet* (*See Textual Note*) ‖ **159** valour ... policies] *stet* (*See Textual Note*) ‖ **168** enemy:–]
~:. ‖ **187** appeare] appreare ‖ **189** Politician] ~, ‖

His waies must not be seene: the superficies   170
Of the greene center must not taste his feet,
When hell is plowd vp with his wounding tracts:
And all his haruest reap't, **from** hellish facts.   [*Exeunt.*]

Finis Actus Quarti.

Actus Quinti   Scena Prima.

Montsurry bare, vnbrac't, pulling Tamyra in,
Comolet, *One bearing light, a standish and paper,*
which sets a Table.

    Com. My Lord remember that your soule must seeke
Her peace, as well as your reuengefull bloud:
You euer, to this houre haue prou'd your selfe
A noble, zealous, and obedient sonne
T'our holy mother: be not an apostate: 5
Your wiues offence serues not (were it the woorst
You can imagine) without greater proofes
To seuer your eternall bonds, and harts;
Much lesse to touch her with a bloudy hand:
Nor is it manly (much lesse husbandly)   10
To expiate any frailty in your wife,
With churlish strokes, or beastly ods of strength:
The stony birth of clowds, will touch no lawrell: /
Nor any sleeper; your wife is your lawrell: [H1]
And sweetest sleeper; do not touch her then: 15
Be not more rude than the wild seed of vapor,
To her that is more gentle than **it** rude;
In whom kind Nature sufferd one offence
But to set of, her other excellence.
    Mont. Good father leaue vs: interrupt no more   20
The course I must run for mine honour sake.

171 feet,] ~: ‖ 173 SD *Exeunt.*] Q2 ‖ V.i.4 sonne] ~, ‖ 6-7 not (were … imagine) … proofes]
Boas; ~, (~ … ~, … ~) ‖ 15 then:] ~ˌ ‖ 17 it] *stet* (*See Textual Note*) ‖ 18 Nature] *N. Brooke*;
nature ‖

His wayes must not be seene, the superficies
Of the greene center must not taste his feet,
When hell is plow'd up with his wounding tracts,
And all his harvest reap't **by** hellish facts.   *Exeunt.*

Finis Actus quarti.

Actus Quinti   Scena Prima.

Montsurry bare, unbrac't, pulling Tamyra in **by the haire,**
Frier, One bearing light, a standish and paper,
which sets a Table.

Tam. O help me Father.
Frier.   Impious Earle forbeare.
Take violent hand from her, or by mine order
The King shall force thee.
Mont.   Tis not violent; –
Come you not willingly?
Tam.   Yes good my Lord.
Frier. My Lord remember that your soule must seek   5
Her peace, as well as your revengefull bloud:
You ever to this houre have prov'd your selfe
A noble, zealous, and obedient sonne
T'our holy mother: be not an Apostate: /   9
Your wives offence serves not (were it the worst   [H3ᵛ]
You can imagine) without greater proofes
To sever your eternall bonds, and hearts;
Much lesse to touch her with a bloudy hand:
Nor is it manly (much lesse husbandly)
To expiate any frailty in your wife,   15
With churlish strokes, or beastly ods of strength:
The stony birth of clowds, will touch no lawrell,
Nor any sleeper; your wife is your lawrell,
And sweetest sleeper; doe not touch her then:
Be not more rude than the wild seed of vapour,   20
To her that is more gentle than **that** rude;
In whom kind Nature suffer'd one offence
But to set off her other excellence.
Mont. Good Father leave us: interrupt no more
The course I must runne for mine honour sake.   25

---

192 feet,] ~; ‖ **V.i.**1 help] Help ‖ **3-4** Tis ... willingly] *Boas; one line* (come) ‖ **4** violent;–] ~;ˏ ‖
5 seek] ~ | *Q2(u)* (*space quad taking ink*); ~, *Q2(c)* ‖ **8** sonne] ~, ‖ **10-11** not (were ... imagine)
... proofes] *Boas;* ~, (~ ... ~, ... ~) ‖ **19** then:] ~ˏ ‖ **21** that] *stet* (*See Textual Note*) ‖ **22**
Nature] *N. Brooke;* nature ‖

Relie on my loue to her, which her fault
Cannot extinguish; will she but disclose
Who was the **hatefull** minister of her loue,
And through what maze he seru'd it, we are friends.   25
   Com. It is a damn'd worke to pursue those secrets,
That would ope more sinne, and prooue springs of slaughter;
Nor is't a path for Christian feete to **touch**;
But out of all way to the health of soules,
A sinne impossible to be forgiuen: 30
Which he that dares commit –
   Mont.   Good father cease:

Tempt not a man distracted; I am apt
To outrages that I shall euer rue:
I will not passe the verge that boundes a Christian,
Nor breake the limits of a man nor husband.   35
   Com. Then **God** inspire **ye** both with thoughts
     and deedes
Worthie his high respect, and your owne soules.

                                             Exit Com.

   Mont. Who shall remooue the mountaine from my **heart**,
Ope the **seuentimes-heat** furnace of my thoughts,
And set fit outcries for a soule in hell?   40
                             Mont. turnes a key.
O now it nothing fits my **cares** to speake,
But thunder, or to take into my throat
The trumpe of Heauen; with whose determinate blasts
The windes shall burst, and the **enraged** seas
Be drunke vp in his soundes; that my hot woes   45
(Vented enough) I might conuert to vapour,
Ascending from my infamie vnseene;
Shorten the world, preuenting the last breath
That kils the liuing, and regenerates death.
   Tam. My Lord, my fault (as you may censure it /   50
With too strong arguments) is past your pardon: [H1ᵛ]
But how the circumstances may excuse mee
God knowes, and your more temperate minde heereafter
May let my penitent miseries make you know.

---

31 commit–] ~—, Q2; ~; ‖ **39** Ope ... furnace] *stet* (See Textual Note) ‖ **50** *Tam.*] *Tamy.* ‖

Rely on my love to her, which her fault
Cannot extinguish: will she but disclose
Who was the **secret** minister of her love,
And through what maze he serv'd it, we are friends.
    Frier. It is a damn'd work to pursue those secrets,   30
That would ope more sinne, and prove springs of slaughter;
Nor is't a path for Christian feet to **tread**;
But out of all way to the health of soules;
A sinne impossible to be forgiven:
Which he that dares commit –
    Mont.   Good Father cease:
    your terrors   35
Tempt not a man distracted; I am apt
To outrages that I shall ever rue:
I will not passe the verge that bounds a Christian,
Nor break the limits of a man nor husband.
    Frier. Then **heaven** inspire **you** both with thoughts
        and deeds   40
Worthy his high respect, and your owne soules.
    Tam. **Father.**
    Frier.   **I warrant thee my dearest daughter**
He will not touch thee; think'st thou him a Pagan?
His honor and his soule lies for thy safety.   *Exit.*
    Mont. Who shall remove the mountaine from my **brest**,   45
Stand the **opening** furnace of my thoughts, /
And set fit out-cries for a soule in hell?   [H4]
                                Mont. turnes a key.

For now it nothing fits my **woes** to speak,
But thunder, or to take into my throat
The trump of Heaven; with whose determinate blasts   50
The windes shall burst, and the **devouring** seas
Be drunk up in his sounds; that my hot woes
(Vented enough) I might convert to vapour,
Ascending from my infamie unseene;
Shorten the world, preventing the last breath   55
That kils the living, and regenerates death.
    Tam. My Lord, my fault (as you may censure it
With too strong arguments) is past your pardon:
But how the circumstances may excuse mee
Heaven knowes, and your more temperate minde hereafter   60
May let my penitent miseries make you know.

---

30 pursue] pnrsue ‖ **35** commit–] ~–. or ~–, (See *Press-Variants*) | cease: your terrors] *stet* (See
Textual Note) ‖ **40** *Frier.*] Com. | heaven ... you] *stet* (See *Textual Note*) ‖ **42-44** *Tam.* Father ...
safety.] *stet* (See *Textual Note*) ‖ **42, 57** *Tam.*] Tamy. ‖ **43** thee;] ~, | Pagan?] ~; ‖ **46** Stand the
opening] *stet* (See *Textual Note*) ‖

Mont. Heereafter? Tis a suppos'd infinite,   55
That from this point will rise eternally:
Fame growes in going; in the scapes of Vertue
Excuses damne her: They be fires in Cities
Enrag'd with those windes that lesse lights extinguish.
Come Syren, sing, and dash against my rockes   60
Thy ruffin Gallie, **laden** for **thy** lust:
Sing, and put all the nets into thy voice,
With which thou drew'st into thy strumpets lappe
The spawne of Venus; and in which ye danc'd;
That, in thy laps steede, I may digge his toombe,   65
And quit his manhoode with a womans sleight,
Who neuer is deceiu'd in her deceit.
Sing (that is, write), and then take from mine eies
The mists that hide the most inscrutable Pandar
That euer lapt vp an adulterous vomit: 70
That I may see the diuell, and suruiue
To be a diuell, and then learne to wiue:
That I may hang him, and then cut him downe,
Then cut him vp, and with my soules beams search
The crankes and cauernes of his braine, and studie   75
The errant wildernesse of a womans face;
Where men cannot get out, for all the Comets
That haue beene lighted at it; though they know
That Adders lie a sunning in their smiles,
That Basilisks drinke their poison from their eies,   80
And no way there to coast out to their hearts;
Yet still they wander there, and are not stai'd
Till they be fetter'd, nor secure before
All cares **distract** them; nor in humane **state**
Till they embrace within their wiues two breasts   85
All Pelion and Cythæron with their beasts.
Why write you not?
     Tam.   O good my Lord forbeare /
In wreake of great **sins**, to engender greater,   [H2]
And make my loues corruption generate murther.
     Mont. It followes needefully as childe and parent;   90
The chaine-shot of thy lust is yet aloft,
And it must murther; tis thine owne deare twinne:
No man can adde height to a womans sinne.
Vice neuer doth her iust hate so prouoke,

---

57 Vertue] *N. Brooke subs.*; vertue ‖ **68** Sing ... write),] ~, ... ~)‚ ‖

Mont. Hereafter? Tis a suppos'd infinite,
That from this point will rise eternally:
Fame growes in going; in the scapes of Vertue
Excuses damne her: They be fires in Cities   65
Enrag'd with those winds that lesse lights extinguish.
Come Syren, sing, and dash against my rocks
Thy ruffin Gally, **rig'd with quench** for lust:
Sing, and put all the nets into thy voice,
With which thou drew'st into thy strumpets lap   70
The spawne of *Venus*; and in which ye danc'd;
That, in thy laps steed, I may digge his tombe,
And quit his manhood with a womans sleight,
Who never is deceiv'd in her deceit.
Sing (that is, write), and then take from mine eyes   75
The mists that hide the most inscrutable Pandar
That ever lapt up an adulterous vomit:
That I may see the devill, and survive
To be a devill, and then learne to wive:
That I may hang him, and then cut him downe,   80
Then cut him up, and with my soules beams search
The cranks and cavernes of his braine, and study
The errant wildernesse of a womans face;
Where men cannot get out, for all the Comets /   84
That have beene lighted at it; though they know   [H4ᵛ]
That Adders lie a sunning in their smiles,
That Basilisks drink their poyson from their eyes,
And no way there to coast out to their hearts;
Yet still they wander there, and are not stay'd
Till they be fetter'd, nor secure before   90
All cares **devoure** them, nor in humane **Consort**
Till they embrace within their wives two breasts
All *Pelion* and *Cythæron* with their beasts.
Why write you not?
    Tam.   O, good my Lord forbeare
In wreak of great **faults** to engender greater,   95
And make my Loves corruption generate murther.
    Mont. It followes needfully as childe and parent;
The chaine-shot of thy lust is yet aloft,
And it must murther; tis thine owne deare twinne:
No man can adde height to a womans sinne.   100
Vice never doth her just hate so provoke,

---

64 Vertue] *N. Brooke subs.*; vertue ‖ **68** rig'd ... for] *stet* (*some copies* rig d) (*See Textual Note and Press-Variants*) ‖ **75** Sing ... write,] ~, ... ~). ‖ **90** secure] secu e *one copy* (*See Press-Variants*) ‖ **91** devoure ... Consort] *stet* (*See Textual Note*) ‖ **93** *Pelion*] Pelion | *Cythæron*] Cythæron ‖

As when she rageth vnder Vertues cloake.   95
Write: For it must be; by this ruthlesse steele,

                                                        [*Touching his sword.*]

By this impartiall torture, [*Pointing to a rack.*] and the
    death
Thy tyrannies haue inuented in my entrailes,
To quicken life in dying, and hold vp
The spirits in fainting, teaching to preserue   100
Torments in ashes, that will euer last.
Speake: Will you write?
    Tam.   Sweete Lord enioine my sinne
Some other penance than what makes it worse:
Hide in some gloomie dungeon my loth'd face,
And let condemned murtherers let me downe   105
(Stopping their noses) my abhorred foode.
Hang me in chaines, and let me eat these armes
That haue offended: Binde me face to face
To some dead woman, taken from the Cart
Of Execution, till death and time   110
In graines of dust dissolue me; Ile endure:
Or any torture that your wraths inuention
Can fright all pittie from the world withall:
But to betray a friend with shew of friendship,
That is too common, for the rare reuenge   115
Your rage affecteth; heere then are my breasts,
Last night your pillowes; heere my wretched armes,
As late the wished confines of your life:
Now breake them as you please, and all the boundes
Of manhoode, noblesse, and religion.   120
    Mont. Where all these haue beene broken, they are kept,
In doing their iustice there:
                                Thine armes haue lost
Their priuiledge in lust, and in their torture
Thus they must pay it. /   [*Stabs her.*]
    Tam.   O Lord.   [H2ᵛ]
    Mont.   Till thou writ'st
Ile write in wounds (my wrongs fit characters)   125
Thy right of sufferance. Write.   [*Stabs her again.*]
    Tam.   O kill me, kill me:
Deare husband be not crueller than death;
You haue beheld some Gorgon: Feele, ô feele

95 Vertues] *Dilke subs.*; vertues ‖ 96 SD *Touching his sword.*] ‖ 97 SD *Pointing to a rack.*] (*See Textual Note*) ‖ 124 SD *Stabs her.*] Q2 ‖ 126 SD *Stabs her again.*] *after D'Urfey* (*See Textual Note*) ‖

As when she rageth under Vertues cloake.
Write; For it must be: by this ruthlesse steele,

                                        [Touching his sword.]

By this impartiall torture, *[Pointing to a rack.]* and the
    death
Thy tyrannies have invented in my entrails,   105
To quicken life in dying, and hold up
The spirits in fainting, teaching to preserve
Torments in ashes, that will ever last.
Speak: Will you write?
    Tam.   Sweet Lord enjoyne my sinne
Some other penance than what makes it worse: 110
Hide in some gloomie dungeon my loth'd face,
And let condemned murtherers let me downe
(Stopping their noses) my abhorred food.
Hang me in chaines, and let me eat these armes
That have offended: Binde me face to face   115
To some dead woman, taken from the Cart
Of Execution, till death and time
In graines of dust dissolve me; Ile endure:
Or any torture that your wraths invention
Can fright all pitie from the world withall: /   120
But to betray a friend with shew of friendship,   [I1]
That is too common for the rare revenge
Your rage affecteth; here then are my breasts,
Last night your pillowes; here my wretched armes,
As late the wished confines of your life: 125
Now break them as you please, and all the bounds
Of manhood, noblesse, and religion.
    Mont. Where all these have bin broken, they are kept,
In doing their justice there **with any shew**
Of the like cruell cruelty: Thine armes have lost   130
Their priviledge in lust, and in their torture
Thus they must pay it.   **Stabs her.**
    Tam.   O Lord.
    Mont.   Till thou writ'st
Ile write in wounds (my wrongs fit characters)
Thy right of sufferance. Write.   *[Stabs her again.]*
    Tam.   O kill me, kill me.
Deare husband be not crueller than death;   135
You have beheld some *Gorgon*: Feele, O feele

---

102 Vertues] *Dilke subs.*; vertues ‖ 103 SD *Touching his sword.*] ‖ 104 SD *Pointing to a rack.*] *(See Textual Note)* ‖ 130 cruell cruelty] *stet (See Textual Note)* ‖ 134 SD *Stabs her again.*] *after D'Urfey (See Textual Note)* ‖ 136 *Gorgon*] Gorgon ‖

How you are turn'd to stone; with my heart blood
Dissolue your selfe againe, or you will grow   130
Into the image of all Tyrannie.
    Mont. As thou art of adulterie, I will **still**
Prooue thee my **like in ill**, being most a monster:
Thus I expresse thee yet.   *[Stabs her again.]*
    Tam.   And yet I liue.
    Mont. I, for thy monstrous idoll is not done yet: 135
This toole hath wrought enough: *[Sheathing his sword.]*
         [Ent. servants and fix her onto a rack.]
                  now, Torture, vse
This other engine on th'habituate powers
Of her thrice damn'd and whorish fortitude.
Vse the most madding paines in her that euer
Thy venoms sok'd through, making most of death;   140
That she may weigh her wrongs with them, and then
Stand, Vengeance, on thy steepest rocke, a victor.
    Tam. O who is turn'd into my Lord and husband?
Husband? My Lord? None but my Lord and husband.
Heauen, I aske thee remission of my sinnes,   145
Not of my paines: husband, ô helpe me husband.
               Ascendit **Comolet.**
    Com. What rape of honour and religion?
O wracke of nature.   *[Falls and dies.]*
    Tam.   Poore man: ô my father,
Father? looke vp; – ô let me downe my Lord,
And I will write.
    Mont.   Author of prodigies!   150
What new flame breakes out of the firmament,
That turnes vp counsels neuer knowne before?
Now is it true, earth mooues, and heauen stands still;
Euen Heauen it selfe must see and suffer ill:
The too huge bias of the world hath swai'd   155
Her backe-part vpwards, and with that she braues /
This Hemisphere, that long her mouth hath mockt: [H3]
The grauitie of her religious face
(Now growne too waighty with her sacriledge
And here discernd sophisticate enough)   160
Turnes to th'Antipodes: and all the formes
That her illusions haue imprest in her,
Haue eaten through her backe: and now all see,

---

134 SD *Stabs her again.*] Q2 (*againe,*) ‖ **136** SD *Sheathing his sword.*] *after Parrott* (*dagger*) | SD *Ent. servants*] Q2 *after l. 136* | *and ... rack.*] *after Dilke* | now, Torture,] ~ˌ ~ˌ ‖ **142** Stand, Vengeance,] ~ˌ ~ˌ | Vengeance] *Parrott*; vengeance ‖ **143, 167** *Tam.*] *Tamy.* ‖ **146** SD *Ascendit Comolet.*] *in left margin opposite ll. 147-48* ‖ **148** SD *Falls and dies.*] Q2 ‖ **149** vp;–] ~;ˌ ‖ **158** face] ~: ‖

How you are turn'd to stone; with my heart blood
Dissolve your selfe againe, or you will grow
Into the image of all Tyrannie.
   Mont. As thou art of adultry, I will **ever**   140
Prove thee my **parallel**, being most a monster:
Thus I expresse thee yet.   ***Stabs her againe.***
   Tam.   And yet I live.
   Mont. I, for thy monstrous idoll is not done yet;
This toole hath wrought enough: –   *[Sheathing his sword.]*
      Ent. **servants** *and fix her onto a rack.*
                 now, Torture, use
This other engine on th'habituate powers   145
Of her thrice damn'd and whorish fortitude.
Use the most madding paines in her that ever
Thy venoms sok'd through, making most of death;
That she may weigh her wrongs with them, and then
Stand, Vengeance, on thy steepest rock a victor.   150
   Tam. O who is turn'd into my Lord and husband?
Husband? My Lord? None but my Lord and husband?
Heaven, I ask thee remission of my sinnes,
Not of my paines: husband, O help me husband. /
      Ascendit **Frier** *with a sword drawne.*   [11ᵛ]
   Frier. What rape of honour and religion?   155
O wrack of nature!   ***Falls and dies.***
   Tam.   Poore man: O my Father,
Father, look up; – O let me downe my Lord,
And I will write.
   Mont.   Author of prodigies!
What new flame breakes out of the firmament,
That turnes up counsels never knowne before?   160
Now is it true, earth moves, and heaven stands still;
Even Heaven it selfe must see and suffer ill:
The too huge bias of the world hath sway'd
Her back-part upwards, and with that she braves
This Hemisphere, that long her mouth hath mockt: 165
The gravity of her religious face
(Now growne too waighty with her sacriledge,
And here discern'd sophisticate enough),
Turnes to th'Antipodes: and all the formes
That her illusions have imprest in her,   170
Have eaten through her back: and now all see,

137 heart] beart ‖ 142 SD *againe.*] ~, ‖ 143 yet;] ~, ‖ 144 enough:–] ~:ˬ | SD *Sheathing his sword.*]
after Parrott (dagger) | SD *Ent. servants*] *after* use (-*s/ defective in some copies*) | SD *and ...
rack.*] *after* Dilke | now, Torture,] ~ˬ ~ˬ ‖ 147 Use] use (*large-fount* u-) ‖ 150 Stand, Vengeance,]
~ˬ ~ˬ | Vengeance] Parrott; vengeance ‖ 151, 175 *Tam.*] Tamy. ‖ 157 Father] Farher | up;–] ~;ˬ ‖
166-68 face ... enough),] ~, ... ~)ˬ ‖

How she is riueted with hypocrisie:
Was this the way? was he the meane betwixt you?   165
    Tam. He was, he was, kind **innocent** man he was.
    Mont. Write, write a word or two.   *[Releasing her.]*
    Tam.   I will, I will.
Ile write, but **in** my bloud that he may see,
These lines come from my wounds and not from me.   *[Writes.]*
    Mont. *[Aside.]* Well might he die for thought: me thinkes
    the frame   170
And shaken ioints of the whole world should crack
To see her parts so disproportionate;
And that his generall beauty cannot stand
Without these staines in the particular man.
Why wander I so farre? heere, heere was she   175
That was a whole world without spot to me:
Though now a world of spots; oh what a lightning
Is mans delight in women! what a bubble,
He builds his state, fame, life on, when he marries!
Since all earths pleasures are so short and small,   180
The way t'nioy it, is t'abiure it all: –
Enough: I must be messenger my selfe,
Disguis'd like this strange creature: *[To Servants.]* in, Ile
    after,
To see what guilty light giues this caue eies,
And to the world sing new impieties.   185
              [Exeunt Servants. He puts Comolet in the vault
              and follows. She wraps her self in the Arras.]

        [Q2 V.ii = Q1 V.iii.1-56, with variant lines.]

---

166 innocent] *stet (See Textual Note)* ‖ **167** SD *Releasing her.] (See Textual Note)* ‖ **169** SD *Writes.]* Q2 ‖ **170** SD *Aside.]* ‖ **175** heere,] Q2; ~ ‖ **178** women!] ~? ‖ **179** marries!] ~? ‖ **181** all:–] ~: ‖ **182-83** I ... creature] *stet (See Textual Note)* ‖ **183** SD *To Servants.] after Lordi* ‖ **185** SD *Exeunt Servants.] Boas; Exeunt./* Q2 | SD *He ... Arras.]* Q2 *(the Frier) (See Textual Note)* ‖

How she is riveted with hypocrisie:
Was this the way? was he the mean betwixt you?
   Tam. He was, he was, kind **worthy** man he was.
   Mont. Write, write a word or two.   *[Releasing her.]*
   Tam.   I will, I will.   175
Ile write, but **with** my bloud that he may see,
These lines come from my wounds and not from me.   **Writes.**
   Mont. [Aside.] Well might he die for thought: me thinks
     the frame
And shaken joynts of the whole world should crack
To see her parts so disproportionate;   180
And that his generall beauty cannot stand
Without these staines in the particular man.
Why wander I so farre? here, here was she
That was a whole world without spot to me,
Though now a world of spots; oh what a lightning   185
Is mans delight in women! what a bubble
He builds his state, fame, life on, when he marries!
Since all earths pleasures are so short and small, /
The way t'enjoy it, is t'abjure it all. –   [I2]
Enough: I must be messenger my selfe,   190
Disguis'd like this strange creature: *[To servants.]* in, Ile
     after,
To see what guilty light gives this Cave eyes,
And to the world sing new impieties.
                   Exeunt *servants.* **He puts the Frier in the vault**
                   and follows. She raps her self in the Arras.

[V.ii.]

           Enter Monsieur **and** *Guise.*
   Mons. Now shall we see that Nature hath no end
In her great works, responsive to their worths,
That she **that** makes so many eyes and soules
To see, and fore-see, is stark blind her selfe,
And as illiterate men say Latine prayers   5
By rote of heart, and dayly iteration,
Not knowing what they **say**; so Nature layes
A **deale** of stuffe together, and by use
Or by the meere necessity of matter
Ends such a work, fills it, or leaves it empty   10
Of strength, or vertue, error, or cleare truth,

---

174 worthy] *stet* (*See Textual Note*) ‖ 175 SD *Releasing her.*] (*See Textual Note*) ‖ 177 and] & ‖ 178 SD *Aside.*] ‖ 186 women!] ~? ‖ 187 marries!] ~? ‖ 189 all.–] ~., ‖ 190-91 I . . . creature:] *stet* (*See Textual Note*) ‖ 191 SD *To servants.*] *after Lordi* ‖ 193 SD *servants*] *Boas* | *follows.*] ~, | *She . . . Arras.*] *stet* (*See Textual Note*) ‖ **V.ii.**] *Boas subs.* (*On the reversal of two scenes, see Textual Note*) ‖ 1 Nature] *Boas; nature* ‖ 3 that] *stet* (*See Textual Note*) ‖ 7 Not . . . say] *stet* (*See Textual Note*) ‖

157

Not knowing what she does, but usually
Gives that which **she calls** merit to a man,
And **beliefe must** arrive him on huge riches,
Honour, and happinesse, that effects his ruine.   15
Even as in ships of warre whole lasts of powder
Are laid (**me thinks**) to make them last and guard,
When a disorder'd spark that powder taking,
Blowes up with sodaine violence and horror
Ships that (kept empty) had sayl'd long with terror.   20
   Gui. He that observes but like a worldly man
That which doth oft succeed, and by th'events
Values the worth of things, will think it true
That Nature works at random, just with you:
But with as much **proportion** she may make   25
A thing that from the feet up to the throat
Hath all the wondrous fabrique man should have,
And leave it headlesse for **a perfect** man;
As give a **full** man valour, vertue, learning,
Without an end more excellent then those   30
On whom she no such worthy part bestowes. /
   Mons. **Yet** shall you see it here, here will be one   [12ᵛ]
Young, learned, valiant, vertuous, and full mann'd,
One on whom Nature spent so rich a hand,
That with an ominous eye she wept to see   35
So much consum'd her vertuous treasurie.
Yet as the winds sing through a hollow tree,
And (since it lets them passe through) **lets** it stand;
But a tree solid (since it gives no way
To their wild **rage**) they rend up by **the** root: 40
So this **whole man**
(That will not wind with every crooked way,
Trod by the servile world) shall reele and fall
Before the frantick puffes of **blinde-borne** Chance,
That pipes **through** empty men, and makes them dance.   45
Not so the Sea raves on the Libian sands,
Tumbling her billowes in each others neck:
Not so the surges of the *Euxine* Sea
(Neere to the frosty pole, where free *Bootes*
From those dark deep waves turnes his radiant teame)   50
Swell (being enrag'd even from their inmost drop)
As Fortune swings about the restlesse state

13-17 she calls ... beliefe must ... me thinks] *stet (See Textual Note)* ‖ **34** Nature] *Q1*; nature ‖
38 lets it] let's it *(See Textual Note)* ‖ **40** rage ... the] *stet (See Textual Note)* ‖ **44** blind-borne]
~ ̬ ̬ | Chance] *N. Brooke*; chance ‖ **48** *Euxine*] euxine *Q1*; Euxian ‖ **50** teame)] ~,) ‖ **52** Fortune]
Q1; fortune ‖

[V.ii.]

D'Ambois with two Pages.

Buss. Sit vp to night, and watch, Ile speake with none
But the old frier, who bring to me.

    Pages.   We will Sir.   *Exeunt Pages.*

    Buss. What violent heat is this? me thinks the fire
Of twenty liues doth on a sudden flash
Through all my faculties: the aire goes high /   5
In this close chamber, and the frighted earth   [*Thunder.*]   [H3ᵛ]
Trembles, and shrinkes beneath me: the whole house
Crackes with his shaken burthen; blesse me, heauen.

                   Enter Vmb. **Comol.**

    Vmb. Note what I want, **my** sonne, and be forewarnd:
O there are bloudy deeds past and to come: 10
I cannot stay, a fate doth rauish me:
Ile meet thee in the chamber of thy loue.   *Exit.*

    Buss. What dismall change is heere? the good old Frier
Is murtherd; being made knowne to serue my loue;

Note what he wants? he wants his **vtmost** weed,   15
He wants his life, and body: which of these
Should be the want he meanes, and may supplie me
With any fit forewarning? this strange vision
(Together with the darke prediction
Vs'd by the Prince of darknesse that was raisd   20
By this embodied shadowe) stir my thoughts
With reminiscion of the Spirits promise;

V.ii.] *N. Brooke (On the reversal of two scenes in Q2, see Textual Note)* ‖ **1** *Buss.*] *D'Amb. (so throughout this scene)* ‖ **2** *Pages.* We] *Dilke; Pa.* We | SD *Exeunt Pages.*] *N. Brooke; Exeunt./ Q2; Exit.* ‖ **6** SD *Thunder.*] Q2 ‖ **10-11** come: ... stay,] ~, ... ~: ‖ **18** vision] ~, ‖

Of vertue, now throwne into all mens hate.

    Enter Montsurry disguis'd, with the murtherers.

[*To Montsurry.*] **Away my Lord, you are perfectly disguis'd,**
Leave us to lodge your ambush.

  Mont.   **Speed me vengeance.**   *Exit.*

  Mons. [*To the Murtherers.*] **Resolve, my Masters, you shall**
    meet with one   56
Will try what proofes your privy coats are made on:
When he is entred, and you heare us stamp,
Approach, and make all sure.

  Murtherers.   **We will my Lord.**   *Exeunt.*

[V.iii.]

    *D'Ambois with two Pages **with Tapers.***

  Buss. Sit up to night, and watch, Ile speak with none
But the old Frier, who bring to me.

  Pages.   We will Sir.   *Exeunt Pages.*

  Buss. What violent heat is this? me thinks the fire
Of twenty lives doth on a suddaine flash
Through all my faculties: the ayre goes high /   5
In this close chamber, and the frighted earth   ***Thunder.*** [13]
Trembles, and shrinks beneath me; the whole house
Nods with his shaken burthen: blesse me, heaven.

    *Enter Vmb. **Frier.***

  Vmb. Note what I want **deare** sonne, and be fore-warn'd.
O there are bloudy deeds past and to come: 10
I cannot stay, a fate doth ravish me:
Ile meet thee in the chamber of thy love.   *Exit.*

  Buss. What dismall change is here? the good old Frier
Is murther'd; being made knowne to serve my love;
And now his restlesse spirit would fore-warne me   15
Of some plot dangerous, and imminent.
Note what he wants? he wants his **upper** weed,
He wants his life, and body: which of these
Should be the want he meanes, and may supply me
With any fit fore-warning? this strange vision   20
(Together with the dark prediction
Us'd by the Prince of darknesse that was rais'd
By this embodied shadow) stirre my thoughts
With reminiscion of the Spirits promise,

---

53 SD *disguis'd*,] ~, ‖ **54** SD *To Montsurry.*] ‖ **56** SD *To the Murtherers.*] | Resolve,] ~, ‖ **59**
Murtherers.] *Murth.* ‖ **V.iii.**] *Boas subs.* ‖ **1** *Buss.*] *D'Amb.* (*so through the rest of this scene*) ‖ **2**
Pages. Wc] *Dilke*; *Pa.* We | SD *Exeunt Pages.*] *N. Brooke*; *Exeunt.* ‖ **8** burthen] *Q2(c)*; burtnen
Q2(u) ‖ **20** vision] ~, ‖

Who told me, that by any inuocation
I should haue power to raise him; though it wanted
The powerfull words, and decent rites of art;   25
Neuer had my set braine such need of spirit,
T'instruct and cheere it; now then, I will claime
Performance of his free and gentle vow,
T'appeare in greater light; and make more plain
His rugged oracle: I long to know   30
How my deare mistresse fares; and be informd
What hand she now holds on the troubled bloud
Of her incensed Lord: me thought the Spirit
(When he had vtterd his perplext presage)
Threw his chang'd countenance headlong into clowdes;   35
His forehead bent, as it would hide his face;
He knockt his chin against his darkned breast,
And strooke a churlish silence through his powrs; –
Terror of darknesse: O thou King of flames,
That with thy Musique-footed horse dost strike   40
The cleere light out of chrystall, on darke earth; /
And hurlst instructiue fire about the world: [H4]
Wake, wake the drowsie and enchanted night,
That sleepes with dead eies in this heauy riddle:
Or thou great Prince of shades where neuer sunne   45
Stickes his far-darted beames: whose eies are made,
To **see** in darknesse: and see euer best
Where **sense is** blindest: open now the heart
Of thy abashed oracle: that for feare,
Of some ill it includes, would faine lie hid,   50
And rise thou with it in thy greater light.
               Surgit Spiritus [Behemoth] cum suis.
   Beh. Thus to obserue my vow of apparition,
In greater light: and explicate thy fate:
I come; and tell thee that if thou obay
The summons that thy mistresse next wil send thee,   55
Her hand shalbe thy death.
   Buss.   When will she send?
   Beh. Soone as I set againe, where late I rose.
   Buss. Is the old Frier slaine?
   Beh.   No, and yet liues not.
   Buss. Died he a naturall death?
   Beh.   He did.
   Buss.   Who then,

---

27 claime] ~, ‖ **29** plain] ~, ‖ **33** Spirit] ~, ‖ **38** powrs] *stet* (pow'rs Q2; *see Textual Note*) |
powrs;–] ~;, ‖ **43** wake the] ~, ~ | night,] ~; ‖ **51** SD Behemoth] Dilke | suis.] ~: ‖ **52** Beh.] Sp.
(*so throughout this scene*) ‖

Who told me, that by any invocation   25
I should have power to raise him; though it wanted
The powerfull words, and decent rites of Art;
Never had my set braine such need of spirit,
T'instruct and cheere it; now then I will claime
Performance of his free and gentle vow,   30
T'appeare in greater light; and make more plain
His rugged Oracle: I long to know
How my deare Mistresse fares; and be inform'd
What hand she now holds on the troubled bloud
Of her incensed Lord: me thought the Spirit   35
(When he had utter'd his perplext presage)
Threw his chang'd countenance headlong into clouds;
His forehead bent, as it would hide his face;
He knockt his chin against his darkned breast,
And struck a churlish silence through his pow'rs. –   40
Terror of darknesse, O thou King of flames,
That with thy Musique-footed horse dost strike /
The cleare light out of chrystall, on dark earth,   [I3ᵛ]
And hurlst instructive fire about the world,
Wake, wake the drowsie and enchanted night,   45
That sleepes with dead eyes in this heavy riddle;
Or thou great Prince of shades where never sunne
Stickes his far-darted beames, whose eyes are made
To **shine** in darknesse, and see ever best
Where **men are** blindest, open now the heart   50
Of thy abashed oracle, that for feare
Of some ill it includes would faine lie hid,
And rise thou with it in thy greater light.
        Thunders. *Surgit Spiritus [Behemoth] cum suis.*
  Beh. Thus to observe my vow of apparition
In greater light, and explicate thy fate,   55
I come; and tell thee that if thou obey
The summons that thy mistresse next will send thee,
Her hand shall be thy death.
  Buss.   When will she send?
  Beh. Soone as I set againe, where late I rose.
  Buss. Is the old Frier slaine?
  Beh.   No, and yet lives not.   60
  Buss. Died he a naturall death?
  Beh.   He did.
  Buss.   Who then

---

40 pow'rs] *stet* (*See Textual Note*) | pow'rs.–] ~., ‖ **45** wake the] ~, ~ ‖ **53** SD *Thunders.*]
Thunders. | *Behemoth*] *Dilke* ‖ **54** *Beh.*] *Sp.* (*so throughout this scene*) ‖

Will my deare mistresse send?
  Beh.   I must not tell thee.   60
  Buss. Who lets thee?
  Beh.   Fate.
  Buss.   Who are Fates ministers?
  Beh. The Guise and Monsieur.
  Buss.   A fit paire of sheeres
To cut the threds of kings, and kingly spirits,
And consorts fit to sound forth harmony,
Set to the fals of kingdomes: shall the hand   65
Of my kinde Mistresse kill me?
  Beh.   If thou yeeld,
To her next summons; y'are faire warnd: farewell.

                                     Exit cum suis.

  Buss. I must fare well, how euer: though I die, /
My death consenting with his augurie;   [H4ᵛ]
Should not my powers obay when she commands,   70
My motion must be rebell to my will:
My will, to life: If when I haue obaid,
Her hand should so reward me, they must arme it,
Binde me **and** force it: or I lay my **soule**
She rather would conuert it, many times   75
On her owne bosome: euen to many deaths:
But were there danger of such violence,
I know tis far from her intent to send:
And who she should send, is as far from thought   79
Since he is dead, whose only meane she vsde.   [*Knocks heard.*]
[*Calls to pages.*] Whose there? looke to the dore: and let
    him in,
Though politicke Monsieur, or the violent Guise.
             Enter Montsurry like the Frier.

  Mont. Haile to my worthy sonne.
  Buss. [*Aside.*] O lying Spirit: –

                  welcome loued father.

---

61 Fates] *Boas*; fates ‖ 67 summons;] ~, | SD *cum suis*] *Spencer* ‖ 68 die,] ~ˏ ‖ 70 obay …
commands,] ~, … ~ˏ ‖ 72 will, to life:] ~: ~ ~, ‖ 73 me,] ~: ‖ 80 SD *Knocks heard.*] *after* Q2 ‖
81 SD *Calls to pages.*] ‖ 84 SD *Aside.*] | Spirit:–] ~:ˏ | father.] ~ˏ ‖

Will my deare mistresse send?
  Beh.   I must not tell thee.
  Buss. Who lets thee?
  Beh.   Fate.
  Buss.   Who are Fates ministers?
  Beh. The *Guise* and Monsieur.
  Buss.   A fit paire of sheeres
To cut the threds of Kings, and kingly spirits,   65
And consorts fit to sound forth harmony,
Set to the fals of Kingdomes: shall the hand
Of my kind Mistresse kill me?
  Beh.   If thou yeeld,   ***Thunders.***
To her next summons; y'are faire warn'd: farewell.

                                Exit cum suis.

  Buss. I must fare well, how ever: though I die, /   70
My death consenting with his augurie;   [I4]
Should not my powers obay when she commands,
My motion must be rebell to my will:
My will to life: if when I have obay'd,
Her hand should so reward me, they must arme it,   75
Binde me **or** force it: or I lay my **life**
She rather would convert it many times
On her owne bosome, even to many deaths:
But were there danger of such violence,
I know 'tis farre from her intent to send: 80
And who she should send is as farre from thought,
Since he is dead, whose only mean she us'd.   ***Knocks heard.***
[*Calls to pages.*] Whose there? look to the dore: and let
    him in,
Though politick Monsieur, or the violent *Guise.*
            Enter Montsurry like the Frier, **with a Letter**
                     written in bloud.
  Mont. Haile to my worthy sonne.
  Buss. [*Aside*]   O lying Spirit!   85
To say the Frier was dead; Ile now beleeve
Nothing of all his forg'd predictions. –
My kinde and honour'd Father, **well reviv'd,**
I have beene frighted with your death, and mine,

---

63 Fates] *Boas;* fates ‖ **64** *Guise*] Guise | sheeres] ~, *?one copy (See Press-Variants)* ‖ **69** SD *cum suis*] *Spencer* ‖ **70** die,] ~. ‖ **74** life:] ~, ‖ **75** me,] ~: ‖ **76** or force] *stet (See Textual Note)* ‖ **82** SD *Knocks heard.*] *Knocks.* ‖ **83** SD *Calls to pages.*] ‖ **84** *Guise*] Guise ‖ **85** SD *Aside.*] ‖ **87** predictions.–] ~., ‖

How fares my **dearest** mistresse?

    Mont.   **Well, as euer**   85

Being well as euer thought on by her **Lord:**
Whereof she sends this witnesse **in** her hand
And praies, for vrgent cause, your **speediest** presence.

                                      [Giving the letter.]

    Buss. What? writ in bloud?
    Mont.   I, tis the inke of louers.
    Buss. O tis a sacred witnesse of her loue.   90
So much elixer of her bloud as this
Dropt in the lightest dame, would make her firme
As heat to fire: and like to all the signes,
Commands the life confinde in all my vaines;
O how it multiplies my bloud with spirit,   95
And makes me apt t'encounter death and hell:
But, come kinde Father; you fetch me to heauen,
And to that end your holy weed was giuen.   *Exit cum Montsurry.*

[V.iii.]

                  Enter Monsieur, Guise **aboue**.
    Mons. Now shall we see, that Nature hath no end,
In her great workes, responsiue to their worths, /
That she **who** makes so many eies, and soules,   [I1]
To see and foresee, is starke blinde herselfe:
And as illiterate men say Latine praiers   5
By roote of heart, and daily iteration;
In whose hot zeale, a man would thinke they knew
What they ranne so away with, and were sure
To haue rewards proportion'd to their labours;
Yet may implore their owne confusions   10
For any thing they know, which oftentimes
It fals out they incurre: So Nature laies
A masse of stuffe together, and by vse,

---

88 SD *Giving the letter.*] ‖ **98** SD *Exit cum Montsurry.*] *Exeunt./* Q2; *Exit.* ‖ **V.iii.**] *N. Brooke* ‖
1 Nature] *Boas*; nature ‖ **12** Nature] Q2; nature ‖

And told my Mistresse hand should be my death   90
If I obey'd this summons.

   Mont.   I beleev'd
Your love had bin much clearer, then to give
Any such doubt a thought, for she is cleare,
And having freed her husbands jealousie,
(Of which her much abus'd hand here is witnesse)   95
She prayes for urgent cause your instant presence.

                                        [*Giving the letter.*]

   Buss. Why then your prince of spirits may be call'd
The prince of lyers.
   Mont.   Holy writ so calls him.
   Buss. What? writ in bloud?
   Mont.   I, 'tis the ink of lovers.
   Buss. O, 'tis a sacred witnesse of her love.   100
So much elixer of her bloud as this
Dropt in the lightest dame, would make her firme
As heat to fire: and like to all the signes, /
Commands the life confinde in all my veines;   [I4ᵛ]
O how it multiplies my bloud with spirit,   105
And makes me apt t'encounter death and hell:
But, come kinde Father; you fetch me to heaven,
And to that end your holy weed was given.   *Exeunt.*

[Q1 V.iii.1-56 = Q2 V.ii, with variant lines.]

91 obey'd] obeyed ‖ 91-92 I . . . give] *Spencer; one line* (your) ‖ 96 SD *Giving the letter.*] ‖

Or by the meere necessitie of matter,
Ends such a worke, fils it, or leaues it emptie 15
Of strength, or vertue, error or cleere truth,
Not knowing what she does; but vsually
Giues that which **wee call** merit to a man,
And **beleeue should** arriue him on huge riches,
Honour, and happinesse, that effects his ruine; 20
Right as in ships of warre, whole lasts of powder
Are laid (**men thinke**) to make them last, and gard **them**;
When a disorder'd sparke that powder taking,
Blowes vp with sudden violence and horror
Ships that, kept emptie, had sail'd long with terror. 25
   Gui. He that obserues, but like a worldly man,
That which doth oft succeede, and by th'euents
Values the worth of things, will thinke it true,
That Nature workes at randome, iust with you:
But with as much **decorum** she may make 30
A thing that from the feete vp to the throat
Hath all the wondrous fabrike man should haue,
And leaue it headlesse for **an absolute** man,
As giue a **whole** man valour, vertue, learning,
Without an end more excellent than those, 35
On whom she no such worthie part bestowes.
   Mons. **Why** you shall see it here, here will be one
Yoong, learned, valiant, vertuous, and full mand;
One on whom Nature spent so rich a hand,
That, with an ominous eie, she wept to see / 40
So much consum'd her vertuous treasurie; [I1ᵛ]
Yet, as the windes sing through a hollow tree,
And (since it lets them passe through) **let** it stand,
But a tree solid, since it giues no way
To their wilde **rages**, they rend vp by **th'**roote: 45
So this **full creature now** shall reele and fall,
Before the franticke pufs of **purblinde** Chance
That pipes **thorow** emptie men, and makes them dance:
Not so the Sea raues on the Lybian sandes,
Tumbling her billowes in each others necke: 50
Not so the surges of the Euxine Sea
(Neere to the frostie Pole, where free Bootes
From those darke-deepe waues turns his radiant Teame)
Swell, being enrag'd euen from their inmost drop,

15 emptie] ~, ‖ 16 truth,] ~; ‖ 18-22 wee call ... beleeue should ... men thinke ... them] *stet* (*See Textual Note*) ‖ 25 that,] ~ₐ ‖ 28 things,] ~; ‖ 29 Nature] *Q2*; nature | randome,] ~ₐ ‖ 43 let] *stet* (*See Textual Note*) | stand,] ~ₐ ‖ 47 Chance] *N. Brooke*; chance ‖ 51 Euxine] euxine ‖ 54 Swell,] ~ₐ | enrag'd] ~, ‖

As Fortune swings about the restlesse state   55
Of vertue, now throwne into all mens hate.

> *Intrat Vmbra* **Comolet to the Countesse,**
> **wrapt in a Canapie.** *[He uncovers her.]*
[*Vmb.*] **Reuiue those** stupid thoughts, and

                                                            sit **not thus,**
Gathering the horrors of your seruants slaughter
(So vrg'd by your hand, and so imminent)
Into an idle fancie; but deuise   60
How to preuent it; watch when he shall rise,
And with a sudden outcrie of his murther,
Blow his retreat before he be **engag'd**.
   Tam. O father, haue my dumbe woes wak'd your death?
When will our humane griefes be at their height?   65
Man is a tree, that hath no toppe in cares;
No roote in comforts; all his power to liue
Is giuen to no end, but t'haue power to grieue.
   Vmb. **Tis** the **iust curse** of our **abus'd** creation,

Which wee must suffer heere, and scape heereafter: 70
He hath the great mind that submits to all,
He sees ineuitable; he the small
That carps at earth, and her foundation shaker,
And rather than himselfe, will mend his maker. /

                                                                  [*Exit.*]
                          D'Amb. at the gulfe.   [12]
   Tam. Away (my loue), away, thou wilt be murther'd.   75

   Buss. Murther'd? I know not what that Hebrew meanes:
That word had ne're beene nam'd had all beene D'Ambois.

56 SD *Vmbra*] *vmbra,* | *He uncovers her.*] *(See Textual Note)* ‖ **57** *Vmb.*] *Shepherd subs.*;
Frier./ Q2 ‖ **58** slaughter] ~, ‖ **59** (So ... imminent)] *stet (See Textual Note)* ‖ **64, 75** *Tam.*] Q2
(*Tamyra.*); *Count. (See Textual Note)* ‖ **74** SD *Exit.*] Q2 *(See Textual Note)* ‖ **75** Away (my
loue),] ~, (~ ~)‚ ‖

[V.iv.]

Thunder. Intrat Vmbra **Frier,** *and discovers* **Tamyra.**

Vmb. **Up with these** stupid thoughts, **still loved daughter,**
And **strike away this heartlesse trance of anguish,**
Be like the Sunne, and labour in eclipses;
Look to the end of woes: oh can you sit
Mustering the horrors of your servants slaughter   5

Before your contemplation, and not study
How to prevent it? watch when he shall rise,
And with a suddaine out-crie of his murther,
Blow his retreat before he be **revenged.**
     Tam. O Father, have my dumb woes wak'd your death?   10
When will our humane griefes be at their height?
Man is a tree, that hath no top in cares;
No root in comforts; all his power to live
Is given to no end, but [t']have power to grieve.
     Vmb. **It is** the **misery** of our creation. **Your**
          true friend,   15

Led by your husband, shadow'd in my weed,
Now enters the dark vault.
     Tam.   **But my dearest Father,**
Why will not you appeare to him your selfe,
And see that none of these deceits annoy him?
     Vmb. **My power is limited, alas I cannot,**   20
All that I can doe — See the Cave opens.   *Exit.*
               D'Amboys at the gulfe.
     Tam. Away (my Love), away, thou wilt be murther'd.
               Enter Monsieur and Guise above.
     Buss. Murther'd? I know not what that Hebrew means:
That word had ne're bin nam'd had all bin *D'Ambois.*

V.iv.] *Boas subs.* ‖ SD *Intrat ... discovers*] stet (*See Textual Note*) ‖ **1** *Vmb.*] *Frier. (so through l. 47)* ‖ **3** eclipses;] ∼, ‖ **5** slaughter] *stet* (*On the omission of a line following this one, see Textual Note to l. 59/–*) ‖ **9** revenged] *stet* (*See Textual Note*) ‖ **10** *Tam.*] *stet* (*See Textual Note*); *Tamyra.* ‖ **14** t'have] *Q1 subs.*; have ‖ **15** It ... friend] *stet* (*See Textual Notes to ll. 70-74/– and –/15-21*) ‖ **15-21** Your ... opens] *stet* (*See Textual Note*) ‖ **16** shadow'd] shadowed ‖ **17** *Tam.*] *Tamyr.* ‖ **19** him?] ∼. ‖ **22** Love),] ∼), ‖ **23** *Buss.*] *D'Amb. (so through l. 48)* ‖

Murther'd? By heauen he is my murtherer
That shewes me not a murtherer; what such bugge
Abhorreth not the very sleepe of D'Ambois?   80
Murther'd? Who dares giue all the roome I see
To D'Ambois reach? or looke with any oddes
His fight i'th' face, vpon whose hand sits death;
Whose sword hath wings, and euerie feather pierceth?

Let in my politique visitants, let them in,   85
Though entring like so many mouing armours,
Fate is more strong than arms, and slie than treason,
And I at all parts buckl'd in my fate:

Dare they not come?
    [*Enter Murtherers at one door, Umbra Comolet at the other.*]

Tam.   They come.
1 Murth.   Come all at once.
Vmb. Backe coward murtherers, backe.
Omnes Murth.   Defend vs heauen.   90
            Exeunt all but the first.
  1 Murth. Come ye not on?
  Buss.   No, slaue, nor goest thou off.
            [Thrusts at him.]
Stand you so firme? [*More thrusts.*] Will it not enter heere?
You haue a face yet: [*Kills him.*] so in thy lifes flame
I burne the first rites to my mistresse fame.
  Vmb. Breath thee braue sonne against the other charge.   95
  Buss. O is it true then that my sense first told mee?
Is my kinde father dead?
  Tam.   He is, my loue.
Twas the Earle my husband in his weede that brought thee.
  Buss. That was a speeding sleight, and well resembled.
Where is that angrie Earle? – my Lord? Come forth   100
And shew your owne face in your owne affaire;
Take not into your noble veines the blood
Of these base villans, nor the light reports

83 i'th'] ith' ‖ **88** fate] Fate ‖ **89** SD *Enter Murtherers*] Q2 | *at one door,*] N. Brooke | *Umbra Comolet at the other.*] Q2 subs. | *1 Murth.*] Q2 subs.; 1. ‖ **90** *Omnes Murth.*] Omn. | SD *all but the first*] Q2 ‖ **91** *1 Murth.*] Dilke subs.; 1. | SD *Thrusts at him.*] Spencer after Neilson ‖ **92** SD *More thrusts.*] *after Boas* ‖ **93** SD *Kills him.*] Parrott after Dilke ‖ **97** He is,] ~ ~ ‖ **100** Earle?–] ~ ‖

Murther'd? By heaven he is my murtherer   25
That shewes me not a murtherer: what such bugge
Abhorreth not the very sleepe of *D'Amboys*?
Murther'd? Who dares give all the room I see
To *D'Ambois* reach? or look with any odds /   29
His fight i'th'face, upon whose hand sits death;   [K1]
Whose sword hath wings, and every feather pierceth?
If I scape Monsieurs Pothecarie Shops,
Foutir for *Guises* Shambles; 'twas ill plotted,
They should have mall'd me here,
When I was rising; I am up and ready.   35
Let in my politique visitants, let them in,
Though entring like so many moving armours,
Fate is more strong than arms, and slie than treason,
And I at all parts buckl'd in my fate.
     Mons., Gui. **Why enter not the coward villains?**   40
     Buss. Dare they not come?
          Enter murtherers at one door with Umbra Frier
                    at the other dore.
Tam.   They come.
1 Murth.   Come all at once.
Vmb. Back coward murtherers, back.
Omnes Murth.   Defend us heaven.
                              Exeunt **all but the first.**

1 Murth. Come ye not on?
Buss.   No, slave, nor goest thou off.
                                        [*Thrusts at him.*]

Stand you so firme? [*More thrusts.*] Will it not enter here?
You have a face yet: [*Kills him.*] so in thy lifes flame   45
I burne the first rites to my Mistresse fame.
     Vmb. Breath thee brave sonne against the other charge.
     Buss. O is it true then that my sense first told me?
Is my kind Father dead?
     Tam.   He is, my Love.
'Twas the Earle my husband in his weed that brought thee.   50
     Buss. That was a speeding sleight, and well resembled.
Where is that angry Earle? – my Lord? Come forth
And shew your owne face in your owne affaire;
Take not into your noble veines the blood
Of these base villaines, nor the light reports   55

---

29 To] T ‖ 30 i'th'] i'th ‖ 32-35 If ... ready] *stet* (*See Textual Note*) ‖ 33 Foutir] ~, ∣ *Guises*]
Guises ∣ *Shambles*; ... plotted,] ~, ... ~ ‖ 35 rising;] ~, ‖ 39 fate.] Fate: ‖ 40 *Mons., Gui.*] Mons.ˌ
Guise. (*See the first Textual Note to* V.iii [*Q1*]; V.ii [*Q2*]) ‖ 41 SD *at one door*] N. Brooke ∣
Umbra Frier] Parrott *subs.*; *Frier* ∣ *1 Murth.*] *Murth.* 1 ‖ 42 *Omnes Murth.*] *Omn.* ‖ 43 *1 Murth.*]
Dilke *subs.*; 1. ∣ SD *Thrusts at him.*] Spencer *after Neilson* ‖ 44 SD *More thrusts.*] *after Boas* ‖
45 SD *Kills him.*] Parrott *after Dilke* ‖ 49 is,] ~ˌ ‖ 52 Earle?–] ~ˌˌ ‖

Of blister'd tongues, for cleere and weightie truth:
But me against the world, in pure defence /   105
Of your rare Ladie, to whose spotlesse name   [I2ᵛ]
I stand heere as a bulwarke, and proiect
A life to her renowne, that euer yet
Hath beene vntainted euen in Enuies eie,
And where it would protect, a sanctuarie.   110
Braue Earle come forth, and keepe your scandall in:
Tis not our fault if you enforce the spot,
Nor the wreake yours if you performe it not.
              *Enter Mont. with **others** [murtherers].*
   Mont. Cowards, a fiend or spirit beat ye off?
They are your owne faint spirits that haue forg'd   115
The fearefull shadowes that your eies deluded:
The fiend was in you; cast him out then thus.
           [Fights with Bussy; D'Ambois hath Montsurry down.]
   Tam. Fauour my Lord, my loue, ô fauour him.
   Buss. I will not touch him: – Take your life, my Lord,
And be appeas'd: –   *[Pistols shot. Bussy falls.]*
        O then the coward Fates   120
Haue maim'd themselues, and euer lost their honour.
   Vmb. What haue ye done slaues? – irreligious Lord?
   Buss. Forbeare them, father; tis enough for me
That Guise and Monsieur, Death and Destinie,
Come behinde D'Ambois: – is my bodie then   125
But penetrable flesh? And must my minde
Follow my blood? Can my diuine part adde
No aide to th'earthly in extremitie?
Then these diuines are but for forme, not fact:
Man is of two sweet Courtly friends compact;   130
A mistresse and a seruant: let my death
Define life nothing but a Courtiers breath.
Nothing is made of nought, of all things made,
Their abstract being a dreame but of a shade.
Ile not complaine to earth yet, but to heauen,   135
And (like a man) looke vpwards euen in death.

---

109 Enuies] *Baskervill*; enuies ‖ **110** protect,] ~ˌ ‖ **113** SD *Mont.*] *Mont*ˌ | *others [murtherers].*] *all the murtherers./ Q2*; *others.* ‖ **117** SD *Fights with Bussy;*] *after D'Urfey* | *D'Ambois ... down.*] *Q2 subs.* ‖ **118** Fauour my Lord,] ~ (~ ~) ‖ **119** him:–] ~:ˌ ‖ **120** appeas'd:–] ~:ˌ | SD *Pistols shot.*] *Pistolls shot within./ Q2 after l.118 (See Textual Note); placed as in Dilke* | *Bussy falls.*] *after D'Urfey* | Fates] *Q2*; fates ‖ **122** slaues?–] ~?ˌ ‖ **124** Death and Destinie] *D'Urfey subs.*; death and destinie | Destinie,] ~ˌ ‖ **125** D'Ambois:–] ~:ˌ ‖ **136** death.] *stet (See Textual Note on ll.–/89-92)* ‖

Of blister'd tongues, for cleare and weighty truth:
But me against the world, in pure defence
Of your rare Lady, to whose spotlesse name
I stand here as a bulwark, and project
A life to her renowne, that ever yet   60
Hath beene untainted even in Envies eye, /
And where it would protect, a Sanctuarie.   [K1ᵛ]
Brave Earle come forth, and keep your scandall in:
'Tis not our fault if you enforce the spot,
Nor the wreak yours if you performe it not.   65
   Enter Mont. with **all the murtherers.**
 Mont. Cowards, a fiend or spirit beat ye off?
They are your owne faint spirits that have forg'd
The fearefull shadowes that your eyes deluded:
The fiend was in you; cast him out then thus.
   Fights with Bussy; **D'Ambois hath Montsurry downe.**
 Tam. Favour my Lord, my Love, O favour him. 70
 Buss. I will not touch him: – Take your life, my Lord,
And be appeas'd: –   **Pistolls shot within.** [*Bussy falls*].
   O then the coward Fates
Have maim'd themselves, and ever lost their honour.
 Vmb. What have ye done slaves? – irreligious Lord?
 Buss. Forbeare them, Father; 'tis enough for me 75
That *Guise* and Monsieur, Death and Destinie,
Come behind *D'Ambois*: – is my body then
But penetrable flesh? And must my mind
Follow my blood? Can my divine part adde
No ayd to th'earthly in extremity?   80
Then these divines are but for forme, not fact:
Man is of two sweet Courtly friends compact;
A Mistresse and a servant: let my death
Define life nothing but a Courtiers breath.
Nothing is made of nought, of all things made, 85
Their abstract being a dreame but of a shade.
Ile not complaine to earth yet, but to heaven,
And (like a man) look upwards even in death. [*Struggles to rise.*]
And if *Vespasian* **thought in majestie**
An Emperour might die standing, why not I? – 90
    She offers to help him.

61 Envies] *Baskervill subs.*; envies ‖ 62 protect,] ~ ‖ 69 SD *Fights with Bussy;*] *after D'Urfey* ‖ 70 Favour my Lord,] ~ (~ ~) ‖ 71 *Buss.*] D'Amb. | him:–] ~:. ‖ 72 appeas'd:–] ~:. | SD *Pistolls shot within.*] *placed as in Dilke after D'Urfey; after l.70 (See Textual Note)* | Bussy falls.] *after D'Urfey* ‖ 74 slaves?–] ~?. ‖ 76 *Guise*] Guise | Death and Destinie] *D'Urfey subs.*; death and destinie | Destinie,] ~ ‖ 77 *D'Ambois*:–] ~:. ‖ 88 SD *Struggles to rise.*] ‖ 89-92 And if ... Groomes] *stet (See Textual Note)* ‖ 90 I?–] I?. | SD *She ... him.*] *placed as in Dilke; in margin opposite ll. 93-94 (to /) (See Textual Note)* ‖

[*Gets up.*] Proppe me, true sword, as thou hast euer done:
The equall thought I beare of life and death,
Shall make me faint on no side; I am vp
Heere like a Roman Statue; I will stand   140
Till death hath made me marble: ô my fame /
Liue in despight of murther; take thy wings   [13]
And haste thee where the gray-eyd Morne perfumes
Her Rosie chariot with Sabæan spices;
Flie, where the Euening from th'Iberean vales,   145
Takes on her swarthy shoulders Heccate
Cround with a groue of oakes: flie where men feele
The burning axeltree: and those that suffer
Beneath the chariot of the Snowy Beare:
And tell them all that D'Ambois now is hasting   150
To the eternall dwellers; that a thunder
Of all their sighes together (for their frailties
Beheld in me) may quit my worthlesse fall
With a fit volley for my funerall.
    Vmb. Forgiue thy murtherers.
    Buss.   I forgiue them all;   155
[*To Montsurry.*] And you my Lord, their fautor; for true signe
Of which vnfain'd remission, take my sword;
Take it, and only giue it motion,
And it shall finde the way to victorie
By his owne brightnesse, and th'inherent valour   160
My fight hath still'd into't, with charmes of spirit.
And let me pray you, that my weighty bloud
Laid in one skale of your impertiall splene
May sway the forfeit of my worthy loue
Waid in the other: and be reconcilde   165
With all forgiuenesse to your matchlesse wife.
    Tam. [*Kneeling by Bussy.*] Forgiue thou me deare seruant,
       and this hand
That lead thy life to this vnworthy end,
Forgiue it, for the bloud with which tis staind
In which I writ the summons of thy death: 170
The forced summons, by this bleeding wound,
By this heere in my bosome: and by this

137 SD *Gets up.*] *D'Urfey* ‖ 139-40 vp … Statue;] *stet* (*See Textual Note*) ‖ 143 Morne] *Parrott subs.*; morne | perfumes] Q2; perfines, (*See Textual Note*) ‖ 144 spices;] ∼, ‖ 145 Euening] *Parrott subs.*; euening ‖ 146 shoulders] ∼, ‖ 156 SD *To Montsurry.*] *Dilke subs.* ‖ 162 And] *N. Brooke*; Now Q2; *Bus.* And (*See Textual Note*) ‖ 167 SD *Kneeling by Bussy.*] ‖

176

Nay without help, in which I will exceed him;
For he died splinted with his chamber Groomes. –
[*Gets up.*] Prop me, true sword, as thou hast ever done:
The equall thought I beare of life and death,
Shall make me faint on no side; I am up   95
Here like a Roman Statue; I will stand /
Till death hath made me Marble: O my fame   [K2]
Live in despight of murther; take thy wings
And haste thee where the gray-ey'd Morn **perfumes**
Her Rosie chariot with Sabæan spices,   100
Fly, where the Evening from th'Iberean vales,
Takes on her swarthy shoulders *Heccate*
Crown'd with a Grove of Oakes: flie where men feele
The burning axeltree: and those that suffer
Beneath the chariot of the Snowy Beare: 105
And tell them all that *D'Ambois* now is hasting
To the eternall dwellers; that a thunder
Of all their sighes together (for their frailties
Beheld in me) may quit my worthlesse fall
With a fit volley for my funerall.   110
    Vmb. Forgive thy murtherers.
    Buss.   I forgive them all;
[*To Montsurry.*] And you my Lord, their fautor; for true signe
Of which unfain'd remission, take my sword;
Take it, and onely give it motion,
And it shall finde the way to victory   115
By his owne brightnesse, and th'inherent valour
My fight hath still'd into't, with charmes of spirit.
Now let me pray you, that my weighty bloud
Laid in one scale of your impertiall spleene,
May sway the forfeit of my worthy love   120
Waid in the other: and be reconcil'd
With all forgivenesse to your matchlesse wife.
    Tam. [*Kneeling by Bussy.*] Forgive thou me deare servant,
       and this hand
That lead thy life to this unworthy end,
Forgive it, for the bloud with which 'tis stain'd,   125
In which I writ the summons of thy death:
The forced summons, by this bleeding wound,
By this here in my bosome: and by this

---

92 Groomes.–] ~. ‖ 93 SD *Gets up.*] *D'Urfey* ‖ 95-96 up ... Statue;] *stet* (See *Textual Note*) ‖
99 Morn] *Parrott*; morn │ perfumes] *stet* (See *Textual Note*) ‖ 101 Evening] *Parrott*; evening ‖
102 shoulders] ~, ‖ 112 SD *To Montsurry.*] *Dilke subs.* ‖ 118 Now] *stet* (See *Textual Note*) ‖
123 SD *Kneeling by Bussy.*] ‖

That makes me hold vp both my hands embrewd
For thy deare pardon.
   Buss.   O, my heart is broken.
Fate, nor these murtherers, Monsieur, nor the Guise,   175
Haue any glorie in my death; but this,
This killing spectacle, this prodigie – /
My sunne is turnd to blood **gainst** whose red beams   [I3ᵛ]
Pindus and Ossa (hid in **endlesse** snow),
Laid on my heart and liuer, from their vains   180
Melt like two hungrie-torrents-eaten rockes
Into the Ocean of all humane life,
And make it bitter, only with my bloud:
O fraile condition of strength, valure: vertue
In me (like warning fire vpon the top   185
Of some steepe Beakon, on a steeper hill)
Made to expresse it: like a falling starre
Silently glanc't, that like a thunderbolt,
Lookt to haue stucke and shooke the firmament.   *[Moritur.]*

[Q2 ll. 146-52 = Q1 ll. 264-70]

   Vmb. *[To Montsurry.]* Son of the earth, whom my vnrested
      soule   190
Rues t'haue begotten in the faith of heauen
(Since thy reuengefull Spirit hath reiected
The charitie it commands, and the remission
To serue and worship, the blind rage of bloud);
Assay to gratulate and pacifie,   195
The soule fled from this worthy by performing
The Christian reconcilement he besought
Betwixt thee and thy Lady, let her wounds
Manlesly digd in her, be easd and cur'd
With balme of thine owne teares: or be assur'd   200
Neuer to rest free from my haunt and horror.

---

174 *Buss.*] *Bus.* | broken.] ~ ‸ ‖ 175 Guise,] ~. ‖ 176-77 death; ... this, ... spectacle, ... prodigie–]
~, ... ~: ... ~: ... ~: (*See Textual Note*) ‖ 179-80 snow), ... liuer, ... vains] ~ ‸ ... ~; ... ~)
(*See Textual Note*) ‖ 181 hungrie-torrents-eaten] hungrie torrents: eating (*See Textual Note*) ‖
184 valure: vertue] ~; ~, (*See Textual Note*) ‖ 189 SD *Moritur.*] *Q2* ‖ 190 SD *To Montsurry.*]
Dilke subs. | soule] ~, ‖ 191-94 heauen ... bloud);] ~; ... ~)‸ (*See Textual Note*) ‖

That makes me hold up both my hands embrew'd
For thy deare pardon.
    Buss.   O, my heart is broken.   130
Fate, nor these murtherers, Monsieur, nor the *Guise*,
Have any glory in my death; but this, /
This killing spectacle, this prodigie –   [K2ᵛ]
My sunne is turn'd to blood **in** whose red beams
Pindus and *Ossa* (hid in **drifts of** snow),   135
Laid on my heart and liver, from their veines
Melt like two hungry-torrents-eaten rocks
Into the Ocean of all humane life,
And make it bitter, only with my bloud:
O fraile condition of strength, valour: vertue   140
In me (like warning fire upon the top
Of some steepe Beacon, on a steeper hill)
Made to expresse it: like a falling starre
Silently glanc't, that like a thunderbolt,   144
Look't to have stuck and shook the firmament.   *Moritur.*
    Vmb. Farewell brave **reliques** of a compleat man.
Look up and see thy spirit made a starre,
Join flames with *Hercules*, and when thou set'st
Thy radiant forehead in the firmament,
Make the vast **chrystall** crack with thy receipt: 150
Spread to a world of fire, and **the** aged skie
Cheere with new sparks of old humanity.
[*To Montsurry.*] Son of the earth, whom my unrested
    soule
Rues t'have begotten in the faith of heaven;

Assay to gratulate and pacifie,   155
The soule fled from this worthy by performing
The Christian reconcilement he besought
Betwixt thee and thy Lady, let her wounds
Manlesly digg'd in her, be eas'd and cur'd
With balme of thine owne teares: or be assur'd   160
Never to rest free from my haunt and horror.

---

130 broken.] ~ₐ ‖ 131 Fate,] ~ₐ *one copy* (*See Press-Variants*) | *Guise*] Guise ‖ 132-33 death; ...
this, ... spectacle, ... prodigie–] ~, ... ~: ... ~: ... ~: (*See Textual Note*) ‖ 135 *Pindus* and
Ossa] Pindus and Ossa ‖ 135-36 snow), ... liver, ... veines] ~ₐ ... ~; ... ~; ... ~) (*See Textual Note*) ‖
137 hungry-torrents-eaten] hungryₐ torrents: eating (*See Textual Note*) ‖ 140 valour:] ~; (*See
Textual Note*) ‖ 146 *Vmb.*] Vmb. Frier. | (*On the transfer of ll. 146-52 from the end of the play, see
Textual Note*) | reliques] *stet* (*See Textual Note to l. 264/146*) ‖ 148 Join ... Hercules] *Q1*; *Jove
... her rules* (*See Textual Note to l. 266/148*) ‖ 150 chrystall crack] *stet* (*See Textual Note to
l. 268/150*) ‖ 153 SD *To Montsurry.*] Dilke *subs.* | Son] *Frier.* Son ‖ 154 heaven;] *stet* (*On the
omission of three lines following this one, see Textual Note to ll. 192-94/–*) ‖

    Mont. See how she merits this: still **sitting** by
And mourning his fall, more than her owne fault.
    Vmb. Remoue, deare daughter, and content thy husband:
So Piety wils thee, and thy seruants peace.   205
    Tam. [*Rising.*] O wretched Piety, that art so distract
In thine owne constancy; and in thy right
Must be vnrighteous: if I right my friend
I wrong my husband: if his wrong I shunne,
The duty of my friend I leaue vndone;   210
Ill plays on both sides; heere and there, it riseth;
No place, no good so good, but ill compriseth;
My soule more scruple breeds, than my bloud, sinne,
Vertue imposeth more than any stepdame:
O had I neuer married but for forme, /   215
Neuer vowd faith but purposd to deceiue: [14]
Neuer made conscience of any sinne,
But clok't it priuately and made it common:
Nor neuer honord beene, in blood, or mind,
Happy had I beene then, as others are   220
Of the like licence; I had then beene honord:
Liu'd without enuy: custome had benumbd
All sense of scruple, and all note of frailty:
My fame had beene vntoucht, my heart vnbroken:
But (shunning all) I strike on all offence.   225
[*Turning indecisively.*] O husband? – deare friend? – O my
    conscience?

    Mont. [*Aside.*] I must not yeeld to pity nor to loue
So seruile and so traiterous: cease my bloud
To wrastle with my honour, fame and iudgement:
[*To Tamyra.*] Away, forsake my house, forbeare complaints   230
Where thou hast bred them: heere all things full
Of their owne shame and sorrow, leaue my house.
    Tam. Sweet Lord forgiue me, and I will be gone,
And till these wounds, that neuer balme shall close
Till death hath enterd at them (so I loue them   235

---

202 sitting] *stet (See Textual Note)* ‖ **205** Piety] piety ‖ **206** *Tam.*] *Tamy.* | SD *Rising.*] | Piety]
N. Brooke; piety ‖ **212** place,] ~: ‖ **224** heart vnbroken] *Q1(u)*; heartvnbroken *Q1(c)* ‖ **225**
offence.] ~, ‖ **226** SD *Turning indecisively.*] | husband?–] ~?. | friend?–] ~?. | *See Textual Note*
for Q2's exits after this line ‖ **227** SD *Aside.*] ‖ **230** SD *To Tamyra.*] ‖ **231** heere] *stet (See Textual*
Note) | full] ~, ‖

Mont. See how she merits this: still **kneeling** by
And mourning his fall, more than her own fault.
  Vmb. Remove, deare daughter, and content thy husband:
So Piety wills thee, and thy servants peace.   165
  Tam. [*Rising.*] O wretched Piety, that art so distract
In thine owne constancie; and in thy right
Must be unrighteous: if I right my friend
I wrong my husband: if his wrong I shunne,
The duty of my friend I leave undone; /   170
Ill playes on both sides; here and there, it riseth;   [K3]
No place, no good so good, but ill compriseth;

O had I never married but for forme,
Never vow'd faith but purpos'd to deceive:
Never made conscience of any sinne,   175
But clok't it privately, and made it common:
Nor never honour'd beene, in blood, or mind,
Happy had I beene then, as others are
Of the like licence; I had then beene honour'd:
Liv'd without envie: custome had benumb'd   180
All sense of scruple, and all note of frailty:
My fame had beene untouch'd, my heart unbroken:
But (shunning all) I strike on all offence.
[*Turning indecisively.*] O husband? – deare friend? – O my
    conscience!
  Mons. [*Aside to Guise.*] **Come let's away, my sences are not
    proofe**   185
Against those plaints. –

> *Exeunt Guise, Mons. above, murtherers below.*
> *Bodies of D'Ambois and 1 Murth. are* **borne off.**

  Mont. [*Aside.*] I must not yeeld to pity nor to love
So servile and so trayterous: cease my bloud
To wrastle with my honour, fame, and judgement:
[*To Tamyra.*] Away, forsake my house, forbeare complaints   190
Where thou hast bred them: here all things full
Of their owne shame and sorrow, leave my house.
  Tam. Sweet Lord forgive me, and I will be gone,
And till these wounds, that never balme shall close
Till death hath enter'd at them, so I love them   195

---

162 kneeling] *stet (See Textual Note)* ‖ 165 Piety] piety ‖ 166 *Tam.] Tamy.* | SD *Rising.*] | Piety]
N. Brooke; piety ‖ 172 place,] ~: | *On the omission of two lines following this one, see Textual
Note to ll. 213-14/–*) ‖ 183 offence.] ~, ‖ 184 SD *Turning indecisively.*] | husband?– ... friend?–]
~?̣ ... ~?̣ ‖ 185 SD *Aside to Guise.*] ‖ 186 SD *above] Boas* | murtherers below.] | *Bodies of
D'Ambois and 1 Murth. are] D'Ambois is* | *On the entire SD, see Textual Note* ‖ 187 SD *Aside.*] ‖
190 SD *To Tamyra.*] ‖ 191 here] *stet (See Textual Note)* | full] ~, ‖ 195 enter'd] enterr'd ‖

Being open'd by your hands), by death be cur'd
I neuer more will grieue you with my sight:
Neuer endure that any roofe shall part
Mine eies and heauen: but to the open deserts
(Like to ⌈a⌉ hunted Tygres) I will flie: 240
Eating my heart, shunning the steps of men,
And looke on no side till I be arriu'd.
   Mont. [*Kneels.*] I do forgiue thee, and vpon my knees
(With hands held vp to heauen) wish that mine honor
Would suffer reconcilement to my loue: 245
But since it will not, – [*Rises.*] Honor, neuer serue
My Loue with flourishing obiect till it sterue:
And as this Taper, though it vpwards looke,

                                        [*Lifting a candle.*]

Downwards must needs consume, so let our loue;
As, hauing lost his hony, the sweet taste   250
Runs into sauor, and will needs retaine
A spice of his first parents, till (like life)
It sees and dies, so let our loue: and lastly, /
As when the flame is sufferd to looke vp   [I4ᵛ]
It keepes his luster: but, being thus turnd downe   255
                                     [*Inverting the candle.*]

(His naturall course of vsefull light inuerted)
His owne stuffe puts it out: so let our loue.
Now turne from me, as heere I turne from thee,
And may both points of heauens strait axeltree
Conioine in one, before thy selfe and me.   260
                 [*Exeunt Montsurry and Tamyra severally.*]
   Vmb. **My terrors are strook inward, and no more**
My pennance will allow they shall enforce
Earthly afflictions but vpon my selfe:
Farewell braue relicts of a compleat man:
Looke vp and see thy spirit made a star,   265
Ioine flames with Hercules: and when thou setst
Thy radiant forhead in the firmament,
Make the vast continent cracke with thy receit,
Spred to a world of fire: and th'aged skie,   269
Chere with new sparkes of old humanity.   [*Exit.*]

           Finis Actus Quinti et vltimi.

---

236 Being] *Q1(u)*; (Being *Q1(c)* | open'd] opened | hands),] ~)‸ ‖ **240** a] *Q2* (*See Textual Note*) ‖
243 SD *Kneels.*] ‖ **244** (With hands held] ‸~ ~ (~ ‖ **246** not,–] ~,‸ | SD *Rises.*] ‖ Honor]
N. Brooke; honor ‖ **248** SD *Lifting a candle.*] ‖ **250** As,] ~‸ ‖ **253** dies,] ~; ‖ **255** SD *Inverting
the candle.*] ‖ **257** loue.] ~, ‖ **260** SD *Exeunt ... severally.*] *N. Brooke* (*See Textual Note*) ‖ **264-
270** Farewell ... humanity.] *stet* (*See Textual Note*) ‖ **264** relicts] *stet* (*See Textual Note*) ‖**268**
continent] ~, (*See Textual Note*) ‖ **270** humanity.] ~‸ ?*some copies* (*See Press-Variants*) | SD
Exit.] (*See Textual Note*) | et] & ‖

(Being open'd by your hands), by death be cur'd
I never more will grieve you with my sight:
Never endure that any roofe shall part
Mine eyes and heaven: but to the open Deserts
(Like to a hunted Tygres) I will flie: 200
Eating my heart, shunning the steps of men,
And look on no side till I be arriv'd.
    Mont. [*Kneels.*] I doe forgive thee, and upon my knees
(With hands held up to heaven) wish that mine honour
Would suffer reconcilement to my Love: 205
But since it will not, – [*Rises.*] Honour, never serve
My Love with flourishing object till it sterve: /
And as this Taper, though it upwards look,   [K3ᵛ]
                                      [*Lifting a candle.*]

Downwards must needs consume, so let our love;
As, having lost his hony, the sweet taste   210
Runnes into savour, and will needs retaine
A spice of his first parents, till (like life)
It sees and dies, so let our love: And lastly,
As when the flame is suffer'd to look up,
It keepes his luster: but, being thus turn'd downe   215
                                      [*Inverting the candle.*]

(His naturall course of usefull light inverted)
His owne stuffe puts it out: so let our love.
Now turne from me, as here I turne from thee,
And may both points of heavens strait axeltree
Conjoyne in one, before thy selfe and me.   220
                                Exeunt severally.

[Q1 ll. 264-70 = Q2 ll. 146-52]

Finis Actus Quinti et ultimi. /

196 open'd] opened | hands),] ~). ‖ **200** a] *stet* (*See Textual Note*) ‖ **203** SD *Kneels.*] ‖ **204** (With hands held] ˏ~ ~ (~ ‖ **206** not,–] ~,ˏ | SD *Rises.*] | Honour] *N. Brooke*; honour ‖ **208** SD *Lifting a candle.*] ‖ **210** As,] ~ˏ ‖ **213** dies,] ~; ‖ **215** SD *Inverting the candle.*] ‖ **217** love.] ~ˏ ‖ **220** SD *Exeunt severally.*] *stet* (*See Textual Note*) | et] & ‖

Epilogue.   [K4]

With many hands you have seene **D'Ambois** *slaine,*
Yet by your grace he may revive againe,
And every day grow stronger in his skill
To please, as we presume he is in will.
The best deserving Actors of the time   5
Had their ascents; and by degrees did clime
To their full height, a place to studie due;
To make him tread in their path lies in you;
Hee'le not forget his Makers; but still prove
His thankfulnesse as you encrease your love.   10

FINIS.

Epilogue] (*See Textual Note*) ‖ **1** *With*] W*1th* ‖ **7** *due;*] ~ ‖

HISTORICAL COLLATION

[Editions collated:

First Quarto (= *Q1*, 1607-8);

Second Quarto (= *Q2*, 1641 etc.);

Dilke (= *D*, in *Old English Plays; Being a Selection from the Early Dramatic Writers*, ed. C. W. Dilke, III, 1814, 234-342; identical re-issue as *Old Plays; Being a Continuation of Dodsley's Collection*, 1816. Based on *Q2*, with little reference to *Q1*, but influenced at times by Thomas D'Urfey's adaptation, *Bussy D'Ambois, or the Husbands Revenge*, 1691; I have collated D'Urfey and include in this record selected readings, especially stage directions [= *Du*]);

Shepherd (= *S*, in *The Works of George Chapman: Plays*, ed. R. H. Shepherd, 1875, pp. 140-77; sheets from the same impression reissued several times with new title pages: e.g., 1889, 1911. Based on his earlier (unsigned) edition in *The Comedies and Tragedies of George Chapman*, II, 1873, 3-96, which purported to be an old-spelling reprint of *Q2*, but was actually a reprint of *Q1* incompletely corrected to agree with *Q2*; I have collated the 1873 edition, known as the Pearson reprint [from its publisher, John Pearson], and record selected readings from it [= *Pe*]);

Phelps (= *Ph*, in *George Chapman*, ed. W. L. Phelps, The Mermaid Series: The Best Plays of the Old Dramatists, 1895, pp. 124-221 [printed by Unwin Brothers, The Gresham Press, Chilworth and London: colophon]; a page-for-page reprint [?1904] from a different setting of type [Printed by Morrison & Gibb Limited, Edinburgh: colophon] is variant in a few respects, and I have accorded it only a partial collation [= *Ph²*]. Based on *Pe*, but modernized after *S*);

Boas (= *B*, in *Bussy D'Ambois and The Revenge of Bussy D'Ambois*, ed. F. S. Boas, The Belles-Lettres Series, 1905, pp. 2-144. An old-spelling edition, with modernized punctuation, of *Q2* – but, judging from a misreading shared with *Pe*, *S*, and *Ph* at III.ii.291/298, perhaps printed from a corrected copy of *Pe*)

Parrott (= *P*, in *The Plays and Poems of George Chapman: The Tragedies*, ed. T. M. Parrott, I, 1910, pp. 3-74; identical reprint as *The Plays of George Chapman*, 1961. 'Essentially' followed *Q2*, but used *S* as copy-text);

Neilson (= *N*, in *The Chief Elizabethan Dramatists Excluding Shakespeare*, ed. W. A. Neilson, 1911, pp. 185-213. Purportedly based on *B*, but used *Ph* as copy-text);

Brooke-Paradise (= *BP*, in *English Drama 1580-1642*, ed. C. F. T. Brooke and
   N. B. Paradise, 1933, pp. 327-60. Purportedly followed *Q2*, but apparently
   used *N* as copy-text);

Rylands (= *R*, in *Elizabethan Tragedy: Six Representative Plays*, ed. George
   Rylands, 1933, pp. 287-386. Essentially a reprint of *Ph²*);

Spencer (= *Sp*, in *Elizabethan Plays*, ed. Hazelton Spencer, 1933, pp. 519-57;
   identical reprint in *Elizabethan and Jacobean Tragedy*, ed. Spencer and
   Robert Ornstein, 1964, pp. 77-115. Purportedly based on *Q2*, but apparently used *N* as copy-text, with corrections from several other editions,
   especially *P*);

Baskervill-Heltzel-Nethercot (= *BHN*, in *Elizabethan and Stuart Plays*, ed.
   C. R. Baskervill, V. B. Heltzel, and A. H. Nethercot, 1934, pp. 725-70;
   apparently identical reprint ['revised' by Nethercot] in *Elizabethan Plays*,
   1971, pp. 705-50. Based on *P*, with corrections from several other editions);

McIlwraith (= *M*, in *Five Stuart Tragedies*, ed. A. K. McIlwraith, The World's
   Classics, 1953, pp. 5-97; reprinted 1959. A reprint of *P*, except for some
   non-textual details);

Pagnini (= *Pg*, in *Bussy D'Ambois*, ed. Marcello Pagnini, Biblioteca Italiana di
   Testi Inglesi, III, 1959, pp. 43-183. Purportedly based on *Q2*, but used *BP*
   as copy-text);

Jacquot (= *J*, in *Bussy D'Ambois*, ed. Jean Jacquot, Collection Bilingue des
   Classiques Étrangers, 1960, pp. 4-160. An old-spelling edition, with page-
   for-page translation into French, of *Q2*, with some emendations. A few
   readings from the translation are cited [= *Jf*]);

Harrier (= *H*, in *The Anchor Anthology of Jacobean Drama*, ed. R. C. Harrier,
   1963, I, 340-428. An old-spelling reprint, purportedly of the Harvard copy
   of *Q2*, but used *J* as copy-text);

Lordi (= *L*, in *Bussy D'Ambois*, ed. R. J. Lordi, Regents Renaissance Drama
   Series, 1964, pp. 3-117. Based on *Q2*);

N. Brooke (= *Br*, in *Bussy D'Ambois*, ed. Nicholas Brooke, The Revels Plays,
   1964, pp. 4-145. Based on *Q1*);

Evans (= *E*, in *Bussy D'Ambois*, ed. Maurice Evans, The New Mermaids,
   1966, pp. 5-78. Based on *Q1*, but printed from a corrected copy of *M*;
   strongly influenced by *Br*);

Fraser (= *F*, in *Drama of the English Renaissance*, ed. R. A. Fraser and Norman
   Rabkin, 1976, II, 271-301. Printed from *E*, with some corrections).

N.B. Several writers, including Pagnini and Jacquot, have incorrectly referred
to an edition of *Bussy D'Ambois* in *Early Seventeenth-Century Plays 1600-
1642*, ed. H. R. Walley and J. H. Wilson, 1930.]

The complexity of the textual problems presented by the two quartos of
Bussy D'Ambois, together with the number of editions collated and the
decision to edit both versions in parallel format, has made desirable certain
modifications of the form of the apparatus that is normal elsewhere in these
pages. Because each quarto contains passages that are absent from the other,
the line-numberings for the two quartos diverge more often than they agree.

Where they diverge, I have keyed entries to both quartos by the use of a dual reference (e.g., '122/122-26'). In all such cases the number to the left of the slash refers to my edition of Q1, that following the slash to my edition of Q2 (in the example cited, the Q2 passage includes four lines that are added to the one common line). An entry keyed to a line that is missing from one of the quartos contains a dash before or after the slash, as appropriate: e.g., '–/126' (line missing from Q1) or '126/–' (line missing from Q2). Except for records of interpolated settings (which are entered following a heading 'SD]'), the lemma in each entry is normally from my text of Q1. A note recording variants to a Q2 reading that has no correspondence in Q1 necessarily takes its lemma from my text of Q2; every such case is signalled by the dash in the line reference (e.g., '–/209') and by the inclusion in the note of '*om. Q1.*'

As stated earlier, all editions before N. Brooke's founded their texts on Q2. Q2+, unless immediately qualified, signifies the agreement of Q2 and all later fully collated editions except those of N. Brooke, Evans, and Fraser. The abbreviation *etc.* indicates that all other fully collated editions not specifically included elsewhere in the entry agree with the edition whose siglum immediately precedes. A hyphen between two sigla indicates the agreement of all fully collated editions found between those two sigla in the above list (for example, *S-P* indicates the agreement of Shepherd, Phelps 1895, Boas, and Parrott, but not necessarily Phelps 1904). Exceptions to the groupings identified in these ways are indicated by their sigla preceded by the abbreviation *exc.* (i.e., except).

As discussed in the Textual Introduction, each quarto contains passages that are omitted from the other. Different editors have made different decisions about including such passages, and when they have included them, they have sometimes emended internal details; my own edition has sometimes departed from its Q1 or Q2 copy-text, as recorded in the footnotes to the text. In order to avoid confusing and cumbersome records in the Historical Collation, I have adopted a system of subsidiary entries to deal with such passages when the internal variants cannot be conveniently recorded as parenthetical exceptions. In such cases, the main entry records the *general* agreement of the editions listed; subsidiary entries, each preceded by an asterisk beneath the main record, show the significant internal variants. Such subsidiary records do not repeat information conveyed in the main entry and ignore editions that omit the passage altogether.

In each entry other than a subsidiary note, any regularly recorded edition not cited by its siglum, or included in a grouping by one of the methods described earlier as having a variant reading, may be taken to agree substantively with the lemma.

Lemmata regularly represent extended passages by printing the first and last word separated by ellipses (...). Variants (other than metrical) are normally printed in full unless they amount to more than about two verse lines; in such cases a reference is supplied to my text of Q1 or Q2, where the full reading will be found. If I have emended the passage, the footnotes to the text record the emendation.

For each variant reading recorded, the accidentals are those of the first text that has that reading. In the interest of simplification, however, I have deleted from all readings (including those in the lemmata) editors' square brackets; in addition, I have not preserved such accidental details as small capitals in speech-prefixes. The stated or implied agreement of any edition with a given reading does not, of course, preclude differences in non-essential details. I have recorded only substantive and semi-substantive variants, including significant variations in metrical arrangement. Variants in expanded or contracted forms (e.g., 'kill us' for 'kill's' or 'she has' for 'sh'as') are not noted when they occur in prose passages. Capitalization variants are recorded when they may involve personification. Resolutions of metrical ambiguities and of ambiguous verbal forms (such as the speech-prefix *Mo.*, which could be either *'Montsurry'* or *'Monsieur'*; or possessives like 'others', which could be either 'other's' or 'others'') are recorded only if editors have resolved them in clearly different ways. In stage directions, I have ignored variations in wording or symbols if the overall meaning was substantially the same: addition or omission of articles and conjunctions, variant names or titles for the same person, equivalent English translations of Latin originals, and even unimportant variants in details: For example, in IV.i.SD, I have treated as equivalent 'The Banquetting-Hall in the Court', 'The Court', and 'A room in the palace'. I have not distinguished those settings printed in the text and those given in notes. In some cases I have adopted from the textual footnotes the abbreviation *subs.* to indicate substantial agreement (despite minor variants) among editions cited. Sometimes I spell out an edition's exceptional minor variants in parentheses following that edition's siglum. I have not normally included palpable errors unless they influenced other editions.

All editorial comments and sigla are printed in italics. When a note records readings that are printed in italics in the earliest edition cited (as is commonly the case with stage directions, for example), the italics are preserved and the readings are set off from the editorial context by a single vertical line (|).

The abbreviation *conj.* indicates a conjectural emendation suggested by the person named: the present editor ('Smith'); previous editors (ordinarily in their editions, but Parrott sometimes in *Englische Studien*, XXXVIII [1907], 359-95); K. Deighton in *The Old Dramatists: Conjectural Readings* (Westminster, 1896), pp. 131-32; J. Le Gay Brereton in *Elizabethan Drama: Notes and Studies* (Sydney, 1909) (reprinted from *Hermes*, 16 Oct., 1905); G. C. Loane, 'Notes on Chapman's Plays,' *MLR*, XXXIII (1938), 340-47; A. S. Ferguson, 'The Plays of George Chapman,' *MLR*, III (1918), 1-24; and some communicated to me privately (by G. Blakemore Evans of Harvard University, Robert C. Roby of Marquette University, Allan Holaday of the University of Illinois, and Gideon Rappaport of San Diego, California).

Dramatis Personae
Dilke (perhaps influenced by the 'Cast' that D'Urfey placed at the head of his adaptation) first supplied a list of characters. Phelps (who wrongly claimed priority for such a list) and all later editors have included one. My list includes historical identifications (which seem not to be integral to Chapman's intentions) from Parrott's notes. The following are the more significant variants –

not spelling variants – among the several lists. The lemma is from my list; Q1, Q2, and S, lacking any such list, must be understood as omitting every entry.

Montsurry, a Count] ~, an Earl *Ph, R*
Beaumond, a courtier] *subs. P, R, Sp, M, Br-F; om. all others. Brereton conjectured that Beaumond and the Nuncius were the same character; see II.i.SD in the Historical Collation, and cf. the Textual Note*
Pyrhot] Pyrlot *D (the first spelling in SD's in both quartos, I.ii.86/94)*
Cartophylax ... underworld] *om. Ph, R*
Beaupre] *in the list of male characters D (See collation of I.ii.SD)*
Pyra ... court] Pyrha, *a maid| Br*

After the list of characters some editors set the scene, as follows:
Scene. – Paris *B-BP, Sp, BHN* (~. Time: *Later sixteenth century*), *H, Br subs.*
(the French Court in the 1570s)

Prologue
Prologue not in Q1; printed in Appendix A in Br
25 *To*] Too *D*

I.i

SD] *A Grove.* | *Du*; *A glade, near the Court.* | *B and subs., N, BP, Sp, Pg;*
   A Forest near Paris | *P, BHN*
SD *Bussy solus.*] *Enter Bussy D'Ambois poore.* | *Q2-F*
1 Reason] reason *D, L*
2 Honor] honour *D, L*
  his] its *Du*
3 monstrous] monstruous *Pg*
  Need] need *D-Ph, N-Sp, Pg, L*
4 humane] *Q1-2, Ph, B, R, J, H;* human *D etc.*
5 incessant] continuall *Q2+*
8 forging] forming *Q2+ exc. S;* frameing *Du*
10 our Tympanouse statists] *Q1, Pe, Br-F;* men meerely great *Q2+*
12 maners] *Q1-2, B, J (Jf:* la cruauté de leurs manières), *H;* Manners, *Du, D;*
   manner's *Pg;* manners' *S etc.*
13 Fortune] fortune *D-Ph, N-Sp, Pg*
20 all their] their *Pe, Ph, R*
   powers] wealth *Q2+;* Studies *Du*
22 tall] stout *Du*
23 Girdle] bridle *Du*
25 glad] *Q1, Pe, S, Ph, N, R, Sp, Br-F;* faine *Q2 etc.*
26 staid] stayed *D*
31 world] earth *Q2+*
32 Vertue] vertue *Q1-D, B, J-L*
   her] our *Du*
33 SD *Procumbit.*] *om. Du*
   SD *two Pages.*] Page. *Du*
34 SD *Aside.*] *Sp; om. Q1-2 etc.*

36 words] worde *Pe*; word *S, Ph, N, R, Sp*

39 tracts] tracks *D*

40 poore] *Q1, Pe, S, Ph, R, Br-F*; meane *Q2 etc.*

42 Nature] *Du, Br*; nature *Q1-2 etc.*

43 likely] possible *Q2+*

44 fit I] good to *Q2+*

53 it.–] *BHN*; ~.ˌ Approaching Bussy. *P, M, L, E*; ~.ˌ *Q1-2 etc.*

54 D'Ambois? . . . aliue?] ~! . . . ~! *Du, B* (*not regularly recorded hereafter*)

56 mote] more *Pe, Ph, R*

57 Think'st] *Q1, Pe, S, Ph, R, and subs. Br-F* (Thinkest *E, F*); Callest *Q2 etc.*
subs. (Call'st *N, BP, Pg*)
state] Place *Du*

59 That] They *H, BP, Pg*

64 Mettall] *Q1-D, B, J, H*; mettle *S etc.*

66 liu'd] liued *Q1, S, Ph, R, E* [*standard in S, Ph, and R for past forms of weak verbs ending in -e, and in E for all weak verbs; BHN and F spell out verbal suffixes but accent those that are syllabic. Hereafter, when such variants are recorded, readings in these editions are normalized according to their intentions: e.g., an -ed spelling in BHN and F is recorded with others reading -'d]*

77 render] renders *P, BP, BHN, M, Pg*

80 doth] *Q1, Pe, S, Ph, R, Br*; doe *Q2 etc.*

82 me doe] *Q1, Du, Br-F*; me *Q2 etc.*

83 liue . . . doe,] ~ˌ . . . ~ˌ *Q1-2, J, Br, F*; ~, . . . ~, *S, Ph, P-Pg*; ~, . . . ~ˌ *E*
as] *Q1, Pe, S, Ph, N, R, Br-F*; where *Q2 etc.*

89 Dame Schoolemistresses] Dames Schoolemistresses *Q1-D, Ph, B, R, J, H, Br, F*; dame's schoolmistresses *N, Sp, BHN*; dames, schoolmistresses *L*; dame-school mistresses *E*

92 portly] *Q1, Pe, Br-F*; humorous *Q2 etc.*

93 a good carriage . . . idle] Apish Cringes . . . wanton *Du*

95 sights] Sighs *Du, D conj.*

102 preacht) . . . Art] ~ˌ . . . ~) *Parrot conj.* (*Englische Studien XXXVIII, 363*), *Loane conj., J, H*

106 I] *Q1-2, B, J, H*; Ay *D etc.* (*not recorded hereafter*)

110 eies] Loves *Q2+*
in-parts] inˌparts *Q1-2, S-B, N, R, Sp, J, H*

112 smother'd] smothered *Q1-2, B, N, Sp, BHN, J, L, E*

113 then.] ~? *P, M*
rude] *Q1, Pe, S, Ph, R, Br-F*; old *Q2 etc.*

117 rul'd] wise *Q2+*

118 SD *Exit . . . Pages.*] *B* (*after l.117*), *P-BP, Sp-Pg, Jf, H-F*; *Exit Mons.* | *Q1-Ph subs., R, J* (*all but D and J after l.117*)
SD *Manet Buss.*] *om. D, N, Sp*; *with previous SD after l.117 B*

119 SD *Rising.*] *om. Q1-2 etc.*

122/122-26 But hee's no husband heere] *Q1, Br*; Like . . . soyl [*as in this ed.*]

Q2 etc. [*See subsidiary note*]
*–/126 his] this *H conj.*
126/130 with] for *Q2+*
128/132 Fortune] fortune *D-Pg, Br-F*
130/134 times] Times *B-BP, Sp-Pg, L-F*
132/136 workes] worketh *D*
140/144 SD *Aside.*] *P, BHN-Pg, Br-F; om. Q1-2 etc.*
     man] wretch *Q2+*
145/149 this:–] *BHN, M, Br-F*; ~. *To Bussy. P, BP, Pg, L;* ~:ˌ *Q1-2 etc.*
148/152 I] I doe *Q2+*
151/155 good] good lordship *Deighton conj.*
152/156 A] His *Q2+*
153/157 good fashion] respect *Q2+ exc. S*
154/158 open'd] opened *Q1-D, B, N, Sp, J-L*
161/165 a] some *Q2+*
163/167 his wise excellencie] your great Masters goodnesse *Q2+*
166/170 tis] it's *R*
     bad] *Q1, Pe, S, Ph, R, Br-F*; rude *Q2 etc.*
175/179 SD *Aside.*] *D, P-BP, Sp-Pg, H, L-F; om. Q1-2 etc.*
176/180 highnes] Graces *Q2+*
178/182 saft;–] *D, P-BP, Sp-Pg, L-F*; ~;ˌ *Q1-2 etc.*
183/187 scholar] *Q1, Pe, S, Ph, N, R, Sp, Br-F*; Poet *Q2 etc.*
188/192 excellence] bounteous Grace *Q2+*; Excellence *Br, E*
189-90/193 your ... Steward] you of long ones *Q2+*
After 190/193] *Pulls him by the Nose.* | *Du; om. Q1-2 etc.*
192/195 SD *Touching his sword.*] *Turnes him about.* | *Du; om. Q1-2 etc.*
193/196 SD *Aside.*] *D, P, BP, Sp-Pg, L-F; om. Q1-2 etc.*
     merrie *Q1, Pe, S, Ph, R, Br-F*; pleasant *Q2 etc.*
     faith] 'faith *S, Ph, P, BP, R, M, Pg, E, F (not recorded hereafter)*
194/197 beleeue it] berlady *Q2+*
196/199 my Lord] *Q1, Pe, S, Ph, R, Br-F*; his Grace *Q2 etc.*
198/201 errant] arrant *BHN, M, Br-F*
204/207 dagger:–] *P, BHN, M, L-F (to him| Br)*; ~:ˌ *Q1-2 etc.*
     Ambo,] *Q1-2, J, H, Br-F*; ~. *D*; ~– *this ed. of Q2*; ~! *S etc.*
–/208-10 *Buss.* How ... D'Amboys.] *om. Q1, Br-F* [*See subsidiary notes*]
     *–/208 I, is] Is *J, H*
     *–/209-10 You ... head] *as prose D*
206/212 Serue God,] If you be thriftie and *Q2-B, N, R, BHN, J-L*
208/214 better.] ~ ... *Jf*
209/215 Rogue.] ~. *Strikes him.* | *Du, B*
211/217 last:] ~. *Strikes again.* | *Du*
215/221 SD *Strikes him.*] *D and subs. P-BP, Sp-Pg, Jf, H-F; Throws him down, kicks him.* | *Du; om. Q1-2 etc.*
216/222 sown] *Q1, Pe, S, Ph, R, Br-F*; set *Q2 etc.*
     their] the *Q2(u)*

I.ii

I.ii] *Scene changes*| *D*; *om. Q1-2, S, Ph, R*

SD] *an Apartment in the Palace.*| *D, B-BP, Sp, BHN, Pg, Jf*

SD *Henry*] *Enter* ~ *D, N, R, H*; *The curtain is drawn disclosing* ~ *P, Sp, Br*

SD *Guise*] ~ ... *playing chess P, N, Sp, BHN, Br-F; cf. ll.67-70*

SD *Montsurry*] *also enter* ~| *Sp*

–/SD *Table ... Tapers.*] *S (Tapers behind the Arras), M, Br subs.; Table Chesbord / & Tapers behind / the Arras.*| *Q2 (opposite I.i.149-51/153-55 [prompter's warning]), Pe (after* respect *in* –/I.i.157*), Ph (as in Pe), BP, Pg (after I.i.149/153), R (as in Pe); om. Q1 etc.*

2 this] that *Q2+*

 SD *Indicating Annable.*] *B note; om. Q1-2 etc.*

4 hand] *Q1, S, Ph, R, Br-F;* the hand *Q2 etc.*

10 form] *Q1, Pe, S, Ph, R, Br-F;* fashion *Q2 etc.*

11 Semi-gods] Demi-gods *Q2+*

–/14-15 No ... Immortality?] *om. Q1, E, F [See subsidiary note]*

  *–/14 Mont.] *Mo.*| *S, Ph, N; Mons.*| *Bp, Pg*

16/18 boast] vaunt *Q2+*

18/20 Rudenesse] Clowneries *Q2+*

19/21 as ... be] (~ ... ~) *D-Ph, N-Sp, Pg*

30/32 deformitie] confusion *Q2+ exc. S*

  sight] eyes *Q2* |

35/37 Subiects] subject's *D-Ph, P-BP, Sp-Pg, L-F;* subjects' *R*

37/39 *Mont.*] *Mo.*| *S, Ph, N;* Mons. *Sp*

38/40 a farre] far *Pg*

40/42 men] Snakes *Du*

42/44 trauell] travail *Sp*

43/45 deliuer'd] deliuered *Q1-D, B, N, Sp, J-L, E*

45/47 first borne] sole heire *Q2+*

51/53 wee] we more *Q2+*

52/54 be ... vanitie] jet in others plumes so haughtely *Q2+, F [See subsidiary note]*

  *others] other's *D;* others' *N, BP, Sp, BHN, Pg, L, F*

53/55 that they] they that *Sp*

–/56 Holding ... vaunts.] *Q2+, F; om. Q1, Br, E*

53/56 SD *D'Ambois.*] ~ *Richly Habited.*| *Du and subs. D, Br, E*

54/57 SD *To Bussy.*] *om. Q1-2 etc.*

55/58 SD *To Henry.*] *subs. P, L; dash for undesignated change N, BP, Sp-M, Br, E; om. Q1-2 etc.*

  this] a *Q2+*

  t'attend you] to court *Q2+*

57-58/60-61 That's ... attire] *as prose Q1-2*

57/60 thinke.] ~. *D'Amboise Kneels and Kisses the Kings hand.*| *Du*

58/61 alter'd] altered *Q1-2, B, N, Sp, J-L, E*

59-61/62-64 I ... I ... we] *Q1, Pe, S, Ph, R, Br-F;* I ... I ... I *Du;* We ... We ... we *Q2 etc.*

59/62 tell you] tell *D*

61/64 Vertue] *Du, Br*; vertue *Q1-2 etc.*

64/67 He] *Q1, Pe, S-B, N, R, Sp, Br-F*; They *Q2 etc.*
    her; shee's not shamelesse.] her. *Q2, D, Pe, Ph, P, BP, R, M-L*

65-67/68-70 I . . . weare him] *as prose Q1-2*

66/69 Rites] dues *Du*; rights *D*

67/70 SD *Henry . . . chess.*] *Jf subs., H; om. Q1-2 etc.; cf. I.ii.SD and collation*
    of l.–/86

68/71 SD *Aside to Bussy.*] *Du; om. Q1-2 etc.*

68-72/71-75 Th'art . . . Graces] *prose as in this ed. D, L-F*; Th'art . . . Duches
    possibly one verse, the rest prose Q1-2; Th'art . . . Duchess / The . . .
    Beaupres / Come . . . many / To . . . friend / That . . . Graces *S-H*

68/71 my loue] sweet heart *Q2+*

70/73 thee;–] *BHN, L*; ~.ˬ *Q2*; ~;ˬ *Q1 etc.*

71/74 Counsell] *Q1-D, B, J, H*; council *S etc.*

–/76 *Buss.* 'Save you Ladyes.] *om. Q1, Du, Br-F*

73/77 Graces] Graces, my Lord *Q2+*

73-74/77-78 thinks . . . behauiour,] *Q1-2, J, H, Br*; ~, . . . ~ˬ *B*; ~ˬ . . . ~ˬ *D etc.*

75/79 *Tam.*] *Beau.| Du*

77/81 *Beaup.*] *Dutch.| Du*

–/84-86 *Henr. . . . extremity.*] *Q2+* (*as verses, the first ending* bashful *S, Ph,*
    N, BP); *om. Q1, Br-F [See subsidiary note]*
       *–/84 SD *Looking . . . board.*] *om. Q2+*

–/86 extremity.] ~. *King goes and sits down at a Table, and beckons Mount*
    Surry to play at Chesse.| Du; cf. collation of l.67/70

83/90 Heere's . . . ripe] *one verse line BP*

85/92 SD *To the Duchess.*] *subs. P, BHN, M, L-F; om. Q1-2 etc.*

86 SD *Enter . . . Pyrhot.*] *Q2+* (*Pyrlot| Q2, D*), *E, F*; *precedes l.108/– Q1*
    (*Pyrlot*), *Br* (*During the last speeches enter . . .*)
    SD *They converse apart.*] *om. Q1-2 etc.*

–/94-104 *Duch.* Soft . . . gamester.] *om. Q1, Br-F [See subsidiary note]*
       *101, 102 porters] porter *D*

87/105 SD *Looking . . . board.*] *Rising from the chess table.| BHN*; Guise
    comes forward.| H; om. Q1-2 etc.

92/110 Saucie] *Aside ~| P-BP, Sp-Pg, H-F*

93/111 Guiserd] guiserd *B, N, BP, Pg*; Guisard *Du, P, Sp-M, L*
    Guiserd. Companion] Guiserd. / Companion [*as if in verse*] *Q1-2*

94/112 Sir] Duke *Q2+*

95/113 that.–] ~.ˬ *Q1-B, R, J*; ~. *To the Duchess.| H, Br*
    Madam] princely Mistresse *Q2+*

96/114 Courtship.] ~. Another Riddle. *Q2+*

99/117 whetstone; . . . Nœuius,] ~, . . . ~! *B and subs. N, BP, Sp, BHN, Pg, L*
    good] *Q1, Pe, S, Ph, R, Br-F*; young *Q2 etc.*

–/120-25 What . . . mine] *See collation at ll.108-13/120-25*

102-15/126-31 Ile . . . distemper] *prose as in this ed. S-B, N-BHN, Pg, L-F*;
    Ile . . . hand [*indeterminate*] / That . . . many / Throates . . . of /
    Many . . . owne. / Come . . . talke? / Talke . . . say, more
    Courtship as you loue it. / *followed by six prose lines that are*

transferred elsewhere in Q2, then |*Gui*. So Sir, so. / *Pyr*.
Heere's ... distemper [*indeterminate*] *Q1*; as *Q1* exc. Talk ...
say. Another Riddle. / *Pyr*. Here's ... distemper [*indeterminate*] *Q2, D*; I'll ... not do't. / Y'ave ... Guise, / And ...
souls, / More ... talk on. / 'Sfoot ... say. / Another riddle
... distemper *Brereton conj., P, M, J, H* [*See collation of
ll. 108-13/120-25*]

105/129 owne.–] *N, BP, Sp, BHN, Pg, L*; ~. To the Duchess| *Br*; ~., *Q1-2 etc.*
106-7/130 more ... it] Another Riddle *Q2+ exc. S*
108-13/120-25 What ... mine] *Q1, Br-F* (*See collation of l. 85/92 SD*); precedes
 Ile doe't by this hand (*l. 102/126*) *Q2+*
108/120 What] *Aside.* ~| *BHN*
110/122 Sfoote] *Aside.* ~| *BHN*
114/– *Gui*. So Sir, so.] *om. Q2+*
117/133 Knights] knights' *D, P, M, L-F*; knight's *S, Ph, N-BHN, Pg*
122/138 Courtship] Courting *Q2+*; prating *Du*
123/139 not.–] ~., *Q1-B, R, J-Br, F*
 say,] ~, *Q1-D, J, H, Br*
128/144 a] *Q1-2, S-N, R, Sp, J, H*; o' *D, P Errata etc.* (*not recorded hereafter*)
130/146 SD *Resumes chess game.*] *BHN subs.; om. Q1-2 etc.*
131/147 SD *To Bussy.*] *P; dash only M, E; om. Q1-2 etc.*
136/152 her!–] *P, Sp-M, L-F*; ~!, *Q1-2 etc.*
136-37/152-53 SD *To Guise.*] *om. Q1-Ph, R*
138/154 SD *Whispers with Duchess.*] *om. Q1-2 etc.*
139/155 SD *Aside.*] *P, BHN, L, Br; dash only M, E, F; om. Q1-2 etc.*
141/157 starr's] *Q1-2*; stars *D, B*; stars' *S etc.*
141-42/157-58 motion, ... light,] ~, (... ~), *L*
142/158 Ardor] Their heat *Q2+*
142-43/158-59 place ... frames;] ~, ... ~; *Q1, S, Ph, R*; ~, ... ~, *Q2, D, B,
 P, BP, Sp, M-H, Br-F*; ~, ... ~, *N, BHN*; ~ (... ~), *L*
143/159 And] but *Q2+*
146/162 setled] quiet *Pg* (*cf. l. 147/163*)
148/164 SD *To Guise.*] *Moving a chess-piece.*| *BP, Pg; om. Q1-2 etc.*
148-49/164-65 You ... more] *as one verse B*
149/165 SD *Rising.*] *om. Q1-2 etc.*
–/165 SD *Flourish short.*] *om. Q1, Br-F*
 SD *After them the Ladies.*] he [Guise] *takes the Dutchess away; then
 Ex. Dutchess Ladies and* Guise. *Du; om. Q1, Pe, S, Ph, R; Exeunt
 Ladies.*| *after l. 169/185 Q2 etc.*
149/165 SD *Barrisor ... whispers.*] *om. Q1-2 etc.*
151/167 shak'd] shaken *Ph², R*
154/170 troe] *Q1-2, B, J, H*; trow ye *D*; trow *S etc.*
155/171 denizond] denizen *D*
156/172 come new] newly drawne *Q2+*
 Mercers] Mercer's *D-Ph, P-Pg, L, E, F*; Mercers' *Br*
159/175 Gallant,] ~, *Q1-D, B, J, H, Br*
163/179 beare] *Q1, Pe, S, Ph, R, L, Br*; bare *Q2 etc.*

roaring] braying *Q2+*
168/184 honour] honour sake *Q2+*
171/187 marie] merry *Pg*
173/189 SD *In mock fright.*] *om. Q1-2 etc.*
174/190 SD *To Barrisor.*] *P*; *om. Q1-2 etc.*
        how] who *B*
176/192 sits] fits *S, Ph, P, R, M-H, E, F*
182/198 SD *Brisac,*] ~ *Q1*
        SD *They listen apart.*] *om. Q1-2 etc.*
183/199 *Pyrh.*] *Bar.| Q2+*
183-85/199-201 O ... you] *prose as in this ed. D-F*; O ... selfe / Such ...
        into / Our [The matter of our *Q2*] ... you *Q1-2*
183/199 strange credulitie] miraculous jealousie *Q2+*
184/200 subiect] object *D*
184/200-1 our] The matter of our *Q2+*
186/202 *Bar.*] *L'An.| Q2+*
188/204 *L'An.*] *Pyr.| Q2+*
        discourse] a discourse *D*
189/205 with] *Q1, Pe, S, Ph, R, Br-F*; in *Q2 etc.*
192/208 laughters] laughter *Pg*
194/210-11 outright] *Q1, Pe, S, Ph, R, Br-F*; outright else *Q2 etc.*
196/213 and] an *D, N, Sp*
200/217 SD *Brisac ... forward.*] *To the* Courtiers *P*; *om. Q1-2 etc.*
207/224 SD *To Brisac.*] *om. Q1-2 etc.*
        Not] Nor *Smith conj.*
208/225 nor] not *D, N, BP, Pg, J*
209/226 SD *To ... Melynell.*] *P*; *om. Q1-2 etc.*
212/229 Come follow] Follow *Q2+*

II.i

SD] *A Room in the Court.| B, P, N, Sp, BHN, Pg·*
SD *Henry*] Enter ~ *S, Ph, N, R, Sp, H, Br*
SD *Beaumond*] *Sp, Br, E*; *Beaumond, Nuncius.| Q1, F*; Montsurry, Beaupre
    D; Montsurry, Beaumond *P, R, BHN, M, Pg*; *Montsurry| Q2 etc.*
SD *and Attendants.*] *om. Q1*
4 Enuie] envy *D-B, N-Sp, Pg*
11 When] *Q1, Pe, S, Ph, R, Br-F*; Where *Q2 etc.*
    filth] faults *Du*
15 of] on *S, Ph, N, R*
19 strait] *Q1-2, B, J, H*; straight *D etc. (not recorded hereafter)*
20 valour] Valour *Q2, J, H, Br*
    giddinesse] Giddiness *Br*
    Iustice Tyrannie] *Q1-2, J, H, Br*; justice tyranny *D etc.*
23 Foe] Foes *Du, Ph, N, R, BHN*
24 SD *Enter Nuncius.*] Nuntius *comes forward.| F*
27 his] *Q1, Pe, S, Ph, R, Br-F*; their *Q2 etc.*
31 and] and from *D*

43 alike;] ~, Q1-2, J, H, Br-F
44 wood] ~: Q1, Br-F; ~, Q2, D, J, H
45 shew'd;] ~, Q1-F
   spirit,] ~; D-Sp, M, Pg, L subs.
47 death] Q2, D, B, J, H; ~; E, F; ~, Q1 etc.
51 Pyrrho's] Pyrrhot's R
60 liues,] Q2, D, J, H; ~; Q1; ~ˌ S etc.
64 others] others' D-Ph, P-M, L-F; other's Pg
70 Sparkl'd] Spakl'd Q2
   much much] much Ph, N, R, Sp
74 Fates] fates D-Ph, N-Sp, Pg
87 scap't;] ~ˌ S
88 deadly bitten] deadly-biting D; deadly-bitten P, BHN, M, E, F
   tugg'd] tuggd'd Q1, Pe
100 yet,] ~ˌ D
101 feare-cold] sere-cold G. B. Evans conj.
105 Beaum.] Mont.| B, N, BP, J, H, L
106 mettall] mettle Br
107 end.–] B, BHN, M, E, F; To the Nuntius. ~ P, L; ~.ˌ Q1-2 etc.
108 felt] fell R
110 furie] Fury L, Br
    [umes] ~, Q1-2, S, Ph, R, J, H
113 Reuenge] revenge D
120 quicke an eie] swift a foot] Q2+
128 the tw'other] th'tw'other Q2, B, Sp, L; th'two other D; tw' other Pg
129 fell ... flew] ~ (... ~) D, B
    spirits] spirit Q2, D, B, J, H
132 others] others' D-Ph, P-M, L-F; other's Pg
133 outright?] outright but hee? Q2-Ph, P, R, BHN, M, J-L
135 feebled] freckled Q2+, Br, E
136 cheekes] Q1, Pe, S, Ph, N, R, Br-F; lips Q2 etc.
137 beares.] ~! Exit Nuntius.| B, N, Pg; cf. l. 206 SD
140 SD They ... Henry.] subs. D, P, BHN-Pg, Jf, H-F; om. Q1-2 etc.
141 Nature] nature D-Ph, N-BHN, Pg
145 the t'one] the one S, Ph, R
    the t'other] the other S; t'other N
163-64 Butchers, ... forgiuen!] subs. B, Bp, Pg, L, E; ~; ... ~? Q1-2 etc.
166 full] true Q2+ (E attributes to Q2 the reading whole; see V.iii.46/V.ii.41)
166-67 men; ... law,] D, B, P, M, L-F; ~, ... ~, Q1-2, J, H; ~ˌ ... ~. S etc.
172 murther'd] murthered Q1-2, B, N, Sp, J-L, E
177-79 man ... men,] ~ˌ ... ~ˌ Q2+, E, F; ~ (... ~) L
178 vprightnesse,] D, B, P, Sp-M, L, E, F; ~; Q1-2 etc.
181 SD Monsieur ... rise.] om. Q1-2 etc.
185 violent] daring Q2+ exc. B
188 a little] as little Du
190 SD Kneels again.] Br; om. Q1-2 etc.
191 craue] ~, B, P, Sp, M-L subs.

193 God] law *Q2, D, B* (Law), *N* (Law), *BHN, J-L*
    nature] Nature *B, P, M, Br-F*
202 a Right] aright *D, S*
    Law ... Nature] *Q1-2, B, J, H, Br-F;* law ... nature *D etc.*
204 no King] no Law *Q2+*
    a King] a Man *Du*
206 SD *Rising.*] *om. Q1-2 etc.*
    SD *Exit ... Beaum.*] *beside ll. 205-6 Q1-2; after l. 205 D, Br*
    SD *Beaum.*] *Montsurry.*| *B, N, BP, Pg-L; Mont.ˌ Beau.* [i.e., Beaupre]
    D (cf. collation of II.i.SD); Beaumond ... *and* Montsurry. *P, BHN;*
    om. Ph, R
    SD *Nuncio*] *subs. Ph, P, R, BHN; om. Q1-2 etc.; cf. collation of l. 137*
    SD *Attendants.*] *D, P, BHN, M subs. (etc.), Br-F; om. Q1-2 etc.*
207 Mort dieu, who] Who *Q2, D, Ph, R, J-L*
209 For] *à Bussy ~ Jf*
210-11/– *Buss.* How ... friend.] *Q1, S, Br-F [See subsidiary note]; om. Q2,*
    Pe, etc.
        211/– SD *Aside.*] *om. Q1 etc.*
211 SD *Exit Mons. with Bussy.*] *Exit.*| *Q1; Exeunt.*| *Br-F; Exit. [after l. –/211]*
    ... Exit. [after l. –/218] Q2+
–/210-18 And ... hated.] *Q2+ (including Pe); om. Q1, Br-F*

II.ii

II.ii] *B-BP, Sp-F; om. Q1 etc.*
SD] *A Room in Montsurry's House.*| *B-BP, Sp, BHN, Pg*
SD *Montsur.*] *Enter Monsieur Q2, D, P, Sp-M, H, L; Enter* Montsurry *Br-F*
SD *Beaupre*] *om. Q2, D, P, BHN, M, H, L*
SD *Pero walking apart with a Book.*] *and Pero with a Booke.*| *Q2, P, BHN,*
    M, H-F; om. Du, D; Pero| *Q1 etc.*
SD *Charlotte, Pyrha*] *om. Q2, D, P, BHN, M, H, L*
1-49/– *Mont.* He ... bloud.] *Q1, Pe, S-B, N-Sp,ˑJ, Br-F; om. Q2 etc. [See*
    subsidiary notes]
        3/– still borne] still-born *Br*
        14/– sleight] slight *S, Ph, N-Sp, Pg*
        24/– Gui.] *om. Q1*
        26/– glorious,] ~ˌ *S, Ph, R*
        31/– SD *Aside.*] *Sp, Jf; om. Q1 etc.*
        33/– SD *Charlotte and Pyrha*] *Br;* Tamyra *and* Pero *remain.*| *Sp;*
            Charlotte *and* Pyrha. Pero *remains reading her book.*| *E, F;*
            om. Q1, S-P, N-R, Pg, J
        37/– stroke] struck *S, Ph, N-Sp, Pg, Br-F*
50 *Mons.* Yet ... vnanswer'd?] *om. Q2, D, P, BHN, M, H, L [See subsidiary*
    note]
        vnanswer'd] vnanswered Q1, Pe, B, Sp, L
59/9 Mine ... mine] My ... my *Du;* My ... mine *N, Sp*
71/21 weighing a dissolute] joyning a lose *Q2+* (loose *all exc. B, J, H*)
76/26 solemne] *Q1, Pe, S, Ph, R, Br-F;* common *Q2 etc.;* Publick *Du*

83/33 For] Your *J, H*
87/37 be] be you *J, H* (*attributing the reading to Q2*)
89/39 SD *Offering a necklace.*] *om.* Q1-2 etc.
93/43 SD *Spurning it.*] *om.* Q1-2 etc.
98/48 loose] lose *Du, S, Ph, N-BHN, Pg*
108/58 SD *Calls.*] *dash only* B, P, Sp-M, L, E, F; *om.* Q1-2 etc.
    SD *To Pero.*] P, M, L, E, F; *Enter* Charlotte. *Du* (*Charlotte has Pero's function in Du*); *Enter* Pero *with a Book.| D* (*before l. 108/58*); *om.* Q1-2 etc.
    you] Q2(c)-F; your Q1, Q2(u)
109/59 taught] thought *Pg*
111/61 good husband] good *husband| D, B, N, Sp, BHN*; 'good husband' *P, BP, M, Pg, H, L, E, F*
    Tam.] *Mont.|* Q1, Pe, S, Ph, N, BP
115/65 husbands] husband's *D, Ph², R, M, Pg, E, F*; husbands' *S, Ph, P-BP, Sp, BHN, L, Br*
117/67 opportunities] importunities *Du, D conj.*; importunacies *D conj.*
122/72 reseruations, ... Parliaments] ~, ... ~, *Q2, D, J, H*; ~ ... ~- *B-BP, Sp-M, E, F*
124/74 Vertues] vertues Q1-2 etc.
131/81 mens] men *D*
134/84 charg'd] charged Q1-B, R, J-L
135/85 profit] honour Q2+
136/86 not] no Q1-2, B, L
140/90 you?] ~: Q1; ~. Q2, S, Ph, N, R, J, H, Br
145/95 SD *Aside.*] *BHN; change marked only with dashes N, BP, Sp, Pg, L, Br; om.* Q1-2 etc.
–/96 In ... another] *om.* Q1, Br
146/97 wane] waue Q1, Pe; wave Q2, Ph, R, BHN, H, F
152/103 SD *To Pero.*] P, L; *change marked only with dashes N, BP, Sp-Pg, Br-F; om.* Q1-2 etc.
    booke I pray:] book; I'll pray, *D*
156/107 SD *Aside.*] P-BP, Sp, BHN, Pg, Jf, H, L, F; *before* I will *D* (*?after Du, who printed |Aside.| in the right margin as if for the whole line*), Br, E (*but with a dash as in* B, M); *change marked only with dashes* B, M; *om.* Q1-2 etc.
157/108 the] Q1, Du, Pe, E, F; yee Q2 etc.
165/116 Time ... Fortune ... Existens] time ... fortune ... existence *Du*; Time ... Fortune ... existence *D, L*
166/117 Makers] maker's *D*
    treasurie] Treasure *Du, S* (treasure)
171/122 that that] that which Q2+
172/123 loue ... againe] lifes meere death loving one that loathes me Q2+ *exc. S*
175/126 SD *The vault opens.*] *opposite* l. 173/124 Q2, D, Br; *om.* Q1, Pe
176/127 the gulfe] a Vault Q2+
176-77/127-31 will ... euer] was never ... blushes Q2+

178/132 SD *Ascendit ... D'Ambois.*] om. Q1

179/133 *Com.*] *Frier.*| Q2+, E, F (*so throughout exc. as noted*)

182/136 adapt] adopt *Pg*

184-86/138-40 know her worths ... know besides] know worths ... know
        her besides *Q2(u)*; know worths ... know besides *Q2(c, first
        state)*

194/148 Moue] Mover *Br conj.*

195/149 Loue] *Q1-2, J, H*; love *D etc.*

209/163 your] you *Ph, R*

215/169 how), I,] ~, ~) *L*

220/174 Loue] *Q1-2, J, H*; love *D etc.*

222/176 honour'd] honoured *Q1-2, B, J, H, L*

225/179 woman] women *Sp*

234/188 foode] blood *BP*

237/191 SD *They stand aside.*] subs. *P, BHN*; om. *Q1-2 etc.*
        SD *Tamyra.*] *Tamyra with a Book.*| *Q2-F*

238/192 Alas] *Aside.* ~ *BP, Pg, Br*

242/196 heart,] ~. *B, N, Sp*

244/198 SD *Advancing with Bussy.*] *advancing*| *P, BHN, L* (*see collation of
        l. 268/222 SD*); om. *Q1-2 etc.*

253/207 houre] ~! *BP, Pg*

255/209 suspicious] suspicion's *S, Ph, R, J* (suspicions; l'ombre du soupçon
        Jf)

262/216 sits] wakes *Q2+*

268/222 Madam] *advancing* ~| *P, L* (*see collation of l. 244/198*)

270/224 Was something troubled] Made some deepe scruple *Q2+*

271/225 hand] honour *Q2+*

274/228-30 which my] his long love / And service, as I heare, being deepely
        vowed / To your perfections, which my ready *Q2+* (vow'd *S,
        Ph, P, R, BHN, M*)

274-75/230-31 presence (Presum'd] ~ˌ ~ *Q1-2*

280/236 comfort] good *Q2+*

286/242 importun'd] importud'd *Q2(u)*

287/243 his owne] his *F*

289/245 SD *Exeunt ... D'Amb.*] *Q2* (*Tamira* [*opposite ll. 288-89/244-45*]),
        D-F; om. *Q1*

290/246 SD *Descendit Com.*] *Descendit Fryar.*| *Q2-F*; om. *Q1*

III.i

SD] *A Room in Montsurry's House.*| *B-BP, Sp, BHN, Pg*

SD *Bucy*] *Enter* ~| *Q2-F*

SD *Tamyra.*] *Tamyra, with a Chaine of Pearle.*| *Q2+*

–/1-2 *Buss.* Sweet ... spice.] om. *Q1, Br-F*

4/6 against] 'gainst *S, Ph, R*

15/17 sin] Sin *P, BHN, M, E*
      gather'd] gathered *Q1-D, B, N, Sp, J-L, E*

25/27 Policy] policy *Q1-B, R, J, H*

26/28 Goddesse] Servile *Q2+, F*
    money] Money *Br*
32/34 our one . . . one] one . . . one *Q2, P, BHN-L*; one . . . in one *D*
    soule, are] ~, ~, *Q1-D, J, H*; ~͵ ~, *Br*; ~͵ ~͵ *S etc.*
33/35 truth] selfe *Q2+*
34/36 Torture . . . Pleasure] *Br*; torture . . . pleasure *Q1-2 etc.*
35/37 men] one *Q2+*
38/40 valure] valour *S, Ph, R*; value *Q1-2 etc.*
–/45-61 Now . . . onely.] *om. Q1, Br-F* [*See subsidiary notes*]
        *–/49 it?] *Q2, J, H*; ~. *D-B, N-Sp, Pg*; ~! *P, BHN, M, L*
        *–/50 SD *Calls.*] *change marked only with dash Q2, S-L*; *om. D*
        *–/51 resolv'd.] ~? *D-R, BHN-Pg, L*
        *–/53 Too . . . stayed] *one verse as in this ed. B, P, Sp-L*; *apparently*
           two verses, the first ending soone? *Q2-Ph, N, BP, R* (*N and*
           BP elsewhere set off verses xcmksn between speeches)
           *stayed] stay'd *S, Ph, P, BP, R, BHN-Pg*
        *–/56 besieg'd] besieged *Q2-B, N, R, Sp, J-L*
        *–/61 SD *Giving a necklace.*] *om. Q2 etc.*
41/61 SD *Exit D'Amb.*] *Descendit Frier and D'Amb.*| *Q2 (after l. 43/62),*
    D-L; *Exit D'Amb.*| *Q1 (opposite ll. 42-43), Br-F*
    SD *Manet Tamy.*] *om. Q2+*; *opposite l. 43/62 Q1*
43/62 It] *Ta.* It *Q1, Pe, S, Ph, R*
47/66 th'whole] the whole *S, Ph, R*
    Nature] nature *S, Ph, P-Pg, L, E, F*
52/71 oppos'd] appos'd *J* (appliquée *Jf*)
62/81 times] fumes *S, Ph, R*
64/83 how] what *Pg*
65/84 orderd] ordered *Q2, D, B, N, Sp, J-L, E*
66/85 passions] *Q1-2, B, J, H*; passion's *D*; passions' *S etc.*
73/92 Sleepe] *Br*; sleepe *Q1-2 etc.*
    thy beauties] thine eyes *Q2+*
78/97 Sleepe] sleepe *Q1-2 etc.*
89/108 Sleepe] *Br*; sleepe *Q1-2 etc.*
98/117 shot] shut *Pg*
99/118 vnderneath the King] under our Kings arme *Q2+*; under the King's
    Arm *Du*

III.ii

III.ii] *om. Q1-Ph, R*
SD] *A Room in the King's Palace.*| *D, B-BP, Sp, BHN, Pg* [*P and others note*
    shift to Monsieur's quarters after l. 281/289; cf. also collation before
    l. 284/291]
SD *Henry*] Enter ~ *Ph, N, R, Sp, H, Br*
SD *Duchess Elenor,*] *Monts. Elenor, Tam. Pero.*| *Q1; cf. collation of l. 59 SD*
SD *Annable*] *om. Q1*
SD *Charlotte*] *om. Q1, D, Br, F*; Beaupre>, ~ *Smith conj.* (*see note in Br*)
SD *Attendants*] *om. Q1*

1 home my] *Q1, Pe, S-B, N, R, Br-F*; home *Q2 etc.*

4 nothing] Sparrowes *Q2+*

6 th'eares] the ears *D-Ph, R*

9, 11 truth] Truth *B, P, M, Br, E*

11 Kings] king's *D, M, Pg*; kings' *S, Ph, P-BHN, L-F*

12 Flatterie] flatterie *Q1-B, R, J, H*

13 Kings] king's *D*; kings' *S, Ph, P-Pg, L-F*

16 truth] *Q1, S, E, F*; Truth *Br*; man *Q2 etc.*

24 trusse] trust *Ph, R*

29 than] by *Q2+ exc. B*

31-32 graduate ... woodmongers (... billets)] ~ (... ~ͺ ... ~) *D and subs. P,*
    BHN, M, L, E, F; ~ͺ ... ~, ... ~ͺ *Ph, N-Sp, Pg*; ~ͺ ... ~ͺ ... ~ͺ *B*

44 rents] rent *B (with space as though a letter had dropped out), M*

49 law] Law *Br*

51 Rapine ... Extortion] rapine ... extortion *S-Pg, L, E, F*

53 learning ... vertue] Learning ... Virtue *Br*
    oppressed] besieged *Q2+*

57 iustice] Justice *Br*

58 tother] rest *Q2+*

59 SD *Enter ... Tamyra, and Pero.*] om. *Q1 (cf. collation of III.ii.SD)*; ~
    ... Tamyra. King and Mont. *talk.*| *Du*

62 Ruffin] *Q1-2, B, J, H*; ruffi'n *Br*; ruffian *Du, D etc.*

64 vapour] slander *Du*

67 charge] bout *Q2+*; Brush *Du*

73 may doe worst?] should do best. *Du*; may do worst. *D*

76 noblie] *Q1-Ph, R, BHN, Pg, L, E, F*; noblier *B, P, M, J, H*; nobler *N etc.*

80 Guiserd] Guisard *P, BHN, M, L*
    SD *To Henry.*] *Du subs.; marked only with a dash Sp;* om. *Q1-2 etc.*

81 face (my Eagle);] ~; (~ ~)ͺ *Q1-D, J, H*; ~; ~ ~, *Br*

83 SD *To Guise.*] om. *Q1-2 etc.*

86 duke] Duke *Q1-2, B, J, H, Br*

88 them,–] *Sp*; ~,ͺ *Q1-2 etc. subs.*
    stay,] ~ͺ *Q1-2, J, H, Br*
    D'Ambois;–] *Sp*; ~;ͺ *Q1-2 etc. subs.*

89 equall] honour'd *Q2+ exc. S*

92 dissentions] dimensions *S, Ph, N, R, Sp*

96 eminence] Empire *Q2+*

98 Nature] nature *Q1-Ph, N-Sp, J, H*

104 out one sticke] one stick out *Q2+*

105 was compris'd] bound our lifes *Q2+*

107 th'ingenuous] th'ingenious *Q2, B, N, BP, BHN, Pg, H, L*; the ingenuous *D*

111 SD *To Guise.*] om. *Q1-2 etc.*

117 prooue ... rodde] hold ... vertue *Q2+*

119 this his] this *Pg*
    SD *Places ... Henry's.*] om. *Q1-2 etc.*

121 Engender not] Decline not to *Q2+*; Incline not to *Du*

126 SD *Places ... theirs.*] om. *Q1-2 etc.*

128 to a] to *Ph²*, *R*

129 your] yours *Q1*, *Q2(u)*; our *Du*

–/131 SD *To the Duchess.*] *subs.* P, M, L; *om.* Q1-2 *etc.*

–/131-38 And ... you?] *om.* Q1, Br-F [*See subsidiary notes*]

          *–/136 SD *To Tamyra.*] P, BHN, L; *marked only with dash* M; *om.* Q2 *etc.*

           *Mistresse] *Q2, D, B, P, M, J-L*; mistress' *S, Ph, N-BHN, Pg*

           *Lady?] *D-Pg, L*; ~. *Q2* (*unclear in many copies; see Press-Variants*), *J, H*

         *–/137 *Tam.*] *Q2-L*; ~ *Scornfully*| *Du*

         *–/138 *Mont.*] *Q2-Pg, H, L*; *Mons.*| *J, Jf*

130/138 SD *Exeunt ... Charlotte,*] Q1 *subs.* (*beside* Q1 *ll.130-33*); *Exeunt Henry, D'Amb. Ladies*| Q2 (*beside* Madam. *and* you?), D (*after* Madam), *S-F*

         SD *and Attendants.*] *om.* Q1-2 *etc.*

132/140 Y'aue] Y'ane *Q1*

         proper] worthy *Q2+*

138/146 ordinance] ordnance *Q2(c), D, BP, Sp, M, Pg, L* (ord'nance), *Br-F*

         implide] imploy'd *Du, D* (employ'd)

141/149 gadding] ranging *Q2+*

144/152 and indeed] for you know *Q2+*

146/154 wise] ~; *Q1, Q2(u)*

         aduantage] advantages *P, BP, M, Pg*

147/155 women, ... may,] *P, BP, BHN-L, E, F*; ~ ... ~ *Q1-2 etc.*

152-53/160-61 being ... choice of] the Hart / (Being old, and cunning in his *Q2+*, *Br*

154/162 discouer'd] discouered *Q1-D, B, N, Sp, Pg-L, E*

155-56/163-64 his ... ruts] (behind some Queich) / He breaks his gall, and rutteth *Q2+, Br* [*See subsidiary note*]

         *–/163 Queich] quitch *S, Ph, N, R, Sp*

159/167 chiefest] safest *Du*

160/168 Ladies] *Q1-2, B, J, H*; lady's *D*; ladies' *S etc.*

         greatest women] chiefest women *Q2+*

163/171 Sharpen] Sharpens *Ph, N, R*

164/172 an excellent] the cunningst *Q2+*

165-67/173-76 our ... your] your ... our *S, Ph, R*; your ... your *N, Sp, BHN*

165-68/173-78 inuestigation. ... discouery.] investigation. / *Mons.* I have broken / The yce to it already with the woman / Of your chast Lady, and conceive good hope, / I shall wade thorow to some wished shore / At our next meeting. / *Monts.* Nay, there's small hope there. *Q2+ exc. as follows: as in Q2 exc.* investigation ... broken *as part of one verse B, N, BP, Sp, BHN, H, Pg; as in B exc. om.* I shall ... shore *J (not Jf); as in Q2 exc.* At our ... hope there *as one verse B-BP, Sp-L*

169/179 *Mont.*] *Guise.*| *Q2+*

         say] 'ssay *Br*

170/180 And we will to the other. / ... Y'are engag'd.] *Q1 (apparently as prose), Q1-F (one verse as in this ed. of Q1); Mons. Starting back? / ... Y'are engag'd indeed. [apparently as prose; I have lined as verse in this ed. of Q2] Q2+ exc. S; And we will to the other. / ... Starting back? / ... Y'are engaged, indeed S (merging Q1 and Q2; apparently as prose)*

170/179 SD *Enter ... Pero.] Q1, Br-F; after* back? *in l.–/180 Q2-B, N-Sp, Pg; after* fitly. *in l.169/179 P etc.*

–/179 SD *Seeing ... go.] om. Q1-2 etc.*

–/180 SD *Stopping Pero.] Takes hold of Charlot.| Du; om. Q1-2 etc.*

170/180 SD *To Charlotte.] Stopping Charlotte.| this ed. of Q2; To Pero. Du; om. Q1-2 etc.*

171/181 An.] *Char.| Q2, D, BP, Pg-L*

171/– SD *To Montsurry.] om. Q1-2 etc.*

171/181 Nay ... seruant] *one verse as in this ed. Br; as prose Q1-2 etc.*
SD *Drawing Annable aside.] Sp; To Anable Du; om. Q1-2 etc.*

172/182 No ... seruice] *as one verse S, Br?; others prose as in this ed. or doubtful*

173/183 SD *To ... aside.] after Sp (see collation of l.175/185); om. Q1-2 etc.*

173-74/183-84 Pray ... expects me] *as one verse S, P, Br?*
Pray] Nay *B*

175/185 Ile] *drawing Charlotte aside. ~| Sp*

175-76/185-86 Ile ... may] *one verse S, Br?*

177/187 SD *To Guise.] om. Q1-2 etc.*

177-81/187-91 Well ... promised] *prose as in this ed. D-Sp, M-L, E, F; as three verses (Well ... hands / Now ... mee / For ... make concerning), the remainder prose Q1 (but beginning* Thy), *Q2; as four verses (Well ... hands / Now ... me / For ... mistress / Speak ... sworn to thee) BHN; as one verse (Well ... hands), the rest prose Br; see verbal variants below*

177/187 said:–] *~:ˌ Q1-2 etc.*

178/188 SD *Aside to Pero.] drawing Pero aside.| Sp, BHN; marked only with dash Br; om. Q1-2 etc.*

179/189 to make] *make N, Sp*
concerning] *of Q2+*

181/190-91 promised] *sworne to thee Q2+*

182/192 you haue sworne] *assurance Q2+*

185-86/195 it bee ... thee] *wee reach our objects Q2+*

189/199 Excellent] *~! Q2, D, P, Sp, M, J-L; ~, S, Ph, N, BP, R, BHN, Pg*

190/199-200 into earth heere] *to perdition Q2+*

192/202 wondring] *watching Q2+*
stole] *stole up Q2+*

194-95/204-5 she set ... banquet] *her selfe reading a letter Q2+*

199/209 No my Lord] *I sweare Q2+*

200/210 SD *Aside.] before* The diuell *P, M subs., Jf, L; after* dam *Sp, H; om. Q1-2 etc. (but see dashes in some eds. at l.205/216)*

201/211-12 infinite] *Why this was the happiest shot that ever flew, the just*

plague of hypocrisie level'd it; Oh the infinite Q2(c)+ (shot? . . .
    flewe, Q2[u], Pe), Br, E
203/214 sleighted] slighted D, P-BP, Sp-Pg, L-F
203/214 freight] fraught Q2+
205/215-16 woman:] ~: never dreaming of D'Amboys.| Q2+
    – deare] P, BP, Sp, M, Pg, Jf, L, Br; ,~ Q1-2 etc.
206/217 SD Aside.] om. Q1-2 etc. (but dashes in some eds. perhaps indicate
    aside)
207/217-18 admiration:–] ~:, Q1-Ph, R, J-L
208/218 his] Q1, D, Pe, S, Ph, R, Br-F; this Q2 etc.
209/219 could] should Q2+
209/220 performed] made Q2+
214/225 SD Whispers with Pero.] subs. P, M, Pg, E, F; om. Q1; Whispers.|
    Q2 etc.
215-18/– Char. I . . . me–] om. Q2, Du, D, B, P, BHN, M, J-L [See
    subsidiary notes]
        *215/– SD Aside to Guise.] om. Q1 etc.
            *to your] to you N
        *218/– SD Whispers with Charlotte.] Whispers.| Br-F; om. Q1 etc.
219/226 SD Aside to Annable.] BHN; om. Q1-2 etc.
219-20/226 27 the Duke . . . wife] as aside Smith conj.
220/227 busie] a busie Q2(u)
223/230 Countesse . . . Lady] Br-F; Lady . . . Countesse Q1; Lady . . .
    Lady Q2+
226/– if she marks it] Q1, Pe, S, Ph, N, R, Br-F; om. Q2 etc.
227/234 SD Aside to Pero.] P, BHN-Pg, L, E, F; om. Q1-2 etc.
    put off] disguise Q2+
    with seeming] seeming Ph, R
228/235 courted;–] B-BP, Sp-Pg, Jf subs., L subs., Br-F; ~;, Q1-2 etc.
    liuer] livor Q2, B, J
228/235 hard] Q1, Pe, S, Ph, P, R, BHN, M, Br-F; dry Q2 etc.
230/237 at] from Q2+
236/243 be] are Q2+
243/249 What . . . portions] as one verse BP
249/255 if] when Q2+
250/256 in] thin B, N
252/258 when tis] when its J
254/260 portion] great portion Q2+
259/265 you] it Q2+
260/266 man, when] man F
    furthest] farthest M, E, F
263-64/269-70 I . . . my mercy] wee . . . our mercies Q2+
264/270 SD Exit . . . Annable.] Exit.| Q1; Exeunt women.| Q2-F
268/274 feele] find Du
270/276 is] Q1, Pe, S, Ph, R, Br-F; is thought Q2 etc.
277/283 horrible] miraculous Q2+
280/286 a sheepe] sheep N, Sp

282/288 And ... confident,] *Aside.* ~ ... ~;– *Du, N, BP, Sp, BHN, Pg*
        my Lord, tis true, and] well my Lord, *Q2+*
–/290 *Gui.* Come ... them.] *om. Q1, Br-F*
Before 284/291] Scene II. Hall. *Re-enter* Monsieur *and* Maffe. *Du;* Scena
        Tertia. *J, II (Jf and H locating new scene in Monsieur's House)*
284/291 O] *Mouns.* ~ *Q2(c)+; Mount.* ~ *Q2(u)*
        bloods] Blood *Du, D*
288/295 monster-formed cloudes] dark and standing foggs *Q2+*
289/296 euer] never *Ph, N, R, Sp, BHN*
291/298 Not] Nor *Pe, S, Ph, B, N, R*
292/299 vailes] veil *E, F*
293-95/– I will ... Caue] *Q1, S (after l.–/304), Br-F; om. Q2 etc.*
–/300-59 But ... humors.] *om. Q1, Br-F [See subsidiary notes]*
        *–/300 cloud] Mine *Du*
        *–/304 would be sure,] ~ˬ ~ ~ˬ *Du, S, Ph, N-R, BHN, Pg;* ~,
            ~ ~, *B, P, Sp, M;* ~ˬ ~, ~, *L*
        *–/314-15 And ... there] *as one line Q2, D*
        *–/315 SD *Calls.*] *change of address marked with dash Sp, L; om.*
            Q2 etc.
        *–/319 your selfe] yourselves *D*
        *–/320 You'l ... Montsurry] *as prose N, BP*
            **Montsurry.*] ~? *S-Pg, L*
        *–/321 *Mons.*] Mont.| *Q2, D, Pe;* Mo.| *S, Ph, N, BHN (Mon.)*
        *–/322 See ... this,] ~, ... ~ˬ *B, P, M, L*
            **this] his *J* (lui *Jf*), *H*
        *–/326 I, and] And *S*
        *–/331 glad–] ~.– *Q2, H;* ~. *J*
        *–/336 Lord–] ~? *Q2, Pe, S, Ph, R, J, H*
        *–/339 D'Ambois–] ~. *J;* ~.– *H*
        *–/340 Precious!] ~!– *Sp;* ~! *Aside.*| *H*
            **Fate] fate *D-Pg, L*
        *–/341 murthered] murther'd *S, Ph, P, R, BHN-Pg*
        *–/342 folly.] ~.– *Sp*
        *–/343 Avant] ~! *D and subs. B, BP, Sp, Pg*
        *–/344 SD *Aside.*] *D, P, Sp, BHN, H, L; marked only with*
            dashes B, N, BP, M, Pg; om. Q2, S, Ph, R, J
        *–/346 D'Ambois.–] ~.ˬ *Q2-B, J-L*
        *–/347 know–] ~.– *Q2, H;* ~. *S, Ph, R*
        *–/348 foole?] *Q2, J, H;* ~; *D;* ~! *S etc.*
        *–/353 Grant thou] ~ˬ ~, *S, Ph, N-BHN, Pg;* ~, ~ˬ *B, P, M, L*
        *–/356 I will then] then I will *Q2(u)*
        *–/357 Natures] nature's *D*
296-98/360-61 It ... strangely, / And ... valour / Vnto] I feare him strangely,
        his advanced valour / Is like *Q2+ exc. S;* It should breathe
        oracles; / ... [*ll.–/305-59*] / I fear him strangely, his advanced
        valour / Is like *S*
297/360 aduanced] advancing *Du*

300/363 learn'd] learned *Ph, R, E*

–/363 SD *Enter Maffe hastily.*] om. *Q1, Br-F*

–/364-69 *Maffe. I . . . endanger'd:*] om. *Q1, Br-F* [*See subsidiary notes*]

       *–/367 SD *Exit.*] subs. *Du, Sp, L;* om. *Q2-R, BHN-H*

              *of death] or death *J* (de ~ *Jf*)

300/369 SD *Enter D'Ambois.*] after at? in l.301/370 *Q2-Ph, R*

–/369 My sweet heart!] om. *Q1, Br-F*

301/370 How] *Mons.* ~ *Q1* (*redundant speech-prefix*)

303/372 head] browes *Q2+*

304/373 you] thou *L*

306/375 Sir] *Q1, Pe, S, Ph, R, Br-F;* Prince *Q2 etc.*

–/378-85 *Buss.* Why . . . appearance.] *Q2+* (overjoy'd *S, Ph, P, R, BHN-Pg*);
      om. *Q1, Br-F*

309/386-87 This . . . doubt] Thy absence so long suffercd oftentimes / Put me
      in some little doubt *Q2+* (suffer'd *S, Ph, BP, R, M, BHN-Pg*)

310/388 for me then] therefore now *Q2+*

312/390 and] an *Ph², R*

      note?] ~, *S*

313/391-94 *Buss.* Come . . . things.] *Q1* (*as prose*), *Br-F* (*verse in E, F; unclear
      in Br*); How . . . yours. [*as in this ed. of Q2 (verse)*] *Q2+* [*See
      subsidiary notes*]

        *–/391 unseasonable] unseasonably *Du, D, S*

             *playest] *Q2, D, B, P, Sp-M, J-L;* play'st *S, Ph, N-R,
             Pg*

314/395 and now by all] to prove which by *Q2+*

316/397-98 affection] still flourishing tree, / With whatsoever may hereafter
      spring *Q2+*

321/403-4 Why] *Mons.* Plaine as truth. / *D'Amb.* Why *Q2+*

331/414 dissection] Description *Du*

333/416 else Sir? come . . . simply] else Sir? come pay me home, ile bide it
      bravely *Q2+*; else Sir? pay me home, ile bide it bravely *P conj., this
      ed. of Q2*; else? come pay me home, ile bide it bravely *Rappaport
      conj.*

334/417 I sweare] swear *Ph, N, R*

336/419 to] so *Q2*

339/422 Iew] ~, *Q1-D, B, P, M, J, H, E, F*

340-41/423-24 possessions, . . . throates] ~ (. . . ~) *B-BP, Sp-Pg, H-Br*

342/425 wife] strumpet *Q2+*

345/428 King:] ~: *Fleeringly.| Du*

346/429 naturals] Animals *Du*

355/438 in that . . . my] in thy . . . the *Q2+*

356/439 I carrie] hath reference *Q2+*

357/440 Th'art] Thou art *S, Ph, R*

359/442 which,] ~ˬ *B, P, M, L, E, F*

364/447 earthie] Earthly *Du*

366/449 liu'st,] *P, Sp, M, E, F;* ~ˬ *L;* ~; *Q1-2 etc. subs.*

367/450 treacheries;] ~, *D, P, Sp, M, L, E, F*

368/451 friends] friends' *S, Ph, P-Pg, L, E, F*; friend's *Br*
    slaughters,] *Q1-2, J, H*; ~; *D*; ~, *S etc.*
369/452 And to] And do *S, Ph, N-Sp, Pg*
370/453 thinkest] think'st *S, Ph, P-Pg, L, E*
376/459 the] your *Du*
382/465 once wrong'd ... y'are] wrong'd ... y'are *Q2(u), E* (wronged), *F*;
    wrong'd ... you are *Q2(c)+*
387/470 that] and *J* (et *Jf*), *H*
390/473 curst] cursed *S, Ph, R, E* (all indeterminate), *F* (syllabic)
394/477 A perfect] *Q1, Pe, S, Ph, R, Br-F*; The purest *Q2 etc.*
395/478 to that wall] equal to *Deighton conj.*
396-97/479-80 tender ... lust;] ~; ... ~, *P, Sp, M, L*
405/488 Vertues] *Br*; vertues *Q1-2 etc.*
410/493 lou'st] lovest *S, Ph, P, R, BHN, M, E, F*
    mee,] ~; *S-Pg subs., E, F*
    SD *Exeunt.*] om. *Q1*

IV.i

SD] *The Banquetting-Hall in the Court.| B-BP, Sp, BHN, Pg*
SD *Henry*] *Enter* ~ *S, Ph, N, R, Sp, H, Br*
SD *Monsieur*] ~ *with a Letter.| Q2-F*
5 fare] foule *Q2+ exc. BP*
7 like,] ~, *Q1-D*
12 light] height *Q2+*
16 images] Idols *Q2+*
–/21 So ... them] *om. Q1, Br-F*
23/24 motions] faculty *Q2+*
25/26 *Buss.*] *Montsur.| Q2+*; *King.| Du*
27/28 predominance] divided Empires *Q2+ exc. S*
27-29/28-30 griefe ... grief's] Grief ... Grief's *Br*
28/29 claime] prove *Q2+*
29/30 And] *D'Amb.* And *Q2+*
    a naturall] natural *D*
32/33 t'a] to a *S, Ph, R*
34/35 SD *To the Duchess.*] subs., *D, P, BHN, M, L, E, F*; om. *Q1-2 etc.*
36/37 Nature] nature *BHN, L*
37/38 tyrannous] priviledge, *Q2, B, J, H*; privilege, *D etc.*; priviledged, *P conj.*
    (*Englische Studien, XXXVIII, 380*)
40/41 Valure] *BHN* (follows a full stop); valure *Q1-2 etc.*
50/51 Schoole of Modesty] *Q1-2, J, H, Br*; school of modesty *D etc.*
52/53 SD *To Bussy.*] *B-BP, Sp, BHN, Pg*; marked only with dash *M, E*; om.
    Q1-2 etc.
    bound] bar *Q2+*
59/60 do they] they do *S, Ph, P, R, BHN, M, E, F*
62/63 enough] ~, *S, P, BP, M, Pg*; ~. *Ph, N, R*
    it.] ~. *Passes from her scornfully.| Du*
63/64 Her] His *P conj.* (*Englische Studien, XXXVIII, 380*), apparently

withdrawn (cf. P ed., p. 556)

64/65 but] *Q1, Pe, S, Ph, N-R, Br-F; and Q2 etc.*

66/67 SD *Draws … converse.*] *aside to Bussy. Sp (so also ll. 69/71, –/77, 73/79, 91/97), Br; marked only with dash M, E; To Bussy. L; om. Q1-2 etc.*

67/68 strike] *not strike Q2+*

69/70 *Buss.*] ~ *aside to Monsieur Sp (so also ll. 71/73, –/77, 76/81)*

69/70-71 No … man] *Q1 (two apparent lines), Br (one verse as in this ed. of Q1), E (as in Q1, but line numbers account for only one verse), F (as in Q1, with line numbers for two lines); If he be wise, not. / Mons. What? not if I should name the Gardener, Q2+*

70-73/72-79 With whom … thee peace] *That I … thee peace [subs. as in this ed. of Q2] Q2+ exc. ll. –/77-78 divided As how? as how? / Perhaps … have / Your … out. / Mons. Peace … thee peace. Q2-Ph, R [See subsidiary note]*

        –/74 jest at] jest that BHN

74/80 that? the] *this to th' Du*

    King?] ~; *Du;* ~. *D;* ~! *B*

77-79/83-85 lawes … Torrents:] ~ (… ~); *Br*

79-81/85-87 glories (… flames, … hammes):] ~ ̭ … ~ ̭ … ~, *B and subs. N, Sp;* ~ (… ~) … ~, *P and subs. BP, BHN-Pg, L*

82-83/88-89 tortures: / All daring] *tortures ̭ / All-daring L*

83/89 you:] ~– *B-BP, BHN-Pg, Br-F*

86/92 toughnesse] *Q1, Du, Sp, Br-F; roughnesse Q2 etc.*

87/93 death] *Death P, BHN, M*

89/95 through] *thorow Q2+ exc. D (throrow Q2[u])*

90/96 aire] *Q1, Du, Br-F; the aire Q2+*

92/98 stild] *still'd Q2, D, B, P, BP, Sp-F; 'still'd S, Ph, N, R*

    Th'Armenian] *the Armenian D*

96/102 Nature] *nature Q1-Ph, N-Sp, J, H*

97/103 spirit] *minde Q2+*

98/104 effect] *desert Q2+*

106/112 is comming to afflict] *steales on to ravish Q2+*

107/113 fate] *Fate Q2, J, H*

111/117 SD *Exit Hen. with*] *Exit. King leaning upon| Du; opposite skie in l. 110/116 Q2*

    SD *Pages*] *om. Q1-2 etc.*

    SD *and Ladies*] *after them the Ladies.| Du; om. Q1*

112/118 SD *Aside to Monsieur.*] *P, BHN, M, E, F; om. Q1-2 etc.*

    Now … brawle] *as prose E (but line numberings do not concur)*

114/120 Lord.] ~. *makes horns at him| Du and subs. D, P-BP, Sp-Pg, H, L, E, F*

115/121 SD *Making horns.*] *Du subs., Jf, Br; om. Q1-2 etc.*

    What,] ~ ̭ *Q1-D, J, H, Br*

118/124 ensignes] *Branches Du*

124/130 noble man] *nobleman S, Ph, P-Pg, L-F*

125/131 SD *Producing a paper.*] *om. Q1-2 etc.*

127/133 mine] *my Ph, N, BP, R, BHN, Pg*

128/132 SD *Ent. Tamy., Pero.*] *after l.126/132 Q2, D, B, P, BP, Sp-L, E, F; om. S, Ph, N, R*
129/134 SD *Exeunt ... Monsieur.*] *om. Q1; after* vnder. *in l.128/134 Q2-F*
132/138 a–] ~. *Q1;* ~.– *Q2*
137/143 plaid] placed *S, Ph, R*
141/147 SD *She ... swoon.*] *om. Q1*
145-46/151-54 Sweete ... enough] *Q1, Br-F;* Sweet Lord, cleare up those
                eyes, unbend that masking forehead, / Whence is it you rush
                upon her with these Irish warres, / More full of sound then
                hurt? but it is enough *Q2, D, Pe, BHN, L; as in Q2, but
                divided as in this ed. of Q2| B, N; as in Q2, but divided* Sweet
                ... is it / You ... wars, / But ... enough *Ph, R; first line as in
                Q1 (*Sweet ... nobless /), *then as in Q2, but divided as in this
                ed. of Q2| S etc. [See subsidiary note]*
                    *145/– shame] love *BP*
                    *146/154 it is] 'tis *S*
150/158 thy] the *Ph, N, R*
151/159 SD *Seeming to recover.*] *om. Q1-2 etc.*
154/162 SD *Aside as she rises.*] Aside.| *D, P, Sp, BHN, H-Br; marked only
                with a dash BP, M, Pg, E, F; om. Q1-2 etc.*
158/166 inform'd:–] ~:ˎ *Q1-B, N-R, Pg-H;* ~. / To her| *Br*
163-64/171-72 merits: ... name ... memorie] ~, ... ~ˎ ... ~, *B, P, Sp, M, E,
                F;* ~, ... ~ˎ ... ~ˎ *BP, Pg, Br;* ~, ... ~, ... ~ˎ *L*
165/173 loth'd] just *Q2+*
172/180 stab'd] stabbed *Ph, R, E*
            SD *Making horns.*] *D, P, M, L, Br-F; om. Q1-2 etc.*
            hand] fingers] *Q2+*
173/181 him?] ~. *S-B, N-R, Pg*
174/182 beautie, ... prooues,] ~, ... ~; *S, Ph, R;* ~, ... ~ˎ *B-BP, Sp-Pg, E, F;*
            ~ (... ~) *L*
179/187 Augean] Egean *Q1-D, B*
181/189 Innocence] *P, BHN, M, Br-F;* innocence *Q1-2 etc.*
182/190 art] are *Q2, D, Pe, B, L*
185/193 teeth ... soile] venom'd teeth from whose curst seed *Q2+*
195/203 See] ~, *B*
196/204 Good] ~, *S, Ph, P, R, M, E*
197-99/205-9 Be ... pawne your honor;] Papers hold ... A hostage for it,
                [as subs. in this ed. of Q2] Q2(c)+ [See subsidiary note]
                    *198/208 your honour] the honour *Q2[u]* (?typographical
                        error for* thy honour)
202/212 much] *Q1, Pe, S, Ph, R, Br-F;* well *Q2 etc.*
206/216 which] that *Pg*
            shouldst] should *D, Pg*
207/217 my Lord] this touch *Q2+*
214/224 Resolue] ~, *D-Ph, N, R*
222/232 Borne] *Q1-2, B, J, H;* Born *D etc.*
            honours?] ~? Montsurry *offers to go.| F*

Ile attend your Lordship] but I will to him *Q2+*
224/234 Speake] Meet *Q2+*
–/236 To ... cursing him.] *om. Q1, Br-F*

IV.ii

IV.ii] *om. Q1-Ph, R*
SD] *A Room in Montsurry's House.| B-BP, Sp, BHN, Pg*
–/SD *Enter ... Frier.] om. Q1, Br-F; cf. collation of l. 7/25*
–/1-18 *Buss. I am ... despaire.] om. Q1, Br-F [See subsidiary notes]*
        *–/4 Mischiefe] *P, Sp-M, L;* mischiefe *Q2 etc.*
        *–/7 enrag'd, ... foming] ~ˌ ... ~, *S, Ph, N, R;* ~ˌ ... ~ˌ *B, P, BP,*
           Sp-Pg, L
        *–/17-18 All ... i'th'earth or aire / Can ... despaire] All ... done, /
           If ... i'the earth or aire / Can ... despaire *B, N, BP*
0/18 SD *Tamyra]* she| *Q1*
    ↝ SD *Pero her maid]* her maid| *Q1, Br;* Pero and her maid| *Q2, Pe, S, Ph,*
    R, L; Pero| *J, H*
1/19 SD *Exit Pero.] om. Q1; after lines Q2-Ph, R, J (but Jf places as in this*
    ed.), Br
–/19 SD *Aside.] marked only with dash Sp; om. Q1-2 etc.*
2/20 Fild] *Q1, Pe;* Fill'd *Q2 etc.*
2-3/20-21 hate) ... them| *subs. D, Sp, L;* ~ˌ ... ~) *Q1-2 and subs. S, Ph, N-R,*
    Pg-H, Br; ~, ... ~, *B etc. subs.*
3/21 his] *Q1, Pe, S, Ph, R, Br-F;* his curst *Q2 etc.*
7/– Father?] *om. Q2, D, B, P, BP, Sp-L*
    SD *Ascendit ... Comolet] Q1, S, Ph, N ('we must suppose that [they]*
    have withdrawn during Pero's presence'), R, Br, E (before Father*), F (as*
    in E); advancing| *P, Sp, BHN, L; om. Q2 etc.*
    SD *in a conjuring robe.]* in a| *Q1(u); om. Q1(c) etc. (cf. collation of*
    l. –/51)
7/25 my] mine *D*
–/27-29 Our ... it.] *Q2(c)+ (*our love is showne *Q2[u]); om. Q1, Br-F*
9-10/30 insensate ... fashion] cold dull Northern brain, what foole but he
    Q2+ exc. S; insensate stock, / Or rude inanimate vapour without
    fashion, / What cold dull northern brain, what fool but he *S (merging*
    words from both quartos)
21/41 within] in *F*
30/50 ye] *Q1, Pe, S, Ph, N, R, Br-F;* you *Q2 etc.*
–/51 SD *He ... robes.] om. Q1 (cf. collation of SD, l. 7/–)*
32/52 spiritalium] *spiritualium| Q2+, E, F*
33/53 Astaroth] Asaroth *Q1-2, B, N, Sp*
34/54 stygis] *Q1-D, Br;* Stygiis| *Du;* Stygis| *S etc.*
35/55 auerni] *Q1-D, Br;* Averni| *S etc.*
36/56 Magnatum] *magnatum| L*
    Noctis] *noctis| D, L*
37/60 SD *Thunder.] Q1 (in left margin opposite* -dita profundissima; *cropped*
    partially in most copies, completely in Huntington copy: hence presumably

Boas's statement that the SD is om. in Q1), Br; after l. 40/60 Q2+, E, F
39/59 spiritali] Spirituali *Du*
40/60 amabili] *amibili| Ph, R*
　　　SD *Ascendit ... Cartophylax*] Ascendit.| Q1-2, S, Ph, R, J; Spirit
　　　riseth.| D
　　　SD *and other spirits*] &c.| M, E; *and other* Devils Br; om. Q1-Ph, R, J
　　　SD *holding torches.*] H (after *Jf |porteurs de torches*), Br; om. Q1-2 etc.
47/67 call'dst] calledst Q1, Q2(*u*), D, B, L
　　　light?] Q1, Q2(*u*); ~, Q2(*c*), D, B, P, BHN, M, J, H, E, F; ~ˌ S etc.
56/76 Articulat] Articular Q2(*u*), D
58/78 one] Q1-2 etc. (*a damaged -e in Q2 caused B and P to attribute to Q2*
　　　the reading on)
63/83 will:–] Sp; ~:ˌ Q1-2 etc.
66/86 I ... darknesse] *two lines* (I will. /) Q1-B, N-R, BHN
71/91 SD *The torch returns.*] subs. Sp, M, H, L, E, F; *Re-enter* Cartophylax
　　　P, BHN, Br; om. Q1-2 etc.
72/92 come;–] Sp; ~;ˌ Q1-2 etc.
74/94 another,] ~ˌ S, Ph, P, R, M, E, F
76/96 SD *To Comolet.*] om. Q1-2 etc.
79/99 SD *apart*] above| P, M; om. Q1-2 etc.; *cf. discussions of alternate*
　　　stagings in B, N, BP, Pg, and Br
　　　SD *Mont.*] Mont. with a paper.| Q2-F
80/100 Beh.] D, F; Mons.| Q1-2, Pe, S (Mo.); Fr.| Ph etc. subs. (Com.| Br)
88/108 Beh.] Pre.| Q1 text, Q2; Per.| Q1 catchword
90/110 SD *Pointing to a paper.*] D subs.; om. Q1-2 etc.
　　　wherein you] where you may Q2+
91/111 Tragedy] Q1-2, J, H, L, Br; tragedy D etc.
102/122 stuffe] lines Q2+
113/133 SD *Enter ... Letter.*] Q2+ (*Enter above*| P, M), Br-F; om. Q1
114/134 Yet stay] Yet Ph², R
116/136 SD *Mont. stabs Pero and exit.*] Exit Mont.| Q1 (*after y'faith. in*
　　　l. 117/137); Exit Mont. and stabs Pero.| Q2 (*after Lord? in l. 116/136*)
117/137 This] That Pe, S, Ph, N, R, Sp
　　　ill] cruelly Q2+
120/140 be, at least, if not a] rather be a bitter Q2+
122/142-43 *Mons. ... Now ... Lord.*] Q1 (*two apparent lines*) *and* (*one verse*
　　　as in this ed. of Q1) Br-F; Guise. To you my Lord. / *Mons.* To
　　　me? Now out upon her. / *Gui.* Let ... Lord. Q2+ (To you ...
　　　upon her *one verse as in this ed. of Q2*| B-BP, Sp-L) [*See sub-*
　　　sidiary notes]
　　　　　*–/142 SD *Takes the letter.*] om. Q1-2 etc.
　　　　　*122/142 SD *Reads.*] L subs.; om. Q1-2 etc.
　　　　　*122/143 see,] ~ˌ Q1-2, H, J, Br
　　　　　　　*Lord.] ~? D
124/145 SD *Calls.*] marked only with dash L; om. Q1-2 etc.
　　　SD *Enter servant.*] om. Q1; *after* Pero? *in l. 123/144* Q2-B, N, R,
　　　Sp, Br

126/147 SD *Mons.*] *Montsurry*| *S, P*

127/148 SD *Servant ... out.*] *P, L (after* rise *in l. 126/147), Br; Lead her out.*|
   Q1-B, N-H, E, F (after rise *in l. 126/147 Q1-Ph, R; after* |Guise.| *in
   l. 126/147 SD B, N, Sp, BHN, J, H*

131/152 stayne] *P conj., Br, E;* stay *Q1, Ph, R;* die *Q2, B, J, H;* dye *D etc.*

132/153 With] In *Q2+*
   his] *Q1-2, Pe, S, Ph, P, R, M, L, Br-F;* her *D etc.*

138/159 let him curb his rage, with policy] curb his valour, with your policies
   *Q2+ (*policy *Smith conj.)*
   SD *suis.*] *the other Spirits.*| *D and subs. E, F; his Devils*| *Br*

143/164 reuoke] invoke *D*

163/184 wait] *Q1-2, B, J, H;* weight *D etc.*

167/188 ruine] raine *Roby conj.*

169/190 Print] taint *Q2+*

172/193 tracts] tracks *D*

173/194 from] by *Q2+*
   SD *Exeunt.*] *om. Q1*

V.i

SD] *A Room in Montsurry's House.*| *B-BP, Sp, BHN, Pg*

SD *Montsurry*] Enter ~ *D, Sp, H, Br*

–/SD *by the haire.*] *om. Q1; with hair dishevel'd*| *Du*

SD *Comolet*] *after them* ~ *Du; followed by the* Friar *D*

SD *Table.*] ~ *and exit.*| *Sp, BHN*

–/1-4 *Tam.* O help ... Lord.] *om. Q1, Br-F [See subsidiary notes]*
   *–/3-4 Tis ... willingly] *as one line Q2-Ph, R*
   *–/3 violent;–] *BHN;* ~;ˌ *Q2 etc.*

6-7/10-11 not (... imagine) ... proofes] *B, P and subs. BP, M, Pg, L, E, F;* ~,
   (... ~, ... ~) *Q1-D, J, H, Br;* ~, ... ~, ... ~, *S etc.*

15/19 then:] ~ˌ *Q1-2, J, H*

17/21 it] that *Q2+*

18/22 Nature] *Br;* nature *Q1-2 etc.*

19/23 of] off *Q2+*

21/25 honour] Honours *Du*

24/28 hatefull] secret *Q2+*

28/32 touch] tread *Q2+*

31/35 commit–] ~; *Q1*
   Good father cease:] Good Father cease: your terrors *Q2, S, Ph, R, L;*
   Good father, ceaseˌ your terrors: *D, B-BP, Sp-H (as separate line in
   Q1-Ph, N-R, BHN, Pg)*

36/40 *Com.*] *Q1-2, Br;* Friar.| *D etc.*
   God] heaven *Q2, D, B, N, BHN, J-L*
   ye] you *Q2+*

–/42-44 *Tam.* Father ... safety.] *om. Q1, Br-F [See subsidiary notes]*
   *–/42 I warrant ... daughter] *printed as if separate line D, S, Ph, R*
   *–/43 Pagan?] ~; *Q2, J, H*

38/45 heart] brest *Q2+*

39/46 Ope the seuentimes-heat] Stand the opening *Q2*, *Ph*, *P*, *BP-L*; Or stand the opening *Du*, *D*; Stand in the opening *B*, *N*; O'restand the opening *Smith conj.*; Ope the seven-times heated *Sp reading of Q1*

40/47 SD *Mont. turnes a key.*] Mont. *locks the door.| Du (after l. 38/45)*

41/48 O] For *Q2+*

    cares] woes *Q2+*

43/50 blasts] blast *Ph*, *N*, *R*

44/51 enraged] devouring *Q2+*

53/60 God] Heaven *Q2-B*, *N*, *R*, *BHN*, *J-L*

57/64 Vertue] *Br*; vertue *Q1-2 etc.*

58/65 Excuses damne her:] ~, ~ ~–! *Du*

60/67 rockes] Rock *Pulls her by the hair.| Du*

61/68 ruffin] *Q1-2*, *B*, *J*, *H*; ruffi'n *Br*; ruffian *Du*, *D etc.*

    laden for thy] rig'd with quench for *Q2+*, *E*

64/71 danc'd] danced *S*, *Ph*, *P*, *R*, *M*, *E*

69/76 inscrutable] instructable *Du*

76/83 face] Heart *Du*

81/88 there to] thereto *D*

84/91 distract] devoure *Q2+*

    humane] human *S*, *P-BP*, *Sp-Pg*, *L-F*

    state] Consort *Q2+*

85/92 wiues] wife's *D-Ph*, *P-Pg*, *E*, *F*; wives' *L*, *Br*

86/93 beasts.] ~.– *B*

87/94 not?] ~– *Dragging her.| Du*

88/95 sins] faults *Q2+*

95/102 Vertues] *D*, *Br*; vertues *Q1-2 etc.*

96/103 SD *Touching his sword.*] om. *Q1-2 etc.*

97/104 SD *Pointing to a rack.*] om. *Q1-2 etc.*

110-11/117-18 Execution, ... me;] ~– ... ~, *B*

117/124 wretched] wreathed *Du*

120/127 noblesse] nobles *D*

122/129-30 there] there with any shew / Of the like cruell cruelty *Q2+ subs.* (*om.* cruell *S*, *P*, *Sp*, *M*, *J*, *H*)

123-24/131-32 Their ... Thus they] Thus their ... They *L*

124/132 SD *Stabs her.*] om. *Q1*

    Lord] Heaven *Du*; lord *B*, *L*

    Lord.] ~– *Du*, *B*

125/133 wrongs] wrongs' *D*, *L*, *Br*; wrong's *S*, *Ph*, *P-Pg*, *E*, *F*

126/134 SD *Stabs her again.*] *Du subs.*; om. *Q1-2 etc.*

131/139 image] very image *Pg*

    Tyrannie] *Q1-2*, *J*, *H*, *Br*; tyranny *D etc.*

132/140 adulterie] Adultery *Du*, *Br*

    still] *Q1*, *Pe*, *S*, *Ph*, *R*, *Br-F*; ever *Q2 etc.*

133/141 like in ill] parallel *Q2+*

134/142 SD *Stabs her again.*] om. *Q1*

136/144 SD *Sheathing his sword.*] *P* (*dagger*), *M* (*dagger [after use]*); om. *Q1-2 etc.*

SD *Ent. servants*] om. *Q1*; at end of this line *Q2-B, N-BHN, Pg,*
H-Br; after *l.138/146 P, M, L-F*; *Ent. servant*| *J* (placed as in *Q2*;
the |-s| is defective in some copies of *Q2*)
SD *and ... rack.*] after *l.138/146 D, P, M, E, F*; at end of this line
with entry *Sp, H-Br*; |with an instrument of torture.| *BP, Pg* (both
placed as in *Sp*); om. *Q1-2 etc.*
now, Torture, vse] ~‸ ~‸ ~‸ *Q1-2, Br*; ~, ~, ~. *S*; ~, ~‸ ~. *Ph, R*
Torture] torture *D-Ph, N-BHN*
141/149 may weigh] weigh *F*
142/150 Stand, Vengeance,] ~‸ ~‸ *Q1-Ph, N, R, BHN, J, H, Br*
Vengeance] vengeance *Q1-B, N-R, J, H*
144/152 and husband.] *Q1, Br*; ~ ~? *Q2, D, J, H*; ~ ~! *S etc.*
–/154 SD *with a sword drawne.*] om. *Q1, Br*
147/155 religion?] ~– *S, Ph, N-BHN, Pg*; ~! *B, P, M, L, E, F*
148/156 SD *Falls and dies.*] *Q2-F* (~ ~ ~ *de saisissement.*| *Jf*); om. *Q1*
161/169 th'Antipodes] the antipodes *D*
165/173 meane] man *Pg*
166/174 innocent] worthy *Q2+*; faithful *Du*
167/175 SD *Releasing her.*] om. *Q1-2 etc.*
168/176 Ile] *aside* ~ *Sp, L*
in] with *Q2+*
169/177 SD *Writes.*] om. *Q1*
170/178 SD *Aside.*] om. *Q1-2 etc.*
173/181 his] this *B conj.*
181/189 all:–] ~:‸ *Q1-2 etc.*
182-83/190-91 I must ... creature] *as aside Smith conj.*
183/191 SD *To Servants.*] *L*; to the body of the Friar *B, Sp*; om. *Q1-2 etc.*
185/193 SD *Exeunt Servants.*] *B-N, Sp-M, H, L, E, F* (follows |in the arras.|
in *B, N,* and *Sp*); om. *Q1*; *Exeunt.*| *Q2 etc.*
SD *He ... Arras.*] *Q2+, Br-F* (*Br* adds |*Curtains closed.*|); om. *Q1*

V.ii (Q1); V.iii (Q2)

V.ii] *Br-F*; om. *Q1-Ph, R*; *Scena Tertia B etc.* In *Q2*, this scene, with added
lines, is transposed to follow *Q1 V.iii.56.*
SD] *D'Ambois' Apartments.*| *D, B-BP, Sp, BHN, Pg*
SD *D'Ambois*] *Enter* ~ *Ph, R, Sp, H-F*
SD *Pages.*] *Pages with Tapers.*| *Q2+, Br*; and *Magician.*| *Du*
V.ii.2/V.iii.2 Pages.] *Pa.*| *Q1-2, S, Ph, N, BP, J*; *Page.*| *Br*
SD *Exeunt Pages.*] *Br*; *Exit.*| *Q1*; *Exeunt.*| *Q2 etc.*
6 SD *Thunder.*] om. *Q1*
8 Crackes] Nods *Q2+*
SD *Enter Vmb. Comol.*] after burthen; *B-BP, Sp-Pg, L, E, F*
9 my] *Q1, Pe, S, Ph, R, Br-F*; deare *Q2 etc.*
13 heere?] ~; *S, Ph, N-BHN, Pg*; ~! *B, P, M, L, E, F*
–/15-16 And now ... imminent.] om. *Q1, Br-F*
15/17 vtmost] upper *Q2+*
25/27 rites] rights *N, BP*

38/40 powrs] *Q1*; pow'rs *Q2, D, B, J-Br*; powers *S etc.*; pores *Smith conj.*
40/42 dost] doth *D*
43/45 night] Night *BHN*
45/47 Or] Oh, *Du, D*
47/49 see in] shine in *Q2+*
48/50 sense is] men are *Q2+ exc. S*
50/52 faine] feign *D*
–/53 SD *Thunders.*] *Q2-F (Thunder.| D); om. Q1*
51/53 SD *cum suis.] om. D; with his* Devils. *Br; with attendant* Spirits.| *H and subs. E, F*
61/63 Fates] *B, P, Sp-Pg, L-F;* fates *Q1-2 etc.*
–/68 SD *Thunders.*] *Q2, J-Br; om. Q1; after* me? *in l.66/68 Pe, S, Ph, R; before |Exit| in l.67/69 D (Thunder), B etc.*
67/69 summons;] ~, *Q1, S, Ph, N, R*
  SD *cum suis.] Sp; with attendant* spirits.| *H; with* Devils. *Br; om. Q1-2 etc.*
68/70 fare well] farewell *S, Ph, R*
70/72 obay ... commands,] ~, ... ~ˌ *Q1, Pe*
72/74 will, to life:] ~: ~ ~, *Q1, Pe*
74/76 me and] me or *Q2+*
  or I] for I *D*
  soule] life *Q2+*
80/82 SD *Knocks heard.] om. Q1; One knocks| P, M, E, F; Knocks.| Q2 etc.*
81/83 SD *Calls to pages.] marked only with a dash Sp, L; om. Q1-2 etc.*
–/84 SD *with ... bloud.] om. Q1*
84/85 SD *Aside.] marked only with dash after* predictions. *in l.–/87 Sp; om. Q1-2 etc.*
  Spirit:–] ~:ˌ *Q1-2 etc.*
84-88/86-96 welcome ... And praies] To say ... She prayes [*subs. as in this ed. of Q2*] *Q2+ [See subsidiary notes]*
  –/87 predictions.–] Sp; ~.ˌ Q2 etc.
  –/90 death] deaths L
  –/91-92 If I ... beleev'd / Your ... give] S-L (divided line not indented in S, Ph, R); If I ... summons. / Monts. I beleev'd ... give Q2 etc.
  –/91 obey'd] obeyed Q2, D, B, BP, Pg-L
88/96 speediest] instant *Q2+*
  SD *Giving the letter.] om. Q1-2 etc.*
–/97-98 *Buss. Why ... him.] om. Q1, Br-F [See subsidiary note]*
  –/98 Mont.] Mons.| D
89/99 What] *Opening the letter* ~ *P, BHN, M, L, E subs.*
96/106 t'encounter] to encounter *D*
  death] Death *P, M, E*
  hell:] ~.– *Sp (for end of an aside?)*
98/108 SD *Exit cum Montsurry.] Exit.| Q1; Exeunt.| Q2 etc.*

V.iii (Q1); V.ii (Q2)

See the first note in the collation to V.ii (V.iii in Q2)

V.iii] *Br-F;* Scena Secunda *B-BP, Sp-L; om. Q1-2 etc.*

SD] *A Room in Montsurry's House.| B-N, Sp, BHN; Location indefinite.|*
BP, Pg

SD/– *aboue.] om. Q2+ (cf. collation of –/V.iv.22 SD)*

V.iii.1/V.ii.1 Nature] nature *Q1-Ph, R, J, H*

3 who] that *Q2+*

6 roote] *Q1, Pe;* rote *Q2 etc.*

7-12/7 In whose … incurre] *Q1, S, BP, Br-F;* Not knowing what they say
Q2 etc.

12/7 Nature] nature *Q1, Pe*

13/8 masse] deale *Q2+*

18/13 wee call] she calls *Q2-Ph, N-R, BHN, L*

19/14 beleeue] beliefe *Q2-B, N, R, BHN, L;* believes *BP (cf. collation of
l. 18/13);* he lief *Deighton conj.;* belive [*?for believe] Brereton conj.*
should] must *Q2-B, N-R, BHN, L*
arriue] arride *Deighton conj.*

20/15 and happinesse] happiness *Pg*

21/16 Right] *Q1, P, M-H;* Even *Q2 etc.*
whole] whose *Pe, S, Ph, N, R, Sp*

22/17 men thinke] me thinks *Q2, D, B, BP, BHN, L*
last, and gard them] last and guard *Q2, D, BHN, L;* last, and guards
Pe, S, Ph, R; lasting guards *Deighton conj.*

25/20 that,] ~ *Q1, S, Ph, N, R, Br*

29/24 Nature] nature *Q1, S, Ph, R*

30/25 decorum] proportion *Q2+*

33/28 an absolute] a perfect *Q2+*

34/29 whole] full *Q2+*

37/32 Why you shall] Yet shall you *Q2+*

38/33 mand] *Q1, D* (man'd); mann'd *Q2 etc.*

39/34 Nature] nature *Q2, D, J, H*

43/38 let it] let's it *Q2, Pe, B;* lets it *D-Ph, N-BHN, Pg*

45/40 rages … th'roote] rage … the root *Q2+*

46/41-43 full creature now] *Q1, Br-F;* whole man / (That will not wind
with every crooked way, / Trod by the servile world) *Q2+ exc. S;*
whole man, so this full creature now, / (That will not wind with
every crooked way, / Trod by the servile world) *S (merging words
from both quartos)*

47/44 purblinde] *Q1, Br-F;* blind borne *Q2, B, J, H;* blind born *D, Pe;*
blind-born *S etc.*
Chance] *Br;* chance *Q1-2 etc.*

48/45 thorow] through *Q2-F*

50/47 others] *Q1-2, B, J, H;* other's *D, N, BP, Sp, BHN, Pg, L, Br;* others'
S etc.
necke] necks *Ph², R*

51/48 Euxine] euxine *Q1;* Euxian *Q2, D, B, J, H, L*

53/50 darke-deepe] *Q1, Br*; dark deep *Q2 etc.*
54/51 Swell, ... enrag'd ... drop,] ∼ˌ ... ∼, ... ∼, *Q1, S, Ph, R, Br*; ∼, ... ∼,
　　... ∼, *P, BHN, M, L, E, F*
55/52 Fortune] fortune *Q2, D, B, J, H*
56/53 vertue] Virtue *Br*
　　mens] man's *F*
–/53 SD *Enter ... murtherers.*] *Q2+ subs. (disguis'd as the* Friar *P, BP,*
　　BHN-Pg, L); *om. Q1, Br-F*
–/54-59 Away ... will my Lord. *Exeunt.*] *om. Q1, Br-F [See subsidiary*
　　notes]
　　　　*-/54 SD *To Montsurry.*] *om. Q2 etc.*
　　　　*-/55 *Mont.*] Guise.| *Du*
　　　　　　*me vengeance] my vengeance *D*; me, vengeance *S-Pg,*
　　　　　　L; us then Vengeance *Du*
　　　　　　*vengeance] Vengeance *Du, Pg, L*
　　　　*-/56 SD *To the Murtherers.*] *om. Q2 etc.*
　　　　*-/59 *Murtherers.*] Murth.| *Q2-Ph, N, BP, Sp, J*; Murderer. *R*

　　　　　　　　V.iii continued (Q1); V.iv (Q2)
–/V.iv] *om. Q1-Ph, R, Br-F*
SD] *A Room in Montsurry's House.*| *B-N, Sp, BHN, Pg*
–/SD *Thunder.*] *om. Q1, D*
SD *Vmbra*] vmbra,| *Q1*
SD *to the Countesse ... He uncovers her.*] to the Countesse, *wrapt in a*
　　Canapie.| *Q1*; £and discovers Tamyra.| *Q2+ exc. D*; Tamyra *is discovered.*|
　　[preceding Umbra's entry] D; and discovers Tamyra, *wrapped in a*
　　canopy.| *Br-F*
V.iii.57/V.iv.1 Reuiue those] Up with these *Q2+*
–/1-4 still loved daughter ... woes:] *om. Q1, Br-F*
57-61/4-7 and sit not thus ... it;] oh can you sit ... it? *Q2+*
58/5 Gathering] Mustering *Q2+*
59/– (So ... imminent)] *om. Q2+ exc. S*
60/6 Into ... deuise] Before your contemplation, and not study *Q2+*
63/9 engag'd] revenged *Q2+*
65/11 humane] human *D, S, P-BP, Sp-Pg, L-F*
68/14 t'haue] have *Q2, J, H*; 't have *Sp*
69/15 Tis the iust curse of our abus'd] It is the misery of our *Q2+ exc. S (J*
　　prints both versions)
70-74/– Which ... maker.] *om. Q2+ exc. S, J (S and J include both ll. 70-74/–*
　　and –/15-21, which are alternatives in other eds.)
–/15-21 Your true friend ... opens.] *om. Q1, Br-F [See subsidiary notes]*
　　　　*-/15 Your true friend] *with* It is ... creation *as one verse as in*
　　　　　　this ed. of Q2| *Q2, D, Sp, L; as separate line S, etc.*
　　　　*-/16 shadow'd] shadowed *Q2, D, B, N, BP, Sp, J-L*
　　　　*-/19 him?] ∼. *Q2, D, J, H*
74/21 SD *Exit.*] *om. Q1, E, F*
　　SD *at the gulfe.*] Ascend from the Vault. *Du*

–/22 SD *Enter ... above.*] *om.* Q1, Br-F (*cf. collation of Q1 V.iii.SD/–*)
81/28 Murther'd? Who] Murder'd͜ who *Ph²*, *R*
–/32-35 If I ... ready.] *om.* Q1, Br-F [*See subsidiary notes*]
      *–/32 I scape] I escape *Du*; I 'scape *D, S, Ph*; i'scape *Ph²*, *R*
      *–/33 plotted,] ~͜ Q2, *S, Ph, R*
      *–/34 They] That *R*
      *–/34-35 They ... ready.] They ... rising. / I ... ready. *P, M*
88/39 fate] *D etc.*; Fate *Q1-2, J, H, Br*
–/40-41 *Mons., Gui.* Why ... villains? / *Buss.*] Q2+ (*aside| Sp*); *om.* Q1, Br-F
89/41 not come?] ~ ~! *D*
      SD *Enter ... other.*] *subs. Jf*, Br-F; *om.* Q1; *Enter murtherers with Frier at the other dore.| Q2 etc.; Enter* Monsieur, *and* Guise *Disguis'd, and* Murderers. *They all fall upon* d'Ambois, *who kills some, and beats out the rest, all but* Monsieur *and* Guise. *Du*
      1. Murth.] 1. Q1; *Mont.| Du*
90/42 *Omnes Murth.*] *Omn.| Q1-2 etc.*
      SD *Exeunt ... first.*] Q2-F (*first* Murtherer *P, BHN, H, L*); *Exeunt.| Q1*
91/43 *1 Murth.*] 1. *Q1-2, S, Ph*; *Guise.| Du*
      ye not] not they *Du*
      SD *Thrusts at him.*] *subs.* N, BP, Sp, Pg; *They fight.| H*; *om. Q1-2 etc.*; *cf. Du*: Fights with Guise *and* Mon.
92/44 SD *More thrusts.*] *subs.*, B, P, BHN, L; *Il lui donne un coupe d'épée, la cotte de maille de l'assassin empéche la lame de pénétrer.| Jf*; *om. Q1-2 etc.*
      Will] –~ *M, E, F*
93/45 SD *Kills him.*] *subs. D* (*after l. 94/46*), P, Sp (*after so*), BHN, M (*end of line*), L, Br (*as D*), E (*as M*), F (*as M*); *Stabs him in the face.| BP, Pg, Jf, H* (*head*); *om. Q1-2 etc.*; *cf. Du*: Disarms Monsieur, *and gets the better of* Guise, *when Three or Four attack him behind, whom he Kills*, Monsieur *and* Guise *Escape out*.
      so] ~! B, P, Sp-M, E, F
94/46 mistresse] *Q1-2, B, J, H*; mistress's *D*; mistress' *S etc.*
100/52 Earle?– my Lord?] *Sp* (Lord,); ~͜ ~ ~? *Q1-Ph, R, Br* (Earl, *S, Ph, R*); ~? ~ ~! *B, P, etc.* (lord, *all but B*)
104/56 truth] Truths *Du*
109/61 Enuies] *BHN, Br*; enuies *Q1-2 etc.*
      eie] Eyes *Du*
113/65 SD *others [murtherers].*] *Q1*; *all the murtherers.| Q2 etc.*
114/66 Cowards] Coward *D*
      off?] ~! *Ph, B, N, R, Sp, L*
117/69 thus.] ~͜ J; ~– Br
      SD *Fights with Bussy.*] *subs. Du*, D, B, P, BHN, M, Jf, H-F; *om. Q1-2 etc.*
      SD *D'Ambois ... down.*] *om. Q1*
118/70 Fauour my Lord,] ~ (~ ~) *Q1-2*; save my Lord, *Du*
119/71 him:–] *Sp*; ~:͜ *Q1-2 etc.*
120/72 SD *Pistols shot.*] *om. Q1*; *Pistolls shot within.| Q2 etc.* (*after l. 118/70*

Q2, S, Ph, R); *They* [i.e., Monsieur and Guise] *rush out behind him,*
and with Pistols shoot him.| Du
    Fates] fates *Q1, Pe*
122/74 slaues?–] *Sp*; ~?ˏ *Q1-2 etc.*
    Lord?] *Q1-D, J-L*; ~! *S etc.*
124/76 Death and Destinie] *Du, P, M, Br, E*; death and destinie *Q1-2 etc.*
    Destinie,] ~ˏ *Q1-D, J, H, Br*
125/77 D'Ambois:–] *Sp, L*; ~:ˏ *Q1-2 etc.*
–/88 SD *Struggles to rise.*] *om. Q1-2 etc.*
–/89-92 And if ... Groomes.] *om. Q1* [See subsidiary note]
        *–/90 SD *She ... him.*] *opposite ll. 137-38/93-94 Q2; after l. –/92*
            Pe, S, Ph, R
137/93 SD *Gets up.*] *Du; om. Q1-2 etc.*
139/95 make] let *Du*
139-40/95-96 vp ... Statue;] *Q1-D, J-Br*; ~, ... ~ˏ *Du, S etc. subs.*
141/97 fame] ~, *S, Ph, P-Pg, L, E, F*
143-45/99-101 Morne ... Euening] *P, BHN, M, Br-F*; morne ... euening
            Q1-2 etc.
143/99 perfumes] perfines, *Q1, Br* (perfines)
148/104 burning] curning *Pe*; cunning *S, Ph, R*
149/105 Beare] bear *D*
156/112 SD *To Montsurry.*] *subs. Du, D, P, M, E, F; om. Q1-2 etc.*
161/117 still'd] 'still'd *N, BP, Pg*
162/118 And] *Bus.* And *Q1*; Now *Q2+*; And now *Du*
167/123 SD *Kneeling by Bussy.*] *om. Q1-2 etc.*
174/130 broken.] ~ˏ *Q1-2, J, H*
175/131 nor these] not these *J (attributing to Dyce copy of Q2), H*
    Guise,] ~. *Q1, Pe*
176/132 death;] ~, *Q1-2 etc.*
177/133 prodigie–] ~: *Q1-2 etc. subs.*
178/134 gainst] in *Q2+*
179-80/135-36 Ossa (... snow), ... liuer, ... vains] *Br*; ~ (... ~ˏ ... ~;...ˏ ~)
        Q1-2; ~ (... ~ˏ ... ~) ... ~ˏ *D and subs. B-N, Sp-L*; ~ˏ ... ~,
        ... ~; ... ~ˏ *S, Ph, R*; ~, ... ~, ... ~, ... ~ˏ *BP, E, F*
179/135 endlesse] drifts of *Q2+*
181/137 Melt ... hungrie-torrents-eaten rockes] Meltˏ ... hungrie torrents:
    eating rockesˏ *Q1-Ph, N, R, Sp, J, H, Br*; Melt, ... hungry torrents
    eating rocks, *B*; Meltˏ ... hungry torrents, eating rocks, *P, BP,*
    BHN-Pg, E, F; Melt (... hungry torrents, eating rocks) *L* [See
    subsidiary note]
        *hungrie-torrents-eaten rockes] hungry, rockes-eating torrents
        Holaday conj.
182/138 humane] *Q1-2, Ph, B, R, J, H*; human *S etc.*
184/140 valure:] ~; *Q1-2*; ~, *Du, D etc.*
    vertue] *Q2, D, B, J-L*; ~, *Q1, S etc.*
187/143 it:] ~ˏ *Br*
189/145 stucke] strucke *B, N*

SD *Moritur.*] *om. Q1*

–/146-52 *Vmb.* Farewell . . . humanity.] *See collation at ll. 261-70/146-52*

190/– *Vmb.*] *Q1-2, Br-F (redundant in Q2); om. D etc.*

190/153 SD *To Montsurry.*] *D, B-BP, Sp, BHN, Pg, Jf, H, L, E subs., F; marked only with dash M; om. Q1-2 etc.*

191/154 t'haue begotten] to have begotted *D*

192-94/– (Since . . . bloud);] *om. Q2, D, B, P, BHN-L*

200/160 balme] blame *Pe, S, Ph, R*

202/162 sitting] *Q1, Pe, S, Ph, R, Br-F;* kneeling *Q2 etc.*

205/165 Piety] piety *Q1-2 etc.*

peace.] ~. *Exit* Umbra *P, Sp, M, Pg*

206/166 SD *Rising.*] *om. Q1-2 etc.*

Piety] *Br;* piety *Q1-2 etc.*

213-14/– My . . . stepdame:] *Q1, Pe, S, Ph, N-Sp, Br-F; om. Q2 etc.*

226/184 SD *Turning indecisively.*] *om. Q1-2 etc.*

husband?– . . . friend?–] ~?ˏ . . . ~?ˏ *Q1-2, J, H, Br;* ~! . . . ~! *D etc.*

conscience?] ~! *Q2-F*

–/185-86 *Mons.* Come . . . plaints.–] *om. Q1, Br-F [See subsidiary notes]*

*·–/185 SD *Aside to Guise.*] *om. Q2 etc.*

*·–/186 plaints.–] *Q2;* ~.ˏ *D etc.*

–/186 SD *Exeunt Guise, Mons.*] *om. Q1, Br-F [See Textual Note]*

SD *aboue.*] *B; om. Q1-2 etc.*

SD *murtherers below.*] *om. Q1-2 etc.*

SD *Bodies of D'Ambois and 1 Murth. are borne off.*] D'Ambois *is borne off.| Q2+; om. Q1, Br-F*

227/187 SD *Aside.*] *om. Q1-2 etc.*

230/190 SD *To Tamyra.*] *marked only with dash N, BP, Sp, BHN, Pg, L; om. Q1-2 etc.*

231/191 heere all things full] here all things are full *D-B, N, R-BHN, F;* here are all things *P* ('The word *are* . . . was probably omitted by mistake after *here*, or joined with that word in pronunciation'), *M;* here are all things full *Pg-H, E;* here're all things full *Br;* here be all things full *F conj.*

236/196 open'd] opened *Q1-2, B, N, Sp, J-L, E*

240/200 a hunted Tygres] *Q2+ exc. S, Ph, R* (tigress *in modern-spelling eds.*); hunted Tygres *Q1, Pe, and subs.* (tigers) *S, Ph, R, Br-F*

243/203 SD *Kneels.*] *om. Q1-2 etc.*

246/206 SD *Rises.*] *om. Q1-2 etc.*

Honor] *Br;* honor *Q1-2 etc.*

Honor,] *Q1-2, S, Ph, R, J, H, Br-F;* ~ˏ *D, etc.*

248/208 SD *Lifting a candle.*] *om. Q1-2 etc.*

253/213 sees] seres *Ferguson conj., J* (se consume *Jf*), *H*

255/215 his] its *Du, D, F*

SD *Inverting the candle.*] *om. Q1-2 etc.*

256-57/216-17 His . . . His] Its . . . Its *Du*

257/217 loue.] ~, *Q1;* ~ˏ *Q2, Br*

260/220 SD *Exeunt . . . severally.*] *Exeunt severally.| Q2+ (this line ending the play in these eds.),* F

261-70/146-52 My ... humanity.] *Q1, Br-F; transferred to follow l.189/145
S, Ph, N-Sp; om. ll.261-63/–, the rest transferred to follow
l.189/145 Q2 etc. [See subsidiary note]*

             *263/– selfe:] ~.– Sp

264/146 braue] drave *Ph* (brave *Ph²*)

         relicts] reliques *Q2+*

266/148 Ioine ... Hercules] *Jove* ... her rules *Q2, D*

268/150 continent cracke ... receit,] ~, ~ ... ~, *Q1;* chrystalḽ crack ...
receit: *Q2+;* continent, crack'd ... receipt, *Br, E;* continenṱ crack ...
receipt. *F*

269/151 th'aged] the aged *Q2, D, B, P, Sp-M, J-L*

270/152 new] the new *D*

         humanity.] ~.– *Sp*

270/– Exit.] *Br-F (this line ending the play in Q1 and these eds.); om. Q1-2 etc.*

Epilogue

Epilogue not in Q1; printed in Appendix A in Br

–/7 due;] ~̭ *Q2-Ph, J, H*

PRESS-VARIANTS

[Variants probably resulting from slipped types are only occasionally recorded, mostly for formes that are otherwise invariant.]

First Quarto

[BL¹ (British Library C.34.c.12); BL² (British Library 644.d.41); Bodl¹ (Bodleian Library Mal. 787); Bodl² (Bodleian Library Mal. 240[8], leaves cropped, sigs. A1 and I4 defective); CLUC (William Andrews Clark Library, University of California at Los Angeles); CSmH¹ (Huntington Library C4966.98515); CSmH² (Huntington Library C4967.87482); CtY (Yale University Library); DFo¹ (Folger Shakespeare Library 4966); DFo² (Folger Shakespeare Library 4967); Dyce (Victoria and Albert Museum 1034.16.Box 4.6); MH¹ (Harvard University Library 14424.13.4*); MH² (Harvard University Library 14424.13.5*); NN (New York Public Library); NNP (Pierpont Morgan Library); Worc (Worcester College Library, Oxford University).]

Sheet A (outer forme)
Corrected: BL², CSmH², CLUC, CtY, DFo², Dyce, MH², Worc
Uncorrected: BL¹, Bodl¹, CSmH¹, DFo¹, MH¹, NN, NNP
Uncertain (title page defective): Bodl²
Sig. A1
  Title page 1608] 1607

Sheet C (outer forme)
[Note: Although there are no stop-press corrections, there is evidence of instability of the types in this forme. With no consistent pattern, the following variants occur in the several copies; I do not identify variant copies, and the form to the left of the bracket is the correct form.]
Sig. C1
  II.i.54 Troy,] Troy͵
Sig. C2ᵛ
  II.i.151 th'account] th account
Sig. C4ᵛ
  II.ii.75 election,] election. [defective inking?]

Sheet D (outer forme)
?Corrected (probably slipped type): NNP
Uncorrected: BL¹, BL², Bodl¹, Bodl², CLUC, CSmH¹, CSmH², CtY, DFo¹, DFo², Dyce, MH¹, MH², NN, Worc

Sig. D1
II.ii.123 essen e] essence

Sheet D (inner forme)

Corrected: CtY
?Uncorrected: BL¹, BL², Bodl¹, Bodl², CLUC, CSmH¹, CSmH², DFo¹,
     DFo², Dyce, MH¹, MH², NN, NNP, Worc
Sig. D1ᵛ
II.ii.156 *Per.*] *Per*: [?]

Sheet E (outer forme)

Corrected: BL¹, Bodl², CSmH¹, CtY (partially cropped), DFo¹, MH¹, MH²,
     NN (partially cropped), NNP
Uncorrected: BL² (point cropped), Bodl¹ (partially cropped), CLUC, DFo²
     (partially cropped), Dyce, Worc (partially cropped)
Uncertain: CSmH² (SD almost wholly cropped)
Sig. E3
III.ii.130 SD *D'Amᵇ.*] *DA'mᵇ.*

Sheet G (inner forme)

First State Corrected: BL¹, BL², Bodl¹, Bodl², CLUC, CSmH¹, CSmH²,
     DFo¹, Dyce, MH¹, NNP, Worc
Uncorrected: DFo², NN
Sig. G2
IV.ii.7 SD *Comolet.*] *Comolet in a*

Second State Corrected: CtY, MH²
Sig. G4
IV.ii.138 SD *suis.*] *suis*:

[Note: Sheet G was incorrectly folded in Bodl¹.]

Sheet I (inner forme)

First State Corrected (pied type): DFo², MH² (type disturbed in V.iii.217 also)
Uncorrected: BL², Bodl¹, CLUC, CSmH¹, CSmH², DFo¹, Dyce, NN, Worc
Sig. I4   i
V.iii.226 consc ence] conscience

Second State Corrected: BL¹, CtY, MH¹, NNP
Sig. I4
V.iii.236 (Being] Being

Third State Corrected (probably pied type): Bodl²
Sig. I4
V.iii.224 heartvnbroken] heart vnbroken

Sheet I (outer forme)

Corrected: BL², Bodl¹, Bodl², CLUC, CSmH¹, CSmH², CtY, DFo¹, DFo²,
     Dyce, MH¹, MH², NN, NNP, Worc

?*Uncorrected*: BL¹
Sig. I4ᵛ
    V.iii.270 humanity.] humanity, [?]
[Note: On sig. I2ᵛ (V.iii.107), several copies appear to have a semicolon rather than a comma after 'bulwarke'; since the upper dot appears to be unstationary, I take it to be a foreign object that took ink for a time.]

Second Quarto

[BL (British Library 644.d.42); Bodl (Bodleian Library, Oxford University Mal. 163[7]); CSmH (Huntington Library DC1941 114344); CtY (Yale University Library; wants A1 and K4); DFo (Folger Shakespeare Library C1941); Dyce (Victoria and Albert Museum Dyce 2035.26.Box 4.7); ICN (Newberry Library); ICU (University of Chicago Library); MB (Boston Public Library); MH (Harvard University Library 14424.13.7*; wants K4); PU (University of Pennsylvania Library; wants K4); TxU¹ (University of Texas Library Ah.C366.B652; sig. A1 defective); TxU² (University of Texas Library Wh.C366.607bc); Worc (Worcester College Library, Oxford University).]

Sheet A (inner forme)
Corrected: Bodl, CSmH, CtY, DFo, Dyce, ICN, ICU, MB, MH, TxU¹,
      TxU², Worc
Uncorrected: BL, PU
Sig. A2
    Prologue 13 *doubting*] *oubting*

Sheet A (outer forme)
Sig. A1
    Title page [Note: The title page exists with three variant dates. I have not collated the later ones. According to Greg, each is a cancel and each is printed from a different setting of type from the original.]

Sheet B (inner forme)
First State Corrected: Bodl, CtY, ICN, MB, MH, Worc
Uncorrected (possibly poor inking): CSmH, DFo
Sig. B3ᵛ
    I.ii.98 *D'Amb.*] *D'Amb*,
Second State Corrected: BL, Dyce, ICU, PU, TxU¹, TxU²
Sig. B2
    I.i.222 their] the
[Note: On B3ᵛ of TxU², the semicolon after 'wife' (I.ii.96) does not print.]

Sheet B (outer forme)
Corrected: BL, Bodl, CSmH, CtY, DFo, ICN, ICU, MB, MH, PU, TxU¹,
      TxU², Worc
Uncorrected: Dyce

Sig. B3
  Signature B3] *omitted*
[Note: Certain other press-variants, occurring intermittently, are probably a result of poor inking rather than correction: (1) Five copies (Bodl, CtY, DFo, MH, Worc) seem to lack the hyphen in 'Demi-gods' on sig. B2ᵛ (I.ii.11); (2) three of those five (DFo, MH, Worc) read 'he' instead of 'the' on sig. B4ᵛ (I.ii.149); and (3) at I.ii.3 (sig. B2ᵛ), CtY has 'you h' for 'youth'.]

Sheet C (inner forme)

  Corrected: BL, CSmH, ICN, MB, PU, TxU¹, TxU²
  Uncorrected: Bodl, CtY, DFo, Dyce, ICU, MH, Worc
Sig. C2
  Catchword *omitted*] Then
[Note: In DFo, ICN, and TxU¹, a quad took ink approximately where the catchword should have been. On C1ᵛ, Worc has a variant presumably due to poor inking: 'Sh' instead of 'She' (II.i.23).]

Sheet C (outer forme)

  Corrected (possibly slipped type): Worc
  Uncorrected: BL, Bodl, CSmH, CtY, DFo, Dyce, ICN, ICU, MB, MH,
        PU, TxU¹, TxU²
Sig. C4ᵛ
  II.ii.23 you] you,
[Note: On sig. C2ᵛ (II.i.93), the apostrophe in 'seal'd' becomes increasingly faint and is not visible in Bodl and DFo.]

Sheet D (inner forme)

  Corrected: BL, Bodl, CtY, Dyce, ICU, MB, MH, PU, TxU¹, TxU², Worc
  Uncorrected: CSmH, DFo, ICN
Sig. D1ᵛ
  II.ii.78 triumph,] triumph.
Sig. D2
  II.ii.95 him,] him.
Sig. D4
  II.ii.242 importun'd] importud'd
  III.i.17 us,] us:
[Note: Poor inking resulted in two defective words in Worc: on sig. D1ᵛ 'fru tlesse' (II.ii.85), on D4 'dea h' (III.i.6).]

Sheet D (outer forme)

  First State Corrected: CSmH, ICN, MH, PU, TxU²
  Uncorrected: DFo
Sig. D1
  II.ii.32 Put-ofs] Puttofs
        44 poyson] poyson,
        58 you are] your are

Sig. D2ᵛ
  II.ii.129 me;] me.
     138, 140 know ... know] know ... know her
Sig. D3
  II.ii.177 any thing] ary[?] thing

Second State Corrected: BL, Bodl, CtY, Dyce, ICU, MB, TxU¹, Worc
Sig. D2ᵛ
  II.ii.138, 140 know her ... know] know ... know

Sheet E (inner forme)

First State Corrected: Bodl, CSmH, Cty, DFo, Dyce, ICN, ICU, MB,
          MH, PU, TxU¹, TxU²
Uncorrected: BL
Sig. E3ᵛ
  III.ii.116 deprave,] deprave:
     129 your] yours
     136   (Lady.   Lady.)
        Mistresse, honour'd] Mistresse (honour'd
     138 Madam.] Madam,
Sig. E4
  III.ii.146 ordnance] ordinance
     154 wise] wise,
        advantage,] advantage˄
     155 worst] woorst
     176 hope,] hope.

?Second State Corrected: Worc
Sig. E2
  III.ii.SD *D'Ambois.* [?]] *D'Ambois,*

[Note: On sig. E2 (III.ii.21) several copies (CtY, Dyce, ICU, MB, PU, Worc) appear to read 'haye' for 'have' because, I assume, of a stray inkmark.]

Sheet E (outer forme)

Corrected: Bodl, CSmH, CtY, Dyce, ICU, MB, MH, PU, TxU¹, TxU²,
     Worc
Uncorrected: BL, DFo, ICN
Sig. E4ᵛ
  III.ii.184 Lord,] Lord?
     190 sure   of] sure| of [inked space quad]
     192 speak :] speak|: [inked space quad]
     211 shot ... flew,] shot? ... flewe˄
     213 and] aud
        heart!] heart:

[Note: Initial letters in III.ii.177-78 (sig. E4ᵛ) are seriously pied in BL, DFo, and ICN and slightly pied in all other copies except Bodl. Poor inking on sig. E3 caused a defective word in Worc: 'disposit on' (III.ii.89).]

Bussy D'Ambois

Sheet F (inner forme)

Corrected: BL, CSmH, ICN, ICU, MB, MH, PU, TxU¹, TxU²

Uncorrected: Bodl, CtY, DFo, Dyce, Worc

Sig. F1ᵛ

III.ii.283 answering;] answering:

Sig. F2

III.ii.291 *Mouns.] Mount.*

299 veiles] vailes

317 *Maffe*] ‖ *Maffe* [preceded by inked M quad]

Sig. F3ᵛ

III.ii.408 heart] heart,

Sig. F4

III.ii.438 dunghill] dnnghill

Sheet F (outer forme)

Corrected: BL, Bodl, CSmH, CtY, DFo, ICN, MB, MH, PU, TxU¹, TxU²,
Worc

Uncorrected: Dyce, ICU

Sig. F1 :

III.ii.214 besides] besides:

227 busie] a busie

Sig. F2ᵛ

III.ii.327 bold] bol

Sig. F3

III.ii.356 I will then] then I will

359 her] the

Sig. F4ᵛ

III.ii.465 you are] y'are

486 and] anp

Sheet G (inner forme)

Corrected: BL, Bodl, CSmH, CtY, DFo, Dyce, ICN, ICU, MB, TxU¹,
TxU², Worc

Uncorrected: MH, PU

Sig. G1ᵛ

IV.i.35 therefore] thereforn

Sig. G2

IV.i.95 thorow] throrow

Sig. G3ᵛ

IV.i.199 resolv'd] resolv d [?]

Sig. G4

IV.i.207 them)] them,

208 your] the

Sheet G (outer forme)

Corrected: BL, Bodl, CSmH, CtY, DFo, Dyce, ICN, ICU, MB, MH,
TxU¹, TxU², Worc

Uncorrected: PU
Sig. G1
  IV.i.SD *Anable,*] *Anable*ˏ
      22 notes)] noteˏ
      26 joyes] joy
Sig. G3
  IV.i.153 her] her,
      154 hurt?] hurt:
Sig. G4ᵛ
  IV.ii.26 and] end
      27 infamy. Our] infamyˏ our
         knowne] showne
      34 consuming] consnming

Sheet H (inner forme)

?Corrected: BL, Bodl, CSmH, CtY, DFo, Dyce, ICN, ICU, MB, MH,
      TxU¹, TxU², Worc
?Uncorrected: PU
Sig. H1ᵛ
  IV.ii.97 acts] acts, [?]

[Note: It is not certain that PU has a comma after 'acts'. In all other copies
there are two spaces after the word; in BL the second space quad took ink.
On sig. H2, MH lacks a point after the speech prefix '*Gui*' (IV.ii.114),
presumably from poor inking. On sig. H3ᵛ, several copies have what could be
a period, rather than a comma, after 'commit –' (V.i.35). On sig. H1ᵛ, CSmH
has 'i ' for 'is' (IV.ii.92), and 'off nded' (IV.ii.106).]

Sheet H (outer forme)

Corrected: Bodl, CtY, DFo, Dyce, ICU, MB, PU, TxU², Worc
Uncorrected: BL, CSmH, ICN, MH, TxU¹
Sig. H1
  IV.ii.67 call'dst ... light,] calledst ... light?
      76 Articulat] Articular
Sig. H2ᵛ
  IV.ii.150 *Frier.*] *Com.*
Sig. H3
  V.i.5 seek,] seek| [space quad taking ink]
[Note: On sig. H4ᵛ, Worc had 'secu e' for 'secure' (V.i.90).]

Sheet I (inner forme)

Corrected: BL, Bodl, CSmH, CtY, DFo, Dyce, ICN, ICU, MB, MH,
      TxU¹, TxU², Worc
Uncorrected: PU
Sig. I3ᵛ
  V.iii.64 sheeres] sheeres, [?]

Sheet I (outer forme)
First State Corrected: BL, DFo, PU
Uncorrected: CSmH, ICN, MH
Sig. I1
Page number 61] *illegible*

Second State Corrected: Bodl, CtY, Dyce, ICU, MB, TxU^1, TxU^2, Worc
Sig. I3
V.iii.8 burthen] burtnen

Sheet K (inner forme)
Corrected: BL, Bodl, CSmH, CtY, DFo, Dyce, ICN, ICU, MB, MH, PU,
TxU^1, TxU^2
?Uncorrected (?poor inking): Worc
Sig. K2
V.iv.131 Fate,] Fate͵

TEXTUAL NOTES

In addition to previous editors of *Bussy D'Ambois*, the scholars whose views are commonly represented in these notes include the following: Parrott (usually his 'Notes on the Text of *Bussy D'Ambois*,' *Englische Studien*, XXXVIII [1907], 359-95; occasionally his edition of Chapman); Berta Sturman ('The 1641 Edition of Chapman's *Bussy D'Ambois*,' *HLQ*, XIV [1951], 171-201); Peter Ure ('Chapman's "Tragedy of Bussy D'Ambois": Problems of the Revised Quarto,' *MLR*, XLVIII [1953], 257-69); A. S. Ferguson ('The Plays of George Chapman,' *MLR*, XIII [1918], 1-24); Robert P. Adams ('Critical Myths and Chapman's Original *Bussy D'Ambois*,' *Renaissance Drama*, IX [1966], 141-61); Albert H. Tricomi ('The Revised *Bussy D'Ambois* and *The Revenge of Bussy D'Ambois*: Joint Performance in Thematic Counterpoint,' *ELN*, IX [1972], 253-62; 'The Revised Version of Chapman's *Bussy D'Ambois*: A Shift in Point of View,' *SP*, LXX [1973], 288-305; and 'The Problem of Authorship in the Revised *Bussy D'Ambois*,' *ELN*, XVII [Sept. 1979], 22-29); R. Corballis ('Bussy D'Ambois: The Textual Problem Once More,' *Journal of the Australasian Universities Language and Literature Association*, XLV [1976], 80-90); Gunilla Florby (*The Painful Passage to Virtue: A Study of George Chapman's* The Tragedy of Bussy D'Ambois *and* The Revenge of Bussy D'Ambois, Lund Studies in English 61 [Lund, 1982]), particularly the chapter called 'The Relationship Between the Original and the Revised Version of *The Tragedy of Bussy D'Ambois*,' pp. 25-69); and E. A. Abbott (*A Shakespearian Grammar*, New Ed. [1874]).

Prologue (Q2 only)

These lines, like the Epilogue also added in Q2, were written for some revival of the play (1634 according to Parrott, 1622-4 according to Freehafer). They do not sound to me like Chapman's work, and no one except Freehafer has claimed them for him. Even if Freehafer's general theory is correct (see my Textual Introduction, p. 12), it does not follow that the Prologue 'must be the work of Chapman, because no living author of Chapman's time is known to have allowed [*sic*] anyone else to revise one of his plays or to write a prologue for one of them.'

I.i

10 Tympanouse statists/men meerely great] All commentators agree that the Q1 reading is 'a typically Chapman phrase' (Sturman), less simple and 'peruiall' (and perhaps therefore less theatrical) than the revision. (For Chapman's rejection of the 'peruiall' in poetry see *The Poems of George Chapman*, ed. Phyllis Bartlett [New York, 1941], p. 49.) 'Statist' is first

cited by the *NED* from 1584 (but was 'very common in 17th c.'); 'tympanous' may have been a Chapman coinage: This usage antedates the first *NED* citation, from Middleton's *A Game at Chess* (1624): 'His proud tympanous master, swell'd with state-wind' – possibly, in its yoking of Chapman's two concepts, an echo of the Q1 reading. Florby puzzled over the change (and the alteration of Q1's 'forging' in l. 8):

> These two phrases are part of Chapman's rendering of a passage from Plutarch's *Moralia*. ... His use of the double sense of 'forge' and his choice of the inkhorn word 'tympanous' bring out the sense of deception and hollowness, integral parts of Chapman's treatment of [the theme of appearance and reality]. ... The phrase replacing the flamboyant 'tympanous' is a closer rendering of the original. ... Had he forgotten the subtlety of 'forge'? It would not be the first instance of forgetfulness on Chapman's part ...

12 maners crueltie] Most modern editors have made 'maners' a possessive, which may be the nearest we can come, in modern punctuation, to Chapman's intention but is not really adequate. The line is structured chiastically with ellipsis: sourness as to countenance; as to manners, cruelty. The relationship is not possessive. Dilke's series (taken from D'Urfey) is impossible.

26 staid] Dilke's spelling, 'stayed', conveys the correct meaning (*NED*, s.b. stay, v^1.20c.; last citation 1590). Fraser's gloss, 'sober,' misses the point, as does Jacquot's translation, 'grave.'

31 world/earth] While it is impossible to determine the reason for the many small changes in Q2, a number (such as this one) seem to have been motivated by a desire to eliminate repetition (here, of the word 'world' from l. 23).

82 wish me doe/wish me] Q1's 'doe' is hypermetrical and unnecessary. I suspect that the manuscript copy for Q1 had a marginal correction, 'doe', for 'doth' (a grammatical slip by Chapman) in l. 80, and that the compositor misinterpreted it as an addition to l. 82. If so, Q2 presents a restoration of Chapman's first intention.

89 Dame] I accept Parrott's emendation from 'Dames' – an easy error because the next word begins with 's-'; cf. *NED*, s.v. 'Dame,' 6.c. Evans's emendation to 'dame-school mistresses' is very appealing. ('Schoolemistresses their' probably = 'schoolmistresses''; see *NED*, s.v. 'Their', B.4) There are various references in Latin to schoolmistresses as teachers of poisoning (e.g., Tacitus, *Annales* XII.13), but Chapman's allusion, which is unidentified, sounds sexual – and contemporary.

119 SD *Rising.*] Bussy gets up from the ground at some point before the scene ends, and, though there is no sure way of knowing when, it should in reason be before Maffe arrives. The hope of advancement offered by Monsieur has removed Bussy's resignation.

–/122-26 Like ... soyl] Except for Sturman, most commentators have found the ring of Chapman in these lines, and Evans adopted them, influenced in part by the reminiscence (discussed by Ferguson and questioned by Jacquot) of Seneca's *Hercules Oetaeus*. N. Brooke rejected the revision 'with misgivings' because he felt (irrelevantly and I think wrongly) that the integration was clumsy. (Harrier's conjecture, 'this … soil' for 'his … soil,' on the ground that Q1 denies Monsieur's husbandry, is misguided.)

126/130 with/for] A fair number of prepositions and other particles are changed in Q2 without evident purpose or effect. Some of them could be the result of transmission errors, but in general Ure is probably right in regarding them as a result of Chapman's fussing with the play.

152/156 A Passe/His Passe] I assume (as Ure seems to have implied) that the Q2 compositor's eye skipped up to the beginning of l. 151/155 by mistake.

183/187 scholar/Poet] Nearly everyone agrees that 'Poet' (Q2) is weaker. Like Parrott and N. Brooke, I suspect corruption by attraction to 'Poetise' in the next line; 'Poet' in l. 165 may also have continued to influence this line.

192/195 SD *Touching his sword.*] Some such threatening gesture is required to give another level of meaning to Bussy's question and justify Maffe's quick reconsideration (and his degrading reference to the Vice's wooden dagger). Cf. 'lead you a dance,' I.ii.214/231. D'Urfey's direction, '*Turnes him about.*', with its implication of physical contact, could reflect stage practice.

196/199 my Lord/His Grace] The revision was perhaps intended to clarify the referent, but some of the many revisions of titles in the play could be transmissional mistakes.

204/207 Ambo] The spelling may reflect Chapman's pronunciation of Bussy's surname (cf. 'oboe' from *hautbois*); see also the notes to ll. –/208-10 and to III.i.SD.

–/208-10 How … mercy *D'Amboys*] Hardly 'comedian's gagging,' as N. Brooke dismissed the lines; I see no gags at all, but mocking sarcasm. It is consistent with Bussy's character not to allow Maffe's distortion of his name (the omission of the honorific 'D'' – not, I think, the pronunciation 'Ambo') to pass unchallenged, as it does in Q1.

206/212 Serue God/If you be thriftie and] Like Ure, I accept Parrott's assumption that Q2's change was made because of a broad interpretation of the Blasphemy Act of 1606, and is therefore without authority.

216/222 sown/set] The metaphor is the same with either reading; see *NED*, s.v. 'Set', *v.*, 12. Q2 'is related more accurately to fruit trees' (Evans); Ure compared *The Tragedie of Byron*, III.i.25-26.

I.ii

SD *Annable*] The name of this English lady in the French court is spelled in various ways in the two quartos, the most recognizable (from an English point of view) being '-bell'.

–/SD *Table, Chesbord, and Tapers.*] I follow Shepherd in transferring this direction from its Q2 location at I.i.149-51/153-55, where it was (as several commentators have said) surely a prompter's warning. Q1, with its sparser indications of theatrical business, has no such notation, although it is clear that a chessgame (with its symbolic accoutrements) occurs in that version as well. See the Textual Note to l. 67/70.

11 Semi-gods/Demi-gods] 'Semi-gods' is a Chapman word (*Hesiod*, I.254).

N. Brooke was probably right in thinking 'Demi-gods' an instance of normalization.

51/53 wee/we more] The addition of 'more' in Q2 was probably a compositor's conscious or unconscious sophistication. The antithesis between 'they' and 'wee' sets up an expectation of a comparative conclusion, but the explanation that follows merely *equates* the faults. (If 'more' is correct, possibly 'and' was marked for deletion.)

–/56 Holding ... vaunts] The Q1 compositor probably left out this line by oversight. Discussion has centered on the issue (ultimately irrelevant to the authorship question) of whether this clarifying addition is 'successful'. I agree with Ure that it is hard to object 'unless we believe that "obscurity in affection of words" is in some way more poetic than the "perviall". But Chapman would not have thought so.'

64/– shee's not shamelesse] I suspect that Q2 cancelled these words inadvertently. I see no other evidence to support Parrott's assumption that Chapman was aiming at greater terseness for Bussy. There are a number of instances, however, in which the compositor's attention to manuscript corrections (in this line 'They' for 'He') apparently caused him to omit nearby matter that was supposed to be retained.

67/70 SD *Henry ... chess.*] That Henry and Guise play a chessgame during this scene is clear from Henry's resignation ('You haue the mate.') in l. 148/164 (which should not be marked, as it is in two editions, by a direction for *Henry* to move a piece). When the game begins is not clear, but Henry's dominant part in the earlier conversation makes it unlikely that he was then playing chess; I follow Jacquot in starting the game here. In D'Urfey's version, the game begins after l. –/85: that is, after the King's final conversational exchange. Guise's angry rebukes to Bussy, of course, come during the game, which ends with Guise declining a rematch (after his ironic victory) and storming offstage.

–/84-86, –/94-104] The bawdy wit and ironic courtliness of these lines are quite consistent with one aspect of Chapman's style, and Ure thought them 'good'. N. Brooke, however, found in them 'nothing distinctive of Chapman' and, like Evans, thought they came from the theater (and thus, by their thinking, not from Chapman). Florby agreed that there is nothing distinctive of Chapman (except for the riddles), but nonetheless thought the interpolation genuine because it coheres with what she found as a 'principle behind the majority of the changes': 'developing an idea, elaborating a phrase or a scene.' (She analyzes the links in imagery with other parts of both versions.) Lines –/84-86, at least, could have been omitted from Q1 by mistake.

86/93 SD *Enter ... Pyrhot.*] The different placement of this entry in the two quartos is insignificant. Bussy's antagonists must enter in time to observe and react to some of the conversation. N. Brooke's vague 'During the last speeches enter ...' is good enough for an editor, but of course a prompt-book would be precise. The quartos do not differ on the placement of the similar entry of Brisac and Melynell below (l. 182/198).

92-95/110-13 Saucie ... for that] Most editors since Parrott mark these words 'aside,' apparently because Bussy refers to Guise in the third person. While possible, this interpretation seems to me less faithful to Chapman's apparent intent than having Bussy audaciously affront Guise. Bussy would not, in Chapman's conception of him, have taken in apparent silence the insulting language of Guise, and the third-person reference (as if talking to others about Guise) heightens the sarcasm.

106-7/130 more Courtship, as you loue it/Another Riddle] The interpolation by Q2 of the same phrase ('Another Riddle') twice within thirteen lines (see l. –/114), in a passage that was considerably marked up (in the copy for Q2) with transpositions and additions, raises the distinct possibility that one of the two interpolations was a mistake.

114/– Gui. So Sir, so.] Probably the beginning of a speech or dialogue that concludes 'Leaue your Courtship/ Courting' (l. 122/138); the middle is in pantomime as we listen to the other courtiers. The present line was omitted from Q2, possibly by accident: The lines just before it were marked for transfer, and the compositor of Q2 could well have failed to notice that seven lines below (as the lines appear on the Q1 page) was a lone line at the bottom of the page not marked for deletion.

141/157 starr's] Apparently the Q1 compositor's (or Chapman's) spelling of 'stars' (here = 'stars''); cf. 'hurl's' and 'Call's' (II.i.8, 20) and see my Textual Introduction, n. 10.

149/165 SD After ... Ladies.] Q1 omits the necessary exit for the ladies. Q2's placement seems, as N. Brooke said, 'quite arbitrary'. G. Blakemore Evans suggests to me that having the women onstage longer gives Bussy something to do while Barrisor, Pyrot, and L'Anou talk among themselves. On the other hand, their conversation is entirely for Bussy's benefit, and he is presumably to be thought of as paying attention to it.

156/172 Mercers] Most editors make the word singular, apparently because of the proverbial reference to 'mercer's books'. But the proverb alludes to a gallant's debts (NED). I think N. Brooke correct in making the word plural, assuming the reference is to mercers' fashion books.

176/192 sits] The word is correct; see NED, s.v. 'Sit', v., 16. More than half of the previous editors emended to 'fits'.

183/199 Pyrh./Bar.] Q2's reassignment of this and the next two speeches could be the result of the collator's error. But the changes seem deliberate and may have been intended to allow Barrisor, leader of the guisards here, to set the tone of antagonism to Bussy: Note that Q2 introduces into Barrisor's speech 'jealousie' in place of Q1's 'credulitie'; thus, the next speaker's jibe at 'jealousie' (spoken by Barrisor in Q1) becomes an echo instead of a new thrust.

II.i

SD Beaumond, and Attendants./Montsurry, and Attendants.] The entry of Nuncius at this point is an obvious mistake presumably derived, as N. Brooke said, from 'Chapman's list of characters for the scene.' The change to

Montsurry in Q2 has been plausibly explained by Parrott as a means of letting him learn of Bussy's pardon, since the lines that serve that purpose in Q1 were cut from II.ii in revision. About half of the previous editors have retained Beaumond as well as Montsurry on the assumption that Beaumond's name was deleted by mistake. The only reason for such an assumption is that *Beau.* appears in Q2 as the speech-prefix for l. 105 and in an exit at l. 206, but the latter is certainly an error (since there is no exit for Montsurry) and the former is probably wrong (since Montsurry is given no speech). Probably the collator (of Q1 with the prompt-book) who prepared the copy for Q2 overlooked the later changes.

27 his/their] Q1's 'his' is grammatically preferable, and 'their' could have resulted from a copyist's or compositor's error by attraction to 'words'. But 'their' is supported by the logic and the psychology of what the Nuntius is saying: He wants a platform as high as mountains, not a particular mountain. The change is probably deliberate.

43-45 resolute alike; ... wood ... spirit,] Q1 punctuates 'alike, ... wood: ... spirit,'; Q2 has commas in all three places. Most editors since Dilke have repointed substantially as I have done. The colon after 'wood' in Q1 is a normal equivalent of the modern comma and should not mislead: It signals the break between the protasis and the apodosis of its sentence and does not (as N. Brooke thought) '[stress] that ll. 45-7 are all expanding the image of [l. 44]' (cf., for example, I.i.27). Still less does it justify Evans's construction of the preposition 'Like' (l. 44) as an adjective modifying 'bonfires' (which he saw as appositional with 'Defendants'); or of 'formes' (l. 47) as the object of 'shew'd', which should be read as intransitive. Each man's demeanor shone with a fire mutually communicated among the three; like mirror reflections, each one manifested identical images ('Like formes') of life and death (i.e., commitment to the same fate). It is, however, typical of Chapman that relationships among subordinate elements can squint in more than one direction.

133 outright?/outright but hee?] The Q2 compositor seems to have made a number of errors in a short space, here duplicating from the next speech the words 'but he'. Parrott saw a problem in having Henry ask about 'All' when he has just been told that Bussy was 'Vntoucht', but 'All' refers to 'others' or, generally, to that large group of dead men.

135 feebled/freckled] As everyone except Sturman and Fraser has agreed, the compositor of Q1 here must have misread copy. *NED* cites Chapman's *Revenge* for the first use of 'freckle' in this sense, and the compositor was probably unfamiliar with the term. Q2 corrected. If I were attempting to establish only one text of *Bussy*, I would follow Q2 here.

163-64 Butchers, ... forgiuen!] Evans claimed credit for emending Q1-2's 'forgiuen?', but the change was first made by Boas and then by three other editors. Interrogation points were frequently used to mark what we punctuate as exclamations. Henry's last line essentially restates his opening, and Monsieur's 'O no' (l. 165) is not an answer to a question, but a disagreement.

166 full men/true men] All recent commentators are agreed that Q1 is more characteristic of Chapman, but the reviser altered both this one and, at V.iii.46/V.ii.41, 'full creature' (to 'whole man'). 'True men' is something of a cliché, but there is only slight difference between 'true' and 'full'.

166 men;] The quartos have commas both here and after 'law' (l. 167), and l. 167 could be construed with what precedes it almost as easily as with what follows. Editors have divided on where to put the stop, but all recent ones point as I do.

193 God/law] This change may have been motivated by censorship, the removal of blasphemy on the stage.

204 King/Law] With the words 'law' and 'king' reverberating through this speech, either reading could be a compositor error by attraction, but the parallels of ll. 203-4 seem to call for 'King' to complete the figure.

207/– Mort dieu,] All commentators agree that the phrase was omitted from Q2 because of censorship.

–/210-18] The substitution by Q2 of nine lines for Q1's two was made in connection with the deletion of fifty lines at the beginning of the following scene; they provide a bridge into what remains of that scene. Sturman and Brooke condemned the style of the new lines, but it is in general not inconsistent with that of Chapman's work in comparable passages of routine business (e.g., V.ii.1-2/V.iii.1-2); in particular, 'deeds of height, / And hard to be atchiev'd' and 'No check in his Rivality' sound to me like Chapman's writing. (Florby, however, called the Q1 version 'brilliant' and Q2 'blurb-like' and 'botched' – not Chapman's.) Sturman also objected that the new passage (especially l. –/213) does violence to the character of Bussy, changing him from a direct man, incapable of intrigue, into a 'deliberately deceitful D'Ambois.' No doubt Bussy's new speech makes things more explicit, but there is in fact no alteration of the main lines of Q1 (even if that were relevant to the authorship question). The correction of this man of 'vertue' has already begun in both versions: To oversimplify, five men died because Bussy did not like some remarks about his clothing! And he pretended to court the Duchess ('for show'), then (one act later) wooed and won Tamyra – in both versions. Corballis, though not denying Chapman's authorship, thought the added confrontation between Bussy and Guise 'clumsily organised' and 'quite detached from what has gone before'; but it seems clear that, here as elsewhere, Chapman was sacrificing one effect for another.

II.ii

SD Pero walking apart with a Book,] The book is not specified in Q1's stage direction, but is certainly present (see l. 108/58). That Pero is onstage during this scene of seduction is surprising to modern sensibilities, and Dilke postponed her entry until she is called (l. 108/58); but Parrott cites comparable situations in All Fooles and Monsieur D'Olive.

1-50/–] The cut in Q2 of fifty lines at the beginning of this scene has occasioned much comment. The omitted passage has essentially three parts:

(1) Montsurry and the ladies, especially Tamyra, discuss Bussy's behavior at court (dramatized in I.ii), and, though all the women comment adversely on his bluntness, Tamyra seems to admire his 'great spirit'; (2) in a brief passage Guise enters in high dudgeon because 'D'Ambois is pardond' (thus fulfilling a prediction made by Montsurry in the first line) and takes Montsurry off to 'consult of this'; (3) left alone, Tamyra expresses her torment that her 'name and house' and her 'religion to this houre obseru'd' cannot any longer withstand her 'licentious fancy', in the gratification of which 'that holy man / That, from my cradle, counseld for my soule' will be an agent. Most editors have printed the passage, even if following Q2 in general, and no later editor has agreed with Dilke's judgment that the omitted lines are 'without intrinsic merit.' Parrott omitted them, however, as lacking 'anything of dramatic importance.' There can be no question, as Parrott said, that the cut, so carefully prepared for by the addition of Montsurry to the list of characters in II.i and by the rewriting of the end of II.i, was deliberate, and I see no reason to doubt that the deliberation was Chapman's.

Ure agreed with Parrott's judgment, and supposed that the reviser was cutting lines (which partly duplicated material in a previous scene) to balance the length of the additions already made in the play. Brooke, however, pronounced Parrott's judgment 'utterly mistaken' and thought the reviser had omitted 'one of Chapman's most interesting achievements' out of 'distaste for Chapman's attitude to passion' and for Q1's 'making the time overlap with the end of II.i.' Sturman argued that the omission alters the character of Bussy and, especially, Tamyra. Ure successfully refuted her argument, and many details demonstrate that Bussy is not 'any more active in [Q2] than in [Q1], or Tamyra any more passive' (Ure). Tricomi has recently argued for significant changes in Tamyra ('The Revised Version of Chapman's *Bussy D'Ambois*'), and Corballis has concluded that the reviser 'meant to shift the responsibility for instigating the affair from Tamyra to Bussy', but both have also recognized that such changes, even if present, do not prove that another mind conceived them.

Florby, who felt that the omission 'does serious damage to the play,' suggested that the lines were removed out of 'deference to religion.' Though in the revised version overall the 'friar retains his role as pander, ... the offending collocations of certain concepts such as tossing temples in the air, bars (i.e. the friar) made engines, "not my name and house nor my religion ... can stand above it," "that holy man ... an agent for my blood," are no more.' Even if such a motive were credited, it would be hard to believe that it would have resulted in a wholesale deletion of the entire passage.

93/43 SD *Spurning it.*] Tricomi is surely wrong in saying that Tamyra offers Bussy 'Monsieur's pearl necklace' at III.i.–/61 ('The Revised Version of Chapman's *Bussy D'Ambois*' and 'The Problem of Authorship'). See her words of rejection at l. 96/46.

111/61 *Mont./Tam.*] Q1's speech-prefix must be wrong. Perhaps it was caused by Chapman's deciding to add this speech after he had written the speech-prefix intended for l. 112/62, and then neglecting to change it.

122/72 Parliaments] Q2 inserts a comma after 'Parliaments', ambiguously allowing construction of the phrase 'after Parliaments' with what follows or what precedes. Along with about half of the previous editors, I have followed Q1 in construing the phrase with the generalizing words that follow. The precise meaning of the passage is not known. It sounds like an echo of some comment relevant to the sparring between Parliament and James in 1604 over their respective prerogatives; see Faith Thompson, *A Short History of Parliaments 1295-1642* (Minneapolis, 1953), pp. 207-11.

–/96 In ... another] Only Brooke, among previous editors, rejected this line, which Ure thought 'strikingly in Chapman's manner.' Q2 may have been restoring an accidental cut in Q1.

146/97 wane] A few editors have restored the quartos' 'waue' (Q2 'wave'), but Tamyra is talking only of diminution, not of undulation. A simple turned letter, I believe, which Q2 followed, provides the best explanation.

157/108 the/yee] Q2 was almost certainly correcting Q1's misunderstanding of the abbreviation 'yᵉ'.

176/127 the gulfe/a Vault] The stage direction added in Q2 ('*The Vault opens.*') could have corrupted its line in some way. I share Florby's sense that Q1's 'gulfe', with its 'dark connotations,' is richer than 'Vault'. (The early placement of the direction in Q2, beside l. 173/124, is perhaps due to the prompter's need of a warning that the trap must be opened.)

176-77/127-31 will ... for euer/was ... blushes] I see no reason to deny Chapman the authorship of Q2's deliberate revision, which Parrott and Ure considered good, and Sturman and Brooke unnecessary. Aesthetically, the Q1 image is more striking, the Q2 passage better. Florby, on the other hand, found Q2 to be in several ways inferior and clumsy but reached no conclusion about the authenticy of the passage: 'Chapman sometimes was clumsy.'

179/133 *Com./Frier.*] The Q2 version deprived Frier of the proper name, Comolet (the name of an actual friar of the period), that had been his in Q1. The reason is unknown, and notably Frier is the most important character who has no name. But he is never addressed by name in either version.

III.i

SD *Bucy/D'Ambois*] The Q1 spelling, *Bucy*, presumably reflects Chapman's pronunciation of the name (to rhyme with 'Lucy'). Speech-prefixes at IV.i.57, 69, 71, 75 (all Q1 references) are related to this spelling.

–/1-2 Sweet ... spice] I agree with N. Brooke in doubting Parrott's suggestion of a common basis in religious topicality for this addition and the revision in V.iii.7-12/V.ii.7. Whatever the motive of the present addition, these lines are among the proofs, as Ure noted, that Sturman wrongly described Q2 as minimizing Tamyra's conflict of conscience. On the other hand, Florby thought the lines a 'glib jingle,' the introduction of which 'before Tamyra's emotional speech is another way of diminishing the pathetic heroine.' The image of the spicy bite of conscience is worthy of Chapman.

32/34 our] The omission of 'our' by Q2 seems clearly to have been a compositor's oversight, understandable in a line that has several three-letter words, three of which begin with 'o-'. I have emended Q2 to agree with Q1.

38/40 valure] Shepherd's emendation. Both quartos have 'value', which is barely possible, since 'value' (*NED*, *sb.*, 5 and 5.b), 'valure' (1.a, c [citing Chapman's *Gentleman Usher*, I.i.13), and 'valour' (2, 3) overlapped in meaning. But 'valure' is 'more appropriate in the mouth of Bussy' (Parrott, who nonetheless followed the quartos), and is certainly a Chapman word – perhaps a Chapman spelling. This page in Q1 (D4) was set by the compositor (B) who in two other instances used (or adopted from copy) the spelling 'valure' rather than 'valour' (A's favorite spelling). If the copy had 'valure' (or its equivalent), a compositor could easily leave out the '-r-' in setting the word. (Cf. *The Conspiracie of Byron*, III.i.79.)

–/45-61 Now let ... love onely] Two consecutive lines in Q1 (ll. 42-43/44, 62) are preceded by headings for Tamyra, the second one (*Ta.*) unusually short. I find almost irresistible Parrott's inference of a cut in Q1. It is, however, possible that the lines added in Q2 represent an addition to the Q1 version (perhaps on an added slip) that did not get transcribed when Q1 was printed. In any case, the lines sound genuine to me, notwithstanding complaints of crudeness or unnecessariness brought by Sturman, Evans, and N. Brooke. They seem no more crude than Tamyra's l. 70/89, which is in both quartos. Florby, in fact, argued persuasively that the crudeness, which Brooke objected to because it 'weakens the context of Tamyra's great speech which follows,' is intended to do just that, and she attached special significance to the ironic uses of the word 'honour'd': 'when we find both the "honour'd daughter" and the "honour'd mistress" in the inserted passage, the appellations are so much in line with Chapman's usage in this and other plays as to warrant the ascription of the passage to him.'

–/49-50 it? ... ho?] Most editors change Q2's queries into exclamations or periods. But the line beginning 'Alas' is best read as a question: in effect, Since I've spent the night here, won't he guess? (Tamyra's 'Come then', l.–/50, = 'Oh well!'). And 'ho' can appropriately be read with a rising intonation (= 'are you there?'). To the extent that these marks heighten our sense of the characters' hypocrisy, they emphasize the more clearly the important development of Bussy's corruption from *virtu* to guilt of the very practices he earlier condemned. Thus, the 'prodigious amount of deceit in the air' about which Corballis complained is precisely the point.

–/51 resolv'd.] Most editors make the line a question. This punctuation works, but I prefer Q2's punctuation, which results in an ironic statement. Tamyra's 'I Father' (l.–/52) need not presuppose a question here.

71/90 loue,/Love,] Both quartos have a query, which is correct by Renaissance punctuation methods, but which might mislead a modern reader: 'love' and 'peace' are in apposition as terms of endearment for Tamyra.

99/118 vnderneath the King/under our Kings arme] Ure and Brooke agreed that the Q2 reading is a weakening, and Florby pronounced the reviser of these words 'clearly not Chapman.' The revision may well relate to staging – if, in III.ii, the King stands with his arm around Bussy's shoulders, say. Cf. D'Urfey's stage direction at IV.i.111/117: 'Exit. *King leaning upon D'ambois.*'

III.ii

1 my Bussy/*Bussy*] About half of the editors follow Q2. It is very likely a compositorial slip, and in a single-text edition I would follow Q1: As G. C. Macauley said in a review of Parrott (*MLR*, VI [1911], 255), Chapman never 'intentionally wrote' such a foot.

16 truth/man] Ure's argument that the Q2 compositor anticipated 'man' of l. 18 is convincing.

76 noblie] Boas emended to 'noblier' (a form last cited by the *NED* from 1602) on the grounds that the 'parallel phrases in the preceding lines are all comparatives' and that 'Bussy, in the second half of this line, cannot mean to deny that Guise is of noble birth.' Parrott accepted Boas's reading as *emendatio certissima*, and it (or a variant, 'nobler') has been adopted by a majority of editors since. (N. Brooke supported the change by saying, questionably, that '"er" could easily be misread as "ie".') But Bussy *does* mean to deny that Guise is noble in Bussy's terms ('merit' rather than 'blood'). The positive form is appropriate to Monsieur, who is correcting Bussy's radical assertion of popular power by the simple statement of Guise's dignity. Bussy's denial of 'gradation' to 'noblesse' in l. 77 could be taken to support a comparative form, but I read it as denying *rank* to anything but merit. This page in Q1 was set by Compositor A, whose predilection for the '-ie' spelling of a final [i] sound caused him on several occasions (though not, to be sure, in l. 78) to spell even the adverbial suffix '-lie'. Hence, we need not assume that he intended to set '-lier'. If Compositor B had set it, emendation would be almost mandatory, because he invariably used the '-ly' spelling.

88 stay, D'Ambois] A handful of editors have followed the quartos in omitting the comma, making it appear that 'D'Ambois' is the object of 'stay'. But Q1 often omits commas before vocatives, and after asking others to stay 'them' (i.e., Guise and Bussy), the King would probably not then ask them to stay one of those two. After 'them', the King addresses Bussy and Guise in turn.

89 equall/honour'd] Q1's 'equall' is not, as Parrott thought, improper for Guise: Henry is trying to cajole Guise into moderation.

104 out one sticke/one stick out] Either Q1 or Q2 could have resulted from compositor error. Q2 is slightly smoother and more expected – and therefore perhaps more likely to be wrong, especially if the compositor relied too heavily on his memory as he made the transition to a new page (l. 104 is the first line on sig. E3ᵛ in Q2).

107 ingenuous/ingenious] A slight majority of editors have followed Q1, which probably best conveys Chapman's intention (*NED*, s.v. 'Ingenuous', 2 and perhaps 3 and 4.b). But the words were often interchanged, and like Brooke I doubt that the change was deliberate.

–/131-38 And hope ... met you] Sturman placed much emphasis on this passage added in Q2, finding it a vulgarization that 'alters the nature of the principal characters.' Ure and Florby, however, argued (successfully, in my opinion) that that is not evidence against Chapman's responsibility – especially since Florby found a pattern of such intentions, coupled with thoroughly Chapmanesque language.

146/154 wise make scapes to please aduantage] The line may be corrupt, in view of the odd semicolon after 'wise' (removed in the corrected state of Q2 with or without authority) and the uncharacteristic metrical deficiency. Moreover, 'to please aduantage' has not yielded a satisfactory explanation. If correct as repunctuated, the sentence may mean, If powerful and clever men commit any transgressions to gratify the occasion that such men have (i.e., if they are going to become vulnerable at all), they'll do it with a woman. Parrott's 'advantages' carries considerable appeal.

–/163 Queich] a seventeenth-century spelling of 'queach'. Shepherd's 'quitch' is wrong; for the distinction, see *NED*.

160/168 greatest women/ chiefest women] I find reasonable, but not compelling, Ure's conjecture that Q2's 'chiefest' is a compositor's error. Several revisions were apparently motivated by a desire to eliminate repetition. Here each alternative involves repetition.

170/– And we will to the other] There is a distinct possibility that the Q2 compositor omitted this half-line through a misunderstanding of the collator's intention: The new speech for Monsieur was taken as a replacement for these words when it may have been meant to be added to them. If it were included in the Q2 version, and if the passage be intended as verse, something would have to be read as a broken line. (N. Brooke was surely right, and alone among editors, to extend the verse portion through l. 171/181.)

–/180 Starting back?] The apparent reluctance of the women to engage with the men (evident in Q1 from Annable's, and then Charlotte's, responses to being approached) is made explicit in Q2 from their first action after they enter. The stage directions that I have interpolated indicate what I believe the stage action to be.

171/181 *An./Char.*] Almost two-thirds of the editors have followed Q1 in assigning this line to Annable, presumably because Montsurry seems to be answering it in the next line. But we are hearing fragments of several conversations, as the pairing-off has already begun.

177/187 said:–] My punctuation of this line reflects what I think happens in the conversation. Up to this point each speech, though aloud, has been addressed to a specific person. 'Well said' is similar, but 'a spirit of Courtship of all hands' is a general but coded speech, signalling to the ladies that an amorous courtly game will now be played, and telling the men to utilize the occasion to elicit whatever information they can.

192/202 wondring/watching] Q2's 'watching', repeating Pero's word from II.ii.156/107, could nonetheless be a compositor's simplification inspired by recollection of that earlier speech.

194-95/204-5 she set close at a banquet/ her selfe reading a letter] As N. Brooke said, Q1 implies a sexual feast. The revised wording (relating directly to Barrisor's letter, II.ii.287/243) is not immediately sexual. But sexual innuendo is still present: Witness the retention in D'Urfey, who tends to vulgarize Chapman's subtleties, of 'reading a Letter'. Q2, often of late accused of the opposite, is actually more subtle here.

200/210 SD *Aside.*] Some part of Monsieur's reaction to Pero's revelation must be aside, since Monsieur presumably does not wish Pero to be privy to all of his motives. Some editors include more or less in the aside, but I include only the overtly hostile words. The second-person pronoun of 'thy Lady' need not imply overt speech.

–/211-12 Why ... Oh the] All editors except Fraser have included this Q2 addition, some (Boas, N. Brooke, and Evans) thinking the passage a restoration of an accidental omission from Q1 (my own view), others (Parrott, like Ure) thinking it a genuine revision.

206/217 *Aside.*] While it is by no means certain that the words 'Gods pretious it transformes me with admiration' are spoken aside, the clause seems to me to be an interruption caused by near speechlessness, not additional words of flattery.

208/218-19 his conueiance/this conveyance] As several editors have noted, two different senses of 'conueiance' are intended in the Q2 version of this line and the next: first, contrivance or trick (*NED*, 11.b.-c.); in l. 209/220, escorting (*NED*, 1). Q1 apparently reduces both to the literal level. Q2's 'his' here is probably a correction of a Q1 error, arising out of the compositor's misunderstanding or by anticipation of 'his' in the next line.

215-18/– *Char.* I ... me–] N. Brooke provided the probable explanation for the accidental omission of these lines from Q2: 'the direction *Whispers* was added [in the copy for Q2] after ll. [214/225] and [218/–], so that the compositor skipped from one to the other.' It does not seem likely that one of the three couples would be left speechless, especially at the cost of what Ure called 'a quite good French joke against the English milord.' In a single-text edition, I would surely include the Q1 passage. I have inserted the two '*Whispers*' stage directions postulated.

223/230 Countesse ... Lady] Q1 reads 'Lady ... Countesse'. I accept Brooke's suggestion that the Q1 compositor transposed the titles, though Chapman could have made the slip himself. Someone recognized that Beaupre is not a countess and corrected the error in the simplest way, so that Q2 has 'Lady' in both positions.

228/235 liuer as hard/livor as dry] Q2's 'livor' is presumably a spelling variant, not the word meaning, figuratively, 'malignity'. Almost half of the editors have followed Q1's 'hard', which makes sense and avoids repetition. But 'dry' is appropriate too.

236/243 be/are] Q2 seems to have normalized the grammar, but 'be' was often used where we would expect 'are' (Abbott, §300).

249/255 if/when] Q2's 'when' is suspect, perhaps an error by attraction to 'when' in the next line.

−/290 *Gui.* Come ... them.] Accidental omission from Q1 is a distinct possibility. N. Brooke thought the line added 'to give Guise an exit line.' Florby agreed but added a structural motive: 'The symmetry of the dealings of the two threesomes ... has been allowed to slacken. ... Now Guise is made to participate in the discoveries ...'

293-301/300-70] The long addition in Q2 has provoked as much controversy as perhaps any other alteration. The Q1 passage consists of four and one-half lines of soliloquy by Monsieur. The substance of the first three and one-half lines is represented in sixty new lines: fifteen lines continuing Monsieur's soliloquy, forty-two lines of largely comic dialogue with his officious steward, Maffe, and twelve lines of another soliloquy by Monsieur (of which five are about servants and seven are a prayer to his 'great starre, and angell of [his] life' for a few days of safety). The remainder of the Q1 passage is then inserted (ll. 296ff./360ff.), slightly reworded to integrate with the context. Finally, six new lines are added in which Maffe announces the sudden arrival of Bussy, and Monsieur reacts to this news. Sturman, N. Brooke, and Evans all found at least large parts of the revised passage effective, but rejected it on various grounds: It violates Chapman's sense of tragic decorum, it merely emphasizes plotting details unnecessarily, it undercuts the 'emotional undercurrents' of what follows, there is no 'positive evidence' that Chapman wrote it even though it is 'striking in Chapman's manner.' Ure wrote a full defense of the scene against Sturman's strictures, concluding that it has the 'true accent of Chapman' (including some specific verbal parallels and rare usages) and that it enriches the characters without radically altering them. Tricomi recently noted ways in which details of this scene mirror earlier moments in the play (Maffe's 'man of bloud', l. −/367, echoing I.i.216/222 and Bussy's bloody duel described in II.i), and concluded (in opposition to Brooke) that the 'reviser understands very well Chapman's work and his methods [and] manifest[s] an artistic sense as well-developed, shall we say, as Chapman's own' ('The Problem of Authorship in the Revised *Bussy D'Ambois*'). Florby also pointed to several Chapmanesque details. At best, in my judgment, those who would deny Chapman's hand have not proved their case. Whoever wrote the Q2 version was a talented writer, and he wrote very much like Chapman; so far as I can determine, he was Chapman.

The presence in Q1 of a redundant speech-prefix at l. 301/370 raises the distinct possibility that the omission there was a cut. If so, in this place at least Q2 would represent an earlier (and longer) version of the play – though it would require subtle reasoning to reconcile that theory with the general relationship of Q2 with prompt-book and of Q1 with foul papers.

−/316 I will speak with none] The parallel between this line and V.ii.1/V.iii.1 (present in both quartos) suggests the care with which the author of the Q2 version approached his task, and his thorough knowledge of the whole play – all of which points to Chapman himself, especially since the parallel sets up a fine contrast between Monsieur's and Bussy's reactions when their desired seclusion is disrupted.

–/317 SD *Exiturus*.] An unusual Latin form that has the earmarks of Chapman's usage, as N. Brooke acknowledges.

333/416 come begin ... simply/pay me home ... bravely] I accept Parrott's conjecture, endorsed by N. Brooke, that Q2 printed 'come' before 'pay' by mistake. The markings in the copy of Q1 that the collator prepared for the Q2 compositor were apparently not always clear, or at least were not accurately interpreted, as to the limits of cuts.

336/419 to] No editor has kept Q2's 'so', which must be a simple misprint.

339/422 Iew] Both quartos place a comma after this word, creating an ambiguity as to whether Chapman means to list two villainous types (slave to a Jew, and English usurer) or one (slave to either a Jew or an English usurer). Like most previous editors, I take 'vsurer' (along with 'Iew') as an object of the preposition 'to' ('slaue to'); see ll. 350-51/433-34, where Monsieur repeats the list of offices: There, he includes 'Slaue' from the earlier list, and omits 'Iew' and 'vsurer'.

340-41/423-24 possessions, ... throates] Boas, followed by most modern editors, made the words 'And cut mens throates' a parenthesis. The relationships in the sentence are ambiguous, but I prefer to construe 'mens throates of morgaged estates' (i.e., the throats of men who have mortgaged estates; cf. a typical possessive construction, 'the king's daughter of France') with 'cut'. Chiastically, the slave forces (seizes) possessions and the hackster cuts throats. But Chapman probably had an impressionistic unity of the whole sequence in mind.

359-60/442-43 which, not to sooth ... Hammon,] Parrott and several other editors removed the comma after 'which', apparently making it the object of 'sooth'; but it probably = 'as to which' (cf. Abbott, §272). Editors seem to have misunderstood the thrust of the context, which is, I believe, an allusion to Plutarch's *Alexander* XXXVII.5, in which the oracle, by Alexander's report, intended to call him παιδιον but glorified him with a slip of the tongue, παιδιοσ (son of Zeus). Jacquot came closest to this gloss, with a reference to Quintus Curtius IV.vii.8, in which Alexander associates *himself* with Jupiter.

382/465 once wrong'd one man, y'are/wrong'd one man, you are] The Q2 omission of 'once' was probably accidental, and the contraction 'y'are' was expanded in the corrected state to compensate.

IV.i

12 light/height] Renaissance astrological treatises spoke of the influence of motion and light, not height. Q2's 'height' is probably an error by the compositor occasioned by the aural/visual similarity of the two words. Cf. the chapter heading in Pico della Mirandola's monumental and influential confutation of astrology, *Disputationes in Astrologiam* (1495): 'praeter commvnem motvs et lvminis influentiam nullam uim cœlestibus peculiarem inesse' (that, except for the general influence of motion and light there is no special power in heavenly bodies) (Georg Olms facsimile [Hildesheim, 1969]

of *Opera Omnia*, I [Basel, 1557], 461). See my article 'John Foxe on Astrology,' *ELR*, I (1971), 210-25. (Aristotle's *Meteorologica*, probably the ultimate source of Renaissance thinking, described the effective forces as motion and *heat*, and 'height' could conceivably be a misreading of 'heat' except that presumably Chapman would not attribute heat to the moon.)

23-27/24-28 motions ... predominance/faculty ... divided Empires] N. Brooke argued that Q2's 'faculty' forgets the moon imagery to which Q1's 'motions' relates. But 'faculty', very apt with 'voluntary' (*NED*, I.4), is relevant also to 'Moones', being the larger term that subsumes both 'light' and 'motion' of l. 12. The change from 'predominance' to 'divided Empires' does abandon the moon image, but (as Ure noted) purposefully, to relate to the contextual images in 'scepters' and 'diademe'. There is no reason to deny Chapman's responsibility for such changes.

25/26 *Buss./Mont.*] N. Brooke was surely right in saying that the lines here assigned to Montsurry were 'conceived as part of Bussy's argument' (hence, Q1's assignment was not a mistake); but there is no reason to think that Chapman did not reassign the lines. Bussy's argument does not suffer: He simply builds on what Montsurry has said. The reassignment need not have been for mechanistic reasons, as Parrott thought ('to give Montsurry a speech' and 'enliven the action on the stage'): The lines are effectively ironic from Montsurry's mouth.

28/29 claime/prove] Parrott and Ure considered Q2's 'prove' a weakening, but it has a logical connection with the demonstrated behavior of the women that is consistent with Chapman's thinking (= 'establish' [*NED*, II.5]).

37/38 tyrannous/priviledge,] Q2 omits the comma, and previous old-spelling editions have concurred, making 'priviledge' an adjective. Parrott defended this interpretation, though it is unprecedented, and sense could be made of the reading (in relation to the legal concept of privilege). Given the way corrections were marked for the printer of Q2, however, it seems more likely that the collator wrote the noun 'priviledge' above Q1's adjective 'tyrannous' and neglected to add the newly needed comma. (Parrott's conjectural emendation to 'privileged' is not necessary.)

64/65 but/and] Q2 may have suffered from confusion over the several meanings of 'nice': e.g., lascivious (*NED*, 2) rather than the correct coy or affectedly shy (*NED*, 5).

74/80 King?] Dilke's period and Boas's exclamation accurately suggest Chapman's intention, but the query of the quartos will suffice since no pointing can adequately convey what must be communicated here by the actor's intonation.

80/86 flames,] Several editors have followed Q1 in omitting the comma, making 'Fed' modify 'flames', and Evans explained the phrase as an allusion to the sacrifice of cocks in the rituals of witchcraft. The concept does not seem to fit the view of Monsieur that Bussy is establishing. Q2's comma, though ambiguous, allows the likelier interpretation: 'Making' and 'Fed' both modifying 'glories'; as Dilke first explained, l. 81/87 describes gestures of servility.

86/92 toughnesse/roughnesse] The Q2 compositor probably misread Q1's 't-'.

90/96 aire/the aire] Q2 looks like a compositor's sophistication.

115/121 SD *Making horns.*] Some editors place this direction early in the preceding line, but Montsurry's anger – and thus, presumably, the action that provokes it – is delayed until the present exchange.

145-46/151-54 Sweete ... creature/Sweet ... hurt] Almost certainly there is some confusion in Q2, as signalled by the metrical chaos of that version. Apparently there was misunderstanding between the collator who prepared the copy and the compositor as to which Q1 words were to be cut. In such circumstances it is not possible to reconstruct with certainty. The most popular editorial practice, first adopted by Shepherd, has been to restore from Q1 'for shame of Noblesse' and to rearrange the lineation of the Q2 addition. I suspect that 'Sweet Lord, cleare up those eyes' should not have been included in the Q2 version: The tone of entreaty, though appropriate to Tamyra's lady-in-waiting, is not consistent with the angry sound of the remainder of her speech.

163-64/171-72 merits: ... name and memorie] Following the punctuation of the quartos, I take 'merits' as the simple object of 'know'; 'name' and 'memorie' are the subjects of an independent clause – not, as in Parrott and some others, appositives with 'merits' in a noun clause that is the object of 'know'. The second clause seems to mean, Your reputation and the memory of what you are (as of now) need to be completely forgotten forever.

165/173 loth'd/just] 'just' = complete (*NED*, 11). The reviser presumably thought Q1's 'loth'd' inappropriate, since the oblivion that Montsurry speaks of is to be desired, not abhorred.

172/180 hand/fingers] Q2 is consistent with l. 187/195 and with the way in which the gesture would be made. I question whether 'hand' survived beyond the foul papers that were the copy for Q1.

179/187 Augean] Q1's 'Egean' was a scribal or compositorial error not caught by the collator who prepared the copy for Q2.

182/190 art/are] Q2 is almost certainly wrong: 'Chapman is not likely, after having written *art*, to have altered it to *are*' (Parrott).

–/205-9 Papers ... for it] N. Brooke agreed with Parrott that 'The philosophical comment contained in the added lines is eminently characteristic of Chapman,' but rejected them ('the new lines fit awkwardly'). Florby elaborated on the Chapmanesque tone, which she associated specifically with the poet's attitude toward his art: 'Not many others would interpolate these abstract musings ... into the worried Tamyra's speech.'

198/208 your honour] The Q2 compositor first printed 'the honour', presumably misreading the collator's manuscript abbreviation 'yʳ' as 'yᵉ'. Possibly, however, what was really written was 'thy' (though 'thine' would be the expected form), which was misprinted 'the' and corrected by guess.

IV.ii

−/SD *Enter D'Ambois and Frier.*] See the notes at IV.ii.7/0 SD.

−/1-18 *Buss. I . . . despaire*] Sturman and N. Brooke found various inconsistencies between this Q2 addition and other parts of the play, but the problems they saw disappear when confronted with certain fundamental dramatic principles. If a character finds reason in one scene to suspect something (in this case, Bussy's suspicion that Monsieur has alerted Montsurry to the liaison), there is no clumsiness in his reacting vigorously when the suspicions are confirmed later (IV.ii.9ff./30ff.). (See my note on ll. 9-13/30-33 below.) Brooke saw the reason for this addition as the necessity of replacing the original musical interlude with dialogue of an equivalent length – speculation concurred in by G. K. Hunter, who pointed out that when Marston's *Malcontent* was transferred from children to adult players, dialogue was augmented 'to entertain a little more time, and to abridge the not received custom of music in our theatre' (*RES*, n.s. XVI [1965], 197). This is a plausible explanation; if correct, it *could* reduce the likelihood that Chapman wrote the new passage, but the evidence is inconclusive. Corballis, in fact, found a different motive for the addition: 'to make it clear that Bussy is already suspicious of Monsieur, and . . . to make Bussy rather than Tamyra the instigator of the conjuring speech which follows' (though the reviser failed to change Frier's later statement, l. 23/43, that he is obeying Tamyra's 'motion'). In any case, I find nothing in the lines foreign to Chapman's style; Ure and Florby pointed to specific linguistic parallels in *The Revenge, The Tragedie of Byron,* and the *Iliad*. (The motive for the addition, according to Florby, was to mark the passage of time while Tamyra writes the letter.)

0/18 SD *Musicke*] If N. Brooke and G. K. Hunter were correct in their speculation that music was cut out when the play was transferred to an adult company (see the preceding note), then the collator's failure to delete the call for music here was an oversight.

0/18 SD *with Pero her maid*] Q1 (followed by N. Brooke) does not name Pero ('*with her maid*'); Q2 adds the name, but refers to two women ('*Pero and her maid*'). Shepherd and his followers (Phelps and Rylands) and, surprisingly, Lordi keep Q2's '*and*'. Tamyra uses the services of only one maid during this scene: to deliver the letter that she said at the end of Act III she would send to Monsieur (l. 1/19). That it is Pero who is sent on this errand is clear: Pero makes the delivery later in this scene as, through Behemoth's powers, Tamyra watches from afar (l. 120/140). There is no reason to suppose another maid is present. The collator added the name that he found in the prompt-book and either he or the compositor assumed that a second woman was intended.

2/20 Fild/Fill'd] Though all editions (except the Pearson reprint) have followed Q2's 'Fill'd', it seems likely that Chapman meant the verb meaning 'To render (materially) foul' or 'To render morally foul or polluted; . . . to corrupt, taint, sully' (*NED*, s.v. 'File', *v.²*, 1 or 3). If so, the collator or the Q2 compositor normalized wrongly.

7/− Father?] It is likely that this word was omitted in Q2 because of careless marking by the collator when he canceled the stage direction at this point in Q1, or because of oversight by the compositor of Q2 occasioned by that cancellation. There is no reason to suppose that Chapman would have left the line metrically deficient.

7/0 SD *Ascendit Bussy/Enter D'Ambois*] The collator struck out the original SD and rewrote it before the lines added in Q2, presumably copying the words exactly from the prompt-book. The change from *Ascendit* to *Enter* may, then, reflect an actual change in stage practice, with Bussy and Frier not entering Tamyra's chamber this time (as they did before) through the secret passageway. If so, there may have been a desire to avoid having them appear from the same trap that later in the scene would produce Behemoth. (Tamyra is obviously unaware of the presence of Bussy and Frier in the Q2 version; thus her speech [ll. 1-6/19-24] is as much a soliloquy there as it is in Q1, when she is genuinely alone, and I have marked it as an aside – which was presumably the intention of Spencer's dash at that point. (I have followed Parrott in having the men 'advance' in Q2.)

7/– SD *in a conjuring robe.*] The uncorrected state of Q1 reads '*in a*', and it is a reasonable guess that the remainder of the stage direction (if it was completed in the manuscript) identified the mystical garb. That Comolet enters already dressed for the ritual is demonstrated by l. 24/44 ('I *haue put on* these exorcising Rites'). It is therefore puzzling that in Q2 he is directed to put on his robes, for Q2 preserves the earlier line describing him as already robed. Indeed, the new lines also include a reference that clearly suggests an already-robed Frier: 'To assume these Magick rites' (l. –/10). If there is merit in some of Sturman's complaints of inconsistencies in the Q2 version of IV.i, the inconsistencies may well relate, not to the question of who wrote the revision, but whether Q2 thoroughly represented all the changes. One may also speculate on the possibility that in this place the Q2 version is earlier than Q1's: If that were the case, Q1 would represent a text that had resolved drafting questions about how to stage the scene.

–/27-29 Our ... it] Ure called the addition 'ill-advised or unlike Chapman,' and N. Brooke objected that it 'belabour[s] the explanation of what is quite clear. ...' Florby, however, concluded on 'circumstantial evidence' that the 'proximity to the new opening lines [of IV.ii] speaks for [Chapman], nothing speaks against him. A 'theatrical reviser' might have put in Tamyra's new lines to fill in a gap left by the author, but would he have changed the first couple of lines of Bussy's outburst so radically?'

9-13/30-33 What ... discouerie?] Corballis found confusion in Q2 resulting from inadequate revision similar to that referred to in the Textual Note to ll. /1-18 above: In Q1, Bussy appears to be asking who betrayed them to Monsieur, and Comolet promises (l. 18/38) to 'take the darkenesse from his face' – i.e., to discover the identity; in Q2, Bussy is not asking for information, but denouncing Monsieur, and Frier's unaltered response is now, Corballis thought, 'nonsense.' If there is a problem, it could be the result, once again, of inadequate collation in the preparation of the copy for Q2. But I do not see a serious problem: In each version, the main thrust of Frier's response is that he will discover what exactly is known, and that is what is most important in fact. When Frier tells Behemoth what information he wants, he says nothing in either version about discovering betrayers (l. 42/62). (Note also that even in Q1 the revelation of Pero's treachery yields no response except Tamyra's question whether she is dead, l. 128/149.)

30/50 ye/you] Q2 is probably an unconscious modernization by the compositor. Cf. 'ye' in both versions of the following line.

–/51 SD *He puts on his robes.*] There is reason to suppose that an editor should excise this Q2 SD. See the note at l. 7/– SD above.

79/99 SD *apart*] Editors are divided on the specific placement of Monsieur and his associates, but are agreed that they are physically separate from the Bussy group. I see no way of determining what happened in the several Renaissance theaters where this play was performed – whether above (least likely, because of sight-lines), behind, or merely on a different part of the main playing area. Hence, I adopt a non-committal 'apart'.

80/100 *Beh.*] Because the quartos' assignment to *Mons.* is patently wrong, nearly all editors since Phelps have assigned the speech to Frier. Only Dilke and Fraser assign it to Behemoth, though several others admit that as a possible emendation. Parrott's arguments notwithstanding (that it is Frier who checks Bussy in l. 81/101 and that up to now Behemoth has communicated directly only with Frier), I follow Dilke because in general Behemoth is in control of the proceedings and knows what can and cannot be done. But there is little material difference.

88/108 *Beh.*] Both quartos have *Pre.* (*Per.* in the Q1 catchword). All editions (except the Pearson reprint) assign the speech to Behemoth. Parrott thought *Pre.* a mere misprint; N. Brooke speculated that it derived from a misreading of *Be.* It is conceivably an abbreviation for some epithet such as Predictor or Prepotent. But the likeliest explanation is that Chapman, engrossed in the contents of the speech, accidentally wrote as a speech-prefix the first three letters of the first word in the line, 'Perswasion', an error that may have been reinforced by his plan to have Pero enter very soon. (The copy for Q1, it will be remembered, was almost surely his foul papers.) When the compositor of Q1 reached the bottom of his printed page, G3, he routinely set as catchword what he saw in the manuscript. When he came to set the actual line on G3^v, he either noticed the problem and guessed at the correct reading by reversing the letters, or set the letters wrong by inadvertence.

131/152 stayne/die] I accept Parrott's conjectural emendation of Q1's 'stay', probably a scribal or compositorial error. Q2's 'die' (i.e., dye) could, of course, be a revision, but it may derive from actors who found it difficult to articulate the contiguous [n] sounds of 'stayne not'. N. Brooke attributed the Q2 reading to an 'editorial emendation', an inherently improbable conclusion. (Phelps and his imitator Rylands, and recently Fraser, followed Q1, which yields no evident meaning; Fraser glossed 'stay' as 'withhold'.)

132/153 his forst bloud] About half of the editors have emended 'his' to 'her' on the assumption that 'bloud' alludes to Tamyra's letter written in blood;

Parrott at first accepted the emendation but in his edition followed quartos. The quartos are right, for, as N. Brooke said, in Act V 'Tamyra clearly regards her hand as guilty of Bussy's death, and so stained with his blood.'

138/159 rage ... policy/valour ... policies] Q2's 'valour' is more apt for Bussy than Q1's 'rage' as an antithesis of 'policy'. There is a distinct possibility, however, that 'policy' was changed to 'policies' by mistake at some point in the transmission of the text, by attraction to the rhyming word 'wise'.

V.i

17/21 than it/ than that] The Q1 commentator probably misread manuscript 'yᵗ' as 'it'; Q2 corrected the mistake.

31/35 cease:/cease: your terrors] Most editors who follow Q2 make 'terrors' the object of 'cease' and thus make 'Tempt' (l. 32/36) an imperative (as in Q1). This is possible, given the method by which the collator marked his corrections in the margins of Q1. Since the Q2 punctuation is perfectly sensible, however, I have elected to follow it. N. Brooke suspects, because of the hypermetrical line, that the collator failed to record the complete revision. As in other places, this is perfectly possible, though it seems an unnecessary assumption here.

36/40 God ... ye/ heaven ... you] One change was an expurgation, the other probably a slip (or a deliberate modernization) by the compositor.

–/42-44 *Tam.* Father ... safety] Parrott supposed that this passage was added to justify Frier's abandonment of Tamyra by having him express assurance of her safety, and subsequent discussion has concerned the effectiveness of the passage given that motivation. I believe that focus is wrong. Tamyra's 'Father' is a poignant expression of fear, and Frier's answer a naive reassurance that the audience knows to be naive: In the game of politics that Bussy has entered, his (and Tamyra's) chief advisor is no match for the adversary who is guided by Guise and Monsieur. This conception is worthy of Chapman's talents.

39/46 Ope the seuentimes-heat/ Stand the opening] Q2 is surely corrupt, probably because of an inadequately marked revision. More significant than the metrical deficiency of the line (which a few editors have attempted to correct by adding a syllable before or after 'Stand') is the substantive inadequacy of the words. Montsurry is seeking relief from pain, which he expresses in the images (thoroughly glossed by Ferguson) of a mountain pressing upon his breast (mythological) and of a fiery furnace (in the Q1 version, certainly the furnace of Nebuchadnezzar [Daniel 3:19] because of the adjective 'seuentimes-heat'). Relief from the mountain would be provided by its removal. In Q1, relief from the furnace is sought in having it opened (cf. *Venus and Adonis*, 331-32: 'An oven that is stopped ... Burneth more hotly'). In Q2, the furnace is already opening (without external agency, apparently), and the concern expressed is for those who are subjected to the escaping heat. In subsequent lines, according to both versions, Montsurry continues to seek relief for himself, but of a different kind: Apparently assuming that the mountain cannot be removed and the heat of the furnace slaked, he asks – since under those conditions ('now') mere speech is insufficient to express his woes – for some musical setting ('outcries') appropriate for one who must remain in hell (the hell presumably related in Chapman's mental processes to the fiery furnace of the preceding line). I cannot believe that Chapman intended to shift the point of view back and forth in this way – even though the biblical passage originally alluded to in l. 39/46 tells us that the men who carried Shadrach, Meshach, and Abednego perished from the heat. Thus, 'opening' certainly and probably 'Stand' as well are misreadings by the Q2 compositor, of the kind that we have seen elsewhere when he was dealing with the collator's manuscript notations – for *something* must have been written in the margin and/or between the lines in the copy of Q1 that went to the Q2 compositor. One can only guess at the correct reading(s). Apparently some form of the verb 'open' was there, perhaps not wholly in manuscript but partly consisting of the letters 'Ope' printed in Q1; there must also have been a word, presumably beginning with 'S-', that could be read as 'Stand'; we seem reasonably safe in assuming that the last four words in the line were correctly preserved from Q1. The most appealing alternative that I have found is 'Open the standing'. Other possibilities for the two key words might be 'Staue', 'Stint', or 'Slake'; and 'unopening'. But no alternative reading is entirely satisfactory. (G. B. Evans has made to me privately the intriguing suggestion that 'Stand' was actually intended to mean 'stet' – i.e., ignore the markings that I have started to make and print the original version.)

61/68 laden for thy/rig'd with quench for] If the rarity of the substantive 'quench' is evidential, the Q2 reading is more clearly Chapman's than some other revisions are: He used the word in *Iliads* XIX.363 and *Revenge* I.ii.28; Parrott, in fact, dated the revision of *Bussy* in part by this parallel with the *Revenge*.

84/91 distract ... state/devoure ... Consort] Ferguson traced 'devoure' to a typical Chapman concern, the desire to echo Horace's *curae edaces*. 'Consort' was a new or very recent word, such as Chapman liked to use at times. (*NED* says that until about 1612 the noun was accented on the second syllable; here it seems to be accented on the first syllable.)

97/104 SD *rack*] The 'other engine' (l. 137/145) need not be a rack, of course (despite the possible pun on 'wracke', l. 148/156, suggested by N. Brooke). Richard Hosley long ago suggested to me that the instrument might be a strappado except that Paul's had no suitable lift.

–/130 cruell cruelty] Parrott, following Shepherd, may well be right in regarding the adjective 'cruell' as a printer's error. The tautology is dramatically effective, however, and may have been intentional, despite the resulting Alexandrine. Most editors have accepted it into their texts.

126/134 SD *Stabs her again.*] D'Urfey's direction ('*Wounds her again.*') is not, I believe, just an added bit of sensationalism for Restoration tastes, but a reflection of Renaissance staging as well. In V.iii.171-73/V.iv.127-39, Tamyra seems to refer to three separate wounds, one in the bosom and two others unlocalized; one of those two may also have been in the bosom, if we may judge from Bussy's reference to Pindus and Ossa as indicating her bleeding breasts (V.iii.179-81/V.iv.135-37). But Q2 (which alone provides directions for the action here) records only two stabbings (ll. 124/132 and 134/142).

166/174 innocent/worthy] Q1's 'innocent' is so absurdly inappropriate that one wonders whether it survived revision in manuscripts written later than the draft that was the copy for Q1. However worthy he was, Comolet was not innocent. It is hard to imagine an audience's thinking the characters' guilt uncertain because of this word, as Parrott suggested.

167/175 SD *Releasing her.*] Tamyra has been under restraint of some sort (I have supposed a rack), and she has asked Montsurry to 'let [her] downe' so that she can write. At the end of the scene, Tamyra does not walk offstage (she '*wraps her self in the Arras*'), and conceivably Chapman conceived of her as remaining under restraint except for her arms. But I am assuming that, though free to move, she is too weakened by torture to walk.

182-83/190-91 I must ... creature] These words could well be an aside, since there is no obvious reason why Chapman would cause them to be addressed to anyone else on stage.

185/193 SD *she wraps her self in the Arras.*] I have interpolated the Q2 direction into my Q1 text, since it is clear from the Q1 stage direction at V.iii.56/V.iv.0 (*Intrat Vmbra Comolet to the Countesse, wrapt in a Canapie.*) that the staging of the two versions was substantially the same. At least in the theater represented in the Q2 version, the arras covered a means of access to the tiring house (cf. the prompter's warning at I.i.153-55 [Q2 numbering], '*Table [etc.] behind the Arras*'). From the audience's perspective, Tamyra remains hidden behind the arras, ashamed and in pain, during the intervening onstage action until Frier 'discovers' her (i.e., uncovers her) in the last scene.

V.ii (Q1)/V.iii (Q2)

For comments on the reversed order of scenes in Q2, see the first note on V.iii (Q1)/V.ii (Q2), following the notes on the present scene.

38/40 powrs/pow'rs] All editions except the Pearson reprint follow Q2 or print the expanded form 'powers'. It is quite likely, however, that Chapman meant 'powres' = pores. *NED* lists 'powre' as a sixteenth-century spelling of 'pore', and at IV.i.210/220, Q1 has 'Powre' for the homophone 'pour'; cf. also, for the [o:] sound followed by a liquid, 'rowl'd' (III.ii.12) and 'Mowle' (III.ii.41). These last three, however, are all on pages probably set by Compositor A. The present page in Q1 was set by Compositor B, who was less disposed to the use of apostrophes than was Compositor A and who may therefore have set his equivalent of 'pow'rs'; on the other hand, he also seems to have followed copy spelling more frequently than A. Note, moreover, that he spelled 'powers' at V.ii.70/V.iii.72.

74/76 and force/ or force] Q2 makes sense, but 'and' works better, and the Q2 compositor may have anticipated 'or' from later in the line.

V.iii (Q1) / V.ii (Q2)

The reversal of scenes by Q2 has evoked much comment. Parrott supposed that stage experience 'showed that this heavy philosophical dialogue between Monsieur and Guise dragged terribly at a time when the audience were eager for the impending catastrophe. It could have been cancelled entirely with no loss to the dramatic effectiveness of the play, but we should then have lost some noble poetry.' Sturman, N. Brooke, and Adams saw the relocation, whatever its motive, as having an enormous effect on the last act. For Brooke, 'the last Act has been turned from tragedy into melodrama (rigged out with tragic trappings),' and Adams, who thought the 'original *Bussy D'Ambois*...' very much superior to the more familiar play,' agreed with him. As Brooke described the change, in Q1 'Monsieur and Guise are detached from the action and turned into first choric figures and then silent Fates. [In Q2] the duologue is brought forward and on to the main stage [possibly, as he speculated a little later, because 'the reviser's theatre did not possess a full balcony'], so that the new rôle of the speakers is obscured; it is followed by a brief addition [–/V.ii.54-59] which revives Monsieur's and Guise's activity as plotters; when [at –/V.iv.23] they re-enter (on the upper stage now [or 'perhaps at windows']), they are twice made to enter the dialogue – once to ask what has happened to the murderers, and then to utter brief exit lines so that they are off-stage before the end. ... Monsieur and Guise are now essentially the master-plotters to the end; the movement in Bussy's speeches towards reflection on Human Destiny is unsupported by the staging, and all the weight falls on the melodramatic plot.' Since 'no significant word of poetry' was altered, Brooke was sure that the vast change in effect was unintentional: The conversion from tragedy into melodrama 'was by sheer inadvertence.' The significance of these observations to the problem of authorship is summarized by Brooke thus: 'the reviser does not delete the inconvenient philosophy; he respects all that Chapman has written; but he does not fully understand it. The one person who could *not* have done this is Chapman himself.'

This is an inspired critical conception, and it is brilliantly argued. But we must break the question down into several component parts: (1) the addition in Q2 of certain lines that show Monsieur and Guise to be actively engaged in the conspiracy against Bussy (and thus, according to Parrott and Sturman, clarify plot details for the audience); (2) the transposition of the two scenes; and (3) the movement of the action of the present scene from an upper stage to the main stage (assuming, as I do along with Brooke, that Q2 has not simply failed to record the word 'above' in the stage direction). To deal first with (2), there is a distinct theatrical advantage in placing the philosophic conversation between Monsieur and Guise earlier, for this arrangement does, as Parrott observed, permit continuity of action during the climactic moments of the play. Surely no one would argue that a concern for such continuity is a concern for the melodramatic. Adams argued that the 'doubly cynical dialogue' between Monsieur and Guise is so placed in Q1 as 'to furnish an ironic frame through which the audience may retrospectively view Bussy's readiness for self-sacrifice and prospectively may prepare to view the hero's imminent destruction by a gangster murder planned by two would-be tyrants.' But placing the dialogue *before* rather than after Bussy's meeting with Behemoth does not alter in any way the thematic relationship between the two scenes – and in fact may enhance the irony of the later scene. If so, that is not merely a *theatrical* advantage, but a *dramatic* advantage. (Cf. Florby's observation that the relocation 'makes the scene in which the false friar urges the hero to obey Tamyra's summons immediately precede the one in which the ghost of the real friar urges the heroine to come to her love's assistance, a nice parallelism.') In short, I see no *special* significance to the rearrangement, least of all to the authorship question; and what change there is in effect I see as a slight but discernible improvement.

The movement of the action to the main stage may indeed have a subtle effect on the audience, but again the difference works in more ways than one. While moving the Monsieur and Guise to a lower (and thus more ordinary) level, and accordingly perhaps reducing the *visual* significance of their superiority to the murderous action on the main stage, the change could have an almost opposite effect: to emphasize the significance of their philosophical discussion. In any case, the alteration seems of slight importance to me, especially since Q2 does bring the two villains back later, almost at the moment of Bussy's murder, to look down on the scene from above. (The reviser's theater had a balcony after all.)

This leaves us, then, with what I take to be Brooke's most considerable objection to this part of Q2: the addition of lines (–/V.ii.54-59 and –/V.iv.40, 185-86) that actively engage Monsieur and Guise in the action onstage. It is, I take it, these additions that indicated to Brooke that the reviser did not 'fully understand' Chapman's philosophy or (by implication) his conception of the play. To deal with this criticism, I must review Brooke's interpretation of what is happening in Act V. The scene (V.ii [Q1]/V.iii [Q2]) in which Bussy recalls Behemoth marks for Brooke the culmination of a movement away from concrete (or, I might say, mundane) conflicts (Bussy vs. Maffe, Bussy vs. a jealous Guise) – conflicts involving issues and philosophies, to be sure, but focusing on particular actions and people – toward an opposition of abstractions. When Behemoth identifies the Guise and Monsieur as Fate's ministers (V.ii.61-62/V.iii.63-64), a suggestion of a 'supernatural presence' is set up; and when Bussy vows later (ll. 71-72/73-74) that he will not allow his 'motion [to be] rebell to [his] will: [His] will, to life', then 'the opposition of Bussy to Guise and Monsieur becomes the opposition of positive life to the negations of fate,' and all the oppositions that Brooke has discussed earlier – 'of health to disease, of freedom to servitude, and so on – are thus associated at the climax in this fundamental sense.' When, in the Q1 version, Guise and Monsieur then enter, 'they have lost their specific identity as conspirators (in Act V that rôle is entirely carried by Montsurry) and taken on ... the abstract quality of choric voices, ... as spectators rather than participants in the final action.' They do not leave the stage as they do in Q2: 'they remain above as detached spectators of all the rest; silent, brooding Fates, reminiscent of the devils who watch Faustus torn to pieces at the end of Marlowe's play (in the text of 1616).' I trust that my abridged summary has not distorted Brooke's complex argument. If I understand it aright, at least a part of what the reviser did not 'fully understand' was that Chapman's conception of the role of Monsieur and Guise in Act V precluded their further active participation in the mortal plot against Bussy. I cannot accept this argument. Even if Chapman's conception of the play in 1604 or 1605 did preclude such participation, and if Q2 is in this part a later recasting, there is no reason why he could not have changed his conception in revision. Guise and Monsieur are Fate's ministers – and are said to be – whether they complain about the tardiness of the murderers or not. I seriously question, however, whether Chapman actually viewed Guise and Monsieur in so restricted a way as Brooke suggests. (Corballis also was 'not wholly convinced' by Brooke's argument: 'Monsieur has been stepping in and out of his choric shoes for most of the play [e.g., IV.i.91-102/97-108]; so it is not remarkable that this happens again in Q2's V.ii. And Guise's views are so consistently wrong-headed that I cannot at any stage regard him as a 'choric' figure.') At the very least, Brooke's argument ignores another important thematic concern of the play – one that is explicitly echoed in the brief additional speeches by Guise and Monsieur in Act V. While this is not the place for a critical analysis of the play, I will note that Bussy's references to his courtly enemies as 'politicke Monsieur' and 'violent Guise', a line present in both plays (V.ii.82/V.iii.84), is no less representative of the play than his characterization of them as 'Fates ministers' (V.ii.61/V.iii.64) or – if he meant the words as appositives – 'Death and Destinie' (V.iii.124/V.iv.76). The conflict between policy and forthright action – and the seemingly inevitable movement toward alliance between them – has been crucial to this play from the outset. It is not without significance that the politician, Monsieur, and the one who has 'cut too many throates alreadie ... and robb'd the Realme of many thousand Soules', Guise, should say *in unison*, 'Why enter not the coward villains?' (–/V.iv.40); or that it is the politician, not the author of the St. Bartholomew Day massacre, who recoils in –/V.iv.185-86. The author of those additional lines – and the reviser who (if we can trust the collator) let stand the intervention of 'a spirit / Rais'd by another' to thwart Bussy's cause (IV.ii.73-75/93-95) – did understand Chapman's play, and understood that there is no contradiction between the theme described by Brooke and the mortal motivations to which I have been referring. (Florby made a different point that is relevant here: Noting that the sudden shift from 'high-pitched praise of Bussy' and 'abstract philosophy' to 'swift arranging of the ambush' creates 'a jarring note,' she concluded that that was precisely the intention: 'what seems important about this new miniature scene is the abrupt change of mood it brings about. Like Tamyra's new lines in [–/]III.i.45[-61] [see note *ad loc.*] it weakens the preceding serious-sounding speeches; the effect is decidedly ironic.') As with other changes in this act, I find the overall difference resulting from the speeches added for Guise and Monsieur to be unrevolutionary, and not finally evidential for the question of authorship.

3 who/that] Q2's compositor may have had a memory failure.

7-12/7 In whose ... incurre/Not knowing what they say] See the note at –/III.i.1-2.

18-22/13-17 wee call ... beleeue should ... men thinke ... gard them/she calls ... beliefe must ... me thinks ... guard] The passage in Q2 can be forced to make Procrustean sense in and of itself, but in context seems manifestly corrupt. In an edition controlled by less conservative principles, I would emend several of its readings here to agree with Q1. I agree with Brooke that the compositor was here following manuscript copy, which he had trouble deciphering. When we consider the unusually high percentage of accidental variants in the early parts of this scene, it seems likely that the collator who prepared the copy for Q2 copied out this passage. But he apparently did not copy out the whole scene, since in later portions there is a much higher degree of formal similarity between Q2 and Q1 than in the earlier lines.

43/38 let it/lets it] I have normalized Q2's 'let's'. It is, of course, grammatically wrong and looks like a simple case of attraction to 'lets' in the parenthesis. The spelling of this form may derive from Chapman himself; see the Textual Introduction, n. 10.

45/40 rages ... th'roote/rage ... the root] Among the other errors by the Q2 compositor in this section, he probably dropped the '-s' from 'rages' and compensated, without authority, by expanding 'th''. Cf. 'rages' in III.i.16.

V.iii continued (Q1)/V.iv (Q2)

56/0 SD *Intrat ...*] See note at V.i.185/193. Q1's *'to the Countesse' 'wrapt in a Canapie'* and Q2's *'discovers Tamyra'* mean the same thing, but the prompt-book underlying Q2 has the technical language of the theater. There is no reason to accept Dilke's change (see Historical Collation), which seems to presuppose the drawing of a curtain before the ghost's entrance.

59/- (So ... imminent)] There is a distinct possibility that Q2 omitted this line by accident. This page was thoroughly marked up by the collator, and the Q2 compositor may once again have been uncertain how much of the printed portion of his copy to delete. On the other hand, it is possible that the line was deliberately removed because of its awkward interruption of the main flow of the sentence – though such considerations seem seldom to have moved Chapman.

63/9 engag'd/revenged] Editors from Dilke on have suspected that 'revenged' is a printer's error for Q1's correct reading, and Ure and Florby (though seeing Chapman's hand in the other revisions in this portion) considered the Q2 reading weaker (Florby: 'To strike out a perfectly suitable martial verb while reinforcing the war imagery elsewhere does not make sense'). Yet 'revenged' in the sense given by Boas ('vengeance is taken on him') is covered by *NED*, *vb.*, 4.b, and revenge in a battlefield context has a long tradition in epic literature and elsewhere.

64/10 *Tam.*] Q1 *Count.*; Q2 *Tamyra.* N. Brooke suggested that Q2's changes in this speech-prefix and in l. 69/15 (Q1 *Vmb.*; Q2 *Frier.*) and in the direction after l. 74/21 (*D'Amb./D'Amboys*) indicate the use of manuscript copy, though 'the reviser continues to be fussy about prefixes for some pages here.' I doubt that that conclusion can be extended beyond the speech-prefixes: The compositor of Q2 was certainly following printed copy at l. 88/39, where he reproduced Q1's colon though that place in Q2 is the end of a speech by Bussy. Q1's speech-prefix here is probably another indication that that text was set from Chapman's foul papers; unless Chapman changed it in the fair copy, the bookkeeper, not the reviser, would have changed this and other headings, in the prompt-book, to make them all consistent. When the collator marked his copy of Q1 for the printer of Q2, he changed many headings to agree with what he saw in the prompt-book. (That he changed many of them unnecessarily – e.g., *Buss.* to *D'Amb.* – contributes to my strong impression that the collator was a mere hireling who did not know the play.)

69/15 creation,/creation. Your true friend] Something appears to be wrong with the line in Q2, for the meter is faulty, despite careful adjustments in the earlier part of the line ('Tis'/'It is'; 'iust curse'/'misery'; 'our abus'd'/'our'). The collator or the compositor may not have recorded the change correctly.

70-74/– Which ... maker] The omission of these lines from Q2 may have been accidental. If (as I believe) the lines added in Q2 were written in the margin of the Q1 copy, there was a special danger in this case of erroneous omission, since the lines omitted from Q2 occur at the very bottom of a page in Q1: When he had set the last manuscript line, the compositor could easily neglect to return to the earlier printed copy. I am not persuaded by Florby's suggestion that religious considerations caused the omission. I am disposed to agree with Evans's comment (used, however, to support a different conclusion) that the viewpoint expressed in the omitted lines 'is so typical of Chapman at the time of writing *The Revenge of Bussy* that it is difficult to believe that he himself could have been the reviser who dropped them.' I do not share Corballis's contention that Bussy's conversion in Q2 into an active instigator of the affair with Tamyra (abetted by the suppression of the roles of Death and Destiny as personified, in Brooke's argument, by Monsieur and Guise) renders these lines inappropriate: Umbra Frier's word 'submit' does not refer to the submission described by Corballis, and the contrast between the 'great mind' and the 'small' does not inevitably apply in this context to Bussy and his adversaries.

–/15-21 Your ... opens] All commentators have agreed that these added lines are suspect. As elsewhere, N. Brooke in particular saw them as attempting to cover up a seeming weakness in the plot (here, the failure of Umbra Frier to do something directly on behalf of Bussy) which in fact 'calls attention to' the weakness without eliminating it. But the relative powerlessness of Umbra Frier has been emphasized in a line common to both versions (V.ii.11/ V.iii.11), and is consistent with the limited powers of the other supernatural beings (IV.ii.73-75/93-95); far from calling attention to a weakness, the added lines re-emphasize something that seems thematically important in the play.

74/21 SD *Exit.*] Q2 marks an exit and (at l. 89/41) a re-entry for Umbra Frier – a spectacular re-entry to confront the murderers and frighten all but one of them into an immediate retreat. Q1 omits directions for both exit and re-entry, but I assume (along with N. Brooke and others who followed Q1) that the stage action of Q1 is substantially similar to that of Q2. The entry even of the murderers is not marked, and the failure to direct an exit and re-entry for

Umbra Comolet must be due to Q1's general carelessness about stage directions in this act. See the note to l. –/186 SD.

–/32-35 If I scape ... ready] Even N. Brooke and Evans, though rejecting these lines, admitted their power and apparent authenticity. Something may have been left out of ll. –/34-35, one of which is metrically deficient. Parrott's arrangement, dividing the lines after 'rising' and thus emphasizing with metrics the powerful statement 'I am up and ready', is appealing.

113/65 SD others [murtherers]/all the murtherers] Q1's vague 'others' is another indication that the copy for Q1 was an authorial manuscript, probably foul papers.

120/72 SD Pistols shot./Pistolls shot within.] In Q2, this direction is placed two lines earlier, and as N. Brooke noted it must be a prompter's warning. Presumably, in fact, some character onstage did the shooting, with the sound effect coming from within. In D'Urfey, it was Monsieur and Guise, but I agree with Brooke in doubting that that was Jacobean stage practice. Most likely it was one of the murderers who fired, but Chapman may well have meant not to reveal the murderer to the audience. I have interpolated a direction for the shooting into the Q1 text, since it is clear that Bussy is also shot there , but I have not specified 'within' since I am even less certain for that version (with Monsieur and Guise on the upper stage watching) what staging Chapman had in mind.

–/89-92 And if Vespasian ... Groomes] All editors have adopted these lines, added in Q2. They probably should have been printed in Q1. Corballis found their source in Grimeston's General Inventory, 'Chapman's favourite source-book at this time.' Cf. Tricomi, 'The Problem of Authorship. ...'

–/90 SD She offers to help him.] Q2 misplaces this direction opposite ll. –/93-94. It cannot have been at that location in the prompt-book from which the collator was correcting the copy of Q1 that he was marking up. Probably the four lines added in the margin made interpretation of the collator's intention difficult for the compositor.

139-40/95-96 I am vp ... Statue] What seems like the natural rhythm of these lines, with a stop after 'vp' and no stop after 'Statue', is belied by the punctuation of the quartos. The quartos' punctuation, however, is not so systematically reliable that we can fault those editors (most of them) who repunctuate.

143/99 perfumes] Q1 'perfines'. Only N. Brooke, assuming a Chapman coinage, has printed Q1's hapax legomenon. The relationship between 'perfumes' and 'Sabæan spices' is so natural, the hypothetical etymology of 'perfines' so strained, and the likelihood of a minim error by the Q1 compositor so credible that it seems pedantic not to emend Q1, as I have done.

162/118 And/Now] The superfluous speech-prefix, Bus., before this line in Q1 arouses suspicions that a speech (by Montsurry?) was omitted from the quarto by mistake – or possibly deleted by Chapman in an early revision of his draft. N. Brooke proposed an ingenious alternative: that ll. 162-66/118-22 were an afterthought 'to make Bussy beg Montsurry to forgive Tamyra, which he could scarcely do later.' Brooke's metrical analysis of l. 167/123 is unconvincing and unnecessary if, for example, before writing anything beyond l. 161/117, Chapman wrote a speech-prefix for an answer to Bussy and then, deciding to add to Bussy's speech, he thoughtlessly changed the speech-prefix to *Bus.* In any case, the superfluous heading is further indication that the copy for Q1 was foul papers.

176-77/132-33 death; . . . prodigie–] I have modernized the pointing to clarify what I think is happening in the syntax. The 'but' (l. 176/132) is a conjunction. Some editors have apparently read it as a preposition (= except): cf. Fraser's note that 'the bleeding Tamyra [is] the only 'glory' accruing to Monsieur and the Guise.' A full stop after 'prodigie' would work, making 'prodigie' (and its appositives) the subject of an elliptical clause, 'this prodigie [has the glory of my death].' I rather think, however, that the three colons in the quartos (reflecting Q1 Compositor B's penchant for the colon in many non-terminal uses) signal an emotional breakdown in Bussy's language caused by the sight of Tamyra's wounds. After proceeding haltingly through three appositional efforts to state the subject of his new clause ('this', 'this killing spectacle', and 'this prodigie'), he is forced into an emotional anacoluthon. In l. 178/134, he successfully begins a wholly different construction involving a metaphorical account of the wounds and their effect on him. (The method of staging Tamyra's wounded and presumably bare breasts with a boy actor presents an interesting question.)

179/135 endlesse snow)/drifts of snow)] In both quartos the parenthesis ends after 'vains' (l. 180/136). A number of editors have ended it after 'liuer' in that line, but I am persuaded by N. Brooke's theory that the bracket after 'vains' was 'accidentally transferred' from the present line. Parrott supposed that Q1's 'endlesse' was altered as being 'an improper epithet in connection with the description of the mountains melting in the beams of the sun, which immediately follows.' Ferguson thought the Q1 reading stronger precisely because of that seeming contradiction: Even the endlessness of the snow could not prevent the melting. According to Ure, one kind of effect was sacrificed in favor of another. The entire passage is so difficult that I am reluctant to try to guess the subtleties that motivated what seems a slight change from a concern that is both temporal and spatial to one that is merely spatial.

181/137 hungrie-torrents-eaten rockes] Q1-2: 'hungrie torrents: eating rockes'. Ferguson's analysis of the received text is so persuasive that one almost forgets that the syntax that would allow his interpretation is all but unsayable: particularly, 'eating rockes', which he sees as lava, apparently in opposition with 'torrents'. The emendation that I have made, adding two hyphens and altering 'eating' to 'eaten', is relatively slight, is conceivable under ordinary processes of textual transmission, and yields a sentence that is meaningful even under the oral conditions of the theater. It also does no damage to a number of the key points in Ferguson's interpretation: the association with Hercules, for instance. The mountains still melt, but now the reason for the snow is clear: Its melting creates the hungry torrents that eat

the rocks of the mountains. The most important association is untouched:
The 'sunne' is still Tamyra, who is 'turnd to blood' because she is wounded,
and the wound 'in [her] bosome' still sets up the image of the two oppressive
and Senecan mountains (hidden in snow because, despite the blood, breasts
are still white). The bitterness of human life (in his imagery, the ocean) is not
from lava, but from the blood of the two lovers (converted from the snow).
Ferguson's assumed volcanoes are sacrificed by the emendation (since the
rocks are eaten by melted snow and not lava), as are the burning mountains
(from Revelation 8:8) inferred by Jacquot. But the allusion to Revelation,
which is plausible, may still be present (in the ocean made bitter by trans-
formation into blood); note that the original reading does not clearly yield a
burning mountain, and the allusion does not depend upon the complete
biblical machinery.

184/140 valure:] Editors have usually changed the quartos' semicolon to a
comma, resulting in a series ('strength, valure, vertue'). But the semicolon
may be meaningful: 'vertue' may be the general term that subsumes 'strength'
and 'valure' – i.e., frail condition of strength and valor, those things that have
been *my* virtue ('vertue / In me').

–/146-52 Farewell ... humanity] See note at ll. 264-70/146-52.

192-94/– (Since ... bloud)] Although it is possible, considering the markings
on this page of Q1 by the collator, that these lines, with their scolding of
Montsurry for rejecting the charity of forgiveness, were omitted in Q2 by
accident, they were probably dropped in revision in order to avoid a sense of
hardening in Montsurry's relationship with his wife. This change is consistent
with the hypothesis that the play was revised to tie in more closely with *The
Revenge of Bussy D'Ambois*; however that my be, it is consistent with the
altered emphasis of the ending, with the transfer of Umbra Frier's eulogy of
Bussy away from its concluding position.

202/162 sitting/kneeling] N. Brooke thought the change to 'kneeling' a
'theatre change'. It seems more likely to mark a deliberate change in
Montsurry's attitude toward the same posture by Tamyra, a softening that is
consistent with the deletion of ll. 192-94/–.

213-14/– My ... stepdame] The omission of these lines by Q2 has no obvious
purpose unless to shorten a bit Tamyra's complaints about her situation.
Chapman may have wished to remove Tamyra's novercal image for 'Vertue'.

–/186 SD *Exeunt Guise, Mons. above*] As with other stage movements in this
act, Q2 is more careful than Q1 about including directions. Indeed, the only
exit marked in Q1 after the end of its V.ii (V.iii in Q2) is the one for the
murderers when they are confronted by Umbra Comolet at V.iii.90/V.iv.42,
and it is inexact (since it does not make clear that one murderer stays
onstage). I have supplied stage directions for Q1 where I was confident that
they represent Chapman's staging, but I have provided no exit for Monsieur
and Guise because its placement seems arbitrary. N. Brooke suggested that
they remain onstage throughout as 'detached spectators', 'silent, brooding
Fates'. Though this is an interesting conception, it takes far too literally a text
that omits exits for other characters who most certainly are intended to exit.

–/186 SD *murtherers ... off.*] Neither quarto provides an exit for the murderers. Q2, however, seems at this point to be clearing the stage for the finale. It provides for the removal of Bussy's body, and I assume that the murderers, exiting at the same time as Guise and Monsieur, perform that task. No mention is made of the body of the dead murderer, but there is no reason to assume that it would be left onstage. Something similar may have happened in the Q1 version, so far as the murderer's body is concerned, but Bussy's body is presumably still onstage as Umbra Comolet pronounces his eulogy over it at the end of the play in the Q1 version. Perhaps Umbra Comolet carried it off when he (presumably) exited at V.iii.270/–, but I have not provided for it there.

231/191 heere/here] Most editors have added 'are' somewhere in the line – perhaps rightly, though 'heere' probably was a way of spelling the contraction 'here're' (as in N. Brooke).

240/200 to a hunted Tygres] Q1 'to hunted Tygres'. Though six editors have followed Q1, both metrics and logic (Tamyra, in her imagination, being a lone fugitive) suggest that its omission of 'a' was a mistake. The earliest citation of 'tigress' in the *NED* is from 1611, close enough to allow the word's existence a few years earlier. N. Brooke argued that *NED* has 'tygres' as a common form of 'tigers' but not for 'tigress' and therefore took Q2's addition of 'a' as a sophistication. His summary of the *NED* testimony is correct, but Q2 itself countervails: By inserting 'a' (whether rightly or wrongly), the Q2 compositor showed that he thought 'Tygres' to be an acceptable form for 'tigress'.

260/220 SD *Exeunt Montsurry and Tamyra severally./Exeunt severally.*] Once again, Q1 makes no provision for getting important characters offstage. I am reasonably confident that Montsurry and Tamyra are not to stay onstage while Umbra Comolet speaks his farewell eulogy to Bussy: Montsurry has prepared (l. 258/218) for their immediate exit ('*Now* turne from me, as *heere* I turne from thee'), and their departure by separate doors, leaving the body of Bussy behind, would make a powerful impact. In Q2, no exit is marked for Umbra Frier, whose last speech in that version (ll. 204-5/164-65) was the advice to Tamyra to leave Bussy's side and rejoin her husband. Parrott and three other editors caused him to exit at that point, but any specific placement (several different ones are defensible) is speculative. I have not resolved the question, except that – if he has stayed during Tamyra's negotiations with her husband – he must be considered as being among those who leave 'severally' (l. 260/220).

264-70/146-52 Farewell ... humanity] The transfer of these lines away from the end in Q2 may have had something to do with the writing of *The Revenge of Bussy D'Ambois*, as N. Brooke and Tricomi have suggested, and it puts the final emphasis on Montsurry and Tamyra rather than on Bussy, 'on the living characters whose affairs are important to the new play' (Brooke). Several recent critics have found the lines much less effective in their Q2 location, but (assuming the changed emphasis is what was desired) removing them from the end leaves the audience with the separate departure of Tamyra and Montsurry as the final powerful image it sees. (I agree with Brooke that the high percentage of errors in Q2's printing of these lines indicates that the compositor was following manuscript: The collator obviously copied out the text from the prompt-book, perhaps being unaware that a printed version of the text was available for cutting and pasting.)

264/146 relicts/reliques] 'reliques' could be a revision (or a correction of a Q1 error), or merely a variant form (since the two words overlapped in meaning).

266/148 Ioine ... Hercules] Q2's '*Jove* ... her rules' makes little sense, and all editors except Dilke have rejected it (as I do). The compositor misread manuscript.

268/150 continent cracke/ chrystall crack] Q2's 'chrystall' is Q2's clarification of Q1's 'continent' (that which contains). N. Brooke's emendation of Q1 to 'continent crack'd' is sound enough on paleographical grounds, but is unnecessary and wrongly makes 'continent' rather than Bussy the subject of 'Spred'. See R. P. Corballis, 'The Apotheosis of Bussy D'Ambois,' *N & Q*, n.s. XXVI (April 1979), 145-46; and my 'On the Date of George Chapman's *Bussy D'Ambois*,' in *Brandeis Essays in Literature*, ed. John Hazel Smith (Waltham, Mass., 1983), pp. 30-36.

Epilogue (Q2 only)

See the note on the Prologue.

The Conspiracie and Tragedie of Charles Duke of Byron, Marshall of France

edited by John B. Gabel

❖

TEXTUAL INTRODUCTION

The several extant documents relating to a notorious performance of Chapman's Byron plays in 1608 have been much discussed by historians of English drama. The basic account of the affair, a portion of a diplomatic dispatch (dated March 29 [O.S.] 1608) from the French ambassador De la Boderie to his superior in Paris, was first printed accurately by J. J. Jusserand in *Modern Language Review* (VI [1911], 203-5) and reprinted by E. K. Chambers in his *Elizabethan Stage* (III, 257-58). Of various other sources of information none is so important as Chapman's letter, presumably to Sir George Buc, Deputy Master of the Revels,[1] concerning the recipient's refusal to grant permission for printing the Byron plays. Because this letter refers to matters significant for the present edition, I give here a transcription drawn directly from Folger MS. V.a. 321, f. 49^r.

> S: I have not deserv'd what I suffer by yor Austeritie; Yf the two or three lynes you crost, were spoken; My vttermost to suppresse them was enough for my discharge; To more then w^{ch}, No promysse can be rackt by reason; I see not myne owne Plaies; Nor carrie the Actors Tongues in my Mouthe; The action of ye mynde is performance sufficient of any dewtie, before the greatest Authoritie[,] wherein I have quitted all yor former favo^{res}, And made them more worthie then any you bestowe on outward observers; Yf the thrice allowance of ye Counsaile for y^e

---

[1] The recipient of the letter is nowhere named. But the function ascribed to him in the letter, the licensing of plays for performance with the consequent censoring of what was objectionable, was specifically Buc's task as Deputy Master of the Revels. (His uncle, Edmund Tilney, the actual Master, performed none of the duties of the office after mid-1607.) When the Byron plays were finally allowed to be printed and were entered in the *Stationers' Register*, it was 'under the hands of Sir George Buc and the wardens.' We can feel confident, therefore, in assuming that Chapman's letter was written to Buc.

Presentment; have not weight enoughe to drawe yo^res after for the Presse; My Breath is a hopeles Adition; Yf you say (for yor Reason) you know not if more then was spoken be now written no No; Nor can you know that, if you had bothe the Copies; Not seeing the first at all: Or if you had seene it presented, yor Memorie could hardly confer wth it so strictly in the Revisall, to descerne the Adition; My short Reason therefore can not sounde yor Severitie; Whosoever it were y^t first plaied the bitter Informer before the frenche Ambassador for a matter so far from offence; And of so muche hono^r for his Maister, as those two partes containe; performd it wth the Gall of a Wulff, and not of a Man; And theise hartie, & secrett vengeances taken for Crost, & Officious humors, are more Politiqu[e] then Christian; W^ch he that hates, will one day discover in ye ope[n] Ruyne of their Aucto^res; And thoughe they be trifles: he yet laies them in Ballance, (as they concerne Iustice, and bewray Appetites to the greatest Tyrannye) wth the greatest; But how easely soever Illiterate Aucthoritie settes vp his Bristles against Povert[ie] Me thinkes yo^res (beinge accompanied wth learninge) should rebate ye pointes of them: And soften the fiercenes of those rude Manners; You know S^r, They are sparkes of the lowest ffier in Nature, that flye out vppon weakenes, wth everie pufft of Power; I desier not, you should drenche yor hand in the least daunger for mee; And therefore (wth entreatie of my Papers returne) I cease ever to trooble you./.

> By the poore subiect of yor
> office for the present./[2]

The composition of the Byron plays, begun after the publication in 1607 of their source, Edward Grimeston's *General Inventorie of the History of France*,[3] must have been completed by about January 1607/8. Chapman's letter to Buc indicates that the plays had been performed before the French ambassador's initial intervention in the matter, which can have been no later (as will be seen below) than about the middle of February. Indeed, Chapman speaks of 'the thrice allowance of ye Counsaile for ye Presentment,'[4] from which it can be inferred that the plays were performed on three different occasions before any trouble developed. Did this set of plays to which the Privy Council gave its blessing and from which Buc cut only 'two or three lynes' contain the scandalous altercation between the French Queen and her husband's mistress, the scene about which the French ambassador complained in the dispatch

---

[2] The letter is reproduced by permission of the Folger Shakespeare Library. A facsimile and transcript have recently been published by A. R. Braunmuller in his *A Seventeenth-Century Letter-Book: A Facsimile Edition of Folger MS. V.a. 321* (Newark, Del.: Univ. of Delaware Press, 1983), pp. 246-7. My transcript varies slightly from Mr Braunmuller's because I have worked from a photocopy of the letter made in the early 1960s when the manuscript had suffered less leaf-edge crumbling (with consequent loss of line endings) than it now has.

[3] In 'The Date of Chapman's *Conspiracy and Tragedy of Byron*,' *MP*, LXVI (1969), 330-2, I took issue with a proposal made some years earlier that the Byron plays derive from Grimeston's manuscript (instead of the printed book) and were written before 1607. For other attempts to date these plays earlier than Chapman's obvious source for them, see Glynne Wickham, *Early English Stages*, II, pt. 1 (New York, 1963), pp. 312-13 fn.; and Robert Wren, 'Salisbury and the Blackfriars Theatre,' *Theatre Notebook*, XXIII (1969), 107-8.

[4] I speculate that the plays were referred to the Privy Council, probably by George Buc himself, because of the potentially offensive nature of any stage portrayal of the reigning monarch of a neighboring nation.

to his government?⁵ I think it patent that it did not. I have argued the case fully elsewhere⁶ and here need only note the two major pieces of evidence, (a) that the French ambassador twice implies that the incident involving the Queen was *added* to the Byron story, and (b) that when the masque (which is part and parcel of the feminine dispute but has nothing to do with the Byron affair) is removed from the printed *Tragedie* and the final act (twice as long as any other) is split in two, the play is revealed to be a tightly constructed, effective drama.

The Byron plays were thus performed several times near the beginning of 1607/8, with no offense to authority beyond the actors' speaking a few lines that had been censored. But then, according to Chapman's letter, an informer carried the news to the French ambassador that the history of the late Marechal de Biron was being staged by English actors. De la Boderie complained to the authorities and secured a prohibition against further performances. His dispatch of March 29 speaks of 'la deffense qui leur avoit esté faicte' and refers to the actors as 'ces certains comédiens à qui j'avois fait deffendre de ne jouer l'histoire du feu mareschal de Biron.'⁷ Jusserand says of the words 'ces certains comédiens' that they 'clearly imply that the ambassador had already written about them.' That earlier dispatch must have reported to Paris the discovery of what the players were about and De la Boderie's success in having the performances stopped.

It is at this point, I believe – perhaps early in February – that Chapman made his first attempt to have the Byron plays published. Since 'Illiterate Aucthoritie' had forbidden further stage performance of the plays, Chapman, in his usual poverty-stricken state, submitted them to Sir George Buc with the hope of securing a license for publication. The copy approved earlier for performance and having the 'two or three lynes' censored was undoubtedly still in the possession of the acting company, the Children of the Revels. What Chapman now sent to Buc would have been either his foul papers (as Fredson Bowers defines that term: 'the author's last complete draft in a shape satisfactory to him to be transferred to a fair copy'⁸) or a newly made fair copy. But the Deputy Master of the Revels refused to grant a license for publication. It appears from the letter that Buc gave no reason for his refusal, and Chapman could only speculate as to what it might be. Buc, he knew, was still angry that the actors had willfully spoken the deleted lines. Chapman

---

⁵ The portion of the dispatch relevant to the Byron plays reads as follows: 'Environ la micaresme ces certains comédiens à qui j'avois fait deffendre de ne jouer l'histoire du feu mareschal de Biron, voyant toutte la cour dehors, ne laissèrent de le faire, et non seulement cela, mais y introduisirent la Royne et Madame de Verneuil, la première traitant celle-cy fort mal de paroles, et luy donnant un soufflet. En ayant eu advis de-là à quelques jours, aussi-tost je m'en allay trouver le Comte de Salsbury et luy fis plainte de ce que non seulement ces compaignons-là contrevenoient à la deffense qui leur avoit esté faicte, mais y adjoustoient des choses non seulement plus importantes, mais qui n'avoient que faire avec le mareschal de Biron, et au partir de-là estoient toutes faulses, dont en vérité il se montra fort courroucé. Et dès l'heure mesme envoya pour les prendre.'
⁶ 'The Original Version of Chapman's *Tragedy of Byron*,' *JEGP*, LXIII (1964), 433-40.
⁷ I have compared Jusserand's transcription with a film of the original, Bibliothèque Nationale MS. Fr. 15984, and find but one error, the omission of 'ne' before 'jouer' in Jusserand's first line.
⁸ *On Editing Shakespeare* (Charlottesville, 1966), p. 13.

wonders whether Buc would be satisfied only if he could compare the first copy he had allowed with the present one, to learn whether 'more then was spoken be now written.' Chapman emphatically denies this to be so, but adds that such a comparison would be meaningless anyway; for it is not what was written in the first copy that matters but what was said on stage – and Buc cannot know what was said, not having seen a stage presentation ('Not seeing the first at all'). And even had he seen the plays performed, he could scarcely remember the spoken words well enough to compare them with the written words in this second copy – this supposed 'Revisall.' Whether Chapman had actual grounds for assigning to Buc these hypothetical objections to licensing the plays for publication, we do not know. It may be that the playwright touches upon a more likely reason for the refusal when he says at the letter's end, 'I desier not, you should drenche yor hand in the least daunger for mee.' Buc would undoubtedly have been justified in hesitating to take responsibility for allowing the publication of plays that had proved offensive to the French ambassador, and he may have wanted considerable time to pass before granting his approval. But Chapman's poverty would not allow him to wait, and so he wrote this testy letter asking for the return of his 'Papers.' Perhaps he hoped at this point to secure permission to print from some other qualified licenser; it is of note that he terms himself at the conclusion of the letter, 'the poore subiect of yor office for the present' – for the present, but not thereafter? Or perhaps Chapman and the managers of the Revels company had already hit upon the idea of an illegal performance of the plays, one that would not merely violate the prohibition against once again staging the Byron history but add to it a sensational portrayal of the French royal family and a related masque. To fit the additions in smoothly and make the consequent cuts necessary elsewhere, Chapman would have needed his own working copy of the text.

The revisions must have been completed by late February, for around Midlent, i.e. March 6 (O.S.), according to the ambassador's dispatch, the notorious performance took place. A few days later De la Boderie heard of it and complained to Robert Cecil, bringing about the arrest of some of the actors, the temporary closing of all the theaters, and a search for the author. A letter from Sir Thomas Lake to Cecil dated March 11 indicates that at that time King James was still intent upon punishing 'the maker' of the offensive plays. Apparently Chapman was given sanctuary by a powerful friend – the Duke of Lennox, it seems[9] – until the affair should blow over.

It is astounding how quickly it did blow over. In the absence of sufficient evidence to enable us to make complete sense of the situation, we can only wonder at the audacity of Chapman and/or the bookseller Thomas Thorpe in

---

[9] From fol. 94^r of the Chapman letterbook cited above, Bertram Dobell published (in *The Athenaeum*, April 6, 1901, p. 433) a fairly accurate transcription of a copy of a letter, almost certainly from Chapman, to one Mr Crane, secretary to the Duke of Lennox. As Dobell notes, the remarks seem actually to be directed beyond the secretary to the Duke. The point of the letter is not clear, but it reflects a situation we can imagine Chapman to have found himself in a week or two after his Mid-Lent trouble. The letter begins thus: 'S^r. Not wearie of my Shelter, but vncertaine, why the Forme of the Clowde, still hovers over me, when the Matter is disperst, I write to intreat yor Resolution. ...'

moving so quickly to publish a work that had outraged the top levels of both the English and French governments. But it is a fact that within three months of the Midlent incident, *The Conspiracie and Tragedie* was in print. That the publication date was no later than the first of June we know from the fortunate survival of the Clark Memorial Library copy of the work, whose first owner noted on the title page the purchase price and date: 'pret 10ᵈ. 1ᵒ. Junii. 1608.' The supreme self-confidence of Chapman and his publisher becomes even more obvious when we realize that it was not until June 5 that the book was entered in the *Stationers' Register*.[10] Chapman may have believed, or known for certain, that the book would enjoy the protection of the influential dedicatee, Sir Thomas Walsingham, who according to the letter of dedication had voiced his 'approbation of these in their presentment.'

The Byron first quarto was printed by George Eld from a manuscript in which the slapping scene of *The Tragedie* was excised but not the masque that relates to it. Because in this mutilated manuscript the masque still occupied the place of the second act (*Finis Actus Secundi* concluded it, but the heading ACTVS II was deleted along with the slapping scene), the remaining scenes could not be distributed as they had been in the original version of *The Tragedie*; consequently the fifth act remained double the normal act-length. Whether the original fourth act of *The Conspiracie*, in which Queen Elizabeth was directly portrayed, was altered at this time in preparation for printing or months earlier at the order of the Privy Council or Buc, when the plays were submitted for a license for 'presentment,' is impossible to say. At any rate, Chapman at some point cut that act by half its length (omitting among other things, I believe, a passage in which Elizabeth spoke to Byron about the fatal ambitions of the Earl of Essex – see *The Tragedie*, V.iii.139ff.) and clumsily recast the direct discourse as indirect.[11]

If the manuscript that Chapman had asked to be returned to him was in fact the one he then revised for the mid-Lent performance, there is a good chance it is also the one in which he made the final necessary cuts and which he then submitted to the printer. The text of Q1 bears all the signs of having come from an author's own papers rather than a manuscript marked for use in the theater. In several places a set of characters is said to enter '*with others*' or '*cum aliis.*' At one point (*Trag.* V.iv.17) there is the direction, '*Enter Byron, a Bishop or two; with all the guards, souldiers with muskets.*', which is

---

[10] On a flyleaf of the Clark copy of Q1, opposite the title page, is the following note by 'B.N.' (Brinsley Nicholson?) concerning the June 5 date of the S.R. entry: 'This compared with date of price on t.p. [i.e. June 1] seems to show that a book was at times first printed & published & then entered.' The case of the Byron plays must be taken into account in future scholarly discussions of the relationship between publication and entry in the *Stationers' Register*.

[11] F. G. Fleay, speaking of these revisions in Act IV and of others he supposed to exist in Act V, said, 'If these alterations were made wholly or partly by Chapman at the order of the Master of the Revels, he has made them intentionally in such a clumsy way as to show where the sutures occur' (*A Biographical Chronicle of the English Drama, 1559-1642* [London, 1891], I, 63-64). I do not find this convincing, and the same applies to Fleay's argument that only in the altered passages is the phrase *Duke of Býron* employed in place of the correct *Duke Býrón*; obvious exceptions to this Fleay must explain away as occurring in 'a doubtfully bombastic passage' or as resulting from 'printer's error.'

quite adequate for a reader, but lacks the specificity necessary for guiding an acting-company.

That Chapman himself was involved in the final stages of the preparation of *The Conspiracie and Tragedie* for publication is evident from his dedicatory letter, where he describes the plays as 'these poore dismemberd Poems.' Indeed, that the author could affix a dedicatory letter at all indicates he had not surrendered complete control of his literary property. I am convinced, from the nature of the one hundred press corrections, that Chapman himself read the proofs. Charlton Hinman, Fredson Bowers, and other close students of the printing of plays in Shakespeare's time have convinced us that correction by printing-house employees was usually done out of a concern for decent typographical form, its chief effect being to remove merely obvious flaws. Proof corrections in the Byron quarto reflect rather an author's concern for literary form and for exactness of expression; specifically, they reflect his second thoughts regarding substantives and his fussiness regarding accidentals. Admittedly, had a printer's man read proof against copy he might have made such corrections as 'Mock'st' for 'Workst' (*Consp.* I.i.155) or 'pace on continuate' for 'place on continuall' (*Consp.* I.ii.142), but it is unlikely for so minor a piece of work as a play quarto that time was taken to read proof against copy. Only the author would have been sufficiently interested to change the slightly ambiguous but otherwise satisfactory 'Sweat' to 'Swette' (*Consp.* I.i.180) and 'Canons' to 'Cannans' (*Consp.* I.i.21, I.ii.34) or to alter the punctuation at several dozen places where the correction makes but little difference in the sense. (All but a few of the sets of punctuation variants involve changes from light to heavy, or from no pointing at all to some mark or other, suggesting an author's anxious concern for clarity as he read through his proofs.) And only the author would, I think, have taken the responsibility for altering in proof 'instrument' to 'Lord' (*Consp.* II.i.70), 'their' to 'his' (*Consp.* III.ii.52), and 'this sute' to 'that' (*Consp.* V.i.68). We know that Chapman corrected the proofs of *The Memorable Masque*, printed by George Eld in 1613, and I think the evidence is clear that he did so for *The Conspiracie and Tragedie*. Consequently, I have adopted the bulk of the corrections in my text. The few exceptions are for obvious reasons – as, for example, when the corrections themselves are patent errors. I have not accepted the one notorious emendation, from 'So long as idle and ridiculus King' (*Consp.* V.ii.5) to 'So long as such as he', this being obviously the product of censorship. Had Chapman been making a change here he would, we can feel confident, at least have produced a complete pentameter line.

Evidence respecting compositor identification is puzzling, and no regular pattern of composition is apparent – perhaps because there is none. A degree of crowding of material on pages 3^v-4^r of three sheets, L, P, and Q, and of stretching on the same pages of N indicate typesetting by forme and from cast-off copy. But there is little evidence for this elsewhere, and indeed strong evidence in some sheets that setting was seriatim by pages. One notices, for instance, at the beginning of sheet H the work of a new compositor, one whose habit it was to use colons after the speech-prefixes and abbreviations. The colons appear regularly on H1^r, 1^v, and 3^v, and irregularly on 2^v; in both K and O they occur on 1ᵛ-3ʳ; in M, N, Q, and R, likewise, they can be found on both inner- and outer-forme pages. Analyses of the recurrence of damaged types and of choices among alternate spellings (in such sets as 'blood'/'bloud', 'power'/'powre', 'valor'/'vallor'/'valour'/'valure', and 'spirit'/'spirrit' and the terminations '-esse'/'-es' and '-ick'/'-ique') reveal nothing that indicates setting by formes. In sheet E and several others in the last half of the book, speeches are frequently concluded with commas and semi-colons, but this correlates with no other typographical or spelling habit.

Two sheets deserve special comment. I suspect that B, inner and outer, was set by a compositor who set nothing beyond this in the quarto. The form 'Fraunce' is peculiar to sheet B; and, with only one exception, here alone is our word 'than' spelled thus instead of 'then'. Furthermore, the type-pages in B are several millimeters wider than elsewhere, indicating that the sheet was composed by someone whose composing-stick was set wider than that of his fellows. Sheet P is curious in that it was printed from type used nowhere else in the book; the type is of the same font but is apparently new, so that it printed very cleanly and evenly. One wonders whether the composition of this single sheet was done in some shop other than Eld's.

It is of considerable interest that in twelve of the sixteen sheets containing the text proper (and thus having headlines) the same skeleton was used for both inner and outer formes. Two of the four sheets for which this is not true, I and R, occur at the ends of the two plays and required adaptation of the skeletons to fit the irregular pagination. Because two plays were involved, it was necessary to make new sets of headlines halfway through the book; thus there is a relatively large number of skeletons, fourteen, for the thirty-two formes in sheets B-R. They occur as follows:

The Conspiracie

I	B inner and outer
II	C inner and outer, F inner and outer
III	D inner and outer, G inner and outer
IV	[with some headlines from B] E inner, H inner
V	E outer, H outer
VI	[with some headlines from H outer] I outer
VII	[with some headlines from I outer] I inner

The Tragedie

VIII	K inner and outer
IX	L inner and outer, O inner and outer
X	M inner and outer, Q inner and outer
XI	N inner and outer [excepting one headline]
XII	[with some headlines from K] P inner and outer
XIII	[with some headlines from P] R inner
XIV	[with some headlines from N outer] R outer

The use of the same skeleton for both formes of so many sheets confirms that composition was, at least in most cases, page by page and indicates that only one press was employed. I conclude that the Byron plays were assigned a low priority in Eld's shop and that typesetting proceeded as the individual compositors had time free from more important projects.

The quality of workmanship in the 1608 edition varies, but on the whole it is satisfactory. Not so that of the 1625 edition. Printed for Thomas Thorpe by 'N.O.,' Nicholas Okes,[12] this quarto is marred by hundreds of literal errors; worse yet, it was printed from an ignorantly edited copy of Q1, resulting in scores of gratuitous changes in word order, tense, number, and lineation, and frequent cavalier substitutions of words. In just one scene, at the beginning of Act V, one finds 'Which' for Q1's 'That', 'It is' for 'Tis', 'at' for 'as', 'Haue' for 'Take', 'hates' for 'loathes', 'How' for 'That', 'sacred' for 'feared', 'imperiall' for 'impartiall', 'many' for 'merry', 'Bryde' for 'Byrde', and so on. Parrott was aware that 'the changes introduced into Q2 are almost always for the worse, and in most cases appear to be either errors, or alterations by some proof-corrector'; but still he supposed Q2 to have a redeeming virtue: 'Here and there, however, I fancy that I see the poet's hand, and it is not impossible that Chapman may have marked a few changes in the copy sent to the printer for the second edition.'[13] What Parrott unfortunately failed to realize was that this copy of Q1 simply consisted of sheets some formes of which were in different states of correction from those in the copies of Q1 he himself worked with. Thus, what he thought to be Chapman's emendations in 1625 were actually only undetected press-variants (frequently in the uncorrected state) of the 1608 edition.[14] It should be noted that, because Parrott was not always careful in correcting the copy of Shepherd's edition he prepared for the press, Parrott's edition contains more Q2 readings than he remarked upon and probably was even aware of.

Shortly after the middle of the nineteenth century, James Russell Lowell prepared an edition of the Byron plays superior to the later ones of Pearson, Shepherd, and Phelps precisely because it was not influenced by the corruptions of Q2. This edition was for some reason never published, but complete page proofs are in the Houghton Library at Harvard University.[15] Lowell was fortunate both in not having worked from Q2 and in being able to consult a copy of Q1 intelligently annotated by his friend C. E. Norton.[16] Most of Norton's emendations Lowell admitted to his text; these, and a few others original with Lowell himself, are shrewd attempts to rectify compositorial errors, and I adopt some of them in the present text and remark upon them in the Textual Notes.

---

[12] For transcriptions of the title pages of the quartos, see W. W. Greg, *A Bibliography of the English Printed Drama to the Restoration*, I (London, 1939), 409-10.

[13] 'The Text of Chapman's *Conspiracy and Tragedy of Charles Duke of Byron*,' *MLR*, IV (1908), 42.

[14] For details on this, see Gabel, 'Some Notable Errors in Parrott's Edition of Chapman's Byron Plays,' *Papers of the Bibliographical Society*, LVIII (1964), 465-68.

[15] Included in this bound volume of proof sheets are not only the Byron plays but Chapman's *Monsieur D'Olive* and a portion of Heywood's *A Woman Killed with Kindness*. According to a handwritten note by C. E. Norton at the beginning of the book, Lowell had intended to edit a series of volumes of old plays; but 'the project seems to have been brought to naught by the interference of greater interests.'

[16] This volume, inscribed 'J. R. Lowell from C. E. Norton,' was for some reason returned to its donor and is now in the Norton Collection at Harvard.

Punctuation in Q1, as in Chapman's letterbook (Folger MS. V.a. 321) is very heavy; colons and semi-colons occur where by modern practice there would be commas or no punctuation at all. I have avoided mere modernization of punctuation and have not attempted even to make Chapman consistent with himself. But where the Q1 pointing would force anyone accustomed to reading seventeenth-century poetry to pause and ponder, where the forward motion of his eye would be more than momentarily halted, I have not hesitated to emend. When an emendation at such a place is derived from an earlier edition, that fact is recorded in the footnotes and, in the case of semi-substantives, in the Historical Collation. But an emendation is not credited to an earlier edition when the agreement between the two readings is merely coincidental, my emendations being the product of an editorial policy quite different from that of Parrott and his predecessors.

In preparation for editing the text of *The Conspiracie and Tragedie* I have collated the twenty-one copies of Q1 named at the head of the list of press-variants; five copies of Q2 from the following institutions: the British Library, Victoria and Albert Museum, Boston Public Library, Folger Shakespeare Library, and Huntington Library; the published editions of Shepherd, Phelps, and Parrott; and the unpublished edition of Lowell. In the list of emendations of the copy-text and in the Textual Notes, I refer not only to the quartos and the modern editions but also to the published notes on these plays cited at the head of the Historical Collation and to the manuscript notes in several copies of Q1 and Q2.

In order to prevent the footnotes in the present edition from bulking even larger than they do, I have frequently had to limit the information in a given note to a single substantival or semi-substantival matter and thus to ignore related 'accidental' information. In the following note, for example,

Diademes.] Q2; ~; Q1

the obvious point at issue is the punctuation: Q2's period has been substituted in the present text for the semi-colon of the Q1 copy-text; but necessarily suppressed is the fact that the spelling of the lemma accords with the 'Diademes' of Q1, not the 'Diadems' of Q2. Further, given the general untrustworthiness of Q2, the footnotes at some points simply do not report its variant readings. Thus, in contrast to the usual practice in this edition of Chapman's plays, the absence of 'Q2' among the sigla in any particular note does *not* imply agreement of Q2's reading with the lemma.[17]

---

[17] Subsequent to completion of the manuscript of the present edition, a modern-spelling version of the Byron plays was published by Garland Press in its Renaissance Drama Series. Any interested reader who compares the tables of Q1 press-variants in that edition and the present one will observe significant differences between the two. In carefully re-examining the evidence, I find that the editor of the Garland edition has overlooked some twenty press-variants; has identified as press-variants a number of what are actually only instances of faintly printed characters, show-through, and type-batter; has reversed the first and second states of correction in one forme; and has failed to perceive that there are two states of correction, not one, in two formes and in another has supposed that there are two states when there is in fact but one.

THE

CONSPIRACIE,

And

TRAGEDIE

OF

CHARLES Duke of BYRON,
Marshall of France.

Acted lately in two playes, at the
Black-Friers.

Written by GEORGE CHAPMAN.

Printed by *G. Eld* for *Thomas Thorppe*, and are to be sold at
the Tygers head in Paules Church-yard.
1608.

[DRAMATIS PERSONAE

Henry IV, King of France
Albert, Archduke of Austria
The Duke of Savoy
The Duke of Byron
D'Auvergne, a French noble allied with Byron
Crequi ⎫
D'Aumont ⎪
Epernon ⎬ French nobles
Nemours ⎪
Soissons ⎭
La Fin, a ruined French noble
Janin, a councilor of the King
Vitry, captain of the King's guard
Bellièvre ⎫
Brulart ⎬ French commissioners to the Archduke
Roiseau, a French gentleman accompanying the commissioners
D'Aumale, a French exile at the Archduke's court
Picoté, a Frenchman in the Archduke's service
Orange ⎫
Mansfield ⎬ nobles in the Austrian court
Roncas, the ambassador of Savoy
Breton ⎫
Rochette ⎬ attendants of the Duke of Savoy
La Brosse, an astrologer

Three ladies of the French court]

Dramatis Personae] *subs. as given by Parrott; first given by Phelps*

To my Honorable and Constant
friend, Sir *Tho: Walsingham*, Knight: and to my much
loued from his birth, the right toward and worthy
Gentleman his sonne *Thomas Walsingham*,
Esquire.

SIR, though I know, you euer stood little affected to these
vnprofitable rites of Dedication; (which disposition in you,
hath made me hetherto dispence with your right in my other
impressions) yet, least the world may repute it a neglect in
me, of so ancient and worthy a friend; (hauing heard your   5
approbation of these in their presentment) I could not but
prescribe them with your name; And that my affection may
extend to your Posteritie, I haue entitled to it, herein,
your hope and comfort in your generous sonne; whom I doubt
not, that most reuerenc'd Mother of *Manly Sciences*; to whose   10
instruction your vertuous care commits him; will so profitably
initiate in her learned labours, that they will make him flor-
ish in his riper life, ouer the idle liues of our ignorant
Gentlemen; and enable him to supply the Honorable places, of
your name; extending your yeares, and his right noble Mothers   15
(in the true comforts of his vertues) to the sight of much,
and most happy Progenie; which most affectionately wishing;
and diuiding these poore dismemberd Poems betwixt you, I desire
to liue still in your gracefull loues; and euer,

The most assured at your commandements
GEORGE CHAPMAN. /

Prologus.

When the vnciuill, ciuill warres of France,
Had pour'd vpon the countries beaten brest,
Her batterd Citties; prest her vnder hils
Of slaughterd carcases; set her in the mouthes

Of *murtherous breaches, and made pale* Despaire   5
Leaue her to Ruine; *through them all,* Byron
Stept to her rescue; tooke her by the hand:
Pluckt her from vnder her vnnaturall presse,
And set her shining in the height of peace.
And now new clensd, from dust, from sweat, and bloud,   10
And dignified with title of a Duke;
As when in wealthy Autumne, *his bright starre*
(Washt in the lofty Ocean) thence ariseth;
Illustrates heauen, and all his other fires
Out-shines and darkens; so admird Byron,   15
All France *exempted from comparison.*
He toucht heauen with his lance; nor yet was toucht
With hellish treacherie: his countries loue,
He yet thirsts: not the faire shades of himselfe:
Of which empoisoned Spring, *when pollicie drinkes,*   20
He bursts in growing great; and rising, sinckes:
Which now behold in our Conspirator,
And see in his reuolt, how honors flood
Ebbes into ayre, when men are Great, not Good. /

5 Despaire] ~, *Q1-2* ‖ 16 France] ~, *Q1-2* ‖ 20 *Spring,*] ~; *Q1-2* ‖

[THE CONSPIRACIE OF
Charles Duke of *Byron*.]

ACTVS 1.   SCAENA 1.

Enter Sauoy, Roncas, Rochette, Breton.

Sau. I would not for halfe *Sauoy*, but haue bound
Fraunce to some fauour, by my personall presence
More than your selfe, (my Lord Ambassadour)
Could haue obtaind; for all Ambassadours
(You know) haue chiefly these instructions;   5
To note the State and chiefe sway of the Court,
To which they are employde; to penetrate
The heart, and marrow of the Kings designes,
And to obserue the countenances and spirites,
Of such as are impatient of rest;   10
And wring beneath, some priuate discontent:
But, past all these, there are a number more
Of these State Critiscismes that our personall view
May profitably make, which cannot fall
Within the powres of our instruction,   15
To make you comprehend; I will doe more
With my meere shadow, than you with your persons.
All you can say against my comming heere,
Is that, which I confesse, may for the time,
Breede strange affections in my brother *Spaine*;   20
But when I shal haue time to make my Cannans,
The long-tong'd Heraulds of my hidden drifts,
Our reconcilement will be made with triumphs.
    Ron. If not, your Highnesse hath small cause to care,
Hauing such worthy reason to complaine   25
Of *Spaines* colde friendship, and his lingring succours,
Who onely entertaines your griefes with hope,
To make your medcine desperate.
    Roch.   My Lord knowes

___

SD *Enter*] Q2 ‖ **13** Critiscismes that] ∼: That *Q1-2* ‖ **21** shal . . . Cannans] *Q1(c)*; shall . . . Canons
Q1(u); shall . . . Cannons Q2 ‖ **23** Our] *Q1(c)*, Q2; Your *Q1(u)* ‖

The Spanish glosse too well; his forme, stuffe, lasting,
And the most dangerous conditions,   30
He layes on them with whome he is in league.
Th'iniustice in the most vnequall dowre, /
Giuen with th'*Infanta*, whome my Lord espousde,   [B1ᵛ]
Compar'd with that her elder sister had,
May tell him how much *Spaines* loue weighs to him;   35
When of so many Globes and Scepters held
By the great King, he onely would bestow
A portion but of six score thousand Crownes
In yeerely pension, with his highnesse wife,
When the *Infanta* wedded by the Archduke   40
Had the *Franch County*, and lowe Prouinces.
   Bret. We should not set these passages of Splene
Twixt *Spaine* and *Sauoy*; to the weaker part,
More good by suffrance growes, than deedes of heart,
The nearer Princes are, the further off   45
In rites of friendship; my aduice had neuer
Consented to this voyage of my Lord,
In which he doth endaunger *Spaines* whole losse,
For hope of some poore fragment heere in *Fraunce*.
   Sau. My hope in *France* you know not, though my counsel,   50
And for my losse of *Spaine*, it is agreede,
That I should sleight it; oft-times Princes rules
Are like the Chymicall Philosophers;
Leaue me then to mine owne proiection,
In this our thriftie Alchymie of state,   55
Yet helpe me thus farre, you that haue beene heere
Our Lord Ambassadour; and, in short informe mee,
What Spirites here are fit for our designes.
   Ron. The new-created Duke *Byron* is fit,
Were there no other reason for your presence,   60
To make it worthie; for he is a man
Of matchlesse valure, and was euer happy
In all encounters, which were still made good,
With an vnwearyed sence of any toyle,
Hauing continewd fourteene dayes together   65
Vpon his horse; his blood is not voluptuous,
Nor much inclinde to women; his desires
Are higher than his state, and his deserts
Not much short of the most he can desire,
If they be weigh'd with what *Fraunce* feeles by them: /   70

---

29 stuffc,] *comma turned Q1* ‖ **35** him;] *Q1(c), Q2;* ~, *Q1(u)* ‖ **41** *Franch County*] Franch County *Q1* ‖ **43** *Sauoy*;] *Q1(c), Q2;* ~, *Q1(u)* ‖ **52** it;] ~, *Q1-2* ‖ **70** If] *followed by turned apostrophe Q1* ‖

He is past measure glorious: And that humour   [B2]
Is fit to feede his Spirites, whome it possesseth
With faith in any errour; chiefly where
Men blowe it vp, with praise of his perfections,
The taste whereof in him so soothes his pallate,   75
And takes vp all his appetite, that oft times
He will refuse his meate, and companie
To feast alone with their most strong conceit;
Ambition also, cheeke by cheeke doth march
With that excesse of glory, both sustain   80
With an vnlimited fancie, That the King,
Nor *Fraunce* it selfe, without him can subsist.
   Sau. He is the man (my Lord) I come to winne;
And that supreame intention of my presence
Saw neuer light till now, which yet I feare,   85
The politike king, suspecting, is the cause
That he hath sent him so farre from my reach,
And made him chiefe in the Commission,
Of his ambassage to my brother Arch-duke,
With whome he is now; and (as I am tolde)   90
So entertaind and fitted in his humour,
That ere I part, I hope he will returne
Prepar'd, and made the more fit for the phisicke
That I intend to minister.
   Ron.   My Lord,
There is another discontented Spirite   95
Now heere in Court, that for his braine, and aptnes
To any course that may recouer him
In his declined and litigious state,
Will serue *Byron*, as he were made for him,
In giuing vent to his ambitious vaine,   100
And that is, *De Laffin.*
   Sau.   You tell me true,
And him I thinke you haue prepar'd for me.
   Ron. I haue my Lord, and doubt not he will prooue,
Of the yet taintlesse fortresse of *Byron*,
A quicke Expugner, and a strong Abider.   105
   Sau. Perhappes the battry will be brought before him, /
In this ambassage, for I am assur'd   [B2ᵛ]
They set high price of him, and are informde
Of all the passages, and means for mines
That may be thought on, to his taking in: 110

---

73 errour;] *Q1(c), Q2*; ~, *Q1(u)* ‖

Enter Henry and Laffin.

The King comes, and *Laffin*: the Kings aspect
Folded in cloudes.
   Hen.   I will not haue my traine,
Made a retreite for Bankroutes, nor my Court,
A hyue for Droanes: prowde Beggars and true Thieues,
That while a forced truth they sweare to me,   115
Robbe my poore subiects, shall giue vp their Arts,
And hencefoorth learne to liue by their desarts;
Though I am growne, by right of Birth and Armes
Into a greater kingdome, I will spreade
With no more shade, then may admit that kingdome   120
Her proper, naturall, and woonted fruites;
Nauarre shall be *Navarre*, and *France* still *France*:
If one may be the better for the other
By mutuall rites, so, neither shall be worse.
Thou arte in lawe, in quarrells, and in debt,   125
Which thou wouldst quit with countnaunce; Borrowing
With thee is purchase, and thou seekst by me
(In my supportance), now our olde warres cease,
To wage worse battells, with the armes of Peace.
   Laf. Peace must not make men Cowherds, nor keepe calme   130
Her pursie regiment with mens smootherd breaths;
I must confesse my fortunes are declinde,
But neither my deseruings, nor my minde:
I seeke but to sustaine the right I found,
When I was rich, in keeping what is left,   135
And making good my honour as at best,
Though it be hard; mans right to euery thing
Wanes with his wealth, wealth is his surest King;
Yet Iustice should be still indifferent.
The ouerplus of Kings, in all their might,   ·140
Is but to peece out the defects of right:
And this I sue for, nor shall frownes and taunts /
(The common Scarre-crowes of all poore mens suites)   [B3]
Nor mis-construction that doth colour still
Licentiate Iustice, punishing good for ill,   145
Keepe my free throate from knocking at the Skie,
If thunder chid mee, for my equitie.
   Hen. Thy equity, is to be euer banisht
From Court, and all societie of noblesse,
Amongst whome thou throwst balls of all dissention;   150

114 Beggars] ~, *Q1-2* ‖ 115 while] with *Q1 2* (*See Textual Note*) ‖ 121 fruites;] -·, *Q1-2* ‖ 128 supportance), ... cease,] ~)ˌ ... ~ˌ *Q1-2* ‖ 130 Cowherds] *stet* (*See Textual Note*) ‖ 147 chid mee] *Q1(c)*; chide me *Q1(u)*; chid me *Q2* | mee,] ~ˌ *Q1-2* ‖

282

Thou arte at peace with nothing but with warre,
Hast no heart but to hurt, and eatst thy heart,
If it but thinke of doing any good:
Thou witchest with thy smiles, suckst bloud with praises,
Mock'st al humanitie; society poisonst;   155
Coosinst with vertue; with religion
Betrayst, and massacrest; so vile thy selfe,
That thou suspectst perfection in others:
A man must thinke of all the villanies
He knowes in all men, to descipher thee,   160
That art the centre to impietie:
Away, and tempt me not.
   Laf.   But you tempt me,
To what, thou Sunne be iudge, and make him see.   *Exit.*
   Sau. Now by my dearest Marquisate of *Salusses*,
Your Maiestie hath with the greatest life   165
Describ'd a wicked man; or rather thrust
Your arme downe through him to his very feete,
And pluckt his inside out, that euer yet,
Mine cares did witnesse; or turnd eares to Eies;
And those strange Characters, writ in his face,   170
Which at first sight, were hard for me to reade,
The Doctrine of your speech, hath made so plaine,
That I run through them like my naturall language:
Nor do I like that mans Aspect, me thinkes,
Of all lookes where the Beames of Starres haue caru'd   175
Their powrefull influences; And (O rare)
What an heroicke, more than royall Spirite
Bewraide you in your first speech, that defies
Protection of vile droanes, that eate the honny /   179
Swette from laborious vertue, and denies   [B3ᵛ]
To giue those of *Nauarre*, though bred with you,
The benefites and dignities of *Fraunce.*
When little Riuers by their greedy currants,
(Farre farre extended from their mother springs)
Drinke vp the forraine brookes still as they runne,   185
And force their greatnesse, when they come to Sea,
And iustle with the Ocean for a roome,
O how he roares, and takes them in his mouth,
Digesting them so to his proper streames,
That they are no more seene, hee nothing raisde   190
Aboue his vsuall bounds, yet they deuour'd,
That of themselues were pleasant, goodly flouds.

---

155 Mock'st al ... poisonst;] *Q1(c)*; Workst all ... ~, *Q1(u)*; Mock'st all ... poysonst; *Q2* ‖
156 vertue;] *Q1(c)*, *Q2*; ~, *Q1(u)* ‖ 171 Which] which' *Q1* ‖ 180 Swette] *Q1(c)*; Sweat *Q1(u)*;
Sweate *Q2* ‖

Hen. I would doe best for both, yet shall not be secure,
Till in some absolute heires my Crowne be setled;
There is so little now betwixt Aspirers   195
And their great obiect in my onely selfe,
That all the strength they gather vnder me,
Tempts combate with mine owne: I therefore make
Meanes for some issue by my marriage,
Which with the great Dukes neece is now concluded,   200
And she is comming; I haue trust in heauen
I am not yet so olde, but I may spring,
And then I hope all traitrous hopes will fade.
    Sau. Else may their whole estates flie, rooted vp
To Ignominie and Obliuion: 205
And (being your neighbor, seruant, and poore kinsman)
I wish your mighty Race might multiply,
Euen to the Period of all Emperie.
    Hen. Thankes to my princely coozen: this your loue
And honour shewne me in your personall presence,   210
I wish to welcome to your full content:
The peace I now make with your brother Archduke,
By Duke *Byron* our Lord Ambassadour,
I wish may happily extend to you,
And that at his returne we may conclude it.   215
    Sau. It shall be to my heart the happiest day
Of all my life, and that life all employd, /
To celebrate the honour of that day.   [B4]
                                                                  Exeunt.

[I.ii]

Enter Roiseau.

Rois. The wondrous honour doone our Duke *Byron*
In his Ambassage heere, in th'Archdukes Court,
I feare will taint his loyaltie to our King,
I will obserue how they obserue his humour,
And glorifie his valure; and how he   5
Accepts and stands attractiue to their ends,
That so I may not seeme an idle spot
In traine of this ambassage, but returne
Able to giue our King some note of all,
Worth my attendance; And see, heere's the man,   10
Who (though a French man, and in *Orleance* borne,

194 setled;] ~, *Q1-2* ‖ 206 neighbor,] *Shepherd*; ~͵ *Q1* ‖ 209 coozen:] ~, *Q1-2* ‖ 212 I now make] *Q1(c), Q2*; now made *Q1(u)* ‖ **I.ii]** *Parrott* ‖ 11 borne,] ~͵ *Q1-2* ‖

Seruing the Arch-duke) I doe most suspect,
Is set to be the tempter of our Duke;
Ile goe where I may see, allthough not heare.   [*Stands aside.*]

    Enter Picoté, with two other spreading a Carpet.

Pic. Spreade heere this historie of *Cateline*,   15
That Earth may seeme to bring forth Roman Spirites;
Euen to his Geniall feete; and her darke breast
Be made the cleare Glasse of his shining Graces;
Weele make his feete so tender, they shall gall
In all paths but to Empire; and therein   20
Ile make the sweete Steppes of his State beginne.

              Exit Picoté with seruants.

    Lowde Musique, and enter Byron.

Byr. What place is this? what ayre? what rhegion?
In which a man may heare the harmony
Of all things moouing? *Hymen* marries heere
Their ends and vses, and makes me his Temple.   25
Hath any man beene blessed, and yet liu'd?
The bloud turnes in my veines, I stand on change,
And shall dissolue in changing; tis so full
Of pleasure not to be containde in flesh:
To feare a violent Good, abuseth Goodnes, /   30
Tis Immortallitie to die aspiring,   [B4ᵛ]
As if a man were taken quicke to heauen;
What will not holde Perfection, let it burst;
What force hath any Cannan, not being chargde,
Or being not dischargde? To haue stuffe and forme,   35
And to lie idle, fearefull, and vnus'd,
Nor forme, nor stuffe shewes; happy *Semele*
That died comprest with Glorie: Happinesse
Denies comparison, of lesse, or more,
And not at most, is nothing: like the shaft   40
Shot at the Sunne, by angry *Hercules*,
And into shiuers by the thunder broken,
Will I be if I burst: And in my heart
This shall be written: yet twas high and right.

        Musique againe.

Heere too? they follow all my steppes with Musique,   45
As if my feete were numerous, and trode sounds
Out of the Center, with *Apolloes* vertue,

---

14 SD *Stands aside.*] *Parrott subs.* ‖ 16 Spirites;] *Q1(c)*; ~, *Q1(u), Q2* ‖ 18 Graces;] ~, *Q1-2* ‖
21 SD *Picoté with seruants*] *Parrott* ‖ 24 heere] ~, *Q1-2* ‖ 34 Cannan] *Q1(c)*; Cannon *Q1(u),*
Q2 ‖ 38 with] *Q1(c), Q2*; in *Q1(u)* ‖ 42 broken,] ~ˌ *Q1-2* ‖

That out of euery thing his ech-part toucht,
Strooke musicall accents: wheresoe're I goe,
They hide the earth from me with couerings rich,   50
To make me thinke that I am heere in heauen.

Enter Picoté in haste.

Pic. This way, your Highnesse.
Byr.   Come they?
Pic.   I, my Lord.

Exeunt.

Enter the other Commissioners of Fraunce,
Belieure, Brulart, with D'Aumall, Orenge.

Bel. My Lord *d'Aumall*, I am exceeding sorie,
That your owne obstinacie to hold out,
Your mortall enmitie against the King,   55
When Duke *du Maine*, and all the faction yeelded,
Should force his wrath to vse the rites of treason,
Vpon the members of your sencelesse Statue,
Your Name and House, when he had lost your person,
Your loue and duety.
Bru.   That which men enforce /   60
By their owne wilfulnesse; they must endure   [C1]
With willing patience, and without complaint.
   D'Aum. I vse not much impatience nor complaint,
Though it offends me much, to haue my name
So blotted with addition of a Traitor,   65
And my whole memory, (with such despight)
Markt and begun to be so rooted out.
   Bru. It was despight that held you out so long,
Whose penance in the King was needfull iustice.
   Bel. Come let vs seeke our Duke, and take our leaues   70
Of th'Archdukes grace.   *Exeunt.*

Enter Byron and Pycoté.

Byr.   Here may we safely breathe?
   Pic. No doubt (my Lord) no stranger knowes this way;
Onely the Arch-duke, and your friend Count *Mansfield*,
Perhaps may make their generall scapes to you,
To vtter some part of their priuate loues,   75
Ere your departure.
Byr.   Then, I well perceiue
To what th'intention of his highnesse tends;

---

51 SD *Picoté*] *Picote Q1-2* ǁ 52 I,] ~ˏ *Q1-2* | SD *with D'Aumall*] *Parrott (after Phelps); Aumall*
Q1-2 ǁ 65 Traitor,] *Shepherd*; ~. *Q1-2* ǁ 66 despight)] ~, *Q1-2* ǁ 67 out.] ~.) *Q1-2* ǁ 71 SD
Pycoté] *Pycotè Q1* ǁ

For whose, and others here, most worthy Lords,
I will become (with all my worth) their seruant,
In any office, but disloyaltie;   80
But that hath euer showd so fowle a monster
To all my Ancestors, and my former life,
That now to entertaine it, I must wholy
Giue vp my habite, in his contrary,
And striue to growe out of priuation.   85
   Pic. My Lord, to weare your loyall habite still,
When it is out of fashion; and hath done
Seruice enough; were rusticke miserie:
The habite of a seruile loyaltie,
Is reckond now amongst priuations,   90
With blindnesse, dumbnesse, deafnesse, scilence, death,
All which are neither natures by themselues
Nor substances, but mere decayes of forme, /
And absolute decessions of nature,   [C1ᵛ]
And so, 'tis nothing, what shall you then loose?   95
Your highnesse hath a habite in perfection,
And in desert of highest dignities,
Which carue your selfe, and be your owne rewarder;
No true powre doth admit priuation,
Aduerse to him; or suffers any fellow   100
Ioynde in his subiect; you, superiors;
It is the nature of things absolute,
One to destroy another; be your Highnesse,
Like those steepe hils that will admit no clowds,
No deawes, nor lest fumes bound about their browes;   105
Because their tops pierce into purest ayre,
Expert of humor; or like ayre it selfe
That quickly changeth; and receiues the sunne
Soone as he riseth; euery where dispersing
His royall splendor; guirds it in his beames,   110
And makes it selfe the body of the light.
Hote, shining, swift, light, and aspiring things,
Are of immortall, and celestiall nature;
Colde, darke, dull, heauie, of infernall fortunes,
And neuer aime at any happinesse: 115
Your excellencie knowes, that simple loyaltie,
Faith, loue, sinceritie, are but words, no things;
Meerely deuisde for forme; and as the Legate,
Sent from his Holinesse, to frame a peace

---

78 whose] *See Textual Note* ‖ 82 former life] *Q2*, formerlife *Q1* ‖ 83 it,] ~; *Q1-2* ‖ 95 nothing]
Q1(c); nothing else *Q1(u)*, *Q2* ‖ 101 you, superiors;] *stet* (*See Textual Note*) ‖ 111 light.] ~;
Q1-2 ‖ 114 heauie,] *Shepherd*; ~ *Q1-2* ‖ 116 knowes,] ~; *Q1-2* ‖

Twixt *Spaine* and *Sauoy*, labour'd feruently,   120
(For common ends, not for the Dukes perticular)
To haue him signe it; he againe endeuours
(Not for the Legates paines, but his owne pleasure)
To gratifie him; and being at last encountred,
Where the flood *Tesyn* enters into *Po*,   125
They made a kinde contention, which of them
Should enter th'others boate; one thrust the other:
One legge was ouer, and another in:
And with a fierie courtesie, at last
Sauoy leapes out, into the Legates armes,   130
And here ends all his loue, and th'others labour; /
So shall these termes, and impositions   [C2]
Exprest before, hold nothing in themselues
Really good; but florishes of forme:
And further then they make to priuate ends   135
None wise, or free, their propper vse intends.
   Byr. O 'tis a dangerous, and a dreadfull thing
To steale prey from a Lyon; or to hide
A head distrustfull, in his opened iawes;
To trust our bloud, in others veines; and hang   140
Twixt heauen and earth, in vapors of their breaths:
To leaue a sure pace on continuate earth,
And force a gate in iumps, from towre to towre,
As they doe that aspire, from height to height;
The bounds of loyaltie are made of glasse,   145
Soone broke, but can in no date be repaird;
And as the Duke *D'Aumall*, (now here in Court)
Flying his countrey, had his Statue torne
Peece-meale with horses; all his goods confiscate,
His Armes of honor, kickt about the streetes,   150
His goodly house at *Annet* rac'd to th'earth,
And (for a strange reproche of his foule treason)
His trees about it, cut off by their wastes;
So, when men flie the naturall clime of truth,
And turne them-selues loose, out of all the bounds   155
Of Iustice, and the straight-way to their ends;
Forsaking all the sure force in themselues
To seeke, without them, that which is not theirs,
The formes of all their comforts are distracted;
The riches of their freedomes forfaited;   160
Their humaine noblesse shamd; the Mansions

---

120 *Sauoy*,] ~; *Q1-2* ‖ 124 encountred,] ~; *Q1-2* ‖ 134 forme:] *Q1(c)*; fame, *Q1(u)*, *Q2* ‖ 142
pace on continuate] *Q1(c)*; place on continuall *Q1(u)*, *Q2* ‖ 148 countrey,] ~; *Q1-2* ‖ 151 earth,]
Q2; ~. *Q1* ‖

Of their colde spirits, eaten downe with Cares;
And all their ornaments, of wit, and valure,
Learning, and iudgement, cut from all their fruites.

               [Enter the Archduke Albert.]

    Alb. O, here were now the richest prize in *Europe*,   165
Were he but taken in affection. *[Embracing Byron.]*
Would we might growe together, and be twins
Of eithers fortune; or that, still embrac't
I were but Ring to such a pretious stone. /   169
    Byr. Your highnesse honors, and high bountie showne me,   [C2ᵛ]
Haue wonne from me, my voluntary powre;
And I must now mooue by your eminent will;
To what particular obiects, if I know
By this mans intercession, he shall bring
My vttermost answere, and performe betwixt vs,   175
Reciprocall, and full intelligence.
    Alb. Euen for your owne deserued roiall good,
Tis ioyfully accepted, vse the loues
And worthy admirations of your friends,
That beget vowes of all things you can wish,   180
And be what I wish: danger saies, no more.   *Exit.*

      Enter Mansfield at another dore. Exit Picoté.

    Mans. Your highnesse makes the light of this Court stoope,
With your so neere departure; I was forc't
To tender to your excellence, in briefe,
This priuate wish, in taking of my leaue;   185
That in some army Roiall, old Cont *Mansfield*,
Might be commanded by your matchles valor,
To the supreamest point of victorie:
Who vowes for that renowne all praier, and seruice:
No more, least I may wrong you.   *Exit Mans:*
    Byr.   Thanke your Lordship.   190

        Enter D'Aumall and Oreng.

    D'Aum. All maiestie be added to your highnesse,
Of which, I would not wish your brest to beare
More modest apprehension then may tread
The high gate of your spirit; and be knowne
To be a fit Bound for your Boundlesse valor.   195

164 SD *Enter ... Albert.*] *Parrott (after Phelps)* ‖ **165** *Alb.*] *Q1(c), Q2; ~ˌ Q1(u)* ‖ **166** affection.]
Q2; ~, Q1 | SD *Embracing Byron.*] *Parrott* ‖ **169** were ... stone.] ~, ... ~: *Q1-2* ‖ **173** obiects,]
~; *Q1-2* ‖ **174** bring] ~: *Q1-2* ‖ **183** departure;] *Shepherd*; ~, *Q1-2* ‖ **193** apprehension ...
tread] ~: ... ~, *Q1-2* ‖ **195** valor.] *Q2; ~; Q1* ‖

Or. So *Oreng* wisheth, and to the desarts
Of your great actions, their most roiall Crowne.

Enter Picoté.

Pic. Away my Lord, the Lords enquire for you.

Exeunt Byron and Picoté.
Manent Oreng, D'Aum. Roiseau.

Or. Would we might winne his valor to our part. /   199
D'Aum. Tis well prepar'd in his entreaty here;   [C3]
With all states highest obseruations:
And to their forme, and words, are added gifts.
He was presented with two goodly horses,
One of which two, was the braue Beast *Pastrana*:
With plate of gold, and a much prized iewell;   205
Girdle and hangers, set with welthy stones:
All which were vallewed, at ten thousand crownes;
The other Lords had suites of tapistry,
And chaines of gold; and euery gentleman
A paire of Spanish Gloues, and Rapire blades: 210
And here ends their entreaty; which I hope
Is the beginning of more good to vs,
Then twenty thousand times their giftes to them.

Enter Alber: Byr: Beli. Mans: Roiseau: with others.

Alb. My Lord, I grieue that all the setting forth,
Of our best welcome, made you more retired: 215
Your chamber hath beene more lou'd then our honors;
And therefore we are glad your time of parting
Is come to set you in the ayre you loue:
Commend my seruice to his Maiestie,
And tell him that this daie of peace with him   220
Ile hold, as holie. All your paines my Lords
I shalbe alwaies glad to gratefie
With any loue and honour your owne hearts
Shall do me grace to wish exprest to you.   224

[Exeunt all but Roiseau.]

Rois. [Advancing.] Here hath beene strange demeaneure, which shall flie,
To the great author of this Ambassy.   *[Exit.]*

FINIS Actus 1.

---

198 SD *Exeunt … Picoté*] *Parrott; Exit Bir· Q1-2* | SD *Manent*] *Manet Q1-2* ‖ **202** gifts.] ~,
Q1-2 ‖ **209** gold;] *Q1(c)*; ~, *Q1(u), Q2* ‖ **223** honour] ~, *Q1-2* ‖ **224** SD *Exeunt … Roiseau.*] ‖
225 *Rois.*] *Ruis. Q1* | SD *Advancing.*] *Parrott* ‖ **226** SD *Exit.*] *Parrott* ‖

ACT. 2 SCE. 1.

Enter Sauoy, Laffin, Roncas, Rochette, Breton.

Sau. Admit no entry, I will speake with none. /
Good signior *de Laffin*, your worth shall finde,   [C3ᵛ]
That I will make a iewell for my cabinet,
Of that the King (in surfet of his store)
Hath cast out, as the sweepings of his hall;   5
I told him, hauing threatned you away,
That I did wonder, this small time of peace,
Could make him cast his armor so securely
In such as you, and as twere set the head
Of one so great in counsailes, on his foote,   10
And pitch him from him with such guardlike strength.
  Laf. He may perhaps finde he hath pitcht away,
The Axeltree that kept him on his wheeles.
  Sau. I told him so, I sweare, in other termes
And not with too much note of our close loues   15
Least so he might haue smokt our practises.
  Laf. To chuse his time, and spit his poison on me,
Through th'eares, and eies of strangers!
  Sau.   So I told him
And more then that, which now I will not tell you:
It rests now then, Noble, and worthy friend,   20
That to our friendship, we draw Duke *Byron*,
To whose attraction there is no such chaine,
As you can fordge, and shake out of your braine.
  Laf. I haue deuisde the fashion and the weight;
To valures hard to draw, we vse retreates;   25
And, to pull shaftes home, (with a good bow-arme)
We thrust hard from vs: since he came from *Flanders*
He heard how I was threatned with the King,
And hath beene much inquisitiue to know
The truth of all, and seekes to speake with me;   30
The meanes he vsde, I answerd doubtfully;
And with an intimation that I shund him,
Which will (I know) put more spur to his charge;
And if his haughty stomacke be preparde,
With will to any act for the aspiring   35
Of his ambitious aimes, I make no doubt
But I shall worke him to your highnesse wish.

SD *Enter*] *Shepherd* ‖ **1** none.] ~, *Q1-2* ‖ **2** *Laffin,*] *Q1(c), Q2;* ~ *Q1(u)* ‖ **11** guardlike] *stet* (*See*
Textual Note) ‖ **14** sweare,] *Q1(c);* ~ *Q1(u), Q2* ‖ **18** strangers!] *Parrott;* ~. *Q1-2* ‖ **27** *Flanders*]
Flanders *Q1-2* ‖ **35** act] ~: *Q1-2* ‖

Sau. But vndertake it, and I rest assur'd: /
You are reported to haue skill in Magick,   [C4]
And the euents of things, at which they reach   40
That are in nature apt to ouerreach:
Whom the whole circkle of the present time,
In present pleasures, fortunes, knowledges,
Can not containe: those men (as broken loose
From humaine limmits) in all violent ends   45
Would faine aspire the faculties of fiends,
And in such ayre breathe his vnbounded spirits,
Which therefore well will fit such coniurations.
Attempt him then by flying; close with him,
And bring him home to vs, and take my dukedome.   50
 Laf. My best in that, and all things, vowes your seruice.
 Sau. Thankes to my deare friend; and the French *Vlisses*.

Exit Sauoy cum suis.

Enter Byron.

 Byr. Here is the man; my honord friend, *Laffin*?
Alone, and heauy countinanc't? on what termes
Stood th'insultation of the King vpon you?   55
 Laf. Why do you aske?
 Byr.   Since I would know the truth.
 Laf. And when you know it; what?
 Byr.   Ile iudge betwixt you,
And (as I may) make euen th'excesse of either.
 Laf. Ahlas my Lord, not all your loyaltie,
Which is in you more then hereditary,   60
Nor all your valure (which is more then humane)
Can do the seruice you may hope on me
In sounding my displeasde integrity;
Stand for the King, as much in policie
As you haue stird for him in deeds of armes,   65
And make your selfe his glorie, and your countries
Till you bee suckt as drie, and wrought as leane,
As my fleade carcase: you shall neuer close
With me, as you imagine.
 Byr.   You much wrong me,
To thinke me an intelligencing Lord. /   70
 Laf. I know not how your so affected zeale,   [C4ᵛ]
To be reputed a true-harted subiect,
May stretch or turne you; I am desperate;
If I offend you, I am in your powre:

---

48 coniurations.] ~, *Q1-2* ‖ **52** SD *cum suis*] Parrott ‖ **59** Ahlas] Ah las *Q1*; Alas *Q2* ‖ **60** you] ~,
Q1 ‖ **61** humane] *Q1(c)*; humaine *Q1(u)*, *Q2* ‖ **70** Lord] *Q1(c)*; instrument *Q1(u)*, *Q2* ‖ **72** true-
harted] ~ᵕ~ *Q1-2* ‖

I care not how I tempt your conquering furie,   75
I am predestin'd to too base an end,
To haue the honor of your wrath destroy me;
And be a worthy obiect for your sword:
I lay my hand, and head too at your feete;
As I haue euer, here I hold it still,   80
End me directly, doe not goe about.
    Byr. [*Aside.*] How strange is this? the shame of his disgrace
Hath made him lunatique.
    Laf.   Since the King hath wrong'd me
He thinkes Ile hurt my selfe; no, no, my Lord:
I know that all the Kings in Christendome,   85
(If they should ioyne in my reuenge) would proue
Weake foes to him, still hauing you to friend:
If you were gone (I care not if you tell him)
I might be tempted then to right my selfe.   *Exit.*
    Byr. He has a will to me, and dares not shew it;   90
His state decai'd, and he disgrac'd, distracts him.

                    Redit Laffin.

    Laf. Change not my words my Lord, I onely said
I might be tempted then to right my selfe:
Temptation to treason, is no treason;
And that word (tempted) was conditionall too: 95
If you were gone. I pray informe the truth.   *Exiturus.*
    Byr. Stay iniur'd man, and know I am your friend,
Farre from these base, and mercenarie reaches,
I am I sweare to you.
    Laf.   You may be so;
And yet youle giue me leaue to be *Laffin*,   100
A poore and expuate humor of the Court:
But what good bloud came out with me, what veines
And sinews of the Triumphs now it makes,
I list not vante; yet will I now confesse,
And dare assume it; I haue powre to adde /   105
To all his greatnesse; and make yet more fixt   [D1]
His bould securitie; Tell him this my Lord;
And this (if all the spirits of earth and aire,
Be able to enforce) I can make good:
If knowledge of the sure euents of things,   110
Euen from the rise of subiects into Kings:
And falles of Kings to subiects, hold a powre

---

79 feete;] ~, *Q1-2* ‖ 82 SD *Aside.*] ‖ 87 him,] ~; *Q1-2* ‖ 90 it;] ~, *Q1-2* ‖ 91 disgrac'd,] *Q2*; ~;
Q1 ‖ 95 too:] ~, *Q1-2* ‖ 96 gone.] ~, *Q1-2* | SD *Exiturus.*] *Shepherd*; *Exitur. Q1-2* ‖ 102 me,] ~;
Q1-2 ‖ 103 Triumphs ... makes,] ~, ... ~; *Q1-2* ‖

Of strength to worke it, I can make it good;
And tell him this to; if in midest of winter
To make black Groues grow greene; to still the thunder;   115
And cast out able flashes from mine eies
To beate the lightning back into the skies,
Proue powre to do it, I can make it good;
And tell him this too; if to lift the Sea
Vp to the Starres, when all the Windes are still;   120
And keepe it calme, when they are most enrag'd:
To make earths driest pallms, sweate humorous springs;
To make fixt rocks walke; and loose shadowes stand;
To make the dead speake: midnight see the Sunne,
Mid-daie turne mid-night; to dissolue all lawes   125
Of nature, and of order, argue powre
Able to worke all, I can make all good,
And all this tell the King.
    Byr.   Tis more then strange,
To see you stand thus at the rapiers point
With one so kinde, and sure a friend as I.   130
    Laf. Who cannot friend himselfe, is foe to any,
And to be fear'd of all, and that is it,
Makes me so skornd, but make me what you can;
Neuer so wicked, and so full of feends,
I neuer yet, was traitor to my friends: 135
The lawes of friendship I haue euer held,
As my religion; and for other lawes,
He is a foole that keepes them with more care,
Then they keepe him, safe, rich, and populare:
For riches, and for populare respects   140
Take them amongst yee Minions, but for safety,
You shall not finde the least flaw in mine armes, /
To pierce or taint me; what will great men be,   [D1ᵛ]
To please the King, and beare authoritie.   *Exit.*
    Byr. How fit a sort were this to hansell fortune?   145
And I will winne it though I loose my selfe;
Though he prooue harder then *Egiptian* Marble,
Ile make him malliable, as th'*Ophyr* gold;
I am put off from this dull shore of Ease,
Into industrious, and high-going Seas;   150
Where, like *Pelides* in *Scamanders* flood,
Vp to the eares in surges, I will fight,
And pluck French *Ilion* vnderneath the waues;

---

113 it,] ~; *Q1 2* ‖ **116** cics] *Phelps*, ~, *Q1-2* ‖ **122** pallms] *stet (See Textual Note)* | springs;] ~͵
Q1-2 ‖ **123** stand;] ~, *Q1-2* ‖ **137** lawes,] ~; *Q1-2* ‖ **146** selfe;] ~, *Q1-2* ‖ **149** Ease] *Parrott*;
East *Q1-2* ‖

If to be highest still, be to be best,
All workes to that end are the worthiest: 155
Truth is a golden Ball, cast in our way,
To make vs stript by falsehood: And as *Spaine*,
When the hote scuffles of *Barbarian* armes
Smotherd the life of *Don Sebastian*,
To guild the leaden rumor of his death   160
Gaue for a slaughterd body (held for his)
A hundred thousand crownes; causd all the state
Of superstitious *Portugall*, to mourne
And celebrate his solemne funerals;
The *Moores* to conquest, thankfull feasts preferre,   165
And all made with the carcasse of a *Switzer*:
So in the Giantlike, and politique warres
Of barbarous greatnesse, raging still in peace,
Showes to aspire iust obiects are laide on
With cost, with labour, and with forme enough,   170
Which onely makes our best acts brooke the light,
And their ends had, we thinke we haue their right;
So wurst workes are made good, with good successe,
And so for Kings, pay subiects carcases.   *Exit.*

[II.ii]

Enter Henry, Roiseau.

Hen. Was he so courted?
  Rois.   As a Cittie Dame,
Brought by her iealous husband, to the Court, /
Some elder Courtiers entertaining him,   [D2]
While others snatch, a fauour from his wife:
One starts from this doore; from that nooke another;   5
With gifts, and iunkets, and printed phrase,
Steale her employment, shifting place by place
Still as her husband comes: so Duke *Byron*
Was woode, and worshipt in the Arch-dukes Court,
And as th'assistants that your Maiestie   10
Ioinde in Commission with him, or my selfe,
Or any other doubted eye appear'd,
He euer vanisht: and as such a dame,
As we compar'd with him before, being wun
To breake faith to her husband, loose her fame,   15

---

157 stript] *stet* (*See Textual Note*) | *Spaine*,] ~. *Q1-2* ‖ 158 armes] ~, *Q1-2* ‖ 165 *Moores*] Moores *Q1-2* ‖ 169 obiects] ~; *Q1-2* ‖ 172 right;] ~, *Q1-2* ‖ II.ii] *Parrott* ‖ SD *Roiseau*] *Q2*; *Roisieau Q1* ‖ 5 another;] ~, *Q1* ‖ 10 Maiestie] ~, *Q1-2* ‖

Staine both their progenies, and comming fresh
From vnderneath the burthen of her shame,
Visits her husband with as chaste a browe,
As temperate, and confirm'd behauiour,
As she came quitted from confession: 20
So from his scapes, would he present a presence,
The practise of his state adulterie,
And guilt that should a gracefull bosome strieke,
Drownde in the set lake, of a hopelesse cheeke.
    Hen. It may be hee dissembled, or suppose,   25
He be a little tainted: men whom vertue
Formes with the stuffe of fortune, great and gratious,
Must needs pertake with fortune in her humor
Of instabilitie: and are like to shafts
Growne crookt with standing, which to rectifie,   30
Must twice as much be bowd another way.
He that hath borne wounds for his worthy parts,
Must for his wurst be borne with: we must fit
Our gouernment to men, as men to it:
In old time, they that hunted sauadge beasts,   35
Are said to clothe themselues in sauage skinnes,
They that were Fowlers when they went on fowling,
Wore garments made with wings resembling Fowles:
To Buls, we must not shew our selues in red, /
Nor to the warlick Elephant in white;   40
In all things gouern'd, their infirmities   [D2ᵛ]
Must not be stird, nor wrought on; Duke *Byron*
Flowes with adust, and melancholy choller,
And melancholy spirits are venemous:
Not to be toucht, but as they may be cur'de: 45
I therefore meane to make him change the ayre,
And send him further from those Spanish vapors,
That still beare fighting sulphure in their brests,
To breath a while in temperate English ayre,
Where lips are spyc'd with free and loyall counsailes,   50
Where policies are not ruinous, but sauing;
Wisdome is simple, valure righteous,
Humaine, and hating facts of brutish forces;
And whose graue natures, scorne the scoffes of *France*,
The empty complements of *Italy*,   55
The any-way encroching pride of *Spaine*,
And loue men modest, harty, iust and plaine.

---

20 confession:] ~. *Q1-2* ‖ 23 strieke] stet (*See Textual Note*) ‖ 27 great] ~, *Q1-2* ‖ 31 way.] ~,
Q1-2 ‖ 40 white;] ~, *Q1-2* ‖ 53 forces;] ~. *Q1* ‖

Enter Sauoy, whispering with Laffin.

Sau. Ile sound him for *Byron*; and what I finde,
In the Kings depth, ile draw vp, and informe,
In excitations to the Dukes reuolt,   60
When next I meete with him.
    Laf.   It must be done
With praising of the Duke; from whom the king
Will take to giue himselfe; which tolde the Duke,
Will take his heart vp into all ambition.
    Sau. I know it (politick friend) and tis my purpose.   65
                                         Exit Laf.

Your Maiestie hath mist a royall sight;
The Duke *Byron*, on his braue beast *Pastrana*,
Who sits him like a full-saild Argosea,
Danc'd with a lofty billow, and as snug
Plyes to his bearer, both their motions mixt;   70
And being considerd in their site together,
They do the best present the state of man,
In his first royaltie ruling; and of beasts
In their first loyaltie seruing (one commanding,
And no way being mou'd; the other seruing, /   75
And no way being compeld) of all the sights   [D3]
That euer my eyes witnest; and they make
A doctrinall and witty Hierogliphick,
Of a blest kingdome: to expresse and teach,
Kings to command as they could serue, and subiects   80
To serue as if they had powre to command.
    Hen. You are a good old horseman I perceiue,
And still out all the vse of that good part:
Your wit is of the true *Pierean* spring,
That can make any thing, of any thing.   85
    Sau. So braue a subiect as the Duke, no king
Seated on earth, can vante of but your Highnesse,
So valiant, loyall, and so great in seruice.
    Hen. No question he sets valour in his height,
And hath done seruice to an equall pitche,   90
Fortune attending him with fit euents,
To all his ventrous and well-laid attempts.
    Sau. Fortune to him was *Iuno* to *Alcides*,
For when, or where did she but open way,
To any act of his? what stone tooke he   95
With her helpe, or without his owne lost bloud?

57 SD *Enter*] *Parrott* ‖ 59 depth,] ~; *Q1-2* ‖ 65 friend)] *Q2*; ~:) *Q1* | purpose.] ~, *Q1-2* ‖ 66 sight;] ~, *Q1-2* ‖ 74-76 seruing (one ... compeld)] *Parrott*; ~; ⁓~ ... ~; *Q1-2* ‖ 93 Fortune] *Q2*; ~? *Q1* | *Iuno*] ~, *Q1-2* ‖

What fort wan he by her? or was not forc't?
What victory but gainst ods? on what Commander
Sleepy, or negligent, did he euer charge?
What Summer euer made she faire to him?   100
What winter, not of one continued storme?
Fortune is so farre from his Creditresse,
That she owes him much; for in him, her lookes
Are louely, modest, and magnanimous,
Constant, victorious; and in his Achieuments,   105
Her cheekes are drawne out with a vertuous rednesse,
Out of his eager spirit to victorie,
And chast contention to conuince with honor;
And (I haue heard) his spirits haue flowd so high,
In all his conflicts against any odds,   110
That (in his charge) his lips haue bled with feruor:
How seru'd he at your famous siege of *Dreux*?
Where the enemie (assur'd of victory) /
Drew out a bodie of foure thousand horse,   [D3ᵛ]
And twice six thousand foote, and like a Crescent,   115
Stood for the signall; you (that show'd your selfe
A sound old souldiar) thinking it not fit
To giue your enemy the ods, and honour
Of the first stroke, commanded *de la Guiche*,
To let flie all his cannans, that did pierse   120
The aduerse thickest squadrons, and had shot
Nine volleies ere the foe had once giuen fire:
Your troope was charg'd, and when your dukes old father
Met with th'assailants, and their Groue of Reiters
Repulst so fiercely, made them turne their beards   125
And rallie vp themselues behind their troopes;
Fresh forces seeing your troopes a little seuerd
From that part first assaulted, gaue it charge,
Which then, this duke made good, seconds his father,
Beates through and through the enemies greatest strength, 130
And breakes the rest like Billowes gainst a rock;
And there the heart of that huge battaile broke.
    Hen. The heart but now came on, in that strong body
Of twice two thousand horse, lead by *Du Maine*,
Which (if I would be glorious) I could say   135
I first encountred.
    Sau.   How did he take in
Beaune in view of that inuincible army

---

116 signall; you] ~, ~: *Q1-2* ‖ 123 father] ~, *Q1-2* ‖ 127 seuerd] ~, *Q1-2* ‖ 131 rock;] ~‸ *Q1-2* ‖
133 body] ~, *Q1-2* ‖ 134 *Maine,*] ~‸ *Q1-2* ‖ 136 in] *Q2*; ~, *Q1* ‖

Lead by the Lord great Constable of *Castile*!
Autun, and *Nuis* in *Burgundy*; chast away,
Vicount *Tauannes* troopes before *Dijon*,   140
And puts himselfe in, and there that was won.
   Hen. If you would onely giue me leaue my Lord,
I would do right to him, yet must not giue –
   Sau. A league from *Fountaine Francois*, when you sent him,
To make discouerie of the *Castile* army,   145
When he descern'd twas it (with wondrous wisdome
Ioinde to his spirit) he seem'd to make retreate,
But when they prest him, and the Barron of *Lux*
Set on their charge so hotely, that his horse,
Was slaine, and he most dangerously engag'd, /   150
Then turnd your braue duke head, and (with such ease   [D4]
As doth an Eccho beate backe violent sounds,
With their owne forces) he, (as if a wall
Start sodainely before them) pasht them all
Flat, as the earth, and there was that field wonne.   155
   Hen. Y'are all the field wide.
   Sau.   O, I aske you pardon,
The strength of that field yet laie in his backe,
Vpon the foes part; and what is to come,
Of this your Marshal, now your worthie Duke,
Is much beyond the rest: for now he sees   160
A sort of horse troopes, issue from the woods,
In number nere twelue hunderd: and retyring
To tell you that the entire armie follow'd,
Before he could relate it, he was forc't
To turne head, and receiue the maine assaulte   165
Of fiue horse troopes: onely with twenty horse:
The first he met, he tumbled to the earth,
And brake through all, not daunted with two wounds,
One on his head, another on his brest,
The bloud of which, drownd all the field in doubte: 170
Your maiesty himselfe was then engag'd,
Your powre not yet arriu'd, and vp you brought
The little strength you had: a cloud of foes,
Ready to burst in stormes about your eares:
Three squadrons rusht against you, and the first,   175
You tooke so fiercely, that, you beate their thoughts
Out of their bosoms, from the vrged fight:
The second, all amazed you ouerthrew,

---

138 *Castile*!] Castile? *Q1-2* ‖ 139 *Nuis in Burgundy*;] ~: ~ Burgundy͵ *Q1-2 (See Textual Note)* ‖
140 *Dijon*] Dijon *Q1-2* ‖ 143 giue–] Parrott; ~. *Q1-2* ‖ 145 *Castile*] Castile *Q1-2* ‖ 148 *Lux*] Lux,
Q1-2 ‖ 159 Duke,] ~͵ *Q1-2* ‖

The third disperst, with fiue and twenty horse
Left of the fourescore that persude the chase: 180
And this braue conquest, now your Marshall seconds
Against two squadrons, but with fifty horse;
One after other he defeates them both,
And made them runne, like men whose heeles were tript,
And pitch their heads, in their great generalls lap: 185
And him he sets on, as he had beene shot
Out of a Cannan: beates him into route, /
And as a little brooke being ouerrunne   [D4ᵛ]
With a black torrent that beares all things downe
His furie ouertakes, his fomy back   190
Loded with Cattaile, and with stackes of Corne,
And makes the miserable Plowman mourne;
So was *du Maine* surchardgd, and so *Byron*
Flow'd ouer all his forces; euery drop
Of his lost bloud, bought with a worthy man;   195
And, onely with a hundred Gentlemen
He wonne the place, from fifteene hundred horse.
  Hen. He won the place?
  Sau.   On my word, so tis sayd.
  Hen. Fie you haue beene extreamely misinform'd.
  Sau. I onely tell your highnesse what I heard,   200
I was not there; and though I haue beene rude,
With wonder of his vallor, and presum'd
To keepe his merit in his full carire,
Not hearing you, when yours made such a thunder;
Pardon my fault, since twas t'extoll your seruant;   205
But, is it not most true, that twixt yee both,
So few achiu'd the conquest of so many?
  Hen. It is a truth, must make me euer thankefull,
But not performd by him, was not I there?
Commanded him, and in the maine assault,   210
Made him but second?
  Sau.   Hee's the capitall souldier,
That liues this day in holy Christendome,
Except your highnesse, alwaies except *Plato*.
  Hen. We must not giue to one, to take from many,
For (not to praise our countrimen) here seru'd,   215
The Generall, Mylor' *Norris*, sent from *England*:
As great a captaine as the world affords:

182 horse;] ~, *Q1-2* ‖ 189 torrent ... downe] ~; ... ~, *Q1-2* ‖ 190 fomy] *Q1(c)*, *Q2*; famy
Q1(u) | back] ~, *Q1-2* ‖ 197 horse.] *Q2*; ~; *Q1* ‖ 198 sayd.] *Q2*; ~: *Q1* ‖ 202 presum'd] ~,
Q1-2 ‖ 207 achiu'd] ~, *Q1-2* ‖ 211 *Sau.*] *Q1(c)*, *Q2*; *San. Q1(u)* ‖ 216 Generall, Mylor'] *Parrott*;
~, *My Lor. Q1* | *England*] *Q2*; *England Q1* ‖

One fit to leade, and fight for Christendome;
Of more experience; and of stronger braine;
As valiant for abiding; In Command,   220
(On any sodaine; vpon any ground
And in the forme of all occasions)
As ready, and as profitably dauntles; /
And heare was then another; Collonell *Williams*,   [E1]
A worthy Captaine; and more like the Duke,   225
Because he was lesse temperate then the Generall;
And being familliar with the man you praise,
(Because he knew him haughty and incapable
Of all comparison) would compare with him,
And hold his swelling valour to the marke   230
Iustice had set in him, and not his will:
And as in open vessells filld with water,
And on mens shoulders borne, they put treene cuppes,
To keepe the wild and slippery element,
From washing ouer: follow all his Swayes   235
And tickle aptnes to exceed his bounds,
And at the Brym containe him: so this knight,
Swum in *Byron*, and held him but to right.
But leaue these hot comparisons, hee's mine owne,
And then what I possesse, Ile more be knowne.   240
   Sau. [*Aside.*] All this shall to the duke, I fisht for this.

                               Exeunt.

        FINIS. Actus Secundi.

ACTVS 3.   SCAENA 1.

Enter La Fin, Byron following vnseene.

   Laf. [*Aside.*] A fained passion in his hearing now,
(Which he thinkes I perceaue not) making conscience,
Of the reuolt that he hath vrdgd to me,
(Which now he meanes to prosecute) would sound,
How deepe he stands affected with that scruple. –   5
As when the Moone hath comforted the Night,
And set the world in siluer of her light,
The Planets, Asterisims and whole state of Heauen,
In beames of gold desending; all the windes,

221-22 (On ... occasions)] *Parrott*; ˌ~ ... ~ˌ *Q1-2* ‖ **223** profitably] ~, *Q1-2* ‖ **228** incapable] ~,
Q1-2 ‖ **230** marke] ~, *Q1-2* ‖ **238** him] ~, *Q1-2* ‖ **240** knowne.] *Q2*; ~, *Q1* ‖ **241** SD *Aside.*]
Parrrott ‖ **III.i.1** SD *Aside.*] *Parrott* ‖ **4** (Which ... prosecute)] *Q1(c), Q2*; ˌ~ ... ~ˌ *Q1(u)* ‖
5 scruple.–] *Parrott*; ~. *Q1-2* ‖

Bound vp in caues, chargd not to driue abrode,   10
Their cloudy heads; an vniuersall peace,
Proclaimd in scilence of the quiet earth;
Soone as her hot and dry fumes are let loose,
Stormes and cloudes mixing, sodainely put out /   14
The eyes of all those glories: The creation,   [E1ᵛ]
Turnd into *Chaos*, and we then desire,
For all our ioye of life, the death of sleepe;
So when the glories of our liues, mens loues,
Cleere consciences, our fames, and loyalties,
That did vs worthy comfort, are eclipsd,   20
Griefe and disgrace inuade vs; and for all
Our night of life besides, our Miserie craues
Darke earth would ope and hide vs in our graues.
    Byr. How Strange is this?
    Laf.   What? did your highnesse heare?
    Byr. Both heard and wonderd, that your wit and spirit,   25
And proffit in experience of the slaueries
Impos'd on vs in those mere politique termes
Of loue, fame, loyalty, can be carried vp
To such a height of ignorant conscience,
Of cowerdise, and dissolution,   30
In all the free-borne powers of royall man.
You that haue made way through all the guards,
Of Ielouse State; and seen on both your sides,
The pikes points chardging heauen to let you passe,
Will you, (in flying with a Scrupulouse wing,   35
Aboue those pikes to heauen-ward) fall on them?
This is like men, that (spirrited with wine,)
Passe dangerouse places safe; and die for feare,
With onely thought of them, being simply sober;
We must (in passing to our wished ends,   40
Through things calld good and bad) be like the ayre,
That euenly interposd betwixt the seas,
And the opposed Element of fire,
At either toucheth, but pertakes with neither;
Is neither hot, nor cold, but with a sleight   45
And harmelesse temper mixt of both th'exstreames.
    Laf. Tis shrode.
    Byr.   There is no truth of any good
To be descernd on earth: and by conuersion,

---

12 earth;] *Parrott*; ~. *Q1-2* ‖ **14** mixing, ... out] ~; ... ~. *Q1-2* ‖ **21** all] *Shepherd*; ~, *Q1-2* ‖
22 craues] *Shepherd*; ~, *Q1-2* ‖ **23** graues.] *Q2*; ~, *Q1* ‖ **25** spirit,] ~. *Q1* ‖ **26** slaueries] ~,
Q1-2 ‖ **27** vs ... termes] *Shepherd*; ~; ... ~, *Q1-2* ‖ **28** vp] ~, *Q1-2* ‖ **29** conscience,] ~; *Q1-2* ‖
43 fire,] ~; *Q1-2* ‖ **45** sleight] ~. *Q1* ‖ **46** exstreames.] *Q2*; ~; *Q1* ‖

Nought therefore simply bad: But as the stuffe,
Prepard for *Arras* pictures, is no Picture, /   50
Till it be formd, and man hath cast the beames,   [E2]
Of his imaginouse fancie through it,
In forming antient Kings and conquerors,
As he conceiues they look't, and were attirde,
Though they were nothing so: so all things here,   55
Haue all their price set downe, from mens concepts,
Which make all terms and actions, good, or bad,
And are but pliant, and wel-coloured threads,
Put into fained images of truth:
To which, to yeeld, and kneele, as truth-pure kings,   60
That puld vs downe with cleere truth of their Ghospell,
Were Superstition to be hist to hell.
  Laf. Beleeue it, this is reason.
  Byr.   T'is the faith,
Of reason and of wisdome.
  Laf.   You perswade,
As if you could create: what man can shunne,   65
The serches, and compressions of your graces?
  Byr. We must haue these lures when we hawke for friends,
And wind about them like a subtle Riuer,
That (seeming onely to runne on his course)
Doth serch yet, as he runnes; and still finds out,   70
The easiest parts of entry on the shore;
Glyding so slyly by, as scarce it toucht,
Yet still eates some thing in it: so must those,
That haue large fields, and currants to dispose.
Come, let vs ioyne our streames, we must runne far   75
And haue but little time: The duke of *Sauoy*,
Is shortly to be gone, and I must needes,
Make you well knowne to him.
  Laf.   But hath your highnes,
Some enterprise of valure ioynd with him?
  Byr. With him and greater persons!
  Laf.   I will creepe   80
Vpon my bosome in your Princely seruice,
Vouch-safe to make me knowne. I heare there liues not,
So kind, so bountyfull, and wise a Prince,
But in your owne excepted excellence. /

60 truth-pure] *Parrott*; ~ ~ *Q1-2* (*See Textual Note*) ‖ **63** reason.] *Q2*; ~; *Q1* ‖ **66** graces?] ~.
Q1-2 ‖ **75** far] *Q2*; ~. *Q1* ‖ **76** of] *Q1(c)*, *Q2*; *om. Q1(u)* | *Sauoy*] Sauoy *Q1-2* ‖ **78** him.] *Q2*; ~,
Q1 ‖ **79** valure] value *Q1-2* (*See Textual Note*) ‖ **80** persons!] ~? *Q1* | creepe] ~. *Q1* ‖

Byr. He shall both know, and loue you: are you mine?   [E2ᵛ]
Laf. I take the honor of it, on my knee,   86
And hope to quite it with your Maiesty.

                                Exeunt.

[III.ii]

Enter Sauoy, Roncas, Rochet, Breton.

  Sau. *La Fin* is in the right; and will obtaine;
He draweth with his weight; and like a plummet
That swaies a dore, with falling of, pulls after.
  Ron. Thus will *Laffin* be brought a Stranger to you,
By him he leads; he conquers that is conquerd,   5
That's sought, as hard to winne, that sues to be wonne.
  Sau. But is my Painter warnd to take his picture,
When he shall see me, and present *Laffin*?
  Roch. He is (my Lord) and (as your highnesse willd)
All we will presse about him, and admire,   10
The royall promise of his rare aspect,
As if he heard not.
  Sau.   Twill enflame him,
Such trickes the Arch-duke vsd t'extoll his greatnes,
Which complements though plaine men hold absurd,
And a meere remedy for desire of Greatnesse,   15
Yet great men vse them, as their state Potatoes,
High Coollises, and potions to excite
The lust of their ambition: and this Duke,
You know is noted in his naturall garb
Extreamely glorious; who will therefore bring   20
An appetite expecting such a baite;
He comes, go instantly, and fetch the Painter.

               Enter Byron, La Fin.

  Byr. All honor to your heighnesse.
  Sau.   Tis most true.   [*Embracing him.*]
All honours flow to me, in you their Ocean;
As welcome worthyest duke, as if my marquisate,   25
Were circkl'd with you in these amorous armes.
  Byr. I sorrow Sir I could not bring it with me, /
That I might so supply the fruitelesse complement,   [E3]

---

87 *Exeunt.*] *Phelps; Exit. Q1-2* ‖ **III.ii**] *Parrott* ‖ SD *Rochet,*] ~. *Q1-2* ‖ **1** *Fin*] ~, *Q1-2* ‖ **3** after.]
Q2; ~, *Q1* ‖ **6** That's] Thats *Q1-2* ‖ **7** picture,] *Q2;* ~. *Q1* ‖ **15** Greatnesse,] ~. *Q1-2* ‖ **16** them,]
~; *Q1-2* | their state] *Q1(c), Q2;* they eate *Q1(u)* ‖ **18** Duke,] ~. *Q1-2* ‖ **22** SD *Byron,*] ~.
Q1-2 ‖ **23** heighnesse.] ~, *Q1-2* | SD *Embracing him.*] *Parrott* ‖ **26** armes.] *Q2;* ~; *Q1* ‖ **27** me,]
~. *Q1-2* ‖

Of onely visiting your excellence,
With which the king now sends me t'entertaine you;   30
Which notwithstanding doth confer this good,
That it hath giuen me some small time to shew,
My gratitude for the many secret bounties,
I haue (by this your Lord Ambassador)
Felt from your heighnesse; and in short, t'assure you,   35
That all my most deserts are at your seruice.
   Sau. Had the king sent me by you halfe his kingdome,
It were not halfe so welcom.
   Byr.   For defect
Of whatsoeuer in my selfe, (my Lord,)
I here commend to your most Princely Seruice   40
This honord friend of mine.
   Sau.   Your name I pray you Sir.
   Laf. Laffin, my Lord.
   Sau.   *Laffin*? [*To Roncas.*] Is this the man,
That you so recommended to my Loue?
   Ron. The same my Lord.
   Sau.   Y'are, next my Lord the duke,
The most desird of all men. [*To Byron.*] O my Lord,   45
The King and I, haue had a mighty conflict,
About your conflicts, and your matchles worth,
In military vertues; which I put
In Ballance with the continent of *France,*
In all the peace and safty it enioyes.   50
And made euen weight with all he could put in
Of all mens else; and of his owne deserts.
   Byr. Of all mens else? would he weigh other mens,
With my deseruings?
   Sau.   I, vpon my life,
The English Generall, the Mylor' *Norris,*   55
That seru'd amongst you here, he paralleld
With you, at all parts, and in some preferd him,
And Collonell *Williams* (a Welch Collonell)
He made a man, that at your most containd you:
Which the Welch Herrald of their praise, the Cucko, /   60
Would scarce haue put, in his monology,   [E3ᵛ]
In iest, and said with reuerence to his merits.
   Byr. With reuerence? Reuerence skornes him: by the spoyle,
Of all her Merits in me, he shall rue it;

30 you;] *Q1(c)*, *Q2*; ~, *Q1(u)* ‖ 35 heighnesse;] *Q1(c)*, *Q2*; ~ˏ *Q1(u)* ‖ 38 welcom.] *Q2*; ~; *Q1* |
defect] ~. *Q1* ‖ 41 mine.] *Q2*; ~; *Q1* ‖ 42 SD *To Roncas.*] *Parrott* ‖ 44 Lord.] *Q2*; ~, *Q1* |
Y'are,] *Shepherd*; ~ˏ *Q1-2* ‖ 45 SD *To Byron.*] *Parrott* ‖ 49 France] *Q2*; France *Q1* ‖ 52 his]
Q1(c), *Q2*; their *Q1(u)* | deserts.] *Q2*; ~, *Q1* ‖ 54 deseruings?] *Q2*; ~.' *Q1(c)*; ~, *Q1(u)* | I,] ~ˏ
Q1-2 ‖ 60 Cucko,] ~. *Q1-2* ‖ 62 merits.] ~, *Q1-2* ‖

Did euer *Curtian* Gullffe play such a part?   65
Had *Curtius* beene so vsed, if he had brook't,
That rauenous whirlepoole, pourd his solide spirrits,
Through earth dissolued sinews, stopt her veines,
And rose with saued *Rome*, vpon his backe,
As I swum pooles of fire, and Gullfs of brasse,   70
To saue my country, thrust this venturous arme,
Beneath her ruines; tooke her on my necke,
And set her safe on her appeased shore?
And opes the king, a fouler bog then this,
In his so rotten bosome, to deuoure   75
Him that deuourd what else had swalloed him,
In a detraction so with spight embrew'd,
And drowne such good in such ingratitude?
My spirrit as yet, but stooping to his rest,
Shines hotly in him, as the Sunne in clowds,   80
Purpled, and made proud with a peacefull Euen:
But when I throughly set to him, his cheekes,
Will (like those clouds) forgoe their collour quite,
And his whole blaze, smoke into endles night.
     Sau. Nay nay, we must haue no such gall my Lord,   85
O'reflow our friendly liuers: my relation,
Onely deliuers my enflamed zeale
To your religious merits; which me thinkes,
Should make your highnes canonizd, a Saint.
     Byr. What had his armes beene, without my arme,   90
That with his motion, made the whole field moue?
And this held vp, we still had victory.
When ouer charg'd with number, his few friends
Retir'd amazed, I set them on assurd,
And what rude ruine seas'd on I confirmed;   95
When I left leading, all his army reeld,
One fell on other foule, and as the *Cyclop*
That hauing lost his eye, strooke euery way, /
His blowes directed to no certaine scope;   [E4]
Or as, the soule departed from the body,   100
The body wants coherence in his parts,
Can not consist, but seuer, and dissolue;
So I remou'd once, all his armies shooke,
Panted, and fainted, and were euer flying,
Like wandring pulses sperst through bodies dying.   105

67 rauenous] *Q2*; rauenons *Q1* ‖ 69 *Rome*] Rome *Q1-2* ‖ 71 country,] ~? *Q1-2* ‖ 76 deuourd ...
him,] *Parrott*; ~, ... ~ˌ *Q1-2* ‖ 77 detraction ... embrew'd] *Parrott*; ~, ... embrewed *Q1-2* ‖
82 him,] *Q2*; ~; *Q1* ‖ 84 night.] *Q2*; ~, *Q1* ‖ 93 friends] *Q2*; ~, *Q1* ‖ 100 as,] ~ˌ *Q1-2* ‖ 105
dying.] *Q2*; ~, *Q1* ‖

Sau. It cannot be denied, tis all so true,
That what seemes arogance, is desert in you.
  Byr. What monstrous humors feed a Princes blood,
Being bad to good men, and to bad men good?
  Sau. Well let these contradictions passe (my lord,)   110
Till they be reconcil'd, or put in forme,
By power giuen to your will, and you present,
The fashion of a perfect gouernment;
In meane space but a word, we haue small time,
To spend in priuate, which I wish may be   115
With all aduantage taken; Lord *Laffin* –
  Ron. Ist not a face of excellent presentment,
Though not so amorouse with pure white, and red,
Yet is the whole proportion singular.
  Roch. That euer I beheld.
  Bret.   It hath good lines,   120
And tracts drawne through it: The purfle, rare.
  Ron. I heard the famous and right learned Earle,
And Archbishop of *Lions*, *Peirse Pinac*,
Who was reported to haue wondrouse Iudgment
In mens euents, and natures, by their lookes: 125
(Vpon his death bed, visited by this duke)
He told his sister, when his grace was gon,
That he had neuer yet obserud a face,
Of worse presage then this: and I will sweare,
That (something seene in Phisiognomy)   130
I do not find in all the rules it giues
One slendrest blemish tending to mishap,
But (on the opposite part) as we may see,
On trees late blossomd, when all frosts are past,
How they are taken, and what wil be fruit: /   135
So, on this tree of Scepters, I discerne   [E4ᵛ]
How it is loden with apparances,
Rules answering Rules; and glances, crownd with glances.
                          He snatches away the picture.
  Byr. What, does he take my picture?
  Sau.   I, my Lord.
  Byr. Your Highnesse will excuse me; I will giue you   140
My likenesse put in Statue, not in picture;
And by a Statuary of mine owne,
That can in Brasse expresse the witte of man,

---

107 you.] *Q2*; ~, *Q1* ‖ **113** perfect] prefect *Q1-2* ‖ **116** *Laffin*–] *Shepherd*; ~. *Q1-2* ‖ **119** singular.] *Q2*; ~; *Q1* ‖ **120** beheld.] *Q2*; ~, *Q1* ‖ **121** purfle] *stet* (*See Textual Note*) | rare.] *Q2*; ~, *Q1* ‖ **123** *Lions*,] *Q2*; ~ˬ *Q1* ‖ **131** it] *Q1(c)*, *Q2*; he *Q1(u)* ‖ **138** glances.] *Q2*; ~; *Q1* ‖ **139** I,] ~ˬ *Q1-2* ‖

And in his forme, make all men see his vertues:
Others, that with much strictnesse imitate,   145
The some-thing stooping carriage of my neck,
The voluble, and milde radiance of mine eyes,
Neuer obserue my Masculine aspect,
And Lyon-like instinct it shaddoweth:
Which Enuie cannot say, is flatterie: 150
And I will haue my Image promist you,
Cut in such matter, as shal euer last;
Where it shall stand, fixt with eternall rootes,
And with a most vnmooued grauitie;
For I will haue the famous mountaine *Oros*,   155
That lookes out of the Dutchy where I gouerne,
(Into your highnesse Dukedome) first made yours,
And then with such inimitable art
Exprest and handled; chieflie from the place
Where most conspicuously, he shewes his face,   160
That though it keepe the true forme of that hill
In all his longitudes, and latitudes,
His height, his distances, and full proportion,
Yet shall it cleerely beare my counterfaite,
Both in my face and all my lineaments: 165
And euery man shall say, this is *Byron*.
Within my left hand, I will hold a Cittie,
Which is the Cittie *Amiens*; at whose siedge
I seru'd so memorably: from my right,
Ile powre an endlesse flood, into a Sea   170
Raging beneath me; which shall intimate /
My ceaselesse seruice, drunke vp by the King   [F1]
As th'Ocean drinkes vp riuers, and makes all
Beare his proude title; *Iuory*, *Brasse* and *Goulde*,
That theeues may purchase, and be bought and sould,   175
Shall not be vsde about me; lasting worth
Shall onely set the duke of *Byron* forth.
    Sau. O that your statuary could expresse you,
With any nerenesse to your owne instructions;
That statue would I prise past all the iewells   180
Within my cabinet of *Beatrice*,
The memorie of my Grandame *Portugall*.
Most roiall duke: we can not longe endure
To be thus priuate, let vs then conclude,
With this great resolution: that your wisedome,   185

145 Others,] *See Textual Note* ‖ **149** instinct] ~, Q1-2 ‖ **152** as shal] Q1(c); it shall Q1(u); as shall Q2 ‖ **172** ceaselesse] Q2; ceaselcsse Q1 ‖ **175** purchase,] ~; Q1-2 ‖ **177** forth.] Q2; ~; Q1 ‖ **182** *Portugall*.] Portugall; Q1-2 ‖

Will not forget to cast a pleasing vaile
Ouer your anger; that may hide each glance,
Of any notice taken of your wronge,
And shew your self the more obsequious.
Tis but the virtue of a little patience,   190
There are so oft attempts made gainst his person,
That sometimes they may speede, for they are plants
That spring the more for cutting, and at last
Will cast their wished shadow; marke ere long –

Enter Nemours, Soisson.

[*Aside to Byron.*] See who comes here my Lord; as now no more;   195
Now must we turne our streame another way. –
My Lord, I humbly thanke his maiesty,
That he would grace my idle time spent here
With entertainement of your princely person;
Which, worthely, he keepes for his owne bosome.   200
My Lord, the duke *Nemours*? and Count *Soisson*?
Your honours haue beene bountifully done me
In often visitation: let me pray you,
To see some iewells now, and helpe my choice:
In making vp a present for the King.   205
  Nem. Your highnesse shall much grace vs.
  Sau.   I am doubtfull
That I haue much incenst the duke *Byron*, /
With praising the Kings worthinesse in armes   [F1ᵛ]
So much past all men.
  Sois.   He deserues it, highly.

               ·*Exit Sauoy with the Lords;*
               manent Byr: Laffin.

  Byr. What wrongs are these, laid on me by the King,   210
To equall others worths in warre, with mine;
Endure this, and be turnd into his Moile
To beare his sumptures: honord friend be true,
And we will turne these torrents. Hence, the King!

                    Exit Laffi.

Enter Henry, Espe: Vitry, Ianin.

  Hen. Why suffer you that ill-aboding vermine,   215
To breede so neere your bosome? bee assurde,
His hants are omenous. Not the throtes of Rauens,
Spent on infected houses; houles of dogges,

---

192 plants] *Q2;* palnts *Q1* ‖ **194** long–] ~, *Q1* | SD *Nemours,*] ~ *Q1-2* ‖ **195** SD *Aside to Byron.*]
Parrott subs. | Lord; . . . more;] ~, . . . ~, *Q1-2* ‖ **196** way.–] *Parrott;* ~; *Q1-2* ‖ **209** SD *Exit . . .*
Lords;] *Parrott;* Exit. *Q1-2* | SD *manent*] manet *Q1-2* ‖ **214** torrents. Hence, the King!] *Parrott;*
~, hence. The King. *Q1* ‖ **215** ill-aboding] ~‿~ *Q1-2* ‖ **217** omenous. Not] ~, not *Q1-2* ‖ **218**
houses;] *Q1(c);* ~, *Q1(u), Q2* ‖

When no sound stirres, at mid-night; apparitions,
And strokes of spirits, clad in black mens shapes: 220
Or ougly womens: the aduerse decrees
Of constellations, nor securitie
In vicious peace, are surer fatall vshers
Of ferall mischiefes, and mortallities,
Then this prodigious feend is, where he fawnes: 225
La fiend, and not *Laffin*, he should be cald.
   Byr. Be what he will, men in themselues entire,
March safe with naked feete, on coles of fire:
I build not outward, nor depend on proppes,
Nor chuse my consort by the common eare: 230
Nor by the Moone-shine, in the grace of Kings:
So rare are true deseruers lou'd or knowne,
That men lou'd vulgarely, are euer none:
Nor men grac't seruilely, for being spots
In Princes traines, though borne euen with their crownes;   235
The Stalion powre, hath such a beesome taile,
That it sweepes all from iustice, and such filth
He beares out in it, that men mere exempt,
Are merely cleerest: men will shortly buie
Friends from the prison, or the pillorie,   240
Rather then honors markets. I feare none, /
But foule Ingratitude, and Detraction,   [F2]
In all the brood of villanie.
   Hen.   No? not treason?
Be circumspect, for to a credulous eye,
He comes inuisible, vail'd with flatterie,   245
And flaterers looke like friends, as Woolues, like Dogges.
And as a glorious Poeme fronted well
With many a goodly Herrald of his praise,
So farre from hate of praises to his face,
That he praies men to praise him, and they ride   250
Before, with trumpets in their mouthes, proclayming
Life to the holie furie of his lines:
All drawne, as if with one eye he had leerd,
On his lou'd hand, and led it by a rule;
That his plumes onely Imp the Muses wings.   255
He sleepes with them, his head is napt with baies,
His lips breake out with *Nectar*, his tunde feete
Are of the great last, the perpetuall motion,
And he puft with their empty breath beleeues

---

219 mid-night;] *Q1(c)*, *Q2*; ~, *Q1(u)* ‖ **222** securitie] ~, *Q1-2* ‖ **224** ferall] *Parrott*; femall *Q1-2* ‖ **232** deseruers] ~, *Q1-2* ‖ **253** leerd] *Q1(c)*, *Q2*; lernd *Q1(u)* ‖ **254** rule;] *Q1(c)*; ~, *Q1(u)*; ~: *Q2* ‖ **255** wings.] ~, *Q1-2* ‖

310

Full merit eas'd those passions of winde,   260
Which yet serue but to praise, and cannot merit,
And so his furie in their ayre expires:
So *de Laffin*, and such corrupted Herralds,
Hirde to encorage, and to glorifie
May force what breath they will into their cheekes,   265
Fitter to blow vp bladders, then full men:
Yet may puff men to, with perswasions
That they are Gods in worth; and may rise Kings
With treading on their noises; yet the worthiest,
From onely his owne worth receiues his spirit   270
And right is worthy bound to any merit;
Which right, shall you haue euer; leaue him then,
He followes none but markt, and wretched men;
And now for *England* you shall goe my lord,
Our Lord Ambassador to that matchlesse Queene;   275
You neuer had a voiage of such pleasure,
Honor, and worthy obiects: Ther's a Queene
Where Nature keepes her state, and State her Court, /
Wisdome her studie, Conntinence her fort,   [F2ᵛ]
Where Magnanimity, Humanitie: 280
Firmnesse in counsaile and Integritie:
Grace to her porest subiects: Maiestie
To awe the greatest, haue respects diuine,
And in her each part, all the vertues shine.
                    Exit Hen. cum suis, manet Byron.
  Byr. Inioy your will a while, I may haue mine.   285
Wherefore (before I part to this ambassage)
Ile be resolu'd by a Magician
That dwells hereby, to whome ile goe disguisde,
And shew him my births figure, set before
By one of his profession, of the which   290
Ile craue his iudgement, fayning I am sent
From some great personage, whose natiuitie,
He wisheth should be censurd by his skill.
But on go my plots, be it good or ill.   *Exit.*

---

260 merit eas'd] ~, ~, *Q1-2* ‖ 261 serue] ~, *Q1-2* | merit,] *Q1(c), Q2*; ~: *Q1(u)* ‖ 262 expires:]
Q1(c), Q2; ~, *Q1(u)* ‖ 265 cheekes,] ~, *Q1-2* ‖ 269 noises;] *Q1(c)*; ~, *Q1(u)*; noses; *Q2* | yet]
Q2; yer *Q1* ‖ 272 euer;] *Q1(c)*; ~, *Q1(u), Q2* ‖ 274 *England*] England *Q1-2* ‖ 276 pleasure,] ~ˏ
Q1-2 ‖ 278 Nature ... State] nature ... state *Q1-2* ‖ 279 Wisdome ... Conntinence] *Wisdome ...
Conntinence Q1-2* ‖ 280 Magnanimity, Humanitie] *Magnanimity, Humanitie Q1-2* ‖ 281
Integritie] integritie *Q1-2* ‖ 284 SD *cum suis*,] *Parrott; & Sau. Q1-2* ‖ 289 before] *Q2*; ~: *Q1* ‖

[III.iii]

Enter La Brosse.

[*Labross.*] This houre by all rules of Astrologie,
Is dangerous to my person, if not deadly.
How haples is our knowledge to fore-tel
And not be able to preuent a mischiefe.
O the strange difference twixt vs and the stars: 5
They worke with inclynations stronge and fatall
And nothing know; and we know all there working
And nought can do, or nothing can preuent!
Rude ignorance is beastly, knowledge wretched:
The heauenly powers enuy what they enioyne: 10
We are commanded t'imitate there natures,
In making all our ends eternitie:
And in that imitation we are plagued,
And worsse then they esteemd, that haue no soules
But in their nostrils, and like beasts expire;   15
As they do that are ignorant of arts,
By drowning there eternall parts in sence,
And sensuall affectations: while wee liue
Our good parts take away, the more they giue. /

Enter Byron solus disguizd like a   [F3]
Carrier of letters.

Byr. [*Aside.*] The forts that fauorites hold in Princes
      hearts,   20
In common subiects loues, and their owne strengths,
Are not so sure, and vnexpugnable,
But that the more they are presum'd vpon,
The more they faile; dayly and hourely proofe,
Tels vs prosperity is at highest degree   25
The founte and handle of calamitie:
Like dust before a whirle-winde those men flie,
That prostrate on the grounds of fortune lye:
And being great (like trees that broadest sproyte)
Their owne top-heauy state grubs vp their roote.   30
These apprehensions startle all my powers,
And arme them with suspition gainst them-selues.
In my late proiects, I haue cast my selfe
Into the armes of others; and will see
If they will let me fall; or tosse me vp   35

III.iii] *Parrott* ‖ 1 *Labross.*] *Shepherd* ‖ 4 mischiefe.] ~, *Q1* ‖ 8 preuent!] ~? *Q1-2* ‖ 10 enioyne]
Enioyne Q1-2 ‖ 14 soules] ~, *Q1-2* ‖ 19 SD *Enter*] *Parrott* ‖ 20 SD *Aside.*] *Parrott* ‖ 21 loues, . . .
strengths,] ~; . . . ~ *Q1-2* ‖ 32 them-selues.] *Phelps*; ~, *Q1-2* ‖ 33 proiects,] ~; *Q1-2* ‖

Into th'affected compasse of a throne. –
God saue you sir.
    Labross.   Y'are welcome friend; what would you?
    Byr. I would entreate you, for some crownes I bring,
To giue your iudgement of this figure cast.
To know by his natiuitie there seene,   40
What sort of end the person shall endure
Who sent me to you, and whose birth it is.
    Labross. Ile herein do my best, in your desire;
                              [He contemplates the figure.]
The man is raisd out of a good descent,
And nothing oulder then your selfe I thinke;   45
Is it not you?
    Byr.   I will not tell you that:
But tell me on what end he shall arriue.
    Labross. My sonne, I see, that he whose end is cast
In this set figure, is of Noble parts,
And by his militarie valure raisde,   50
To princely honors; and may be a king,
But that I see a *Caput Algol* here, /
That hinders it I feare.   [F3ᵛ]
    Byr.   A *Caput Algol*?
What's that I pray?
    Labross.   Forbeare to aske me, sonne,
You bid me speake, what feare bids me conceale.   55
    Byr. You haue no cause to feare, and therefore speake.
    Labross. Youle rather wish you had beene ignorant,
Then be instructed in a thing so ill.
    Byr. Ignorance is an idle salue for ill,
And therefore do not vrge me to enforce,   60
What I would freely know: for by the skill
Showne in thy aged hayres, ile lay thy braine
Here scattered at my feete, and seeke in that,
What safely thou must vtter with thy tongue,
If thou deny it.
    Labross.   Will you not allow me   65
To hold my peace? what lesse can I desire?
If not, be pleasd with my constrained speech.
    Byr. Was euer man yet punisht for expressing
What he was chargde? be free, and speake the wurst.
    Labross. Then briefly this; the man hath lately done   70
An action that will make him loose his head.

---

36 throne.–] *Parrott*; ~.ˌ *Q1-2* ‖ **40** seene,] ~; *Q1-2* ‖ **41** endure] ~, *Q1-2* ‖ **43** SD *He … figure.*]
Parrott ‖

Byr. Curst be thy throte and soule, Rauen, Shriech-owle,
    hag.   *[Beating La Brosse.]*
Labross. O hold, for heauens sake hold.
  Byr.   Hold on, I will,
Vault, and contractor of all horrid sounds,
Trumpet of all the miseries in hell,   75
Of my confusions; of the shamefull end
Of all my seruices; witch, fiend, accurst
For euer be the poison of thy tongue,
And let the black fume of thy venomd breath,
Infect the ayre, shrinke heauen, put out the starres,   80
And raine so fell and blew a plague on earth,
That all the world may falter with my fall.
    Labross. Pitty my age, my Lord.
  Byr.   Out prodigie,
Remedy of pitty, mine of flint,
Whence with my nailes and feete, ile digge enough /   85
Horror, and sauadge cruelty, to build   [F4]
Temples to Massacre: dam of deuils take thee,
Hadst thou no better end to crowne my parts?
The Buls of *Colchos*, nor his triple neck,
That howles out Earthquakes: the most mortall vapors,   90
That euer stifled and strooke dead the fowles,
That flew at neuer such a sightly pitch,
Could not haue burnt my bloud so.
    Labross.   I told truth,
And could haue flatterd you.
  Byr.   O that thou hadst;
Would I had giuen thee twenty thousand crownes   95
That thou hadst flatterd me: there's no ioy on earth,
Neuer so rationall, so pure, and holy,
But is a Iester, Parasite, a Whore,
In the most worthy parts, with which they please
A drunkennesse of soule, and a disease.   100
    Labross. I knew you not.
  Byr.   Peace, dog of *Pluto*, peace,
Thou knewst my end to come, not me here present:
Pox of your halting humane knowledges;
O death! how farre off hast thou kild? how soone
A man may know too much, though neuer nothing?   105
Spight of the Starres, and all Astrologie,
I will not loose my head: or if I do,

---

72 SD *Beating La Brosse.*] *Parrott* ‖ 85 enough] ~, *Q1-2* ‖ 88 parts?] ~. *Q1-2* ‖ 89 *Colchos*]
Q1(c), Q2; Calchos Q1(u) ‖ 99 please] ~, *Q1-2* ‖

A hundred thousand heads shall off before.
I am a nobler substance then the Starres,
And shall the baser ouer-rule the better?   110
Or are they better, since they are the bigger?
I haue a will, and faculties of choise,
To do, or not to do: and reason why,
I doe, or not doe this; the starres haue none,
They know not why they shine, more then this Taper,   115
Nor how they worke, nor what: ile change my course,
Ile peece-meale pull, the frame of all my thoughts,
And cast my will into another mould:
And where are all your *Caput Algols* then?
Your Plannets all, being vnderneath the earth, /   120
At my natiuitie: what can they doe?   [F4ᵛ]
Malignant in aspects? in bloudy houses?
Wilde fire consume them; one poore cup of wine,
More then I vse, then my weake braine will beare,
Shall make them drunke and reele out of their spheres,   125
For any certaine act they can enforce.
O that mine armes were wings, that I might flie,
And pluck out of their hearts, my destinie!
Ile weare those golden Spurres vpon my heeles,
And kick at fate; be free all worthy spirits,   130
And stretch your selues, for greatnesse and for height:
Vntrusse your slaueries, you haue height enough,
Beneath this steepe heauen to vse all your reaches,
'Tis too farre off, to let you, or respect you.
Giue me a spirit that on this lifes rough sea,   135
Loues t'haue his sailes fild with a lustie winde,
Euen till his Sayle-yeards tremble, his Masts crack,
And his rapt ship runne on her side so lowe
That she drinkes water, and her keele plowes ayre;
There is no danger to a man, that knowes   140
What life and death is: there's not any law,
Exceeds his knowledge; neither is it lawfull
That he should stoope to any other lawe.
He goes before them, and commands them all,   144
That to him-selfe is a law rationall.   *Exeunt.*

---

124 then my] *Parrott* (than); that my *Q1-2* ‖ 137 tremble,] ~; *Q1-2* ‖ 145 SD *Exeunt.*] *Exit.*
Q1-2 ‖

ACTVS 4.   SCE. 1.

Enter D'Aumont, with Crequi.

[*D'Aum.*] The Duke of *Byron* is return'd from *England*,
And (as they say) was Princely entertainde,
Schoold by the matchlesse Queene there, who I heare
Spake most diuinely; and would gladly heare,
Her speech reported.
    Cre.   I can serue your turne,   5
As one that speakes from others, not from her,
And thus it is reported at his parting: /
Thus *Monsieur Du Byron* you haue beheld,   [G1]
Our Court proportion'd to our little kingdome,
In euery entertainment; yet our minde,   10
To do you all the rites of your repaire,
Is as vnbounded as the ample ayre.
What idle paines haue you bestowd to see
A poore ould woman? who in nothing liues
More, then in true affections, borne your king;   15
And in the perfect knowledge she hath learn'd,
Of his good knights, and seruants of your sort.
We thanke him that he keepes the memory
Of vs and all our kindnesse; but must say,
That it is onely kept; and not laid out   20
To such affectionate profit as we wish;
Being so much set on fire with his deserts,
That they consume vs; not to be restorde
By your presentment of him, but his person:
And we had [not] thought, that he whose vertues flye   25
So beyond wonder, and the reach of thought,
Should check at eight houres saile, and his high spirit
That stoopes to feare, lesse then the Poles of heauen,
Should doubt an vnder billow of the Sea,
And (being a Sea) be sparing of his streames: 30
And I must blame all you that may aduise him;
That (hauing helpt him through all martiall dangers)
You let him stick, at the kinde rites of peace,
Considering all the forces I haue sent,
To set his martiall seas vp in firme walls,   35
On both his sides for him to passe at pleasure;
Did plainly open him a guarded way
And led in Nature to this friendly shore.

---

1 D'Aum.] Q2; *om.* Q1 ‖ 7 parting:] Q2; ~, Q1 ‖ 24 him,] ~; Q1-2 ‖ 25 not] *Parrott* (*See Textual Note*) ‖ 28 heauen,] ~; Q1-2 ‖ 38 shore.] ~, Q1-2 ‖

But here is nothing worth his personall sight,
Here are no walled Cities; for that Christall   40
Sheds, with his light, his hardnesse and his height
About our thankfull person, and our Realme;
Whose onely ayde, we euer yet desirde;
And now I see, the helpe we sent to him,
Which should haue swum to him in our owne bloud, /   45
Had it beene needfull; (our affections   [G1ᵛ]
Being more giuen to his good, then he himselfe)
Ends in the actuall right it did his state,
And ours is sleighted; all our worth is made,
The common-stock, and banck; from whence are seru'd   50
All mens occasions; yet (thankes to heauen)
Their gratitudes are drawne drye; not our bounties.
And you shall tell your King, that he neglects
Ould friends for new; and sets his soothed Ease
Aboue his honor; Marshals policie   55
In ranck before his iustice; and his profit
Before his royalty: his humanitie gone,
To make me no repaiment of mine owne.
    D'Aum. What answered the Duke?
    Cre.   In this sort.
Your highnesse sweete speech hath no sharper end,   60
Then he would wish his life, if he neglected
The least grace you haue nam'd; but to his wish,
Much powre is wanting: the greene rootes of warre,
Not yet so close cut vp, but he may dash
Against their relickes to his vtter ruine,   65
Without more neere eyes, fixt vpon his feete,
Then those that looke out of his countries soyle,
And this may well excuse his personall presence,
Which yet he oft hath long'd to set by yours:
That he might immitate the Maiestie,   70
Which so long peace hath practisde, and made full,
In your admir'd apparance; to illustrate
And rectifie his habite in rude warre.
And his will to be here, must needs be great,
Since heauen hath thron'de so true a royaltie here,   75
That he thinkes no king absolutely crownde,
Whose temples haue not stood beneath this skie,
And whose height is not hardned with these starres,
Whose influences for this altitude,

---

41 Sheds, ... hardnesse] *Parrott*; ~ˌ ... ~, *Q1-2* ‖ 59 D'Aum.] *D'Au. Q1 (through l.122)* ‖ 61
life, ... neglected] ~; ... ~, *Q1-2* ‖

Distild, and wrought in with this temperate ayre,   80
And this diuision of the Element
Haue with your raigne, brought forth more worthy spirits, /
For counsaile, valour, height of wit, and art,   [G2]
Then any other region of the earth:
Or were brought forth to all your ancestors.   85
And as a cunning Orator reserues
His fairest similies, best-adorning figures,
Chiefe matter, and most mouing arguments
For his conclusion; and doth then supply
His ground-streames layd before, glides ouer them,   90
Makes his full depth seene through; and so takes vp,
His audience in Aplawses past the clowds:
So in your gouernment, conclusiue Nature,
(Willing to end her Excellence in earth
When your foote shall be set vpon the starres)   95
Showes all her Soueraigne Beauties, Ornaments,
Vertues, and Raptures; ouertakes her workes
In former Empires, makes them but your foyles,
Swels to her full Sea, and againe doth drowne
The world, in admiration of your crowne.   100
   D'Aum. He did her (at all parts) confessed right.
   Cre. She tooke it yet, but as a part of Court-ship,
And sayd, he was the subtle Orator,
To whom he did too gloriously resemble
Nature in her, and in her gouernment.   105
He said, he was no Orator, but a Souldier,
More then this ayre, in which you breath hath made me,
My studious loue of your rare gouernment,
And simple truth, which is most eloquent.
Your Empire is so amply absolute,   110
That euen your Theaters show more comely rule,
True noblesse, royaltie, and happinesse
Then others courts: you make all state before
Vtterly obsolete; all to come, twice sod.
And therefore doth my royall Soueraigne wish   115
Your yeares may proue, as vitall, as your virtues,
That (standing on his Turrets this way turn'd,
Ordring and fixing his affaires by yours)
He may at last, on firme grounds, passe your Seas,
And see that Maiden-sea of Maiestie, /   120
In whose chaste armes, so many kingdomes lye.   [G2ᵛ]

85 ancestors.] ~, *Q1-2* || 86 Orator] ~, *Q1-2* || 92 clowds:] ~. *Q1-2* || 93 Nature] nature *Q1-2* || 100 crowne] *Q2*; erowne *Q1* || 104 resemble] ~, *Q1-2* || 105 gouernment.] ~, *Q1-2* || 106 He . . . Souldier,] *See Textual Note* || 108 loue] ~, *Q1-2* || 109 eloquent.] ~, *Q1-2* ||

D'Aum. When came she to her touch of his ambition?
  Cre. In this speech following, which I thus remember.
If I hold any merit worth his presence,
Or any part of that, your Courtship giues me,   125
My subiects haue bestowd it; some in counsaile,
In action some, and in obedience all;
For none knowes, with such proofe as you my Lord,
How much a subiect may renowne his Prince,
And how much Princes of their subiects hold;   130
In all the seruices that euer subiect
Did for his Soueraigne, he that best deseru'd
Must (in comparison) except *Byron*;
And to winne this prise cleere, without the maimes
Commonly giuen men by ambition,   135
When all their parts lye open to his view,
Showes continence, past their other excellence:
But for a subiect to affect a kingdome,
Is like the Cammell, that of *Ioue* begd hornes,
And such mad-hungrie men, as well may eate,   140
Hote coles of fire, to feede their naturall heate;
For, to aspire to competence with your king
What subiect is so grose, and Gyantly?
He hauing now a *Daulphine* borne to him,
Whose birth, ten dayes before, was dreadfully   145
Vsherd with Earth-quakes, in most parts of *Europe*,
And that giues all men, cause enough to feare
All thought of competition with him.
Commend vs good my Lord, and tell our Brother
How much we ioy, in that his royall issue,   150
And in what prayers, we raise our heart to heauen,
That in more terror to his foes, and wonder,
He may drinke Earthquakes, and deuoure the thunder:
So we admire your valure, and your vertues,
And euer will contend, to winne their honor.   155
Then spake she to *Crequie*, and Prince *D'Auergne*,
And gaue all gracious farewels; when *Byron*
Was thus encountred by a Councellor /
Of great and eminent name, and matchlesse merit: [G3]
I thinke (my Lord) your princely *Daulphin* beares   160
Arion on his Cradle, through your kingdome,
In the sweete Musique ioy strikes from his birth.
He answerd; And good right; the cause commands it.

132 Soueraigne,] ~; *Q1-2* ‖ 133 except] ~, *Q1-2* ‖ 134 cleere,] ~; *Q1-2* ‖ 137 excellence:] *Q1(c)*,
Q2; ~, *Q1(u)* ‖ 152 wonder,] ~ˏ *Q1-2* ‖ 153 thunder:] *Q1(c)*; ~, *Q1(u)*; ~ˏ *Q2* ‖ 161 on] *Q1(c)*,
Q2; in *Q1(u)* ‖ 163 And] and *Q1-2* ‖

But (said the other) had we a fift *Henry*,
To claime his ould right: and one man to friend,   165
Whom you well know my Lord, that for his friendship
Were promist the Vice-royaltie of *France*,
We would not doubt of conquest, in despight
Of all those windy Earth-quakes. He replyed;
Treason was neuer guide to English conquests,   170
And therefore that doubt shall not fright our *Daulphine*;
Nor would I be the friend to such a foe,
For all the royalties in Christendome.
Fix there your foote (sayd he) I onely giue
False fire, and would be lothe to shoote you of: 175
He that winnes Empire with the losse of faith,
Out-buies it; and will banck-route; you haue layde
A braue foundation, by the hand of virtue:
Put not the roofe to fortune: foolish statuaries,
That vnder little Saints suppose great bases,   180
Make lesse, to sence, the Saints; and so where fortune,
Aduanceth vile mindes, to states great and noble,
She much the more exposeth them to shame,
Not able to make good, and fill their bases,
With a conformed structure; I haue found,   185
(Thankes to the blesser of my searches) that counsailes,
Held to the lyne of Iustice, still produce
The surest states, and greatest, being sure,
Without which fit assurance, in the greatest –
As you may see a mighty promontorie   190
More digd and vnder-eaten, then may warrant
A safe supportance to his hanging browes,
All passengers auoide him, shunne all ground
That lyes within his shadow, and beare still
A flying eye vpon him: so great men   195
Corrupted in their grounds and building out /
Too swelling fronts, for their foundations;   [G3ᵛ]
When most they should be propt, are most forsaken,
And men will rather thrust into the stormes
Of better grounded States, then take a shelter   200
Beneath their ruinous, and fearefull weight;
Yet they so ouersee their faultie bases,
That they remaine securer in conceipt:
And that securitie, doth worse presage

178 virtue] *Q1(c)*, *Q2*; victorie *Q1(u)* ‖ 179 fortune:] *Q1(c)*, *Q2*; ~, *Q1(u)* ‖ 180 suppose great bases,] ~, ~ ~, *Q1-2* ‖ 183 the] *Q1(c)*, *Q2*; *om. Q1(u)* ‖ 187 Iustice, still produce] ~; ~ ~, *Q1-2* ‖ 189 greatest–] *Parrott*; ~, *Q1-2* ‖ 191 warrant] ~, *Q1-2* ‖ 192 supportance] ~, *Q1-2* ‖ 195 him:] ~, *Q1-2* ‖ 196 grounds] *Q1(c)*, *Q2*; ground, *Q1(u)* | out] ~. *Q1* ‖ 202 they so ouersee] ~, ~ ~, *Q1-2* ‖

Their nere distructions, then their eaten grounds;   205
And therefore heauen it selfe is made to vs
A perfect Hierogliphick to expresse,
The Idlenesse of such securitie,
And the graue labour, of a wise distrust,
In both sorts of the all-enclyning starres;   210
Where all men note this difference in their shyning,
As plaine as they distinguish either hand;
The fixt starres wauer, and the erring, stand.
  D'Aum. How tooke he this so worthy admonition?
  Cre. Grauely applied (said he) and like the man,   215
Whome all the world saies, ouerrules the starres;
Which are diuine bookes to vs; and are read
By vnderstanders oncly, the true obiects,
And chiefe companions of the truest men;
And (though I need it not) I thanke your counsaile,   220
That neuer yet was idle, but spherelike,
Still mooues about, and is the continent
To this blest Ile.

ACT. 5. SCEN. 1.

Enter Byron, D'Auergne, Laffin.

  Byr. The Circkle of this ambassie is closde,
For which I long haue long'd, for mine owne ends;
To see my faithfull, and leaue courtly friends,
To whom I came (me thought) with such a spirit,
As you haue seene, a lusty courser showe,   5
That hath beene longe time at his manger tied;
High fead, alone, and when (his headstall broken) /
Hee runnes his prison, like a trumpet neighs,   [G4]
Cuts ayre, in high curuets, and shakes his head:
(With wanton stoopings, twixt his forelegs) mocking   10
The heauy center; spreds his flying crest,
Like to an Ensigne, hedge and ditches leaping,
Till in the fresh meade, at his naturall foode
He sees free fellowes, and hath met them free:
And now (good friend) I would be faine inform'd,   15
What our right Princely Lord, the duke of *Sauoy*
Hath thought on, to employ my comming home.

<hr>

210 enclyning] *Q2*; enclying *Q1* ‖ 213 wauer] *Q2*; mauer *Q1* ‖ 214 worthy] *Q2*; worrhy *Q1* ‖
216 ouerrules] *stet* (*See Textual Note*) ‖ 221 but] *Q2*; But *Q1* ‖ **V.i.**10 stoopings] stopings *Q1-2*
(*See Textual Note*) ‖ 12 hedge] ~, *Q1-2* ‖ 13 meade] *Brereton conj.*; meate *Q1-2* (*See Textual
Note*) ‖

Laf. To try the Kings trust in you, and withall,
How hot he trailes on our conspiracie:
He first would haue you, begge the gouernment,   20
Of the important Citadell of *Bourg*:
Or to place in it, any you shall name:
Which wilbe wondrous fit, to march before,
His other purposes; and is a fort
Hee rates, in loue, aboue his patrimonie;   25
To make which fortresse worthie of your suite:
He vowes (if you obtaine it) to bestowe
His third faire daughter, on your excellence,
And hopes the King will not deny it you.
    Byr. Denie it me? deny me such a suite?   30
Who will he grant, if he deny it me?
    Laf. He'le finde some politique shift to do't, I feare.
    Byr. What shift? or what euasion can he finde,
What one patch is there in all policies shop,
(That botcher vp of Kingdomes) that can mend   35
The brack betwixt vs, any way denying?
    D'Au. That's at your perill.
    Byr.   Come, he dares not do't.
    D'Au. Dares not? presume not so; you know (good duke)
That all things hee thinkes fit to do, he dares.
    Byr. By heauen I wonder at you, I will aske it,   40
As sternely, and secure of all repulse
As th'antient *Persians* did when they implorde,
Their idoll fire to grant them any boone;
With which they would descend into a flood, /   44
And threaten there to quench it, if they faild,   [G4ᵛ]
Of that they ask't it.
    Laf.   Said like your Kings King;
Cold hath no act in depth, nor are suites wrought
(Of any high price) that are coldly sought:
Ile hast, and with your courage, comfort *Sauoy.*   *Exit Laffin.*
    D'Au. I am your friend (my Lord) and will deserue   50
That name, with following any course you take;
Yet (for your owne sake) I could wish your spirit
Would let you spare all broade termes of the King,
Or, on my life you will at last repent it.
    Byr. What can he doe?
    D'Au.   All that you can not feare.   55

---

21 *Bourg*] Bourg *Q1-2* ‖ 31 me?] ~. *Q1-2* ‖ 36 denying?] ~. *Q1-2* ‖ 37 That's] Thats *Q1-2* |
perill.] *Q2*; ~: *Q1* ‖ 42 *Persians*] Persians *Q1-2* ‖ 46 it.] ~: *Q1-2* ‖ 54 it.] *Q2*; ~: *Q1* ‖

Byr. You feare too much, be by, when next I see him,
And see how I will vrge him in this suite.
He comes; marke you, that thinke he will not grant it.

Enter Henry, Esp. Soiss. Ia.

I am become a suiter to your highnesse.
   Hen. For what, my Lord, tis like you shall obtaine.   60
   Byr. I do not much doubt that; my seruices,
I hope haue more strength in your good conceite
Then to receiue repulse, in such requests.
   Hen. What is it?
   Byr. That you would bestowe on one whom I shall name,   65
The keeping of the Citadell of *Bourg*.
   Hen. Excuse me sir, I must not grant you that.
   Byr. Not grant me that?
   Hen.   It is not fit I should;
You are my gouernor in *Burgundy*,
And Prouince gouernors, that command in chiefe,   70
Ought not to haue the charge of fortresses;
Besides, it is the chiefe key of my kingdome,
That opens towards *Italie*, and must therefore,
Be giuen to one that hath imediatly   74
Dependance on vs. /
   Byr.   These are wondrous reasons,   [H1]
Is not a man depending on his merits
As fit to haue the charge of such a key
As one that meerely hangs vppon your humors?
   Hen. Do not enforce your merits so your self;
It takes away their luster, and reward.   80
   Byr. But you will grant my suite?
   Hen.   I sweare I cannot,
Keeping the credit of my braine and place.
   Byr. Will you deny me then?
   Hen.   I am inforcst;
I haue no power, more then your selfe in things
That are beyond my reason.
   Byr.   Then my selfe?   85
That's a strange sleight in your comparison;
Am I become th'example of such men
As haue lest power? Such a diminitiue?
I was comparatiue in the better sort;

---

57 suite.] ~, *Q1-2* ‖ 58 He ... it.] *Shepherd*; He ... thinke/ He ... it. *Q1-2* | comes;] ~, *Q1-2* ‖
66 *Bourg.*] Bourg, *Q1* ‖ 68 that] *Q1(c)*, *Q2*; this sute *Q1(u)* ‖ 69 *Burgundy*] Burgundy *Q1-2* ‖ 73
Italie] Italie *Q1-2* ‖ 75 *Byr.*] ~: *Q1* (*colon in all speech-prefixes through l.118 and in V.ii.29 and
ll.101-27*) ‖ 79 enforce ... self] *Q1(c)*; inferre ... selfe *Q1(u)*; enforce ... selfe *Q2* ‖ 81 cannot,]
Q2; ~. *Q1* ‖ 88 lest ... diminitiue] *Q1(c)*, *Q2*; best ... dininitiue *Q1(u)* ‖

And such a King as you, would say I cannot   90
Do such or such a thing, were I as great
In power as he; euen that indefinite he,
Exprest me full: This Moone is strangely chang'd.
   Hen. How can I helpe it? would you haue a King
That hath a white beard, haue so greene a braine?   95
   Byr. A plague of braine; what doth this touch your braine?
  You must giue me more reason or I sweare –
   Hen. Sweare; what do you sweare?
   Byr.   I Sweare you wrong me,
And deale not like a King, to iest, and sleight,
A man that you should curiously reward;   100
Tell me of your gray beard? it is not gray
With care to recompence me, who eas'd your care.
   Hen. You haue beene recompenc't, from head to foote.
   Byr. With a distrusted dukedome: Take your dukedome
Bestow'd on me againe; It was not giuen   105
For any loue, but feare, and force of shame.
   Hen. Yet twas your honor; which if you respect not,
Why seeke you this Adition? /
   Byr.   Since this honour,   [H1ᵛ]
Would shew you lou'd me to, in trusting me,
Without which loue, and trust, honor is shame;   110
A very Pageant, and a propertie:
Honor, with all his Adiuncts, I deserue,
And you quit my deserts, with your gray beard.
   Hen. Since you expostulate the matter so;
I tell you plaine; Another reason is   115
Why I am mou'd to make you this deniall
That I suspect you to haue had intelligence
With my vowd enimies.
   Byr.   Miserie of vertue,
Ill is made good, with worse? This reason poures
Poyson, for Balme, into the wound you made;   120
You make me madde, and rob me of my soule,
To take away my try'd loue, and my Truth;
Which of my labors, which of all my woundes,
Which ouerthrow, which Battayle wonne for you,
Breedes this suspition? Can the blood of faith,   125
(Lost in all these to finde it proofe, and strength)
Beget disloyalty? all my raine is falne,
Into the horse-fayre; springing pooles and myre;

90 cannot] ~, *Q1-2* ‖ **91** Do such ... thing,] ~ ~; ... ~; *Q1-2* ‖ **93** chang'd.] *Q2*; ~; *Q1* ‖ **95** beard,] ~; *Q1-2* ‖ **97** sweare–] *Shepherd*; ~ͺ *Q1* ‖ **106** shame.] *Q2*; ~; *Q1* ‖ **110** trust,] ~; *Q1-2* ‖

And not in thankfull grounds, or fields of fruite;
Fall then before vs, O thou flaming Christall,   130
That art the vncorrupted Register
Of all mens merits: And remonstrate heere,
The fights, the dangers, the affrights and horrors,
Whence I haue rescu'd this vnthankefull King:
And shew (commixt with them) the ioyes, the glories   135
Of his state then: Then his kind thoughts of me:
Then my deseruings: Now my infamie:
But I will be mine owne King: I will see,
That all your Chronicles be fild with me,
That none but I, and my renowned Syre   140
Be said to winne the memorable fieldes
Of *Arques* and *Deepe*: and none but we of all
Kept you from dying there, in an Hospitall;
None but my selfe, that wonne the day at *Dreux*:
A day of holy name, and needes no night: /   145
Nor none but I at *Fountaine Francois* burst,   [H2]
The heart strings of the leaguers; I alone,
Tooke *Amiens* in these armes, and held her fast,
In spight of all the Pitchy fires she cast,
And clowds of bullets pourd vpon my brest,   150
Till she showd yours; and tooke her naturall forme;
Onely my selfe (married to victory)
Did people *Artois*, *Douay*, *Picardie*,
Bethune, and Saint *Paule*, *Bapaume*, and *Courcelles*,
With her triumphant issue.
   Hen.   Ha ha ha!   155
                             Exit Henry cum suis.
              Byron drawing and is held by D'Au.
   D'Au. O hold my Lord; for my sake, mighty Spirrit.
                                   Exeunt.

[V.ii]

Enter Byron, D'Au. following vnseene.

   Byr. Respect, Reuendge, slaughter, repaie for laughter!
What's graue in Earth, what awfull? what abhord?
If my rage be ridiculouse? I will make it,
The law and rule of all things serious.
So long as idle and riduculus Kings   5

134 rescu'd] Q2; rsscu'd Q1 ‖ 145 needes] Q2; ~, Q1 ‖ 151 forme;] ~, Q1-2 ‖ 155 issue.] Q2;
~; Q1 | ha!] ~, Q1 | SD *Exit … suis.*] *Exit,* Q1 ‖ 156 SD *Exeunt.*] *Phelps; Exit.* Q1-2 ‖ **V.ii**]
Parrott ‖ SD *Byron, D'Au.*] ~, *Dau* Q1-2 ‖ 1 laughter!] ~, Q1-2 ‖ 2 What's] Q2; Whats' Q1 ‖
5 idle … Kings] *Shepherd*; idle … King Q1(u), Q2; such as he Q1(c) ‖

325

Are suffered, soothed and wrest all right to safty,
So long is mischiefe gathering massacres,
For their curst kingdomes; which I will preuent.
Laughter? Ile fright it from him, farre as he,
Hath cast irreuocable shame; which euer,   10
Being found is lost and lost returneth neuer;
Should Kings cast of their bounties, with their dangers?
He that can warme at fires, where vertue burnes,
Hunt pleasure through her torments; nothing feele,
Of all his subiects suffer; but long hid   15
In wants, and miseries, and hauing past
Through all the grauest shapes, of worth and honor,
(For all *Heroique* fashions to be learned,
By those hard lessons) shew an antique vizard –
Who would not wish him rather hewd to nothing,   20
Then left so monstrous? slight my seruices? /
Drowne the dread noises of my sword, in laughter?   [H2ᵛ]
(My blowes, as but the passages of shadowes,
Ouer the highest and most barraine hills)
And vse me like no man, but as he tooke me   25
Into a desart, gasht with all my wounds,
Sustaind for him, and buried me in flies?
Forth vengeance then, and open wounds in him
Shall let in *Spaine*, and *Sauoy*.

        Offers to draw and D'Au: againe holds him.

D'Au.   O my Lord,
This is to large a licence giuen your furie;   30
Giue time to it; what reason, sodainely,
Can not extend, respite doth oft supplie.
   Byr. While respite holds reuenge, the wrong redoubles,
And so the shame of sufferance; it torments me,
To thinke what I endure, at his shrunke hands,   35
That skornes the guift, of one pore fort to me:
That haue subdu'd for him, O iniurie,
Forts, Citties, Countries, I, and yet my furie –

                                        Exiturus.

---

6 right to safty,] ~, ~ ~ ~ *Q1-2* ‖ 8 preuent.] ~, *Q1-2* ‖ 15 long hid] (~ ~) *Q1-2* ‖ 18-19 (For . . . lessons)] *stet* (*See Textual Note*) ‖ 19 vizard–] *Parrott;* ~, *Q1-2* ‖ 22 dread] *Deighton conj.;* dead *Q1-2* (*See Textual Note*) ‖ 23-24 (My . . . hills)] *Parrott;* ~ . . . ~, *Q1-2* (*See Textual Note*) ‖ 25 me like no man,] ~, ~, ~ ~; *Q1-2* ‖ 27 flies?] ~; *Q1-2* ‖ 29 *Spaine,* and *Sauoy*] *Q2;* Spaine, and Sauoy *Q1* ‖ 31 it;] ~, *Q1-2* ‖ 33 respite] *Q2;* ~, *Q1* ‖ 34 sufferance;] ~, *Q1-2* ‖ 37 him,] ~; *Q1* ‖ 38 furie–] *Parrott;* ~. *Q1-2* | SD *Exiturus.*] *Parrott;* Exieunt. *Q1-2* | SD *Enter Henry.*] *Parrott* ‖

[Enter Henry.]

Hen. Byron?

D'Au.   My Lord? the King calls.

Hen.   Turne I pray.

How now? from whence flow these distracted faces?   40

From what attempt returne they? as disclayming,

Their late *Heroique* bearer? what, a pistall?

Why, good my Lord, can mirth make you so wrathfull?

    Byr. Mirth? twas mockerie, a contempt; a scandall

To my renowne for euer: a repulse,   45

As miserably cold, as Stygian water,

That from sincere earth issues, and doth breake

The strongest vessells, not to be containde,

But in the tough hoofe of a pacient Asse.

    Hen. My Lord, your iudgement is not competent   50

In this dissention; I may say of you,

As Fame saies of the antient *Eleans*,

That, in th'Olimpian contentions,

They euer were the iustest Arbitrators,

If none of them contended, nor were parties; /   55

Those that will moderate disputations well,   [H3]

Must not themselues affect the coronet;

For as the ayre, contain'd within our eares:

If it be not in quiet; nor refrains,

Troubling our hearing, with offensiue sounds;   60

(But our affected instrument of hearing,

Repleat with noise, and singings in it selfe)

It faithfully receiues no other voices;

So, of all iudgements, if within themselues

They suffer spleene, and are tumultuous,   65

They can not equall differences without them;

And this winde, that doth sing so in your eares,

I know, is no disease bred in your selfe;

But whisperd in by others; who in swelling

Your vaines with emptie hope of much, yet able,   70

To performe nothing; are like shallow streames,

That make themselues so many heauens to sight;

Since you may see in them, the Moone, and Starres,

The blew space of the ayre; as farre from vs,

(To our weake sences) in those shallow streames   75

As if they were as deepe, as heauen is high;

39 calls.] Q2; ~, *Q1* | pray.] ~, *Q1-2* ‖ 50 competent] ~, *Q1-2* ‖ 51 dissention; ... you,] ~, ...
~; *Q1-2* ‖ 52 *Eleans*] Eleans *Q1-2* ‖ 59 refrains] *Q1(c)*, Q2; refaine *Q1(u)* ‖ 60 sounds] *Q1(c)*,
Q2; sound *Q1(u)* ‖ 61-62 (But ... selfe)] *Parrott*; ̗~ ... ~, *Q1(c)*, Q2; ̗~ ... ~: *Q1(u)* ‖ 65
tumultuous,] ~; *Q1-2* ‖ 72 heauens] ~; *Q1-2* ‖ 74 space] *Q1(c)*, Q2; sphare *Q1(u)* ‖ 75 sences)]
Q1(c), Q2; ~, *Q1(u)* ‖

Yet with your middle finger onely, sound them,
And you shall pierce them to the very earth;
And therefore leaue them, and be true to me
Or yow'le be left by all; or be like one   80
That in cold nights will needes haue all the fire,
And there is held by others, and embrac't
Onely to burne him: your fire wilbe inward,
Which not another deluge can put out:

                     Byron kneeles while the King goes on.

O Inocence the sacred amulet,   85
Gainst all the poisons of infirmitie:
Of all misfortune, iniurie, and death,
That makes a man, in tune still in himselfe;
Free from the hell to be his owne accuser,
Euer in quiet, endles ioy enioying;   90
No strife, nor no sedition in his powres:
No motion in his will, against his reason, /
No thought gainst thought, Nor (as twere in the confines   [H3^v]
Of wishing, and repenting) doth possesse
Onely a wayward, and tumultuose peace,   95
But (all parts in him, friendly and secure,
Fruitefull of all best thinges in all worst Seasons)
He can with euery wish, be in their plenty,
When the infectious guilt of one foule crime,
Destroyes the free content of all our time.   100
    Byr. Tis all acknowlegd, and, (though all to late)
Heere the short madnesse of my anger ends:
If euer I did good I lockt it safe
In you, th'impregnable defence of goodnesse:
If ill, I presse it with my penitent knees   105
To that vnsounded depth, whence naught returneth.
    Hen. Tis musique to mine eares: rise then, for euer
Quit of what guilt soeuer, till this houre,
And nothing toucht in honnor or in spirit,
Rise without flattery, rise by absolute merit.   110

             Enter Esp: to the King, Byron etc.
             Enter Sauoy with three Ladies.

    Esp. Sir if it please you to bee taught any Courtship take
you to your stand: *Sauoy* is at it with three Mistresses at once;
he loues each of them best, yet All differently.
    Hen. For the time he hath beene here, he hath talkt a

---

82 others] *Q1(c), Q2;* other *Q1(u)* ‖ **99** When] ~, *Q1-2* ‖ **107** then, for euer] ~ ~~, *Q1-2* ‖ **110**
SD *Enter … Byron]* ~: … ~: *Q1* ‖ **112** once;] ~ *Q1* ‖

Volume greater then the *Turkes* Alcaron; stand vp close; his   115
lips go still.   [*Retiring with Byron and the Lords.*]
   Sau. Excuse me, excuse me; The King has ye all.
   1. True Sir, in honorable subiection.
   2. To the which we are bound by our loyallty.
   Sau. Nay your excuse, your excuse; intend me for affection?   120
you are all bearers of his fauours; and deny him not your
opposition by night.
   3. You say rightly in that; for therein we oppose vs to his
command.
   1. In the which he neuer yet prest vs.   125
   2. Such is the benediction of our peace.
   Sau. You take me still in flat misconstruction, and conceiue /
not by me.   [H4]
   1. Therein we are strong in our owne purposes; for it were
something scandalous for vs to conceiue by you.   130
   2. Though there might be question made of your fruitfulnes,
yet drie weather in haruest dooes no harme.
   Hen. They will talke him into *Sauoy*; he beginnes to hunt
downe.
   Sau. As the King is, and hath beene, a most admired, and   135
the most vnmatchable souldier, so hath he beene, and is, a sole
excellent, and vnparalelld Courtier.
   Hen. [*Aside.*] *Pouvre Amy Merciè.*
   1. Your highnes does the king but right sir.
   2. And heauen shall blesse you for that iustice, with plentiful   140
store of want in Ladies affections.
   Sau. You are cruell, and wil not vouchsafe me audience to
any conclusion.
   1. Beseech your grace conclude, that we may present our
curtsies to you, and giue you the adiew.   145
   Sau. It is saide, the king wil bring an army into *Sauoy*.
   2. Truely we are not of his counsaile of warre.
   Sau. Nay but vouchsafe me.
   3. Vouchsafe him, vouchsafe him, else there's no play in't.
   1. Well I vouchsafe your Grace.   150
   Sau. Let the king bring an army into *Sauoy*, and Ile finde him
sport for fortie yeares.
   Hen. [*Aside.*] Would I were sure of that, I should then haue
a long age, and a merry.
   1. I thinke your Grace woulde play with his army at   155
Balloone.

115 *Turkes*] Turkes *Q1-2* ‖ 116 still.] *Q2*; ~ *Q1* | SD *Retiring … Lords.*] *Parrott* ‖ 117 all.] *Q2*;
~; *Q1* ‖ 118, 119, 123 *1. … 2. … 3.*] *1. … 2. … 3. Q1-2 (so throughout scene)* ‖ 120 excuse,
your excuse;] ~; ~ ~, *Q1-2* ‖ 131 *2.*] *2, Q1* ‖ 136 the] *Q1(c)*; om. *Q1(u), Q2* ‖ 138 SD *Aside.*]
Parrott ‖ 140-41 And … affections.] *Shepherd*; And … iustice,/ With … affections. *Q1-2* ‖ 147
2.] *2 Q1* ‖ 153 SD *Aside.*] *Parrott* ‖ 154 age] *Q1(u), Q2*; gae *Q1(c) (See Textual Note)* ‖

2. My faith, and that's a martiall recreation.

3. It is next to impious courting.

Sau. I am not hee that can set my Squadrons ouer-night,
by midnight leape my horse, curry seauen miles, and by three,   160
leape my mistris; returne to mine armie againe, and direct as
I were infatigable, I am no such tough souldier.

1. Your disparitie is beleeu'd sir.

2. And tis a peece of virtue to tell true. /   164

3. Gods me, the king!   [*Discovering Henry.*]   [H4ᵛ]

Sau. Well, I haue said nothing that may offend.

1. Tis hop't so.

2. If there be any mercie in laughter.

Sau. Ile take my leaue.

[*To Henry.*] After the tedious stay my loue hath made,   170
(Most worthy to command our earthly zeale)
I come for pardon, and to take my leaue;
Affirming though I reape no other good,
By this my voiage, but t'haue seene a Prince
Of greatnes, in all grace so past report,   175
I nothing should repent me; and to shew,
Some token of my gratitude, I haue sent,
Into your treasury, the greatest Iewells,
In all my Cabinet of *Beatrice,*
And of my late-deceased wife, th'Infanta.   180
Which are two Basigns, and their Ewrs of christall,
Neuer yet vallewd for their workmanship,
Nor the exceding riches of their matter.
And to your stable (worthy duke of *Byron*)
I haue sent in two of my fayrest horses.   185

  Byr. Sent me your horses? vpon what desert?
I entertaine no presents, but for merits;
Which I am farre from at your highnes hands;
As being of all men to you the most stranger.
There is as ample bounty in refusing;   190
As in bestowing, and with this I quit you.

  Sau. Then haue I lost nought but my poore good will.

  Hen. Well cosine, I with all thankes, welcome that;
And the rich arguments with which you proue it,
Wishing I could, to your wish welcome you;   195
Draw, for your marquisate, the articles

---

165 king!] ~, *Q1* | SD *Discovering Henry.*] *Parrott* ‖ **167** hop't] *Q1(c)*, *Q2*; hapt *Q1(u)* | so.]
Q2; ~, *Q1* ‖ **170** SD *To Henry.*] *Parrott (at end of line 169)* ‖ **174** voiage,] ~; *Q1-2* ‖ **175** report,]
~; *Q1-2* ‖ **176** me;] ~, *Q1-2* ‖ **178** treasury] *Q1(c)*; treasure *Q1(u)*, *Q2* ‖ **179-80** In ... *Beatrice,/*
And ... *Infanta.*] *Q1(c)*, *Q2*; *order of lines reversed Q1(u)* ‖ **179** *Beatrice,*] Beatrice. *Q1* ‖ **180** th']
Q1(c), *Q2*; the' *Q1(u)* ‖ **183** matter.] matter‸ *Q1(c)*, *Q2*; mattr‸ *Q1(u)* ‖ **184** stable (worthy ...
Byron)] *Q2*; ~, (~ ... ~, *Q1* ‖ **188** your] *Q2*; yout *Q1* ‖ **189** stranger.] ~, *Q1-2* ‖ **192** will.] *Q2*;
~, *Q1* ‖ **196** articles] ~; *Q1* ‖

Agreed on in our composition,
And it is yours, but where you haue propos'd,
(In your aduices) my designe for *Millane*,
I will haue no warre with the king of *Spaine*,   200
Vnlesse his hopes proue weary of our peace;
And (Princely cosine) it is farre from me, /
To thinke your wisedome, needeful of my counsaile,   [I1]
Yet loue, oft-times must offer things vnneedeful;
And therefore I would counsaile you to hold   205
All good termes, with his Maiestie of *Spaine*:
If any troubles should be stirr'd betwixt you,
I would not stirre therein, but to appease them;
I haue too much care of my royal word,
To breake a Peace so iust and consequent,   210
Without force of precedent iniurie:
Endles desires are worthles of iust Princes,
And onely proper to the swinge of tyrants.
    Sau. At al partes spoke like the most christian king.
I take my humblest leaue, and pray your Highnes,   215
To holde me as your seruant, and poore kinsman,
Who wisheth no supreamer happines
Than to be yours: To you (right worthy Princes)
I wish for all your fauours powr'd on me
The loue of al these Ladies mutually,   220
And (so they please their Lordes) that they may please
Themselues by all meanes. And be you assurde
(Most louely Princesses) as of your liues,
You cannot be true women, if true wiues.   *Exit.*
    Hen. Is this he *Espernon*, that you would needes perswade   225
vs courted so absurdly?
    Esp. This is euen he sir, howsoeuer he hath studied his Parting
Courtship.
    Hen. In what one point seemde hee so ridiculous as you
would present him?   230
    Esp. Behold me sir, I beseech you behold me, I appeare to
you as the great Duke of *Sauoy* with these three Ladies.
    Hen. Well sir, we graunt your resemblance.
    Esp. He stole a carriage sir, from Count *d'Auuergne* heere.
    D'Au. From me sir?   235
    Esp. Excuse me sir, from you I assure you: heere sir, he
lies at the Lady *Antoniette*, iust thus, for the worlde, in the
true posture of Count *d'Auuergne*.

---

197 composition] *Q1(c)*, *Q2*; compsition *Q1(u)* ‖ 198 propos'd] *Q2*; porpos'd *Q1(c)*; purposed
Q1(u) (*See Textual Note*) ‖ 199 *Millane*] Millane *Q1-2* ‖ 200 *Spaine*] Spaine *Q1-2* ‖ 214 king.] ~,
Q1 ‖ 225-26 Is ... absurdly?] *Shepherd*; Is ... needes/ Perswade ... absurdly. *Q1-2* ‖

D'Au. Y'are exceeding delightsome.

Hen. Why is not that wel? it came in with the organ hose. /   240

Esp. Organ hose? a pox an't; let it pipe it selfe into contempt;   [I1ᵛ]
hee hath stolne it most felloniously, and it graces him like a
disease.

Hen. I thinke he stole it from *D'Auuergne* indeed.

Esp. Well, would he had robd him of all his other diseases,   245
he were then the soundest lord in *France*.

D'Au. As I am sir, I shall stand all wethers with you.

Esp. [*To Henry.*] But sir, he has praisd you aboue th'inuention
of Rimers.

Hen. Wherein? or how?   250

Esp. He tooke vpon him to describe your victories in warre,
and where hee should haue sayd, you were the most absolute
souldier in Christendome, (no Asse could haue mist it) hee
deliuerd you for as pretty a fellow of your hands, as any was
in *France*.   255

Hen. Marry, God dild him.

Esp. A pox on him.

Hen. Well, (to be serious) you know him well
To be a gallant Courtier: his great wit
Can turne him into any forme he lists,   260
More fit to be auoyded then deluded.
For my Lord Duke of *Byron* here well knowes,
That it infecteth, where it doth affect:
And where it seemes to counsaile, it conspires.
With him go all our faults, and from vs flie,   265
(With all his counsaile) all conspiracie.

Finis Actus Quinti,
et ultimi.

---

241 an't] ant *Q1-2* ‖ **242** stolne it] *Q1(c)*; stolneit *Q1(u)* ‖ **246** he] *Q2*; He *Q1* ‖ **248** SD *To Henry.*] ‖ **256** Marry,] ~. *Q1-2* ‖ **261** auoyded] *Q2*; ~, *Q1* ‖ **262** here] ~, *Q1-2* ‖

[DRAMATIS PERSONAE

Henry IV, King of France
The infant Dauphin
The Duke of Byron
D'Auvergne, a French noble allied with Byron
D'Escures
Epernon
Montigny } French nobles
Soissons
La Fin, a ruined French noble
The Chancellor
The Vidame
Janin, a councilor of the King
Fleury
Harlay } judges
Potier
The ambassador of Spain
Prâlin
Vitry } captains of the King's guard
A captain of Byron's guard
Varennes, a member of Byron's guard
La Brunel, a captain under Byron

A bishop
A messenger
A soldier
The Hangman
The nurse of the Dauphin
A lady
Byron's sister

Figures in the Masque:
Chastity, impersonated by Marie de Medici, Queen of France
Liberality, impersonated by Mademoiselle d'Entragues, mistress
  of the King
Four other Virtues
Cupid]

Dramatis Personae] *subs. as given by Parrott; first given by Phelps*

THE TRAGEDIE OF
Charles Duke of *Byron*.

ACTVS, 1. SCENA, 1.

Enter Henry, Vidame, D'escures, Espernon, Ianin.

Hen. Byron fallne in so tratrous a relaps,
Aleadgd for our ingratitude: what offices,
Titles of honor, and what admiration,
Could *France* afford him that it pourd not on?
When he was scarce arriu'd at forty yeares,   5
He ranne through all chiefe dignities of *France.*
At fourteene yeares of age he was made Colonell
To all the *Suisses* seruing then in *Flanders*;
Soone after he was marshall of the campe.
And shortly after, marshall Generall: 10
He was receiued high Admirall of *France*
In that our Parlament we held at *Tours*;
Marshall of *France* in that we held at *Paris*.
And at the Siege of *Amiens* he acknowledgd,
None his Superiour but our selfe, the King;   15
Though I had there, the Princes of the blood
I made him my Lieutennant Generall,
Declard him Ioyntly the prime Peere of *France*,
And raisd his Barony into a Duchy.
   Ian. And yet (my Lord) all this could not allay   20
The fatall thirst of his ambition,
For some haue heard him say he would not die,
Till on the wings of valour he had reacht
One degree heigher; and had seene his head,
Set on the royall Quarter of a crowne;   25
Yea at so vnbeleeu'd a pitch he aymd,
That he hath said his heart would still complaine,

I.i SD *Enter*] Q2 ‖ 4 *France*] Q2; France *Q1* ‖ 8 *Suisses*] Suisses Q1-2 | *Flanders*] Q2; Flanders
Q1 ‖ 19 Duchy.] Q2; ~, *Q1* ‖ 21 thirst] Q2; thrist *Q1* ‖

Till he aspird the style of Soueraigne. /
And from what ground my Lord rise all the leuyes   [13ᵛ]
Now made in *Italy*? from whence should spring   30
The warlike humor of the Count *Fuentes*?
The restles stirrings of the Duke of *Sauoye*?
The discontent the Spaniard entertaind,
With such a threatning fury, when he heard
The preiudiciall conditions,   35
Propos'd him, in the treaty held at *Veruins*?
And many other braueries, this way ayming,
But from some hope of inward ayd from hence?
And that, all this derectly aymes at you,
Your highnes hath by one intelligence,   40
Good cause to thinke; which is your late aduice,
That the Sea army, now prepard at *Naples*,
Hath an intended Enterprise on *Prouence*,
Although the cunning Spaniard giues it out,
That all is for *Algier*.
    Hen.   I must beleeue,   45
That without treason bred in our owne brests,
Spaines affayres are not in so good estate,
To ayme at any action against *France*:
And if *Byron* should be their instrument,
His altred disposition could not growe,   50
So far wide in an instant; Nor resigne,
His valure to these lawles resolutions
Vpon the sodaine; nor without some charms,
Of forreigne hopes and flatteries sung to him:
But far it flyes my thoughts, that such a spirrit,   55
So actiue, valiant, and vigilant;
Can see it selfe transformed with such wild furies.
And like a dreame it shewes to my conceipts,
That he who by himselfe hath wonne such honor:
And he to whome his father left so much,   60
He that still dayly reapes so much from me,
And knowes he may encrease it to more proofe
From me, then any other forreigne King;
Should quite against the streame of all religion,
Honor, and reason, take a course so foule, /   65
And neither keepe his Oth, nor saue his Soule.   [14]
Can the poore keeping of a Citadell
Which I denyed, to be at his disposure,

28 Soueraigne.] ~, *Q1-2* ‖ **37** braueries] *Q2*; beaueries *Q1* ‖ **43** *Prouence,*] ~? *Q1-2* ‖ **47** *Spaines*]
Spaines, *Q1* ‖

336

Make him forgoe the whole strength of his honours?
It is impossible; though the violence,   70
Of his hot spirrit made him make attempt
Vpon our person for denying him,
Yet well I found his loyall iudgment seru'd,
To keepe it from effect: besides, being offer'd
Two hundred thousand crownes in yearely pention,   75
And to be Generall of all the forces
The *Spaniards* had in *France*, they found him still,
As an vnmatcht *Achilles* in the warres,
So a most wise *Vlisses* to their words,
Stopping his eares at their enchanted sounds;   80
And plaine he tould them that although his blood
(Being mou'd by Nature) were a very fire
And boyld in apprehension of a wrong;
Yet should his mind hold such a scepter there,
As would containe it from all act and thought   85
Of treachery or ingratitude to his Prince.
Yet do I long, me thinkes, to see *La Fin*,
Who hath his heart in keeping; since his state,
(Growne to decay and he to discontent)
Comes neere the ambitious plight of Duke *Byron*.   90
My Lord *Vidame*, when does your Lordship thinke,
Your vnckle of *La Fin* will be arriu'd?
    Vid. I thinke (my Lord) he now is neere ariuing;
For his particular iourny and deuotion,
Voud to the holy Lady of *Loretto*,   95
Was long since past and he vpon returne.
    Hen. In him, as in a christall that is charm'd,
I shall descerne by whome and what designes,
My rule is threatened: and that sacred power
That hath enabled this defensiue arme,   100
(When I enioyd but an vnequall Nooke,
Of that I now possesse) to front a King
Farre my Superiour: And from twelue set battailes, /
March home a victor: ten of them obtaind,   [14ᵛ]
Without my personall seruice; will not see   105
A traitrous subiect foile me, and so end
What his hand hath with such successe begunne.

---

70 impossible;] ~, *Q1-2* ‖ 71 spirrit] spiritit *Q1*; spirit *Q2* ‖ 72 him,] ~; *Q1-2* ‖ 74-77 besides, being offer'd ... *France*,] *Parrott*; ~ ~~, ... ~; *Q1-2* ‖ 75 pention,] ~. *Q1-2* ‖ 82 mou'd by Nature)] ~) ~~, *Q1-2* ‖ 92 arriu'd?] ~. *Q1-2* ‖ 93 ariuing;] ~, *Q1-2* ‖ 101 but an] *Q2*; but in an *Q1* ‖ 104 March] Marcht *catchword on preceding page of Q1-2* ‖

Enter a Ladie, and a Nursse bringing
the Daulphine.

Esp. See the yong *Daulphin* brought to cheere your highnes.
Hen. My royall blessing, and the King of heauen,
Make thee an aged, and a happie King: 110
Helpe Nurse to put my sword into his hand;
Hold Boy, by this; and with it may thy arme
Cut from thy tree of rule, all traitrous branches,
That striue to shadow and eclips thy glories;
Haue thy old fathers angell for thy guide,   115
Redoubled be his spirit in thy brest;
Who when this State ranne like a turbulent sea,
In ciuill hates and bloudy enmity,
Their wrathes and enuies, like so many windes,
Setled and burst: and like the Halcions birth,   120
Be thine to bring a calme vpon the shore,
In which the eyes of warre may euer sleepe,
As ouerwacht with former massacres,
When guiltie [lust], made Noblesse, feed on Noblesse;
All the sweete plentie of the realme exhausted;   125
When the nak't merchant, was pursude for spoile,
When the pore Pezants frighted neediest theeues
With their pale leanenesse; nothing left on them
But meager carcases sustaind with ayre,
Wandring like Ghosts affrighted from their graues,   130
When with the often and incessant sounds
The very beasts knew the alarum bell,
And (hearing it) ranne bellowing to their home:
From which vnchristian broiles and homicides,
Let the religious sword of iustice free   135
Thee and thy kingdomes gouern'd after me.
O heauen! or if th'vnsettled bloud of *France*,
With ease, and welth, renew her ciuill furies: /
Let all my powers be emptied in my Sonne   [K1]
To curb, and end them all, as I haue done.   140
Let him by vertue, quite cut of from fortune
Her fetherd shoulders, and her winged shooes,
And thrust from her light feete, her turning stone;
That she may euer tarry by his throne.
And of his worth, let after ages say,   145
(He fighting for the land; and bringing home
Iust conquests, loden with his enimies spoiles)

108 *Daulphin*] Daulphin *Q1*; Dolphin *Q2* ‖ 123 ouerwacht] *Shepherd subs.*; ouermacht *Q1*
(*See Textual Note*) ‖ 124 guiltie] *Q2*; gultie *Q1* | lust] *Parrott* (*See Textual Note*) ‖ 137 *France*]
France *Q1-2* ‖ 141 cut of from fortune] *Shepherd subs.*; out ~ ~ ~, *Q1-2* ‖

His father past all *France* in martiall deeds,
But he, his father twenty times exceedes.

[*Exeunt.*]

[I.ii]

*Enter the Duke of Byron, D'Auuergne
and Laffin.*

Byr. My deare friends *D'Auuergne,* and *Laffin,*
We neede no coniurations to conceale
Our close intendments, to aduance our states
Euen with our merits; which are now neclected;
Since *Britaine* is reduc't, and breathlesse warre   5
Hath sheath'd his sword, and wrapt his Ensignes vp;
The King hath now no more vse of my valure,
And therefore I shall now no more enioy
The credite that my seruice held with him;
My seruice that hath driuen through all extreames,   10
Through tempests, droughts, and through the deepest floods;
Winters of shot: and ouer rockes so high
That birds could scarce aspire their ridgy toppes.
The world is quite inuerted: vertue throwne
At Vices feete: and sensuall peace confounds   15
Valure, and cowardise: Fame, and Infamy;
The rude and terrible age is turnd againe:
When the thicke ayre hid heauen, and all the starres,
Were drown'd in humor, tough, and hard to peirse,
When the red Sunne held not his fixed place;   20
Kept not his certaine course, his rise and set /
Nor yet distinguisht with his definite boundes;   [K1ᵛ]
Nor in his firme conuersions, were discernd
The fruitfull distances of time and place,
In the well varyed seasons of the yeare;   25
When th'incomposd incursions of floods
Wasted and eat the earth; and all things shewed
Wilde and disordred: nought was worse then now.
Wee must reforme and haue a new creation
Of State and gouernment; and on our *Chaos*   30
Will I sit brooding vp another world.
I who through all the dangers that can siege
The life of man, haue forcst my glorious way
To the repayring of my countries ruines,

---

148 *France*] France *Q1-2* ‖ 149 SD *Exeunt.*] *Phelps* ‖ *I.ii*] *Parrott* ‖ 2 conceale] ~: *Q1-2* ‖ 5 *Britaine*] Britaine *Q1-2* ‖ 13 toppes.] ~; *Q1* ‖ 15 confounds] ~, *Q1-2* ‖ 28 now.] ~; *Q1-2* ‖

Will ruine it againe, to re-aduance it;   35
Romaine *Camyllus*, safte the State of *Rome*
With farre lesse merite, then *Byron* hath *France*;
And how short of his is my recompence.
The king shall know, I will haue better price
Set on my seruices; in spight of whome   40
I will proclaime and ring my discontents
Into the farthest eare of all the world.
   Laf. How great a spirit he breaths? how learnd? how wise?
But (worthy Prince) you must giue temperate ayre,
To your vnmatcht, and more then humaine winde;   45
Else will our plots be frost-bit, in the flowre.
   D'Au. Betwixt our selues we may giue liberall vent
To all our fiery and displeas'd impressions;
Which nature could not entertaine with life,
Without some exhalation; A wrongd thought   50
Will breake a rib of steele.
   Byr.   My Princely friend,
Enough of these eruptions; our graue Councellor
Well knowes that great affaires will not be forg'd
But vpon Anuills that are linde with wooll;
We must ascend to our intentions toppe   55
Like Clowdes that be not seene till they be vp!
   Laf. O, you do too much rauish; And my soule
Offer to Musique in your numerous breath; /
Sententious, and so high, it wakens death;   [K2]
It is for these parts, that the Spanish King   60
Hath sworne to winne thee [ouer] to his side
At any price or perrill; That great *Sauoy*,
Offers his princely daughter, and a dowry,
Amounting to fiue hundred thousand crownes;
With full transport of all the Soueraigne rights   65
Belonging to the State of *Burgondie*;
Which marriage will be made, the onely Cyment
T'effect and strengthen all our secret Treaties;
Instruct me therefore, (my assured Prince)
Now I am going to resolue the King   70
Of his suspitions, how I shall behaue me.
   Byr. Go my most trusted friend, with happy feete:
Make me a sound man with him; Go to Court
But with a little traine; and be prepar'd
To heare, at first, tearmes of contempt and choller,   75

---

36 *Rome*] Rome *Q1-2* ‖ **37** *France*] France *Q1-2* ‖ **38** his] *Loane conj.*; this *Q1-2* (*See Textual Note*) ‖ **43** *Laf.*] *Laff:* Q1 (*colon in all speech-prefixes through I.iii.44, except I.ii.43, 52, 89*) ‖ **56** vp!] vp? *Q1*; vp. *Q2* ‖ **61** thee ouer] them *Q1-2* (*See Textual Note*) ‖ **66** *Burgondie*] Burgondie *Q1-2* ‖ **69** therefore] *Q2*; thererfore *Q1* ‖

Which you may easily calme, and turne to grace,
If you beseech his highnesse to beleeue
That your whole drift and course for *Italy*,
(Where he hath heard you were) was onely made
Out of your long-well-knowne deuotion   80
To our right holy Lady of *Lorretto*,
As you haue told some of your friends in Court:
And that in passing *Mylan* and *Thurin*,
They charg'd you to propound my marriage
With the third daughter of the Duke of *Sauoy*;   85
Which you haue done, and I reiected it,
Resolu'd to build vpon his royall care
For my bestowing, which he lately vowd.
   Laf. O, you direct, as if the God of light
Sat in each nooke of you; and pointed out   90
The path of Empire; Charming all the dangers
On both sides arm'd, with his harmoniouse finger.
   Byr. Besides let me intreat you to dismisse,
All that haue made the voyage with your Lordship,
But specially the Curate: And to locke   95
Your papers in some place of doubtlesse safety; /
Or sacrifize them to the God of fire;   [K2ᵛ]
Considering worthily that in your handes
I put my fortunes, honour, and my life.
   Laf. Therein the bounty that your Grace hath showne me,   100
I prize past life, and all thinges that are mine;
And will vndoubtedly preserue, and tender
The merit of it, as my hope of heauen.
   Byr. I make no question; farewell worthy friend.

                                   Exeunt.

[I.iii]

Enter Henry, Chancellor, Laffin, D'Escures, Ianin,
Henry hauing many papers in his hand.

   Hen. Are these proofes of that purely Catholike zeale
That made him wish no other glorious title,
Then to be calld the scourge of *Huguenots*?
   Chan. No question sir, he was of no religion;
But (vpon false groundes, by some Courtiers laid)   5
Hath oft bene heard to mocke and iest at all.

---

76 grace,] ~. *Q1-2* ‖ **78** *Italy*] Italy *Q1-2* ‖ **83** *Mylan* and *Thurin*] Mylan and Thurin *Q1-2* ‖ **84** marriage] *Q2*; marrriage *Q1* ‖ **85** *Sauoy*] Sauoy *Q1-2* ‖ **104** SD *Exeunt.*] *Exit. Q1-2* ‖ I.iii] *Parrott* ‖ SD *Enter*] ‖ **1** Catholike] *Q2*; Chatholike *Q1* ‖

Hen. Are not his treasons haynous?
All.   Most abhord.
  Chan. All is confirmd that you haue heard before,
And amplified with many horrors more.
  Hen. Good *De Laffin*; you were our golden plummet,   10
To sound this gulphe of all ingratitude;
In which you haue with excellent desert
Of loyalty and pollicie, exprest
Your name in action; and with such apparence
Haue prou'd the parts of his ingratefull treasons,   15
That I must credit, more then I desir'd.
  Laf. I must confesse my Lord, my voyages
Made to the Duke of *Sauoy* and to *Mylan*;
Were with indeauour, that the warres returnd,
Might breed some trouble to your Maiestie;   20
And profit those by whome they were procur'd;
But since, in their disseignes, your sacred person
Was not excepted (which I since haue seene)
It so abhord me, that I was resolu'd
To giue you full intelligence thereof; /   25
And rather chus'd to fayle in promises,   [K3]
Made to the seruant; then infringe my fealty
Sworne to my royall Soueraigne and Maister.
  Hen. I am extreamely discontent to see,
This most vnnaturall conspiracie;   30
And would not haue the Marshall of *Byron*,
The first example of my forced Iustice;
Nor that his death should be the worthy cause,
That my calme raigne, (which hetherto hath held
A cleare and cheerefull skie aboue the heads   35
Of my deare subiects) should so sodainely
Be ouercast with clowdes of fire, and thunder;
Yet on submission, I vow stil his pardon.
  Ian. And still our humble counsayles, (for his seruice)
Would so resolue you, if he will imploy   40
His honourd valure as effectually,
To fortifie the State, against your foes;
As he hath practis'd bad intendments with them.
  Hen. That vow shall stand; and we will now addresse,
Some messengers to call him home to Court;   45
Without the slendrest intimation,
Of any ill we know; we will restraine

---

7 Most] − ~ *Q1-2* | abhord.] *Q2*; ~; *Q1* ‖ 10 *De*] *De' Q1* ‖ 16 desir'd.] *Q2*; ~, *Q1* ‖ 18 *Sauoy*
... *Mylan*] Sauoy ... Mylan *Q1-2* ‖ 28 Maister.] *Q2*; ~; *Q1* ‖ 30 vnnaturall] *Q2*; vnaturall *Q1* ‖

(With al forgiuenes, if he will confesse)
His headlong course to ruine; and his taste,
From the sweete poyson of his friendlike foes: 50
Treason hath blisterd heeles, dishonest Thinges
Haue bitter Riuers, though delicious Springs;
Descures haste you vnto him, and informe,
That hauing heard by sure intelligence,
Of the great leuies made in *Italie,*   55
Of Arms and soldiers, I am resolute,
Vpon my frontiers to maintaine an Army;
The charge whereof I will impose on him;
And to that end, expresly haue commanded,
De Vic, our Lord Ambassador in *Suisse,*   60
To demand leuie of six thousand men:
Appointing them to march where Duke *Byron*
Shall haue directions; wherein I haue follow'd, /
The counsaile of my Constable his Gossip;   [K3ᵛ]
Whose lik't aduice, I made him know by letters,   65
Wishing to heare his owne, from his owne mouth,
And by all meanes coniure, his speediest presence;
Do this with vtmost hast.
   D'Esc.   I will my Lord.   *Exit Desc.*
   Hen. My good Lord Chancellor, of many Peeces,
More then is here, of his conspiracies   70
Presented to vs, by our friend, *Laffin;*
You, onely, shall reserue these seauen and twenty,
Which are not those that most conclude against him;
But mention only him; since I am loth,
To haue the rest of the conspirators, knowne.   75
   Chan. My Lord, my purpose is to guard all these,
So safely from the sight of any other:
That in my doublet I will haue them sow'd;
Without discouering them to mine owne eies,
Till neede, or opportunitie requires.   80
   Hen. You shall do well my Lord, they are of weight;
But I am doubtfull that his conscience
Will make him so suspitious of the worst,
That he will hardly be induc't to come.
   Ian. I much should doubt that to, but that I hope   85
The strength of his conspiracie, as yet
Is not so readie, that he dare presume,

---

48 With al] *Shepherd;* Withal *Q1* ‖ **53** *Descures*] *See Textual Note* ‖ **55** *Italie*] Italie *Q1-2* ‖ **56**
soldiers,] *Q2;* ~; *Q1* ‖ **60** *Suisse*] Suisse *Q1-2* ‖ **65** him] *Q2;* him him *Q1* ‖ **66** owne,] ~; *Q1-2* ‖
73 most] *Shepherd;* must *Q1-2* ‖ **82** doubtfull] *Q2;* ~; *Q1* ‖

By his refusall to make knowne so much
Of his disloialtie.
   Hen.   I yet conceiue
His practises are turnd to no bad end,   90
And good *Laffin*, I pray you wright to him,
To hasten his repaire: and make him sure,
That you haue satisfied me to the full,
For all his actions, and haue vtterd nought,
But what might serue to banish bad impressions.   95
   Laf. I will not faile my Lord.
   Hen.   Conuaie your letters
By some choice friend of his: or by his brother:
And for a third excitement to his presence, /
Ianin, your selfe shall goe, and with the powre   [K4]
That both the rest employ to make him come,   100
Vse you the strength of your perswasions.
   Ian. I will my Lord, and hope I shall present him.

                                  Exit Ian.

[ACTVS 2.]

      Enter Esper. Soisson, Vitry, Pralin, etc.
               to the King.

   Esp. Wil't please your Maiestie to take your place,
The Maske is comming.
   Hen.   Roome my Lords, stand close.

     Musique and a Song, aboue, and Cupid *enters*
       with a Table written, hung about his neck;
     after him two Torch-bearers; after them Mary,
      D'Entragues, *and* 4. *Ladies more with their*
         Torch-bearers, etc. Cupid *speakes.*

   Cup. My Lord, these Nimphs, part of the scatterd traine,
Of friendlesse Vertue (liuing in the woods
Of shady *Arden*: and of late not hearing   5
The dreadfull sounds of Warre; but that sweete Peace,
Was by your valure lifted from her graue,
Set on your royall right hand: and all vertues
Summond with honor, and with rich rewards,
To be her hand-maides): These I say, the vertues,   10
Haue put their heads out of their Caues and Couerts,

89 conceiue] ~; *Q1-2* ‖ **96** letters] ~; *Q1-2* ‖ **98** presence,] ~; *Q1-2* ‖ **ACTVS 2.**] *Parrott; see
Textual Note* ‖ SD *to the King.*] *Parrott* ‖ **1** *Esp.*] Espa. *Q1-2* | Wil't] Wilt *Q1-2* ‖ **2** SD *aboue*]
Q2; ahoue *Q1* ‖ **4** Vertue] vertue *Q1-2* ‖

To be her true attendants in your Court:
In which desire, I must relate a tale,
Of kinde and worthy emulation,
Twixt these two vertues, leaders of the traine.   15
This on the right hand is *Sophrosyne*,
Or *Chastitie*: this other *Dapsyle*
Or *Liberaltie*: their Emulation
Begat a iarre, which thus was reconcil'd.
I, (hauing left my Goddesse mothers lap,   20
To hawlke, and shoote at Birds in *Arden* groues,)
Beheld this Princely Nimph, with much affection,
Left killing Birds, and turn'd into a Birde, /
Like which I flew betwixt her Iuory brests,   [K4ᵛ]
As if I had beene driuen by some Hawlke,   25
To sue to her for safety of my life;
She smilde at first, and sweetly shadowd me,
With soft protection of her siluer hand;
Some-times she tyed my legges in her rich hayre,
And made me (past my nature, libertie)   30
Proud of my fetters: As I pertly sat,
On the white pillowes of her naked brests,
I sung for ioy; she answered note for note,
Relish for relish, with such ease and Arte,
In her diuine diuision, that my tunes,   35
Showd like the God of Shepheards to the Sunnes,
Comparde with hers: ashamd of which disgrace,
I tooke my true shape, Bowe, and all my shafts,
And lighted all my torches at her eyes,
Which set about her, in a golden ring,   40
I followd Birds againe, from Tree to Tree,
Kild, and presented, and she kindely tooke.
But when she handled my triumphant Bowe,
And saw the beauty of my golden shafts,
She begd them of me; I, poore boy replyed,   45
I had no other Riches; yet was pleasde
To hazard all, and stake them gainst a kisse,
At an old game I vsde, call'd Penny-prick.
She priuie to her owne skill in the play,
Answerd my challenge, so, I lost my armes: 50
And now my Shafts are headed with her lookes,
One of which Shafts she put into my Bowe,
And shot at this faire Nimph, with whom before

15 vertues] Vertues *Q1-2* ‖ 26 safety] *Q2*; saftety *Q1* ‖ 40 set ... ring,] (~ ... ~) *Q1-2* ‖

I tolde your Maiestie, she had some iarre.
The Nimph did instantly repent all parts   55
She playd in vrging that effeminate warre,
Lou'd and submitted; which submission
This tooke so well, that now they both are one:
And as for your deare loue, their discords grew,
So for your loue, they did their loues renew.   60
And now to prooue them capable of your court, /
In skill of such conceipts, and quallities   [L1]
As here are practisde; they will first submit
Their grace in dancing to your highnesse doome,
And pray the prease to giue their meisures roome.   65

Musique, Dance, etc. which done Cupid *speakes.*

If this suffice, for one Court complement,
To make them gratious, and entertainde;
Behold another parcell of their Court-ship,
Which is a rare dexteritie in riddles,
Showne in one instance, which is here inscrib'd.   70
Here is a Riddle, which if any Knight
At first sight can resolue; he shall enioy
This Iewell here annext; which though it show
To vulgar eyes, no richer then a Peble;
And that no Lapydarie, nor great man   75
Will giue a Soulz for it; 'tis worth a kingdome:
For 'tis an artificiall stone composde,
By their great Mistresse, Vertue: and will make
Him that shall weare it, liue with any little,
Suffizde, and more content then any king.   80
If he that vndertakes cannot resolue it;
And that these Nimphs can haue no harbor here;
(It being considered, that so many vertues
Can neuer liue in Court) he shall resolue
To leaue the Court, and liue with them in *Arden*.   85
   Esp. Pronounce the riddle: I will vndertake it.
   Cup. 'Tis this sir.
      What's that a faire Lady, most of all likes,
      Yet euer makes shew she least of all seekes?
      That's euer embrac'd, and affected by her,   90
      Yet neuer is seene to please or come nigh her:
      Most seru'd in her night-weeds: does her good in a corner,
      But a poore mans thing, yet doth richly adorne her:
      Most cheape, and most deare, aboue all worldly pelfe,
      That is hard to get in, but comes out of it selfe.   95

65 pray] *stet* (*See Textual Note*) | roome.] ~, *Q1* ‖ **72** sight] *Q2*; fight *Q1* ‖ **85** *Arden.*] *Q2*; ~,
Q1 ‖ **88-123** *What's that . . . and so*] *See Textual Note* ‖

Esp. Let me peruse it, *Cupid.*
Cup.   Here it is.
Esp. Your Riddle is *Good Fame.* /
Cup. Good fame? how make you that good?   [L1ᵛ]
Esp. Good fame is that a good Lady most likes I am sure.
Cup. That's graunted.   100
Esp. Yet euer makes showe she least of all seekes: for shee
likes it onely for the vertue, which is not glorious.
Hen. That holds well.
Esp. Tis euer embrac't and affected by her: for she must
perseuer in vertue or fame vanishes. Yet neuer is seene to please   105
or come nye her: for fame is Inuisible.
Cup. Exceeding right.
Esp. Most serued in her night weeds: for Ladies that most
weare their Nightweeds come lest abrode, and they that come
least abrode serue fame most; according to this; *Non forma sed*   110
fama in publicum exire debet.
Hen. Tis very substantiall.
Esp. Does her good in a corner: that is, in her most retreate
from the world, comforts her; but a poore mans thing: for
euery poore man may purchase it, yet doth richly adorne   115
a Lady.
Cup. That all must grant.
Esp. Most cheape for it costs nothing, and most deare,
for gould can not buy it; aboue all worldly pelffe; for that's
transitory, and fame eternall. It is hard to get in; that is,   120
hard to get: But comes out of it selfe; for when it is vertuosely
deserud with the most inward retreate from the world,
it comes out in spight of it, and so *Cupid* your iewell is
mine.
Cup. It is: and be the vertue of it, yours.   125
Wee'l now turne to our daunce, and then attend
Your heighnes will, as touching our resort,
If Vertue may be entertaind in Court.
Hen. This show hath pleased me well, for that it figures
The reconcilement of my Queene and Mistris: 130
Come, let vs in and thanke them and prepare,
To entertaine our trusy friend *Byron.*

                                                        Exeunt.

                    Finis Actus Secundi. /

97 *Good*] good *Q1-2* ‖ 99 sure.] *Q2*; ~; *Q1* ‖ 100 That's graunted.] *Q2*; Thats ~; *Q1* ‖ 104
must] ~, *Q1-2* ‖ 105-6 Yet ... Inuisible.] *Q2*; *set off in single line Q1* ‖ 106 Inuisible.] *Q2*; ~,
Q1 ‖ 113 is,] ~‿ *Q1-2* ‖ 119 that's] *Q2*; thats *Q1* ‖ 120 is,] ~‿ *Q1-2* ‖ 126 attend] ~, *Q1* ‖ 128
Vertue] vertue *Q1-2* | Court.] *Q2*; ~, *Q1* ‖ 129 figures] ~. *Q1-2* ‖ 131 Come, let] ~‿ Let *Q1-2* ‖

ACTVS 3.   SCENA 1.   [L2]

Enter Byron. D'Auuer.

  Byr. Deare friend, we must not be more true to kings,
Then Kings are to their subiects; there are schooles,
Now broken ope in all parts of the world,
First founded in ingenious *Italy*,
Where some conclusions of estate are held,   5
That for a day preserue a Prince, and euer,
Destroy him after: from thence men are taught,
To glyde into degrees of height by crafte,
And then lock in them-selues by villanie:
But God, who knowes kings are not made by art,   10
But right of Nature, nor by trechery propt,
But simple vertue, once let fall from heauen,
A branch of that greene tree, whose root is yet,
Fast fixt aboue the starrs: which sacred branch,
Wee well may liken to that Lawrell spray,   15
That from the heauenly Eagles golden seres,
Fell in the lap of great *Augustus* wife:
Which spray once set, grew vp into a tree,
Whereof were Girlonds made, and Emperors,
Had their estates and foreheads crownd with them: 20
And as the armes of that tree did decay,
The race of great *Augustus* wore away;
Nero being last of that imperiall line,
The tree and Emperor together died.
Religion is a branch, first set and blest   25
By heauens highe finger in the hearts of kings,
Which whilelome grew into a goodly tree;
Bright Angels sat and sung vpon the twigs,
And royall branches for the heads of Kings,
Were twisted of them; but since squint-ey'd enuye,   30
And pale suspicion, dasht the heads of kingdomes,
One gainst another: two abhorred twins,
With two foule tayles, sterne Warre and Libertie,
Entred the world. The tree that grew from heauen /   34
Is ouerrunne with mosse; the cheerfull musique,   [L2ᵛ]
That heeretofore hath sounded out of it,
Beginnes to cease; and as she casts her leaues,
(By small degrees) the kingdomes of the earth
Decline and wither: and looke, whensoeuer

III.i SD *D'Auur.*] *D'Auer. Q1* ‖ **2** subiects;] ~, *Q1-2* ‖ **4** *Italy*] Italy *Q1-2* ‖ **22** away;] ~, *Q1-2* ‖
27 tree;] ~, *Q1-2* ‖ **30** them;] ~ᵕ *Q1-2* | enuye,] ~: *Q1* ‖ **33** tayles,] ~: *Q1-2* ‖ **34** heauen] ~.
Q1-2 ‖ **39** looke,] ~ᵕ *Q1-2* ‖

That the pure sap in her, is dried vp quite,   40
The lamp of all authoritie goes out,
And all the blaze of Princes is extinkt;
Thus as the Poet sends a messenger
Out to the stage, to shew the summe of all,
That followes after: so are Kings reuolts,   45
And playing both waies with religion,
Fore-runners of afflictions imminent,
Which (like a Chorus) subiects must lament.
    D'Au. My Lord I stand not on these deepe discourses,
To settle my course; to your fortunes mine   50
Are freely and inseperablie linckt:
And to your loue my life.
    Byr.   Thankes Princely friend,
And whatsoeuer good shall come of me,
Pursu'd by al the Catholike Princes aydes
With whom I ioyne, and whose whole states proposde   55
To winne my valure, promise me a throne:
All shall be, equall with my selfe, thine owne.

                            [*Enter La Brunel.*]

    La Brun. My Lord here is *D'escuris* sent from the King,
Desires accesse to you.
    Byr.   Attend him in.

                            Enter D'escuris.

    D'Esc. Helth to my Lord the Duke.
    Byr.   Welcome *D'escuris,*   60
In what helth rests our royall Soueraigne?
    D'Esc. In good helth of his bodie, but his minde,
Is something troubled with the gathering stormes,
Of forreigne powres; that as he is inform'd
Addresse themselues into his frontier townes;   65
And therefore his intent, is to maintaine /
The body of an armie on those parts;   [L3]
And yeeld their worthie conduct to your valure.
    Byr. From whence heares he that any stormes are rising?
    D'Esc. From *Italy*; and his intelligence,   70
No doubt is certaine, that in all those partes
Leuies are hotly made; for which respect,
He sent to his Ambassador *De Vic,*
To make demand in *Switzerland,* for the raising

40 quite,] ~; *Q1-2* ‖ 48 lament.] *Q2*; ~: *Q1* ‖ 50 course; ... fortunes] *Loane conj.*; ~͵ ... ~;
Q1-2 ‖ 55 proposde] ~, *Q1-2* ‖ 57 be, ... selfe,] *Shepherd*; ~͵ ... ~; *Q1* | SD *Enter La Brunel.*]
Parrott ‖ 59 SD *Enter D'escuris.*] *Parrott; follows La Brunel's speech Q1-2* ‖ 60 Duke.] *Q2*; ~:
Q1 ‖ 61 Soueraigne?] ~. *Q1-2* ‖ 66 maintaine] ~: *Q1-2* ‖ 70 *Italy*] Italy *Q1-2* ‖ 74 *Switzerland*]
Switzerland *Q1-2* ‖

349

With vtmost dilligence of sixe thousand men; 75
All which shall bee commanded to attend,
On your direction; as the Constable
Your honord Gossip gaue him in aduice;
And hee sent you by wrighting: of which letters,
He would haue answere, and aduice from you 80
By your most speedie presence.
    Byr.   This is strange,
That when the enimie is t'atempt his frontiers,
He calls me from the frontiers: does he thinke,
It is an action worthie of my valure
To turne my back, to an approching foe? 85
    D'Esc. The foe is not so nere, but you may come,
And take more strickt directions from his highnesse,
Then he thinkes fit his letters should containe,
Without the least attainture of your valure;
And therefore good my Lord, forbeare excuse 90
And beare your selfe on his direction;
Who well you know hath neuer made designe
For your most worthy seruice, where he saw
That any thing but honour could succede.
    Byr. I will not come I sweare.
    D'Esc.   I know your grace, 95
Will send no such vnsauorie replie.
    Byr. Tell him that I beseech his Maiesty,
To pardon my repaire till th'end be knowne
Of all these leuies now in *Italie*.
    D'Esc. My Lord I know that tale will neuer please him; 100
And wish you as you loue his loue and pleasure,
To satisfie his summons speedily: /
And speedily I know he will returne you. [L3ᵛ]
    Byr. By heauen it is not fit: if all my seruice
Makes me know any thing: beseech him therefore, 105
To trust my iudgement in these doubtfull charges,
Since in assur'd assaults it hath not faild him.
    D'Esc. I would your Lordship now, would trust his iudgement.
    Byr. Gods precious, y'are importunate past measure,
And (I know) further then your charge extends; 110
Ile satisfie his highnesse, let that serue;
For by this flesh and bloud, you shall not beare,
Any replie to him, but this from me.

88 containe,] *Q2;* ~; *Q1* ‖ **95** sweare.] *Q2;* ~: *Q1* ‖ **97** beseech] *Q2;* besecch *Q1* ‖ **99** *Italie*] Italie *Q1-2* ‖ **103** you.] *Q2;* ~; *Q1* ‖ **110** further] *Q2;* ~, *Q1* | extends;] ~, *Q1-2* ‖

D'Esc. Tis nought to me my Lord, I wish your good,   114
And for that cause haue beene importunate.   *Exit Desc:*
    La Brun. By no meanes goe my Lord, but with distrust,
Of all that hath beene said or can be sent;
Collect your friends, and stand vpon your gard,
The Kings faire letters, and his messages
Are onely Golden Pills, and comprehend   120
Horrible purgatiues.
    Byr.   I will not goe,
For now I see th'instructions lately sent me,
That something is discouerd, are too true,
And my head rules none of those neighbor Nobles,
That euery Pursiuant brings beneath the axe: 125
If they bring me out, they shall see ile hatch
Like to the Black-thorne, that puts forth his leafe,
Not with the golden fawnings of the Sunne,
But sharpest showers of haile, and blackest frosts:
Blowes, batteries, breaches, showers of steele and bloud,   130
Must be his doun-right messengers for me,
And not the misling breath of policie:
He, he himselfe, made passage to his Crowne
Through no more armies, battailes, massacres,
Then I will aske him to arriue at me;   135
He takes on him, my executions,
And on the demolitions, that this arme,
Hath shaken out of forts and Citadells,
Hath he aduanc't the Tropheys of his valor;
Where I, in those assumptions may skorne, /   140
And speake contemptuously of all the world,   [L4]
For any equal yet, I euer found;
And in my rising, not the Syrian Starre
That in the Lyons month, vndaunted shines,
And makes his braue ascension with the Sunne,   145
Was of th'Egiptians, with more zeale beheld,
And made a rule to know the circuite
And compasse of the yeare, then I was held
When I appeard from battaile; the whole sphere,
And full sustainer of the state we beare;   150
I haue *Alcides*-like gone vnder th'earth
And on these showlders borne the weight of *France*:
And (for the fortunes of the thankles King)
My father (all know) set him in his throne,

116 Lord,] ~; *Q1-2* ‖ 144 month] *Parrott*; mouth *Q1-2* ‖ 148 yeare,] ~; *Q1-2* ‖ 151 *Alcides*]
Alcides *Q1-2* ‖ 152 *France*] *Q2*; France *Q1* ‖

And if he vrge me, I may pluck him out.   155

                        Enter Mess:

  Mes. Here is the president *Ianin*, my Lord;
Sent from the King, and vrgeth quick accesse.
  Byr. Another Pursiuant? and one so quick?
He takes next course with me, to make him stay:
But, let him in, let's here what he importunes.   160

                               [Exit La Brunel.]

                        Enter Ianin.

  Ian. Honor, and loyall hopes to Duke *Byron*.
  Byr. No other tooch me: say how fares the King?
  Ian. Farely my Lord; the cloud is yet farre off
That aimes at his obscuring, and his will,
Would gladly giue the motion to your powers   165
That should disperse it; but the meanes, himselfe,
Would personally relate in your direction.
  Byr. Still on that hante?
  Ian.   Vpon my life, my Lord,
He much desires to see you, and your sight
Is now growne necessarie to suppresse   170
(As with the glorious splendor of the Sunne)
The rude windes that report breaths in his eares,
Endeuoring to blast your loialtie.
  Byr. Sir, if my loyaltie, stick in him no faster
But that the light breath of report may loose it,   175
(So I rest still vnmoou'd) let him be shaken.
  Ian. But these aloofe abodes, my Lord bewray, /
That there is rather firmnesse in your breath,   [L4ᵛ]
Then in your heart; Truth is not made of glasse,
That with a small touch, it should feare to breake,   180
And therefore should not shunne it; beleeue me
His arme is long, and strong; and it can fetch
Any within his will, that will not come:
Not he that surfets in his mines of gold,
And for the pride thereof, compares with God,   185
Calling (with almost nothing different)
His powers inuincible, for omnipotent,
Can back your boldest Fort gainst his assaults;
It is his pride, and vaine ambition,
That hath but two staires in his high designes   190

---

155 SD *Enter Mess:*] *in right margin of Q1-2 after* out ‖ **160** SD *Exit La Brunel.*] *Parrott* | SD *Enter Ianin.*] *in right margin of Q1-2 after* importunes ‖ **190** designes] ~; *Q1-2* ‖

(The lowest enuie, and the highest bloud)
That doth abuse you; and giues mindes too high,
Rather a will by guiddinesse to fall,
Then to descend by iudgement.
    Byr.   I relye
On no mans back nor belly; but the King   195
Must thinke that merit, by ingratitude crackt,
Requires a firmer sementing then words.
And he shall finde it a much harder worke
To soder broken hearts, then shiuerd glasses.
    Ian. My Lord, 'tis better hold a Soueraignes loue   200
By bearing iniuries; then by laying out
Stirre his displeasure; Princes discontents
(Being once incenst) are like the flames of *Ætna*,
Not to be quencht, nor lessend: and be sure,
A subiects confidence in any merit,   205
Against his Soueraigne, that makes him presume
To flie too high; approoues him like a clowd,
That makes a show as it did hawlke at kingdomes,
And could command all raisd beneath his vapor:
When sodainly, the Fowle that hawlkt so faire,   210
Stoopes in a puddle, or consumes in ayre.
    Byr. I flie with no such ayme, nor am opposde,
Against my Soueraigne; but the worthy height
I haue wrought by my seruice, I will hold, /   214
Which if I come away, I cannot do;   [M1]
For if the enimie should inuade the Frontier,
Whose charge to guard, is mine, with any spoile,
(Although the King in placing of another
Might well excuse me) yet all forraine Kinges
That can take note of no such secret quittance,   220
Will lay the weakenesse here, vpon my wants;
And therefore my abode is resolute.
    Ian. I sorrow for your resolution,
And feare your dissolution, will succeed.
    Byr. I must indure it.
    Ian.   Fare you well my Lord.   225
                          [*Exit Ianin.*]

    Byr. Farewell to you;

                    Enter La Brun.

      Captaine what other newes?

---

209 command] ~, *Q1-2* ‖ **219** yet] Yet *Q1-2* ‖ **223** *Ian.*] ~: (*colon in all speech-prefixes through l. 248*) ‖ **225** it.] *Q2*; ~; *Q1* | Lord.] *Q2*; ~; *Q1* | SD *Exit Ianin.*] *Q2* ‖ **226** SD *Enter La Brun.*] *Enter Brun. Q1-2* (*in right margin after* you;) ‖

La Brun. *La Fin* salutes you. [*Giving letters.*]

    Byr. Welcome good friend; I hope your wisht arriuall,
Will giue some certaine end to our disseignes.

    La Brun. I know not that, my Lord; reports are rais'd   230
So doubtfull and so different, that the truth
Of any one can hardly be assur'd.

    Byr. Good newes, *D'Avuergne*; our trusty friend *La Fin*,
Hath clear'd all scruple with his Maiestie,
And vtterd nothing but what seru'd to cleare   235
All bad Suggestions.

    La Brun.   So he sayes, my Lord,
But others say, *La Fins* assurances
Are meere deceipts; and wish you to beleeue;
That when the *Vidame*, nephew to *La Fin*,
Met you at *Autune*, to assure your doubts   240
His vncle had said nothing to the King
That might offend you, all the iournies charge,
The King defraid; besides, your truest friendes
Willd me to make you certaine that your place
Of gouernment is otherwise dispos'd;   245
And all aduise you, for your latest hope,
To make retreat into the *Franch County*.

    Byr. I thanke them all, but they touch not the depth,
Of the affaires, betwixt *La Fin* and me, /
Who is returnd contented to his house,   250
Quite freed, of all displeasure or distrust;   [M1ᵛ]
And therefore, worthy friends wele now to Court.

    D'Au. My Lord, I like your other friends aduices,
Much better then *Laffins*; and on my life
You can not come to Court with any saftie.   255

    Byr. Who shall infringe it? I know, all the Court,
Haue better apprehension of my valure;
Then that they dare lay violent hands on mee;
If I haue onely meanes to drawe this sword,
I shall haue powre enough to set me free,   260
From seasure, by my proudest enemie.

                                                 Exeunt.

227 you.] *Q2*; ~; *Q1* | SD *Giving letters.*] *Parrott* ‖ **229** disseignes.] *Q2*; ~; *Q1* ‖ **230-32** I . . . assur'd.] *Shepherd*; *as prose Q1-2* (so . . . of) ‖ **236** Lord,] ~‿ *Q1-2* ‖ **240-42** doubts . . . you,] *Parrott*; ~, . . . ~; *Q1-2* ‖ **246** And all] Andall *Q1* ‖ **249** me,] ~. *Q1-2* ‖ **253** *D'Au.*] ~‿ ‖ **261** SD *Exeunt.*] *Phelps*; *Exit. Q1-2* ‖

[III.ii]

Enter Esper: Vyt: Pral:

Esp. He will not come I dare engage my hand.
Vit. He will be fetcht then, ile engage my head.
Pra. Come, or be fetcht, he quite hath lost his honor,
In giuing these suspicions of reuolt
From his allegiance: that which he hath wunne,   5
With sundry wounds, and perrill of his life;
With wonder of his wisdome, and his valure,
He looseth with a most enchanted glorie:
And admiration of his pride, and folly.
Vit. Why, did you neuer see a fortunate man,   10
Sodainely rais'd to heapes of welth and honor?
Nor any rarely great in guifts of nature,
As valure, wit, and smooth vse of the tongue,
Set strangely to the pitch of populare likings?
But with as sodaine falls the rich and honord,   15
Were ouerwhelmd by pouertie and shame,
Or had no vse of both aboue the wretched?
Esp. Men neuer are satisfi'd with that they haue;
But as a man, matcht with a louely wife,
When his most heauenly Theorye of her beauties,   20
Is duld and quite exhausted with his practise:
He brings her forth to feasts, where he ahlas,
Falls to his viands with no thought like others,
That thinke him blest in her, and they (poore men) /   24
Court, and make faces, offer seruice, sweate,   [M2]
With their desires contention, breake their braines
For iests, and tales: sit mute, and loose their lookes,
(Far out of wit, and out of countenance)
So all men else, do what they haue transplant,
And place their welth in thirst of that they want.   30

Enter Henry, Chanc: Vyd: Desc: Ianin.

Hen. He will not come; I must both grieue and wonder,
That all my care to winne my subiects loue
And in one cup of friendship to comix,
Our liues and fortunes; should leaue out so many
As giue a man (contemptuous of my loue,   35

III.ii] *Parrott* ‖ SD *Enter*] *Q2* ‖ 10 Why,] ~, *Q1-2* ‖ 16 pouertie and shame,] *Q2*; ~, ~ ~, *Q1* ‖
17 wretched?] ~. *Q1-2* ‖ 35 contemptuous] *Q2*; comtemptuous *Q1* ‖

And of his owne good, in the Kingdomes Peace)
Hope, in a continuance so vngratefull,
To beare out his designes in spight of me;
How should I better please all, then I do?
When they suppos'd, I would haue giuen some,   40
Insolent garisons; others Citadells,
And to all sorts, encrease of miseries;
Prouince by Prouince, I did visit all
Whom those iniurious rumors had diswaide;
And shew'd them how, I neuer sought to build,   45
More forts for me, then were within their hearts;
Nor vse more sterne constraints, then their good wills,
To succor the necessities of my crowne;
That I desird to ad to their contents
By all occasions, rather then subtract;   50
Nor wisht I, that my treasury should flow,
With gold that swum in, in my subiects teares;
And then I found no man, that did not blesse,
My few yeares raigne, and their triumphant peace;
And do they now so soone, complaine of ease?   55
He will not come!

          Enter Byron, D'Auuergne; brother,
                 with others.

Esp.   O madnesse! he is come.
Chan. The duke is come my Lord.
Hen.   Oh Sir, y'are welcome, /
And fitly, to conduct me to my house.   [M2ᵛ]
   Byr. I must beseech your Maiesties excuse,
That (Ielouse of mine honor) I haue vsd,   60
Some of mine owne commandment in my stay,
And came not with your heighnesse soonest summons.
   Hen. The faithfull seruant right in holy writ;
That said he would not come and yet he came:
But come you hether; I must tell you now,   65
Not the contempt you stood to in your stay,
But the bad ground that bore vp your contempt,
Makes you arriue at no port, but repentance,
Despayre, and ruine.
   Byr.   Be what port it will,
At which your will, will make me be ariued,   70
I am not come to iustifie my selfe,

---

48 crowne;] ~, *Q1-2* ‖ 54 raigne, … peace;] ~; … ~, *Q1-2* ‖ 56 He … come!] *Q2 subs.*; *Hen.*
He will not come? *Q1 (See Textual Note)* | SD Enter … others.] *placement as in Q2, in right
margin of Q1 following* come? | madnesse! … come.] ~? … ~, *Q1* ‖ 57 Lord.] *Q2*; ~: *Q1* ‖
58 house.] *Q2*; ~; *Q1* ‖ 69 ruine.] *Q2*; ~; *Q1* ‖

To aske you pardon nor accuse my friends.
    Hen. If you conceale my enemies you are one,
And then my pardon shall be worth your asking,
Or else your head be worth my cutting of.   75
    Byr. Being friend and worthy fautor of my selfe,
I am no foe of yours, nor no empayrer,
Since he can no way worthely maintaine
His Princes honor that neglects his owne:
And if your wil haue beene to my true reason   80
(Maintaining still the truth of loyalty)
A checke to my free nature and mine honor,
And that on your free iustice I presum'd
To crosse your will a little, I conceiue
You will not thinke this forfaite worth my head.   85
    Hen. Haue you maintaind your truth of loyalty,
When since I pardoned foule ententions,
Resoluing to forget eternally,
What they apperd in, and had welcomd you
As the kind father doth his riotous son?   90
I can approuc facts fowler then th'intents,
Of deepe disloyalty and highest treason.
    Byr. May this right hand be thunder to my brest,
If I stand guilty of the slendrest fact,
Wherein the lest of those two can be prooued, /   95
For could my tender conscience but haue toucht,   [M3]
At any such vnnaturall relaps;
I would not with this confidence haue runne,
Thus headlong in the furnace of a wrath,
Blowne, and thrice kindled: hauing way enough,   100
In my election both to shunne and sleight it.
    Hen. Y'are grosely and vain gloriously abus'd,
There is no way in *Sauoy* nor in *Spaine*,
To giue a foole that hope of your escape,
And had you not (euen when you did) arriued,   105
(With horror to the proudest hope you had)
I would haue fetcht you.
    Byr.   You must then haue vs'd
A power beyond my knowledge, and a will,
Beyond your iustice. For a little stay
More then I vsd would hardly haue beene worthy,   110
Of such an open expedition;
In which to all the censures of the world,

72 friends.] Q2; ~, *Q1* ‖ 80 reason] ~, *Q1-2* ‖ 83 presum'd] Q2; presum,d *Q1* ‖ 84 conceiue] ~,
Q2; conceine, *Q1* ‖ 85 head.] Q2; ~; *Q1* ‖ 86 loyalty,] ~? *Q1-2* ‖ 88-90 Resoluing . . . son?]
Shepherd (*with comma after* son); Resoluing . . . in,/ And . . . son. *Q1-2* (as) ‖ 92 treason.] Q2;
~; *Q1* ‖ 101 it.] Q2; ~, *Q1* ‖ 105 arriued,] Q2; ~. *Q1* ‖ 107 vs'd] ~. *Q1* ‖

My faith and Innocence had beene fouly foyld;
Which I protest by heauens bright wittnesses
That shine farr, farr, from mixture with our feares,   115
Retaine as perfect roundnes as their spheares.
    Hen. Tis well my Lord, I thought I could haue frighted
Your firmest confidence: some other time,
We will (as now in priuate) sift your actions,
And poure more then you thinke into the siue,   120
Alwaies reseruing clemency and pardon
Vpon confession, be you nere so foule.
Come let's cleere vp our browes; shall we to tennis?
    Byr. I, my Lord, if I may make the match.
The Duke *Espernon* and my selfe will play,   125
With you and Count *Soissons.*
    Esp.   I know my Lord
You play well but you make your matches ill.
    Hen. Come tis a match.   *Exit.*
    Byr.   [*To Espernon.*] How like you my ariuall?
    Esp. Ile tell you as your friend in your eare.
You haue giuen more preferment to your courage, /   130
Then to the prouident counsailes of your friends.   [M3ᵛ]
    D'Au. I told him so my Lord, and much was grieu'd
To see his bold approach, so full of will.
    Byr. Well I must beare it now, though but with th'head,
The shoulders bearing nothing.
    Esp.   By Saint *Iohn,*   135
Tis a good headlesse resolution.   *Exeunt.*

ACTVS. 4.   SCEN. 1.

Enter Byron. D'Auuergne.

    Byr. O the most base fruites of a setled peace!
In men, I meane; worse then their durty fields,
Which they manure much better [then] them-selues:
For them they plant, and sowe, and ere they grow
Weedie, and choakt with thornes, they grub and proyne,   5
And make them better then when cruell warre,
Frighted from thence the sweaty labourer:
But men them-selues, in steed of bearing fruites,

---

114 I protest] *Shepherd*; (~ ~) *Q1-2* ‖ 115 feares,] *Q2*; ~. *Q1* ‖ 116 spheares.] *Q2*; ~; *Q1* ‖ 117, 128 *Hen.*] ~ *Q1* ‖ 119 actions,] *Q2*; ~. *Q1* ‖ 122 foule.] ~, *Q1-2* ‖ 123 let's] lets *Q1-2* | browes; . . . tennis?] ~ . . . ~. *Q1-2* ‖ 124 I, my Lord,] ~ ~ ~ *Q1-2* ‖ 126 *Soissons.*] *Q2*; ~; *Q1* | Lord] ~. *Q1-2* ‖ 128 SD *To Espernon.*] *Parrott* ‖ 129 Ile . . . eare.] *stet (See Textual Note)* ‖ IV.i SD *Enter*] *Q2* ‖ 3 then] *Q2* ‖ 4 grow] ~, *Q1-2* ‖ 6 better] ~, *Q1-2* ‖

Growe rude, and foggie, ouer-growne with weedes,
Their spirits, and freedomes smootherd in their ease;   10
And as their tyrants and their ministers,
Growe wilde in prosecution of their lusts,
So they grow prostitute, and lye (like whores)
Downe and take vp, to their abhord dishonors:
The friendlesse may be iniur'd and opprest;   15
The guiltlesse lead to slaughter, the deseruer
Giuen to the begger; right be wholy wrongd,
And wrong be onely honor'd; till the strings
Of euery mans heart, crack; and who will stirre,
To tell authority, that it doth erre?   20
All men cling to it, though they see their blouds
In their most deare associates and Allyes,
Pour'd into kennels by it: and who dares
But looke well in the breast, whom that impayres?
How all the Court now lookes askew on me?   25
Go by without saluting, shun my sight,
Which (like a March sunne) agues breeds in them,
From whence of late, 'twas health to haue a beame. /
      D'Au. Now none will speake to vs, we thrust our selues   [M4]
Into mens companies, and offer speech,   30
As if not made, for their diuerted eares,
Their backs turnd to vs, and their words to others,
And we must like obsequious Parasites,
Follow their faces, winde about their persons,
For lookes and answers: or be cast behinde,   35
No more viewd then the wallet of their faults.

                    Enter Soisson.

      Byr. Yet here's one views me, and I thinke will speake.
      Soiss. My Lord, if you respect your name and race,
The preseruation of your former honors,
Merites and vertues; humbly cast them all,   40
At the kings mercy; for beyond all doubt,
Your acts haue thether driuen them: he hath proofes
So pregnant, and so horride, that to heare them,
Would make your valure in your very lookes,
Giue vp your forces, miserably guilty: 45
But he is most loth (for his ancient loue
To your rare vertues: and in their empaire,
The full discouragement of all that liue,

13 and lye] *Q1(c)*, *Q2*; andlye *Q1(u)* ‖ 16 lead] *stet* (*See Textual Note*) ‖ 20 erre?] ~. *Q1-2* ‖ 27 March] *Q2*; march *Q1* ‖ 47 vertues:] ~:) *Q1* ‖

To trust or fauour any gifts in Nature)
T'expose them to the light; when darknesse may   50
Couer her owne broode, and keepe still in day,
Nothing of you but that may brooke her brightnesse:
You know what horrors these high strokes do bring,
Raisd in the arme of an incensed King.

   Byr. My Lord, be sure the King cannot complaine   55
Of any thing in me, but my true seruice,
Which in so many dangers of my death,
May so approoue my spotlesse loyaltie;
That those quite opposite horrors you assure,
Must looke out of his owne ingratitude;   60
Or the malignant enuies of my foes,
Who powre me out in such a Stygian flood,
To drowne me in my selfe, since their deserts
Are farre from such a deluge; and in me
Hid like so many riuers in the Sea. /   65
   Soiss. You thinke I come to sound you; fare you wel.   [M4ᵛ]
                                                      Exit.

         Enter Chancellor, Espernon, Ianin, Vidame,
           Vitry, Pralin, whisperinge by couples, etc.

   D'Au. See see, not one of them will cast a glaunce
At our eclipsed faces.
   Byr.   They keepe all
To cast in admiration on the King:
For from his face are all their faces moulded.   70
   D'Au. But when a change comes; we shall see them all
Chang'd into water, that will instantly
Giue looke for looke, as if it watcht to greete vs;
Or else for one, they'l giue vs twenty faces,
Like to the little specks on sides of glasses.   75
   Byr. Is't not an easie losse to lose theyr lookes,
Whose hearts so soone are melted?
   D'Au.   But me thinks,
(Being Courtiers) they should cast best looks on men,
When they thought worst of them.
   Byr.   O no my Lord,
They n'ere dissemble but for some aduantage;   80
They sell theyr looks, and shadowes; which they rate
After theyr markets, kept beneath the State;
Lord what foule weather theyr aspects do threaten?
See in how graue a Brake he sets his vizard:

66 *Soiss.*] ~: *Q1 (colon in all speech-prefixes through l. 92)* | wel.] ~, *Q1* || **68** faces.] *Q2*; ~;
Q1 || **68-69** They . . . King:] *Shepherd; one line Q1-2* (to) || **75** glasses.] *Q2*; ~; *Q1* ||

360

Passion of nothing; See, an excellent Iesture: 85
Now Courtship goes a ditching in theyr fore-heads;
And we are falne into those dismall ditches;
Why euen thus dreadfully would they be rapt,
If the Kings butterd egges, were onely spilt.

                    Enter Henry.

Hen. Lord Chancellor.
Chan.   I, my Lord.
Hen.   And lord *Vidame.*   90
                    Exit Henry with Chancellor
                          and Vidame.

Byr. And not *Byron?* here's a prodigious change.
D'Au. He cast no Beame on you.
Byr.   Why now you see
From whence theyr countenances were copyed. /

        Enter the captaine of Byrons guard   [N1]
              with a letter.

D'Au. See, here comes some newes, I beleeue my Lord.
Byr. What saies the honest captaine of my guard?   95
Cap. I bring a letter from a friend of yours.
Byr. Tis welcome then.
D'Au.   Haue we yet any friends?
Cap. More then yee would I thinke: I neuer saw,
Men in their right mindes so vnrighteous
In their owne causes.
Byr.   See what thou hast brought.   100
                        [*He reads the letter.*]

Hee wills vs to retire our selues my Lord,
And makes as if it were almost too late.
What saies my captaine; shall we goe or no?
  Cap. I would your daggers point, had kist my heart,
When you resolu'd to come.
  Byr.   I pray thee why?   105
  Cap. Yet, doth that sencelesse Apoplexy dull you?
The diuell or your wicked angell blinds you,
Bereauing all your reason of a man
And leaues you but the spirit of a horse,
In your brute nostrills: onely powre to dare.   110
  Byr. Why, dost thou think, my comming here hath brought me
To such an vnrecouerable danger?

---

90 Chancellor.] *Q2;* ~; *Q1* | I, my Lord.] ~, ~ ~; *Q1* | Vidame.] *Q2;* ~: *Q1* | SD *Henry . . .*
Vidame] Phelps subs. ‖ **91** change.] *Q2;* ~; *Q1* ‖ **92** you.] *Q2;* ~; *Q1* ‖ **97** then.] *Q2;* ~: *Q1* ‖
100 brought.] ~, *Q1-2* | SD *He reads the letter.*] ‖ **102** late.] ~, *Q1-2* ‖ **105** thee] *Q2;* the *Q1* ‖
106 Apoplexy] Apopelxy *Q1-2* ‖

    Cap. Iudge by the strange Ostents that haue succeeded,
Since your arriuall: the kinde fowle, the wilde duck,
That came into your cabinet, so beyond   115
The sight of all your seruants, or your selfe:
That flew about, and on your shoulder sat
And which you had so fed, and so attended,
For that dum loue she shew'd you; iust as soone,
As you were parted, on the sodaine died.   120
And to make this no lesse then an Ostent;
Another that hath fortun'd since, confirmes it:
Your goodly horse *Pastrana*, which the Archduke,
Gaue you at *Bruxells*; in the very houre,
You left your strength, fel mad, and kild himselfe;   125
The like chanc't to the horse the great duke sent you:
And, with both these, the horse the duke of *Lorraine*, /
Sent you at *Vimie* made a third presage,   [N1ᵛ]
Of some Ineuitable fate that toucht you,
Who like the other pin'd away and died.   130
    Byr. All these together are indeed ostentfull,
Which by another like, I can confirme:
The matchlesse Earle of *Essex* who some make,
(In their most sure diuinings of my death)
A parallell with me in life and fortune,   135
Had one horse like-wise that the very howre,
He sufferd death, (being well the night before)
Died in his pasture. Noble happy beasts,
That die, not hauing to their wills to liue:
They vse no deprecations, nor complaints,   140
Nor sute for mercy: amongst them the Lion,
Serues not the Lion; nor the horse the horse,
As man serues man. When men shew most their spirrits,
In valure and their vtmost dares to do;
They are compard to Lions, Woolues, and Bores;   145
But by conuersion, none will say a Lyon,
Fights as he had the Spirrit of a man.
Let me then in my danger now giue cause,
For all men to begin that *Simile*.
For all my huge engagement, I prouide me,   150
This short sword onely; which if I haue time,
To show my apprehendor, he shall vse,
Power of tenne Lions if I get not loose.

                                  [Exeunt.]

114 wilde duck] wildeduck *Q1* ‖ **116** seruants] *Q2*; seruanrs *Q1* ‖ **118** attended,] ~; *Q1-2* ‖ **124** *Bruxells*] Bruxells *Q1-2* ‖ **125** fel mad] fel-mad *Q1* ‖ **127** *Lorraine*] Lorraine *Q1-2* ‖ **128** at] ~, *Q1-2* ‖ **130** died.] *Q2*; ~, *Q1* ‖ **140** complaints,] *Q2*; ~. *Q1* ‖ **143** man. When] ~: when *Q1-2* ‖ **145** Bores;] ~, *Q1-2* ‖ **146** conuersion,] *Q2*; ~; *Q1* | none] None *Q1-2* ‖ **153** SD *Exeunt.*] *Phelps* ‖

[IV.ii]

Enter Henry, Chancellor, Vidame, Ianin,
Vitry, Pralin.

Hen. What shall we doe with this vnthankefull man?
Would he (of one thing) but reueale the truth,
Which I haue proofe of, vnderneath his hand,
He should not tast my Iustice. I would giue,
Two hundred thousand crownes, that he would yeeld   5
But such meanes for my pardon, as he should;
I neuer lou'd man like him: would haue trusted,
My Sonne in his protection, and my Realme:
He hath deseru'd my loue with worthy seruice, /   9
Yet can he not deny, but I haue thrice,   [N2]
Sau'd him from death: I drew him of the foe
At *Fountaine Francoise* where he was engag'd,
So wounded, and so much amazd with blowes,
That (as I playd the souldier in his rescue,)
I was enforc't to play the Marshall [too],   15
To order the retreat: because he said,
He was not fit to do it nor to serue me.
    Chan. Your maiesty hath vsd your vtmost meanes,
Both by your owne perswasions, and his friends,
To bring him to submission, and confesse   20
(With some signe of repentance) his foule fault:
Yet still he stands prefract and insolent.
You haue in loue and care of his recouery
Beene halfe in labour to produce a course,
And resolution, what were fit for him.   25
And since so amply it concernes your crowne,
You must by law cut of, what by your grace,
You cannot bring into the state of safety.
    Ian. Begin at th'end my Lord and execute,
Like *Alexander* with *Parmenio.*   30
Princes (you knowe) are Maisters of their lawes,
And may resolue them to what forms they please,
So all conclude in iustice; in whose stroke,
There is one sort of manadge for the Great;
Another for inferiour: The great Mother,   35
Of all productions (graue Necessity)
Commands the variation: And the profit,
So certenly fore-seene, commends the example.

IV.ii] *Parrott* ‖ **5** yeeld] *Q2*; ~, *Q1* ‖ **11** foe] ~. *Q1* ‖ **15** too] *Brereton conj. (See Textual Note)* ‖ **17** me.] *Q2*; ~, *Q1* ‖ **19** friends,] *Q2*; ~. *Q1* ‖ **20** to] *Q2*; ro *Q1* ‖ **25** what] *stet (See Textual Note)* ‖ **28** safety.] *Q2*; ~, *Q1* ‖

Hen. I like not executions so informall,
For which my predecessors haue beene blam'd: 40
My Subiects and the world shall knowe, my powre
And my authority by lawes vsuall course
Dares punish; not the deuilish heads of treason,
But there confederates be they nere so dreadfull.
The decent ceremonies of my lawes,   45
And their solemnities shall be obserued,
With all their Sternenes and Seueritie. /
   Vit. Where will your highnes haue him apprehended?   [N2ᵛ]
   Hen. Not in the Castle (as some haue aduis'd)
But in his chamber.
   Pral.   Rather in your owne,   50
Or comming out of it; for tis assur'd
That any other place of apprehension,
Will make the hard performance, end in blood.
   Vit. To shun this likely-hood, my Lord tis best
To make the apprehension neere your chamber;   55
For all respect and reuerence giuen the place.
More then is needfull, to chastice the person,
And saue the opening of to many veines,
Is vain and dangerous.
   Hen.   Gather you your guard,
And I will finde fit time to giue the word,   60
When you shall seaze on him and on *D'Auuergne*.
   Vit. Wee will be readie to the death (my Lord).

                               Exeunt all but Henry.

   Hen. O thou that gouernst the keene swords of Kings,
Direct my arme in this important stroke,
Or hold it being aduanc't; the weight of blood,   65
Euen in the basest subiect, doth exact
Deepe consultation, in the highest King;
For in one subiect, deaths vniust affrights,
Passions, and paines, (though he be n'ere so poore)
Aske more remorse, then the voluptuous spleenes   70
Of all Kings in the world, deserue respect;
Hee should be borne grey-headed that will beare
The sword of Empire; Iudgement of the life,
Free state, and reputation of a man,
(If it be iust and worthy) dwells so darke   75
That it denies accesse to Sunne and Moone;
The soules eye sharpned with that sacred light,

---

41 knowe, my powre] ~; ~ ~, *Q1*; ~ˌ ~ ~ˌ *Q2* ‖ 48 *Vit.*] ~: *Q1 (colon in all speech-prefixes through l.109, except l.96)* ‖ 50 chamber.] *Q2*; --; *Q1* ‖ 56 place.] ~, *Q1-2 (See Textual Note)* ‖ 58 veines,] ~; *Q1-2* ‖ 61 *D'Auuergne.*] *Q2*; ~; *Q1* ‖ 62 death (my Lord).] ~; (~ ~)ˌ *Q1-2* | SD *all but Henry*] *Parrott* ‖

Of whome the Sunne it selfe is but a beame,
Must onely giue that iudgement; O how much
Erre those Kings then, that play with life and death,   80
And nothing put into their serious States,
But humor and their lusts! For which alone
Men long for kingdomes; whose huge counterpoise /
In cares and dangers, could a foole comprise,   [N3]
He would not be a King but would be wise.   85

> *Enter Byron talking with the Queene:*
> *Esp: with D'Entragues, D'Av: with an-*
> *other Lady, Montigny, others attending.*

Heere comes the man, with whose ambitious head
(Cast in the way of *Treason*) we must stay
His full chace of our ruine and our Realme;
This houre shall take vpon her shady winges
His latest liberty and life to Hell.   90
   D'Au. [*Aside to Byron.*] We are vndonc!   [*Exit.*]
   Qu.   Whats that?
   Byr.   I heard him not.
   Hen. Madam y'are honord much, that Duke *Byron*
Is so obseruant; Some, to cardes with him,
You foure, as now you come, sit to *Primero*;
And I will fight a battayle at the *Chesse.*   95
   Byr. A good safe fight beleeue me; Other warre
Thirsts blood, and wounds, and his thirst quencht, is thankles.
   Esp. Lift, and then cut.
   Byr.   Tis right the end of lifting,
When men are lifted to their highest pitch,
They cut of those that lifted them so high.   100
   Qu. Apply you all these sports so seriously?
   Byr. They first were from our serious acts deuis'd,
The best of which, are to the best but sports
(I meane by best, the greatest); for their ends,
In men that serue them best, are their owne pleasures.   105
   Qu. So, in those best mens seruices, their ends
Are their owne pleasures; passe.
   Byr.   I vy't.
   Hen.   [*Aside.*] I see't;
And wonder at his frontles impudence.   *Exit Hen:*
   Chan. How speedes your Maiestie?
   Qu.   Well; the Duke instructs me

---

85 wise.] ~; *Q1-2* | SD *Esp: with*] *Phelps*; *Esp: Q1-2* | SD *Montigny,*] *Phelps* ‖ **86** Heere] *Q2*;
Hen: Heere *Q1* ‖ **91** SD *Aside to Byron.*] *Parrott* | vndone!] ~? *Q1-2* | SD *Exit.*] *Phelps* |
not.] *Q2*; ~; *Q1* ‖ **95** *Chesse.*] *Q2*; ~; *Q1* ‖ **97** thankles.] *Q2*; ~; *Q1* ‖ **98** cut.] *Q2*; ~; *Q1* ‖
103-4 sports … greatest);] ~; … ~). *Q1-2* ‖ **107** vy't.] *Q2*; ~; *Q1* | SD *Aside.*] *Parrott* ‖ **108**
impudence.] *Q2*; ~; *Q1* ‖

With such graue lessons of morallitie /   110
Forc't out of our light sport; that if I loose,   [N3ᵛ]
I cannot but speed well.
   Byr.   Some idle talke,
For Courtship sake, you know does not amisse.
   Chan. Would we might heare some of it.
   Byr.   That you shall,
I cast away a card now, makes me thinke,   115
Of the deceased worthy King of *Spaine*.
   Chan. What card was that?
   Byr.   The King of hearts (my Lord)
Whose name yeelds well the memorie of that King,
Who was indeed the worthy King of hearts,
And had, both of his subiects hearts, and strangers,   120
Much more then all the Kings of Christendome.
   Chan. He wun them with his gold.
   Byr.   He wun them chiefely,
With his so generall Pietie and Iustice:
And as the little, yet great *Macedon*,
Was sayd with his humane philosophy,   125
To teach the rapefull *Hyrcans*, mariage;
And bring the barbarous *Sogdians*, to nourish,
Not kill their aged Parents, as before;
Th'incestuous *Persians* to reuerence
Their mothers, not to vse them as their wiues;   130
The *Indians* to adore the Grecian Gods,
The *Scythians* to inter, not eate their Parents;
So he, with his diuine Philosophy,
(Which I may call his, since he chiefely vsd it)
In *Turky*, *India*, and through all the world,   135
Expell'd prophane idolatry; and from earth,
Raisd temples to the highest: whom with the word,
He could not winne, he iustly put to sword.
   Chan. He sought for gold, and Empire.
   Byr.   Twas Religion,
And her full propagation that he sought; /   140
If gold had beene his end, it had beene hoorded,   [N4]
When he had fetcht it in so many fleetes:
Which he spent not on Median Luxurie,
Banquets, and women; Calidonian wine,
Nor deare Hyrcanian fishes, but emploid it,   145

---

110 morallitie] *Shepherd*; mortallitie *Q1 (See Textual Note)* ‖ 116 *Spaine*] Q2; Spaine *Q1* ‖ 124
Macedon] Macedon *Q1-2* ‖ 128 Parents, as before;] ~; ~ ~, *Q1* ‖ 131 Grecian] *Grecian Q1-2* ‖
138 sword.] Q2; ~, *Q1* ‖ 143 Median] *Median Q1-2* ‖ 144 Calidonian] *Calidonian Q1-2* ‖ 145
Hyrcanian] *Hyrcanian Q1-2* ‖

To propagate his Empire; and his Empire
Desird t'extend so, that he might withall,
Extend Religion through it, and all nations
Reduce to one firme constitution,
Of Pietie, Iustice, and one publique weale;   150
To which end he made all his matchles subiects
Make tents their castles, and their garisons;
True Catholikes, contrimen and their allies;
Heretikes, strangers and their enemies.
There was in him the magnanimity –   155
 Montig. To temper your extreame applause (my Lord)
Shorten, and answere all things in a word:
The greatest commendation we can giue
To the remembrance of that King deceast;
Is, that he spar'd not his owne eldest sonne,   160
But put him iustly to a violent death,
Because, hee sought to trouble his estates.
 Byr. Ist so?
 Chan.   [*Aside to Montigny.*] That bit
 (my Lord) vpon my life,
Twas bitterly replied, and doth amaze him.

   The King sodainely enters hauing determined
      what to doe.

 Hen. It is resolud, a worke shall now be done,   165
Which, while learnd *Atlas* shall with starres be crownd,
While th'Ocean walkes in stormes his wauy round,
While Moones at full, repaire their broken rings: /
While *Lucifer* fore-shewes *Auroras* springs,   [N4ᵛ]
And *Arctos* stickes aboue the Earth vnmou'd,   170
Shall make my realme be blest, and me belou'd;
Call in the count *D'Auuergne.*

     Enter D'Au.

    A word my Lord.
Will you become as wilfull as your friend?
And draw a mortall iustice on your heads,
That hangs so blacke and is so loth to strike?   175
If you would vtter what I knowe you knowe,
Of his inhumaine treason; one Stronge Barre,
Betwixt his will, and duty were dissolud.
For then I know he would submit himselfe;

---

148 nations] ~, *Q1-2* ‖ 153 Catholikes, contrimen ... allies;] *Parrott*; ~ ~; ... ~, *Q1-2* ‖ 154
strangers] *Parrott*; ~, *Q1-2* ‖ 155 magnanimity–] *Parrott*; ~. *Q1-2* ‖ 157 word:] ~, *Q1-2* ‖ 163
SD *Aside to Montigny.*] *Parrott* ‖ 165 It ... done,] *Shepherd*; It is resolud,/ A ... done, *Q1-2* ‖
166 while] (~ *Q1-2* ‖ 168 their] *Q2*; theit *Q1* ‖ 171 belou'd] beloued *Q1-2* ‖ 172 SD *Enter
D'Au.*] *in right margin of Q1 following D'Auuergne* ‖ 177 one] *Shepherd*; on *Q1-2* ‖

Thinke you it not as stronge a point of faith,   180
To rectifie your loyalties to me,
As to be trusty in ech others wrong?
Trust that deceiues our selues is treachery,
And Truth that truth conceales an open lie.
   D'Au. My Lord if I could vtter any thought,   185
Instructed with disloyalty to you,
And might light any safty to my friend;
Though mine owne heart came after, it should out.
   Hen. I knowe you may, and that your faiths affected
To one another, are so vaine and faulce,   190
That your owne Strengths will ruine you: ye contend,
To cast vp rampiers to you in the sea,
And striue to stop the waues that runne before you.
   D'Au. All this my Lord to me is mistery.
   Hen. It is? Ile make it plaine enough. Beleeue me.   195
Come my Lord Chancellor let vs end our mate.

Enter Varennes, whispering to Byron.

   Var. You are vndone my Lord.   *Exit.*
   Byr.   Is it possible?
   Qu. Play, good my Lord: whom looke you for?
   Esp.   Your mind,
Is not vpon your Game.
   Byr.   Play, pray you play.
   Hen. Enough, tis late, and time to leaue our play, /   200
On all hands; all forbeare the roome. My Lord,   [O1]
Stay you with me.   *[Exeunt all but Henry and Byron.]*
       Yet is your will resolued,
To dewty, and the maine bond of your life?
I sweare (of all th'Intrusions I haue made,
Vpon your owne good, and continew'd fortunes)   205
This is the last; informe me yet the truth,
And here I vow to you, (by all my loue;
By all meanes showne you, euen to this extreame,
When all men else forsake you) you are safe.
What passages haue slipt twixt count *Fuentes*,   210
You, and the Duke of *Sauoye?*
   Byr.   Good my Lord,
This nayle is driuen already past the head,

183 is] *Shepherd*; in *Q1-2* ‖ **184** lie.] *Q2*; ~; *Q1* ‖ **188** after,] ~ *Q1-2* | out.] *Q2*; ~; *Q1* ‖ **189** faiths] faith's *Q1-2* ‖ **193** you.] *Q2*; ~, *Q1* ‖ **194** mistery] *Shepherd*; misery *Q1-2* ‖ **195** is?] ~; *Q1* | enough *Q2*; enouge *Q1* ‖ **197** Lord.] *Q2*; ~; *Q1* ‖ **198** Play,] ~ *Q1-2* ‖ **199** Game.] *Q2*; ~, *Q1* | play.] *Q2*; ~, *Q1* ‖ **201** roome. My Lord,] ~ ~, my ~? *Q1-2* ‖ **202** me.] ~; *Q1-2* | SD *Exeunt ... Byron.*] *Parrott* (*in line 201 following* roome) | Yet] yet *Q1-2* ‖ **209** safe.] *Q1(c)*; ~, *Q1(u)*; ~: *Q2* ‖ **211** Lord,] *Q2*; ~. *Q1* ‖

You much haue ouerchargd, an honest man:
And I beseech you yeeld my Inocence iustice,
(But with my single valure) gainst them all,   215
That thus haue poisoned your opinion of me,
And let me take my vengeance by my sword:
For I protest, I neuer thought an Action,
More then my tongue hath vtterd.
    Hen.   Would twere true;
And that your thoughts and deeds, had fell no fouler.   220
But you disdaine submission, not remembring,
That (in intentes vrdgd for the common good)
He that shall hould his peace being chardgd to speake:
Doth all the peace and nerues of Empire breake;   224
Which on your conscience lie, adieu, good night.   *Exit.*
   Byr. Kings hate to heare what they command men speake;
Aske life, and to desert of death ye yeeld.
Where Medicins loath, it yrcks men to be heald.

       Enter Vitry, with two or three of the Guard,
        Espernon, Vidame, following. Vytry
          layes hand on Byrons sword.

   Vit. Resigne your sword (my Lord) the King commands it.
   Byr. Me to resigne my sword? what king is he,   230
Hath vsd it better for the realme then I?
My sword, that all the warres within the length,
Breadth and the whole dimensions of great *France*,
Hath sheathd betwixt his hilt and horrid point? /   234
And fixt ye all in such a florishing Peace?   [O1ᵛ]
My sword that neuer enimie could inforce,
Bereft me by my friendes? Now, good my Lord,
Beseech the King, I may resigne my sword,
To his hand onely.

              Enter Ianin.

   Ian.   [*To Vitry.*] You must do your office,
The King commands you.
   Vit.   Tis in vaine to striue,   240
For I must force it.
   Byr.   Haue I n'ere a friend,
That beares another for me? All the Guard?
What, will you kill me? will you smother here

___

213 ouerchargd] *Q1(c), Q2*; ouerchragd *Q1(u)* ‖ 214 beseech] *Q1(c), Q2*; besech *Q1(u)* ‖ 218 Action] *Q1(c), Q2*; Acton *Q1(u)* ‖ 219 vtterd.] *Q1(c), Q2*; ~, *Q1(u)* | true;] *Q2*; ~. *Q1* ‖ 224 breake;] ~, *Q1-2* ‖ 225 night] *Q1(c), Q2*; might *Q1(u)* ‖ 226 speake;] ~, *Q1-2* ‖ 228 heald.] *Q2*; ~, *Q1* | SD Espernon] Esper *Q1* ‖ 239 Ian.] Ianin: *Q1 (colon in all speech-prefixes through V.i.37, except IV.ii.291)* | SD To Vitry.] *Parrott* ‖ 240 you.] *Q2*; ~; *Q1* ‖ 241 it.] *Q2*; ~; *Q1* ‖ 243 What,] ~. *Q1-2* ‖

His life that can command, and saue in field,
A hundred thousand liues? For man-hood sake;   245
Lend something to this poore forsaken hand;
For all my seruice, let me haue the honor
To dye defending of my innocent selfe,
And haue some little space to pray to God.

Enter Henry.

  Hen. Come, you are an Atheist *Byron*, and a Traytor,   250
Both foule and damnable; Thy innocent selfe?
No Leper is so buried quicke in vlcers
As thy corrupted soule: Thou end the war?
And settle peace in *France*? what war hath rag'd,
Into whose fury I haue not expos'd   255
My person, with as free a spirit as thine?
Thy worthy Father, and thy selfe, combinde,
And arm'd in all the merits of your valors;
(Your bodyes thrust amidst the thickest fights)
Neuer were bristeld with so many battayles,   260
Nor on the foe haue broke such woods of Launces
As grew vpon my thigh; and I haue Marshald –
I am asham'd to bragge thus; [but] where enuy
And arrogance, their opposit Bulwarke raise;
Men are allowd to vse their proper praise;   265
Away with him.   *Exit Henry:*
  Byr.   Away with him? liue I? /
And here my life thus sleighted? cursed man,   [O2]
That euer the intelligensing lights
Betraid me to mens whorish fellowships;
To Princes Moorish slaueries; To be made   270
The Anuille, on which onely blowes, and woundes
Were made the seed, and wombs of others honors;
A property for a Tyrant, to set vp,
And puffe downe, with the vapour of his breath;
Will you not kill me?
  Vit.   No; we will not hurt you,   275
We are commanded onely to conduct you
Into your lodging.
  Byr.   To my lodging? where?
  Vit. Within the Cabynet of Armes my Lord.
  Byr. What to a prison? Death! I will not go.

254 *France*] *Q2*; France *Q1* ‖ 255 expos'd] ~, *Q1-2* (*See Textual Note*) ‖ 256 person, with]
Shepherd; ~; wich is *Q1* (*See Textual Note*) ‖ 262 Marshald–] *Parrott*; ~; *Q1-2* ‖ 263 but] *See
Textual Note* ‖ 266 him.] *Q2*; ~; *Q1* ‖ 277 lodging.] *Q2*; ~; *Q1* ‖ 278 Lord.] *Q2*; ~: *Q1* ‖ 279
Death! ... go.] ~; ... ~; *Q1* ‖

Vit. Weele force you then.
Byr.   And take away my sword;   280
A proper point of force; ye had as good,
Haue rob'd me of my soule; Slaues of my Starrs,
Partiall and bloody; O that in mine eyes
Were all the Sorcerous poyson of my woes,
That I might witch ye headlong from your height,   285
And trample out your execrable light.
    Vit. Come will you go my Lord? this rage is vaine.
    Byr. And so is all your graue authority;
And that all *France* shall feele before I Die;
Ye see all how they vse good Catholiques.   290
                                              [*Exit Byron guarded.*]

    Esp. Farewell for euer; so haue I desern'd
An exhalation that would be a Starre
Fall when the Sunne forsooke it, in a sincke.
Shooes euer ouerthrow that are too large,
And hugest canons, burst with ouercharge.   295

                    Enter D'Avuergne, Pralin, following
                              with a Guard.

    Pra. My Lord I haue commandment from the King,
To charge you go with me, and aske your sword.
    D'Au. My sword, who feares it? it was n'ere the death
Of any but wilde Bores; I prithee take it; /   299
Hadst thou aduertis'd this when last we met,   [O2ᵛ]
I had bene in my bed, and fast asleepe
Two houres ago; lead; ile go where thou wilt.

                                              Exit guarded.

    Vid. See how he beares his crosse, with his small strength,
On easier shoulders then the other *Atlas.*
    Esp. Strength to aspire, is still accompanied   305
With weakenes to indure; All popular gifts,
Are coullors, that will beare no vineger;
And rather to aduerse affaires, betray,
Then arme against them; his State still is best
That hath most inward worth; and that's best tryed,   310
That neither glories, nor is glorified.   [*Exeunt.*]

---

280 then.] *Q2*; ~; *Q1* ‖ 286 out your execrable] *Q2*; ou't, your execrable *Q1* ‖ 287 vaine.] *Q2*;
~; *Q1* ‖ 289 *France*] *Q2*; France *Q1* ‖ 290 Catholiques.] *Q2*; ~; *Q1* | SD *Exit Byron guarded.*]
Parrott ‖ 294 Shooes] *stet* (*See Textual Note*) ‖ 295 SD *Enter*] *Q2* ‖ 297 sword.] *Q2*; ~; *Q1* ‖
302 ago] *Q2*; a goe *Q1* | lead; ile] *Q1(c)*; ~‚ ~; *Q1(u)*; ~, ~ *Q2* | wilt.] *Q2*; ~: *Q1* | SD
guarded] *Parrott* ‖ 307 that] *Parrott* (*Deighton conj.*); it *Q1-2* ‖ 308 betray,] ~; *Q1-2* ‖ 309
Then] *Loane conj.* (Than); Thine *Q1-2* | is] *Q2*; his *Q1* ‖ 311 SD *Exeunt.*] *Q2* ‖

ACTVS. 5. SCÆNA. 1.

Enter Henry, Soissons, Ianin, Descures, cum aliis.

Hen. What shall we thinke (my Lords) of these new forces
That (from the King of *Spaine*) hath past the Alps?
For which (I thinke) his Lord Ambassador,
Is come to Court, to get their passe for *Flanders*?
    Ian. I thinke (my Lord) they haue no end for *Flanders*;   5
Cont *Maurice* being allready entred *Brabant*
To passe to *Flanders*, to relieue *Ostend*,
And th'Arch-duke full prepar'd to hinder him;
And sure it is that they must measure forces,
Which (ere this new force could haue past the Alps)   10
Of force must be incountred.
    Soiss.   Tis vnlikely,
That their march hath so large an ayme as *Flanders*.
    D'Esc. As these times sort, they may haue shorter reaches;
That would pierce further.
    Hen.   I haue bene aduertis'd,
That Cont *Fuentes* (by whose meanes this army   15
Was lately leuied; And whose hand was strong,
In thrusting on *Byrons* conspiracie)
Hath caus'd these cunning forces to aduance,
With coullor onely to set downe in *Flanders*;
But hath intentionall respect to fauor /   20
And countnance his false Partizans in *Bresse*,   [O3]
And friendes in *Burgondie*; to giue them hart
For the full taking of their hearts from me;
Be as it will; we shall preuent theyr worst;
And therefore call in *Spaines* Ambassador.   25

Enter Ambassador with others.

What would the Lord Ambassador of *Spaine*?
    Amb. First (in my maisters name) I would beseech
Your highnes hearty thought; That his true hand,
(Held in your vowd amities) hath not toucht,
At any least point in *Byrons* offence;   30
Nor once had notice of a cryme so foule;
Whereof, since he doubts not, you stand resolu'd,
He prayes your Leagues continuance in this fauor;

ACTVS. 5. SCÆNA. 1.] *Q2*; Actus. 5. Scæna. 1. *Q1* ‖ SD *Enter*] *Parrott* ‖ 2 *Spaine*] *Q2*; Spaine *Q1* ‖
4 *Flanders*] *Q2*; Flanders *Q1* ‖ 5 *Flanders*] *Q2*; Flanders *Q1* ‖ 6 *Brabant*] *Q2*; Brabant *Q1* ‖ 7
Flanders ... Ostend] *Q2*; Flanders ... Ostend *Q1* ‖ 12 *Flanders.*] *Q2*; Flanders; *Q1* ‖ 14 further.]
Q2; ~, *Q1* ‖ 19 *Flanders*] *Q2*; Flanders *Q1* ‖ 21 *Bresse*] *Q2*; Bresse *Q1* ‖ 22 *Burgondie*] *Q2*;
Burgondie *Q1* ‖ 25 *Spaines* Ambassador.] *Q2*; Spaines ~, *Q1* ‖ 26 Lord] *Q1(c)*, *Q2*; Lord of
Q1(u) | *Spaine*] *Q2*; Spaine *Q1* ‖ 33 continuance] *Q1(c)*, *Q2*; continnuance *Q1(u)* ‖

That the army he hath rais'd to march for *Flanders*,
May haue safe passage by your frontier townes,   35
And finde the Riuer free, that runs by *Rhosne*.
    Hen. My Lord my frontiers shall not be disarm'd,
Till, by araignment of the Duke of *Byron*,
My scruples are resolu'd; and I may know
In what account to hold your Maisters faith,   40
For his obseruance of the League betwixt vs;
You wish me to beleeue that he is cleare
From all the proiects caus'd by Cont *Fuentes*,
His speciall Agent; But where deedes pull downe,
Words may repaire no faith; I scarce can thinke   45
That his gold was so bounteously employd,
Without his speciall counsaile, and command:
These faint proceedings in our Royall faiths,
Make subiects proue so faithlesse. If, because
We sit aboue the danger of the lawes,   50
We likewise lift our Armes aboue their iustice;
And that our heauenly Soueraigne, bounds not vs
In those religious confines; out of which
Our iustice and our true lawes are inform'd;
In vaine haue we expectance that our subiects,   55
Should not as well presume to offend their Earthly,
As we our Heauenly Soueraigne. And this breach
Made in the Forts of all Society, /
Of all celestiall, and humane respects,   [O3ᵛ]
Makes no strengths of our bounties, counsailes, armes,   60
Hold out against their treasons; and the rapes
Made of humanitie, and religion,
In all mens more then *Pagan* liberties,
Atheismes, and slaueries will deriue their springs
From their base Presidents, copied out of kings.   65
But all this, shall not make me breake the commerce,
Authorisde by our treaties; let your Armie
Take the directest passe, it shall goe safe.
    Amb. So rest your highnesse euer; and assurde
That my true Soueraigne, lothes all opposite thoughts.   70
                                                                    [*Exit cum suis.*]

    Hen. Are our dispatches made to all the kings,
Princes, and Potentates, of Christendome?

---

34 *Flanders*] Q2; Flanders Q1 ‖ 36 *Rhosne*] Q2; Rhosne Q1 ‖ 43 *Fuentes*] Q1(c), Q2; *Fluentes*
Q1(u) ‖ 44 where] ~, Q1-2 ‖ deedes] Q2; ~, Q1 ‖ 45 Words] Q2; ~, Q1 ‖ repaire] ~, Q1-2 ‖
49 faithlesse. If, because] Parrott subs.; ~: ~ ~, Q1; ~; if ~, Q2 ‖ 55 expectance] Q1(c), Q2;
epectance Q1(u) ‖ 57 Soueraigne.] ~? Q1-2 ‖ 58 Society,] ~; Q1-2 ‖ 60 counsailes,] Q2; ~ Q1 ‖
70 SD *Exit cum suis.*] Parrott subs. ‖

Ambassadors and Prouince gouernors,
T'enforme the truth of this conspiracie?

    Ian. They all are made my Lord, and some giue out,   75
That 'tis a blow giuen to religion,
To weaken it, in ruining of him,
That said, he neuer wisht more glorious title,
Then to be call'd the scourge of *Hugenots.*

    Soiss. Others that are like fauourers of the fault,   80
Said 'tis a politique aduise from *England,*
To breake the feared Iauelins, both together.

    Hen. Such shut their eyes to truth, we can but set
His lights before them, and his trumpet sound
Close to their eares; their partiall wilfulnesse,   85
In resting blinde, and deafe, or in peruerting,
What their most certaine sences apprehend,
Shall naught discomfort our impartiall Iustice,
Nor cleere the desperat fault that doth enforce it.

Enter Vyt.

    Vit. The Peeres of *France* (my Lord) refuse t'appeare,   90
At the arraignement of the Duke *Byron.*

    Hen. The Court may yet proceed; and so command it,
'Tis not their slacknesse to appeare shall serue,
To let my will t'appeare in any fact,
Wherein the bouldest of them, tempts my iustice.   95
I am resolu'd, and will no more endure,
To haue my subiects make what I command, /
The subiect of their oppositions,   [O4]
Who euer-more slack their allegiance,
As kings forbeare their pennance; how sustaine   100
Your prisoners their strange durance?

    Vit.   One of them,
(Which is the Count *D'Avuergne*) hath merry spirits,
Eates well, and sleepes: and neuer can imagine,
That any place where he is, is a prison;
Where on the other part, the Duke *Byron,*   105
Enterd his prison, as into his graue,
Reiects all food, sleepes not, nor once lyes downe:
Furie hath arm'd his thoughts so thick with thornes,
That rest can haue no entry: he disdaines
To grace the prison with the slendrest show,   110
Of any patience, least men should conceiue,
He thought his sufferance in the lest sort fit;

---

82 feared] *stet (See Textual Note)* ‖ **88** Iustice,] *Q2; ~. Q1* ‖ **89** SD *Enter Vyt.*] *in right margin of Q1-2 following it.* ‖ **112** lest] *Parrott* (least); *best Q1-2* ‖

And holds his bands so worthlesse of his worth,
That he empaires it, to vouchsafe to them,
The lest part of the peace, that freedom owes it: 115
That patience therein, is a willing slauerie,
And (like the Cammell) stoopes to take the load:
So still he walkes: or rather as a Byrde,
Enterd a Closet, which vnwares is made,
His desperate prison (being pursude) amazd, 120
And wrathfull beates his brest from wall to wall,
Assaults the light, strikes downe himselfe, not out,
And being taken, struggles, gaspes, and bites,
Takes all his takers strokings, to be strokes,
Abhorreth food, and with a sauadge will, 125
Frets, pines, and dyes, for former libertie.
So fares the wrathfull Duke; and when the strength
Of these dumbe rages, breake out into sounds,
He breaths defiance, to the world, and bids vs,
Make our selues drunke, with the remaining bloud 130
Of fiue and thirty wounds receiud in fight,
For vs and ours; for we shall neuer brag,
That we haue made his spirits check at death:
This rage in walkes and words; but in his lookes /
He coments all: and prints a world of bookes. 135
   Hen. Let others learne by him to curb their spleenes, [O4ᵛ]
Before they be curbd; and to cease their grudges:
Now I am setled in my Sunne of height,
The circulare splendor and full Sphere of State
Take all place vp from enuy: as the sunne, 140
At height, and passiue ore the crownes of men,
His beames diffusd, and downe-right pourd on them,
Casts but alittle or no shade at all,
So he that is aduanc'd aboue the heads,
Of all his Emulators, with high light, 145
Preuents their enuies, and depriues them quite.

                                    Exeunt.

[V.ii]

Enter the Chancellor, Harlay, Potiers, Fleury,
in scarlet gownes, Laffin, Descures, with
other officers of state.

   Chan. I wonder at the prisoners so long stay.

---

115 lest] *Parrott* (least); best *Q1-2* (See Textual Note) ‖ 128 breake] *stet* (See Textual Note) ‖ 135 bookes.] *Q2;* ~, *Q1* ‖ 139 splendor ... State] *Parrott;* ~, ... ~. *Q1-2* ‖ 143 Casts] Cast *Q1-2* (See Textual Note) ‖ 146 quite.] *Q2;* ~, *Q1* ‖ **V.ii**] *Parrott* ‖ SD Descures] *Q1 (second state corrected), Q2;* Desɔures *Q1 (first state corrected);* Deesɔures *Q1(u)* ‖ 1 stay.] *Q2;* ~, *Q1* ‖

Har. I thinke it may be made a question,
If his impacience will let him come.
    Pot. Yes, he is now well stayd: Time and his Iudgment,
Haue cast his passion and his feuer of.   5
    Fleu. His feuer may be past, but for his passions,
I feare me we shall find it spic'd to hotly,
With his ould poulder.
    D'Esc.   He is sure come forth;
The Carosse of the Marquis of *Rhosny*
Conducted him along to th'Arcenall,   10
Close to the Riuer-side: and there I saw him,
Enter a barge couered with Tapistry,
In which the kings gards waited and receiued him.
Stand by there, cleere the place!
    Chan.   The prisoner comes.
My Lord *Laffin* forbeare your sight a while,   15
It may incense the prisoner: who will know,
By your attendance nere vs, that your hand,
Was chiefe in his discouery; which as yet,
I thinke he doth not doubt.
    Laf.   I will forbeare,   19
Till your good pleasures call me.   *Exit Laf.* /
    Har.   When he knowes   [P1]
And sees *Laffin*, accuse him to his face,
The Court I thinke will shake with his distemper.

       Enter Vitry, Byron, with others and a guarde.

    Vit. You see my Lord, 'tis in the golden chamber.
    Byr. The golden chamber? where the greatest Kings
Haue thought them honor'd to receiue a place: 25
And I haue had it; am I come to stand
In ranke and habite here of men arraignd,
Where I haue sat assistant, and beene honord,
With glorious title of the chiefest vertuous,
Where the Kings chiefe Solicitor hath said,   30
There was in *France*, no man that euer liu'd,
Whose parts were worth my imitation;
That, but mine owne worth, I could imitate none:
And that I made my selfe inimitable,
To all that could come after; whom this Court   35
Hath seene to sit vpon the Flower de Lice
In recompence of my renowned seruice.

---

2 Har.] ~: *Q1* ‖ **4** now] *Q1(c), Q2;* new *Q1(u)* ‖ **9** *Rhosny*] *Q1(c), Q2; Rhosuy Q1(u)* ‖ **14** there, ... place!] ~ͺ ... ~, *Q1* ‖ **19** doubt.] *Q2;* ~, *Q1* ‖ **20** pleasures] *Q1(c), Q2;* plesures *Q1(u)* | me.] *Q2;* ~, *Q1* | Har.] *Q2;* Hen. *Q1* ‖ **33** worth,] ~; *Q1-2* ‖

Must I be sat on now, by petty Iudges?
These Scarlet robes, that come to sit and fight
Against my life; dismay my valure more,   40
Then all the bloudy Cassocks *Spaine* hath brought
To field against it.
    Vit.   To the barre my Lord.
                         He salutes, and stands to the barre.

    Har. Read the inditement.
    Chan.   Stay, I will inuert
(For shortnesse sake) the forme of our proceedings,
And out of all the points the processe holds,   45
Collect fiue principall, with which we charge you.
    1. First you conferd with one, cald *Picoté*,
At *Orleance* borne, and into *Flanders* fled,
To hold intelligence by him with the Archduke,
And for two voyages to that effect,   50
Bestowd on him, fiue hundred, fiftie crownes.
    2. Next you held treaty with the Duke of *Sauoy*,
Without the Kings permission; offering him
All seruice and assistance gainst all men, /   54
In hope to haue in marriage, his third daughter.   [P1ᵛ]
    3. Thirdly you held intelligence with the Duke,
At taking in of *Bourge*, and other Forts;
Aduising him, with all your preiudice,
Gainst the Kings armie, and his royall person.
    4. The fourth is; that you would haue brought the King, 60
Before Saint *Katherines* Fort, to be there slaine:
And to that end writ to the Gouernor,
In which you gaue him notes to know his highnesse.
    5. Fiftly, you sent *Laffin* to treate with *Sauoy*,
And with the Count *Fuentes*, of more plots,   65
Touching the ruine of the King and realme.
    Byr. All this (my Lord) I answer, and deny:
And first for *Picoté*; he was my prisoner,
And therefore I might well conferre with him:
But that our conference tended to the Arch-duke,   70
Is nothing so; I onely did employ him
To Captaine *La Fortune*, for the reduction
Of *Seurre*, to the seruice of the King,
Who vsd such speedy dilligence therein,
That shortly 'twas assur'd his Maiestie.   75
    2. Next, for my treaties with the Duke of *Sauoy*,

---

40 dismay] *Q2*; dsmay *Q1* ‖ 45 points] ~, *Q1-2* ‖ 47 *Picoté*] Picote *Q1-2* ‖ 73 King,] ~. *Q1-2* ‖
75 Maiestie.] *Q2*; ~, *Q1* ‖

Roncas his Secretarie, hauing made
A motion to me, for the Dukes third daughter,
I tolde it to the King; who hauing since,
Giuen me the vnderstanding by *La Force*   80
Of his dislike; I neuer dreamd of it.
  3. Thirdly, for my intelligence with the Duke,
Aduising him against his Highnesse armie:
Had this beene true, I had not vndertaken
Th'assault of *Bourg*, against the Kings opinion,   85
Hauing assistance but by them about me:
And (hauing wunne it for him) had not beene
Put out of such a gouernment so easily.
  4. Fourthly, for my aduise to kill the King;
I would beseech his Highnesse memory,   90
Not to let slip, that I alone diswaded
His viewing of that Fort; informing him, /
It had good marke-men; and he could not goe,   [P2]
But in exceeding danger, which aduise
Diuerted him: the rather, since I said,   95
That if he had desire to see the place
He should receiue from me a Plot of it;
Offering to take it with fiue hundred men,
And I my selfe would go to the assault.
  5. And lastly, for intelligences held,   100
With *Sauoy* and *Fuentes*: I confesse,
That being denyed to keepe the Cytadell,
Which with incredible perill I had got,
And seeing another, honor'd with my spoiles,
I grew so desperate that I found my spirit,   105
Enrag'd to any act, and wisht my selfe,
Couer'd with bloud.
    Chan.   With whose bloud?
    Byr.   With mine owne;
Wishing to liue no longer, being denyed,
With such suspition of me, and set will,
To rack my furious humor into bloud.   110
And for two moneths space, I did speake, and wright,
More then I ought; but haue done euer well,
And therefore your enformers haue beene false,
And (with intent to tyranize) subornd.
    Fleu. What if our witnesses come face to face,   115
And iustifie much more then we alledge?

113 false,] ~. *Q1-2* ‖

Byr. They must be hyrelings then, and men corrupted.
Pot. What thinke you of *La Fin*?
Byr. I hold *La Fin*,
An honor'd Gentleman, my friend and kinsman.
Har. If he then aggrauate, what we affirme, 120
With greater accusations to your face,
What will you say?
Byr. I know it can not be.
Chan. Call in my Lord *La Fin*.
Byr. Is he so neere?
And kept so close from me? can all the world, 124
Make him a treacher?

Enter La Fin. /

Chan. I suppose my Lord, [P2ᵛ]
You haue not stood within, without the eare
Of what hath heere beene vrgd against the Duke;
If you haue heard it, and vpon your knowledge
Can witnesse all is true, vpon your soule;
Vtter your knowledge.
Laf. I haue heard my Lord, 130
All that hath past here; and vpon my soule,
(Being chargd so vrgently in such a Court)
Vpon my knowledge I affirme all true;
And so much more: as had the prisoner liues
As many as his yeares, would make all forfaite. 135
Byr. O all yee vertuous powers, in earth and heauen,
That haue not put on hellish flesh and blood,
From whence these monstrous issues are produc'd,
That cannot beare in execrable concord,
And one prodigious subiect, contraries; 140
Nor (as the Ile that of the world admirde
Is seuerd from the world) can cut your selues
From the consent and sacred harmonie
Of life, yet liue; of honor, yet be honord;
As this extrauagant, and errant roge, 145
From all your faire *Decorums*, and iust lawes,
Findes powre to doe: and like a lothesome wen,
Sticks to the face of nature, and this Court;
Thicken this ayre, and turne your plaguie rage,
Into a shape as dismall as his sinne. 150
And with some equall horror teare him of

---

125 treacher?] Q2; ~. Q1 | Chan.] ~ Q1 ‖ **126** within,] Q2; ~; Q1 ‖ **140** subiect,] Q1(u); ~; Q1(c), Q2 ‖ **141** (as ... of] Q1(c), Q2; ~ ... (of Q1(u) | admirde] ~) Q1-2 ‖ **143** harmonie] hermonie Q1; harmony Q2 ‖

From sight and memory: let not such a court,
To whose fame all the Kings of Christendome,
Now laie their eares, so crack her royall Trumpe,
As to sound through it, that here vanted iustice   155
Was got in such an incest: is it iustice
To tempt, and witch a man, to breake the law,
And by that witch condemne him? let me draw
Poison into me with this cursed ayre,
If he bewitcht me, and transformd me not;   160
He bit me by the eare, and made me drinke /
Enchanted waters; let me see an Image   [P3]
That vtterd these distinct words; *Thou shalt dye,*
O wicked King; and if the diuill gaue him
Such powre vpon an Image; vpon me   165
How might he tyrannize? that by his vowes
And othes so Stygian, had my Nerues and will,
In more awe then his owne? What man is he
That is so high, but he would higher be?
So roundly sighted, but he may be found,   170
To haue a blinde side, which by craft persude,
Confederacie, and simply trusted treason,
May wrest him past his Angell, and his reason?
   Chan. Witchcraft can neuer taint an honest minde.
   Har. True gold, will any triall stand, vntoucht.   175
   Pot. For coulours that will staine when they are tryed,
The cloth it selfe is euer cast aside.
   Byr. Some-times, the very Glosse in any thing,
Will seeme a staine; the fault not in the light,
Nor in the guilty obiect, but our sight.   180
My glosse, raisd from the richnesse of my stuffe,
Had too much splendor for the Owly eye,
Of politique and thanklesse royaltie:
I did deserue too much; a plurisie
Of that blood in me is the cause I dye.   185
Vertue in great men must be small and sleight:
For poore starres rule, where she is exquisite.
Tis tyrannous, and impious policie,
To put to death by fraude and trecherie;
Sleight is then royall, when it makes men liue,   190
And if it vrge faults, vrgeth to forgiue.
He must be guiltlesse, that condemnes the guiltie;
Like things, do nourish like, and not destroy them:

---

154 laie] laid *Q1-2* | eares,] *Q2*; ~; *Q1* ‖ **164** *O wicked King*] *Q1(c)*, *Q2*; O wicked King *Q1(u)* ‖
168 owne? What] ~: what *Q1-2* ‖ **171** craft] ~, *Q1-2* ‖ **187** exquisite.] ~, *Q1-2* ‖ **192** guiltie;] ~,
Q1-2 ‖

Mindes must be sound, that iudge affaires of weight,
And seeing hands cut corosiues from your sight.   195
A Lord intelligencer? hangman-like,
Thrust him from humaine fellowship, to the desarts
Blowe him with curses; shall your iustice call
Treacherie her Father? would you wish her weigh /   199
My valure with the hisse of such a viper?   [P3ᵛ]
What I haue done to shunne the mortall shame,
Of so vniust an opposition
(My enuious starres cannot deny me this,
That I may make my Iudges witnesses;
And that my wretched fortunes haue reseru'd   205
For my last comfort) yee all know (my Lords).
This body gasht with fiue and thirty wounds,
Whose life and death you haue in your award,
Holds not a veine that hath not opened beene,
And which I would not open yet againe,   210
For you and yours; this hand that writ the lines
Alledgd against me, hath enacted still,
More good then there it onely talkt of ill.
I must confesse my choller hath transferd
My tender spleene to all intemperate speech: 215
But reason euer did my deeds attend
In worth of praise, and imitation.
Had I borne any will to let them loose,
I could haue flesht them with bad seruices,
In *England* lately, and in *Swizerland*:   220
There are a hundred Gentlemen by name,
Can witnesse my demeanure in the first;
And in the last Ambassage I adiure
No other testimonies then the Seigneurs
De Vic, and *Sillerie*; who amply know,   225
In what sort, and with what fidelitie
I bore my selfe; to reconcile and knit,
In one desire so many wills disioynde,
And from the Kings allegiance quite with-drawne.
My acts askt many men, though done by one.   230
And [though] I were but one, I stood for thousands,
And still I hold my worth, though not my place:
Nor sleight me, Iudges, though I be but one;
One man, in one sole expedition,
Reduc'd into th'imperiall powre of *Rome*,   235

195 hands] ~, *Q1-2* ‖ 202 opposition] ~; *Q1-2* ‖ 203-6 (My ... comfort)] ‚~ ... ~; *Q1 (See Textual Note)* ‖ 206 Lords).] ~) *Q1-2* ‖ 212 me,] ~; *Q1-2* ‖ 216-17 attend ... imitation.] *Parrott (Brereton conj.)*; ~. ... ~, *Q1* ‖ 231 though] *Shepherd (See Textual Note)* ‖ 233 one;] ~, *Q1-2* ‖

381

Armenia, Pontus, and *Arabia*,
Syria, Albania, and *Iberia*,
Conquerd th'*Hyrcanians*; and to *Caucasus*,
His arme extended; the *Numidians* /
And *Affrick* to the shores Meridionall,   240
His powre subiected; and that part of *Spaine*   [P4]
Which stood from those parts that *Sertorius* rulde,
Euen to the *Atlantique* Sea he conquered.
Th'*Albanian* kings, he from their kingdoms chac'd,
And at the *Caspian* Sea, their dwellings plac'd: 245
Of all the Earths globe, by powre and his aduice,
The round-eyd Ocean saw him victor thrice:
And what shall let me (but your cruell doome,)
To adde as much to *France*, as he to *Rome*?
And to leaue Iustice neither Sword nor word,   250
To vse against my life, this Senate knowes,
That what with one victorious hand I tooke,
I gaue to all your vses, with another:
With this I tooke, and propt the falling kingdome,
And gaue it to the King: I haue kept   255
Your lawes of state from fire; and you your selues,
Fixt in this high Tribunall; from whose height
The vengefull Saturnales of the League
Had hurld yee head-long; doe yee then returne
This retribution? can the cruell King,   260
The kingdome, lawes, and you, (all sau'd by me)
Destroy their sauer? What (aye me) I did
Aduerse to this; this damnd Enchanter did,
That tooke into his will, my motion;
And being banck-route both of wealth and worth,   265
Pursued with quarrels, and with suites in law;
Feard by the kingdome; threatned by the king;
Would raise the loathed dung-hill of his ruines,
Vpon the monumentall heape of mine:
Torne with possessed whirle-winds may he dye,   270
And dogs barke at his murtherous memory.
  Chan. My Lord, our liberall sufferance of your speech,
Hath made it late; and for this Session,
We will dismisse you; take him back my Lord.
                                                   Exeunt Vit. and Byron.

  Har. You likewise may depart.   *Exit Laffin.*
  Chan.   What resteth now   275

236-37 *Armenia … Iberia,*] *Shepherd*; *one line Q1-2* ‖ **244** their] *Parrott*; the *Q1-2* ‖ **249** *Rome?*]
~, *Q1-2* ‖ **251** life,] *Parrott*; ~; *Q1-2* ‖ **258** Saturnales] Saturnals *Q1-2* (*See Textual Note*) ‖ **262**
What] what *Q1-2* ‖ **271** memory.] *Q2*; ~, *Q1* ‖ **274** *Exeunt*] Exit *Q1-2* ‖

To be decreed gainst this great prisoner?
A mighty merit, and a monstrous crime, /
Are here concurrent; what by witnesses,   [P4ᵛ]
His letters, and instructions, we haue prou'd,
Himselfe confesseth, and excuseth all   280
With witch-craft, and the onely act of thought.
For witch-craft I esteeme it a meere strength
Of rage in him conceiu'd gainst his accuser;
Who being examinde hath denied it all;
Suppose it true, it made him false; But wills   285
And worthy mindes, witch-craft can neuer force.
And for his thoughts that brake not into deeds;
Time was the cause, not will; the mindes free act
In treason still is Iudgd as th'outward fact.
If his deserts haue had a wealthy share,   290
In sauing of our land from ciuill furies:
Manlius had so that saft the Capitoll;
Yet for his after traiterous factions,
They threw him head-long from the place he sau'd.
My definite sentence then, doth this import: 295
That we must quench the wilde-fire with his bloud,
In which it was so traiterously inflam'd;
Vnlesse with it, we seeke to incence the land.
The King can haue no refuge for his life,
If his be quitted: this was it that made   300
Lewis th'eleuenth renounce his countrymen,
And call the valiant *Scots* out of their kingdome,
To vse their greater vertues, and their faiths,
Then his owne subiects, in his royall guarde:
What then conclude your censures?
    Omnes.   He must dye.   305
    Chan. Draw then his sentence, formally, and send him;
And so all treasons in his death attend him.

                                          Exeunt.

[V.iii]

Enter Byron, Espernon, Soisson, Ianin,
Vidame, Descures.

    Vid. I ioy you had so good a day my Lord.
    Byr. I wone it from them all: the Chancellor
I answerd to his vttermost improuements:

---

278 witnesses,] ~; *Q1* ‖ 279 letters, ... prou'd,] ~ˌ ... ~ˌ *Q1-2* ‖ 281 thought.] *Q1(c)*, *Q2*; ~,
Q1(u) ‖ 291 furies] *Q1(c)*, *Q2*; friends *Q1(u)* ‖ 298 land.] *Shepherd*; ~, *Q1-2* ‖ V.iii] *Parrott* ‖ 1
Vid.] *Vit. Q1-2* ‖

I mou'd my other Iudges to lament
My insolent misfortunes; and to lothe / 5
The pockie soule, and state-bawde, my accuser. [Q1]
I made replie to all that could be said,
So eloquently, and with such a charme,
Of graue enforcements, that me thought I sat,
Like *Orpheus* casting reignes on sauage beasts; 10
At the armes end (as twere) I tooke my barre
And set it farre aboue the high tribunall,
Where like a Cedar on Mount *Lebanon*,
I Grew, and made my iudges show like Box-trees;
And Boxtrees right, their wishes would haue made them, 15
Whence boxes should haue growne, till they had strooke
My head into the budget: but ahlas,
I held their bloudy armes, with such strong reasons;
And (by your leaue) with such a iyrck of wit:
That I fetcht bloud vpon the Chancelors cheekes. 20
Me thinkes I see his countinance as he sat;
And the most lawierly deliuery
Of his set speeches: shall I play his part?
   Esp. For heauens sake, good my Lord.
   Byr.   I will ifaith.
Behold a wicked man: A man debaucht, 25
A man, contesting with his King; A man,
On whom (my Lords) we are not to conniue,
Though we may condole: A man:
That *Læsa Maiestate*, sought a lease,
Of *Plus quam satis*. A man that *vi et armis* 30
Assaild the King; and would *per fas et nefas*,
Aspire the kingdome: here was lawiers learning.
   Esp. He said not this my Lord, that I haue heard.
   Byr. This or the like, I sweare. I pen no speeches.
   Soiss. Then there is good hope of your wisht acquitall. 35
   Byr. Acquitall? they haue reason; were I dead
I know they can not all supply my place;
Is't possible the King should be so vaine,
To thinke he can shake me with feare of death?
Or make me apprehend that he intends it? 40
Thinkes he to make his firmest men, his clowds?
The clowdes (obseruing their Æriall natures)
Are borne aloft, and then to moisture chang'd, /
Fall to the earth; where being made thick, and cold, [Q1ᵛ]

---

6 accuser.] ~, *Q1-2* ‖ **13** *Lebanon*] Lebanon *Q1-2* ‖ **20** cheekes.] ~, *Q1-2* ‖ **23** part?] *Shepherd*; part? *Enter Soiss: Esp: Q1* ‖ **24, 33** *Esp.*] ~: *Q1* ‖ **24** ifaith.] ~, *Q1-2* ‖ **38** Is't] Ist *Q1-2* ‖ **43** chang'd] *Shepherd*; hang'd *Q1-2* ‖

They loose both al their heate, and leuitie;   45
Yet then againe recouering heate and lightnesse,
Againe they are aduanc't: and by the Sunne
Made fresh and glorious; and since clowdes are rapt
With these vncertainties: now vp, now downe,
Am I to flit so with his smile, or froune?   50
   Esp. I wish your comforts, and incoradgments,
May spring out of your saftie; but I heare
The King hath reasond so against your life,
And made your most friends yeeld so to his reasons,
That your estate is fearefull.
   Byr.   Yeeld t'his reasons?   55
O how friends reasons, and their freedomes stretch,
When powre sets his wide tenters to their sides!
How, like a cure, by mere opinion,
It workes vpon our bloud? like th'antient Gods
Are *Moderne* Kings, that liu'd past bounds themselues,   60
Yet set a measure downe, to wretched men:
By many Sophismes, they made good, deceipt;
And, since they past in powre, surpast in right:
When Kings wills passe, the starres winck, and the Sunne,
Suffers eclips: rude thunder yeelds to them   65
His horrid wings: sits smoothe as glasse englazd,
And lightning sticks twixt heauen and earth amazd:
Mens faiths are shaken: and the pit of truth
O'reflowes with darkenesse, in which Iustice sits,
And keepes her vengeance tied to make it fierce;   70
And when it comes, th'encreased horrors showe,
Heauens plague is sure, though full of state, and slowe.
   Sist. [*Within.*] O my deare Lord and brother, O the Duke?
   Byr. What sounds are these my Lord? hark, hark, me thinks
I heare the cries of people.
   Esp.   Tis for one,   75
Wounded in fight here at Saint *Anthonies* Gate.
   Byr. Sfoote, one cried the Duke: I pray [you] harken
Againe, or burst your selues with silence – no!
What contriman's the common headsman here? /
   Soiss. He's a Bourgonian.   [Q2]
   Byr.   The great deuill he is!   80
The bitter wizerd told me, a Burgonian,
Should be my headsman; strange concurrences:

---

63 surpast] ~, *Q1-2* ‖ 64 passe,] *Q2*; ~; *Q1* ‖ 66 englazd] *Parrott*; engazd *Q1-2* ‖ 73 SD *Within.*]
Q2 | O my ... Duke?] *Shepherd*; O my ... brother,/ O the Duke? *Q1-2* ‖ 76 Gate.] ~: *Q1-2* ‖
77 you] *See Textual Note* | harken] ~, *Q1-2* ‖ 78 silence – no!] *Parrott*; ~, ~: *Q1-2* ‖ 80 is!]
~, *Q1-2* ‖

S'death whose here?

                    Enter 4. Vshers bare, Chanc: Har: Pot:
                         Fleur: Vit: Pralin, with others.

                   O then I am but dead,
Now, now ye come all to pronounce my sentence.
I am condemn'd vniustly: tell my kinsfolkes,   85
I die an innocent: if any friend
Pittie the ruine of the States sustainer
Proclaime my innocence; ah Lord Chancelor,
Is there no pardon? will there come no mercie?
I, put your hat on, and let me stand bare,   90
Showe your selfe right a Lawier.
  Chan.   I am bare,
What would you haue me do?
  Byr.   You haue not done,
Like a good iustice; and one that knew
He sat vpon the precious bloud of vertue;
Y'aue pleasd the cruell King, and haue not borne,   95
As great regard to saue as to condemne;
You haue condemn'd me, my Lord Chancelor,
But God acquites me; he will open lay
All your close treasons against him, to collour
Treasons layd to his truest images;   100
And you my Lord shall answere this iniustice,
Before his iudgement seate: to which I summon
In one yeare and a daie your hot apparanse;
I goe before, by mens corrupted domes;
But they that caus'd my death, shall after come   105
By the imaculate iustice of the highest.
  Chan. Well, good my Lord, commend your soule to him,
And to his mercie, thinke of that, I pray.
  Byr. Sir, I haue thought of it, and euery howre,
Since my affliction, askt on naked knees   110
Patience to beare your vnbeleeu'd Iniustice:
But you, nor none of you haue thought of him,
In my euiction: y'are come to your benches,
With plotted iudgements; your linckt eares so lowd, / 114
Sing with preiudicate windes, that nought is heard, [Q2ᵛ]
Of all, pore prisoners vrge gainst your award.
  Har. Passion, my Lord, transports your bitternes,
Beyond all collour; and your propper iudgement:

86-87 I ... sustainer] *Shepherd*; I ... innocent:/ If ... sustainer *Q1-2* (pittie) ‖ **116** award.] *Q2*;
~; *Q1* ‖

No man hath knowne your merits more then I;
And would to God your great misdedes had beene,   120
As much vndone, as they haue beene concealde;
The cries of them for iustice (in desert)
Haue beene so lowd and piersing; that they deafned
The eares of mercie; and haue labord more,
Your Iudges to compresse then to enforce them.   125
   Pot. We bring you here your sentence, will you reade it?
   Byr. For heauens sake, shame to vse me with such rigor;
I know what it imports, and will not haue,
Mine eare blowne into flames with hearing it;
[*To Fleury.*] Haue you beene one of them that haue condemn'd
    me?   130
   Fleu. My Lord I am your Orator: God comfort you.
   Byr. Good Sir, my father lou'd you so entirely,
That if you haue beene one, my soule forgiues you;
It is the King (most childish that he is
That takes what he hath giuen) that iniures me: 135
He gaue grace in the first draught of my fault,
And now restraines it: grace againe I aske;
Let him againe vouchsafe it: send to him,
A post will soone returne: the Queene of *England*,
Told me that if the wilfull Earle of *Essex*,   140
Had vsd submission, and but askt her mercie,
She would haue giuen it, past resumption;
She (like a gratious Princesse) did desire
To pardon him: euen as she praid to God,
He would let doune a pardon vnto her;   145
He yet was guiltie, I am innocent:
He still refusd grace, I importune it.
   Chan. This askt in time (my Lord) while he besought it,
And ere he had made his scucrity knowne,
Had (with much ioye to him) I know beene granted.   150
   Byr. No, no, his bountie, then was misery,
To offer when he knew twould be refusde; /
He treads the vulgar pathe of all aduantage,   [Q3]
And loues men, for his vices, not for their vertues;
My seruice would haue quickn'd gratitude,   155
In his owne death, had he beene truely royall;
It would haue stirr'd the image of a King,
Into perpetuall motion to haue stood
Neere the conspiracie restraind at *Mantes*;

126 it?] ~. *Q1-2* ‖ 130 SD *To Fleury.*] *Parrott* ‖ 131 *Fleu.*] *Flen. Q1* ‖ 137 restraines] *Q2*; restaines *Q1* ‖ 139 *England*] England *Q1-2* ‖ 140 *Essex*] *Q2*; Essex *Q1* ‖ 150 granted.] *Q2*; ~; *Q1* ‖ 154 not] *Q2*; nor *Q1* ‖ 158 motion] *Parrott*; ~; *Q1-2* ‖ 159 *Mantes*] *Q2*; Mantes *Q1* ‖

And in a danger, that had then the Woulfe,   160
To flie vpon his bosome, had I onely held
Intelligence with the conspirators;
Who stuck at no check but my loyaltie,
Nor kept life in their hopes, but in my death;
The seege of *Amiens*, would haue softned rocks,   165
Where couer'd all in showers of shot and fire,
I seem'd to all mens eyes a fighting flame
With bullets cut, in fashion of a man;
A sacrifize to valure (impious King)
Which he will needes extinguish, with my bloud;   170
Let him beware, iustice will fall from heauen,
In the same forme I serued in that seege,
And by the light of that, he shall decerne,
What good, my ill hath brought him; it will nothing,
Assure his State: the same quench he hath cast   175
Vpon my life, shall quite put out his fame;
This day he looseth, what he shall not finde,
By all daies he suruiues; so good a seruant,
Nor *Spaine* so great a foe; with whom, ahlas,
Because I treated am I put to death?   180
Tis but a politique glose: my courage rais'd me,
For the deare price of fiue and thirtie skarres,
And that hath ruin'd me, I thanke my Starres:
Come ile goe where yee will, yee shall not lead me.

                                                    [*Exit Byron.*]

    Chan. I feare his frenzie. Neuer saw I man   185
Of such a spirit so amaz'd at death.
    Har. He alters euery minute: what a vapor
The strongest minde is to a storme of crosses!

                        Exeunt   Chancellor,   Harlay,   Potier,
                        Fleury, Vitry. Manent Esper: Soisson,
                        Ianin, Vidame, D'escures.

    Esp. O of what contraries consists a man!
Of what impossible mixtures? vice and vertue, /   190
Corruption, and eternnesse, at one time,   [Q3ᵛ]
And in one subiect, let together, loosse?
We haue not any strength but weakens vs,
No greatnes but doth crush vs into ayre.
Our knowledges, do light vs but to erre,   195
Our Ornaments are Burthens: Our delights

160 then] *stet (See Textual Note)* ‖ **165** *Amiens*] Q2; Amiens Q1 ‖ **179** *Spaine*] Q2; Spaine Q1 ‖
181 but] *Shepherd*; put Q1-2 ‖ **184** SD *Exit Byron.*] *Parrott* ‖ **185-86** I ... death.] *Shepherd*;
I ... frenzie,/ Neuer ... death. Q1-2 (of) ‖ **187-88** vapor/ ... crosses!] ~?/ ... ~. Q1-2 | SD
Chancellor ... Vitry] | SD *Soisson, Ianin,*] Q2; ~: ~: Q1 ‖ **189** *Esp.*] ~: Q1 ‖ **196** delights]
Q2; delightss Q1 ‖

388

Are our tormentors; fiendes that (raisd in feares)
At parting shake our Roofes about our eares.
   Soiss. O Vertue, thou art now farre worse then Fortune!
Her gifts stucke by the Duke, when thine are vanisht,   200
Thou brau'st thy friend in Neede: Necessity,
That vsd to keepe thy welth, Contempt, thy loue,
Haue both abandond thee in his extreames,
Thy powers are shadowes, and thy comfort, dreames.
   Vid. O reall Goodnesse, if thou be a power   205
And not a word alone, in humaine vses,
Appere out of this angry conflagration,
Where this great Captaine (thy late Temple) burns,
And turne his vicious fury to thy flame,
From all earths hopes mere guilded with thy fame: 210
Let Pietie enter with her willing crosse,
And take him on it; ope his brest and armes,
To all the Storms, Necessity can breath,
And burst them all with his embraced death.
   Ian. Yet are the ciuille tumults of his spirits,   215
Hot and outragiouse: not resolued, ahlas,
(Being but one man) t'endure the kingdomes dome;
He doubts, stormes, threatens, rues, complains, implores;
Griefe hath brought all his forces to his lookes,
And nought is left to strengthen him within,   220
Nor lasts one habite of those greeu'd aspects:
Blood expells palenesse, palenes Blood doth chace,
And sorrow errs through all forms in his face.
   D'Esc. So furiouse is he, that the Politique law,
Is much to seeke, how to enact her sentence: 225
Authority backt with arms, (though he vnarmd)
Abhorrs his furie, and with doubtfull eyes,
Views on what ground it should sustaine his ruines, /
And as a Sauadge Bore that (hunted longe,   [Q4]
Assayld and set vp) with his onely eyes,   230
Swimming in fire, keepes of the baying hounds;
Though suncke himselfe, yet houlds his anger vp,
And snowes it forth in foame; houlds firme his stand,
Of Battalouse Bristles: feedes his hate to die,
And whets his tuskes with wrathfull maiesty: 235
So fares the furious Duke, and with his lookes,

---

199 Vertue] vertue *Q1-2* ‖ 202 Contempt] contempt *Q1-2* ‖ 204 dreames.] *Q2*; ~, *Q1* ‖ 205
Goodnesse, ... power] goodnesse ... ~! *Q1-2* ‖ 211 Pietie] pietie *Q1-2* ‖ 214 death.] *Q2*; ~, *Q1* ‖
215 *Ian.*] ~, *Q1* ‖ 216 ahlas] *Q2*; *Ahlas Q1* ‖ 217 t'endure] *Loane conj.*; render *Q1-2* ‖ 218
implores;] ~, *Q1* ‖ 223 face.] *Q2*; ~, *Q1* ‖ 226 Authority] *Q2*; Authoriy *Q1* ‖ 229 Sauadge]
Q2; *Sauadge Q1* ‖ 231 fire, ... hounds;] ~, ... ~, *Q1-2* ‖ 234 Bristles] *Bristles Q1* ‖ 235
maiesty:] *Q2*; ~. *Q1* ‖

Doth teach death horrors; makes the hangman learne
New habites for his bloody impudence;
Which no habituall horror from him driues,
Who for his life shunns death, by which he liues.   240
                                         [Exeunt.]

[V.iv]

Enter Chauncellor, Harlay, Potier, Fleury,
Vitry, Pralin, D'Escures.

  Vit. Will not your Lordshippe haue the Duke distinguisht
From other prisoners, where the order is,
To giue vp men condemd into the hands
Of th'executioner? He would be the death,
Of him that he should die by, ere he sufferd,   5
Such an abiection.
  Chan.   But to bind his hands,
I hold it passing needefull.
  Har.   Tis my Lord,
And very dangerous to bring him loose.
  Pra. You will in all dispaire and fury plunge him,
If you but offer it.
  Pot.   My Lord by this,   10
The prisoners Spirit is some-thing pacified,
And tis a feare that th'offer of those bands,
Would breed fresh furies in him, and disturbe,
The entry of his soule into her peace.
  Chan. I would not that, for any possible danger,   15
That can be wrought, by his vnarmed hands,
And therefore in his owne forme bring him in.

Enter Byron, a Bishop or two; with all the
guards, souldiers with muskets.

  Byr. Where shall this weight fall? on what rhegion,
Must this declining prominent poure his lode?
Ile breake my bloods high billows gainst my starrs;   20
Before this hill be shooke into a flat, /
All *France* shall feele an earthquake; with what murmur,   [Q4ᵛ]
This world shrinkes into Chaos?
  Bish.   Good my Lord,
Forgoe it willingly; and now resigne,

---

239 no] *Loane conj.*; now *Q1-2* ‖ **240** liues.] *Q2*; ~, *Q1* | SD *Exeunt.*] *Parrott* ‖ **V.iv**] *Parrott* ‖
SD *Vitry, Pralin, D'Escures.*] *Vitry. Q1-2* ‖ **2-4** prisoners, … executioner? He] *Parrott*; ~? …
~; he *Q1-2* ‖ **6** abiection.] *Q2*; ~, *Q1* ‖ **7** needefull.] *Q2*; ~, *Q1* ‖ **9** *Pra.*] ~: *Q1* ‖ **14** peace.]
Q2; ~, *Q1* ‖ **17** in.] *Q2*; ~, *Q1* ‖ **20** starrs;] ~, *Q1-2* ‖ **22** *France*] *Q2*; France *Q1* ‖ **23** *Bish.*]
Parrott; *Arch. Q1-2* ‖

Your sensuall powers entirely to your soule.   25
  Byr. Horror of death, let me alone in peace,
And leaue my soule to me, whome it concernes;
You haue no charge of it; I feele her free,
How she doth rowze, and like a Faulcon stretch
Her siluer wings; as threatening Death, with death;   30
At whom I ioyfully will cast her off:
I know this bodie but a sinck of folly,
The ground-work, and rais'd frame of woe and frailtie:
The bond, and bundle of corruption;
A quick corse, onely sensible of griefe,   35
A walking sepulcher, or household thiefe:
A glasse of ayre, broken with lesse then breath,
A slaue bound face to face to death, til death:
And what say all you more? I know, besides
That life is but a darke and stormy night,   40
Of sencelesse dreames, terrors, and broken sleepes;
A Tyranie, deuising paines to plague
And make man long in dying, racks his death;
And death is nothing, what can you say more?
I being a large Globe, and a little earth,   45
Am seated like earth betwixt both the heauens:
That if I rise, to heauen I rise; if fall
I likewise fall to heauen; what stronger faith,
Hath any of your soules? what say you more?
Why lose I time in these things? talke of knowledge,   50
It serues for inward vse. I will not die
Like to a Clergie man; but like the Captaine,
That prayd on horse-back and with sword in hand,
Threatend the Sunne, commanding it to stand;
These are but ropes of sand.
  Chan.   Desire you then,   55
To speake with any man?
  Byr. I would speake with *La Force*, and *Saint Blancart.* /
Vit. [They are not in the city.]   [R1]
  Byr.   Do they flie me?
Where is *Preuost*, controwler of my house?
  Pral. Gone to his house ith' countrie three daies since.   60
  Byr. He should haue stayd here, he keepes all my blancks;
O all the world forsakes me! wretched world,
Consisting most of parts, that flie each other:

---

30 Death,] death, *Q1-2* || 38 to face] ~ ~, *Q1-2* || 39 say] *Deighton conj.*; sayd *Q1-2* (*See Textual Note*) || 45 being a large] *Parrott*; bring a long *Q1-2* (*See Textual Note*) || 47 rise,] ~; *Q1-2* || 57 *Saint*] Saint *Q1* || 58 *Vit.* ... city.] *Parrott* (*See Textual Note*) || 60 ith'] *Q2*; ith *Q1* ||

A firmnesse, breeding all inconstancy,
A bond of all disiunction; like a man   65
Long buried, is a man that long hath liu'd;
Touch him, he falls to ashes; for one fault,
I forfeite all the fashion of a man;
Why should I keepe my soule in this dark light?
Whose black beames lighted me to loose my selfe.   70
When I haue lost my armes, my fame, my minde,
Friends, brother, hopes, fortunes, and euen my furie?
O happie were the man, could liue alone,
To know no man, nor be of any knowne!
    Har. My Lord, it is the manner once againe   75
To read the sentence.
    Byr.   Yet more sentences?
How often will yee make me suffer death,
As yee were proud to heare your powreful domes?
I know and feele you were the men that gaue it,
And die most cruellie to heare so often   80
My crimes and bitter condemnation vrdg'd:
Suffize it, I am brought here; and obey,
And that all here are priuie to the crimes.
    Chan. It must be read my Lord, no remedie.
    Byr. Reade, if it must be, then, and I must talke.   85
    Har. The processe being extraordinarily made and examin'd
by the Court, and chambers assembled –
    Byr. Condemn'd for depositions of a witch?
The common deposition, and her whoore
To all whorish periuries and treacheries.   90
Sure he cal'd vp the diuill in my spirits,
And made him to vsurpe my faculties:
Shall I be cast away now he's cast out?
What Iustice is in this? deare countrey-men, /
Take this true euidence, betwixt heauen and you,   95
And quit me in your hearts.   [R1ᵛ]
    Chan.   Go on.
    Har. Against *Charles Gontalt* of *Byron*: knight of both the
orders; Duke of *Byron*, peere and marshall of *France*; Gouernor
of *Burgondy*, accus'd of treason in a sentence was giuen the 22.   100
of this month, condemning the said Duke of *Byron* of heigh
treason, for his direct conspiracies against the kings person;
enterprises against his state –
    Byr. That is most false; let me for euer be,

---

71 minde] *Parrott (Deighton conj.)*; winde *Q1-2* ‖ 76 sentence.] *Q2*; ~? *Q1* ‖ 77 death,] ~?
Q1-2 ‖ 103 state–] ~.——— *Q1* ‖

Depriued of heauen, as I shall be of earth,   105
If it be true: knowe worthy country-men,
These two and twenty moneths I haue bene clere,
Of all atempts against the king and state.
    Har. Treaties and trecheries with his Enemies, being marshall
of the Kings army, for reparation of which crimes they depriued   110
him of all his estates, honors and dignities, and condemned him
to lose his head vpon a Scaffold at the Greaue –
    Byr. The Greaue? had that place stood for my dispatch
I had not yeelded; all your forces should not,
Stire me one foote; wild horses should haue drawne,   115
My body peece-meale, eare you all had brought me.
    Har. Declaring all his goods moueable and inmoueable whatsoeuer
to be confiscate to the King: the Signeury of *Byron* to loose the
title of Duchy and Peere for euer.
    Byr. Now is your forme contented?
    Chan.   I, my Lord   120
And I must now entreat you to deliuer,
Your order vp, the king demands it of you.
    Byr. And I restore it, with my vow of safty
In that world, where both he and I are one,
I neuer brake the oth I tooke to take it.   125
    Chan. Wel now my Lord wee'l take our latest leaues,
Beseeching heauen to take as clere from you,
All sence of torment in your willing death:
All loue and thought of what you must leaue here,
As when you shall aspire heauens highest sphere.   130
    Byr. Thankes to your Lordship and let me pray to,
That you will hold good censure of my life, /
By the cleere witnesse of my soule in death,   [R2]
That I haue neuer past act gainst the King,
Which if my faith had let me vndertake,   135
He had bene three yeares since, amongst the dead.
    Har. Your soule shall finde his safety in her owne.
Call the executioner.   [*Exeunt the Chancellor and Harlay.*]
    Byr.   Good sir I pray,
Go after and beseech the Chancellor
That he will let my body be interrd,   140
Amongst my predecessors at *Byron.*
    D'Esc. I go my Lord.   *Exit.*
    Byr.   Go, go? can all go thus?

---

106 it] Q2; It *Q1* | -men,] Q2; ~. *Q1* ‖ 112 Greaue–] ~. *Q1* ‖ 120 contented?] Q2; ~, *Q1* | I,] ~͵
Q1-2 ‖ 123 safty] ~, *Q1-2* ‖ 125 it.] Q2; ~, *Q1* ‖ 126 Wel] Q2; W'el *Q1* ‖ 130 sphere.] Q2; ~,
Q1 ‖ 136 He] *Parrott*; They *Q1-2* | dead.] Q2; ~; *Q1* ‖ 137 Har.] *Harl: Q1 (colon in all
speech-prefixes through l. 224)* | owne.] ~, *Q1-2* ‖ 138 executioner.] Q2; ~: *Q1* | SD *Exeunt ...
Harlay.] Parrott* ‖ 141 Byron.] Q2; ~: *Q1* ‖ 142 Lord.] Q2; ~: *Q1* ‖

And no man come with comfort? farewell world:
He is at no end of his actions blest,
Whose ends will make him greatest, and not best;   145
They tread no ground, but ride in ayre on stormes,
That follow State, and hunt their empty formes;
Who see not that the Valleys of the world,
Make euen right with the Mountains! that they grow
Greene, and lye warmer; and euer peacefull are,   150
When Clowdes spit fire at Hilles, and burne them bare!
Not Valleys part, but we should imitate Streames,
That run below the Valleys, and do yeeld
To euery Mole-hill; euery Banke imbrace
That checks their Currants; and when Torrents come,   155
That swell and raise them past their naturall height,
How madde they are, and trubl'd! like low stremes
With Torrents crownd, are men with Diademes.
    Vit. My Lord tis late; wil't please you to go vp?
    Byr. Vp? tis a faire preferment, ha ha ha!   160
There should go showtes to vp-shots; not a breath
Of any mercy, yet? come, since we must.

[He mounts the scaffold.]

[Enter the Hangman.]

Whose this?
    Pral.   The executioner, my Lord.
    Byr. Death slaue, downe, or by the blood that moues me
Ile plucke thy throat out; goe, Ile call you straight.   165
Hold, boy; and this.

[Casting his handkerchief and doublet to a boy.]
    Hang.   Soft, boy, ile barre you that.

[Seizing the doublet.]
    Byr. Take this then, yet I pray thee that againe. /

*[Casting his hat to the boy and
recovering his handkerchief.]*

I do not ioy in sight of such a Pageant   [R2ᵛ]
As presents death; Though this life haue a cursse;
Tis better then another that is worse.   170

[He blindfolds his own eyes.]
    Bish. My Lord, now you are blinde to this worlds sight,

---

148 the Valleys] *Q1(c), Q2;* they Valleys *Q1(u)* ‖ 149 Mountains!] ~? *Q1* ‖ 151 bare!] ~? *Q1* ‖
157 trubl'd!] ~? *Q1* | stremes] *Shepherd subs.;* straines *Q1-2* ‖ 158 Diademes.] *Q2;* ~; *Q1* ‖ 159
wil't] wilt *Q1-2* ‖ 160 ha!] ~, *Q1-2* ‖ 162 must.] ~; *Q1-2* | SD *He ... scaffold.] Parrott* | SD
Enter the Hangman.] Parrott (after Phelps) ‖ 163 Lord.] ~; *Q1* ‖ 165 straight.] ~, *Q1-2* ‖ 166
Hold, ... this. *Hang.* Soft, ... that.] *in a single line Q1* | Hold, ... this.] ~ˏ ... ~, *Q1* | SD
Casting ... boy.] Parrott | Soft, boy, ... that.] ~ˏ ~ˏ ... ~ˏ *Q1* | SD *Seizing the doublet.]* ‖ 167
thee that againe.] ~, ~ ~ˏ *Q1* | SD *Casting ... handkerchief.]* ‖ 170 another ... worse.] *Q2;* ~,
... ~; *Q1* | SD *He ... eyes.] Parrott* ‖ 171 Bish.] *Parrott;* Arch. *Q1-2* ‖

394

Looke vpward to a world of endles light.
   Byr. I, I, you talke of vpward still to others,
And downwards looke, with headlong eyes your selues.   174
[*To the Hangman.*] Now come you vp sir; But not touch me yet;
Where shall I be now?
   Hang.   Heere my Lord.
   Byr.   Where's that?
   Hang. There, there, my Lord.
   Byr.   And where, slaue, is that there?
Thou seest I see not, yet speakst as I saw;
Well, now is't fit?
   Hang.   Kneele, I beseech your Grace,
That I may do mine office with most order.   180
   Byr. Do it, and if at one blow thou art short,
Giue one and thirty, Ile indure them all.
Hold; stay alittle; comes there yet no mercy?
High Heauen curse these exemplarie proceedings,
When Iustice failes, they sacrifize our example.   185
   Hang. Let me beseech you, I may cut your haire.
   Byr. Out vgly Image of my cruell Iustice;
Yet wilt thou be before me? Stay my will,
Or by the will of Heauen Ile strangle thee!
   Vit. My Lord you make to much of this your body,   190
Which is no more your owne.
   Byr.   Nor is it yours;
Ile take my death, with all the horride rites
And representments, of the dread it merits;
Let tame Nobilitie, and nummed fooles
That apprehend not what they vndergo,   195
Be such exemplarie, and formall sheepe;
I will not haue him touch me, till I will;
If you will needs racke me beyond my reason,
Hell take me, but Ile strangle halfe that's here,
And force the rest to kill me. Ile leape downe /   200
If but once more they tempt me to dispaire;   [R3]
You wish my quiet, yet giue cause of fury:
Thinke you to set rude windes vpon the Sea,
Yet keepe it calme? or cast me in a sleepe,
With shaking of my chaines about myne eares?   205
O honest Soldiers, you haue seene me free,

---

172 light.] *Q2*; ~; *Q1* ‖ 175 SD *To the Hangman.*] *Parrott subs.* ‖ 176 Lord.] *Q2*; ~; *Q1* |
Where's] Wheres *Q1*; Wher's *Q2* ‖ 177 Lord.] *Q2*; ~; *Q1* ‖ 178 not, yet speakst] *Parrott*; ~? ~
I speake *Q1* ‖ 179 is't] ist *Q1*; 'ist *Q2* ‖ 180 order.] *Q2*; ~; *Q1* ‖ 185 example.] *Q2*; ~; *Q1* ‖
186 haire.] *Q2*; ~; *Q1* ‖ 188 me? Stay] ~, stay *Q1-2* ‖ 189 thee!] *Q2*; ~; *Q1* ‖ 191 owne.] *Q2*;
~; *Q1* ‖ 199 that's] *Q2*; thats *Q1* ‖

From any care, of many thousand deathes!
Yet, of this one, the manner doth amaze me.
View, view, this wounded bosome, how much bound
Should that man make me, that would shoote it through;   210
Is it not pitty I should lose my life,
By such a bloody and infamous stroake?
   Soldi. Now by thy spirit, and thy better Angell,
If thou wert cleere, the Continent of *France*,
Would shrinke beneath the burthen of thy death,   215
Ere it would beare it.
   Vit.   Whose that?
   Soldi.   I say well:
And cleere your Iustice, here is no ground shrinks,
If he were cleere it would: And I say more,
Clere, or not cleere, If he with all his foulenesse,
Stood here in one Skale, and the Kings chiefe Mynion,   220
Stood in another, here: Put here a pardon,
Here lay a royall gift; this, this, in merit,
Should hoyse the other Mynion into ayre.
   Vit. Hence with that franticke!
   Byr.   This is some poore witnes
That my desert, might haue out-weighed my forfeyt: 225
But danger, hauntes desert, when he is Greatest;
His hearty ills, are prou'd out of his glaunces,
And Kings suspicions, needes no Ballances;
So her's a most decreetall end of me:
Which I desire, in me, may end my wrongs;   230
Commend my loue, I charge you, to my brothers,
And by my loue, and misery command them,
To keepe their faiths that bind them to the King,
And proue no stomakers of my misfortunes;
Nor come to Court, till time hath eaten out, /   235
The blots, and skarres of my opprobrious death;   [R3ᵛ]
And tell the Earle, my deare friend of *D'Auuergne*,
That my death vtterly were free from griefe,
But for the sad losse of his worthy friendship;
And if I had beene made for longer life,   240
I would haue more deseru'd him in my seruice,
Beseeching him to know I haue not vsde
One word in my arraignement that might touch him,
Had I no other want then so ill meaning:
And so farewell for euer: neuer more   245

---

214 *France*] France *Q1* ‖ 216 it.] ~; *Q1* ‖ 222 gift;] ~, *Q1-2* ‖ 223 ayre.] *Q2*; ~: *Q1* ‖ 224 franticke!] ~: *Q1-2* ‖ 237 *D'Auuergne*] *Q2*; *D'Auergne Q1* ‖ 243 arraignement] ~; *Q1-2* ‖

Shall any hope of my reuiuall see mee;
Such is the endlesse exile of dead men.
Summer succeeds the spring; Autumne the Summer,
The Frosts of Winter, the falne leaues of Autumne:
All these, and all fruites in them yearely fade,   250
And euery yeare returne: but cursed man,
Shall neuer more renew, his vanisht face;
Fall on your knees then, Statists ere yee fall,
That you may rise againe: knees bent too late,
Stick you in earth like statues: see in me   255
How you are powr'd downe from your cleerest heauens;
Fall lower yet: mixt with th'vnmoued center,
That your owne shadowes may no longer mocke yee.
Stricke, stricke, O stricke; flie, flie commanding soule,
And on thy wings for this thy bodies breath,   260
Beare the eternall victory of death.

FINIS.

248 Autumne] *Q2*; *Autumne Q1* ‖ 249 Autumne] *Autumne Q1-2* ‖ 253 knees then,] ~, ~
Q1-2 ‖ 259 Stricke ... soule] *Shepherd*; Stricke ... stricke;/ Flie ... soule *Q1* (*See Textual Note*) ‖

HISTORICAL COLLATION

[Editions collated: Shepherd (*S*, in *The Works of George Chapman: Plays*, 1874, pp. 214-74); Phelps (*Ph*, in *George Chapman*, 1895, pp. 319-479); and Parrott (*P*, in *The Plays and Poems of George Chapman: The Tragedies*, 1910, pp. 149-271). The siglum *Q1* represents the quarto of 1608; *Q2*, that of 1625. *Q(c)* and *Q(u)* represent the corrected and uncorrected states, respectively, of *Q1*. Reference is also made to notes on these plays by K. Deighton (*The Old Dramatists: Conjectural Readings*, 1896, pp. 133-38), J. Brereton ('Notes on the Text of Chapman's Plays,' *MLR*, III, 1907, 60-61), T. M. Parrott ('The Text of Chapman's Conspiracy and Tragedy of Charles Duke of Byron,' *MLR*, IV, 1908, 40-64), and G. Loane ('Notes on Chapman's Plays,' *MLR*, XXXIII, 1938, 251-52; and 'More Notes on Chapman's Plays,' *MLR*, XXXVIII, 1943, 344-45).

Lemmata are taken from the present text; where the lemma represents the reading of the copy-text (Q1), omission of any given siglum indicates that particular edition's agreement with the lemma. Only substantive and semi-substantive variants are recorded. The occurrence of several sigla following a reading indicates an agreement in the substantival point at issue, not necessarily in accidentals. Purposely omitted are the modern editors' choices for handling the *finis* tags at the ends of acts; Shepherd translates these into English, Parrott gives them in Latin, and Phelps omits them altogether.]

Title Page

Black-Friers.] *Blacke-Friers, and other publique Stages. Q2*

Prologue

Prologus.] PROLOGVE. *Q2*
19 *faire shades*] *fierce hates Deighton conj.*

The Conspiracie

I.i

SCAENA I.] SCENA I Paris. *A Room in the Court P*
SD *Enter*] Q2, S, Ph, P; *om.* Q1
22 long] loud *S*
23 Our] *Q1(c)*; Your *Q1(u)*
41 *Franch County*] Franch County *Q1, S, Ph*; French Bounty *Q2*; Franche-Comté *P*

43 *Sauoy*;] *Q1(c)*; ~, *Q1(u)*, S, Ph; ~: P
54 proiection] protection *Q2*
112 my] any *Q2*
115 while] with *Q1-2*, S, Ph, P
116 their] the *Q2*
130 Cowherds] Cowards *Q2*, S, Ph, P
145 Licentiate] Licentiary *Q2*, S, Ph
147 chid] *Q1(c)*; chide *Q1(u)*
148 is] it is *Q2*
149 noblesse] noblenesse *Q2*
154 praises] prayse *Q2*
155 Mock'st *Q1(c)*; Workst *Q1(u)*
163 be] to S, Ph
165 life] *om.* *Q2*
169 Mine] My *Q2*, S, Ph, P
184 farre] faire *Q2*
201 haue] *om.* *Q2*
203 traitrous] traytors *Q2*, S, Ph
206 neighbor,] S, Ph, P; ~ *Q1*; neighbours *Q2*
212 I now make] *Q1(c)*; now made *Q1(u)*, P

I.ii

I.ii] SCENA II *Brussels. A Room in the* Archduke's *Court* P; *om. Q1-2*, S, Ph
13 set] sent *Q2*
14 SD *Stands aside.*] *Retires* P; *om. Q1-2*, S, Ph
21 Steppes] steppe *Q2*
   SD *Picoté with seruants*] P; *om. Q1-2*, S, Ph
38 with] *Q1(c)*; in *Q1(u)*
52 SD *with D'Aumall*] P; D'AUMALE Ph; *Aumall, Q1-2*, S
64 offends] offend *Q2*, S, Ph
66 my] by *Q2*
71 SD *Pycoté*] Picoté *above* P
95 nothing] *Q1(c)*; nothing else *Q1(u)*, *Q2*
98 carue] craue *Q2*
101 you, superiors;] ~ ~, P
127 others] other *Q2*
131 others] other *Q2*
134 forme] *Q1(c)*; fame *Q1(u)*, *Q2*
142 pace on continuate] *Q1(c)*; place on continuall *Q1(u)*, *Q2*
161 noblesse] noblenesse *Q2*
164 SD *Enter ... Albert.*] P; Enter ALBERT. Ph; *om. Q1-2*, S
166 SD *Embracing Byron.*] P; *om. Q1-2*, S, Ph
175 vttermost] vtmost *Q2*, S, Ph
179 your] our *Q2*
181 saies,] ~ *Q2*
183 departure;] S, Ph, P; ~, *Q1-2*
198 SD *Exeunt ... Picoté.*] P; *Exit Bir: Q1-2*, S, Ph

SD *Manent*] *Manet Q1-2, S, Ph, P*
213 SD *Enter Alber: ... Mans: Roiseau: with others.*] *Enter below* Albert ... Mansfield, *with others P*
221 Ile hold] Is held *Q2, S, Ph*
224 SD *Exeunt ... Roiseau.*] *Exeunt P; om. Q1-2, S, Ph*
225 SD *Advancing.*] *P; om. Q1-2, S, Ph*
226 SD *Exit.*] *P; om. Q1-2, S, Ph*

II.i

SCE. I.] SCENA I *A Room in the House of* Nemours *at* Paris *P*
SD *Enter*] *S, Ph, P; om. Q1-2*
4 Of] Or *Q2*
11 guardlike] guardless *P*
16 haue] *om. Q2*
51 seruice] servant *P*
52 SD *cum suis*] *P; om. Q1-2, S, Ph*
68 fleade] flea'd *S, Ph*; flay'd *P*
70 Lord] *Q1(c)*; instrument *Q1(u), Q2, S, Ph, P*
96 SD *Exiturus.*] *S, Ph, P; Exitur. Q1-2*
102 But] By *Q2*
116 eies] *Ph, P;* ~, *Q1-2, S*
122 pallms] plains *P*
133 so] *om. Q2*
142 mine] my *S, Ph, P*
149 Ease] *P;* East *Q1-2, S, Ph*

II.ii

II.ii] SCENA II *A room in the Court P; om. Q1-2, S, Ph*
23 strieke] strike *Q2, S, Ph, P*
47 from] then *Q2*
57 SD *Enter*] *P; om. Q1-2, S, Ph*
58-61 Ile ... him.] *as aside P*
61-64 It ... ambition.] *as aside P*
65 I ... purpose.] *as aside P*
97 was not] not was *Q2*
128 part first] first part *Q2*
139 *Nuis in Burgundy;*] ~: ~ Burgundy˰ *Q1-2, P;* ~, ~ Burgundy, *S, Ph*
141 that was] was that *Q2*
143 yet] yet you *Q2*
149 charge] change *Q2*
172 and] then *Q2*
180 of] all *Q2*
181 this] his *Q2*
182 but with] with but *Deighton conj.*
187 beates] beares *Q2*
190 ouertakes,] ouer-takes˰ *Q2*
216 Mylor'] *P; My Lor. Q1; My Lord Q2; Mylor S, Ph*

221-22 (On ... occasions)] *P*; ͵~ ... ~͵ *Q1-2, S, Ph*
241 SD *Aside.*] *P*; *om. Q1-2, S, Ph*

III.i

SCAENA I.] SCENA I *A Room in* Byron's *House P*
1 SD *Aside.*] *P*; *om. Q1-2, S, Ph*
22 besides,] ~͵ *P*
24 *Byr.*] *Byr. advancing P*
27 vs ... termes] *S, Ph, P*; ~; ... ~, *Q1-2*
34 points] poynt *Q2*
39 of] on *Q2*
44 At] As *Q2*
65 could] would *Q2*
76 of] *Q1(c)*; *om. Q1(u)*
79 valure] value *Q1-2, S, Ph, P*
87 quite] quit *Q2*
   SD *Exeunt.*] *Ph, P*; *Exit. Q1-2, S*

III.ii

III.ii] SCENA II *A Room in the Court P*; *om. Q1-2, S, Ph*
6 sought] fought *S, Ph*
16 their state] *Q1(c)*; they eate *Q1(u)*
23 SD *Embracing him.*] *P*; *om. Q1-2, S, Ph*
42 SD *To Roncas.*] *P*; *om. Q1-2, S, Ph*
44 Y'are,] *S, Ph, P*; ~͵ *Q1-2*
45 SD *To Byron.*] *P*; *om. Q1-2, S, Ph*
52 his] *Q1(c)*; their *Q1(u)*
76-77 him,/ In a detraction] *P*; ~͵/ ~ ~ ~, *Q1-2, S, Ph*
98 strooke] stroke *Q2*
121 purfle] profile *P*
131 it] *Q1(c)*; he *Q1(u)*
152 as] *Q1(c)*; it *Q1(u)*
170 powre] power *Q2*
195 SD *Aside to Byron.*] aside (*following* Lord) *P*; *om. Q1-2, S, Ph*
209 SD *Exit ... Lords;*] *P*; *Exit. Q1-2, S, Ph*
213 sumptures] sumpteres *Q2*
214 torrents. Hence, the King!] *P*; ~, hence. *The King. Q1*; ~, hence. *En.*
   the King. Q2; ~ hence. *Enter the* King. *S, Ph*
224 ferall] *P*; femall *Q1-2, S, Ph*
253 leerd] *Q1(c)*; lernd *Q1(u)*
254 led] let *Q2*
258 last] blast *Deighton conj.*
260 eas'd] caused *Deighton conj.*
284 SD *cum suis*] *P*; & *Sau. Q1-2, S, Ph*
291 fayning] saying *Q2*

III.iii

III.iii] SCENA III *The House of the* Astrologer *P*; *om.* Q1-2, S, Ph
13 imitation] intimation Q2
19 SD *Enter*] *P*; *om.* Q1-2, S, Ph
20 SD *Aside.*] *P*; *om.* Q1-2, S, Ph
29 sproyte] sproote Q2
32-33 them-selues./ In ... proiects,] Ph, P; ~,/ ~ ... ~; Q1-2, S
43 SD *He ... figure.*] *P*; *om.* Q1-2, S, Ph
64 must] may'st S, Ph
72 Shriech] Scriech Q2, S, Ph, P
   SD *Beating La Brosse.*] *P*; *om.* Q1-2, S, Ph
124 then my] *P* (than my); that my Q1-2, S, Ph
145 SD *Exeunt.*] *Exit.* Q1-2, S, Ph, P

IV.i

SCE. I.] SCENA I *A Room in the Court P*
1 *D'Aum.*] Q2, S, Ph, P; *om.* Q1
25 had not] *P*; had Q1-2, S, Ph; not *Brereton conj.*
38 led] let Q2
41 Sheds, ... hardnesse] *P*; ~ ... ~, Q1-2, S, Ph
47 good] blood S, Ph
87 similies] smiles Q2; similes S, Ph, P
112 noblesse, royaltie] noblenesse, royally Q2
113 others] other Q2
161 on] *Q1(c)*; in *Q1(u)*
165 claime] proclaime Q2
178 virtue] *Q1(c)*; victorie *Q1(u)*
183 the] *Q1(c)*; *om. Q1(u)*
186 searches] search Q2, S, Ph, P
196 grounds] *Q1(c)*; ground *Q1(u)*
216 ouerrules] ouer-rule Q2
220 it] *om.* Q2

V.i

SCEN. I] SCENA I *A Room in the Court P*
7 fead] fed Q2
10 stoopings] stopings Q1-2; stoppings S, Ph, P
13 meade] *Brereton conj.*; meate Q1-2, S, Ph, P
68 that] *Q1(c)*; this sute *Q1(u)*
79 enforce] *Q1(c)*; inferre *Q1(u)*
88 lest] *Q1(c)*; best *Q1(u)*
104 distrusted] distrust Q2
136 his kind] this kind Q2
155 SD *Exit ... suis.*] *Exit,* Q1-2, S, Ph, P
156 SD *Exeunt.*] *Ph*; *Exit.* Q1-2, S; *Exit* Byron *followed by* D'Auvergne *P*

V.ii

V.ii] SCENA II *Another Room in the Court* P; *om.* Q1-2, S, Ph
5 idle ... Kings] S, Ph, P; idle ... King *Q1(u)*, Q2; such as he *Q1(c)*
18-19 (For ... lessons)] ˏ~ ... ~, S, Ph; ˏ~ ... ~ˏ P
22 dread] *Deighton conj.*; dead Q1-2, S, Ph, P
23-24 (My ... hills)] P; ˏ~ ... ~, Q1-2, S, Ph
38 SD *Exiturus.*] P; *Exieunt.* Q1; *Exeunt* Q2, Ph; *om.* S
   SD *Enter Henry.*] P; *om.* Q1-2, S, Ph
50-51 competent ... dissention;] P; ~, ... ~, Q1-2; ~; ... ~ˏ S, Ph
54 They] That S, Ph
60 sounds] *Q1(c)*; sound *Q1(u)*
66 without] with Q2
70 vaines] veines Q2
74 space] *Q1(c)*; sphare *Q1(u)*
82 others] *Q1(c)*; other *Q1(u)*
84 not another] an other Q2
110 SD *Enter Sauoy ... Ladies.*] *follows Henry's speech, line 116* P
120 affection?] ~: Q2; ~; S, Ph, P
130 for vs] *om.* Q2
136 the] *Q1(c)*; *om.* *Q1(u)*, S, Ph, P
138 SD *Aside.*] P; *om.* Q1-2, S, Ph
145 curtsies] curtesies Q2
149 there's] there is Q2, S, Ph
153 SD *Aside.*] P; *om.* Q1-2, S, Ph
   then] *om.* Q2
165 SD *Discouering Henry.*] P; *om.* Q1-2, S, Ph
170 SD *To Henry.*] P (*at end of line 169*); *om.* Q1-2, S, Ph
178 treasury] *Q1(c)*; treasure *Q1(u)*, Q2
179-80 In ... Beatrice,/ And ... Infanta.] *Q1(c)*; *order of lines reversed Q1(u)*
198 propos'd] Q2, S, Ph, P; porpos'd *Q1(c)*; purposed *Q1(u)*
248 SD *To Henry.*] *om.* Q1-2, S, Ph, P
252 most absolute] absolut'st Q2

The Tragedie

I.i

SCENA, I.] SCENA I *A Room in the Court* P
SD *Enter*] Q2, S, Ph; *om.* Q1, P
8 then] them Q2
33 Spaniard] Spaniards Q2
74-77 besides, being offer'd ... France,] P; ~ˏ ~ ~, ... ~; Q1-2, S, Ph
101 but an] Q2, S, Ph, P; but in an Q1
120 the] *om.* Q2
123 ouerwacht] overwatch'd S, Ph; ouermacht Q1; ouermatcht Q2; overmatch'd P
124 guiltie [lust], made Noblesse, feed] P; gultie, made Noblesse, feed Q1-2, Ph; guilty mad noblesse, feed S; guilty, mad Noblesse fed *Deighton conj.*
141 cut] S, P; out Q1-2, Ph

149 *Exeunt.*] *Ph, P; om. Q1-2, S*

I.ii

I.ii] SCENA II *At Dijon P; om. Q1-2, S, Ph*
20 his] her *Q2*
38 his] *Loane conj.;* this *Q1-2, S, Ph, P*
45 winde] minde *Deighton conj.*
59 wakens] weakens *Q2*
61 thee ouer] them *Q1-2, S, Ph, P*
67 Cyment] Clyment *Q2*
79 hath] had *Q2*
82 your] my *Q2*
92 sides arm'd,] ~, ~͵ *S, Ph*
104 SD *Exeunt.*] *Exit. Q1-2, S, Ph; Exit* Byron *with the others P*

I.iii

I.iii] SCENA III *A Room in the Court P; om. Q1-2, S, Ph*
SD *Enter*] *om. Q1-2, S, Ph, P*
48 With al] with al *S, Ph, P;* Withal *Q1;* Withall *Q2*
73 most] *S, Ph, P;* must *Q1-2*
  against] 'gainst *Q2*

II.

ACTVS 2.] ACTUS II *A Room in the Court P; om. Q1-2, S, Ph*
SD *to the King.*] *P; om. Q1-2, S, Ph*
12 her] your *S, Ph, P*
27 sweetly] quickly *S*
45 of] off *Q2; S, Ph, P*
65 pray] play *Q2, S;* play; *Ph*
102 the] *om. Q2, S, Ph, P*
105 is seene] seene *Q2, S, Ph*
126-27 and ... will,] *om. Q2*

III.i

SCENA I.] SCENA I *At Dijon P*
SD *Enter Byron. D'Auuer.*] ~ ~. *D'Auer. Q1; Enter the Duke of Byron, D'Auergne. Q2, S; Enter the* Duke *of* BYRON, D'AUVERGNE, BRUN. *Ph*
50 course; ... fortunes] *Loane conj.;* ~͵ ... ~; *Q1-2, S, Ph, P*
57 be, ... selfe,] *S, Ph, P;* ~͵ ... ~; *Q1;* ~͵ ... ~, *Q2*
  SD *Enter La Brunel.*] *P; om. Q1-2, S, Ph*
59 SD *Enter D'escuris.*] *P; follows La Brunel's speech Q1-2, S, Ph*
121 purgatiues.] ~. *Exit* BRUN. *Ph*
127 his] its *Ph*
144 month] *P;* mouth *Q1-2, S, Ph*
160 SD *Exit La Brunel.*] *P; om. Q1-2, S, Ph*
190 staires] starres *Q2*
204 nor] no nor *Q2*
225 SD *Exit Ianin.*] *Q2, S, Ph, P; om. Q1*

234 scruple] scruiples Q2
240-42 doubts ... you,] P; ~, ... ~; Q1-2, S, Ph
247 *Franch*] French Q2
261 SD *Exeunt.*] Ph; *Exit.* Q1-2, S; *Exit* Byron *with the others* P

III.ii

III.ii] SCENA II *A Room in the Court* P; *om.* Q1-2, S, Ph
SD *Enter*] Q2, S, Ph, P
11-14 honor? ... likings?] ~, ... ~, P
29 else, do] ~ ̭ ~; Ph
39 should] shall Q2
44 diswaide] dismay'd P
56 He ... come!] Q2 *subs.*, S, Ph, P; *preceded by speech head* 'Hen.' Q1
    SD *Enter ... others.*] *follows first half of line 56* Q1-2, S, Ph, P
60 Ielouse] Iealousie Q2
81 of] and Q2
86-90 loyalty,/ When ... son?] ~?/ ~ ... ~. Q1-2; ~?/ ~ ... ~, S, Ph; ~,/
    ~, ... ~, P
90 the] a Q2
92 treason.] Q2, S, Ph; ~; Q1; ~? P
107 must then] then must Q2
111 expedition] exhebition Q2
116 as perfect] a perfect Q2
128 SD *To Espernon.*] P; *om.* Q1-2, S, Ph

IV.i

SCEN. I.] SCENA I *A Room in the Court* P
SD *Enter Byron*] *Byron* Q1, P; *Enter the Duke of Byron* Q2, S, Ph
2 meane] meant Q2
3 then] Q2, S, Ph, P; *om.* Q1
31 diuerted] deliuered Q2
33 must] most Q2
46 most] *om.* Q2
61 Or] *om.* S
66 fare you wel.] farwel Q2
82 kept] keepe Q2
84 Brake] Barke Q2
90 I,] *om.* Q2
    SD *Exit ... Vidame.*] P; *Exit.* Q1-2, S; *Exit, with* CHANCELLOR, *etc.* Ph
100 SD *He ... letter.*] *showing the letter* P (*at beginning of line*); *om.* Q1-2,
    S, Ph
101 wills] will S, Ph
153 SD *Exeunt.*] Ph, P; *om.* Q1-2, S

IV.ii

IV.ii] SCENA II *Another Room in the Court* P; *om.* Q1-2, S, Ph
3 of] off Q2

15 Marshall too] *Brereton conj.*; Marshall *Q1-2, P*; Marechal, *S, Ph*
25 what] that *Q2, P*
41 knowe, my powre] ~; ~ ~, *Q1*; ~ˌ ~ ~ˌ *Q2, P*; ~ˌ ~ ~, *S, Ph*
56 place.] ~, *Q1-2, S, Ph, P*
59 you] then *Q2*
61 on] *om. Q2*
62 SD *all but Henry*] *P; om. Q1-2, S, Ph*
85 SD *Esp: with*] *Ph*; *Esp: Q1-2, S, P*
   SD *Montigny,*] *Ph, P; om. Q1-2, S*
86 Heere] *Q2, P*; *Hen:* Heere *Q1, S, Ph*
89 winges] winge *Q2, S*
91 SD *Aside to Byron.*] *P; om. Q1-2, S, Ph*
   SD *Exit.*] *Exit* D'AUVERGNE. *Ph, P; om. Q1-2, S*
97 thankles.] thankless. Byron, *The* Queen, Epernon *and* Montigny *play at cards P*
107 SD *Aside.*] *P; om. Q1-2, S, Ph*
109 *Chan.*] *Chan. To the* Queen *P*
110 morallitie] *S, Ph*; mortallitie *Q1-2, P*
119 the] that *Q2*
124 as] as be *Q2*
130 to] *om. Q2*
134 his] it *S, Ph*
163 SD *Aside to Montigny.*] *P; om. Q1-2, S, Ph*
175 blacke] back *Loane conj.*
177 one] *S, Ph, P*; on *Q1-2*
183 is] *S, Ph, P*; in *Q1-2*
184 an] and *Q2*
194 mistery] *S, Ph, P*; misery *Q1-2*
202 SD *Exeunt ... Byron.*] *P (in line 201 following* roome); *om. Q1-2, S, Ph*
227 Aske] As *Q2*
239 SD *To Vitry.*] *P; om. Q1-2, S, Ph*
256 with] *S, P*; wich is *Q1-2, Ph*
258 of] or *Q2*
263 but] *om. Q1-2, S, Ph, P*
272 others] other *S, Ph*
273 A property] Properties *Q2*
286 And] So *Q2, S, Ph*
290 SD *Exit Byron guarded.*] *P; om. Q1-2, S, Ph*
295 SD *Enter*] *Q2, S, Ph, P; om. Q1*
302 SD *guarded*] *P; om. Q1-2, S, Ph*
307 that] *Deighton conj., P*; it *Q1-2, S, Ph*
308 aduerse] aduise *Q2*
309 Then] *Loane conj.* (Than); Thine *Q1-2, S, Ph, P*
   is] *Q2, S, Ph, P*; his *Q1*
310 That] As *Q2*
311 That] As *Q2*
   SD *Exeunt.*] *Q2, S, Ph, P; om. Q1*

V.i

SCÆNA. 1.] SCENA I *The Council Chamber P*
SD *Enter*] *P; om. Q1-2, S, Ph*
2 That] Which *Q2*
9 And] For *Q2, S, Ph*
11 Tis] It is *Q2*
12 as] at *Q2*
15 That] How *Q2, S, Ph, P*
38 Till] Vntill *Q2*
60 counsailes,] *Q2, S, Ph, P;* ~ *Q1*
68 Take] Haue *Q2*
70 lothes] hates *Q2*
SD *Exit cum suis.*] *Exit the* Ambassador *P; om. Q1-2, S, Ph*
71 *Hen.*] Hen. [*To* Janin] *P; om. Q1-2, S, Ph*
76 That] How *Q2*
82 feared] sacred *Q2, S, Ph, P*
88 impartiall] imperiall *Q2, Ph*
91 Duke] Duke of *Q2, S, Ph*
92 it] *om. Q2*
93 'Tis] It is *Q2*
99 slack] make slack *Q2, S, Ph*
102 merry] many *Q2*
112 lest] *P* (least); best *Q1-2, S, Ph*
114 That] As *Q2*
115 lest] *P* (least); best *Q1-2, S, Ph*
116 That] So *Q2*
117 load:] ~, *S, Ph*
118 Byrde] Bryde *Q2*
119 vnwares] vnawares *Q2, S, Ph*
122 out] it *Deighton conj.*
143 Casts] Cast *Q1-2, S, Ph, P*

V.ii

V.ii] SCENA II *The Golden Chamber in the Palace of Justice P; om. Q1-2, S, Ph*
5 of] off *Q2, S, Ph, P*
20 Till] Vntil *Q2*
Har.] *Q2, S, Ph, P;* Hen. *Q1*
60 The fourth is;] Fourthly, *Q2*
76 treaties] treaty *Q2, S, Ph*
87 for] from *Q2*
117 then] *om. Q2*
122 you] you then *Q2*
I know] *om. Q2*
151 of] off *Q2, S, Ph, P*
154 laie] laid *Q1-2, S, Ph, P*
169 That] Which *Q2*
172 simply ... treason,] simple ... reason, *Q2*
176 they are] th'are *Q2*

180 Nor] Not *Q2*
188 Tis] It is *Q2*
191 vrge] urges *Ph*
194 sound] found *S, Ph*
196 Lord intelligencer? hangman-like,] lord, ~! ~-~? *P*
197 desarts] desert *S, Ph*
201 I haue] haue I *Q2, S, Ph*
202 opposition] ~; *Q1-2*; ~? *S, Ph*; ~, *P*
203-6 (My ... comfort)] ‸~ ... ~; *Q1-2, S, Ph, P*
203 My] Mine *Q2*
206 Lords).] ~)‸ *Q1-2*; ~, *S, Ph, P*
216-17 attend ... imitation.] *Brereton conj., P*; ~. ... ~, *Q1, S, Ph*; ~, ...
    ~, *Q2*
231 though] *S; om. Q1-2, Ph, P*
236 and] *om. Q2*
244 their] *P*; the *Q1-2, S, Ph*
249 *Rome?*] ~, *Q1-2, S, Ph*; ~. *P*
251 life,] *P*; ~; *Q1-2, S, Ph*
258 Saturnales] Saturnals *Q1-2, S, Ph, P*; Saturnalians *Deighton conj.*
262 sauer] sauor *Q2*
274 SD *Exeunt*] *Exit Q1-2, S, Ph, P*
291 furies] *Q1(c)*; friends *Q1(u)*

V.iii

V.iii] SCENA III Byron's *Cell in the Bastile P; om. Q1-2, S, Ph*
1 *Vid.*] *S, Ph, P; Vit. Q1-2*
14 my] *om. Q2*
23 part?] *S, Ph, P*; part? *Enter Soiss: Esp: Q1-2 (in line 22 in Q2)*
27 Lords] lord *S, Ph, P*
28 Though] Although *Deighton conj.*
43 chang'd] *S, Ph, P*; hang'd *Q1-2*
66 englazd] *P*; engazd *Q1-2, S, Ph*
73 SD *Within.*] *Q2, S, Ph, P; om. Q1*
77 you] *om. Q1-2, S, Ph, P*
78 your selues] you selfe *Q2*
83 SD *Vshers bare,*] ~, ~‸ *S*
    SD *Vit:*] *om. Q2*
91 right a] a right *Q2, S, Ph*
129 blowne] blow *Q2*
130 SD *To Fleury.*] *P; om. Q1-2, S, Ph*
134-35 he is ... giuen) that] ~ ~) ... ~, and *Q2*
137 restraines] *Q2, S, Ph, P*; restaines *Q1*
154 his vices, not for] *P*; his vices, nor for *Q1*; their vices, not for *Q2, Ph*;
    their vices, not *S*
158 motion] *P*; ~; *Q1-2, S, Ph*
181 but] *S, Ph, P*; put *Q1-2*
184 SD *Exit Byron.*] *P; om. Q1-2, S, Ph*
188 SD *Chancellor ... Vitry*] *om. Q1-2, S, Ph, P*

SD *Manent*] *Manet* S, Ph
198 At] As Q2
210 guilded] guided Q2
217 t'endure] *Loane conj.*; render Q1-2, S, Ph; under *Deighton conj.*, P
231 of] off Q2, S, Ph, P
239 no] *Loane conj.*; now Q1-2, S, Ph, P
240 SD *Exeunt*] P; *om.* Q1-2, S, Ph

V.iv

V.iv.] SCENA IV *The Courtyard of the Bastile. A Scaffold* P; *om.* Q1-2, S, Ph
SD *Vitry, Pralin, D'Escuris.*] *Vitry.* Q1-2, S; *Vitry, Pralin* Ph, P
2-4 prisoners, . . . executioner? He] P; ~? . . . ~; he Q1-2, S, Ph
23 Bish.] P; *Arch.* Q1-2, S, Ph
39 say] *Deighton conj.*; sayd Q1-2, S, Ph, P
45 being a large Globe, and a little earth] P; bring a long Globe, and a little earth Q1-2, S, Ph; being a blown globe of a little breath *Deighton conj.*; being a lone Globe, and a little earth *Brereton conj.*
58 *Vit.* . . . city.] P; *om.* Q1-2, S, Ph
71 minde] *Deighton conj.*, P; winde Q1-2, S, Ph
77 yee] you Q2
86 *Har.*] *Har. [reads the sentence]* P (*not hereafter recorded*)
88-89 depositions . . . deposition] dispositions . . . disposition Q2
94 is] *om.* Q2
100 treason in a] treason, a P
136 He] P; They Q1-2, S, Ph
137 her] his Q2
138 SD *Exeunt* . . . *Harlay.*] P; *om.* Q1-2, S, Ph
148 the Valleys] Q1(c); they Valleys Q1(u)
149 the] *om.* Q2, S
157 stremes] streams S, Ph, P; straines Q1-2
162 SD *He . . . scaffold.*] P; *om.* Q1-2, S, Ph
SD *Enter the Hangman.*] P; *The* HANGMAN *enters.* Ph; *om.* Q1-2, S
166 SD *Casting . . . boy.*] P; *om.* Q1-2, S, Ph
SD *Seizing the doublet.*] *om.* Q1-2, S, P; *Blindfolds him.* Ph
167 SD *Casting . . . handkerchief.*] *om.* Q1-2, S, Ph, P
170 SD *He . . . eyes.*] P; *om.* Q1-2, S, Ph
171 Bish.] P; *Arch:* Q1-2, S, Ph
175 SD *To the Hangman.*] *To the* Executioner P; *om.* Q1-2, S, Ph
178 not, yet speakst] P; not? yet I speake Q1, S, Ph; not, yet I speake Q2
200 kill] *om.* Q2
206 Soldiers,] soldiers, *To the* Guard P; *om.* Q1-2, S, Ph
221 another, here] another place P
227 hearty] hearts Q2

PRESS VARIANTS IN Q1

The Conspiracie

[Copies collated: BL[1] (British Library C.30.e.2), BL[2] (C.12.g.5 [3]), Bodl (Bodleian Library), CLUC (Wm. Andrews Clark Memorial Library, University of California, Los Angeles), CSmH (Huntington Library), CtY[1] (Elizabethan Club, Yale University), CtY[2] (Beinecke Rare Book and Manuscript Library, Yale University), DFo (Folger Shakespeare Library), Dyce (Victoria and Albert Museum), IU[1] (University of Illinois Library, *Consp.* and *Trag.*), IU[2] (*Consp.* only), MB (Boston Public Library), MH (Houghton Library, Harvard University), MWiWC (Chapin Library, Williams College), PU (University of Pennsylvania Library), TxU[1] (University of Texas Library, Ah C366 B652; wants leaves A1-2, B1, B4, and H2; B2-3 and L1-2 defective), TxU[2] (Wh C366 608c), TxU[3] (Ah C366 608ca), TxU[4] (Ah C366 608c; *Consp.* only; lacks leaf A1), Worc[1] (Library of Worcester College, Oxford; wants leaves A1-2; R1-3 defective), Worc[2] (*Consp.* only).]

Sheet B (inner forme)

Corrected: BL[2], Bodl, CLUC, CSmH, CtY[1], CtY[2], Dyce, IU[1], IU[2], MB, MH, MWiWC, PU, Txu[1], TxU[3], TxU[4], Worc[1], Worc[2] [defective, wants all but items in I.i.43 and 212 below]
Uncorrected: BL[1], DFo, TxU[2]
Sig. B1[v]
  I.i.35 him;] him,
    43 *Sauoy*;] *Sauoy,*
Sig. B2[r]
  I.i.73 errour;] errour,
Sig. B3[v]
  I.i.180 Swette] Sweat
    212 I now make] now made
Sig. B4[r]
  I.ii.16 Spirites;] Spirites,

Sheet B (outer forme)

Corrected: BL[1], BL[2], Bodl, CSmH, CtY[2], DFo, Dyce, IU[1], IU[2], MB, MH, MWiWC, TxU[1] [defective, wants all but items in I.i.155 and 156 below], TxU[3], TxU[4], Worc[1], Worc[2]
Uncorrected: CLUC, CtY[1], PU, TxU[2]

Sig. B1[r]
  I.i.21 shal ... Cannans] shall ... Canons
    23 Our] Your
Sig. B3[r]
  I.i.147 chid mee] chide me
    155 Mock'st al ... poisonst;] Workst all ... poisonst,
    156 vertue;] vertue,
Sig. B4[v]
  I.ii.34 Cannan] Cannon
    38 with] in

Sheet C (inner forme)

Corrected: BL[1], BL[2], Bodl, CLUC, CSmH, CtY[1], CtY[2], DFo, Dyce, IU[1],
      IU[2], MB, MH, MWiWC, PU, TxU[1], TxU[2], TxU[3], Worc[2]
Uncorrected: TxU[4], Worc[1]
Sig. C1[v]
  I.ii.95 nothing] nothing else
Sig. C2[r]
  I.ii.134 forme:] fame,
    142 pace on continuate] place on continuall
    165 *Alb.*] *Alb*
Sig. C3[v]
  II.i.2 *Laffin,*] *Laffin*
    14 sweare,] sweare
Sig. C4[r]
  II.i.61 humane] humaine
    70 Lord] instrument

Sheet C (outer forme)

First State Corrected: DFo, IU[1], IU[2], MB, MWiWC, TxU[1], TxU[3], TxU[4],
      Worc[1]
Uncorrected: BL[1], Bodl, CLUC, CSmH, CtY[1], CtY[2], Dyce, MH, PU,
      TxU[2], Worc[2]
Sig. C4[v]
  (catchword) To] TO
Second State Corrected: BL[2]
Sig. C3[r]
  I.ii.209 gold;] gold,

Sheet D (outer forme)

Corrected: BL[1], BL[2], Bodl, CSmH, CtY[2], IU[1], IU[2], MH, MWiWC, TxU[2],
      TxU[4], Worc[2]
Uncorrected: CLUC, CtY[1], DFo, Dyce, MB, PU, TxU[1], TxU[3], Worc[1]
Sig. D4[v]
  II.ii.190 fomy] famy
    211 *Sau.*] *San.*

Sheet E (inner forme)

Corrected: BL¹, BL², Bodl, CLUC, CtY¹, CtY², DFo, Dyce, IU¹, IU², MB,
MH, MWiWC, PU, TxU¹, TxU², TxU³, TxU⁴, Worc²

Uncorrected: CSmH, Worc¹

Sig. E2ʳ

III.i.76 of] *om*.

Sig. E4ʳ

III.ii.131 it] he

Sheet E (outer forme)

Corrected: BL¹, BL², Bodl, CLUC, CtY¹, CtY², DFo, Dyce, IU¹, IU², MH,
MWiWC, PU, TxU¹, TxU², TxU⁴, Worc²

Uncorrected: CSmH, MB, TxU³, Worc¹

Sig. E1ʳ

III.i.4 (Which ... prosecute)] Which ... prosecute

Sig. E2ᵛ

III.ii.16 their state] they eate

Sig. E3ʳ

III.ii.30 you;] you,
   35 heighnesse;] heighnesse
   52 his] their
   54 deseruings.'] deseruings,

Sig. E4ᵛ

III.ii.152 as shal] it shall

Sheet F (inner forme)

First State Corrected: TxU²

Uncorrected: CLUC, CtY¹, PU

Sig. F2ʳ

III.ii.253 leerd] lernd
   254 rule;] rule,
   261 merit,] merit:
   262 expires:] expires,
   269 noises;] noises,
   272 euer;] euer,

Sig. F4ʳ

III.iii.89 *Colchos*] *Calchos*

Second State Corrected: BL¹, BL², Bodl, CSmH, CtY², DFo, Dyce, IU¹,
IU², MB, MH, MWiWC, TxU¹, TxU³, TxU⁴,
Worc¹, Worc²

Sig. F1ᵛ

III.ii.218 houses;] houses,
   219 mid-night;] mid-night,

Sheet G (outer forme)

Corrected: BL¹, BL², Bodl, CLUC, CtY¹, CtY², DFo, Dyce, IU¹, IU², MH,
MWiWC, PU, TxU¹, TxU², TxU⁴, Worc²

Uncorrected: CSmH, MB, TxU³, Worc¹
Sig. G2ᵛ
  IV.i.137 excellence:] excellence,
      153 thunder:] thunder,
Sig. G3ʳ
  IV.i.161 on] in
      178 virtue] victorie
      179 fortune:] fortune,
      183 the] *om.*
      196 grounds] ground,
Sig. G4ᵛ
  V.i.68 that] this sute

Sheet H (inner forme)

Corrected: BL¹, CLUC, CSmH, CtY¹, CtY², DFo, Dyce, IU², MB, MH,
      MWiWC, PU, TxU¹ [defective, wants item in V.ii.5 below],
      TxU³, Worc¹
Uncorrected: BL², Bodl, IU¹, TxU², TxU⁴, Worc²
Sig. H2ʳ
  V.ii.5 such as he] idle and riduculus King
Sig. H4ʳ
  V.ii.136 the] *om.*
      154 gae] age

Sheet H (outer forme)

Corrected: BL¹, BL², Bodl, CSmH, CtY², DFo, Dyce, IU¹, IU², MB, MH,
      MWiWC, TxU¹, TxU², TxU³, TxU⁴, Worc¹, Worc²
Uncorrected: CLUC, CtY¹, PU
Sig. H1ʳ
  V.i.79 enforce ... self] inferre ... selfe
      88 lest ... diminitiue] best ... dininitiue
Sig. H3ʳ
  V.ii.59 refrains] refaine
      60 sounds] sound
      62 selfe,] selfe:
      74 space] sphare
      75 sences)] sences,
      82 others] other
Sig. H4ᵛ
  V.ii.167 hop't] hapt
      178 treasury] treasure
      179-80 In ... Beatrice./ And ... Infanta.] And ... Infanta./ In ... Beatrice.
      180 th'] the'
      183 matter] mattr
      197 composition] compsition
      198 porpos'd] purposed

Sheet I (inner forme)

Corrected: BL¹, BL², Bodl, CSmH, CtY¹, CtY², DFo, Dyce, IU¹, IU², MB,
        MH, MWiWC, PU, TxU¹, TxU², TxU³, TxU⁴, Worc¹, Worc²
Uncorrected: CLUC
Sig. I1ᵛ
    V.ii.242 stolne it] stolneit
        243 disease] diseas e
        246 *France.*] *France .*
        247 wethers] weᵗhers
        249 Rimers] Rim ers

The Tragedie

[Copies collated: same as those for *The Conspiracie* with the exception of IU²,
TxU⁴, and Worc², which want *The Tragedie*]

Sheet M (inner forme)

Corrected: BL², Bodl, CLUC, CSmH, CtY¹, DFo, Dyce, IU¹, MB, MH,
        PU, TxU¹, TxU², TxU³, Worc¹
Uncorrected: BL¹, CtY², MWiWC
Sig. M3ᵛ
    IV.i.13 and lye] andlye

Sheet N (outer forme)

Corrected: BL¹, BL², Bodl, CLUC, CSmH, CtY¹, CtY², DFo, Dyce, IU¹,
        MB, MH, MWiWC, TxU¹, TxU², TxU³, Worc¹
Uncorrected: PU
Sig. N3ʳ
    IV.ii.85 SD *Queene:*] *Queene:*ʳ
            another] anothe

Sheet O (outer forme)

First State Corrected: MWiWC
Uncorrected: CtY²
Sig. O1ʳ
    IV.ii.213 ouerchargd] ouerchragd
        214 beseech] besech
        219 vtterd.] vtterd,
        225 night] might
Sig. O2ᵛ
    IV.ii.302 lead; ile] lead ile;
Sig. O3ʳ
    V.i.26 Lord] Lord of
        33 continuance] continnuance
        43 *Fuentes]* *Fluentes*
        55 expectance] epectance

Sig. O4ᵛ
  V.ii.SD *Desɔures*] *Deesɔures*
    4 now] new
    20 pleasures] plesures
  Second State Corrected: BL¹, BL², Bodl, CLUC, CSmH, CtY¹, DFo, Dyce,
                             IU¹, MB, MH, PU, TxU¹, TxU², TxU³, Worc¹
Sig. O1ʳ
  IV.ii.209 safe.] safe,
      218 Action] Acton
Sig. O4ᵛ
  V.ii.SD *Descures*] *Desɔures*
    9 *Rhosny*] *Rhosuy*
[When the first-state corrections were made in this forme, type was disturbed
in the top two lines of sig. O3ʳ. The resulting irregularity, evident in MWiWC,
was set right when the second-state corrections were made.]

Sheet P (outer forme)

First State Corrected: Bodl
Uncorrected: MH
Sig. P4ᵛ
  V.ii.291 furies] friends
  Second State Corrected: BL¹, BL², CLUC, CSmH, CtY¹, CtY², DFo, Dyce,
                             IU¹, MB, MWiWC, PU, TxU¹, TxU², TxU³, Worc¹
Sig. P2ᵛ
  V.ii.140 subiect;] subiect,
      141 (as the Ile that of] as the Ile that (of
Sig. P3ʳ
  V.ii.164 *O wicked King*] O wicked King
Sig. P4ᵛ
  V.ii.281 thought.] thought,
      283 accuser;] accuser;

Sheet R (inner forme)

First State Corrected: BL²
Uncorrected: MB
Sig. R1ᵛ
  V.iv.115 drawne,] drawne,
  Second State Corrected: BL¹, Bodl, CLUC, CSmH, CtY¹, CtY², DFo,
                             Dyce, IU¹, MH, MWiWC, PU, TxU¹, TxU²,
                             TxU³, Worc¹
Sig. R2ʳ
  V.iv.148 the Valleys] they Valleys

TEXTUAL NOTES

The Conspiracie

I.i

115 while] The 'with' of the quartos illogically makes the 'forced truth' sworn to the King the means by which the dishonest courtiers rob the King's subjects. The emendation makes the swearing of fealty and robbing of subjects occur simultaneously, a hypocritical situation which understandably angers Henry. The word 'truth' should perhaps be emended to 'troth'; but the *NED* does attest the use of 'truth' in the seventeenth century to mean 'faith, trust, confidence.'

130 Cowherds] The word should not, in modern-spelling editions, without some thought be emended to Q2's 'Cowards', for which it is admittedly a legitimate spelling variant. 'Cowherds' can plausibly be taken as denoting keepers of cattle, to be contrasted in their lowly security with adventuresome military captains. Byron employs this contrast in *The Tragedie*, IV.i.1-10.

I.ii

78 whose] There is some temptation to emend to 'whom', the objective case making somewhat better sense than the possessive. But 'whose' can be understood as referring back to 'th'intention' of 'his highnesse', to which intention Byron is willing to become a 'seruant'.

101 you, superiors;] Parrott punctuates so as to make the phrase a direct address to superior persons. But the quarto pointing can be understood as producing the sense 'You do not suffer any superiors', thus paralleling but contrasting with the sense of the preceding statement, 'No true powre .../ ... suffers any fellow/ Ioynde in his subiect; ...'

II.i

11 guardlike] If emendation were to be required, 'godlike' would be a more likely possibility than Parrott's 'guardless'. But the *NED* gives 'a posture of defense' as one sense of 'guard' current in Chapman's time; the phrase 'guardlike strength' would thus mean 'a strong posture of defense'.

122 pallms] Parrott takes this word in Q1 'to be a misprint for *plains*', which Q2 has 'still further distorted' to 'palms'. But the metaphor intended, I think, is the homely one of the sweating palms of the hands.

157 stript] C. E. Norton, in the copy of Q1 now in the Norton Collection at the Houghton Library, emended the word to 'tript'; but as a note at this

place in the Folger copy indicates, 'stript' equals 'outstripped,' a sense current in Chapman's time.

II.ii

23 strieke] All editions subsequent to Q1 emend to 'strike'. The word is rather a variant spelling of 'streak,' a word which both makes sound sense here and rhymes with 'cheeke' in the next line.

139 *Nuis in Burgundy*] That '*in Burgundy*' modifies '*Nuis*' instead of 'chast' is obvious from Chapman's source for this passage in Grimeston: ' ... the Marshall of *Biron* hauing taken *Beaune* in view of this great armie of the Constable of *Castille*, *Autun* & *Nuys* in *Bourgongne*, hee puts himselfe into *Dijon* ...' (p. 781C).

III.i

60 truth-pure] The tautology in lines 60-61 makes me suspect that 'truth pure' in Q1 is not correct, that the compositor's eye caught 'truth' in either the preceding or following line of his copy and that he substituted it unconsciously in line 60 for some other monosyllable. But I would not venture to guess, out of a myriad of possibilities, what the correct word is.

79 valure] The reading 'value' of Q1 is certainly not impossible. But 'valure' is a common spelling of 'valor' in Chapman's work, and 'some enterprise of valure' would appropriately be what Laffin is ascribing to the vainglorious Byron.

III.ii

121 purfle] Parrott emends to 'profile' on the ground that 'purfle' means, inappropriately, 'a decorated, or embroidered border.' But it also means, or meant (according to the *NED*) 'the contour or outline of anything' and was at the beginning of the seventeenth century 'a new adoption from Fr. ... Soon superseded by *profile*.'

145 Others,] The comma appears, faintly, in some but not all copies in which the outer forme of sheet E is in the corrected state. Though it may represent a genuine stop-press correction in that forme, I am not sufficiently certain of that to include it in the register of press variants. The defective type sort that produced it seems to have been used again in IV.i.154 of *The Conspiracie* (sig. G2ᵛ).

IV.i

25 not] As Parrott points out, a negative lacking in Q1 is necessary in this sentence, and I have adopted the 'not' he inserts before 'thought'. Admittedly, '*we'd* not thought' would be more satisfactory metrically, but Chapman was not scrupulous about superfluous unaccented syllables. And 'we'd not' would have been less likely to be misread as 'we had' than would 'we had not'. It may be, of course, that a question is involved: 'who had thought ...?'

106 He ... Souldier,] Lowell reordered this line in order to place 'no Orator' adjacent to 'More then this ayre' in the following line, to which it is logically

related; thus Lowell's reading, 'He said he was a soldier, "but no orator,/ More than this air ... hath made me. ..."'

216 ouerrules] As to whether Q1's 'ouerrules' or Q2's 'ouer-rule' is correct, Parrott was of contradictory opinions. In his general notes on *The Conspiracie* he paraphrases the line as 'Whom the stars direct and govern,' which implies that the plural verb is required; but in his Text Notes he opts for the singular when he says of Q2's emendation, 'This change may have been made to make the verb agree with its supposed subject *starres*; but the true subject is *whom*, attracted into the objective to agree with its antecedent.' I concur in this reasoning and, as Parrott does in his text, maintain Q1's 'ouerrules'.

V.i

10 stoopings] This reading can be found in an anonymous article on Chapman's tragedies in *The Retrospective Review*, IV (1821), 371, in Norton's annotated copy, and in Lowell's unpublished edition. But all later editors of the play have taken Q1's 'stopings' to mean 'stoppings.' It seems obvious that the 'stoopings' of the horse's head 'twixt his forelegs' are what Chapman intended.

13 meade] I accept Brereton's conjecture in place of Q1's 'meate'. Parrott's proposal of the meaning 'meal' or 'repast' does little to justify the retention of 'meate'.

V.ii

18-19 (For ... lessons)] It is essential that the round brackets of Q1 be preserved here in this complicated sentence to make clear that the subject of 'shew' is not 'fashions' but 'that' (line 13): 'He that can warme ... Hunt ... nothing feele, ... but ... shew ... – Who would not wish him rather hewd to nothing ...?' The parenthetic phrase modifies 'shew', 'for' having the sense of 'despite'.

22 dread] Parrott rejects this conjecture of Deighton (which also occurs as a manuscript emendation in the Norton copy) as being 'rather tame'. He takes 'dead' to mean 'past,' 'extinct,' or (perhaps) 'deadly.' There seems to me to be no justification whatever for the last of these; and what is explicitly past or extinct would scarcely need to be drowned.

23-24 (My ... hills)] Lowell placed these two lines immediately after line 21, thus making 'blowes' parallel to 'seruices', both of them things being 'slighted' by the King.

154 age] There is no question that 'age' occurs in the uncorrected state of the forme, 'gae' in the corrected. The type here was apparently dislocated in the process of making corrections elsewhere in the forme and then reset erroneously.

198 propos'd] The press correction 'porpos'd' in Q1 is itself an error for 'propos'd'. According to Grimeston, the Duke of Savoy presented Henry with 'his first proposition of the Empire and Duchie of *Millan*' (p. 900F), the latter a 'dessein' (p. 901B) involving war between France and Spain. 'propos'd ... my designe' means 'proposed a scheme for me'.

The Tragedie

I.i

123 ouerwacht] Shepherd was right, I am confident, in emending 'ouermacht' to 'overwatch'd'. According to the *NED* 'overwatch' means 'To fatigue or wear out with excessive watching; to weary or exhaust by keeping awake or by want of sleep.' Shakespeare uses the word several times in these senses.

124 lust] Parrott's emendation strikes me as the best of a number that have been suggested for this troublesome line. It is interesting that Deighton's conjectural reading 'When guilty, mad Noblesse fed on Noblesse' was anticipated by Charles Lamb in *Specimens of English Dramatic Poets* (1808), by the author of the article on Chapman's tragedies in *The Retrospective Review*, IV (1821), 373, and by Lowell in his unpublished edition.

I.ii

38 his] The seventeenth-century hand whose jottings fill the margins of the 'Earl of Pembroke's' copy of Q2 (British Library, C.45.b.9) emended 'this' to 'his', which Parrott terms a 'rather plausible suggestion' but does not incorporate in his text. I adopt the emendation, because the demonstrative 'this' of Q1 has no proper antecedent.

61 thee ouer] This manuscript emendation of 'them' in the Norton copy repairs both the sense and the meter. There is a redundancy in the version of Q1 and all later editions: 'It is for these parts, that the Spanish King/ Hath sworne to winne them [i.e. these parts] to his side.'

I.iii

53 Descures] The name 'D'Escures' receives a variety of spellings in the quartos. In the speech headings I have silently reduced all forms to 'D'Esc.'; in the text and stage directions I have allowed the variant spellings to stand.

II.

ACTVS 2.] What constitutes the present second act of *The Tragedie* is, as was indicated in the Textual Introduction, a portion of the material Chapman interpolated into the completed play. To make room for it, he combined the original fourth and fifth acts into a new fifth act and redesignated the original second the new third act and the original third the new fourth act. The interpolated material included the infamous altercation between Henry's queen and his mistress and the masque celebrating the ladies' reconciliation, but only the masque was allowed to see print. One possibility for the present edition would have been to restore the pristine form of the play and to print the masque scene as an appendix. But all in all it seemed best to maintain the structure of *The Tragedie* as Chapman saw it into print in 1608 and as every succeeding edition has presented it.

65 pray] The second letter of 'pray' became sufficiently deformed in the printing of Q1 that in some copies the word looks like 'play'. Thus Shepherd's reading, adopted by Phelps.

88-123 What's that ... and so] Lowell omitted the whole of the riddle sequence, presumably because of its salacious overtones.

III.ii

56 He ... come!] In Q1 'He will not come?' is assigned to '*Hen.*'; in all later editions the speech-prefix is omitted and the words made part of Henry's long speech immediately preceding. Perhaps the Q1 compositor mistakenly omitted a speech lying between the long one and this exclamation of Henry's; less likely would be that he misread copy and assigned the exclamation to the wrong speaker. In the absence of evidence on the point, I feel obliged to accept Q2's solution.

129 Ile .... . eare.] In the Norton copy of Q1 a manuscript 'here' has been inserted after 'friend'. The meter would profit from some such monosyllabic interpolation, but 'here' rhymes too grossly with 'eare' to make me willing to lay it to Chapman's charge.

IV.i

16 lead] This is a variant spelling of the past tense 'led,' as 'fead' (*Consp.* V.i.7) is of 'fed.'

IV.ii

15 too] To provide the extra syllable necessary in the quarto version of this line, Shepherd and Phelps print 'Marechal' for 'Marshall'; and Parrott says in a note that 'Marshall' must be 'pronounced here as a word of three syllables.' I believe that the 'too' Brereton would interpolate was indeed in Chapman's manuscript, it being the equivalent of the 'also' in the source for this passage in Grimeston: '... as I played the Souldiar to saue him, I also plaid the Marshall to make the Retreat ...' (p. 970C).

25 what] Parrott thinks the 'that' of Q2 a 'better reading' than the 'what' of Q1, but there is no reason to suppose that Chapman did not write the latter.

56 place.] All previous editions punctuate in such a fashion as to make 'respect and reuerence' appear to be the subject of 'is' in line 59. The actual subject of that verb, I am sure, is 'More then is needful' in line 57. Line 56 constitutes a prepositional phrase modifying 'tis best' in line 54.

110 morallitie] Parrott was tempted by the 'morality' of Shepherd, Phelps, and Deighton, but retained in his text Q1's 'mortallitie' as meaning 'human life,' 'human nature.' But inasmuch as Byron is throughout this passage drawing morals from the actions of the participants in the games, I concur in the emendation.

255 expos'd] In none of the copies I have examined do the apostrophes actually appear that I have put into 'expos'd' in this line, 'arm'd' in line 258, and 'asham'd' in line 263. But in each case there is a space between the final *d* and the letter preceding, which suggests that the compositor intended an apostrophe but mistakenly set a space instead.

256 person, with] The Q1 reading is not impossible, but it implausibly equivalences Henry's 'person', which he has exposed in warfare, to his spirit.

Shepherd's attractive emendation – 'with' for 'wich is' – makes the free spirit a characteristic of the person. If the Q1 compositor did indeed misread 'with' in his copy as 'wich', he might well have supplied 'is' in an attempt to make sense of the passage.

263 but] This interpolation by C. E. Norton in his copy of Q1 strikes me as a word so obviously useful that probably it was in Chapman's manuscript. The sense of the passage calls for an adversative here, and a natural accenting of 'enuy' is made possible by the additional syllable.

294 Shooes] Parrott emends to 'shows' on the grounds that 'the homely figure "too big shoes upset their wearer," would not be at all in his "heightened style,"' and that context demands an intransitive verb. The meaning he derives is thus 'pageants overturn.' The argument from context is not credible: two sentences are involved here, and 'Shooes euer ouerthrow' and 'hugest canons, burst' of the second sentence do not, as does 'exhalation ... Fall' of the first, depend upon 'so haue I desern'd'. And I think it particularly risky to say what George Chapman would *not* do, even in his 'heightened style.'

<h2 style="text-align:center">V.i</h2>

82 feared] There is no reason to accept Q2's 'sacred' in place of Q1's 'feared', as earlier editors do. There are a number of such unnecessary emendations in the first scene of this act in Q2.

115 lest] Lines 113-15 constitute one of the most difficult passages in the play, and the choice of 'best' or 'lest' (= least) in line 115 depends upon one's understanding of several ambiguous pronouns. The antecedent of 'it' in line 114 I take to be 'sufferance'; of 'them', 'men'; and of 'it' in line 115, 'worth'. Consonant with these interpretations 'lest' seems to be required in line 115 (as it is in line 112); thus I find the following sense in the passage: 'he makes his suffering worse in order to offer to men observing him the very slightest show of the personal contentment that would be his if he were free.' The noun clause of lines 116-17 parallels 'The lest part ... ,' both being objects of 'to vouchsafe'.

128 breake] Logically, the form of this verb should be singular, 'breakes', its subject being 'strength' in line 127. But the plural is there by attraction of the plural noun 'rages' immediately preceding it; because this is a common construction in writing of the time, I allow 'breake' to stand.

143 Casts] Previous editors have accepted Q1's 'Cast', apparently supposing 'beames' to be its subject. I take 'sunne' in line 140 to be the subject and line 142 to be a parenthetic absolute.

<h2 style="text-align:center">V.ii</h2>

203-6 (My ... comfort)] I have introduced the round brackets to make clear that the passage is parenthetic, and that (despite the lack in Q1 of a period at the end of line 206) the object of 'yee all know' is the 'what' clause in lines 201-2, not the 'This body gasht' clause of lines 207-11.

231 though] Parrott rejects Shepherd's interpolation on the ground that 'the syncopated first foot' makes it unnecessary for the meter. But the sense of

the line requires 'though'; and because Chapman does use the word in line 233 in what is a specific echo of line 231, I follow Shepherd in the interpolation. Lowell too inserted 'though'.

258 Saturnales] Deighton proposed 'Saturnalians' for Q1's 'Saturnals', presumably as a means of gaining the necessary extra syllable in the line. On the basis of the spelling in the passage in Grimeston which was Chapman's source here (p. 977D), I emend to 'Saturnales.'

V.iii

77 you] In the Norton copy of Q1, 'out' is interpolated after 'cried' and 'you' after 'pray'. The latter emendation is likely in that it does away with the necessity of accenting 'harken' on the second syllable. The former I reject because the expletive 'Sfoote' is undoubtedly supposed to be accented, and the line thus begun has no place for 'out.'

160 then] The annotator of the Norton copy emends to 'been', which is plausible. I allow 'then' to stand because sense can be made of 'that had then the Woulfe,/ To flie vpon his bosome' if 'that' is taken to be the subject of 'had' and the latter be understood as meaning 'had as an element in it'.

V.iv

39 say] Parrott rejects this conjecture of Deighton for Q1's 'sayd', but the change is clearly necessary. Byron is telling his would-be spiritual advisers that he knows all any man can know about death – what more can they say to him? Note the present tense in the parallel 'what can you say more?' (line 44) and 'what say you more?' (line 49).

45 being a large] Parrott's emendation of Q1's 'bring a long' strikes me as precisely what is called for here. 'Byron, then, calls himself, ... at once "a large map and a microcosm."'

58 *Vit. . . . city.*] That a speech of Vitry's was omitted in the composition of Q1 is evident from the catchword *Vyt.* at the bottom of the preceding page. Parrott has re-constructed the speech from a passage in Grimeston: 'Hee sayd that he desired to see *La Forse* and Saint *Blancart.* They tould him that they were not in the Cittie ...' (p. 988C). At this place in his unpublished edition Lowell supplied the half-line 'My Lord, they have left Paris.'

259 Stricke . . . soule] Because the two halves of line 259 are printed in Q1 as separate lines, Parrott wonders whether perhaps 'Chapman meant Byron's speech to terminate with the word *strike*, and gave the last words of the play to another speaker. Grimeston says (p. 991) that Biron's head was struck off while he was still speaking.' But what he was speaking, according to Grimeston, was 'his last prayer to recommend his Soule vnto God'; and that I think is what the final lines represent.

In British Museum copy C.30.e.2, in a secretary hand, is written under the final line of the play, 'He Strikes his heade of ——', which echoes Grimeston's marginal note, 'He cuts of his heade' (p. 991E).

The Revenge of Bussy D'Ambois

Edited by Robert J. Lordi

❧

TEXTUAL INTRODUCTION

The Revenge of Bussy D'Ambois was entered, together with *The Widow's Tears*, to John Browne in the *Stationers' Register* on April 17, 1612. It survives in a single quarto (1613), comprising forty unnumbered leaves.[1] Greg identifies the printer as Thomas Snodham on the basis of the initials on the title page,[2] and the identification is strengthened by Snodham's publishing ventures with John Browne and Matthew Lownes in 1611(?).[3] Greg calls attention to the unusual form of the imprint, 'in that the printer, though apparently the responsible party, is indicated by his initials only', and suggests the possibility that Browne, the holder of the copy, rather than Snodham, was the actual publisher. Greg supports his suggestion in pointing out that the address of Browne, as well as that of John Helme, the bookseller, was St Dunstan's Churchyard, and that later records show clearly that Browne retained control of the stock. An entry in the *Stationers' Register* for February 17, 1623, notices that the widow of Browne 'assigned over' title to *The Revenge*, together with several other titles, to John Marriott. An entry for May 3, 1651, notices the transfer of 'all title to copy of over 30 works, one of which is *The Revenge of D'Amboys*' from John Marriott to his son Richard; and one for December (?)12, 1653, the transfer of *The Revenge* (along with ten other titles) from R. Marriott to H. Moseley. 'Since Moseley later advertised [*The Revenge*] although he never printed it, he would appear to have acquired the remaining stock of the original edition.'[4]

Apparently *The Revenge* enjoyed no greater success with the reading public than it had with audiences at Whitefriars (see facsimile title page) soon

---

[1] For bibliographical description, see W. W. Greg, *A Bibliography of the English Printed Drama to the Restoration* (London, 1939), I, 448 (no. 307).
[2] *Ibid.*
[3] R. B. McKerrow, *A Dictionary of Printers and Booksellers in England, Scotland and Ireland ... 1557-1640* (London, 1910), p. 135.
[4] Greg, pp. 448-449.

after its composition late in 1610, or early in 1611. In 'The Epistle Dedicatorie', addressed to Sir Thomas Howard, Chapman himself concedes that 'the Scænicall presentation [met] with some maligners'. And although the edition was probably not a large one, as is implied by the fact that the pressman tended to get ahead of the compositor, it was still not completely sold off at least as late as the 1650s when Moseley attempted to sell the remaining stock of the original edition.[5]

Although the provenance of the copy from which the 1613 quarto was set is uncertain, the manuscript was undoubtedly a very good one, perhaps the prompt-book released for printing because of the play's limited stage success, as Parrott suggests,[6] perhaps even a Chapman holograph (as I shall argue), but almost certainly a fair copy (judging from the quarto's relative freedom from error). The dedication, the marginal glosses, and the stage directions all imply that Chapman carefully prepared the manuscript from which the quarto was set. Indeed, one stop-press correction raises the distinct possibility that Chapman may even have proofread at least one of the formes.

'The Epistle Dedicatorie' to Sir Thomas Howard is the most immediate indication of Chapman's official involvement in the printing of his play. The practice recently adopted by Ben Jonson of elevating the status of plays by officially dedicating them to worthy patrons of the arts was a growing, but by no means a usual, one by 1613.[7] Chapman had dedicated only one earlier two-part play, *The Conspiracie and Tragedie of Charles Duke of Byron* (1608), before he dedicated *The Revenge* and *The Widdowes Teares* in 1613. The tentative tone that characterizes the dedication of *The Revenge* betrays his conscious effort to increase his patron's esteem for this unsuccessful play.

The three marginal glosses in the body of the text point to a similar desire to elevate *The Revenge* from a commodity to the dignity of a serious 'work'. Although glosses are commonplace in Chapman's non-dramatic work, among his plays, they appear only in *The Revenge*.[8] These glosses are all clearly authorial in origin and 'literary' in character. Two of them (at II.i.134-142, 156) cite specified classical sources which are echoed by lines in the text, and the third (at II.i.181) calls attention to a simile in the text. Moreover, two are in Latin and one in Latin and Greek. Not only are they clearly aimed at the learned reader, but they are so devoid of theatrical value that it is all but inconceivable that they even appeared in the manuscript originally submitted by Chapman to the bookkeeper to be used in preparation of the prompt-book. The inference is that almost certainly Chapman added them later when preparing a manuscript of the play for printing.

[5] *Ibid.*, p. 449.
[6] '... it may be that [the play's] slight success was one of the reasons which led to its being surrendered by the company ... to the author, who published it with this apologetic dedication' (T. M. Parrott, *The Plays of George Chapman: The Tragedies* (London, 1910), p. 577).
[7] 'It is plain that Chapman, like Jonson, revolted against the low esteem in which the acted drama was held by scholarly and literary circles in his day, and by these references [in the dedication to *The Widow's Tears* and *The Revenge*] to the aristocratic and courtly patronage in Italy hoped to raise them to a juster estimate of the contemporary drama in England' (T. M. Parrott, *The Plays of George Chapman: The Comedies* (London, 1914), p. 807).
[8] Glosses appear also in *The Masque of the Middle Temple*, written especially for the court festivities attendant upon the marriage of the Elector Palatine to Princess Elizabeth on February 14, 1613.

Several characteristics of the stage directions, although not always without ambiguity, also suggest on the whole Chapman's hand rather than that of the prompter. All but six of the entrances (at I.i.144; I.ii.120; IV.iii.90; V.iv.37; V.v.5, 161) are generally centered and set each on a separate line; and all except three exits (at III.ii.178; IV.iii.87; V.v.119) and all other directions except two (at III.ii.161; IV.iv.12) are flush right, all of which is consistent with the usual arrangement of such directions in Elizabethan prompt-books.⁹ But most of the exceptions, it seems to me, suggest that the author re-worked the manuscript in an effort to increase the readability of the play. For example, the minor entrance '[*Intr. Ancil.*]' at IV.iii.90, as also the direction '[*Exit Ancil.*]' three lines earlier, is placed mid-speech at the precise point at which the action is called for. The total theatrical context, including the Countess's command before her maid leaves and her reference to the jewels in the cabinet at the point where the maid returns with it, would, it seems to me, make these directions in the quarto unnecessary in the prompt-book. If they had been considered necessary in the theater, they would probably have appeared in imperative form in the right margin, not, as in the quarto, in the indicative in square brackets and in Latin. The square brackets are perhaps an indication that these and two later, similarly bracketed directions (at III.ii.161, 178) were inserted by Chapman in preparing the manuscript for the press: all four use Latin (only one of them conventionally), a Chapman trademark,¹⁰ and the square brackets (perhaps supplied by the compositor) suggest that they were somehow marked for insertion. The intention behind them seems to be to make imaginatively present to the reader minor actions that were readily apparent in the playhouse. Especially is this true of '[*osculatur*]' (III.ii.161), a piece of stage business not clear from the text that Chapman might have felt would otherwise be missed by the reader.

The four principal entrances at the right margin with no break in the text (at I.i.144; V.iv.37; V.v.5, 161) can be explained by a similar hypothesis; each of them is clearly anticipated by what is said by the actors already on the stage. In fact, in the first one (at I.i.144) in which the King and others are directed to enter, the King never actually enters the scene at all. Apparently, in the theater he showed himself long enough for Monsieur to be seen taking leave of him, but since Baligny does not mention the King (as he does Monsieur, Guise, and Clermont) at this point in the text of the play, Chapman again may have felt a need to make clear to the reader what was apparent to the auditor's eyes, namely that Monsieur was taking leave of the King.¹¹

Most of the other directions except for terse 'entrances' or 'exits' are

⁹ W. W. Greg, *Dramatic Documents from the Elizabethan Playhouses* (Oxford, 1931), pp. 206-207.
¹⁰ In one or more stage directions in each of his plays, Chapman uses Latin unconventionally; i.e., besides his conventional use of Latin for directions such as '*Exit*' and '*Exeunt*', Chapman puts many directions in Latin which ordinarily would be in English, e.g., '*Procumbit.*' at I.i.33 in *Bussy D'Ambois*, and '*Exiturus.*' at II.i.96 in *The Conspiracie of Byron*.
¹¹ It is of course possible that Chapman had already added this entrance and the other three entrances in the right margin of the fair copy that he submitted to the acting company as an aid to understanding by the actors, but their placement flush right suggests that they were after-thoughts and thus later additions to the manuscript.

generally literary (i.e., of a kind originating with the author rather than a bookkeeper) both in style and grammatical construction. They usually describe action on the stage in an indicative[12] rather than an imperative manner. Often they are elliptical, omitting altogether the major verb[13] or using a participial form of the verb,[14] both of which constructions are more consistent with a literary than theatrical purpose. Also probably literary (in the sense that they derive from Chapman) are the several directions in Latin,[15] as are the Latin notations marking the beginning and ending of each act. In this connection, the direction '*Ascendit Vmbra Bussi.*' (V.v.1) is especially apropos, since 'Bussy' has been so properly Latinized.

This inventory leaves a few stage directions that may possibly suggest prompt copy. Five specify properties;[16] three call for sound effects;[17] two refer to costumes;[18] and one may be imperative.[19] In addition, three stage directions are non-permissive[20] to the extent that they specify a definite number of minor, otherwise nameless, characters who in an author's manuscript may well have been left indefinite in number, as indeed they often are in the 1613 quarto.[21] In most of these directions, it should be noted, indications of prompt copy are slight, and as good a case can be posited for attributing them to the author as to a bookkeeper. The specifying of properties, except at IV.iv.1, may be attributable to Chapman's desire to enhance the readability of the play. Two of the directions calling for sound effects (at III.i.58; V.v.119) are unspecific and less 'technically precise' than we might expect from a bookkeeper.[22] Both of the costumes are disguises, the mention of which seems more consistent with a literary than a theatrical aim, especially since neither is phrased as a warning. The one possible imperative direction '*Fight.*' (V.v.67) may be viewed as an elliptical indicative in the light of comparable constructions in the same scene (V.v.85, 110). Further, it might be argued that '*two Souldiers*' are specified in two directions (III.iii.1; III.iv.149) because they have individual speaking parts in the play. The few remaining directions – especially the specifications of '*pen, incke, and paper*' (IV.iv.1) and of '*sixe of the Guard*' (V.ii.1) – may indeed be prompt-notes, but even these may be questioned in the light of the preponderance of evidence that emphatically suggests an authorial manuscript, and the absence of any unambiguous prompt copy evidence such as warnings or anticipatory directions.

One more direction remains to be considered, particularly for its support of the supposition that Chapman re-worked his manuscript for the press, but also because it strengthens the hypothesis that he occasionally read

---

[12] I.ii.24, 115, 138; III.i.58; III.ii.161; IV.iii.96, 107; V.i.1, 32; V.iii.22, 38; V.iv.35, 36, 37, 72; V.v.5, 29, 44, 85, 87, 110, 111, 119, 161.
[13] I.ii.1; II.i.1; III.i.1, 59; III.iv.7; IV.i.1, 6, 10, 39; V.v.85, 119.
[14] I.i.144; III.i.1, 60; III.ii.1; III.iv.1; IV.i.1, 10, 40; V.iii.18; V.v.119, 203.
[15] I.ii.1, 115; III.ii.161; III.iv.7, 165; IV.iii.87, 90; IV.iv.12; V.i.1.
[16] I.ii.120; III.ii.61; IV.iv.1; IV.v.49, 64; V.iii.1.
[17] III.i.58, 59; V.v.119.
[18] III.iv.149; V.iii.1.
[19] V.v.67.
[20] III.iii.1; III.iv.149; V.ii.1.
[21] III.i.1; III.ii.1; IV.i.41; IV.v.1, 64; V.iv.37; V.v.215.
[22] See Greg, *Dramatic Documents*, p. 213.

proof.[23] It appears on the inner forme of sheet H, which survives in four states: the first state is preserved in one, the second in ten, the third in six, and the fourth in one, of the eighteen extant copies of the quarto. The uncorrected state (i.e., the first of the four states) has the direction *'Hee raises her, and / Exe. leades her out.'* in the right margin at IV.iii.107, and 'san'd' (for 'sau'd') in l. 108. The first corrected state (i.e., the second of the four states) shows just one change, 'san'd' corrected to 'sau'd'. Survival of the first (i.e., the uncorrected state) in only one copy, when one considers the proofreader's failure to notice the obviously misplaced *'Exe.'* in the stage direction immediately above, suggests that sheet H was subjected to a somewhat cursory proofreading rather early in the press run (perhaps even at the press).

The misplaced *'Exe.'* was, however, noticed in a second, more careful proofreading, which presumably occurred roughly midway through the press-run; for the second corrected state, in which *'Exe.'* is removed to the end of the direction where it belongs, survives in only one-third of the extant copies. In the third and final state of correction, the descriptive part of the direction (*'He raises / her, and / leades her / out.'*) is set in new type[24] and located in the left margin opposite ll. 107-109, whereas *'Exe.'* (expanded to *'Exeunt.'*) remains in the right margin after l. 107.

The one plausible explanation of how these four states came about implies the proposition we have been pursuing: that Chapman re-worked his manuscript for the press. The misprinting of 'san'd' for 'sau'd', which identifies the uncorrected state, is easily explained as a compositor's error; thus it would seem that the first corrected state accurately reflects what appeared in the manuscript and that the compositor – who, as we shall later see, was generally a careful workman – set the direction precisely as he read it there. What probably happened was this: When Chapman began to prepare his manuscript for the printer, the *'Exe.'* was already in place after l. 107 but without the rest of the stage business (*'Hee raises her, and leades her out.'*). It is highly unlikely that the prompter inserted this descriptive direction in an already crowded right margin,[25] especially since the action is so obviously called for by the prone position of the Countess on the stage. Its literary flavor points instead to the author and his desire to enhance the readability of his play by describing an action not visibly apparent to the reader. Thus Chapman probably added it in the only space available to him in his manuscript, that is, over and around the already present *'Exe.'* This version the compositor set first. The resulting awkwardness of the direction, however, was readily observed in the belated second proofreading, whereupon the

---

[23] Much of the following analysis of this proof correction appears in my 'Proofreading of *The Revenge of Bussy D'Ambois,*' *ELN,* X (Mar., 1973), 188-197, where I discuss some of the wider implications for bibliographical studies of the proofreading of *The Revenge.*

[24] I am indebted for this observation to the late James G. McManaway, Consultant in Literature and Bibliography at the Folger Shakespeare Library, who kindly looked at the four states of this stage direction at my request. The variant spelling 'He' is one sign of the new setting.

[25] The unusually long (because almost entirely monosyllabic) line spoken by the Usher, together with his *'Exit.'* (l. 108), must have left as little space at this point in the manuscript as there is in the quarto.

'*Exe.*' was moved to its correct position at the end of the descriptive part of the direction.

How the fourth state came about is a matter of conjecture, but that it is the fourth and not the third state is indicated by the new type used in setting the direction. Also, it probably occurred very late in the press-run, since it survives in only one of the extant copies. The belatedness of this change from one corrected state to a further state of correction (with no additional changes anywhere in sheet H) invites the interesting speculation that Chapman himself may have occasionally read proof, and in this case requested the removal of the descriptive part of the direction to the left margin, a shift that enjoyed the advantage of balancing with the stage direction '*Auersus.*', already in the left margin several lines below, and also of relieving the crowding in the right margin.

Any alternate theory of how the third state of correction of sheet H came about does not alter the basic proposition we have been arguing: that the manuscript used by the printer of the quarto was one prepared by Chapman. The stage directions, the glosses, and the dedication all strongly suggest this conclusion. One further bit of evidence in corroboration is the list of 'The Actors names', also probably added by Chapman for the printing.

The evidence thus far adduced to establish Chapman's official stamp on the manuscript used by the printer does not fully exclude the possibility that the manuscript was at one time a theatrical copy, which was subsequently returned to Chapman after the play met with little applause.[26] Though the theatrical copy (perhaps annotated by the bookkeeper) could have been either Chapman's fair copy, or a transcription thereof, there is some, however inconclusive, evidence that the manuscript placed in the hands of the printer was a holograph rather than a transcription.

The punctuation, lineation, and elisions in the quarto suggest a holographic copy. The punctuation, with relatively few exceptions, is heavy and systematic, and provides a generally reliable guide to meaning, even when obscured by Chapman's characteristically involved syntax. The use of parentheses (a Chapman trademark) is common, and in some places where we find parentheses enclosing less heavy punctuation (e.g. I.i.12, 170, 248, 364; II.i.11, 199; V.i.12, 46), the parentheses would seem to indicate that Chapman had sought to increase the clarity of his completed manuscript by making additions to the punctuation already there. The lineation of the verse of the quarto, which with the exception of two brief passages (see Textual Notes) presents no real metrical problems, suggests that the compositor set from a carefully written manuscript. Elisions, especially those involving the endings of past participles (see Textual Note, V.iii.2), are so consistently used and prove to be so trustworthy a guide to the meter that it is virtually impossible to ascribe them to anyone but Chapman.

The omission of two stage directions that probably would be necessary in a prompt copy but not in one meant for reading also suggests holographic copy. The King's exit is not marked after his entrance at I.i.144, nor is his

---

[26] This is Parrott's theory. See note 6 above.

entrance precisely marked after he shows himself at V.iv.37.[27] Both of these omissions are the result of directions which, as we argued earlier, were probably added by Chapman for the reader. What has been added is important to someone who is reading the play but not to someone who is watching it in the theater; and what has been omitted is important in the theater, but offers little or no difficulty to the reader.

Perhaps also suggestive of holographic copy (or of a scribal copy thereof) are the inconsistencies in speech prefixes in the quarto (e.g. *Coun.*, *Count.*; *Gui.*, *Guise.*; *Char.*, *Charl.*; *Ren.*, *Rene.*; *Tam.*, *Tamy.*; *Mon.*, *Mont.*; *Esp.*, *Esper.*; *Mail.*, *Maill.*; *Mess.*, *Messen.*; *Soul.*, *Sould.*). Some few of these inconsistencies (which have been normalized in this edition) derive from the compositor's need to justify his lines. Others might reflect the spelling habits of different compositors, but since, as we will show below, only one compositor almost certainly set this entire work, they are more likely attributable to Chapman himself, or to a scribal copy of his holograph.

The first indication that a single compositor set the quarto is the general consistency and uniformity of pattern in the signatures, the catchwords, the headings for each act (in roman font and set off from the text by double rules), the speech-prefixes (always in italic, except for the first one which is centered to allow for an ornamental capital to head the opening line of the play), and the stage directions (always in italic and, as we have seen, with entrances normally centered and exits and other directions normally in the right margin). The text itself is printed throughout in a single roman font, except for seven words in italics, two of which are Latin expressions, and three others the names of classical figures.

Analysis of its spelling characteristics also indicates that the quarto was set by a single compositor. All variant spellings of frequently used words (e.g., 'he,' 'hee'; 'she,' 'shee'; 'we,' 'wee'; 'ye,' 'yee'; 'me,' 'mee') occur arbitrarily throughout the entire printed text in nearly every possible combination, mixed ('he,' 'shee'; 'we,' 'yee'; etc.) and/or paired ('he,' 'hee'; 'she,' 'shee'; etc.). For instance, we always find several mixed combinations and some paired combinations in both formes of each sheet from B through K. We find a mixed or paired combination in nearly every page of the text, often in adjacent lines; and in some cases (necessarily few since the possibilities of such occurrences are small), paired combinations occur in the same line (see II.i.266; IV.iii.17, 80; V.i.128; V.ii.11, 21).[28] Besides these frequently used words, there are no other pairs of spelling variants that occur with sufficient frequency or consistency to suggest that their occurrence is other than accidental. On the other hand, the frequency and consistency with which a number of particular spellings occurs suggest that these forms reflect the orthographic habits of one man. 'Ile', 'goe', and 'doe' (except in the two places where 'doe' appears in the contracted form, 'doo't') are invariable

---

[27] The third omission is '*Manet Bal.*' at IV.iv.56.
[28] Compositors during this period would readily vary spellings in order to justify a line; but since *The Revenge* is almost entirely in verse (only the anonymous letter which Clermont receives runs over a single line of prose), justification was scarcely a problem for the compositor except in a few places where a lengthy stage direction in the margin caused crowding.

throughout the text. 'Onely' is also invariable, and so are the suffixes '-lesse' and '-nesse', except for two cases of '-nes' in V.iv.37 on I4ᵛ where crowding necessitated the shorter forms. Doubling of consonants is common (as in 'winne,' 'comming,' 'pennance'), especially of final '-l' (as in 'loyall,' 'needfull,' 'equall'). Double 'l' is found also where we would expect it (in 'ill,' 'wall,' 'tell'); but, unexpectedly, when a final '-s' is added to such words, the spelling almost always becomes 'ils,' 'wals,' 'tels,' 'swels,' 'bels,' 'wils,' 'dwels,' 'kils.'

Final '-e' is a preferred spelling, not only in the already mentioned 'Ile,' 'doe,' 'goe,' '-nesse,' '-lesse,' but also in such words as 'finde,' 'owne,' 'warre.' Even some words that normally appear without a final '-e' (e.g. 'law,' 'say,' 'stay') regularly have an 'e' added to their plural or third person singular forms (e.g., 'lawes,' 'sayes,' 'stayes'). This preference for a final or silent '-e' may account for the very common final '-ie' instead of '-y' in such words as 'satisfie,' 'busie,' 'pittie.'

The variation between '-y' and '-ie' endings is one of the constant features of the spelling, and if at first sight the choice between these endings seems arbitrary, analysis indicates a remarkable degree of consistency in the choice. In adverbs ending in '-ly', '-ie' is never substituted for the '-y', and final '-y' is invariable after a vowel ('toy,' 'prey,' 'decay') and in such commonly used pronouns as 'any,' 'many,' and 'every.' Of the more than 255 other words in the text that might end in either '-y' or '-ie', over three-fourths end in '-ie'. With but six exceptions, every word of more than two syllables which could feasibly end in '-ie' (e.g., 'policie') does so; and to diminish the possibility that the exceptions may be a sign of two different compositors' spelling habits, one should note that four of these exceptions appear in variant spellings, in one instance ('victorie,' 'victory') the first form and its variant occurring on the same page (I4). Moreover, except for three which end in '-yes' (e.g., 'Countryes'), all regular plural nouns end in '-ies'; and two of the exceptions occur with the expected '-ies' as well as the '-yes' ending. In one instance, both 'Ladies' and 'Ladyes' occur on the same page (E4).

The exceptional spellings in the latter instance (i.e., 'Ladyes' instead of 'Ladies') may be the product of a common tendency to prefer an internal 'y' (where modern spelling practice would most often require an 'i') in nearly every possible position (e.g., 'sayles,' 'reynes,' 'voyce,' 'Tyger,' 'Heroycall,' 'lye,' 'lyes'). The only sizeable group of exceptions to this tendency involves six one-syllable words ('lie,' 'die,' 'trie,' 'flie,' 'slie,' 'skie'), appearing a total of sixteen times. But of these sixteen, which represent less than half of the total appearances of such words, ten are accounted for by only two words ('lie,' 'die'), and these are balanced by nine appearances of their counterparts ('lye,' 'dye'). Furthermore, since these variant spelling forms are so few, no significant grouping occurs on any page that might warrant attributing the variation to a change in compositors. These variations are more likely a result of differences between the spelling habits of the compositor and of the author, whose spellings occasionally may have influenced the compositor's.[29]

---

[29] 'We may thus regard it as a general rule ... that in common words and in words misread as

That the proofreading of the quarto was carried out with a notable concern for accuracy in small as well as important matters is evidenced by an analysis of the press-variants preserved in the eighteen extant copies.[30] Although the thirty-five press-variants are distributed through ten of the twenty formes, twenty-one occur in only two of the formes, eleven in outer C and ten in inner G. The reason for the rather heavy proof correction in these two formes is a matter of conjecture, but it may be that Chapman himself read proof on these formes after the regular proofing.[31] I have suggested that perhaps Chapman requested the change in position of the stage direction that appears in three states in H(i). Who more readily than Chapman could have spotted the incorrect speech-prefixes *Mons.* for *Mont.* throughout C(o), especially since the proofreader, if he proofread C(i), had already missed nine earlier settings of *Mont.* for *Mons.* in that forme, which, as we shall see below, was machined first?

Moreover, the correction in F1 might well be attributed to Chapman, and if not to Chapman, then to a proofreader with a most scrupulous concern for textual accuracy. For the line (III.ii.188) makes perfectly good sense without the addition of 'rang'd' (which is redundant), and might be accepted as metrically sound by anyone unfamiliar with the trisyllabic accent of the Italian borrowing, 'Battailia'. Despite its redundancy, however, Chapman apparently felt that 'rang'd' was needed in the line for metrical purposes, and we can be reasonably certain that the correction is authorial,[32] that is, that it

---

common words, the compositor would follow his own spelling; in rare ones, or words which are not words at all, the spelling of the MS. or what he believed to be its spelling' (R. B. McKerrow, *An Introduction to Bibliography* [Oxford, 1927], p. 249). Barring the authority of McKerrow, my own not entirely successful attempts to discern Chapman's spelling habits by examining copies of those documents fairly certainly written and signed by him (several letters in the Dobell MSS and two entries in Henslowe) and those of his works probably set from his own manuscripts (i.e., all his nondramatic works) would warrant only a thoughtful guess that the spellings of *The Revenge* are largely those of the compositor. Furthermore, the spelling habits observed in my analysis of the four other dramatic texts printed by Thomas Snodham at about the time when he printed *The Revenge* (*The Atheist's Tragedy*, 1611/1612; *The Alchemist*, 1612; *Thomas Lord Cromwell*, 1613; *The Insatiate Countess*, 1613) were found not to be sufficiently distinct from those in *The Revenge* to aid in distinguishing Chapman's spelling habits from those of the compositor, who very likely had a hand in the setting of all these plays.

[30] See the list of 'Press-Variants in Q (1613)'.

[31] Percy Simpson presents unmistakable evidence that Chapman read proof (albeit belatedly) on *The Masque of the Middle Temple* (1613), with the result that he caused insertions to be made of two notes (which should have appeared in the text proper) immediately following the preliminary description of *The Masque* with this apology for their misplacement:

> These following [i.e., the two notes] should in duty haue had their proper places, after euery fitted speech of the Actors; but being preuented by the vnexpected haste of the Printer, which he neuer let me know, and neuer sending me a proofe, till he had past those speeches; I had no reason to imagine hee could have been so forward. His fault is therfore to be supplied by the obseruation, and reference of the Reader, who will easily perceiue, where they were to bee inserted.

(*Proof-Reading in the Sixteenth, Seventeenth and Eighteenth Centuries* [London, 1935], p. 5). See also, G. Blakemore Evans, ed. *The Memorable Masque* in *The Plays of George Chapman: The Comedies* (Urbana, Illinois, 1970), gen. ed. Allan Holaday.

[32] The certainty is based on the locution 'rang'd in Battailia' which Chapman uses *mutatis mutandi* in three other places in the play (III.iv.78, 153-154; IV.iii.30). He also uses 'put' or 'set' (instead of 'rang'd') with 'Battaile(s)' in three places (II.i.24; III.i.60; III.iii.13), but nowhere except in the redundant locution does he use 'rang'd,' and 'put' or 'set' together with a form of 'Battaile'.

was either in the printer's manuscript (which means that the proofreader referred to manuscript), or that Chapman caught the metrical irregularity while reading proof and ordered the correction. Significantly, the other three semi-substantive changes in this forme also suggest Chapman's intervention. The insertion and removal of commas in two of these in order to increase clarity[33] again argue a fidelity to copy that is difficult to reconcile with ordinary proofreading practices. Such proofreading by the author is, of course, entirely possible, especially in the light of the remaining proof-corrections, all of which in varying degrees suggest a similar special concern for the kind of accuracy we have been associating with Chapman.

Detailed in what follows are the results of an analysis of reappearing types[34] made in conjunction with analyses of the running titles and of the press-corrections. The evidence provided by these analyses proves conclusively (1) that the printer's copy of the manuscript was cast off (probably because of a short type supply), and (2) that the quarto (except for sheet H) was set by formes and probably[35] by a single compositor. The reappearing types generally provide ample evidence (except in the case of sheets D and K) that the formes were machined in the following order: B(o), B(i), C(i), C(o), D(o), D(i), E(i), E(o), F(o), F(i), G(i), G(o), H(o), H(i), I(i), I(o), K(i), K(o).

The running titles (RT's) support the earlier conclusion that a single compositor set the quarto throughout. The first two sheets of the text (B and C) use four different combinations of seven different titles, with each succeeding forme using from one to three titles from the preceding forme. That is, no two of the first four formes use a common skeleton. Skeleton 1, made up of four of the seven titles used in the first four formes, appears first as a complete unit in C(o) and then again in D(o), from which point it continues to print each succeeding forme to the completion of sheet F. Skeleton 2, made up from the three titles remaining from the seven used in the first four formes plus a newly set title, appears first in G(i), and then immediately again in G(o). Sheet H uses Skeleton 1 in its outer forme and

---

[33] Two editors of the play, Boas and Parrott, fell easy victims to the confusion occasioned by their use of the uncorrected reading. See Textual Notes.

[34] The collation of types was accomplished at the British Library, the only library with three copies of the quarto. The method used was to inspect each letter of the text of the quarto with a magnifying glass to find any distinctive irregularity (such as might result from wear, breaking, or bending) in the type that impressed it, and then to compare that letter with the same letter in the second and third copies of the quarto to rule out irregularities due to poor inking, the introduction of foreign matter (such as a hair or dust), etc. When verified as distinctive, the type was recorded as a lemma reading identified by page and line number, and this process was repeated throughout the text as each new type was identified. When one of the types thus recorded was discovered in a later forme, it was also recorded by page and line number with the proper lemma reading only after it too had been verified by comparing it with its counterparts in the other two copies of the quarto, and also by cross-comparing it with the impression by which it was originally identified. After I had located and duly recorded every identifiable type either as a new lemma reading or as a reappearance of an earlier lemma reading, I made a list of every re-appearing type that fulfilled two conditions: (1) if it was identified with the highest degree of certainty attainable, and (2) if it was significant for studying the relationships among formes (e.g., a type migrating from B(o) to K(i) is generally non-significant). I then sought to explain the observable patterns of migration of the types in my list from one forme to another.

[35] This hedging word is meant only to restrict the evidence supplied by the analyses cited here. The spelling analysis proves that there was only one compositor.

Skeleton 2 in its inner forme. Sheet I uses Skeleton 1 in both formes, and sheet K uses Skeleton 2 in both formes.

Analysis of its reappearing types and of its RT's indicates that sheet B was set by formes, with B(o) precedent. B(o) was certainly machined before B(i), for fifteen of its distinctive types appear in both formes of sheet C. On the other hand, I found no type from B(i) in sheet C, whereas eight of its types appear in the last four pages (3, 3^v, 4, 4^v) of sheet D.

Neither of the two skeleton formes of sheet B is completely distinct. B(o) was imposed with three RT's (B1, the first page of the text has no RT but a head title instead.). The RT's in B(o), labelled III, IV, V representing the order in which they were identified, occur respectively on 2^v, 3, and 4^v. RT's IV and V are used again in B(i) on 4 and 3^v respectively, and two new RT's, labelled I and II, appear respectively on 1^v and 2. This use of part of the skeleton of B(o) for that of B(i) indicates that sheet B was set by formes, that B(o) was set first and that at least two pages of B(i) were set and imposed with their RT's before RT's IV and V became available from B(o). This procedure also suggests that press-work was a good deal more rapid than composing, probably because the number of press pulls was small.

Analysis of reappearing types offers little help in determining whether sheet C was set seriatim or by formes. Types from B(o), apparently distributed before the setting of sheet C began, are found in both formes of C; whereas no type from B(i) is found in either forme of C. But the make-up of the distinct skeletons used in the two formes of C, and a set of press corrections in C(o), together with the failure to correct identical errors in C(i), serve to indicate that sheet C was probably set by formes, with C(i) precedent.

First of all, the two distinct skeletons used in sheet C have only seven different titles. RT III, the one title of B(o) not being used in B(i), is used in both skeletons of C. Skeleton I (made up of titles I, II, III, V) is used for the first time as a complete unit in C(o). Three of its titles come directly from B(i). The skeleton used for C(i) is made up of RT III and RT IV (taken from B[i]) and two new titles, VI and VII. The use of RT III in both formes of C confirms our earlier impression that press-work proceeded at a faster pace than composition. But its use in the first page (1, 1^v) of both formes is more noteworthy since this would immediately rule out the possibility of seriatim setting, at least if we can assume that the compositor imposed each page, as he completed setting it, with its RT. The assumption is a fair one if we look at the relation of RT's to pages in C(i), remembering that B(i) was probably still on the press during the early stages of the setting of sheet C. RT III is imposed with C1^v; RT VI, with C2; RT VII, with C3^v; and RT IV, with C4. This pattern would seem to indicate that C1^v was set first and imposed with the only RT (i.e., RT III) then available. For the next two pages set, two new titles (VI and VII) had to be made up, and by the time C4 was completely set, B(i) had been wrought off so that one of its RT's (IV) became available for imposition with C4.

However, the assumption that the compositor always imposed each page as he completed it with its RT meets with difficulty when we consider the make-up of Skeleton I, first used as a unit in C(o). Three of its titles (I, V, II), used to impose respectively pages C4^v, C3, C2^v, were readily available from the recently distributed B(i); but the occurrence in C1 of RT III, the title which was also used to impose C1^v of the inner forme, which presumably had gone to press, would destroy that assumption unless we argue either that C(i) was wrought off before the setting of C(o) began, or that the setting of C(o) proceeded in reverse order and that C(i) was completely wrought off some time just before the compositor finished composing C1, the last page set for C(o).

That RT III migrated from C(i) to C(o), and not vice versa, is strongly implied by a set of proof corrections in C(o) and the lack of any correction of identical errors in C(i), the implication being that C(i) had been completely wrought off before the first impression of C(o) was available for proof-reading. On pages 2^v, 3, and 4^v of C(o), in seven instances (four in speech-prefixes, three in stage directions) *Mons.* has been corrected to *Mont.*; whereas on pages 3^v and 4 of C(i), in nine instances (eight in speech-prefixes, one a catchword) *Mons.* remains uncorrected (and incorrect).[36] The inference from the proofreading of sheet C is that C(i) must have been precedent, and the proofreading evidence combined with that from the make-up of the skeletons suggests that sheet C was set by formes.

The distinctive types that I have identified as migrating from sheet C to sheet D do not provide a sufficiently clear pattern for determining how sheet D was set, but there is some evidence to suggest that it was set by formes with the outer forme precedent. Nine distinctive types from C(i) are found reappearing in sheet D, all in the pages of D(o), except one in D4. Ten types from C(o) are found reappearing in sheet D, all in D(i), but, oddly, only in the first two pages (eight in 1^v, two in 2).

No explanation of this complex pattern is available that does not give rise to almost as many questions as it answers. It would seem, for example, that C(i) was distributed first and its types used to set at least the first two pages of D(o), whereupon B(i) was distributed to complete the last two pages, and that later C(o) was distributed, probably during the setting of D1^v and D2. But, assuming this to be the order of distribution of the three formes whose types were apparently used in the setting of sheet D, why do we find only one type from C(i), distributed first, in D(i), set last? Why do we find no B(i) types in the first two pages of C(i)? And why no C(o) types in the last two pages of D(i)? We may find our answer to the last question if we assume the order of setting of D(i) to be from last to first, i.e., 4, 3^v, 2, 1^v. Hypothesizing this reverse order has the added advantage of explaining how we find B(i) types in the last two pages of both D formes, even if it leaves unexplained our puzzling failure to find B(i) types in the first two pages of D(i). The failure to find types where we might expect to find them is, of course, no proof that such types are not there. In all likelihood, they are, but their number may be so small as to render even the most exhaustive search fruitless.

---

[36] The repeated error in setting *Mons.* for *Mont.* should not be construed as a sign of great carelessness on the part of the compositor, for not only on paleographical grounds is the manuscript reading *Mont.* likely to be misread for *Mons.*, but Monsieur's appearance as a character in the preceding scene had necessitated the compositor's setting the speech-prefix *Mons.* sixteen times in the last four pages of sheet B.

The RT's offer no evidence for determining which forme of sheet D was precedent, since the same set of RT's (I, II, III, V) which imposed the last forme off the press, C(o), was used to impose both formes of sheet D. Nor are there any proof corrections in this sheet to aid in this determination. But since we find a number of types from D(o) in both formes of sheet E, and a number of types from D(i) exclusively in E(o), the evidence that D(o) must have been precedent is presumable here and will become clearer in our analysis of the next two sheets.

An analysis of the migration of distinctive types from the D formes to the E formes indicates that sheet E was set by formes, with E(i) precedent. We find ten distinctive types from D(o), which the compositor presumably distributed before he began setting E(i), in one or the other forme of sheet E. Most of the ten appear in E(i), as might be expected, since the types on top of the piles in the cases would quite naturally be taken first. On the other hand, we find no type from D(i) in E(i), but do find six of its types in E(o), though none of the six appears before E2^v, which fact, together with the two types from D(o) that we find in E1, suggests that D(i) was distributed soon after the composition of E1. The reappearance of seven types from E(i) in the precedent outer forme of sheet F indicates that E(i) was distributed before E(o); this order of distribution further suggests that E(i) was precedent in sheet E.

The same set of RT's (I, II, III, V) used in sheet D reappears in both formes of sheet E. There are press variants in each forme, one in the inner, three in the outer. The one in E(i), the SD 'Exit.' for 'Eit.', could have been easily observed and corrected without reference to manuscript; but of the three in E(o), that in 2^v is substantive and must have required reference to manuscript; and the two in 4^v, though they are at most semi-substantive and could have been made without reference to manuscript, nevertheless indicate extremely conscientious proofreading.

That sheet F was set by formes with F(o) precedent is indicated by the identification of seven distinctive types from E(i), precedent in sheet E, that reappear in F(o); no type from E(o) has been found to appear before sheet G. Interestingly, all of the seven types identified in E(i) are found in the two top pages (3^v, 4) of the forme as it would lie on the bench, and none of these seven is found in F1. This pattern may suggest that the distribution of E(i) began soon after F1 was set, and that only the first two pages of E(i) were stripped and distributed before the compositor resumed and finally completed the setting of F(o). The precedence of F(o) is also indicated by the fact that six of its types can be identified in G(o), whereas no F(i) type reappears before sheet I.

The same set of RT's (I, II, III, V) used in C(o) and in both formes of sheets D and E was used in both formes of sheet F. Of the four press corrections in F(o), on three different pages, the first is substantive, and, if it is not by Chapman, could only have been made with reference to manuscript; and of the other three, two, involving the insertion of commas that remove the possibility of ambiguous readings, indicate extremely careful proofreading.

Sheet G was set by formes, with G(i) precedent. From the five distinctive types from F(o) that reappear in G(o), it would seem that G(o) was precedent;

but the absence of any distinctive type from sheet F in G(i) is an indication that G(i) was probably completely set before F(o) was distributed.

Apparently both formes of sheet F were distributed somewhat later than had been normal up to this point in the work. No type from F(i) has been found before sheet I, and none from F(o) before the second page of G(o), findings which would mean that five pages of sheet G were set before distribution of the precedent forme of sheet F had begun. Further evidence for the precedence of G(i) is indicated by the reappearance of fourteen of its distinctive types in sheet H, whereas no type from G(o) has been found before sheet I.

That G(i) was completely set before either of the F formes was distributed is implied by the use of a completely new set of RT's (IV, VI, VII, VIII) in both formes of sheet G. Why the compositor did not return to the skeleton with which he had printed the preceding seven formes is not clear. Probably there was some delay in the machining of F(i) so that its skeleton was not immediately available when the pages of G(i) were ready for imposition. Some such delay seems likely because, up to this point, the compositor had had difficulty in keeping up with the press, as is clear from his use of the same skeleton to impose the preceding seven formes. When he completed setting G(i), he imposed it with the three RT's (IV, VI, VII) that had lain on the bench unused since the machining of C(i) and with one new RT (VIII) that he made up to complete the skeleton. He used this new skeleton again in G(o), and later also in H(i) and in both formes of sheet K. The new RT (VIII) also indicates that G(i) was precedent, for it was set very loosely, with an abnormal amount of space between the 'of' and 'Bussy', and then reset with the space closed in G(o) and in its later appearances.

Eleven press corrections make sheet G the most heavily corrected sheet in the entire quarto. Only one occurs in G(o), and that – the supplying of the signature 'G3' – is non-substantive, and of a kind that perhaps was caught by the press-man. Of the ten in G(i), all are substantive or semi-substantive, indicating extremely careful proofreading and very probably reference to manuscript.

Contrary to what, up to this point, had been the usual practice, sheet H was probably set seriatim, with H(o) precedent. Sheet H was composed mostly of types available from the distribution of F(o) and of G(i). Of the nine distinctive types from F(o) found in sheet H, seven appear in the first two pages (1, 1ᵛ), four in the outer forme, three in the inner forme; and of fourteen individual types from G(i) found in sheet H, only one is found in H1ᵛ and the others in each of the final six pages (2, 2ᵛ, 3, 3ᵛ, 4, 4ᵛ). Such a pattern strongly suggests that after the completion of G(o), the compositor began setting sheet H seriatim, with much of the type coming from F(o), the most recently distributed forme. When his supply ran low, somewhere about midway through H1ᵛ, he stopped to distribute G(i), which as we have seen, was precedent. Why he chose to distribute G(i) rather than F(i), which was still lying on his bench, is not clear; but this distribution indicates that press-work was again running well ahead of composition, since G(i), despite the considerable time that must have been used in its extensive press correcting, was wrought off before the compositor had completed the first two pages of sheet H.

Our supposition that sheet H was composed seriatim is further corroborated by its being the first sheet since C to use two sets of RT's. H(o) uses Skeleton I (I, II, III, V) and H(i) Skeleton II (IV, VI, VII, VIII). Apparently there was no immediate need to get either forme ready for the press, possibly because part of another book was being machined. Had such a need existed, setting by formes, which had been usual up to this point, would have been in order, since composition was always behind press-work. But from sheet D on, the same set of RT's used in the first forme machined was used again in the second forme. Apparently with seven of the eight pages before him, the compositor imposed the inner forme with the RT's from G(o), recently off the press, and then, immediately or after composing the eighth page, imposed the outer forme with the RT's from the still undistributed F(i). The fact that we find the latter set of RT's (I, II, III, V) in both formes of sheet I, which was set by formes, suggests that H(o) was precedent.

The three press corrections in sheet H have been discussed in detail earlier.

Sheet I was set by formes, with I(i) precedent. The I formes are filled with types from F(i), G(o), and from parts of H(i) and H(o). F(i) apparently was belatedly distributed just before composition of I(i) began; for one of its types appears as early as line 8 in 1^v of the I forme. In all, seven individual types from F(i) have been identified in sheet I, three in the inner, four in the outer forme, presumptive evidence of seriatim setting. And the distinctive types from G(o) reappearing in both formes of I would seem to confirm this presumption; but a closer analysis of the evidence from reappearing types reveals an interesting pattern which suggests, quite unexpectedly, that instead sheet I was set by formes.

First of all, the fact that three types of F(i) are distributed over three pages of I(i), whereas all four of the types from F(i) occur in I1 is, I think, a cause for suspicion. And the types from G(o) reappearing in sheet I confirm this suspicion. For, of the twelve distinctive types of G(o) that reappear in sheet I, four appear in the first two pages (1, 2^v) of I(o), whereas the other eight are distributed through three of the pages of I(i) – presumptive evidence, when taken together with the distribution of the types in F(i), that all of I(i) was composed from the types distributed from F(i) and G(o), leaving sufficient type only for the first two pages of I(o).

The individual types migrating from sheet H form an unusual pattern that fairly well clinches the case for the setting of sheet I by formes. Ten types from sheet H have been identified as reappearing in I(o), whereas no type from sheet H has been found in I(i). Of the ten types, five are from only two pages (1^v, 4) of H(i), and the other five are from only one page (2^v) of H(o); and even more interesting is that all ten of them migrate only to the last two pages (3, 4^v) of I(o). This somewhat anomalous pattern is explainable if we recall that apparently there was sufficient type from the distribution of F(i) and G(o) for the composition of I(i) and the first two pages of I(o), which were then set after the distribution of three pages (1^v, 2^v, 4) of sheet H. It is not at all clear why the compositor should have distributed only one page of

H(o), which was certainly available, since it was precedent in sheet H, and then turned to distributing only two pages of H(i), which became available by the time H2^v was distributed. But our assumption that this is what he did is fairly well supported by the types from the other pages in sheet H that reappear in sheet K. Of the nineteen distinctive types from both formes of sheet H identified as reappearing in sheet K, all but two are from the five pages (1, 2, 3, 3^v, 4^v) of sheet H that had not been distributed earlier.

There are no press corrections in sheet I, and the RT's offer no additional evidence for determining the order of setting and machining the sheet. As indicated in the discussion of sheet H, the RT's from H(o) (I, II, III, V) reappear in both formes of sheet I. But crowding on both I4 and I4^v corroborates my assumption that the setting was by formes. I4 is the only page in the text with thirty-nine lines, one more than the norm; and the penultimate line in I4^v has three words ('greatnes,' 'goodness,' 'wher') abbreviated to make room for the two stage directions in the margin at the very end of the page. Otherwise, without exception, every word ending in '-ness' is spelled '-nesse'; and 'where' is normally spelled with its final '-e'.

Sheet K presents a number of problems for which no satisfactory solution has been found. Since no types from either forme of sheet I are found in sheet K, it is unlikely that the type from sheet I was distributed before sheet K was completely set. Usually, when no types from one sheet can be found in its successor, it is extremely difficult, if not impossible, to determine by type analysis how the succeeding sheet was set and in what order the formes were machined. However, since five type-pages of sheet H were distributed after composition of sheet I, but before composition of sheet K, we may consider sheet K as the immediate successor of at least these five pages of sheet H.

As mentioned earlier, nineteen distinctive types from the five pages of sheet H reappear in both formes of sheet K, forming a pattern consistent with an hypothesis that sheet K was set by formes. Nine of these types derive from H(i), and of these, seven are from the two pages (2, 3^v) of H(i) not distributed earlier; but they appear in only the first two pages (3^v, 4) of K(i). The remaining ten types from sheet H all derive from the last three pages (1, 3, 4^v) of H(o) not distributed earlier, and all appear in only the first three pages (1^v, 2, 3^v) of K(i). Thus, the types from the five pages in sheet H form a neat pattern, all those from the inner forme migrating to K(o) and all those from the outer forme to K(i); in fact, the pattern is so neat as to be mystifying. For, if one set of pages, say the two in H(i), were distributed first, why do we find types from these pages only in the first two pages and not in the last two pages of K(o)? And even more unusual, why does none show up in any of the pages of K(i), where we could expect at least a few to appear? Alternatively, a similar question arises if we assume that the other set of pages from H(o) was distributed first. Here we find types from these three pages of H(o) migrating to the first three pages of K(i), but none in the last page, none in K(o), and not even a type from H2^v (distributed earlier) in any one of the eight pages of sheet K. Search and research of the pages in question have yielded no further type identifications that might resolve the mystery. One possibility is that the pages from H(i) and those from H(o) were distributed into different cases. This assumption would explain why the types from the pages of H(i) and those of H(o) appear exclusively in K(o) and K(i) respectively. But it would not explain why no types from H(i) appear in K3 and K4^v, nor why no types from H(o) appear in K4, nor why no types from H2^v appear in any of the pages of sheet K.

There is one other possibility that may explain the type facts we have thus far presented, a possibility supported by some additional type identifications and a series of assumptions about the reason for our failure to make type identifications in certain pages. Before beginning composition of K(i), which was probably precedent, the compositor distributed the three pages (1, 3, 4^v) of H(o) which were still standing, a procedure which would account for the frequent use of types from these three pages in the first three pages (1^v, 2, 3^v) of K(i), but which still leaves unexplained why no types from those pages in H(o) are found in the last page (4) of K(i). The answer to this mystery is that there probably is such type in K4 but not enough to be readily discoverable. In other words, most of those types from the three pages of H(o), lying, as we should expect, at the the tops of the heaps in their respective sort compartments, would be used in the composition of the first three pages of H(o). This assumption is corroborated by the fact that some of the types left over from the earlier distribution of H1^v and H4 (we have identified two) appear in the last two pages of K(i), and also by the appearance of several types from sheets E, F, G (distributed much earlier) in K(i), particularly in K4. The fact that none of these types from earlier sheets makes a known appearance between its respective sheet and K(i) is *prima facie* evidence that the supply of type in the cases was running low.

In earlier, similar situations, the compositor had interrupted composition to distribute more type because the resultant delay in getting his immediate forme to the press was made up in the setting of subsequent formes. But since he was here at work on the last sheet, with no future gain in time in prospect, he completed the entire forme and got it ready for the press before distributing the two remaining pages (2, 3^v) of H(i) for use in the setting of K(o). After this distribution, his supply of type was sufficient for composition of the first two pages (1, 2^v) of K(o). Most of the rest of the type for the last two pages (3^v, 4) came, predictably enough, from sheets E, F, and G, distributed much earlier.

One other indication that sheet K was set by formes, with K(i) precedent, is the crowding at the bottom of K1. The page ends with the stage direction 'Enter Monts. and Tamyra.', followed by two brief speeches by these two characters printed in a single line of type. The page has the usual thirty-eight lines but would have been longer than average if the compositor had not squeezed in the stage direction which starts the scene without the usual spacing above and below. (Only four other pages depart from the thirty-eight-line norm: the first and last half-pages; I3, which has thirty-six lines but ends a scene; and I4, which has thirty-nine.)

As might be expected, since neither of the I formes was distributed before composition of sheet K, the RT's used in both formes of sheet K are those used in H(i), that is IV, VI, VII, VIII.

The insertion of a colon in K1 represents the single press correction in this sheet. Since this correction increases textual clarity, it corroborates our assumption that the quarto was proofread with care.

THE
REVENGE

OF
Bussy D'Ambois.

A
TRAGEDIE.

As it hath beene often presented at the priuate Play-house in the White-Fryers.

Written

By GEORGE CHAPMAN, Gentleman.

LONDON:
Printed by *T.S.* and are to be solde by IOHN HELME,
at his Shop in S. Dunstones Church-yard,
in *Fleetstreet.* 1 6 1 3.

TO THE RIGHT   [A3]
VERTVOVS, AND
truely Noble Knight, S^{r.}
Thomas Howard, &c.

Sir,   5

Since Workes of this kinde haue beene lately
esteemed worthy the Patronage of some of our worthiest
Nobles, I haue made no doubt to preferre this of mine
to your vndoubted Vertue, and exceeding true Noblesse:
as contayning matter no lesse deseruing your reading,   10
and excitation to Heroycall life, then any such late
Dedication. Nor haue the greatest Princes of Italie,
and other Countries, conceiued it any least diminution
to their greatnesse, / to haue their Names wing'd with   [A3ᵛ]
these Tragicke Plumes, and disperst by way of Patron-   15
age, through the most Noble Notices of Europe.

Howsoeuer therefore in the Scænicall presentation,
it might meete with some maligners, yet considering,
euen therein, it past with approbation of more worthy
iudgements; the Ballance of their side (especially   20
being held by your impartiall hand) I hope will to no
graine abide the out-weighing. And for the autenticall
truth of eyther person or action, who (worth the respecting)
will expect it in a Poeme, whose subiect is not truth,
but things like truth? Poore enuious soules they are   25
that cauill at truths want in these naturall fictions:
materiall instruction, elegant and sententious excitation
to Vertue, and deflection from her contrary; being the
soule, lims, and limits of an autenticall Tragedie.
But whatsoeuer merit of your full countenance and   30
fauour suffers defect in this, I shall soone supply
with some other of more generall account: wherein your
right vertuous Name made / famous and preserued to pos-   [A4]
teritie, your future comfort and honour in your present

---

4 *Howard,*] ~. ‖

442

acceptation, and loue of all vertuous and diuine expression;   35
may be so much past others of your Rancke encreast, as
they are short of your Iudiciall Ingenuitie, in their
due estimation.

For, howsoeuer those Ignoble and sowre-brow'd
Worldlings are carelesse of whatsoeuer future, or   40
present opinion spreads of them; yet (with the most
diuine Philosopher, if Scripture did not confirme it)
I make it matter of my Faith; that we truely retaine an
intellectuall feeling of Good or Bad after this life;
proportionably answerable to the loue or neglect we   45
beare here to all Vertue, and truely-humane Instruction:
In whose fauour and honour I wish you most eminent;
And rest euer.

Your   true   Vertues
most true obseruer,   50
Geo. Chapman.

39 sowre-brow'd] ~-/~ ‖

The Actors names. [A4ᵛ]

Henry, the King.
Monsieur, his Brother.
Guise, a Duke.
Renel, a Marquesse.
Mont sureau, an Earle. 5
Baligny, Lord Lieutenant.
Clermont D'Ambois.
Maillard.
Challon. } Captaines.
Aumal. 10
Espernone.

Soissone.
Perricot.
[An Usher to the Countess.
A Messenger.] 15
The Guard.
Souldiers.
Seruants.

The ghost of {
Bussy.
Monsieur. 20
Guise.
Card. Guise.
Shattilion.

Countesse of Cambray.
Tamyra, wife to Mont sureau. 25
Charlotte, wife to Baligny.
Rioua, a Seruant.

---

3 a Duke] *Parrott*; *D.* ‖ **5** *Mont sureau*] *Q(c)*; *Mont surrau Q(u)* ‖ **7** *Clermont*] ~, ‖ **14** An ... Countess] *Parrott* ‖ **15** A *Messenger*] *Boas* ‖

THE REVENGE
OF
Bussy D'Ambois.
A
TRAGEDIE.

Actus primi   Scæna prima.

Enter Baligny, Renel.

Bal. To what will this declining Kingdome turne,
Swindging in euery license, as in this
Stupide permission of braue D'Ambois Murther?
Murther made paralell with Law? Murther vs'd
To serue the Kingdome, giuen by sute to men   5
For their aduancement? suffered scarcrow-like
To fright adulterie? what will policie
At length bring vnder his capacitie?
   Ren. All things: for as when the high births of Kings,
Deliuerances, and Coronations,   10
We celebrate with all the Cities Bels
(Iangling together in vntun'd confusion:)
All order'd Clockes are tyed vp: so when Glory,
Flatterie, and smooth applauses of things ill,
Vphold th'inordinate swindge of downe-right power,   15
Iustice, and truth, that tell the bounded vse,
Vertuous, and well distinguisht formes of Time, /
Are gag'd and tongue-tide; but wee haue obseru'd   [B1ᵛ]
Rule in more regular motion: things most lawfull
Were once most royall; Kings sought common good,   20
Mens manly liberties, though ne'er so meane,
And had their owne swindge so: more free, and more,
But when pride enter'd them, and Rule by power,
All browes that smil'd beneath them, frown'd; hearts grieu'd,

SD *Enter*] Enter ‖ 1 *Bal.*] *Baligny. (centered above l. 1)* ‖ 9 Kings,] ~ ‖ 18 tongue-tide;] ~-~, ‖
20 royall;] ~, | good,] ~ ‖

445

By imitation; vertue quite was vanisht,   25
And all men studi'd selfe-loue, fraud, and vice;
Then no man could be good but he was punisht:
Tyrants being still more fearefull of the good
Then of the bad; their subiects vertues euer
Manag'd with curbs, and dangers, and esteem'd   30
As shadowes, and detractions to their owne.
    Bal. Now all is peace, no danger: now what followes?
Idlenesse rusts vs; since no vertuous labour
Ends ought rewarded: Ease, Securitie
Now all the Palme weares; wee made warre before   35
So to preuent warre; men with giuing gifts
More then receiuing, made our Countrey strong;
Our matchlesse race of Souldiers then would spend
In publike warres, not priuate brawles, their spirits;
In daring Enemies, arm'd with meanest armes;   40
Not courting strumpets, and consuming birth-rights
In Apishnesse, and enuy of attire.
No labour then was harsh, no way so deepe,
No rocke so steepe, but if a Bird could scale it,
Vp would our youth flie to. A Foe in armes   45
Stirr'd vp a much more lust of his encounter,
Then of a Mistresse neuer so be-painted:
Ambition then, was onely scaling walles;
And ouer-topping turrets: Fame was wealth;
Best parts, best deedes, were best Nobilitie;   50
Honour with worth; and wealth well got or none.
Countries we wonne with as few men as Countries.
Vertue subdu'd all.
    Ren.   Iust: and then our Nobles
Lou'd vertue so, they prais'd and vs'd it to; /   54
Had rather doe, then say; their owne deedes hearing   [B2]
By others glorified, then be so barraine,
That their parts onely stood in praising others.
    Bal. Who could not doe, yet prais'd, and enui'd not;
Ciuile behauiour flourisht; Bountie flow'd;
Auarice to vpland Boores, slaues, hang-men banisht.   60
    Ren. Tis now quite otherwise; but to note the cause
Of all these foule digressions, and reuolts
From our first natures, this tis in a word:
Since good Arts faile, crafts and deceits are vs'd;
Men ignorant are idle; idle men   65

---

26 vice;] ~, ‖ **35** weares;] ~, ‖ **36** warre;] ~, ‖ **55** hearing] *stet* (*See Textual Note*) ‖ **59** flow'd;] ~,
‖ **60** slaues,] ~‸ ‖ **64** vs'd;] ~: ‖

Most practise what they most may doe with ease,
Fashion, and fauour; all their studies ayming
At getting money, which no wise man euer
Fed his desires with.
    Bal.   Yet now none are wise
That thinke not heauen's true foolish, weigh'd with that.   70
Well thou most worthy to be greatest Guise,
Make with thy greatnesse a new world arise.
Such deprest Nobles (followers of his)
As you, your selfe, my Lord will finde a time
When to reuenge your wrongs.
    Ren.   I make no doubt: 75
In meane time, I could wish, the wrong were righted
Of your slaine Brother in law, braue Bussy D'Ambois.
    Bal. That one accident was made my charge.
My Brother Bussy's Sister (now my wife)
By no suite would consent to satisfie   80
My loue of her, with marriage, till I vow'd,
To vse my vtmost to reuenge my Brother:
But Clermont D'Ambois (Bussy's second Brother)
Had (since his apparition, and excitement)
To suffer none but his hand in his wreake,   85
Which hee hath vow'd, and so will needes acquite
Me of my vow, made to my wife, his Sister,
And vndertake himselfe Bussy's reuenge;
Yet loathing any way to giue it act,
But in the noblest and most manly course, /   90
(If th'Earle dares take it) he resolues to send   [B2ᵛ]
A Challenge to him, and my selfe must beare it,
To which deliuerie I can vse no meanes;
He is so barricado'd in his house,
And arm'd with guard still.
    Ren.   That meanes lay on mee,   95
Which I can strangely make. My last lands sale,
By his great suite, stands now on price with him,
And hee (as you know) passing couetous,
(With that blinde greedinesse that followes gaine)
Will cast no danger, where her sweet feete tread.   100
Besides, you know, his Lady by his suite,
(Wooing as freshly, as when first loue shot
His faultlesse arrowes from her rosie eyes)
Now liues with againe, and shee, I know,

---

70 heauen's true] heauens true (*See Textual Note*) ‖ 74 your selfe] *Parrott*; my selfe (*See Textual Note*) ‖ 84 (since ... excitement)] (~) ... ~, (*See Textual Note*) ‖ 90 course,] ~. ‖

Will ioyne with all helps, in her friends reuenge.   105
   Bal. No doubt (my Lord) and therefore let me pray you
To vse all speede; for so on needels points
My wifes heart stands with haste of the reuenge:
Being (as you know) full of her brothers fire,
That shee imagines I neglect my vow;   110
Keepes off her kinde embraces, and still askes;
When, when, will this reuenge come? when perform'd
Will this dull vow be? And, I vow to Heauen,
So sternely, and so past her sexe she vrges
My vowes performance; that I almost feare   115
To see her, when I haue a while beene absent,
Not showing her before I speake, the bloud
She so much thirsts for, freckling hands and face.
   Ren. Get you the Challenge writ, and looke from me,   119
To heare your passage clear'd no long time after.   *Exit Ren.*
   Bal. All restitution to your worthiest Lordship,
Whose errand I must carrie to the King,
As hauing sworne my seruice in the search
Of all such Malecontents, and their designes,
By seeming one, affected with their faction,   125
And discontented humours gainst the state:
Nor doth my brother Clermont scape my counsaile /
Giuen to the King, about his Guisean greatnesse,   [B3]
Which (as I spice it) hath possest the King
(Knowing his daring spirit) of much danger,   130
Charg'd in it to his person: though my conscience
Dare sweare him cleare of any power to be
Infected with the least dishonestie:
Yet that sinceritie, wee Politicians
Must say, growes out of enuie, since it cannot   135
Aspire to policies greatnesse: and the more
We worke on all respects of kinde, and vertue,
The more our seruice to the King seemes great,
In sparing no good that seemes bad to him:
And the more bad, we make the most of good,   140
The more our policie searcheth; and our seruice
Is wonder'd at for wisedome and sincerenesse.
Tis easie to make good suspected still,
Where good, and God, are made but cloakes for ill.

    Enter Henry, Monsieur, Guise, Clerm., Espernone, Soisson.
       Monsieur taking leaue of the King.

---

113 And, ... Heauen,] ~ͺ ... ~. ‖ **118** face.] ~, ‖ **127** Clermont] *Clermont* ‖ **130** danger,] ~: ‖
144 SD *Enter ... King.*] *in right margin opposite ll.145-49* | SD *Clerm.,*] ~.ͺ | SD *Soisson*]
Shepherd; *Foisson* ‖

See Monsieur taking now his leaue for Brabant,   [*Exit Henry.*]
The Guise, and his deare Minion, Clermont D'Ambois,   146
Whispering together, not of state affaires
I durst lay wagers, (though the Guise be now
In chiefe heate of his faction) but of some thing,
Sauouring of that which all men else despise,   150
How to be truely noble, truely wise.
   Mons. See how hee hangs vpon the eare of Guise,
Like to his Iewell.
   Esp.   Hee's now whisp'ring in
Some doctrine of stabilitie, and freedome,
Contempt of outward greatnesse, and the guises   155
That vulgar great ones make their pride and zeale,
Being onely seruile traines, and sumptuous houses,
High places, offices.
   Mons.   Contempt of these
Does he read to the Guise? Tis passing needfull,
And hee, I thinke, makes show t'affect his doctrine.   160
   Esp. Commends, admires it.
   Mons.   And pursues another.
Tis fine hypocrisie, and cheape, and vulgar,/
Knowne for a couert practise, yet belecu'd   [B3ᵛ]
(By those abus'd soules, that they teach and gouerne)
No more then Wiues adulteries, by their Husbands,   165
They bearing it with so vnmou'd aspects,
Hot comming from it; as twere not [at] all,
Or made by custome nothing. This same D'Ambois
Hath gotten such opinion of his vertues,
(Holding all learning but an Art to liue well,)   170
And showing hee hath learn'd it, in his life,
Being thereby strong in his perswading others;
That this ambitious Guise, embracing him,
Is thought t'embrace his vertues.
   Esp.   Yet in some
His vertues are held false for th'others vices: 175
For tis more cunning held, and much more common,
To suspect truth then falshood: and of both,
Truth still fares worse; as hardly being beleeu'd,
As tis vnvsuall, and rarely knowne.
   Mons. Ile part engendring vertue. Men affirme   180
Though this same Clermont hath a D'Ambois spirit,
And breathes his brothers valour; yet his temper

---

145 SD *Exit Henry.*] *Lordi (after Parrott)* ‖ **161** another.] ~, ‖ **167** at] *Shepherd* ‖ **174** t'embrace]
t'mbrace ‖

Is so much past his, that you cannot moue him:
Ile try that temper in him. Come, you two
Deuoure each other with your vertues zeale,   185
And leaue for other friends, no fragment of yee:
I wonder Guise, you will thus rauish him
Out of my bosome, that first gaue the life
His manhood breathes, spirit, and meanes and luster.
What doe men thinke of me, I pray thee Clermont?   190
Once giue me leaue (for tryall of that loue
That from thy brother Bussy thou inherit'st)
T'vnclaspe thy bosome.
    Cler.   As how sir?
    Mons. Be a true glasse to mee, in which I may
Behold what thoughts the many-headed beast,   195
And thou thy selfe breathes out concerning me,
My ends, and new vpstarted state in Brabant,
For which I now am bound, my higher aymes,
Imagin'd here in France: speake man, and let /   199
Thy words be borne as naked as thy thoughts: [B4]
O were braue Bussy liuing!
    Cler.   Liuing my Lord?
    Mons. Tis true, thou art his brother, but durst thou
Haue brau'd the Guise: mauger his presence, courted
His wedded Lady; emptied euen the dregs
Of his worst thoughts of mee, euen to my teeth;   205
Discern'd not me his rising soueraigne
From any common groome: but let me heare
My grossest faults, as grosse-full as they were.
Durst thou doe this?
    Cler.   I cannot tell: A man
Does neuer know the goodnesse of his stomacke   210
Till hee sees meate before him. Were I dar'd,
Perhaps as he was, I durst doe like him.
    Mons. Dare then to poure out here thy freest soule,
Of what I am.
    Cler.   Tis stale, he tolde you it.
    Mons. He onely iested, spake of splene and enuie;   215
Thy soule more learn'd, is more ingenuous,
Searching, iudiciall; let me then from thee
Heare what I am.
    Cler.   What but the sole support,
And most expectant hope of all our France,
The toward victor of the whole Low Countryes?   220

---

195 many-headed beast] ~ ͺ ~-~ ‖ **220** Low] low ‖

450

Mons. Tush, thou wilt sing Encomions of my praise.
Is this like D'Ambois? I must vexe the Guise,
Or neuer looke to heare free truth; tell me,
For Bussy liues not: hee durst anger mee,
Yet for my loue, would not haue fear'd to anger   225
The King himselfe. Thou vnderstand'st me, dost not?
   Cler. I shall my Lord, with studie.
   Mons. Dost vnderstand thy selfe? I pray thee tell me,
Dost neuer search thy thoughts, what my designe
Might be to entertaine thee and thy brother?   230
What turne I meant to serue with you?
   Cler. Euen what you please to thinke.
   Mons.   But what thinkst thou?
Had I no end in't think'st?
   Cler.   I thinke you had.
   Mons. When I tooke in such two as you two were, /   234
A ragged couple of decaid Commanders,   [B4ᵛ]
When a French-crowne would plentifully serue
To buy you both to any thing i'th'earth.
   Cler. So it would you:
   Mons.   Nay bought you both out-right,
You and your Trunkes: I feare me, I offend thee.
   Cler. No not a iot.
   Mons.   The most renowmed Souldier   240
Epaminondas (as good Authors say)
Had no more suites then backes, but you two shar'd
But one suite twixt you both, when both your studies
Were not what meate to dine with; if your Partridge,
Your Snipe, your Wood-cocke, Larke, or your red Hering,   245
But where to begge it, whether at my house,
Or at the Guises (for you know you were
Ambitious beggars,) or at some Cookes-shop,
T'eternize the Cookes trust, and score it vp.
Dost not offend thee?
   Cler.   No sir. Pray proceede.   250
   Mons. As for thy Gentry, I dare boldly take
Thy honourable othe: and yet some say
Thou and thy most renowmed noble Brother,
Came to the Court first in a Keele of Sea-coale;
Dost not offend thee?
   Cler.   Neuer doubt it, sir.   255
   Mons. Why doe I loue thee then? why haue I rak'd thee
Out of the dung-hill? cast my cast Ward-robe on thee?

---

241 Epaminondas] *Epaminondas* ‖

451

Brought thee to Court to, as I did thy Brother?
Made yee my sawcy bon companions?
Taught yee to call our greatest Noble men   260
By the corruption of their names; Iack, Tom?
Haue I blowne both for nothing to this bubble?
Though thou art learn'd; th'ast no enchanting wit,
Or were thy wit good, am I therefore bound
To keepe thee for my Table?
    Cler.   Well Sir, 'twere   265
A good Knights place. Many a proud dubb'd Gallant
Seekes out a poore Knights liuing from such Emrods.
    [*Mons.*] Or what vse else should I designe thee to?
Perhaps you'll answere me, to be my Pander. /
    Cler. Perhaps I shall.   [C1]
    Mons.   Or did the slie Guise put thee   270
Into my bosome, t'vndermine my proiects?
I feare thee not; for though I be not sure
I haue thy heart, I know thy braine-pan yet
To be as emptie a dull piece of wainscot
As euer arm'd the scalpe of any Courtier;   275
A fellow onely that consists of sinewes;
Meere Swisser, apt for any execution.
    Cler. But killing of the King.
    Mons.   Right: now I see
Thou vnderstand'st thy selfe.
    Cler.   I, and you better.
You are a Kings sonne borne –   280
    Mons. Right.
    Cler.   And a Kings brother –
    Mons. True.
    Cler. And might not any foole haue beene so too,
As well as you?   285
    Mons. A poxe vpon you.
    Cler.   You did no Princely deedes
Ere you're borne (I take it) to deserue it;
Nor did you any since that I haue heard;
Nor will doe euer any, as all thinke.   290
    Mons. The Diuell take him. Ile no more of him.
    Guise. Nay: stay my Lord, and heare him answere you.
    Mons. No more I sweare. Farewell.   *Ex. Mons.*
                                                Esper. Soiss.

    Guise.   No more: Ill fortune.

---

263 th'ast] thast ‖ **268** *Mons.*] Boas ‖ **279-87** *Cler.* ... deedes] *Cler.* ... King. / *Mons.* ... see / Thou ... selfe. / *Cler.* ... better. / You ... Right. / *Cler.* ... True. / *Cler.* ... too, / As ... you. / *Cler.* ... deedes (*See Textual Note*) ‖ **280** borne–] ~. ‖ **282** brother–] ~. ‖

I would haue giuen a million to haue heard
His scoffes retorted: and the insolence   295
Of his high birth and greatnesse (which were neuer
Effects of his deserts, but of his fortune)
Made show to his dull eyes, beneath the worth
That men aspire to by their knowing vertues,
Without which Greatnesse is a shade, a bubble.   300
   Cler. But what one great man dreames of that, but you?
All take their births and birth-rights left to them
(Acquir'd by others) for their owne worths purchase,
When many a foole in both, is great as they:
And who would thinke they could winne with their worths   305
Wealthy possessions, when wonne to their hands, /
They neyther can iudge iustly of their value,   [C1ᵛ]
Nor know their vse; and therefore they are puft
With such proud tumours as this Monsieur is:
Enabled onely by the goods they haue,   310
To scorne all goodnesse: none great fill their fortunes,
But as those men that make their houses greater,
Their housholds being lesse, so Fortune raises
Huge heapes of out-side in these mightie men,
And giues them nothing in them.
   Guise.   True as truth: 315
And therefore they had rather drowne their substance
In superfluities of brickes and stones;
(Like Sysiphus, aduancing of them euer,
And euer pulling downe) then lay the cost
Of any sluttish corner, on a man,   320
Built with Gods finger, and enstil'd his Temple.
   Bal. Tis nobly said, my Lord.
   Guise.   I would haue these things
Brought vpon Stages, to let mightie Misers
See all their graue and serious miseries, plaid,
As once they were in Athens, and olde Rome.   325
   Cler. Nay, we must now haue nothing brought on Stages,
But puppetry, and pide ridiculous Antickes:
Men thither come, to laugh, and feede foole-fat,
Checke at all goodnesse there, as being prophan'd:
When wheresoeuer goodnesse comes, shee makes   330
The place still sacred; though with other feete
Neuer so much tis scandal'd, and polluted.
Let me learne any thing that fits a man,

---

311 great] ~, ‖ 318 Sysiphus] *Sysiphus* ‖

In any Stables showne, as well as Stages.
  Bal. Why? is not all the world esteem'd a Stage?   335
  Cler. Yes: and right worthily: and Stages too
Haue a respect due to them: if but onely,
For what the good Greeke Moralist sayes of them;
Is a man proud of greatnesse, or of riches?
Giue me an expert Actor; Ile shew all,   340
That can within his greatest glory fall.
Is a man fraid with pouertie and lownesse? /
Giue me an Actor, Ile shew euery eye   [C2]
What hee laments so, and so much doth flye,
The best and worst of both: if but for this then,   345
To make the proudest out-side that most swels,
With things without him, and aboue his worth,
See how small cause hee has to be so blowne vp,
And the most poore man, to be grieu'd with poorenesse,
Both being so easily borne by expert Actors.   350
The Stage and Actors are not so contemptfull,
As euery innouating Puritane,
And ignorant sweater, out of zealous enuie,
Would haue the world imagine. And besides
That, all things haue beene likened to the mirth,   355
Vs'd vpon Stages, and for Stages fitted.
The splenatiue Philosopher that euer
Laught at them all, were worthy the enstaging:
All obiects, were they ne'er so full of teares,
He so conceited, that he could distill thence   360
Matter that still fed his ridiculous humour.
Heard he a Lawyer, neuer so vehement pleading,
Hee stood and laught. Heard hee a Trades-man swearing
Neuer so thriftily (selling of his wares);
Hee stood and laught. Heard hee an holy brother,   365
For hollow ostentation at his prayers
Ne'er so impetuously; hee stood and laught.
Saw hee a great man neuer so insulting,
Seuerely inflicting, grauely giuing lawes,
Not for their good, but his; hee stood and laught.   370
Saw hee a youthfull widow
Neuer so weeping, wringing of her hands,
For her lost Lord, still the Philosopher laught:
Now whether hee suppos'd all these presentments,
Were onely maskeries, and wore false faces: 375

---

338 Moralist] *Shepherd*; Moralists ‖ 348 vp,] ~; ‖ 353 sweater,] ~ˌ (*See Textual Note*) ‖ 354-55 besides That,] ~, ~ˌ ‖ 364 (selling ... wares);] (~ ... ~;) (*See Textual Note*) ‖

Or else were simply vaine, I take no care,
But still hee laught, how graue soere they were.
   Guise. And might right well (my Clermont) and for this
Vertuous digression, wee will thanke the scoffes
Of vicious Monsieur. But now for the maine point /   380
Of your late resolution for reuenge   [C2ᵛ]
Of your slaine friend.
   Cler.   I haue here my Challenge,
Which I will pray my Brother Baligny
To beare the murtherous Earle.
   Bal.   I haue prepar'd
Meanes for accesse to him, through all his Guard.   385
   Guise. About it then, my worthy Baligny,
And bring vs the successe.
   Bal.   I will my Lord.   *Exeunt*.

[I.ii]

Tamyra sola.

   Tam. Reuenge, that euer red sitt'st in the eyes
Of iniur'd Ladies, till we crowne thy browes
With bloudy Lawrell; and receiue from thee
Iustice for all our honors iniurie,
Whose wings none flye, that Wrath or Tyrannie   5
Haue ruthlesse made, and bloudy: enter here,
Enter, O enter: and, though length of time
Neuer lets any scape thy constant iustice,
Yet now preuent that length. Flye, flye, and here
Fixe thy steele foot-steps: Here, O here, where still   10
Earth (mou'd with pittie) yeelded and embrac'd
My Loues faire figure, drawne in his deare bloud,
And mark'd the place, to show thee where was done
The cruell'st murther that ere fled the Sunne.
O Earth! why keep'st thou not as well his spirit,   15
To giue his forme life? No, that was not earthly:
That (rarefying the thinne and yeelding ayre)
Flew sparkling vp into the Sphære of fire,
Whence endlesse flames it sheds in my desire:
Here be my daily pallet, here all nights   20
That can be wrested from thy riuals armes;
(O my deare Bussy) I will lye, and kisse
Spirit into thy bloud, or breathe out mine

---

382 friend] *stet* (*See Textual Note*) ‖ I.ii] *Boas* ‖ 4 honors] *Shepherd subs*.; humors ‖ 6 bloudy:
enter] bloudy. Enter ‖

In sighes, and kisses, and sad tunes to thine.   *She sings.*

Enter Montsur.

Mont. Still on this hant? Still shall adulterous bloud /   25
Affect thy spirits? Thinke, for shame, but this,   [C3]
This bloud that Cockatrice-like thus thou brood'st
To dry is to breede any quench to thine.
And therefore now (if onely for thy lust
A little couer'd with a vaile of shame)   30
Looke out for fresh life, rather then witch-like,
Learne to kisse horror, and with death engender.
Strange crosse in nature, purest virgine shame
Lies in the bloud, as lust lyes; and together
Many times mixe too: and in none more shamefull   35
Then in the shamefac't. Who can then distinguish
Twixt their affections; or tell when hee meetes
With one not common? Yet, as worthiest Poets
Shunne common and plebeian formes of speech,
Euery illiberall and affected phrase   40
To clothe their matter: and together tye
Matter and forme, with Art and decencie;
So worthiest women should shunne vulgar guises,
And though they cannot but flye out for change,
Yet modestie, the matter of their liues,   45
Be it adulterate, should be painted true
With modest out-parts; what they should doe still
Grac'd with good show, though deedes be ne'er so ill.
Tam. That is so farre from all yee seeke of vs,
That (though your selues be common as the ayre)   50
We must not take the ayre, wee must not fit
Our actions to our owne affections:
But as Geometricians (you still say)
Teach that no lines, nor superficies,
Doe moue themselues, but still accompanie   55
The motions of their bodies; so poore wiues
Must not pursue, nor haue their owne affections,
But to their husbands earnests, and their iests,
To their austerities of lookes, and laughters,
(Though ne'er so foolish and iniurious)   60
Like Parasites and slaues, fit their disposures.
Mont. I vsde thee as my soule, to moue and rule me.
Tam. So said you, when you woo'd. So Souldiers tortur'd /

---

24 SD *Montsur.*] *Q(c)*; *Monsieur. Q(u)* ‖ 25 *Mont.*] *Q(c)*; *Mons. Q(u)* ‖ 28 dry] *Q(c)*; dye *Q(u)* ‖
32 engender.] *Q(c)*; ~. *Q(u)* ‖ 42 decencie;] ~. ‖ 52 affections] affectons ‖ 54 lines] *Q(c)*; liues
Q(u) ‖ 62 *Mont.*] *Q(c)*; *Mons. Q(u)* ‖

With tedious sieges of some wel-wall'd Towne,   [C3ᵛ]
Propound conditions of most large contents,   65
Freedome of Lawes, all former gouernment;
But hauing once set foote within the Wals,
And got the reynes of power into their hands,
Then doe they tyrannize at their owne rude swindges,
Seaze all their goods, their liberties, and liues,   70
And make aduantage, and their lusts, their lawes.
    Mont. But loue me, and performe a Wifes part yet,
(With all my loue before) I sweare forgiuenesse.
    Tam. Forgiuenesse! that grace you should seeke of mee:
These tortur'd fingers, and these stab'd-through armes   75
Keepe that law in their wounds yet, vnobseru'd,
And euer shall.
    Mont.   Remember their deserts.
    Tam. Those with faire warnings might haue beene reform'd,
Not these vnmanly rages. You haue heard
The fiction of the North winde and the Sunne,   80
Both working on a Traueller, and contending
Which had most power to take his cloake from him:
Which when the Winde attempted, hee roar'd out
Outragious blasts at him to force it off,
That wrapt it closer on. When the calme Sunne   85
(The Winde once leauing) charg'd him with still beames,
Quiet, and feruent, and therein was constant,
Which made him cast off both his cloake and coate:
Like whom should men doe. If yee wish your Wiues
Should leaue dislik'd things, seeke it not with rage;   90
For that enrages: what yee giue, yee haue:
But vse calme warnings, and kinde manly meanes,
And that in Wiues most prostitute will winne
Not onely sure amends; but make vs Wiues
Better then those that ne'er led faultie liues.   95

Enter a Souldier.

    Sould. My Lord.
    Mont.   How now; would any speake with me?
    Sould. I, Sir.
    Mont.   Peruerse, and traiterous miscreant:
Where are your other fellowes of my Guard? /
Haue I not told you, I will speake with none,   [C4]
But Lord Renel?
    Sould.   And tis hee that stayes you.   100

---

72 *Mont.*] *Shepherd; Mons.* ‖ 77 *Mont.*] *Shepherd; Mons.* ‖ 96-97 *Sould.* ... miscreant:] *Boas;*
Sould. My Lord. / *Mons.* ... Sir. / *Mons.* ... miscreant:* ‖ 96 *Mont.*] *Shepherd; Mons.* ‖ 97 *Mont.*]
Shepherd; Mons. ‖

Mont. O, is it he? Tis well: attend him in.   [*Exit Souldier.*]
I must be vigilant: the Furies haunt mee.
Doe you heare dame?

Enter Renel, with the Souldier.

Ren. [*Aside to the Souldier.*] Be true now, for your Ladies iniur'd sake,
Whose bountie you haue so much cause to honour: 105
For her respect is chiefe in this designe,
And therefore serue it, call out of the way
All your confederate fellowes of his Guard,
Till Monsieur Baligny be enter'd here.
Sould. Vpon your honour, my Lord shall be free   110
From any hurt you say?
Ren. Free as my selfe. Watch then, and cleare his entrie.
Sould. I will not faile, my Lord.   *Exit Souldier.*
Ren.   God saue your Lordship.
Mont. My noblest Lord Renel! past all men welcome.
Wife, welcome his Lordship.   *Osculatur.*
Ren.   I much ioy   115
In your returne here.
Tam.   You doe more then I.
Mont. Shee's passionate still, to thinke we euer parted,
By my too sterne iniurious Ielousie.
Ren. Tis well your Lordship will confesse your errour
In so good time yet.

Enter Baligny with a Challenge.

Mont.   Death! Who haue wee here?   120
Ho! Guard! Villaines!
Bal.   Why exclaime you so?
Mont. Negligent Trayters! Murther, murther, murther.
Bal. Y'are mad. Had mine entent beene so, like yours,
It had beene done ere this.
Ren.   Sir, your intent,
And action too, was rude to enter thus.   125
Bal. Y'are a decaid Lord to tell me of rudenesse,
As much decaid in manners as in meanes.
Ren. You talke of manners, that thus rudely thrust
Vpon a man that's busie with his Wife.
Bal. And kept your Lordship then the dore?
Ren.   The dore?   130
                          [*Draws his sword.*] /

101 *Mont.*] *Shepherd*; *Mons.* | SD *Exit Souldier.*] *Boas* ‖ 104 SD *Aside ... Souldier.*] *Boas* ‖ 111
say?] ~. ‖ 114 *Mont.*] *Shepherd*; *Mons.* | Renel] *Renel* ‖ 115-16 Wife ... I.] *Boas*; Wife ...
Lordship. / *Ren. ... here. / Tamy. ... I. Q* (in) ‖ 117 *Mont.*] *Shepherd*; *Mons.* ‖ 120 SD *Enter ...
Challenge.*] *flush right* | *Mont.*] *Shepherd*; *Mons.* ‖ 121 So?] ~. ‖ 122 *Mont.*] *Shepherd*; *Mons.* ‖
123 Y'are] *Shepherd*; Ye'are ‖ 130 the dore?] ~ ~. | SD *Draws his Sword.*] *Lordi* ‖

Mont. [*To Renel.*] Sweet Lord forbeare. [*To Baligny.*] Show, show
    your purpose sir,   [C4ᵛ]
To moue such bold feete into others roofes.
    Bal. This is my purpose sir, from Clermont D'Ambois
I bring this Challenge.
    Mont.   Challenge! Ile touch none.
    Bal. Ile leaue it here then.
    Ren.   Thou shalt leaue thy life first.   135
    Mont. Murther, Murther!
    Ren.   Retire my Lord; get off.
Hold, or thy death shall hold thee. Hence my Lord.
    Bal. There lye the Chalenge.   *They all fight and Bal. driues*
                            in Mont. Exit Mont.

    Ren.   Was not this well handled?
    Bal. Nobly my Lord. All thankes.   *Exit Bal.*
    Tam.   Ile make him reade it.   *Exit Tamy.*
    Ren. This was a sleight well maskt. O what is man,   140
Vnlesse he be a Politician!   *Exit.*

Finis Actus primi.

Actus secundi   Scæna prima.

Henry, Baligny.

    Hen. Come Baligny, we now are priuate: Say,
What seruice bring'st thou? make it short; the Guise
(Whose friend thou seem'st) is now in Court, and neare,
And may obserue vs.
    Bal.   This sir, then in short.
The faction of the Guise (with which my policie,   5
For seruice to your Highnesse seemes to ioyne)
Growes ripe, and must be gather'd into hold;
Of which my Brother Clermont being a part
Exceeding capitall, deserues to haue
A capitall eye on him. And (as you may   10
With best aduantage, and your speediest charge,)
Command his apprehension: which (because
The Court, you know, is strong in his defence)
Wee must aske Country swindge and open fields.
And therefore I haue wrought him to goe downe /   15

---

131 *Mont.*] Q(c); *Mons.* Q(u) | SD *To Renel.*] Parrott | SD *To Baligny.*] Parrott subs. | sir,] ~. ‖
133 *Bal.*] Q(c); *Mons.* Q(u) ‖ 134-36 I ... off.] Boas; I ... Challenge. / Mon. ... then. / Ren. ...
murther! / Ren. ... off. ‖ 134 *Mont.*] Shepherd; *Mon.* ‖ 136 *Mont.*] Q(c); *Mons.* Q(u) ‖ 138 SD
Mont.] Q(c); *Mons.* Q(u) | SD *Mont.*] Q(c); *Mons.* Q(u) ‖

To Cambray with me (of which Gouernment   [D1]
Your Highnesse bountie made mee your Lieutenant)
Where when I haue him, I will leaue my house,
And faine some seruice out about the confines,
When in the meane time, if you please to giue   20
Command to my Lieutenant, by your Letters,
To traine him to some muster, where he may
(Much to his honour) see for him, your forces
Put into Battaile; when hee comes, hee may
With some close stratageme be apprehended: 25
For otherwise your whole powers there will faile
To worke his apprehension: and with that
My hand needes neuer be discern'd therein.
   Hen. Thankes honest Baligny.
   Bal.   Your Highnesse knowes
I will be honest; and betray for you   30
Brother and Father: for, I know (my Lord)
Treacherie for Kings is truest Loyaltie;
Nor is to beare the name of Treacherie,
But graue, deepe Policie. All acts that seeme
Ill in particular respects, are good   35
As they respect your vniuersall Rule.
As in the maine sway of the vniuerse
The supreame Rectors generall decrees,
To guard the mightie Globes of Earth and Heauen,
Since they make good that guard to preseruation   40
Of both those in their order and first end,
No mans particular (as hee thinkes) wrong
Must hold him wrong'd: no, not though all mens reasons,
All Law, all conscience, concludes it wrong.
Nor is comparison a flatterer   45
To liken you here to the King of kings;
Nor any mans particular offence
Against the worlds sway, to offence at yours
In any subiect; who as little may
Grudge at their particular wrong (if so it seeme),   50
For th'vniuersall right of your estate;
As (being a Subiect of the Worlds whole sway /
As well as yours; and being a righteous man   [D1ᵛ]
To whom Heauen promises defence, and blessing,
Brought to decay, disgrace, and quite defencelesse)   55
Hee may complaine of Heauen for wrong to him.

48 sway,] ~; ‖ **50** wrong (... seeme),] ~; ... ~‸‸ ‖ **51** estate;] ~. ‖

Hen. Tis true: the Simile at all parts holds,
As all good Subiects hold, that loue our fauour.
   Bal. Which is our Heauen here; and a miserie
Incomparable, and most truely Hellish   60
To liue depriu'd of our Kings grace and countenance,
Without which best conditions are most cursed:
Life of that nature, howsoeuer short,
Is a most lingering, and tedious life;
Or rather no life, but a languishing,   65
And an abuse of life.
   Hen.   Tis well conceited.
   Bal. I thought it not amisse to yeeld your Highnesse
A reason of my speeches; lest perhaps
You might conceiue I flatter'd: which (I know)
Of all ils vnder heauen you most abhorre.   70
   Hen. Still thou art right, my vertuous Baligny,
For which I thanke and loue thee. Thy aduise
Ile not forget: Haste to thy Gouernment,
And carry D'Ambois with thee. So farewell.   *Exit.*
   Bal. Your Maiestie fare euer like it selfe.   75

Enter Guise.

Guise. My sure Friend Baligny!
Bal.   Noblest of Princes!
Guise. How stands the State of Cambray?
Bal.   Strong, my Lord,
And fit for seruice: for whose readinesse
Your creature Clermont D'Ambois, and my selfe
Ride shortly downe.
   Guise.   That Clermont is my loue;   80
France neuer bred a nobler Gentleman
For all parts: he exceedes his Brother Bussy.
   Bal. I, my Lord?
   Guise.   Farre: because (besides his valour) /
Hee hath the crowne of man, and all his parts,   [D2]
Which Learning is; and that so true and vertuous,   85
That it giues power to doe, as well as say
What euer fits a most accomplisht man;
Which Bussy, for his valours season, lackt;
And so was rapt with outrage oftentimes
Beyond Decorum; where this absolute Clermont,   90
Though (onely for his naturall zeale to right)
Hee will be fiery, when hee sees it crost;

And in defence of it; yet when he lists
Hee can containe that fire, as hid in Embers.
    Bal. No question, hee's a true, learn'd, Gentleman.   95
    Guise. He is as true as Tides, or any Starre
Is in his motion: And for his rare learning,
Hee is not (as all else are that seeke knowledge)
Of taste so much deprau'd, that they had rather
Delight, and satisfie themselues to drinke   100
Of the streame troubled, wandring ne'er so farre
From the cleare fount, then of the fount it selfe.
In all; Romes Brutus is reuiu'd in him,
Whom hee of industry doth imitate.
Or rather, as great Troys Euphorbus was   105
After Pithagoras; so is Brutus, Clermont.
And (were not Brutus a Conspirator) –
    Bal. Conspirator, my Lord? Doth that empaire him?
Cæsar beganne to tyrannize; and when vertue,
Nor the religion of the Gods could serue   110
To curbe the insolence of his proud Lawes,
Brutus would be the Gods iust instrument.
What said the Princesse (sweet Antigone)
In the graue Greeke Tragedian, when the question
Twixt her and Creon is, for lawes of Kings?   115
Which when he vrges, shee replies on him;
Though his Lawes were a Kings, they were not Gods;
Nor would shee value Creons written Lawes
With Gods vnwrit Edicts: since they last not
This day and the next, but euery day and euer;   120
Where Kings Lawes alter euery day and houre, /
And in that change imply a bounded power.   [D2ᵛ]
    Guise. Well, let vs leaue these vaine disputings what
Is to be done, and fall to doing something.
When are you for your Gouernment in Cambray?   125
    Bal. When you command, my Lord.
    Guise.   Nay, that's not fit.
Continue your designements with the King,
With all your seruice; onely if I send
Respect me as your friend, and loue my Clermont.
    Bal. Your Highnesse knowes my vowes.
    Guise.   I, tis enough.   130
                         Exit Guise. Manet Bal.
    Bal. Thus must wee play on both sides, and thus harten
In any ill those men whose good wee hate.

107 Conspirator)–] ~)‿ ‖

Kings may doe what they list: and for Kings, Subiects,
Eyther exempt from censure or exception:
For, as no mans worth can be iustly iudg'd
But when he shines in some authoritie;
So no authoritie should suffer censure
But by a man of more authoritie.
Great vessels into lesse are emptied neuer,
There's a redoundance past their continent euer.
These *virtuosi* are the poorest creatures;
For looke how Spinners weaue out of themselues
Webs, whose strange matter none before can see;
So these, out of an vnseene good in vertue,
Make arguments of right, and comfort, in her,
That clothe them like the poore web of a Spinner.

Αμηχανον δε
παντος &c. 135
Impossible est
viri cognoscere
mentem ac
voluntatem,
priusquam in
Magistratibus
apparet. 140
Sopho. Antig.

145

Enter Clermont.

Cler. Now, to my Challenge. What's the place, the weapon?
Bal. Soft sir: let first your Challenge be receiued.
Hee would not touch, nor see it.
  Cler.   Possible!
How did you then?
  Bal.   Left it, in his despight. 150
But when hee saw mee enter so expectlesse,
To heare his base exclaimes of murther, murther,
Made me thinke Noblesse lost, in him quicke buried. /
  Cler. They are the breathing Sepulchres of Noblesse: [D3]
No trulier noble men, then Lions pictures 155
Hung vp for signes, are Lions. Who knowes not, *Quo mollius degunt, eo*
That Lyons the more soft kept, are more seruile? *seruilius.* Epict.
And looke how Lyons close kept, fed by hand,
Lose quite th'innatiue fire of spirit and greatnesse
That Lyons free breathe, forraging for prey; 160
And grow so grosse, that mastifes, curs, and mungrils
Haue spirit to cow them: So our soft French Nobles
Chain'd vp in ease and numbd securitie,
(Their spirits shrunke vp like their couetous fists,
And neuer opened but Domitian-like, 165
And all his base obsequious minions
When they were catching, though it were but flyes),
Besotted with their pezzants loue of gaine,
Rusting at home, and on each other preying,
Are for their greatnesse but the greater slaues, 170

---

134 *Αμηχανον ... Antig.*] *here placed subs. as in Boas; in left margin in* Q ‖ **164-67** (Their ... flyes),] *Parrott;* ⸲~ ... ~⸲· ‖

And none is noble but who scrapes and saues.
   Bal. Tis base, tis base; and yet they thinke them high.
   Cler. So Children mounted on their hobby-horse,
Thinke they are riding, when with wanton toile
They beare what should beare them. A man may well   175
Compare them to those foolish great-spleen'd Cammels,
That to their high heads, beg'd of Ioue hornes higher;
Whose most vncomely, and ridiculous pride
When hee had satisfied, they could not vse,
But where they went vpright before, they stoopt,   180
And bore their heads much lower for their hornes;   *Simil.*
As these high men doe, low in all true grace,
Their height being priuiledge to all things base.
And as the foolish Poet that still writ
All his most selfe-lou'd verse in paper royall,   185
Or Partchment rul'd with Lead, smooth'd with the Pumice;
Bound richly vp, and strung with Crimson strings;
Neuer so blest as when hee writ and read
The Ape-lou'd issue of his braine; and neuer
But ioying in himselfe; admiring euer: 190
Yet in his workes behold him, and hee show'd /
Like to a ditcher. So these painted men,   [D3ᵛ]
All set on out-side, looke vpon within,
And not a pezzants entrailes you shall finde
More foule and mezel'd, nor more steru'd of minde.   195
   Bal. That makes their bodies fat. I faine would know
How many millions of our other Nobles
Would make one Guise. There is a true tenth Worthy,
Who (did not one act onely blemish him) –
   Cler. One act? what one?
   Bal.   One, that (though yeeres past done)   200
Stickes by him still, and will distaine him euer.
   Cler. Good Heauen! wherein? what one act can you name
Suppos'd his staine, that Ile not proue his luster?
   Bal. To satisfie you, twas the Massacre.
   Cler. The Massacre? I thought twas some such blemish.   205
   Bal. O it was hainous.
   Cler.   To a brutish sense,
But not a manly reason. Wee so tender
The vile part in vs, that the part diuine
We see in hell, and shrinke not. Who was first
Head of that Massacre?
   Bal.   The Guise.
   Cler.   Tis nothing so.   210

181 hornes;] ~. | *Simil.*] Simil. ‖ **199** him)–] ~.) ‖

Who was in fault for all the slaughters made
In Ilion, and about it? Were the Greekes?
Was it not Paris rauishing the Queene
Of Lacedæmon? Breach of shame and faith?
And all the lawes of Hospitalitie?   215
This is the Beastly slaughter made of men,
When Truth is ouer-throwne, his Lawes corrupted;
When soules are smother'd in the flatter'd flesh,
Slaine bodies are no more then Oxen slaine.
    Bal. Differ not men from Oxen?
    Cler.   Who sayes so?   220
But see wherein; In the vnderstanding rules
Of their opinions, liues, and actions;
In their communities of faith and reason.
Was not the Wolfe that nourisht Romulus /   224
More humane then the men that did expose him?   [D4]
    Bal. That makes against you.
    Cler.   Not sir, if you note
That by that deede, the actions difference make
Twixt men and beasts, and not their names nor formes.
Had faith, nor shame, all hospitable rights
Beene broke by Troy, Greece had not made that slaughter.   230
Had that beene sau'd (sayes a Philosopher)
The Iliads and Odysses had beene lost;
Had Faith and true Religion beene prefer'd,
Religious Guise had neuer massacerd.
    Bal. Well sir, I cannot when I meete with you   235
But thus digresse a little, for my learning,
From any other businesse I entend.
But now the voyage, we resolu'd for Cambray,
I told the Guise beginnes; and wee must haste.
And till the Lord Renel hath found some meane   240
(Conspiring with the Countesse) to make sure
Your sworne wreake on her Husband (though this fail'd)
In my so braue Command, wee'll spend the time,
Sometimes in training out in Skirmishes,
And Battailes, all our Troopes and Companies;   245
And sometimes breathe your braue Scotch running horse,
That great Guise gaue you, that all th'horse in France
Farre ouer-runnes at euery race and hunting
Both of the Hare and Deere. You shall be honor'd
Like the great Guise himselfe, aboue the King.   250
And (can you but appease your great-spleen'd Sister,

---

214 Lacedæmon] Lacædemon ‖ 224 Romulus] *Romulus* ‖ 232 lost;] ~, ‖ 234 massacerd.] ~, ‖
240 Renel] *Renel* ‖

465

For our delaid wreake of your Brothers slaughter)
At all parts you'll be welcom'd to your wonder.
   Cler. Ile see my Lord the Guise againe before
Wee take our iourney.
   Bal.   O sir, by all meanes,   255
You cannot be too carefull of his loue,
That euer takes occasion to be raising
Your virtues, past the reaches of this age,
And rankes you with the best of th'ancient Romanes.
   Cler. That praise at no part moues mee, but the worth /   260
Of all hee can giue others spher'd in him.   [D4ᵛ]
   Bal. Hee yet is thought to entertaine strange aymes.
   Cler. He may be well; yet not as you thinke strange.
His strange Aymes are to crosse the common Custome
Of Seruile Nobles; in which hee's so rauisht,   265
That quite the Earth he leaues, and vp hee leapes,
On Atlas shoulders, and from thence lookes downe,
Viewing how farre off other high ones creepe:
Rich, poore of reason, wander; All pale looking,
And trembling but to thinke of their sure deaths,   270
Their liues so base are, and so rancke their breaths.
Which I teach Guise to heighten, and make sweet
With lifes deare odors, a good minde and name;
For which, hee onely loues me, and deserues
My loue and life, which through all deaths I vow: 275
Resoluing this, (what euer change can be)
Thou hast created, thou hast ruinde mee.   *Exeunt.*

Finis Actus secundi.

Actus tertij   Scæna prima.

A march of Captaines ouer the Stage.
Maillard, Chalon, Aumall following with Souldiers.

   Mail. These Troopes and companies come in with wings:
So many men, so arm'd, so gallant Horse,
I thinke no other Gouernment in France
So soone could bring together. With such men
Me thinkes a man might passe th'insulting Pillars   5
Of Bacchus and Alcides.
   Chal.   I much wonder

---

277 SD *Exeunt.*] Parrott; *Exit.* ‖

Our Lord Lieutenant brought his brother downe
To feast and honour him, and yet now leaues him
At such an instance.
    Mail.   Twas the Kings Command:
For whom he must leaue Brother, Wife, friend, all things. /   10
    Aum. The confines of his Gouernment, whose view   [E1]
Is the pretext of his Command, hath neede
Of no such sodaine expedition.
    Mail. Wee must not argue that. The Kings Command
Is neede and right enough: and that he serues,   15
(As all true Subiects should) without disputing.
    Chal. But knowes not hee of your Command to take
His Brother Clermont?
    Mail.   No: the Kings will is
Expressely to conceale his apprehension
From my Lord Gouernour. Obseru'd yee not?   20
Againe peruse the Letters. Both you are
Made my assistants, and haue right and trust
In all the waightie secrets like my selfe.
    Aum. Tis strange a man that had, through his life past,
So sure a foote in vertue and true knowledge,   25
As Clermont D'Ambois, should be now found tripping,
And taken vp thus, so to make his fall
More steepe and head-long.
    Mail.   It is Vertues fortune,
To keepe her low, and in her proper place.
Height hath no roome for her: But as a man   30
That hath a fruitfull wife, and euery yeere
A childe by her, hath euery yeere a month,
To breathe himselfe: where hee that gets no childe
Hath not a nights rest (if he will doe well);
So, let one marry this same barraine Vertue,   35
She neuer lets him rest: where fruitfull vice
Spares her rich drudge, giues him in labour breath;
Feedes him with bane, and makes him fat with death.
    Chal. I see that good liues neuer can secure
Men from bad liuers. Worst men will haue best   40
As ill as they, or heauen to hell they'll wrest.
    Aum. There was a merit for this, in the fault
That Bussy made; for which he (doing pennance)
Proues that these foule adulterous guilts will runne
Through the whole bloud, which not the cleare can shunne.   45
    Mail. Ile therefore take heede of the bastarding /
Whole innocent races; tis a fearefull thing.   [E1ᵛ]

34 well);] ~.) ‖

And as I am true Batcheler, I sweare,
To touch no woman (to the coupling ends)
Vnlesse it be mine owne wife or my friends.   50
I may make bold with him.
    Aum.   Tis safe and common.
The more your friend dares trust, the more deceiue him.
And as through dewie vapors the Sunnes forme
Makes the gay Rainebow, girdle to a storme,
So in hearts hollow, Friendship (euen the Sunne   55
To all good growing in societie)
Makes his so glorious and diuine name hold
Collours for all the ill that can be told.   *Trumpets within.*
    Mail. Harke, our last Troopes are come.   *Drums beate.*
    Chal.   Harke, our last foote.
    Mail. Come, let vs put all quickly into battaile,   60
And send for Clermont, in whose honour, all
This martiall preparation wee pretend.
    Chal. Wee must bethinke vs, ere wee apprehend him,
(Besides our maine strength) of some stratageme
To make good our seuere Command on him;   65
As well to saue bloud, as to make him sure:
For if hee come on his Scotch horse, all France
Put at the heeles of him, will faile to take him.
    Mail. What thinke you if wee should disguise a brace
Of our best Souldiers in faire Lackies coates,   70
And send them for him, running by his side,
Till they haue brought him in some ambuscado
We close may lodge for him; and sodainely
Lay sure hand on him, plucking him from horse.
    Aum. It must be sure and strong hand: for if once   75
Hee feeles the touch of such a stratageme,
Tis not the choisest brace of all our Bands
Can manacle, or quench his fiery hands.
    Mail. When they haue seaz'd him, the ambush shal make in.
    Aum. Doe as you please; his blamelesse spirit deserues   80
(I dare engage my life) of all this, nothing.
    Chal. Why should all this stirre be then? /
    Aum.   Who knowes not   [E2]
The bumbast politie thrusts into his Gyant,
To make his wisedome seeme of size as huge,
And all for sleight encounter of a shade,   85
So hee be toucht, hee would haue hainous made?

58 SD *Trumpets within.*] *Boas; after* come *(l. 59)* ‖ 59 SD *Drums beate.*] *Parrott; after* foote *(l. 59)* ‖

Mail. It may be once so; but so euer, neuer;
Ambition is abroad, on foote, on horse;
Faction chokes euery corner, streete, the Court;
Whose faction tis you know: and who is held   90
The fautors right hand: how high his aymes reach,
Nought but a Crowne can measure. This must fall
Past shadowes waights; and is most capitall.
    Chal. No question; for since hee is come to Cambray
The malecontent, decaid Marquesse Renel,   95
Is come, and new arriu'd; and made partaker
Of all the entertaining Showes and Feasts
That welcom'd Clermont to the braue Virago
His manly Sister. Such wee are esteem'd
As are our consorts. Marquesse malecontent   100
Comes where hee knowes his vaine hath safest vent.
    Mail. Let him come at his will, and goe as free,
Let vs ply Clermont, our whole charge is hee.   *Exeunt.*

[III.ii]

Enter a Gentleman Vsher before Clermont: Renel,
Charlotte, with two women attendants, with others:
Showes hauing past within.

    Char. This for your Lordships welcome into Cambray.
    Ren. Noblest of Ladies, tis beyond all power
(Were my estate at first full) in my meanes
To quit or merit.
    Cler.   You come something latter
From Court my Lord then I: And since newes there   5
Is euery day encreasing with th'affaires,
Must I not aske now, what the newes is there?
Where the Court lyes? what stirre? change? what auise
From England, Italie?
    Ren.   You must doe so,
If you'll be cald a Gentleman well quallified, /   10
And weare your time and wits in those discourses.   [E2ᵛ]
    Cler. The Locrian Princes therefore were braue Rulers;
For whosoeuer there came new from Countrie,
And in the Citie askt, what newes? was punisht:
Since commonly such braines are most delighted   15
With innouations, Gossips tales, and mischiefes:
But as of Lyons it is said and Eagles,

---

89 Court;] ~, ‖ **103** SD *Exeunt.*] *Phelps; Exit. Q(c); Eit. Q(u)* ‖ **III.ii**] *Boas* ‖ **9** Italie?] ~. ‖ **12** Rulers] *Shepherd;* Rubers ‖ **16** innouations, Gossips] *Q(c);* innouations, of Gossips *Q(u)* ‖

That when they goe, they draw their seeres and tallons
Close vp, to shunne rebating of their sharpnesse:
So our wits sharpnesse, which wee should employ   20
In noblest knowledge, wee should neuer waste
In vile and vulgar admirations.
   Ren. Tis right: but who, saue onely you, performes it,
And your great brother? Madame, where is he?
   Char. Gone a day since, into the Countries confines,   25
To see their strength, and readinesse for seruice.
   Ren. Tis well: his fauour with the King hath made him
Most worthily great, and liue right royally.
   Cler. I: Would hee would not doe so. Honour neuer
Should be esteem'd with wise men, as the price   30
And value of their virtuous Seruices,
But as their signe or Badge: for that bewrayes
More glory in the outward grace of goodnesse,
Then in the good it selfe; and then tis said:
Who more ioy takes, that men his good aduance,   35
Then in the good it selfe, does it by chance.
   Char. My brother speakes all principle; what man
Is mou'd with your soule? or hath such a thought
In any rate of goodnesse?
   Cler.   Tis their fault.
We haue examples of it, cleare and many.   40
Demetrius Phalerius, an Orator,
And (which not oft meete) a Philosopher,
So great in Athens grew, that she erected
Three hundred Statues of him; of all which,
No rust, nor length of time corrupted one;   45
But in his life time, all were ouerthrowne.
And Demades (that past Demosthenes /
For all extemporall Orations)   [E3]
Erected many Statues, which (he liuing)
Were broke, and melted into Chamber-pots.   50
Many such ends haue fallen on such proud honours,
No more because the men on whom they fell
Grew insolent, and left their vertues state;
Then for their hugenesse, that procur'd their hate:
And therefore little pompe in men most great,   55
Makes mightily and strongly to the guard
Of what they winne by chance, or iust reward.
Great and immodest braueries againe,

---

43 she] *Deighton*; he (*See Textual Note*) ‖

Like Statues, much too high made for their bases,
Are ouerturn'd as soone, as giuen their places.   60

Enter a Messenger with a Letter.

Mess. Here is a Letter sir deliuer'd mee,
Now at the fore-gate by a Gentleman.
   Cler. What Gentleman?
   Mess.   Hee would not tell his name;
Hee said, hee had not time enough to tell it,
And say the little rest hee had to say.   65
   Cler. That was a merry saying; he tooke measure
Of his deare time like a most thriftie husband.
   Char. What newes?
   Cler.   Strange ones, and fit for a Nouation;
Waightie, vnheard of, mischieuous enough.
   Ren. Heauen shield: what are they?
   Cler.   Read them, good my Lord.   70
   Ren. You are betraid into this Countrie. Monstrous!
   Char. How's that?
   Cler. Read on.
   Ren. Maillard, your brothers Lieutenant, that yesterday
inuited you to see his Musters; hath Letters and strickt Charge   75
from the King to apprehend you.
   Char. To apprehend him?
   Ren. Your Brother absents himselfe of purpose.
   Cler. That's a sound one.
   Char. That's a lye. /   80
   Ren. Get on your Scotch horse, and retire to your strength; [E3ᵛ]
you know where it is, and there it expects you: Beleeue this
as your best friend had sworne it. Fare-well if you will.
Anonymos. What's that?
   Cler. Without a name.   85
   Char. And all his notice too, without all truth.
   Cler. So I conceiue it Sister: ile not wrong
My well knowne Brother for Anonymos.
   Char. Some foole hath put this tricke on you, yet more
T'vncouer your defect of spirit and valour,   90
First showne in lingring my deare Brothers wreake.
See what it is to giue the enuious World
Aduantage to diminish eminent virtue.
Send him a Challenge? Take a noble course
To wreake a murther, done so like a villaine?   95

---

74 your] *Shepherd*; you | Lieutenant] Leiutenant ‖ 88 Anonymos.] ~, ‖ 90 valour,] ~. ‖

Cler. Shall we reuenge a villanie with villanie?
Char. Is it not equall?
Cler.   Shall wee equall be
With villaines? Is that your reason?
Char.   Cowardise euermore
Flyes to the shield of Reason.
Cler.   Nought that is
Approu'd by Reason, can be Cowardise.   100
    Char. Dispute when you should fight. Wrong, wreaklesse sleeping,
Makes men dye honorlesse: One borne, another
Leapes on our shoulders.
    Cler.   Wee must wreake our wrongs
So, as wee take not more.
    Char.   One wreakt in time
Preuents all other. Then shines vertue most   105
When time is found for facts; and found, not lost.
    Cler. No time occurres to Kings, much lesse to Vertue;
Nor can we call it Vertue that proceedes
From vicious Fury. I repent that euer
(By any instigation in th'appearance   110
My Brothers spirit made, as I imagin'd)
That e'er I yeelded to reuenge his murther. /
All worthy men should euer bring their bloud   [E4]
To beare all ill, not to be wreakt with good:
Doe ill for no ill: Neuer priuate cause   115
Should take on it the part of publike Lawes.
    Char. A D'Ambois beare in wrong so tame a spirit!
    Ren. Madame, be sure there will be time enough
For all the vengeance your great spirit can wish.
The course yet taken is allow'd by all,   120
Which being noble, and refus'd by th'Earle,
Now makes him worthy of your worst aduantage:
And I haue cast a proiect with the Countesse
To watch a time when all his wariest Guards
Shall not exempt him. Therefore giue him breath;   125
Sure Death delaid is a redoubled Death.
    Cler. Good Sister trouble not your selfe with this:
Take other Ladyes care; practise your face.
There's the chaste Matron, Madame Perigot,
Dwels not farre hence; Ile ride and send her to you,   130
Shee did liue by retailing mayden-heads
In her minoritie: but now shee deales

---

98 With ... euermore] *Parrott*; With villaines? / Is ... reason? / *Char.* ... euermore ‖ **101**
Wrong,] *Shepherd*; ~ͺ ‖ **130** hence;] ~, ‖

472

In whole-sale altogether for the Court.
I tell you, shee's the onely fashion-monger
For your complexion, poudring of your haire,   135
Shadowes, Rebatoes, Wires, Tyres, and such trickes,
That Cambray, or I thinke, the Court affords:
She shall attend you Sister, and with these
Womanly practises emply your spirit;
This other suites you not, nor fits the fashion.   140
Though shee be deare, lay't on, spare for no cost,
Ladies in these haue all their bounties lost.
 Ren. Madame, you see, his spirit will not checke
At any single danger; when it stands
Thus merrily firme against an host of men,   145
Threaten'd to be [in] armes for his surprise.
 Char. That's a meere Bugge-beare, an impossible mocke.
If hee, and him I bound by nuptiall faith
Had not beene dull and drossie in performing
Wreake of the deare bloud of my matchlesse Brother, / 150
What Prince? what King? which of the desperat'st Ruffins, [E4ᵛ]
Outlawes in Arden, durst haue tempted thus
One of our bloud and name, be't true or false?
 Cler. This is not caus'd by that: twill be as sure
As yet it is not, though this should be true.   155
 Char. True? tis past thought false.
 Cler.   I suppose the worst,
Which farre I am from thinking; and despise
The Armie now in battaile that should act it.
 Char. I would not let my bloud vp to that thought,
But it should cost the dearest bloud in France.   160
 Cler. Sweet Sister, (*osculatur*) farre be both off as the fact
Of my fain'd apprehension.
 Char.   I would once
Strip off my shame with my attire, and trie
If a poore woman, votist of reuenge
Would not performe it, with a president   165
To all you bungling foggy-spirited men;
But for our birth-rights honour, doe not mention
One syllable of any word may goe
To the begetting of an act so tender,
And full of sulphure as this Letters truth: 170
It comprehends so blacke a circumstance
Not to be nam'd, that but to forme one thought,

---

134 fashion-monger] ~-~, ‖ 139 emply] *See Textual Note* ‖ 146 in] *Shepherd* ‖ 151 Ruffins]
Shepherd subs.; Ruffings ‖ 152 Arden] *Shepherd*; Acden ‖ 153 false?] ~. ‖ 159 *Char.*]
Shepherd; *Cler.* ‖ 161 (*osculatur*)] [~] ‖ 162 would] Would ‖ 167 honour,] *Q(c)*; ~. *Q(u)* ‖ 171
circumstance] *Q(c)*; ~, *Q(u)* ‖ 172 nam'd,] ~; ‖

It is, or can be so, would make me mad:
Come my Lord, you and I will fight this dreame   174
Out at the Chesse.
    Ren.   Most gladly, worthiest Ladie.   *Exeunt Char. and Ren.*

Enter a Messenger.

    Mess. Sir, my Lord Gouernours Lieutenant prayes
Accesse to you.
    Cler.   Himselfe alone?
    Mess.   Alone, sir.
    Cler. Attend him in. (*Exit Mess.*) Now comes this plot to tryall,
I shall descerne (if it be true as rare)
Some sparkes will flye from his dissembling eyes.   180
Ile sound his depth. /

Enter Maillard with the Messenger.   [F1]

    Mail.   Honour, and all things noble.
    Cler. As much to you good Captaine. What's th'affaire?
    Mail. Sir, the poore honour we can adde to all
Your studyed welcome to this martiall place,
In presentation of what strength consists   185
My Lord your Brothers Gouernment is readie.
I haue made all his Troopes and Companies
Aduance, and put themselues rang'd in Battailia,
That you may see, both how well arm'd they are;
How strong is euery Troope and Companie;   190
How ready, and how well prepar'd for seruice.
    Cler. And must they take mee?
    Mail.   Take you, sir? O Heauen!
    Mess. Beleeue it sir, his count'nance chang'd in turning.
    Mail. What doe you meane sir?
    Cler.   If you haue charg'd them,
You being charg'd your selfe, to apprehend mee,   195
Turne not your face: throw not your lookes about so.
    Mail. Pardon me sir. You amaze me to conceiue
From whence our wils to honour you, should turne
To such dishonour of my Lord your Brother.
Dare I, without him, vndertake your taking?   200
    Cler. Why not? by your direct charge from the King?
    Mail. By my charge from the King? would he so much
Disgrace my Lord, his owne Lieutenant here,
To giue me his Command without his forfaite?
    Cler. Acts that are done by Kings, are not askt why.   205

---

173 so,] ~; ‖ **175** SD *Exeunt*] Boas; *Exit* ‖ **178** SD (*Exit Mess.*)] [~ ~.] ‖ **182** affaire?] ~. ‖ **188** rang'd] Q(c); *om.* Q(u) ‖ **191** seruice.] ~, (*See Textual Note*) ‖

Ile not dispute the case, but I will search you.
   Mail. Search mee? for what?
   Cler.   For Letters.
   Mail.   I beseech you,
Doe not admit one thought of such a shame
To a Commander.
   Cler.   Goe to: I must doo't.
Stand and be searcht; you know mee.
   Mail.   You forget /   210
What tis to be a Captaine, and your selfe.   [F1ᵛ]
   Cler. Stand, or I vow to heauen, Ile make you lie
Neuer to rise more.
   Mail.   If a man be mad
Reason must beare him.
   Cler.   So coy to be searcht?
   Mail. Sdeath sir, vse a Captaine like a Carrier?   215
   Cler. Come, be not furious; when I haue done
You shall make such a Carrier of me
If't be your pleasure: you're my friend I know,
And so am bold with you.
   Mail.   You'll nothing finde
Where nothing is.
   Cler.   Sweare you haue nothing.   220
   Mail. Nothing you seeke, I sweare. I beseech you,
Know I desir'd this out of great affection,
To th'end my Lord may know out of your witnesse,
His Forces are not in so bad estate
As hee esteem'd them lately in your hearing: 225
For which he would not trust me with the Confines;
But went himselfe to witnesse their estate.
   Cler. I heard him make that reason, and am sorie
I had no thought of it before I made
Thus bold with you; since tis such Ruberb to you.   230
Ile therefore search no more. If you are charg'd
(By Letters from the King, or otherwise)
To apprehend me, neuer spice it more
With forc'd tearmes of your loue, but say: I yeeld;
Holde; take my sword; here; I forgiue thee freely;   235
Take; doe thine office.
   Mail.   Sfoote, you make m'a hang-man:
By all my faith to you, there's no such thing.
   Cler. Your faith to mee?
   Mail.   My faith to God: All's one,

---

215 Carrier?] ~. ‖ 221 sweare.] ~, ‖ 233 me,] ~; ‖ 234 but ... yeeld] *See Textual Note* ‖

Who hath no faith to men, to God hath none.
    Cler. In that sense I accept your othe, and thanke you.   240
I gaue my word to goe, and I will goe.   *Exit Cler.*
    Mail. Ile watch you whither. /   *Exit Mail.*
    Mess.   If hee goes, hee proues   [F2]
How vaine are mens fore knowledges of things,
When heauen strikes blinde their powers of note and vse;
And makes their way to ruine seeme more right,   245
Then that which safetie opens to their sight.
Cassandra's prophecie had no more profit
With Troyes blinde Citizens, when shee fore-tolde
Troyes ruine: which succeeding, made her vse
This sacred Inclamation; God (said shee)   250
Would haue me vtter things vncredited:
For which now they approue what I presag'd;
They count me wise, that said before I rag'd.   [*Exit.*]

[III.iii]

Enter Challon with two Souldiers.

    Chal. Come Souldiers: you are downe-wards fit for lackies;
Giue me your Pieces, and take you these Coates,
To make you compleate foot-men: in whose formes
You must be compleate Souldiers: you two onely
Stand for our Armie.
    1 [*Sould.*] That were much.
    Chal.   Tis true,   5
You two must doe, or enter, what our Armie
Is now in field for.
    2 [*Sould.*]   I see then our guerdon
Must be the deede it selfe, twill be such honour:
    Chal. What fight Souldiers most for?
    1 [*Sould.*]   ˙ Honour onely.
    Chal. Yet here are crownes beside.
    Ambo.   We thanke you Captaine.   10
    2 [*Sould.*] Now sir, how show wee?
    Chal.   As you should at all parts.
Goe now to Clermont D'Ambois, and informe him,
Two Battailes are set ready in his honour,
And stay his presence onely for their signall,
When they shall ioyne: and that t'attend him hither,   15
Like one wee so much honour, wee haue sent him –

---

253 SD *Exit.*] *Boas* ‖ **III.iii**] *Boas* ‖ **5** 1 [*Sould.*]] 1 (*not hereafter recorded*) ‖ **7** 2 [*Sould.*]] 2 (*not hereafter recorded*) ‖ **16** him–] *Shepherd*; ~. ‖

1 [*Sould.*] Vs two in person.
Chal.   Well sir, say it so. /
And hauing brought him to the field, when I   [F2ᵛ]
Fall in with him, saluting, get you both
Of one side of his horse, and plucke him downe,   20
And I with th'ambush laid, will second you.
   1 [*Sould.*] Nay, we shall lay on hands of too much strength
To neede your secondings.
   2 [*Sould.*]   I hope, we shall.
Two are enough to encounter Hercules.   24
   Chal. Tis well said worthy Souldiers: hast, and hast him.   [*Exeunt.*]

[III.iv]

Enter Clermont, Maillard close following him.

Cler. [*Aside to himself.*] My Scotch horse to their Armie –
Mail.   Please you sir?
Cler. Sdeath you're passing diligent.
Mail.   Of my soule
Tis onely in my loue to honour you
With what would grace the King: but since I see
You still sustaine a iealous eye on mee,   5
Ile goe before.
   Cler.   Tis well; Ile come; my hand.
   Mail. Your hand sir? Come, your word, your choise be vs'd.   *Exit.*

Clermont solus.

   Cler. I had an auersation to this voyage,
When first my Brother mou'd it; and haue found
That natiue power in me was neuer vaine;   10
Yet now neglected it. I wonder much
At my inconstancie in these decrees,
I euery houre set downe to guide my life.
When Homer made Achilles passionate,
Wrathfull, reuengefull, and insatiate   15
In his affections; what man will denie,
He did compose it all of industrie,
To let men see, that men of most renowne,
Strong'st, noblest, fairest, if they set not downe
Decrees within them, for disposing thcsc,   20
Of Iudgement, Resolution, Vprightnesse,
And certaine knowledge of their vse and ends, /

25 SD *Exeunt.*] *Phelps* ‖ **III.iv**] *Boas* ‖ **1** SD *Aside to himself.*] *Parrott subs.* | Armie–] *Boas*; ~. ‖
22 knowledge] ~, | ends,] ~‸ ‖

Mishap and miserie no lesse extends [F3]
To their destruction, with all that they pris'd,
Then to the poorest, and the most despis'd? 25

Enter Renel.

Ren. Why, how now friend? retir'd? take heede you proue not
Dismaid with this strange fortune: all obserue you.
Your gouernment's as much markt as the Kings.
What said a friend to Pompey?
  Cler.   What?
  Ren.   The people
Will neuer know, vnlesse in death thou trie, 30
That thou know'st how to beare aduersitie.
  Cler. I shall approue how vile I value feare
Of death at all times: but to be too rash,
Without both will and care to shunne the worst,
(It being in power to doe, well and with cheere) 35
Is stupid negligence, and worse then feare.
  Ren. Suppose this true now.
  Cler.   No, I cannot doo't.
My sister truely said; there hung a taile
Of circumstance so blacke on that supposure,
That to sustaine it thus, abhorr'd our mettall. 40
And I can shunne it too, in spight of all:
Not going to field: and there to, being so mounted
As I will, since I goe.
  Ren.   You will then goe?
  Cler. I am engag'd both in my word, and hand;
But this is it, that makes me thus retir'd, 45
To call my selfe t'account, how this affaire
Is to be manag'd if the worst should chance:
With which I note, how dangerous it is,
For any man to prease beyond the place,
To which his birth, or meanes, or knowledge ties him; 50
For my part, though of noble birth, my birth-right
Had little left it, and I know tis better
To liue with little; and to keepe within
A mans owne strength still, and in mans true end, / 54
Then runne a mixt course. Good and bad hold neuer [F3ᵛ]
Any thing common: you can neuer finde
Things outward care, but you neglect your minde.
God hath the whole world perfect made and free;

His parts to th'vse of th'All; men then that be
Parts of that All, must as the generall sway   60
Of that importeth, willingly obay
In euery thing without their power to change.
Hee that vnpleas'd to hold his place, will range,
Can in no other be contain'd that's fit,
And so resisting th'All, is crusht with it.   65
But he that knowing how diuine a Frame
The whole world is: and of it all, can name
(Without selfe-flatterie) no part so diuine,
As hee himselfe; and therefore will confine
Freely, his whole powers, in his proper part,   70
Goes on most God-like. Hee that striues t'inuert
The Vniuersals course with his poore way,
Not onely dust-like shiuers with the sway,
But crossing God in his great worke, all earth
Beares not so cursed, and so damn'd a birth.   75
    Ren. Goe, on; Ile take no care what comes of you;
Heauen will not see it ill, how ere it show:
But the pretext to see these Battailes rang'd
Is much your honour.
    Cler.   As the world esteemes it.
But to decide that, you make me remember   80
An accident of high and noble note,
And fits the subiect of my late discourse,
Of holding on our free and proper way.
I ouer-tooke, comming from Italie,
In Germanie, a great and famous Earle   85
Of England; the most goodly fashion'd man
I euer saw: from head to foote in forme
Rare, and most absolute; hee had a face
Like one of the most ancient honour'd Romanes,
From whence his noblest Familie was deriu'd;   90
He was beside of spirit passing great, /
Valiant, and learn'd, and liberall as the Sunne,   [F4]
Spoke and writ sweetly, or of learned subiects,
Or of the discipline of publike weales;
And t'was the Earle of Oxford: and being offer'd   95
At that time, by Duke Cassimere, the view
Of his right royall Armie then in field,
Refus'd it, and no foote was mou'd, to stirre
Out of his owne free fore-determin'd course:
I wondring at it, askt for it his reason,   100

59 All] all | be] *Deighton conj.*; are (*See Textual Note*) ‖ 60 All] all ‖ 74 worke,] ~; ‖ 80 that,] ~;
‖ 97 field,] ~; ‖

It being an offer so much for his honour.
Hee, all acknowledging, said, t'was not fit
To take those honours that one cannot quit.
   Ren. Twas answer'd like the man you haue describ'd.
   Cler. And yet he cast it onely in the way,   105
To stay and serue the world. Nor did it fit
His owne true estimate how much it waigh'd,
For hee despis'd it; and esteem'd it freer
To keepe his owne way straight, and swore that hee
Had rather make away his whole estate   110
In things that crost the vulgar, then he would
Be frozen vp, stiffe, like a sir Iohn Smith
(His Countrey-man) in common Nobles fashions;
Affecting, as the end of Noblesse were
Those seruile obseruations.
   Ren.   It was strange.   115
   Cler. O tis a vexing sight to see a man
Out of his way, stalke proud, as hee were in;
Out of his way to be officious,
Obseruant, wary, serious, and graue,
Fearefull, and passionate, insulting, raging,   120
Labour with iron Flailes, to thresh downe feathers
Flitting in ayre.
   Ren.   What one considers this,
Of all that are thus out? or once endeuours,
Erring, to enter on mans Right-hand path?
   Cler. These are too graue for braue wits: giue them toyes,   125
Labour bestow'd on these is harsh and thriftlesse.
If you would Consull be (sayes one) of Rome, /
You must be watching, starting out of sleepes;   [F4ᵛ]
Euery way whisking; gloryfying Plebeians,
Kissing Patricians hands, Rot at their dores;   130
Speake and doe basely; euery day bestow
Gifts and obseruance vpon one or other:
And what's th'euent of all? Twelue Rods before thee,
Three or foure times sit for the whole Tribunall;
Exhibite Circean Games; make publike feasts: 135
And for these idle outward things (sayes he)
Would'st thou lay on such cost, toile, spend thy spirits?
And to be voide of perturbation
For constancie (sleepe when thou would'st haue sleepe,
Wake when thou would'st wake, feare nought, vexe for nought),   140

---

117 stalke proud,] ~, ~ˏ ‖ **124** Erring, to enter] *Boas*; ~ˏ ~ ~, ‖ **134** Tribunall;] ~. ‖ **135** feasts:]
~, ‖ **137** spirits?] ~. ‖ **139-40** constancie (. . . nought),] ~: . . . ~ˏ, ‖

No paines wilt thou bestow? no cost? no thought?
   Ren. What should I say? as good consort with you,
As with an Angell: I could heare you euer.
   Cler. Well; in, my Lord, and spend time with my Sister;
And keepe her from the Field with all endeauour;   145
The Souldiers loue her so; and shee so madly
Would take my apprehension, if it chance,
That bloud would flow in riuers.
   Ren.   Heauen forbid;
And all with honour your arriuall speede.   *Exit.*

       Enter Messenger with two Souldiers like Lackies.

   Mess. Here are two Lackies sir, haue message to you.   150
   Cler. What is your message? and from whom, my friends?
   1 [*Sould.*] From the Lieutenant Colonell, and the Captaines,
Who sent vs to informe you, that the Battailes
Stand ready rang'd, expecting but your presence,
To be their honor'd signall when to ioyne,   155
And we are charg'd to runne by, and attend you.
   Cler. I come. I pray you see my running horse
Brought to the backe-gate to mee.
   Mess.   Instantly.   *Exit Mess.*
   Cler. Chance what can chance mee; well or ill is equall
In my acceptance, since I ioy in neyther;   160
But goe with sway of all the world together. /
In all successes, Fortune and the day   [G1]
To mee alike are; I am fixt, be shee
Neuer so fickle; and will there respose,   164
Farre past the reach of any Dye she throwes.   *Ex. cum Pediss.*

             Finis Actus tertij.

Actus quarti   Scæna prima.

       Alarum within: Excursions ouer the Stage.
The Souldiers disguised like Lackies running, Maillard following them.

   Mail. Villaines, not hold him when ye had him downe.
   1 [*Sould.*] Who can hold lightning? Sdeath a man as well
Might catch a Canon Bullet in his mouth,
And spit it in your hands, as take and hold him.
   Mail. Pursue; enclose him; stand, or fall on him,   5

---

152 Lieutenant Colonell] *Q(c)*; ~, ~ *Q(u)* (See Textual Note) ‖ **IV.i** SD *the*] *thee* | SD *Souldiers disguised like*] Boas subs. ‖

And yee may take him. Sdeath, they make him guards. *Exit with the Lackies.*

Alarum still, and enter Chalon with two Souldiers.

Chal. Stand Cowards, stand, strike, send your bullets at him.

1 [*Sould.*] Wee came to entertaine him sir, for honour.

2 [*Sould.*] Did ye not say so?

Chal. Slaues, hee is a traitor; 9

Command the horse troopes to ouer-runne the traitor. *Exeunt.*

Showts within. Alarum still, and Chambers shot off.
Then enter Aumall.

Aum. What spirit breathes thus, in this more then man,
Turnes flesh to ayre possest, and in a storme,
Teares men about the field like Autumne leaues?
He turnd wilde lightning in the Lackies hands,
Who, though their sodaine violent twitch vnhorst him, 15
Yet when he bore himselfe, their saucie fingers
Flew as too hot off, as hee had beene fire.
The ambush then made in, through all whose force,
Hee draue as if a fierce and fire-giuen Canon
Had spit his iron vomit out amongst them. / 20
The Battailes then, in two halfe-moones enclos'd him, [G1ᵛ]
In which he shew'd, as if he were the light,
And they but earth, who wondring what hee was,
Shruncke their steele hornes, and gaue him glorious passe:
And as a great shot from a towne besieg'd, 25
At foes before it, flyes forth blacke and roring,
But they too farre, and that with waight opprest,
(As if disdaining earth) doth onely grase,
Strike earth, and vp againe into the ayre;
Againe sinkes to it, and againe doth rise, 30
And keepes such strength that when it softliest moues,
It piece-meale shiuers any let it proues:
So flew braue Clermont forth, till breath forsooke him,
Then fell to earth, and yet (sweet man) euen then
His spirits conuulsions made him bound againe, 35
Past all their reaches; till all motion spent,
His fixt eyes cast a blaze of such disdaine,
All stood and star'd, and vntouch'd let him lie,
As something sacred fallen out of the skie. *A cry within.*
O now some rude hand hath laid hold on him! 40

---

6 SD *with the Lackies.*] Parrott | SD *with two Souldiers.*] Parrott ‖ 8 1 [*Sould.*]] *See Textual Note* ‖ 10 SD *Exeunt.*] Boas; *Exit.* | SD *still,*] ~. ‖ 23 was,] ~; ‖ 24 passe:] Q(c); ~, Q(u) ‖ 28 grase] Q(c); grasse Q(u) ‖

Enter Maillard, Chalon leading Clermont, Captaines and
Souldiers following.

See, prisoner led, with his bands honour'd more,
Then all the freedome he enioy'd before.
   Mail. At length wee haue you sir.
   Cler.   You haue much ioy too,
I made you sport yet, but I pray you tell mee,
Are not you periur'd?
   Mail.   No: I swore for the King.   45
   Cler. Yet periurie I hope is periurie.
   Mail. But thus forswearing is not periurie;
You are no Politician: not a fault,
How foule soeuer, done for priuate ends,
Is fault in vs sworne to the publike good: 50
Wee neuer can be of the damned crew,
Wee may impolitique our selues (as t'were)
Into the Kingdomes body politique, /
Whereof indeede we're members: you misse terme's.   [G2]
   Cler. The things are yet the same.   55
   Mail. Tis nothing so: the propertie is alter'd:
Y'are no Lawyer. Or say that othe and othe
Are still the same in number, yet their species
Differ extreamely, as for flat example,
When politique widowes trye men for their turne,   60
Before they wed them, they are harlots then,
But when they wed them, they are honest women:
So, priuate men, when they forsweare, betray,
Are periur'd treachers, but being publique once,
That is, sworne, married to the publique good –   65
   Cler. Are married women publique?
   Mail.   Publique good;
For marriage makes them, being the publique good,
And could not be without them. So I say
Men publique, that is, being sworne or married
To the publique good, being one body made   70
With the Realmes body politique, are no more
Priuate, nor can be periur'd, though forsworne,
More then a widow, married for the act
Of generation, is for that an harlot,
Because for that shee was so, being vnmarried: 75

54 we're] *Shepherd;* we'are | misse terme's] *stet (See Textual Note)* ‖ **64** once] *stet (See Textual Note)* ‖ **65** sworne, married] *Q(c);* sworne-married *Q(u)* | good–] ~. ‖ **66** good;] *Q(c);* ~, *Q(u)* ‖ **69** sworne or married] *Q(c);* sworne-married *Q(u)* ‖ **70** publique good] good publique *(See Textual Note)* ‖ **73-74** widow, married ... generation,] *Parrott;* ~ ̬ ~, ... ~ ̬ ‖

An argument *a paribus.*
    Chal.   Tis a shrow'd one.
    Cler. Who hath no faith to men, to God hath none:
Retaine you that Sir? who said so?
    Mail.   Twas I.
    Cler. Thy owne tongue damne thy infidelitie.
But Captaines all you know me nobly borne,   80
Vse yee t'assault such men as I with Lackyes?
    Chal. They are no Lackyes sir, but Souldiers,
Disguis'd in Lackyes coates.
    1 [*Sould.*]   Sir, wee haue seene
The enemie.
    Cler.   Auant yee Rascols, hence.
    Mail. Now leaue your coates.   [*Exeunt Souldiers.*]
    Cler.   Let me not see them more.   85
    Aum. I grieue that vertue liues so vndistinguisht
From vice in any ill, and though the crowne
Of Soueraigne Law, shee should be yet her foot-stoole, /
Subiect to censure, all the shame and paine   [G2ᵛ]
Of all her rigor.
    Cler.   Yet false policie   90
Would couer all, being like offenders hid,
That (after notice taken where they hide)
The more they crouch and stirre, the more are spide.
    Aum. I wonder how this chanc'd you.
    Cler.   Some informer,
Bloud-hound to mischiefe, vsher to the Hangman,   95
Thirstie of honour for some huge state act,
Perceiuing me great with the worthy Guise
(And he, I know not why, held dangerous),
Made me the desperate organe of his danger,
Onely with that poore colour: tis the common   100
And more then whore-like tricke of treacherie,
And vermine bred to rapine, and to ruine:
For which this fault is still to be accus'd,
Since good Arts faile, crafts and deceits are vs'd.
If it be other neuer pittie mee.   105
    Aum. Sir, we are glad, beleeue it, and haue hope
The King will so conceit it.
    Cler.   At his pleasure.
In meane time, what's your will Lord Lieutenant?
    Mail. To leaue your owne horse, and to mount the trumpets.

81 Lackyes?] ~. ‖ **83-85** Disguis'd ... more.] Disguis'd ... coates. / 1 ... enemie. / *Cler.* ...
hence. / *Mail.* ... coates. / *Cler.* ... more. Q (the) ‖ **85** SD *Exeunt Souldiers.*] *Lordi* ‖ **88** Law,]
~; ‖ **97-98** Guise (... he, ... why, ... dangerous),] ~: ... ~ (... ~) ... ~, ‖ **104** Arts] *Parrott
conj.*; acts (*See Textual Note*) ‖

Cler. It shall be done: this heauily preuents   110
My purpos'd recreation in these parts;
Which now I thinke on, let mee begge you sir,
To lend me some one Captaine of your Troopes,
To beare the message of my haplesse seruice,
And miserie, to my most noble mistresse,   115
Countesse of Cambray: to whose house this night
I promist my repaire, and know most truely,
With all the ceremonies of her fauour,
She sure expects mee.
    Mail.   Thinke you now on that?
    Cler. On that, sir? I, and that so worthily,   120
That if the King in spight of your great seruice,
Would send me instant promise of enlargement,
Condition I would set this message by, /
I would not take it, but had rather die.   [G3]
    Aum. Your message shall be done sir: I my selfe   125
Will be for you a messenger of ill.
    Cler. I thanke you sir, and doubt not yet to liue
To quite your kindnesse.
    Aum.   Meane space vse your spirit
And knowledge for the chearfull patience
Of this so strange and sodaine consequence.   130
    Cler. Good sir, beleeue that no perticular torture
Can force me from my glad obedience
To any thing the high and generall Cause,
To match with his whole Fabricke, hath ordainde,
And know yee all (though farre from all your aymes,   135
Yet worth them all, and all mens endlesse studies)
That in this one thing, all the discipline
Of manners, and of manhood is contain'd;
A man to ioyne himselfe with th'Vniuerse,
In his maine sway, and make (in all things fit)   140
One with that All, and goe on, round as it;
Not plucking from the whole his wretched part,
And into straites, or into nought reuert,
Wishing the compleate Vniuerse might be
Subiect to such a ragge of it as hee: 145
But to consider great Necessitie
All things, as well refract as voluntarie,
Reduceth to the prime celestiall Cause,
Which he that yeelds to with a mans applause,

---

112 on,] ~: ‖ 133 Cause] *Shepherd*; cause ‖ 141 All] *Shepherd*; all ‖ 146 Necessitie] *Shepherd*;
necessitie ‖ 147 things, ... refract ... voluntarie,] *Boas*; ~ˬ ... ~, ... ~ˬ ‖ 148 Cause] cause ‖

And cheeke by cheeke goes, crossing it no breath,   150
But like Gods Image, followes to the death,
That man is truely wise, and euery thing,
(Each cause, and euery part distinguishing)
In Nature, with enough Art vnderstands,
And that full glory merits at all hands,   155
That doth the whole world at all parts adorne,
And appertaines to one celestiall borne.   *Exeunt omnes.*

[IV.ii]

Enter Baligny, Renel.

Bal. So foule a scandall neuer man sustain'd, /
Which caus'd by th'King, is rude and tyrannous: [G3ᵛ]
Giue me a place, and my Lieutenant make
The filler of it.
   Ren.   I should neuer looke
For better of him; neuer trust a man,   5
For any Iustice, that is rapt with pleasure:
To order armes well, that makes smockes his ensignes,
And his whole Gouernments sayles: you heard of late,
Hee had the foure and twenty wayes of Venerie
Done all before him.
   Bal.   Twas abhorr'd and beastly.   10
   Ren. Tis more then natures mightie hand can doe
To make one humane and a Letcher too.
Looke how a Wolfe doth like a Dogge appeare,
So, like a friend is an Adulterer;
Voluptuaries, and these belly-gods,   15
No more true men are, then so many Toads.
A good man happy, is a common good;
Vile men aduanc'd liue of the common bloud.
   Bal. Giue and then take like children.
   Ren.   Bounties are
As soone repented as they happen rare.   20
   Bal. What should Kings doe, and men of eminent places;
But as they gather, sow gifts to the Graces?
And where they haue giuen, rather giue againe,
(Being giuen for vertue) then like Babes and fooles,
Take and repent Gifts; why are wealth and power?   25
   Ren. Power and wealth moue to tyranny, not bountie;
The Merchant for his wealth is swolne in minde,

---

150 cheeke by cheeke goes,] ~, ~ ~, ~; | ıt] ~, ‖ **IV.ii]** *Boas* ‖ **2** by th'] by' th ‖ **14** Adulterer;]
~, ‖ **15** belly-gods,] ~-~; ‖ **22** Graces?] *Q(c)*; graces, *Q(u)* ‖

When yet the chiefe Lord of it is the Winde.
   Bal. That may so chance to our State-Merchants too:
Something performed, that hath not farre to goe.   30
   Ren. That's the maine point, my Lord; insist on that.
   Bal. But doth this fire rage further? hath it taken
The tender tynder of my wifes sere bloud?
Is shee so passionate?
   Ren.   So wilde, so mad,
Shee cannot liue, and this vnwreakt sustaine. /   35
The woes are bloudy that in women raigne.   [G4]
The Sicile gulfe keepes feare in lesse degree;
There is no Tyger, not more tame then shee.
   Bal. There is no looking home then?
   Ren.   Home? Medea
With all her hearbs, charmes, thunders, lightnings,   40
Made not her presence, and blacke hants more dreadfull.
   Bal. Come, to the King, if he reforme not all,
Marke the euent, none stand where that must fall.   *Exeunt.*

[IV.iii]

Enter Countesse, Rioua, and an Vsher.

Vsh. Madame, a Captaine come from Clermont D'Ambois
Desires accesse to you.
   Count.   And not himselfe?
   Vsh. No, Madame.
   Count.   That's not well. Attend him in.   *Exit Vsh.*
The last houre of his promise now runne out
And he breake? some brack's in the frame of nature   5
That forceth his breach.

Enter Vsher and Aumal.

   Aum.   Saue your Ladiship.
   Count. All welcome. Come you from my worthy seruant?
   Aum. I, Madame, and conferre such newes from him –
   Count. Such newes? what newes?
   Aum. Newes that I wish some other had the charge of.   10
   Count. O what charge? what newes?
   Aum. Your Ladiship must vse some patience
Or else I cannot doe him that desire,
He vrg'd with such affection to your Graces.
   Count. Doe it; for heauens loue doe it; if you serue   15

---

40 lightnings] *Q(c)*; lightning *Q(u)* ‖ **IV.iii]** *Boas* ‖ **2-3** Desires ... in.] *Boas*; Desires ... you. /
Count. ... Madame. / Coun. ... in. ‖ **5** he breake? some brack's] *Q(c)*; hee breake, some brack
Q(u) ‖ **8** him–] ~. ‖ **9, 11** Such ... newes?] *See Textual Note* ‖ **10** had] *Q(c)*; had had *Q(u)* ‖ **15**
doe it;] ~ ~, ‖

His kinde desires, I will haue patience.
Is hee in health?
   Aum.   He is.
   Count.   Why, that's the ground
Of all the good estate wee hold in earth;
All our ill built vpon that, is no more
Then wee may beare, and should; expresse it all.   20
   Aum. Madame, tis onely this; his libertie –
   Count. His libertie! Without that, health is nothing. /
Why liue I, but to aske in doubt of that,   [G4ᵛ]
Is that bereft him?
   Aum.   You'll againe preuent me.
   Count. No more, I sweare; I must heare, and together   25
Come all my miserie. Ile hold though I burst.
   Aum. Then madame, thus it fares; he was enuited
By way of honour to him, to take view
Of all the Powers his brother Baligny
Hath in his gouernment; which rang'd in battailes,   30
Maillard, Lieutenant to the Gouernour,
Hauing receiu'd strickt Letters from the King,
To traine him to the musters, and betray him,
To their supprise, which, with Chalon in chiefe,
And other Captaines (all the field put hard   35
By his incredible valour for his scape)
They haplesly and guiltlesly perform'd,
And to Bastile hee's now led prisoner.
   Count. What change is here? how are my hopes preuented?
O my most faithfull seruant; thou betraid?   40
Will Kings make treason lawfull? Is Societie
(To keepe which onely Kings were first ordain'd)
Lesse broke in breaking faith twixt friend and friend,
Then twixt the King and Subiect? let them feare,
Kings Presidents in licence lacke no danger.   45
Kings are compar'd to Gods, and should be like them,
Full in all right, in nought superfluous;
Nor nothing straining past right, for their right:
Raigne iustly, and raigne safely. Policie
Is but a Guard corrupted, and a way   50
Venter'd in Desarts, without guide or path.
Kings punish Subiects errors with their owne.
Kings are like Archers, and their Subiects, shafts:
For as when Archers let their arrowes flye,

---

20 should;] *Q(c)*; ~‸ *Q(u)* ‖ 21 libertie–] *Boas*; ~. ‖ 22 that,] *Parrott*; ~‸ ‖ 25 sweare;] ~, ‖ 31 Maillard] Mailiard ‖

They call to them, and bid them flye or fall,   55
As if twere in the free power of the shaft
To flye or fall, when onely tis the strength,
Straight shooting, compasse giuen it by the Archer,
That makes it hit or misse; and doing eyther,
Hee's to be prais'd or blam'd, and not the shaft: /   60
So Kings to Subiects crying, doe, doe not this;   [H1]
Must to them by their owne examples strength,
The straightnesse of their acts, and equall compasse,
Giue Subiects power t'obey them in the like;
Not shoote them forth with faultie ayme and strength,   65
And lay the fault in them for flying amisse.
   Aum. But for your seruant, I dare sweare him guiltlesse.
   Count. Hee would not for his Kingdome traitor be;
His Lawes are not so true to him, as he.
O knew I how to free him, by way forc'd   70
Through all their armie, I would flye, and doe it:
And had I, of my courage and resolue,
But tenne such more, they should not all retaine him;
But I will neuer die, before I giue
Maillard an hundred slashes with a sword,   75
Chalon an hundred breaches with a Pistoll.
They could not all haue taken Clermont D'Ambois,
Without their treacherie; he had bought his bands out
With their slaue blouds: but he was credulous;
Hee would beleeue, since he would be beleeu'd;   80
Your noblest natures are most credulous.
Who giues no trust, all trust is apt to breake;
Hate like hell mouth, who thinke not what they speake.
   Aum. Well, Madame, I must tender my attendance
On him againe. Will't please you to returne   85
No seruice to him by me?
   Count.   Fetch me straight
My little Cabinet. (*Exit Ancil.*) Tis little, tell him,
And much too little for his matchlesse loue:
But as in him the worths of many men
Are close contracted; (*Intr. Ancil.*) so in this are Iewels   90
Worth many Cabinets. Here, with this (good sir)
Commend my kindest seruice to my seruant,
Thanke him, with all my comforts; and, in them
With all my life for them: all sent from him
In his remembrance of mee, and true loue: 95

66 amisse.] ~, ‖ 87 (*Exit Ancil.*)] [~ ~.] | little,] ~ˏ ‖ 90 (*Intr. Ancil.*)] [~. ~.] ‖

And looke you tell him, tell him how I lye   *She kneeles downe*
Prostrate at feet of his accurst misfortune, /   *at his feete.*
Pouring my teares out, which shall euer fall,   [H1ᵛ]
Till I haue pour'd for him out eyes and all.
   Aum. O Madame, this will kill him: comfort you   100
With full assurance of his quicke acquitall;
Be not so passionate: rise, cease your teares.
   Count. Then must my life cease. Teares are all the vent
My life hath to scape death: Teares please me better,
Then all lifes comforts, being the naturall seede   105
Of heartie sorrow. As a tree fruit beares,
So doth an vndissembled sorrow, teares.   *He raises her, and leades*
                                  her out. Exeunt.
   Vsh. This might haue beene before, and sau'd much charge.   *Exit.*

[IV.iv]

Enter Henry, Guise, Baligny, Esp. Soisson.
Pericot with pen, incke, and paper.

   Guise. Now sir, I hope your much abus'd Eyes see
In my word for my Clermont, what a villaine
Hee was that whisper'd in your iealous eare
His owne blacke treason in suggesting Clermonts:
Colour'd with nothing but being great with mee.   5
Signe then this writ for his deliuerie,
Your hand was neuer vrg'd with worthier boldnesse:
Come, pray sir, signe it: why should Kings be praid
To acts of Iustice? tis a reuerence
Makes them despis'd, and showes they sticke and tyre   10
In what their free powers should be hot as fire.
   Hen. Well, take your will sir, (*Auersus.*) Ile haue mine ere long. –
But wherein is this Clermont such a rare one?
   Guise. In his most gentle, and vnwearied minde,
Rightly to vertue fram'd; in very nature;   15
In his most firme inexorable spirit,
To be remou'd from any thing hee chuseth
For worthinesse; or beare the lest perswasion
To what is base, or fitteth not his obiect;
In his contempt of riches and of greatnesse;   20
In estimation of th'Idolatrous vulgar;

---

107 SD *He ... Exeunt.*] Q(c) (*See Introduction, pp. 426-28, and list of Press-Variants*) ‖ 108
sau'd] Q(c); san'd Q(u) ‖ **IV.iv.**] *Boas* ‖ **1** your] *Shepherd*; you're ‖ **5** mee.] ~, ‖ **12** SD
(*Auersus.*)] *Auersus.* Q(c) (*in left margin*); Auersus. Q(u) (*in left margin*) | long.–] *Boas*; ~.ˏ ‖

His scorne of all things seruile and ignoble,
Though they could gaine him neuer such aduancement;
His liberall kinde of speaking what is truth, /   24
In spight of temporising; the great rising,   [H2]
And learning of his soule, so much the more
Against ill fortune, as shee set her selfe
Sharpe against him, or would present most hard,
To shunne the malice of her deadliest charge;
His detestation of his speciall friends,   30
When he perceiu'd their tyrannous will to doe,
Or their abiection basely to sustaine
Any iniustice that they could reuenge;
The flexibilitie of his most anger,
Euen in the maine careere and fury of it,   35
When any obiect of desertfull pittie
Offers it selfe to him; his sweet disposure
As much abhorring to behold, as doe
Any vnnaturall and bloudy action;
His iust contempt of Iesters, Parasites,   40
Seruile obseruers, and polluted tongues:
In short, this Senecall man is found in him,
Hee may with heauens immortall powers compare,
To whom the day and fortune equall are,
Come faire or foule, what euer chance can fall,   45
Fixt in himselfe, hee still is one to all.
   Hen. Showes he to others thus?
   Omnes.   To all that know him.
   Hen. And apprehend I this man for a traitor?
   Guise. These are your Macheuilian Villaines,
Your bastard Teucers, that their mischiefes done,   50
Runne to your shield for shelter: Cacusses,
That cut their too large murtherous theueries,
To their dens length still: woe be to that state
Where treacherie guards, and ruine makes men great.
   Hen. Goe, take my Letters for him, and release him.   55
   Omnes. Thankes to your Highnesse, euer liue your Highnesse.
                                 Exeunt. Manet Bal.

   Bal. Better a man were buried quicke, then liue
A propertie for state, and spoile, to thriue.   *Exit.*

---

26 And] and | learning] *stet (See Textual Note)* ‖ **51** Cacusses] *Boas;* Caucusses ‖ **56** SD *Manet Bal.*] *Parrott subs.* ‖

[IV.v]

Enter Clermont, Mail. Chal. with Souldiers.

Mail. Wee ioy you take a chance so ill, so well.
Cler. Who euer saw me differ in acceptance /
Of eyther fortune?   [H2ᵛ]
    Chal.   What, loue bad, like good?
How should one learne that?
    Cler.   To loue nothing outward,
Or not within our owne powers to command;   5
And so being sure of euery thing we loue,
Who cares to lose the rest? if any man
Would neyther liue nor dye in his free choise,
But as hee sees necessitie will haue it,
(Which if hee would resist, hee striues in vaine)   10
What can come neere him, that hee doth not well,
And if in worst euents, his will be done;
How can the best be better? all is one.
    Mail. Me thinkes tis prettie.
    Cler.   Put no difference
If you haue this, or not this; but as children   15
Playing at coites, euer regard their game,
And care not for their coites; so let a man
The things themselues that touch him not esteeme,
But his free power in well disposing them.
    Chal. Prettie from toyes.
    Cler.   Me thinkes this double disticke   20
Seemes prettily too, to stay superfluous longings:
Not to haue want, what riches doth exceede?
Not to be subiect, what superiour thing?
He that to nought aspires, doth nothing neede;
Who breakes no Law is subiect to no King.   25
    Mail. This goes to mine eare well I promise you.
    Chal. O, but tis passing hard to stay one thus.
    Cler. Tis so; rancke custome raps men so beyond it,
And as tis hard, so well mens dores to barre
To keepe the cat out, and th'adulterer;   30
So tis as hard to curbe affections so
Wee let in nought to make them ouer-flow.
And as of Homers verses, many Critickes
On those stand, of which times old moth hath eaten,
The first or last feete, and the perfect parts   35

IV.v] *Boas* || **7** rest?] ~: || **11** well] *stet (See Textual Note)* || **31** so] *Boas;* ~, || **35** parts] ~, ||

Of his vnmatched Poeme sinke beneath, /
With vpright gasping, and sloath dull as death: [H3]
So the vnprofitable things of life,
And those we cannot compasse, we affect;
All that doth profit, and wee haue, neglect,   40
Like couetous, and basely getting men,
That gathering much, vse neuer what they keepe;
But for the least they loose, extreamely weepe.
    Mail. This prettie talking and our horses walking
Downe this steepe hill, spends time with equall profit.   45
    Cler. Tis well bestow'd on ye, meate and men sicke
Agree like this, and you; and yet euen this
Is th'end of all skill, power, wealth, all that is.
    Chal. I long to heare sir, how your Mistresse takes this.

Enter Aumal with a Cabinet.

    Mail. Wee soone shall know it: see Aumall return'd.   50
    Aum. Ease to your bands sir.
    Cler.   Welcome worthy friend.
    Chal. How tooke his noblest Mistresse your sad message?
    Aum. As great rich men take sodaine pouertie.
I neuer witness'd a more noble loue,
Nor a more ruthfull sorrow: I well wisht   55
Some other had beene master of my message.
    Mail. Y'are happy sir, in all things, but this one,
Of your vnhappy apprehension.
    Cler. This is to mee, compar'd with her much mone,
As one teare is to her whole passion.   60
    Aum. Sir, shee commends her kindest seruice to you,
And this rich Cabinet.
    Chal.   O happy man.
This may enough hold to redeeme your bands.
    Cler. These clouds I doubt not, will be soone blowne ouer.

Enter Baligny with his discharge: Renel, and others.

    Aum. Your hope is iust and happy, see sir both   65
In both the looks of these.
    Bal.   Here's a discharge
For this your prisoner, my good Lord Lieutenant. /
    Mail. Alas, sir, I vsurpe that stile enforc't,   [H3�v]
And hope you know it was not my aspiring.
    Bal. Well sir, my wrong aspir'd past all mens hopes.   70
    Mail. I sorrow for it sir.
    Ren.   You see sir there

36 Of] of ‖ 43 weepe.] ~, ‖ 53 pouertie.] ~, ‖

Your prisoners discharge autenticall.
    Mail. It is sir, and I yeeld it him with gladnesse.
    Bal. Brother, I brought you downe to much good purpose.
    Cler. Repeate not that sir: the amends makes all.   75
    Ren. I ioy in it, my best and worthiest friend,
O y'haue a princely fautor of the Guise.
    Bal. I thinke I did my part to.
    Ren.   Well, sir; all
Is in the issue well: and (worthiest Friend)   *[Giving Clermont letters.]*
Here's from your friend the Guise; here from the Countesse,   80
Your Brothers Mistresse, the contents whereof
I know, and must prepare you now to please
Th'vnrested spirit of your slaughtered brother,
If it be true, as you imagin'd once,
His apparition show'd it; the complot   85
Is now laid sure betwixt vs; therefore haste
Both to your great friend (who hath some vse waightie
For your repaire to him) and to the Countesse,
Whose satisfaction is no lesse important.
    Cler. I see all, and will haste as it importeth.   90
[To Aumal.] And good friend, since I must delay a little
My wisht attendance on my noblest Mistresse,
Excuse me to her, with returne of this,
And endlesse protestation of my seruice;
And now become as glad a messenger,   95
As you were late a wofull.
    Aum.   Happy change!
I euer will salute thee with my seruice.   *Exit.*
    Bal. Yet more newes Brother; the late iesting Monsieur
Makes now your Brothers dying prophesie equall
At all parts, being dead as he presag'd.   100
    Ren. Heauen shield the Guise from seconding that truth,
With what he likewise prophesied on him. /
    Cler. It hath enough, twas grac'd with truth in one,   [H4]
To th'other falshood and confusion.
Leade to th' Court sir.
    Bal.   You Ile leade no more,   105
It was to ominous and foule before.   *Exeunt.*

Finis Actus quarti.

---

75 all.] -: ‖ 79 SD *Giving Clermont letters.*] *Parrott subs.* ‖ 91 SD *To Aumal.*] ‖ 96 change!] ~, ‖
104 To th'] To'th ‖ 105 to th'] to'th ‖

Actus quinti Scæna prima.

Ascendit Vmbra Bussi.

Vmb. Vp from the Chaos of eternall night,
(To which the whole digestion of the world
Is now returning) once more I ascend,
And bide the cold dampe of this piercing ayre,
To vrge the iustice, whose almightie word   5
Measures the bloudy acts of impious men,
With equall pennance, who in th'act it selfe
Includes th'infliction, which like chained shot
Batter together still; though (as the thunder
Seemes, by mens duller hearing then their sight, .   10
To breake a great time after lightning forth,
Yet both at one time teare the labouring cloud,)
So men thinke pennance of their ils is slow,
Though th'ill and pennance still together goe.
Reforme yee ignorant men, your manlesse liues   15
Whose lawes yee thinke are nothing but your lusts;
When leauing, but for supposition sake,
The body of felicitie, Religion
(Set in the midst of Christendome, and her head
Cleft to her bosome; one halfe one way swaying,   20
Another th'other), all the Christian world
And all her lawes, whose obseruation,
Stands vpon faith, aboue the power of reason:
Leauing (I say) all these, this might suffice,
To fray yee from your vicious swindge in ill, /   25
And set you more on fire to doe more good: [H4ᵛ]
That since the world (as which of you denies?)
Stands by proportion, all may thence conclude,
That all the ioynts and nerues sustaining nature,
As well may breake, and yet the world abide,   30
As any one good vnrewarded die,
Or any one ill scape his penaltie.   *The Ghost stands close.*

Enter Guise, Clermont.

Guise. Thus (friend) thou seest how all good men would thriue,
Did not the good thou prompt'st me with preuent,
The iealous ill pursuing them in others.   35
But now thy dangers are dispatcht, note mine:
Hast thou not heard of that admired voyce,

---

4 ayre,] ~. ‖ 17 leauing,] ~ ͕ ‖ 18-21 felicitie, Religion (Set ... swaying, ... th'other),] *Parrott subs.*; ~ (~) ͕ ~ ... ~ ͕ ... ~: ‖ 27 denies?] ~ ͕ ‖

That at the Barricadoes spake to mee,
(No person seene) Let's leade my Lord to Reimes?
   Cler. Nor could you learne the person?
   Guise.   By no meanes.   40
   Cler. Twas but your fancie then, a waking dreame:
For as in sleepe, which bindes both th'outward senses,
And the sense common to; th'imagining power
(Stird vp by formes hid in the memories store,
Or by the vapours of o'er-flowing humours   45
In bodies full and foule; and mixt with spirits,)
Faines many strange, miraculous images,
In which act, it so painfully applyes
It selfe to those formes, that the common sense
It actuates with his motion; and thereby   50
Those fictions true seeme, and haue reall act:
So, in the strength of our conceits, awake,
The cause alike, doth oft like fictions make.
   Guise. Be what it will, twas a presage of something
Waightie and secret, which th'aduertisements   55
I haue receiu'd from all parts, both without,
And in this Kingdome, as from Rome and Spaine,
Lorraine and Sauoye, giues me cause to thinke,
All writing that our plots Catastrophe,
For propagation of the Catholique cause, /   60
Will bloudy proue, dissoluing all our counsailes.   [I1]
   Cler. Retyre then from them all.
   Guise.   I must not doe so.
The Arch-Bishop of Lyons tels me plaine
I shall be said then to abandon France
In so important an occasion: 65
And that mine enemies (their profit making
Of my faint absence) soone would let that fall,
That all my paines did to this height exhale.
   Cler. Let all fall that would rise vnlawfully:
Make not your forward spirit in vertues right,   70
A property for vice, by thrusting on
Further then all your powers can fetch you off.
It is enough, your will is infinite
To all things vertuous and religious,
Which within limits kept, may without danger,   75
Let vertue some good from your Graces gather,
Auarice of all is euer nothings father.

---

39 my Lord] *Boas*; (~ ~) ‖ **53** oft] *Boas*; of ‖ **57** Spaine,] ~ˌ ‖ **58** Lorraine] *Boas*; Soccaine ‖

Vmb. [*Advances and addresses Clermont.*] Danger (the spurre of
    all great mindes) is euer
The curbe to your tame spirits; you respect not
(With all your holinesse of life and learning)   80
More then the present, like illiterate vulgars;
Your minde (you say) kept in your fleshes bounds,
Showes that mans will must rul'd be by his power:
When (by true doctrine) you are taught to liue
Rather without the body, then within;   85
And rather to your God still then your selfe:
To liue to him, is to doe all things fitting
His Image, in which, like himselfe we liue;
To be his Image, is to doe those things,
That make vs deathlesse, which by death is onely   90
Doing those deedes that fit eternitie,
And those deedes are the perfecting that Iustice,
That makes the world last, which proportion is
Of punishment and wreake for euery wrong,
As well as for right a reward as strong: 95
Away then, vse the meanes thou hast to right
The wrong I suffer'd. What corrupted Law /
Leaues vnperform'd in Kings, doe thou supply,   [I1ᵛ]
And be aboue them all in dignitie.   *Exit.*
   Guise. Why stand'st thou still thus, and applyest thine eares,   100
And eyes to nothing?
     Cler.   Saw you nothing here?
   Guise. Thou dream'st awake now; what was here to see?
   Cler. My Brothers spirit, vrging his reuenge.
   Guise. Thy Brothers spirit! pray thee mocke me not.
   Cler. No, by my loue and seruice.
   Guise.   Would he rise,   105
And not be thundring threates against the Guise?
   Cler. You make amends for enmitie to him,
With tenne parts more loue, and desert of mee;
And as you make your hate to him no let
Of any loue to mee; no more beares hee   110
(Since you to me supply it) hate to you:
Which reason and which Iustice is perform'd
In Spirits tenne parts more then fleshy men,
To whose fore-sights our acts and thoughts lie open:
And therefore since hee saw the treacherie   115
Late practis'd by my brother Baligny,

---

78 SD *Advances ... Clermont.*] *Lordi (after Parrott)* ‖ 81 vulgars;] ~, ‖ 90 onely] *Boas;* ~; (*See
Textual Note*) ‖ 102 dream'st] *Shepherd;* ~, ‖ 109 him] ~, ‖ 111 you:] ~. ‖ 113 men,] ~. ‖

Hee would not honor his hand with the iustice
(As hee esteemes it) of his blouds reuenge,
To which my Sister needes would haue him sworne,
Before she would consent to marry him.   120
    Guise. O Baligny, who would beleeue there were
A man, that (onely since his lookes are rais'd
Vpwards, and haue but sacred heauen in sight)
Could beare a minde so more then diuellish
As, for the painted glory of the countenance,   125
Flitting in Kings, doth good for nought esteeme,
And the more ill hee does, the better seeme?
    Cler. Wee easily may beleeue it, since we see
In this worlds practise few men better be.
Iustice to liue doth nought but Iustice neede,   130
But Policie must still on mischiefe feede.
Vntruth for all his ends, truths name doth sue in;
None safely liue, but those that study ruine. /
A good man happy, is a common good;   [I2]
Ill men aduanc'd liue of the common bloud.   135
    Guise. But this thy brothers spirit startles mee,
These spirits seld or neuer hanting men,
But some mishap ensues.
    Cler.   Ensue what can:
Tyrants may kill, but neuer hurt a man;
All to his good makes, spight of death and hell.   140

Enter Aumall.

    Aum. All the desert of good, renowne your Highnesse.
    Guise. Welcome Aumall.
    Cler.   My good friend, friendly welcome.
How tooke my noblest mistresse the chang'd newes?
    Aum. It came too late sir, for those loueliest eyes
(Through which a soule look't so diuinely louing,   145
Teares nothing vttering her distresse enough)
She wept quite out, and like two falling Starres
Their dearest sights quite vanisht with her teares.
    Cler. All good forbid it.
    Guise.   What euents are these?
    Cler. All must be borne my Lord; and yet this chance 150
Would willingly enforce a man to cast off
All power to beare with comfort, since hee sees
In this, our comforts made our miseries.
    Guise. How strangely thou art lou'd of both the sexes;
Yet thou lou'st neyther, but the good of both.   155

---

124 diuellish] ~? ‖ **125** As,] ~ ‖ **127** seeme?] ~. ‖ **141** good, renowne] *stet* (*See Textual Note*) ‖

Cler. In loue of women, my affection first
Takes fire out of the fraile parts of my bloud;
Which till I haue enioy'd, is passionate,
Like other louers: but fruition past,
I then loue out of iudgement; the desert   160
Of her I loue, still sticking in my heart,
Though the desire, and the delight be gone,
Which must chance still, since the comparison
Made vpon tryall twixt what reason loues,
And what affection, makes in mee the best   165
Euer preferd; what most loue, valuing lest. /
   Guise. Thy loue being iudgement then, and of the minde,   [I2ᵛ]
Marry thy worthiest mistresse now being blinde.
   Cler. If there were loue in mariage so I would;
But I denie that any man doth loue,   170
Affecting wiues, maides, widowes, any women:
For neither Flyes loue milke, although they drowne
In greedy search thereof; nor doth the Bee
Loue honey, though the labour of her life
Is spent in gathering it; nor those that fat   175
On beasts, or fowles, doe any thing therein
For any loue: for as when onely nature
Moues men to meate, as farre as her power rules,
Shee doth it with a temperate appetite,
(The too much men deuoure, abhorring nature;   180
And in our most health, is our most disease)
So, when humanitie rules men and women,
Tis for societie confinde in reason.
But what excites the beds desire in bloud,
By no meanes iustly can be construed loue;   185
For when loue kindles any knowing spirit,
It ends in vertue and effects diuine;
And is in friendship chaste, and masculine.
   Guise. Thou shalt my Mistresse be; me thinkes my bloud
Is taken vp to all loue with thy vertues.   190
And howsoeuer other men despise
These Paradoxes strange, and too precise,
Since they hold on the right way of our reason,
I could attend them euer. Come, away;
Performe thy brothers thus importun'd wreake;   195
And I will see what great affaires the King
Hath to employ my counsell, which he seemes
Much to desire, and more and more esteemes.   *Exeunt.*

---

176 On] *Shepherd*; Or ‖ 180-81 (The ... disease)] ͜~ ... ~: ‖ 182 women,] ~. ‖ 198 SD *Exeunt.*]
Phelps; *Exit.* ‖

[V.ii]

Enter Henry, Baligny, with six of the Guard.

Hen. Saw you his sawcie forcing of my hand
To D'Ambois freedome?
   Bal.   Saw, and through mine eyes
Let fire into my heart, that burn'd to beare /
An insolence so Giantly austere.   [I3]
   Hen. The more Kings beare at Subiects hands, the more   5
Their lingring Iustice gathers; that resembles
The waightie, and the goodly-bodied Eagle,
Who (being on earth) before her shady wings
Can raise her into ayre, a mightie way
Close by the ground she runnes; but being aloft,   10
All shee commands, she flyes at; and the more
Death in her Seres beares, the more time shee stayes
Her thundry stoope from that on which shee preyes.
   Bal. You must be then more secret in the waight
Of these your shadie counsels, who will else   15
Beare (where such sparkes flye as the Guise and D'Ambois)
Pouder about them. Counsels (as your entrailes)
Should be vnpierst and sound kept; for not those,
Whom you discouer, you neglect; but ope
A ruinous passage to your owne best hope.   20
   Hen. Wee haue Spies set on vs, as we on others;
And therefore they that serue vs must excuse vs,
If what wee most hold in our hearts, take winde;
Deceit hath eyes that see into the minde.
But this plot shall be quicker then their twinckling,   25
On whose lids Fate, with her dead waight shall lie,
And Confidence that lightens ere she die.
Friends of my Guard, as yee gaue othe to be
True to your Soueraigne, keepe it manfully:
Your eyes haue witnest oft th'Ambition   30
That neuer made accesse to me in Guise
But Treason euer sparkled in his eyes:
Which if you free vs of, our safetie shall
You not our Subiects, but our Patrons call.
   Omnes. Our duties binde vs, hee is now but dead.   35
   Hen. Wee trust in it, and thanke ye. Baligny,
Goe lodge their ambush, and thou God that art
Fautor of Princes, thunder from the skies,
Beneath his hill of pride this Gyant Guise.   *Exeunt.* /

V.ii] Boas ‖ SD *Guard*] guard ‖ 23 winde;] ~, ‖

[V.iii]

Enter Tamyra with a Letter, Charlotte in mans attire.　　　[13ᵛ]

Tam. I see y'are Seruant, sir, to my deare sister,
The Lady of her lou'd Baligny.
　　Char. Madame I am bound to her vertuous bounties,
For that life which I offer in her seruice,
To the reuenge of her renowned brother.　　　　　　　　　　5
　　Tam. She writes to mee as much, and much desires,
That you may be the man, whose spirit shee knowes
Will cut short off these long and dull delayes,
Hitherto bribing the eternall Iustice:
Which I beleeue, since her vnmatched spirit　　　　　　　　10
Can iudge of spirits, that haue her sulphure in them;
But I must tell you, that I make no doubt,
Her liuing brother will reuenge her dead,
On whom the dead impos'd the taske, and hee,
I know, will come t'effect it instantly.　　　　　　　　　15
　　Char. They are but words in him; beleeue them not.
　　Tam. See; this is the vault, where he must enter:
Where now I thinke hee is.

Enter Renel at the vault, with the Countesse being blinde.

Ren.　　　　　　　　God saue you Lady.
What Gentleman is this, with whom you trust
The deadly waightie secret of this houre?　　　　　　　　20
　　Tam. One that your selfe will say, I well may trust.
　　Ren. Then come vp Madame.　　　　*He helps the Countesse vp.*
　　　　　　　　　See here honour'd Lady,
A Countesse that in loues mishap doth equall
At all parts, your wrong'd selfe; and is the mistresse
Of your slaine seruants brother; in whose loue,　　　　　25
For his late treachrous apprehension,
She wept her faire eyes from her Iuory browes,
And would haue wept her soule out, had not I
Promist to bring her to this mortall quarrie,
That by her lost eyes for her seruants loue,　　　　　　30
She might coniure him from this sterne attempt,
In which, (by a most ominous dreame shee had) /
Shee knowes his death fixt, and that neuer more　　　　　[14]
Out of this place the Sunne shall see him liue.
　　Char. I am prouided then to take his place,　　　　35
And vndertaking on me.
　　Ren.　　　　　　　You sir, why?

V.iii] *Boas* ‖ **2** lou'd] *stet* (*See Textual Note*) ‖ **4** her seruice] *Shepherd*; her vertuous seruice (*See Textual Note*) ‖ **25** loue,] ∼ˌ ‖

Char. Since I am charg'd so by my mistresse,
His mournfull sister.
  Tam.   See her Letter sir.   *Hee reades.*
Good Madame, I rue your fate, more then mine,
And know not how to order these affaires,   40
They stand on such occurrents.
  Ren.   This indeede,
I know to be your Lady mistresse hand,
And know besides, his brother will, and must
Indure no hand in this reuenge but his.

      Enter Vmbr. Bussy.

  Vmb. Away, dispute no more; get vp, and see,   45
Clermont must auchthor this iust Tragedie.
  Count. Who's that?
  Ren.   The spirit of Bussy.
  Tam.   O my seruant!
Let us embrace.
  Vmb.   Forbeare. The ayre, in which
My figures liknesse is imprest, will blast;
Let my reuenge for all loues satisfie,   50
[*To the Countess.*] In which (dame) feare not, Clermont shall
  not dye:
No word dispute more, vp, and see th'euent.   *Exeunt Ladyes.*
Make the Guard sure Renel; and then the doores
Command to make fast, when the Earle is in.   *Exit Ren.*
The blacke soft-footed houre is now on wing,   55
Which for my iust wreake, Ghosts shall celebrate,
With dances dire, and of infernall state.   *Exit.*

      [V.iv]

      Enter Guise.

  Guise. Who sayes that death is naturall, when nature
Is with the onely thought of it, dismaid?
I haue had Lotteries set vp for my death,
And I haue drawne beneath my trencher one,
Knit in my hand-kerchiefe another lot,   5
The word being; Y'are a dead man if you enter; /
And these words, this imperfect bloud and flesh,   [14ᵛ]
Shrincke at in spight of me; their solidst part
Melting like snow within mee, with colde fire:

47-48 *Count. … which*] *Boas*; *Coun. … Bussy. / Tam. … embrace. / Vmb. … which* Q (let) ‖
49 blast;] ~, ‖ **51** SD *To the Countess.*] ‖ **V.iv**] *Boas* ‖ **6** enter;] ~, ‖

I hate my selfe, that seeking to rule Kings,   10
I cannot curbe my slaue. Would any spirit
Free, manly, Princely, wish to liue to be
Commanded by this masse of slauerie,
Since Reason, Iudgement, Resolution,
And scorne of what we feare, will yeeld to feare?   15
While this same sincke of sensualitie swels,
Who would liue sinking in it? and not spring
Vp to the Starres, and leaue this carrion here,
For Wolfes, and Vultures, and for Dogges to teare?
O Clermont D'Ambois, wert thou here to chide   20
This softnesse from my flesh, farre as my reason,
Farre as my resolution, not to stirre
One foote out of the way, for death and hell.
Let my false man by falshood perish here,
There's no way else to set my true man cleere.   25

              Enter Messenger.

Mess. The King desires your Grace to come to Councill.
  Guise. I come. [*Exit Messenger.*] It cannot be: hee will not dare
To touch me with a treacherie so prophane.
Would Clermont now were here, to try how hee
Would lay about him, if this plot should be: 30
Here would be tossing soules into the skie.
Who euer knew bloud sau'd by treacherie?
Well, I must on, and will; what should I feare?
Not against two Alcides? against two
And Hercules to friend, the Guise will goe.   35

     He takes vp the Arras, and the Guard enters vpon him:
               hee drawes.

Holde murtherers. (*They strike him downe.*) So then, this is
   confidence
In greatnes, not in goodnes: wher is the King?

     The King comes in sight with Es. Sois. Aum. and others.

Let him appeare to iustifie his deede, /
In spight of my betrai'd wounds, ere my soule   [K1]
Take her flight through them, and my tongue hath strength   40
To vrge his tyrannie.
  Hen.   See sir, I am come
To iustifie it before men, and God,
Who knowes with what wounds in my heart for woe

---

27 SD *Exit Messenger.*] ‖ **34** two Alcides] *Shepherd*; ~, ~ ‖ **36** Holde] *Parrott*; *Guise.* Holde |
(*They … downe.*)] ~ … ~. ‖ **37** King] king | SD *The … others.*] *in right margin* | SD *King*]
king | SD *Aum.*] *Walley* ‖ **38** deede,] ~. ‖ **39** wounds,] ~; ‖

Of your so wounded faith, I made these wounds,
Forc't to it by an insolence of force   45
To stirre a stone, nor is a rocke oppos'd
To all the billowes of the churlish sea,
More beate, and eaten with them, then was I
With your ambitious mad Idolatrie;
And this bloud I shed, is to saue the bloud   50
Of many thousands.
   Guise.   That's your white pretext,
But you will finde one drop of bloud shed lawlesse,
Will be the fountaine to a purple sea:
The present lust, and shift made for Kings liues
Against the pure forme, and iust power of Law,   55
Will thriue like shifters purchases; there hangs
A blacke Starre in the skies, to which the Sunne
Giues yet no light, will raine a poyson'd shower
Into your entrailes, that will make you feele
How little safetie lies in treacherous steele.   60
   Hen. Well sir, Ile beare it; y'haue a Brother to,
Bursts with like threates, the skarlet Cardinall:
Seeke, and lay hands on him; and take this hence,
Their blouds, for all you, on my conscience.   *Exit.*
   Guise. So sir, your full swindge take; mine, death hath curb'd.   65
Clermont, farewell: O didst thou see but this!
But it is better, see by this the Ice
Broke to thine owne bloud, which thou wilt despise,
When thou hear'st mine shed. Is there no friend here
Will beare my loue to him?
   Aum.   I will, my Lord.   70
   Guise. Thankes with my last breath: recommend me then
To the most worthy of the race of men.   *Dyes. Exeunt.*

[V.v]

Enter Monts. and Tamyra.

   Mont. Who haue you let into my house?
   Tam.   I, none. /
   Mont. Tis false, I sauour the rancke bloud of foes   [K1ᵛ]
In euery corner.
   Tam.   That you may doe well,
It is the bloud you lately shed, you smell.

---

66 this!] *Shepherd*; ~: Q(c); ~ �‚ Q(u) ‖ **V.v**] *Boas* ‖

Mont. Sdeath the vault opes.   *The gulfe opens.*
Tam.   What vault? hold your sword.   5

                          Clermont ascends.

Cler. No, let him vse it.
Mont.   Treason, murther, murther.
Cler. Exclaime not; tis in vaine, and base in you,
Being one, to onely one.
Mont.   O bloudy strumpet!
Cler. With what bloud charge you her? it may be mine
As well as yours; there shall not any else   10
Enter or touch you: I conferre no guards,
Nor imitate the murtherous course you tooke;
But single here, will haue my former challenge,
Now answer'd single, not a minute more
My brothers bloud shall stay for his reuenge,   15
If I can act it; if not, mine shall adde
A double conquest to you, that alone
Put it to fortune now, and vse no ods.
Storme not, nor beate your selfe thus gainst the dores,
Like to a sauage vermine in a trap: 20
All dores are sure made, and you cannot scape,
But by your valour.
Mont.   No, no, come and kill mee.   *[Lies down.]*
Cler. If you will die so like a beast, you shall,
But when the spirit of a man may saue you,
Doe not so shame man, and a Noble man.   25
Mont. I doe not show this basenesse, that I feare thee,
But to preuent and shame thy victory,
Which of one base is base, and so Ile die.
Cler. Here then.
Mont.   Stay, hold, one thought hath harden'd me,

                                                   He starts vp.
And since I must afford thee victorie,   30
It shall be great and braue, if one request
Thou wilt admit mee.
Cler.   What's that?
Mont.   Giue me leaue
To fetch and vse the sword thy Brother gaue mee
When he was brauely giuing vp his life.
Cler. No, Ile not fight against my brothers sword,   35
Not that I feare it, but since tis a tricke, /
For you to show your backe.   [K2]
Mont.   By all truth, no:

---

5 SD *Clermont ascends.*] *in right margin* ‖ 22 SD *Lies down.*] *Parrott subs.* ‖ 28-29 Which . . .
me,] *Boas*; Which . . . then. / *Mon.* . . . me, ‖

505

Take but my honourable othe, I will not.

    Cler. Your honourable othe! plaine truth no place has

Where othes are honourable.

    Tam.   Trust not his othe.   40

Hee will lie like a Lapwing; when shee flyes

Farre from her sought nest, still here tis shee cryes.

    Mont. Out on thee damme of Diuels. I will quite

Disgrace thy braues conquest, die, not fight.   *Lyes downe.*

    Tam. Out on my fortune to wed such an abiect.   45

Now is the peoples voyce, the voyce of God;

Hee that to wound a woman vants so much,

(As hee did mee) a man dares neuer touch.

    Cler. Reuenge your wounds now madame, I resigne him

Vp to your full will, since hee will not fight.   50

First you shall torture him (as hee did you,

And Iustice wils) and then pay I my vow.

Here, take this Ponyard.

    Mont.   Sinke Earth, open Heauen,

And let fall vengeance.

    Tam.   Come sir, good sir hold him.

    Mont. O shame of women, whither art thou fled!   55

    Cler. Why (good my Lord) is it a greater shame

For her then you? come, I will be the bands

You vs'd to her, prophaning her faire hands.

    Mont. No sir, [*Rises.*] Ile fight now, and the terror be

Of all you Champions to such as shee.   60

I did but thus farre dally: now obserue,

O all you aking fore-heads that haue rob'd,

Your hands of weapons, and your hearts of valour,

Ioyne in mee all your rages, and rebutters,

And into dust ram this same race of Furies,   65

In this one relicke of the D'Ambois gall,

In his one purple soule shed, drowne it all.   *Fight.*

Now giue me breath a while.

    Cler.   Receiue it freely.

    Mont. What thinke y'a this now?

    Cler.   It is very noble, /   69

Had it beene free (at least) and of your selfe;   [K2ᵛ]

And thus wee see (where valour most doth vant)

What tis to make a coward valiant.

    Mont. Now I shall grace your conquest.

    Cler.   That you shall.

39 othe!] ~, ‖ **41** Lapwing;] ~, ‖ **44** braues] *stet (See Textual Note)* ‖ **59** SD *Rises.*] *Lordi* ‖ **66** D'Ambois] *Parrott*; Ambois ‖ **68** Now] *Parrott*; *Mont.* Now ‖ **69** noble,] ~. ‖ **70** selfe;] ·~, ‖ **73-74** *Mont. . . . fortune.*] *Boas*; *Mont. . . . conquest. / Cler. . . . it. / Cler. . . . fortune.* ‖

Mont. If you obtaine it.
Cler.   True sir, tis in fortune.
Mont. If you were not a D'Ambois, I would scarce   75
Change liues with you, I feele so great a change
In my tall spirits breath'd, I thinke, with the breath
A D'Ambois breathes here, and necessitie
(With whose point now prickt on, and so, whose helpe
My hands may challenge, that doth all men conquer,   80
If shee except not you, of all men onely)
May change the case here.
Cler.   True as you are chang'd,
Her power in me vrg'd, makes y'another man,
Then yet you euer were.
Mont.   Well, I must on.
Cler. Your Lordship must by all meanes.
Mont.   Then at all.   85
                   Fights, and D'Ambois hurts him.

     Charlotte appears aboue with Renel and the Countess.

Char. Death of my father: what a shame is this,
Sticke in his hands thus?
Ren. [*Tries to stop Charlotte.*] Gentle sir forbeare.   *She gets downe.*
Count. Is he not slaine yet?
Ren.   No Madame, but hurt
In diuers parts of him.
Mont.   Y'haue giuen it me,
And yet I feele life for another vennie.   90

           Enter Charlotte below.

Cler. What would you sir?
Char.   I would performe this Combat.
Cler. Against which of vs?
Char.   I care not much if twere
Against thy selfe: thy sister would haue sham'd,
To haue thy Brothers wreake with any man
(In single combat) sticke so in her fingers.   95
Cler. My Sister? know you her?
Tam.   I sir, shee sent him,
With this kinde Letter, to performe the wreake /
Of my deare Seruant.   [K3]
Cler.   Now alas good sir,
Thinke you you could doe more?
Char.   Alas? I doe,

---

85 SD *Charlotte ... Countess.*] *Phelps subs.*; *Charlotte aboue.* ‖ **87-89** Sticke ... me,] *Boas*;
Sticke ... forbeare. / *Coun.* ... yet? / *Ren.* ... him. / *Mont.* ... me, Q (in) ‖ **87** SD *Tries ...*
Charlotte.] *Boas subs.* | SD *She gets downe.*] *Lordi; after* yet? (*l.* 88) ‖ **90** vennie.] ~, | SD *below*]
Boas ‖

And wer't not, I, fresh, sound, should charge a man   100
Weary, and wounded, I would long ere this,
Haue prou'd what I presume on.
    Cler.   Y'haue a minde
Like to my Sister, but haue patience now,
If next charge speede not, Ile resigne to you.
    Mont. Pray thee let him decide it.
    Cler.   No, my Lord,   105
I am the man in fate, and since so brauely
Your Lordship stands mee, scape but one more charge,
And on my life, Ile set your life at large.
    Mont. Said like a D'Ambois, and if now I die,   109
Sit ioy and all good on thy victorie.   *Fights, and fals downe.*
Farewell, I hartily forgiue thee – Wife,   *Hee giues his hand to Cler.*
And thee; let penitence spend thy rest of life.   *and his Wife.*
    Cler. Noble and Christian.
    Tam.   O it breakes my heart.
    Cler. And should, for all faults found in him before,
These words, this end, makes full amends and more.   115
Rest worthy soule, and with it the deare spirit
Of my lou'd Brother, rest in endlesse peace:
Soft lie thy bones, Heauen be your soules abode,
And to your ashes be the earth no lode.

        Musicke, and the Ghost of Bussy enters, leading the Ghost
        of the Guise; Monsieur, Cardinall Guise, and Shattilion,
          they dance about the dead body, and Exeunt.

How strange is this? the Guise amongst these spirits,   120
And his great Brother Cardinall, both yet liuing,
And that the rest with them, with ioy thus celebrate
This our reuenge? This certainely presages
Some instant death both to the Guise and Cardinall.
That the Shattilions Ghost to should thus ioyne   125
In celebration of this iust reuenge, /
With Guise, that bore a chiefe stroke in his death,   [K3ᵛ]
It seemes that now he doth approue the act,
And these true shadowes of the Guise and Cardinall,
Fore-running thus their bodies, may approue   130
That all things to be done, as here wee liue,
Are done before all times in th'other life.
That Spirits should rise in these times yet are fables,

---

111 Farewell] *Shepherd; Mon.* Farewell | thee–] ~. *(See Textual Note)* | SD *Hee ... Wife.*] *after*
life *(l. 112)* ‖ **112** thee;] ~, ‖ **118** bones,] ~ˎ ‖ **120** How] *Cler.* How ‖ **125** Shattilions] Shattilians ‖
133 fables,] ~; ‖

Though learnedst men hold that our sensiue spirits
A little time abide about the graues   135
Of their deceased bodies; and can take
In colde condenc't ayre, the same formes they had,
When they were shut vp in this bodies shade.

Enter Aumall.

  Aum. O Sir, the Guise is slaine.
  Cler.   Auert it Heauen.
  Aum. Sent for to Councill, by the King, an ambush   140
(Lodg'd for the purpose) rusht on him, and tooke
His Princely life; who sent (in dying then)
His loue to you, as to the best of men.
  Cler. The worst, and most accurst of things creeping
On earths sad bosome. Let me pray yee all   145
A little to forbeare, and let me vse
Freely mine owne minde in lamenting him.
Ile call yee straight againe.
  Aum.   We will forbeare,
And leaue you free sir.   *Exeunt.*
  Cler.   Shall I liue, and hee
Dead, that alone gaue meanes of life to me?   150
There's no disputing with the acts of Kings,
Reuenge is impious on their sacred persons:
And could I play the worldling (no man louing
Longer then gaine is reapt, or grace from him)
I should suruiue, and shall be wondred at,   155
Though (in mine owne hands being) I end with him:
But Friendship is the Sement of two mindes,
As of one man the soule and body is,
Of which one cannot seuer, but the other
Suffers a needfull separation.   160
  Ren. I feare your seruant, Madame: let's descend.
Descend Ren. and Coun. /
  Cler. Since I could skill of man, I neuer liu'd   [K4]
To please men worldly, and shall I in death
Respect their pleasures, making such a iarre
Betwixt my death and life, when death should make   165
The consort sweetest; th'end being proofe and crowne
To all the skill and worth wee truely owne?
Guise, O my Lord, how shall I cast from me
The bands and couerts hindring me from thee?

---

144 accurst] *stet* (*See Textual Note*) ‖ **148-49** Ile ... hee] *Boas*; Ile ... againe. / *Aum.* ... sir. /
Cler. ... hee Q (and) ‖ **156** Though (in] (~͵ ~ ‖ **161** SD *Descend ... Coun.*] *after ll. 160-61* ‖ **163**
death] ~, ‖

The garment or the couer of the minde,   170
The humane soule is; of the soule, the spirit
The proper robe is; of the spirit, the bloud;
And of the bloud, the body is the shrowd.
With that must I beginne then to vnclothe,
And come at th'other. Now then as a ship,   175
Touching at strange, and farre remoued shores;
Her men a shore goe, for their seuerall ends,
Fresh water, victuals, precious stones, and pearle,
All yet intentiue (when the master cals,
The Ship to put off ready) to leaue all   180
Their greediest labours, lest they there be left,
To theeues, or beasts, or be the Countries slaues:
So, now my master cals, my ship, my venture
All in one bottome put, all quite put off,
Gone vnder saile, and I left negligent,   185
To all the horrors of the vicious time,
The farre remou'd shores to all vertuous aimes;
None fauouring goodnesse; none but he respecting
Pietie or man-hood. Shall I here suruiue,
Not cast me after him into the sea,   190
Rather then here liue, readie euery houre
To feede theeues, beasts, and be the slaue of power?
I come my Lord, Clermont thy creature comes.   *Hee kils himselfe.*

Enter Aumal, Tamyra, Charlotte.

Aum. What? lye and languish, Clermont? Cursed man
To leaue him here thus: hee hath slaine himselfe.   195
    Tam. Misery on misery! O me wretched Dame
Of all that breath! all heauen turne all his eyes, /
In harty enuie, thus on one poore dame.   [K4ᵛ]
    Char. Well done my Brother: I did loue thee euer,
But now adore thee: losse of such a friend   200
None should suruiue, [or] of such a Brother;
With my false husband liue, and both these slaine?
Ere I returne to him, Ile turne to earth.

Enter Renel leading the Countesse.

Ren. Horror of humane eyes, O Clermont D'Ambois!
Madame, wee staid too long, your seruant's slaine.   205
    Count. It must be so, he liu'd but in the Guise,
As I in him. O follow, life, mine eyes.

179 (when the] ‸~ (~ ‖ 197 breath!] ~, ‖ 201 or] *See Textual Note* ‖ 202 slaine?] *Shepherd;* ~: ‖
207 follow, life,] ~‸ ~‸ ‖

Tam. Hide, hide thy snakie head, to Cloisters flie,
In pennance pine, too easie tis to die.
 Char. It is. In Cloisters then let's all suruiue.   210
Madame, since wrath nor griefe can helpe these fortunes,
Let vs forsake the world, in which they raigne,
And for their wisht amends to God complaine.
 Count. Tis fit and onely needfull: leade me on,   214
In heauens course comfort seeke, in earth is none.   *Exeunt.*

    Enter Henry, Espernone, Soissone, and others.

 Hen. Wee came indeede too late, which much I rue,
And would haue kept this Clermont as my crowne.
Take in the dead, and make this fatall roome
(The house shut vp) the famous D'Ambois Tombe.   *Exeunt.*

       FINIS.

210 *Char.*] *Shepherd; Cler.* ‖

HISTORICAL COLLATION

[Editions collated: Shepherd (= S, in *The Works of George Chapman: Plays*, I, 1874, pp. 178-213); Phelps (= *Ph*, in *The Best Plays of the Old Dramatists, the Mermaid Series*, 1895, pp. 223-317); Boas (= *B*, in *The Belles-Lettres Series* edition of *Bussy D'Ambois and The Revenge of Bussy D'Ambois*, 1905, pp. 164-306); Parrott (= *P*, in *The Plays of George Chapman: The Tragedies*, 1910, pp. 75-148, 571-590; Walley and Wilson (= *W*, in *Early Seventeenth-Century Plays, 1600-1642*, 1930, pp. 459-527); Lordi (= *L*, in *The Revenge of Bussy D'Ambois*, 1977, pp. 39-229). In addition, emendations suggested by K. Deighton in *The Old Dramatists: Conjectural Readings* (Westminster, 1896), pp. 132-133, and by G. G. Loane in 'More Notes on Chapman's Plays,' *MLR*, XXXVIII (1943), 343, are also included. Only substantive and semi-substantive variants are recorded; obvious errors are not recorded. Lemmata are taken from the present text. Where lemma represents the reading of Q copy-text or of Q (corrected), omission of siglum indicates agreement with lemma.]

The Actors names.

1 *Henry*, the King] Henry III, King of France *W*
3 a Duke] *P, W, L; D. Q*; Duke *S, Ph, B*
6 Lieutenant] Lieutenant of Cambray *B, P, L*; Lord-Lieutenant, of Cambrai *W*
7 *Clermont D'Ambois*] Clermont d'Ambois, Brother of the Dead Bussy d'Ambois *W*
11 *Espernone*] Epernon ⎫ *courtiers L*
12 *Soissone*] Soisson ⎭
    Soissone] Soissons *W (not hereafter recorded)*
13 *Perricot*] Perricot, An *Usher B*; Perricot, *an Usher to Guise P, W, L*
14 An ... Countess] *P, W, L; om. Q, S, Ph, B*
15 A *Messenger*] *B, L; om. Q, S, Ph, P, W*
21 ghost] ghost[s] *B, P, W, L*
26 *Charlotte*] *Charlotte D'Ambois B*
27 Seruant] Servant to the Countess *B, L*
    After this list of *The Actors names*, *W* has: Scene. – *Paris, Cambrai, and the vicinity.*

I.i

Actus ... prima.] ~ ... ~. *A Room at the Court in Paris. B*; ~ ... ~ˌ *A Room in the Court P, W*

22 so:] ~‸ B, P, W, L

60 slaues,] S, Ph, B, P, W, L; ~‸ Q

70 heauen's true] S, Ph, W, L; heauens true Q, B; heaven's tru[th] P

74 your selfe] P, W, L; my selfe Q, S, Ph, B

121 All] [To Renel leaving.] All L

144 SD Enter ... King.] B, P, W, L; opposite ll. 145-49; after l. 145 S, Ph, Q
    SD Soisson] S, Ph, B, P, W, L; Foisson Q

145 SD Exit Henry.] L; om. Q, S, Ph, B; after l. 144 P, W

167 at] S, Ph, Deighton conj., B, P, W, L; om. Q

181 D'Ambois] D'Ambois' S, Ph, P, W

184 him] om. Ph
    him. Come] him. [To Guise and Clermont] Come P, L; him. – Come W

216 ingenuous] ingenious P, W

250 Dost] Does't P, W

255 Dost] Does't P, W

265 Cler.] om. S, Ph

268 Mons.] B, P, W, L; om. Q, S, Ph

288 you're] you were S, Ph, B

302 births] birth, S, Ph

338 Moralist] S, Ph, B, P, W, L; Moralists Q

353 sweater, out] ~‸ ~ Q, S, Ph, B; ~-~ P, W, L

358 them all,] them. All W

364 (selling ... wares);] (~ ... ~;) Q; , ~ ... ~, S, Ph; ‸~ ... ~, B, P, W;
    (~ ... ~), L

382 friend] brother S, Ph, P, W

I.ii

I.ii] L; om. Q, S, Ph; Scæna Secunda. A Room in Montsurry's house. B, P, W

4 honors] S, Ph, B, P, W, L; humors Q

6 Haue] Hath S, Ph, W

14 ere] e'er S, Ph, P, W, L

24 SD Montsur.] Q(c); Monsieur. Q(u)

25 Mont.] Q(c); Mons. Q(u)

28 dry] Q(c); dye Q(u)

54 lines] Q(c); liues Q(u)

62 Mont.] Q(c); Mons. Q(u)

72 Mont.] S, Ph, B, P, W, L; Mons. Q

76 wounds yet,] ~, ~, S, Ph; ~‸ ~‸ B

77 Mont.] S, Ph, B, P, W, L; Mons. Q

96 Mont.] S, Ph, B, P, W, L; Mons. Q

97 Mont.] S, Ph, B, P, W, L; Mons. Q

100 tis] it is B

101 Mont.] S, Ph, B, P, W, L; Mons. Q
    SD Exit Souldier.] B, L; om. Q, S, Ph, P, W

104 SD Aside ... Souldier.] B, P, W, L; om. Q, S, Ph

114 Mont.] S, Ph, B, P, W, L; Mons. Q

115 Osculatur.] Renel salutes her. W

Ren.] Ren. [*to Tam.*] B
117 Mont.] S, Ph, B, P, W, L; *Mons.* Q
120 Mont.] S, Ph, B, P, W, L; *Mons.* Q
122 Mont.] S, Ph, B, P, W, L; *Mons.* Q
130 SD *Draws his Sword.*] L; *om.* Q, S, Ph, B, P, W
131 Mont.] Q(c); *Mons.* Q(u)
     SD *To Renel.*] P, W, L; *om.* Q, S, Ph, B
     SD *To Baligny.*] P subs., W, L; *om.* Q, S, Ph, B
133 Bal.] Q(c); *Mons.* Q(u)
134 Mont.] *Mon.* Q
136 Mont.] Q(c); *Mons.* Q(u)
137 Hold] [*To Baligny*] Hold P, L
138 SD *They ... in Mont.*] *after* off (*l. 136*) B
     SD *Exit Mont.*] *after* Challenge (*l. 138*) B
     SD *Mont.*] Q(c); *Mons.* Q(u)
     SD *Mont.*] Q(c); *Mons.* Q(u)
     Finis Actus primi.] *om.* W

II.i

Actus ... prima.] ~ ... ~. *A Room at the Court.* B; ~ ... ~ˌ *A Room in the Court* P, W
     SD *Henry, Baligny*] Enter Henry *and* Baligny W
50 at] *om.* S
74 SD *Exit.*] Exit Henry. W
120 the] *om.* S, Ph
130 SD *Manet Bal.*] *om.* W
181 *Simil.*] *om.* W
255 iourney.] ~? B
277 SD *Exeunt.*] P, W, L; *Exit.* Q, S, Ph, B
     Finis Actus secundi.] *om.* W

III.i

Actus ... prima.] ~ ... ~. *A Parade-Ground near Cambrai.* B; ~ ... ~ˌ *A Field near Cambrai* P, W
58 SD *Trumpets within.*] B, P, W, L; *after* come (*l. 59*) Q, S, Ph
59 SD *Drums beate.*] P, W, L; *after* foote (*l. 59*) Q, S, Ph; *before* Harke (*l. 59*) B
83 thrusts] thrust S, Ph
103 SD *Exeunt.*] Ph, B, P, W, L; *Exit.* Q(c), S; *Eit.* Q(u)

III.ii

III.ii] L; *om.* Q, S, Ph; ~.~ *A Room in the Governor's Castle at Cambrai.* B; ~.~ *A Room in the Castle* P; ~.~ *A Room in the Castle at Cambrai.* W
12 Rulers] S, Ph, B, P, W, L; Rubers Q
16 innouations, Gossips] Q(c); innouations, of Gossips Q(u)
43 she] *Deighton conj.*, L; he Q, S, Ph, B, P, W; they *Loane conj.*

67 husband.] husband. [*Reads*] *P, W*
71 *Ren.*] *Ren.* [*reads*] *P, W*
74 your] *S, Ph, B, P, W, L*; you *Q*
145 an] a *S, Ph*
146 in] *S, Ph, B, P, W, L*; *om. Q*
151 Ruffins] Ruffings *Q, B*; ruffians *S, Ph, P, W, L*
152 Arden] *S, Ph, B, P, W, L*; Acden *Q*
159 *Char.*] *S, Ph, B, P, W, L*; *Cler. Q*
161 SD *osculatur*] *after* apprehension (*l. 162*) *P*; *salutes her.* (*after* apprehension *l. 162*) *W*
175 SD *Exeunt*] *B, P, L*; *Exit Q, S, Ph, W*
188 rang'd] *Q(c)*; *om. Q(u), B*
192 Heauen!] heaven! [*turning away*] *P, W*
193 *Mess.*] *Mess.* [*aside to Clermont*] *B, P, W, L*
234 say] stay *S*
236 m'a] me a *S, Ph*
253 SD *Exit.*] *B, P, W, L*; *om. Q, S, Ph*

III.iii

III.iii] *L*; *om. Q, S, Ph*; ~.~ *A Camp near Cambrai. B*; ~.~ *In the Camp P*; ~.~ *The Camp near Cambrai. W*
10 *Ambo.*| *1st Ph*; *Both. W*
25 *Exeunt.*] *Ph, B, P, W, L*; *om. Q, S*

III.iv

III.iv] *L*; *om. Q, S, Ph*; ~.~ *A Room in the Governor's Castle at Cambrai. B*; ~.~ *A Room in the Castle P, W*
1 SD *Aside to himself.*] *P subs., W, L*; *om. Q, S, Ph, B*
7 *Exit.*] *Exit* Maillard. *W*
  SD *Clermont solus.*] *om. W*
35 doe,] *Q(c)*; ~ *Q(u), B*
59 be] *Deighton conj., P, W, L*; are *Q, S, Ph, B*
114 as] as't *B*
124 Erring, to enter] *B, P, W, L*; ~ ~ ~, *Q, S, Ph*
135 Circean] Circene *P, W*
149 SD *Exit.*] *Exit* Renel. *W*
151 friends] friend *S, Ph*
152 Lieutenant Colonell] *Q(c)*; ~, ~ *Q(u), B, P, W*; ~-~ *S, Ph*
165 SD *Ex. cum Pediss.*] *Exeunt. W*
  SD *Finis Actus tertij.*] *om. W*

IV.i

Actus ... prima.] ~ ... ~. *A Parade-Ground near Cambrai. B*; ~ ... ~ *A Field near Cambrai P, W*
  SD *Souldiers disguised like*] *B, P, L*; *om. Q, S, Ph*; Soldiers *disguised as W*
6 SD *with the Lackies.*] *P, L*; *om. Q, S, Ph, B*; Maillard. *W*

SD *with two Souldiers.*] P, L; *om.* Q, S, Ph, B, W
10 SD *Exeunt.*] B, P, W, L; *Exit.* Q, S, Ph
28 grase] Q(c); grasse Q(u), B
34 Then ... then] *om.* S, Ph
44 sport] ~. B
54 terme's] terms S, Ph, B, P, W
57 Y'are] You are S, Ph, W
65 sworne, married] Q(c); sworne-married Q(u), B
　good–] S, Ph, B, P, W, L; ~. Q
69 sworne or married] Q(c); sworne-married Q(u), B
70 publique good] L; good publique Q, S, Ph, B, P, W
73-74 widow, married ... generation,] P, W, L; ~ˏ ~, ... ~ˏ Q, S, Ph, B
79 thy] thine S, Ph
85 SD *Exeunt Souldiers.*] L; *om.* Q, S, Ph, B, P, W
104 Arts] P *conj.*, L; acts Q, S, Ph, B, P, W
157 SD *omnes.*] *om.* W

IV.ii

IV.ii] L; *om.* Q, S, Ph; ~.~ *A Room at the Court in Paris.* B; ~.~ *A Room
　in the Court* P, W
40 lightnings] Q(c); lightning Q(u), B

IV.iii

IV.iii] L; *om.* Q, S, Ph; ~.~ *A Room in the House of the Countess of
　Cambrai.* B, P, W
5 he breake? some brack's] Q(c); hee breake, some brack Q(u); hee breake,
　some brack's B
10 had] Q(c); had had Q(u)
20 should;] Q(c); ~ˏ Q(u)
21 libertie–] B, P, W, L; ~. Q, S, Ph
44 feare,] ~ˏ B; ~. P; ~; W
87 SD *Ancil.*] Riova. (*in right margin*) W
90 SD *Intr. Ancil.*] Re-enter Riova *with the cabinet.* (*centered after l. 90*) W
107 SD *Exeunt.*] Riova *following.* W
108 sau'd] Q(c); san'd Q(u)

IV.iv

IV.iv] L; *om.* Q, S, Ph; ~.~ *A Room at the Court in Paris.* B; ~.~ *A Room
　in the Court* P, W
1 your] S, Ph, P, W, L; you're Q, B
12 SD *Auersus.*] L; *before Hen.* Q; *after* long S, Ph, B, P; [Aside.] (*after
　sir*) W
　long.–] B, P, W, L; ~.ˏ Q, S, Ph
18 lest] best S, Ph
26 learning] leaning *Loane conj.*

51 Cacusses] *B, P, L*; Caucusses *Q*; Caucuses *S, Ph*; Cacuses *W*
56 SD *Manet Bal.*] *P subs., W, L*; *om. Q, S, Ph, B*

IV.v

IV.v] *L*; *om. Q, S, Ph*; ~.~ *A Country Road, between Cambrai and Paris.*
    B; ~.~ *On the Road to Paris P, W*
11 well] will *P, W*
28 raps] wraps *S, Ph, W*
57 Y'are] You're *S, Ph*
68 vsurpe] usurp'd *S, Ph, W*
79 SD *Giving Clermont letters.*] *P subs., W, L*; *om. Q, S, Ph, B*; *after*
    mistress (*l. 81*) *P, W*
91 SD *To Aumal.*] *om. Q, S, Ph, B, P, W, L*
93 this,] this, [*Gives cabinet to* Aumale. *W*
97 SD *Exit.*] *Exit* Aumale. *W*
106 SD *Finis Actus quarti.*] *om. W*

V.i

Actus ... prima.] ~ ... ~. *A Room in the Palace of the Duke of Guise. B*;
    ~ ... ~ˌ *A Room in the House of Guise P, W*
    SD *Ascendit Vmbri Bussi.*] *The* Ghost *of* Bussy *arises. W*
32 SD *close.*] *apart. W*
39 my Lord] *B, P, W, L*; (~ ~) *Q*; , ~ ~, *S, Ph*
53 oft] *B, P, W, L*; of *Q, S, Ph*
58 Lorraine] *B, P, W, L*; Soccaine *Q, S, Ph*
78 SD *Advances ... Clermont.*] *L*; *om. Q, S, Ph, B*; *advancing P, W*
90 onely] *B, P, W, L*; ~; *Q, S, Ph*
98 SD *Exit.*] *Exit* Ghost. *W*
102 dream'st] *S, Ph, B, P, W, L*; ~, *Q*
141 good, renowne] ~ˌ ~, *P, W, L*
155 lou'st] lovest *S, Ph*
171 maides] maid *S, P*
176 On] *S, Ph, B, P, W, L*; Or *Q*
198 SD *Exeunt.*] *Ph, B, P, W, L*; *Exit. Q, S*

V.ii

V.ii] *L*; *om. Q, S, Ph*; ~.~ *A Room at the Court. B*; ~.~ *A Room in the*
    Court P, W

V.iii

V.iii] *L*; *om. Q, S, Ph*; ~.~ *A Room in Montsurry's House. B, P, W*
2 lou'd] loued *S, Ph, B, P, W*
4 her seruice] *S, B, P, W, L*; her vertuous seruice *Q, Ph*
18 SD *being*] *om. W*
44 SD *Vmbr.*] *the* Ghost *of W*
45 *Vmb.*] Ghost. *W*

48 *Vmb.*] *Ghost. W*
51 SD *To the Countess.*] om. Q, S, Ph, B, P, W, L

V.iv

V.iv] L; om. Q, S, Ph; ~.~ *An Ante-room to the Council-Chamber.* B;
   ~.~ *An Ante-room in the Palace* P, W
8 solidst] solidest S, Ph
27 SD *Exit Messenger.*] L subs.; om. Q, S, Ph, B, P, W
34 two Alcides] S, Ph, P, W; ~, ~ Q, B, L
36 Holde] P, L; *Guise.* Holde Q, S, Ph, B, W
   SD *They ... downe.*] *after* confidence S, Ph, B, P, W
37 SD *Aum.*] W, L; om. Q, S, Ph, B, P
46 is] as S, Ph
61 y'haue] ye have S, Ph
64 SD *Exit.*] *Exit* Henry. W
72 SD *Exeunt.*] *Exeunt* [*the* guard *with the body*] P, L; *Exeunt with the body.* W

V.v

V.v] L; om. Q, S, Ph; ~.~ *A Room in Montsurry's House.* B, P, W
5 opes] opens B
22 SD *Lies down.*] P subs., W, L; om. Q, S, Ph, B
29 then.] ~. [*Offers to kill* Montsurry] P, W, L
44 braues] bravos B; braver's P, W
59 SD *Rises.*] L; om. Q, S, Ph, B, P, W
66 D'Ambois] P, W, L; *Ambois* Q, S, Ph, B
67 SD *Fight.*] *They fight.* W
68 Now] P, W, L; *Mont.* Now Q, S, Ph, B
77 spirits breath'd,] ~; ~, S, Ph, P; ~, ~, W
85 SD *Fights.*] *They fight.* W
   SD *Charlotte ... Countess.*] Ph subs., B, P, W, L; *Charlotte aboue.* Q, S
87 SD *Tries ... Charlotte.*] B subs., P, W, L; om. Q, S, Ph
   SD *She gets downe.*] L; *after* yet? (*l.* 88) Q, S, Ph; *after* thus? (*l.* 87) B;
   Charlotte *gets down* (*after* yet? *l.* 88) P; Charlotte *descends.* (*after* yet?
   l. 88) W
90 SD *below.*] B, P, W, L; om. Q, S, Ph
91 *Cler.*] ~. [*To* Charlotte] P, W
105 *Mont.*] *Mont.* [*To* Clermont] P, L
111 Farewell] S, Ph, B, P, W, L; *Mon.* Farewell Q
   thee–] L; ~. Q; ~, S, Ph, W; ~; B, P
   SD *Hee ... Wife.*] L; *after* life (*l.* 112) Q, S, Ph, B, P, W
119 SD *Ghost ... Guise*] *Ghosts ... Guise* B, P, W, L
120 How] *Cler.* How Q, S, Ph, B, P, W, L
149 SD *Exeunt.*] *Exeunt all but* Clermont. W
161 SD *Descend ... Coun.*] Renel *and the* Countess *descend.* W
201 or] L; om. Q, S, Ph, B, P, W
   Brother] brother [none] B, P, W

202 slaine?] *S, Ph, W, L;* ~: *Q;* ~! *B, P*

210 *Char.*] *S, Ph, B, P, W, L; Cler. Q*

216 much] *om. L*

219 SD *Exeunt.*] *Exeunt [with the bodies] P, W*

PRESS-VARIANTS IN Q (1613)

[Copies collated: BL¹ (British Library C. 34. c. 16); BL² (British Library Ashley 381); BL³ (British Library C. 12.g.6); Bodl (Bodleian Library Malone 240 [9]); CLUC (William A. Clark Library); CtY (Yale University Library); CSmH (Henry E. Huntington Library); DFo¹ (Folger Shakespeare Library, Copy 1); DFo² (Folger Shakespeare Library, Copy 2, wants sheet A); Dyce (Dyce Collection, Victoria and Albert Museum); Eton (Eton College Library); Fors (Forster Collection, Victoria and Albert Museum: original sheet A wanting; Title-page is a cancel; 'The Epistle Dedicatorie' and 'The Actors names' are supplied in a nineteenth-century hand); ICU (University of Chicago Library); LC (Library of Congress); MB (Boston Public Library); MH (Harvard University Library); Pforz (The Carl H. Pforzheimer Library); TxU (University of Texas Library).]

Sheet A (outer forme)

Corrected: BL², BL³, CLUC, CSmH, CtY, DFo¹, ICU, MB, MH, Pforz, TxU
Uncorrected: BL¹, Bodl, Dyce, Eton, LC
Sig. A4ᵛ
  l. 5 *Mont sureau*] *Mont surrau*

Sheet C (outer forme)

Corrected: BL¹, BL², BL³, Bodl, CLUC, CSmH, DFo², Dyce, Eton, Fors, LC, MH
Uncorrected: CtY, DFo¹, ICU, MB, Pforz, TxU
Sig. C2ᵛ
  I.ii.24 SD *Montsur.*] *Monsieur.*
    25 *Mont.*] *Mons.*
Sig. C3
  I.ii.28 dry] dye
    32 engender.] engender‸
    54 lines] liues
    62 *Mont.*] *Mons.*
Sig. C4ᵛ
  I.ii.131 *Mont.*] *Mons.*
    133 *Bal.*] *Mons.*
    136 *Mont.*] *Mons.*
    138 SD *Mont.*] *Mons.*
    138 SD *Mont.*] *Mons.*

Sheet E (outer forme)

Corrected: BL¹, BL², BL³, Bodl, CSmH, CtY, DFo¹, DFo², Dyce, Eton, Fors, ICU, LC, MB, MH, Pforz, TxU
Uncorrected: CLUC
Sig. E2ᵛ
   III.ii.16 innouations, Gossips] innouations, of Gossips
Sig. E4ᵛ
   III.ii.167 honour,] honour˛
      171 circumstance] circumstance,

Sheet E (inner forme)

Corrected: BL¹, BL², BL³, Bodl, CSmH, CtY, DFo¹, DFo², Dyce, Eton, Fors, ICU, LC, MB, MH, Pforz, TxU
Uncorrected: CLUC
Sig. E2
   III.i.103 SD *Exit.*] *Eit.*

Sheet F (outer forme)

Corrected: Bodl, CLUC, CSmH, Eton, Fors, LC
Uncorrected: BL¹, BL², BL³, CtY, DFo¹, DFo², Dyce, ICU, MB, MH, Pforz, TxU
Sig. F1
   III.ii.188 themselues rang'd in] themselues in
Sig. F3
   III.iv.35 doe,] doe˛
      40 thus,] thus˛
Sig. F4ᵛ
   III.iv.152 Lieutenant] Lieutenant,

Sheet G (outer forme)

Corrected: BL², BL³, Bodl, CLUC, CtY, DFo¹, Eton, Fors, ICU, LC, MB, Pforz, TxU
Uncorrected: BL¹, CSmH, DFo², Dyce, MH
Sig. G3
  Sig. G3] *om.*

Sheet G (inner forme)

Corrected: BL², BL³, Bodl, CLUC, CtY, Eton, Fors, ICU, LC, MB, Pforz, TxU
Uncorrected: BL¹, CSmH, DFo¹, DFo², Dyce, MH
Sig. G1ᵛ
   IV.i.24 passe:] passe,
      28 grase] grasse
Sig. G2
   IV.i.65 sworne, married] sworne-married
      66 good;] good,
      69 sworne or married] sworne-married

Sig. G3ᵛ
  IV.ii.22 Graces?] graces,
Sig. G4
  IV.ii.40 lightnings] lightning
  IV.iii.5 he breake? some brack's] hee breake, some brack
        10 had] had had
        20 should;] should‸

Sheet H (inner forme)

First State Corrected: BL², BL³, Bodl, CLUC, CtY, Eton, MB, MH, Pforz,
        TxU

Uncorrected: LC
Sig. H1ᵛ
  IV.iii.108 sau'd] san'd
Second State Corrected: BL¹, CSmH, DFo², Dyce, Fors, ICU
Sig. H1ᵛ
  IV.iii.107 SD *Hee raises her, and/ leades her out. Exe. (in right margin)*]
        Hee raises her, and/ Exe. leades her out. (in right margin)
Third State Corrected: DFo¹
Sig. H1ᵛ
  IV.iii.107 SD *He raises/ her, and/ leades her/ out. (in left margin) Exeunt.
        (in right margin)*] *Hee raises her, and/ leades her out. Exe. (in
        right margin)*
  IV.iv.12 *Auersus*] Auersus

Sheet K (outer forme)

Corrected: BL¹, BL², BL³, Bodl, CLUC, CtY, CSmH, DFo¹, DFo², Dyce,
        Eton, ICU, LC, MB, MH, Pforz, TxU
Uncorrected: Fors
Sig. K1
  V.iv.66 this:] this‸

TEXTUAL NOTES

[Full references to the emendations and readings of earlier editors and commentators cited here will be found in the headnote to the Historical Collation, except for one reading from J. Brereton, for which see his 'Notes on the Text of Chapman's Plays,' *MLR*, III (1907), 59.]

I.i

55 hearing] Parrott notes that 'strict syntax would seem to demand *hear*, but Chapman's syntax is far from strict.' Compare 'ayming' (l. 67).

70 heauen's true] Parrott alone among the editors emends to 'heaven's truth', but 'true' was commonly used in Chapman's time as an adverb (meaning 'truly,' 'really,' 'genuinely') alone or in combination with substantives, present or past participles, or, as here, with other adjectives (e.g., 'true-sweet,' 'true-noble').

74 your selfe] The Q 'my selfe' may be correct if we consider it as a subject in series with 'my Lord' (i.e., Guise). Chapman uses 'my selfe' as a subject in l. 92 of this same speech.

84 (since ... excitement)] Though the emended punctuation here does not resolve the syntactic difficulty of Q's punctuation, it does serve to show the connection between 'Had' (l. 84) and its object 'To suffer ...' (l. 85).

279-87 *Cler.* ... deedes] No satisfactory metrical arrangement seems possible for these lines other than the one adopted here. The arrangement and punctuation presented are intended to suggest that Clermont takes little notice of Monsieur's 'interpolations' (which I have numbered as separate lines [281, 283, 286] as falling outside the metrical scheme). Clermont's speech thus is continuous, and metrically regular (cf. IV.iii.9, 11), as indicated by the aligning of l. 282 with l. 280 and of l. 287 with l. 285.

353 sweater,] My emendation of punctuation here makes the phrase 'out ... enuie' adverbial modifying 'Would haue ... imagine' (l. 354), but the phrase 'of ... enuie' may instead be adjectival modifying the compound 'sweater-out', which is Parrott's reading.

364 (selling ... wares)] Parrott notes that 'Q encloses these words in a parenthesis. If this be taken to indicate the construction, *thriftily* modifies *swearing*. Possibly this is right, but I have found the use of parentheses so often plainly wrong in old copies of Chapman, that I have preferred in this case to follow [Boas] and take *thriftly* as modifying *selling*.' Parrott's objection that parentheses are misused in Chapman misses the point. What is faulty is not the placement of the phrase in a parenthesis (which indeed is one of Chapman's trademarks), but the placement of the phrase in the sentence.

Chapman often places a parenthetical phrase at some remove from the word it modifies. Here the phrase in question modifies, not 'swearing', but 'Trades-Man' in the previous line, and 'thriftily' modifies 'swearing' as Q indicates it does. 'Thriftily' is not used in its current sense of 'frugally,' 'sparingly,' as Boas and Parrott assume, but in its obsolete sense of 'in a becoming or seemly manner, properly; worthily, handsomely, finely; hence, thoroughly, soundly, well' (*NED*). The obsolete sense conforms well with the intended irony of the speech, which irony is heightened by 'Neuer so', which is used, as it is here, 'in conditional clauses, denoting unlimited degree or amount' (*NED*).

382 friend] Of the early editors, only Boas accepts this Q reading. Parrott follows Shepherd and Phelps in emending to 'brother' on the grounds that the emendation is 'required by both metre and context. The allusion is to Clermont's brother, *Bussy*. The Q *friend* is probably due to an officious proofreader, who noticed the word *brother* applied to Baligny in l. [383], and thought that the phrase *slaine brother* was wrong'. The meter would be improved by the emendation, but not necessarily the context. It is perfectly clear from the conversation of Baligny and Renel earlier in the scene (ll. 76-88) who has been slain and who has resolved to revenge him. Also, the outer forme of sheet C (in which the disputed word occurs) has eleven press corrections in it. If the compositor set 'brother', the supposed reading of his manuscript, only to have an officious proofreader change it to 'friend', then we might expect one of the eighteen extant copies of Q to preserve the reading 'brother'. Besides, all eleven corrections in sheet C were most probably made with reference to manuscript, revealing a careful concern, surely not officiousness, on the part of the proofreader with regard to his manuscript. Finally, the *NED* gives a possible, if extraordinary, meaning for *friend* as 'a kinsman or near relation'.

III.ii

43 she] Deighton alone emends the Q reading 'he' to 'she' referring to Athens. Although Loane's emendation to 'they = the Athenians' is technically correct since it was 'the Athenians [who] raised 360 brazen statues to [Demetrius Phalerius's] honor' (see *Lemprière's Classical Dict.*, p. 200), 'she' makes good sense and is more likely to have been the manuscript reading mistaken for 'he'.

139 emply] i.e., employ = imply, or 'involve,' 'contain,' *NED*, 5b.

191 seruice.] Maillard's speech here seems to be completed, but it is possible that Clermont's abrupt question in l. 192 is meant to interrupt it, in which case the comma after 'seruice' in Q may be intended to indicate the broken-off speech.

234 but … yeeld] i.e., simply declare your duty and I will willingly surrender.

III.iv

57 Things … care] Deighton reads 'Things outward *worth* care'; Brereton reads 'things out [i.e., outward] worth care.' There is no need to emend when

we take the meaning of 'care' to be 'an object or matter of concern.' The sentence thus should read 'you can never find outward (i.e., external) things a matter of concern without neglecting your mind.'

59 be] Deighton and Parrott substitute 'be' for Q's 'are' to restore the apparently intended rhyme with 'free' in the preceding line. Clermont's speech from l. 56 to the end is in rhymed couplets and, as Parrott notes, from l. 58 to the end is, with only three minor changes, identical with the first eighteen lines of 'Pleas'd with thy place', an earlier poem by Chapman appended to his translation of *Petrarchs Seven Penitentiall Psalms*. The relevant lines in the earlier version begin:

> God hath the whole world perfect made, & free;
> His parts to th'vse of all. Men then, that be ...
> (P. B. Bartlett, *Poems*, 1941, p. 237)

152 Lieutenant Colonell] Shepherd, who is followed by Phelps, has 'lieutenant-colonel' because his copy of Q had the corrected reading. Boas, unaware of the corrected reading, justifies the uncorrected reading by referring to a statement in the source: 'D'Eurre ... entreated the Count of Auvergne [i.e., the historical counterpart of Clermont] to see [the muster] to the ende ... that all his companions should be wonderfully honored with the presence of their coronell'. Parrott accepts Boas's reading, but I have adopted the corrected reading. The Count of Auvergne may have been the regiment's 'coronell', but Baligny, not Clermont, is the colonel of the regiment referred to in the play, and Maillard is Baligny's 'Lieutenant Colonell'. The word 'lieutenant' is generally applied to an officer who acts as a substitute for a superior, as can be seen when Baligny refers to himself as the King's 'Lieutenant' and to Maillard, a Captain, as his 'Lieutenant' (II.i.17, 21); when Maillard refers twice to Baligny as a 'Lord Lieutenant' (III.i.7; III,ii.203) who is also a 'Commander' (III.ii.204, 209), or Colonel; and when Renel refers to Maillard as a 'Lieutenant' (III.ii.74). Baligny, as the immediate commander of the regiment, is a Colonel, but, as a substitute for the King, the ultimate commander, he is a Lieutenant, or Lord Lieutenant (cf. IV.v.66-69). Maillard is a Captain, but as a substitute commander for Baligny, who is absent, he quite properly is accorded the designation of 'Lieutenant Colonell'. Furthermore, most of the press corrections were carefully made with reference to manuscript.

IV.i

8 1 [*Sould.*] This soldier and '2 [*Sould.*]' (l. 9) are not to be confused with '*The Souldiers disguised like Lackies*' in the opening lines of this scene.

54 misse terme's] All previous editors read 'miss terms', but the *NED* lists several readings for *Misterm* during Chapman's time with the meaning 'to term incorrectly, to apply a wrong term or name to'. The context makes clear that the intended meaning is 'you misterm us'. Further, this reading occurs on a page which itself and the forme G(i), in which it appears, show signs of heavy and careful proofreading, probably carried out with reference to manuscript. (But compare the next two Textual Notes calling attention to readings on the same page which, if incorrect as suggested, were missed by the proofreader.)

64 once] The Q reading 'once' is retained here, but not without a strong inclination to emend to 'ones'. 'ones' could easily have been misread by the compositor as 'once', and probably better fits the context. It would seem that the emphasis is more on the contrast between 'priuate men' (l. 63) and 'publique ones' than on the temporal aspects of Maillard's argument raised in ll. 60-63.

70 publique good] Q and all previous editors have 'good publique' but the emendation is called for by meter, sense, and the established form of the noun phrase in ll. 50, 65, 66, and 67.

104 Arts] The Q reading 'acts' could well be, as Parrott conjectures, 'a misprint for arts', especially since 'Arts' is used in an otherwise identical line in the play:

> Since good Arts faile, crafts and deceits are vs'd;
>
> (I.i.64)

Here 'Arts' provides a sharp contrast to 'crafts and deceits'. To sharpen the contrast and to distinguish 'Arts' (i.e., as applied to learning and the behavior consequent upon learning) from possible confusion with crafts and deceits with which words it shares common meanings, 'good' is supplied as a qualifier.

IV.iii

9, 11] These prose lines, which interrupt the regular blank verse of Aumal's speech, should be compared with those by Monsieur in I.i.281, 283, 286.

IV.iv

26 learning] Loane is alone in reading 'leaning' here.

IV.v.

11 well] Parrott alone among the editors emends to 'will' on the grounds that 'the context, especially l. 12, seems to show *will* is required.' The context seems rather to support the Q reading if we take 'doth' to mean 'fare' and note the relation of 'well' to 'best' and 'better' in l. 13.

V.i

90 onely] Boas and Parrott delete the semi-colon in Q after 'onely' without explanation. The emendation depends on the meaning of 'by death', which phrase I take to mean, following definitions of *by* in *NED*, 'because of or on account of the inevitability of death'.

141 good, renowne] Parrott, Walley, and Lordi here read 'good renown,', taking 'renowne' as a noun rather than a verb.

V.iii

2 lou'd] All editors agree in expanding Q's 'lou'd' to 'loued,' as Parrott explains, 'metris causa!' I have not accepted the emendation because (1) there are other defective lines in the play (e.g., I.i.227, 231, 371; I.ii.103; IV.i.55; V.v.201) and (2) because Chapman's general practice is to spell the endings

of his past participles in such a manner as to indicate whether or not they should receive a metrical accent. In the play, we find two classes of '-ed' endings for past participles, those that by themselves or as part of a syllable would naturally receive an accent (e.g., 'rewarded,' 'affected,' 'troubled,' 'glorified') and those that would not ordinarily receive an accent but nevertheless do (e.g., 'cursed,' III.iv.75; 'admired,' V.i.37; 'vnmatched,' V.iii.10). Whenever a past participle ending is not to be given an accent, Chapman's almost invariable practice is to spell the ending so that all possibility of an extra accent is removed (e.g., 'usde,' 'forc't,' 'learn'd,' 'lou'd,' 'distinguisht').

4 her seruice] Shepherd's silent emendation (accepted by all editors) is ratified by Boas on the grounds that 'vertuous, which is obviously hypermetrical, has been repeated by mistake from the previous line'.

V.v

44 braues] Boas emends to 'bravos' and Parrott to 'braver's', but the Q reading is superior to both. In his translation of the *Iliads*, Chapman had already used *braues* with the meaning 'warrior' or 'soldier':

> ... advance / Thy braves against his single power:
> (III.462-63)

In our text, its meaning is closer to 'champion', a word Montsurry uses in reference to Clermont in l. 60 of this scene.

111 thee–] There is no agreement on how to punctuate here. After 'thee', Q places a period, Shepherd and Phelps place a comma, and Boas and Parrott a semi-colon. The adopted punctuation has been chosen as a means of indicating that 'Wife' as well as 'thee' (Clermont) is the direct object of 'forgiue'. The SD at l. 111 lends support to this view. Apparently Montsurry *'giues his hand to Cler.'* at the point of interruption in the speech, and then turns and *'giues his hand to ... his Wife'* after the second 'thee' (l. 112).

144 accurst] All earlier editors read 'accursed' without explanation. This emendation does not improve the meter (unless we give 'of' a main accent) and it is contrary to Chapman's habitual practice in spelling the endings of past participles that do not receive an accent (see Textual Note at V.iii.2).

201 or] Boas and Parrott mended the obviously faulty line here by adding 'none' after 'brother', an emendation that can be defended as making sense of the passage, and as supplying rhetorical and metrical balance. But if we are to assume that the compositor left out a word, it seems preferable to assume it was 'or', which would have the MS read 'or of such a Brother'? Such a reading would improve the meter. Alternatively, we might accept the emendation of 'or' for Q's 'of': given the phrase 'of such a friend' in the line above, it would have been an easy matter for the compositor to set 'of such a Brother' for 'or such a Brother'.

Caesar and Pompey

edited by
Thomas L. Berger and Dennis G. Donovan

❖

TEXTUAL INTRODUCTION

Caesar and Pompey (Greg, *Bibliography*, no. 444) was entered to Thomas
Harper in the *Stationers' Register* on 18 May 1631:

> Entred for his copye vnder the handes of Sir HENRY HERBERT Knight
> and Master Harrison Warden a Playe called CAESAR AND POMPEY by
> GEORGE CHAPMAN ... vj^{d} [1]

[1] The play itself was written much earlier, as Chapman admits in his dedicatory epistle to the
Earl of Middlesex. Parrott's date of 1612-1613 has been accepted by Chambers, *Elizabethan
Stage*, III, 259, and others. Ennis Rees, *The Tragedies of George Chapman* (Cambridge, Mass.,
1954), pp. 128-133, dates the play around 1604-1605, as does Elias Schwartz, 'The Dates and
Order of Chapman's Tragedies,' *MP*, LVII (1959-1960), 80-82. J. E. Ingledew, 'The Date and
Composition of Chapman's *Caesar and Pompey*,' *RES*, n.s. XII (1961), 144-159, sets limits of
1597-1607 on the composition, giving 1605 as a probable date. He would, however, date II.i at
1610-1611. Robert Ornstein, 'The Dates of Chapman's Tragedies, Once More,' *MP*, LIX (1961-
1962), 61-64, questions the traditional identification of Bellamont in *Northward Ho* (IV.i.6-10)
as Chapman and retains Parrott's date. Albert H. Tricomi, 'The Dates of the Plays of George
Chapman,' *ELR*, XII (1982), 242-266, dates the play in the middle of 1604, 'after Bussy and
before *The Widow's Tears*' (p. 258). Tricomi accepts the identification of Bellamont in *Northward
Ho* as Chapman, noting especially the speech in V.i: 'I can in the writing of a tragedy, make
Caesar speake better then euer his ambition could: when I write of *Pompey* I haue *Pompeies*
soule within me.' Tricomi observes that 'Bellamont's description of his tragedy corresponds to
the actual play Chapman wrote. Chapman's Pompey *is* a man who discovers a Stoic heroism in
defeat and in Chapman's conception Caesar does speak better than his ambition could' (p. 256).
Tricomi notes as well that the passage in II.i.171-182 of *Caesar and Pompey* 'does not require
any inference about [Edmund] Tilney's impending death to make good sense' and thus the scene
need not be dated around the time of Tilney's death in 1610 (p. 257). He argues that the play was
staged, probably in 1604, and that its staging 'exhibits remarkable similarities to *Bussy D'Ambois*,
indicating that both plays were ... written with the same stage conditions in mind' (p. 257). If
the play was not performed, then, as John Russell Brown observes ('Chapman's *Caesar and
Pompey*: An Unperformed Play?' *MLR*, XLIX [1954], 469), normally 'it would be necessary to
choose between ... two dates for *Caesar and Pompey*, but a play that is never performed is often
a play which is never finished, for until publication the author is given no spur to finish his work
– a work which may have presented problems unforetold when it was started. There are signs of
rewriting or changes of intention in *Caesar and Pompey*, and there seems to be no difficulty in
dating its composition in 1605 and in 1612 or 1613.'

Harper printed a quarto edition of the play in the same year.[2] The *Register* discloses no transfer of the copyright, although the play was reissued with a new cancel title leaf (A2) in 1652 and again in 1653 with yet another cancel title leaf.[3] Nine of the thirty-nine extant 1631 copies have a variant title page, *The Warres of Pompey and Caesar*, which was changed in the course of printing sheet A to *Caesar and Pompey*.[4] The 1631 quarto in its three issues comprises the only seventeenth-century edition of the play.[5]

Although some characteristics of the quarto might suggest two compositors, in the final analysis, the most compelling evidence clearly suggests that one man set type for the entire volume. We offer first the case for a single compositor. An abundance of distinctive spellings proves especially convincing. Throughout the text one finds exclusively the forms 'goe', 'doe', 'be', 'we', 'she', 'warre', 'farre', 'poyson', 'Ile', 'here', 'murther', 'O', 'cowherd', and 'publique'. Furthermore, the typesetter emphatically prefers 'me' (106) to 'mee' (1), 'he' (100) to 'hee' (1), 'blood' (17) to 'bloud' (1), and 'only' (29) to 'onely' (5).[6]

Terminal spellings also suggest one compositor. For example, he prefers terminal '-y' to '-ie'; after B, the first full sheet of text, he never employs terminal '-ie' more than once in a sheet. And in each instance where the terminal '-ie' does occur, it belongs to a word that he has not set before, and thus comes at a point where he might be expected to follow his copy closely.[7] A marked preference throughout for terminal '-all' over '-al' also is consistent with the one-compositor theory, although this characteristic may again reflect the spelling of the copy rather than that of the compositor.[8]

The general uniformity of printing practices in all parts of the volume also suggests a single compositor. Treatment of the catchword is consistent throughout. Before a page that begins with a speech-prefix, the compositor

[2] Harper printed from 1614 to 1655/6. He was apprenticed to Melchisedeck Bradwood on 29 July 1604 and gained his freedom on 29 October 1611. His first entry in the *Register* was on 2 July 1614 (Arber, III, 29, 549). His career is marked by few irregularities. He was fined for printing the Psalms in 1637 (Jackson, *Records*, p. 286) and was involved in litigations with George Wood and William Lee over the press of Thomas Snodham (Jackson, *Records*, p. xvi; Arber, III, 703). During the early years of the rebellion he was in trouble for printing pamphlets against Parliament (Plomer, *Dictionary*, p. 91).
[3] The 1653 title page maintains that the text is printed 'As it was Acted at the *Black-Fryers*', in contradiction to Chapman's insistence in the dedicatory epistle that the play was never staged.
[4] Additionally, 'G.C.' was expanded to 'GEORGE CHAPMAN'. See Greg, *Bibliography*, II, 442-443. The inner forme of sheet A exists in two states of correction. On A3ᵛ 'such defects' is corrected to 'old defects'. The uncorrected state exists in three of the forty-three extant pages, two of which have *The Warres of Pompey and Caesar* on the title page, A2, which is wanting in the University of Toronto copy. For a full description, see our 'A Note on the Text of Chapman's *Caesar and Pompey*,' PBSA, LXV (1971), 267-268. It is likely that sheet A was composed and printed last.
[5] The text collates A-I4, K2. The title page is on A2; A1, A1ᵛ, and A2ᵛ are blank. A3-A4 are taken up with the dedicatory epistle, A4ᵛ with the argument. The text itself begins on B1 and ends on K2; K2ᵛ is a blank. The play is divided into five acts; the only scenic division occurs at the beginning of each act, when the first scene is indicated. See Greg, *Bibliography*, II, 594-595.
[6] Less convincing preferences are 'Ayre' (9) to 'Aire' (3), 'battaile' (16) to 'battell' (6), and 'neare' (9) to 'neere' (4).
[7] The five instances of terminal '-ie' after sheet B are 'lasie' (C3), 'navie' (D4), 'alacritie' (F2), 'justifie' (G2ᵛ), and 'pietie' (I2).
[8] For example, 'naturall', 'martiall', 'Imperiall', 'peecemeall'.

uses as his catchword only the speech-prefix, never the speech-prefix and the first word of the speech. He regularly indents speech-prefixes, except where justification makes indentation impossible.[9] And he is careful about the number of lines on a page; most pages contain thirty-seven lines. Those on which an act begins (B1, C3, E3^v, F3^v, and H2) naturally fall short of thirty-seven; the compositor also shortened three others (B2^v, H3, K1) to thirty-six lines to avoid starting a stage direction at the bottom of one page and continuing it on the next. But nowhere do we find the kind of distinctive variation that might suggest the presence of a new compositor. And finally, the occurrence of several identifiable types throughout the volume provides additional corroboration of the one-compositor theory.[10]

Evidence for two or more compositors is at best slight. If there were two, they had the same spelling preferences and other idiosyncrasies discussed above. Minor inconsistencies can be detected in the composition of sheets B-D and E-K. The abbreviated form 'Hee's' (used twice) disappears after sheet D and is replaced by 'He's' (used six times). Similarly, 'honour' and 'honor' are used non-preferentially through sheet D. 'Honour' disappears in sheets E-K. Wrong fount italic 'Y' is introduced in sheet E, and wrong fount italic 'I' and 'O' make their first appearance in sheet F. Swash italic 'E' and 'D' appear first in sheet E.[11] But this evidence more convincingly suggests a work interruption after sheet D than a change in compositors. And the running titles corroborate such an interpretation; those from D(o) shift to E(i) and those from D(i) move to E(o).[12]

A rudimentary analysis indicates that two skeletons were used in printing the play. Skeleton I (identified by its set of titles) printed both formes of sheet B (inner first)[13] and the outer formes of C-D. Skeleton II printed the inner formes of C-D. For sheets E-G, skeleton I printed the inner formes and skeleton II the outer. In other words, skeleton I printed both formes of B, outer C and D, and inner E, F, and G. Skeleton II printed inner C-D and outer E-G. At sheet H seven of the eight titles are exchanged when stop-press corrections are made in both formes.[14] The pattern assumes some degree of

---

[9] We find no evidence in the speech-prefixes themselves of more than one compositor.

[10] See Robert K. Turner, Jr., 'Reappearing Types as Bibliographical Evidence,' *SB*, XIX (1966), 198-209. D. F. McKenzie's caveats in 'Printers of the Mind: Some Notes on Bibliographical Theories and Printing-House Practices,' *SB*, XXII (1969), 1-75, have been taken into consideration here and throughout the textual introduction.

[11] Regular italic and swash italic 'A', 'C', 'P', 'M', 'G', 'V', and 'R', however, are mixed from the beginning of the play.

[12] The Petworth House Library copy of *The Warres of Pompey and Caesar*, with the inner forme of sheet D unprinted and with D3 and D4^v of the outer forme imperfectly printed, may serve as additional evidence of such a stoppage.

[13] The precedence of the inner forme in sheet B is easily proved, for the ascender of 'f' in 'of' is present on B1^v of all copies. It is present in only ten of the copies on B2^v and does not print in the remaining thirty-four copies. The breakage, however, is not clean. A press variant on B2^v demonstrates that the uncorrected state of the text appears with the broken 'f'. Thus the ascender degenerates in the course of the printing and does not break cleanly at one point. If sheet B were set by formes, B(o), with its head title and correspondingly lesser amount of text, could be supposed to precede B(i) in terms of composition and presswork. Here B(i) is clearly first through the press.

[14] After the presswork was completed on G(i), three of the running titles were transferred to H(o) and a new title was introduced; G(o) was still at press. When H(o) was removed from the

regularity in sheet I, only to be interrupted again at sheet K, a half sheet. Here, though he made no corrections *per se*, the printer, during the run, exchanged one set of titles for another as we discover from ten of the extant copies. The order through the press, then, can be postulated as G(i), G(o), H(o), H(i), I(i), I(o), and K.[15] The University of Pennsylvania copy raises additional problems by introducing eight new titles in sheets I and K. A supposition that this copy was assembled from uncorrected proof sheets seems improbable, particularly since it includes both formes of sheet I in corrected state. Possibly it was made from type left standing in expectation that a few extra sheets of I and K, the last sheets of text, would be needed to fill out the edition.[16]

Apparently, much of the play was set by formes. The printer's use of two skeletons and their accompanying running titles is, of course, quite consistent with this assumption as is the fact that the whole play was set as verse and thus simplified the task of casting off copy.[17] But indications of type shortages in the later sheets provide the most convincing support for our theory.[18] In sheet E wrong fount italic '*Y*' appears only in the inner forme; in sheet F wrong fount italic '*Y*', '*I*', and '*O*' are also confined to the inner forme. Wrong fount italic '*O*' and '*I*' continue to appear in the inner forme of sheet G, and wrong fount italic '*I*' appears in the inner forme of sheet H. Sheets E-H, therefore, were probably set by formes, the outer preceding the inner in order of composition.[19] In sheet I wrong fount italic '*I*' appears in both formes but more plentifully in the outer. That the inner forme of this sheet was set first is implied by the occurrence of wrong fount roman 'C' in the outer forme only and by the running titles.

On the other hand, we find no evidence to suggest that sheets B-D were set by formes; in fact, the running titles in sheet B suggest seriatim setting.[20]

---

press for corrections, it was unlocked, stripped of its titles, corrected, and given the titles of the now wrought off G(o). After the printing of H(o) had been completed and it was removed from the press, three of its 'corrected' titles and one 'uncorrected' title were transferred to H(i), now ready for press. When H(i) was removed from the press for resetting, three of its titles were changed and one remained the same. A remaining title from H(o) and three 'uncorrected' titles from H(i) comprise the set for I(i). I(o), which followed I(i) through the press, is made up of one title from H(o) and three titles from 'corrected' H(i).

[15] It is not possible that the running titles from uncorrected H(o) went to print the half-sheet K. The persistence of an unchanged title in H(i) after correction makes a printing order of H, K, and I impossible.

[16] Mrs Neda Westlake, Rare Book Librarian at the University of Pennsylvania, has assured us that there has been no external inking or tampering with the running titles. The University of Texas copy of the 1631 issue, on the other hand, has had some thirty-one of its titles marred by hand inking.

[17] The prose passages in II.i. and V.i. were set as verse. With capitalization of common nouns and capitalization following colons, the passages probably looked like verse to the compositor, and, altering a few lower case letters to upper case, he set them as such.

[18] See G. W. Williams, 'Setting by Formes in Quarto Printing,' *SB*, XI (1958), 39-52, for the standard discussion of type shortages and setting by formes.

[19] The running titles indicate that the presswork for sheet G was done with the inner forme preceding the outer.

[20] Though it is reasonable to assume that 'once he started to set by formes the odds are that a compositor would continue to set by formes as long as the press kept pace with him' (Robert K. Turner, Jr., 'The Printing of Beaumont and Fletcher's *The Maid's Tragedy*, Q1 [1619],' *SB*, XIII [1960], 207), the assumption need not apply to earlier sheets when later ones were set by formes.

Evidence from reappearing types is at best tentative, and though, as we noticed, it suggests one compositor, it proves of no help in distinguishing passages set seriatim from those set by formes.

The nature of the copy behind the quarto has been fully discussed by John Russell Brown and shown to be a manuscript in Chapman's autograph.[21] In his dedication Chapman tells the Earl of Middlesex that the play was never staged, but on the title page of the 1653 reissue, the play is said to have been acted at the Blackfriars Theatre.

In his investigations of the copy-text, Parrott noted that the stage directions were quite full, something unusual in Chapman, and concluded that the quarto 'was printed from a stage copy which had been carefully marked for performance.'[22] In order to reconcile Chapman's statement with the existence of prompt-copy, Parrott was forced into a complicated hypothesis:

> The only hypothesis, I think, which acquits Chapman of inveracity is that he wrote this play with no thought of the stage, and that it was nevertheless obtained by the players at Blackfriars and rehearsed for performance, at which time the directions would naturally be inserted. If we are to take Chapman's words seriously, we must imagine that he interfered, withdrew the play before any performance, kept it by him for years, and toward the close of his life, sent the interpolated manuscript to the printer, hoping to turn an honest penny by an almost forgotten work.[23]

Brown, in taking issue with Parrott, sees no sign of the prompt-book in the quarto (p. 467). Indeed, the number of entrants is often vague (p. 467), and those stage directions which seem to indicate a prompt-book origin (Cato's carrying a book in IV.vi.15 and V.ii.0, the Lentuli reading letters, V.i.0) are derived from Chapman's sources and are not pertinent to the action (pp. 467-468).[24] Along with certain textual corruptions (II.i.86, IV.iv.90, and V.i.214) and inconsistencies in plotting and characterization, the unwieldy *dramatis personae*, Brown maintains, would prevent a performance:

> A cast would need twenty men, four boys, and about twelve supers; this is allowing for the maximum amount of doubling, with twenty-one changes in character, disregarding those of the supers. These requirements are greater than those of any other Chapman tragedy; *The Tragedy of Byron* is the nearest, requiring fourteen men, three boys, and about eight supers (p. 468).

Though the dedication suggests that *Caesar and Pompey* was never performed, Chapman had the stage in mind during composition (p. 469). Directions at II.i.86, III.ii.107, IV.ii.0, IV.iii.0, IV.vi.0, and V.ii.161 refer to specific parts of the stage.

---

[21] 'Chapman's "Caesar and Pompey": an Unperformed Play?' *MLR*, XLIX (1954), 466-469. Subsequent references will appear in text.
[22] T. M. Parrott, *The Plays and Poems of George Chapman: The Tragedies* (London, 1910), p. 656.
[23] Parrott, *Tragedies*, pp. 656-657.
[24] Further evidence for authorial copy is seen in the speech-prefix used when both Lentuli speak. The Latin (and authorial) abbreviation *Amb.* is used rather than the English (and prompter's) *Both.*

The text of the quarto has been called 'corrupt'[25] and 'troublesome.'[26] Much of the poetry is circuitous, convoluted, and syntactically difficult. The play is as much a philosophical set piece as it is drama, and Chapman often loses himself in his own neo-Stoic wanderings. It is surprising, in fact, that the compositor was able to decipher the copy as well as he did. Most of the errors occur in the accidentals.

Determination of the press variants derives from collation of forty-five copies of the quarto in its three issues, all that are known to exist.[27] Variants were discovered in eight of the ten sheets. For the most part corrections are slight, more are typographical than substantive, and they appear to be non-authorial. One page, H4, was completely reset in the course of printing.

The play was included in the 1873 Pearson reprint of *The Comedies and Tragedies of George Chapman*, in Shepherd's *The Works of George Chapman* (1874), and in Parrott's edition of *The Tragedies* (1910). It was edited as a Master's thesis at Reading University in 1954 by J. E. Ingledew, but the edition has not been published.[28]

---

[25] Millar MacLure, *George Chapman* (Toronto, 1966), p. 51; Charlotte Spivack, *George Chapman* (New York, 1957), p. 144.

[26] Parrott, *Tragedies*, p. 677.

[27] There is no copy of the 1653 reissue in the Chapin Library of Williams College, as Greg maintains (*Bibliography*, II, 595). The National Library of Scotland copy of the 1631 *The Warres of Pompey and Caesar*, listed in Carl J. Stratman, *Bibliography of English Printed Tragedy, 1565-1900* (Carbondale, Ill., 1966), p. 100, is reported missing.

[28] Though not included in the historical collation, Mr Ingledew's thesis has been consulted. All of his textual notes have been considered, and several have necessitated emendations in the text. Akihiro Yamada's analysis of the text of the play, 'Bibliographical Studies of George Chapman's *Caesar and Pompey* (1631),' *Studies in English Literature* (Japan), 1977, pp. 3-31, has proved helpful in many instances.

THE
VVARRES
OF
POMPEY *and* CAESAR.

Out of whofe euents is euicted this
Propofition.

Only a iuft man is a freeman.

By G. C.

LONDON:
Printed by THOMAS HARPER, and are to be
fold by *Godfrey Emondfon,* and *Thomas Alchorne.*
M.DC.XXXI.

CAESAR

AND

POMPEY:

A Roman Tragedy, declaring their VVarres.

Out of whofe euents is euicted this
Propofition.

Only a iuft man is a freeman.

By GEORGE CHAPMAN.

LONDON:
Printed by THOMAS HARPER, and are to be
fold by *Godfrey Emondfon*, and *Thomas Alchorne*.
M. DC. XXXI.

Julius Cæsar

Pompey

Sextus, his son

Marcus Cato

Porcius, his son

Marc Anthony

Marcus Brutus

The King of Iberia

The King of Thessaly

The King of Cicilia

The King of Epirus

The King of Thrace

Minutius }
Metellus } Tribunes

The two Consuls

Marcellus }
Gabinius }
Vibius } Roman nobles
Demetrius }
The two Lentuli }

Athenodorus, a philosopher

Statilius, a disciple of Cato

Cleanthes, the physician of Cato

Crassinius }
Acilius } souldiers of Caesar

Achillas }
Septimius } murderers
Salvius }

Fronto, a ruined knave

Ophioneus, a devil

Marcilius }
Butas } servants of Cato

Drusus, servant of Cornelia

Nuntius

Soothsayer

Master of a ship

Sentinel

Senators, Scouts, Lords and Citizens of Rome and Utica, Ushers, Souldiers, Sailors, Ruffians, Pages, Notary, Trumpeter

Cornelia, wife of Pompey

Cyris, his daughter

Telesilla }
Lælia } maids of Cornelia]

Dramatis Personae] *first given by Parrott; here rearranged and expanded*

TO
THE RIGHT HONO-
rable, his exceeding good Lord, the
Earle of *Middlesex*, &c.

Though (my good Lord) this martiall History suffer
the diuision of Acts and Scenes, both for the more
perspicuity and height of the celebration, yet neuer toucht
it at the Stage; or if it had (though some may perhaps
causelesly empaire it) yet would it, I hope, fall vnder no 5
exception in your Lordships better-iudgeing estimation, since
scenicall representation is so farre from giuing iust cause of
any least diminution, that the personall and exact life it
giues / to any History, or other such delineation of humane [A3ᵛ]
actions, ads to them luster, spirit and apprehension, which 10
the only section of Acts and Scenes makes mee stand vpon thus
much, since that only in some precisianismes will require a
little preuention: And the hasty prose the stile auoides,
obtaine to the more temperate and stai'd numerous elocution,
some assistance to the acceptation and grace of it. Though 15
ingeniously my gratitude confesseth (my Lord) it is not
such as hereafter I vow to your honor, being written so long
since, and had not the timely ripenesse of that age that
(I thank God) I yet finde no fault withall for any old defects.

Good my Lord vouchsafe your idle minutes may admit 20
some slight glances at this, till some worke of more
nouelty and / fashion may conferre this the more liking [A4]
of your honors more worthy deseruings; To which his bounden
affection vowes all seruices.

Euer your Lordships
GEO. CHAPMAN. /

---

8 *diminution,*] ∼; ‖ 17 *hereafter*] here- after | *honor,*] ∼; ‖ 18 *since,*] ∼; ‖ 19 *old*] *Q(c)*; *such Q(u)*
(*See Textual Note*) ‖

The Argument.

Pompey and *Cæsar* bring their Armies so neare *Rome*,
that the Senate except against them. *Cæsar* vnduly
and ambitiously ‖ commanding his forces. *Pompey* more for
feare of *Cæsars* violence to the State, then mou'd with
any affectation of his own greatnesse. Their opposite   5
pleadings, out of which admirable narrations are made,
which yet not conducing to their ends, warre ends them.
In which at first *Cæsar* is forc't to fly, whom *Pompey*
not pursuing with such wings as fitted a speeding Conqueror,
his victory was preuented, and he vnhappily dishonor'd.   10
Whose ill fortune his most louing and learned wife *Cornelia*
trauailde after, with paines solemne and carefull enough;
whom the two *Lentuli* and others attended, till she
miserably found him, and saw him monstrously murthered.
Both the Consuls and *Cato* are slaughterd with their   15
owne invincible hands; and *Cæsar* (in spight of all his
fortune) without his victory, victor. /

---

9 Conqueror,] ~; ‖ **13** *Lentuli*] *Lentnli* ‖

ONELY A IVST MAN
IS A FREE MAN.

[B1]

Act I.   Scene I.

Cato, Athenodorus, Porcius, Statilius.

Cat. Now will the two Suns of our Romane Heauen
(*Pompey* and *Cæsar*) in their Tropicke burning,
With their contention, all the clouds assemble
That threaten tempests to our peace and Empire,
Which we shall shortly see poure down in bloud,   5
Ciuill and naturall, wilde and barbarous turning.
  Ath. From whence presage you this?
  Cat.   From both their Armies,
Now gathered neere our *Italie*, contending
To enter seuerally: *Pompey's* brought so neere
By *Romes* consent, for feare of tyranous *Cæsar*,   10
Which *Cæsar* fearing to be done in fauour
Of *Pompey*, and his passage to the Empire,
Hath brought on his for interuention.
And such a flocke of Puttocks follow *Cæsar*,
For fall of his ill-disposed Purse   15
(That neuer yet spar'd Crosse to Aquiline vertue)
As well may make all ciuill spirits suspicious.
Looke how against great raines, a standing Poole
Of Paddockes, Todes, and water-Snakes put vp /   19
Their speckl'd throates aboue the venemous Lake,   [B1ᵛ]
Croking and gasping for some fresh falne drops
To quench their poisond thirst, being neere to stifle
With clotterd purgings of their owne foule bane;
So still, where *Cæsar* goes, there thrust vp head,
Impostors, Flatterers, Fauorites, and Bawdes,   25
Buffons, Intelligencers, select wits,

---

8 *Italie*] Italie ‖ 9 *Pompey's*] *Pompeys* ‖ 10 *Romes*] Romes | consent,] ~; ‖ 12 Empire,] ~; ‖ 15 fall] *stet (See Textual Note)* ‖ 22 thirst,] ~; ‖ 26 wits,] ~; ‖

541

Close Murtherers, Montibanckes, and decaied Theeues,
To gaine their banefull liues reliefes from him.
From *Britaine*, *Belgia*, *France*, and *Germanie*,
The scum of either Countrie, (chus'd by him,   30
To be his blacke Guard, and red Agents here)
Swarming about him.
   Por.   And all these are said
To be suborn'd, in chiefe, against your selfe;
Since *Cæsar* chiefly feares, that you will sit
This day his opposite, in the cause for which   35
Both you were sent for home; and he hath stolne
Accesse so soone here; *Pompeys* whole rest raisde
To his encounter; and on both sides, *Rome*
In generall vproare.
   Stat. [*To Athenodorus.*] Which Sir, if you saw,
And knew, how for the danger, all suspect   40
To this your worthiest friend (for that knowne freedome
His spirit will vse this day, 'gainst both the Riuals;
His wife and familie mourne, no food, no comfort
Allowd them, for his danger) you would vse
Your vtmost powrs to stay him from the Senate,   45
All this daies Session.
   Cat.   Hee's too wise, *Statilius*,
For all is nothing.
   Stat.   Nothing Sir? I saw
Castor and *Pollux* Temple, thrust vp full,
With all the damn'd crew you haue lately nam'd:
The market place and suburbs swarming with them: 50
And where the Senate sit, are Ruffians pointed
To keepe from entring the degrees that goe /
Vp to the Bench all other but the Consuls,   [B2]
Cæsar and *Pompey*, and the Senators,
And all for no cause, but to keepe out *Cato*,   55
With any violence, any villanie;
And is this nothing Sir? Is his One life,
On whom all good liues, and their goods depend,
In *Romes* whole Empire! All the Iustice there
That's free, and simple; all such virtues too,   60
And all such knowledge; Nothing, nothing, all?
   Cat. Away *Statilius*; how long shall thy loue
Exceede thy knowledge of me, and the Gods,
Whose rights thou wrongst for my right? haue not I

---

29 *Britaine*, *Belgia*, *France*, and *Germanie*] Britaine, Belgia, France, and Germanie ‖ 35 opposite,] ~; ‖ 38 *Rome*] Rome ‖ 39 SD *To Athenodorus.*] *Parrott* ‖ 42 Riuals;] ~, ‖ 53 Bench] ~; ‖ 59 *Romes*] Romes ‖ 63 Gods,] ~? ‖

Their powers to guard me, in a cause of theirs? 65
Their iustice, and integrity included,
In what I stand for? he that feares the Gods,
For guard of any goodnesse, all things feares;
Earth, Seas, and Aire; Heauen, darknesse, broade day-light;
Rumor, and Silence, and his very shade: 70
And what an Aspen soule hath such a creature?
How dangerous to his soule is such a feare?
In whose cold fits, is all heauens iustice shaken
To his faint thoughts; and all the goodnesse there
Due to all good men, by the gods owne vowes, 75
Nay, by the firmenesse of their endlesse Being,
All which shall faile as soone as any one
Good to a good man in them: for his goodnesse
Proceeds from them, and is a beame of theirs.
O neuer more, *Statilius*, may this feare 80
Taint thy bould bosome, for thy selfe, or friend,
More then the gods are fearefull to defend.
  Ath. Come; let him goe, *Statilius*; and your fright;
This man hath inward guard, past your yong sight.

                                        Exeunt. Manet Cato.

                    Enter Minutius.

  Cat. Welcome; come stand by me in what is fit 85
For our poore Cities safety; nor respect
Her proudest foes corruption, or our danger /
Of what seene face soeuer.   [B2ᵛ]
  Min.   I am yours.
But what alas, Sir, can the weaknesse doe
Against our whole State, of vs only two? 90
You know our Statists spirits are so corrupt
And seruile to the greatest, that what crosseth
Them, or their owne particular wealth, or honor,
They will not enterprise to saue the Empire.
  Cat. I know it; yet let vs doe like our selues. 95
                                        Exeunt.

68 goodnesse,] ~; ‖ 69 day-light;] ~, ‖ 84 SD *Exeunt. ... Minutius.*] *Exeunt / Enter Minutius, manet Cato.* ‖ 88 face] Q(c); faec Q(u) ‖ 90 State,] ~ₐ ‖ 92 greatest,] ~; ‖ 93 honor,] ~; ‖

543

[I.ii]

Enter some bearing Axes, bundles of rods, bare, before two
Consuls; Cæsar and Metellus, Anthonius and Marcellus in
couples; Senators, People, Souldiers, etc. following. The
Consuls enter the Degrees, with Anthonius and Marcellus:
Cæsar staying a while without with Metellus, who hath a
paper in his hand.

Cæs. Moue you for entring only *Pompeys* army;
Which if you gaine for him, for me, all iustice
Will ioyne with my request of entring mine.
   Met. Tis like so, and I purpose to enforce it.
   Cæs. But might we not win *Cato* to our friendship   5
By honoring speeches, nor perswasiue gifts?
   Met. Not possible.
   Cæs.   Nor by enforciue vsage?
   Met. Not all the violence that can be vsde,
Of power, or set authority can stirre him,
Much lesse faire words win, or rewards corrupt him;   10
And therefore all meanes we must vse to keepe him
From off the Bench.
   Cæs.   Giue you the course for that,
And if he offer entry, I haue fellowes
Will serue your will on him, at my giuen signall.

                                   They ascend. /

Enter Pompey, Gabinius, Vibius, Demetrius, with   [B3]
papers. Enter the Lists, ascend and sit. After whom
enter Cato, Minutius, Athenodorus, Statilius, Porcius.

   Cat. He is the man that sits so close to *Cæsar,*   15
And holds the law there, whispering; see the Cowherd
Hath guards of arm'd men got, against one naked.
Ile part their whispering virtue.
   1 [*Cit.*]   Hold, keepe out.
   2 [*Cit.*] What? honor'd *Cato*? enter, chuse thy place.
   Cat. Come in;

       Cato drawes Minutius in and sits betwixt Cæsar
                and Metellus.

     – Away vnworthy groomes.
   3 [*Cit.*]   No more.   20

I.ii] *Parrott subs.* | SD *bare,*] ~; | SD *Consuls;*] ~, | SD *Metellus, Anthonius*] ~; ~, | SD
Anthonius] ~, ‖ 2 him,] ~; ‖ 9 authority] authoitry ‖ 18 1 [*Cit.*]] 1 (*speech-prefixes similarly*
expanded in lines 19, 20, 23, 25, 27) ‖ 20 SD *Cato drawes Minutius*] He drawes him (*See Textual*
Note) ‖

Cæs. What should one say to him?
Met.   He will be Stoicall.
Cat. Where fit place is not giuen, it must be taken.
4 [*Cit.*] Doe, take it *Cato*; feare no greatest of them;
Thou seek'st the peoples good; and these their owne.
5 [*Cit.*] Braue *Cato*! what a countenance he puts on?   25
Let's giue his noble will, our vtmost power.
6 [*Cit.*] Be bould in all thy will; for being iust,
Thou maist defie the gods.
Cat.   Said like a God.
Met. We must endure these people.
Cæs.   Doe; begin.
Met. Consuls, and reuerend Fathers; And ye people,   30
Whose voyces are the voyces of the Gods;
I here haue drawne a law, by good consent,
For entring into *Italy*, the army
Of *Romes* great *Pompey*: that his forces here,
As well as he, great *Rome* may rest secure   35
From danger of the yet still smoking fire
Of *Catilines* abhorr'd conspiracy:
Of which the very chiefe are left aliue,
Only chastisde but with a gentle prison.
  Cat. Put them to death then, and strike dead our feare, /   40
That well you vrge, by their vnfit suruiuall,   [B3ᵛ]
Rather then keepe it quick, and two liues giue it,
By entertaining *Pompeys* army too,
That giues as great cause of our feare, as they.
For their conspiracy, onely was to make   45
One Tyrant ouer all the State of *Rome*.
And *Pompeys* army, sufferd to be entred,
Is, to make him, or giue him meanes to be so.
  Met. It followes not.
  Cat.   In purpose, clearely Sir,
Which Ile illustrate, with a cleare example.   50
If it be day, the Sunne's aboue the earth;
Which followes not (youle answere) for 'tis day
When first the morning breakes; and yet is then
The body of the Sunne beneath the earth;
But he is virtually aboue it too,   55
Because his beames are there; and who then knowes not
His golden body will soone after mount?
So *Pompeys* army entred *Italy*,

35 *Rome*] ~, ‖ 36 fire] ~, ‖ 39 chastisde] ~, ‖ 41 suruiuall,] ~. ‖ 42 quick,] ~; ‖ 43 too,] ~. ‖ 49
purpose,] ~; ‖ 57 mount?] ~. ‖

545

Yet *Pompey's* not in *Rome*; but *Pompey's* beames
Who sees not there? and consequently, he   60
Is in all meanes enthron'd in th'Emperie.
   Met. Examples proue not, we will haue the army
Of *Pompey* entred.
   Cat.   We? which we intend you?
Haue you already bought the peoples voices?
Or beare our Consuls or our Senate here   65
So small loue to their Country, that their wills
Beyond their Countrys right are so peruerse,
To giue a Tyrant here entire command?
Which I haue prou'd as cleare as day, they doe,
If either the Conspirators suruiuing   70
Be let to liue; or *Pompeys* army entred;
Both which, beat one sole path; and threat one danger.
   Cæs. Consuls, and honor'd Fathers; The sole entry
Of *Pompeys* army, Ile not yet examine:
But for the great Conspirators yet liuing, /   75
(Which *Cato* will conclude as one selfe danger,   [B4]
To our deare Country; and deterre all therefore
That loue their Country, from their liues defence)
I see no reason why such danger hangs
On their sau'd liues, being still safe kept in prison;   80
And since close prison, to a Roman freedome,
Ten fold torments more, then directest death,
Who can be thought to loue the lesse his Country,
That seekes to saue their liues? And lest my selfe
(Thus speaking for them) be vniustly toucht   85
With any lesse doubt of my Countryes loue,
Why (reuerend Fathers) may it be esteem'd
Selfe praise in me, to proue my selfe a chiefe
Both in my loue of her, and in desert
Of her like loue in me? For he that does   90
Most honour to his Mistrisse, well may boast
(Without least question) that he loues her most.
And though things long since done, were long since known,
And so may seeme superfluous to repeat;
Yet being forgotten, as things neuer done,   95
Their repetition needfull is, in iustice,
T'enflame the shame of that obliuion:
For hoping it will seeme no lesse empaire
To others acts, to truely tell mine owne;

66 Country,] Courtry; ‖ 78 defence)] ~. ‖ 80 liues,] ~; ‖ 89 her,] ~; ‖ 91 Mistrisse,] ~; ‖

Put all together; I haue past them all   100
That by their acts can boast themselues to be
Their Countries louers: first in those wilde kingdomes
Subdu'd to *Rome*, by my vnwearied toyles,
Which I dissauag'd and made nobly ciuill.
Next, in the multitude of those rude Realmes   105
That so I fashiond, and to *Romes* yong Empire
Of old haue added: Then the battailes numbred
This hand hath fought, and wonne for her, with all
Those infinites of dreadfull enemies
I slue in them: Twice fifteene hundred thousand   110
(All able Souldiers) I haue driuen at once
Before my forces: and in sundry onsets, /
A thousand thousand of them, put to sword: [B4ᵛ]
Besides, I tooke in lesse then ten yeares time,
By strong assault, aboue eight hundred Cities,   115
Three hundred seuerall Nations, in that space,
Subduing to my Countrey; all which seruice,
I trust, may interest me in her loue,
Publique, and generall enough, to aquit me
Of any selfe-loue, past her common good: 120
For any motion of particular iustice
(By which her generall Empire is maintaind)
That I can make for those accused prisoners,
Which is but by the way, that so the reason
Metellus makes for entring *Pompeys* armie   125
May not more weighty seeme, then to agree
With those imprison'd nobles vitall safeties;
Which granted, or but yeelded fit to be,
May well extenuate the necessity
Of entring *Pompeys* armie.
   Cat.   All that need   130
I tooke away before; and reasons gaue
For a necessity to keepe it out,
Whose entry (I thinke) he himselfe affects not,
Since I as well thinke he affects not th'Empire.
And both those thoughts hold; since he loues his Country,   135
In my great hopes of him, too well to seeke
His sole rule of her, when so many soules,
So hard a taske approue it; nor my hopes
Of his sincere loue to his Country build
On sandier grounds then *Cæsars*; since he can   140

103 toyles,] ~. ‖ 106 fashiond,] ~; ‖ 110 I] *Parrott*; (~ ‖ 111 (All] *Parrott*; ˏ~ ‖ 120 selfe-loue,]
~; ‖ 124 way,] ~; ‖ 125 armie] ~, ‖ 127 nobles] ~, | safeties;] ~. ‖ 132 out,] ~ˏ ‖ 133 not,] ~. ‖
134 Empire.] ~, ‖ 136 him,] ~ˏ ‖ 139 Country] ~, ‖

As good Cards shew for it as *Cæsar* did,
And quit therein the close aspersion
Of his ambition, seeking to imploy
His army in the breast of *Italy*.
   Pom. Let me not thus (imperiall Bench and Senate)   145
Feele myselfe beat about the eares, and tost
With others breathes to any coast they please,
And not put some stay to my errors in them. /
The gods can witnesse that not my ambition   [C1]
Hath brought to question th'entry of my army;   150
And therefore not suspected the effect,
Of which that entry is supposde the cause:
Which is a will in me, to giue my power
The rule of *Romes* sole Empire, that most strangely
Would put my will in others powers; and powers   155
(Vnforfeit by my fault) in others wills.
My selfe-loue, out of which all this must rise:
I will not wrong the knowne proofes of my loue
To this my natiue Cities publique good,
To quit, or thinke of; nor repeat those proofes   160
Confirm'd in those three triumphs I haue made,
For conquest of the whole inhabited world;
First *Affrick*, *Europe*, and then *Asia*,
Which neuer Consull but my selfe could boast.
Nor can blinde Fortune vaunt her partiall hand,   165
In any part of all my seruices,
Though some haue said, she was the page of *Cæsar*,
Both sayling, marching, fighting, and preparing
His fights in very order of his battailes:
The parts she plaid for him inuerting nature,   170
As giuing calmnesse to th'enraged sea;
Imposing Summers weather on sterne winter;
Winging the slowest foot he did command,
And his most Cowherd making fierce of hand.
And all this euer when the force of man   175
Was quite exceeded in it all; and she
In th'instant adding her cleare deity.
Yet, her for me, I both disclaime and scorne;
And where all fortune is renounc't, no reason
Will thinke one man transferd with affectation   180
Of all *Romes* Empire; for he must haue fortune
That goes beyond a man; and where so many

---

147 please,] ~: ‖ 154 Empire,] ~; ‖ 161 made,] ~; ‖

Their hand-fulls finde with it; the one is mad
That vndergoes it: and where that is clear'd,
Th'imputed meanes to it, which is my sute /   185
For entry of mine army, I confute.   [C1ᵛ]
    Cat. What rests then, this of all parts being disclaimd?
    Met. My part, Sir, rests, that let great *Pompey* beare
What spirit he lists; 'tis needfull yet for *Rome*,
That this Law be establisht for his army.   190
    Cæs. Tis then as needfull to admit in mine;
Or else let both lay downe our armes; for else
To take my charge off, and leaue *Pompey* his,
You wrongfully accuse me to intend
A tyranny amongst ye; and shall giue   195
Pompey full meanes to be himselfe a tyrant.
    Ant. Can this be answer'd?
    1 *Cons.*   Is it then your wils
That *Pompey* shall cease armes?
    Ant.   What else?
    Omn.   No, no.
    2 *Cons.* Shall *Cæsar* cease his armes?
    Omn.   I, I.
    Ant.   For shame!
Then yeeld to this cleare equity, that both   200
May leaue their armes.
    Omn.   We indifferent stand.
    Met. Read but this law, and you shall see a difference
Twixt equity and your indifferency;
All mens obiections answered; Read it Notary.
    Cat. He shall not read it.
    Met.   I will read it then.   205
    Min. Nor thou shalt read it, being a thing so vaine,
Pretending cause for *Pompeys* armies entry,
That only by thy Complices and thee,
Tis forg'd to set the Senate in an vproare.
                                [He snatches the bill.]
    Met. I haue it Sir, in memory, and will speake it.   210
    Cat. Thou shalt be dumbe as soone.
    Cæs.   Pull downe this *Cato*,
Author of factions, and to prison with him.
                       He drawes, and all draw.
    Sen. Come downe Sir.
    Pom.   Hence ye mercenary Ruffians. /

---

184 clear'd,] ~; ‖ 193 his,] ~; ‖ 196 tyrant.] ~, ‖ 199 shame!] ~‸ ‖ 208 thee,] ~; ‖ 209 SD *He snatches the bill.*] *Parrott* ‖ 212 SD *He drawes, and all draw.*] *Parrott; after Sir., l. 213* ‖ 213 *Sen.*] *Parrott; Gen. (See Textual Note)* ‖

1 *Cons.* What outrage shew you? sheath your insolent swords,   [C2]

Or be proclaim'd your Countreys foes and traytors.   215

   Pom. How insolent a part was this in you,

To offer the imprisonment of *Cato*?

When there is right in him (were forme so answer'd

With termes and place) to send vs both to prison,

If, of our owne ambitions, we should offer   220

Th'entry of our armies; for who knowes

That, of vs both, the best friend to his Country,

And freest from his owne particular ends

(Being in his power), would not assume the Empire,

And hauing it, could rule the State so well   225

As now 'tis gouern'd, for the common good?

   Cæs. Accuse your selfe, Sir (if your conscience vrge it),

Or of ambition, or corruption,

Or insufficiency to rule the Empire,

And sound not me with your Lead.

   Pom.   Lead? tis Gold,   230

And spirit of Gold too, to the politique drosse

With which false *Cæsar* sounds men; and for which

His praise and honour crownes them; who sounds not

The inmost sand of *Cæsar*? for but sand

Is all the rope of your great parts affected.   235

You speake well, and are learn'd; and golden speech

Did Nature neuer giue man, but to guild

A copper soule in him; and all that learning

That heartily is spent in painting speech,

Is merely painted, and no solid knowledge.   240

But y'aue another praise for temperance,

Which nought commends your free choice to be temperate.

For so you must be; at least in your meales,

Since y'aue a malady that tyes you to it,

For feare of daily fals in your aspirings.   245

And your disease the gods nere gaue to man,

But such a one, as had a spirit too great

For all his bodies passages to serue it,

Which notes th'excesse of your ambition. /   249

The malady chancing where the pores and passages   [C2ᵛ]

Through which the spirit of a man is borne,

So narrow are, and straight, that oftentimes

They intercept it quite, and choake it vp.

And yet because the greatnesse of it notes

---

219 prison,] ~? ‖ **223** ends] ~; ‖ **224** power),] ~)͵ ‖ **226** gouern'd] gouer'nd ‖ **227** Sir] ~, | it),] ~)͵ ‖ **231** too,] ~; ‖ **237** man,] ~; ‖ **244** it,] ~; ‖ **246** man,] ~; ‖

A heat mere fleshly, and of bloods ranck fire,   255
Goates are of all beasts subiect'st to it most.
    Cæs. Your selfe might haue it then, if those faults cause it;
But deales this man ingeniously, to tax
Men with a frailty that the gods inflict?
    Pom. The gods inflict on men, diseases neuer,   260
Or other outward maimes, but to decipher,
Correct, and order some rude vice within them:
And why decipher they it, but to make
Men note, and shun, and tax it to th'extreame?
Nor will I see my Countryes hopes abusde,   265
In any man commanding in her Empire;
If my more tryall of him, makes me see more
Into his intricasies; and my freedome
Hath spirit to speake more, then obseruers seruile.
    Cæs. Be free, Sir, of your insight and your speech;   270
And speak, and see more, then the world besides;
I must remember I haue heard of one,
That fame gaue out, could see thorow Oke and stone:
And of another set in *Sicily*,
That could discerne the Carthaginian Nauy,   275
And number them distinctly, leauing harbor,
Though full a day and nights saile distant thence:
But these things (Reuerend Fathers) I conceiue,
Hardly appeare to you worth graue beliefe:
And therefore since such strange things haue beene seene   280
In my so deepe and foule detractions,
By only Lyncean *Pompey*, who was most
Lou'd and beleeu'd of *Romes* most famous whore,
Infamous *Flora*; by so fine a man
As *Galba*, or *Sarmentus*; any iester   285
Or flatterer may draw through a Ladyes Ring; /
By one that all his Souldiers call in scorne   [C3]
Great *Agamemnon*, or the king of men;
I rest vnmou'd with him; and yeeld to you
To right my wrongs, or his abuse allow.   290
    Cat. My Lords, ye make all *Rome* amaz'd to heare.
    Pom. Away, Ile heare no more; I heare it thunder.
My Lords, all you that loue the good of *Rome*,
I charge ye, follow me; all such as stay,
Are friends to *Cæsar*, and their Countreys foes.   295
    Cæs. Th'euent will fall out contrary, my Lords.

---

258 ingeniously] *stet* (*See Textual Note*) ‖ 261 maimes,] ~; ‖ 282 *Pompey*,] ~; ‖ 292-93 thunder./
My Lords, all] *Parrott*; ~./ ~ ~; All ‖

551

1 *Cons.* Goe, thou art a thiefe to *Rome*, discharge thine army,
Or be proclaim'd, forthwith, her open foe.
    2 *Cons. Pompey*, I charge thee, helpe thy iniur'd Country
With what powers thou hast arm'd, and leuy more.   300
    The Ruffians. Warre, warre, O *Cæsar.*
    Sen. and Peop.   Peace, peace, worthy *Pompey.*
                                                         [*Exeunt.*]

Act II.   Scene I.

Enter Fronto all ragg'd, in an ouergrowne red Beard,
black head, with a Halter in his hand, looking about.

    [*Fro.*] Warres, warres, and presses, fly in fire about;
No more can I lurke in my lasie corners,
Nor shifting courses: and with honest meanes
To rack my miserable life out, more,
The rack is not so fearefull; when dishonest   5
And villanous fashions faile me, can I hope
To liue with virtuous? or to raise my fortunes
By creeping vp in Souldierly degrees?
Since villany varied thorow all his figures,
Will put no better case on me then this;   10
Despaire! come sease me: I had able meanes; /
And spent all in the swinge of lewd affections;   [C3ᵛ]
Plung'd in all riot, and the rage of blood;
In full assurance that being knaue enough,
Barbarous enough, base, ignorant enough,   15
I needs must haue enough, while this world lasted;
Yet, since I am a poore, and ragged knaue,
My rags disgrace my knauery so, that none
Will thinke I am knaue; as if good clothes
Were knacks to know a knaue, when all men know   20
He has no liuing? which knacks since my knauery
Can shew no more; and only shew is all
That this world cares for; Ile step out of all
The cares 'tis steept in.   *He offers to hang himselfe.*

    Thunder, and the Gulfe opens, flames issuing; and
    Ophioneus ascending, with the face, wings, and taile
    of a Dragon; a skin coate all speckled on the throat.

301 SD *Exeunt.*] ‖ **II.i.1** *Fro.*] *Shepherd subs.* ‖ **6** me,] ~; ‖ **18** disgrace] disgace ‖ **20** knaue,] ~; ‖

Oph. Hold Rascall, hang thy selfe in these dayes? The   25
only time that euer was for a Rascall to liue in?

Fro. How chance I cannot liue then?

Oph. Either th'art not rascall nor villaine enough; or
else thou dost not pretend honesty and piety enough to
disguise it.   30

Fro. That's certaine, for euery asse does that. What
art thou?

Oph. A villaine worse then thou.

Fro. And dost breathe?

Oph. I speake, thou hear'st, I moue, my pulse beates   35
fast as thine.

Fro. And wherefore liu'st thou?

*Oph.*The world's out of frame, a thousand Rulers
wresting it this way, and that, with as many Religions;
when, as heauens vpper Sphere is mou'd onely by one, so   40
should the Sphere of earth be, and Ile haue it so. /

Fro. How canst thou? what art thou?   [C4]

Oph. My shape may tell thee.

Fro. No man?

Oph. Man? no spawne of a clot, none of that cursed   45
Crew, damn'd in the masse it selfe, plagu'd in his birth,
confinde to creepe below, and wrestle with the Elements;
teach himselfe tortures; kill himselfe, hang himselfe;
no such gally slaue, but at warre with heauen; spurning
the power of the gods, command the Elements.   50

Fro. What maist thou be then?

Oph. An endlesse friend of thine; an immortall deuill.

Fro. Heauen blesse vs.

Oph. Nay then, forth, goe, hang thy selfe, and thou
talk'st of heauen once.   55

Fro. I haue done; what deuill art thou?

Oph. Read the old stoick *Pherecides*, that tels thee
me truly, and sayes that I *Ophioneus* (for so is my name) –

Fro. Ophioneus? what's that?

25-26 Hold ... in?] *Shepherd*; Hold ... dayes?/ The ... in? ‖ **28-30** Either ... it.] *Shepherd*;
Either ... enough;/ Or ... honesty/ And ... it. ‖ **31-32** That's ... thou?] *Shepherd*; That's ...
that./ What ... thou? ‖ **35-36** I ... thine.] *Shepherd*; I ... beates/ Fast ... thine. ‖ **35** speake,] ~ ‖
38-41 The ... so.] *Shepherd*; The ... Rulers/ Wresting ... many/ Religions ... mou'd/ Onely ...
and/ Ile ... so. ‖ **40** one,] ~; ‖ **45-50** Man ... Elements.] *Shepherd*; Man ... cursed/ Crew ...
birth,/ Confinde ... Elements;/ Teach ... hang himselfe;/ No ... heauen;/ Spurning ...
Elements. ‖ **45** no] ~, (*See Textual Note*) ‖ **46** selfe,] ~; ‖ **50** command] *stet* (*See Textual Note*) |
Elements.] ~: ‖ **54-55** Nay ... once.] *Shepherd*; Nay ... talk'st/ Of ... once. ‖ **57-58** Read ...
name)–] *Shepherd*; Read ... thee/ Me ... is/ My name.) ‖ **57** *Pherecides*] Pherecides ‖

Oph. Deuilish Serpent, by interpretation; was generall   60
Captaine of that rebellious host of spirits that wag'd
warre with heauen.

Fro. And so were hurl'd downe to hell.

Oph. We were so; and yet haue the rule of earth; and
cares any man for the worst of hell then?   65

Fro. Why should he?

Oph. Well said; what's thy name now?

Fro. My name is *Fronto.*

Oph. Fronto? A good one; and has *Fronto* liu'd thus
long in *Rome*? lost his state at dice? murther'd his   70
Brother for his meanes? spent all? run thorow worse
Offices since? beene a Promoter? a Purueyor? a Pander?
a Sumner? a Sergeant? an Intelligencer? and at last
hang thy selfe?

Fro. [Aside.] How the deuill knowes he all this?   75

Oph. Why thou art a most greene Plouer in policy,
I perceiue; and maist drinke Colts-foote, for all thy /
horse-mane beard: S'light, what need hast thou to hang   [C4ᵛ]
thy selfe? as if there were a dearth of hangmen in the
land? Thou liu'st in a good cheape State, a man may be   80
hang'd here for a little, or nothing. What's the reason
of thy desperation?

Fro. My idle dissolute life, is thrust out of all
his corners by this searching tumult now on foot in
Rome.   85

———— ———— ———— *Cæsar* now and *Pompey*
Are both for battaile: *Pompey* (in his feare
Of *Cæsars* greater force) is sending hence
His wife and children, and he bent to fly.

> *Enter Pompey running ouer the Stage with his*
> *wife and children; Gabinius, Demetrius, Vibius,*
> *Pages; other Senators, the Consuls and all following.*

See, all are on their wings; and all the City   90
In such an vproare, as if fire and sword
Were ransacking, and ruining their houses.
No idle person now can lurke neare *Rome*,
All must to armes; or shake their heeles beneath
Her martiall halters; whose officious pride   95

60-62 Deuilish ... heauen.] *Shepherd*; Deuilish ... generall/ Captaine ... that/ Wag'd ... heauen.
|| 64-65 We ... then?] *Shepherd*; We ... cares/ Any ... then? || 69-74 *Fronto* ... selfe?] *Shepherd*;
Fronto ... long/ In ... his/ Brother ... worse/ Offices ... Pander?/ A Sumner? ... last/ Hang
... selfe? || 75 SD *Aside.*] *Parrott* || 76-82 Why ... desperation?] *Shepherd*; Why ... I/ Perceiue
... thy/ Horsemane ... hast/ Thou ... dearth/ Of ... cheape/ State ... or/ Nothing ...
desperation? || 78 horse-mane] *catchword*; horsemane *(text)* || 83-85 My ... *Rome.*] *Shepherd*;
My ... corners/ By ... *Rome.* || 86 ———— ———— ————] *stet (See Textual Note)* || 89 SD
children;] ~, || 92 houses.] ~, ||

Ile shun, and vse mine owne swinge: I be forc't
To helpe my Countrey, when it forceth me
To this past-helping pickle?

   Oph. Goe to, thou shalt serue me; chuse thy profession;
and what cloth thou wouldst wish to haue thy Coat cut   100
out on.

   Fro. I can name none.

   Oph. Shall I be thy learn'd Counsaile?

   Fro. None better.

   Oph. Be an Archflamen then, to one of the Gods.   105

   Fro. Archflamen? what's that?

   Oph. A Priest.

   Fro. A Priest? that nere was Clerke?

   Oph.   No Clerke? what then?
The greatest Clerks are not the wisest men. /   109
Nor skils it for degrees in a knaue, or a fooles preferment;   [D1]
Thou shalt rise by fortune: let desert rise leisurely
enough, and by degrees; fortune preferres headlong, and
comes like riches to a man; huge riches being got with little
paines, and little with huge paines. And for discharge of
the Priesthood, what thou wantst in learning, thou shalt   115
take out in goodfellowship: thou shalt equiuocate with
the Sophister, prate with the Lawyer, scrape with the Vsurer,
drinke with the Dutchman, sweare with the French man,
cheat with the English man, brag with the Scot, and turne
all this to Religion, *Hoc est regnum Deorum Gentibus.*   120

   Fro. All this I can doe to a haire.

   Oph. Very good, wilt thou shew thy selfe deepely
learn'd too, and to liue licentiously here, care for
nothing hereafter?

   Fro. Not for hell?   125

   Oph. For hell? soft, Sir; hop'st thou to purchase hell
with only dicing or whoring away thy liuing? murthering
thy brother, and so forth? No, there remaine works of a
higher hand and deeper braine, to obtaine hell. Thinkst
thou earths great Potentates haue gotten their places   130
there with any single act of murther, poysoning, adultery,
and the rest? No; tis a purchase for all manner of

99-101 Goe ... on.] *Parrott*; Goe ... profession;/ And ... Coat/ Cut ... on. ‖ **110-120** Nor ...
Gentibus.] *Shepherd*; Nor ... preferment,/ Thou ... leisurely/ Enough ... headlong,/ And ...
being/ Got ... And/ For ... wantst/ In ... goodfellowship:/ Thou ... with/ The Lawyer ...
with the/ Dutchman ... cheat/ With ... and/ Turne ... *regnum/ Deorum Gentibus.* ‖ **110**
preferment;] ~, ‖ **114** paines,] ~; ‖ **122-124** Very ... hereafter?] *Shepherd*; Very ... too,/ And
... hereafter? ‖ **126-134** For ... pleasure.] *Shepherd*; For ... hell/ With ... liuing?/ Murthering ...
there/ Remaine ... braine,/ To ... great/ Potentates ... with/ Any ... adutery,/ And ... manner/
Of ... priuiledg'd/ By ... enioyd/ With pleasure. ‖ **126** soft,] ~. ‖ **128** No,] ~. ‖ **131** adultery]
adutery ‖

villany; especially, that may be priuiledg'd by Authority, coulourd with holinesse, and enioyd with pleasure.

Fro. O this were most honourable and admirable. 135

Oph. Why such an admirable honorable villane shalt thou be.

Fro. Is't possible?

Oph. Make no doubt on't; Ile inspire thee. 139

Fro. Sacred and puissant. *He kneeles.*

Oph. Away; Companion and friend, giue me thy hand; say, dost not loue me? art not enamourd of my acquaintance? /

Fro. Protest I am. [D1ᵛ]

Oph. Well said, protest and tis enough. And 145 know for infallible; I haue promotion for thee; both here, and hereafter; which not one great one amongst millions shall euer aspire to. *Alexander*, nor great *Cyrus*, retaine those titles in hell, that they did on earth. 150

Fro. No?

Oph. No: he that sold Seacoale here, shall be a Baron there; he that was a cheating Rogue here, shall be a Iustice of peace there; a knaue here, a knight there. In the meane space, learne what it is to liue; 155 and thou shalt haue Chopines at commandment to any height of life thou canst wish.

Fro. I feare my fall is too low.

Oph. Too low foole? hast thou not heard of *Vulcans* falling out of heauen? Light a thy legges, and no matter 160 though thou halt'st with thy best friend euer after; tis the more comely and fashionable. Better goe lame in the fashion with *Pompey*, then neuer so vpright, quite out of the fashon, with *Cato*.

Fro. Yet you cannot change the old fashion (they 165 say) and hide your clouen feet.

Oph. No? I can weare Roses that shall spread quite ouer them.

Fro. For loue of the fashion doe then.

Oph. Goe to; I will hereafter. 170

---

133 Authority,] ~; ‖ 136-137 Why ... be.] *Shepherd*; Why ... shalt/ Thou be. ‖ 141-143 Away ... acquaintance?] *Shepherd*; Away ... thy/ Hand ... enamourd/ Of ... acquaintance? ‖ 145-150 Well ... earth.] *Shepherd*; Well ... for/ Infallible ... and/ Hereafter ... amongst/ Millions ... great/ *Cyrus* ... did/ On earth: ‖ 152-157 No ... wish.] *Shepherd*; No ... be/ A ... cheating/ Rogue ... there;/ A knaue ... meane/ Space ... shalt/ Haue ... height/ Of ... wish. ‖ 159-164 Too ... *Cato*.] *Shepherd*; Too ... falling/ Out ... matter/ Though ... tis/ The ... lame/ In ... vpright,/ Quite ... *Cato*. ‖ 164 fashon,] ~ ‖ 165-166 Yet ... feet.] *Shepherd*; Yet ... say)/ And ... feet. ‖ 167-168 No ... them.] *Shepherd*; No ... quite/ Ouer them. ‖

Fro. But for the Priesthood you offer me, I affect it not.

Oph. No? what saist thou to a rich office then?

Fro. The only second meanes to raise a rascall in the earth.   175

Oph. Goe to; Ile helpe thee to the best ith' earth then: And that's in *Sicilia*, the very storehouse of the Romanes, where the Lord chiefe Censor there lyes now a dying; whose soule I will haue; and thou shalt haue his office.   180

Fro. Excellent; was euer great office better supplied?

                                                                     Exeunt. /

[II.ii]

Nuntius.   [D2]

[*Nuntius.*] Now is the mighty Empresse of the earth
(Great *Rome*) fast lockt vp in her fancied strength,
All broke in vproares; fearing the iust gods
In plagues will drowne her so abuscd blessings.
In which feare, all without her wals, fly in,   5
By both their iarring Champions rushing out;
And those that were within, as fast fly forth;
The Consuls both are fled without one rite
Of sacrifice submitted to the gods,
As euer heretofore their custome was   10
When they began the bloody frights of warre.
In which our two great Souldiers now encountring,
Since both left *Rome*, oppos'd in bitter skirmish,
Pompey (not willing yet to hazard battaile,
By *Catos* counsaile, vrging good cause) fled: 15
Which firing *Cæsars* spirit, he pursu'd
So home, and fiercely, that great *Pompey* skorning
The heart he tooke, by his aduised flight,
Despisde aduice as much as his pursuite.
And as in *Lybia*, an aged Lion,   20
Vrg'd from his peacefull couert, feares the light
With his vnready and diseas'd appearance,
Giues way to chace a while, and coldly hunts,

174-175 The ... earth.] *Shepherd*; The ... rascall/ In ... earth. ‖ 176-180 Goe ... office.]
Shepherd; Goe ... then:/ And ... the/ Romanes ... there/ Lyes ... and/ Thou ... office. ‖ 176
ith'] ith ‖ 177 *Sicilia*,] ~; ‖ II.ii] *Parrott subs.* ‖ 1 Nuntius.] *Shepherd* ‖ 5 in,] ~; ‖ 16 spirit,] ~; ‖

Till with the youthfull hunters wanton heat,
He all his coole wrath frets into a flame: 25
And then his sides he swinges with his Sterne,
To lash his strength vp, lets downe all his browes
About his burning eyes, erects his mane,
Breakes all his throat in thunders, and to wreake
His hunters insolence, his heart euen barking, 30
He frees his fury, turnes, and rushes back
With such a gastly horror, that in heapes,
His proud foes fly, and he that station keepes:
So *Pompeys* coole spirits, put to all their heat / 34
By *Cæsars* hard pursuit, he turnd fresh head, [D2ᵛ]
And flew vpon his foe with such a rapture
As tooke vp into furies, all friends feares;
Who fir'd with his first turning, all turnd head,
And gaue so fierce a charge, their followers fled,
Whose instant issue on their both sides, see, 40
And after set out such a tragedy,
As all the Princes of the earth may come
To take their patternes by the spirits of *Rome*.

[*Exit.*]

[II.iii]

Alarme, after which enter Cæsar following Crassinius
calling to the Souldiers.

Crass. Stay cowherds, fly ye *Cæsars* fortunes?
Cæs. Forbeare foolish *Crassinius*, we contend in vaine
To stay these vapours, and must raise our Campe.
Crass. How shall we rise (my Lord) but all in vproares,
Being still pursude?

Enter Acilius.

[*Acil.*]   The pursuit stayes, my Lord, 5
Pompey hath sounded a retreat, resigning
His time to you to vse, in instant raysing
Your ill-lodg'd army, pitching now where fortune
May good amends make for her fault to day.
Cæs. It was not fortunes fault, but mine, *Acilius*, 10
To giue my foe charge, being so neare the sea,
Where well I knew the eminence of his strength,
And should haue driuen th'encounter further off;

27 strength] strenth | lets] let's ‖ 28 eyes,] ∼; ‖ 30 barking,] ∼; ‖ 35 pursuit,] ∼ˏ ‖ 43 SD *Exit.*]
Parrott subs. ‖ **II.iii**] *Parrott subs.* ‖ 1 cowherds] *Shepherd*; cowherd (*See Textual Note*) ‖ 2
foolish] *stet* (*See Textual Note*) ‖ 5 *Acil.*] *Parrott* ‖ 10 mine,] ∼ˏ ‖

Bearing before me such a goodly Country,
So plentifull, and rich, in all things fit   15
To haue suppli'd my armies want with victuals,
And th'able Cities too, to strengthen it,
Of *Macedon* and *Thessaly*, where now
I rather was besieg'd for want of food,
Then did assault with fighting force of armes. /   20

Enter Anthony, Vibius, with others.   [D3]

Ant. See, Sir, here's one friend of your foes recouer'd.
Cæs. *Vibius*? In happy houre.
Vib.   For me vnhappy.
Cæs. What? brought against your will?
Vib.   Else had not come.
Ant. Sir, hee's your prisoner, but had made you his,
Had all the rest pursu'd the chace like him;   25
He draue on like a fury; past all friends,
But we that tooke him quick in his engagement.
     Cæs. O *Vibius*, you deserue to pay a ransome
Of infinite rate, for had your Generall ioyn'd
In your addression, or knowne how to conquer,   30
This day had prou'd him the supreame of *Cæsar*.
     Vib. Knowne how to conquer? His fiue hundred Conquests
Atchieu'd ere this day, make that doubt vnfit
For him that flyes him; for, of issues doubtfull,
Who can at all times put on for the best?   35
If I were mad, must hee his army venture
In my engagement? Nor are Generalls euer
Their powers disposers, by their proper Angels,
But trust against them, oftentimes, their Counsailes,
Wherein, I doubt not, *Cæsars* selfe hath err'd   40
Sometimes, as well as *Pompey*.
     Cæs.   Or done worse,
In disobeying my Counsaile (*Vibius*)
Of which, this dayes abused light is witnesse;
By which I might haue seene a course secure
Of this discomfiture.
     Ant.   Amends sits euer   45
Aboue repentance, what's done, wish not vndone;
But that prepared patience that you know
Best fits a souldier charg'd with hardest fortunes;
Asks still your vse, since powers still temperate kept

---

30 conquer,] ~; ‖ 34 doubtfull,] ~. ‖

Ope still the clearer eyes by one faults sight /   50
To place the next act, in the surer right.   [D3ᵛ]
 Cæs. You prompt me nobly Sir, repayring in me
Mine owne stayes practice, out of whose repose
The strong convulsions of my spirits forc't me
Thus farre beyond my temper; but good *Vibius*,   55
Be ransom'd with my loue, and haste to *Pompey*,
Entreating him from me, that we may meet,
And for that reason which I know this day
Was giuen by *Cato*, for his pursutes stay
(Which was preuention of our Romane blood)   60
Propose my offer of our hearty peace.
That being reconcil'd, and mutuall faith
Giuen on our either part, not three dayes light
May further shew vs foes, but (both our armies
Disperst in Garisons) we may returne   65
Within that time to *Italy*, such friends
As in our Countryes loue, containe our splenes.
 Vib. Tis offerd, Sir, 'boue the rate of *Cæsar*
In other men, but in what I approue
Beneath his merits: which I will not faile   70
T'enforce at full to *Pompey*, nor forget
In any time the gratitude of my seruice.
      Vib. salutes Ant. and the other, and exit.
 Cæs. [*To Vibius.*] Your loue, Sir, and your friendship.
 Ant.   This prepares
A good induction to the change of fortune,
In this dayes issue, if the pride it kindles   75
In *Pompeys* vaines, makes him deny a peace
So gently offerd: for her alterd hand
Works neuer surer from her ill to good
On his side she hath hurt, and on the other
With other changes, then when meanes are vsde   80
To keepe her constant, yet retire refusde.
 Cæs. I try no such conclusion, but desire
Directly peace. In meane space Ile prepare
For other issue in my vtmost meanes;
Whose hopes now resting at *Brundusium*,   85
In that part of my army, with *Sabinus*,
I wonder he so long delaies to bring me, /
And must in person haste him, if this Euen   [D4]
I heare not from him.
 Crass.   That (I hope) flyes farre

59-60 Was ... blood]] *Parrott*; (Was ... stay/ Which ... blood) ‖ **67** splenes.] ~‸ ‖ **72** SD *Vib.*]
Vi. ‖ **73** SD *To Vibius.*] ‖ **73-74** This ... fortune,] *Shepherd*; *one line in* Q ‖

Your full intent, my Lord, since *Pompeys* navie, 90
You know, lies houering all alongst those seas,
In too much danger, for what ayde soeuer
You can procure, to passe your person safe.
  Acil. Which doubt may proue the cause that stayes *Sabinus*;
And, if with shipping fit to passe your army, 95
He yet straines time to venture, I presume
You will not passe your person with such Conuoy
Of those poore vessels, as may serue you here.
  Cæs. How shall I helpe it? shall I suffer this
Torment of his delay? and rack suspitions 100
Worse then assur'd destructions through my thoughts?
  Ant. Past doubt he will be here; I left all orderd,
And full agreement made with him to make
All vtmost haste, no least let once suspected.
  Cæs. Suspected? what suspection should feare a friend 105
In such assur'd streights from his friends enlargement?
If twere his souldiers safeties he so tenders,
Were it not better they should sinke by sea,
Then wrack their number, King and cause ashore?
Their stay is worth their ruine, should we liue, 110
If they in fault were? if their leader! he
Should dye the deaths of all; in meane space, I
That should not, beare all; fly the sight in shame,
Thou eye of nature, and abortiue night
Fall dead amongst vs: with defects, defects 115
Must serue proportion; iustice neuer can
Be else restor'd, nor right the wrongs of man. *Exeunt.*

[II.iv]

Pompey, Cato, Gabinius, Demetrius, Athenodorus,
Porcius, Statilius.

  Pom. This charge of our fierce foe, the friendly gods
Haue in our strengthen'd spirits beaten back /
With happy issue, and his forces lessen'd, [D4ᵛ]
Of two and thirty Ensignes forc't from him,
Two thousand souldiers slaine.
  Cat.   O boast not that, 5
Their losse is yours, my Lord.
  Pom.   I boast it not,

---

93 procure,] ~ˌ ‖ 101 thoughts?] ~. ‖ 105 suspection] *stet* (*See Textual Note*) ‖ 106 enlargement?]
~. ‖ 112 Should] *Pearson*; Sould (*See Textual Note*) ‖ 113 all;] ~, ‖ **II.iv**] *Parrott subs.* ‖ **1**
friendly] firiendly ‖ **2** strengthen'd] stregthen'd ‖

But only name the number.
   Gab.   Which right well
You might haue raisde so high, that on their tops
Your Throne was offer'd, euer t'ouerlooke
Subuerted *Cæsar*, had you beene so blest   10
To giue such honor to your Captaines Counsailes
As their alacrities did long to merit
With proofefull action.
   Dem.   O twas ill neglected.
   Stat. It was deferr'd with reason, which not yet
Th'euent so cleare is to confute.
   Pom.   If twere,   15
Our likeliest then was, not to hazard battaile,
Th'aduenture being so casuall; if compar'd
With our more certaine meanes to his subuersion.
For finding now our army amply storde
With all things fit to tarry surer time,   20
Reason thought better to extend to length
The warre betwixt vs; that his little strength
May by degrees proue none; which vrged now
(Consisting of his best and ablest souldiers),
We should haue found at one direct set battaile   25
Of matchlesse valours, their defects of victuall
Not tyring yet enough on their tough nerues;
Where, on the other part, to put them still
In motion, and remotion, here and there;
Enforcing them to fortifying still   30
Where euer they set downe; to siege a wall,
Keepe watch all night in armour: their most part
Can neuer beare it, by their yeares oppression,
Spent heretofore too much in those steele toyles. /   34
   Cat. I so aduisde, and yet repent it not,   [E1]
But much reioyce in so much saued blood
As had beene pour'd out in the stroke of battaile,
Whose fury thus preuented, comprehends
Your Countreys good, and Empires; in whose care,
Let me beseech you that in all this warre,   40
You sack no City subiect to our Rule,
Nor put to sword one Citizen of *Rome*,
But when the needfull fury of the sword
Can make no fit distinction in maine battaile;
That you will please still to prolong the stroke   45

---

18 subuersion.] ~? ‖ **23** now] ~, ‖ **24** souldiers),] ~). ‖ **26** valours,] ~; ‖ **27** nerues;] ~, ‖ **33** oppression,] ~; ‖ **39** care,] *Q(u)*; ~ *Q(c)* (*See Textual Note*) ‖ **41** City] ~, ‖ **42** *Rome*,] ~; ‖ **44** battaile;] ~, ‖

Of absolute decision to these iarres,
Considering you shall strike it with a man
Of much skill and experience, and one
That will his Conquest sell at infinite rate,
If that must end your difference; but I doubt   50
There will come humble offer on his part,
Of honor'd peace to you, for whose sweet name
So cryed out to you in our late-met Senate,
Lose no fit offer of that wished treaty.
Take pity on your Countreys blood as much   55
As possible may stand without the danger
Of hindering her iustice on her foes,
Which all the gods to your full wish dispose.
    Pom. Why will you leaue vs? whither will you goe
To keepe your worthyest person in more safety   60
Then in my army, so deuoted to you?
    Cat. My person is the least, my Lord, I value;
I am commanded by our powerfull Senate,
To view the Cities, and the kingdomes scituate
About your either army, that which side   65
Soeuer conquer, no disordered straglers
Puft with the Conquest, or by need impeld,
May take their swinge more then the care of one
May curb and order in these neighbor confines;
My chiefe passe yet resolues for *Vtica*.   70
    Pom. Your passe (my truest friend, and worthy Father) /
May all good powers make safe, and alwayes answer   [E1ᵛ]
Your infinite merits, with their like protection;
In which, I make no doubt but we shall meet
With mutuall greetings, or for absolute conquest   75
Or peace preuenting that our bloody stroke.
[*To Athenodorus.*] Nor let our parting be dishonor'd so,
As not to take into our noblest notice
Your selfe (most learned and admired Father)
Whose merits, if I liue, shall lack no honor.   80
Porcius, Statilius, though your spirits with mine
Would highly chere me, yet ye shall bestow them
In much more worthy conduct; but loue me,
And wish me conquest, for your Countreys sake.
    Stat. Our liues shall seale our loues, Sir, with worst deaths   85
Aduentur'd in your seruice.
    Pom.   Y'are my friends.
                  Exeunt Cat., Athen., Por., Stat.

---

54 Lose] *Parrott*; Lost (*See Textual Note*) ‖ **69** confines;] ∼ ‖ **70** *Vtica*] Vtica ‖ **73** protection;]
∼. ‖ **76** stroke.] ∼, ‖ **77** SD *To Athenodorus.*] *Parrott subs.* ‖ **86** SD *Exeunt Cat., Athen., Por.,*]
∼. ∼., ∼., ∼., | SD *Stat.*] *Sat.* ‖

These friends thus gone, tis more then time we minded
Our lost friend *Vibius*.
   Gab.   You can want no friends,
See, our two Consuls, Sir, betwixt them bringing
The worthy *Brutus*.

Enter two Consuls leading Brutus betwixt them.

   1 Cons.   We attend (my Lord)   90
With no meane friend, to spirit your next encounter,
Six thousand of our choice Patrician youths
Brought in his conduct.
   2 Cons.   And though neuer yet
He hath saluted you with any word
Or looke of slendrest loue in his whole life,   95
Since that long time since, of his fathers death
By your hand authord; yet see, at your need
He comes to serue you freely for his Country.
   Pom. His friendly presence, making vp a third
With both your persons, I as gladly welcome,   100
As if *Ioues* triple flame had guilt this field, /
And lightn'd on my right hand, from his shield.   [E2]
   Bru. I well assure my selfe, Sir, that no thought
In your ingenious construction, touches
At the aspersion that my tendred seruice   105
Proceeds from my despaire of elsewhere safety.
But that my Countreys safety owning iustly
My whole habilities of life and fortunes,
And you the ablest fautor of her safty,
Her loue, and (for your loue of her) your owne   110
Only makes sacred to your vse my offering.
   Pom. Farre fly all other thought from my construction,
And due acceptance of the liberall honor,
Your loue hath done me, which the gods are witnesse,
I take as stirr'd vp in you by their fauours,   115
Nor lesse esteeme it then an offering holy;
Since, as of all things, man is said the measure,
So your full merits measure forth a man.
   1 Cons. See yet, my Lord, more friends.
   2 Cons.   Fiue Kings, your seruants.

Enter fiue Kings.

   Iber. Conquest and all grace crowne the gracious *Pompey*,   120
To serue whom in the sacred Romane safety,

---

104 ingenious] *stet (See Textual Note, I.ii.258)* || **120** *Iber.*] *Shepherd*; *Hib.* ||

My selfe, *Iberias* King, present my forces.
    Thess. And I that hold the tributary Throne
Of Grecian *Thessaly*, submit my homage,
To *Rome*, and *Pompey*.
    Cil.   So *Cilicia* too.   125
    Epir. And so *Epirus*.
    Thra.   Lastly I from *Thrace*
Present the duties of my power and seruice.
    Pom. Your royall aides deserue of *Rome* and *Pompey*
Our vtmost honors. O may now our fortune
Not ballance her broad breast twixt two light wings,   130
Nor on a slippery globe sustaine her steps,
But as the Spartans say, the Paphian Queene /
(The flood *Eurotas* passing) laid aside   [E2ᵛ]
Her Glasse, her Ceston, and her amorous graces,
And in *Lycurgus* fauor, arm'd her beauties   135
With Shield and Iaueline, so may fortune now,
The flood of all our enemies forces passing
With her faire Ensignes, and arriu'd at ours,
Displume her shoulders, cast off her wing'd shooes,
Her faithlesse, and still-rowling stone spurne from her,   140
And enter our powers as she may remaine
Our firme assistent: that the generall aydes,
Fauours, and honors you performe to *Rome*,
May make her build with you her endlesse home.
    Omn. The gods vouchsafe it; and our causes right.   145
    Dem. What suddaine Shade is this? obserue my Lords,
The night, me thinks, comes on before her houre.
                               Thunder and lightning.
    Gab. Nor trust me if my thoughts conceiue not so.
    Bru. What thin clouds fly the winds, like swiftest shafts
Along aires middle region.
    1 Cons.   They presage   150
Vnusuall tempests.
    2 Cons.   And tis their repaire,
That timelesse darken thus the gloomy ayre.
    Pom. Let's force no *omen* from it, but avoid
The vapors furies now by *Ioue* employd.   [*Exeunt.*]

---

135 fauor,] ~; ‖ **154** SD *Exeunt.*] *Parrott* ‖

[II.v]

Thunder continued, and Cæsar enters disguisde.

[*Cæs.*] The wrathfull tempest of the angry night,
Where hell flyes mufl'd vp in clouds of pitch,
Mingl'd with Sulphure, and those dreadfull bolts,
The *Cyclops* Ram in *Ioues* Artillery,
Hath rousde the furies, arm'd in all their horrors,   5
Vp to the enuious seas, in spight of *Cæsar*.
O night, O ielous night, of all the noblest
Beauties, and glories, where the gods haue stroke
Their foure digestions from thy gastly Chaos, /   9
Blush thus to drowne them all in this houre sign'd   [E3]
By the necessity of fate for *Cæsar*.
I that haue ransackt all the world for worth,
To forme in man the image of the gods,
Must like them haue the power to check the worst
Of all things vnder their celestiall Empire,   15
Stoope it, and burst it, or breake through it all,
With vse and safety, till the Crowne be set
On all my actions; that the hand of nature
In all her worst works ayming at an end,
May in a master-peece of hers be seru'd   20
With tops, and state fit for his virtuous Crowne:
Not lift arts thus farre vp in glorious frame,
To let them vanish thus in smoke and shame.
This riuer *Anius* (in whose mouth now lyes
A Pynnace I would passe in, to fetch on   25
My armies dull rest from *Brundusium*)
That is at all times else exceeding calme
(By reason of a purling winde that flyes
Off from the shore each morning, driuing vp
The billows farre to sea), in this night yet,   30
Beares such a terrible gale, put off from sea,
As beats the land wind back, and thrusts the flood
Vp in such vproare, that no boat dare stirre.
And on it is disperst all *Pompeys* nauy
To make my perill yet more enuious.   35
Shall I yet shrinke for all? were all, yet more?
There is a certaine need that I must giue
Way to my passe; none, knowne, that I must liue.

Enter Master of a ship with Sailors.

II.v] *Parrott subs.* ‖ **1** *Cæs.*] *Parrott* ‖ **4** *Cyclops*] Cyclops | Ram] *stet* (*See Textual Note*) ‖ **9**
digestions] ~, ‖ **27** calme] ~, ‖ **30** sea),] ~)ˌ ‖ **31** gale,] ~; ‖ **38** SD *Sailors.*] ~ˌ ‖

Mast. What battaile is there fought now in the ayre,
That threats the wrack of nature?
    Cæs.   Master? come.   40
Shall we thrust through it all?
    Mast.   What lost man /
Art thou in hopes and fortunes, that dar'st make   [E3ᵛ]
So desperate a motion?
    Cæs. Launch man, and all thy feares fraight disauow,   44
Thou carriest *Cæsar* and his fortunes now.   [*Exeunt.*]

Act III.   Scene I.

Pompey, two Consuls, fiue Kings, Brutus, Gabinius,
Demetrius.

[*Pom.*] Now to *Pharsalia*, where the smarting strokes
Of our resolu'd contention must resound,
(My Lords and friends of *Rome*) I giue you all
Such welcome as the spirit of all my fortunes,
Conquests, and triumphs (now come for their crowne)   5
Can crowne your fauours with, and serue the hopes
Of my deare Country, to her vtmost wish;
I can but set vp all my being to giue
So good an end to my forerunning Acts,
The powers in me that formd them hauing lost   10
No least time since, in gathering skill to better,
But like so many Bees haue brought me home,
The sweet of whatsoeuer flowers haue growne
In all the meades, and gardens of the world.
All which hath growne still, as the time encreasd   15
In which twas gather'd, and with which it stemm'd,
That what decay soeuer blood inferr'd,
Might with my mindes store, be suppli'd, and cher'd:
All which, in one fire of this instant fight
Ile burne, and sacrifice to euery cinder   20
In sacred offering to my Countreys loue;
And therefore what euent soeuer sort,
As I no praise will looke for, but the good
Freely bestow on all (if good succeed); /   24
So if aduerse fate fall, I wish no blame,   [E4]
But th'ill befalne me, made my fortunes shame,

---

39 ayre,] ~. ‖ 41 man] ~, ‖ 43 motion?] ~. ‖ 45 SD *Exeunt.*] *Parrott* ‖ **III.i.1** *Pom.*] *Shepherd* ‖ 8
I can] Ican ‖ 9 Acts,] ~; ‖ 11 better,] ~; ‖ 13 sweet] fweet ‖ 15 encreasd] *Parrott (Brereton conj.*);
encrease (*See Textual Note*) ‖ 16 stemm'd,] ~. ‖ 18 cher'd:] ~, ‖ 21 loue;] ~, ‖ 24 all] ~; ‖
succeed);] ~). ‖

Not mine, nor my fault.
  1 Cons.   We too well loue *Pompey*,
To doe him that iniustice.
  Bru.   Who more thirsts
The Conquest, then resolues to beare the foile?
  Pom. Said *Brutus*-like, giue seuerall witnesse all,   30
That you acquit me whatsoeuer fall.
  2 Cons. Particular men particular fates must beare,
Who feeles his owne wounds lesse, to wound another?
  Thess. Leaue him the worst whose best is left vndone,
He only conquers whose minde still is one.   35
  Epir. Free mindes, like dice, fall square, what ere the cast.
  Iber. Who on him selfe sole stands, stands solely fast.
  Thra. He's neuer downe, whose minde fights still aloft.
  Cil. Who cares for vp or downe, when all's but thought?
  Gab. To things euents doth no mans power extend.   40
  Dem. Since gods rule all, who any thing would mend?
  Pom. Ye sweetly ease my charge, your selues vnburthening.
Return'd not yet our trumpet, sent to know
Of *Vibius* certaine state?
  Gab.   Not yet, my Lord.
  Pom. Too long protract we all meanes to recouer   45
His person quick or dead, for I still thinke
His losse seru'd fate, before we blew retreat,
Though some affirme him seene soone after, fighting.
  Dem. Not after, Sir (I heard), but ere it ended.
  Gab. He bore a great minde to extend our pursuit   50
Much further then it was; and seru'd that day
(When you had, like the true head of a battaile,
Led all the body in that glorious turne)
Vpon a farre-off Squadron that stood fast
In conduct of the great *Marc Anthony*,   55
When all the rest were fled, so past a man
That in their tough receipt of him, I saw him
Thrice breake thorow all with ease, and passe as faire /
As he had all beene fire, and they but ayre.   [E4ᵛ]
  Pom. He stuck at last, yet, in their midst, it seem'd.   60
  Gab. So haue I seene a fire drake glide at midnight
Before a dying man to point his graue,
And in it stick and hide.
  Dem.   He comes yet safe.

      A Trumpet sounds, and enters before Vibius,
            with others.

---

36 square] sqare ‖ **37** *Iber.*] *Ibir.* ‖ **39** thought?] ∼. ‖ **41** mend?] ∼. ‖ **47** retreat,] ∼; ‖ **48** seene
soone after,] ∼, ∼ ∼ˌ ‖ **49** Sir (I heard),] ∼, (∼ ∼)ˌ ‖ **60** last,] ∼ˌ ‖

Pom. O *Vibius*, welcome; what, a prisoner?
With mighty *Cæsar*, and so quickly ransom'd?   65
    Vib. I, Sir, my ransome needed little time,
Either to gaine agreement for the value,
Or the disbursment, since in *Cæsars* grace
Were both concluded.
    Pom.   Was his grace so free?
    Vib. For your respect, Sir.
    Pom.   Nay, Sir, for his glory: 70
That the maine Conquest he so surely builds on
(Which euer is forerun with petty fortunes),
Take not effect, by taking any friend
From all the most my poore defence can make,
But must be compleat, by his perfect owne.   75
    Vib. I know, Sir, you more nobly rate the freedome
He freely gaue your friend, then to peruert it
So past his wisdome: that knowes much too well
Th'vncertaine state of Conquest, to raise frames
Of such presumption on her fickle wings,   80
And chiefely in a losse so late, and grieuous.
Besides, your forces farre exceeding his,
His whole powers being but two and twenty thousand,
And yours full foure and forty thousand strong:
For all which yet, he stood as farre from feare   85
In my enlargement, as the confident glory
You please to put on him; and had this end
In my so kinde dismission, that as kindely /
I might solicite a sure peace betwixt you.   [F1]
    Pom. A peace? Is't possible?
    Vib.   Come, doe not shew   90
This wanton incredulity too much.
    Pom. Beleeue me I was farre from such a thought
In his high stomack: *Cato* prophecied then.
What thinke my Lords our Consuls, and friend *Brutus*?
    Amb. Cons. An offer happy!
    Bru.   Were it plaine and hearty.   95
    Pom. I, there's the true inspection to his prospect.
    Bru. This streight of his perhaps may need a sleight
Of some hid stratagem, to bring him off.
    Pom. Deuices of a new fordge to entrap me?

---

64 welcome; what,] ~, ~. | 66 I,] ~. | ransome] ~, ‖ 69 Were] *Parrott conj.*; We (*See Textual Note*) | free?] ~. ‖ 70 glory:] ~. ‖ 71 on] ~, ‖ 72 fortunes),] ~). ‖ 74 most] ~, ‖ 77 friend,] ~; ‖ 79 Conquest,] ~; ‖ 83 thousand,] ~: ‖ 90-91 A peace ... much.] *Parrott*; A peace ... possible?/ *Vib.* Come ... this ... much. ‖ 91 much.] *Q(u)*; om. *Q(c)* (*See Textual Note, II.iv.39*) ‖ 94 Brutus?] *Q(u)*; Bru *Q(c)* ‖ 95 Amb. Cons.] *Parrott subs.*; Omn. | happy!] ~: ‖ 96 inspection] inspecton ‖ 97 sleight] *Q(u)*; sleig *Q(c)* ‖

I rest in *Cæsars* shades? walke his strow'd paths?   100
Sleepe in his quiet waues? Ile sooner trust
Hibernian Boggs, and quicksands; and hell mouth
Take for my sanctuary: in bad parts
That no extreames will better, natures finger
Hath markt him to me, to take heed of him.   105
What thinks my *Brutus*?
   Bru.   Tis your best and safest.
   Pom. This offer'd peace of his is sure a snare
To make our warre the bloodier, whose fit feare
Makes me I dare not now (in thoughts maturer
Then late enclin'de me) put in vse the Counsaile   110
Your noble father *Cato* (parting) gaue me,
Whose much too tender shunning innocent blood,
This battaile hazards now, that must cost more.
   1 *Cons.* It does, and therefore now no more deferre it.
   Pom. Say all men so?
   Omn.   We doe.
   Pom.   I grieue ye doe,   115
Because I rather wish to erre with *Cato*
Then with the truth goe of the world besides;
But since it shall abide this other stroke,
Ye gods that our great Romane *Genius*
Haue made, not giue vs one dayes conquest only,   120
Nor grow in conquests for some little time, /
As did the *Genius* of the *Macedons*;   [F1ᵛ]
Nor be by land great only, like *Laconians*;
Nor yet by sea alone, as was th'*Athenians*;
Nor slowly stirr'd vp, like the Persian Angell;   125
Nor rockt asleepe soone, like the Ionian spirit;
But made our Romane *Genius*, fiery, watchfull,
And euen from *Romes* prime, ioynd his youth with hers,
Grow as she grew, and firme as earth abide,
By her encreasing pomp, at sea, and shore,   130
In peace, in battaile; against *Greece* as well
As our Barbarian foes; command yet further
Ye firme and iust gods, our assistfull Angell
For *Rome*, and *Pompey*, who now fights for *Rome*;
That all these royall Lawes, to vs, and iustice   135
Of common safety, may the self-loue drowne
Of tyrannous *Cæsar*; and my care for all
Your Altars crowne with endlesse festiuall.   *Exeunt.*

---

118 stroke,] ~. ‖ **126** spirit;] ~. ‖ **138** crowne] *Parrott*; crown'd (*See Textual Note*) ‖

[III.ii]

Cæsar, Anthony, a Soothsayer, Crassinius, Acilius,
with others.

Cæs. Say (sacred Southsayer) and informe the truth,
What liking hast thou of our sacrifice?
   Sooth. Imperiall *Cæsar*, at your sacred charge,
I drew a milke-white Oxe into the Temple,
And turning there his face into the east   5
(Fearefully shaking at the shining light),
Downe fell his horned forehead to his hoofe;
When I began to greet him with the stroke,
That should prepare him for the holy rites,
With hydeous roares he laid out such a throat   10
As made the secret lurkings of the god
To answer ecco-like, in threatning sounds:
I stroke againe at him, and then he slept,
His life-blood boyling out at euery wound
In streames as cleare as any liquid Ruby;   15
And there began to alter my presage, /
The other ill signes, shewing th'other fortune   [F2]
Of your last skirmish, which farre opposite now,
Proues ill beginnings good euents foreshew.
For now the beast cut vp, and laid on th'Altar,   20
His lims were all lickt vp with instant flames,
Not like the Elementall fire that burnes
In houshold vses, lamely struggling vp,
This way and that way winding as it rises,
But (right and vpright) reacht his proper sphere   25
Where burnes the fire eternall and sincere.
   Cæs. And what may that presage?
   Sooth.   That euen the spirit
Of heauens pure flame flew downe and rauisht vp
Your offerings blaze in that religious instant,
Which shewes th'alacritie and cheerefull virtue   30
Of heauens free bounty, doing good in time,
And with what swiftnesse true deuotions clime.
   Omn. The gods be honor'd.
   Sooth.   O behold with wonder,
The sacred blaze is like a torch enlightned,
Directly burning iust aboue your campe!   35

III.ii] *Parrott subs.* ‖ **4** milke-white] ~‿~ ‖ **5** east] ~, ‖ **6** light),] ~). ‖ **7** hoofe;] ~, ‖ **15** Ruby;] ~, ‖
17 fortune] ~, ‖ **18** now,] ~‿ ‖ **19** Proues] ~, ‖

Omn. Miraculous.
  Sooth.   Beleeue it, with all thanks:
The Romane *Genius* is alterd now,
And armes for *Cæsar*.
  Cæs.   Soothsayer be for euer
Reuerenc't of *Cæsar*. O *Marc Anthony*,
I thought to raise my camp, and all my tents   40
Tooke downe for swift remotion to *Scotussa*.
Shall now our purpose hold?
  Ant.   Against the gods?
They grace in th'instant, and in th'instant we
Must adde our parts, and be in th'vse as free.
  Crass. See Sir, the scouts returne.

Enter two scouts.

  Cæs.   What newes, my friends?   45
  1 Scou. Arme, arme, my Lord; the voward of the foe
Is rang'd already. /
  2 Scou.   Answer them, and arme: [F2ᵛ]
You cannot set your rest of battell vp
In happyer houre; for I this night beheld
A strange confusion in your enemies campe,   50
The souldiers taking armes in all dismay,
And hurling them againe as fast to earth,
Euery way routing; as th'alarme were then
Giuen to their army. A most causelesse feare
Disperst quite through them.
  Cæs.   Then twas *Ioue* himselfe   55
That with his secret finger stirr'd in them.
  Crass. Other presages of successe (my Lord)
Haue strangely hapn'd in th'adiacent Cities,
To this your army: for in *Tralleis*,
Within a Temple, built to Victory,   60
There stands a statue of your forme and name,
Neare whose firme base, euen from the marble pauement,
There sprang a Palme tree vp, in this last night,
That seemes to crowne your statue with his boughs,
Spred in wrapt shadowes round about your browes.   65
  Cæs. The signe, *Crassinius*, is most strange and gracefull,
Nor could get issue, but by power diuine;
Yet will not that, nor all abodes besides
(Of neuer such kinde promise of successe)
Performe it without tough acts of our owne.   70

---

40 tents] ~, ‖ **45** SD *Enter two scouts.*] *in right margin, opposite* returne. ‖ **52** earth,] ~. ‖

No care, no nerue the lesse to be emploid;
No offering to the gods, no vowes, no prayers:
Secure and idle spirits neuer thriue
When most the gods for their aduancements striue.
And therefore tell me what abodes thou buildst on   75
In any spirit to act, enflam'd in thee,
Or in our Souldiers seene resolu'd addresses?
   Crass. Great and firy virtue. And this day
Be sure (great *Cæsar*) of effects as great
In absolute conquest; to which are prepar'd   80
Enforcements resolute, from this arm'd hand,
Which thou shalt praise me for aliue or dead. /
   Cæs. Aliue (ye gods vouchsafe) and my true vowes   [F3]
For life in him (great heauen) for all my foes
(Being naturall Romans) so farre ioyntly heare   85
As may not hurt our Conquest, as with feare
Which thou already strangely hast diffusde
Through all their army; which extend to flight
Without one bloody stroke of force and fight.
   Ant. Tis time, my Lord, you put in forme your battell.   90
   Cæs. Since we must fight then, and no offerd peace
Will take with *Pompey*: I reioyce to see
This long-time lookt for, and most happy day,
In which we now shall fight, with men, not hunger,
With toyles, not sweats of blood through yeares extended,   95
This one day seruing to decide all iarres
Twixt me and *Pompey*. Hang out of my tent
My Crimsine coat of armes, to giue my souldiers
That euer-sure signe of resolu'd-for fight.
   Crass. These hands shall giue that signe to all their longings.   100
                                             Exit. Crass.

   Cæs. [*To Anthony.*] My Lord, my army, I thinke best to order
In three full Squadrons: of which let me pray
Your selfe would take on you the left wings charge;
My selfe will lead the right wing, and my place
Of fight elect in my tenth legion: 105
My battell by *Domitius Calvinus*
Shall take direction.

       The Cote of Armes is hung out, and the Souldiers
                 shoute within.

  Ant.   Heark, your souldiers shoute
For ioy to see your bloody Cote of Armes

---

76 any] *Pearson*; an ‖ 86 Conquest,] ~; ‖ 95 not] *stet* (*See Textual Note*) ‖ 101 SD *To Anthony.*]
Parrott ‖

Assure their fight this morning.
   Cæs.   A blest Euen
Bring on them worthy comforts. And ye gods   110
Performe your good presages in euents
Of fit crowne for our discipline, and deeds
Wrought vp by conquest; that my vse of it /
May wipe the hatefull and vnworthy staine   [F3ᵛ]
Of Tyrant from my Temples, and exchange it   115
For fautor of my Country; ye haue giuen
That title to those poore and fearefull fowles
That euery sound puts vp, in frights and cryes,
Euen then, when all *Romes* powers were weake and heartles,
When traiterous fires, and fierce Barbarian swords,   120
Rapines, and soule-expiring slaughters fild
Her houses, Temples, all her ayre, and earth.
To me then (whom your bounties haue enform'd
With such a spirit as despiseth feare;
Commands in either fortune, knowes, and armes   125
Against the worst of fate; and therefore can
Dispose blest meanes, encourag'd to the best)
Much more vouchsafe that honor; chiefely now,
When *Rome* wants only this dayes conquest giuen me
To make her happy, to confirme the brightnesse   130
That yet she shines in ouer all the world:
In Empire, riches, strife of all the Arts,
In gifts of Cities, and of kingdomes sent her,
In Crownes laid at her feet, in euery grace
That shores, and seas, floods, Islands, Continents,   135
Groues, fields, hills, mines, and metals can produce;
All which I (victor) will encrease, I vow
By all my good, acknowledg'd giuen by you.   *[Exeunt.]*

Act IV.   Scene I.

Pompey in haste, Brutus, Gabinius, Vibius following.

   [*Pom.*] The poyson steep't in euery vaine of Empire,
In all the world, meet now in onely me,
Thunder and lighten me to death; and make
My senses feed the flame, my soule the crack. /   4
Was euer soueraigne Captaine of so many   [F4]
Armies and Nations, so opprest as I,

---

115 Temples,] ~; ‖ **116** Country;] ~, ‖ **118** cryes,] ~; ‖ **119** heartles,] Q(c); heartle Q(u) ‖ **131** world:] ~; ‖ **133** her,] ~, ‖ **138** SD *Exeunt.*] *Parrott* ‖ **IV.**] IIII ‖ **1** *Pom.*] *Shepherd* ‖

With one hosts headstrong outrage? vrging fight,
Yet fly about my campe in panick terrors;
No reason vnder heauen suggesting cause.
And what is this but euen the gods deterring   10
My iudgement from enforcing fight this morne?
The new-fled night made day with Meteors,
Fir'd ouer *Cæsars* campe, and falne in mine,
As pointing out the terrible euents
Yet in suspence; but where they threat their fall   15
Speake not these prodigies with fiery tongues,
And eloquence that should not moue but rauish
All sound mindes, from thus tempting the iust gods,
And spitting out their faire premonishing flames
With brackish rheumes of ruder and brainsick number?   20
What's infinitely more, thus wild, thus mad
For one poore fortune of a beaten few,
To halfe so many staid, and dreadfull souldiers?
Long train'd, long foughten? able, nimble, perfect
To turne and winde aduantage euery way?   25
Encrease with little, and enforce with none?
Made bold as Lyons, gaunt as famisht wolues,
With still-seru'd slaughters, and continuall toyles.
   Bru. You should not, Sir, forsake your owne wise Counsell,
Your owne experienc't discipline, owne practise,   30
Owne god-inspired insight to all changes,
Of Protean fortune, and her zany, warre,
For hosts, and hels of such; What man will thinke
The best of them, not mad; to see them range
So vp and downe your campe, already suing   35
For offices falne, by *Cæsars* built-on fall,
Before one stroke be struck? *Domitius, Spinther,*
Your father *Scipio* now preparing friends
For *Cæsars* place of vniuersall Bishop?
Are you th'obserued rule, and voucht example,   40
Who euer would commend Physitians, /
That would not follow the diseas'd desires   [F4ᵛ]
Of their sick patients; yet incurre your selfe
The faults that you so much abhorre in others?
   Pom. I cannot, Sir, abide mens open mouthes,   45
Nor be ill spoken of; nor haue my counsels
And circumspections, turnd on me for feares,
With mocks and scandals that would make a man

20 ruder and] ruderand | number?] ~, ‖ 22 few,] ~; ‖ 40 example,] ~; ‖ 43 patients;] ~? ‖ 44 others?] ~. ‖

Of lead, a lightning, in the desperat'st onset
That euer trampled vnder death, his life.   50
I beare the touch of feare for all their safeties,
Or for mine owne? enlarge with twice as many
Selfe-liues, selfe-fortunes? they shall sinke beneath
Their owne credulities, before I crosse them.
Come, haste, dispose our battaile.
    Vib.   Good my Lord,   55
Against your *Genius* warre not for the world.
    Pom. By all worlds he that moues me next to beare
Their scofs and imputations of my feare
For any cause, shall beare this sword to hell.
Away, to battaile; good my Lord, lead you   60
The whole six thousand of our yong Patricians,
Plac't in the left wing to enuiron *Cæsar.*
My father *Scipio* shall lead the battaile;
Domitius the left wing; I the right
Against *Marc Anthony.* Take now your fils   65
Ye beastly doters on your barbarous wills.   *Exeunt.*

[IV.ii]

    Alarme, excursions, of al: The fiue Kings driuen
    ouer the Stage, Crassinius chiefely pursuing: At
    the dore enter againe the fiue Kings. The battell
                continued within.

    Epir. Fly, fly, the day was lost before twas fought.
    Thess. The Romans feard their shadowes.
    Cil.   Were there euer
Such monstrous confidences, as last night
Their Cups and musique shew'd? Before the morning /   4
Made such amazes ere one stroke was struck?   [G1]
    Iber. It made great *Pompey* mad, which who could mend?
The gods had hand in it.
    Thra.   It made the Consuls
Run on their swords to see't. The braue Patricians
Fled with their spoyled faces, arrowes sticking
As shot from heauen at them.
    Thess.   Twas the charge   10
That *Cæsar* gaue against them.
    Epir.   Come, away,
Leaue all, and wonder at this fatall day.   *Exeunt.*

---

49 lightning,] ~; ‖ **51-54** I beare . . . crosse them.] *stet* (*See Textual Note*) ‖ **60** Lord,] ~ ‖ **IV.ii**
Parrott subs. ‖ **7** *Thra.*] *Parrott subs.*; *Tra.* ‖

[IV.iii]

*The fight neerer; and enter Crassineus, a sword,
as thrust through his face; he fals. To him Pompey
and Cæsar fighting: Pompey giues way, Cæsar
follows, and enters at another dore.*

Cæs. Pursue, pursue; the gods foreshew'd their powers,
Which we gaue issue, and the day is ours.
Crassineus? O looke vp: he does, and shewes
Death in his broken eyes; which *Cæsars* hands
Shall doe the honor of eternall closure.   5
Too well thou keptst thy word, that thou this day
Wouldst doe me seruice to our victory,
Which in thy life or death I should behold,
And praise thee for; I doe, and must admire
Thy matchles valour; euer euer rest   10
Thy manly lineaments, which in a tombe
Erected to thy noble name and virtues,
Ile curiosly preserue with balmes, and spices,
In eminent place of these Pharsalian fields,
Inscrib'd with this true scroule of funerall.   15

Epitaph:

Crassineus *fought for fame, and died for* Rome,
Whose publique weale springs from this priuate tombe. /

Enter some taking him off, whom Cæsar helps. [G1ᵛ]

[IV.iv]

*Enter Pompey, Demetrius, with black robes in their
hands, broad hats, etc.*

Pom. Thus haue the gods their iustice, men their wils,
And I, by mens wils rulde, my selfe renouncing,
Am by my Angell and the gods abhorr'd;
Who drew me, like a vapour, vp to heauen
To dash me like a tempest 'gainst the earth: 5
O the deserued terrors that attend
On humane confidence! had euer men
Such outrage of presumption to be victors
Before they arm'd? To send to *Rome* before
For houses neare the market place, their tents   10
Strowd all with flowers, and nosegayes; tables couer'd

IV.iii] *(See Textual Note)* ‖ SD *enter*] ~, ‖ **15** scroule] *Parrott (Deighton conj.)*; soule *(See Textual Note)* ‖ **16** died for] *diedfor* ‖ **IV.iv**] ‖ **2** rulde,] ~; ‖

With cups and banquets; bayes and mirtle garlands,
As ready to doe sacrifice for conquest
Rather then arme them for fit fight t'enforce it;
Which when I saw, I knew as well th'euent   15
As now I feele it, and because I rag'd
In that presage, my *Genius* shewing me clearely
(As in a mirror) all this cursed issue,
And therefore vrg'd all meanes to put it off
For this day, or from these fields to some other,   20
Or from this ominous confidence, till I saw
Their spirits settl'd in some grauer knowledge
Of what belong'd to such a deare decision;
They spotted me with feare, with loue of glory,
To keepe in my command so many Kings,   25
So great an army; all the hellish blastings
That could be breath'd on me, to strike me blinde
Of honor, spirit and soule: And should I then
Saue them that would in spight of heauen be ruinde?
And, in their safeties, ruine me and mine   30
In euerlasting rage of their detraction?
    Dem. Your safety and owne honor did deserue /
Respect past all their values; O my Lord   [G2]
Would you—
    Pom.   Vpbraid me not; goe to, goe on.
    Dem. No; Ile not rub the wound. The misery is,   35
The gods for any error in a man
Which they might rectify (and should; because
That man maintain'd the right) should suffer wrong
To be thus insolent, thus grac't, thus blest!
    Pom. O the strange carriage of their acts, by which   40
Men order theirs, and their deuotions in them;
Much rather striuing to entangle men
In pathlesse error, then with regular right
Confirme their reasons, and their pieties light.
For now Sir, whatsoeuer was foreshowne   45
By heauen, or prodigy (ten parts more for vs,
Forewarning vs, deterring vs, and all
Our blinde and brainlesse frenzies, then for *Cæsar*),
All yet will be ascribde to his regard
Giuen by the gods for his good parts, preferring   50
Their glosse (being starck impostures) to the iustice,
Loue, honor, piety, of our lawes and Countrey;

14 t'enforce] t'enfore ‖ 18 issue,] ~; ‖ 21 ominous] om nous ‖ 30 safeties,] ~ˎ ‖ 31 detraction?]
~. ‖ 34 you—] *Parrott;* ~? (*See Textual Note*) ‖ 37 Which ... rectify (and] (·~ ... ~, ~ (*See
Textual Note*) ‖ 39 blest!] ~? ‖ 41 theirs,] ~; ‖ 46-48 prodigy (ten ... *Cæsar*),] ~; ~ ... ~;ˎ ‖ 52
Countrey;] ~. ‖

Though I thinke these are arguments enow
For my acquitall, that for all these fought.
   Dem. Y'are cleare, my Lord.
   Pom.   Gods helpe me, as I am;   55
What euer my vntoucht command of millions
Through all my eight and fifty yeares, hath woonne,
This one day (in the worlds esteeme) hath lost,
So vile is praise and dispraise by euent.
For I am still my selfe in euery worth   60
The world could grace me with, had this dayes Euen
In one blaze ioyn'd, with all my other Conquests.
And shall my comforts in my well-knowne selfe
Faile me for their false fires, *Demetrius*?
   Dem. O no, my Lord.
   Pom.   Take grief for them, as if   65
The rotten-hearted world could steepe my soule /
In filthy putrifaction of their owne;   [G2ᵛ]
Since their applauses faile me, that are hisses
To euery sound acceptance? I confesse,
That till th'affaire was past, my passions flam'd,   70
But now tis helplesse, and no cause in me;
Rest in these embers my vnmoued soule,
With any outward change, this dystick minding:
No man should more allow his owne losse, woes,
(Being past his fault) then any stranger does.   75
And for the worlds false loues, and ayry honors,
What soule that euer lou'd them most in life
(Once seuer'd from this breathing sepulchre),
Againe came and appearde in any kind
Their kinde admirer still, or did the state   80
Of any best man here, associate?
And euery true soule should be here so seuer'd
From loue of such men, as here drowne their soules
As all the world does? *Cato* sole excepted,
To whom Ile fly now, and my wife in way   85
(Poore Lady, and poore children, worse then fatherlesse)
Visit, and comfort. Come *Demetrius*,   *They disguise themselues.*
We now must sute our habites to our fortunes
And since these changes euer chance to greatest,
Nor desire to be   90
(Doe fortune, to exceed it, what she can)
A *Pompey*, or a *Cæsar*, but a man.   *Exeunt.*

---

58 lost,] ~. ‖ **67** owne;] ~? ‖ **68** me,] ~? ‖ **71** me;] ~, ‖ **73** minding:] ~; ‖ **77** life] ~, ‖ **78** sepulchre),] ~)‿ ‖ **84** excepted] *Shepherd*; accepted (*See Textual Note*) ‖ **89** greatest,] ~. ‖ **90** Nor desire to be] *See Textual Note* ‖

[IV.v]

Enter Cæsar, Anthony, Acilius, with souldiers.

Cæs. O We haue slaine, not conquerd! Roman blood
Peruerts th'euent, and desperate blood let out
With their owne swords. Did euer men before
Enuy their owne liues, since another liu'd
Whom they would willfully conceiue their foe,   5
And forge a Tyrant merely in their feares
To iustifie their slaughters? Consuls? furies.
   Ant. Be, Sir, their faults their griefes! The greater number /
Were only slaues, that left their bloods to ruth,   [G3]
And altogether, but six thousand slaine.   10
   Cæs. How euer many; gods and men can witnesse
Themselues enforc't it, much against the most
I could enforce on *Pompey* for our peace.
Of all slaine, yet, if *Brutus* only liu'd,
I should be comforted, for his life sau'd   15
Would weigh the whole six thousand that are lost.
But much I feare his death, because the battell
Full stricken now, he yet abides vnfound.
   Acil. I saw him fighting neare the battels end,
But suddainly giue off, as bent to fly.   20

Enter Brutus

   Ant. He comes here, see Sir.
   Bru.   I submit to *Cæsar*
My life and fortunes.
   Cæs.   A more welcome fortune
Is *Brutus*, then my conquest.
   Bru.   Sir, I fought
Against your conquest, and your selfe; and merit
(I must acknowledge) a much sterner welcome.   25
   Cæs. You fought with me, Sir, for I know your armes
Were taken for your Country, not for *Pompey*:
And for my Country I fought, nothing lesse
Then he, or both the mighty-stomak't Consuls;
Both whom (I heare) haue slaine themselues before   30
They would enioy life in the good of *Cæsar*.
But I am nothing worse, how ill soeuer
They, and the great authority of *Rome*
Would faine enforce me by their mere suspitions.

IV.v] ‖ **1** conquerd!] ~, ‖ **9** bloods] *Q(c)*: blood *Q(u)* ‖

Lou'd they their Country better then her *Brutus*?   35
Or knew what fitted noblesse, and a Romane,
With freer soules then *Brutus*? Those that liue
Shall see in *Cæsars* iustice, and what euer
Might make me worthy both their liues and loues, /   39
That I haue lost the one without my merit,   [G3ᵛ]
And they the other with no Roman spirit.
Are you empair'd to liue, and ioy my loue?
Only requite me, *Brutus*, loue but *Cæsar*,
And be in all the powers of *Cæsar*, *Cæsar*.
In which free wish, I ioyne your father *Cato*;   45
For whom Ile haste to *Vtica*, and pray
His loue may strengthen my successe to day.   *Exeunt.*

[IV.vi]

Porcius in haste, Marcillius bare, following.
Porcius discouers a bed, and a sword hanging
by it, which he takes downe.

  Mar. To what vse takc you that (my Lord)?
  Por.   Take you
No note that I take it, nor let any seruant,
Besides your selfe, of all my fathers nearest,
Serue any mood he serues, with any knowledge
Of this or any other. *Cæsar* comes   5
And giues his army wings to reach this towne,
Not for the townes sake, but to saue my father;
Whom iustly he suspects to be resolu'd
Of any violence to his life, before
He will preserue it by a Tyrants fauour.   10
For *Pompey* hath miscaried, and is fled.
Be true to me, and to my fathers life;
And doe not tell him; nor his fury serue
With any other.
  Mar.   I will dye, my Lord,
Ere I obserue it.
  Por.   O my Lord and father.   15

Cato, Athenodorus, Statilius. Cato with
a booke in his hand.

  Cat. What feares fly here on all sides? what wilde lookes
Are squinted at me from mens mere suspicions /

---

36 Romane,] ~. ‖ 37 *Brutus*?] ~. ‖ **IV.vi**] ‖ 1 Lord)?] ~?) ‖ 6 towne,] ~. ‖ 7 father;] ~. ‖

That I am wilde my selfe, and would enforce [G4]
What will be taken from me by the Tyrant?
    Ath. No: Would you only aske life, he would thinke 20
His owne life giuen more strength in giuing yours.
    Cat. I aske my life of him?
    Stat.   Aske what's his owne?
Of him he scornes should haue the least drop in it
At his disposure.
    Cat.   No, *Statilius.*
Men that haue forfeit liues by breaking lawes, 25
Or haue beene ouercome, may beg their liues,
But I haue euer beene in euery iustice
Better then *Cæsar*, and was neuer conquer'd,
Or made to fly for life, as *Cæsar* was;
But haue beene victor euer, to my wish, 30
'Gainst whomsoeuer euer hath opposde;
Where *Cæsar* now is conquer'd in his Conquest,
In the ambition, he till now denide,
Taking vpon him to giue life, when death
Is tenfold due to his most tyrannous selfe. 35
No right, no power giuen him to raise an army,
Which in despight of *Rome* he leades about
Slaughtering her loyall subiects, like an outlaw,
Nor is he better. Tongue, shew, falshood are,
To bloodiest deaths his parts so much admir'd, 40
Vaineglory, villany; and at best you can,
Fed with the parings of a worthy man.
My fame affirme my life receiu'd from him?
Ile rather make a beast my second father.
    Stat. The gods auert from euery Roman minde 45
The name of slaue to any Tyrants power.
Why was man euer iust, but to be free,
'Gainst all iniustice? and to beare about him
As well all meanes to freedome euery houre,
As euery houre he should be arm'd for death, 50
Which only is his freedome?
    Ath.   But *Statilius*, /
Death is not free for any mans election, [G4ᵛ]
Till nature, or the law, impose it on him.
    Cat. Must a man goe to law then, when he may
Enioy his owne in peace? If I can vse 55
Mine owne my selfe, must I of force, reserue it

---

19 Tyrant?] ~. ‖ **21** yours.] ~ˌ ‖ **29** was;] ~. ‖ **33** denide,] ~; ‖ **51** *Statilius*,] ~ˌ ‖

To serue a Tyrant with it? All iust men
Not only may enlarge their liues, but must,
From all rule tyrannous, or liue vniust.
 Ath. By death must they enlarge their liues?
 Cat.   By death.   60
 Ath. A man's not bound to that.
 Cat.   Ile proue he is.
Are not the liues of all men bound to iustice?
 Ath. They are.
 Cat.   And therefore not to serue iniustice:
Iustice it selfe ought euer to be free,
And therefore euery iust man being a part   65
Of that free iustice, should be free as it.
 Ath. Then wherefore is there law for death?
 Cat.   That all
That know not what law is, nor freely can
Performe the fitting iustice of a man
In kingdomes common good, may be enforc't.   70
But is not euery iust man to him selfe
The perfect'st law?
 Ath.   Suppose.
 Cat.   Then to himselfe
Is euery iust mans life subordinate.
Againe, Sir; Is not our free soule infus'd
To euery body in her absolute end   75
To rule that body? in which absolute rule
Is she not absolutely Empresse of it?
And being Empresse, may she not dispose
It, and the life in it, at her iust pleasure?
 Ath. Not to destroy it.
 Cat.   No; she not destroyes it 80
When she disliues it; that their freedomes may /
Goe firme together, like their powers and organs, [H1]
Rather then let it liue a rebell to her,
Prophaning that diuine coniunction
Twixt her and it; nay, a disiunction making   85
Betwixt them worse then death, in killing quick
That which in iust death liues: being dead to her
If to her rule dead; and to her aliue,
If dying in her iust rule.
 Ath.   The body liues not
When death hath reft it.
 Cat.   Yet tis free, and kept 90

70 be enforc't] beenforc't ‖ 86 death,] ~; ‖

583

Fit for reiunction in mans second life;
Which dying rebell to the soule, is farre
Vnfit to ioyne with her in perfect life.
    Ath. It shall not ioyne with her againe.
    Cat.   It shall.
    Ath. In reason shall it?
    Cat.   In apparant reason;   95
Which Ile proue clearely.
    Stat.   Heare, and iudge it Sir.
    Cat. As nature works in all things to an end,
So in th'appropriate honor of that end,
All things precedent haue their naturall frame;
And therefore is there a proportion   100
Betwixt the ends of those things and their primes:
For else there could not be in their creation,
Always, or for the most part, that firme forme
In their still like existence; that we see
In each full creature. What proportion then   105
Hath an immortall with a mortall substance?
And therefore the mortality to which
A man is subiect, rather is a sleepe,
Then bestiall death; since sleepe and death are call'd
The twins of nature. For if absolute death   110
And bestiall sease the body of a man,
Then is there no proportion in his parts,
His soule being free from death, which otherwise /
Retaine diuine proportion. For as sleepe   [H1ᵛ]
No disproportion holds with humane soules,   115
But aptly quickens the proportion
Twixt them and bodies, making bodies fitter
To giue vp formes to soules, which is their end:
So death (twin-borne of sleepe) resoluing all
Mans bodies heauy parts, in lighter nature   120
Makes a reunion with the spritely soule;
When in a second life their beings giuen,
Holds their proportion firme, in highest heauen.
    Ath. Hold you our bodies shall reuiue, resuming
Our soules againe to heauen?
    Cat.   Past doubt, though others   125
Thinke heauen a world too high for our low reaches,
Not knowing the sacred sence of him that sings:
Ioue can let downe a golden chaine from heauen,

---

108 subiect,] ~; ‖ **114** Retaine] Q(c); Retaines Q(u) (*also as catchword in both states*) (*See Textual Note*) ‖ **120** parts,] ~; ‖ **126** reaches,] ~. ‖ **127** sings:] ~, ‖

Which tyed to earth, shall fetch vp earth and seas;
And what's that golden chaine, but our pure soules,   130
A golden beame of him, let downe by him,
That gouern'd with his grace, and drawne by him,
Can hoist this earthy body vp to him,
The sea, and ayre, and all the elements
Comprest in it: not while tis thus concret,   135
But fin'd by death, and then giuen heauenly heat.
   Ath. Your happy exposition of that place
(Whose sacred depth I neuer heard so sounded)
Euicts glad grant from me you hold a truth.
   Stat. Is't not a manly truth, and mere diuine?   140
   Cat. Tis a good chearefull doctrine for good men.
But (sonne and seruants) this is only argu'd
To spend our deare time well, and no life vrgeth
To any violence further then his owner
And grauer men hold fit. Let's talke of *Cæsar*,   145
He's the great subiect of all talke, and he
Is hotly hasting on. Is supper ready?
   Mar. It is, my Lord.
   Cat.   Why then let's in and eat; /
Our coole submission will quench *Cæsars* heat.   [H2]
   Stat. Submission? here's for him.   *[Draws his sword.]*
   Cat.   *Statilius,*   150
My reasons must not strengthen you in error,
Nor learn'd *Athenodorus* gentle yeelding.
Talke with some other deepe Philosophers,
Or some diuine Priest of the knowing gods,
And heare their reasons; in meane time come sup.   155
                     Exeunt, Cato going out arme in
                     arme betwixt Athen. and Statilius.

Act V.   Scene I.

   Enter Vshers, with the two Lentuli, and Sextus
   before Cornelia; Cyris, Telesilla, Lælia, Drusus,
   with others, following, Cornelia, Sextus and the
       two Lentuli reading letters.

   Cor. So may my comforts for this good newes thriuc
As I am thankfull for them to the Gods.
Ioyes vnexpected, and in desperate plight,

---

145 Let's] Lets ‖ 150 SD *Draws his sword.*] | *Statilius*] Statilus ‖ 155 SD *Exeunt,*] ~. ‖ **V.i**] SD
Sextus] Parrott; *Septimius* (See Textual Note) | SD *Sextus*] Parrott; *Septimius* ‖

Are still most sweet, and proue from whence they come,
When earths still Moonelike confidence, in ioy, 5
Is at her full, true ioy descending farre
From past her sphere, and from that highest heauen
That moues and is not mou'd: how farre was I
From hope of these euents, when fearefull dreames
Of Harpies tearing out my heart? of armies 10
Terribly ioyning? Cities, kingdomes falling,
And all on me? prou'd sleepe, not twin to death,
But to me, death it selfe? yet waking then,
These letters, full of as much chearefull life,
I found closde in my hand. O gods how iustly 15
Ye laugh at all things earthly? at all feares /
That rise not from your iudgements? at all ioyes, [H2ᵛ]
Not drawne directly from your selues, and in ye!
Distrust in man is faith, trust in him ruine.
Why write great learned men? men merely rapt 20
With sacred rage, of confidence, beleefe?
Vndanted spirits? inexorable fate
And all feare treading on? tis all but ayre,
If any comfort be, tis in despaire.
   1 Len. You learned Ladies may hold any thing. 25
   2 Len. Now madam is your walk from coach come neare
The promontory, where you late commanded
A Sentinell should stand to see from thence
If either with a nauy, brought by sea,
Or traine by land, great *Pompey* comes to greet you 30
As in your letters, he neare this time promisde.
   Cor. O may this Isle of *Lesbos*, compast in
With the *Ægæan* sea, that doth diuide
Europe from *Asia* (the sweet literate world
From the Barbarian) from my barbarous dreames 35
Diuide my dearest husband and his fortunes.
   2 Len. He's busied now with ordering offices.
By this time, madam, sits your honor'd father

                                 He looks in his letter.

In *Cæsars* chaire of vniuersall Bishop.
Domitius Ænobarbas is made Consull, 40
Spynther his Consort; and *Phaonius*
Tribune, or Pretor.

                Sextus with a letter.

  Sex.   These were only sought

---

4 come,] ~; ‖ 6 full, true] ~. True ‖ 13 waking] *Pearson*; making ‖ 14 letters,] ~; ‖ 18 ye!] ~, ‖
30 land,] ~; ‖ 34 *Asia*] ~. | the] The ‖ 40 *Ænobarbas*] ~, ‖ 42 SD *Sextus*] *Parrott*; *Septimius* |
Sex.] *Parrott*; *Sep.* ‖

Before the battaile, not obtaind; nor mouing
My father but in shadowes.
    Cor.   Why should men
Tempt fate with such firme confidence? seeking places   45
Before the power that should dispose could grant them?
For then the stroke of battaile was not struck.
    1 Len. Nay, that was sure enough. Physitians know /
When sick mens eyes are broken, they must dye.   [H3]
Your letters telling you his victory   50
Lost in the skirmish, which I know hath broken
Both the eyes and heart of *Cæsar*: for as men
Healthfull through all their liues to grey-hayr'd age,
When sicknesse takes them once, they seldom scape:
So *Cæsar* victor in his generall fights   55
Till this late skirmish, could no aduerse blow
Sustaine without his vtter ouerthrow.

              [Enter a Sentinel, above.]

    2 Len. See, madam, now; your Sentinell: enquire.
    Cor. Seest thou no fleet yet (Sentinell) nor traine
That may be thought great *Pompeys*?
    Sent.   Not yet, madame.   60
    1 Len. Seest thou no trauellers addrest this way?
In any number on this Lesbian shore?
    Sent. I see some not worth note; a couple comming
This way, on foot, that are not now farre hence.
    2 Len. Come they apace? like messengers with newes?   65
    Sent. No, nothing like (my Lord) nor are their habites
Of any such mens fashions, being long mantles,
And sable hew'd; their heads all hid in hats
Of parching *Thessaly*, broad brimm'd, high crown'd.
    Cor. These serue not our hopes.
    Sent.   Now I see a ship,   70
A kenning hence, that strikes into the hauen.
    Cor. One onely ship?
    Sent.   One only, madam, yet.
    Cor. That should not be my Lord.
    1 Len.   Your Lord? no madam.
    Sent. She now lets out arm'd men vpon the land.
    2 Len. Arm'd men? with drum, and colours?
    Sent.   No, my Lord,   75
But bright in armes, yet beare halfe pikes, or beadhookes.
    1 Len. These can be no plumes in the traine of *Pompey*.

---

48 Physitians] *Physitians* ‖ 51 Lost] *stet* (*See Textual Note*) ‖ 57 SD *Enter ... above.*] *Parrott*
subs. ‖ 67 fashions,] ~; ‖ 71 hence,] ~; ‖ 76 yet] *stet* (*See Textual Note*) ‖

Cor. Ile see him in his letter, once again.

Sent. Now, madam, come the two I saw on foot. /

Enter Pompey and Demetrius. [H3ᵛ]

Dem. See your Princesse, Sir, come thus farre from the   80
City in her coach, to encounter your promist comming
about this time in your last letters.

Pom. The world is alterd since *Demetrius*.

Offer to goe by.

1 *Len.* See, madam, two Thessalian Augurs it seemes
by their habits. Call, and enquire if either by their   85
skils or trauels, they know no newes of your husband.

Cor. My friends? a word.

Dem. With vs, madam?

Cor. Yes. Are you of *Thessaly*?

Dem. I, madam, and all the world besides.   90

Cor. Your Country is great.

Dem. And our portions little.

Cor. Are you Augures?

Dem. Augures, madam? yes a kinde of Augures, *alias*
Wizerds, that goe vp and downe the world, teaching how   95
to turne ill to good.

Cor. Can you doe that?

Dem. I, madam, you haue no worke for vs, haue you? No
ill to turne good, I meane?

Cor. Yes; the absence of my husband.   100

Dem. What's he?

Cor. *Pompey* the great.

Dem. Wherein is he great?

Cor. In his command of the world.

Dem. Then he's great in others. Take him without his   105
addition (great) what is he then?

Cor. *Pompey*.

Dem. Not your husband then?

Cor. Nothing the lesse for his greatnesse.

Dem. Not in his right, but in your comforts he is.   110

Cor. His right is my comfort.

Dem. What's his wrong?

Cor. My sorrow. /

Dem. And that's ill. [H4]

Cor. Yes.   115

80-82 See ... letters.] *Shepherd*; See ... the/ City ... comming/ About ... letters. ‖ **83**
Demetrius.] ∼; | SD *Offer*] (*offer* ‖ **84-86** See ... husband.] *Shepherd*; See ... seemes/ By ...
their/ Skils ... husband. ‖ **94-96** Augures ... good.] *Shepherd*; Augures ... *alias*/ Wizerds ...
teaching/ How ... good. ‖ **105-106** Then ... then?] *Shepherd*; Then ... his/ Addition ... then? ‖
110 right,] ∼; ‖

Dem. Y'are come to the vse of our Profession, madam:
Would you haue that ill turnd good? that sorrow turnd
comfort?

Cor. Why, is my Lord wrong'd?

Dem. We professe not that knowledge, madam: Supose he   120
were.

Cor. Not I.

Dem. Youle suppose him good.

Cor. He is so.

Dem. Then must you needs suppose him wrong'd; for all   125
goodnesse is wrong'd in this world.

Cor. What call you wrong?

Dem. Ill fortune, affliction.

Cor. Thinke you my Lord afflicted?

Dem. If I thinke him good (madam) I must. Vnlesse   130
he be worldly good, and then, either he is ill, or has
ill: Since, as no sugar is without poyson, so is no
worldly good without ill, euen naturally nourisht in
it, like a houshold thiefe, which is the worst of all
theeues.   135

Cor. Then he is not worldly, but truly good.

Dem. He's too great to be truly good; for worldly
greatnes is the chiefe worldly goodnesse; and all worldly
goodnesse (I prou'd before) has ill in it, which true
good has not.   140

Cor. If he rule well with his greatnesse, wherein
is he ill?

Dem. But great Rulers are like Carpenters that weare
their Rules at their backs still: and therefore to make
good your true good in him, y'ad better suppose him little,   145
or meane. For in the meane only is the true good.

Pom. But euery great Lady must haue her husband
great still, or her loue will be little.

Cor. I am none of those great Ladyes.

1 Len. She's a Philosophresse, Augure, and can turne   150
ill to good as well as you.

116-118 Y'are ... comfort?] *Shepherd*; Y'are ... madam,/ Would ... that/ Sorrow ... comfort? ‖
116 madam:] ~, ‖ 119 Why,] ~ˏ ‖ 120-121 We ... were.] *Shepherd*; We ... madam:/ Supose ...
were. ‖ 120 Supose] *Q(u)*; Suppose *Q(r)* ‖ 125-126 Then ... world.] *Shepherd*; Then ... for/ All
... world. ‖ 130-135 If ... theeues.] *Shepherd*; If ... he/ Be ... ill:/ Since ... worldly/ Good ...
a/ Houshold ... theeues. ‖ 131 good,] *Q(u)*; ~; *Q(r)* ‖ 132 poyson,] ~: ‖ 133 ill, euen] ~. Euen ‖
137-140 He's ... not.] *Shepherd*; He's ... greatnes/ Is ... goodnesse/ (I ... not. ‖ 139 it,] ~: ‖
141 greatnesse,] ~; ‖ 143-146 But ... good.] *Shepherd*; But ... their/ Rules ... your/ True ...
meane./ For ... good. ‖ 143 Carpenters] *Q(u)*; ~, *Q(r)* ‖ 145 little,] *Q(u)*; ~ˏ *Q(r)* ‖ 146 meane.]
Q(u); ~, *Q(r)* ‖ 147-148 But ... little.] *Shepherd*; But ... husband/ Great ... little. ‖ 150-151
She's ... you.] *Shepherd*; She's ... turne/ Ill ... you. ‖ 150 Philosophresse,] ~ˏ ‖

Pom. I would then, not honor, but adore her: could you submit your selfe chearefully to your husband, / supposing him falne?   [H4ᵛ]

Cor. If he submit himselfe chearfully to his fortune.   155

Pom. Tis the greatest greatnes in the world you vndertake.

Cor. I would be so great, if he were.

Pom. In supposition.

Cor. In fact.   160

Pom. Be no woman, but a Goddesse then; and make good thy greatnesse; [*Reveals himself.*] I am chearfully falne; be chearfull.

Cor. I am: and welcome, as the world were closde
In these embraces.

Pom.   Is it possible?   165
A woman, losing gretnesse, still as good,
As at her greatest? O gods, was I euer
Great till this minute?

Amb. Len.   *Pompey?*

Pom.   View me better.

Amb. Len. Conquerd by *Cæsar?*

Pom.   Not I, but mine army.
No fault in me, in it: no conquest of me.   170
I tread this low earth as I trod on *Cæsar.*
Must I not hold my selfe, though lose the world?
Nor lose I lesse; a world lost at one clap,
Tis more then *Ioue* euer thundred with.
What glory is it to haue my hand hurle   175
So vast a volley through the groning ayre?
And is't not great, to turne griefes thus to ioyes,
That breake the hearts of others?

Amb. Len.   O tis *Ioue*-like.

Pom. It is to imitate *Ioue*, that from the wounds
Of softest clouds, beats vp the terriblest sounds.   180
I now am good, for good men still haue least,
That twixt themselues and God might rise their rest.

Cor. O *Pompey, Pompey*: neuer Great till now.

Pom. O my *Cornelia*: let vs still be good,
And we shall still be great: and greater farre   185
In euery solid grace, then when the tumor
And bile of rotten obseruation sweld vs. /
Griefes for wants outward, are without our cure,   [I1]

152-154 I ... falne?] *Shepherd*; I ... you/ Submit ... husband,/ Supposing ... falnc? ‖ 161-163
Be ... chearfull.] *Shepherd*; Be ... greatnesse;/ I ... chearfull. ‖ 162 SD *Reveals himself.*] *Parrott
subs.* ‖ 179 *Pom.*] *Pom,* ‖

590

Greatnesse, not of it selfe, is neuer sure.
Before, we went vpon heauen, rather treading   190
The virtues of it vnderfoot, in making
The vicious world our heauen, then walking there
Euen here, as knowing that our home, contemning
All forg'd heauens here raisde, setting hills on hills.
Vulcan from heauen fell, yet on's feet did light,   195
And stood no lesse a god then at his height;
At lowest, things lye fast: we now are like
The two Poles propping heauen, on which heauen moues;
And they are fixt, and quiet; being aboue
All motion farre, we rest aboue the heauens.   200
   Cor. O, I more ioy, t'embrace my Lord thus fixt,
Then he had brought me ten inconstant conquests.
   1 *Len.* Miraculous standing in a fall so great,
Would *Cæsar* knew, Sir, how you conquerd him
In your conuiction.
   Pom.   Tis enough for me   205
That *Pompey* knows it. I will stand no more
On others legs: nor build one ioy without me.
If euer I be worth a house againe,
Ile build all inward: not a light shall ope
The common outway: no expence, no art,   210
No ornament, no dore will I vse there,
But raise all plaine, and rudely, like a rampier,
Against the false society of men
That still batters
All reason peecemeale. And for earthy greatnesse   215
All heauenly comforts rarifies to ayre,
Ile therefore liue in darke, and all my light,
Like ancient Temples, let in at my top.
This were to turne ones back to all the world,
And only looke at heauen. *Empedocles*   220
Recur'd a mortall plague through all his Country,
With stopping vp the yawning of a hill,
From whence the hollow and vnwholsome South /
Exhald his venomd vapor. And what else   [I1ᵛ]
Is any King, giuen ouer to his lusts,   225
But euen the poyson'd cleft of that crackt mountaine,
That all his kingdome plagues with his example?
Which I haue stopt now, and so cur'd my Country
Of such a sensuall pestilence:

---

192 heauen,] ~; ‖ 193 home,] ~; ‖ 194 raisde,] ~; ‖ 198 moues;] Q(u); ~ˏ Q(c) (*See Textual Note, II.iv.39*) ‖ 199 quiet;] ~, ‖ 200 farre,] *Parrott;* ~; ‖ 203 1 *Len.*] ~ ~ˏ ‖ 215 peecemeale. And] stet (*See Textual Note*) ‖ 216 ayre,] stet (*See Historical Collation*) ‖

591

When therefore our diseas'de affections   230
Harmefull to humane freedome, and stormelike
Inferring darknesse to th'infected minde
Oppresse our comforts: tis but letting in
The light of reason, and a purer spirit,
Take in another way; like roomes that fight   235
With windowes gainst the winde, yet let in light.
   Amb. Len. My Lord, we seru'd before, but now adore you.
   Sent. My Lord, the arm'd men I discou'rd lately
Vnshipt, and landed, now are trooping neare.
   Pom. What arm'd men are they?
   1 *Len.*   Some, my Lord, that lately   240
The Sentinell discouer'd, but not knew.
   Sent. Now all the sea (my Lords) is hid with ships,
Another Promontory flanking this,
Some furlong hence, is climb'd, and full of people,
That easily may see hither, it seemes, looking   245
What these so neare intend: Take heed, they come.

        Enter Achillas, Septimius, Saluius, with souldiers.

   Ach. Haile to *Romes* great Commander; to whom *Ægypt*
(Not long since seated in his kingdome by thee,
And sent to by thee in thy passage by)
Sends vs with answer: which withdraw and heare.   250
   Pom. Ile kisse my children first.
   Sex.   Blesse me, my Lord.
   Pom. I will, and *Cyris*, my poore daughter too.
Euen that high hand that hurld me downe thus low,
Keepe you from rising high: I heare: now tell me.
I thinke (my friend) you once seru'd vnder me: 255

        Septimius only nods with his head. /

Nod onely? not a word daigne? what are these?   [12]
Cornelia? I am now not worth mens words.
   Ach. Please you receiue your ayde, Sir?
   Pom.   I, I come.
                  Exit Pom. They draw and follow.
   Cor. Why draw they? See, my Lords; attend them vshers.
               [*Exeunt the two Lentuli, and Demetrius,*
                    with the Ushers.]
   Sent. O they haue slaine great *Pompey*.
   Cor.   O my husband.   260

---

231 freedome,] ~; ‖ **239** landed,] ~; ‖ **245** hither,] ~; | seemes,] ~ ‖ **246** SD *Septimius*] *Parrott*;
Septius (See Textual Note) | souldiers.] ~, ‖ **251** *Sex.*] *Parrott*; *Sep.* ‖ **255** SD *Septimius*] *Parrott*;
Septius ‖ **256** Nod] *Pom.* ~ ‖ **257** words.] ~: ‖ **258** SD *They*] Q(c); *The* Q(u) ‖ **259** SD *Exeunt
... Ushers.*] *Parrott* ‖

Sex., Cyr. Mother, take comfort.

Enter Pompey bleeding.

O my Lord and father.

Pom. See heauens your sufferings; is my Countries loue,
The iustice of an Empire, pietie,
Worth this end in their leader? last yet life,
And bring the gods off fairer: after this 265
Who will adore, or serue the deities?

He hides his face with his robe.

Enter the Murtherers.

Ach. Helpe hale him off: and take his head for *Cæsar.*
Sex. Mother? O saue vs; *Pompey?* O my father.

[Exeunt the Murtherers with Pompey.]

Enter the two Lentuli and Demetrius bleeding,
and kneele about Cornelia.

1 Len. Yet fals not heauen? Madam, O make good
Your late great spirits; all the world will say, 270
You know not how to beare aducrse euents,
If now you languish.
Omn. Take her to her coach.

They beare her out.

[V.ii]

Cato with a booke in his hand.

[*Cat.*] O Beastly apprehenders of things manly,
And merely heauenly: they with all the reasons
I vsde for iust mens liberties, to beare
Their liues and deaths vp in their owne free hands,
Feare still my resolution, though I seeme / 5
To giue it off like them: and now am woonne [12ᵛ]
To thinke my life in lawes rule, not mine owne,
When once it comes to death; as if the law
Made for a sort of outlawes, must bound me
In their subiection; as if I could 10
Be rackt out of my vaines, to liue in others;
As so I must, if others rule my life;
And publique power keepe all the right of death,
As if men needes must serue the place of iustice,
The forme, and idoll, and renounce it selfe? 15

---

261 *Sex.,*] *Parrott subs.*; *Sept.* ‸ ‖ 262 sufferings;] ~, | Countries loue,] *Q(c)*; Countres ~‸ *Q(u)* ‖ 263 Empire, pietie,] ~; ~; ‖ 264 leader?] ~: ‖ 268 *Sex.*] *Parrott*; *Sep.* | SD *Exeunt ... Pompey.*] *Parrott subs.* ‖ **V.ii**] *Parrott subs.* ‖ 1 *Cat.*] *Parrott subs.* ‖ 4 hands,] ~; ‖ 5 resolution,] ~‸ ‖ 14 iustice,] ~; ‖

Our selues, and all our rights in God and goodnesse?
Our whole contents and freedomes to dispose,
All in the ioyes and wayes of arrant rogues?
No stay but their wilde errors, to sustaine vs?
No forges but their throats to vent our breaths?   20
To forme our liues in, and repose our deaths?
See, they haue got my sword. Who's there?

Enter Marcillius bare.

Mar.   My Lord.
     Cat. Who tooke my sword hence? Dumb? I doe not aske
For any vse or care of it: but hope   24
I may be answered. Goe Sir, let me haue it.   *Exit Mar.*
Poore slaues, how terrible this death is to them?
If men would sleepe, they would be wroth with all
That interrupt them: Physick take to take
The golden rest it brings: both pay and pray
For good, and soundest naps, all friends consenting   30
In those kinde inuocations; praying all
Good rest, the gods vouchsafe you; but when death
(Sleepes naturall brother) comes (that's nothing worse,
But better, being more rich, and keepes the store;
Sleepe euer fickle, wayward still, and poore),   35
O how men grudge, and shake, and feare, and fly
His sterne approaches? all their comforts taken
In faith, and knowledge of the blisse and beauties /
That watch their wakings in an endlesse life,   [13]
Dround in the paines and horrors of their sense   40
Sustainde but for an houre; be all the earth
Rapt with this error, Ile pursue my reason,
And hold that as my light and fiery pillar,
Th'eternall law of heauen and earth no firmer.
But while I seeke to conquer conquering *Cæsar*,   45
My soft-splen'd seruants ouerrule and curb me.

He knocks, and Butas enters.

Where's he I sent to fetch and place my sword
Where late I left it? Dumb to? Come another!

Enter Cleanthes.

Where's my sword hung here?
     Cle.   My Lord, I know not.

Ent. Marcilius.

     Cat. The rest, come in there. Where's the sword I charg'd you   50

---

23 *Cat.*] *Cat,* ‖ 30 naps,] ~; ‖ 33 comes] ~; ‖ 34 better,] ~; | rich,] ~; ‖ 35 poore),] ~). ‖ 39 life,]
~: ‖ 46 SD *Butas*] *Parrott*; *Brutus* (*See Textual Note*) ‖ 48 SD *Enter Cleanthes.*] *in right margin
in Q* ‖ 49 not.] ~, | SD *Ent. Marcilius.*] *in right margin in Q* ‖

To giue his place againe? Ile breake your lips ope;
Spight of my freedome, all my seruants, friends,
My sonne and all, will needs betray me naked
To th'armed malice of a foe so fierce
And Beare-like, mankinde of the blood of virtue.   55
O gods, who euer saw me thus contemn'd?
Goe call my sonne in; tell him, that the lesse
He shewes himselfe my sonne, the lesse Ile care
To liue his father.

          Enter Athenodorus, Porcius: Porcius kneeling;
             Butas, Cleanthes and Marcilius by him.

  Por.   I beseech you, Sir,
Rest patient of my duty, and my loue;   60
Your other children think on, our poore mother,
Your family, your Country.
  Cat.   If the gods
Giue ouer all, Ile fly the world with them.
Athenodorus, I admire the changes
I note in heauenly prouidence. When *Pompey*   65
Did all things out of course, past right, past reason, /
He stood inuincible against the world: [13ᵛ]
Yet, now his cares grew pious, and his powers
Set all vp for his Countrey, he is conquered.
  Ath. The gods wills secret are, nor must we measure   70
Their chast-reserued deepes by our dry shallowes.
Sufficeth vs, we are entirely such
As twixt them and our consciences we know
Their graces, in our virtues, shall present
Vnspotted with the earth, to th'high throne   75
That ouerlookes vs: for this gyant world
Let's not contend with it, when heauen it selfe
Failes to reforme it: why should we affect
The least hand ouer it, in that ambition?
A heape tis of digested villany;   80
Virtue in labor with eternall Chaos
Prest to a liuing death, and rackt beneath it,
Her throwes vnpitied, euery worthy man
Limb by limb sawne out of her virgine wombe,
To liue here peecemeall tortur'd; fly life then;   85
Your life and death made presidents for men.   *Exit.*
  Cat. Ye heare (my masters) what a life this is,
And vse much reason to respect it so.

---

51 ope;] ~, ‖ 52 freedome,] *Shepherd*; ~; | friends,] ~; ‖ 59 SD *Butas*] *Parrott*; *Brutus* ‖ 64 changes] ~, ‖ 75 earth, to th'] ~; to' th ‖ 82 it,] ~. ‖ 83 vnpitied,] ~; ‖ 85 tortur'd;] ~, ‖

But mine shall serue ye. Yet restore my sword,
Lest too much ye presume, and I conceiue   90
Ye front me like my fortunes. Where's *Statilius*?
   Por. I think Sir, gone with the three hundred Romans
In *Lucius Cæsars* charge, to serue the victor.
   Cat. And would not take his leaue of his poore friend?
Then the Philosophers haue stoop't his spirit,   95
Which I admire, in one so free, and knowing,
And such a fiery hater of base life,
Besides being such a vow'd and noted foe
To our great Conqueror. But I aduisde him
To spare his youth, and liue.
   Por.   My brother *Brutus*   100
Is gone to *Cæsar*.
   Cat.   *Brutus*? Of mine honor /
(Although he be my sonne in law) I must say   [I4]
There went as worthy, and as learned a President
As liues in *Romes* whole rule, for all lifes actions;
And yet your sister *Porcia* (his wife)   105
Would scarce haue done this. But (for you my sonne)
Howeuer *Cæsar* deales with me, be counsailde
By your experienc't father, not to touch
At any action of the publique weale,
Nor any rule beare neare her politique sterne: 110
For, to be vpright, and sincere therein
Like *Catos* sonne, the times corruption
Will neuer beare it: and, to sooth the time,
You shall doe basely, and vnworthy your life;
Which, to the gods I wish, may outweigh mine   115
In euery virtue; howsoeuer ill
You thriue in honor.
   Por.   I, my Lord, shall gladly
Obey that counsell.
   Cat.   And what needed you
Vrge my kinde care of any charge that nature
Imposes on me? haue I euer showne   120
Loues least defect to you? or any dues
The most indulgent father (being discreet)
Could doe his dearest blood? doe you me right
In iudgement, and in honor; and dispence
With passionate nature: goe, neglect me not,   125
But send my sword in. Goe, tis I that charge you.

98 Besides] ~, ‖ **105** *Porcia*] Q(c); *Porcea* Q(u) ‖ **107** me,] ~; ‖ **111** vpright] Q(c); vbright Q(u) ‖
122 indulgent] Q(c); iddulgent Q(u) ‖

Por. O my Lord, and father; [*To the others.*] come, aduise me.

Exeunt. [*Manet Cato.*]

Cat. What haue I now to thinke on in this world?
No one thought of the world, I goe each minute
Discharg'd of all cares that may fit my freedome. 130
The next world, and my soule, then let me serue
With her last vtterance; that my body may
With sweetnesse of the passage drowne the sowre
That death will mix with it: the Consuls soules
That slew themselues so nobly, scorning life 135
Led vnder Tyrants Scepters, mine would see. /
For we shall know each other; and past death [I4ᵛ]
Retaine those formes of knowledge learn'd in life;
Since, if what here we learne, we there shall lose,
Our immortality were not life, but time. 140
And that our soules in reason are immortall,
Their naturall and proper obiects proue;
Which immortallity and knowledge are.
For to that obiect euer is referr'd
The nature of the soule, in which the acts 145
Of her high faculties are still employde.
And that true obiect must her powers obtaine
To which they are in natures aime directed,
Since twere absurd to haue her set an obiect
Which possibly she neuer can aspire. 150

Enter a Page with his sword taken out before.

Pag. Your sword, my Lord.
  Cat.   O is it found? lay downe
Vpon the bed (my boy).   *Exit Pa.*
                    Poore men; a boy
Must be presenter; manhood at no hand
Must serue so foule a fact; for so are calde
(In common mouths) mens fairest acts of all. 155
Vnsheath; is't sharpe? tis sweet. Now I am safe,
Come *Cæsar*, quickly now, or lose your vassall.
Now wing thee, deare soule, and receiue her, heauen.
The earth, the ayre, and seas I know, and all
The ioyes, and horrors of their peace and warres, 160
And now will see the gods state, and the starres.

*He fals vpon his sword, and enter Statilius at
another side of the Stage with his sword drawne,
Porcius, Butas, Cleanthes and Marcilius holding
his hands.*

127 father;] ~, | SD *To the others.*] *Parrott* | SD *Manet Cato.*] ‖ 148 directed,] ~. ‖ 152 boy).]
~). ‖ 158 her,] ~. ‖ 161 SD *Butas*] *Parrott*; *Brutus* ‖

Stat. *Cato?* my Lord?
Por.   I sweare (*Statilius*) /
He's forth, and gone to seeke you, charging me   [K1]
To seeke elsewhere, lest you had slaine your selfe;
And by his loue entreated you would liue.   165
    Stat. I sweare by all the gods, Ile run his fortunes.
    Por. You may, you may; but shun the victor now,
Who neare is, and will make vs all his slaues.
    Stat. He shall himselfe be mine first, and my slaues.   *Exit.*
    Por. Looke, looke in to my father, O (I feare)   170
He is no sight for me to beare and liue.   *Exit.*
    Omn. 3. O ruthfull spectacle!
    Cle.   He hath ript his entrals.
    But. Search, search; they may be sound.
    Cle.   They may, and are.
Giue leaue, my Lord, that I may sew them vp,
Being yet vnperisht.
    Cat.   Stand off; now they are not.   175
                    He thrusts him back, and plucks out
                    his entrals.

Haue he my curse that my lifes least part saues.
Iust men are only free, the rest are slaues.   [*Dies.*]
    But. Myrror of men.
    Mar.   The gods enuied his goodnesse.

Enter Cæsar, Anthony, Brutus, Acilius, with
Lords and Citizens of Vtica.

    Cæs. Too late, too late; with all our haste. O *Cato,*
All my late Conquest, and my lifes whole acts,   180
Most crownde, most beautified, are basted all
With thy graue lifes expiring in their scorne.
Thy life was rule to all liues; and thy death
(Thus forcibly despising life) the quench
Of all liues glories.
    Ant.   Vnreclaimed man?   185
How censures *Brutus* his sterne fathers fact?
    Bru. Twas not well done.
    Cæs.   O censure not his acts,
Who knew as well what fitted man, as all men. /

Enter Achillas, Septimius, Salvius, with   [K1ᵛ]
Pompeys head.

172 3.] 3ˬ | spectacle!] ~? ‖ 173 *But.*] *Parrott; Bru.* | sound] *stet* (*See Textual Note*) ‖ 174 vp,] ~ˬ ‖
175 SD *He ... entrals.*] *Shepherd; He ... & (after* unperisht.*)/ plucks ... entrals. (after* not.) ‖
177 SD *Dies.*] *Parrott* ‖ 178 *But.*] *Parrott; Bru.* ‖ 181 basted] *stet* (*See Textual Note*) ‖ 187
acts,] ~; ‖ 188 SD *Achillas*] *Parrott; Achilius* (*See Textual Note*) ‖

All kneeling. Your enemies head great *Cæsar.*
Cæs.   Cursed monsters,
Wound not mine eyes with it, nor in my camp   190
Let any dare to view it; farre as noblesse
The den of barbarisme flies, and blisse
The bitterest curse of vext and tyrannisde nature,
Transferre it from me. Borne the plagues of virtue,
How durst ye poyson thus my thoughts? to torture   195
Them with instant rapture.
    Omn. 3.   Sacred *Cæsar.*
    Cæs. Away with them; I vow by all my comforts,
Who slack seemes, or not fiery in my charge,
Shall suffer with them.
    All the souldiers.   Out base murtherers;
Tortures, tortures for them.   *Hale them out.*
    Omn. [3.]   Cruell *Cæsar.*   200
    Cæs. Too milde with any torture.
    Bru.   Let me craue
The ease of my hate on their one curst life.
    Cæs. Good *Brutus* take it; O you coole the poyson
These villaines flaming pour'd vpon my spleen
To suffer with my lothings. If the blood   205
Of euery common Roman toucht so neare,
Shall I confirme the false brand of my tyranny
With being found a fautor of his murther
Whom my deare Country chusde to fight for her?
    Ant. Your patience Sir, their tortures well will quit you.   210
    Bru. Let my slaues vse, Sir, be your president.
    Cæs. It shall, I sweare: you doe me infinite honor.
O *Cato,* I enuy thy death, since thou
Enuiedst my glory to preserue thy life.
Why fled his sonne and friend *Statilius*?   215
So farre I fly their hurt, that all my good
Shall fly to their desires. And (for himselfe) /
My Lords and Citizens of *Vtica,*   [K2]
His much renowne of you, quit with your most.
And by the sea, vpon some eminent rock,   220
Erect his sumptuous tombe; on which aduance
With all fit state his statue; whose right hand
Let hold his sword, where, may to all times rest
His bones as honor'd as his soule is blest.   [*Exeunt.*]

FINIS.

---

194 virtue,] ~, ‖ 196 Them with] *stet* (See *Textual Note*) ‖ 200 them.] ~: | SD *Hale*] hale | *Omn.*
3.] *Parrott*; *Omn.* ‖ 204 pour'd] pou'rd ‖ 206 neare,] ~; ‖ 224 SD *Exeunt.*]

HISTORICAL COLLATION

[Editions collated: Pearson (= *Pe*, in *The Comedies and Tragedies of George Chapman*, III, 1873, pp. 123-194; readings recorded only where they differ from Q); Shepherd (=*S*, in *The Works of George Chapman: Plays*, 1875, pp. 351-380); and Parrott (=*P*, in *The Plays and Poems of George Chapman: The Tragedies*, 1910, pp. 339-400). The siglum Q identifies the quarto of 1631, with Q(c) and Q(u) designating corrected and uncorrected states and Q(r) indicating the reset page, H4. In addition, emendations suggested by K. Deighton, *The Old Dramatists: Conjectural Readings* (Westminster, 1896), pp. 141-143; J. Brereton, 'Notes on the Text of Chapman's Plays,' *MLR*, III (1907), 63-64; T. M. Parrott, 'Notes on the Text of Chapman's Plays,' *Anglia*, XXX (1907), 501-522; G. G. Loane, 'Notes on Chapman's Plays,' *MLR*, XXXIII (1938), 253-254; and G. G. Loane, 'More Notes on Chapman's Plays,' *MLR* XXXVIII (1943), 347, are also included. Only substantive and semi-substantive variants are recorded; obvious errors are not recorded. Lemmata are taken from the present text. Where lemma represents the reading of Q copy-text, omission of a siglum indicates agreement with lemma.]

Dedication

19 old] Q(c); *such* Q(u), S, P

Argument

12 trauailde] travelled *S*

I.i

SD Scene I.] ~ ~. *A Room in* Cato's *House P*
SD *Porcius*] Portius *P* (*not hereafter recorded*)
15 For ... Purse] For fall of his so ill-disposed purse *Brereton conj.*; For fallings of his ill-disposed purse *P*
39 SD *To Athenodorus*] *P*; om. *Q, S*
42 Riuals;] ~) *P*
44 danger)] ~, *P*
82 then] that *P conj.*
84 SD *Exeunt. ... Minutius.*] *Exeunt./ Enter Minutius, manet Cato. Q, S; Exeunt* Portius, Athenodorus, *and* Statilius/ *Enter* Minutius, *manet* Cato *P*

I.ii

I.ii] *P*; *om. Q, S*
SD I.ii] ~.~ *The Forum, before the Temple of Castor and Pollux P*
SD *Anthonius*] *Antonius S*; Antony *P* (*not hereafter recorded*)
1 *Cæs.*] ~. *aside to* Metellus *P*
  entring] entering *S* (*so regularly; not hereafter recorded*)
4 *Met.*] ~. *aside to* Cæsar *P*
18-27 1 [*Cit.*], etc.] *P subs.*; 1st Co., 2nd Co., etc. *S*; I, 2, 3, etc. *Q*
20 *Cat.* Come in] *Cato*, come in *Brereton conj.*; Cato [*To his friends.*] Come
  in *P*
20 SD *Cato drawes Minutius*] *He drawes him Q, S, P*
29 *Met.*] ~. *rising P*
99-100 owne; ... together;] ~, ~, *P*
110 I] *P*; (~ *Q, S*
111 (All] *P*; ˏ~ *Q, S*
180 transferd] transformed *Deighton conj.*; transfused *Deighton conj.*
193 To] You *P conj.*
201 armes] armies *P conj.*
209 SD *He ... bill.*] *P*; *om. Q, S*
212 SD *He ... draw.*] *P*; *after* Sir, *l. 213, Q*; *after* Ruffians, *l. 213, S*
213 *Sen.*] *P*; *Gen. Q, S*
221 Th'entry] The entry *S*
256 subiect'st] subject *S*
258 ingeniously] ingenuously *P*
291 Lords] Lord *S*
292-293 thunder./ My Lords,] *P*; ~ˏ/ ~ ~; *Q, S*
297 1 *Cons.*] ~ ~. *to* Caesar *P*
301 SD *Exeunt.*] *om. Q, S, P*

II.i

SD Scene I.] ~ ~. *Before the Walls of Rome P*
1 *Fro.*] *S, P*; *om. Q*
19 am knaue] ~ a ~ *S, P*
33 A] O *Pe*
45 no] ~, *Q, S, P*
50 command] commanding *P*; I ~ *P conj.*
75 SD *Aside.*] *P*; *om. Q, S*
79 were] was *S*
83 *Fro.*] *Gro. Pe*
161 though] Thou *Pe*

II.ii

II.ii] *P*; *om. Q, S*
11 frights] sights *P conj.*; fights *P conj.*; rites *P conj.*
12 encountring] encountering *S*
43 SD *Exit.*] *om. Q, S*; ~ Nuntius *P*

II.iii

II.iii] *P*; *om. Q, S*

SD II.iii] ~.~ *A Battlefield near Dyrrhachium P*
1-2 Stay cowherds ... foolish *Crassinius*] S; ~ cowherd ... ~ ~ Q; ~
    foolish cowards ... Crassinius P
5 *Acil.*] P; *om.* Q, S
23 had] I'd P *conj. (Anglia)*
39 Counsailes] counsels S; councils P
42 Counsaile] counsel S; council P
59-60 Was ... stay/ (Which ... blood)] P; (Was ... stay/ Which ... blood)
    Q, S
68 'boue] aboue S, P
73 SD *To Vibius.*] P; *om.* Q, S
105 suspection] suspect P *(Brereton conj.)*
111 were?] ~; P
    leader!] ~, S, P
112 Should] *Pe*, S, P; Sould Q
    all;] S; ~, Q; ~. P

II.iv

II.iv] P; *om.* Q, S
SD II.iv] ~.~ *The Camp of Pompey P*
54 Lose] P *(Deighton conj.)*; Lost Q, S
58 dispose.] ~. going P
77 SD *To Athenodorus.*] *after* selfe, *l.79*, P; *om.* Q, S
95 slendrest] slenderest S, P
104 ingenious] ingenuous P
120 *Iber.*] S, P; *Hib.* Q

II.v

II.v] P; *om.* Q, S
SD II.v] ~.~ *The Bank of the River Anius P*
1 *Cæs.*] P; *om.* Q, S
4 Ram] ram S, P
9 foure] sour *Deighton conj.*
22 Not] Nor S
44 fraight] straight S
45 SD *Exeunt.*] P; *om.* Q, S

III.i

SD Scene I.] ~ ~. *The Camp of* Pompey P
1 *Pom.*] S, P; *om.* Q
15 encreasd] P *(Brereton conj.)*; encrease Q, S
69 Were] P *conj.*; We Q, S
91 much.] Q(*u*), P; *om.* Q(*c*), S
94 *Brutus?*] Q(*u*), S, P; *Bru* Q(*c*)
95 *Amb. Cons.*] *Omn.* Q, S; *Both Consuls* P
97 sleight] Q(*u*), S, P; sleig Q(*c*)
98 Of] Or P *conj.*
138 crowne] P; crown'd Q, S

III.ii

III.ii] *P*; *om. Q, S*
SD III.ii] ~.~ *The Camp of* Cæsar *P*
12 threatning] threatening *S*
58 th'adiacent] the adjacent *Pe, S, P*
61 of] with *S, P*
76 any] *Pe, S, P*; an *Q*
84-85 in him ... farre] in him – great heaven, for all my foes,/ Being natural
     Romans! – so far *P*
90 *Ant.*] *Cnth. Pe*; *Crass. S*
95 not] nor *Loane conj.*
101 SD *To Anthony.*] *P*; *om. Q, S*
109 A] O *Pe*
117 fowles] sowles *Pe, S*
119 heartles,] *Q(c), S, P*; heartle *Q(u)*
127 blest] best *S*
138 SD *Exeunt.*] *P*; *om. Q, S*

IV.i

SD Scene I.] ~ ~. *The Camp of* Pompey *P*
1 *Pom.*] *S, P*; *om. Q*
20 ruder] rude *S*
49 lightning,] ~; *Q, S*; ~ˌ *P*
    desperat'st] desperatest *S*
52 Or] Not *Deighton conj.*
    enlarge] enlarged *Deighton conj.*

IV.ii

IV.ii] *P*; *om. Q, S*
SD IV.ii] ~.~ *The Battlefield of Pharsalia P*
7 *Thra.*] *P*; *Tra. Q, S*

IV.iii

IV.iii] *om. Q, S, P*
15 scroule] *P* (*Deighton conj.*); soule *Q, S*

IV.iv

IV.iv] Scene III *Another Part of the Battlefield P*; *om. Q, S*
34 you–] *P*; ~? *Q, S*
37 Which ... rectify (and] (~ ... ~, ~ *Q, S, P*
84 excepted] *S, P*; accepted *Q*
88-89 We ... fortunes/ And ... greatest,] And ... greatest,/ We ... fortunes
    Deighton conj.
90 Nor desire to be] ****** nor desire to be *P*

IV.v

IV.v] SCENE II *S*; SCENE IV *Another Part of the Field P*; *om. Q*

9 bloods] Q(c), S, P; blood Q(u)
14 slaine, yet,] ~, ~ˬ S; ~ˬ ~, P

IV.vi

IV.vi] SCENE III S; SCENE V *A Room in* Cato's *House in Utica* P; *om.* Q
15 SD *Cato*] *Enter* Cato P
39 Tongue, shew] Tongue-show *Deighton conj.*
40 To] The *Deighton conj.*
114 Retaine] Q(c); Retaines Q(u), S, P
123 their] this *Pe*
150 SD *Draws his sword.*] *om.* Q, S, P

V.i

SD Scene I.] ~ ~. *The Island of Lesbos, near the shore* P
SD *Sextus*] P; *Septimius* Q, S
SD *Sextus*] P; *Septimius* Q, S
6 full, true] P; ~. True Q, S
8 mou'd:] moved, S; mou'd. P
13 waking] *Pe*, S, P; making Q
42 SD *Sextus with a letter.*] Sextus *comes forward with a letter* P
      SD *Sextus*] P; *Septimius* Q, S
      Sex.] P; Sep. Q, S
51 Lost] Left P
57 SD *Enter a Sentinel, above.*] *Enter a Sentinel* P; *om.* Q, S
76 yet] that P
79 SD *Demetrius.*] Demetrius *disguised* P
83 SD *Offer*] They offer P
120 *Dem.*] Cor. *Pe*
      professe] possess S, P
162 SD *Reveals himself.*] Revealing himself P; *om.* Q, S
174 *Ioue* euer] *Ioue* hath euer *Brereton conj.*
200 farre,] P; ~; Q, S
215 peecemeale. And] ~, and P
216 ayre,] ~. P
246 SD *Achillas*] *Acilius* S
      SD *Septimius*] P; *Septius* Q, S
247 Ach.] Arch. *Pe*
251 Sex.] P; Sep. Q, S
255 SD *Septimius*] P; *Septius* Q, S
256 Nod] P; Pom. Nod Q, S
258 SD *They*] Q(c), S, P; *The* Q(u)
259 SD *Exeunt ... Ushers.*] P; *om.* Q, S
260 Sent.] Sex. P
261 Sex.] P; Sept. Q, S
267 Helpe] ~! S
268 Sex.] P; Sep. Q, S
      SD *Exeunt ... Pompey.*] Exeunt Murderers *with* Pompey P; *om.* Q, S

V.ii

V.ii] *P*; *om. Q, S*
SD V.ii] ~.~ *A Room in* Cato's *House in Utica P*
1 *Cat.*] *P*; *om. Q, S*
20 No] ~, *S*
46, 59, 161 SD *Butas*] *P*; *Brutus Q, S*
49 SD *Ent. Marcilius.*] *After* there, *l. 50, P*
52 freedome,] *S, P*; ~; *Q*
75 th'] the *S*
105 *Porcia*] *Q(c), S*; *Porcea Q(u)*; *Portia P*
111 vpright] *Q(c), S, P*; vbright *Q(u)*
122 indulgent] *Q(c), S, P*; iddulgent *Q(u)*
127 *Por.*] *Cor. Pe*; *Co. S*
    SD *To the others.*] *P*; *om. Q, S*
    SD *Manet Cato.*] *om. Q, S, P*
130 fit] let *P conj.*
151 lay] lay't *S*
173, 178 *But.*] *P*; *Bru. Q, S*
173 sound] found *S, P*
177 SD *Dies.*] *P*; *om. Q, S*
181 basted] blasted *Pe, S, P*
188 SD *Achillas*] *P*; *Achilius Q*; *Acilius S*
189 *All kneeling.*] *All three kneeling P*
196 Them with] With them with *P*; Bear them with *Brereton conj.*
200 SD *Hale them out.*] *After* torture, *l. 201, P*
    Omn. 3.] *P*; *Omn. Q, S*
224 SD *FINIS.*] *om. S*

PRESS-VARIANTS

[Copies collated: BL¹ (British Library C.30.e.6), BL² (British Library C.12.g.5(2)), BL³ (British Library Ashley 383), BL⁴ (British Library C.34.g.4), BL⁵ (British Library E714/17 (1653 reissue)), Bodl¹ (Bodleian Malone 241 (5)), Bodl² (Bodleian Malone 164(6)), CLUC (W. A. Clark Library, the University of California at Los Angeles), CSmH¹ (Huntington Library C4993 98544), CSmH² (Huntington Library C4992 98552), CtY¹ (Yale University 631), CtY² (Yale University 631b), CtYEC (Yale Elizabethan Club), DFo¹ (Folger Shakespeare Library 482), DFo² (Folger Shakespeare Library cs 163), DLC¹ (Library of Congress PR 2447), DLC² (Library of Congress, Longe Collection), Dyce¹ (Victoria and Albert Museum Dyce Collection 2051/26 Box 5.y), Dyce² (Victoria and Albert Museum Forster Collection), Dyce³ (Victoria and Albert Museum Lennard Bequest F.D. 15./17), Dyce⁴ (Victoria and Albert Museum Dyce Collection (1653 reissue)), Eton (Eton College), ICU (University of Chicago), IU (University of Illinois), MB (Boston Public Library), MH¹ (Harvard University 14424.13.13.2), MH² (Harvard University 14424.13.14), MH³ (Harvard University (1652 reissue)), MWiWc (Chapin Collection of Williams College), NLS (National Library of Scotland, wants K2), NN (New York Public Library), NPf (Carl H. Pforzheimer Library), Ph¹ (Petworth House Library, Sussex), Ph² (Petworth House Library, Sussex (wants inner forme of sheet D, D3 and D4ᵛ imperfectly printed)), PU (University of Pennsylvania), RDG (Reading University), RLS (Royal Library of Sweden), Soanes (Sir John Soanes Library, London (wants D1, D2, D3)), Taylor (private copy of Robert H. Taylor, Princeton, N.J.), TCC (Trinity College, Cambridge (1653 reissue, wants A3, A4)), TxU¹ (University of Texas 366/631wa), TxU² (University of Texas (1652 reissue, wants A3)), UTor (University of Toronto, wants A2), Worc¹ (Worcester College, Oxford 6.24.(3)), Worc² (Worcester College, Oxford 2.5.(2)). Though not strictly press variants, the variants in the resetting of H4 and the variants in the running titles in sheets H-K have been recorded.]

Sheet A (inner forme)

First State Corrected: BL⁵, Bodl¹, CSmH², CtY¹, Dyce⁴, MH², MH³, MWiWc, PH², Taylor, TCC, TxU²

Uncorrected: BL⁴, Dyce¹, UTor

Sig. A3ᵛ
  Epistle Dedicatory
  19 *old*] *such*
  Second State Corrected: BL¹, BL², BL³, Bodl², CLUC, CSmH¹, CtY²,

CtYEC, DFo¹, DFo², DLC¹, DLC², Dyce², Dyce³,
Eton, ICU, IU, MB, MH¹, NLS, NN, NPf, PH¹,
PU, RDG, RLS, Soanes, TxU¹, Worc¹, Worc²

Sig. A2

Title page CAESAR] The
ᴀɴᴅ] WARRES
POMPEY:] OF
A Roman Tragedy, de-] POMPEY and CAESAR.
claring their Warres.] Out of whofe euents is euicted this
Out of whofe euents is euicted this] Propofition.
Propofition.] *Only a iuft man is a freeman.*
Only a iuft man is a freeman.]

By GEORGE CHAPMAN.] By *G.C.*
(blank)] title-page ornament

Sheet B (outer forme)

Corrected: BL¹, BL², BL⁴, BL⁵, Bodl¹, Bodl², CLUC, CSmH², CtY¹,
CtYEC, DFo², DLC², Dyce¹, Dyce³, Dyce⁴, Eton, ICU, IU,
MB, MH¹, MH², MH³, MWiWc, NPf, PH¹, PH², PU, RDG,
RLS, Soanes, Taylor, TxU¹, TxU², UTor, Worc¹

Uncorrected: BL³, CSmH¹, CtY², DFo¹, DLC¹, Dyce², NLS, NN, TCC,
Worc²

Sig. B2ᵛ

I.i.88 face] faec

Sheet E (outer forme)

Corrected [*Pied*; *see Textual Note*, II.iv.39]: BL¹, BL³, BL⁵, CSmH², CtY²,
DFo², DLC¹, Dyce⁴, IU

Uncorrected: BL², BL⁴, Bodl¹, Bodl², CLUC, CSmH¹, CtY¹, CtYEC, DFo¹,
DLC², Dyce¹, Dyce², Dyce³, Eton, ICU, MB, MH¹, MH²,
MH³, MWiWc, NLS, NN, NPf, PH¹, PH², PU, RDG,
RLS, Soanes, Taylor, TCC, TxU¹, TxU², UTor, Worc¹,
Worc²

Sig. E1

II.iv.39 care] care,

Sheet F (outer forme)

Corrected [*Pied*; *see Textual Note*, II.iv.39]: BL², Bodl¹, CSmH², Dyce¹,
Dyce³, MWiWc, PH², TxU², UTor

Uncorrected: BL¹, BL³, BL⁴, BL⁵, Bodl², CLUC, CSmH¹, CtY¹, CtY²,
CtYEC, DFo¹, DFo², DLC¹, DLC², Dyce², Dyce⁴, Eton,
ICU, IU, MB, MH¹, MH², MH³, NLS, NN, NPf, PH¹, PU,
RDG, RLS, Soanes, Taylor, TCC, TxU¹, Worc¹, Worc²

Sig. F1

III.i.91 too] too much.
94 *Bru*] *Brutus?*

97 sleig] sleight

Sheet F (inner forme)

Corrected: BL¹, BL³, BL⁵, Bodl², CLUC, CSmH¹, CtY¹, CtY², CtYEC, DFo¹, DFo², DLC¹, Dyce¹, Dyce⁴, IU, MB, MH¹, MH³, NLS, NN, PH¹, Soanes, TCC, TxU¹, Worc¹, Worc²

Uncorrected: BL², BL⁴, Bodl¹, CSmH², DLC², Dyce², Dyce³, Eton, ICU, MH², MWiWc, NPf, PH², PU, RDG, RLS, Taylor, TxU², UTor

Sig. F3ᵛ

III.ii.119 heartles,] heartle

Sheet G (outer forme)

Corrected: BL¹, BL², BL³, BL⁴, BL⁵, Bodl¹, Bodl², CLUC, CSmH¹, CSmH², CtY¹, CtY², CtYEC, DFo¹, DFo², DLC¹, DLC², Dyce¹, Dyce², Dyce³, Dyce⁴, Eton, ICU, IU, MB, MH¹, MH³, MWiWc, NLS, NN, NPf, PH¹, PH², PU, RDG, RLS, Soanes, TCC, TxU¹, TxU², Worc¹, Worc²

Uncorrected: MH², Taylor, UTor

Sig. G3

IV.v.9 bloods] blood

Sheet H (outer forme)

Corrected: BL¹, BL³, BL⁴, BL⁵, Bodl¹, CSmH², CtY¹, CtY², CtYEC, DLC¹, Dyce¹, Dyce², Dyce³, Dyce⁴, ICU, MB, MH², MH³, MWiWc, NLS, NPf, PH¹, PH², PU, RDG, RLS, Taylor, TCC, TxU², UTor

Uncorrected: BL², Bodl², CLUC, CSmH¹, DFo¹, DFo², DLC², Eton, IU, MH¹, NN, Soanes, TxU¹, Worc¹, Worc²

Sig. H1 running title (*See Textual Introduction, p. 532*)

IV.vi.82 organs] orgens

Sig. H2ᵛ running title

Sig. H3 running title

Sig. H4ᵛ running title

Sheet H (inner forme)

First State Corrected (reset): BL⁴, Bodl¹, CSmH², CtY¹, Dyce¹, MH², MWiWc, PH², RDG, Taylor, UTor

Uncorrected: BL¹, BL², BL³, BL⁵, Bodl², CLUC, CSmH¹, CtY², CtYEC, DFo¹, DFo², DLC¹, DLC², Dyce², Dyce⁴, Eton, ICU, IU, MB, MH¹, MH³, NLS, NN, NPf, PH¹, PU, RLS, Soanes, TCC, TxU¹, Worc¹, Worc²

Sig. H2 running title (*See Textual Introduction, p. 532*)

Sig. H3ᵛ running title

Sig. H4 running title

V.i.114 Dem.] *D*em.

115 Cor.] *Cor.*
117 Would] would
     Sorrow] sorrow
118 comfort?] comfort?
119 Cor.] *Cor.*
120 Supose] Suppose
122 Cor.] *Cor.*
     I.] I
123 *Dem.*] *Dem.*
124 Cor.] *Cor.*
127 Cor.] *Cor.*
     wrong?] wrong?
128 *Dem.*] *Dem.*
129 Cor.] *Cor.*
     afflicted?] afflicted?
130 *Dem.*] *Dem.*
131 good,] good;
138 *Is*] Is
139 *I*] I
141 *If*] If
142 ill?] ill?
143 *Dem.*] *Dem.*
     Carpenters] Carpenters,
145 little,] little˷
146 meane.] meane,
149 Cor. *I*] *Cor.* I
150 I *Len.*] I *Lent.*
151 *Ill*] Ill
152 *Pom. I*] *Pom.* I
  Second State Corrected: Dyce³, TxU²
Sig. H1ᵛ
  IV.vi.115 retaine] retaines

Sheet I (outer forme)

First State Corrected [*Pied*; *see Textual Note*, II.iv.39]: BL¹, BL⁵, CSmH¹,
          DFo², DLC², MH³, NLS, NPf, RLS, TxU¹, Worc¹,
          Worc²
Uncorrected: BL², BL³, BL⁴, Bodl¹, Bodl², CLUC, CSmH², CtY¹, CtY²,
          CtYEC, DFo¹, DLC¹, Dyce¹, Dyce², Dyce³, Dyce⁴, Eton,
          ICU, IU, MB, MH¹, MH², MWiWc, NN, PH¹, PH²,
          RDG, Soanes, Taylor, TCC, TxU², UTor
Sig. I1
  V.i.198 moues] moues;
  Second State Corrected: PU
Sig. I2ᵛ running title (*See Textual Introduction, p. 532*)
Sig. I4ᵛ running title

Sheet I (inner forme)

First State Corrected: BL¹, BL², BL³, BL⁵, Bodl², CLUC, CSmH¹, CtY²,
CtYEC, DFo¹, DFo², DLC¹, DLC², Dyce², Dyce³,
Dyce⁴, Eton, ICU, IU, MB, MH¹, MH², MH³, NLS,
NN, NPf, PH¹, RDG, RLS, Soanes, Taylor,
TCC, TxU¹, TxU², Worc¹, Worc²

Uncorrected: BL⁴, Bodl¹, CSmH², CtY¹, Dyce¹, MWiWc, PH², UTor

Sig. I1ᵛ
  V.i.250 Sₑnds] Sends
Sig. I2
  V.i.258 SD *They*] *The*
      262 Countries loue,] Countres loue͜
Sig. I3ᵛ
  V.ii.86 men.] men˙
Sig. I4
  V.ii.105 *Porcia*] *Porcea*
      111 vpright] vbright
      122 indulgent] iddulgent
Second State Corrected: PU
Sig. I1ᵛ running title (*See Textual Introduction, p. 532*)
Sig. I2 running title
Sig. I3ᵛ running title

Sheet K (outer and inner formes)

First State Corrected: BL⁴, Bodl¹, CSmH², CtY¹, DFo², Dyce¹, MH²,
MWiWc, PH², UTor

Uncorrected: BL¹, BL², BL³, BL⁵, Bodl², CLUC, CSmH¹, CtY², CtYEC,
DFo¹, DLC¹, DLC², Dyce², Dyce³, Dyce⁴, Eton, ICU, IU,
MB, MH¹, MH³, NLS, NN, NPf, PH¹, RDG, RLS, Soanes,
Taylor, TCC, TxU¹, TxU², Worc¹, Worc²

Sig. K1 running title (*See Textual Introduction, p. 532*) (DFo¹, Soanes titles
  clipped)
Sig. K1ᵛ running title (DFo¹, Dyce⁴, Soanes titles clipped)
Sig. K2 running title (Dyce⁴, Worc² titles clipped; NLS wants K2)
Second State Corrected: PU
Sig. K1 running title (*See Textual Introduction, p. 532*)
Sig. K1ᵛ running title
Sig. K2 running title

TEXTUAL NOTES

Dedication

19 *old*] This is the reading of the corrected forme, and there is reason to believe it is authorial. Although '*such defects*' makes perfectly good sense, '*old defects*' frees Chapman from any blame in the present for defects of the past. See *Textual Introduction*, note 4.

I.i

15 For fall of his ill-disposed Purse] The reading of the quarto is satisfactory, though it is a syllable short of the pentameter line. To correct this deficiency, Brereton conjectured 'For fall of his so ill-disposed purse' and Parrott emended to 'For fallings of his ill-disposed purse'. Retaining Q's 'fall' adds another paradox to the many Cato utters in the play, Caesar's rise depending on his fall.

I.ii

20 *Cat.* Come in;/ *Cato drawes Minutius*] Brereton suggests emending the line to read '*Cato*, come in', assuming the compositor mistook Cato's name, as he is addressed by the Citizen, for a speech-prefix. J. E. Ingledew notes that the quarto line is satisfactory, following Plutarch in detail. For clarity, we emend the '*He*' of the following stage direction to '*Cato*', the '*him*' to '*Minutius*'.

213 *Sen.*] Q's '*Gen.*' is emended by Parrott, who notes that 'there is no character in the play to whom this abbreviation will apply' (*Tragedies*, p. 678). Assigning the speech to the Senators reveals their opposition to Caesar and their support for Pompey before the final speeches of the scene, when they openly side with Pompey against Caesar. Ingledew disagrees: 'It seems more likely that *Gen.* is the leader of Caesar's hirelings, echoing his order *Pull downe this Cato*, and addressing Cato. Moreover, there is no historical evidence that Caesar was armed, and he is unlikely to have offered violence himself with a gang of armed men hired for the purpose. This is reinforced by ll. 12-14 where he tells Metellus that he has *fellowes/ Will serue your will on him, at my giuen signall*' (p. 226). The stage direction begins after the speech to '*Gen.*' because there is no room for it in the preceding line. Further, there is no evidence that Caesar was unarmed; indeed, given his character and the situation at this point in the play, he should be armed. Finally, what is the 'giuen signall' of l. 14 but Caesar's drawing of his sword?

258 ingeniously] Parrott emends to 'ingenuously.' Citing an example from

Bussy D'Ambois, he states that the 'two are mere variants of the same word in Elizabethan English' (*Tragedies*, p. 565). This is clearly not the case, as the *NED* records examples of the two words being mistaken for each other in the sixteenth and seventeenth centuries. While the meaning here, and at II.iv.104, is 'ingenous,' we retain the Q reading in both instances. The confusion was most likely in Chapman's mind, not in the compositor's. Hooker and Shakespeare both use the words in this confused sense.

II.i

45 no spawne of a clot] The comma after 'no' in Q, accepted by Shepherd and Parrott, makes it appear that Ophioneus is addressing Fronto as a spawn of a clot. Rather, he is saying that he himself is 'no spawne of a clot', just as he is 'none of that cursed Crew'.

50 command the Elements] Retaining the Q reading over Parrott's 'commanding', though making the participle non-parallel with 'spurning', gives the advantage of leaving 'command' open either for an assumed 'I' (In spurning the power of the gods, I command the elements), which Parrott considers but rejects, or an assumed infinitive phrase (spurning the powers of the gods in order to command the elements).

86] ⸻ ⸻ ⸻] The first of several textual hiatuses, the three dashes in the quarto indicate Chapman's breaking off prose and beginning a section of verse. Presumably they reflect the copy behind the quarto, perhaps serving as a visual device to Chapman, reminding him to write a transitional half line when he revised the play.

II.iii

1-2 Stay ... *Crassinius*] That 'cowherds' is plural is borne out by the preceding stage direction and the use of 'ye,' almost always in this play a second person plural pronoun. Parrott's emendation, 'Stay foolish cowherds, ... Forbeare *Crassinius*', making the cowards, not Crassinius, foolish, is unnecessary. It is less foolish to be a coward than it is to attempt to stop the flight of cowards, as Crassinius is doing at the opening of this scene.

105 suspection] Parrott's emendation to 'suspect' is not necessary. According to *NED*, 'suspection' is an obsolete form of 'suspicion.'

112 Should] Q's 'Sould' is a perfectly acceptable northernism, according to *NED*, but as Chapman rarely uses this form and never uses it in this play, we take 'sould' to be a compositorial error.

II.iv

39 care,] The uncorrected state of Q retains the comma. The 'corrected' state omits it, or, rather, the comma has pied. Evidently the furniture surrounding the outer forme was loose or ill-fitting, especially around page E1. There is evidence of pied type again on sigs. F1 (III.i.91, 94, 97) and I1 (V.i.198). The running titles of the University of Pennsylvania copy for sheet I, also possessing a pied I1, reveal that 'moves;' is the uncorrected state, 'moves ' the pied or 'corrected' state.

54 Lose] Considering the lines that follow, Parrott's emendation to the imperative, conjectured by Deighton, seems valid. The e/t misreading is common. Perhaps the compositor thought the 'name' of l. 52 to refer not to 'honor'd peace' but to Caesar.

II.v

4 Ram] Q's reading leaves little doubt that the word in question is a noun. Shepherd's use of the lower-case 'r' suggests that 'ram' may be a verb, which it is not.

III.i

15 encreasd] The past tenses 'gather'd' and 'stemm'd' of l. 16 demand a past tense for encrease; the e/d misreading is not unusual.

69 Were] Parrott's conjecture has merit, and we have emended Q's 'We'; Parrott's gloss, '"We [i.e. Caesar and I] both came to an agreement in his free remission of my ransom"' (*Tragedies*, p. 670) shows the difficulty involved in trying to retain the Q reading. 'Were both concluded' emphasizes the power of Caesar's grace both in its 'value' and its 'disbursment'.

138 crowne] In this instance 'drowne' of l. 136 demands the same verb construction for 'crowne' (Parrott's emendation).

III.ii

95 not] Loane urges 'nor', seeing toils and sweats of blood as approximately the same. This emendation destroys the parallelism with the preceding line's 'with men, not hunger'.

IV.i

51-54 I beare ... crosse them.] The passage is difficult, and the Q reading has been retained. Deighton suggests replacing 'Or' and 'enlarge' of l. 52 with 'Not' and 'enlarged' respectively. Ingledew rejects Deighton's 'Not' but retains his 'enlarged'; at the same time Ingledew emends 'Selfe-liues' of l. 53 to 'Self-loues', noting that *NED* 'gives only one example of "self-life", where it has the meaning of "self-existence", clearly inappropriate here' (p. 229). Self-existence is appropriate here. Pompey asks two questions in these lines, then answers both. Shall I let men slander me by saying that I am afraid in order to save these people or to save myself? Should I enlarge the self-fortunes they have been seeking (IV.i.33-37) with twice as many of my lives, if I had two? No, they shall perish first.

IV.iii

IV.iii] Shepherd and Parrott treat this scene as a continuation of the preceding scene, which it clearly is not. For the most part the scenes in the play alternate between Caesar and Pompey or between Caesar and Cato. After IV.ii, a scene dealing with Pompey's defeat, Chapman shifts to Caesar and the dead Crassinius, only to return in IV.iv to Pompey and Demetrius.

15 scroule] Parrott's emendation of Q's 'soule', based on Deighton's conjecture, 'makes sense of an otherwise unintelligible passage' (*Tragedies*, p. 679).

IV.iv

34 you—] Parrott's emendation; the dash following 'you' indicates that Pompey interrupts Demetrius's speech in the following line. Q's question mark need not be read as interrogative but rather as exclamatory; perhaps Chapman indicated the speech break with a dash, which the compositor misread as a question mark.

37-38 Which they might rectify (and should; because/ That man maintain'd the right)] Placing the parentheses around 'and ... right' restores the meaning, the gods suffering (allowing) wrong to be insolent, even when they might rectify it.

84 excepted] Along with II.iii.1-2, this provides evidence that the compositor was setting several lines at a time. Here he retained the sound (accepted) but made a common homonymic error.

90 Nor desire to be] This provides additional evidence, along with II.i.86, of the nature of the copy, Chapman failing to revise the text and complete the line.

IV.vi

114 Retaine] The corrected state is found in only two of the extant quartos. Parrott, not knowing the corrected state, explains 'Retaines', the uncorrected state, as 'the so-called northern plural, agreeing with its subject *parts*' (*Tragedies*, p. 673).

V.i

SD *Sextus*] The compositor obviously misread Chapman's abbreviation 'Se.' for Septimius. Parrott makes the emendation to '*Sextus*', noting that 'it is not at all likely that such a scholar as Chapman confused Sextus Pompey with Septimius the murderer' (*Tragedies*, p. 680).

51 Lost] Parrott's emendation to 'Left' is unnecessary. The letters need not be broken off, as Parrott maintains. Rather, the letters telling of the final victory were lost in the turmoil of the skirmish.

76 yet] Parrott's emendation to 'that' is based on an assumption that the compositor misread the 'yᵗ' abbreviation as 'yet'. In the preceding line one of the Lentuli has asked two questions. The sentinel answers the second question first, the first second.

215 peecemeale. And] Parrott's emendation to 'peecemeale, and' makes it appear that the false society of men not only batters all reason piecemeal but rarifies all heavenly comforts to air; this is not the case.

246 SD *Septimius*] Again, as at the beginning of the act, the compositor has misread Chapman's abbreviation.

V.ii

46 SD *Butas*] This is the first appearance of Butas. The compositor, either through an oversight or from misreading Chapman's abbreviation, set '*Brutus*'.

173 sound] Parrott follows Shepherd's misreading of Q and prints 'found'. In none of the copies collated does the horizontal bar on the 's' cross the vertical bar and make the letter appear like an 'f'. The 'vnperisht' nature of the entrails (l. 175) affirms the reading 'sound'.

181 basted] The emendation in Pearson to 'blasted' is followed by Shepherd and Parrott. Ingledew notes that 'the verb "baste", meaning "to beat thoroughly, get the better of", fits the sense here' (p. 232).

188 SD *Achillas*] The compositor, thinking of Acilius, who entered at l. 178, set '*Achilius*', a combination of both names.

196 Them with] Parrott's emendation is unnecessary. Philosophically or morally, Caesar is tortured by the instant rapture the thought of Pompey's death brings him, aware that such instant rapture will soon pass and that Pompey's death will bring remorse to Rome politically and to him personally. Lines 196-197 make it clear that Achillas, Septimius, and Salvius will be physically tortured for the (impending) mental torture they inflict on Caesar by bringing him Pompey's head. Ingledew's emendation, dropping the 'to' of l. 195, is also unnecessary (p. 232).

The Tragedie
of
Chabot Admirall of France

edited by G. Blakemore Evans

❧

TEXTUAL INTRODUCTION

The Tragedie of Chabot Admirall of France has survived in a single quarto edition (= Q) printed by Thomas Cotes for Andrew Crooke and William Cooke in 1639. Together with a comedy called *The Ball*, it was entered, without any reference to George Chapman, on the *Stationers' Register* 24 October 1638 to Crooke and Cooke under the hands of Wikes and Rothwell:

> Entred for their Copie vnder the hands of Master Wykes
> and Master Rothwell warden a Booke called PHILLIP
> CHALBOTT Admirall of Ffrance and *the Ball.* by James
> Shirley ... vj^d.[1]

W. W. Greg in his *Bibliography of the English Printed Drama to the Restoration* (II [London, 1951], no. 550) offers a full descriptive collation of Q, recording the missigning of sig. A3 as B3 and the loss of 'e' in the catchword 'He' on A4^v in most copies, but fails to note the absence of a catchword on H2 in all copies.

Chapman's name, preceding that of James Shirley, appears on the title page,[2] and there is no question that the main hand in the play is his. There is also no question that Shirley's hand may be detected sporadically throughout the play as it appears in Q, but the extent of his involvement is impossible to determine with any exactness. Aside from these 'verities,' which would include the entry on the *Register*, only two other facts are incontrovertible:

---

[1] *A Transcript of the Registers of the Company of Stationers of London; 1554-1640*, ed. Edward Arber, IV (London, 1877), 415.
[2] As Greg (*Bibliography*) points out, the title page of *Chabot* employs the same setting of type, apart from the titles of the two plays, as the title page of *The Ball*, the play entered with *Chabot* on the *Stationers' Register*. The arrangement of the material for *The Ball* suggests to me that the *Chabot* title page is the earlier.

(1) *Chabot* cannot have been composed in any form before 1611, the year in which the play's principal source, the enlarged edition of Etienne Pasquier's *Les Recherches de la France*, was published (another edition, 1621);[3] (2) the play, as represented in Q, was licensed by Sir Henry Herbert, Master of the Revels, on 29 April 1635.[4] Otherwise, we are faced with a mountain of speculation and conjecture. When was *Chabot* originally composed and for what occasion (if any)? Was it from the first a joint work by Chapman and Shirley? Or does the Q text represent a later revision by Chapman and Shirley or by Shirley alone? If there was such a revision, when was it undertaken? These questions have received widely different answers from both editors and critics and none of the proposed answers offers more than a hypothetical solution.

Suggested dates for the original composition of *Chabot* vary between 1611-12, 1612-13, 1621-24, most recent opinion favoring a date between 1611 and 1613, a period that neatly links *Chabot* with Chapman's interest in French history and, particularly, with the Byron plays (1607-8) and *The Revenge of Bussy D'Ambois* (1610-11). The much later date of 1621-24 was advanced by Mrs Norma Dobie Solve,[5] who interpreted *Chabot* as a kind of political allegory, written by Chapman in an attempt to effect the release of his patron the Earl of Somerset from his imprisonment in the Tower, where he had been held prisoner ever since his indictment and conviction in 1616 for alleged complicity in the notorious murder of Sir Thomas Overbury. According to Mrs Solve's scenario, then, Somerset was portrayed as Chabot; Villiers, by then Duke of Buckingham, who, as the new favorite, had replaced Somerset in King James's affection, as the Constable (Montmorency); King James as the King (Francis I); Francis Bacon, who, conniving with James, had played a major role in the conviction of Somerset and who, after becoming Lord Chancellor in 1618, was himself tried and condemned for bribery in 1621, as the Chancellor; Sir Edward Coke, the Lord Chief Justice, who like Bacon had been a central figure in Somerset's trial, as the Proctor General (or Advocate); Sir Ralph Winwood as the Treasurer; and Sir Henry Montagu as the Secretary.

Mrs Solve's case for dating was accepted by T. M. Parrott, who had earlier[6] proposed 1612-13, though he narrowed the date to 1621-22 on the grounds that Somerset, though not finally pardoned until 1624, had been released from the Tower in January of 1622, a date that stood firm (accepted by G. E. Bentley)[7] until 1960, when Irving Ribner[8] reverted to Parrott's original date (1612-13)[9] and suggested that a Chapman/Shirley revision, adapting the

---

[3] A few copies of the 1611 *Recherches* carry a 1610 date on the title page.
[4] *The Dramatic Records of Sir Henry Herbert*, ed. J. Q. Adams (New Haven, 1917), p. 36.
[5] *Stuart Politics in Chapman's 'Tragedy of Chabot'* (Ann Arbor, Michigan, 1928).
[6] *The Plays and Poems of George Chapman: The Tragedies* (London, 1910), p. 633. Parrott accepted Mrs Solve's dating, with the noted narrowing, in his review of her monograph in *JEGP*, XXIX (1930), 300-304.
[7] *The Jacobean and Caroline Stage*, V (Oxford, 1956), 1088-91.
[8] 'The Meaning of Chapman's *Tragedy of Chabot*,' *MLR*, LV (1960), 321-31. The substance of the article is essentially repeated in Ribner's *Jacobean Tragedy: The Quest for Moral Order* (New York, 1962).
[9] Ribner silently alters the proposed date to 1614 in his *Jacobean Tragedy*.

play to comment on the Somerset/Bacon relationship, was made some time after 1621, the year of Bacon's trial and conviction. In 1965, Thelma Herring,[10] taking strong issue with Ribner's interpretation of *Chabot* as 'a tragic study of the pride and delusion of fallen man' (p. 171), a Christian allegory, suggests that Chapman, with the Somerset/Villiers parallel in mind, composed, or began to compose, the play at some time during the second half of his Hitchin retreat (1614-19), during which time he was in danger of being arrested for debt,[11] that he later, after 1621, revised it with the Bacon trial as an incentive, and that Shirley only entered the picture at some point after 1630-34. Most recently, the case for dating has been examined by A. H. Tricomi.[12] He supports Parrott's original early date, though preferring 1611-12 on the evidence that all but one (1613) of the verbal echoes between *Chabot* and other Chapman works cluster around those years – as he admits a circumstantial argument[13] – and dismisses Mrs Solve's argument for a political allegory on the grounds of 'her extreme selectivity and occasional misconstruction of the historical details chosen to support the thesis' (p. 261). Although Tricomi points out a number of real difficulties in Mrs Solve's presentation of the historical evidence,[14] he does not convince me that there is nothing to her case, particularly if we do not accept as complete a character for character identification as she argues for. Of the several views advanced,

---

[10] 'Chapman and an Aspect of Modern Criticism,' *Renaissance Drama*, ed. S. Schoenbaum, VIII (1965), 167-79.

[11] C. J. Sisson and Robert Butman, 'George Chapman, 1612-22: Some New Facts,' *MLR*, XLVI (1951), 185-90.

[12] 'The Dates of the Plays of George Chapman,' *English Literary Renaissance*, XII (1982), 261-64.

[13] The danger inherent in this kind of argument, particularly when applied to an allusively repetitive poet like Chapman, apart from the instance in *Eugenia* (1613), which Tricomi notes, is further shown by a hitherto unnoticed close parallel between *Chabot* (IV.i.425-29) and (a) a passage in Chapman's Dedicatory Epistle to the first twelve books of his *Odysses* addressed to Somerset and written late in 1614: 'And as we see / The Sunne, all hid in clouds, at length got free, / Through some forc't couert, over all the wayes / Neare and beneath him, shootes his vented rays / Farre off and stickes them in some little Glade, / All woods, fields, rivers left besides in shade:' (*Chapman's Homer*, ed. Allardyce Nicoll, 1956, II, 7); and (b) another passage in Chapman's Dedication of his *Georgicks of Hesiod* to Francis Bacon written in 1618: '. . . no Lustre being so Sun like, as that which passeth aboue al clouds vnseen, ouer Fields, Turrets, & Temples; and breaks out, in free beams, on some humblest Cotage' (sig. A3). The passage in *Chabot* is obviously closer verbally to the second and later of these parallels, but it would be dangerous to infer that the *Chabot* passage is therefore later than passage (a), though admittedly tempting. Another slighter parallel with *Chabot* (II.iii.138) also occurs in the 1618 Bacon dedication: 'Nor were those *Greeks* so circular in their elegant vtterance, but their inward Iudgements and learnings, were as round and solid' (sig. A2'), and an 'echo' of *Chabot* (II.iii.154) may perhaps be recognized in Chapman's Dedication to Somerset of *The Hymns of Homer* (1624; ll. 19-20): 'Nor virtue shines more in a louely Face; / Then true desert, is stuck off with Disgrace.'

[14] One point in Tricomi's argument against associating Chabot with Somerset is certainly mistaken (p. 263). It is not Chabot who in V.iii.129-31 is appointed as the King's Secretary; it is Allegre, Chabot's faithful servant. In arguing for an early date, Tricomi also fails to note that one of the arguments against a 1621-22 date (that 'Chapman's dramatic activity appears to have come to an end after the first decade of the Jacobean period' [p. 265]) is no longer tenable. William Wells (*N & Q*, CLIV [1928], 6-9) and D. J. Jump, in his edition of *Rollo Duke of Normandy* (London, 1948), a play written between 1622 and 1624, establish Chapman's hand in three stretches of the text (III.i.1-263, 331-420; IV.iii), an ascription strongly endorsed by Cyrus Hoy ('The Shares of Fletcher and His Collaborators in the Beaumont and Fletcher Canon (VI),' *SB*, XIV [1961], 62-63).

Miss Herring's reconstruction of the order of events seems to me the most persuasive: (1) the first draft of the play in finished or partially finished form perhaps around 1616 when the Somerset affair was reaching its crisis; (2) a revision by Chapman shortly after May of 1621 to take advantage of the trial and disgrace of Bacon;[15] (3) a second revision of (2) some ten or more years later by Shirley to make the play more appealing to a Caroline audience.

Parrott, on the basis of an early date of 1612-13, offers a neatly argued provenance which explains how Chapman's manuscript finally came to Shirley's attention. He suggests that the play was originally written for the Queen's Revels, the children's company which had acted Chapman's earlier plays and which was amalgamated at just about this time (1612-13) with the Lady Elizabeth's company, the personal link being the actor Nathan Field, a friend of Chapman's, who, in the new alignment, became the manager and leading actor of the Lady Elizabeth's company. The manuscript then would have remained in the archives of the Lady Elizabeth's company, which in 1625 became known as Her Majesty's Servants, the same company, as the title page of Q indicates, that performed a revised version of *Chabot* at some time shortly after it had been licensed by Sir Henry Herbert, Master of the Revels, on 29 April 1635. A slight readjustment of Parrott's argument will bring it into line with Miss Herring's proposed order of events. If Chapman began or completed a play on the Chabot story some time before 1621-22, or first composed the play in 1621-22, as Mrs Solve suggests, it would in either case have been only natural for him to offer it to the Lady Elizabeth's company with which, earlier, he had been so closely associated. It is true that his friend Field left that company to join the King's Men around 1616, but if we are willing to accept the play's political thrust, particularly the quite damaging portrait it offers of King James, any possibility of production by the King's Men, even with Field there to promote it, would surely have been out of the question. On the whole, moreover, it seems to me likely that *Chabot* was never either completed (if begun) or offered to a company for production until 1621-22,[16] by which time Field was dead. From 1614 to 1619 Chapman's position was very precarious as a wanted debtor and he had already had brushes with the authorities over *Eastward Ho!* and the Byron plays, not to mention the very unfavorable criticism his fulsome poem, *Andromeda Liberata* (1614), celebrating the marriage of Somerset and the former Lady Essex, had incurred. Even by 1621-22 it would have been a daring attempt. It was one thing to dedicate to Somerset the *Odysses* (1614-16), the *Pro Vere* (1622), and the *Hymnes of Homer* (1624, just before Somerset's pardon), quite another thing to try to influence public opinion

---

[15] It should be noticed, of course, that a scene of the Chancellor's trial was almost certainly a part of the play even if written before 1621, since Pasquier reports Poyet's trial, conducted by the same judges who had earlier under Poyet's threats condemned Chabot.

[16] The dedication of his translation of *The Georgicks of Hesiod* to Bacon in 1618, 'a bid for favor' as Mrs Solve (p. 30) describes it, would perhaps have been unlikely had Chapman recently been trying to offer *Chabot* for actual production. In any event, it is only fair to point out that, given Chapman's unflagging support of Somerset (see below), this dedication may be considered as a point against any identification with Bacon in the character of the Chancellor, at least before 1621-22.

through a play. That there is no record of any performance of *Chabot* at this time or earlier is scarcely surprising.

At exactly what point James Shirley entered the picture is not known. He wrote his first play in 1624/5 for the Lady Elizabeth's company and continued to write almost exclusively for that company, after it became Her Majesty's Servants, until 1636. Most agree that any collaboration between Chapman and Shirley in the earlier 1620s is simply unthinkable. The most likely supposition is that he revised Chapman's play just shortly before it was licensed in April of 1635. If so, it seems unlikely that Chapman, who died 12 May 1634, had any part in the revision. Supporting a 1635 date, as Parrott has noticed, are some interesting echoes of *Chabot* in Shirley's *The Duke's Mistress*, which was licensed 18 January 1635/6. He also suggests, however, that Rogero's mock indictment of Depazzi in Shirley's *The Traitor* (licensed 4 May 1631), III.i, is an imitation of the Proctor-General's (Advocate's) speeches in *Chabot* III.ii and V.ii, which would seem to indicate a knowledge of Chapman's manuscript four or five years earlier.[17] Possibly so, but evidence of Chapman's influence is limited essentially to a similarity in situation and may be nothing more than coincidence. In any case, it only means that Shirley may have glanced through *Chabot* some years before he revised it and does not prove any personal relationship between Shirley and Chapman at that time. At any rate, by the early 1630s the presumed official objections to the political implications of the play that could have been raised ten or more years earlier would presumably have been largely forgotten, especially since all the principals supposedly shadowed there were dead: Villiers/Buckingham (assassinated 1628), King James (1625), Bacon (1626), Coke (1634) – only Somerset, the one person who might not have found the play offensive, was ironically still alive. Like the date or dates of Chapman's own involvement with the story of Chabot, the date of Shirley's revision must remain hypothetical.

There is general agreement that *Chabot* even in its revised form is basically the work of Chapman. His philosophical emphasis, characteristic vocabulary, and tortuously involved syntax are apparent in almost every scene. Parrott's analysis of Shirley's part in the revision, though challenged on details,[18] is, I believe, essentially correct and has received support from Cyrus Hoy's comparative study of Chapman's and Shirley's use of a variety of contracted forms.[19] Chapman uses such forms very rarely in writing tragedy (freely in his comedies); Shirley, on the other hand, makes extensive use of contracted forms throughout his work. A study of the contractions in the play shows that they fall most heavily in those parts where Parrott thinks Shirley's hand to be most clearly marked. Parrott's most controversial statement is his suggestion that the characters of the Queen and Chabot's Wife were 'entirely composed, or greatly enlarged, by Shirley to add a feminine interest' (p. 641).

[17] Parrott, p. 463.
[18] Robert S. Forsythe, *The Relations of Shirley's Plays to the Elizabethan Drama* (New York, 1914), pp. 417-19.
[19] 'The Shares of Fletcher and His Collaborators in the Beaumont and Fletcher Canon (VI),' *SB*, XIV (1961), 61-63; 'The Shares of Fletcher and His Collaborators in the Beaumont and Fletcher Canon (IV),' *SB*, XII (1959), 109-10.

He thus sees II.i (wholly) and III.i (almost wholly) as Shirley's, both scenes connected with the Queen's jealousy of Chabot's Wife's position, the second showing the sudden change of heart through which she becomes Chabot's defender. As we shall see, there is internal evidence for thinking that the Queen's role has been 'fattened,' but that Shirley invented either character, especially that of Chabot's Wife, is now considered questionable. Parrott also finds Shirley's hand strongly marked in IV.i (first 120 lines), V.i (revised by Shirley, lines 39-81 wholly his), and V.iii (a substratum of Chapman heavily overlaid by Shirley). Chapman's hand is most clearly evident he thinks in I.i (almost pure Chapman), I.ii (mostly Chapman, but with touches of Shirley), II.ii (essentially Chapman, with some Shirley, particularly in the first ten lines), II.iii (essentially Chapman, with perhaps some cutting by Shirley), III.ii (almost wholly Chapman), and V.ii (mainly, if not completely, Chapman).

Three apparent dislocations in the text may be seen as evidence of revision. Two of them are concerned with the role of the Queen. In IV.i and V.i the answer to a speech by the Queen (IV.i.31-35; V.i.11-15) is clearly directed to the Constable, suggesting that speeches originally belonging to the Constable have been reassigned.[20] The third, in III.ii, is more serious and may have resulted either from accidental misplacement of a sheet of the printer's manuscript copy[21] or from an attempt by Shirley to break up the Proctor-General's very long prose speech (here ll. 89-143), which, in turn, produced a similar, and obviously incorrect, division of Chabot's defense (ll. 168-209 in the present text; the break in Q coming at l. 197). The textual dislocation in Chabot's defense was first pointed out by G. C. Macaulay in his review of Parrott's edition,[22] but the correct disposition of lines 116-143 we owe to A. S. Ferguson.[23] The Macaulay/Ferguson order is here followed.

The precise nature of the copy behind Q is uncertain. Nothing in Q supports a theatre or prompt-book provenance, nor is there any significant indication (from characteristic Chapman spellings) that the manuscript was partly in Chapman's autograph.[24] Considering the amount of Shirley's presumed revision, this last is not surprising. The most likely source for the copy, therefore, would seem to be a transcript made from Chapman's manuscript ('foul papers' or 'fair copy') after it had been worked over by Shirley (? and Chapman). If Shirley himself made such a transcript, it would help to explain the intrusion, *currente calamo*, of some Shirleian contractions in sections of the text that otherwise appear to carry the strong mark of Chapman's hand.

Thomas Cotes's printing establishment seems to have exercised little care in producing Q. Some but not very much press-correction was done, but nothing that necessarily suggests consultation of copy by the proof-corrector,

---

[20] See the Textual Notes.
[21] A. S. Ferguson, 'Chapman, *The Tragedy of Chabot*, Act III, Sc. ii, ll. 147-68,' *MLR*, XXIII (1928), 46.
[22] *MLR*, VI (1911), 256.
[23] See note 20 above.
[24] See, however, the Textual Note on II.iii.207.

while a number of obvious errors were allowed to pass unnoticed. Moreover, the quality of the press-work was careless, raised quads and spaces frequently being permitted to leave ugly traces between words and at the beginning and end of lines. It is difficult to determine whether one or more compositors were responsible for setting the text. Charles Pennel[25] believes that Q was set seriatim by two compositors: Compositor A, sheets A and B; Compositor B, sheets D through I. He is uncertain about sheet C. Unfortunately, the only distinguishing evidence for Compositors A and B lies in the variant use of the speech-prefix *Kin.* (Compositor A) and *King.* (Compositor B); spelling tests or idiosyncratic handling of stage directions and punctuation yield nothing that may serve as a further guide in separating Compositor A from B. It must, moreover, be observed that the distribution of the *Kin./King.* speech-prefixes is not entirely consistent. Only in sheets D and F through I is *King.* used throughout. In sheets A and B, where Compositor A is supposed to favor *Kin.*, *King.* occurs once in each (A4, B4ᵛ); in sheet C, where Compositor B is supposed to favor *King.*, *Kin.* occurs three times (C2, C3ᵛ [twice]); and in sheet E *Kin.* appears once (E4ᵛ) and *King.* not at all, which might be interpreted to mean that Compositor A set signature E. It may further be noticed that in I.i the King's first speech immediately following his entry (at l. 116, A3ᵛ) is assigned to *Kin.* and that in three later cases *Kin.* is the form employed at the beginning of a new scene (II.i, B4; II.iii, C2; IV.i, E4ᵛ), the last two supposedly in work by Compositor B. From this it may be inferred, I think, that the manuscript copy favored *Kin.* On the other hand, the *Kin. /King.* variation in Q may simply reflect a similar variation in the use of this speech-prefix in the copy itself without any necessary reference to compositorial preference. Thus, though Pennel may be correct in postulating two compositors with extraordinarily similar spelling habits who are otherwise distinguished by *Kin.* or *King.*, the nature of the evidence for two compositors seems to me at best ambiguous and I lean to the view that a single compositor set the whole of Q. One other piece of evidence may, perhaps, help to support the presence of a single compositor. So far as I am competent to judge, Q was set from a single case of type. This is suggested in part by the frequent appearance on virtually every page of a form of 'e' with a short bar above it (i.e. 'ē', the bar being the English form of the tilde). The two forms ('e' and 'ē') are mixed indiscriminately and 'ē' is never employed, even in prose, to perform its recognized function (indicating the omission of a following 'm' or 'n').[26] Since the 'tilde' in 'ē' sometimes prints comparatively clearly and sometimes very faintly,[27] one may suspect that some attempt has

[25] Professor Pennel has kindly allowed me to make use of an unpublished modern-spelling edition of *Chabot* which he prepared some years ago.

[26] The same mixture of 'e' and 'ē' occurs in *The Ball*, the play that was entered on the *Stationers' Register* in company with *Chabot* (see above, p. 617). See note 2, above, for another printing house connection between the two plays. The same type-case was employed by Thomas Cotes in John Fletcher's *Wit without Money* (1639).

[27] Occasionally the 'ē' form seems to occur without the 'tilde' in some copies. It is possible that a few of these represent stop-press variants, but I think it more likely that most such cases arise from type-settling or weak impressions of individual sheets. No examples are included in the List of Press-Variants.

been made to file the 'tilde' down in order to increase the supply of regular 'e's. While it is, of course, possible that Cotes had more than one type-case furnished with this unusual mixture of 'e' sorts, it may, I believe, be considered at least unlikely. The present text makes no attempt to preserve the distinction between 'e' and 'ē'.

Q employs two skeleton formes (I and II) for the headlines (i.e. '*The Admirall of France.*', used throughout, except for A4ᵛ and B4ᵛ, which read '*The French Admirall.*'). Skeleton I imposed formes A-outer (three headlines), B-outer (fourth headline added), C-inner, C-outer (with one headline reset ['*The French Admirall.*' changed to '*The Admirall of France.*']), D-inner, E-outer, F-inner, G-inner, H-inner, and I-inner (three headlines). Skeleton II imposed formes A-inner (two headlines), B-inner (third and fourth headlines added, those from A-outer being turned: the headline from A3ᵛ used for B1ᵛ, that for A4 for B2), D-outer, E-inner, F-outer, G-outer, H-outer, and I-outer (three headlines). The pattern here emerging appears to be consistent with seriatim composition and the use of either one or two presses.[28] Several headlines seem to have been loosely locked in the chase, that on E2 gradually dividing in the middle in the course of printing off, while some headlines (on B2, E3ᵛ, E4, G1, G3, H1, I1) show slight variation in some copies in their positioning relative to the text below, variations that do not appear to have any necessary correlation to proof-correction.

Aside from the confused arrangement of the Proctor-General's and Chabot's speeches in III.ii (discussed above), a number of obvious compositorial misreadings, and rather chaotic punctuation, Q affords an adequate text, one that probably reproduces the manuscript copy with some competence. Entrances are usually carefully observed, sometimes with considerable descriptive detail; exits (and some re-entries) less so. This is what we might expect in a text printed from a manuscript without stage provenance. Speeches are accurately distributed, except at V.iii.210, where the Queen is given the concluding lines which clearly and properly belong to the King, an error that may, I think, be attributed to an error in the copy. In any case, it seems impossible to associate this error with revision and the two cases discussed earlier (IV.i.31-35; V.i.11-15), where speeches by the Queen would appear originally to have belonged to the Constable. The form of the speech-prefixes is unusually consistent, with two exceptions, *Kin.* and *King.* (already discussed) and *Pro.* (i.e. Proctor-General) in II.ii and *Adv.* (i.e. Advocate) in IV.i and V.ii, two distinct forms for the same character, which, in expanded forms, also occur in the stage directions in these scenes. In line with editorial policy in normalizing speech-prefixes (except for *Asall.* at I.i.1), *King.* has been adopted throughout, but the variant *Pro.* and *Adv.* speech-prefixes have been retained, since they may have some bearing on the problem of revision, either Chapman's postulated earlier revision or Shirley's later revision.

Q offers a special problem in punctuation. The comma is used throughout

---

[28] I am especially grateful to Professor John H. Smith for material help in analyzing the Q headlines, as also for his kindness in checking errors in Ezra Lehman's reprint (1906) of a copy of Q (822.C37t) in the University of Pennsylvania Library.

with wild abandon and can often lead to misreading, particularly when Chapman's tortuous syntax is involved. I have, therefore, felt forced to emend the punctuation rather more frequently than our editorial policy ordinarily allows.

A list of the earlier edited texts of *Chabot* which have been collated or consulted for the present edition may be found in the head-note to the Historical Collation.

THE
TRAGEDIE
OF
CHABOT
ADMIRALL OF
FRANCE:

As it vvas prefented by her
Majefties Servants, at the private
Houfe in *Drury* Lane.

✠✠✠✠✠✠✠✠✠✠✠✠✠✠✠✠✠✠✠✠✠✠✠✠✠✠✠✠✠✠✠✠✠✠✠✠

Written by ⟨ *George Chapman,*
and
James Shirly. ⟩

✠✠✠✠✠✠✠✠✠✠✠✠✠✠✠✠✠✠✠✠✠✠✠✠✠✠✠✠✠✠✠✠✠✠✠✠

LONDON,
Printed by *Tho. Cotes,* for *Andrew Crooke,*
and *William Cooke.*
1639.

Asall [a gentleman in waiting].
Allegre [a servant of the Admiral].
King [Francis I, King of France].
Queene [wife of Francis I].
Treasuror
Chancellor [Guillaume Poyet].
Admirall [Philip Chabot, Admiral of France].
Father [Father-in-law of the Admiral].
[*Wife* of the Admiral].
[*Proctor-*] *Generall* [or *Advocate*].
Iudges [First and Second].
Officers.
Secretary.
Vshers.
Constable [Montmorency, Lord High Constable of France].
Courtiers.
Porter.
[*Captain of the*] *Guard.*
[*Notary.*]
[*Petitioners.*]

---

1 *Asall*] *See Textual Note for comments on the list of* 'Speakers.'

THE TRAGEDIE OF PHILIP CHABOT, [A2]
ADMIRALL of FRANCE.

Actus Primus.   [Scena I.]

Enter Asall, and Allegre.

Asall. Now *Phillip Chabot*, Admirall of *France*,
The great, and onely famous Favorite
To *Francis* first of that Imperiall name,
Hath found a fresh competitor in glory
(Duke *Montmorancie*, Constable of *France*),   5
Who drinkes as deepe as he of the streame Royall,
And may in little time convert the strength
To raise his spring, and blow the others fall.
   Al. The world would wish it so, that will not patiently
Endure the due rise of a vertuous man.   10
   As. If he be vertuous, what is the reason
That men affect him not, why is he lost /
Toth'generall opinion, and become   [A2ᵛ]
Rather their hate than love?
   Al.   I wonder you
Will question it, aske a ground or reason   15
Of men bred in this vile degenerate age;
The most men are not good, and it agrees not
With impious natures to allow what's honest;
Tis an offence enough to be exalted
To regall favours; great men are not safe   20
In their owne vice, where good men by the hand
Of Kings are planted to survey their workings;
What man was ever fixt ith'Sphere of honour,
And precious to his Soveraigne, whose actions,
Nay very soule was not expos'd to every   25
Common and base dissection? and not onely

Scena I.] *Parrott (after Dyce)* ‖ 4-5 glory … *France*),] ~, … ~)ˏ ‖ 18 what's] whats | honest;]
~, ‖ 20 favours;] ~, ‖ 23 ith'] 'ith ‖

That which in Nature hath excuse, and in
Themselves is priviledg'd by name of frailtie,
But even Vertues are made crimes, and doom'd
Toth'fate of Treason.
    As.   A bad age the while.   30
I aske your pardon Sir, but thinkes your judgement,
His love to Justice, and Corruptions hate
Are true and hearty?
    Al.   Iudge your selfe by this
One argument, his hearty truth to all,
For in the heart hath anger his wisest seate,   35
And gainst unjust suites such brave anger fires him,
That when they seeke to passe his place and power,
Though mov'd, and urg'd by the other minion,
Or by his greatest friends, and even the King
Leade them to his allowance with his hand,   40
First given in Bill, assign'd, even then his spirit
(In nature calme as any Summers evening),
Puts up his Whole powers like a Winters sea,
His bloud boyles over, and his heart even cracks
At the injustice, and he teares the Bill,   45
And would doe, were he for't to be torne in peeces.
    As. Tis brave I sweare. /
    Al.   Nay it is worthy your wonder,   [A3]
That I must tell you further, there's no Needle
In a Sunne Diall plac'd upon his steele
In such a tender posture, that doth tremble,   50
The timely Diall being held amisse,
And will shake ever, till you hold it right,
More tender than himselfe in any thing
That he concludes in Iustice for the State:
For as a fever held him, hee will shake   55
When he is signing any things of weight,
Least humane frailty should misguide his justice.
    As. You have declar'd him a most noble Iusticer.
    Al. He truely weighes and feeles Sir, what a charge
The subjects livings are (being even their lives   60
Laid on the hand of power,) which abus'd,
Though seene blood flow not from the justice seate,
Tis in true sence as grievous, and horrid.
    As. It argues nothing lesse, but since your Lord
Is diversly reported for his parts,   65

30 while.] ~, ‖ **41-2** spirit ... evening),] ~, ... ~), **47** wonder,] ~‸ ‖ **48** there's] theres ‖ **50** tremble,] ~‸ ‖ **52** right,] ~‸ ‖ **61** abus'd,] ~‸ ‖ **62** seene] ~, | flow not] flownot ‖

What's your true censure of his generall worth,
Vertue and Iudgement?
   Al. As of a Picture wrought to opticke reason,
That to all passers by, seemes as they move
Now woman, now a Monster, now a Divell,   70
And till you stand, and in a right line view it,
You cannot well judge what the maine forme is,
So men that view him but in vulgar passes,
Casting but laterall, or partiall glances
At what he is, suppose him weake, unjust,   75
Bloody, and monstrous, but stand free and fast,
And judge him by no more than what you know
Ingenuously, and by the right laid line
Of truth, he truely, will all stiles deserve
Of wise, just, good, a man both soule and nerve.   80
   As. Sir, I must joyne in just beleefe with you,
But what's his rivall the Lord high Constable?
   Al. As just, and well inclin'd when hee's himselfe,
(Not wrought on with the counsells, and opinions /   84
Of other men) and the maine difference is,   [A3ᵛ]
The Admirall is not flexible nor wonne
To move one scruple, when he comprehends
The honest tract and justnesse of a cause;
The Constable explores not so sincerely
The course hee runnes, but takes the minde of others   90
(By name Iudiciall) for what his owne
Iudgement, and knowledge should conclude.
   As.   A fault
In my apprehension: anothers knowledge
Applied to my instruction, cannot equall
My owne soules knowledge, how to informe Acts;   95
The Sunnes rich radiance shot through waves most faire,
Is but a shaddow to his beames ith'ayre,
His beames that in the ayre we so admire,
Is but a darkenesse to his flame in fire,
In fire his fervour but as vapour flies   100
To what his owne pure bosome rarifies:
And the Almighty wisedom, having given
Each man within himselfe an apter light
To guide his acts, than any light without him
(Creating nothing not in all things equall)   105
It seemes a fault in any that depend

---

66 What's] Whats ‖ 67 Iudgement?] ~. ‖ 73 passes,] ~ₐ ‖ 74 glances] ~, ‖ 82 what's] whats ‖ 88 cause;] ~, ‖ 93 apprehension:] ~, ‖

On others knowledge, and exile their owne.
   Al. Tis nobly argued, and exemplified,
But now I heare my Lord, and his young rivall
Are to be reconcil'd, and then one light   110
May serve to guide them both.
   As. I wish it may, the King being made first mover
To forme their reconcilement, and enflame it
With all the sweetnesse of his praise and honour.
   Al. See, tis dispatch'd I hope, the King doth grace it.   115

Loud Musicke, and Enter Vshers before, the Secretary,
Tresuror, Chancellor; Admirall, Constable hand
in hand, the King following, others attend.

   King. This doth expresse the noblest fruit of peace.
   Cha. Which when the great begin, the humble end
In joyfull imitation, all combining /
A *Gordian* beyond the *Phrigian* knot,   [A4]
Past wit to lose it, or the sword; be still so.   120
   Tre. Tis certaine Sir, by concord least things grow
Most great, and flourishing like trees that wrap
Their forehead in the skies, may these doe so.
   King. You heare my Lord, all that is spoke contends
To celebrate with pious vote the attonement   125
So lately, and so nobly made betweene you.
   Adm. Which for it selfe Sir, [I] resolve to keepe
Pure, and inviolable, needing none
To encourage or confirme it, but my owne
Love and allegiance to your sacred counsell.   130
   King. Tis good, and pleases, like my dearest health.
[*To the Constable.*] Stand you firme on that sweete simplicitie?
   Con. Past all earth pollicie that would infringe it.
   King. Tis well, and answers all the doubts suspected. –

Enter one that whispers with the Admirall.

And what moves this close message *Phillip*?   135
   Adm. My wives Father Sir, is closely come to Court.
   King. Is he come to the Court, whose aversation
So much affects him, that he shunnes and flies it?
What's the strange reason that he will not rise
Above the middle region he was borne in?   140
   Adm. He saith Sir, tis because the extreame of height
Makes a man lesse seeme to the imperfect eye
Then he is truely, his acts envied more,

115 SD *Chancellor;*] ~, ‖ **116** *King.*] Kin. (*throughout scene, except at l. 137*) ‖ **119** *Gordian*] *Dyce*; gardian ‖ knot,] ~. ‖ **120** sword;] ~, ‖ **127** I resolve] *Dyce*; resolve ‖ **131** health.] ~, ‖ **132** SD *To the Constable.*] *Parrott* ‖ simplicitie?] ~. ‖ **134** suspected.–] *Dyce*; ~., ‖ **138** it?] ~, ‖

And though he nothing cares for seeming, so
His being just stand firme twixt heaven and him,   145
Yet since in his soules jealousie, hee feares
That he himselfe advanced, would undervalue
Men plac'd beneath him, and their businesse with him,
Since height of place oft dazles height of judgement,
He takes his toppe-saile downe in such rough stormes,   150
And apts his sailes to ayres more temperate.
   King. A most wise soule he has: how long shall Kings
Raise men that are not wise till they be high?
You haue our leave, but tell him *Phillip* wee   154
Would have him neerer. /
   Con.   Your desires attend you.   [A4ᵛ]
                                  [*Exit the Admiral.*]

                Enter another.

   King. We know from whence you come: say to the Queene,
We were comming to her, tis a day of love
And she seales all perfection.   *Exit with Attendants.*
   Tre.   My Lord,
We must beseech your stay.
   Con.   My stay?
   Cha.   Our Counsells
Have led you thus farre to your reconcilement,   160
And must remember you, to observe the end
At which in plaine I told you then wee aim'd at:
You know we all urg'd the attonement, rather
To enforce the broader difference betweene you,
Then to conclude your friendshippe, which wise men   165
Know to be fashionable, and priviledg'd pollicie,
And will succeede betwixt you, and the Admirall
As sure as fate, if you please to get sign'd
A sute now to the King with all our hands,
Which will so much increase his precise justice,   170
That weighing not circumstances of politicke State,
He will instantly oppose it, and complaine,
And urge in passion, what the King will sooner
Punish than yeeld too, and so render you
In the Kings frowne on him, the onely darling,   175
And mediate power of *France.*
   Con.   My good Lord Chancellor,
Shall I so late atton'd, and by the Kings

---

148 plac'd] *Parrott*; placed ‖ 152 has:] ∼, ‖ 155 SD *Exit the Admiral.*] *Parrott subs.* ‖ 156 come:]
∼, ‖ 158 SD *Exit with Attendants.*] *Parrott*; Exit ‖ 162 at:] ∼, ‖ 164 betweene] bet weene ‖

Hearty and earnest motion, fall in peeces?
   Cha. Tis he, not you that breake.
   Tre.   Ha not you patience
To let him burne himselfe in the Kings flame?   180
   Cha. Come, be not Sir infected with a spice
Of that too servile equitie, that renders
Men free borne slaves, and rid with bits like horses,
When you must know my Lord, that even in nature
A man is *Animall politicum*,   185
So that when he informes his actions simply /
He does in both 'gainst pollicie and nature,   [B1]
And therefore our soule motion is affirm'd
To be like heavenly natures circular,
And circles being call'd ambitious lines,   190
We must like them become ambitious ever,
And endles in our circumventions;
No tough hides limiting our cheverill mindes.
   Tre. Tis learnedly, and past all answer argued:
Y'are great, and must grow greater still, and greater,   195
And not be like a dull and standing lake,
That settles, putrifies, and chokes with mudde,
But like a river gushing from the head,
That windes through the undervailes, what checkes ore flowing
Gets strength still of his course,   200
Till with the Ocean meeting, even with him
In sway, and title, his brave billowes move.
   Con. You speake a rare affection, and high soules,
But give me leave great Lords, still my just thankes
Remembred to your counsells and direction,   205
I seeking this way to confirme my selfe
I undermine the columnes that support
My hopefull glorious fortune, and at once
Provoke the tempest, though did drowne my envie,
With what assurance shall the King expect   210
My faith to him, that breake it for another?
He has engag'd our peace, and my revenge
Forfits my trust with him, whose narrow sight
Will penetrate through all our mists, could we
Vaile our designe with clouds blacker than night;   215
But grant this danger over, with what Iustice,
Or satisfaction to the inward Iudge,
Shall I be guiltie of this good mans ruine,

---

187 in] *stet* (*See Textual Note*) ‖ **194** argued:] ~, ‖ **195** Y'are] Yare ‖ **211** another?] ~, ‖ **218** guiltie] gultie ‖

Though I may still the murmuring tongues without me,
Loud conscience has a voyce to shadder greatnesse.   220
  Sec. A name to fright, and terrifie young statists.
There is necessitie my Lord, that you
Must lose your light, if you ecclipse not him:
Two starres so Lucide cannot shine at once /
In such a firmament, and better you   [B1ᵛ]
Extinguish his fires, then be made his fuell,   226
And in your ashes give his flame a Trophy.
  Cha. My Lord, the league that you have vow'd of friendship,
In a true understanding not confines you,
But makes you boundlesse; turne not edge at such   230
A liberty, but looke to your owne fortune;
Secure your honour: a Precisian,
In state, is a rideculous miracle;
Friendship is but a visor, beneath which
A wise man laughes to see whole families   235
Ruinde, upon whose miserable pile
He mounts to glory. Sir you must resolve
To use any advantage.
  Con.   Misery
Of rising Statesmen, I must on! I see
That 'gainst the politicke, and priviledg'd fashion,   240
All justice tasts but affectation.
  Cha. [*Aside to the Secretary and Treasurer.*] Why so? we shall
    do good on him ith'end.   *Exeunt.*

[I.ii]

Enter Father and the Admirall.

  Adm. You are most welcome.
  Fa.   I wish your Lordships safetie,
Which whilst I pray for, I must not forget
To urge agen the wayes to fixe you where
No danger has accesse to threaten you.
  Adm. Still your old argument, I owe you love for't.   5
  Fa. But fortified with new and pregnant reasons,
That you should leave the Court.
  Adm.   I dare not Sir.
  Fa. You dare be undone then.
  Adm.   I should be ingratefull

220 shadder] *stet (See Textual Note)* ‖ 221 statists.] ~, ‖ 223 him:] ~, ‖ 230 boundlesse;] ~, ‖ 232
honour:] ~, ‖ 233 miracle;] ~, ‖ 237 glory.] ~, ‖ 239 Statesmen,] ~ˌ | on!] ~, ‖ 242 SD *Aside ...
Treasurer.*] ‖ **I.ii**] *Dyce* ‖ **5** for't] fort ‖

To such a master, as no subject boasted,
To leave his services when they exact   10
My chiefest dutie, and attendance Sir.
   Fa. Would thou wert lesse, degraded from thy titles,
And swelling offices, that will ith'end
Engulfe thee past a rescue. I had not come
So farre to trouble you at this time, but that   15
I doe not like the loud tongues o'the world, /
That say the King has tane another favorite,   [B2]
The Constable, a gay man, and a great,
With a huge traine of faction too, the Queene,
Chancellor, Treasurer, Secretary, and   20
An army of state warriers, whose discipline
Is sure, and subtile to confusion;
I hope the rumour's false, thou art so calme.
   Adm. Report has not abus'd you Sir.
   Fa.   It has not,
And you are pleas'd? then you doe meane to mixe   25
With unjust courses, the great Constable
And you combining, that no suite may passe
One of the graples of your eithers rape.
I that abhorr'd, must I now entertaine
A thought, that your so straight, and simple custome   30
To render Iustice, and the common good,
Should now be patch'd with pollicy, and wrested
From the ingenious step you tooke, and hang
Vpon the shoulders of your enemy
To beare you out in what you shame to act?   35
   Adm. Sir, We both are reconciled.
   Fa. It followes then that both the acts must beare
Like reconcilement, and if hee will now
Maligne and mallice you for crossing him
Or any of his faction in their suites,   40
Being now atton'd, you must be one in all,
One in corruption, and twixt you two millstones
New pickt, and put together, must the graine
Of good mens needfull meanes to live be ground
Into your choking superfluities;   45
You both too rich, they ruinde.
   Adm.   I conceive Sir
Wee both may be enrich'd, and raise our fortunes
Even with our places in our Soveraignes favour:

9 boasted,] ~ˌ ‖ 10 services] *Parrott*; service ‖ 12 lesse,] *Parrott*; ~ˌ ‖ 14 rescue.] ~, ‖ 18 Constable,] ~ˌ ‖ 19 huge] *Dyce*; hugh | traine] rraine ‖ 22 confusion;] ~, ‖ 25 pleas'd?] ~, ‖ 28 rape.] ~, ‖ 33 tooke, and hang] *Shepherd*; ~, / And ~ ‖ 35 act?] ~. ‖ 44 live] ~, ‖

Though past the height of others, yet within
The rules of Law and Iustice, and approove   50
Our actions white and innocent. /
    Fa.   I doubt it: [B2ᵛ]
White in forc'd shew perhaps, which will I feare
Prove in true substance but a Millers whitenesse,
More sticking in your clothes then conscience.
    Adm. Your censure herein tasts some passion Sir,   55
And I beseech you nourish better thoughts,
Then to imagine that the Kings meere grace
Sustaines such prejudice by those it honours;
That of necessitie we must pervert it
With passionate enemies, and ambitious boundlesse   60
Avarice, and every licence incident
To fortunate greatnesse, and that all abuse it
For the most impious avarice of some.
    Fa. As if the totall summe of favorites frailties
Affected not the full rule of their Kings   65
In their owne partially dispos'd ambitions,
And that Kings doe no hazard infinitely
In their free realties of rights and honours,
Where they leave much for favourites powers to order.
    Adm. But wee have such a master of our King   70
In the Imperiall art, that no power flies
Out of his favour, but his policie ties
A criance to it, to containe it still;
And for the reconcilement of us Sir,
Never were two in favour, that were more   75
One in all love of Iustice, and true honour,
Though in the act and prosecution
Perhaps we differ. Howsoever yet
One beame us both creating, what should let
That both our soules should both one mettle beare,   80
And that one stampe, one word, one character?
    Fa. I could almost be won to be a Courtier,
There's some thing more in's composition,
Then ever yet was favourites.

Enter a Courtier.

What's hee?

    Cour. I bring your Lordship a sign'd bill, to have   85
The addition of your honor'd hand; the counsell /

---

51 it:] ~ˏ ‖ **52** White in forc'd] *Shepherd*; While inforc'd ‖ **66** dispos'd] *Parrott*; disposed ‖ **75**
more] ~ˏ ‖ **78** Perhaps] *Dyce*; Pehaps ‖ **81** character?] ~. ‖ **83** There's] Theres ‖ **84** What's] Whats
‖ **86** hand;] ~, ‖

Have all before subscribed, and full prepar'd it.   [B3]

    Adm. It seemes then they have weigh'd the importance of it,
And know the grant is just.
    Cour.   No doubt my Lord,
Or else they take therein the Constables word,   90
It being his suite, and his power having wrought
The King already to appose his hand.
    Adm. I doe not like his working of the King,
For if it be a suite made knowne to him,
And fit to passe, he wrought himselfe to it;   95
However my hand goes to no such grant,
But first I'le know and censure it my selfe.
    Cour. [*Aside.*] *Até*, if thou beest goddesse of contention
That *Iove* tooke by the haire, and hurl'd from heaven,
Assume in earth thy empire, and this bill   100
Thy firebrand make to turne his love, thus tempted,
Into a hate, as horrid as thy furies.
    Adm. Does this beare title of his Lordships suite?
    Cour. It does my Lord, and therefore he beseech'd
The rather your dispatch.
    Adm.   No thought the rather,   105
But now the rather all powers against it,
The suite being most injust, and he pretending
In all his actions justice, on the sudden
After his so late vow not to violate it,
Is strange and vile, and if the King himselfe   110
Should owne and urge it, I would stay and crosse it,
For tis within the free power of my office,
And I should straine his kingdome if I past it.
I see their poore attempts, and giddy malice;
Is this the reconcilement that so lately   115
He vow'd in sacred witnesse of the King?
Assuring me, he never more would offer
To passe a suite unjust, which I well know
This is, above all, and have often beene urg'd
To give it passage. – Be you Sir the Judge.   120
    Fa. I wonot meddle
With any thing of state, you knew long since. /
    Adm. Yet you may heare it Sir.   [B3ᵛ]
    Fa.   You wonot urge
My opinion then, go to.
    Adm.   An honest merchant

---

95 it;] ~, ‖ **98** SD *Aside.*] *Parrott (after Dyce)* | *Até*] *Dyce*; A he ‖ **99** heaven,] ~ₐ ‖ **101** tempted,]
~ₐ ‖ **113** it.] ~, ‖ **120** passage. – Be] *Dyce*; ~, ₐ be ‖

Presuming on our league of *France* with *Spaine*,   125
Brought into *Spaine* a wealthy ship, to vent
Her fit commodities to serve the country,
Which, in the place of suffering their saile
Were seas'd to recompence a *Spanish* ship
Priz'd by a *French man*, ere the league was made;   130
No suites, no letters of our Kings could gaine
Our merchants first right in it, but his letters
Vnreverently received, the Kings selfe scandall,
Beside the leagues breach, and the foule injustice
Done to our honest merchant, who endured all,   135
Till some small time since (authoris'd by our counsell,
Though not in open Court) he made a ship out,
And tooke a *Spaniard*, brings all home, and sues
To gaine his full prov'd losse, full recompence
Of his just prize; his prize is staid and ceaz'd,   140
Yet for the Kings disposure, and the *Spaniard*
Makes suite to be restor'd her, which this bill
Would faine get granted, faining (as they hop'd)
With my allowance, and way given to make
Our Countrey mans in *Spaine* their absolute prize.   145
  Fa. 'Twere absolute injustice.
  Adm.   Should I passe it?
  Fa. Passe life, and state before.
  Adm.   If this would seeme
His Lordships suite, his love to me, and justice
(Including plots upon me, while my simplenesse
Is seriously vow'd to reconcilement),   150
Love him good vulgars, and abhorre me still,
For if I court your flatterie with my crimes,
Heavens love before me fly, till in my tombe
I sticke pursuing it, and for this bill,
Thus say twas shiver'd. Blesse us equall heaven!   155
                                      [Tears the bill.] Exit.

  Fa. This could I cherish now, above his losse. – /
You may report as much, the bill discharg'd Sir.   *Exeunt.*   [B4]

---

130 made;] ~, ‖ 133 selfe scandall] *stet* (*See Textual Note*) ‖ 140 prize;] ~, ‖ 146 it?] ~. ‖ 149-50
(Including ... reconcilement),] ͺ~ ... ~ͺ; ‖ 155 shiver'd. Blesse] ~, blesse | SD *Tears the bill.*]
Dyce ‖ 156 cherish now,] *Dyce*; ~, ~ͺ | losse.–] *Dyce*; ~,ͺ ‖

Actus Secundus. [*Scena I.*]

Enter King and Queen, Secretary with the Torne bill.

King. Is it ene so.

Qu.   Good heaven how tame you are?
Doe Kings of *France* reward foule Traitors thus?

King. No Traitor, y'are too loude, *Chabot*'s no Traitor,
He has the passions of a man about him,
And multiplicitie of cares may make   5
Wise men forget themselves, come be you patient.

Qu. Can you be so, and see your selfe thus torne?

King. Our selfe?

Qu. [*Showing the torn bill.*] There is some left, if you dare owne
Your royall character; is not this your name?

King. Tis *Francis* I confesse.

Qu.   Be but a name   10
If this staine live upon't. Affronted, by
Your subject, shall the sacred name of King,
A word to make your nation bow and tremble,
Be thus profain'd? are lawes establish'd
To punish the defacers of your image,   15
But dully set by the rude hand of others
Vpon your coine, and shall the character
That doth include the blessing of all *France*,
Your name, thus written by your royall hand,
Design'd for Justice, and your Kingdomes honour,   20
Not call up equall anger to reward it?
Your Counsellors of state contemn'd, and slighted,
As in this braine more circumscrib'd all wisedome,
And pollicy of Empire, and your power,
Subordinate and subject to his passion.   25

King. Come, it concernes you not.

Qu.   Is this the consequence
Of an attonement made so lately betweene /
The hopefull *Mountmorencie*, and his Lordship,   [B4ᵛ]
Vrg'd by your selfe with such a precious sanction?
Come, he that dares doe this, wants not a heart,   30

Scena I.] *Parrott (after Dyce)* ‖ **1** *King.*] *Kin. (throughout scene, except at l. 48)* ‖ **3** *Chabot's*]
Chabots ‖ **7** torne?] ~. ‖ **8** selfe?] ~. | SD *Showing ... bill.*] *Parrott* | owne] ~, ‖ **9** character;] ~,
‖ **11** upon't. Affronted] ~, affronted ‖ **14** profain'd?] ~, ‖ **19** hand,] ~ˌ ‖ **22** slighted,] ~ˌ ‖ **23**
this braine more] *stet (See Textual Note)* ‖ **28** Lordship,] ~ˌ ‖ **29** Vrg'd] *Dyce subs.*; V̆rge |
sanction?] ~; ‖

But opportunitie.
   King.   To doe what?
   Qu.   To teare
Your crowne off.
   King.   Come your language doth taste more
Of rage and womanish flame than solid reason
Against the Admirall. What commands of yours,
Not to your expectation obey'd   35
By him, is ground of your so keene displeasure?
   Qu. Commands of mine? he is too great, and powerfull
To stoope to my employment, a *Colossus*,
And can stride from one Province to another
By the assistance of those offices   40
You have most confidently impos'd upon him;
Tis he, not you take up the peoples eyes
And admiration, while his Princely wife –
   King. Nay then I reach the spring of your distaste,
He has a wife, —

     Enter Chancellor, Treasurer, and whisper with
               the King.

   Qu. [*Aside.*]   Whom for her pride I love not,   45
And I but in her husbands ruine can
Triumph ore her greatnesse.
   King. Well, well, Ile thinke on't?   *Exit.*
   Cha.   He beginnes to incline. –
Madam you are the soule of our great worke.
   Qu. Ile follow, and imploy my powers upon him.   50
   Tre. We are confident you will prevaile at last,
And for the pious worke oblige the King to you.
   Cha. And us your humblest creatures.
   Qu.   Presse no further.
                      Exit Que.

   Cha. Let's seeke out my Lord Constable.
   Tre.   And inflame him –
   Cha. To expostulate with *Chabot*, something may   55
Arise from thence, to pull more weight upon him.   *Exeunt.*

31-32 teare / Your] *Parrott*; ~ your ‖ 34 Admirall. What] ~, what | yours,] ~ ‖ 38 a] *a* ‖ 41 him;]
~, ‖ 43 wife–] *Dyce*; ~. ‖ 45 SD *Aside.*] *Parrott* ‖ 46-47 can / Triumph] *Parrott*; Can triumph ‖
48 incline.–] *Dyce*; ~, ‖ 53 *Cha.*] ~, | SD *Exit*] ~. ‖ 54 Let's] Lets | him–] *Dyce subs.*; ~. ‖

[II.ii]

Enter Father and Allegre.

Fa. How sorts the businesse? how tooke the King /
The tearing of his bill? [C1]
  Al.   Exceeding well,
And seem'd to smile at all their grimme complaints,
Gainst all that outrage to his highnesse hand,
And said in plaine, he sign'd it but to try 5
My Lords firme Iustice.
  Fa.   What a sweete King tis?
  Al. But how his rivall the Lord Constable
Is labour'd by the Chancellor, and others to retort
His wrong with ten parts more upon my Lord,
Is monstrous? 10
  Fa. Neede hee their spurres?
  Al.   I Sir, for hee's afraid
To beare himselfe too boldly in his braves
Vpon the King (being newly entred Mynion)
Since tis but patience sometime they thinke
(Because the favor spending in two streames, 15
One must runne low at length) till when he dare
Take fire in such flame, as his faction wishes,
But with wise feare containes himselfe, and so
Like a greene faggot in his kindling smoakes,
And where the Chancellor his chiefe *Cyclops* findes 20
The fire within him apt to take, he blowes,
And then the faggot flames, as never more
The bellowes needed, till the too soft greenenesse
Of his state habit shewes his sappe still flowes,
Above the solid timber, with which, then 25
His blaze shrinkes head, he cooles, and smoakes agen.
  Fa. Good man he would be, wod the bad not spoile him.
  Al. True sir, but they still ply him with their arts,
And as I heard have wrought him, personally
To question my Lord with all the bitternesse 30
The galls of all their faction can powre in,
And such an expectation hangs upon't,
Through all the Court as twere with child, and long'd
To make a mirror of my Lords cleare blood,
And therein see the full ebbe of his flood, 35
And therefore if you please to counsell him /

II.ii] *Dyce* ‖ 6 Iustice.] ~, ‖ 11 hee's] hees ‖ 14 thinke] ~; *(See Textual Note)* ‖ 15 (Because] ˌ~ ‖
16 length)] *Parrott*; ~, ‖ 20 *Cyclops*] Cyclops ‖ 24 habit] ~, ‖ 33 Through] *Brereton conj.*;
Though ‖

You shall performe a fathers part. [C1ᵛ]
   Fa.   Nay since
Hee's gone so farre, I wod not have him feare
But dare e'm, and yet ile not meddle in't.

                 Enter Admirall.

Hee's here, if he have wit to like his cause,   40
His spirit wonot be asham'd to die in't.   *Exit.*
   Al. My Lord retire, y'are way-laid in your walkes,
Your friendes are all fallen from you, all your servants
Suborn'd by all advantage to report
Each word you whisper out, and to serve you   45
With hat and knee, while other have their hearts.
   Adm. Much profit may my foes make of such servants,
I love no enemy I have so well,
To take so ill a bargaine from his hands.
   Al. Their other oddes yet shun, all being combinde,   50
And lodg'd in ambush, ariv'd to doe you mischiefe
By any meanes past feare of law, or soveraigne.
   Adm. I walke no desart, yet goe arm'd with that,
That would give wildest beasts instincts to rescue,
Rather then offer any force to hurt me;   55
My innocence is, which is a conquering justice,
As weares a shield, that both defends and fights.
   Al. One against all the world.
   Adm.   The more the oddes,
The lesse the conquest, or if all the world
Be thought an army fit to employ gainst one,   60
That one is argued fit to fight gainst all;
If I fall under them, this breast shall beare
Their heape digested in my sepulchre:
Death is the life of good men, let e'm come.

       Enter Constable, Chancellor, Treasurer, Secretary.

   Con. I thought my Lord our reconcilement perfect;   65
You have exprest what sea of gall flow'd in you,
In tearing of the bill I sent to allow.
   Adm. Dare you confesse the sending of that bill?
   Con. Dare, why not?
   Adm.   Because it breake your oath /   69
Made in our reconcilement, and betrayes   [C2]
The honour, and the chiefe life of the King
Which is his justice.

---

38 Hee's] Hees ‖ 39 in't] int ‖ 40 Hee's] Hees ‖ 41 in't] int ‖ 47 *Adm.*] ~, ‖ 51 ambush,] ~ ‖
56-57] *stet* (See *Textual Note*) ‖ 58 *Al.*] *All.* ‖ 63 sepulchre:] ~, ‖ 65 perfect;] ~, ‖ 68 bill?] ~. ‖

Con. Betraies?
Adm.   No lesse, and that Ile prove to him.
Omnes. You can not.
Tre. I would not wish you offer at an action   75
So most impossibly, and much against
The judgement, and favour of the King.
    Adm. His judgement nor his favour I respect,
So I preserve his Iustice.
    Cha.   Tis not Iustice,
Which I'le prove by law, and absolute learning.   80
    Adm. All your great law, and learning are but words,
When I plead plainely, naked truth, and deedes,
Which though you seeke to fray with state, and glory,
I'le shoote a shaft at all your globe of light;   84
If lightning split it, yet twas high and right.   *Exit.*
    Con. Brave resolution so his acts be just,
He cares for gaine nor honour.
    Cha.   How came he then
By all his infinite honour and his gaine?
    Tre. Well said my Lord.
    Sec.   Answer but onely that.
    Con. By doing justice still in all his actions.   90
    Sec. But if this action prove unjust, will you
Say all his other may be so as well,
And thinke your owne course fitter farre than his?
    Con. I will ———   *Exit.*
    Cha. He cooles, we must not leave him, we have no   95
Such engine to remove the Admirall.   *Exeunt.*

[II.iii]

Enter King and the Admirall.

    King. I prethee *Philip* be not so severe
To him I favour; tis an argument
That may serve one day to availe your selfe,
Nor Does it square with your so gentle nature,
To give such fires of envie to your bloud;   5
For howsoeuer out of love to Iustice, /
Your Iealousie of that doth so incense you,   [C2ᵛ]
Yet they that censure it will say tis envy.
    Adm. I serve not you for them, but for your selfe,
And that good in your Rule, that Iustice does you,   10

---

74 Omnes.] ~ˌ ‖ **84** light;] ˌ·, ‖ **85** split it] (*See Textual Note*) ‖ **87** nor] *Brereton conj.*; not ‖ **93** his?] ~. ‖ **94** Con.] ~, ‖ **II.iii**] *Dyce* ‖ **1** King.] Kin. (*again at ll. 82, 98*) ‖ **2** favour;] ~, ‖

And care not this [*snapping his fingers*] what others say, so you
Please but to doe me right for what you know.
   King. You will not doe your selfe right, why should I
Exceede you to your selfe?
   Adm.   My selfe am nothing
Compar'd to what I seeke: tis justice onely   15
The fount and flood, both of your strength and kingdomes.
   King. But who knowes not, that extreame justice is
(By all ruld lawes) the extreame of injurie,
And must to you be so; the persons that
Your passionate heate calls into question   20
Are great, and many, and may wrong in you
Your rights of kinde, and dignities of fortune,
And I advanc'd you not to heape on you
Honours, and fortunes, that by strong hand now
Held up, and over you, when heaven takes off   25
That powerfull hand, should thunder on your head,
And after you crush your surviving seedes.
   Adm. Sir, your regards to both are great, and sacred,
But if the innocence, and right that rais'd me
And meanes for mine, can finde no friend hereafter   30
Of him that ever lives, and ever seconds
All Kings just bounties with defence, and refuge
In just mens races, let my fabricke ruine,
My stocke want sap, my branches by the roote
Be torne to death, and swept with whirlewindes out.   35
   King. For my love no relenting?
   Adm.   No my leige,
Tis for your love, and right that I stand out.
   King. Be better yet advis'd.
   Adm.   I cannot Sir
Should any Oracle become my counsell,
For that I stand not out, thus of set will,   40
Or pride of any singular conceite, /
My enemies, and the world may clearely know;   [C3]
I taste no sweetes to drowne in others gall,
And to affect in that which makes me lothed,
To leave my selfe and mine expos'd to all   45
The dangers you propos'd, my purchas'd honours,
And all my fortunes in an instant lost,
That many cares, and paines, and yeares have gather'd,
How mad were I to rave thus in my wounds,

---

11 SD *snapping his fingers*] ‖ 15 seeke:] ~, ‖ 18 (By] (by ‖ 19 so;] ~, ‖ 26 hand, should] *Dyce*;
hand 'should ‖ 36 relenting?] ~. ‖ 42 know;] *Parrott*; ~, ‖ 48 many] *Brereton conj.*; mony, ‖

Vnlesse my knowne health felt in these forc'd issues   50
Were sound, and fit, and that I did not know
By most true proofes, that to become sincere
With all mens hates, doth farre exceede their loves,
To be as they are, mixtures of corruption?
And that those envies that I see pursue me   55
Of all true actions are the naturall consequents
Which being my object, and my resolute choise
Not for my good but yours, I will have justice.
   King. You will have justice? is your will so strong
Now against mine? your power being so weake   60
Before my favour gave them both their forces:
Of all that ever shar'd in my free graces,
You *Philip Chabot* a meane Gentleman
Have not I rais'd you to a supremest Lord,
And given you greater dignities than any?   65
   Adm. You have so.
   King.   Well sed, and to spurre your dullnesse
With the particulars to which I rais'd you,
Have not I made you first a Knight of the Order,
Then Admirall of *France*, then *Count Byzanges*,
Lord, and Livetenant generall of all   70
My country, and command of *Burgandy*;
Livetenant generall likewise of my sonne
Daulphine, and heire, and of all *Normandy*,
And of my chiefely honor'd privy Counsell,
And cannot all these powers weigh downe your will?   75
   Adm. No Sir, they were not given me to that end,
But to uphold my will, my will being just.
   King. And who shall judge that Justice, you or I? /
   Adm. I Sir, in this case; your royall thoughts are fitly   [C3ᵛ]
Exempt from every curious search of one,   80
You have the generall charge with care of all.
   King. And doe not generalls include particulars?
May not I Iudge of any thing compriz'd
In your particular as well as you?
   Adm. Farre be the misery from you, that you may!   85
My cares, paines, broken sleepe therein made more
Than yours should make me see more, and my forces
Render of better judgement.
   King.   Well Sir, grant
Your force in this, my odds in benefits

---

59 justice?] ~, ‖ **61** forces:] ~ˌ ‖ **71** *Burgandy*] *Burgady* ‖ **79** case;] *Dyce*; ~ˌ ‖ **85** may!] ~, ‖ **89** this,] ~ˌ ‖

Paid for your paines, put in the other scale,   90
And any equall holder of the ballance
Will shew my merits hoist up yours to aire
In rule of any doubt or deed betwixt us.
   Adm. You merit not of me for benefits
More than my selfe of you for services.   95
   King. Is't possible?
   Adm.   Tis true.
   King.   Stand you on that?
   Adm. I to the death, and will approve to all men.
   King. I am deceiv'd but I shall finde good Judges
That will finde difference.
   Adm.   Finde them, being good.
   King. Still so? what if conferring   100
My bounties, and your services to sound them,
We fall foule on some licences of yours?
Nay, give me therein some advantage of you.
   Adm. They cannot.
   King. Not in sifting their severe discharges   105
Of all your offices?
   Adm.   The more you sift
The more you shall refine mee.
   King.   What if I
Grant out against you a commission
Ioyn'd with an extraordinary processe
To arrest, and put you in lawes hands for triall? /   110
   Adm. Not with lawes uttermost.   [C4]
   King.   Ile throw the dice.
   Adm. And Ile endure the chance, the dice being square,
Repos'd in dreadlesse confidence, and conscience,
That all your most extreames shall never reach,
Or to my life, my goodes or honours breach.   115
   King. Was ever heard so fine a confidence?
Must it not prove presumption, and can that
Scape brackes and errors in your search of law?
I prethee weigh yet, with more soule that danger,
And some lesse passion.
   Adm.   Witnesse heaven, I cannot,   120
Were I dissolv'd, and nothing else but soule.
   King. [*Aside.*] Beshrew my blood, but his resolves amaze me. –
Was ever such a Iustice in a subject,
Of so much office left to his owne swinge,

---

96 Is't] Ist | possible?] ~. ‖ **98** deceiv'd] *Shepherd*; ~, ‖ **99** them,] ~ͺ ‖ **102** yours?] ~, ‖ **110** triall?]
~. ‖ **112** chance, the] *Shepherd*; ~, / The ⌈ square,] ~. ‖ **113** Repos'd] *Dyce*; *Adm.* Repos'd (*See
Textual Note*) ‖ **118** law?] ~, ‖ **119** that] *Pennel conj.*; than ‖ **120** cannot,] ~. ‖ **122** SD *Aside.*]
Parrott (after Dyce) | Beshrew] Be shrew | me.–] *Parrott (after Dyce)*; ~;ͺ ‖ **124** swinge,] ~ͺ ‖

That left to law thus, and his Soveraignes wrath,   125
Could stand cleare spight of both? let reason rule it
Before it come at law: a man so rare
In one thing cannot in the rest be vulgar,
And who sees you not in the broad high-way
The common dust up in your owne eyes beating,   130
In quest of riches, honours, offices,
As heartily in shew as most beleeve?
And he that can use actions with the vulgar,
Must needes embrace the same effects, and cannot informe him
Whatsoever he pretends, [or] use them with such   135
Free equitie, as fits one just and reall,
Even in the eyes of men, nor stand at all parts
So truly circular, so sound, and solid,
But have his swellings out, his crackes and crannies,
And therefore in this, reason, before law   140
Take you to her, least you affect and flatter
Your selfe with mad opinions.
    Adm.   I were mad
Directly Sir, if I were yet to know
Not the sure danger, but the certaine ruine /   144
Of men shot into law from Kings bent brow,   [C4ᵛ]
There being no dreame from the most muddie braine
Vpon the foulest fancie, that can forge
More horrour in the shaddowes of meere fame,
Then can some Lawyer in a man expos'd
To his interpretation by the King,   150
But these grave toyes I shall despise in death,
And while I live will lay them open so
(My inocence laid by them) that like foiles
They shall sticke off my merits tenne times more,
And make your bounties nothing, for who gives   155
And hits ith'teeth, himselfe payes with the glory
For which he gave, as being his end of giving,
Not to crowne merits, or doe any good,
And so no thankes is due but to his glory.
    King. Tis brave I sweare.
    Adm.   No Sir, tis plaine, and rude,   160
But true, and spotlesse, and where you object
My hearty, and grosse vulgar love of riches,
Titles, and honours, I did never seeke them
For any love to them, but to that justice

---

127 law:] ~, ‖ 130 eyes beating,] *Dyce*; ~, ~ͺ ‖ 132 beleeve?] ~, ‖ 134 informe him] *stet* (*See Textual Note*) ‖ 135 or use] use ‖ 140 this,] *Parrott*; ~ͺ ‖ 154 off] *Brereton conj.*; of ‖ 156 ith'] ith ‖ 160 rude,] ~ͺ ‖

You ought to use in their due gift to merits,   165
To shew you royall, and most open handed,
Not using for hands talons, pincers, grapples;
In whose gripes, and upon whose gord point,
Deserts hang sprawling out their vertuous limbs.
  King. Better and better.
  Adm.   This your glory is,   170
My deserts wrought upon no wretched matter,
But shew'd your royall palmes as free, and moist,
As *Ida*, all enchast with silver springs,
And yet my merit still their equall sings.
  King. Sing till thou sigh thy soule out, hence, and
    leave us.   175
  Adm. My person shall, my love and faith shall never.
  King. Perish thy love, and faith, and thee for ever;

                              [Exit the Admiral.]

Whose there?

                   Enter Asall.

    Let one goe for the Chancellor. /
  As. He's here in Court Sir.   *[D1]*
  King.   Haste and send him hither.

                                [Exit Asall.]
This is an insolence I never met with: 180
Can one so high as his degrees ascend,
Clime all so free, and without staine?

                Enter Chancellor.

                   My Lord
Chancellor, I send for you about a service
Of equall price to me, as if againe
My ransome came to me from *Pavian* thraldome,   185
And more, as if from forth a subjects fetters,
The worst of servitudes, my life were rescued.
  Cha. You fright me with a Prologue of much trouble.
  King. Me thinkes it might be: tell me out of all
Your famous learning, was there ever subject   190
Rais'd by his Soveraignes free hand from the dust,
Vp to a height above Ayres upper region,
That might compare with him in any merit
That so advanc'd him? and not shew in that
Grosse over-weening worthy cause to thinke   195
There might be other over-sights excepted

---

169 limbs.] ∼, ‖ 170 is,] ∼, ‖ 175 out,] ∼, ‖ 177 SD *Exit the Admiral.*] *Dyce subs.* ‖ 179 hither.]
∼, | SD *Exit Asall.*] *Dyce* ‖ 180 with:] ∼, ‖ 182 staine? My Lord] staine? / My Lord | SD *Enter
Chancellor.*] *as Dyce; followes* My Lord ‖ 187 servitudes,] ∼, ‖ 189 be:] ∼, ‖

Of capitall nature in his sifted greatnesse?
   Cha. And past question Sir, for one absurd thing granted,
A thousand follow.
   King.   You must then employ
Your most exact, and curious art to explore   200
A man in place of greatest trust, and charge,
Whom I suspect to have abus'd them all,
And in whom you may give such proud veines vent,
As will bewray their boyling bloud corrupted
Both gainst my crowne and life.   205
   Cha. And may my life be curst in every act,
If I explore him not to every fiuer.
   King. It is my Admirall.
   Cha.   Oh my good Leige
You tempt, not charge me with such search of him.
   King. Doubt not my heartiest meaning: all the troubles   210
That ever mov'd in a distracted King, /
Put in just feare of his assaulted life,   [D1ᵛ]
Are not above my sufferings for *Chabot.*
   Cha. Then I am glad, and proud that I can cure you,
For he's a man that I am studied in,   215
And all his offices, and if you please
To give authoritie –
   King.   You shall not want it.
   Cha. If I discharge you not of that disease,
About your necke growne, by your strange trust in him,
With full discovery of the foulest treasons –   220
   King. But I must have all prov'd with that free justice –
   Cha. Beseech your Majestie doe not question it.
   King. About it instantly, and take me wholly
Vpon your selfe.
   Cha.   How much you grace your servant?
   King. Let it be fiery quicke.
   Cha.   It shall have wings,   225
And every feather shew the flight of Kings.   [*Exeunt.*]

---

197 greatnesse?] ~. ‖ **198** absurd] absur'd ‖ **206** life be] *Shepherd*; life / Be ‖ **207** fiuer] *Pennel conj.*; finer (*See Textual Note*) ‖ **210** meaning:] ~, ‖ **212** life,] ~. ‖ **217** authoritie–] *Dyce*; ~. **220** treasons–] *Dyce*; ~. ‖ **221** justice–] *Pennel*; ~. **226** SD *Exeunt.*] *Dyce* ‖

Actus Tertius. [*Scena I.*]

*Enter Chancellor attended, the Proctor generall
whispering in his eare. Two Iudges following.
They past, enter Chabot in his gowne, a guard
about him, his father and his wife on each side.
Allegre is supported over the stage.*

Adm. And have they put my faithfull servant to the racke?
Heaven arme the honest man.

    Fa. Allegre feeles the malice of the Chancellor.

    Adm. Many upon the torture have confest
Things against truth, and yet his paine sits neerer   5
Than all my other feares. [*To his Wife.*] Come don't weepe.

    Wif. My Lord, I doe not grive out of a thought,
Or poore suspition, they with all their malice
Can staine your honour, but it troubles me,
The King should grant this licence to your enemies,   10
As he were willing to heare *Chabot* guilty. /

    Adm. No more, the King is just, and by exposing me   [D2]
To this triall, meanes to render me
More happy to his subjects, and himselfe;
His sacred will be obey'd. Take thy owne spirit,   15
And let no thought infringe thy peace for me,
I goe to have my honours all confirm'd;
Farewell, thy lip [*kisses her*]; my cause has so much innocence,
It shanot neede thy prayer. [*To Father.*] I leave her yours
Till my returne; oh let me be a sonne   20
Still in your thoughts. – Now Gentlemen set forward.

                      Exit with Guards. Manent Father and Wife.

    Fa. See you that trust in greatnesse, what sustaines you;
These hazards you must looke for, you that thrust
Your heads into a cloud, where lie in ambush
The souldiers of state in privy armes   25
Of yellow fire, jealous, and mad at all
That shoote their foreheads up into their forges,
And pry into their gloomy Cabbinets;
You like vaine Citizens that must goe see
Those ever-burning furnaces, wherein   30
Your brittle glasses of estate are blowne;
Who knowes not you are all but puffe, and bubble

Scena I.] Parrott (after Dyce) ‖ SD *past, enter*] past. / Enter | SD *guard*] gaurd | SD *side.*] ~, |
SD *Allegre is … stage.*] Pennel subs.; *Allegre.* ‖ 1 racke?] ~, ‖ 6 feares. Come] ~, come | SD *To
his Wife.*] Parrott ‖ 14 himselfe;] ~. ‖ 15 obey'd. Take] ~, take ‖ 16 infringe] in fringe ‖ 18
Farewell, thy lip;] ~. ~ ~, | SD *kisses her*] Dyce ‖ 19 prayer.] ~, | SD *To Father.*] Parrott ‖ 21
thoughts. – Now] Dyce; ~, now | SD *with Guards*] Parrott subs. | SD *Manent*] Manente (See
Textual Note) ‖ 22 you;] ~, ‖ 26 fire,] ~. ‖ 30 ever-burning] ~.~ ‖

Of breath, and fume forg'd, your vile brittle natures
Cause of your dearenesse? were you tough and lasting,
You would be cheape, and not worth halfe your face.   35
Now daughter Plannet strooke?
    Wif.   I am considering
What forme I shall put on, as best agreeing
With my Lords fortune.
    Fa.   Habit doe you meane,
Of minde or body?
    Wif.   Both wod be apparell'd.
    Fa. In neither you have reason yet to mourne.   40
    Wif. Ile not accuse my heart of so much weakenesse.
Twere a confession gainst my Lord.   The Queene!

       Enter Queene, Constable, Treasurer, Secretary.

She has exprest 'gainst me some displeasure.
    Fa. Let's this way through the Gallery.   *[They retire.]* /
    Qu.   Tis she!   [D2ᵛ]
Doe you my Lord say I wod speake with her.   45
[*To the Treasurer.*] And has *Allegre*, one of chiefest trust with
    him
Suffered the racke? the Chancellor is violent;
And what's confest?
    Tre.   Nothing, he contemn'd all
That could with any cruelst paine explore him,
As if his minde had rob'd his nerves of sence,   50
And through them diffus'd fiery spirits above
All flesh and blood; for as his limbs were stretch'd,
His contempts too extended.
    Qu.   A strange fortitude!
    Tre. But we shall lose th'arraignement.
    Qu.   The successe
Will soone arrive.
    Tre.   Youle not appeare, my Lord then?   55
    Con. I desire your Lordship wod excuse me.
    Tre. We are your servants.   *Exeunt Tre. and Sec.*
    Con. [*Bringing Wife forward, who kneels.*] She attends you
    Madam.
    Qu. This humblenesse proceedes not from your heart;
Why, you are a Queene your selfe in your owne thoughts,
The Admiralls wife of *France* cannot be lesse;   60
You have not state enough, you shold not move

---

35 face.] ~, ‖ **36** strooke?] ~. ‖ **44** Let's] Lets | SD *They retire.*] *Parrott* | she!] ~, ‖ **45** her.] ~? ‖
46 SD *To the Treasurer.*] *Parrott* ‖ **48** what's] whats ‖ **56** desire your] *Parrott*; ~ / Your ‖ **57** SD
Exeunt] *Exiunt.* | SD *Bringing … kneels.*] *Dyce subs.* ‖ **58** heart;] ~, ‖ **60** lesse;] ~, ‖

Without a traine of friends and servants.
  Wif.   There is some mystery
Within your language Madam; I woud hope
You have more charitie than to imagine
My present condition worth your triumph,   65
In which I am not so lost, but I have
Some friends and servants with proportion
To my Lords fortune, but none within the list
Of those that obey mee can be more ready
To expresse their duties, than my heart to serve   70
Your just commands.
  Qu.   Then pride will ebbe I see,
There is no constant flood of state, and greatnesse;
The prodigie is ceasing when your Lord /
Comes to the ballance; hee whose blazing fires,   [D3]
Shot wonders through the Kingdome, will discover   75
What flying and corrupted matter fed him.
  Wif. My Lord?
  Qu.   Your high and mighty Justicer,
The man of conscience, the Oracle
Of State, whose honorable titles
Would cracke an Elephants backe, is now turn'd mortall, 80
Must passe examination, and the test
Of Law, have all his offices rip'd up,
And his corrupt soule laid open to the subjects:
His bribes, oppressions, and close sinnes that made
So many grone, and curse him, now shall finde   85
Their just reward, and all that love their country,
Blesse heaven, and the Kings Iustice, for removing
Such a devouring monster.
  Fa. [*To the Constable, coming forward.*] Sir your pardon. –
Madam you are the Queene, she is my daughter,
And he that you have character'd so monstrous,   90
My sonne in Law, now gon to be arraign'd;
The King is just, and a good man, but't does not
Adde to the graces of your royall person
To tread upon a Lady thus dejected
By her owne griefe; her Lord's not yet found guilty,   95
Much lesse condemn'd, though you have pleas'd to execute
    him.
  Qu. What sawcy fellow's this?
  Fa.   I must confesse

---

63 Madam;] ~, ‖ 72 greatnesse;] ~, ‖ 74 ballance;] ~, ‖ 83 subjects:] ~, ‖ 88 SD *To ... forward.*]
Parrott subs. | pardon.–] *Dyce;* ~. ‖ 91 arraign'd;] ~, ‖ 95 griefe;] ~, ‖

I am a man out of this element,
No Courtier, yet I am a gentleman
That dare speake honest truth to the Queenes eare,   100
(A duty every subject wonot pay you)
And justifie it to all the world, there's nothing
Doth more ecclipse the honours of our soule,
Than an ill-grounded, and ill-followed passion,
Let flie with noise, and license against those   105
Whose hearts before are bleeding.
    Con.   Brave old man.
    Fa. Cause you are a Queene, to trample ore a woman, /
Whose tongue and faculties are all tied up!   [D3ᵛ]
Strike out a Lyons teeth, and pare his clawes,
And then a dwarfe may plucke him by the beard,   110
Tis a gay victory.
    Qu. [*To the Constable.*] Did you heare, my Lord?
    Fa. I ha done.
    Wif. [*Rises.*]   And it concernes me to beginne:
I have not made this pause through servile feare
Or guiltie apprehension of your rage,
But with just wonder of the heates, and wildnesse   115
Has prepossest your nature gainst our innocence;
You are my Queene, unto that title bowes
The humblest knee in *France*, my heart made lower
With my obedience, and prostrate duty,
Nor have I powers created for my use,   120
When just commands of you expect their service;
But were you Queene of all the world, or something
To be thought greater, betwixt heaven and us
That I could reach you with my eyes and voyce,
I would shoote both up in defence of my   125
Abused honour, and stand all your lightning.
    Qu. So brave.
    Wif.   So just and boldly innocent,
I cannot feare arm'd with a noble conscience
The tempest of your frowne, were it more frightfull
Then ever fury made a womans anger,   130
Prepar'd to kill with deaths most horrid ceremony,
Yet with what freedome of my soule I can
Forgive your accusation of my pride.
    Qu. Forgive? what insolence is like this language?
Can any action of ours be capable   135

---

98 element,] ~̭ ‖ 104 ill-grounded, and ill-followed] ~̭~, ~ ~̭~ ‖ 107 Queene,] ~̭ ‖ 108 up!]
~, ‖ 111 *Qu.*] ~, | SD *To the Constable.*] *Parrott subs.* | heare,] ~̭ ‖ 112 SD *Rises.*] *Parrott*
subs. | beginne:] ~, ‖ 116 innocence;] ~, ‖ 130 ever] *Shepherd*; every ‖

Of thy forgivenesse? dust! how I dispise thee?
Can we sinne to be object of thy mercie?
   Wif. Yes, and have don't already, and no staine
To your greatnesse Madam, tis my charity
I can remit: when soveraigne Princes dare   140
Doe injury to those that live beneath them,
They turne worth pitty, and their pray'rs, and tis /
In the free power of those whom they oppresse   [D4]
To pardon e'm; each soule has a prerogative,
And priviledge royall that was sign'd by heaven,   145
But though ith'knowledge of my disposition
Stranger to pride, and what you charge me with,
I can forgive the injustice done to me,
And striking at my person, I have no
Commission from my Lord to cleere you for   150
The wrongs you have done him, and till he pardon
The wounding of his loyaltie, with which life
Can hold no ballance, I must take just boldnesse
To say ———
   Fa.   No more. Now I must tell you daughter
Least you forget your selfe, she is the Queene,   155
And it becomes not you to vie with her
Passion for passion: if your Lord stand fast
To the full search of Law, Heaven will revenge him,
And give him up precious to good mens loves;
If you attempt by these unruly wayes   160
To vindicate his justice, Ime against you,
Deere as I wish your husbands life and fame;
Subjects are bound to suffer, not contest
With Princes, since their Will and Acts must be
Accounted one day to a Judge supreme.   165
   Wif. I ha done. If the devotion to my Lord,
Or pietie to his innocence have led me
Beyond the awfull limits to be observ'd
By one so much beneath your sacred person,
I thus low crave your royall pardon Madam;   170
[*Kneels.*] I know you will remember in your goodnesse,
My life blood is concern'd while his least veine
Shall runne blacke and polluted, my heart fed
With what keepes him alive, nor can there be
A greater wound than that which strikes the life   175
Of our good name, so much above the bleeding

138 don't] dont ‖ 140 remit:] ∼, ‖ 141 injury] in jury ‖ 144 e'm;] ∼, ‖ 146 ith'] ith ‖ 151 till] *Shepherd*; still ‖ 153 take] *Dyce*; talke ‖ 154 more. Now] ∼, now ‖ 157 passion:] ∼, ‖ 159 loves;] ∼, ‖ 162 fame;] ∼, ‖ 163 Subjects] *Dyce*; Suffer ‖ 166 done. If] ∼, if ‖ 171 SD *Kneels.*] *Dyce* ‖

Of this rude pile wee carry, as the soule
Hath excellence above this earth-borne frailty:
My Lord, by the Kings will is lead already /
To a severe arraignement, and to Iudges,   [D4ᵛ]
Will make no tender search into his tract   181
Of life and state; stay but a little while,
And *France* shall eccho to his shame or innocence.
This suit I begge with teares; I shall have sorrow
Enough to heare him censur'd foule and monstrous,   185
Should you forbeare to antidate my sufferings.
    Qu. Your conscience comes about, and you incline
To feare he may be worth the lawes condemning.
    Wif. I sooner will suspect the starres may lose
Their way, and cristall heaven returne to Chaos;   190
Truth sits not on her square more firme than he;
Yet let me tell you Madam, were his life
And action so foule as you have character'd,
And the bad world expects, though as a wife
Twere duty I should weepe my selfe to death,   195
To know him falne from vertue, yet so much
I a fraile woman love my King and Country,
I should condemne him too, and thinke all honours,
The price of his lost faith, more fatall to me,
Than *Cleopatra's* aspes warme in my bosome,   200
And as much boast their killing.
    Qu. [*Aside.*]   This declares
Another soule than was deliver'd me,
My anger melts, and I beginne to pitty her.
How much a Princes eare may be abus'd? –
Enjoy your happie confidence, at more leasure   205
You may heare from us.
    Wif. [*Rises.*]   Heaven preserve the Queene,
And may her heart be charitable.
    Fa. You blesse and honour your unworthy servant.
                             [*Exeunt Father and Wife.*]
    Qu. My Lord, did you observe this?
    Con.   Yes great Madam,
And read a noble spirit, which becomes   210
The wife of *Chabot*; their great tie of marriage
Is not more strong upon em, than their vertues.
    Qu. That your opinion? I thought't your judgement
Against the Admirall: doe you thinke him honest? /

---

182 state;] ~, ‖ 183 innocence.] ~, ‖ 184 teares;] ~, ‖ 194 expects] expe cts ‖ 198 honours,] ~ˏ ‖
199 faith,] ~ˏ ‖ 201 SD *Aside.*] *Parrott (after Dyce)* ‖ 203 her.] ~, ‖ 204 abus'd?-] *Dyce*; ~?ˏ ‖ 206
SD *Rises.*] ‖ 208 *Exeunt … Wife.*] *Dyce subs.* ‖ 211 *Chabot*;] ~, ‖ 213 thought't] thought ‖ 214
Admirall:] ~, ‖

Con. Religiously, a true, most zealous Patriot,   [E1]
And worth all royall favour.
    Qu.   You amaze me;   216
Can you be just your selfe then, and advance
Your powers against him?
    Con.   Such a will be farre
From *Montmoranzie!* Pioners of state
Have left no art to gaine me to their faction,   220
And tis my misery to be plac'd in such
A sphere where I am whirl'd by violence
Of a fierce raging motion, and not what
My owne will would encline me. I shall make
This appeare Madam, if you please to second   225
My free speech with the King.
    Qu.   Good heaven protect all,
Haste to the King, Iustice her swift wing needes:
Tis high time to be good, when vertue bleedes.   *Exeunt.*

[III.ii]

Enter Officers before the Chancellor, Iudges, the
Proctor generall, whispering with the Chancellor;
they take their places.
To them
Enter Treasurer and Secretary who take their places
prepared on one side of the Court.
To them
The Captaine of the Guard, the Admirall following,
who is plac'd at the barre.

Cha. Good Mr. Proctor generall begin.
    Pro. It is not unknowne to you my very good Lords
the Iudges, and indeed to all the world, for I will
make short worke, since your honourable eares neede
not to be enlarged (I speake by a figure) with prolixe   5
ennumeration how infinitly the King hath favoured
this ill-favoured Traitor; and yet I may worthily
too insist and prove that no grace hath beene so
large and voluminous, as this, that he hath appointed
such upright Iudges at this time, and the chiefe   10
of this Triumvirie, our Chancellor by name *Poyet,*
which deriveth from the Greeke his Etymology from
Poyein, which is to make, to create, to invent matter

---

216 me;] ~, ‖ 219 *Montmoranzie!*] ~, ‖ 227 needes:] ~, ‖ **III.ii**] Dyce ‖ SD *Chancellor;*] ~, ‖ 2
Pro.] ~, ‖ 5 enlarged (I . . . figure)] ~, ~ . . . ~ ‖ 7 ill-favoured] ~,~ ‖ 13 *Poyein*] Dyce; *Poyeni* ‖

that was never extant in nature, from / whence also [E1ʳ]
is the name and dignitie of *Poeta*, which I will not 15
insist upon, in this place, although I am confident
his Lordshippe wanteth no facultie in making of Verses:
but what addition I say is it to the honour of this
Delinquent, that he hath such a Iudge, a man so learned,
so full of equity, so noble, so notable in the progresse 20
of his life, so innocent, in the manage of his office
so incorrupt, in the passages of State so wise, in
affection to his country so religious, in all his services
to the King so fortunate, and exploring, as envie it
selfe cannot accuse, or malice vitiate, whom all lippes 25
will open to commend, but those of *Philip*; and in their
hearts will erect Altars, and Statues, Columnes, and
Obeliskes, Pillars and Pyramids, to the perpetuitie of
his name and memory. What shall I say? but conclude for
his so great and sacred service, both to our King and 30
Kingdome, and for their ever lasting benefit, there may
everlastingly be left here one of his loynes, one of his
loynes ever remaine I say, and stay upon this Bench, to
be the example of all Iustice, even while the North and
South Starre shall continue. 35
    Cha. You expresse your Oratory Mr. Proctor,
I pray come presently to the matter.
    Pro. Thus with your Lordships pardon, I proceede,
and the first thing I shall glance at, will be worth
your Lordships reflection, his ingratitude, and to 40
whom? to no lesse person than a King, and to what King?
his owne, and our generall Soveraigne, *Proh deum
atque hominum fidem*; a King, and such a King, the
health, life, and soule of us all, whose very mention
drawes this salt water from my eyes; for hee indeede 45
is our eye, who wakes and watches for us when we
sleepe, and who will not sleepe for him? I meane
not sleepe, which the Philosophers call, a naturall
cessation of the common and consequently of all the
exterior sences, caused first and immediatly by a 50
detension of spirits, which can have no communication,
since the way is obstructed, by which these spirits
should commearce, by vapours ascending from the
stomacke to the head, by which evaporation the rootes
of the nerves are filled, through which the animall 55
spirits [use] to be powred into the dwellings of the

---

22 incorrupt,] ~; ‖ 28 Obeliskes] *Dyce*; Obelishes ‖ 31 ever lasting] *possibly one word in Q* ‖ 34
be the] *Q(c)*; bethe *Q(u)* ‖ 37 pray] *Q(c)*; ray *Q(u)* ‖ 41 King?] ~, ‖ 42 Soveraigne,] So- /
veraigne‿ ‖ 47 him?] ~, ‖ 55-56 animall spirits use] *Parrott (after Dyce)*; annuall spirits, ‖

externall sences; but sleepe / I take for death,   [E2]
which all know to be *Vltima linea*. Who will not
sleepe eternally for such a King as wee enjoy? If
therefore in generall as hee is King of us all,   60
all sharing and dividing the benefits of this our
Soveraigne, none should be so ingratefull as once
to murmure against him, what shall be said of
the ingratitude more monstrous in this *Chabot*?
for our *Francis* hath loved, not in generall and   65
in the croud with other subjects, but particularly
this *Philip*, advanc'd him to the supreme dignitie
of a Statsman, lodg'd him in his very heart, yet
Monstrum horrendum! even to this *Francis* hath *Philip*
beene ingratefull. *Brutus* the loved sonne hath   70
stabbed *Cæsar* with a Bodkin: Oh what brute may be
compared to him? and in what particulars may this
crime be exemplified? hee hath, as wee say, chopt
Logicke with the King, nay to the very teeth of his
Soveraigne advanc'd his owne Gnat-like merits, and   75
justified with *Luciferous* pride, that his services
have deserved more than all the bounty of our
Munificent King hath paid him.

   Cha. Observe that my Lords.

   Pro. Nay he hath gone further, and most traiterously   80
hath committed outrage and impiety to the Kings owne
hand, and royall character, which presented to him
in a bill from the whole counsell, hee most violently
did teare in peeces, and will doe the very body and
person of our King, if your Justice make no   85
timely prevention, and strike out the Serpentine
teeth of this high, and more than horrible monster.

   Tre. This was enforced home.

   Pro. In the next place I will relate to your
honours his most cruell exactions upon the subject,   90
the old vantcurriers of rebellions. In the yeare
1536. and 37. this oppressour, and this extortioner,
under pretext of his due taxation, being Admirall,
impos'd upon certaine Fishermen, (observe I beseech
you the circumstance of their persons, Fishermen)   95
who poore *Iohns* were embarqued upon the cost of
Normandy, and fishing there for Herrings (which some
say is the king of Fishes) he impos'd I say twenty
souse, and upon every boate six *liuers*: oh intollerable

---

58 *linea*. Who] ~, who ‖ **62** none should] noneshould ‖ **64** *Chabot?*] ~, ‖ **67** *Philip*,] ~ ‖ **69**
horrendum!] ~; ‖ **73** exemplified?] ~; ‖ **75** advanc'd] *Dyce subs.*; advance ‖ **81** committed]
commitred ‖ **85** our ... your] *Q(c)*; your ... our *Q(u)* ‖ **92** 1536.] *Q(c)*; 15.6. *Q(u)* | 37. this]
37. This ‖ **93** Admirall,] ~ ‖ **99** *liuers*:] ~, ‖

exaction! enough not onely to alienate the hearts of   100
these miserable people from their King, which
Ipso facto is high treason, but an occasion of a
greater inconveni / ence, for want of due provision   [E2ᵛ]
of fish among the subjects, for by this might ensue
a necessitie of mortall sins, by breaking the   105
religious fast upon Vigils, Embers, and other dayes
commanded by sacred authority, besides the miserable
rut that would follow, and perhaps contagion, when
feasting and flesh should be licenced for every
carnall appetite. —— I could urge many more   110
particulars of his dangerous insatiate and boundlesse
Avarice, but the improvement of his estate in so few
yeares, from a private Gentlemans fortune, to a great
Dukes revenewes, might save our Soveraigne therein
an Orator to enforce and prove faulty even to   115
gyantisme against heaven. / And how this great   [[E3]]
and mighty fortune hath exalted him to pride
is apparant, not onely in his braves and
bearings to the King, the fountaine of all this
increase, but in his contempt and scorne   120
of the subject, his vast expences in buildings,
his private bounties, above royall to souldiers
and schollers, that he may be the Generall and
Patron, and protector of armes and arts; the
number of domesticke attendants, an army of   125
Grashoppers and gay Butterflies able to devoure
the Spring; his glorious wardrobes, his stable of
horses that are prick'd with provender, and will
enforce us to weede up our Vineyards to sow Oates
for supply of their provision, his caroches shining   130
with gold, and more bright than the chariot of
the Sunne, wearing out the pavements; nay, he is
of late so transcendently proud, that men must be
his Mules, and carry him up and downe as it were   134
in a Procession for men to gaze / at him till   [[E3ᵛ]]
their chines crackes with the weight of his
insupportable pride, and who knowes but this may
prove a fashion? But who grones for this? the subject,
who murmure, and are ready to beginne a rebellion,
but the tumultuous saylers, and water-rats, who runne   140
up and downe the citie, like an overbearing tempest,

---

114 Soveraigne] soveraigne ‖ 116-143 And how ... countrymen.] *arranged as by Ferguson; Pro.*
And how ... countrymen. *(following l.196 in Q) (See Textual Note)* ‖ 141 overbearing] over- /
bearing ‖

cursing the Admirall, who in duty ought to undoe
himself for the generall satisfaction of his countrymen. /

Iudg. This is but a noise of words. [E2ᵛ]

Pro. To the foule outrages so violent, let us adde 145
his Commissions granted out of his owne presum'd
authoritie (his Majestie neither inform'd or respected),
his disloyalties, infidelities, contempts, oppressions,
extortions, with innumerable abuses, offences, and
forfeits, both to his Majesties most royall person, 150
crowne, and dignitie, yet notwithstanding all these
injustices, this unmatchable, unjust delinquent
affecteth to be thought inculpable, and incomparable
just; but alas my most learned Lords, none knowes
better than your selves, how easie the sinceritie 155
of Iustice is pretended, how hard it is to be
performed, and how common it is for him that hath
least colour of title to it, to be thought the very
substance and soule of it: he that was never true
scholler in the least degree, longs as a woman with 160
child to be great with scholler, she that was never
with child longs *Omnibus vijs et modis* to be got with
child, and will weare a cushion to seeme with child,
and hee that was never just, will fly in the Kings
face to be counted just, though for all he be nothing, 165
but just, a Traytor.

Sec. The Admirall smiles.

Iudg. Answer your selfe my Lord.

Adm.   I shall, and briefely:
The furious eloquence of my accuser hath
Branch'd my offences hainous to the King, 170
And then his subject, a most vast indictment,
That to the King I have justified my merit,
And services; which conscience of that truth, /
That gave my actions life when they are questioned, [E3]
I ought to urge agen, and doe without 175
The least part of injustice; for the Bill,
A foule, and most unjust one, and prefer'd
Gainst the Kings honour, and his subjects priviledge,
And with a policie to betray my office,
And faith to both, I doe confesse I tore it, 180
It being prest immodestly, but without
A thought of disobedience to his name,

---

146 Commissions] Com- / mission s ‖ 147 authoritie (his . . . respected),] ~, ‿~ . . . ~‿ | inform'd]
Dyce subs.; infround ‖ 154 Lords] *Dyce*; Lord ‖ 159 it:] ~, ‖ 168 briefely:] ~, ‖ 176 Bill,] ~‿ ‖

To whose mention I bow, with humble reverence,
And dare appeale to the Kings knowledge of me,
How farre I am in soule from such a rebell;   185
For the rest my Lord, and you my honour'd Iudges,
Since all this mountaine all this time in labour
With more than mortall fury gainst my life,
Hath brought forth nought but some ridiculous vermine,
I will not wrong my right, and innocence,   190
With any serious plea in my reply,
To frustrate breath, and fight with terrible shaddowes
That have beene forg'd, and forc'd against my state,
But leave all, with my life to your free censures;
Onely beseeching all your learned judgements   195
Equall and pious conscience to weigh /
The varietie, and wonder now presented   [[E3ᵛ]]
To your most noble notice, and the worlds,
That all my life and actions, and offices,
Explor'd with all the hundred eyes of Law   200
Lighted with lightning, shot out of the wrath
Of an incenst, and commanding King,
And blowne with foes, with farre more bitter windes,
Then Winter from his Easterne cave exhailes,
Yet nothing found, but what you all have heard,   205
And then consider if a peere of State
Should be expos'd to such a wild arraignement
For poore complaints, his fame, faith, life, and honours
Rackt for no more.
   Cha.   No more? good heaven, what say
My learned assistants?   210
   1 *Iudg.* My Lord, the crimes urg'd here for us to censure
As capitall, and worth this high arraignement
To me seeme strange, because they doe not fall
In force of Law, to arraigne a Peere of State,
For all that Law can take into her power   215
To sentence, is the exaction of the Fishermen.
   2 *Iudg.* Here is no majesty violated, I consent
To what my Brother has exprest.
   Cha.   Breake then in wonder,
My frighted words out of their forming powers,
That you no more collect, from all these forfeits   220
That Mr. Proctor generall hath opened,

---

185 rebell;] ~, ‖ 192 shaddowes] *Dyce*; shaddow ‖ 196 weigh] *Macaulay conj.*; ~. ‖ 197-209 The
varietie ... more.] *arranged as by Macaulay*; *Adm.* The varietie ... more. (*following l. 143 in Q*)
(*See Textual Note to ll. 116-143*) ‖ 205 Yet] *Q(c)*; Yeh *Q(u)* ‖ 206 State] ~, ‖ 210 assistants?] ~. ‖
217-18 consent / To] *Shepherd*; ~ to ‖ 218 *Cha.*] ~, ‖

With so apparant, and impulsive learning,
Against the rage and madnesse of the offender,
And violate Majestie (my learned assistants)
When Majestie's affronted and defied, /   225
(It being compar'd with? and in such an onset   [E4]
As leap'd into his throate? his life affrighting?)
Be justified in all insolence, all subjects,
If this be so considered, and insult
Vpon your priviledg'd malice! Is not Majestie   230
Poyson'd in this wonder! and no felony set
Where royaltie is rob'd, and [violate]?
Fie how it fights with Law, and grates upon
Her braine and soule, and all the powers of Reason! –
Reporter of the processe, shew the sedule.   235
    No. Here my good Lord.
    1 *Judg.*   No altering it in us.
    2 *Judg.* Farre be it from us Sir.
    Cha.   Here's silken Iustice!
It might be altered, mend your sentences.
    Both. Not wee my Lord.
    Cha.   Not you? The King shall know
You slight a duty to his will, and safety.   240
Give me your pen, it must be capitall.
    1 *Judg.* Make what you please my Lord, our doome shall stand.
    Cha. Thus I subscribe, now at your perills follow.
    Both. Perills my Lord? threates in the Kings free justice?
    Tre. I am amaz'd they can be so remisse.   245
    Sec. Mercifull men, pittifull Iudges certaine.
    1 *Judg.* [*Aside to 2 Judge.*] Subscribe, it matters nothing
      being constrain'd;
On this side [*V*], and on this side, this capitall *I*,
Both which together put, import plaine *Vi*;
And witnesse we are forc'd.
    2 *Judg.* [*Aside to 1 Judge.*]   Enough,   250
It will acquit us when we make it knowne,
Our names are forc'd.
    Cha.   If traiterous pride
Vpon the royall person of a King
Were sentenc'd unfelloniously before,
Ile burne my Bookes and be a Iudge no more.   255

---

225 Majestie's] Majesties ‖ 226-27 (It being ... affrighting?)] *Parrott subs.*; ‿ ~ / ... ~?‿ (*See Textual Note*) ‖ 228 subjects,] ~‿ ‖ 230 malice! Is] *Dyce*; ~, is ‖ 232 and violate?] *Parrott (after Dyce)*; and ‖ 234 Reason!–] *Dyce*; ~,‿ ‖ 236 1 *Judg.*] *Dyce*; 1. (*throughout rest of scene*) ‖ 237 2 *Judg.*] *Dyce*; 2. (*throughout rest of scene*) | Here's] Heres | Iustice!] ~, ‖ 240 safety.] ~, ‖ 245 *Tre.*] ~, ‖ 247 SD *Aside to 2 Judge.*] *Parrott (aside)* | constrain'd;] ~‿ ‖ 248 side *V*,] *Lehman*; side, | *I*] I ‖ 250 SD *Aside to 1 Judge.*] *Parrott (aside)* ‖

Both. Here are our hands subscrib'd.
Cha.   Why so, it joyes me,
You have reform'd your justice and your judgement; /
Now have you done like Iudges and learned Lawyers,   [E4ᵛ]
The King shall thanke, and honour you for this.
Notary read.   260
    No. We by his sacred Majestie appointed Judges,
upon due triall, and examination of *Philip Chabot*
Admirall of *France* declare him guiltie of high
treasons, etc.
    Cha. Now Captaine of the guard,   265
Secure his person, till the King signifie
His pleasure for his death. This day is happy
To *France*, thus reskued from the vile devourer.

                        A shoute within.

Harke how the votes applaud their blest deliverance!
[*To the Admiral.*] You that so late did right and conscience
        boast,   270
Heavens mercy now implore, the Kings is lost.   *Exeunt.*

                Actus Quartus.   [*Scena I.*]

            Enter King, Queene, and Constable.

    King. You raise my thoughts to wonder, that you Madam,
And you my Lord, unite your force to pleade
Ith'Admiralls behalfe; this is not that
Language you did expresse, when the torne Bill
Was late pretended to us; it was then   5
Defiance to our high prerogative,
The act of him whose proud heart would rebell
And arm'd with faction, too soone attempt
To teare my crowne off.
    Qu.   I was ignorant
Then of his worth, and heard but the report   10
Of his accusers, and his enemies,
Who never mention in his character
Shadowes of any vertue in those men,
They would depresse: like Crowes, and carrion birds,
They fly ore flowrie Meades, cleare Springs, faire Gardens,   15

---

257 judgement;] ∼, ‖ **261-64** We by ... etc.] *as prose, Parrott; as verse,* Q (We ... appointed /
Judges ... examination / Of ... *France* / Declare ... &c.) ‖ **265-66** guard, / Secure ... till] gaurd,
secure ... / Till ‖ **267** death. This] ∼, this ‖ **269** deliverance!] ∼, ‖ **270** SD *To the Admiral.*]
Parrott subs. ‖ *Scena I.*] *Parrott (after Dyce)* ‖ **1** *King.*] *Kin. (otherwise / King. / throughout
scene)* | thoughts] thoughrs ‖ **3** behalfe;] ∼, ‖ **5** us;] ∼, ‖ **14** depresse:] *Dyce;* ∼. ‖

And stoope at carcasses; for your owne honour /
Pitty poore *Chabot.* [F1]
  King. Poore and a *Colossus?*
What could so lately straddle ore a Province,
Can he be fallen so low, and miserable,
To want my pitty, who breakes forth like day, 20
Takes up all peoples eyes, and admiration?
It cannot be; he hath a Princely wife too.
  Qu. I interpose not often Sir, or presse you
With unbecomming importunitie,
To serve the profitable ends of others: 25
Conscience, and duty to your selfe inforce
My present mediation; you have given
The health of your owne state away, unlesse
Wisedome in time recover him.
  King. If he proove
No adulterate gold, triall confirmes his value. 30
  Qu. Although it hold in mettle gracious Sir,
Such fiery examination, and the furnace
May wast a heart that's faithfull, and together
With that you call the *feces,* something of
The precious substance may be hazarded. 35
  King. [*To the Constable.*] Why, you are the chiefe engine rais'd
    against him,
And in the worlds Creede labour most to sinke him,
That in his fall, and absence every beame
May shine on you, and onely guild your fortune;
Your difference is the ground of his arraignement, 40
Nor were we unsollicited by you,
To have your bill confirm'd, from that, that spring,
Came all these mighty and impetuous waves,
With which he now must wrastle; if the strength
Of his owne innocence can breake the storme, 45
Truth wonot lose her servant, her wings cover him,
He must obey his fate.
  Con. I would not have
It lie upon my fame, that I should be
Mentioned in Story his unjust supplanter
For your whole Kingdome. I have beene abused, 50
And made beleeve my suite was just and necessary: /
My walkes have not beene safe, my closet prayers, [F1ᵛ]

---

17 *Colossus*] Colossus ‖ 22 be;] ~, ‖ 25 others:] ~ˏ ‖ 27 mediation;] ~, ‖ 33 that's] thats ‖ 36 SD
To the Constable.] *Parrott (See Textual Note)* ‖ 39 fortune;] ~, ‖ 42 that, that spring,] ~ˏ ~ ~ˏ ‖
44 wrastle;] ~, ‖ 50 Kingdome.] ~, ‖ 51 necessary:] ~, ‖

But some plot has persued me, by some great ones
Against your noble Admirall; they have frighted
My fancy into my dreames with their close whispers,   55
How to uncement your affections,
And render him the fable, and the scorne
Of *France*.
    Qu.   Brave *Montmorancie*.
    King.   Are you serious?
    Con. Have I a soule? or gratitude, to acknowledge
My selfe your creature, dignified and honor'd   60
By your high favours? with an equall truth,
I must declare the justice of your Admirall
(In what my thoughts are conscious) and will rather
Give up my claime to birth, title, and offices,
Be throwne from your warme smile, the top and crowne   65
Of subjects happinesse, then be brib'd with all
Their glories to the guilt of *Chabots* ruine.
    King. Come, come, you over act this passion,
And if it be not pollicie it tasts
Too greene, and wants some counsell to mature it: 70
His fall prepares your triumph.
    Con.   It confirmes
My shame alive, and buried will corrupt
My very dust, make our house-genious grone,
And fright the honest marble from my ashes:
His fall prepare my triumph? turne me first   75
A naked exile to the world.
    King.   No more,
Take heede you banish not your selfe, be wise,
And let not too much zeale devoure your reason.

Enter Asall.

    As. Your Admirall is condemn'd Sir!
    King.   Ha? strange! no matter,
Leave us. [*Exit Asall.*] A great man I see may be   80
As soone dispatch'd, as a common subject.
    Qu. No mercy then for *Chabot*. /

Enter Wife and Father.   [F2]

    Wif.   From whence came
That sound of *Chabot*? then we are all undone:
[*Kneels.*] Oh doe not heare the Queene, she is no friend

---

54 Admirall;] ~, ‖ 58 serious?] ~. ‖ 61 favours?] *Dyce*; ~ ‖ 70 it:] ~, ‖ 73 house-genious] *Q(c)*; house genious *Q(u)* ‖ 78 zeale] *Q(c)*; eale *Q(u)* ‖ 79 Admirall is] *Shepherd*; ~ / Is | Sir!] ~? ‖ 80 us. A] ~, a | SD *Exit Asall.*] *Dyce* ‖ 84 SD *Kneels.*] *Parrott subs.* ‖

666

To my poore Lord, but made against his life, 85
Which hath too many enemies already.
  Con. [*To Father.*] Poore soule, shee thinkes the Queene is still
    against him,
Who employeth all her powers to preserve him.
  Fa. Say you so my Lord? daughter the Queen's our friend.
  Wif. Why doe you mocke my sorrow! can you flatter 90
Your owne griefe so? [*To the King.*] Be just, and heare me sir,
And doe not sacrifice a subjects blood
To appease a wrathfull Queene; let mercy shine
Vpon your brow, and heaven will pay it backe
Vpon your soule: be deafe to all her prayers. 95
  King. Poore heart, she knowes not what she has desir'd.
  Wif. I begge my *Chabots* life, my sorrowes yet
Have not destroid my reason.
  King.   He is in the power
Of my Lawes, not mine.
  Wif.   Then you have no power,
And are but the emptie shadow of a King. 100
To whom is it resign'd? where shall I begge
The forfeit life of one condemn'd by Lawes
Too partiall doome?
  King.   You heare he is condemn'd then?
  Fa. My sonne is condemn'd sir.
  King.   You know for what too.
  Fa. What the Iudges please to call it, 105
But they have given't a name, Treason they say.
  Qu. I must not be denied.
  King.   I must deny you.
  Wif. Be blest for ever for't.
  Qu.   Grant then to her.
  King. Chabot condemn'd by law?
  Fa.   But you have power
To change the rigor, in your breast there is 110
A Chancellor above it. [*Kneels.*] I nere had
A suite before, but my knees joyne with hers /
To implore your royall mercy to her Lord, [F2ᵛ]
And take his cause to your examination:
It cannot wrong your Iudges, if they have 115
Beene steer'd by conscience.
  Con.   It will fame your Iustice.
  King. I cannot be prescrib'd, you kneele in vaine;

---

87 SD *To Father.*] *Parrott* ‖ 91 so? Be] ~, be | SD *To the King.*] *Parrott* ‖ 93 Queene;] ~, ‖ 95
soule:] ~, ‖ 98-99 power / Of] *Parrott*; ~ of ‖ 100 King.] ~, ‖ 103 Too] *Dyce*; To ‖ 108 for't]
fort ‖ 111 it.] ~, | SD *Kneels.*] *Parrott subs.* ‖ 114 examination:] ~, ‖ 117 vaine;] ~, ‖

You labour to betray me with your teares
To a treason above his, gainst my owne Lawes.

[*The Wife faints.*]

Looke to the Lady ———

Enter Asall.

As.   Sir the Chancellor.   120
King. Admit him. – Leave us all.   *Exeunt all but the King.*

Enter Chancellor.

How now my Lord?

You have lost no time, and how thrive the proceedings?
   Cha. Twas fit my gracious Soveraigne, time should leave
His motion made in all affaires beside,
And spend his wings onely in speed of this.   125
   King. You have shew'd diligence, and what's become
Of our most curious Iusticer, the Admirall?
   Cha. Condemn'd sir utterly, and all hands set
To his conviction.
   King.   And for faults most foule?
   Cha. More than most impious, but the applausive issue   130
Strooke by the concourse of your ravish'd subjects
For joy of your free Iustice, if there were
No other cause to assure the sentence just
Were proofe convincing.
   King.   Now then he sees cleerely
That men perceive how vaine his Iustice was,   135
And scorne him for the foolish net he wore
To hide his nakednesse; is't not a wonder
That mens ambitions should so blinde their reason
To affect shapes of honesty, and take pride
Rather in seeming, then in being just?   140
   Cha. Seeming has better fortune to attend it
Then being sound at heart, and vertuous.
   King. Professe all? nothing doe, like those that live /
By looking to the Lamps of holy Temples,   [F3]
Who still are busie taking off their snuffes,   145
But for their profit sake will adde no oyle;
So these will checke and sentence every flame,
The blaze of riotous blood doth cast in others,
And in themselves leave the fume most offensive:
But he to doe this? more deceives my judgement   150

---

119 Lawes.] ∼, | SD *The Wife faints.*] *Parrott subs.* ‖ 121 him. – Leave] *Dyce*; ∼, ‸ leave | SD
Exeunt ... King.] *Dyce*; *Exeunt.* (*following* Lady ——— *in l.120*) ‖ 122 proceedings?] ∼. ‖
123 *Cha.*] *Q(c)*; *King. Q(u)* ‖ 126 what's] whats ‖ 137 is't] ist ‖ 140 just?] ∼. ‖ 147 flame] *Parrott*;
fame ‖ 149 offensive:] ∼, ‖

668

Than all the rest whose nature I have sounded.
   Cha. I know Sir, and have prov'd it.
   King.   Well my Lord
To omit circumstance, I highly thanke you
For this late service you have done me here,
Which is so great and meritorious   155
That with my ablest power I scarce can quit you.
   Cha. Your sole acceptance (my dread Soveraigne)
I more rejoyce in, than in all the fortunes
That ever chanc'd me, but when may it please
Your Highnesse to order the execution?   160
The haste thus farre hath spar'd no pinions.
   King. No my Lord, your care
Hath therein much deserv'd.
   Cha.   But where proportion
Is kept toth'end in things, at start so happy,
That end set on the crowne.
   King.   Ile speede it therefore.   165
   Cha. Your thoughts direct it, they are wing'd.   *Exit.*
   King.   I joy
This boldnesse is condemn'd, that I may pardon,
And therein get some ground in his opinion
By so much bounty as saves his life,
And me thinks that weigh'd more, should sway the ballance   170
Twixt me and him, held by his owne free Iustice,
For I could never finde him obstinate
In any minde he held, when once he saw
Th'error with which he laboured, and since now
He needs must feele it, I admit no doubt,   175
But that his alteration will beget
Another sence of things twixt him and me;
Whose there?

Enter Asall. /

          Goe to the Captaine of my guard,   [F3ᵛ]
And will him to attend his condemn'd prisoner   179
To me instantly.
   As.   I shall sir.   [*Exit.*]

Enter Treasurer and Secretary.

   King. My Lords, you were spectators of our Admirall.

---

157 Soveraigne] soveraigne ‖ 164 happy,] ~. ‖ 166-67 I joy / This] *Dyce*; ~ ~ this ‖ 177 twixt]
Q(c); twit *Q(u)* ‖ 178-79 guard, / And ... to] ~, and ... / To ‖ 179-80 prisoner / To] ~ to ‖ 180
SD *Exit.*] *Dyce* ‖

669

Tre. And hearers too of his most just conviction,
In which we witnest over-weight enough
In your great bounties, and as they there were weigh'd
With all the feathers of his boasted merits.   185
   King. Has felt a scorching triall, and the test
(That holds fires utmost force) we must give mettalls
That will not with the hammer, and the melting
Confesse their truth, and this same sence of feeling
(Being ground to all the sences) hath one key   190
More than the rest to let in through them all
The mindes true apprehension, that thence takes
Her first convey'd intelligence. I long
To see this man of confidence agen:
How thinke you Lords, will *Chabot* looke on mee,   195
Now spoild of the integrity, he boasted?
   Sec. It were too much honour to vouchsafe your sight.
   Tre. No doubt my Leige, but he that hath offended
In such a height against your crowne and person,
Will want no impudence to looke upon you.   200

Enter Asall, Captaine, Admirall.

   Cap. Sir, I had charge given me by this Gentleman
To bring your condemn'd prisoner to your presence.
   King. You have done well, and tell the Queene, and our
Lord Constable we desire their presence. [*To Asall.*] Bid
Our Admiralls Lady, and her father too   205
Attend us here, they are but new withdrawne.
   As. I shall sir!   [*Exeunt Asall and Captain.*]
   Tre. [*Aside to the Secretary.*]   Doe you observe this confidence?
He stands as all his triall were a dreame.
   Sec. [*Aside to the Treasurer.*] Hele finde the horrour waking,
     the King's troubled;
Now for a thunder-clap: the Queene and Constable.   210

Enter Captain and Asall with Queene, Constable, Wife and Father.

   Tre. [*Aside to the Secretary.*] I doe not like their mixture.
   King.   My Lord
   Admirall, /
You made it your desire to have this triall   [F4]
That late hath past upon you;
And now you feele how vaine is too much faith
And flattery of your selfe, as if your brest   215

---

198 Leige] *Dyce*; Leigh ‖ 203 *King.*] ~, ‖ 204 presence. Bid] ~, bid | SD *To Asall.*] (*See Textual Note*) ‖ 207 SD *Exeunt ... Captain.*] | SD *Aside ... Secretary.*] ‖ 209 SD *Aside ... Treasurer.*] ‖ 210 SD *Enter Captain and Asall with Queene,*] *Enter Queene,* ‖ 211 SD *Aside ... Secretary.*] | *King.*] ~, ‖

Were proofe gainst all invasion; tis so slight
You see it lets in death. What's past, hath beene
To satisfie your insolence, there remaines
That now we serve our owne free pleasure, therefore
By that most absolute power, with which all right   220
Puts in my hands, these issues, turnes, and changes,
I here in eare of all these, pardon all
Your faults and forfeits, whatsoever sensur'd,
Againe advancing, and establishing
Your person in all fulnesse of that state   225
That ever you enjoy'd before th'attainder.
  Tre. Wonderfull, pardon'd!
  Wif.   Heaven preserve the King.
  Qu. Who for this will deserve all time to honour him.
  Con. And live Kings best example.
  Fa.   Sonne y'are pardon'd,
Be sure you looke hereafter well about you.   230
  Adm. Vouchsafe great Sir to assure me what you said,
You nam'd my pardon.
  King.   And agen declare it,
For all crimes past, of what nature soever.
  Adm. You cannot pardon me Sir.
  King.   How's that *Philip*?
  Adm. It is a word carries too much relation   235
To an offence, of which I am not guilty,
And I must still be bold where truth still armes,
In spight of all those frownes that would deject me,
To say I neede no pardon.
  King.   Ha, howe's this?
  Fa. Hee's mad with over-joy, and answers nonsense.   240
  King. Why, tell me *Chabot*, are not you condemn'd?
  Adm. Yes, and that justifies me much the more,
For whatsoever false report hath brought you,
I was condemn'd for nothing that could reach /   244
To prejudice my life, my goods or honour,   [F4ᵛ]
As first in firmenesse of my conscience,
I confidently told you, not alas
Presuming on your slender thred of favour,
Or pride of fortunate and courtly boldnesse,
But what my faith and justice bade me trust too,   250
For none of all your learned assistant Judges,
With all the malice of my crimes could urge,

---

216 invasion;] ~, ‖ 217 death. What's] ~, whats ‖ 221 issues,] ~. ‖ 229 y'are] yare ‖ 238 frownes]
Q(c); frounes Q(u) | me,] ~. ‖ 239 howe's] howes ‖ 240 Hee's] Hees ‖

Or felony or hurt of sacred power.
   King. Doe any heare this, but my selfe? My Lords,
This man still justifies his innocence: 255
What prodigies are these? have not our Lawes
Past on his actions? have not equall Iudges
Certified his arraignement, and him guilty
Of capitall Treason? and yet doe I heare
Chabot accuse all these, and quit himselfe.   260
   Tre. It does appeare distraction sir.
   King.   Did we
Seeme so indulgent to propose our free
And royall pardon without suite or prayer,
To meete with his contempt?
   Sec.   Vnhear'd of impudence!
   Adm. I were malicious to my selfe, and desperate   265
To force untruths upon my soule, and when
Tis cleare, to confesse a shame to exercise
Your pardon sir. Were I so foule and monstrous
As I am given to you, you would commit
A sinne next mine, by wronging your owne mercy   270
To let me draw out impious breath: it will
Release your wonder, if you give command
To see your processe, and if it prove other
Than I presume to informe, teare me in peeces.
   King. Goe for the Processe, and the Chancellor,   275
With the assistant Iudges. I thanke heaven   *Exit As.*
That with all these inforcements of distraction
My reason stayes so cleare to heare, and answer,
And to direct a message. This inversion
Of all the loyalties, and true deserts /   280
That I beleev'd I govern'd with till now   [G1]
In my choice Lawyers, and chiefe Counsellors
Is able to shake all my frame of reason.
   Adm. I am much griv'd.
   King.   No more! [*Aside.*] I doe incline
To thinke I am abus'd, my Lawes betrai'd   285
And wrested to the purpose of my Judges:
This confidence in *Chabot* turnes my judgement;
This was too wilde a way to make his merits
Stoope and acknowledge my superior bounties,
That it doth raise, and fixe e'm past my art   290
To shadow all the shame and forfeits mine.

---

255 innocence:] ~, ‖ **257** actions?] ~, ‖ **268** sir. Were] ~, were ‖ **271** breath:] ~, ‖ **281** with] ~, ‖ **284** more!] ~, | SD *Aside.*] *Parrott* ‖ **286** Judges:] ~, ‖ **287** judgement;] ~, ‖ **290** art] ~, ‖ **291** forfeits] *stet* (*See Textual Note*) ‖

Enter Asall, Chancellor, Iudges.

As. The Chancellor and Judges Sir.

Tre. [*Aside to the Secretary.*]   I like not
This passion in the King, the Queene and Constable
Are of that side.

King.   My Lord, you dare appeare then?

Cha. Dare Sir, I hope.

King.   Well done, hope still, and tell me,   295
Is not this man condemn'd?

Cha.   Strange question Sir,
The processe will declare it, sign'd with all
These my assistant brothers reverend hands
To his conviction in a publike triall.

King. You said for foule and monstrous facts prov'd by him?   300

Cha. The very words are there sir.

King.   But the deedes
I looke for sir, name me but one that's monstrous?

Cha. His foule comparisons, and affronts of you,
To me seem'd monstrous.

King.   I told you them sir,
Nor were they any that your so vast knowledge,   305
Being a man studied in him, could produce
And prove as cleare as heaven; you warranted
To make appeare such treasons in the Admirall,
As never all Lawes Volumes yet had sentenc'd,
And *France* should looke on, having scap'd with wonder. /   310
What in this nature hath beene cleerely prov'd   [G1ᵛ]
In his arraignement?

1 Judg.   Nothing that we heard
In slendrest touch urg'd by your Advocate.

King. Dare you affirme this too?

2 Judg.   Most confidently.

King. No base corruptions charg'd upon him?

1 Judg.   None sir.   315

Tre. [*Aside to the Secretary.*] This argues *Chabot* has corrupted
    him.

Sec. [*Aside to the Treasurer.*] I doe not like this.

1 Judg.   The summe
    of all
Was urg'd to prove your Admirall corrupt,
Was an exaction of his officers,

---

292 SD *Aside ... Secretary.*] ‖ 300 him?] ~. ‖ 302 that's] thats ‖ 307 heaven;] ~, ‖ 309 Lawes] ~, ‖
310 wonder.] ~. ‖ 312 arraignement?] ~. | 1 *Judg.*] *Dyce*; 1. (*throughout scene*) ‖ 314 2 *Judg.*]
Dyce; 2. (*throughout scene*) ‖ 315 *King.*] ~, | him?] ~. ‖ 316 SD *Aside ... Secretary.*] ‖ 317 SD
Aside ... Treasurer.] ‖

Of twenty *souse* taken from the Fishermen,   320
And for every boate [sixe *liuers*,]
That fish'd the *Normand* coast.
    King.   And was this all
The mountaines, and the marvells promist me,
To be in cleere proofe made against the life
Of our so hated Admirall?
    Iudges.   All sir,   325
Vpon our lives and consciences.
    Cha. [*Aside.*]   I am blasted.
    King. How durst you then subscribe to his conviction?
    1 *Judg.* For threats by my Lord Chancellor on the Bench,
Affirming that your Majestie would have it
Made capitall treason, or account us traitors.   330
    2 *Judg.* Yet sir, we did put to our names with this
Interposition of a note in secret
In these two letters *V*, and *I*, to shew
Wee were enforc'd to what we did, which then
In Law is nothing.
    Fa. [*Aside to the Chancellor.*]   How doe you feele your
        Lordship?   335
Did you not finde some stuffing in your head,
Your braine should have beene purg'd.
    Cha. [*Aside.*]   I fall to peeces.
Would they had rotted on the Bench.
    King. And so you sav'd the peace of that high Court,
Which otherwise his impious rage had broken,   340
But thus am I by his malicious arts /
A party rendred, and most tyrannous spurre   [G2]
To all the open course of his base envies,
A forcer of my Iudges, and a thirst
Of my nobilities blood, and all by one,   345
I trusted to make cleere my love of Iustice.
    Cha. I beseech your Majestie, let all my zeale
To serve your vertues, with a sacred value
Made of your royall state, to which each least
But shade of violence in any subject   350
Doth provoke certaine death –
    King.   Death on thy name
And memory for ever! One command
Our Advocate attend us presently.
    As. He waites here.

---

320 Fishermen,] ~ˌ ‖ 321-22 And for … *liuers*, / That] For every boate, and that (*See Textual Note*) ‖ 325 Admirall?] ~. | *Iudges.*] *Dyce*; *Iud.* ‖ 326 SD *Aside.*] *Parrott* ‖ 327 conviction?] ~. ‖ 335 SD *Aside … Chancellor.*] | Lordship?] ~, ‖ 337 SD *Aside.*] | peeces.] ~, ‖ 339 Court,] ~. ‖ 342 party] *Dyce*; parly ‖ 351 death–] *Dyce*; ~. ‖ 352 ever! One] ~, one ‖

King. But single death shall not excuse thy skinne   355
Torne ore thine eares, and what else can be inflicted,
If thy life with the same severity
Dissected cannot stand so many fires.
   Sec. Tre. Be mercifull great Sir.   *[They kneel.]*
   King.   Yet more amaze?
Is there a knee in all the world beside   360
That any humane conscience can let bow
For him? y'are traitors all that pitty him.
   Tre. *[Aside to the Secretary.]* This is no time to move.
   King.   Yet twas
     my fault
To trust this wretch, whom I knew fierce and proud
With formes of tongue and learning. What a prisoner   365
Is pride of the whole flood of man? for as
A humane seede is said to be a mixture
And faire contemperature extracted from
All our best faculties, so the seede of all
Mens sensuall frailty, may be said to abide,   370
And have their confluence in onely pride;
It stupifies mans reason so, and dulls
True sence of any thing, but what may fall
In his owne glory, quenches all the spirits
That light a man to honour and true goodnesse.   375
   As. Your Advocate.

              Enter Advocate [Proctor-General]. /

King.   Come hither.   *[G2ᵛ]*
Adv.   My most gracious Soveraigne.
                  [King talks with him aside.]
   Adm. Madam you infinitely oblige our duty.
   Qu. I was too long ignorant of your worth my Lord,
And this sweete Ladies vertue.
   Wif.   Both your servants.
   Adm. I never had a feare of the Kings Iustice,   380
And yet I know not what creepes ore my heart,
And leaves an ice beneath it. My Lord Chancellor,
You have my forgivenesse, but implore heavens pardon
For wrongs to equall justice; you shall want
No charitie of mine to mediate   385
To the King for you.
   Cha.   Horrour of my soule

---

355 excuse] *Parrott*; ~, ‖ 356 inflicted,] ~ ̭ ‖ 359 SD *They kneel.*] *Dyce* ‖ 362 him?] ~, | y'are]
yare ‖ 363 SD *Aside ... Secretary.* ‖ 365 learning. What] ~, what ‖ 371 pride;] ~, ‖ 376 SD *Enter
Advocate*] *in right margin opposite* Advocate | SD *Proctor-General*] | SD *King ... aside.*]
Parrott ‖ 381 know] Know ‖ 382 it. My] ~, my ‖ 384 justice;] ~, ‖

Confounds my gratitude.
   Con. [*To the Admiral.*] To me now most welcome.
   Adv. [*To the King.*] It was my allegiance sir, I did enforce,
But by directions of your Chancellor;
It was my office to advance your cause   390
Gainst all the world, which when I leave to execute,
Flea me, and turne me out a most raw Advocate.
   King. You see my Chancellor.
   Adv.   He has an ill looke with him.
   King. It shall be your province now, on our behalfe
To urge what can in justice be against him;   395
His riot on our Lawes, and corrupt actions
Will give you scope and field enough.
   Adv.   And I
Will play my law prize, never feare it sir,
He shall be guilty of what you please; I am studied
In him sir, I will squeeze his villanies,   400
And urge his acts so whom into his bowells,
The force of it shall make him hang himselfe,
And save the Lawes a labour.
   King.   Iudges, for all
The poisonous outrage, that this viper spilt
On all my royall freedome and my Empire,   405
As making all but servants to his malice, /
I will have you revise the late arraignement,   [G3]
And for those worthy reasons, that already
Affect you for my Admiralls acquitall,
Employ your justice on this Chancellor.   410
Away with him!
Arrest him Captaine of my guard to answer
All that due course of Law against him can
Charge both his Acts and life.
   Cap.   I doe arrest thee
Poyet Lord Chancellor in his Highnesse name,   415
To answer all that equall course of Law
Can charge thy acts and life with.
   Cha.   I obey.
                         [*Exit Chancellor guarded.*]
   King. How false a heart corruption has, how base
Without true worth are all these earth-bred glories?
Oh blessed justice, by which all things stand,   420
That stills the thunder, and makes lightning sinke

---

387 SD *To the Admiral.*] *Parrott subs.* ‖ **388** SD *To the King.*] *Parrott* ‖ **389** Chancellor;] ~, ‖
395 him;] ~, ‖ **399** please;] ~, ‖ **401** whom] *stet* (*See Textual Note*) ‖ **409** acquitall,] ~. ‖ **410-11**
Chancellor. / Away with him!] ~, away ~ ~, ‖ **417** obey] Obey ‖ SD *Exit Chancellor guarded.*]
Parrott ‖

Twixt earth and heaven amaz'd, and cannot strike,
Being prov'd so now in wonder of this man,
The object of mens hate, and heavens bright love;
And as in cloudy dayes, we see the Sunne   425
Glide over turrets, temples, richest fields,
All those left darke, and slighted in his way,
And on the wretched plight of some poore shed,
Powres all the glories of his golden head;
So heavenly vertue, on this envied Lord,   430
Points all his graces, that I may distinguish
Him better from the world.
    Tre.   You doe him right.
    King. But away Iudges, and pursue the arraignement
Of this polluted Chancellor with that swiftnesse,
His fury wing'd against my Admirall,   435
And be you all, that sate on him compurgators
Of me against this false Iudge.
    Iudges.   We are so.
    King. [*To the Secretary and Treasurer.*] Be you two joyn'd in
      the commission,
And nothing urg'd but justly, of me learning
This one more lesson out of the events   440
Of these affaires now past, that whatsoever /   [G3ᵛ]
Charge or Commission Iudges have from us,
They ever make their ayme ingenuous Iustice,
Not partiall for reward, or swelling favour,
To which if your King steere you, spare to obey;   445
For when his troubled blood is cleere, and calme,
He will repent that he pursued his rage,
Before his pious Law, and hold that Iudge
Vnworthy of his place, that lets his censure
Flote in the waves of an imagin'd favour: 450
This shipwracks in the haven, and but wounds
Their consciences that sooth the soone-ebb'd humours
Of their incensed King.
    Con. Tre.   Royall and sacred.
    King. Come *Philip*, shine thy honour now for ever,
For this short temporall ecclipse it suffer'd   455
By th'interpos'd desire I had to try thee,
Nor let the thought of what is past afflict thee,
For my unkindnesse; live still circled here,
The bright intelligence of our royall spheere.   *Exeunt.*

---

431 distinguish] dinstinguish ‖ 437 *Iudges.*] Dyce; *Iud.* ‖ 438 SD *To ... Treasurer.*] ‖ 450 favour:]
~, ‖ 452 soone-ebb'd] ~ˬ~ ‖ 458 unkindnesse;] ~, ‖

Actus Quintus. [*Scena I.*]

Enter Queene, Constable, Father.

Qu. The Admirall sicke?

Fa.   With danger at the heart,
I came to tell the King.

Con.   He never had
More reason in his soule, to entertaine
All the delights of health.

Fa.   I feare my Lord,
Some apprehension of the Kings unkindnesse,   5
By giving up his person, and his offices
To the Lawes gripe and search, is ground of his
Sad change, the greatest soules are thus oft wounded;
If he vouchsafe his presence, it may quicken
His fast decaying spirits, and prevent /   10
The hasty ebbe of life.   [G4]

Qu.   The King is now
Fraught with the joy of his fresh preservation,
The newes so violent, let into his eare,
May have some dangerous effect in him:
I wod not counsell sir to that.

Fa.   With greater reason   15
I may suspect they'le spread my Lord, and as
A river, lift his curl'd and impetuous waves
Over the bankes, by confluence of streames
That fill and swell their channell, for by this time
He has the addition of *Allegres* suffering,   20
His honest servant, whom I met, though feeble
And worne with torture, going to congratulate
His Masters safetie.

Qu.   It seemes he much
Affected that *Allegre.*

Con.   There will be
But a sad interview and dialogue.   25

Qu. Does he keepe his bed?

Fa.   In that alone
He shewes a fortitude, he will move, and walke
He sayes while his owne strength or others can
Support him, wishing he might stand and looke
His destiny in the face at the last summons,   30

Scena I.] *Parrott (after Dyce)* ‖ **8** soules] *Dyce*; foules | wounded;] ~, ‖ **14** him:] ~, ‖ **16** they'le
... Lord] (*See Textual Note*) ‖ **17** river, lift] *Dyce*; ~ left ‖ **19** their] *Dyce*; her ‖ **21** met,] ~ ‖ **30**
summons] *Dyce*; summon ‖

Not sluggishly exhaile his soule in bed,
With indulgence, and nice flattery of his limbs.
   Qu. Can he in this shew spirit, and want force
To wrastle with a thought?
   Fa.   Oh Madam, Madam,
We may have proofe against the sword, and tyranny   35
Of boysterous warre that threatens us, but when
Kings froune, a Cannon mounted in each eye,
Shoote death to apprehension, ere their fire
And force approach us.

Enter King.

   Con.   Here's the King.
   Qu.   No words
To interrupt his quiet. /
   Fa.   Ile begon then.   [G4ᵛ]
   King. Our Admiralls father! call him backe.   41
   Qu. I wonot stay to heare e'm.   *Exit.*
   Con.   Sir, be prudent,
And doe not for your sonne fright the Kings health.   *Exit.*
   King. What, ha they left us? how does my Admirall?
   Fa. I am forbid to tell you sir.
   King.   By whom?   45
   Fa. The Queene and my Lord Constable.
   King.   Are there
Remaining seedes of faction? have they soules
Not yet convinc'd ith'truth of *Chabots* honour,
Cleare as the christall heaven, and bove the reach
Of imitation?
   Fa.   Tis their care of you,   50
And no thought prejudiciall to my sonne.
   King. Their care of me?
How can the knowledge of my Admiralls state
Concerne their feares of me? I see their envie
Of *Chabots* happinesse, whose joy to be   55
Rendr'd so pure and genuine to the world
Doth grate upon their conscience and affright 'em;
But let 'em vexe, and bid my *Chabot* still
Exalt his heart, and triumph, he shall have
The accesse of ours; the kingdome shall put on   60
Such joyes for him as she would bost to celebrate

---

45 whom?] ~. ‖ 48 ith'] ith ‖ 50 imitation?] ~. ‖ 54 me?] ~, ‖ 60 ours;] ~, ‖

Her owne escape from ruine.

  Fa. [*Aside.*]   He is not
In state to heare my sad newes I perceive.

  King. That countenance is not right, it does not answer
What I expect. Say, how is my Admirall?   65
The truth upon thy life.

  Fa.   To secure his,
I would you had.

  King.   Ha? Who durst oppose him?

  Fa. One that hath power enough hath practised on him
And made his great heart stoope.

  King.   I will revenge it / 69
With crushing, crushing that rebellious power   [H1]
To nothing, name him.

  Fa.   He was his friend.

  King. A friend to malice, his owne blacke impostume
Burne his blood up! what mischiefe hath ingendred
New stormes?

  Fa.   Tis the old tempest.

  King.   Did not we
Appease all horrors that look'd wilde upon him?   75

  Fa. You drest his wounds I must confesse, but made
No cure, they bleede a fresh; pardon me sir,
Although your conscience have clos'd too soone,
He is in danger, and doth want new surgerie;
Though he be right in fame, and your opinion,   80
He thinkes you were unkinde.

  King.   Alas poore *Chabot*,
Doth that afflict him?

  Fa.   So much, though he strive
With most resolv'd and Adamantine nerves,
As ever humane fire in flesh and blood
Forg'd for example, to beare all, so killing   85
The arrowes that you shot were (still your pardon)
No *Centaures* blood could rancle so.

  King.   If this
Be all, ile cure him: Kings retaine
More Balsome in their soule then hurt in anger.

  Fa. Farre short sir, with one breath they uncreate, 90
And Kings with onely words more wounds can make
Then all their kingdome made in balme can heale;
Tis dangerous to play to wilde a descant

---

62 SD *Aside.*] *Parrott (after Dyce)* ‖ **62-63** not / In ... I] *Shepherd*; ~ in ... / ~ ‖ **65** expect. Say] *Shepherd*; ~, / ~ ‖ **66-67** his, / I] *Parrott*; ~, ~ ‖ **67** *King.*] ~. ‖ **70** crushing, crushing] *stet (See Textual Note)* ‖ **70-71** power / To nothing, name] ~ to ~, / Name ‖ **73** up!] ~, ‖ **77** fresh;] ~, ‖ **79** surgerie;] *Dyce*; ~ ‖ **82** him?] ~. ‖ **84** blood] ~, ‖ **87** *Centaures*] Centaures ‖ **88** him:] ~, ‖ **92** heale;] ~, ‖

On numerous vertue, though it become Princes
To assure their adventures made in every thing: 95
Goodnesse confin'd within poore flesh and blood,
Hath but a queazie and still sickly state;
A musicall hand should onely play on her
Fluent as ayre, yet every touch command.
   King. No more, 100
Commend us to the Admirall, and say, /
The King will visite him, and bring [him] health. [H1ᵛ]
   Fa. I will not doubt that blessing, and shall move
Nimbly with this command. *Exeunt.*

[V.ii]

   Enter Officers before, Treasurer, Secretary, and Iudges,
   attended by Petitioners, the Advocate [Proctor-General]
   also with many papers in his hand; they take their places.
   The Chancellor with a guard, and plac'd at the Barre.

   Tre. Did you beleeve the Chancellor had beene
So foule?
   Sec.   Hec's lost toth' people, what contempts
They throw upon him? but we must be wise.
   1 Iudg. Were there no other guilt, his malice shew'd
Vpon the Admirall, in orebearing justice, 5
Would well deserve a sentence.
   Tre.   And a deepe one.
   2 Iudg. If please your Lordships to remember that
Was specially commended by the King,
As being most blemish to his royall person,
And the free justice of his state.
   Tre.   Already 10
He has confest upon his examinations
Enough for sensure, yet to obey forme ——
Mr. Advocate if you please ——
   Adv. I am ready for your Lordships: It hath beene
said, and will be said agen, and may truely be 15
justified, *Omnia ex lite fieri.* It was the position
of Philosophers, and now proved by a more Philosophycall
sect, the Lawyers, that *Omnia ex lite fiant,* we are
all made by Law, made I say, and worthily if we be

95 thing:] ∼, ‖ 97 state;] ∼, ‖ 98 play on] *Q(c)*; pla yon *Q(u)* ‖ 102 bring him] *Dyce*; bring ‖ **V.ii]**
Dyce ‖ SD *Advocate [Proctor-General]*] *Advocate* | SD *hand;*] ∼, | 17 Philosophycall] *Q(c)*;
Phylosophycall *Q(u)* ‖

just; if we be unjust, marr'd, though in marring   20
some, there is necessitie of making others, for if
one fall by the Law, tenne to one but another is
exalted by the execution of the Law, since the
corruption of one must conclude the generation
of another, though not alwayes in the same profession; 25
the corruption of an Apothecary may be the generation
of a Doctor of Physicke; the corruption of a Citizen
may beget a Courtier, and a Courtier may very well
beget an Alderman; the corruption of an Alderman
may be the generation of a Country Iustice, whose   30
corrupt ignorance easily may beget a tumult; /
a tumult may beget a Captaine, and the corruption   [H2]
of a Captaine may beget a Gentleman-Vsher, and a
Gentleman-Vsher may beget a Lord, whose wit may
beget a Poet, and a Poet may get a thousand pound   35
a yeare, but nothing without corruption.

   Tre. Good Mr. Advocate be pleas'd to leave
All digressions, and speake of the Chancellor.

   Adv. Your Lordship doth very seasonably premonish,
and I shall not neede to leave my subject corruption,   40
while I discourse of him, who is the very fenne and
Stigian abisse of it: five thousand and odde hundred
foule and impious corruptions (for I will be briefe)
have beene found by severall examinations, and by
oathes prov'd against this odious and polluted   45
Chancelor, a man of so tainted, and contagious a
life, that it is a miracle any man enjoyeth his
nostrills, that hath lived within the sent of
his offices; he was borne with teeth in his head,
by an affidavit of his Midwife, to note   50
his devouring, and hath one toe on his left foote
crooked, and in the forme of an Eagles talon, to
foretell his rapacitie: What shall I say?
branded, mark'd, and design'd in his birth for
shame and obloquie, which appeareth further by a   55
mole under his right eare, with only three
Witches haires in't, strange and ominous
predictions of nature.

   Tre. You have acquainted your selfe but very lately
With this intelligence, for as I remember   60
Your tongue was guilty of no such character,

---

20 just;] ~, | unjust] un just ‖ **26** Apothecary] ~, ‖ **29** Alderman;] ~, ‖ **31** tumult;] ~, ‖ **37-38**
Good ... Chancellor.] *as prose,* Q (all) ‖ **37** pleas'd] pleased ‖ **42** *Stigian*] stigian | it:] ~, ‖ **43** (for
... briefe)] ‚~ ... ~; ‖ **48** within] with- / in ‖ **57** in't] int ‖

When hee sat Iudge upon the Admirall,
A pious incorrupt man, a faithfull and fortunate
Servant to his King, and one of the greatest
Honours that ever the Admirall received,   65
Was that he had so noble and just a Iudge;
This must imply a strange volubilitie in
Your tongue, or conscience: I speake not to discountenance
Any evidence for the King, but to put you
In minde, Mr. Advocate that you had then   70
A better opinion of my Lord Chancellor.

    Adv. Your Lordship hath most aptly interpos'd,
and with a word I shall easily satisfie all your
judgements; He was then / a Judge, and *in Cathedra*,   [H2ᵛ]
in which he could not erre; it may be your Lordships   75
cases: out of the chaire and seate of Iustice, he
hath his frailties, is loos'ed and expos'd to the
conditions of other humane natures; so every Iudge,
your Lordships are not ignorant, hath a kinde of
priviledge while he is in his state, office and   80
being, and although hee may *quoad se*, internally
and privately be guilty of bribery of Iustice, yet
quoad nos, and in publike he is an upright and
innocent Iudge: we are to take no notice, nay, we
deserved to suffer, if wee should detect or staine   85
him; for in that we disparage the Office, which is
the Kings, and may be our owne, but once remov'd
from his place by just dishonour of the King, he
is no more a Iudge but a common person, whom the law
takes hold on, and wee are then to forget what hee   90
hath beene, and without partialitie to strip and
lay him open to the world, a counterfeit and
corrupt Iudge, as for example, hee may and ought
to flourish in his greatnesse, and breake any mans
necke, with as much facilitie as a jeast, but the   95
case being altered, and hee downe, every subject
shall be heard; a Wolfe may be appareld in a
Lamb-skinne; and if every man should be afraid to
speake truth, nay and more than truth, if the good
of the subject which are clients sometime require   100
it, there would be no remove of Officers, if no
remove no motions, if no motion in Court no heate,
and by consequence but cold Termes; take away this

65-66 received, / Was that] ~, was That ‖ 66-71 Iudge; / . . . Chancellor.] ~, this must / Imply
. . . or / Conscience, . . . any / Evidence . . . in minde, / Mr. . . . opinion / Of . . . Chancellor. ‖
74 *in*] in ‖ 76 cases:] ~, ‖ 84 Iudge:] ~, ‖ 89 but] hut ‖ 97 heard;] ~, ‖ 98 Lamb-skinne]
Lamb- / skinne ‖

moving, this removing of Iudges, the Law may bury
it selfe in Buckram, and the kingdome suffer for   105
want of a due execution; and now I hope your
Lordships are satisfied.

    Tre. Most learnedly concluded to acquit your selfe.

    1 *Iudg.* Mr. Advocate, please you to urge for satisfaction
Of the world, and clearing the Kings honour, how   110
Injustly he proceeded against the Admirall.

    Adv. I shall obey your Lordship ——— So vast,
so infinite hath beene the impudence of this
Chancellor, not onely toward the subject, but even
the sacred person of the King, that I tremble as   115
with a Palsie to remember it. This man, or rather
this monster, having power and commission trusted
for the examination of the Lord Admirall, a man
perfect in all honour and justice, indeede the very
ornament and second / flower of *France* (for the   [H3]
Flower de lis is sacred and above all flowers,   121
and indeede the best flower in our garden), having
used all wayes to circumvent his innocence by
suborning and promising rewards to his betrayers,
by compelling others by the cruelty of tortures, as   125
namely Mounsieur *Allegre* a most honest and faithfull
servant to his Lord, tearing and extending his
sinewes upon the racke to force a confession to his
purpose, and finding nothing prevaile upon the invincible
vertue of the Admirall –   130

    Sec. [*Aside to the Treasurer.*] How he would flatter him?

    Adv. Yet most maliciously proceeded to arraigne
him; to be short, against all colour of Iustice
condemn'd him of high treasons; oh thinke what the
life of man is, that can never be recompenced; but   135
the life of a just man, a man that is the vigour
and glory of our life and nation to be torne to
death, and sacrifis'd beyond the mallice of
common persecution. What Tiger of *Hercanian* breede
could have beene so cruell? but this is not all!   140
he was not guilty onely of murder, guilty I may
say *In foro conscientiæ*, though our good Admirall
was miraculously preserv'd, but unto this he added
a most prodigious and fearefull rape, a rape even
upon Iustice it self, the very soule of our state,   145

---

119 justice,] ~; ‖ **120-22** (for ... garden), having] ˏ~ ... ~. Having ‖ **121** *lis*] ~, ‖ **130** Admirall–]
Dyce subs.; ~. ‖ **131** SD *Aside ... Treasurer.*] *Parrott subs.* ‖ **133** short,] ~ˏ ‖ **140** all!] ~? ‖ **142**
conscientiae] *cōscientiæ Q(c)*; *cōsctieniæ Q(u)* ‖

for the rest of the Iudges upon the Bench, venerable
images   of   *Astræa*,   he   most   tyranously
compel'd   to   set   their   hands   to   his   most   unjust
sentence; did ever story remember the like outrage
and injustice? what forfeit, what penalty can be   150
enough   to   satisfie   this   transcendent   offence?
and yet my good Lords, this is but veniall to the
sacriledge which now followes, and by him committed:
not content with this sentence, not satisfied with
horrid violence upon the sacred Tribunall, but hee   155
proceedes and blasphemes the very name and honour
of   the   King   himselfe   (observe   that),   making   him
the author and impulsive cause of all these rapines,
justifying   that   he   mov'd   onely   by   his   speciall
command to the death, nay the murder of his most   160
faithfull   subject,   translating   all   his   owne
blacke and damnable guilt upon the Kings heires:
a traytor to his Country, first, he conspires the death
of one whom the King loves, and whom every subject ought
to honour, and then makes it no conscience to   165
proclaime it the Kings act, and by consequence
declares him a / murderer of his owne, and of   [H3ᵛ]
his best subjects.

 Within. An Advocate, an Advocate, teare him in
peeces, teare the Chancellor in peeces.   170

 Tre. The people have deepe sence of the Chancellors injustice.

 Sec. We must be carefull to prevent their mutiny.

 1 *Iudg.* It will become our wisedomes to secure
The court and prisoner.

 Tre.   Captaine of the guard.

 2 *Judg.* What can you say for your selfe Lord Chancellor?   175

 Cha. Againe, I confesse all, and humbly fly to
The royall mercy of the King.

 Tre.   And this
Submission is the way to purchase it.

 Cha. Heare me great Iudges, if you have not lost
For my sake all your charities, I beseech you,   180
Let the King know my heart is full of penitence,
Calme his high-going sea, or in that tempest
I ruine to eternitie: oh my Lords,
Consider your owne places, and the helmes
You sit at; while with all your providence   185

---

146 rest of] restof ‖ 147 *Astræa*] *Dyce*; *Austria* ‖ 150 injustice?] ~; ‖ 153 committed:] ~, ‖ 157 himselfe (observe that),] ~, ˌ~ ~ˌ, ‖ 162 heires:] ~, (*See Textual Note*) ‖ 169 SD *Within.*] ~, ‖ 170 peeces, teare] ~, / Teare ‖ 173-74 secure / The court and] *Dyce*; ~ the ~ / And ‖ 175 2 *Judg.*] *Dyce*; 2. | Chancellor?] ~. ‖ 177-78 this / Submission] *Parrott*; ~ submission ‖ 183 eternitie:] ~, ‖ 185 at;] ~, ‖

You steere, looke forth and see devouring quicksands.
My ambition now is punish'd, and my pride
Of state and greatnesse falling into nothing,
I that had never time through vast employments
To thinke of heaven, feele his revengefull wrath,   190
Boyling my blood, and scorching up my entrills;
There doomesday is my conscience, blacke and horrid,
For my abuse of Iustice, but no stings
Pricke with that terrour as the wounds I made
Vpon the pious Admirall: some good man   195
Beare my repentance thither, he is mercifull,
And may encline the King to stay his lightning
Which threatens my confusion; that my free
Resigne of title, office, and what else
My pride look'd at, would buy my poore lives safety,   200
For ever banish me the court, and let
Me waste my life farre off in some Village.
   Adv. How? Did your Lordships note his request to
you? he would direct your sentence to punish him with
confining / him to live in the country, like the   [H4]
Mouse in the Fable, that having offended to deserve   206
death, beg'd he might be banished into a Parmisan.
I hope your Lordships will be more just to the
nature of his offences.
   Sec. I could have wish'd him fall on softer ground   210
For his good parts.
   Tre.   My Lord, this is your sentence:
For your high misdemeanours against his Majesties
Iudges, for your unjust sentence of the most equall Lord
Admirall, for many and foule corruptions and abuse of
your office, and that infinite staine of the Kings   215
person, and honour, we in his Majesties name,
deprive you of your estate of Chancellor, and
declare you uncapeable of any judiciall office, and
besides condemne you in the sum of two hundred thousand
crownes; whereof one hundred thousand to the King,   220
and one hundred thousand to the Lord Admirall, and
what remaineth of your estate to goe to the restitution
of those you have injur'd, and to suffer perpetuall
imprisonment in the Castle.
So take him to your custody.   225
Your Lordships have beene mercifull in his sentence.

                                                Exit.

186 quicksands.] ~, ‖ **191** entrills;] ~, ‖ **192** conscience,] ~. ‖ **194** Pricke] *Dyce*; Prickt ‖ **195** Admirall:] ~, ‖ **198** confusion;] ~, ‖ **204** you?] ~, ‖ **211-12** sentence: / For] ~. for ‖ **212** your] *Dyce*; you ‖ **217** Chancellor,] ~: (?) ‖ **224-25** Castle. / So] *Dyce subs.*; ~, so ‖ **225-26** custody. / Your] ~. ~ ‖

[*Cha.*] They have spar'd my life then, that some cure
　　may bring;
Ile spend it in my prayers for the King.　　　　　　　　　*Exeunt.*

[V.iii]

Enter Admirall in his Gowne and Cap, his Wife.

Adm. Allegre! I am glad he hath so much strength,
I prethee let me see him.
　Wif. 　　　　　　It will but
Enlarge a passion ——— my Lord hee'le come
Another time and tender you his service.
　Adm. Nay then ———　　　　　　　　　　　　　　　　5
　Wif. Although I like it not, I must obey.　　　　　　*Exit.*

Enter Allegre supported.

　Adm. Welcome my injur'd servant, what a misery
Ha they made on thee?
　Al. 　　　　　　Though some change appeare
Vpon my body, whose severe affliction
Hath brought it thus to be sustained by others,　　　　　10
My hart is still the same in faith to you,
Not broken with their rage.
　Adm. 　　　　　　Alas poore man! /
Were all my joyes essentiall, and so mighty　　　　　　　[H4ᵛ]
As the affected world beleeves I taste,
This object were enough to unsweeten all;　　　　　　　　15
Though in thy absence I had suffering,
And felt within me a strong sympathy,
While for my sake their cruelty did vexe,
And fright thy nerves with horrour of thy sence,
Yet in this spectacle I apprehend　　　　　　　　　　　　20
More griefe than all my imagination
Could let before into me; didst not curse me
Vpon the torture?
　Al. 　　　　　Good my Lord, let not
The thought of what I suffer'd dwell upon
Your memory, they could not punish more　　　　　　　　25
Then what my duty did oblige to beare
For you and Iustice, but there's some thing in
Your lookes, presents more feare than all the mallice
Of my tormentors could affect my soule with:

---

227 *Cha.* They] *Dyce*; They | bring;] ~, ‖ 228 Ile] *Dyce subs.*; I ‖ **V.iii**] *Dyce* ‖ 1 *Allegre!*] ~ˌ ‖ 11
hart] *Dyce subs.*; hurt ‖ 15 all;] ~, ‖ 27 there's] theres ‖ 29 with:] ~, ‖

That palenesse, and the other formes you weare,   30
Would well become a guilty Admirall, and one
Lost to his hopes and honour, not the man
Vpon whose life the fury of unjustice
Arm'd with fierce lightning, and the power of thunder,
Can make no breach. I was not rack'd till now,   35
There's more death in that falling eye, than all
Rage ever yet brought forth. What accident sir can blast,
Can be so blacke and fatall to distract
The calme? the triumph that should sit upon
Your noble brow? Misfortune could have no   40
Time to conspire with fate, since you were rescued
By the great arme of providence, nor can
Those garlands that now grow about your forehead
With all the poyson of the world be blasted.   ·
    Adm. Allegre, thou dost beare thy wounds upon thee,   45
In wide and spacious characters, but in
The volumne of my sadnesse thou dost want
An eye to reade; an open force hath torne
Thy manly sinewes which sometime may cure; /   49
The engine is not seene that wounds thy Master,   [I1]
Past all the remedy of art or time,
The flatteries of Court, of fame or honours:
Thus in the Sommer a tall flourishing tree,
Transplanted by strong hand, with all her leaves
And blooming pride upon her makes a shew   55
Of Spring, tempting the eye with wanton blossome,
But not the Sunne with all her amorous smiles,
The dewes of morning, or the teares of night,
Can roote her fibers in the earth agen,
Or make her bosome kinde, to growth and bearing,   60
But the tree withers, and those very beames
That once were naturall warmth to her soft verdure
Dry up her sap and shoote a feaver through
The barke and rinde, till she becomes a burthen
To that which gave her life: so *Chabot, Chabot*.   65
    Al. Wonder in apprehension, I must
Suspect your health indeede.
    Adm.   No, no, thou shanot
Be troubled, I but stirr'd thee with a morrall
That's empty, containes nothing: I am well,
See I can walke; poore man, thou hast not strength yet.   70
                                                              [*Exit.*]

35 breach.] ~, ‖ 36 There's] Theres ‖ 37 forth. What] ~, what ‖ 40 brow? Misfortune] ~, misfortune ‖
48 reade; . . . force] *Dyce*; ~ˌ . . . ~, ‖ 49 cure;] ~ˌ ‖ 52 honours:] ~, ‖ 56 wanton blossome,] Q(c); ~,
~ˌ Q(u) ‖ 58 morning] *Dyce*; mornings ‖ 60 growth] Q(c); groweth Q(u) ‖ 67 No,] ~ˌ ‖ 68 morrall] ~,
‖ 69 That's] Thats | empty, containes nothing:] ~ˌ ~ ~, ‖ 70 walke;] ~ˌ | SD *Exit.*] *Dyce* ‖

688

Al. What accident is ground of this distraction?

Enter Admirall.

Adm. Thou hast not heard yet what's become oth' Chancellor?
Al. Not yet my Lord.
Adm.   Poore gentleman, when I thinke
Vpon the King, I've balme enough to cure
A thousand wounds, have I not *Allegre*?   75
Was ever bountious mercy read in story,
Like his upon my life, condemn'd for sacrifice
By Law, and snatch'd out of the flame unlooked for,
And unpetitioned? but his justice then
That wod not spare whom his owne love made great,   80
But give me up to the most cruell test
Of Iudges, for some boldnesse in defence
Of my owne merits, and my honest faith to him,
Was rare, past example. /

Enter Father.   [I1ᵛ]

Fa.   Sir, the King
Is comming hither.
Al.   It will   85
Become my duty sir to leave you now.
Adm. Stay by all meanes *Allegre*, 'tshall concerne you.
I'me infinitely honor'd in his presence.

Enter King, Queene, Constable, and Wife.

King. Madam be comforted, Ile be his Phisitian.
Wif. Pray heaven you may.   [*The Admiral kneels.*
                                      The King raises him.]
King.   No ceremoniall knees,   90
Give me thy heart, my deare, my honest *Chabot*,
And yet in vaine I chalenge that, tis here
Already in my owne, and shall be cherish'd
With care of my best life; [no] violence
Shall ravish it from my possession,   95
Not those distempers that infirme my blood
And spirits shall betray it to a feare;
When time and nature joyne to dispossesse
My body of a cold and languishing breath,
No stroake in all my arteries, but silence   100
In every faculty, yet dissect me then,
And in my heart, the world shall read thee living,

---

72 what's] whats ‖ 73 *Adm.*] ~, ‖ 83 him,] ~ˌ ‖ 84 rare, past] Q(c); ~ ~, Q(u) ‖ 87 *Adm.*] ~, |
you.] ~, ‖ 90 SD *The Admiral … him.*] *Parrott subs.* ‖ 92 that,] ~ˌ ‖ 94 life; no violence] *Dyce*;
life, violence ‖ 97 feare;] ~, ‖

689

And by the vertue of thy name writ there,
That part of me shall never putrifie,
When I am lost in all my other dust.   105
   Adm. You too much honour your poore servant sir,
My heart dispares so rich a monument;
But when it dies ———
   King.   I wonot heare a sound
Of any thing that trenched upon death:
He speakes the funerall of my crowne that prophesies   110
So unkinde a fate; weele live and die together,
And by that duty which hath taught you hitherto
All loyall and just services I charge thee,
Preserve thy heart for me and thy reward,
Which now shall crowne thy merits.
   Adm.   I have found /   115
A glorious harvest in your favour sir,   [I2]
And by this overflow of royall grace,
All my deserts are shadowes and flie from mee;
I have not in the wealth of my desires,
Enough to pay you now, yet you encourage me   120
To make one suite.
   King.   So soone as nam'd possesse it.
   Adm. You would be pleas'd take notice of this Gentleman,
A Secretary of mine.
   Con.   Mounsieur *Allegre,*
He that was rack'd sir for your Admirall.
   Adm. His limbs want strength to tender their full duty,   125
An honest man that suffers for my sake.
   King. He shall be deare to us. [*To Allegre.*] For what has
      past sir
By the unjustice of our Chancellors power,
Weele study to recompence; ith'meane time that office
You exercis'd for *Chabot* we translate   130
To our selfe, you shall be our Secretary.
   Al.   This is
An honour above my weake desert, and shall
Oblige the service of my life to satisfie it.
   Adm. You are gracious, and in this act have put
All our complaints to silence. You *Allegre,*   135

Enter Tresuror, Secretary, one of them gives
the King the sentence of the Chancellor.

Cherish your health, and feeble limbs which cannot

---

103 writ] *Dyce;* write ‖ **109** trenched] *stet (See Textual Note)* | death:] ~, ‖ **111** fate;] ~, ‖ **112** hitherto] ~, ‖ **118** mee;] ~, ‖ **127** us. For] ~, for | SD *To Allegre.*] *Parrott* ‖ **129** recompence;] ~, ‖ **135** silence. You] ~, you | SD *one ... Chancellor*] *Parrott subs.* ‖

Without much prejudice be thus employ'd;
All my best wishes with thee.
   Al.   All my prayers
Are duties to your Lordship ———   *Exit, supported.*
   King.   Tis too little,
Can forfeit of his place, wealth, and a lasting   140
Imprisonment purge his offences to
Our honest Admirall? had our person beene
Exempted from his mallice, he did persecute
The life of *Chabot* with an equall wrath;
You should have powr'd death on his treacherous head,   145
I revoke all your sentences, and make
Him that was wrong'd full Master of his destiny. /
[*To the Admiral.*] Be thou his judge.   [12ᵛ]
   Adm.   O farre be such injustice,
I know his doome is heavie, and I begge
Where mercy may be let into his sentence   150
For my sake you would soften it; I have
Glory enough to be set right in yours,
And my deare countries thought, and by an act
With such apparent notice to the world.
   King. Expresse it in some joy then.
   Adm.   I will strive   155
To shew that pious gratitude to you but ———
   King.   But what?
   Adm. My frame hath lately sir beene tane a peeces,
And but now put together, the least force
Of mirth will shake and unjoynt all my reason,
Your patience royall sir.
   King.   Ile have no patience,   160
If thou forget the courage of a man.
   Adm. My strength would flatter me.
   King.   Phisitians!
Now I begin to feare his apprehension;
Why how is *Chabots* spirit falne?
   Qu.   Twere best
He were convei'd to his bed.
   Wif.   How soone turn'd widdow.   165
   Adm. Who would not wish to live to serve your goodnes?
[*To those supporting him.*] Stand from me, you betray me with
     your feares:
The plummets may fall off that hang upon

---

139 SD *Exit, supported.*] *Exit.* ‖ 142 Admirall?] ~, ‖ 144 wrath;] ~, ‖ 147 destiny.] ~, ‖ 148 SD *To the Admiral.*] *Parrott subs.* ‖ 151 it;] ~, ‖ 156 *King.*] *Kng.* | what?] ~, ‖ 162 Phisitians!] ~, ‖ 163 apprehension;] ~, ‖ 166 goodnes?] ~, ‖ 167 SD *To ... him.*] *Parrott* | feares:] ~, ‖

691

My heart, they were but thoughts at first, or if
They weigh me downe to death, let not my eyes   170
Close with another object then the King,
Let him be last I looke on.
   King. I would not have him lost for my whole Kingdome.
   Con. He may recover sir.
   King.   I see it fall,
For Iustice being the proppe of every Kingdome   175
And mine broke, violating him that was
The knot and contract of it all, in him
Is already falling in my eare; /
Pompey could heare it thunder, when the Senate   [13]
And Capitoll were deafe to heavens loud chiding.   180
Ile have another sentence for my Chancellor,
Vnlesse my *Chabot* live. In a Prince
What a swift executioner is a frowne,
Especially of great and noble soules? –
How is it with my *Philip?*
   Adm.   I must begge   185
One other boone.
   King.   Vpon condition
My *Chabot* will collect his scatter'd spirits,
And be himselfe agen, he shall divide
My Kingdome with me.
   Fa.   Sweete King.
   Adm.   I observe
A fierce and killing wrath engendred in you;   190
For my sake, as you wish me strength to serve you,
Forgive your Chancellor, let not the story
Of *Philip Chabot* read hereafter draw
A teare from any family; I beseech
Your royall mercy on his life, and free   195
Remission of all seasure upon his state,
I have no comfort else.
   King.   Endeavour but
Thy owne health, and pronounce generall pardon
To all through *France.*
   Adm.   Sir I must kneele to thanke you,
It is not seal'd else. [*Kneels.*] Your blest hand, live happy, 200
May all you trust have no lesse faith then *Chabot,*

---

177 all, in him] *Lordi conj.*; ~ˎ ~ ~, ‖ 178 Is] *Lordi conj.*; It | eare;] ~, ‖ 180 deafe to] *Brereton conj.*; ~, so | chiding.] ~, ‖ 182 live. In] ~, / ~ ‖ 184 soules?–] *Dyce*; ~;ˎ ‖ 188 divide] *Q(c)*; dvide *Q(u)* ‖ 190 killing] kllling ‖ 194 family;] ~, ‖ 197-98 Endeavour but / Thy] *Parrott*; ~ / But thy | 200 else. Your] ~, your | SD *Kneels.*] *Parrott* | hand,] ~ˎ ‖

Oh.   [*Dies.*]
   Wif.   His heart is broken.
   Fa.   And kneeling sir,
As his ambition were in death to shew
The truth of his obedience.
   Con.   I feard this issue.
   Tre. Hee's past hope.
   King.   He has a victory in's death,   205
This world / deserv'd him not; how soone he was   [13ᵛ]
Translated to glorious eternitie!
Tis too late to fright the ayre with words,
My teares embalme him.
   Wif.   What can become of me?
   King. Ile be your husband Madam, and with care   210
Supply your childrens father, to your father
Ile be a sonne; in what our love or power
Can serve his friends, *Chabot* shall nere be wanting;
The greatest losse is mine, past scale or recompence.
We will proceede no further gainst the Chancellor,   215
To the charitie of our Admirall he owes
His life which ever banish'd to a prison,
Shall not beget in us, or in the subject
New feares of his injustice; for his fortunes
Great and acquir'd corruptly, tis our will   220
They make just restitution for all wrongs
That shall within a yeare be prov'd against him;
O *Chabot* that shall boast as many monuments
As there be hearts in *France*, which as they grow,
Shall with more love enshrine thee, Kings they say,   225
Die not, or starve succession: oh why
Should that stand firme, and Kings themselves despaire,
To finde their subject still in the next heire?

                                           Exeunt.

                FINIS.

202 SD *Dies.*] *Dyce* ‖ 205 Hee's] Hees | in's] ins ‖ 205-09 death, / ... My] ~, this world / Deserv'd him not, how ... translated / To glorious eternitie, tis too late / To ... words, my ‖ 210 *King.*] *Dyce*; *Qu.* ‖ 212 sonne;] ~, ‖ 213 wanting;] ~, ‖ 214 recompence.] ~, ‖ 217 prison,] *Q(c)*; ~. *Q(u)* ‖ 219 injustice;] ~, ‖ 223-28 O *Chabot* ... heire?] *See Textual Note* ‖ 226 succession:] ~, ‖ 228 heire?] ~. ‖

HISTORICAL COLLATION

[Editions collated: Dyce (and Gifford) (= *D*, in *The Dramatic Works and Poems of James Shirley*, 1833, Vol. VI, pp. 85-167); Shepherd (= *S*, in *The Works of George Chapman: Plays*, 1874, pp. 519-50; not included in R. H. Shepherd's old-spelling reprint, *Chapman's Dramatic Works*, 1873); Parrott (= *P*, in *The Plays and Poems of George Chapman: The Tragedies*, 1910, pp. 273-337). The following have also been consulted for readings and emendations: Ezra Lehman, ed., *The Tragedie of Chabot Admirall of France*, 1906 (= *L*; an undependable and misleading reprint of a copy of Q in the University of Pennsylvania Library [822 C37t]); J. Brereton, 'Notes on the Text of Chapman's Plays,' *MLR*, III (1907-8), 67-68; G. C. Macaulay, review of Parrott in *MLR*, VI (1911), 256; A. S. Ferguson, 'Chapman, *The Tragedy of Chabot*, Act III, Sc. ii, ll. 147-68,' *MLR*, XXIII (1928), 46; G. G. Loane, 'Notes on the Text of Chapman's Plays,' *MLR*, XXXIII (1938), 252-53, and 'More Notes on Chapman's Plays,' *MLR*, XXXVIII (1943), 345-46; Charles Pennel (= *Pen*), an unpublished, modern-spelling edition of *Chabot* (here used with Professor Pennel's permission); Robert J. Lordi, unpublished conjectures, privately offered to the editor. Only substantive and semi-substantive variants are recorded; obvious errors are not recorded. Lemmata are taken from the present text. Where lemma represents the reading of Q copy-text, omission of siglum indicates agreement with the lemma. Since Dyce, Shepherd, and Parrott all reproduce the corrected state of Q in their texts of *Chabot*, the corrected and uncorrected states of Q (see Press-Variants, pp. 704-706) have been omitted from the Historical Collation.]

I.i

I.i] *P*; *Actus Primus. Q*; ACT I. SCENE I. *An Apartment in the Palace. D*;
    ACT THE FIRST. *S*; *setting in P: A Room in the Court*
13 Toth'] To the *D*, *S*; To th' *P* (*not hereafter recorded*)
23 ith'] i' the *D*; i' th' *S*, *P* (*not hereafter recorded*)
38-41 Though ... assign'd,] (Though ... assign'd) *P*
47 worthy] worth *S*, *P*
56 any things] any thing *D*; anything *S*
57 humane] human *D*, *S*, *P* (*throughout*)
63 and] ~ as *S*
69 by, seemes] ~ˌ ~, *D*, *S*, *P*
88 tract] track *D*
107 others] other's *D*, *S*; others' *P*
113 enflame] inflame *D*, *S*, *P*

115 SD *and ... Secretary*] *Enter Ushers, Secretary D; and enter* Ushers
   before Secretary *S*
   SD *others attend.*] *Attendants, &c. D*
119 *Gordian*] *D, S, P;* gardian *Q*
   Phrigian] '*hrigian L (misreading of a damaged 'P')*
120 lose] loose *S, P*
127 I] *D, S, P; om. Q*
132 SD *To ... Constable.*] *P; om. Q, D, S*
133 *Con.*] *Mont. D, P (throughout);* Mo. *S (throughout)*
   earth] earth[ly] *D*
134 SD *Enter ... Admirall.*] *Enter an Attendant, who whispers Chabot, and
   exit. D*
136 *Adm.*] *Chab. D, S, P (throughout)*
140 borne] born *D, S, P*
148 plac'd] *P;* placed *Q, D, S*
155 SD *Exit the Admiral.*] *P subs.; om. Q, D, S*
   SD *Enter another.*] *Enter an Attendant. D*
158 SD *with Attendants.*] *P; and Att. S; om. Q, S*
170 increase] incense *S*
176 mediate] 'mediate *D, S*
179 Ha] Have *D (throughout);* Ha' *S, P (throughout)*
183 free borne] free born *S, P*
187 in] it *S, P*
188 soule] soul's *D*
189 natures] Nature's *D;* nature *S;* natures' *P*
195 Y'are] *S, P;* Yare *Q;* You are *D*
206 I] I[n] *P*
209 envie,] ~. *D, S, P*
220 shadder] shudder *D, S, P;* shatter *or* shadow *L conj.*
239 Statesmen, ... on!] ~, ..., *Q;* ~! ... ~, *D;* ~! ...; *S, P*
242 SD *Aside ... Treasurer.*] *om. Q, D, S, P*

I.ii

I.ii] SCENE II. *Another Apartment in the Same. D;* SCENA II *Another
   Room in the Court P; om. Q, S*
8 ingratefull] ungrateful *D*
10 services] *P;* service *Q, D, S*
12 lesse,] *P;* lesse‿ *Q, D, S*
19 huge] *D, S, P;* hugh *Q*
22 subtile] subtle *P*
33 ingenious] ingenuous *D, P*
52 White in forc'd] *S, P;* While inforc'd *Q;* While enforc'd *D*
60 ambitious boundlesse] ~, ~ *S;* ambitions ~, *P (Brereton conj.)*
66 dispos'd] *P;* disposed *Q, D, S*
67 no] not *P conj.;* so *conj.*
68 realties] realities *P (error corrected in Text Notes)*
78 Perhaps] *D, S, P;* Pehaps *Q*

86 counsell] Council *D, S, P (throughout in this sense)*
98 SD *Aside.*] *P (after D); om. Q, S*
    Até] *D, S, P*; A he *Q*
    beest] be'st *D*
105 No] ∼, *D, S*
106 powers] power's *D, S*; the powers *L*; [my] power's *P conj.*
107 injust] unjust *D, S, P*
121 wonot] will not *D, S (throughout)*; wo' not *P (throughout)*
124 then,] ∼? *D, S, P*
128 saile] sale *D, S, P*
133 received] receiv'd *P*
    scandall] scandal'd *Pen conj.*
135 endured] endur'd *P*
139 full prov'd] full-prov'd *D*; full-proved *S*
146 Twere] I were *L (misreading of a damaged 'T')*
155 SD *Tears the bill.*] *D; om. Q, S, P*
156 cherish now,] *D, S, P*; ∼, ∼ₐ *Q*

II.i

II.i] *P; Actus Secundus. Q*; ACT II. SCENE I. *An Apartment in the Palace.*
    D; ACT THE SECOND. *S; setting in P: A Room in the Court*
3 y'are] you're *D, S*
8 SD *Showing ... bill.*] *P; om. Q, D, S*
23 this braine more] his brain were *S, P*
27 lately] late *S*
29 Vrg'd] *after* Urged *D, S, P*; Vrge *Q*
31 opportunitie.] opportunity – *D, S, P*
45 SD *Aside.*] *P (after D); om. Q, S*
48 *King.*] *King.* [*To Chancellor*] *P; om. Q, D, S*
54 him–] *S, P*; ∼. *Q*; ∼, – *D*

II.ii

II.ii] SCENE II. *Another Apartment in the Same. D*; SCENA II *Another*
    Room in the Court P; om. Q, S
10 monstrous?] ∼. *D, S, P*
11 I] Ay *D, S, P*
14 Since] (Since *P*
    they thinke] ∼ ∼; *Q, D, S*; [he] think[s] *P*
15 (Because] ₐ∼ *Q, D, S, P*
16 length)] *P*; ∼, *Q, D, S*
27 wod] would *D, S, P (throughout)*
33 Through] *Brereton conj., P*; Though *Q, D, S*
39 e'm] them *D, S (throughout unless otherwise noted)*; 'em *P (throughout)*
42 y'are] you're *D*
43 fallen] fall'n *S*
46 other] others *S, P (P corrects in* Text Notes)
51 ariv'd] arm'd *P conj.*

53 walke] wake *L* (*misreading a weak-printing* 'l')
56 innocence is, which] innocence which *S*; innocence, which *P*
57 As weares] As 'twere *Brereton conj.*; A[nd] wears *P*
60 gainst] against *D*; 'gainst *S*
64 e'm] them *D*; 'em *S, P*
69 breake] brake *D, P*; breaks *S*
77 and] ~ the *S, P* (*P corrects in* Text Notes)
87 nor] *Brereton conj., P*; not *Q, D, S*
94 will———] will. *D, S, P*

II.iii

II.iii] SCENE III. *Another Apartment in the Same. D*; SCENA III *Another
    Room in the Court P*; *om. Q, S*
11 SD *snapping his fingers*] *om. Q, D, S, P*
16 kingdomes] kingdom's *P*
42 know;] *P*; know, *Q, D, S*
43 gall,] gall; *D, S*
44 lothed] loath'd *D*; loathed *S, P*
48 many] *Brereton conj., P*; mony, *Q*; money, *D, S*
54 corruption?] ~; *P*
71 *Burgandy*] *Burgady Q*; Burgundy *D, S, P*
86 slccpc] sleepes *conj.*
97 I] Λy *D, S, P*
98 deceiv'd] *S, P*; ~, *Q*; ~; *D*
102-03 yours? Nay,] *S, P*; yours, / Nay, *Q*; your's? / Nay, *D*; yours / May
    P conj.
113 Repos'd] *D, S, P*; *Adm.* Repos'd *Q*
119 that] *Pen conj.*; than *Q, D*; the *S, P*
122 SD *Aside.*] *P* (*after D, S*); *om. Q*
124 swinge] swing *D*
130 eyes beating,] *D, S, P*; ~, ~ *Q*
134 informe him] (inform him), *P*
135 or use] use *Q, D, S, P*
154 off] *Brereton conj., P*; of *Q, D, S*
177 SD *Exit the Admiral.*] *D, S, P subs.*; *om. Q*
179 SD *Exit Asall.*] *D, S, P*; *om. Q*
207 fiuer] *Pen conj.*; finer *Q*; fibre *D, S, P*
217 authoritie–] *D, S, P*; ~. *Q*
220 treasons–] *D, S, P*; ~. *Q*
221 justice–] *Pen*; ~. *Q, D, S, P*
226 SD *Exeunt.*] *D, S, P*; *om. Q*

III.i

III.i] *P*; *Actus Tertius. Q*; ACT III. SCENE I. *A Gallery. D*; ACT THE
    THIRD. *S*; *setting in P*: A Gallery
SD past] pass. *D*
SD *a guard about him,*] ~ gaurd ~ ~, *Q*; guarded, followed by *D*
SD *his wife ... side*] Wife *on each side of D*

SD *Allegre ... stage.*] *Allegre.* Q, D, S; Allegre [*guarded*] P; Allegre [*passes*].
 Pen
6 SD *To his Wife.*] P; *om.* Q, D, S
 don't] do not S
18 Farewell, thy] ~ˬ ~ Q; ~; ~ D, S, P
 SD *kisses her*] D, P; *om.* Q, S
19 shanot] shall not D, S; sha' not P
 SD *To Father.*] P; *om.* Q, D, S
21 SD *Exit with Guards.*] P *subs.*; *Exit.* Q, S; *Exeunt all but Fath. and
 Wife.* D
 SD *Manent*] Manente Q, S, P; *see above for* D
30 ever-burning] D, S, P; ~ˬ~ Q
35 face] fare *conj.*
43 'gainst] against S; gainst P
44 SD *They retire.*] P; *om.* Q, D, S
46 SD *To the Treasurer.*] P; *om.* Q, D, S
 of] of the S
47 Suffered] Suffer'd S, P
50 rob'd] robb'd D, S, P
53 contempts] contempt's S
54 th'] the D
57 SD *Bringing ... kneels.*] *Chabot's Wife approaches the Queen, and kneels.*
 D; *Approaching with* Wife *who kneels* P (*after end of l. 57*); *om.* Q, S
88 SD *To ... forward.*] P *subs.*; *om.* Q, D, S
98 this] his L *conj.*
104 ill-grounded, and ill-followed] ~ˬ~, ~ ~ˬ~ Q; ~-~, ~ ill-follow'd D;
 ~-~ˬ ~ ill-follow'd S; ~-~ˬ ~ ~-~ P
111 SD *To the Constable.*] P *subs.*; *om.* Q, D, S
 heare,] D, S, P; ~ˬ Q
112 SD *Rises.*] *rising* P; *om.* Q, D, S
130 ever] S, P; every Q, D
142 pray'rs] prayers D, S
151 till] S, P; still Q, D
153 ballance,] ~. D
 take] D, S, P; talke Q
163 Subjects] D, S, P; Suffer Q
171 SD *Kneels.*] D; *Kneeling* P; *om.* Q, S
172 life blood] ~-~ D, S, P
178 earth-borne] earth-born D, S, P
181 tract] track D
186 antidate] antedate S, P
189 *Wif.*] *Wife.* [*rising.*] D; *om.* Q, S, P
201 SD *Aside.*] P (*after* D); *om.* Q, S
206 SD *Rises.*] *om.* Q, D (*see l. 189*), S, P
207 SD *Exeunt ... Wife.*] D, P *subs.*; *om.* Q, S
213 thought't] thought Q, D, S, P; thought 'twas *conj.*
219 Pioners] Pioneers D, P

III.ii

III.ii] SCENE II. *A Court of Justice. D*; SCENA II *A Court of Justice P*;
   om. Q, S
SD *Enter*] ~, *on one side, D*
   To them] *then D*
   To them *The*] *On the other side, enter D*
1 Mr.] master *D (throughout)*; Master *S, P (throughout)*
7 ill-favoured] *D, S, P*; ~ ˌ ~ *Q*
13 *Poyein*] *D, S*; *Poyeni Q*; ποιεῖν *P*
20-21 notable ... life,] ~, ... ~ ˌ *Brereton conj., P*
28 Obeliskes] *D, S, P*; Obelishes *Q*
29 memory.] ~? *D, S*
36-37 You ... matter.] *as prose, P*
37 pray] pray you *conj.*
42 *Proh*] pro *S, P*
55-56 animall spirits use] *P*; annuall spirits, *Q*; animal spirits ˌ *D, S*
62 ingratefull] ungrateful *D*
70 ingratefull] ungrateful *D, S*
75 advanc'd] advance *Q*; advanced *D, S, P*
96 cost] coast *D, S, P*
116-43 And how ... countrymen.] *arranged as by Ferguson*; Pro. And how
   ... countrymen. *Q (following l.196), D, S, P; following l.166,
   Macaulay conj.*
136 crackes] crack *D, S, P (P corrects in* Text Notes)
   his] *om. S*
138 this? the] this, [but] the *D*
144 *Iudg.*] 1 *Judge. D*
147 inform'd] infround *Q*; informed *D, S, P*
   respected] suspected *L conj.*
154 Lords] *D, S, P*; Lord *Q*
158 least] lost *L (misreading owing to hole in page of copy used)*
166 just, a] ~ ˌ ~ *D, S, P*
173 conscience] conscious *L conj.*
174 questioned] question'd *D, S*
178 subjects] subject's *D*; subjects' *S, P*
192 shaddowes] *D, S, P*; shaddow *Q*
196 weigh] *Macaulay conj.*; ~. *Q, D, S*; ~ – *P*
197-209 The varietie ... more.] *arranged as by Macaulay*; Adm. The varietie
   ... more. *Q (following l.143), D, S, P*
202 incenst] incensed *D, S*; incens'd *P*
210 learned] learn'd *S, P*
226-27 (It ... affrighting?)] *P subs.*; It ... onset / As ... Affrighting? *Q*; It
   ... onset / As ... affrighting! *D, S*
232 rob'd] robb'd *D, S, P*
   and violate?] *P*; and *Q, S*; and [violate]! *D*; and – *Pen*
236 1 *Judg.*] *D, S, P (throughout)*; 1. *Q*

237 2 *Judg.*] D, S, P (*throughout*); 2. Q
247 SD *Aside to 2 Judge.*] *aside* P; *om.* Q, D, S
248 side V] L, P; side Q, D, S
250 forc'd] forced D, S
    SD *Aside to 1 Judge.*] *aside* P; *om.* Q, D, S
252 forc'd] forced D, S
261-64 We ... treasons, etc.] *as prose*, P; *as verse*, Q, D, S (... appointed /
    ... examination / ... France / ... &c.)
270 SD *To the Admiral.*] P *subs.; om.* Q, D, S

IV.i

IV.i] P; *Actus Quartus.* Q; ACT IV. SCENE I. *An Apartment in the Palace.*
    D; ACT THE FOURTH. S; *setting in* P: *A Room in the Court*
14 depresse:] D, S, P; ~ Q
18 What] That P
19 fallen] fall'n S
25 others:] ~ Q; ~. D, S, P
31 *Qu.*] *Montmorency.* Pen (*after Loane conj.*)
    mettle] metal D, S, P
36 SD *To the Constable.*] P; *om.* Q, D, S
55 into] in S
61 favours?] D, S, P; ~ Q
80 SD *Exit Asall.*] D, P; *om.* Q, S
81 dispatch'd] dispatched D, S
84 SD *Kneels.*] *Kneeling* P; *om.* Q, D, S
85 made] mad P *conj.*
87 SD *To Father.*] P; *om.* Q, D, S
91 SD *To the King.*] P; *om.* Q, D, S
103 Too] D, S, P; To Q
104 too.] ~? D, S, P
111 SD *Kneels.*] *Kneeling* P; *om.* Q, D, S
119 SD *The Wife faints.*] P *subs.; om.* Q, D, S
121 SD *Exeunt ... King.*] D, S, P; *Exeunt.* Q (*following* Lady —— *in*
    l. 120)
136 wore] wove *conj.*
147 flame] P; fame Q, D, S
150 this?] ~, D, S, P
161 hath] has S, P
165 set] sets Brereton (*and Loane*) *conj.*
180 SD *Exit.*] D; *om.* Q, S, P
184 and] *om.* P
185 merits.] merits – Pen (*reading* bounties; *in l. 184*)
198 Leige] Leigh Q; liege D, S; Liege P
200 SD *Captaine,*] *with* Captain *and* D
201-02 Sir ... presence.] *as prose*, Pen
204 SD *To Asall.*] *om.* Q, D, S, P

207 SD *Exeunt ... Captain.*] *Exit. D*; om. Q, S, P
    SD *Aside ... Secretary.*] om. Q, D, S, P
209 SD *Aside ... Treasurer.*] om. Q, D, S, P
210 SD *Asall with*] om. Q, D, S, P
211 SD *Aside ... Secretary.*] *Pen*; om. Q, D, S, P
221 issues, turnes] D, S, P; ~ ͜ ~ Q; issues' turnes *conj.*
229 y'are] P; yare Q; you're D, S
240 over-joy] ~ ͜ ~ D, S, P
251 learned] learn'd S, P
252 the malice] their malice, *conj.*
264 Vnhear'd of] Unheard of D; Unheard-of S, P
270 mine] time S (*error*)
276 SD *Exit As.*] *after Iudges. D, S, P*
284 SD *Aside.*] P; om. Q, D, S
291 shadow ... forfeits] ~ ͜ ... forfeit's D, S; ~; ... forfeit's *Brereton conj.*, P
291 SD *Asall,*] *Asall, with D*
292 SD *Aside ... Secretary.*] *aside P*; om. Q, D, S
295 Sir, I hope.] ~? ~ ~ – D, S, P
309 Lawes Volumes] ~, ~ Q; law's ~ D, S, P
313 slendrest] slenderest D, S
316 SD *Aside ... Secretary.*] *aside P*; om. Q, D, S
317 SD *Aside ... Treasurer.*] *aside P*; om. Q, D, S
321 And for ... sixe *liuers,*] For every boat, and Q; For every boat D, S, P
322 *Normand*] Norman D, S, P
325 *Iudges.*] D, S, P; *Iud.* Q
326 SD *Aside.*] P; om. Q, D, S
335 SD *Aside ... Chancellor.*] om. Q, D, S, P
336 head,] head? D, S, P
337 SD *Aside.*] om. Q, D, S, P
342 party] D, S, P; parly Q
344 a thirst] athirst P *conj.*
351 death–] D, S, P; ~. Q
355 excuse] P; ~, Q; excuse; D, S
359 SD *They kneel.*] D; *Kneeling. P*; om. Q, S
362 y'are] P; yare Q; You're D, S
363 SD *Aside ... Secretary.*] *Aside P*; om. Q, D, S
365 prisoner] poisoner *Loane conj.*
366 Is pride of] Of pride is *Brereton conj.*
369 our] out L
376 SD *Proctor-General*] om. Q, D, S, P
    SD *King ... aside.*] P; om. Q, D, S
387 SD *To the Admiral.*] *P subs.*; om. Q, D, S
388 SD *To the King.*] P; om. Q, D, S
401 whom] home D, S, P
412 my] the S
417 SD *Exit Chancellor guarded.*] P; om. Q, D, S
437 *Iudges.*] D, P; *Iud.* Q; *Ju.* S

438 SD *To ... Treasurer.*] om. Q, D, S, P
452 soone-ebb'd] D, S, P; ~ ~ Q
453 *Con.*] *Sec. conj.*

V.i

V.i] P; *Actus Quintus.* Q; ACT V. SCENE I. *An Apartment in the Palace.*
  D; ACT THE FIFTH. S; *setting in P: A Room in the Court*
1-15 With danger ... to that.] *Loane suggests shifting the Queen's second*
  speech (ll. 11-15) to follow the Father's first speech (ll. 1-2) and assigning
  ll. 9-11 (first half) to the Constable.
8 soules] D, S, P; foules Q
11 *Qu.*] *Con. Lordi conj.*
17 river, lift] D, S, P; ~ left Q
19 their] D, S, P; her Q
30 summons] D, S, P; summon Q
62 SD A*side.*] P (*after* D); om. Q, S
67 had.] had it. *Loane conj.*
70 crushing, crushing] ~ D, S, P
77 a fresh] afresh D, S, P
78 too] soe *conj.*
79 surgerie;] D, S, P; ~ Q
102 bring him] D, S, P; bring Q

V.ii

V.ii] SCENE II. *A Court of Justice.* D; SCENA II *A Court of Justice* P;
  om. Q, S
SD *attended by Petitioners*] *Petitioners following* D
SD *guard,*] ~, *is then brought in* D; ~ [*is led in*], P
1 *Tre.*] *Treas.* [*aside*] P
2 *Sec.*] *Sec.* [*aside*] P
7 If] If't D, S
35 pound] pounds D
37 pleas'd] pleased Q, D, S, P
49 borne] born D, S, P
59-71 You ... Chancellor.] *as prose,* D, S, P
81 and although] although P
98 Lamb-skinne] lamb's skin D, S; ~ ~ P
109-11 Mr. Advocate ... Admirall.] *as prose,* S, P
111 Injustly] Unjustly D
131 SD *Aside ... Treasurer.*] aside P; om. Q, D, S
147 Astræa] D, S, P; Austria Q
162-63 Kings heires: a] ~ ~, ~ Q; King. Here's a D, S, P
169 SD *Within.*] [*Voices*] *within.* P; [*The People*] *within.* Pen
191 entrills] entrails D, S, P
192 There doomesday is] There's doomsday in D, S; ~ ~ ~ - Brereton *conj.*
194 Pricke] D, P; Prickt Q; Prick'd S
198 confusion; that] ~, ~ Q; ~. That D, S, P
200 lives safety,] life's safety! D, S, P

202 farre] afar *P conj.*
    some] some [mean] *D*
212 your] *D, S, L, P;* you *Q*
218 uncapeable] incapable *D*
226 SD *Exit.*] *Exeunt all except the* Chancellor *and guards. Pen*
227 *Cha.*] *D, S, L, P; om. Q*
228 Ile] I['ll] *D, S, P;* I *Q*

V.iii

V.iii] SCENE III. *A Room in* Chabot's *House. D;* SCENA III *A Room in*
    Chabot's *House P; om. Q, S*
SD *Enter ... Wife.*] *Enter* Wife *and* Chabot, *in his gown and cap. D*
11 hart] hurt *Q;* heart *D, S, P*
33 unjustice] injustice *D, S, P*
37 can blast] *om. S*
48 reade;] *D, S, P;* ~ˏ *Q*
49 sometime] some time *D, S, P*
56 blossome] blossomes *conj.*
58 morning] *D, S, P;* mornings *Q*
67 shanot] shalt not *D, S;* sha' not *P*
70 walke;] *D, S, P;* ~ˏ *Q*
    SD *Exit.*] *D, S, P; om. Q*
72 oth'] o' the *D, S;* o' th' *P*
78 unlooked for] unlook'd for *D;* unlook'd-for *S*
79 unpetitioned] unpctition'd *D, S*
90 SD *The Admiral ... him.*] *P subs.; om. Q, D, S*
94 no] *D, S, P; om. Q*
103 writ] *D, S, P;* write *Q*
109 trenched] trencheth *D, S, P*
127 SD *To Allegre.*] *P; om. Q, D, S*
128 unjustice] injustice *D, S*
135 SD *one ... Chancellor*] *P subs.; om. Q, D, S*
139 SD *supported*] *om. Q, D, S, P*
144 *Chabot* with] ~. With *P conj.*
148 SD *To the Admiral.*] [*Turning to* Chabot] *P; om. Q, D, S*
157 tane] ta'en *D, S, P;* torn *Lordi conj.*
    a peeces] apieces *D;* a-pieces *S, P*
162 me.] me. [*Swoons. D*
167 SD *To ... him.*] *P; om. Q, D, S*
178 Is] *Lordi conj.;* It *Q;* It [is] *D, S, P*
180 to] *Brereton conj., P;* so *Q, D, S*
198 Thy] thine *D, S*
200 SD *Kneels.*] *P; om. Q, D, S*
202 SD *Dies.*] *D, S, P; om. Q*
210 *King.*] *D, S, P; Qu. Q*
225 thee,] thee! *D, P;* thee: *S*
230 SD *FINIS.*] *om. D, S*

PRESS-VARIANTS

[Copies collated: BL (British Library 644.d.54), Chi (University of Chicago Library PR 2249 T5), CSmH[1] (Huntington Library C 4996 98553), CSmH[2] (Huntington Library 98539), CtY (Yale University Library Ih 0366 639), DFo[1] (Folger Shakespeare Library 4996 copy 1), DFo[2] (Folger Shakespeare Library 4996 copy 2, with Thomas Dring's advertising slip on sig. A1ᵛ), Dyce (Victoria and Albert Museum 2055 25 c.16), MB (Boston Public Library 149. 591), MH (Harvard University Library 14424.17), NNP (Pierpont Morgan Library), TxU (University of Texas Library 61. 4681), Vir (University of Virginia Library), Worc (Worcester College Library, Oxford)]

Sheet E (inner forme)

Corrected: BL, Chi, CSmH[2], CtY, DFo[1], DFo[2], Dyce, MB, MH, NNP, TxU, Vir, Worc
Uncorrected: CSmH[1]

Sig. E1ᵛ
   III.ii.34 be the] bethe
       37 I pray] I ray
Sig. E2
   III.ii.85 our King, if your] your King, if our
       92 yeare 1536.] yeare 15.6.
Sig. E3ᵛ
   III.ii.205 Yet] Yeh

Sheet F (outer forme)

First State Corrected: CSmH[2], DFo[2], Vir
Uncorrected: MH
Sig. F2ᵛ
   IV.i.134 *King.* Now] ■ *King.* Now
Sig. F3
   IV.i.177 twixt] twit
   Second State Corrected: BL, Chi, CSmH[1], CtY, DFo[1], Dyce, MB, NNP, TxU, Worc
Sig. F2ᵛ
   IV.i.123 *Cha.* Twas] *King.* Twas

Sheet F (inner forme)

Corrected: BL, Chi, CSmH¹, CSmH², CtY, DFo¹, DFo², Dyce, MB,
    NNP, TxU, Vir, Worc
Uncorrected: MH

Sig. F1ᵛ
    IV.i.73 house-genious] house genious
        78 zeale] eale
Sig. F3ᵛ
    IV.i.210 SD *Wife and*] Wife⎮*and*
Sig. F4
    IV.i.238 frownes] frounes

Sheet H (outer forme)

Corrected: BL, Chi, CSmH², CtY, Dfo¹, DFo², Dyce, MB, MH, NNP,
    TxU, Vir, Worc
Uncorrected: CSmH¹

Sig. H1
    V.i.98 play on] pla yon
Sig. H3
    V.ii.142 *cōscientiæ*] *cōsctieniæ*
        151 satisfie this] satisfie⎮this⎮

Sheet H (inner forme)

Corrected: BL, Chi, CsmH², CtY, DFo², Dyce, MB, MH, NNP, TxU,
    Vir, Worc
Uncorrected: CSmH¹, DFo¹

Sig. H1ᵛ
    V.ii.17 Philosophycall] Phylosophycall
Sig. H3ᵛ
    V.ii.199 Resigne] Resigne (*indented*)
Sig. H4
    V.ii.219 sum of] sum⎮of

Sheet I (outer forme)

Corrected: BL, Chi, CSmH¹, CSmH², CtY, DFo¹, DFo², Dyce, MB,
    NNP, TxU, Vir, Worc
Uncorrected: MH

Sig. I1
    V.iii.51 *line moved slightly to left*] *line even with one above*
        56 wanton blossome,] wanton, blossome
        60 growth] groweth
        84 rare, past] rare past,
Sig. I3
    V.iii.188 divide] dvide

Sheet I (inner forme)

Corrected: BL, Chi, CSmH[1], CSmH[2], CtY, DFo[1], DFo[2], Dyce, MB, NNP, TxU, Vir, Worc

Uncorrected: MH

Sig. I3[v]

V.iii.217 prison,] prison.

TEXTUAL NOTES

Speakers.

1 *Asall*] The list of 'Speakers.' in Q is both inaccurate and incomplete. Parrott suggests that the omission of Chabot's Wife may indicate that she was not originally included as a character in Chapman's pre-revision version of the play. But this seems highly unlikely (see Introduction, pp. 621-22) and we may note that the Queen, whom Parrott also suggests as a possible addition, does figure in the list of 'Speakers.' The bracketed characters and character descriptions are taken from either Dyce or Parrott. Chabot appears twice, first as *Admirall.* and a second time as *Chabot.*, following *Generall.*, a designation Parrott explains as an error for [*Proctor-*]*Generall.*, a character later called *Advocate* in IV.i and V.ii. No *Porter.* appears in the play in its revised form. The character has been retained as a possible vestige of the pre-Shirley revision, though Parrott temptingly suggests that it is merely a compositor's misreading of *Proctor*. Following Parrott, I have added *Petitioners*. They are mentioned in the opening SD to V.ii and, though they have no part in the scene as it now stands, may have figured in the scene as originally written.

I.i

187 does ... nature] i.e. acts against both aspects of his nature (as a creature ['*Animall*'] and as a creature socially motivated ['*politicum*']). Shepherd's emendation of 'in' to 'it' makes the sense more obvious but does not seem to be absolutely necessary.

220 shadder] A variant of 'shalder' (= to crumble or break up, *NED*). Dyce's 'shudder' is therefore unnecessary.

I.ii

133 selfe scandall] i.e. the obloquy accruing to the King's own self (as a result of the way in which his letters had been ignored). Pennel's conjecture 'selfe scandal'd' is, however, appealing, since Chapman employs 'scandald' in *The Revenge of Bussy D'Ambois*, I.i.332, and in the 'Dialogue' (l. 9) appended to his *Justification of Andromeda Liberata* (1614).

II.i

23 As in this ... wisedome] As if in this more circumscribed mind (i.e. Chabot's) were (to be found) all wisdom. See Historical Collation for suggested emendation.

II.ii

14 they thinke] i.e. the members of his faction (cf. l. 17) think. Parrott's emendation ('he thinks') is, nevertheless, tempting.

56-57 My innocence ... fights.] My innocence, which is a conquering justice, is such as wears a shield that both defends me and fights for me. See Historical Collation for suggested emendations.

85 split it] i.e. split the 'shaft' of l. 84 aimed at the Chancellor's 'globe of light' (his 'state, and glory', l. 83). The image is based on the story of Hercules bending his bow against the sun when fetching away the oxen at Tartessus (see Parrott, pp. 641-42).

II.iii

113 Repos'd] The duplicated speech-prefix *Adm.* preceding this line in Q is difficult to account for, since l. 113 depends on the first half of l. 112, making the period after 'square' in Q wrong. Possibly an interjection by the King, interrupting Chabot, has been omitted.

134-35 cannot informe him ... or use] 'informe him' is extra-metrical and may represent either Chapman's first thought which remained undeleted or, as Parrott suggests, the result of untidy cutting. If so, the omission of 'informe him', with a comma added after 'cannot', makes good sense of the passage. But some sort of sense can be wrung out of the text as it stands by taking 'informe him' to mean 'give him his essential quality or character (as a good man)' (see *NED* II.b; and compare the use of 'informe' and 'informes' in I.i.95, 186), and inserting 'or' before 'use' seems better than to omit 'informe him' or to leave it dangling in parentheses as Parrott does. Brereton's conjecture that 'cannot informe him' was a marginal comment by the printer indicating that someone could not tell him what word was missing after 'and' is rightly dismissed by Parrott, who points out that 'cannot' is required to go with 'use'.

207 fiuer] i.e. sinew. Pennel's conjecture of 'fiuer' for Q 'finer' has been accepted in preference to Dyce's emendation 'fibre' (i.e. fiber) because (a) Chapman uses the variant form 'fiuer' for 'fiber' (see *Bussy D'Ambois*, II.i.100; 'A Hymne to Our Saviour on the Crosse,' l. 134; and the *Odysses*, XVIII, 5) and (b) Q 'finer' is an easy minim misreading of a manuscript 'fiuer' (i.e. fiver). The later appearance of 'fibers' (V.iii.59) should not influence the choice of reading here.

III.i

21 SD *Manent*] Q '*Manente*', though retained by Shepherd and Parrott, is grammatically unacceptable and, so far as I know, occurs nowhere else in or out of Chapman. Either '*Manentibus*' or '*Manentes*' would be required by the context. '*Manent*' is, of course, commonly used in stage directions at this period.

III.ii

116-143, 197-209] The rearrangement of these lines from their position in Q is discussed in the Introduction, p. 622.

226-27 (It being ... affrighting?)] The sense of these lines is far from clear. Parrott's parentheses help somewhat and the three question marks may be read as exclamation marks. 'It' presumably refers back to 'violate Majestie' (l. 224), but what is being 'compar'd' is certainly not obvious, though the two following statements or exclamations seem to be intended as a comment on the Proctor-General's reaction to Chabot's supposedly horrendous crimes, or, less likely, I think, to Chabot's reaction to the Proctor-General's verbal attack.

IV.i

36 SD *To the Constable.*] The King's speech appears to be directed as an answer to the preceding speech (ll. 31-35) by the Queen, but it is clearly addressed to the Constable. Loane's conjecture that ll. 31-35 should be assigned to the Constable is, therefore, tempting, but since we are here dealing with a problem reflecting probable revision (see the Introduction, p. 622), it seems preferable to retain the text as it stands, with the addition of Parrott's stage direction. A parallel textual situation, again involving the Queen and Constable, arises with the Father's speech in V.i.15-23.

204 SD *To Asall.*] There seems to be some confusion, possibly the result of carelessness in revision, as to whom the King is addressing in ll. 203-06. Lines 203-04 ('You have ... presence.') seem to be addressed to the Captain, evidenced by 'and' in l. 203, but only Asall (l. 207) acknowledges the orders ('I shall sir!'). To clarify the situation, the present text makes the King turn from the Captain to Asall at 'Bid' (l. 204) and then exits both the Captain and Asall at l. 207 SD, re-entering them at l. 210 SD, since both are required later in the scene.

291 To shadow ... forfeits mine] i.e. to portray all the shame and losses that are mine (as a result of the 'wilde' method I chose to test Chabot's merit). See Historical Collation for suggested emendations.

321-22 And for ... *liuers,* / That] Dyce and later editors have been satisfied simply to delete Q 'and' following 'boate,', but the present arrangement, with the insertion of 'six *liuers*' after 'boate' and the transposition of 'and' to precede 'for', brings these lines into agreement with the original account of the incident in III.ii.97-99 and thus concludes the speech with a half-line that is completed by the half-line beginning the King's rejoinder.

401 whom] Dyce's reading 'home' is unnecessary; 'whom' is a recognized variant spelling of 'home'.

V.i

16 they'le ... Lord] See the Textual Note to IV.i.36 SD.

70 crushing, crushing] Although Parrott acknowledges that this kind of repetition is in Chapman's manner, he follows Dyce in omitting the second

'crushing'. The present rearrangement of ll. 70-71 preserves 'crushing, crushing' and furnishes a more adequate half-line to be completed by the Father's answer (even so, l. 71 is a foot short).

V.ii

162-63 the Kings heires: a traytor] Editors all follow Dyce in emending to 'the King. Here's a traitor', certainly a persuasive emendation. I have retained the original, however, with a colon after 'heires' instead of the Q comma, because there appears to be a reference to 'heires' in 'murderer of his owne' (l. 167) and some connection with the concluding lines of the play, enigmatic as they are (V.iii.225-28). See the Textual Note on V.iii.223-28.

V.iii

109 trenched upon] i.e. touched upon (*NED* III.6). Dyce's emendation 'trencheth upon' gives a more natural tense sequence but is not absolutely necessary.

223-28 O *Chabot* ... heire?] The final lines (225-28: 'Kings ... heire?') taken in isolation have tended to induce despair among commentators (Parrott, for example, who quite mistakenly, I think, attributes them to Shirley); they should, however, be considered in the context of the immediately preceding lines, of which, syntactically, they may be taken as a part. My colleague John Klause suggests the following paraphrase of ll. 223-28: 'O Chabot, your authority over the hearts of Frenchmen will not die, but increase, even as time passes. Just as Kings die not (otherwise the concept of 'succession' is meaningless), and as a King need not fear to lose authority, after his death, over his heir and successor, so you may be assured that your "rule" over our hearts, your heirs, will never lapse.' (Note that 'or starve succession' here is taken to mean 'or the concept of succession would also die'.) Such an interpretation has the great virtue of tying ll. 225-28 directly to Chabot, which another suggested paraphrase of these lines by John Spring (requiring the emendation of 'their' in l. 228 to either 'them' or 'they're') fails to do: 'Kings, they say, may not die before they provide for a successor, lest they starve the succession. Oh, why should this be, and why must kings be left to despair at the discovery that they, alone of men, are subjects to kings unborn?' (*N & Q*, CCXII (1977), 523). A third paraphrase of ll. 225-28, which also applies these lines to Chabot, has been suggested to me by Professor Allan Holaday: 'It is said that kings don't die because, if they did (i.e. if the line of kings ended) the concept of succession would die. Oh why, if that stands firm (i.e. if that notion is true) should kings despair of finding the same continuity (i.e. like the succession of kings) in subjects? That is, why should I despair of finding among my future subjects an heir of Chabot (i.e. another subject as worthy as Chabot)?'

Sir Gyles Goosecappe, Knight

edited by John F. Hennedy

❉

TEXTUAL INTRODUCTION

There are two seventeenth-century quarto editions of *Sir Gyles Goosecappe*. The first (Q1) was printed in 1606 by John Windet for Edward Blount; the second (Q2) in 1636 for Hugh Perry. Although no printer's name appears on the title page of the second edition, W. W. Greg, who gives a full bibliographical description of the two quartos, surmises from the printer's device that it was printed by John Norton, the younger, and either Nicholas or John Okes.[1]

The text of Q2 derives from that of Q1. From signature B, the beginning of the text, through G4, Q2 is a nearly line for line reprint of Q1; from G4ᵛ through L2, the last page of the text, it becomes as well a page for page reprint. Certain errors in the second quarto result from peculiarities in the Q1 text which misled the Q2 compositor, as the following three examples will illustrate. At the beginning of I.i.57, the name '*Wil*' appears in parentheses in Q1 to indicate direct address. The compositor of Q2, supposing the name to be a speech-prefix, placed a period after the word 'Commendations', which ends line 56; indented *Will* at the beginning of the next line; and capitalized the 'i' of the following 'is', thus muddling the sense of the speech. Secondly, between 'wit' and 'a good bustling gallant' (I.i.126) in Q1, rather than a mark of punctuation, which the construction clearly requires, there appears a gap, which probably contained at some time the appropriate pointing. Q2 closes the gap, but follows Q1 in placing no punctuation between 'wit' and the following 'a'. Finally, in Q1 at I.ii.66-67, where the lines end respectively 'familiare' and 'shall', the comma after 'familiare' was dropped to the end of the line below, just as the final 'l' on 'shall' was dropped to the end of the following line. Q2, while replacing the needed comma after 'familiare', repeats the misplaced comma after 'shall', which, as we have seen, was produced by a printing error in Q1.

[1] W. W. Greg, *A Bibliography of the English Printed Drama to the Restoration* (London, 1951), I, No. 228.

Since Q1 provides our only substantive text of the play, one would like to determine the kind of manuscript that served as printer's copy. A piece of external evidence – the entry of Q1 in the *Stationers' Register* for Edward Blount on January 10, 1606 – is pertinent to this question:

> Entred for his Copie vnder the handes of Master WILSON and Master **ffield** warden An Comedie called *Sir GYLES GOOSECAP* PROVIDED that yt be printed accordinge to the Copie wherevnto master WILSONS hand ys at ....[2]

One might conclude that the ecclesiastical licenser, John Wilson, had read with some thoroughness the copy from which Q1 was printed and that this copy had been somehow revised to meet his approval.

The play, as we know it, contains evidence of such revision. At the end of the second act (II.i. 353-355), Eugenia invites her guests, Lord Tales and Sir Cutbert Kingcob, to accompany her to supper that evening at the home of Lord and Lady Furnifall. Later (III.i.178-188), Captain Foulweather, in describing this unusual couple to his companion, Rudesby, reveals that Lady Furnifall, who normally terrorizes her husband, becomes 'sociable' when she gets 'typsie' and that Lord Furnifall, to display this remarkable change in his wife's disposition, often invites guests to his home. Foulweather concludes by promising that Rudesby will be able to see her perform that same evening when they eat supper with the Furnifalls. After such an introduction, one naturally expects to find a later scene which dramatizes Lady Furnifall's antics.[3]

Although no such scene exists in the version of the play which was printed, it seems probable that one was present in an earlier version. IV.ii takes place at Lord Furnifall's home; and although we never meet Lady Furnifall, an apparent reference to her occurs at the close of the scene. The page Will's remark, 'Another Crashe in my Ladies Celler yfaith *monsieur*.' (IV.ii.229-230), is unrelated to anything that precedes it in this scene, but could easily refer to Lady Furnifall's behavior as previously described by Foulweather. This line probably survives from an earlier version of the scene in which Lady Furnifall appeared and displayed her drinking humor, an episode to which the licenser, Wilson, apparently objected. Its deletion and possibly other changes produced another 'copy' which he approved for publication.

Such a supposition invites speculation about the printer's copy. R. B. McKerrow, arguing for the frequent use of authors' dramatic manuscripts as printer's copy, and recognizing that the author or bookseller would probably submit to the licenser a 'tidy and readable' copy, conjectures that plays which had already been licensed for performance would not be reread by the licenser for the press before printing.[4] Since *Sir Gyles Goosecappe* is our

---

[2] *A Transcript of the Registers of the Company of Stationers of London: 1554-1640 A.D.*, ed. Edward Arber (London, 1876), III, 133.

[3] T. M. Parrott discusses this possibility in 'The Authorship of "Sir Gyles Goosecappe,"' *MP*, IV (1906), 34 and in his 'Introduction' to *The Plays of George Chapman: The Comedies*, p. 892. He bases his argument on the earlier descriptions of Lady Furnifall, failing to notice the reference to her at the end of IV.ii.

[4] 'The Elizabethan Printer and Dramatic Manuscripts,' *Library*, XII, Ser. 4, No. 3 (December, 1931), 253-275.

most certain example of a play which a licenser actually read,[5] we might conclude, if we follow McKerrow's logic, that it was printed from fair copy, possibly a prompt-copy. It is improbable that already untidy 'foul papers,' further marked up by the author as he revised to satisfy the licenser, would have been submitted for the licenser's final approval.

Yet on the basis of internal evidence, it seems unlikely that a prompt-copy lies behind the printed text. None of the characteristics associated with this type of copy appears in *Sir Gyles Goosecappe*: there are no references to stage properties, for example, nor any mention of an actor's name along with that of the character he represents.

On the other hand, characteristics associated with an 'autograph manuscript not corrected and made uniform by a stage-reviser for prompt-copy or by a scribe for purposes of a private transcript'[6] are evident. Irregularities in speech-prefixes, for example, occur throughout the play. The speech-prefix for Goosecappe, normally *Goos.* or *Go.*, occurs once as *Giles.* Some speeches are incorrectly assigned. In two instances (III.i.62-63; IV.iii.1 and 5), the same prefix occurs before two adjacent speeches, the second of which obviously belongs to another speaker; for one short speech (V.ii.57) no prefix is supplied. The erroneous substitution of *King.* for *Rud.* (III.i.184) apparently illustrates the author's tendency to confuse these closely associated characters. We learn from Will at III.i.161-165, only a few lines before this confusion of headings, that Sir Cutbert (as his name is most often spelled) Kingcob is Sir Cutbert Rudesby's uncle. Although the *dramatis personae* lists Kingcob's first name as 'Clement', throughout the play he is called 'Cutbert', the inconsistency possibly resulting from an inadvertent switch by the author. That the dramatist might have recognized this confusion and may also have intended to change Rudesby's first name is suggested by two references to him as 'Sir Moyle' (III.i.15 and 62), although Moyle may simply be a nickname for Rudesby. A further instance of the confusion of these names deserves mention, although it may have resulted from a compositor's error. The speech-prefix, *Cud.*, which occurs for Rudesby at IV.ii.124, is possibly a mixture of the abbreviated first name, *Cut.*, and the normal heading, *Rud.*

Other errors in the text which may have resulted from the compositor's use of an imperfect holograph manuscript also occur. Sir Gyles's oath, 'to God' (III.i.95), seems to be missing a word such as 'would'.[7] A few lines later (III.i.99-100), the double occurrence of an oath, 'Ile be sworne,' may exemplify the kind of repetition often found in an author's rough draft.[8] The obviously bad line of verse, 'Ile now make her now amends with Adoration.' (V.ii.291), could be accounted for in the same way. Similarly, the line, 'I will not write, my friend shall speake for me.' (III.ii.29), appears in Q2 as 'I will not writ, Our my friend shall speake for me.' Q1, while omitting 'our',

---

[5] F. P. Wilson, 'Shakespeare and the "New Bibliography,"' *The Bibliographical Society, 1892-1942: Studies in Retrospect* (London, 1949), pp. 88, 109.

[6] Wilson, p. 107.

[7] The oath 'would to God' appears twice in this play (I.iv.151; V.ii.150).

[8] The single 'Ile be sworne' appears eight times, on three occasions spoken by Goosecappe.

contains between 'write' and 'my' no pointing and a gap of at least four spaces. If this gap results from a correction in Q1, we can conclude that the 'our' in Q2 derives from an uncorrected state of this forme in Q1. Such an interpretation fits the evidence.[9] Thus, the meaningless juxtaposition of 'our' and 'my' in the uncorrected version of Q1 could well have been caused by the printer's reliance on the author's rough draft in which the dramatist had revised 'our' to 'my'.

Only those stage directions designating entrances are stated in the imperative, the usual form employed by both author and stage-reviser for this type of direction. The others – '*He daunceth speaking.*' (II.i.76-77), '*He reads and comments.*' (III.ii.91-92), '*He writes and she dictates.*' (IV.i.150-151), and '*He drawes the Curtaines and sits within them.*' (V.ii.132) – appear to be the author's work rather than that of a reviser preparing prompt-copy. The occurrence of '*Clarence Solus.*' at the start of Act II is also consistent with Chapman's fondness for Latin stage directions.

Thus, internal evidence, which implies that the printer of Q1 had in hand the author's foul papers, seemingly contradicts external evidence, which suggests that he did not. As noted before, the licenser's having read the copy from which Q1 was set implies that this was some form of fair copy; yet the Q1 text exhibits characteristics usually associated with foul papers. A conclusion which takes into account both types of evidence is that the version lying behind Q1 is a copy especially prepared for the licenser based on the author's original manuscript. In it Chapman had presumably made the revisions and deletions required by the licenser, but failed to eliminate all the confusions existing in the original draft.

Seventy-eight press-variants occur in the ten copies of Q1 that I have examined. From our knowledge of Chapman's concern for the accuracy of his printed works and from the nature of these changes, it appears that some of them may have originated with the author himself. We know from a passage in his introduction to *The Memorable Masque* that Chapman did in one instance receive proofs from the printer.[10]

Although Windet, the printer of Q1 of *Sir Gyles Goosecappe*, showed concern for accuracy in his 1597 folio edition of Richard Hooker's *Lawes of Ecclesiastical Politie*,[11] he failed to satisfy Chapman in his first printing of a Chapman work. In 1598 Windet printed Chapman's two earliest translations of Homer – first *The Seauen Bookes of the Iliades of Homere, Prince of Poets* and later *Achilles Shield*. Chapman's concern about the accuracy of the printing is evidenced by the addition of an errata list to *The Seauen Bookes* and his complaint about Windet's 'extreame false printing' in the introduction 'to the understander' of *Achilles Shield*. This earlier experience might have

---

[9] In Q1 the line in question occurs in signature E, which also contains the readings 'merrit' (III.ii.27) and 'mourner' (III.ii.28), corrupted to 'merry' and 'manner' in Q2. In the copies of Q1 which I have examined, no press-variants occur in this signature. Since variants appear in seven of the nine other sheets, the exceptions being the first two, A and B, it is highly probable that these corruptions in Q2 originate from an uncorrected state of one or both formes of E.

[10] See Vol. I of the present edition, p. 568, ll. 143-149.

[11] Percy Simpson, *Proof-reading in the Sixteenth, Seventeenth, and Eighteenth Centuries* (Oxford, 1935), pp. 76-79.

caused Chapman to check Windet's printing of *Sir Gyles Goosecappe* closely, just as it might have made Windet eager to afford Chapman such an opportunity.

The nature of several stop-press corrections in Q1 does, indeed, suggest that Chapman himself originated them. The substitution, for example, of 'sweet' for 'dear' (I.iv.164) and the addition of two stage directions, '*He daunceth speaking.*' (II.i.76-77) and '*He reads and comments.*' (III.ii.91-92), would not be likely to result from the usual printshop procedures. Although the revisions of 'bindes' to 'buildes' (I.iv.133), 'rightest' to 'richest' (I.iv.147), 'good' to 'od' (V.i.75), and 'shippards' to 'sheppards' (V.i.106) could have been initiated by a proofreader other than the author, it seems more likely that Chapman was responsible for these also. Thus, except for five obviously wrong revisions,[12] the corrected readings seem to be authoritative and have been adopted in the present text.

Q1 was printed with probably three sets of running-titles: set I in sheets B (outer and inner), D (outer), E (outer), H (outer), and I (inner); set II in sheets C (outer and inner), E (inner), F (inner), G (outer), and H (inner); and set III in sheets D (inner), F (outer), G (inner), and I (outer).

From a list included in a report to the Master and Wardens of the Stationers' Company, we know that as early as July, 1586, Windet owned three presses;[13] we should expect, therefore, that he would normally employ more than one compositor. It appears that three compositors, here identified as X, Y, and Z, worked on *Sir Gyles Goosecappe*. Compositor X set sheets A and B, Compositor Y worked from the beginning of sheet C to the end of H, and Compositor Z set sheets I and K. Compositors X and Y are clearly distinguishable; Compositor Z shared several of the characteristics of both X and Y.

Patterned variations between final '-y' and final '-ie' spellings are the most numerous of several orthographic characteristics that distinguish sheets A-B from the rest of the quarto. In both A and B, final '-y' spellings exceed in number final '-ie' spellings; in all other sheets, the situation is reversed. Thus a preference for final '-y' over final '-ie' identifies Compositor X; Compositors Y and Z both prefer final '-ie'. Variations among '-es' and '-esse' spellings of the suffix '-ess' show a similar pattern. Compositor X favored the '-es' form: it appears seven times to only one '-esse' in the first two sheets. The middle six signatures, the work of Compositor Y, contain twenty-nine '-esse' spellings, but only nineteen '-es' forms. Compositor Z, who used each form five times, shows no preference. The words 'dear', 'year', and 'clear' vary in their spellings between '-eare' and '-eere'. Compositor X used seven '-eare' to three '-eere' spellings, while Y favored '-eere' over '-eare' twenty to eleven; the three examples appearing in Z's section (one '-eare' and two '-eere' spellings) provide insufficient evidence to determine his preference. The most marked variation in spelling is that between '-ould' and '-ood'[14] in 'should',

---

[12] I.iv.116 and 168; II.i.60, 66, and 193.
[13] Arber, V, lii.
[14] Exceptions are 'shudd' (II.i.109), 'shoold' (III.i.22), and 'cud' (III.i.264).

'could', and 'would'. In this case the X form, '-ould', continues through signature C into the first three pages of D. From A2 through D2 there are thirty-eight '-ould' forms to seven '-ood' spellings; in the rest of the text there are seven '-ould' and eighty-eight '-ood' forms. Since all other significant variants show the first shift in compositors as coming between signatures B and C, I can only suggest the possibility that Compositor X was following his copy in the predominance of '-ould' spellings and that Y also began by following the copy, until at D2^v he started substituting his characteristic '-ood' spellings. Z also favored the '-ood' forms.

In two other instances, variant spellings help to define the work stints of each compositor. 'These' occurs as 'theis' six times in signatures A and B and three times as 'these'. In signatures C through H, 'these' occurs nine times and 'theis' twice. Signatures I and K contain two instances of each form. In the first two signatures, the variable 'hir' appears five times along with eighteen 'her' spellings; in the middle six, 'hir' appears only once together with fifty-eight 'her' forms; in the last two, 'hir' again appears once among thirty instances of 'her'.

Though the punctuation proves of limited help in defining each compositor's portion of the text, evidence from the capitalization pattern of three recurrent words, 'sir', 'knight', and 'ile', corroborates that from the spelling practices. A tabulation reveals that Compositor Z employed upper case for these words less often than X and more often than Y. For example, 'sir' occurs forty-nine times in the first two signatures and fifteen in the last two for a total of sixty-four occurrences within the work stints of Compositors X and Z; and in only one instance does it begin with lower-case 's'. But Compositor Y uses lower-case 's' for this word from three to ten times in each of the middle six signatures. In the cases of 'knight' and 'ile', however, Z's practice is closer to Y's than it is to X's. The word 'knight', which occurs in every signature except C and I, begins with an upper-case 'k' only three times, once in A and twice in B. The contraction 'ile' begins with an upper-case 'i' seven times and with a lower-case 'i' only once in signatures A and B. All other signatures, except D and E, show either a predominance of 'ile' over 'Ile' or an even distribution of both forms. Variations in the running-titles, though not providing decisive evidence, seem also to indicate a break between sheets A and B and the other sheets in Q1.

After the 1636 quarto, *Sir Gyles Goosecappe* was not reprinted until 1884, when A. H. Bullen included it in his *Collection of Old English Plays*. Though Bullen apparently consulted Q1, he derived his old-spelling text principally from Q2; as a result it contains numerous errors. Yet some of his emendations plausibly resolve cruxes in Q1. His correction of the second 'verbe' to 'adverbe' (I.ii.95), his reading of 'on't' (II.i.214) for the 'one' of Q1 and the 'on' of Q2, and his emendations of 'all' to 'add' (IV.iii.80) and 'Weend' to 'Weeud' (V.ii.163), for example, are adopted in the present text.

The only other edition of *Sir Gyles Goosecappe* – that appearing in Thomas Marc Parrott's *The Plays of George Chapman: The Comedies* (1914) – despite its modernized spelling and punctuation, is superior to Bullen's. First, because Parrott used Q1 as his copy-text, he avoided Bullen's practice of accepting corrupt readings from Q2. And, by comparing three different copies of Q1,[15] Parrott discovered many of the press-variants recorded in this edition.

---

[15] A Bodleian Library copy, a British Library copy (facsimile in *Tudor Facsimile Texts*, ed. J. S. Farmer, 1912), and Willy Bang's and Rudolph Brotanek's reprint of a copy of Q1 from the K. und K. Hof-Bibliothek at Vienna, which appeared in *Materialien zur Kunde des älteren Englischen Dramas*, XXVI (1909).

SIR

GYLES GOOSECAPPE
Knight.

A Comedie prefented by the Chil:
of the Chappell.

AT LONDON.
Printed by *Iohn Windet* for
Edward Blount. 1606.

[DRAMATIS PERSONAE]

Eugenia, A widowe, and a Noble Ladie.   [A1ᵛ]

Hyppolita,
Penelope, } Ladie-virgines, and Companions to Eugenia.

Wynnifred, gentlewoman to Eugenia.

[Anabell, waiting woman to Eugenia.]   5

Momford, A Noble Man, vnkle to Eugenia.

Clarence, Gentleman, friend to Momford.

Fowlewether, a french affected Trauayler, and a Captaine.

Sir Giles Goosecap, a foolish knight.

Sir Cuthbert Rudsbie, a blunt knight.   10

Sir Clement Kingcob, a knight.

Lord Tales.

Lord Furnifall.

Bullaker, a french Page.

Iack
Will } Pages.   15

[Doctor Versey.]

[Horatio, a singer.]

[Messenger.]

[Musicians.]   20

DRAMATIS PERSONAE] Parrott ‖ 5 Anabell, … Eugenia.] Parrott ‖ 6 Momford] Q2; Monford Q1 (See Textual Note) ‖ 7 Momford] Q2; Monf. Q1 ‖ 9 Goosecap,] Q2; ∼: Q1 ‖ 11 Clement] stet (See Textual Note) | Kingcob] Q2; kingcob Q1 ‖ 16 Pages.] Q2; ∼. Q1 ‖ 17-20 Doctor Versey … Musicians.] Parrott ‖

SIR GYLES GOOSECAPPE, KNIGHT. [A2]

ACTVS PRIMVS, SCÆNA PRIMA

Enter Bullaker with a Torche.

Bullaker.

This is the Countesse *Eugenias* house I thinke, I can
neuer hit of theis same English Cittie howses, tho I
were borne here: if I were in any Citty in Fraunce, I
coulde find any house there at midnight.

Enter Iacke, and Will.

Ia. Theis two strange hungrie knights (*Wil*) make   5
the leanest trenchers that euer I waited on.

Will. A plague on them *Iack*, they leaue vs no fees
at all, for our attendance, I thinke they vse to sett
their bones in siluer they pick them so cleane; see,
see, see *Iack* what's that?   10

Ia. A my worde (*Will*) tis the great Baboone, that
was to be seene in Southwarke.

Will. Is this he? gods my life what beastes were we,
that we wood not see him all this while; neuer trust mee
if hee looke not somewhat like a man, see how pretely hee   15
holds the torche in one of his forefeete; where's his
keeper trowe, is he broke loose?

Ia. Hast euer an Apple about thee (*Will*)? weele
take him vp sure, we shall get a monstrous deale of
mony with him. /   20

Will. That we shall yfaith boy, and looke thou here,   [A2ᵛ]
here's a red-cheekt apple to take him vp with.

Ia. Excellent fit a my credit, let's lay downe our
prouant, and to him.

Bul. [*Aside.*] Ile let them alone a while.   25

---

9 cleane;] ~, *Q1-2* ‖ 10 what's] whats *Q1-2* ‖ 11 *Ia.*] *Many of the several speech-prefixes in this
scene (as here) lack a period; not hereafter recorded for this or other speech-prefixes in this scene.* ‖
14 while;] ~, *Q1-2* ‖ 16 forefeete;] ~, *Q1-2* | where's] wheres *Q1-2* ‖ 18 (*Will*)?] (~). *Q1-2* ‖ 21
yfaith] yfath *Q1-2* ‖ 22 here's] heres *Q1-2* | red-cheekt] red cheekt *Q1-2* ‖ 23 let's] lets *Q1-2* ‖ 25
SD *Aside.*] *Parrott* ‖

721

Ia. Giue me the apple to take vp *Iacke*, because my
name is *Iacke*.

Will. Hold thee *Iacke*, take it.

Ia. Come *Iacke*, come *Iacke*, come *Iacke*.

Bul. I will come to you Sir, Ile *Iacke* ye a my worde,   30
Ile *Iacke* ye.

Will. Gods me he speakes *Iacke*, O pray pardon vs
Sir.

Bul. Out ye *mopede monckies* can yee not knowe a man
from a *Marmasett*, in theis Frenchified dayes of ours?   35
nay ile *Iackefie* you alittle better yet.

Both. Nay good Sir, good Sir, pardon vs –

Bul. Pardon vs, out ye home-bred peasants, plain
english, pardon vs? if you had parled, and not spoken,
but said *pardonne moy*, I wood haue pardon'd you, but   40
since you speake, and not parley, I will cudgell ye better
yet.

Ambo. O *pardonne moy mounsieur.*

Bul. Bien *ie vous remercie*, ther's *pardonnne pour
vous* Sir now.   45

Will. Why I thanke ye for it Sir, you seeme to bee
a Squire of our order Sir.

Ia. Whose page might you be Sir?

Bul. I am now the great French Traualers page –

Will. Or rather the french Traualers great page.   50
Sir, on, on.

Bul. Hight Captaine *Fouleweather*, alias Comendations;
whose valour's within here at super with the Countes
Eugenia, whose propper eaters I take you two to be.

Will. You mistake vs not Sir.   55

Ia. This captain *Fouleweather*, alias Commendations
(*Wil*) is the gallant that wil needs be a sutor to our
Countes.

Will. Faith and if *Fouleweather* be a welcome suiter
to a faire Ladie, has good lucke.   60

Ia. O Sir, beware of one that can showre into the
lapps of Ladies. Captaine *Fowleweather*? why hee's a /
Captinado, or Captaine of Captaines, and will lie in   [A3]
their ioyntes that giue him cause to worke vppon them,
so heauylie that hee will make their hartes ake I   65
warrant him; Captaine *Fowleweather*? why hee will make

30 you] Q2; your Q1 ‖ 37 *Both.*] *both*, Q1; *both*. Q2 | vs–] ~, Q1; ~. Q2 ‖ 39 vs?] Q2; ~, Q1 ‖ 40 *moy*,] ~; Q1-2 ‖ 43 *Ambo.*] ~. Q1-2 ‖ 44 ther's] thers Q1-2 ‖ 48 Sir?] ~. Q1-2 ‖ 49 page–] *Parrott*; ~. Q1-2 ‖ 51 on.] Q2; ~. Q1 ‖ 52, 56 *Fouleweather*] Q2; Fouleweather] Q1 ‖ 53 valour's] valours Q1-2 ‖ 58 Countes.] Q2; ~. Q1 ‖ 59 *Fouleweather*] Fouleweather Q1-2 ‖ 62 Ladies.] *Bullen*; ~, Q1-2 | *Fowleweather*] Fowleweather Q1-2 | hee's] hees Q1-2 ‖ 66 *Fowleweather*] Fowleweather Q1-2 ‖ 64-65 them, so heauylie] *Parrott*; ~ ~ ~ ~, Q1-2 ‖

the cold stones sweate for feare of him, a day or two
before he come at them. Captaine *Fowleweather*? why
he does so dominere, and raigne ouer women –

Will. A plague of Captaine *Fowleweather*, I remember 70
him now *Iack*, and know him to be a dull moist-braind
Asse.

Ia. A Southerne man I thinke.

Will. As fearefull as a Hare, and a will lye like a
Lapwing, and I know how he came to be a Captain, and to 75
haue his Surname of Commendations.

Ia. How I preethee *Will*?

Will. Why Sir he serued the great Ladie *Kingcob*,
and was yeoman of her wardroppe, and because a cood brush
vp her silkes lustely, she thought hee would curry the 80
enemies coates as soundly, and so by her commendations,
he was made Captaine in the lowe Countries.

Ia. Then being made Captaine onely by his Ladies
commendations, without any worth also of his owne, he
was euer after surnamde Captaine Commendations? 85

Will. Right.

Bul. I Sir right, but if he had not said right,
my Captaine shoulde haue taken no wrong at his handes,
nor yours neither I can tell ye.

Ia. What are those two Knights names, that are thy 90
captaines *Comrades*, and within at supper with our Lady?

Bul. One of their names Sir, is, Sir *Gyles Goosecappe*,
the other's Sir *Cutt. Rudseby*.

Will. Sir *Gyles Goosecappe*? what's he, a gentleman?

Bul. I that he is at least if he be not a noble 95
man, and his chiefe house is in Essex.

Ia. In Essex? did not his Auncestors come out of
London?

Bul. Yes that they did Sir, the best *Goosecappes* / in [A3ᵛ]
England, comes out of London I assure you. 100

Will. I but Sir these must come into it before they
come out on't I hope, but what countriman is Sir *Cutt.*
Rudesby?

Bul. A Northern man, or a Westernman I take him,
but my Captaine is the Emphaticall man; and by that 105
pretty word Emphaticall you shall partly know him; for
tis a very forcible word in troth, and yet he forces it

68 *Fowleweather*] Fowleweather *Q1-2* ‖ **69** women–] ~. *Q1-2* ‖ **70** *Fowleweather,*]
Fowleweather. *Q1 (possible semicolon very faint)*; Fowleweather. *Q2* ‖ **71** moist-braind] *Q2*;
moist braind *Q1* ‖ **75** Lapwing] Lap- / wing *Q1-2* ‖ **78** *Kingcob*] Kingcob *Q1-2* ‖ **93** other's]
others *Q1-2* ‖ **94** Goosecappe?] ~. *Q1* | what's] *Q2*; whats *Q1* | he,] ~. *Q1-2* ‖ **98** London?]
Londō. *Q1*; ~. *Q2* ‖ **99** *Goosecappes*] Gosecappes *Q1-2* ‖ **102** on't] ont *Q1-2* ‖ **103** *Rudesby*]
Q2; *Rudeby Q1* ‖

too much by his fauour; mary no more then he does all
the rest of his wordes; with whose multiplicitie often
times he trauailes himselfe out of all good company.   110

Ia. Like enough; he trauaild for nothing else.

Will. But what qualities haunt Sir *Gyles Goosecap*
now Sir?

Bul. Sir *Gyles Goosecap* has alwayes a deathes head
(as it were) in his mouth, for his onely one reason for   115
euery thing is, because wee are all mortall; and therefore
hee is generally cald the mortall knight; then hath
he another prettie phrase too, and that is, he will
tickle the vanitie an't still in euery thing, and this
is your *Summa totalis* of both their virtues.   120

Ia. Tis enough, tis enough, as long as they haue
land enough, but now muster your thirde person afore
vs I beseech you.

Bul. The thirde person and second knight blunt Sir
Cutt. Rudesby, is indeed blunt at a sharpe wit, and   125
sharpe at a blunt wit; a good bustling gallant talkes
well at Rouers; he is two parts souldier; as slouenlie
as a Switzer, and somewhat like one in face too; for
he weares a bush beard wil dead a Cannon shott better
then a woolpacke: hee will come into the presence like   130
yor Frenchman in foule bootes: and dares eate garlik as
a preparatiue to his Courtship; you shall knowe more of
him hereafter; but good wags let me winne you now, for
the Geographicall parts of your Ladies in requitall.

Will. That you shall Sir, and the Hydrographicall   135
too and you will; first my Ladie the widowe, and Countes /
Eugenia, is in earnest, a most worthy Ladie, and indeede   [A4]
can doe more then a thousand other Ladies can doe I can
tell ye.

Bul. What's that I pray thee?   140

Ia. Mary Sir, he meanes she can do more then sleep,
and eate and drinke; and play at noddy, and helpe to
make hir selfe readie.

Bul. Can she so?

Will. She is the best scholler of any woman but one   145
in England, she is wise and vertuous.

Ia. Nay shee has one strange qualitie for a woman
besides, tho these be strange enough that hee has
rekoned.

110 himselfe] Q2; himsele *Q1* ‖ 119 an't] ant *Q1-2* ‖ 123 you.] Q2; ~, *Q1* ‖ 126 wit;] ~ *Q1-2* ‖
130 woolpacke] wool-/packe *Q1-2* ‖ 132 preparatiue] *Bullen*; prepra-/tiue *Q1-2* ‖ 140 What's]
Q2; Whats *Q1* ‖ 146 vertuous.] Q2; ~, *Q1* ‖

Bul. For Gods sake what's that?   150

Ia. She can loue reasonable constantly, for she loued her husband only, almost a whole yeere togeather.

Bul. That's strange indeed, but what is youre faire Ladie Sir?

Ia. My Ladie Sir, the Ladie *Hippolita* –   155

Will. That is as chast as euer was *Hippolitus.*

Ia. (True my prettie *Parenthesis*) is halfe a maid, halfe a wife, and halfe a widdowe.

Bul. Strange tale to tell; howe canst thou make this good my good *Assumpsit.*   160

Ia. Thus Sir, she was betroathed to a gallant young gentleman that lou'de hir with such passion and admiration that he neuer thought he could bee so blessed as to enioy her in full marriage, till the minister was marrying them, and euen then when he was saying I *Charles*   165 take thee *Hippolita*, with extreame ioy he began to looke pale, then going forwardes saying to my wedded wife, he lookt paler, and, then pronouncing, for richer for poorer as long as we both shall liue, he lookt extreame pale; Now sir when she comes to speake her parte, and said, I   170 *Hippolita* take thee *Charles*, hee began to faint for ioy, then saying to my wedded husband, hee began to sinke, but then going forth to for better for worse, he / coulde   [A4ᵛ] stand no longer, but with veric conceit it seemd, that shee whome hee tendred as the best of all thinges, shoulde   175 pronounce the worst, and for his sake too, hee suncke downe right, and died sodenly: And thus being halfe married, and her halfe husband wholy dead, I hope I may with discretion affirme her, halfe a maide, halfe a wife, and halfe a widdowe; do ye conceiue me Sir?   180

Bul. O Lord Sir, I deuoure you quicke; and now Sir I beseech you open vnto me your tother Ladie, what is shee?

Will. Ile answere for her, because I know her Ladiship to be a perfect maide indeed.   185

Bul. How canst thou know that?

Will. Passing perfectly I warrant ye.

Ia. By measuring her necke twice, and trying if it will come about hir forehead, and slyp ouer her nose?

Will. No Sir no, by a rule that wil not slip so, I   190 warrant you, which for hir honours sake I wil let slip

---

150 what's] whats *Q1-2* ‖ 153 That's] Thats *Q1-2* ‖ 155 *Hippolita*–] *Bullen*; ~. *Q1-2* ‖ 162 lou'de] loude *Q1-2* ‖ 166 *Hippolita*,] *Parrott*; ~; *Q1*; ~ˏ *Q2* ‖ 171 *Hippolita*] *Q2*; *Hippolota Q1* ‖ 173 to] *Parrott*; too *Q1-2* ‖ 174 longer,] *Q2*; ~ˏ *Q1* ‖ 190 so,] *Parrott*; ~ˏ *Q1-2* ‖

vnto you; gods so *Iack*, I thinke they haue supt.

Ia. Bir Ladie we haue waited wel the while.

Will. Well though they haue lost their attendance,
let not vs lose our Suppers *Iack*.   195

Ia. I doe not meane it; come Sir you shall goe
in and drinke with vs yfaith.

Bul. Pardonne moy mounsieur.

Both. No pardoning in trueth Sir.   199

Bul. Ie vous remercy de-bon Ceur.   *Exeunt.*

[I.ii]

*Enter Goosecappe, Rudesby, Fouleweather, Eugenia,
Hippol., Penelope, Wynne.*

Rud. A plague on you sweete Ladies, tis not so late,
what needed you to haue made so short a supper?

Goos. In truth Sir *Cutt.* we might haue tickled the
vanitie an't, an howre longer if my watch be trustible.

Foul. I but how should theis bewties knowe that Sir   5
Gyles? your watch is mortall, and may erre. /

Goos. That's sooth Captain, but do you hear honest   [B1]
friend, pray take a light, and see if the moone shine,
I haue a Sunne diall will resolue presently.

Foul. Howsoeuer belieue it Ladies, tis vnwholesome,   10
vncourtlie, vnpleasant to eate hastelie, and rise sodainly,
a man can shew no discourse, no witt, no stirring, no
varietie, no prettie conceits, to make the meate goe down
emphaticaly.

Eug. Winnefred.   15

Win. Madam.

Eug. I prethie goe to my vnkle the Lord *Momford*, and
intreat him to come quicken our eares with some of his
pleasant Spirit; This same *Fowleweather* has made me so
melanchollie; prethie make haste.   20

Win. I will madam.   *Exit.*

Hip. We will bid our guests good night madam, this
same *Fowleweather* makes me so sleepie.

Pen. Fie vppon it, for Gods sake shut the Casements,
here's such a fulsome aire comes into this chamber; in   25
good faith madame you must keepe your house in better
reparations, this same *Fowlweather* beats in so filthily.

192 you;] ~, *Q1-2* ‖ **196** it;] ~, *Q1-2* ‖ **199** *Both.*] both ~ *Q1*; both. *Q2* ‖ **I.ii**] *Bullen* ‖ SD
Goosecappe, Rudesby, Fouleweather, Eugenia, Hippol.,] ~ ~. ~. ~. ~. ~. *Q1-2* ‖ **2** supper?] ~.
Q1-2 ‖ **4** an't] ant *Q1-2* ‖ **7** That's] Thats *Q1-2* ‖ **14** emphaticaly.] *Q2*; ~? *Q1* ‖ **20** melanchollie;]
Parrott; ~, *Q1-2* ‖ **25** here's] heres *Q1-2* ‖

Eug. Ile take order with the Porter for it Ladie –
good night gentlemen.

Rud. Why good night and be hangd, and youl needs be gon. 30

Goos. God giue you good night madams, thanke you
for my good-cheere; weele tickle the vanitie an't, no
longer with you at this time, but ile indite your Ladyship
to supper at my lodging one of these mornings; and that
ere long too, because we are all mortall you know. 35

Eug. Light the Ladie *Penelope*, and the Ladie *Hippolita*
to their chambers – good night faire Ladies.

Hip. Good night madam, I wish you may sleepe well
after your light supper.

Eug. I warrant you Ladie I shall neuer be troubled 40
with dreaming of my French Suter.   *Exeunt the ladies.*

Rud. Why how now my Frenchified captain *Fowlweather*?
by gods ludd thy Surname is neuer thought vpon here, I
perceiue heere's no bodie giues thee any commendations.

Foul. Why this is the vntrauaild rudnes of our grose 45
Eng-/lish Ladies now; would any French Ladie vse a man thus [B1ᵛ]
thinke ye? be they any way so vnciuil, and fulsome?
they say they weare fowle smockes, and course smockes;
I say they lie, and will die in't.

Rud. I, doe so, pray thee, thou shalt die in a very 50
honorable cause, thy countries generall quarrell right.

Foul. Their smockes quoth you? a my worde you shal
take them vp so white, and so pure, so sweet, so Emphaticall,
so moouing –

Rud. I marry Sir, I think they be continually mouing. 55

Foul. But if their smockes were Course or foule –

Rud. Nay I warrant thee thou carest not, so thou
wert at them.

Foul. S'death they put not all their virtues in
their smockes, or in their mockes, or in their stewde 60
cockes as our Ladies doe.

Rud. But in their stewde pox, there's all their
gentilitie.

Goos. Nay good Sir *Cutt.* doe not agrauate him no
more. 65

Foul. Then are they so kinde, so wise, so familiare,

---

28 Ladie–] ~, *Q1-2* ‖ **32** cheere;] ~, *Q1-2* | an't] ant *Q1-2* ‖ **33** Ladyship] La: *Q1*; La. *Q2* ‖ **37**
chambers–] ~, *Q1-2* ‖ **41** SD *Exeunt the ladies.*] *Parrott*; *Exeunt̪ Q1*; *Exeunt. Q2* ‖ **44** heere's]
heeres *Q1-2* ‖ **46** Eng-/lish] *catchword Q1*; Eng-/lesh *Q1 (text)* ‖ **48** smockes;] ~, *Q1-2* ‖ **49**
in't] int *Q1-2* ‖ **54** moouing–] *Q2*; ~. *Q1* ‖ **56** foule–] *Parrott*; ~. *Q1-2* ‖ **62** there's] theres
Q1-2 ‖ **66** familiare,] *Q2*; ~ˎ *Q1 (comma slipped to end of next line)* ‖

727

so noble, so sweet in entertainment, that when you shall
haue cause to descourse or sometimes to come neerer
them; if your breath bee ill, your teeth ill, or any thing
about you ill, why they will presently breake with ye,   70
in kind sort, good termes, pretty experiments, and tell
you plaine this; thus it is with your breath Sir, thus
it is with your teeth Sir, this is your disease, and
this is your medicine.

Goos. As I am true mortall Knight, it is most superlatiuely   75
good, this.

Foul. Why this is Courtly now, this is sweete, this
plaine, this is familiar, but by the Court of France,
our peuishe dames are so proud, so precise, so coy, so
disdainfull, and so subtill, as the *Pomonean* Serpent,   80
mort dieu the Punck of Babilon was neuer so subtill.

Rud. Nay doe not chafe so Captaine. /

Foul. Your Frenchman wood euer chafe Sir *Cutt.* being   [B2]
thus moude.

Rud. What? and play with his beard so?   85

Foul. I and brystle, it doth expresse that passion
of anger very full and emphaticall.

Goos. Nay good knight if your French wood brystle,
let him alone; introth our Ladies are a little too coy
and subtill Captaine indeed.   90

Foul. Subtle Sir *Giles Goosecappe*? I assure your
Soule, they are as subtill with their suters, or loues,
as the Latine Dialect where the nominatiue Case, and the
verbe, the Substantiue, and the Adiectiue, the verbe,
and the adverbe, stand as far a sunder, as if they were   95
perfect strangers one to another; and you shall hardly
find them out, but then learne to Construe, and perse
them, and you shall find them prepard, and acquainted,
and agree together, in Case, gender, and number.

Goos. I detest, Sir *Cutt.*, I did not thinke hee had   100
bin halfe the quintissence of a scholler he is.

Foul. Slydd there's not one of them truely emphatical.

Goos. Yes Ile ensure you Captaine, there are many
of them truely Emphaticall: but all your French Ladies
are not fatt? are they Sir?   105

Foul. Fatt, Sir? why doe yee thinke Emphaticall is
fatt, Sir *Giles*?

67 shall] *Bullen*; shal, *Q1* (*second l slipped to end of next line*); shall, *Q2* ‖ **68** neerer] *Q2*; neererl
Q1 ‖ **85** so?] *Q2*; ~. *Q1* ‖ **89** let him] lethim *Q1-2* ‖ alone;] ~, *Q1-2* ‖ **95** adverbe] *Bullen*; verbe
Q1-2 (*See Textual Note*) ‖ **100** detest,] *Bullen*; ~‸ *Q1-2* ‖ Cutt.] ~‸ *Q1-2* ‖ **102** there's] *Q2*;
theres *Q1* ‖ **104** Emphaticall:] *Q2*; ~‸ *Q1* ‖ **106** Fatt, Sir?] ~‸ ~, *Q1*; ~‸ ~? *Q2* ‖ **107** fatt, Sir]
~‸ ~ *Q1-2* ‖

Rud. Gods my life brother knight, didst thou thinke
so? hart I know not what it is my selfe, but yet I
neuer thought it was fatt, Ile be sworne to thee.   110

Foul. Why if any true Courtly dame had had but this
new fashioned sute, to entertaine any thing indifferently
stuffed, why you should haue had her more respectiue by
farre.

Rud. Nay there's some reason for that Captaine, me   115
thinks a true woman should perpetually doate vppon a new
fashion.

Foul. Why y'are i'th'right Sir *Cutt. In noua fert
Animus mutatas dicere formas.* Tis the mind of man, and   119
wo-/man to affect new fashions; but to our Mynsatiues for   [B2ᵛ]
sooth, if he come like to your *Besognio,* or your bore,
so he bee rich, or emphaticall, they care not; would I
might neuer excell a dutch Skipper in Courtshippe, if
I did not put distaste into my cariage of purpose; I
knew I should not please them. *Lacquay? allume le torche.*   125

Rud. Slydd, here's neither Torch, nor Lacquay me
thinks.

Foul. O *mon dew.*

Rud. O doe not sweare Captaine.

Foul. Your Frenchman euer sweares Sir *Cutt.,* vpon   130
the lacke of his Lacquay I assure you.

Goos. See heere he comes, and my Ladies two pages,
they haue bin tickling the vanitie on't yfaith.

SCÆNA TERTIA.

Enter to them Iack, Bullaker, Will.

Ia. Captaine *Fowleweather,* my Ladie the Countes
Eugenia commends hir most kindly to you, and is determined
to morrowe morning earely if it be a frost to take
her Coach to *Barnet* to bee nipt; where if it please you,
to meet her, and accompany her homewarde, ioyning your   5
wit with the frost, and helpe to nippe her, she does
not doubt but tho you had a sad supper, you will haue
a ioyfull breakefast.

Foul. I shall indeed my deare youth.

Rud. Why Captaine I abusd thee, I see: I said the   10

---

112 indifferently] *Q2;* in differently *Q1* ‖ 115 there's] theres *Q1-2* ‖ 118 i'th'right] i'thright
Q1-2 ‖ 119 Tis] *Q2;* tis *Q1* ‖ 126 here's] heres *Q1-2* ‖ 130 *Cutt.*] ~, *Q1-2* ‖ 133 on't] ont *Q1;*
ant *Q2* ‖ I.iii.1 *Fowleweather*] *Q2;* Fowleweather *Q1* ‖ 4 *Barnet*] Barnet *Q1-2* | nipt;] *Q2;* ~,
Q1 ‖ 6 her, she] *Q2;* ~. She *Q1* ‖ 9 deare] *Q2;* deeare *Q1* ‖

Ladies respected thee not, and now I perceiue the widowe
is in loue with thee.

Foul. Sblood knight I knew I had strucke her to
the quicke, I wondred shee departed in that extrauagant
fashion: I am sure I past one *Passado* of Courtship vppon   15
her, that has hertofore made a lane amongst the French
Ladies like a Culuering Shot, Ile be sworne; and I
think Sir *Gyles* you saw how she fell vnder it.

Goos. O as cleare as candlelight, by this day-light.

Rud. O good knight a the post, heele sweare any thing.   20

Will. The other two Ladies commend them no lesse
kindly to you two knights too; and desire your worships
wood meete them at *Barnet* ith' morning with the Captaine.

Foul. Goos. Rud. O good Sir. /

Goos. Our worships shal attend their Ladiships   [B3]
thether.   26

Ia. No Sir *Giles* by no meanes, they will goe priuately
thether, but if you will meet them there –

Rud. Meet them? weele die for't, but weele meet them.

Foul. Let's goe thether to night knights, and you   30
bee true gallants.

Rud. Content.

Ia. [*To Will.*] How greedely they take it in Sirra.

Goos. No it is too farre to goe to night, weele bee
vp betimes ith'morning, and not goe to bedd at all.   35

Foul. Why it's but ten miles, and a fine cleere night
S. *Gyles*.

Goos. But ten miles? what doe ye talke Captaine?

Rud. Why doost thinke it's any more?

Goos. I, Ile laie ten pounds it's more then ten mile,   40
or twelue either.

Rud. What to *Barnet*?

Goos. I, to *Barnet*.

Rud. Slidd, Ile laie a hundred pound with thee, if
thou wilt.   45

Goos. Ile laie fiue hundred, to a hundred. Slight
I will not be outborne with a wager, in that I know; I
am sure it was foure yeares agon ten miles thether, and
I hope tis more now. Slidd doe not miles growe thinke
you, as well as other *Animals*?   50

Ia. O wise Knight!

21 *Will.*] Q2; *Will* Q1 (*used often as speech-prefix without a period; not hereafter recorded*) ||
23 *Barnet*] Barnet Q1-2 | ith'] ith Q1-2 || **24** *Rud.*] Q2; ~, Q1 | O] Q2; ~. Q1 || **28** there–]
Parrott; ~. Q1-2 || **29** them?] Q2; ~, Q1 | for't] fort Q1-2 || **30** Let's] Lets Q1-2 || **33** SD *To
Will.*] Parrott subs. || **35** ith'] ith Q1-2 || **36, 39, 40** it's] its Q1-2 || **37** *Gyles.*] Q2; ~ Q1 || **43**
Barnet.] Q2; ~? Q1 || **46** hundred.] ~ Q1-2 || **47** know;] ~, Q1; ~: Q2 || **49** now.] *Bullen*; ~,
Q1-2 || **50** *Animals?*] Q2; ~. Q1 ||

Goos. I neuer Innd in the Towne but once, and then
they lodged me in a Chamber so full of theise Ridiculus
Fleas, that I was faine to lie standing all night, and
yet I made my man rise, and put out the candle too, because   55
they should not see to bite me.

Foul. A prettie proiect.

Bul. Intruth Captain if I might aduise you, you
should tarrie, and take the morning afore you.

Foul. How? *O mon Diew,* how the villaine *poulltroune,*   60
dishonours his trauaile? you *Buffonly Mouchroun,* are
you so mere rude, and English to aduise your Captaine?

Rud. Nay I prethie *Fouleweather* be not tempesteous
with thy poore Lacquay.

Foul. Tempesteous Sir *Cutt.*? will your Frenchman   65
thinke you, suffer his Lacquay to aduise him? /

Goos. O God you must take heed Lacquy how you aduise   [B3ᵛ]
your captain, your French lacquay would not haue don it.

Foul. He would haue bin poxt first: *Allume le
torche,* sweet pages commend vs to your Ladies, say wee   70
kisse their white handes, and will not faile to meete
them: knights which of you leades?

Goos. Not we Sir, you are a Captaine, and a leader.

Rud. Besides, thou art commended for the better man,
for thou art very Commendations it selfe, and Captaine   75
Commendations.

Foul. Why, what tho I be Captaine Commendations?

Rud. Why and Captain Commendations, is hartie
commendations, for Captaines are hartie I am sure, or
else hang them.   80

Foul. Why, what if I bee harty Commendations? come,
come, sweete knights leade the way.

Rud. O Lorde Sir, alwaies after my hartie Commendations.

Foul. Nay then you conquer mee with president, by   85
the Autenticall forme of all Iustice letters. *Alloun.*

*Exeunt [Foulweather,
Goosecap, Rudesby].*

Ia. Here's a most sweet Gudgeon swallowed, is there
not?

Will. I but how will they disgest it thinkest thou?
when they shall finde our Ladies not there?   90

---

65 *Cutt.*?] ~‸, *Q1*; ~‸? *Q2* ‖ **78** Commendations] *Q2*; commendations *Q1* | hartie] *Q2*; ~? *Q1* ‖
80 them.] *Q2*; ~, *Q1* ‖ **81** Commendations?] ~, *Q1-2* ‖ **86** SD *Exeunt ... Rudesby.*] *Exeunt.*
Q1-2 ‖ **87** Here's] *Q2*; Heres *Q1* ‖

Ia. I haue a vaunt-Curriing deuise shall make them
digest it most healthfully.   *Exeunt.*

SCÆNA QVARTA.

Enter Clarence, Musicians.

Cla. Worke on sweet loue, I am not yet resolud
T'exhaust this troubled spring of vanities
And nurse of perturbations, my poore life,
And therefore since in euery man that holds
This being deare, there must be some desire   5
Whose power to'enioy his obiect may so maske /
The Iudging part that in her radyant eyes   [B4]
His estimation of the world may seeme
Vpright, and worthy, I haue chosen loue
To blind my Reason with his mistie handes   10
And make my estimatiue power beleiue
I haue a proiect worthy to imploy
What worth so euer my whole man affordes:
Then sit at rest my Soule, thou now hast found
The ende of thy infusion; in the eyes   15
Of thy diuine *Eugenia* looke for heauen.   *A song to the Violls.*
[*To the Musicians.*] Thanks gentle friends.
Is your good Lord and mine, gon vp to bedd yet?

Enter Momford.

Mom. I do assure ye not Sir, not yet, nor yet, my
deep, and studious friend, not yet musicall *Clarence.*   20
   Cla. My Lord?
   Mom. Nor yet, thou sole deuider of my Lordshippe.
   Cla. That were a most vnfit diuision
And farre aboue the pitche of my lowe plumes;
I am your bold and constant guest my Lord.   25
   Mom. Far, far from bold, for thou hast known me long
Almost theis twentie yeares, and halfe those yeares
Hast bin my bedfellow; long time before
This vnseene thing, this thing of nought indeed
Or *Atome*, cald my Lordshippe shinde in me,   30
And yet thou makst thy selfe as little bould
To take such kindnes, as becomes the Age
And truth of our indissolable loue
As our acquaintance sprong but yesterday,

I.iv SD *Clarence,*] Q2; ~ Q1 ‖ **15** infusion;] *Bullen;* ~, Q1-2 ‖ **16** SD *A … Violls.*] *after l.17*
Q1-2 ‖ **17** SD *To the Musicians.*] | Thanks] *Bullen; Cla.* ~ Q1 | friends.] Q2; ~ Q1 ‖ **18** Is]
Q2; is Q1 ‖ **22** *Mom.*] Q2; ~, Q1 ‖ **24** plumes,] Q2; ~ Q1 ‖ **30** *Atome,* cald] *Parrott;* - -, Q1-2
‖ **34** yesterday,] Q2; ~ Q1 ‖

Such is thy gentle and too tender Spirit.   35
   Cla. My Lord, my want of Courtship makes me feare
I should be rude, and this my meane estate
Meetes with such enuie, and detraction,
Such misconstructions, and resolud misdoomes
Of my poore worth, that should I be aduaunc'd /   40
Beyond my vnseene lowenes, but one haire,   [B4ᵛ]
I should be torne in peeces with the Spirits
That flye in ill-lungd tempests through the world,
Tearing the head of vertue from her shoulders
If she but looke out of the ground of glorie.   45
Twixt, whome, and me, and euery worldlie fortune
There fights such sowre, and Curst *Antipathy,*
So waspishe, and so petulant a Starre,
That all things tending to my gracc or good
Are rauisht from their obiect, as I were   50
A thing created for a wildernes
And must not thinke of any place with men.
   Mom. O harke you Sir, this waiwarde moode of yours
Must syfted be, or rather rooted out,
Youle no more musick Sir?
   Cla.   Not now my Lord.   55
   Mom. Begon my masters then, to bedd, to bedd.
   Cla. I thanke you honest friends.   *Exeunt Musicians.*
   Mom. Hence with this book, and now *Mounsieur Clarence,*
methinks plaine and prose friendship would do excellent
well betwixt vs: come thus Sir, or rather thus, come: 60
[*Embracing him.*] Sir tis time I trowe that we both liu'd like
one bodie, thus, and that both our sides were slit, and
Concorporat with *Organs* fit to effect an indiuiduall passage
euen for our very thoughts; suppose wee were one bodie
now, and I charge you beleeue it, whereof I am the hart,   65
and you the liuer.
   Cla. Your Lordship might well make that diuision
if you knew the plaine song.
   Mom. O Sir, and why so I pray?
   Cla. First because the heart, is the more worthy   70
entraile, being the first that is borne, and moues, and
the last that moues, and dies; and then being the fountaine
of heate too, for wheresoeuer our heate does not
flowe directly from the hart to the other Organs, there,

38 detraction,] Q2; ~‸ Q1 || 41 haire,] Q2; ~‸ Q1 || 47 fights] Q2; fiights Q1 | *Antipathy,*] Q2;
~‸ Q1 || 54 Must] must Q1-2 || 55 Youle] youle Q1-2 | Lord.] Q2; ~, Q1 || 56 then,] ~‸ Q1-2 ||
57 friends.] Q2; ~‸ Q1 || 60 vs:] Q2; ~‸ Q1 || 61 SD *Embracing him.*] *Parrott* || 65 it,] *Parrott;*
~; Q1-2 ||

their action must of necessitie cease, and so without   75
you I nether would nor could liue. /

Mom. Wel Sir for these reasons I may be the heart,   [C1]
why may you be the liuer now?

Cla. I am more then ashamde, to tell you that my
Lord.   80

Mom. Nay, nay be not too suspitious of my iudgement
in you I beseech you: asham'd friend? if your loue ouercome not that shame, a shame take that loue I saie. Come
sir why may you be the liuer?

Cla. The plaine and short truth is (my Lord) because   85
I am all liuer, and tournd louer.

Mom. Louer?

Cla. Louer yfaith my Lord.

Mom. Now I prethee let me leape out of my skin for
ioy: why thou wilt not now reviue the sociable mirth   90
of thy sweete disposition? wilt thou shine in the world
a new? and make those that haue sleighted thy loue,
with the Austeritie of thy knowledge, doate on thee againe
with thy commaunding shaft of their humors?

Cla. Alas my Lord they are all farre out of my aime;   95
and onely to fit my selfe a little better to your friendshippe,
haue I giuen these wilfull raygnes to my affections.

Mom. And yfaith is my sower friend to all worldlie
desires ouertaken with the hart of the world, Loue? I
shall be monstrous proud now, to heare shee's euerie way   100
a most rare woman that I know thy spirit, and iudgement
hath chosen; is she wise? is she noble? is she capable
of thy vertues? will she kisse this forehead with
iudiciall lipps? where so much iudgement and vertue
deserues it? Come brother Twinn, be short I charge you,   105
and name me the woman.

Cla. Since your Lordship will shorten the length
of my follies relation, the woman that I so passionatelie
loue, is no worse Ladie then your owne Neece, the too
worthie Countesse *Eugenia.*   110

Mom. Why so, so, so, you are a worthie friend are
you not to conceale this loue-mine in your head, and /
would not open it to your hart? now beshrow my hart, if   [C1ᵛ]
my hart dance not for ioy tho my heeles do not, and they
doe not, because I will not set that at my heeles that   115

---

81 Nay,] *Q2;* ~‿ *Q1* | iudgement] *Q2;* ~, *Q1* ‖ 83-84 Come ... liuer?] *as separate line Q1-2* ‖
90 ioy:] *Q2;* ~‿ *Q1* ‖ 93 thee] *Q2;* the *Q1* ‖ 95 Alas] *Q2;* A las *Q1* ‖ 99 world, Loue?] *Q2;* ~? ~‿
Q1 ‖ 100 shee's] shees *Q1-2* ‖ 102 chosen;] ~, *Q1-2* ‖ 104 so much] somuch *Q1-2* ‖ 113 hart?]
Q2; ~, *Q1* ‖

my friend sets at his hart; what? friend and Nephew
both? nephew is a far inferior title to friend I confesse,
but I wil preferre thee backwards (as many friends
doe) and leaue their friends woorse then they found them.

Cla. But my noble Lo. it is almost a prodegie, that   120
I being onely a poore Gentleman and farre short of that
state and wealth that a Ladie of her greatnesse in both
will expect in her husband –

Mom. Hold thy doubt friend, neuer feare any woman,
vnlesse thy selfe be made of strawe, or some such drie   125
matter, and she of lightning. *Audacitie* prospers aboue
probabilitie in all worldlie matters. Dost not thou
knowe that Fortune gouernes them without order, and
therefore reason the mother of order is none of her
counsaile? why should a man desiring to aspire an   130
vnreasonable creature which is a woman, seeke her
fruition by reasonable meanes? because thy selfe
buildes vppon reason, wilt thou looke for congruitie
in a woman? why? there is not one woman amongst one
thousand, but will speake false Latine, and breake   135
Priscians head. Attempt nothing that you may with great
reason doubt of, and out of doubt you shall obtaine
nothing. I tell thee friend the eminent confidence of
strong spirits is the onely wich-craft of this world,
Spirits wrastling with spirits, as bodies with bodies: 140
this were enough to make thee hope well, if she were one
of these painted communities, that are rauisht with
Coaches, and vpper hands, and braue men of durt: but
thou knowest friend shee's a good scholler, and like
enough to bite at the rightest reason, and reason euermore   145
Ad optima hortatur: to like that which is best, not
that which is brauest, or richest, or greatest, and so
consequently worst. But proue what she can, we will
turne her, and winde her, and / make her so plyant that   [C2]
we will drawe her through a wedding ring yfaith.   150

Cla. Would to god we might my Lord.
Mom. Ile warrant thee friend.

116-17 friend sets ... hart; what? friend ... Nephew both?] frends ~ ... ~, ~? ~ ... Nephews
~? *Q1(c)*; friends set ... heart, ~? friende ... Nephew? ~ *Q1(u)*; ~ ~ ... heart? friend, ...
Nephews ~? *Q2* ‖ 118 thee] *Q1(c), Q2*; the *Q1(u)* ‖ 119 them.] *Q2*; ~, *Q1* ‖ 122 greatnesse]
Q1(c); greatnesses *Q1(u), Q2* ‖ 123 husband–] *Bullen*; ~. *Q1-2* ‖ 126 lightning.] *Q2*; ~, *Q1* ‖
127 matters. Dost] *Q2*; ~, dost *Q1* ‖ 130 counsaile?] *Q2*; ~, *Q1* ‖ 131 woman,] *Q2*; ~? *Q1* ‖
132 meanes?] *Q2*; ~, *Q1* ‖ 133 buildes] *Q1(u)*; bindes *Q1(u), Q2* ‖ 136 head. Attempt] *Q2*; ~,
attempt *Q1* ‖ 137 nothing.] *Q2*; ~, *Q1* ‖ 138 eminent] *Q1(c), Q2*; enminent *Q1(u)* ‖ 140 bodies
... bodies:] *Q2*; ~? ... ~ *Q1(c)*; ~? ... ~? *Q1(u)* ‖ 141 thee] *Q1(c), Q2*; the *Q1(u)* ‖ 144 shee's]
shees *Q1-2* ‖ 146 *hortatur*] *Q2*; *hortetur Q1* ‖ 147 richest] *Q1(c)*; rightest *Q1(u), Q2* ‖ 148
worst.] *Q2*; ~, *Q1* ‖

Enter Messenger.

Mes. Here is mistris *Winnyfred* from my Lady *Eugenia*
desires to speake with your Lordshippe.

Mom. Marrie enter mistris *Winnifred* euen here I   155
pray thee; – from the Ladie *Eugenia*, doe you heare friend?

Cla. Very easilie on that side my Lord.

Mom. Let me feele. Does not thy heart pant apace?
by my hart well labor'd *Cupid*, the field is yours sir
God, and vppon a verie honourable composition. I am   160
sent for now I am sure, and must euen trusse and to her:

Enter Winnyfred.

wittie mistris *Winnifred*, nay come neere woman. I am
sure this Gentleman thinkes his chamber the sweeter
for your sweet presence.

Win. My absence shall thanke him my Lord.   165

Mom. What, rude, Mistris *Winnifred*? nay faith you
shall come to him, and kisse him, for his kindenesse.

Win. Nay good my Lord, Ile neuer goe to the market
for that ware, I can haue it brought home to my dore.

Mom. O *Winnifred*, a man may know by the   170
market-folkes how the market goes.

Win. So you may my Lord, but I knowe fewe Lords
that thinke scorne to go to that market themselues.

Mom. To goe to it *Winnifred*? nay to ride to it
yfaith.   175

Win. That's more then I knowe my Lord.

Mom. Youle not belieue it then till you are a horse-
backe, will ye?

Win. Come, come, I am sent of a message to you, wil
you heare it?   180

Mom. Stoppe, stoppe, faire *Winnifred*, would you
haue audience so soone, there were no state in that
yfaith; this faire gentlewoman sir –

Win. Now we shall haue a fiction I beleiue.

Mom. Had three Suiters at once. /   185

Win. Youle leaue out none my Lord.   [C2ᵛ]

Mom. No more did you *Winnifred*: you enterferde
with them all in truth.

153 Here] *Q2*; here *Q1(c)*; Where *Q1(u)* | *Winnyfred* from] *Bullen*; ~; ~ *Q1(c)*; ~; for *Q1(u)*,
Q2 ‖ **156** thee;–] *Bullen*; ~,ˏ *Q1-2* ‖ **158** feele. Does ... apace?] *Bullen*; ~? does ... ~, *Q1*; ~.
does ... ~? *Q2* ‖ **160** composition.] ~, *Q1-2* ‖ **162** woman.] *Q1(c)*, *Q2*; ~ˏ *Q1(u)* ‖ **164** sweet]
Q1(c); deare *Q1(u)*, *Q2* ‖ **165** *Win.*] *Q2*; ~, *Q1* ‖ **166** What, rude,] *Parrott*; ~ˏ ~, *Q1*; ~ˏ ~? *Q2* ‖
168 market] *Q1(u)*, *Q2*; ~, *Q1(c)* ‖ **169** ware,] *Q2*; ~, *Q1* | dore.] *Q1(c)*, *Q2*; ~ˏ *Q1(u)* ‖ **171**
market-folkes] *Q2*; mar-./ket-folkes *Q1* ‖ **174** *Winnifred*?] *Q2*; ~, *Q1* ‖ **176** That's] Thats
Q1-2 ‖ **177** then till you are] *Q1(c)*; till you are then *Q1(u)*, *Q2* ‖ **179** you,] *Q2*; ~ˏ *Q1* ‖ **181**
stoppe,] ~ˏ *Q1-2* ‖ **183** sir–] *Bullen*; ~. *Q1-2* ‖ **187** *Mom.*] *Q2*; ~, *Q1* | *Winnifred*:] *Q2*; ~ˏ *Q1* ‖

Win. O Monstrous, Lord, by this light!

Mom. Now Sir to make my tale short I will doe that   190
which she did not; vz. leaue out the two first; the
third comming the third night for his turne –

Win. My Lord, my Lord, my Ladie does that, that no
bodie else does, desires your companie, and so fare you well.

Mom. O stay a little sweet *Winnifred*, helpe me but   195
to trusse my pointes againe, and haue with you.

Win. Not I by my truth my Lord, I had rather see
your hose about your heeles, then I would helpe you to
trusse a point.

Mom. O wittie *Winnifred*? for that Iest, take thy   200
pasport, and tell thy Ladie thou leftst me with my hose
about my heeles.

Win. Well, well my Lord, you shall sit till the
mosse grow about your heeles, ere I come at you againe.   *Exit.*

Mom. She cannot abide to heare of her three Suiters;   205
but is not this verie fit my sweete *Clarence*? Thou seest
my rare Neece cannot sleep without me; but for thy company
sake, she shall to night; and in the morning I
will visit her earely; when doe thou but stand in that
place, and thou maiest chance heare, (but art sure to   210
see) in what subtill, and farre fetcht manner Ile
solicite her about thee.

Cla. Thanks worthie Lord.   *Exeunt.*

Finis Actus Primi.

ACTVS SECVNDI   SCÆNA PRIMA

Clarence Solus.

Cla. I That haue studied with world-skorning thoughts
The waie of heauen, and how trew heauen is reacht, /
To know how mightie, and how many are   [C3]
The strange affections of inchaunted number,
How to distinguish all the motions   5
Of the Celestiall bodies, and what powre
Doth seperate in such forme this massie Rownd:
What is his Essence, Efficacies, Beames?

189 Monstrous, Lord,] *Parrott*; ~ˌ ~ˌ *Q1-2* ‖ 191 first;] ~, *Q1-2* ‖ 192 turne–] *Bullen*; ~. *Q1-2* ‖
194 companie,] *Q2*; ~ˌ *Q1* ‖ 201 Ladie] *Bullen*; Ladies *Q1-2* ‖ 203 Lord,] ~ˌ *Q1-2* ‖ 204 about]
Q2; a bout *Q1* | SD *Exit.*] *Q2*; *æxit. Q1* ‖ 213 Cla.] *Q2*; ~, *Q1* | SD *Exeunt.*] *Q2*; *exeunt. Q1* |
SD *Finis Actus Primi.*] *Q2*; ~. ~ *Primis*ˌ *Q1* ‖ **II.i** SCÆNA] SCENA *Q2*; SÆNA *Q1* ‖ 2 The]
the *Q1-2* | reacht,] *Parrott*; ~ˌ *Q1-2* ‖ 4 number,] ~ˌ *Q1*; ~. *Q2* ‖ 7 Doth] *Q2*; doth *Q1* ‖

Footesteps, and Shadowes? what Eternesse is,
The world, and Time, and Generation?   10
What Soule, the worldes Soule is? what the blacke Springes
And vnreueald Originall of Things,
What their perseuerance? what is life and death,
And what our Certaine Restauration?
Am with the staid-heads of this Time imployd   15
To watch with all my Nerues a Female shade.   [*Retires.*]

Enter Wynnefred, Anabell, with their sowing workes
and sing: After their song Enter Lord Momford.

Mom. Witty Mistrisse *Wynnefred*, where is your
Countesse I pray?
Win. Faith your Lordship is bould enough to seeke
her out, if she were at her vrinall!   20

[*Enter Eugenia.*]

Mom. Then Sh'as done it seemes, for here she comes
to saue mee that labour; away wenches, get you hence
wenches.   *Exeunt Wynnifred and Anabell.*
Eug. What, can you not abide my maides vnkle?
Mom. I neuer cood abide a maid in my life Neece, but   25
either I draw away the maid, or the maidenhead with a wet
finger.
Eug. You loue to make your selfe worse then you are
stil.
Mom. I know fewe mend in this world Madam. For   30
the worse the better thought on, the better the worse
spoken on euer amongst women.
Eug. I wonder where you haue binne all this while
with your sentences.
Mom. Faith where I must be again presently. I   35
cannot stay long with you my deere Neece. /
Eug. By my faith but you shall my Lorde; Gods pittie   [C3ᵛ]
what wil become of you shortly, that you driue maids
afore you, and offer to leaue widowes behind you, as
mankindelie, as if you had taken a surfet of our Sex   40
lately, and our very sight turnd your stomacke?
Mom. Gods my life, She abuses her best vnkle; neuer
trust mee if it were not a good reuenge to helpe her to
the losse of her widowhead.
Eug. That were a reuenge and a halfe, indeed.   45
Mom. Nay twere but a whole reuenge Neece, but such

9 Eternesse is,] *Bullen*; Eternesses ~. *Q1-2* ‖ 16 with all] *Bullen*; withall *Q1-2* | SD *Retires.*]
Parrott ‖ 20 vrinall!] ~? *Q1-2* | SD *Enter Eugenia.*] *Parrott subs.* ‖ 22 labour;] ~, *Q1-2* ‖ 23 SD
Exeunt Wynnifred and Anabell.] *Exeunt. Q1-2* ‖ 30 Madam.] ~, *Q1-2* ‖ 37 Lorde;] ~, *Q1-2* ‖
41 stomacke?] *Q2*; ~. *Q1* ‖

a reuenge as woulde more then obserue the true rule of
a reuenge.

Eug. I know your rule before you vtter it, *Vlciscere
Inimicos sed sine tuo incommodo.*   50

Mom. O rare Neece, you may see, what tis to bee a
scholler now: Learning in a woman is like waight in gold,
or Luster in Diamants, which in no other Stone is so
rich or refulgent.

Eug. But say deere Vnckle how could you finde in   55
your heart to stay so long from me?

Mom. Why alas Neece, y'are so smeard with this
willfull-widdowes-three-yeeres blacke weede, that I
neuer come to you, but I dreame of Courses, and Sepulchres,
and Epitaphs, all the night after, and therefore adew   60
deere Neece.

Eug. Beshrew my hearte my Lorde, if you goe theis
three houres.

Mom. Three houres? nay Neece, if I daunce attendance
three hours (alone in her chamber) with any Lady so   65
neere alide to me, I am verie idle ifaith; [*Aside.*] marie with
such an other I woulde daunce, one, two, three, foure,
and fiue, tho it cost me tenne shillings; and now I am
in, haue at it, my head must deuise something while
my feet are pidling thus, that may bring her to some fit   70
consideration of my friend, who indeed is only a great
scholler, and all his honours, and riches lie in his mind.

Eug. Come, Come, pray tell me vnckle, how does my /
cosen *Momford*?   [C4]

Mom. Why, well, verie well Neece, and so is my friend   75
Clarence well too, and then is there a worthie gentleman   *He daunceth*
well as any is in England I can tell ye.   *speaking.*

Eug. But when did you see my Cosen?

Mom. [*Aside.*] And tis pittie but he should do well, and he
shall do well too, if all my wealth will make him well.   80

Eug. [*Aside.*] What meanes hee by this, tro? – your Lo: is
verie dancitiue me thinkes.

Mom. I, and I could tel you a thing would make your
Ladiship verie dancitiue, or else it were verie dunsatiue
yfaith. [*Aside.*] O how the skipping of this Christmas blocke   85

---

48 reuenge] *stet* (*See Textual Note*) ‖ 50 *Inimicos*] *Parrott*; *Inimico Q1-2* ‖ 51-52 a scholler] a a
~ *Q1-2* ‖ 52 now:] ~, *Q1-2* ‖ 54 refulgent.] *Q2* ~. *Q1* ‖ 56 me?] *Q1(c)*, *Q2*; ~. *Q1(u)* ‖ 60
Epitaphs] *Q1(c)*, *Q2*; Epitaths *Q1(u)* | adew] *Q1(u)*, *Q2*; dew *Q1(c)* ‖ 65 hours] *Q1(c)*, *Q2*;
houres *Q1(u)* | any] *Q1(c)*, *Q2*; an *Q1(u)* ‖ 66 alide to] *Q2*; alideto *Q1* | ifaith;] iafith; *Q1(c)*;
ifaith, *Q1(u)*; yfaith, *Q2* | SD *Aside.*] *Parrott* ‖ 67 other] *Bullen*; ~; *Q1-2* ‖ 76-77 SD *He
daunceth speaking.*] ~ *daunceih* ~. *Q1(c)*; *om. Q1(u)*, *Q2* ‖ 79 SD *Aside.* ‖ 80 do] *Q1(c)*; be
Q1(u), *Q2* ‖ 81 SD *Aside.*] *Parrott* | this, tro] ~, ~ *Q1-2* | tro?–] ~?. *Q1(c)*; ~, yee, *Q1(u)*, *Q2* ‖
85 SD *Aside.*] *Parrott* ‖

of ours moues the blockheded heart of a woman? and indeed any thing that pleaseth the foolish eye which presently runnes with a lying tale of Excellence to the mind.

Eug. But I pray tell me my Lord, could you tell me of a thing would make me dance say you? 90

Mom. Wel, farewell sweet Neece, I must needs take my leaue in earnest.

Eug. Lord blesse vs, here's such a stir with your farewels.

Mom. I wil see you againe within these two or three 95
dayes a my word Neece.

Eug. [*Aside.*] Gods pretious, two or three dayes? why this Lord is in a maruailous strange humor. – Sit downe sweet Vnckle, yfaith I haue to talke with you about greate matters. 100

Mom. Say then deere Neece, bee shorte, vtter your mind quickly now.

Eug. But I pray tell me first, what's that would make me daunce yfaith?

Mom. Daunce, what daunce? hetherto your dauncers 105
legges bow for-sooth, and Caper, and Ierke, and Firke, and dandle the bodie aboue them, as it were their great childe; though the speciall Ierker bee aboue this place I hope, here lies that shudd fetch a perfect woman ouer the Coles yfaith. 110

Eug. Nay good Vnckle, say what's the thing you /
could tel me of? [C4ᵛ]

Mom. No matter, no matter: But let mee see a passing prosperous forehead of an exceeding happie distance betwixt the eye browes; a cleere lightning eye; a temperate 115
and freshe bloud in both the cheekes; excellent markes, most excellent markes of good fortune.

Eug. Why, how now Vnckle did you neuer see mee before?

Mom. Yes Neece; but the state of these thinges at this instant must bee specially obserued, and these 120
outwarde signes being now in this cleere eleuation, showe your vntroubled mind is in an excellent power, to preferre them to act forth then a litle, deere Neece.

Eug. This is excellent.

Mom. The Crises here are excellent good; The proportion 125

---

86 blockheded] *Q1(c)*; blockhead *Q1(u)*, *Q2* | woman?] *Q1(c)*; ~, *Q1(u)*, *Q2* ‖ **89** Lord,] ~ₐ *Q1-2* ‖ **91** Neece,] *Q2*; ~ₐ *Q1* ‖ **93** here's] heres *Q1-2* ‖ **96** word] *Q1(c)*, *Q2*; woord *Q1(u)* ‖ **97** SD *Aside.*] ‖ **98** maruailous] *Q1(c)*; marualous *Q1(u)*; maruallous *Q2* | humor.–] ~ₐ *Q1-2* ‖ **101** shorte,] ~ₐ *Q1-2* ‖ **103** what's] *Q2*; whats *Q1* ‖ **108** childe;] *Q1(c)*; ~, *Q1(u)*, *Q2* ‖ **111** Vnckle, say what's] ~ₐ ~ whats *Q1-2* ‖ **112** of?] *Q2*; ~. *Q1* ‖ **114** an exceeding] *Q2*; anexcceeding *Q1* ‖ **123** litle,] ~ₐ *Q1-2* ‖ **125** Crises] *Q2*; Creses *Q1* (*See Textual Note*) ‖

of the chin good; the little aptnes of it to sticke out; good. And the wart aboue it most exceeding good. Neuer trust me, if all things bee not answerable to the prediction of a most diuine fortune towards her; now if shee haue the grace to apprehend it in the nicke; ther's all.   130

Eug. Well my Lorde, since you will not tell me your secret, ile keepe another from you; with whose discouerie, you may much pleasure mee, and whose concealement may hurt my estate. And if you bee no kinder then to see mee   135 so indangered, ile bee very patient of it I assure you.

Mom. Nay then it must instantly foorth. This kind coniuration euen fires it out of me; and (to be short) gather all your Iudgment togeather, for here it comes. Neece; *Clarence, Clarence,* rather my Soule then my friend,   140 *Clarence* of too substantiall a worth, to haue any figures cast about him, (notwithstanding, no other woman with Empires could stirre his affections) is with your vertues most extreamely in loue; and without your requitall dead. And with it Fame shall sound this golden   145 disticke through the world of you both. /

> *Non illo melior quisquam nec amantior æqui*   [D1]
> *Vir fuit, aut illa reuerentior vlla Dearum.*

Eug. Ay me poore Dame, O you amase me Vnckle, Is this the wondrous fortune you presage?   150 What man may miserable women trust?

Mom. O peace good Ladie, I come not to rauishe you to any thing. But now I see how you accept my motion: I perceiue (how vpon true triall) you esteeme me. Haue I ridd al this Circuite to leuie the powers of   155 your Iudgment, that I might not prooue their strength too sodainly with so violent a charge: And doe they fight it out in white bloud, and showe me their hearts in the soft Christall of teares?

Eug. O vnckle you haue wounded your selfe in charging   160 me that I should shun Iudgement as a monster, if it woulde not weepe; I place the poore felicitie of this worlde in a woorthie friende, and to see him so vnworthely reuolted, I shedd not the teares of my Brayne, but the teares of my soule. And if euer nature made teares   165

---

130 ther's] thers *Q1-2* ‖ 136 indangered,] ~; *Q1-2* ‖ 138 coniuration] con/iuration *Q1-2* ‖ 140 *Clarence, Clarence*] ~ ̣ ~ *Q1-2* | friend,] ~ ̣ *Q1-2* ‖ 158 bloud, and] *Q2*; ~. And *Q1* ‖ 159 teares?] *Q2*; ~ ̣ *Q1* ‖

th'effects of any worthie cause, I am sure I now shedde them worthelie.

Mom. [*Aside.*] Her sensuall powers are vp yfaith, I haue thrust her soule quite from her Tribunall. This is her *Sedes vacans* when her subiects are priueledged to libell 170 against her, and her friends. – But weeps my kind Neece for the wounds of my friendshippe? and I toucht in friendship for wishing my friende doubled in her singular happinesse?

Eug. How am I doubl'd? when my honour, and good 175 name, two essentiall parts of mee, woulde bee lesse, and lost?

Mom. In whose Iudgment?

Eug. In the iudgment of the world.

Mom. Which is a fooles boult. *Nihil a virtute nec a veritate remotius quam Vulgaris opinio*: But my deare 180 Neece, / it is most true that your honour and good name [D1ᵛ] tendred as they are the species of truth are worthilie two essentiall parts of you; But as they consist only in ayrie titles and corrupteble blood (whose betternes *sanitas et non nobilitas efficit*) and care not how many 185 base and execrable acts they commit, they touch you no more then they touch eternitie. And yet shal no nobilitie you haue in either, be impaired neither.

Eug. Not to marrie a poore gentleman?

Mom. Respect him not so; for as he is a gentleman 190 he is noble; as he is welthilie furnished with true knowledge, he is rich and therein adorn'd with the exactest complements belonging to euerlasting noblenesse.

Eug. Which yet will not maintaine him a weeke: Such kinde of noblenesse giues no cotes of honour nor can 195 scarse gette a cote for necessitie.

Mom. Then is it not substantiall knoweledge (as it is in him) but verball and fantasticall for *Omnia in illa ille complexu tenet*.

Eug. Why seekes he me then? 200

Mom. To make you ioynt partners with him in all thinges, and there is but a little partiall difference betwixt you, that hinders that vniuersall ioynture: The bignesse of this circle held too neer our eye keepes it from the whole Spheare of the Sunne; but could we sustaine 205

---

166 th'effects] *Q2*; theffects *Q1* ‖ 168 SD Aside.] *Parrott* ‖ 171 friends.–] *Parrott*; ∼. *Q1-2* ‖ 176 mee,] *Parrott*; ∼; *Q1-2* ‖ 179 *virtute*] *Q1(c, 1st state)*, *Q2*; *vertute Q1(u)* (*See Textual Note*) ‖ 180 *veritate*] *Q2*; *viritate Q1* (*See Textual Note*) ‖ 184 betternes] *Loane conj.*; bitternes *Q1-2* (*See Textual Note*) ‖ 192 exactest] *Q2*; exa-/ctest *Q1(c)*; exa-/test *Q1(u)* ‖ 193 noblenesse.] *Q1(u)*, *Q2*; ∼ *Q1(c)* ‖ 196 necessitie.] *Q2*; ∼. *Q1* ‖ 199 *complexu tenet*] *Q1(c)*, *Q2*; *complexutenet Q1(u)* ‖ 205 Sunne; but] *Q1(c)*, *Q2*; ∼, ∼; *Q1(u)* ‖

it indifferently betwixt vs and it, it would then without
checke of one beame appeare in his fulnes.

Eug. Good Vnckle be content, for now shall I neuer
dreame of contentment.

Mom. I haue more then done Ladie, and had rather   210
haue suffer'd an alteration of my being then of your
Iudgement; but (deere neece) for your owne honours
sake repaire it instantly.

Enter Hippolita. Penelope. Jack. Will.

See heere comes the Ladies; make an Aprill day on't   214
deare loue and be sodainely cheere-/full. God saue   [D2]
you more then faire Ladies, I am glad your come, for my
busines will haue me gone presently.

Hip. Why my Lord *Momford* I say? wil you goe before
dinner?

Mom. No remedie sweete Bewties, for which rudenesse   220
I lay my hands thus lowe for your pardons.

Pen.   O Courteous Lord *Momford!*

Mom. Neece? *Mens est quæ sola quietos,*
        Sola facit claros, mentemque honoribus ornat.   [*Retires.*]

Eug.   *Verus honos Iuuat at mendax infamia terret.*   225

Mom. [*To Clarence.*] Mine owne deare nephew?

Cla. What successe my Lord?

Mom. Excellent; excellent; come Ile tell thee all.

                                                                      Exeunt.

Hip. Doe you heare madam, how our youthes here
haue guld our three suiters?   230

Eug. Not I Ladie, I hope our suiters are no fit meat
for our Pages.

Pen. No madam, but they are fit sawce for anie mans
meat Ile warrant them.

Eug. What's the matter *Hippolita?*   235

Hip. They haue sent the knightes to *Barnet* madam
this frostie morning to meete vs their.

Eug. Is't true youths, are knights fit subiects for
your knaueries?

Will. Pray pardon vs madam, we would be glad to please   240
anie body.

Ia. I indeed madam and we were sure we pleas'd them
highly to tell them you were desirous of their companie.

---

208 content,] *Q2;* ~ *Q1* ‖ **212** honours] *Q2;* honour *Q1* ‖ **214** on't] *Bullen;* one *Q1;* on *Q2* ‖ **215**
cheere-/full.] *Q2;* ~ *Q1* ‖ **221** pardons.] *Q2;* ~: *Q1* ‖ **223-24** est quæ ... quietos, ... claros,] *Q2;*
estquæ ... ~. ... ~ *Q1* ‖ **224** ornat.] *Q1(c), Q2;* ~ *Q1(u)* | SD *Retires.*] *Parrott; exit* *Q1-2* ‖ **225,**
231 Eug.] *Q2;* ~ *Q1* ‖ **226** Mom.] *Q2;* Mon. *Q1* | SD *To Clarence.*] *Parrott subs.* ‖ **228** SD *Exeunt.*]
Q2; exeunt *Q1* ‖ **231** Not] *Q2;* not *Q1* ‖ **236** Hip.] *Q2;* Hp. *Q1* ‖ **238** Eug.] *Q2;* Eiug. *Q1* | Is't]
Parrott; I'st *Q1-2* ‖

Hip. O twas good, *Eugenia*, their liuers were too hot, you know, and for temper sake they must needes haue a cooling carde plaid vpon them.   245

Will. And besides madam we wood haue them knowe that your two little Pages, which are lesse by halfe / then two leaues, haue more learning in them then is in all their three volumnes.   [D2ᵛ]   250

Ia. I yfaith *Will*, and putt their great pagicall index to them too.

Hip. But how will ye excuse your abuses wags?

Will. We doubt not madam, but if it please your Ladiship to put vp their abuses –   255

Ia. Trusting they are not so deere to you, but you may.

Will. Wee shall make them gladly furnishe their pockets with them.

Hip. Well, children, and foules, agree as you will, and let the world knowe now, women haue nothing to doe with you.   260

Pen. Come madam I thinke your dinner bee almost readie.

Enter Tales, Kingcob.

Hip. And see, here are two honorable guestes for you, the Lord *Tales*, and Sir *Cutberd Kingcob*.   265

Tal. Lacke you any guests madam?

Eug. I my Lord such guests as you.

Hip. There's as common an answere, as yours was a question my Lord.

King. Why? al things shood be common betwixt Lords and Ladies, you know.   270

Pen. Indeed Sir *Cutberd Kingcob*, I haue heard, you are either of the familie of Loue, or of no religion at all.

Eug. Hee may well be said to be of the family of Loue, he does so flowe in the loues of poore ouerthrowne Ladies.   275

King. You speake of that I wood doe madam, but in earnest, I am now suing for a newe mistres; looke in my hand sweet Ladie, and tell mee what fortune I shall haue with her.   280

Eug. Doe you thinke me a witch, Sir *Cutberd*?

---

244 good,] ~‸ *Q1-2* ‖ 251 I yfaith] *Q2*; I faith *Q1* ‖ 255 abuses–] *Parrott*; ~, *Q1*; ~. *Q2* ‖ 258 *Will.*] ~‸ *Q1*; *Wil. Q2* ‖ 263 readie.] *Q2*; ~, *Q1* | SD *Tales*,] *Q2*; ~‸ *Q1* ‖ 268 *Hip.*] *Q2*; *Hip*‸ *Q1* | There's] Theres *Q1-2* ‖ 270-71 Lords and Ladies,] *Parrott*; ~, ~ ~‸ *Q1*; ~, ~ ~, *Q2* ‖ 272 *Cutberd Kingcob*] *Q2*; *Kutberd Cingcob Q1(c, 2nd state)*; *Kutberd* ~ *Q1(c, 1st state)*; *Kutberd Bingcob Q1(u)* ‖

King. Pardon mee Madam, but I know you to bee learnd
in all thinges.

Eug. Come on, let's see. /   285

Hip. He does you a speciall fauour Ladie, to giue   [D3]
you his open hand, for tis commonly shut they say.

King. What find you in it madam?

Eug. Shut it now, and ile tell yee.

King. What now Ladie?   290

Eug. Y'aue the worst hand that euer I saw knight
haue; when tis open, one can find nothing in it, and
when tis shutt one can get nothing out on't.

King. The age of letting goe is past madam, wee
must not now let goe, but strike vp mens heeles, and   295
take am as they fall.

Eug. A good Cornish principle belieue it Sir *Cuttberd*.

Tal. But I pray tell me Ladie *Penelope*, how entertaine
you the loue of my Cosen Sir *Gyles Goosecappe*?

Pen. Are the *Goosecaps* akin to you my Lord?   300

Tal. Euen in the first degree madam. And Sir *Gyles*
I can tell ye, tho he seeme something simple, is composd
of as many good parts as any knight in England.

Hip. He shood be put vp for concealement then, for
he shewes none of them.   305

Pen. Are you able to reckon his good parts my Lord?

Tal. Ile doe the best I can Ladie, first, hee daunces
as comely and lightly as any man, for vpon my honour, I
haue seene him daunce vpon Egges, and a has not broken
them.   310

Pen. Nor crackt them neither?

Tal. That I know not, indeed I wood bee loath to lie though
he be my kinsman, to speake more then I know by him.

Eug. Well forth my Lord.

Tal. He has an excelent skil in al maner of perfumes,   315
and if you bring him gloues from fortie pence, to forty
Shillings a paire, he will tell you the price of them to
two pence.

Hip. A prettie sweet qualitie belieue me.

Tal. Nay Ladie hee will perfume you gloues him   320
selfe most delicately, and giue them the right Spanish
Titillation. /

---

285 on,] Q2; ~. Q1 | let's] lets Q1-2 || 292 haue;] ~, Q1-2 || 293 on't] ont Q1-2 || 298, 320 *Tal.*]
Tales. Q1; *Tales.* Q2 || 299 *Goosecappe?*] ~. Q1-2 || 300 Lord?] Q2; ~. Q1 || 301 Euen] Q1(c,
2nd state), Q2; Fuen Q1 (u, c, 1st state) || 304 *Hip.*] Q2; ~, Q1 || 311 neither?] ~. Q1-2 || 312
loath] ~, Q1-2 || 316 gloues from] Q1(c, 2nd state), Q2; glones fro Q1(u, c, 1st state) || 317
paire,] Q2; ~, Q1 || 321 selfe] Q2; ~; Q1 | delicately] Q2; dilicately Q1 ||

Pen. Titillation, what's that my Lord? [D3ᵛ]

Tal. Why Ladie tis a pretty kinde of terme newe come
vp in perfuming, which they call a Titillation. 325

Hip. Very well expounded my Lord; forth with your
kınsmans parts I pray.

Tal. Hee is the best Sempster of any woman in England,
and will worke you needle worke edgings, and French purles
from an Angell to foure Angells a yearde. 330

Eug. That's pretious ware indeed.

Tal. He will worke you any flower to the life, as
like it as if it grewe in the verie place, and being a
delicate perfumer, hee will giue it you his perfect and
naturall sauor. 335

Hip. This is wonderful; forth sweet Lord *Tales.*

Tal. He will make you flyes and wormes, of all sortes
most liuely, and is now working a whole bed embrodred,
with nothing but glowe wormes; whose lightes a has so
perfectly done, that you may goe to bed in the chamber, 340
doe any thing in the Chamber, without a Candle.

Pen. Neuer trust me if it be not incredible; forth
my good Lord.

Tal. Hee is a most excellent Turner, and will turne
you wassel-bowles, and posset Cuppes caru'd with Libberdes 345
faces, and Lyons heades with spoutes in their mouthes,
to let out the posset Ale, most artificially.

Eug. Forth good Lord *Tales.*

Pen. Nay good my Lord no more, you haue spoken for
him thoroughly I warrant you. 350

Hip. I lay my life *Cupid* has shott my sister in loue
with him out of your lipps my Lord.

Eug. Wel, come in my Lords, and take a bad dinner
with me now, and wee will all goe with you at night to a
better supper with the Lord, and Ladie *Furnifall.* 355

King. Tal. We attend you honorable Ladies. *Exeunt.*

ACTVS TERTII   SCÆNA PRIMA. [D4]

Enter Rudesby, Goosecappe.

Rud. Bullaker.

Bul. [*Within.*] I Sir.

Rud. Ride and catch the Captaines horse.

---

323 *Pen.*] Pene. *Q1 (as catchword only)* –2 | Titillation,] ~ ˏ *Q1-2* | what's] *Q2*; whats *Q1* ‖ 331
That's] *Q2*; Thats *Q1* ‖ III.i SD *Rudesby,*] *Q2*; ~ ˏ *Q1* ‖ 2, 4 SD *Within.*] *Parrott* ‖

Bul. [*Within.*] So I doe Sir.

Rud. I wonder Sir *Gyles* you wood let him goe soe,   5
and not ride after him.

Goos. Wood I might neuer be mortall Sir *Cutt*: if I
ridd not after him, till my horse sweat, so that he had
nere a drie thread on him, and hollod and hollod to him to
stay him, till I had thought my fingers ends wood haue   10
gon off with hollowings, Ile be sworn to ye; and yet he ran
his way like a *Diogenes*, and would neuer stay for vs.

Rud. How shall wee doe to get the lame Captaine to
London, now his horse is gone?

Goos. Why hee is but a lame Iade neither Sir *Moyle*,   15
we shal soone our'take him I warrant ye.

Rud. And yet thou saist thou gallopst after him as
fast as thou coodst, and coodst not Catch him; I lay my
life some Crabfishe has bitten thee by the tongue, thou
speakest so backward still.   20

Goos. But here's all the doubt Sir *Cutt*: if nobodie
shoold catch him now, when hee comes at London, some
boy or other wood get vppe on him and ride him hotte into
the water to washe him; Ile bee sworne I followed one
that ridd my horse into the Thames, till I was vppe tooth'   25
knees hetherto; and if it had not beene for feare of
going ouer shooes, because I am troubled with the rheume,
I wood haue taught him to washe my horse when hee was
hott yfaith;

Enter Foul.

how now sweet Captaine, dost feele any ease in thy payne   30
yet? /

Rud. Ease in his paine quoth you, has good lucke if   [D4ᵛ]
he feele ease in paine I thinke, but wood any asse in
the world ride downe such a hill as Highgate is, in
such a frost as this, and neuer light?   35

Foul. Gods pretious Sir *Cutt.* your Frenchman neuer
lights I tell ye.

Goos. Light Sir *Cutt.*, Slight and I had my horse
again, there's nere a paltrie English frost ͜an them all
shood make me light.   40

Rud. Goe too, you French Zanies you, you wil follow
the french steps so long, till you be not able to set
one Sound Steppe oth' ground all the daies of your life.

8 after] Q2; aftter Q1 ‖ 11 hollowings, . . . ye;] *Parrott*; ~; . . . ~ Q1; ~; . . . ~, Q2 ‖ 14 horse is]
Q2; horseis Q1 ‖ 21 here's] heres Q1-2 ‖ 25 tooth'] tooth Q1-2 ‖ 29-31 yfaith . . . yet?] *see list of
Press-Variants for corrected and uncorrected states of Q1; Q2 follows Q1(c)* ‖ 29 yfaith] Q2;
yfath Q1(c,u) | SD *Enter Foul.*] *as in Q1(c), Q2; after was l.28 Q1(u)* ‖ 30 Captaine,] Q2;
Captain͜ Q1(c); Captaine͜ Q1(u) | ease in] Q1(u), Q2; easein Q1(c) ‖ 35 light?] ~͜ Q1; ~. Q2 ‖
38 Cutt.] ~͜ Q1-2 ‖ 39 there's] theres Q1-2 ‖ 41 too,] ~͜ Q1-2 ‖ 43 oth'] oth Q1-2 ‖

Goos. Why Sir *Cut*: I care not if I be not sound so
I be well, but we were iustly plaugde by this hill, for   45
following women thus.

Foul. I and English women too sir *Giles*.

Rud. Thou art still prating against English women,
I haue seene none of the French dames I confesse, but
your greatest gallants, for men in *Fraunce*, were here   50
lately I am sure, and methinkes there should be no more
difference betwixt our Ladies and theirs, then there is
betwixt our Lordes and theirs, and our Lords are as farr
beyond them yfaith, for person, and Courtshippe, as they
are beyond ours for phantasticallitie.   55

Foul. O Lord sir *Cut.*, I am sure our Ladies hold our
Lords tack for Courtshippe, and yet the french Lords
put them downe, you noted it sir *Gyles*.

Goos. O God sir, I stud and heard it, as I sat ith'
presence.   60

Rud. How did they put them downe I pray thee?

Foul. Why for wit, and for Court-shippe Sir *Moile*.

Rud. As how good lefthandded *Francois*?

Foul. Why Sir when *Monsieur Lambois* came to your
mistris the Ladie *Hippolita* as she sate in the presence, –   65
sitt downe here good Sir *Gyles Goosecappe*, – hee kneeld me
by her thus Sir, and with a most queint French *starte* in
his speech of ah *bellissime*, I desire to die now saies
hee for / your loue that I might be buried here.   [E1]
                                                                 70
Rud. A good pickt-hatch complement by my faith;
but I prethee what answer'd she?

Foul. She, I scorne to note that I hope; then did
he vie it againe with an other hah.

Rud. That was hah, hah, I wood haue put the third
hah to it, if I had been as my mistris, and hah, hah,   75
haht him out of the presence yfaith.

Foul. Hah saies he, theis faire eyes, I wood not for
a million they were in *Fraunce*, they wood renewe all our
ciuill-wars againe.

Goos. That was not so good me thinkes captaine.   80

---

44 *Cut:*] *Q1(c, 1st state);* ~. *Q1(u);* ~. *Q2* ‖ **45** well,] *Q1(c, 1st state), Q2;* ~. *Q1(u)* | plaugde . . .
hill,] *Q1(c, 1st state), Q2;* ~, . . . ~. *Q1(u)* ‖ **47** women] *Q1(c, 1st state), Q2;* weomen *Q1(u)* ‖ **48**
art] *Q1(c, 2nd state), Q2;* arr *Q1(u, c, 1st state)* | women,] *Q2;* ~. *Q1* ‖ **50** gallants,] *Q1(c, 1st
state), Q2;* ~. *Q1(u)* ‖ **56** *Cut.*,] *Cut, Q1; Cut. Q2* ‖ **57** french Lords] *Q1(c, 2nd state), Q2;* ~
Lodrs *Q1(u, c, 1st state)* ‖ **58** sir] *Q2;* sir *Q1* ‖ **59** ith'] ith *Q1-2* ‖ **63** *Rud.*] *Bullen;* Foul. *Q1-2* |
Francois?] ~. *Q1-2* ‖ **64** *Monsieur*] *Q1 (c, 2nd state), Q2;* Meuusieur *Q1(u, c, 1st state)* ‖ **65-66**
presence, – . . . *Goosecappe*, –] *Bullen;* ~, . . . ~, . *Q1-2* ‖ **67** *starte*] *Q1(c, 2nd state), Q2;* ftarte
Q1(c, 1st state); Arte *Q1(u)* ‖ **67-69** in . . . for] *repeated in Q1 (See Textual Note)* ‖ **70** pickt-hatch]
Q2; pick-thacht *Q1* ‖ **71** she?] ~. *Q1-2* ‖ **72** hope;] ~, *Q1-2* ‖ **76** yfaith.] *Q2;* ~, *Q1* ‖

748

Rud. Well iudgd yfaith, there was a little wit in
that I must confesse, but she put him down far, and aunswered
him with a question and that was whether he wood seem a
louer or a iester, if a louer a must tel her far more
lykelier then those, or else she was far from belieuing   85
them, if a Iester, she cood haue much more ridiculous iests
then his of twenty fooles that followed the court, and
told him she had as lieue be courted with a brush faggot
as with a frenchman, that spent it selfe al in sparks,
and would sooner fire ones chimney then warme the house,   90
and that such sparkes were good enough yet to set thatcht
dispositions a fire, but hers was tild with sleight, and
respected them as sleightly.
  Goos. Why so Captaine, and yet you talke of your
great frenchmen, [wood] to God little England had neuer   95
knowne them I may say.
  Foul. What's the matter sir *Giles,* are you out of
loue with frenchmen now of a sodaine?
  Goos. Slydd captaine wood not make one, Ile be
sworne? Ile be sworne, they tooke away a mastie dogge   100
of mine by commission; now I thinke on't makes my teares
stand in my eyes with greefe; I had rather lost the
dearest friend that euer I lay withal in my life, by
this light; neuer stir if / hee fought not with great   [E1ᵛ]
Sekerson foure hours to one, foremoste take vp hindmoste,   105
and tooke so many loaues from him, that hee sterud him
presently: So at last the dogg cood doe no more then a
Beare cood doe, and the beare being heauie with hunger
you know, fell vppon the dogge, broke his backe, and the
dogge neuer stird more.   110
  Rud. Why thou saist the frenchmen tooke him away.
  Goos. Frenchmen, I, so they did too, but yet and
hee had not bin kild, twood nere a greeud me.
  Foul. O excellent vnitie of speach.

        Enter Will and Iacke at seuerall doores.

Will. Saue ye knights.   115
Ia. Saue you Captaine.
Foul. Pages, welcome my fine pages.

---

81 Well iudgd] *Q2;* Welliudgd *Q1* ‖ 84 iester] iestter *Q1;* jester *Q2* ‖ 90 sooner fire] *Q2;*
sooner-/fire *Q1* ‖ 95 wood] *Bullen;* om. *Q1-2* ‖ 98 sodaine?] *Q2;* ~. *Q1* ‖ 99 wood] Wood
Q1-2 ‖ 100 sworne?] ~, *Q1;* ~. *Q2* ‖ 101-102 commission; now ... greefe;] ~, ~, ... ~, *Q1-2* ‖
103-104 withal ... life, ... light;] ~, ... ~, ... ~, *Q1;* ~, ... ~, ... ~, *Q2* ‖ 103 by] *Parrott;* be
Q1-2 ‖ 104 if] *Q2;* if / if *Q1* ‖ 114 SD *Will*] ~, *Q1-2* ‖ 117 *Foul.*] *Q2; Faul. Q1* ‖

Rud. Welcome boyes.

Goos. Welcome sweet *Will*, good *Iacke*.

Foul. But how chaunce you are so farre from London   120
now pages? is it not almost dinner time?

Will. Yes indeed Sir, but we left our fellowes to
wait for once, and cood not chuse in pure loue to your
worships, but we must needs come and meet you, before you
mett our Ladies, to tell you a secret.   125

Omnes. A secrett, what secret I pray thee?

Ia. If euer your worships say any thing, we are
vndone for euer.

Omnes. Not for a world beleue it.

Will. Why then this it is; wee ouerheard our Ladies   130
as they were talking in priuate say they refusde to meet
you at *Barnet* this morning of purpose, because they wood
try which of you were most patient.

Ia. And some said you, Sir *Gyles*, another you Sir [*Cutt.*]
and the third you Captaine.   135

Omnes. This was excellent.

Will. Then did they sweare one another not to
excuse themselues to you by any meanes, that they might
trie you the better; now if they shal see you say nothing in   139
the / worlde to them, what may come of it, when Ladies   [E2]
begin to trie their suters once, I hope your wisedomes
can iudge a little.

Foul. O ho my little knaue let vs alone now yfaith;
wood I might be Casheird, if I say any thing.

Rud. Faith and I can forbeare my Tongue as well as   145
another I hope.

Goos. Wood I might be degraded if I speake a word,
Ile tell them I care not for loosing my labour.

Foul. Come knights, shall we not reward the pages?

Rud. Yes I prethee doe, Sir *Gyles* giue the boyes   150
something.

Goos. Neuer stirre Sir *Cutt.*, if I haue euer a groat
about me but one three pence.

Foul. Well knights ile lay out for's all; – here my
fine pages.   155

Will. No in deed an't please your worshippe.

Foul. O pages refuse a gentlemans bountie?

Ia. Crie you mercy Sir, thanke you sweete Captaine.

---

121 pages? ... time?] *Q2;* ~, ... ~. *Q1* ‖ **126, 129** *Omnes.*] *Q2;* ~ *Q1* ‖ **127** thing,] *Q2;* ~. *Q1* ‖
134 *Cutt.*] *Bullen; om. Q1-2 (See Textual Note)* ‖ **135** Captaine.] *Q2;* ~, *Q1* ‖ **139** better;]
Bullen; ~, *Q1-2* ‖ **143** yfaith;] *Bullen;* ~, *Q1-2* ‖ **149** knights,] ~ *Q1-2* ‖ **152** *Cutt.*] ~ *Q1;*
Cut. Q2 ‖ **154** for's all;] fors all, *Q1-2* ‖ **156** an't] ant *Q1-2* ‖ **157** bountie?] *Q2;* ~. *Q1* ‖ **158**
Captaine.] *Q2;* ~, *Q1* ‖

Foul. And what other newes is stirring my fine
villiacos?   160

Will. Marrie Sir they are inuited to a greate supper
to night to your Lords house Captaine, the Lord *Furnifall*,
and there will bee your great cosen Sir *Gyles Goosecappe*,
the Lorde *Tales*, and your vnckle Sir *Cutt. Rudesby*, Sir
Cutbert Kingcob.   165

Foul. The Lord *Tales*, what countriman is hee?

Ia. A kentish Lord Sir, his auncestors came forth
of Canterburie.

Foul. Out of Canterburie?

Will. I indeed, Sir, the best *Tales* in England are your   170
Canterburie *Tales*, I assure ye.

Rud. The boy tels thee true Captaine.

Ia. Hee writes his name Sir, *Tales*, and hee being the
tenth sonne his father had, his father Christned him *Decem*   174
Tales, and so his whole name is the / Lord *Decem Tales*.   [E2ᵛ]

Goos. A my mortallitie the boy knowes more then I
doe of our house.

Rud. But is the Ladie *Furnifall* (Captaine) still
of the same drinking humor she was wont to be?

Foul. Still of the same, knight, and is neuer in any   180
sociable vaine till she be typsie, for in her sobrietie
shee is madd, and feares my good little old Lord out of
all proportion.

Rud. And therefore as I hear he will earnestly
inuite guestes to his house, of purpose to make his wife   185
dronk, and then dotes on her humor most prophanely.

Foul. Tis very true knight; wee will suppe with them
to night; and you shall see her; and now I thinke on't,
ile tell you a thing knights, wherein perhaps you may
exceedinly pleasure me.   190

Goos. What's that good Captain?

Foul. I am desirous to helpe my Lord to a good
merrie Foole, and if I cood help him to a good merry one,
he might doe me very much credit I assure ye.

Rud. Sblood thou speakest to vs as if wee cood   195
serue thy turne.

Foul. O *Fraunce*! Sir *Cutt*: your Frenchman wood not
haue taken me so, for a world, but because Fooles come
into your companies many times to make you merrie –

---

160 villiacos?] ~. *Q1-2* ‖ 168 of] *Parrott;* off *Q1-2* ‖ 169 Canterburie?] ~. *Q1-2* ‖ 170 indeed,
Sir,] *Q2;* ~‸ ~‸ *Q1* ‖ 171 *Tales*] *Q2;* tales *Q1* ‖ 172 The] *Q2;* the *Q1* ‖ 174 had,] ~; *Q1-2* ‖ 179
be?] *Q2;* ~. *Q1* ‖ 180 same,] *Q2;* ~‸ *Q1* ‖ 184 *Rud.*] *Bullen; King. Q1-2* ‖ 188 on't] ont *Q1-2* ‖
191 What's . . . Captain?] *Q2;* Whats . . . ~. *Q1* ‖ 197 *Fraunce*!] *Parrott;* ~‸ *Q1-2* ‖ 199 merrie–]
~‸ *Q1;* ~. *Q2* ‖

Rud. As thou doost.   200

Goos. Nay good Sir *Cutt*: you know fooles doe come
into your companies.

Rud. I and thou knowst it too, no man better.

Foul. Beare with Choller Sir *Gyles*.

Will. But wood you helpe your Lord to a good foole   205
so faine Sir?

Foul. I my good page exceeding faine.

Ia. You mean a wench, do you not Sir, a foolish
wench?

Foul. Nay I wood haue a man foole, for his Lord: 210
page.

Will. Does his Lord: loue a foole, so wel I pray?

Foul. Assure thy selfe page, my Lord loues a foole
as / he loues himselfe.   [E3]

Ia. Of what degree wood you haue your Foole Sir?   215
for you may haue of all maner of degrees.

Foul. Faith I wood haue him a good Emphaticall foole,
one that wood make my Lorde laugh well, and I carde not.

Will. Laugh well (vm) then wee must know this Sir,
is your Lorde Costiue of laughter, or laxatiue of laughter?   220

Foul. Nay he is a good merrie little Lorde, and
indeed something Laxatiue of Laughter.

Will. Why then Sir the lesse witt will serue his
Lordships turne; marrie if he had bin Costiue of laughter,
hee must haue had two or three drams of witt the more in   225
his foole, for we must minister according to the quantity
of his Lord: humor you know, and if he shood haue as
much Witt in his foole being Laxatiue of laughter, as if
hee were Costiue of Laughter, why he might laugh himselfe
into an *Epilepsie*, and fall down dead sodainly, as   230
many haue done with the extremitie of that passion; and
I know your Lord cares for nothing, but the health of a
foole.

Foul. Th'art ith'right my notable good page.

Ia. Why, and for that health Sir we will warrant his   235
Lordship, that if he should haue all Bacon *de sanitate
tuenda* reade to him, it shood not please his Lordship so
well as our foole shall.

Foul. Remercy my more then English pages.

Goos. A my word I haue not seene pages haue so much   240
witt, that haue neuer bin in *Fraunce* Captain.

---

206 Sir?] *Q2; ~. Q1* ‖ **212** pray?] *Q2; ~. Q1* ‖ **215** Sir?] *Q2; ~, Q1* ‖ **218** not.] *Bullen; ~, Q1;*
no I. *Q2* ‖ **221** a] *Q2;* om. *Q1* ‖ **224** turne;] ~, *Q1-2* ‖ **229** himselfe] *Q2;* himsele *Q1* ‖ **234**
Th'art ith'] Thart ith *Q1-2* ‖ **236** Bacon] *Parrott; Bacon Q1-2* ‖ **239** *Remercy*] Remercy *Q1-2* ‖
241 *Fraunce*] Fraunce *Q1;* France *Q2* ‖

Foul. Tis true indeed Sir *Gyles,* well then my almost french Elixers, will you helpe my Lord to a foole, so fitt for him as you say?

Will. As fitt, Ile warrant you Captain, as if he were made for him, and hee shall come this night to supper, and foole where his Lord: sits at table.   245

Foul. Excellent fitt, faile not now my sweet pages. /

Ia. Not for a world sir, we will goe both, and seeke   [E3ᵛ]
him presently.   250

Foul. Doe so my good wagges.

Will. Saue you knights.

Ia. Saue you Captaine.   *Exeunt Will and Jack.*

Foul. Farewell my prettie knaues; come knights, shall we resolue to goe to this Supper?   255

Rud. What else?

Goos. And let's prouide torches for our men to sit at dore withall captaine.

Foul. That we will I warrant you sir *Giles.*

Rud. Torches? why the Moone will shine man.   260

Goos. The moone Sir *Cut*: I scorne the moone yfaith. Slydd sometimes a man shal not get her to shine and if he wood giue her a couple of Capons, and one of them must be white too. God forgiue me I cud neuer abide her since yesterday, she seru'de me such a trick tother night.   265

Rud. What trick sir *Gyles?*

Goos. Why sir *Cut*: cause the daies be mortall and short now you knowe, and I loue daie light well; I thought it went awaie faster then it needed, and run after it into *Finsburie*-fieldes ith'calme euening to see the   270
winde-mils goe; and euen as I was going ouer a ditch the moone by this light of purpose runnes me behind a cloud, and lets me fall into the ditch, by heauen.

Rud. That was ill done in her in deed sir *Giles.*

Goos. Ill done sir *Cut*:? Slydd a man may beare, and   275
beare, but and she haue noe more good manners, but to make euery black slouenly cloude a pearle in her eye, I shall nere loue English moone againe, while I liue Ile besworne to ye.

Foul. Come knights to London: horse, horse, horse.   280
                        [Exeunt Foulweather and Goosecap.]

Rud. In what a case he is with the poore English moone, because the french moones (their torches) wil- / be   [E4]

243 Elixers,] *Parrott;* ~. *Q1;* ~ˌ *Q2* ‖ 244 say?] ~. *Q1-2* ‖ 251 wagges.] ~ˌ *Q1-2* ‖ 253 SD *Will and Jack*] *Parrott subs.;* ‖ 254 knaues;] ~ˌ *Q1-2* ‖ 256 else?] *Q2;* ~. *Q1* ‖ 261 yfaith.] ~ˌ *Q1-2* ‖ 264 too.] ~ˌ *Q1-2* | forgiue] *Q2;* for giue *Q1* ‖ 269 awaie] a waie *Q1;* away *Q2* ‖ 270 ith'] ith *Q1-2* ‖ 271 goe;] *Q2;* ~? *(question mark reversed) Q1* ‖ 273 ditch,] ~ˌ *Q1-2* ‖ 275 Cut:?] ~:ˌ *Q1; Cut? Q2* ‖ 277 eye,] ~ˌ *Q1-2* ‖ 280 Come] *Q2;* come *Q1* | London:] *Bullen;* ~ˌ *Q1-2* | SD *Exeunt ... Goosecap.*] *Parrott* ‖

the lesse in fashion, and I warrant you the Captaine will
remember it too, tho hee say no thing; hee seconds his
resolute chase so and followes him, Ile lay my life you   285
shall see them the next cold night, shut the mooneshine
out of their chambers, and make it lie without doores all
night. I discredit my witt with their companies now I
thinke on't, plague a god on them; Ile fall a beating
on them presently.   290
                                                             Exit.

[III.ii]

Enter Clarence, Horatio;
Lorde Momford following behind.

Cla. Sing, good *Horatio*, while I sigh and write.
According to my master *Platos* minde
The Soule is musick, and doth therefore ioy
In accents musicall, which he that hates
With points of discorde is togeather tyed   5
And barkes at *Reason*, Consonant in sence.
Diuine *Eugenia* beares the ocular forme
Of musicke and of *Reason*, and presents
The Soule exempt from flesh in flesh inflam'd;
Who must not loue hir then, that loues his soule?   10
To her I write; my friend, the starre of friends
Wil needs haue my strange lines greet her strange eies
And for his sake ile powre my poore Soule forth
In floods of Inke; but did not his kind hand
Barre me with violent grace, I wood consume   15
In the white flames of her impassionate Loue
Ere my harsh lipps shood vent the odorous blaze.
For I am desperate of all worldly Ioyes
And there was neuer man so harsh to men;
When I am fullest of digested life   20
I seeme a liuelesse *Embrion* to all
Each day rackt vp in nightlike Funerall.
Sing, good *Horatio*, whilst I sigh and write.

Canto. /
The Letter.   [E4ᵛ]

Suffer him to loue that suffers not louing; my
loue is without passion and therefore free from alteration. 25

284 thing;] ~, *Q1-2* ‖ **III.ii**] *Bullen* ‖ SD *Enter ... behind.*] ~ *Lorde Momford and Clarence. /*
Clarence Horatio. Q1-2 (Clarence, Horatio. Q2) ‖ **1** Sing,] ~. *Q1-2* ‖ **7** *Eugenia*] ~, *Q1-2* ‖ **9**
inflam'd;] *Q2*; ~, *Q1* ‖ **11** write;] ~, *Q1-2* ‖ **15** consume] *Bullen*; ~. *Q1-2* ‖ **19** men;]
~, *Q1-2* ‖ **23** Sing,] ~. *Q1-2* ‖ **24** louing;] ~, *Q1-2* ‖

Prose is too harsh, and verse is poetrie.
Why shood I write then? merrit clad in Inke
Is but a mourner, and as good as naked.
I will not write, my friend shall speake for me.
Sing one staue more my good *Horatio*.   30

Canto.

I must remember I knowe whom I loue,
A dame of learning, and of life exemt
From all the Idle fancies of her sex,
And this that to an other dame wood seeme
Perplext and foulded in a redelesse vaile   35
Wilbe more cleere then ballads to her eye.
Ile write, if but to satisfie my friend.
Your third stance sweet *Horatio* and no more.

Canto.   [*Exit Horatio.*]

How vainely doe I offer my strange loue?
I marrie, and bid states, and entertaine   40
Ladies with tales and iests, and Lords with newes
And keepe a house to feast *Acteons* hounds
That eate their maister, and let ydell guests
Drawe me from serious search of things diuine
To bid them sit, and welcome, and take care   45
To sooth their pallats with choyce kytchin-stuff,
As all must doe that marrie and keepe house
And then looke on the left side of my yoake
Or on the right perhaps and see my wife
Drawe in a quite repugnant course from me   50
Busied to starch her french purles, and her puffs
When I am in my *Anima reflexa*
Quid sit fælicitas, quæ origo rerum?
And make these beings that are knowne to be
The onely serious obiects of true men   55
Seeme shadowes; with substantiall stir she keepes
About her shadowes, which if husbands loue /
They must belieue, and thus my other selfe   [F1]
Brings me another bodie to dispose
That haue alreadie much too much of one,   60
And must not looke for any Soule of her
To helpe to rule two bodies.
   Mom.   Fie for shame.

---

26 poetrie.] ~ ͜ *Q1-2* ‖ 28 naked.] *Q2*; ~ *Q1* ‖ 29 write, . . . me.] *Q2*; ~ ͜ . . . ~ *Q1* ‖ 32 A dame]
Adame *Q1*; a ~ *Q2* ‖ 35 redelesse] *Parrott*; rudelesse *Q1-2* (*See Textual Note*) ‖ 36 eye.] *Q2*; ~ ͜
Q1 ‖ 38 stance] *Q2*; stauce *Q1* | SD *Exit Horatio.*] ‖ 46 kytchin-stuff,] *Q2*; ~ *Q1* ‖ 48 side] *Q2*;
sid *Q1* ‖ 53 *Quid*] quid *Q1-2* ‖ 56 shadowes;] ~, *Q1-2* ‖ 58 They] the *catchword in Q1* ‖ 62 to
rule two] *Q2*; two ~ to *Q1* ‖

I neuer heard of such an antedame.
Doe women bring no helpe of soule to men?
Why, friend, they either are mens soules themselues   65
Or the most wittie Imitatrixes of them
Or prettiest sweet apes of humaine Soules,
That euer Nature fram'd; as I will proue.
For first they be *Substantiæ lucidæ*
And purer then mens bodies, like their soules,   70
Which mens harsh haires both of their brest and chinne
Occasiond by their grose and ruder heate
Plainely demonstrates: Then like soules they doe,
Mouere corpora, for no power on earth
Moues a mans bodie, as a woman does!   75
Then doe they *Dare formas corpori*
Or adde faire formes to men, as their soules doe:
For but for women, who wood care for formes?
I vowe I neuer wood washe face, nor hands
Nor care how ragg'd, or slouenlie I went,   80
Wer't not for women, who of all mens pompes
Are the true finall causes: Then they make
Men in their Seedes imortall like their Soules
That els wood perish in a spanne of time.
Oh they be Soulelike-Creatures, and my Neece   85
The Soule of twentie rare Soules stild in one.
   Cla. That, that it is my Lord, that makes me loue.
   Mom. Oh are ye come Sir, welcome to my Neece
As I may say at midnight; gentle friend
What haue you wrott I pray?
   Cla.   Strange stuffe my Lord.   90
   Mom. Indeed the way to belieue is to loue   *He reads and*
And the right way to loue is to belieue. /   *comments.*
This I will carry now with pen and Incke   [F1ᵛ]
For her to vse in answere, see, sweet friend
She shall not stay to call, but while the steele   95
Of her affection is made softe and hott,
Ile strike and take occasion by the browe.
Blest is the wooing that's not long a dooing.   *Exit.*
   Cla. Had euer man so true, and noble friend?
Or wood men thinke this sharpe worlds freezing Aire   100
To all true honour and iudiciall loue
Wood suffer such a florishing pyne in both
To ouerlooke the boxe-trees of this time?

---

65 Why, friend,] *Q2;* ∼ˏ ∼ˏ *Q1* ‖ **70** bodies,] ∼ˏ *Q1-2* ‖ **80** went,] *Q2;* ∼ˏ *Q1* ‖ **89** midnight;] ∼ˏ *Q1;* ∼-, *Q2* ‖ **91-92** SD *He ... comments.] Q1(c), Q2; om. Q1(u)* ‖ **92** belieue.] ∼̂ *Q1-2* ‖ **98** that's] thats *Q1-2* ‖

When the learnd mind hath by impulsion wrought
Her eyes cleere fire into a knowing flame,   105
No elementall smoke can darken it
Nor Northen coldnes nyppe her *Daphnean* flower.
O sacred friendshippe thanks to thy kind power
That being retir'd from all the faithles worlde
Appearst to me in my vnworldly friend,   110
And for thine owne sake let his noble mind
By mouing presedent to all his kind
(Like iust *Deucalion*) of earths stonie bones
Repaire the world with humane bloud and flesh   114
And dying vertue with new life refresh.   *Exit.*

ACTVS QVARTVS [SCÆNA PRIMA].

Enter Tales, Kingcob, Eugenia, Hippolita,
Penelope, Winnifred.

King. Tis time to leaue your Chests Ladies, tis too
studious an exercise after dinner.

Tal. Why is it cal'd Chests?

Hip. Because they leane vppon their Chests that
play at it.   5

Tal. I wood haue it cald the strife of wittes, for
tis a game so wittie, that with strife for maisterie,
wee hunt it eagerly. /

Eug. Specially where the wit of the *Goosecaps* are   [F2]
in chase my Lord.   10

Tal. I am a *Goosecappe* by the mothers side madam,
at least my mother was a *Goosecappe.*

Pen. And you were her white sonne, I warrant my Lord.

Tal. I was the yongest, Ladie, and therefore must be
her white sonne ye know; the youngest of tenne I was.   15

Hip. And the wisest of Fifteene.

Tal. And sweet Ladie will ye cast a kind eye now
vpon my Cosin, Sir *Gyles Goosecappe*?

Pen. Pardon, my Lord, I haue neuer a spare eye to cast
away I assure ye.   20

Tal. I wonder you shood Count it cast away Ladie
vppon him, doe you remember those fewe of his good
partes I rehearst to you?

Pen. Verie perfectly my Lord, amongst which one of

105 flame,] ~. *Q1*; ~; *Q2* || 107 flower.] ~, *Q1-2* || **IV.i** SCÆNA PRIMA] *Parrott* || **1** Ladies,]
Q2; ~ *Q1* || **6** *Tal.*] *Q2*; ~ *Q1*; || **9** *Eug.*] *Q1* (catchword) -2; *Eug* *Q1* || **14** yongest,] *Q2*; ~
Q1 || **15** know;] ~ *Q1-2* || **18** *Goosecappe*?] ~. *Q1-2* || **19** Pardon, my Lord,] ~ ~ ~ *Q1*; ~
~ ~, *Q2* || **23** you?] *Q2*; ~. *Q1* ||

them was, that he is the best Sempster of any woman in   25
England; pray let's see some of his worke.

Hip. Sweet Lord let's see him sowe a little.

Tal. You shall a mine honour Ladie.

Eug. Hee's a goodly greate knight indeed; and a little
needle in his hand will become him prettelie.   30

King. From the Spanish pike to the Spanish needle,
he shall play with any knight in England Ladie.

Eug. But not *è conuerso*, from the Spanish needle to
the Spanish pike.

King. I thinke he be too wise for that indeed madam,   35
for he has 20. miles length in land lies togeather, and
hee wood bee loath to bring it all to the length of a pike.

Hip. But no man commends my blount Seruant Sir *Cutt:
Rudesby* methinks.

King. Hee is a kind gentleman Ladie though hee bee   40
blunt, and is of this humor: the more you presume vppon
him without Ceremonie, the more / he loues you; if he knowe   [F2ᵛ]
you thinke him kinde once and will say nothing but still
vse him, you may melt him into any kindenesse you will;
he is right like a woman, and had rather, you shood   45
bluntlie take the greatest fauour you can of him, then
shamefastly intreat it.

Eug. He saies wel to you *Hippolita*.

Hip. I madam, but they saie, he will beat one in
Iest, and byte in kindenesse, and teare ones ruffes in   50
Courtshippe.

King. Some that he makes sport withall perhappes,
but none that he respects I assure ye.

Hip. And what's his liuing sir *Cutbeard*?

King. Some two thousand a yeare Ladie.   55

Hip. I pray doe not tell him that I ask't, for I
stand not vpon liuing.

King. O Good Ladie who can liue without liuing?

Enter Momford.

Mom. Still heere Lordings? good companions yfaith,
I see you come not for vittles.   60

Tal. Vittles, my Lord? I hope we haue vittles at
home.

Mom. I but sweet Lord, there is a principle in the

---

25 woman] *Q1(c)*, *Q2*; women *Q1(u)* ‖ **26** England] *Q1(c)*, *Q2*; Eugland *Q1(u)* | England;] ~,
Q1-2 | worke.] ~? *Q1-2* ‖ **26, 27** let's] lets *Q1-2* ‖ **29** Hee's] Hees *Q1-2* ‖ **41** humor:] ~, *Q1-2* ‖
42 you;] ~, *Q1-2* ‖ **48** *Eug.*] *Q2*; ~ˌ *Q1* ‖ **49** *Hip.*] *Q2*; ~ˌ *Q1* ‖ **53** assure ye] *Q2*; assureye *Q1* ‖
54 what's] *Q2*; wha'ts *Q1* ‖ **58** *King.*] *Q2*; ~ˌ *Q1* ‖ **59** *Mom.*] *Q2*; ~ˌ *Q1* ‖ **61** Lord?] *Q2*; ~ˌ *Q1* ‖

Polititians phisicke, Eat not your meat vpon other mens
trenchers, and beware of surfits of your owne coste: 65
manie good companions cannot abide to eate meate at
home ye know. And how faires my noble Neece now, and
her faire Ladie Feeres?

    Eug. What winde blowes you hether troe?

    Mom. [*To Eugenia.*] Harke you madam, the sweete gale   70
of one *Clarences* breath, with this his paper sayle blowes
me hether.   [*Offering her a letter.*]

    Eug. [*To Momford.*] Aye me, stil in that humor? beshrowe
my hart if I take anie Papers from him.

    Mom. [*To Eugenia.*] Kinde bosome doe thou take it then. /   75

    Eug. [*To Momford.*] Nay then neuer trust me.   [F3]

    Mom. [*To Eugenia.*] Let it fall then, or cast it awaie you
were best, that euerie bodie may discouer your loue suits,
doe; there's sombodie neare if you note it, – and how haue
you spent the time since dinner nobles?   80

    King. At chests my Lord.

    Mom. [*To Eugenia.*] Read it neece.

    Eug. [*To Momford.*] Heere, beare it backe I pray.

    Mom. [*To Eugenia.*] I beare you on my backe to heare
you; – and how play the Ladies sir *Cuthbert*, what men doe   85
they play best withall, with knights or rookes?

    Tal. With knights my Lord.

    Mom. T'is pitty their boord is no broader, and that
some men caled guls are not added to their game.

    King. Why my Lo. it needs not, they make the   90
knights guls.

    Mom. That's pretty sir *Cuthbert*; [*To Eugenia.*] you haue
begon I know Neece, forth I commaund you.

    Eug. [*To Momford.*] O y'are a sweete vnckle.

    Mom. I haue brought her a little *Greeke*, to helpe   95
me out withal, and shee's so coy of her learning for sooth
she makes it strange: Lords, and Ladies, I inuite you
al to supper to night, and you shal not denie me.

    All. We will attend your Lordshippe.

    Tal. Come Ladies let's into the gallerie a little.   100
                                       Exeunt.

    Mom. And now what saies mine owne deare neece yfaith?

64-65 Eat not ... trenchers] *stet* (*See Textual Note*) ‖ **65** coste:] *Q2*; ~ ˏ *Q1* ‖ **70** SD *To Eugenia.*]
‖ **72** SD *Offering ... letter.*] *Parrott* ‖ **73** SD *To Momford.*] | me, stil] *Parrott*; ~ ˏ ~, *Q1-2* ‖ **75**
SD *To Eugenia.*] ‖ **76** SD *To Momford.*] ‖ **77** SD *To Eugenia.*] ‖ **79** there's] theres *Q1-2* | it,–]
Bullen; ~ ˏ *Q1-2* ‖ **81** Lord.] *Q2*; Lords, *Q1* ‖ **82** SD *To Eugenia.*] *Parrott subs.* ‖ **83** SD *To
Momford.*] *Parrott subs.* | Heere,] *Bullen*; ~ ˏ *Q1-2* ‖ **84** SD *To Eugenia.*] *Parrott subs.* ‖ **85**
you;–] ~ ˏ *Q1-2* ‖ **89** game.] *Q2*; ~ ˏ *Q1* ‖ **92** Mom.] *Q2*; ~ ˏ | That's] *Q2*; Thats *Q1* | SD *To
Eugenia.*] *Parrott subs.* ‖ **94** SD *To Momford.*] *Parrott subs.* | y'are] yare *Q1-2* ‖ **96** shee's] shees
Q1-2 ‖ **100** SD *Exeunt.*] *Q2*; *exeunt* ˏ *Q1* ‖

Eug. What shood she saie to the backside of a paper?

Mom. Come, come, I knowe you haue byn a'the bellie side.

Eug. Now was there euer Lord so prodigall, of his owne honor'd blood, and dignity?

105

Mom. Away with these same horse-faire alligations, will you answere the letter?

Eug. Gods my life you goe like a cuning spokes man; / answere vnckle? what doe ye thinke me desperate of a husband?

[F3ᵛ]
111

Mom. Not so neece, but carelesse of your poore vnkle.

Eug. I will not write that's certaine.

Mom. What wil you haue my friend and I perrish? doe you thirst our bloods?

115

Eug. O y'are in a mightie danger noe doubt on't.

Mom. If you haue our bloods beware our ghostes I can tell ye, come will ye write?

Eug. I will not write yfaith.

120

Mom. Yfaith dame, then I must be your secretarie I see; here's the letter, come, doe you dictate and Ile write.

Eug. If you write no otherwise then I dictate, it will scarce proue a kinde answere I beleeue.

125

Mom. But you will be aduis'de I trust. Secretaries are of counsaile with their countesses; thus it begins. *Suffer him to loue, that suffers not louing.* What answere you to that?

Eug. He loues extreamely that suffers not in loue.

130

Mom. He answeres you for that presentlie, his loue is without passion, and therefore free from alteration, for *Pati* you know is *in Alterationem labi*; he loues you in his soule he tels you, wherein there is no passion. Saie dame what answere you?

135

Eug. Nay if I answere anie thing –

Mom. Why, verie well, ile answere for you.

Eug. You answere? shall I set my hand to your answere?

Mom. I by my faith shall ye.

140

---

102 paper?] *Q2*; ~. *Q1* ‖ 109 man] *Q2*; man, / man *Q1* | man;] ~, *Q1-2* ‖ 111 husband?] *Q2*; ~, *Q1* ‖ 115 perrish?] *Q2*; ~, *Q1* ‖ 117 y'are] yare *Q1-2* ‖ 121 Yfaith] yfaith *Q1*; yFaith *Q2* ‖ 122 see;] ~, *Q1-2* | here's] heres *Q1-2* ‖ 127 countesses;] *Bullen*; ~, *Q1-2* ‖ 128 *Suffer ... louing.*] *The quoted parts of both letters are in roman in Q1-2; here, and below, given in italics as in Bullen.* | louing. What] *Bullen*; louing, what *Q1-2* ‖ 133 *in*] *Q2*; in *Q1* ‖ 134-135 passion. Saie] *Bullen*; ~, saie *Q1-2* ‖ 135 you?] *Q2*; ~. *Q1* ‖ 136 thing–] *Bullen*; ~. *Q1-2* ‖ 137 Why,] ~? *Q1-2* ‖

Eug. By my faith, but you shal answere as I wood
haue you then.

Mom. Alwaies put in with aduice of your secretarie,
neece; come, what answere you? /   144
[F4]

Eug. Since you needes will haue my Answere, Ile
answere briefely to the first, and last part of his letter.

Mom. Doe so Neece, and leaue the midst for him-/ selfe
a gods name: what is your answeare?

Eug. 1 cannot but suffer you to loue, if you do loue.   149

Mom. Why very good, thcre it is, *and will requit*   *He writes and*
your loue; say you so?   *she dictates.*

Eug. Beshrowe my lipps then my Lord.

Mom. Beshrowe my fingers but you shall; what, you
may promise to requite his loue, and yet not promise him
marriage I hope; wel, *and will requite your loue.*   155

Eug. Nay good my Lord hold your hand, for ile bee
sworne, ile not set my hand too't.

Mom. Well hold of your hand good madam till it
shood come on, Ile be readie for it anon, I warrant ye:
now forth; *my Loue is without passion, and therefore*   160
free from alteration; what answere you to that madam?

Eug. Euen this my Lorde, *your Loue being mentall,*
needes no bodely Requitall.

Mom. I am Content with that, and here it is; *but in*
hart.   165

Eug. What but in hart?

Mom. Hold of your hand yet I say; *I doe embrace and*
repaie it.

Eug. You may write vnckle, but if you get my hand
to it –   170

Mom. Alas Neece this is nothing; is't any thing to
a bodely marriage, to say you loue a man in Soule if
your harts agree and your bodies meet not? simple
marriage rites, now let vs foorth: hee is in the way
to felicitie, and desires your hand.   175

Eug. My hand shall alwaies signe the way to felicitie.

Mom. Very good, may not any woman say this now?
Conclude now sweet Neece.

Eug. And so God prosper your Iourney.

Mom. Charitably concluded, though farre short of   180

---

144 neece;] ~, *Q1-2* ‖ 146 answere] *Q2*; Answere *Q1* ‖ 148 name:] *Q2*; ~, *Q1* ‖ 151 SD *dictates*]
Q2; *dictatcs Q1* ‖ 161 *alteration*;] alteration, *Q1-2* ‖ 166 What] *Q2*; ~, *Q1* ‖ 167 say;] *Bullen*;
~, *Q1-2* ‖ 168 it.] *Q2*; ~, *Q1* ‖ 170 it–] *Bullen*; ~, *Q1*; ~. *Q2* ‖ 171 nothing; is't] ~, ist *Q1-2* ‖
174 marriage] *Q2*; marriarge *Q1* ‖ 177 now?] ~. *Q1-2* ‖ 178 Conclude] *Q2*; Conclud *Q1* ‖

that loue I wood haue showen to any friend of yours /
Neece I sweare to you; your hand now, and let this little   [F4ᵛ]
stay his appetite.

 Eug. Read what you haue writ my Lord.

 Mom. What needs that madam, you remember it I am sure.   185

 Eug. Well if it want sence in the Composition, let
my secretarie be blam'd for't; their's my hand.

 Mom. Thanks gentle Neece, now ile reade it.

 Eug. Why now, more then before I pray?

 Mom. That you shall see straite. *I cannot but suffer*   190
you to loue if you doe loue, and wil requite your loue.

 Eug. Remember that requitall was of your own putting
in, but it shal be after my fashion, I warrant ye.

 Mom. Interrupt me no more; *your loue being mentall*
needs no bodely requitall, but in hart I embrace and repay   195
it; my hand shall alwaies signe the way to felicitie, and
my selfe, knit with you in the bandes of marriage, euer
walke with you in it, and so God prosper our iourney:
            Eugenia.

 Eug. Gods me life, tis not thus I hope.   200

 Mom. By my life but it is Neece.

 Eug. By my life but tis none of my deed then.

 Mom. Doe you vse to set your hand to that which is
not your deed? your hand is at it Neece, and if there
be any law in England, you shall performe it too.   205

 Eug. Why, this is plaine dishonoured deceit.
Does all your truest kindnes end in lawe?

 Mom. Haue patience Neece, for what so ere I say
Onely the lawes of faith, and thy free loue
Shall ioyne my friend and thee, or naught at al,   210
By my friends loue, and by this kisse it shall.

 Eug. Why, thus did false *Accontius* snare *Cydippe.*

 Mom. Indeed deere loue his wile was something like,
And then tis no vnheard-of trecherie
That was enacted in a goddes Eye: 215
Accontius worthie loue feard not *Diana* /
Before whome he contriu'de this sweete deceite.   [G1]

 Eug. Wel there you haue my hand, but ile be sworne
I neuer did thing so against my will.

 Mom. T'will proue the better madam, doubt it not.   220

---

182 you;] ~, *Q1-2* | and let] *Q2*; andlet *Q1* || 187 for't;] ~, *Q1-2* | their's] theirs *Q1*; thers *Q2* ||
190 straite.] ~, *Q1-2* || 191 loue,] *Q2*; ~ *Q1* || 192-193 putting in] *Q2*; putning it *Q1* || 193
fashion,] *Q2*; ~ *Q1* || 194 more;] ~, *Q1-2* | *mentall*] *Q2*; men-/ toll *Q1* || 197 selfe, . . .
marriage,] *Parrott*; ~ . . . ~, *Q1-2* || 198 you] *Parrott*; ~, *Q1-2* || 204 deed?] ~, *Q1-2* || 205 too.]
Q2; ~: *Q1* || 206 Why,] Wh,y *Q1*; ~? *Q2* || 213 like,] *Q2*; ~ *Q1* || 215 Eye:] *Q2*; ~, *Q1* || 217
deceite.] *Q2*; ~ *Q1* || 218 be sworne] besworne *Q1-2* ||

And to allay the billows of your blood,
Rais'de with my motion bold and opposite,
Deere neece suppe with me, and refresh your spirites:
I haue inuited your companions
With the two guests that dinde with you to daie,   225
And will send for the old Lord *Furnifall*,
The Captaine, and his mates and (tho at night)
We will be merrie as the morning *Larke*.
   Eug. No, no my Lord, you will haue *Clarence* there.
   Mom. Alas poore gentleman I must tell you now   230
Hee's extreame sicke, and was so when he writt,
Tho he did charge me not to tell you so;
And for the world he cannot come abroade.
   Eug. Is this the man that without passion loues?
   Mom. I doe not tell you he is sicke with loue;   235
Or if he be tis wilfull passion,
Which he doth choose to suffer for your sake
And cood restraine his sufferance with a thought;
Vppon my life he will not trouble you;
And therefore worthie neece faile not to come.   240
   Eug. I will on that condition.
   Mom.   Tis perform'd:
For were my friend well and cood comfort me,
I wood not now intreate your companie,
But one of you I must haue, or I die,   244
Oh such a friend is worth a monarchie.   *Exeunt.*

[IV.ii]

Enter Lord Furnifall. Rudsbie. Goosecappe.
Fowlweather. Bullaker.

   Fur. Nay my gallants I will tell you more.
   All. Forth good my Lord.
   Fur. The euening came and then our waxen stars
Sparkled about the heauenly court of *Fraunce.*
When I then young and readiant as the sunne /   5
Gaue luster to those lampes, and curling thus   [G1ᵛ]
My golden foretoppe, stept into the presence,
Where set with other princely dames I found
The Countesse of *Lancalier* and her neece

---

222 opposite,] Q2; ~ QI ‖ 226 *Furnifall*,] Q2; ~ QI ‖ 227 Captaine,] Q1(c), Q2; Captaines
Q1(u) ‖ 230 Alas] Q2; A las QI ‖ 231 Hee's] Hees QI; He's Q2 | writt,] Q2; ~ QI ‖ 234
loues?] Q2; ~ QI ‖ 236 passion,] ~. Q1-2 ‖ 238 thought;] ~, Q1-2 ‖ 241-245 I … monarchie.]
Bullen; as prose Q1-2 (for … but … oh) ‖ 242 me,] Q2; ~; QI ‖ **IV.ii**] *Bullen* ‖ 4 *Fraunce*]
Fraunce *QI*; *France Q2* ‖

Who as I told you cast so fix'd an eye   10
On my behauiours talking with the king.
    All. True my good Lord.
    Fur. They rose when I came in, and all the lights
Burnd dim for shame, when I stood vp and shind.
    Foul. O most passionate description Sir *Cutt*:   15
    Rud. True of a candles end.
    Goos. The passingst description of a candle, that
euer liu'd Sir *Cutt*:
    Fur. Yet aymd I not at them, nor seemd to note
What grace they did me, but found courtly cause   20
To talke with an accomplisht gentleman
New come from *Italie*; in quest of newes
I spake *Italian* with him.
    Rud.   What so young?
    Fur. O *rarissime volte cadono nel parlar nostro*
familiare.   25
    Foul. Slidd, a cood speake it knight, at three yeare
        old.
    Fur. Nay gentle Captaine doe not set me forth;
I loue it not, in truth I loue it not.
    Foul. Slight my Lord but truth is truth you know.
    Goos. I dare ensure your Lordship, Truth is truth, and   30
I haue heard in *Fraunce*, they speake *French* as well as
their mother tongue my Lord.
    Fur. Why tis their mother tonge my noble knight.
But (as I tell you) I seem'd not to note
The Ladies notes of me, but held my talke,   35
With that Italionate Frenchman, and tooke time
(Still as our conference seru'd) to shew my Courtship
In the three quarter legge, and setled looke,
The quick kisse of the toppe of the forefinger
And other such exploytes of good Accost;   40
All which the Ladies tooke into their eyes
With such attention that their fauours swarm'de /
About my bosome, in my hart, mine eares,   [G2]
In skarffes about my thighes, vpon mine armes,
Thicke on my wrystes, and thicker on my hands,   45
And still the lesse I sought, the more I found.
All this I tell to this notorious end,
That you may vse your Courtship with lesse care

11 king.] ~: *Q1*; King. *Q2* || 22 *Italie*;] *Bullen*; ~, *Q1-2* || 22-23 *Italie ... Italian*] *Q2*; Italie ...
Italian *Q1* || 27 forth;] *Q2*; ~ *Q1* || 28 it not,] *Q1(c)*, *Q2*; in ~, *Q1(u)* || 31 *Fraunce ... French*]
Fraunce ... French *Q1*; *France ... ~ Q2* | well] ~, *Q1-2* || 33 knight.] *Q2*; ~ *Q1* || 36 With]
Q2; with *Q1* || 42 swarm'de] *Q1(c)*, *Q2*; ~. *Q1(u)* || 43 hart] *Q2*; hatt *Q1* || 44 armes,] ~ *Q1-2* ||

To your coy mistresses; As when we strike
A goodly Sammon, with a little line, 50
We doe not tugge to hale her vp by force
For then our line wood breake, and our hooke lost;
But let her carelesse play alongst the streame
As you had left her, and sheele drowne her selfe.
    Foul. A my life a most rich comparison. 55
    Goos. Neuer stirre, if it bee not a richer Caparison,
then my Lorde my Cosine wore at tilt, for that was
brodred with nothing but mooneshine ith' the water, and
this has Sammons in't; by heauen a most edible Caparison.
    Rud. Odious thou woodst say, for Comparisons are 60
odious.
    Foul. So they are indeede sir *Cut*: all but my Lords.
    Goos. Bee Caparisons odious Sir *Cutt*:? what, like
flowers?
    Rud. O asse they be odorous. 65
    Goos. A botts athat stincking worde odorous, I can
neuer hitt on't.
    Fur. And how like you my Court-counsaile, gallants
ha?
    Foul. Out of all proportion excellent my Lord: and 70
beleeue it for Emphaticall Courtship, your Lordship
puts downe all the Lords of the Court.
    Fur. No, good Captaine no.
    Foul. By *Fraunce* you doe my Lord for Emphaticall
Courtship. 75
    Fur. For Emphaticall Courtship indeed I can doe
somewhat.
    Foul. Then does your merrie entertainment become
you so festifally, that you haue all the brauerie of a
Saint *Georges* day about ye when you vse it. 80
    Fur. Nay that's too much, in sadnes, Captaine.
    Goos. O good my Lord, let him prayse you, what so
ere / it costs your Lordshippe. [G2ᵛ]
    Foul. I assure your Lordshippe your merrie behauiour
does so festifally showe vpon you, that euery high 85
holliday when Ladies wood bee most bewtifull, euery one
wishes to God shee were turnd into such a little Lord
as you, when y'are merrie.
    Goos. By this fire they doe my Lord, I haue heard
am. 90

---

50 line,] Q2; ~ Q1 ‖ **58** ith'] ith Q1; it'h Q2 ‖ **62** *Cut*:] Q1(c); ~ Q1(u); ~. Q2 ‖ **63** *Cutt*:?] ~:
Q1; *Cut*? Q2 | what,] ~ Q1-2 ‖ **68** Court-counsaile,] ~ Q1-2 ‖ **73** No,] ~ Q1-2 ‖ **74** *Fraunce*]
Fraunce Q1; *France* Q2 ‖ **76** For] Q1(c), Q2; Eor Q1(u) ‖ **81** that's] thats Q1-2 | much, in
sadnes,] Q2; ~ ~ ~ Q1 ‖ **86** bewtifull,] *Bullen*; ~; Q1-2 ‖

Fur. Marrie God forbid, knight, they shood be turnd
into me; I had rather be turnd into them amine honor.

Foul. Then for your Lordships quippes, and quick iests,
why *Gesta Romanorum* were nothing to them a my vertue.

Fur. Well, well, well, I will heare thee no more,   95
I will heare thee no more, good Captaine. Th'ast an
excellent witt, and thou shalt haue Crownes amine honour;
and now knights and Captain, the foole you told me of,
do you al know him?

Goos. I know him best my Lord.   100

Fur. Doe you Sir *Gyles*? to him then good knight, and
be here with him, and here, and here, and here againe;
I meane paint him vnto vs Sir *Gyles*, paint him liuely,
liuely now, my good knightly boy.

Goos. Why my good Lord? hee will nere be long from   105
vs, because we are all mortall you know.

Fur. Verie true.

Goos. And as soone as euer wee goe to dinner, and
supper togeather –

Rud. Dinner and supper togeather, when's that troe?   110

Goos. A will come you in amongst vs, with his Cloake
buttond, loose vnder his chinne.

Rud. Buttond loose my Lord?

Goos. I me Lord buttond loose still, and both the
flaps cast ouer before, both his shoulders afore him.   115

Rud. Both shouldiers afore him?

Fur. From before him hee meanes; forth good Sir *Gyles*.

Goos. Like a potentate my Lord?

Rud. Much like a Potentate indeed.

Goos. For all the world like a Potentate S. *Cut*: ye   120
know. /

Rud. So Sir.   [G3]

Goos. All his beard nothing but haire.

Rud. Or something else.

Goos. Or something else as you say.   125

Foul. Excellent good.

Goos. His Mellons, or his Apricocks, Orrenges alwaies
in an vncleane hand-kerchiffe very cleanely I warrant you
my Lord.

Fur. A good neate foole Sir *Gyles* of mine honour.   130

Goos. Then his fine words that hee sets them in,

---

91 forbid, knight,] *Q2*; ~ˏ ~ˏ *Q1* ‖ **94** vertue.] *Q2*; ~ˏ *Q1* ‖ **96** Captaine.] ~, *Q1-2* | Th'ast]
Tha'st *Q1*; Tha's *Q2* ‖ **97** honour;] ~, *Q1-2* ‖ **98** of] off *Q1-2* ‖ **99** him?] *Q1(c)*, *Q2*; ~. *Q1(u)* ‖
101 *Gyles*?] ~, *Q1-2* ‖ **103** meane paint] *Q1(c)*, *Q2*; ~ haint *Q1(u)* ‖ **107** true.] *Q2*; ~, *Q1* ‖
109 togeather–] *Bullen*; ~, *Q1*; ~. *Q2* ‖ **110** when's] whens *Q1-2* ‖ **118** my] *Q2*; My *Q1* ‖ **124**
Rud.] *Parrott*; Cud. *Q1-2* ‖ **127** Orrenges] *Q1(c)*, *Q2*; Orrrenges *Q1(u)* ‖

concaticall, a fine Annisseede wenche foole, vppon ticket
and so forth.

Fur. Passing strange wordes belieue me.

Goos. Knoth euery man at the table, though he neuer   135
saw him before, by sight, and then will he foole you so
finely my Lorde, that hee will make your hart ake, till
your eyes runne ouer.

Fur. The best that euer I heard; gramercy good
knight for thy merrie description. Captaine, I giue thee   140
twentie companies of commendations, neuer to bee casheird.

Enter Iacke and Will on the other side.

Ambo. Saue your Lordship.

Fur. My prettie cast of *Merlins*, what prophecies
with your little maistershippes?

Ia. Things that cannot come to passe my Lord, the   145
worse our fortunes.

Foul. Why what's the matter pages?

Rud. How now, my Ladies foysting hounds.

Goos. M. *Iack*, M. *Iacke*; how do ye M. *William*?
frolick?   150

Will. Not so frolicke, as you left vs Sir *Gyles*.

Fur. Why wags, what news bring you a Gods name?

Ia. Heauie newes indeed my Lord, pray pardone vs.

Fur. Heauie newes? not possible your little bodies
cood bring am then; vnload those your heauie newes I   155
beseech ye!

Will. Why my Lord, the foole we tooke for your Lord: is
thought too wise for you, and we dare not present him. /

Goos. Slydd pages, youle not cheate's of our foole   [G3ᵛ]
wil ye?   160

Ia. Why sir *Giles*, hee's too dogged and bitter for
you in truth, we shall bring you a foole to make you
laugh, and he shall make all the world laugh at vs.

Will. I indeed sir *Giles*, and he knowes you so wel
too.   165

Goos. Knowe me? slight he knowes me no more then
the begger knowes his dish.

Ia. Faith he begs you to be content sir *Giles*, for
he wil not come.

Goos. Begg me? slight I wood I had knowne that;   170

132 foole,] *Bullen*; ∼, *Q1-2* ‖ 134 me.] *Q2*; ∼, *Q1* ‖ 136 sight,] *Q2*; ∼, *Q1* ‖ 139 heard;] ∼, *Q1-2*
| gramercy] *Parrott*; gray mercy *Q1-2* ‖ 140 description.] *Q2*; ∼, *Q1* ‖ 142 Ambo.] *Am. Q1-2* |
Lordship.] *Q2*; ∼, *Q1* ‖ 147 what's] whats *Q1-2* ‖ 148 now,] ∼, *Q1-2* ‖ 149 William?] *Q2*; ∼,
Q1 ‖ 152 name?] *Q2*; ∼. *Q1* ‖ 155 then;] ∼, *Q1-2* ‖ 156 ye!] ∼? *Q1-2* ‖ 157 Lord,] ∼, *Q1-2* ‖
158 him.] *Q2*; ∼, *Q1* ‖ 159 cheate's] *Parrott*; cheates *Q1-2* ‖ 161 hee's] hees *Q1-2* ‖ 165 too.]
Q2; ∼, *Q1* ‖ 166 Goos.] *Giles, Q1-2* ‖ 170 that;] ∼, *Q1-2* ‖

tother daie, I thought I had met him in Paules, and he had
byn anie body else but a piller, I wood haue runne him
through by heauen, beg me?

Foul. He begges you to be content sir *Giles*, that
io, he praies you.   175

Goos. O does he praise me? then I commend him.

Fur. Let this vnsutable foole goe sir *Giles*, we
will make shift without him.

Goos. That we wil a my word my Lord, and haue him
too for all this.   180

Will. Doe not you say so sir *Giles*, for to tell you
true that foole is dead.

Goos. Dead? Slight that cannot be man, I knowe he
wood ha writ to me an't had byn so.

Fur. Quick or dead let him goe sir *Giles*.   185

Ia. I my Lord, for we haue better newes for you to
harken after.

Fur. What are they my good Nouations?

Ia. My Lord *Momford* intreates your Lordship and
these knights and captaine to accompany the countesse   190
Eugenia, and the other two Ladies at his house at supper
to night.

Will. All desiring your Lo: to pardon them, for not
eating your meat to night.

Fur. With all my hart wagges, and their's amends; my   195
harts, now set your courtshippe a'the last, a'the
tainters, and pricke vp your selues for the Ladies. /

Goos. O braue sir *Cut.*, come let's prick vp the Ladies!   [G4]

Fur. And wil not the knights two noble kinsemen be
there?   200

Ia. Both will be their my Lord.

Fur. Why there's the whole knot of vs then, and there
shall wee knocke vppe the whole triplicitie of your
nuptials.

Goos. Ile make my Lord my Cosin speake for me.   205

Foul. And your Lordship will be for me I hope.

Fur. With tooth and naile Captaine, a my Lordship.

Rud. Hang am Tytts, ile pommell my selfe into am.

Ia. Your Lo: your Cosin Sir *Gyles* has promist the
Ladies they shall see you sowe.   210

Goos. Gods mee, wood I might neuer be mortall if I
doe not carry my worke with me.

176 me?] ~, *Q1*; ~ *Q2* ‖ **184** an't] ont *Q1*; ant *Q2* ‖ **188** What] *Q2*; what *Q1* ‖ **189** Lordship]
Q2; Lorship *Q1* ‖ **195** With all] *Parrott*; Withall *Q1-2* | their's] theirs *Q1*; thers *Q2* ‖ **198** *Cut.*,]
~.. *Q1*; ~. *Q2* | let's] lets *Q1-2* ‖ **202** there's] theres *Q1-2* ‖ **207** a] A *Q1-2* | Lordship] *Q2*;
Lord *Q1* ‖ **208** Tytts,] *Q2*; ~ *Q1* ‖

Fur. Doe so Sir *Gyles*, and withall vse meanes
To taint their high blouds with the shafte of Loue.
Sometimes a fingers motion woundes their minds;   215
A iest, a Iesture, or a prettie laugh:
A voyce, a present; ah, things done ith' nick
Wound deepe, and sure, and let flie your gold
And we shall nuptialls haue; hold belly hold.
    Goos. O rare Sir *Cutt*: we shall eate nut-shells.   220
Hold belly hold.   *Exeunt Furnifall and the Knights.*
    Ia. O pittifull knight, that knowes not nuptialls
from nutshells.
    Will. And now *Comme porte vous monsieur?*
    Bul. Porte bien vous remercy.   225
    Ia. We may see it indeed Sir, and you shall goe afore
with vs.
    Bul. No, good *monsieurs.*
    Will. Another Crashe in my Ladies Celler yfaith
monsieur.   230
    Bul. Remercy de bon ceur monsieurs.   *Exeunt.*

[IV.iii]

Enter Clarence, Mumford.   [G4ᵛ]

    Mom. How now my friend, does not the knowing beames
That through thy common sence glaunce through thy eyes
To reade that letter, through thine eyes retire
And warme thy heart with a tryumphant fire?
    Cla. My Lord I feele a treble happines   5
Mix in one soule, which proues how eminent
Things endlesse are aboue things temporall,
That are in bodies needefully confin'de;
I cannot suffer their dementions pierst
Where my immortall part admits expansure   10
Euen to the comprehension of two more
Commixt substantially with her meere selfe.
    Mom. As how my strange, and riddle-speaking friend?
    Cla. As thus my Lord: I feele my owne minds ioy
As it is separate from all other powers,   15
And then the mixture of an other soule
Ioyn'de in direction to one end, like it,
And thirdly the contentment I enioy,

---

214 Loue.] *Bullen;* ~, *Q1;* love, *Q2* ‖ 216 laugh:] *Q2;* ~. *Q1* ‖ 217 present;] *Bullen;* ~, *Q1-2* |
ith'] ith *Q1-2* ‖ 219 haue;] ~, *Q1;* ~ *Q2* ‖ 221 Hold] hold *Q1-2* | hold.] ~ *Q1-2* | SD *Exeunt
... Knights.] Parrott; Exeunt. Q1-2* ‖ 222 knowes] *Q2;* koowes *Q1* ‖ 225 *Bul.] Q2; Bull˳ Q1* ‖
228 No,] *Parrott;* ~˳ *Q1-2* ‖ 229 *Will.]* ~: *Q1;* Wil. *Q2* ‖ **IV.iii**] *Bullen* ‖ SD *Clarence,] Q2;* ~˳
Q1 ‖ 1 friend,] *Q2;* ~˳ *Q1* ‖ 5 *Cla.] Parrott; Mom. Q1-2* ‖ 14 Lord:] ~, *Q1-2* ‖

As we are ioynd, that I shall worke that good
In such a noble spirit as your neece,   20
Which in my selfe I feele for absolute;
Each good minde dowbles his owne free content
When in an others vse they giue it vent.
   Mom. Said like my friend, and that I may not wrong
Thy full perfections with an emptier grace,   25
Then that which showe presents to thy conceits,
In working thee a wife worse then she seemes;
Ile tell thee plaine a secret which I knowe.
My neece doth vse to paint herselfe with white
Whose cheekes are naturally mixt with redd   30
Either because she thinks pale-lookes moues most:
Or of an answereable nice affect
To other of her modest qualities;
Because she wood not with the outward blaze
Of tempting bewtie tangle wanton eies;   35
And so be troubled with their tromperies: /
Which construe as thou wilt, I make it knowne   [H1]
That thy free comment may examine it,
As willinger to tell truth of my neece,
Then in the least degree to wrong my friend.   40
   Cla. A ielous part of friendshippe you vnfold;
For was it euer seene that any dame
Wood chainge of choice a well mixt white and redd
For bloodles palenes, if she striu'd to moue?
Her painting then is to shunn motion,   45
But if she mended some defect with it
Breedes it more hate then other ornaments
(Which to supplie bare nature) Ladies weare?
What an absurd thing is it to suppose
(If Nature made vs either lame or sick,)   50
We wood not seeke for sound lymmes, or for health
By Art the Rector of confused Nature?
So in a face if Nature be made lamer
Then Art can make it, is it more offence
To helpe her want there then in other limmes?   55
Who can giue instance where dames faces lost
The priuiledge their other parts may boast?
   Mom. But our most Court-receiued Poet saies
- That painting is pure chastities abator.
   Cla. That was to make vp a poore rime to Nature,   60

---

19 ioynd,] *Q2*; ~͵ *Q1* ‖ **45** Her] *Q1(c, 2nd state), Q2*; He *Q1(u, c, 1st state)* ‖ **47** ornaments] ~;
Q1-2 ‖ **49** What] *Q1(c, 1st state), Q2*; ⅄hat *Q1(u)* | suppose] *Parrott*; ~; *Q1-2* ‖ **53** lamer] *Q1(c,
2nd state)*; lame *Q1(u, c, 1st state), Q2* ‖ **57** boast?] ~. *Q1-2* ‖ **58** Court-receiued] *Parrott*; Court
receiued *Q1-2* | Poet] *Parrott*; Poets *Q1-2 (See Textual Note)* ‖ **60** Nature,] *Parrott*; ~. *Q1-2* ‖

And farre from any Iudgment it confered;
For lightnes comes from harts, and not from lookes,
And if inchastitie possesse the hart,
Not painting doth not race it, nor being cleare
Doth painting spot it,   65
Omne bonum naturaliter pulchrum.
For outward fairenes beares the diuine forme,
And moues beholders to the Act of loue;
And that which moues to loue is to be wisht
And eche thing simplie to be wisht is good.   70
So I conclude mere painting of the face
A lawfull and a commendable grace.
   Mom. What paradox dost thou defend in this? /
And yet through thy cleare arguments I see   [H1ᵛ]
Thy speach is farr exempt from flatterie,   75
And how illiterate custome groslie erres
Almost in all traditions she preferres.
Since then the doubt I put thee of my neece,
Checks not thy doubtlesse loue, forth my deare friend.
And to add force to those impressions,   80
That now haue caru'd her phantasie with loue,
I haue invited her to supper hecre,
And told her thou art most extreamelie sick,
Which thou shalt counterfeit with all thy skill,
   Cla. Which is exceeding smale to counterfeit.   85
   Mom. Practise a little, loue will teach it thee,
And then shall doctor *Versey* the phisitian,
Come to thee while her selfe is in my house,
With whome as thou confer'st of thy disease,
Ile bring my neece with all the Lords and Ladies   90
Within your hearing vnder fain'd pretext,
To shew the pictures that hang neere thy chamber,
Where when thou hearst my voyce, know she is there.
And therefore speake that which may stir her thoughts,
And make her flie into thy opened armes.   95
Ladies whome true worth cannot moue to ruth
Trew louers must deceue to shew their truth.   *Exeunt.*

Finis Actus Quarti.

61 confered;] *Parrott;* ~ ͺ *Q1-2* ‖ 62 lookes,] *Q2;* ~ ͺ *Q1* ‖ 63 hart,] ~; *Q1-2* ‖ 73 this?] *Q2;* ~ ͺ
Q1 ‖ 76 erres] ~? *Q1-2* ‖ 80 add] *Bullen;* all *Q1-2* ‖ 82 heere,] ~. *Q1-2* ‖ 83 sick,] *Bullen;* ~.
Q1-2 ‖ 85 *Cla.*] *Q2; Cla: Q1* | counterfeit.] ~, *Q1;* ~ ͺ *Q2* ‖ 88 house,] *Bullen;* ~. *Q1-2* ‖ 90 with
all] *Q2;* withall *Q1* | Ladies] *Bullen;* ~. *Q1-2* ‖ 94 speake] *Q1(c), Q2;* speske *Q1(u)* ‖ 97 truth.]
Q2; ~ ͺ *Q1* ‖

ACTVS QVINTI SCÆNA PRIMA.

Enter Momford, Furnifall, Tales, Kingcob, Rudesbie,
Goosecap, Foulweather, Eugenia, Hippolita, Penelope,
Winnifred.

Mom. Where is Sir *Gyles Goosecappe* here?

Goos. Here my Lord.

Mom. Come forward knight, t'is you that the Ladies
admire at working a mine honor. /   4

Goos. A little at once my Lorde for Idlenes sake.   [H2]

Fur. Sir *Cut.*, I say, to her captaine.

Pen. Come good seruant let's see what you worke.

Goos. Why looke you mistris I am makeing a fine drie
sea, full of fishe, playing in the bottome, and here ile
let in the water so liuely, that you shall heare it rore.   10

Eug. Not heare it Sir *Giles.*

Goos. Yes in sooth madam with your eyes.

Tal. I Ladie; for when a thing is done so exceedeingly
to the life, as my knightlie cosen does it, the eye
oftentimes takes so strong a heede of it, that it cannot   15
containe it alone, and therefore the eare seemes to take
part with it.

Hip. That's a verie good reason my Lord.

Mom. [*Aside.*] What a Iest it is, to heare how seriouslie he
striues to make his foolish kinsmans answeres wise ones.   20

Pen. What shall this be seruant?

Goos. This shall be a great whale mistris, at all
his bignesse spouting huge hils of salt-water afore him,
like a little water squirt, but you shall not neede to
feare him mistris, for he shalbe silke and gould, he shall   25
doe you noe harme, and he be nere so liuely.

Pen. Thanke you good seruant.

Tal. Doe not thinke Ladie, but he had need tell you
this a forehand: for a mine honor, he wrought me the
monster *Caucasus* so liuely, that at the first sight I   30
started at it.

Mom. The monster *Caucasus* my Lord? *Caucasus* is a
mountaine; *Cacus* you meane.

Tal. Cacus indeede my Lorde, crie you mercie.

Goos. Heere ile take out your eye, and you wil   35
mistris.

---

3 knight,] ~͵ Q1-2 ‖ **5** Goos.] Q2; Goos: Q1 (*a number of speech-prefixes, through l. 103, are so*
pointed; not hereafter recorded) ‖ **6** Cut.,] ~͵ Q1; ~.͵ Q2 ‖ **19** SD Aside.] ‖ **20** kinsmans] Q1(c),
Q2; uinsmans Q1(u) ‖ **29** forehand:] Q2; ~͵ Q1 ‖

Pen. No by my faith Seruant t'is better in. /
Goos. Why Ladie, Ile but take it out in iest, in   [H2ᵛ]
earnest.
Pen. No, something else there, good seruant.   40
Goos. Why then here shall be a Camell, and he shall
haue hornes, and he shall looke (for al the world) like
a maide without a husband.
Hip. O bitter sir *Giles.*
Tal. Nay he has a drie wit Ladie I can tell ye.   45
Pen. He bobd me there indeede my Lord.
Fur. Marry him sweet Lady, to answere his bitter
bob.
King. So she maie answere him with hornes indeed.
Eug. See what a pretie worke he weares in his   50
boote-hose.
Hip. Did you worke them your selfe sir *Gyles,* or
buy them?
Goos. I bought am for nothing madam in th'exchange.
Eug. Bought am for nothing?   55
Tal. Indeed madam in th'exchange they so honor him
for his worke that they will take nothing for anie thing
he buies on am; but where's the rich night-cappe you
wroght cosen? if it had not byn too little for you, it
was the best peece of worke, that euer I sawe.   60
Goos. Why my Lord, t'was bigg enough, when I wrought
it, for I wore pantables then you knowe.
Tal. Indeede the warmer a man keepes his feete the
lesse he needes weare vppon his head.
Eug. You speake for your kinsman the best, that euer   65
I heard my Lord.
Goos. But I beleeue madam, my Lord my cosen has not
told you all my good parts.
Tal. I told hir so I warrant you cosen.
Hip. What doe you thinke he left out Sir *Giles?*   70
Goos. Marrie madam I can take tobacco now, and I haue
bought glow-wormes to kindle it withall, better / then   [H3]
all the burning glasses ith'world.
Eug. Glowe-wormes sir *Giles?* will they make it burne?
Goos. O od, madam, I feed am with nothing but fire,   75
a purpose; Ile besworne they eat me fiue faggots a-weeke
in charcoale.

---

37 in.] Q2; ~ Q1 ‖ 40 there,] Q1(c, 2nd state); ~ Q1(u, c, 1st state), Q2 ‖ 42 (for al the world)]
Q1(c, 2nd state); ~ all ~~ Q1(u, c, 1st state), Q2 ‖ 54 th'exchange.] Q2; th'exange Q1 ‖ 55
nothing?] Q2; ~. Q1 ‖ 58 am;] Q1(c, 2nd state); ~, Q1(u, c, 1st state), Q2 | where's] wheres
Q1-2 ‖ 59 wroght] Q2; wrohgt Q1 ‖ 69 hir] him Q1-2 ‖ 73 ith'] ith Q1-2 ‖ 74 Giles?] Q2; ~
Q1 ‖ 75 od] Q1(c, 2nd state); good Q1(u, c, 1st state), Q2 (See Textual Note) | od, madam,] ~
~ Q1-2 ‖ 76 purpose;] ~, Q1-2 | a-weeke] a-/weeke Q1-2 ‖

Tal. Nay he has the strangest deuices Ladies that euer you heard I warrant ye.

Fur. That's a strange deuice indeed my Lord.　　　　80

Hip. But your sowing sir *Gyles* is a more gentlewoman-like qualitie I assure you.

Pen. O farr away, for now seruant, you neede neuer marrie, you are both husband, and wife your selfe.

Goos. Nay indeede mistris, I wood faine marrie for　　85
all that, and ile tell you my reason, if you will.

Pen. Let's heare it good seruant.

Goos. Why madam we haue a great match at foot-ball towards, married men against batchellers, and the married men be al my friends, so I wood faine marrie to take the　　90
married mens parts in truth.

Hip. The best reason for marriage that euer I heard sir *Gyles.*

Goos. I pray will you keepe my worke a little mistris; I must needes straine a little courtsie in truth.　　95

　　　　　　　　　　　　　　　　　Exit Sir Gyles.

Hip. Gods my life I thought he was a little to blame.

Rud. Come, come, you heare not me dame.

Fur. Well said sir *Cut.*, to her now; we shall heare fresh courting.

Hip. Alas sir *Cut.*, you are not worth the hearing,　　100
euery bodie saies you cannot loue, how soeuer you talke on't.

Rud. Not loue dame? slydd what argument woodst haue of my loue tro? lett me looke as redde as scarlet a fore I see thee, and when thou comst in sight, if the sunne of　　105
thy bewtie doe not white me like a sheppards holland, I am a Iewe to my Creator. /

Hip. O excellent.　　　　　　　　　　　　　　[H3ᵛ]

Rud. Let mee burst like a Tode, if a frowne of thy browe has not turnd the verie heart in my bellie, and　　110
made mee readie to bee hangd by the heeles for a fortnight to bring it to the right againe.

Hip. You shood haue hangd longer Sir *Cut:*, tis not right yet.

Rud. Zounes, bid me cut off the best lymme of my bodie　　115
for thy loue, and ile lai't in thy hand to proue it; doost thinke I am no Christian, haue I not a Soule to saue?

81 more] *Q1(c, 2nd state)*; most *Q1(u, c, 1st state)*, *Q2* (*See Textual Note*) ‖ **85** mistris,] *Q2*; ~̣ *Q1* ‖ **98** *Cut.*,] ~̣, *Q1*; ~·̣ *Q2* | now;] *Q2*; ~̣ *Q1* ‖ **100** Alas] *Q2*; A las *Q1* | *Cut.*,] ~̣, *Q1-2* ‖ **103** loue] *Q1(c, 1st state)*, *Q2*; ~? *Q1(u)* ‖ **105** sight,] *Parrott*; ~̣ *Q1-2* ‖ **106** bewtie] *Parrott*; ~, *Q1*; beauty, *Q2* | sheppards] *Q1(c, 2nd state)*; shippards *Q1(u, c, 1st state)*, *Q2* | holland,] *Q2*; ~̣ *Q1* ‖ **111** fortnight] fort-/night *Q1-2* ‖ **113** *Cut:*,] ~:̣ *Q1-2* ‖ **114** yet.] *Q2*; ~, *Q1* ‖ **115** Zounes] *Parrott*; Zonnes *Q1-2* ‖ **116** it;] ~, *Q1-2* ‖

Hip. Yes tis to saue yet, I warrant it, and wilbe
while tis a soule if you vse this.

Fur. Excellent Courtship of all hands, only my   120
Captaines Courtshippe is not heard yet; good madam giue
him fauour to court you with his voyce.

Eug. What shood he Court me withall else my Lord?

Mom. Why, I hope madam there be other things to Court
Ladies withall besides voyces.   125

Fur. I meane with an audible sweete song madam.

Eug. With all my heart my Lorde, if I shall bee so
much indebted to him.

Foul. Nay I will be indebted to your eares Ladie for
hearing me sound musicke.   130

Fur. Well done Captaine, proue as it wil now.

Enter Messenger.

Mes. My Lord, Doctor *Versey* the Physitian is come to
see master *Clarence*.

Mom. Light and attend him to him presently.

Fur. To master *Clarence*? what is your friend sicke?   135

Mom. Exceeding sicke.

Tal.   I am exceeding sorrie.

King. Neuer was sorrow worthier bestowed
Then for the ill state of so good a man.

Pen. Alas poore gentleman; good my Lord let's see him.

Mom. Thankes gentle Ladie, but my friend is loth /   140
To trouble Ladies since he cannot quitt them   [H4]
With any thing he hath that they respect.

Hip. Respect my Lord; I wood hold such a man
In more respect then any Emperor
For he cood make me Empresse of my selfe   145
And in mine owne rule comprehend the world.

Mom. How now, young dame? what sodainly inspird?
This speech hath siluer haires, and reuerence asks,
And soner shall haue dutie done of me
Then any pompe in temperall Emperie.   150

Hip. Good madam get my Lord to let vs greet him.

Eug. Alas we shall but wrong and trouble him.
His Contemplations greet him with most welcome.

Fur. I neuer knew a man of so sweet a temper,
So soft and humble, of so high a Spirit.   155

---

118 yet,] *Parrott;* ~ͻ *Q1-2* ‖ 121 Courtshippe] ~, *Q1-2* | yet;] ~, *Q1-2* ‖ 123 withall] with all
Q1-2 ‖ 132 *Mes.*] *Me. Q1-2* | Lord,] *Q2;* ~ͻ *Q1* ‖ 139 let's] lets *Q1-2* ‖ 141 them] ~. *Q1-2* ‖ 147
now,] *Parrott;* ~ͻ *Q1-2* | inspird?] *Q2;* ~ͻ *Q1* ‖ 148 asks,] *Q2;* ~ͻ *Q1* ‖ 154 temper,] *Q2;* ~ͻ *Q1* ‖

Mom. Alas my noble Lord he is not rich,
Nor titles hath, nor in his tender cheekes
The standing lake of *Impudence* corrupts,
Hath nought in all the world, nor nought wood haue,
To grace him in the prostituted light.   160
But if a man wood consort with a Soule
Where all mans Sea of gall and bitternes
Is quite evaporate with hir holy flames,
And in whose powers a Doue-like Innocence
Fosters her owne deserts, and life and death,   165
Runnes hand in hand before them, All the Skies
Cleere and transparent to her piercing eyes,
Then wood my friend be something, but till then
A *Cipher*, nothing, or the worst of men.
    Foul. Sweet Lord let's goe visit him.   170

Enter Gooscappe.

    Goos. Pray, good my Lord, what's that you talke on?
    Mom. Are you come from your necessarie busines Sir
Gyles? we talke of the visiting of my sicke friend *Clarence.*
    Goos. O good my Lord let's visit him, cause I knowe
his brother.   175
    Hip. Know his brother, nay then Count doe/not denie him. [H4ᵛ]
    Goos. Pray, my Lord, whether was eldest, he or his
elder brother?
    Mom. O! the younger brother eldest, while you liue
Sir *Gyles.*   180
    Goos. I say so still my Lord, but I am so borne down
with truth as neuer any knight ith'world was I thinke.
    Tal. A man wood thinke he speakes simplie now; but
indeed it is in the will of the parents, to make which
child they will youngest, or eldest: For often we see the   185
younger inherite, wherein he is eldest.
    Eug. Your Logicall wit my Lorde is able to make any
thing good.
    Mom. Well come sweet Lords, and Ladies, let vs spend
The time till supper-time with some such sights   190
As my poore house is furnished withall,
Pictures and Iewels; of which implements
It may be I haue some wil please you much.
    Goos. Sweet Lord let's see them.   *Exeunt.*

166 them,] *Bullen*; ~: *Q1-2* ‖ **170** let's] lets *Q1-2* ‖ **171** Pray,] *Bullen*; ~ₐ *Q1-2* | what's] *Q2*;
whats *Q1* | you] *Q1(c), Q2*; yon *Q1(u)* ‖ **174** let's] lets *Q1-2* | knowe] *Q1(c), Q2*; konwe
Q1(u) ‖ **177** Pray, ... Lord,] ~ₐ ... ~ₐ *Q1-2* ‖ **182** ith'] ith *Q1-2* ‖ **191** withall,] *Q2*; ~ₐ *Q1* ‖ **194**
let's] lets *Q1-2* ‖

[V.ii]

Enter Clarence and Doctor.

Do. I thinke your disease Sir, be rather of the
mind then the bodie.

Cla. Be there diseases of the mind Doctor?

Do. No question Sir, euen as there be of the bodie.

Cla. And cures for them too?   5

Do. And cures for them too, but not by Phisick.

Cla. You will haue their deseases, greifes? wil ye
not?

Do. Yes, oftentimes.

Cla. And doe not greifes euer rise out of passions?   10

Do. Euermore.

Cla. And doe not passions proceed from corporall
distempers?

Do. Not the passions of the mind, for the mind many
times is sicke, when the bodie is healthfull.   15

Cla. But is not the mindes-sicknes of power to make
the bodie sicke?

Do. In time, certaine. /

Cla. And the bodies ill affections able to infect   [I1]
the mind?   20

Do. No question.

Cla. Then if there bee such a naturall commerce of
Powers betwixt them, that the ill estate of the one offends
the other, why shood not the medicines for one cure the
other?   25

Do. Yet it will not, you see. *Hei mihi quod nullis
amor est medicabilis herbis.*

Cla. Nay then Doctor, since you cannot make any
reasonable Connexion of these two contrarieties, the minde
and the bodie, making both subiect to passion, wherein you   30
confound the substances of both, I must tell you there is
no disease of the mind but one, and that is *Ignorance.*

Do. Why what is loue? is not that a disease of the
mind?

Cla. Nothing so: for it springs naturally out of the   35
bloode, nor are wee subiect to any disease, or sorrowe,
whose causes or effects simply and natiuely concerne the
bodie, that the mind by any meanes partaketh, nor are

V.ii] *Bullen* ‖ **26** not,] ~, *Q1-2* | *Hei mihi*] *Q1(c), Q2; Heimihi Q1(u)* | *nullis*] *Q2; nullus Q1* ‖
29 contrarieties,] *Parrott*; ~, *Q1-2* ‖

there any passions in the Soule, for where there are no
affections, there are no passions: And *Affectus* your   40
master *Gallen* refers *parti irascenti*, For *illic est anima
sentiens vbi sunt affectus*: Therefore the Rationall Soule
cannot be there also.

Do. But you know we vse to say, my mind giues mee
this or that, euen in those addictions that concerne the   45
bodie.

Cla. We vse to say so indeed, and from that vse comes
the abuse of all knowledge, and her practize, for when
the obiect in question onely concerns the state of the
bodie, why shood the soule bee sorry or glad for it? if   50
she willingly mixe her selfe, then shee is a foole, if of
necessitie and against her will, a slaue, and so, far
from that wisdome, and freedome that the Empresse of
Reason, and an eternall Substance shood comprehend.

Do. Diuinely spoken Sir, but verie Paradoxicallie. /   55

Enter, above, Momford, Tales, Kingcob, Furnif: Rudes: Goos: Foul: [I1ᵛ]
Eugenia, Penelope, Hippolita, Winnifrid.

Mom. Who's there?

[Enter Servant.]

[Serv.] I, my Lord.
Mom. Bring hether the key of the gallerie, me thought
I heard the Doctor and my friend.
Fur. I did so, sure.
Mom.   Peace then a while my Lord,   60
We will be bold to evesdroppe; For I know
My friend is as respectiue in his chamber
And by himselfe, of any thing he does
As in a *Criticke Synods* curious eyes
Following therein *Pythagoras* golden rule: 65
Maximè omnium teipsum reuerere.
Cla. Knowe you the Countesse *Eugenia* Sir?
Do. Exceeding wel Sir, she's a good learned scholler.
Cla. Then I perceiue you know her well indeed.
Do. Me thinks you two shood vse much conference.   70
Cla. Alas sir, we doe verie seldome meet,
For her estate, and mine are so vnequall,
And then her knowledge passeth mine so farre
That I hold much too sacred a respect,

50 bodie,] ~? *Q1*; ~; *Q2* ‖ 52 a . . ., and] A . . ., And *Q1*; A . . ., and *Q2* ‖ 55 SD *Enter, above,*] *Parrott; Enter Q1-2* | SD *Furnif: Rudes:*] ~; ~. *Q1; Furnifall, Rudesby, Q2* ‖ 56 SD *Enter Servant.*] ‖ 57 *Serv.*] *Parrott (See Textual Note)* ‖ 60 so,] *Parrott;* ~ *Q1-2* | Lord,] ~ *Q1-2* ‖ 65 rule:] ~. *Q1-2* ‖ 74 too] *Q2;* to *Q1* ‖

Of hir high vertues to let mine attend them.   75
   Do. Pardon me Sir, this humblenes cannot flowe
Out of your iudgment but from passion.
   Cla. Indeed I doe account that passion,
The verie high perfection of my mind,
That is excited by her excellence,   80
And therefore willingly, and gladly feele it.
For what was spoken of the most chast Queene
Of riche *Pasiaca* may be said of her:
Anteuenit sortem moribus virtutibus Annos,
Sexum animo, morum Nobilitate Genus.   85
   Do. A most excellent *Distick.*
   Mom. Come Lords away, let's not presume too much
Of a good nature; not for all I haue
Wood I haue him take knowledge of the wrong /   89
I rudely offer him: come then ile shewe   [I2]
A few rare Iewels to your honour'd eyes,
And then present you with a common supper.
   Goos. Iewells my Lord? why is not this candlesticke
one of your iewells pray?
   Mom. Yes marrie is it Sir *Gyles,* if you will.   95
   Goos. Tis a most fine candlesticke in truth, it
wants nothing but the languages.
   Pen. The languages, seruant, why the languages?
   Goos. Why mistris; there was a lattin candlestick
here afore, and that had the languages I am sure.   100
   Tal. I thought he had a reason for it Ladie.
   Pen. I and a reason of the Sunne too my Lord, for
his father wood haue bin ashamed on't.   *Exeunt Momford and the rest.*
   Do. Well master *Clarence* I perceiue your mind
Hath so incorparate it selfe with flesh   105
And therein rarified that flesh to spirit,
That you haue need of no Phisitians helpe.
But good Sir euen for holy vertues health
And grace of perfect knowledge, doe not make
Those ground-workes of eternitie you lay   110
Meanes to your ruine, and short being here:
For the too strict and rationall Course you hold
Will eate your bodie vp; and then the world,
Or that small point of it, where virtue liues
Will suffer Diminution: It is now   115

77 iudgment] *Q2;* udgment *Q1* ‖ **83** her:] ~. *Q1-2* ‖ **86** *Distick] Q2; Dictick Q1* ‖ **87** let's] lets
Q1-2 ‖ **88** nature;] ~, *Q1-2* ‖ **91** to your] *Q2;* toyour *Q1* ‖ **93** Iewells] *Q2;* I ewells *Q1* | Lord?]
Bullen; ~, *Q1-2* ‖ **95** marrie] *Q2;* marrre *Q1* | *Gyles,] Q2;* ~. *Q1* ‖ **96** *Goos.] Q2;* ~: *Q1* | fine]
Q2; sine *Q1* ‖ **98** languages,] ~. *Q1-2* ‖ **103** SD *Exeunt ... rest.] Parrott; Exeunt. Q1-2* ‖ **110**
eternitie] *Bullen;* ~, *Q1-2* ‖

Brought almost to a simple vnitie,
Which is, (as you well know) *Simplicior puncto.*
And if that point faile once, why, then alas
The vnitie must onely be suppos'd.
Let it not faile then, most men else haue sold it;   120
Tho you neglect your selfe, vphould it,
So with my reuerend loue I leaue you Sir.   *Exit.*
   Cla. Thanks worthie Doctour, I do amply quite you.
I proppe poore vertue, that am propt my selfe,
And onely by one friend in all the world,   125
For vertues onely sake I vse this wile, /
Which otherwise I wood despise and scorne;   [I2ᵛ]
The world should sinke and all the pompe she hugs
Close in her hart, in her ambitious gripe,
Ere I sustaine it, if this slendrest ioynt   130
Mou'd with the worth that worldlings loue so well
Had power to saue it from the throate of hell.

     He drawes the Curtaines and sits within them.
       Enter Eugenia, Penelope, Hippolita.

   Eug. Come on faire Ladies I must make you both
Familiar witnesses of the most strange part
And full of impudence that ere I plaide.   135
   Hip. What's that good madam?
   Eug. I that haue bene so more then maiden-nice
To my deare Lord and vnkle not to yeeld
By his importunate suite to his friends loue
In looke, or almost thought; will of my selfe   140
Farre past his expectation or his hope
In action, and in person greete his friend,
And comfort the poore gentlemans sick state.
   Pen. Is this a part of so much Impudence?
   Eug. No but I feare me it will stretch to more.   145
   Hip. Mary, madam, the more the merrier.
   Eug. Marrie Madam? what shood I marrie him?
   Hip. You take the word me thinkes as tho you would,
And if there be a thought of such kind heate
In your cold bosome, wood to God my breath   150
Might blowe it to the flame of your kind hart.
   Eug. Gods pretious, Ladie, knowe ye what you say,
Respect you what I am, and what he is,
What the whole world wood say, and what great Lords

119 suppos'd.] *Q2*; ~, *Q1* ‖ 123 you.] ~ˬ *Q1-2* ‖ 127 scorne;] ~, *Q1-2* ‖ 129 gripe,] *Q2*; ~ˬ *Q1* ‖ 132 hell.] *Q2*; ~ˬ *Q1* ‖ 136 What's] *Q2*; Whats *Q1* ‖ 137 then maiden-nice] *Q2*; thenmaiden-nice *Q1* ‖ 145 more.] *Q2*; ~ˬ *Q1* ‖ 146 Mary, madam,] ~ˬ ~ˬ *Q1-2* ‖ 148 take the] *Q2*; takethe *Q1* ‖ 152 pretious,] *Bullen*; ~ˬ *Q1-2* ‖

I haue refused and might as yet embrace,   155
And speake you like a friend, to wish me him?
  Hip. Madam I cast all this, and know your choyse
Can cast it quite out of the christall dores
Of your Iudiciall eyes: I am but young
And be it said without all pride I take /   160
To be a maid, I am one, and in deed   [I3]
Yet in my mothers wombe to all the wiles
Weeud in the loomes of greatnes, and of state:
And yet euen by that little I haue learn'd
Out of continuall conference with you,   165
I haue cride haruest home of thus much iudgment
In my greene sowing time, that I cood place
The constant sweetnes of good *Clarence* mind,
Fild with his inward wealth and noblenes,
(Looke madam) here, when others outward trashe   170
Shood be contented to come vnder here.
  Pen. And so say I vppon my maidenhead.
  Eug. Tis well said Ladies, thus we differ then,
I to the truth-wise, you to worldly men:
And now sweet dames obserue an excellent iest   175
(At least in my poore iesting.) Th'Erle my vnckle
Will misse me straite, and I know his close drift
Is to make me, and his friend *Clarence* meete
By some deuice or other he hath plotted.
Now when he seekes vs round about his house   180
And cannot find vs, for we may be sure
He will not seeke me in his sicke friends chamber,
(I haue at al times made his loue so strange,)
He straight will thinke, I went away displeas'd,
Or hartelie careles of his hartiest sute.   185
And then I know there is no greife on earth
Will touch his hart so much, which I will suffer
To quite his late good pleasure wrought on me,
For ile be sworne in motion and progresse
Of his friends suite, I neuer in my life   190
Wrastled so much with passion or was mou'd
To take his firme loue in such Ielouse part.
  Hip. This is most excellent madam, and will proue
A neecelike, and a noble frends Reuenge.
  Eug. Bould in a good cause, then let's greet his friend.   195

     [*She opens the curtains and discloses Clarence.*]

---

160 take] ~, *Q1-2* ‖ 163 Weeud] *Bullen;* Weend *Q1-2 (See Textual Note)* ‖ 169 noblenes,]
Parrott; ~; *Q1-2* ‖ 170 (Looke madam) here,] (~ ~ ~,) *Q1-2* ‖ 182 friends] *Q2;* ftiends *Q1* ‖
195 let's ... friend.] lets ... ~, *Q1-2* | SD *She ... Clarence.*] *Parrott subs.* ‖

781

Where is this sickly gentleman, at his booke?
Now in good troth I wood theis bookes were burnd /
That rapp men from their friends before their time.   [13ᵛ]
How does my vnckles friend? no other name
I need giue him, to whome I giue my selfe.   200
 Cla. O madam let me rise that I may kneele,
And pay some dutie to your soueraigne grace.
 Hip. Good *Clarence* doe not worke your selfe disease,
My Ladie comes to ease and comfort you.
 Pen. And we are handmaides to her to that end.   205
 Cla. Ladies my hart will breake, if it be held
Within the verge of this presumtuous chaire.
 Eug. Why, *Clarence* is your iudgement bent to show
A common louers passion? let the world,
That liues without a hart, and is but showe,   210
Stand on her emtie, and impoisoned forme,
I knowe thy kindenesse, and haue seene thy hart,
Cleft in my vnckles free, and friendly lippes,
And I am onely now to speake and act,
The rites due to thy loue: oh I cood weepe   215
A bitter showe of teares for thy sick state,
I cood giue passion all her blackest rites,
And make a thousand vowes to thy deserts,
But these are common, knowledge is the bond,
The seale and crowne of our vnited mindes.   220
And that is rare, and constant, and for that,
To my late written hand I giue thee this.
See heauen, the soule thou gau'st is in this hand.
This is the knot of our eternitie,
Which fortune, death, nor hell, shal euer loose.   225
        [She draws the curtains.]

    Enter Bullaker. Iack. Wil.

 Ia. What an vnmannerly trick is this of thy countesse,
to giue the noble count her vnckle the slippe thus?
 Will. Vnmannerlie, you villayne? O that I were
worthie to weare a dagger to anie purpose for thy sake?
 Bul. Why young gentlemen, vtter your anger with your   230
fists. /
 Will. That cannot be, man, for all his fists are shut you   [I4]
know, and vtter nothing, and besides I doe not thinke

196 gentleman,] ~ˌ *Q1-2* ‖ **198** time.] *Bullen;* ~, *Q1-2* ‖ **199** friend?] ~, *Q1-2* ‖ **200** selfe.] *Q2;* ~, *Q1* ‖ **203** *Hip.*] *Q2; Hip: Q1 (a number of speech-prefixes through l.314 so pointed; not hereafter recorded)* | disease,] ~ˌ *Q1-2* ‖ **211** Stand] stand *Q1-2* ‖ **213** Cleft] *Parrott (Bullen conj.);* Clest *Q1-2 (See Textual Note)* | lippes,] *Bullen;* ~ˌ *Q1-2* ‖ **215** rites] rit'es *Q1-2* | weepe] *Bullen;* ~. *Q1-2* ‖ **217** rites,] ~. *Q1* ‖ **222** this.] *Bullen;* ~, *Q1-2* ‖ **225** SD *She ... curtains.*] *Parrott subs.* ‖ **232** be,] *Bullen;* ~ˌ *Q1-2* ‖

782

my quarrell iust for my Ladies protection in this cause,
for I protest she does most abhominablie miscarrie her   235
selfe.

Ia. Protest you sawsie Iack you! I shood doe my
countrie and court-shippe good seruice to beate thy
coalts teeth out of thy head, for suffering such a
reuerend worde to passe their guarde; why, the oldest   240
courtier in the world man, can doe noe more then protest.

Bul. Indeede page, if you were in *Fraunce*, you wood
bee broken vpon a wheele for it, there is not the best
Dukes sonne in *Fraunce* dares saie I protest, till hee
bee one and thirtie yeere old at least, for the inheritance   245
of that worde is not to bee possest before.

Will. Well, I am sorie for my presumtion then, but
more sorie for my Ladies, marie most sorie for thee good
Lorde *Momforde*, that will make vs most of all sorie for
our selues, if wee doe not fynde her out.   250

Ia. Why alas what shood wee doe? all the starres of
our heauen see, wee seeke her as fast as wee can, if shee
bee crept into a rush wee will seeke her out or burne her.

Enter Momford.

Mom. Villaines, where are your Ladies? seeke them out;
Hence, home ye monsters, and stil keep you there   255
Where leuitie keepes, in her inconstant Spheare.   *Exeunt Pages.*
Awaie you pretious villaines. What a plague
Of varried tortures is a womans hart?
How like a peacockes taile with different lightes,
They differ from them selues; the very ayre   260
Alters the aspen humors of their bloods. /
Now excellent good, now superexcellent badd.   [14ᵛ]
Some excellent good, some? but one of all:
Wood anie ignorant babie serue her friend
Such an vnciuill part? Sblood what is learning?   265
An artificiall cobwebbe to catch *flies*,
And nourish *Spiders*? cood she cut my throate
With her departure I had byn her calfe,
And made a dish at supper for my guests
Of her kinde charge; I am beholding to her.   270
Puffe, is there not a feather in this ayre

---

237 you!] *Bullen*; ∼, *Q1-2* ‖ 241 protest.] *Q2*; ∼, *Q1* ‖ 242 page,] ∼ ͵ *Q1-2* ‖ 242, 244 *Fraunce*]
Fraunce Q1; *France Q2* ‖ 254 Villaines, ... out] *Bullen*; ∼ ͵ ... them / Out *Q1-2* | Ladies?] ∼,
Q1-2 ‖ 255 Hence] hence *Q1-2* | and] *Q2*; nad *Q1* ‖ 256 inconstant] *Q2*; in constant *Q1* |
Spheare.] ∼, *Q1-2* | SD *Exeunt Pages*.] *Q2*; ∼. ∼. (*with* Pages *on line below*) *Q1* ‖ 257
villaines. What] ∼, what *Q1-2* | plague] ∼, *Q1-2* ‖ 264 friend] ∼, *Q1-2* ‖ 267 *Spiders*?] *Q2*; ∼,
Q1 | throate] ∼, *Q1-2* ‖ 268 With] *Q1(c)*, *Q2*; W with *Q1(u)* ‖ 270 charge; ... her.] *Bullen*; ∼;
... ∼, *Q1-2* ‖

A man may challenge for her? what? a feather?
So easie to be seene; so apt to trace
In the weake flight of her vnconstant wings?
A mote, man, at the most, that with the sunne,   275
Is onely seene, yet with his radiant eye,
We cannot single so from other motes,
To say this mote is shee; passion of death,
She wrongs me past a death; come, come my friend
Is mine, she not her owne, and there's an end.   280

             [*Eugenia opens the curtains.*]

  Eug. Come vnckle shall we goe to supper now?
  Mom. Zounes to supper? what a dorr is this?
  Eug. Alas what ailes my vnckle? Ladies see.
  Hip. Is not your Lordshippe well?
  Pen.   Good, speake my Lord.
  Mom. A sweete plague on you all, ye wittie rogues;   285
Haue you no pittie in your villanous iests,
But runne a man quite from his fifteene witts?
  Hip. Will not your Lord-shippe see your friend, and
    neece?
  Mom. Wood I might sinke if I shame not to see her.
Tush t'was a passion of pure Ielosie,   290
Ile make her now amends with Adoration.
Goddes of learning and of constancie,
Of friendshippe and euerie other vertue –
  Eug. Come, come, you haue abus'de me now I know
And now you plaister me with flatteries.   295
  Pen. My Lord the contract is knit fast betwixt them. /
  Mom. Now all heauens quire of Angels sing Amen,   [K1]
And blesse theis true borne nuptials with their blisse,
And Neece tho you haue Cosind me in this,
Ile vnckle you yet in an other thing,   300
And quite deceiue your expectation.
For where you think you haue contracted harts
With a poore gentleman, he is sole heire
To all my Earledome, which to you and yours
I freely, and for euer here bequeath;   305
Call forth the Lords, sweet Ladies, let them see
This sodaine and most welcome Noueltie;

273 trace] *Parrott*; ~; *Q1-2* ‖ 275 mote, man,] ~ ̣ ~ ̣ *Q1-2* ‖ 277 We] *Q2*; we *Q1* ‖ 278 shee;] ~,
Q1-2 ‖ 279 death;] ~, *Q1-2* | friend] *Q2*; ~, *Q̂1* ‖ 280 there's] theres *Q1-2* | SD *Eugenia ...
curtains.*] *Parrott subs.* ‖ 283 Alas] *Q2*; A las *Q1* | vnckle?] *Q2*; ~, *Q1* ‖ 284 Good,] *Bullen*; ~ ̣
Q1-2 ‖ 285 rogues;] ~ ̣ *Q1-2* ‖ 286-287 Haue ... witts?] *Bullen*; *as prose Q1-2* (haue ... but) ‖ 288
Will ... neece?] *Parrott*; *as prose Q1-2* ‖ 289 *Mom.*] *Q1(c)*, *Q2*; *Mnm. Q1(u)* | her.] ~ *Q1-2* ‖ 291
Ile make] *Bullen*; ~ now ~ *Q1-2* | amends] a mends *Q1-2* ‖ 293 vertue–] ~. *Q1-2* ‖ 296 them.]
~ ̣ *Q1-2* ‖ 306 Ladies,] ~ ̣ *Q1-2* ‖

But crie you mercy Neece, perhaps your modestie
Will not haue them pertake this sodaine matche.
    Eug. O vnckle thinke you so? I hope I made   310
My choyce with too much Iudgment to take shame
Of any forme I shall performe it with.
    Mom. Said like my Neece, and worthy of my friend.

Enter Furnifal, Tal: King: Goos: Rud: Foul: Ia:
Will, Bullaker.

My Lords, take witnes of an absolute wonder,
A marriage made for vertue, onely vertue: 315
My friend, and my deere neece are man and wife.
    Fur. A wonder of mine honour, and withall
A worthie presedent for al the world;
Heauen blesse you for it Ladie, and your choyce.
    Ambo. Thankes my good Lord.   320
    Tal. An Accident that will make pollicie blushe,
And all the Complements of wealth and state,
In the succesfull and vnnumbred Race
That shall flowe from it, fild with fame and grace.
    King. So may it speed, deere Countesse, worthy *Clarence.*   325
    Ambo. Thankes good Sir *Cutberd.*
    Fur. Captaine be not dismaid; Ile marrie thee,
For while we liue, thou shalt my consort be.
    Foul. By *Fraunce* my Lord, I am not grieu'd a whit,
Since *Clarence* hath her; he hath bin in *Fraunce,*   330
And therefore merits her if she were better. /
    Mom. Then knights ile knit your happie nuptial knots,   [K1ᵛ]
I know the Ladies minds better then you;
Tho my rare Neece hath chose for vertue onlie,
Yet some more wise then some, they choose for both   335
Vertue, and wealth.
    Eug.   Nay unckle then I plead
This goes with my choyce, *Some more wise then some,*
For onely vertues choise is truest wisedome.
    Mom. Take wealth, and vertue both amongst you then;
They loue ye knights extreamely, and Sir *Cutt:*   340
I giue the chast *Hippolita* to you,
Sir *Gyles* this Ladie –
    Pen.   Nay stay there my Lord,
I haue not yet prou'd all his knightly parts;

---

310 so?] ~, *Q1-2* || 314 My] *Mom:* ~ *Q1-2* || 315 vertue:] *Bullen;* ~, *Q1-2* || 320 *Ambo.*] ~ˌ
Q1-2 || 325 speed,] *Bullen;* ~ˌ *Q1-2* || 326 *Ambo.*] ~ˌ *Q1-2* || 327 dismaid;] ~, *Q1-2* || 329, 330
Fraunce] Fraunce *Q1;* *France Q2* || 339 then;] ~, *Q1-2* || 342 Ladie–] *Bullen;* ~; *Q1;* ~. *Q2* ||
343 parts;] ~ˌ *Q1-2* ||

I heare he is an excellent Poet too.

Tal. That I forgot sweet Ladie; good Sir *Gyles,*   345
Haue you no sonnet of your penne about ye?

Goos. Yes, that I haue I hope, my Lord my Cosen.

Fur. Why, this is passing fit.

Goos. Ide be loth to goe without paper about me
against my mistris; hold my worke againe, a man knows   350
not what neede he shall haue perhaps.

Mom. Well remembred a mine honour Sir *Gyles.*

Goos. Pray read my Lorde, I made this sonnet of my
mistris.

Rud. Nay reade thy selfe man.   355

Goos. No intruth Sir *Cut*: I cannot reade mine owne
hande.

Mom. Well I will reade it.

Three things there be which thou shouldst only craue,
Thou Pomroy, or thou apple of mine eye;   360
Three things there be, which thou shouldst longe to haue,
And for which three, each modest dame wood crie;
Three things there be, that shood thine anger swage,
An English mastife, and a fine french page.

Rud. Sblood Asse, there's but two things, thou shamst   365
thy selfe. /

Goos. Why Sir *Cutt*: that's *Poetica licentia*; the verse   [K2]
wood haue binne too long, and I had put in the third.
S'light you are no Poet I perceiue.

Pen. Tis excellent seruant.

Mom.   Keepe it Ladie then,   370
And take the onely knight of mortall men.

Goos. Thanke you good my Lord as much as tho you had
giuen me twentie shillings in truth, now I may take the
married mens parts at footeball.

Mom. All comforts crowne you all; and you Captaine,   375
For merrie forme sake let the willowe crowne;
A wreath of willow bring vs hither straite.

Fur. Not for a world shood that haue bin forgot.
Captaine it is the fashion, take this crowne.

Foul. With all my hart my Lord, and thanke ye too;   380
I will thanke any man that giues me crownes.

Mom. Now will we consecrate our readie supper
To honourd *Hymen* as his nuptiall rite,

---

345 *Gyles,*] ~‸ *Q1-2* ‖ 347 hope,] *Bullen*; ~‸ *Q1-2* ‖ 350 mistris;] ~, *Q1-2* ‖ 352 *Gyles.*] *Q2*; ~: *Q1* ‖ 365 there's] theres *Q1-2* ‖ 367 *Goos.*] catchword *Q1*; om. *Q1* (text) | that's ... *licentia*;] thats ... ~, *Q1-2* | *Poetica licentia*] *Q2*; *Poeticalicentia Q1* ‖ 368 third.] ~, *Q1-2* ‖ 375 Captaine,] ~‸ *Q1-2* ‖ 378 forgot.] ~‸ *Q1-2* ‖ 380 too;] ~, *Q1*; ~, *Q2* ‖

In forme whereof first daunce faire Lords and Ladies
And after sing, so we will sing and daunce,   385
And to the skies our vertuous ioyes aduance.

The Measure.

Now to the song, and doe this garland grace.

Canto.

> *Willowe, willowe, willowe,*
>   *our captaine goes downe:*
> *Willowe, willowe, willowe,*   390
>   *his vallor doth crowne.*
> *The rest with Rosemarie we grace.*
>   *O Hymen let thy lights*
> *With richest rayes guild euerie face,*
>   *and feast harts with delights.*   395
> *Willowe, willowe, willow,*
>   *we chaunt to the skies:*
> *And with blacke and yellowe,*
>   *giue courtship the prize.*

FINIS.

HISTORICAL COLLATION

[Editions collated: Q2 (1636), Harvard and Library of Congress copies; Bullen (= B, in *A Collection of Old English Plays*, III [1884], pp. 1-94); and Parrott (= P, in *The Plays and Poems of George Chapman: The Comedies* [1914], pp. 607-70). The siglum Q1 identifies the quarto of 1606, with *Q1(c)* and *Q1(u)* designating corrected and uncorrected states of that text. In addition, emendations suggested by George G. Loane in 'More Notes on Chapman's Plays,' *MLR*, XXXVIII (1943), 340-347, are also included. Only substantive and semi-substantive variants are recorded; obvious errors are not recorded. Lemmata are taken from the present text. Where lemma represents the reading of Q1 copy-text, omission of a siglum indicates agreement with lemma. Q1 press-variants not included when Q2, B, P read with *Q1(c)*.]

I.i

ACTVS ... PRIMA] ~ ... ~ *Before the House of* Eugenia P
18 (*Will*)?] B, P; (~)ˬ Q1-2
19 vp] ~; B
25 SD *Aside.*] P; *om.* Q1-2, B
30 you] Q2, B, P; your Q1
39 vs?] Q2, B, P; ~, Q1
49 page–] P; ~. Q1-2, B
50-51 page. Sir,] ~, ~; B, P
56 Commendations] ~. Q2; ~ – B; ~, P
57 (*Wil*)] *used as speech-prefix* B
59 *Will.*] Bul. B
64-65 them, so heauylie] P; ~ˬ ~ ~, Q1-2, B
69 women–] ~. Q1-2, B, P
70 *Fowleweather*,] B; ~ˬ Q1-2; ~! P
74 and a will] and will Q2, B
94 *Goosecappe*?] B; ~ˬ Q1-2; ~! P
100 comes] come Q2, B
111 trauaild] travelled P
119 an't] on't P
126 wit;] B, P; ~ˬ Q1-2
132 preparatiue] B, P; prepra-/tiue Q1-2
139 ye] you Q2, B
155 *Hippolita*–] B, P; ~. Q1-2
166 *Hippolita*, ... extreame] P; ~; ... ~ Q1; ~ˬ ... ~, Q2, B
173 to] P; too Q1-2; too, B

174 longer,] Q2, B, P; ~ Q1
195 not vs] us not P
    Suppers] Supper Q2, B

I.ii

I.ii] B; om. Q1-2; SCENA II A Room in Eugenia's House P
14 emphaticaly.] Q2, B, P; ~? Q1
41 SD Exeunt the ladies.] P; Exeunt Q1; Exeunt. Q2
43 gods] Cods Q2, B
52 you?] ~; Q2
54 moouing–] Q2, B; ~. Q1, P
56 foule–] P; ~. Q1-2, B
77-78 this plaine] ~ is ~ P
95 adverbe] B, P; verbe Q1-2
97 Construe] Conster Q2, B
104 Emphaticall:] Q2, B, P; ~ Q1
106 Sir?] Q2, B, P; ~, Q1
125 Lacquay?] Lacquays, P
133 on't] P; ant Q2; ont Q1, B

I.iii

4 nipt;] Q2, B, P; ~ Q1
6 her, she] Q2, B, P; ~. She Q1
18 how] om. Q2, B
28 there–] P; ~. Q1-2, B
33 SD To Will.] om. Q1-2, B; aside P
    Sirra.] ~? Q2, B, P
40 mile] miles Q2, B
43 Barnet.] Q2, B; ~? Q1; ~! P
47 know;] P; ~, Q1; ~: Q2, B
61 trauaile] travel P

I.iv

SCÆNA QUARTA.] ~ ~ A Room in Momford's House P
17 SD To the Musicians.] om. Q1-2, B, P
    Thanks] B, P; Cla. ~ Q1-2
24 plumes;] Q2, B, P; ~ Q1
30 Atome, cald] P; ~ ~, Q1-2; ~ ~ B
34 yesterday,] Q2; ~ Q1; ~; B, P
60 vs:] Q2, B, P; ~ Q1
60-61 come: Sir] ~. ~ Q2; ~. ~, B; ~, ~; P
61 SD Embracing him.] P; om. Q1-2, B
74 Organs, there,] ~ ~, Q2, B; ~, ~ P
81 iudgement] Q2, B, P; ~, Q1
90 ioy:] Q2, B; ~ Q1; ~. P
99 worlde, Loue?] Q2, B, P; ~? ~ Q1
113 hart?] Q2, B; ~, Q1; ~! P

116-17 friend sets ... hart; what, friend ... Nephew both?] frends ~ ... ~,
  ~? ~ ... Nephews ~? *Q1(c)*; friends set ... heart, ~? friende ...
  Nephew? ~ *Q1(u)*; ~ ~ ... heart? friend, ... Nephews ~? *Q2, B*;
  ~ ~ ... ~. What, ~ ... ~ ~? *P*
122 greatnesse] *Q1(c)*; greatnesses *Q1(u), Q2*
123 husband–] *B, P*; ~. *Q1-2*
130 counsaile?] *Q2, B, P*; ~, *Q1*
131 woman,] *Q2, B, P*; ~? *Q1*
132 meanes?] *Q2, B, P*; ~, *Q1*
133 buildes] *Q1(c)*; bindes *Q1(u), Q2, B*
136 head. Attempt] *Q2, B, P*; ~, attempt *Q1*
140 bodies ... bodies:] *Q2, B*; ~? ... ~ *Q1(c)*; ~? ... ~? *Q1(u)*; ~ ...
  ~; *P*
146 *hortatur*] *Q2, B, P*; *hortetur Q1*
147 richest] *Q1(c)*; rightest *Q1(u), Q2, B*
153 *Winnyfred* from] *B, P*; ~; ~ *Q1(c)*; ~; for *Q1(u), Q2*
164 sweet] *Q1(c)*; deare *Q1(u), Q2, B*
166 rude,] *P*; ~ *Q1*; ~? *Q2, B*
168-69 market ... ware,] *Q2, B, P*; ~, ... ~ *Q1(c)*; ~ ... ~ *Q1(u)*
177 then till you are] *Q1(c)*; till you are then *Q1(u), Q2, B*
183 sir–] *B, P*; ~. *Q1-2*
187 *Winnifred*:] *Q2, B*; ~ *Q1*; ~; *P*
192 turne–] *B, P*; ~. *Q1-2*
201 Ladie] *B, P*; Ladies *Q1-2*
213 SD *Primi*] *Q2, B, P*; *Primis Q1*

II.i

ACTVS ... PRIMA] ~ ... ~ *A Room in* Eugenia's *House P*
4 number,] *P*; ~ *Q1*; ~. *Q2*; ~; *B*
8 Beames?] ~, *Q2, B, P*
9 Eternesse] *B, P*; Eternesses *Q1-2*
  is,] *B, P*; ~ *Q1-2*
13 what is] what's *Q2, B*
14 Restauration?] ~: *Q2, B*; ~ – *P*
16 with all] *B, P*; withall *Q1-2*
  SD *Retires*.] *P*; om. *Q1-2, B*
20 SD *Enter Eugenia*.] om. *Q1-2, B*; *after* labour *l. 22 P*
48 reuenge] reuenger *Q2, B, P*
50 *Inimicos*] *P*; *Inimico Q1-2, B*
60 adew] *Q1(u), Q2, B, P*; dew *Q1(c)*
66 ifaith;] ~, *Q1(u), Q2*; iafith; *Q1(c)*; ~ – *B*; ~! *P*
  SD *Aside*.] *P*; om. *Q1-2, B*
67 other] *B, P*; ~; *Q1-2*
76-77 SD *He daunceth speaking*] ~ *daunceih* ~ *Q1(c)*; om. *Q1(u), Q2*
79 SD *Aside*.] om. *Q1-2, B, P*
80 do] *Q1(c)*; be *Q1(u), Q2, B*
81 SD *Aside*.] *P*; om. *Q1-2, B*

tro?] *Q1(c)*; ~‸ yee, *Q1(u)*, *Q2*
　Lo:] Lo. *Q2*; Lord *B*; lordship *P*
85 SD *Aside.*] *P*; *om.* *Q1-2, B*
86 blockheded] *Q1(c)*; blockhead *Q1(u), Q2, B, P*
97 SD *Aside.*] *om.* *Q1-2, B, P*
108 childe;] *Q1(c)*; ~, *Q1(u), Q2*
　aboue] about *Q2*
109 hope,] ~‸ *B*; ~: *P*
113 see a] ~. [*Studying her face*] A *P*
125 Crises] *Q2, B, P*; Creses *Q1*
140-41 friend, *Clarence*] ~‸ ~ *Q1-2*; ~‸ ~, *B, P*
148 *Dearum*] *Deorum Q2, B, P*
168 SD *Aside.*] *P*; *om.* *Q1-2, B*
180 *veritate*] *Q2, B, P*; *viritate Q1*
184 betternes] *Loane conj.*; bitternes *Q1-2, B, P*
206 vs and it, it would] ~, and it would *Q2, B*
212 honours] *Q2, B*; honour *Q1*; honour's *P*
214 day on't] *B, P*; ~ one *Q1*; ~, on *Q2*
224 SD *Retires.*] *P*; exit‸ *Q1-2*; *om. B*
226 SD *To Clarence.*] *om. Q1-2, B*; *aside to* Clarence *P*
255 abuses–] *P*; ~, *Q1*; ~. *Q2, B*
263 SD *Enter Tales, Kingcob.*] ~ Lord ~, Sir Clement ~ *P*
265 *Cutberd*] *Clement P* (*throughout; not noted hereafter*)
292 haue;] *B, P*; ~, *Q1-2*
321 selfe] *Q2, B, P*; ~; *Q1*

III.i

SD ACTVS ... PRIMA.] ~ ... ~‸ *Near Barnet P*
2, 4, SD *Within.*] *P*; *om. Q1-2, B*
11 hollowings, ... ye;] *P*; ~; ... ~‸ *Q1*; ~; ... ~, *Q2, B*
15 Why] ~? *Q2, B*; ~, *P*
　Moyle] Cut. *P*; *also at III.i.62*
48 women,] *Q2, B*; ~‸ *Q1*; ~; *P*
63 *Rud.*] *B, P*; Foul. *Q1-2*
70 pickt-hatch] *Q2, B, P*; pick-thacht *Q1*
72 hope;] *B*; ~‸ *Q1-2*; ~. *P*
84 a must] he ~ *Q2*
95 wood] *B, P*; *om. Q1-2*
99 wood] would't *P*
　one,] *Q2, B*; ~? *P*
99-100 Ile be sworne?] *B*; ~ ~ ~, *Q1*; ~ ~ ~. *Q2*; *om. P*
101 commission; now] ~‸ ~, *Q1-2*; ~: ~ *B*; ~, ~ *P*
103-4 withal ... life, ... light;] ~, ... ~‸ ... ~, *Q1*; ~, ... ~, ... ~, *Q2*;
　　~‸ ... ~‸ ... ~; *B*; ~‸ ... ~, ... ~! *P*
103 by] *P*; be *Q1-2, B*
121 not] *om. Q2, B*
134 *Cutt.*] *B, P*; *om. Q1-2*

157 bountie?] Q2, B, P; ~. Q1
184 *Rud.*] B, P; *King.* Q1-2
197 *Fraunce!*] P; ~ Q1-2; ~, B
199 merrie–] ~ Q1; ~. Q2, B, P
204 Beare] ~ off Q2, B
218 not.] B, P; ~, Q1; no I. Q2
219 (vm)] (~): B; hum! P
222 something] sometimes Q2, B
243 Elixers,] P; ~. Q1; ~ Q2, B
253 SD *Exeunt Will and Iack.*] *Exeunt.* Q1-2, B; *Exeunt Pages* P
266 What] Why Q2
275 *Cut:?*] *Cut?* Q2, B; *Cut.?* P; *Cut:* Q1
280 London:] B; ~ Q1-2; ~! P
    SD *Exeunt ... Goosecap.*] P; *om.* Q1-2, B
284 too, ... thing;] P; ~, ... ~, Q1-2; ~: ... ~, B

III.ii

III.ii] B; *om.* Q1-2; SCENA SECUNDA *A Room in* Momford's *House* P
    SD *Enter ... behind.*] ~ *Lorde Momford and Clarence. Clarence*
    Horatio. Q1-2, B; ~ Lord Momford *and* Clarence, [*and*] Horatio P
11 starre] state Q2
13 powre] power Q2, B
19 men;] ~, Q1-2; ~. B, P
27 merrit] merry Q2
28 mourner] manner Q2
29 write, ... me.] Q2, B, P; ~ ... ~ Q1
35 redelesse] P; rudelesse Q1-2, B
38 SD *Exit Horatio.*] *om.* Q1-2, B, P
42 feast] feed P
44 diuine] ~? Q2, B
48 side] Q2, B, P; sid Q1
53 *sit*] *est* Q2, B
56 shadowes;] ~, Q1-2, B; ~ P
62 to rule two] Q2, B, P; two ~ to Q1
    bodies.] ~? B
63 antedame] antheame Q2; antidame P
75 does!] ~. Q2, B; ~; P
89 midnight;] B; ~ Q1; ~, Q2; ~. P
90 *Cla.*] ~. [*giving Momford the letter*] P
105 flame,] P; ~. Q1; ~; Q2, B

IV.i

ACTVS ... PRIMA.] ~ ... ~ *A Room in* Eugenia's *House* P
42 you;] B; ~, Q1-2; ~. P
64 not] hot B *conj.*
65 coste:] Q2; ~ Q1; ~. B, P
70 SD *To Eugenia.*] *om.* Q1-2, B, P

72 SD *Offering ... letter.*] *P*; *om.* Q1-2, B
73 SD *To Momford.*] *om.* Q1-2, B, P
75 SD *To Eugenia.*] *om.* Q1-2, B, P
76 SD *To Momford.*] *om.* Q1-2, B, P
77 SD *To Eugenia.*] *om.* Q1-2, B, P
77-78 awaie ... best,] ~, ... ~‸ Q2; ~, ... ~, B, P
79 neare if you] ~, ~ ~ Q2; neare, you B
    it, – and] ~, – And B; ~, ~ Q1-2; ~! – And P
81 Lord.] Q2, B, P; Lords, Q1
82 SD *To Eugenia.*] *om.* Q1-2, B; *aside to* ~ P
83 SD *To Momford.*] *om.* Q1-2, B; *aside to* ~ P
84 SD *To Eugenia.*] *om.* Q1-2, B; *aside to* ~ P
85 you;–] ~;‸ Q1-2; ~.‸ B; ~. – P
92 SD *To Eugenia.*] *om.* Q1-2, B; *Aside to* ~ P
94 SD *To Momford.*] *om.* Q1-2, B; *aside* P
100 SD *Exeunt.*] ~‸ *all but* Momford *and* Eugenia P
136 thing–] B, P; ~. Q1-2
137 Why,] P; ~? Q1-2, B
158, 167 of] off Q2, B, P
166 What] Q2, B, P; ~, Q1
170 it–] B, P; ~, Q1; ~. Q2
187 hand.] ~. [*She signs*] P
190 straite.] B; ~, Q1-2; ~. [*Reads.*] P
200 me] my P
206 Why,] ~? Q2, B

<h2 style="text-align:center">IV.ii</h2>

IV.ii] B; *om.* Q1-2; SCENA SECUNDA *A Room in* Lord Furnifall's
    House P
22 *Italie*;] B, P; Italie, Q1; *Italie,* Q2
26 yeare] yeeres Q2, B
43 hart] Q2, B, P; hatt Q1
68 Court-counsaile,] B, P; ~‸ Q1-2
101 *Gyles?*] B, P; ~, Q1-2
109 togeather–] B, P; ~, Q1; ~. Q2
114 me] my Q2, B, P
123 haire.] ~ – P
124 *Rud.*] P; *Cud.* Q1-2, B
132 foole,] B, P; ~‸ Q1-2
139 gramercy] P; gray mercy Q1-2, B
143 cast of] cast-of Q2, B
166 *Goos.*] P; *Giles*‸ Q1-2, B
195 With all] P; Withall Q1-2, B
198 Ladies!] ~, Q2; ~. B, P
207 a] B; A Q1-2; o' P
    Lordship] Q2, B, P; Lord Q1
221 SD *Exeunt ... Knights.*] P; *Exeunt.* Q1-2, B

IV.iii

IV.iii] *B*; *om*. *Q1-2*; SCENA TERTIA *A Room in* Momford's *House P*
5 *Cla.*] *P*; *Mom. Q1-2, B*
9 I] And *Loane conj.*
46 defect] defects *Q2, B*
53 lamer] *Q1(c)*; lame *Q1(u), Q2, B*
58 Poet] *P*; Poets *Q1-2, B*
61 confered;] *P*; ~‸ *Q1-2, B*
63 hart,] *P*; ~; *Q1-2, B*
73 this?] *Q2, B, P*; ~‸ *Q1*
76 erres] *B, P*; ~? *Q1-2*
80 add] *B, P*; all *Q1-2*
84 skill,] ~. *Q2, B, P*
90 with all] *Q2, B, P*; withall *Q1*
   Ladies] *B, P*; ~. *Q1-2*

V.i

SD ACTVS ... PRIMA.] ~ ... ~‸ *A Room at* Lord Momford's *House P*
3 knight,] ~‸ *Q1-2*; ~; *B, P*
11 *Giles.*] ~? *Q2, B, P*
19 SD *Aside.*] *om. Q1-2, B, P*
20 ones.] ~? *Q2, B*
29 forehand:] *Q2, B*; ~‸ *Q1*; ~, *P*
32 *Caucasus* my Lord?] ~? ~ ~, *Q2, B*; ~, ~ ~? *P*
42 (for ... world)] *Q1(c)*; ‸~ all ... ~‸ *Q1(u), Q2, B, P*
50 in] on *P*
58 am;] *Q1(c)*; ~, *Q1(u), Q2*; ~. *P*
69 hir] him *Q1-2, B*; 'em *P*
75 od] *Q1(c)*; good *Q1(u), Q2, B, P*
81 more] *Q1(c)*; most *Q1(u), Q2, B, P*
96 Gods] Cods *Q2*
98 now;] *Q2, B, P*; ~‸ *Q1*
106 sheppards] *Q1(c)*; shippards *Q1(u), Q2, B*
115 Zounes] *P*; Zonnes *Q1-2, B*
123 withall] *B, P*; with all *Q1-2*
147 inspird?] *Q2, B, P*; ~‸ *Q1*

V.ii

V.ii] *B*; *om. Q1-2*; SCENA SECUNDA *Another Room in* Lord Momford's
   House P
7 ye] you *Q2, B*
26 *nullis*] *Q2, B, P*; *nullus Q1*
55 SD *Enter, above,*] *P*; Enter *Q1-2, B*
   SD *Winnifred.*] ~‸ *and a* Servant *P*; *om. Q1-2, B*
56 SD *Enter Servant.*] *om. Q1-2, B, P*
57 *Serv.*] *P*; *om. Q1-2*; Fur. *B*

83 *Pasiaca*] *Phasiaca P*

84 *Anteuenit ... virtutibus*] *Moribus Antevenit sortem virtibus Q2*; *Moribus Antevenit sortem,* ~ *B, P*

86 *Distick*] *Q2, B*; *Dictick Q1*; distich *P*

95 marrie] *Q2, B, P*; marrre *Q1*

103 SD *Exeunt Momford and the rest.*] *P*; *Exeunt. Q1-2, B*

110 eternitie] *B, P*; ~, *Q1-2*

123 you.] *P*; ~ₐ *Q1-2*; ~; *B*

152 Gods] Cods *Q2*

160 take] *B, P*; ~, *Q1-2*

163 Weeud] *B, P*; Weend *Q1-2*

170 (Looke madam) here,] *B*; (~ ~ ~,) *Q1-2*; ₐ~ ~, ~; *P*

174 truth-wise] truth-wife *Q2, B*

195 SD *She ... Clarence.*] *om. Q1-2, B*; *Drawing the curtains, and disclosing* ~ₐ *P*

196 gentleman, at] ~ₐ ~ *Q1*; ~ ~? *Q2*; ~? ~ *B, P*

213 Cleft] *P (B conj.)*; Clest *Q1-2, B*

225 SD *She ... curtains.*] *om. Q1-2, B*; ~ *... * ~ₐ *concealing* Clarence, *herself, and her attendants P*

228 villayne] villaynes *Q2, B*

238 beate] beare *B*

245 yeere] yeeres *Q2*

252 can,] ~ₐ *Q2, B*; ~; *P*

254 Villaines, ... out] *B, P*; ~ₐ *... * them / Out *Q1-2*

261 Alters] Alter *Q2, B*

267 *Spiders?*] *Q2, B, P*; ~, *Q1*

273 trace] *P*; ~; *Q1-2*; ~, *B*

275 mote, man, at] *B*; ~ₐ ~ₐ ~ *Q1-2*; ~, ~, with *P*

278 shee;] ~, *Q1-2*; ~. *B, P*

279 friend] *Q2, B, P*; ~, *Q1*

280 SD *Eugenia ... curtains.*] *om. Q1-2, B*; ~ *draws ... * ~ₐ *disclosing* Clarence, *herself and her attendants P*

284 Good,] *B, P*; ~ₐ *Q1-2*

291 Ile make] *B, P*; ~ now ~ *Q1-2*

293 vertue–] ~. *Q1-2, B*; ~ₐ *P*

298 blisse] blesse *Q2*

367 *Goos.*] *catchword Q1*; *om. Q1 (text)*

376 forme] form's *P*

393 *lights*] *light Q2, B, P*

395 *delights*] *delight Q2, B, P*

PRESS-VARIANTS

[Copies collated: BL (British Library 643 d. 29, wants K2); Bodl (Bodleian Library); Dyce (Victoria and Albert Museum); DFo (Folger Shakespeare Library); MH (Harvard University Library); CSmH (Huntington Library); DLC (Library of Congress); MB (Boston Public Library); NNP (Pierpont Morgan Library); CtY (Yale University Library)]

Sheet C (inner forme)

Corrected: Dyce, DFo, MH, CSmH, NNP, CtY
Uncorrected: BL, Bodl, DLC, MB

Sig. C1ᵛ

I.iv.116 frends sets] friends set
        hart] heart
        friend] friende
  116-17 Nephews both?] Nephew? both͐
  118 thee] the
  122 greatnesse] greatnesses
  133 buildes] bindes
  138 eminent] enminent
  140 with bodies] with bodies?
  141 thee] the
  147 richest] rightest

Sig. C2

I.iv.153 here] Where
        from] for
  162 woman.] woman͐
  164 sweet] deare
  168 market,] market͐
  169 dore.] dore͐
  177 then till you are] till you are then

Sig. C3ᵛ

II.i.56 me?] me.
  60 dew] adew
      Epitaphs] Epitaths
  65 hours] houres
      any] an
  66 iafith;] ifaith,

Sig. C4

II.i.76-77 SD *He daunceih speaking.*] om.

80 do] be
81 tro?] tro yee,
86 blockheded] blockhead
   womā?] woman,
96 word] woord
98 maruailous] marualous
108 childe;] childe,

Sheet D (outer forme)

First State Corrected: MH
Uncorrected: MB
Sig. D1
  II.i.179 *virtute*] *vertute*
Sig. D2ᵛ
  II.i.272 *Kingcob*] *Bingcob*
Sig. D4ᵛ
  III.i.44 *Cut*:] *Cut*ˏ
    45 well,] well ˏ
      plaugde] plaugde,
      hill,] hill ˏ
    47 women] weomen
    50 gallants,] gallants ˏ
    67 *ſtarte*] *Arte*
Second State Corrected: BL, Bodl, Dyce, DFo, CSmH, DLC, NNP,
                       CtY
Sig. D2ᵛ
  II.i.272 *Kutberd Cingcob*] *Kuttberd Kingcob*
Sig. D3
  II.i.301 Euen] Fuen
    316 gloues frō] glones fro
Sig. D4ᵛ
  III.i.48 art] arr
    57 french Lords] french Lodrs
    64 *Monsieur*] *Meuusieur*
    67 *starte*] *ſtarte*

Sheet D (inner forme)

Corrected: BL, Bodl, Dyce, DFo, CSmH, DLC, NNP, CtY
Uncorrected: MH, MB
Sig. D1ᵛ
  II.i.192 exa-/ctest] exa-/test
    193 noblenesse] noblenesse.
    199 *complexu tenet*] *complexutenet*
    205 Sunne; but] Sunne but;
Sig. D2
  II.i.224 ornat.] ornat ˏ

Sig. D4

    III.i.29-31 yfath; / how now sweet Captain dost feele any easein thy
           payne / yet?] yfath; how now sweet Captaine dost feele any
           ease / in thy payne yet?

Sheet F (outer forme)

Corrected: BL, Bodl, Dyce, DFo, CSmH, DLC, MB, NNP, CtY
Uncorrected: MH

Sig. F1

    III.ii.91-92 SD *He reads and comments.*] om.

Sheet F (inner forme)

Corrected: BL, Bodl, Dyce, DFo, DLC, MB, NNP, CtY
Uncorrected: MH, CSmH

Sig. F2

    IV.i.25 woman] women
       26 England] Eugland

Sheet G (outer forme)

Corrected: BL, Dyce, MH, NNP, MB
Uncorrected: Bodl, DFo, CSmH, DLC, CtY

Sig. G1

    IV.i.227 Captaine,] Captaines

Sig. G2ᵛ

    IV.ii.99 him?] him.
       103 meane paint] meane haint

Sig. G3

    IV.ii.127 Orrenges] Orrrenges

Sheet G (inner forme)

Corrected: BL, NNP, MB
Uncorrected: Bodl, Dyce, DFo, MH, CSmH, DLC, CtY

Sig. G1ᵛ

    IV.ii.28 it not,] in not,
       42 swarm'de] swarm'de.

Sig. G2

    IV.ii.62 *Cut*:] *Cut*
       76 For] Eor

Sheet H (outer forme)

First State Corrected: NNP
Uncorrected: Bodl, Dyce, CSmH, DLC, CtY

Sig. H1

    IV.iii.49 What] Mhat

Sig. H3

    V.i.103 loue] loue?
Second State Corrected: BL, DFo, MH, MB

Sig. H1
  IV.iii.45 Her] He
      53 lamer] lame
Sig. H2ᵛ
  V.i.40 there,] there͏ͅ
     42 (for al the world)] ͏ͅfor all the world͏ͅ
     58 am;] am,
Sig. H3
  V.i.75 od] good
     81 more] most
    106 sheppards] shippards

Sheet H (inner forme)

Corrected: BL, MH, NNP, MB
Uncorrected: Bodl, Dyce, DFo, CSmH, DLC, CtY
Sig. H1ᵛ
  IV.iii.94 speake] speske
Sig. H2
  V.i.20 kinsmans] uinsmans
Sig. H4
  V.i.171 you] yon
    174 knowe] konwe

Sheet I (outer forme)

Corrected: Bodl, Dyce, DFo, DLC, NNP
Uncorrected: BL, MH, CSmH, MB, CtY
Sig. I1
  V.ii.26 *Hei mihi*] *Heimihi*
Sig. I4ᵛ
  V.ii.268 With] W with
    289 *Mom.*] *Mnm.*

TEXTUAL NOTES

Dramatis Personae

6 Momford] In Q1 this name is spelled here '*Monford*' (along with the abbreviation '*Monf.*' in the next line), but throughout the play as '*Momford*'.

11 *Sir Clement Kingcob*] This character is named Cutbert Kingcob in the text. For a discussion of the possible cause of this alteration, see the Textual Introduction.

I.ii

95 adverbe] Though both Q1 and Q2 read 'verbe', Bullen's emendation to 'adverbe' makes sense out of an otherwise meaningless phrase.

II.i

48 reuenge] Former editors emend to 'reuenger', but there does not seem to be sufficient cause for such a change.

125 Crises] The present reading follows Q2 and all subsequent editions, which emend the 'Creses' of Q1. Confusion between 'e' and 'i' is common in Q1. Two stop-press revisions of the Q1 text involve these letters: '*vertute*' to '*virtute*' (II.i.179) and 'shippards' to 'sheppards' (V.i.106). Similarly, Q2 corrects two other errors: '*viritate*' to '*veritate*' (II.i.180) and 'dilicately' to 'delicately' (II.i.321). Loane's emendation of 'bitternes' to 'betternes' (II.i.184), adopted by the present edition, falls into the same category. One definition of 'crisis' recorded in the *NED*, with this passage from *Sir Gyles Goosecappe* cited as an example, is 'a point by which to judge, token, sign.' Such a meaning fits the context much better than the possibility that Momford discovers and remarks on 'creses' in the face of his young and beautiful niece.

179-180 *virtute ... veritate*] Apparently, the first 'i' and 'e' in these words were reversed in the uncorrected state of Q1. The corrected version changes '*vertute*' to '*virtute*', but leaves '*viritate*', which Q2 emends to '*veritate*'.

184 betternes] Loane's suggestion that Q1's 'bitternes' be emended to 'betternes' helps to make sense out of a difficult passage. Other confusions between 'e' and 'i', noted above in the discussion of 'Crises', and Chapman's use of 'betternes' in his *Commentarius* on Book II of his translation of Homer's *Iliads* support this emendation.

III.i

67-69 in ... for] These words, occurring at the bottom of D4ᵛ, are repeated (reading 'he' for 'hee') at the top of E1. Such repetitions were not unusual, according to McKerrow ('The Use of the Galley in Elizabethan Printing,' *The Library*, II, ser. iv, 1921-1922, 100).

134 Sir *Cutt.*] Although Q1 omits the proper name, a blank space large enough to include it occurs after 'Sir'. Since Goosecappe, in this same speech, is called 'Sir *Gyles*', it seems probable that Rudesby would be addressed as 'Sir *Cutt.*'

III.ii

35 redelesse] The reading, 'rudelesses', of Q1 does not appear in *NED*. Parrott emends to 'redelesse', as he states, in the sense of 'indecipherable,' 'impossible to pierce through.' The only meaning for 'redelesse' listed in *NED* is 'devoid or destitute of counsel; *esp.* of persons, having no resource in a difficulty or emergency, not knowing what to do.' The term, as used in the present context, could have been derived from 'rede' in the sense of 'plan, design, or scheme.'

IV.i

64-65 Eat not ... trenchers] Bullen suggests a possible emendation of 'not' to 'hot', and Parrott thinks that these words should be stated affirmatively for them to make sense in this context. The statement is correct as it stands when one reads it not as an independent, imperative clause, but as a subordinate, conditional clause.

IV.iii

58 Poet] Although all editions before Parrott read 'Poets', there seems little doubt, as Parrott claims, that this is meant as a specific reference to Samuel Daniel, who, in his 'Complaint of Rosamond,' calls 'the adulterate beauty of a false cheek,' 'chastity's abator' (l. 41), which he rhymes two lines later with 'nature'. Thus, Clarence replies to Momford's statement by claiming that the 'most Court-receiued Poet' called 'painting' 'chastities abator' only 'to make vp a poore rime to Nature'.

V.i

75 od] Although all later editions follow the uncorrected state, 'good', the corrected 'od' as a 'minced form of God' (*NED*) is just as plausible.

81 more] Later editions follow the uncorrected state, 'most'. Because of the comparison of Sir Gyles' sewing to his other hobbies, however, the corrected reading, 'more', is the appropriate one. Penelope's following phrase, 'O farr away', also indicates the intended comparison in Hippolita's statement.

V.ii

57 *Serv.*] Q1 and Q2 omit a speech-prefix here. Bullen's assignment of these words to Furnifall is improbable in view of the manner in which Momford orders the unidentified speaker in the following speech. Parrott's assignment of this speech to a servant, even though no such character is mentioned anywhere else, seems a more plausible emendation.

163 Weeud] Since this word is clearly a part of the metaphor continued in the phrase 'loomes of greatnes', we may be fairly certain that the 'Weend' of Q1 and Q2 resulted from a turned 'u.'

213 Cloft] No such word as 'Clest', the reading of Q1 and Q2, appears in *NED*. This seems to be another example of a confusion between long-s and 'f'. 'Cleft' is used here as the past participle of 'cleave,' meaning 'to stick fast or adhere to' (*NED*).